ADMINISTRATIVE LAW

Australia
The Law Book Company
Brisbane, Sydney, Melbourne, Perth

Canada
Carswell
Ottawa, Toronto, Calgary, Montreal, Vancouver

AGENTS

India
N.M. Tripathi (Private) Ltd
Bombay

Eastern Law House (Private) Ltd
Calcutta

M.P.P. House
Bangalore

Universal Book Traders
Delhi

Aditya Books
Delhi

Israel
Steimatzky's Agency Ltd
Tel Aviv

Pakistan
Pakistan Law House
Karachi, Lahore

ADMINISTRATIVE LAW

Third Edition

P. P. CRAIG

Reader in Law
Worcester College, Oxford

LONDON
SWEET & MAXWELL
1994

First Edition 1983
Second Edition 1989

Published by Sweet & Maxwell Limited of
South Quay Plaza, 183 Marsh Wall, London E14 9FT
Typeset by Advance Typesetting Ltd, Oxford
Printed by Information Press, Eynsham, Oxford

No natural forests were destroyed to make this product;
only farmed timber was used and replanted.

A CIP catalogue record for this book is available from
the British Library

ISBN 0 421 51000 5

© P. P. Craig 1994

To my mother
and
the memory of my father

PREFACE TO THE FIRST EDITION

This book has taken shape over several years during which my ideas on administrative law have developed. I am indebted to a number of people with whom I have discussed the subject during that period. I would like to thank Jack Beatson and John Evans, both of whom found time to read large parts of the manuscript despite having heavy commitments of their own. I have profited from discussion of particular aspects of administrative law with Harry Arthurs, Peter Cane, Michael Elliott, Dennis Galligan, Martin Matthews and Stephen Parry. The work was expedited by the grant of sabbatical leave by Worcester College, Oxford and the University of Oxford, and I am grateful also to Osgoode Hall Law School and the University of Virginia for making the sabbatical so rewarding. A special note of thanks is due to Francis Reynolds, my former tutor and present colleague, who first stimulated my interest in law.

Sweet & Maxwell Ltd. has provided constant support and encouragement. I cannot apologise enough to all those who have had to read my appalling handwriting, and who have succeeded in producing wonderful typescripts in the face of such adversity.

The law is as stated on May 31, 1983.

P. P. Craig
Worcester College
Oxford

PREFACE TO THE THIRD EDITION

There have been considerable developments in administrative law since the second edition of this book. First, the whole nature of our administrative system has changed dramatically with the implementation of the Next Steps initiative, contracting-out and the like. Secondly, EC law has become ever more important within this field, both as a source of governing rules and also as a mechanism whereby aggrieved individuals can challenge domestic governmental action. Thirdly, important changes have taken place in the context of judicial review: there have been significant decisions in particular areas such as natural justice, jurisdiction, discretion and standing; the courts have become more explicit as to the power of the common law to protect individual rights and to fashion principles of good administration; and the case law concerning remedies has grown considerably over the past five years. These developments have led to the following major modifications since the second edition.

(1) Chapter 1 has been recast to take account of shifts in doctrinal thinking as to the purpose and aim of administrative law.
(2) The discussion of the administrative system has been altered to reflect the bureaucratic changes which have occurred. The implications of the Next Steps regime and contracting-out are considered in Chapter 3, while privatisation and regulation are considered within that Chapter and in Chapter 6.
(3) EC law has been dealt with in two ways. There is a new Chapter 5 which deals with the general structure of EC institutions, the legislative process, supremacy, direct effect and the like. Other topics from EC law, such as proportionality, fundamental rights, reasons, damages and public procurement, have been integrated into the relevant chapters of the book concerned with those issues.
(4) The chapters covering judicial review have all been updated and expanded, most notably Chapter 11, concerning discretion.
(5) The volume of case law on Order 53 has necessitated the addition of a separate Chapter 15 to cover this subject.

I would like to thank those at Sweet & Maxwell for all their support and help in the production of this new edition. Their efficiency during the production process was greatly appreciated.

The law is as stated on May 31, 1994.

P. P. Craig
Worcester College
Oxford
June 1, 1994

CONTENTS

PART 2: JUDICIAL REVIEW

PART 4: REMEDIES II

TABLE OF CASES

Alphabetical List

European Court

TABLE OF LEGISLATION

UK Statutes

European Union Treaties
and Conventions

PART 1

THE ADMINISTRATIVE SYSTEM

1. THE NATURE AND PURPOSE OF ADMINISTRATIVE LAW

Section 1. Introduction[1]

What is administrative law? A perusal of the literature presents the reader with considerable diversity of opinion. Description and prescription are not easily separated. For some it is the law relating to the control of government power, the main object of which is to protect individual rights. Others place greater emphasis upon rules which are designed to ensure that the administration effectively performs the tasks assigned to it. Yet others see the principal objective of administrative law as ensuring governmental accountability, and fostering participation by interested parties in the decision-making process.

None of these is right or wrong in some absolute sense. All are, however, incomplete. An adequate understanding of the nature and purpose of administrative law requires us to probe further into the way in which our society is ordered. At the most basic level it requires us to articulate more specifically the type of democratic society in which we live and to have some vision of the political theory which that society espouses. The role of more particular legal topics which constitute administrative law, such as natural justice, judicial review and the like can only be adequately assessed within such a framework. Concepts such as accountability, participation and rights do not possess only one interpretation which can be analysed by a purely "factual" inquiry. Nor can the place of such ideas be understood by pointing to their general connections with a democratic society. The very meaning and importance of such concepts will differ depending upon the *type* of democratic regime within which they subsist. Or to put the same point in a different way, every democratic society will have some ideas of rights, participation and accountability, but these will differ depending upon the nature of that society.

Administrative law is easier to understand when such background ideas are revealed, precisely because the rationale for the topics which make up the subject and the manner in which they interrelate, become clearer. Any attempt to discuss particular topics without considering these background ideas evidences a series of implicit assumptions about such ideas which are concealed and untested. This chapter will therefore be organised in the following manner. Two different pictures of the democratic state will be presented. The consequences that each has for the nature of administrative

---

[1] Footnotes have been deliberately kept to a minimum within this chapter.

law, and for the interpretation to be accorded to its main component parts will be examined. The defects which exist within each will be made apparent.

Section 2. Dicey, Unitary Democracy and the Ultra Vires Principle

1. *The Basis of the Traditional Model*

(1) UNITARY DEMOCRACY

It is a commonplace among administrative lawyers that Dicey is responsible for the subject having a "bad name" in this country. This is indeed a fact brought home to most constitutional law students early in their legal career after tackling the rule of law. Dicey's dislike of administrative law is of course readily apparent from the *Law of the Constitution*. We have, however, to push further if we are to understand in more detail how Dicey's views have coloured administrative law. What did this scholar actually do which was to have such a lasting effect on our subject? What Dicey actually did was to base his view of administrative law on a certain view of democracy which can be termed unitary. This is not a difficult idea and may be explained as follows.

First, all students are aware of the sovereignty of Parliament in the sense that Parliament is omnicompetent. It can in theory ban smoking in Paris, or repeal the grant of independence to former colonies. Less well known is an equally important aspect of sovereignty which may be termed *parliamentary monopoly*. This means that all governmental power should be channelled through Parliament in order that it might be subject to legitimation and over-sight by the Commons. There was a belief in the nineteenth century, albeit not universally shared but held by Dicey, that the Commons could and did control the executive; *and* that all public power should be subject to legislative oversight.[2]

Second, Dicey then used the rule of law to reinforce sovereignty in the sense of parliamentary monopoly.[3] How did he achieve this? The Diceyan rule of law has what may be termed both a descriptive and a normative content. In *descriptive terms* it was assumed that the regular law predominated, that exercise of broad discretionary power was absent and that all people were subject to the ordinary law of the realm. All public power did in fact reside with Parliament. In *normative terms* it was assumed that this was indeed a better system than that which existed in France, where special rules and a distinct regime existed for public law matters. It was "good" that all law should be regular law, duly enacted and legitimated by Parliament.

Thus democracy was for Dicey unitary, in the sense that all public power was channelled through Parliament. This democratic system was also "self-correcting", in that Dicey believed that the Commons accurately reflected

---

[2] See the discussion below, pp. 5-7, and see Dicey, *Introduction to the Study of the Law of the Constitution* (10th ed., 1959), pp. 73, 83, 84, 433.
[3] *Ibid.* pp. 188, 193.

the will of the people and controlled the executive. The all-powerful Parliament would not therefore be likely to pass legislation which was contrary to the wishes of the electorate.

(2) UNITARY DEMOCRACY, THE ULTRA VIRES PRINCIPLE AND ADMINISTRATIVE LAW

It was this conception of democracy which provided the framework within which to place administrative law. Dicey did not give any extensive attention to this, principally because he misconceived the scope of administrative power which actually existed when he wrote. Notwithstanding this error, it was the conceptual foundation of unitary democracy, buttressed by the rule of law, that provided a fitting base to legitimate the judicial power which the courts were in fact exercising in this area. The connection can be expressed as follows.

It is readily apparent that the execution of legislation may in fact require the grant of discretionary power to a minister or agency. Parliament may not be able to foresee all eventualities and flexibility may be required to implement the legislation. The legislature will of necessity grant power subject to conditions. For example *if* a house is unfit for habitation a minister may order its demolition. Herein lies the modern conceptual justification for judicial intervention. It was designed to ensure that the sovereign will of Parliament was not transgressed by those to whom such grants of power were made. If authority had been delegated to a minister to perform certain tasks on certain conditions, the courts' function was to check that only those tasks were performed and only where the conditions were present. For the courts not to have intervened would have been to accord a legislative power to the minister or agency by allowing them to "legislate" in areas not specified by the real legislature, Parliament.

The less well known face of sovereignty, that of parliamentary monopoly, thus demanded an institution to *police* the boundaries which Parliament had stipulated, and the *ultra vires* principle was the doctrinal tool used to achieve this end. This principle expresses two related ideas. One is that those to whom power has been granted should only exercise that power within their designated area. In this narrow sense the *ultra vires* principle expresses the idea that the agency must have the legal capacity to act in relation to the topic in question: an institution given power by Parliament to adjudicate on employment matters should not take jurisdiction over non-employment issues. In a broader sense the *ultra vires* principle has connoted the existence of a number of constraints upon the way in which the power given to the administrative agency has been exercised: the agency must comply with rules of fair procedure, it must exercise its discretion to attain only proper and not improper purposes, it must act on relevant and not irrelevant considerations and it must not act unreasonably.

Now it would be mistaken to assume that the judiciary originally conceived of intervention in these terms. The origins of judicial review are complex, and are interwoven with the intricacies of the prerogative writs.[4]

---

[4] de Smith, "The Prerogative Writs" (1951) 11 C.L.J. 40, and "Wrongs and Remedies in Administrative Law" (1952) M.L.R. 189; Jaffe and Henderson, "Judicial Review and the Rule

The motivation behind early judicial review resided principally in the desire to ensure the predominance of the High Court over "inferior jurisdictions", and to provide remedies to those whom the established judiciary felt had been unjustly or illegally treated by such authorities. In striving to attain these objectives the court could indeed often come into direct conflict with the legislative will.

Notwithstanding this continuing tension, the rationale for judicial review was slowly transformed in the nineteenth century. The twin rationales for early judicial review continued to exist. They were, however, supplemented by a growing tendency to relate the exercise of judicial power to the will of Parliament. The *ultra vires* principle became the justification for judicial intervention, and set the boundaries for that intervention. It did so in two distinct albeit related ways.

On the one hand, the judiciary began to justify the exercise of jurisdictional control more specifically and explicitly in terms of ensuring that the tribunal in question did not usurp or extend the area over which the legislature had granted it jurisdiction. The objective was to ensure that the agency did not act *ultra vires* by regulating behaviour or legislating in areas outside of those delegated to it by Parliament. Conflicting cases were reconciled by reasoning that the legislature had intended differing agencies to possess different amounts of power and that this was evident in the empowering legislation.[5] This explanation was generally unconvincing. Reference to the particular statutory grants of power in the conflicting cases gives no indication that the results could be reconciled by differences in legislative intent. The questionable nature of the reasoning did not destroy the utility of the conceptual tool. The courts would simply police the boundaries made manifest by the particular legislative grant of authority, preventing the agency from entering in areas where the real legislature, Parliament, had forbidden it to tread. The courts acquired a malleable tool through which to justify intervention with administrative behaviour.

On the other hand, the courts became more aware, in form at least, of the legitimate limits to the exercise of judicial power. If the administrative agency *was* within its assigned area, then it was performing tasks allocated to it by the legislature. It was not contravening the legislative monopoly possessed by Parliament which had chosen to delegate this function to the agency. The courts should be wary of substituting their view for that of the chosen agency, and many of the judicial limits on the way in which discretion could be used were justified as applications of statutory intent.[6]

The connection between this approach by the courts and Dicey's rule of law was a natural one. The flexibility inherent in the idea of legislative intent preserved the veneer that the courts were simply applying the legislative mandate when controlling "inferior" jurisdictions. Dicey's rule of law added respectability to this exercise of power by entrenching the idea that it was natural, right and a matter of constitutional principle that the

---

of Law: Historical Origins" (1956) 72 L.Q.R. 345; Henderson, *Foundations of English Administrative Law* (1963); Rubinstein, *Jurisdiction and Illegality* (1975).
[5] See below, pp. 352-353.
[6] See pp. 405-409.

ordinary courts should be supreme and that the ordinary law should be all pervasive. The consequences of this model will now be assessed.

2. The Implications of the Traditional Ultra Vires Model

(1) ULTRA VIRES: THE FORM OF JUDICIAL INTERVENTION

The model outlined above helped to shape the very form of judicial intervention in the following way. There is a distinction between appeal and review. The former is concerned with the merits of the case, in the sense that the appellate court can substitute its own opinion for that of the initial decision-maker. Appeals can lie on fact and law, or simply upon law. Such rights of appeal are statutory, and the courts possess no inherent appellate jurisdiction. Review is, at least in theory, different from this. It is concerned not with the merits of the decision, but with its "validity" or with the "scope" of the agency's power. The courts' power of review is not based upon statute, but upon an inherent jurisdiction within the superior courts.

An interesting and important question is why the courts possess this inherent power. It is by no means novel. Indeed the texts of early administrative cases are replete with the language of review and jurisdiction. The original rationale for this inherent jurisdiction was obviously linked to the reasons given above for the development of judicial review: a desire by the courts to control inferior agencies and to protect the individual from illegalities committed by them. Nonetheless the development of the traditional model in the nineteenth century served *both* to strengthen the rationale for this inherent jurisdiction *and* to reinforce the division between review and appeal.

It achieved the former by linking the basis for intervention to the enforcement of the legislative will. All grants of power by Parliament can be expressed in the following terms: if X exists, you may or shall do Y. For example, if an employee is injured at work a tribunal may or shall grant compensation. The inherent jurisdiction of the court was therefore strengthened by the insistence that it was simply deciding whether X did exist and what considerations could be taken into account when determining Y. The courts, it could now be argued, must possess this inherent jurisdiction to safeguard the legislative monopoly of Parliament.

It achieved the latter by insisting that when the court was enforcing the legislative will it was only undertaking review and not appeal. The court was simply determining the "validity" of the agency behaviour. The merits were for the agency itself which had been assigned the task by Parliament. This may all appear to be conceptually neat, if not elegant. It has however produced a host of problems which will be examined more fully below.

(2) ULTRA VIRES: THE SHAPE AND SCOPE OF JUDICIAL INTERVENTION

The traditional model has had a profound effect upon the shape and scope of judicial intervention in three distinct ways.

First, it has accorded centre stage to control by the courts of administrative agencies. This is regarded as the main purpose of administrative law. The vigorous assertion of the supremacy of the ordinary law, which is seen as the vehicle through which to vindicate Parliament's legislative monopoly, is directed towards *controlling* or *containing* the bureaucratic organs of the state. Such agencies are viewed with implicit distrust and there is dissatisfaction with the role of the state which is producing this abundance of administrative institutions. External control through the courts is seen as the principal means of containing agency power.[7]

A second consequence of the traditional model has been to foster a *generalist* as opposed to a *functionalist* approach to judicial intervention and to administrative law more generally. There has been a reluctance to admit special regimes. The legacy of the rule of law has been that all rules of the legal system should be equally applicable to all. General rules did not, on the whole, have to be modified when thinking of social welfare as opposed to industrial disputes, or tax as opposed to competition law. This is not to say that the courts would never take account of such differences. A generalist rather than functionalist approach is nonetheless implied by the traditional model.

A third consequence of this model has been to foster judicial activism in the following sense. The basic thrust behind this approach is, as we have seen, that the ordinary courts and the ordinary law are superior to all else, and that these are the organs which will safeguard the legislative monopoly of Parliament by policing the boundaries of legislative intent through the *ultra vires* principle. In the event of a difference of opinion between the courts and an agency as to the meaning which should be given to one of these legislative conditions, the tendency of the traditional model is to prefer the opinion of the reviewing court, provided that this can be reconciled with the idea of review on the grounds of "validity". The distinction between "validity" and the "merits" is, as we shall see,[8] an elusive one. Almost any scope of judicial intervention can be formally reconciled with the idea that the courts are thereby effectuating the intent of the legislature and simply intervening to determine the validity of the agency's decision.

Our previous example can be used to demonstrate this quite simply. Parliament has passed a statute which states that "if an employee is injured at work, he or she may be granted compensation." This statute contains three legislative conditions: the existence of an employee, the presence of an injury, the occurrence of which happens at work. Let us imagine that the court differs from the agency in the meaning to be given to one of these phrases, even though the agency interpretation is a reasonable one. Is this an error and if so does it go to the validity of the agency's power? This is, as we shall see, a difficult question, the answer to which depends ultimately upon whose interpretation of the particular terms is to be given precedence. The courts themselves have differed radically in their answer to this question over the years.[9] However, a court which does wish to intervene can do so with ease. It can argue that the interpretation of any question of law, or mixed fact and law, is one which the legislature intended to be for

---

[7] See also, Harlow and Rawlings, *Law and Administration* (1984), Chap. 1.
[8] Chap. 10.
[9] See pp. 350-362.

the court; that the courts are the arbiters on all such issues and that any such error therefore goes to the validity of the agency's decision.

(3) THE RANGE OF PROTECTED INTERESTS: THE AMBIT OF NATURAL JUSTICE AND STANDING

We have thus far considered the ways in which the traditional model and the *ultra vires* principle have affected both the form and scope of judicial intervention. They have also had an effect upon the range of interests which are regarded as coming within the ambit of administrative law. This can be explained as follows.

Administrative law has what may be regarded as certain *gateways*, methods of getting *into* the system. Thus the rules of natural justice tell us who is entitled to be heard before an agency makes its decision; and the rules of standing inform us as to who should be able to complain to the court that an agency has overstepped its powers. A notable feature of administrative law has been the insistence that only those who possessed private rights in the traditional sense of a cause of action in contract or tort, etc., were to be allowed into the system. The gateways were barred to those who did not possess such rights.[10]

There is no doubt that the preoccupation of the common law with traditional rights is a partial explanation of this phenomenon. However the judicial attitude fitted well with the traditional model. The judicial function was to police the boundaries of the legislative intent through the *ultra vires* principle, with the consequence that the private autonomy of the individual was protected by confining the public body to its assigned area. The only types of private autonomy which the courts would recognise were however rights derived from contract, tort, etc. Only those who had such rights could use the gateways. The idea that the ordinary law was being applied by the ordinary courts was reinforced by this restriction on the range of protected interests. It strengthened the belief that the court was doing no more than applying standard notions of contract or tort to cases where the defendant happened to be a public body.

We should pause here to notice a tension inherent in the traditional model which explains much of the complex case law on natural justice and standing: the twin objectives of policing the frontiers of legislative intent and protecting only traditional private rights could conflict. This important point can be simply demonstrated. Imagine that the court is faced with licensing legislation which does not give those affected rights in the traditional sense. A disappointed applicant could not construct a case in contract or tort, etc. The court may, however, be eager to fulfil its policing role. Something has to give. *Either* the court gives up its policing role in this area, *or* it relaxes the definition of "right" and thereby widens the gateways available to the citizen. Which of these occurred? The answer is both, or more accurately the courts sometimes did one and sometimes the other, hence the resulting complexity in the case law.[11]

---

[10] See pp. 479-485.
[11] *Loc. cit.*

(4) THE TYPE OF PROCEDURAL PROTECTION

The traditional model has also had an influence upon the very meaning which should be given to "procedural rights". When lawyers think of procedural rights, they tend to think of the rules of natural justice. The twin elements of this idea are a right to be heard and a right to an unbiased hearing. An individual should be entitled to such rights before certain types of decision are made which affect him or her. These are the rules which the courts have generally imposed upon administrative agencies. They assume a method of decision-making which lawyers call adversarial adjudication. The parties will present their arguments to the relevant agency which will judge which party has the better case.

The traditional model has helped to shape this notion of process rights in the following way. If we assume, as the traditional model does, that the ordinary law is being applied by the ordinary courts to cases involving administrative agencies, then it becomes natural to assume also that the type of process rights which such agencies should have to follow will be the same as those which are employed by the ordinary courts. The procedure in these courts is the epitome of adversarial adjudication. Barristers present their arguments and do battle with their adversaries before an unbiased judge. Agencies should therefore have to comply with the same type of procedure. Three consequences follow from this reasoning:

First, it helps to explain the prevalence of the distinction between "administrative" and "judicial" proceedings which is a prominent feature of some of the mid-twentieth century case law.[12] If the procedure before an agency was to assume the form of adversarial adjudication then certain courts felt that this was only suitable if the agency was itself in some sense "judging" a matter between two opposing litigants. If it could not be said to be doing this and was only engaged in "administration", then no procedural rights should be available to these parties.

Secondly, and more importantly, the traditional model helps us to understand the unwillingness of the courts to grant process rights in "legislative" contexts. Courts have been generally reluctant to interfere when an agency is, for example, making a rule of a generalised nature rather than engaging in individualised adjudication. In particular the courts have been largely negative when faced with pleas to grant interested parties hearing rights before the agency makes the rule, unless the legislature has specifically authorised this.[13] The flaws in this reasoning will be examined later. The judicial response did, however, fit the "logic" of the traditional model in a double sense.

On the one hand, it might be difficult to apply process rights which were designed for "judging", to a situation when someone was "legislating". On the other hand, even to accept that any process rights might be necessary would be to challenge the foundation of the unitary vision of democracy. Let us remember that this embraced the idea that all public power was exercised by Parliament, either directly or indirectly through ideas such as ministerial responsibility. Parliament was the sole body which legislated,

---

[12] See pp. 283-285.
[13] Some change in this attitude is evident in more recent case law, see pp. 256-258.

and all such legislation was legitimated through parliamentary processes. The public participated through the vote and then indirectly and vicariously through their MP. To admit that the agencies might make rules of a legislative nature and that people should be given process rights to participate in their formation, would be to challenge the whole idea that our democracy really was unitary. It would be to accept the idea that bodies outside Parliament legislated, and that the ordinary parliamentary processes could not adequately control such norms.

The third consequence of modelling procedural rights after those of the ordinary courts has been to constrict experimentation with other types of process right. The essence of this important theme is not difficult and can be explained here.[14] If the courts always insist that the process rights before an agency are to be mirrored on those of the ordinary courts even if in a modified way, then it also follows that the agency is presumed to be in some way "judging" between two sides. The type of decision-making is adjudication and the species of process rights reflects this. Now we might decide that certain types of agency decision-making should not take the form of judging, but should rather, for example, be like arbitration, resort to chance[15] or managerial discretion. Distinctive process rights which protect and reflect these types of decision-making will be required. The traditional model with its assumption that process rights must be like those of the ordinary courts impedes such experimentation.

(5) TORT, CONTRACT AND PUBLIC BODIES

The final way in which the traditional model has had an impact upon present legal doctrine is in one sense the most obvious. This concerns the way in which the ordinary principles of tort, contract and estoppel should be applied to public bodies. It will be remembered that the specific focus of Dicey's attack upon the French system related to the way in which he perceived it as giving advantageous treatment to public officials if and when they committed a wrong. The situation in England was different. The ordinary law applied to all. Special regimes did not exist. If a public officer committed a wrong then standard principles of tortious liability were applied.

How far the ordinary principles of tortious or contractual liability ought to be modified when dealing with public bodies is a topic which continues to divide commentators. The Diceyan legacy was, however, to preclude, or at least forestall, reasoned discussion on this issue by insisting that any such distinctive regime would be contrary to the rule of law. When such discourse did surface in the case law it assumed a defensive, almost apologetic, air. This has changed recently as the courts have become more willing to articulate and assess what the justifiable, distinct needs of the public body might in fact be.[16] It would however be wrong to assume that the approach engendered by the traditional model has been completely shed.

---

[14] See pp. 302-304.
[15] Not as odd as it might seem. The allocation of scarce resources, such as college housing, is often by ballot, which is an example of decision-making by resort to chance.
[16] See Chaps. 17-19.

3. *The Deficiencies of the Traditional Ultra Vires Model*

(1) INTRODUCTION

Certain of the deficiencies of the traditional model have already been touched upon in the preceding discussion. A more structured survey of these and other difficulties is however warranted.

At the most basic level the traditional view was flawed because the premises about the way in which democratic society operated were themselves false. The idea of unitary democracy and legislative monopoly in which all public power was channelled through Parliament, and in which Parliament controlled the executive, was upset by two realisations. On the one hand, there was the growing awareness that the legislature did not in fact control the executive but vice versa. Legislation became the prerogative of the executive and parliamentary acquiescence was ensured by the managers of the party machine. On the other hand, there was an increasing realisation that Parliament did not in fact wield all public power, and that many institutions outside of Parliament exercised some species of public authority. These themes will be developed more fully later. Let us now consider their general implications for the traditional model.

(2) MISTAKE AVOIDANCE AND THE DISTRUST OF THE ADMINISTRATIVE STATE

The traditional model is based upon a distrust of the administrative state. The growth of administrative law was directly connected with the extension of governmental functions relating to the poor, the unemployed, trade regulation and the like. It became impossible to separate an evaluation of the agencies applying these laws from a value judgment of the social policies in the laws themselves. Those who disliked such social intervention, including Dicey, tended to view the agencies applying such laws with suspicion. The predominance accorded to the "ordinary law" applied by the "ordinary courts" was envisaged as a means of controlling these agencies and of maintaining judicial supervision over the substantive policies which they applied. The paramount function of the courts was essentially negative, to ensure that the agency did not make mistakes by exceeding the power granted to it.

These twin themes of mistake avoidance and distrust came to be challenged as a direct consequence of changing attitudes towards the social policies which the agencies were applying. People came to perceive the positive contributions of such policies, and academics such as Robson approached the study of administrative justice without "any ready-made assumption that every tribunal which does not at the moment form part of the recognised system of judicature must necessarily and inevitably be arbitrary, incompetent, unsatisfactory, injurious to the freedom of the citizen and to the welfare of society."[17] The consequences of this change in attitude were important. Administrative agencies were not now viewed as perfect. Defects in their operation were readily apparent. However it was no longer taken for granted that the justice dispensed by the ordinary

---

[17] Robson, *Justice and Administrative Law* (1928), p. XV.

courts and the ordinary law was necessarily better than that of agencies; nor was it felt that the sole object of administrative law was to ensure that the agency avoided making mistakes by overstepping its boundaries. A more positive desire that the agency should successfully fulfil the policy assigned to it became the focus of discussion and the courts were perceived as but one factor in fulfilling this objective.

(3) FORM AND SCOPE OF INTERVENTION: THE INDETERMINACY OF THE ULTRA VIRES PRINCIPLE

The basis of the traditional model was that the courts would preserve the legislative monopoly of Parliament by the judicial insistence that the agency remained within the area assigned to it by the legislature, and that the courts would achieve this through the *ultra vires* principle. Three problems can be identified, all of which relate to the indeterminacy of legislative intent.

The *first* problem is the difficulty of defining the scope of an institution's designated area. This has been touched upon already. The flexibility inherent in the *ultra vires* concept could preserve the veneer that the courts were simply obeying the legislative mandate, but it was precisely this flexibility which ultimately robbed the reasoning of any conviction.

This can be simply demonstrated by returning to our example of the employee who is injured at work and seeks compensation. In one obvious sense all these legislative conditions define the scope of the agency's power. There must be "an employee", "who is injured", "at work", before the agency can give any compensation. However to allow the reviewing court to substitute its opinion on all such matters would mean that the agency then only has power when the court agrees with the agency's findings, not otherwise. Any distinction between review which goes to "validity", and appeal which goes to the "merits" disappears. Courts have been aware of this conundrum and have defined jurisdictional error in differing ways, some broad, some narrow.[18] The central point for present purposes is that *almost any* such justification can be formally reconciled with legislative intent. It can always, for example, be argued that Parliament intended all questions of law to reside with the ordinary courts, or by way of contrast, that Parliament intended only that certain "preliminary" conditions be judicially reviewed. Legislative intent could legitimate almost all types of judicial control, and therefore lost its potency to legitimate any particular one.

It is this very malleability of the *ultra vires* principle which has led Sir John Laws to the conclusion that the principle is merely a tautology, in the following sense: that because the principle does not of itself indicate what is to count as a want of power, invocation of the principle amounts to saying no more than that the court will strike down what it chooses to strike down.[19] In the same vein the author notes that the *ultra vires* principle is in reality a fig-leaf, enabling the courts to intervene in decisions "without

---

[18] See pp. 350-362.
[19] Sir John Laws, "Illegality: The Problem of Jurisdiction", *Judicial Review* (Supperstone Q.C. and Goudie Q.C. eds., 1992), p. 52.

an assertion of judicial power which too nakedly confronts the established authority of the Executive or other public bodies."[20]

A *second* related problem, is that the traditional model came under particular strain when the legislation which emerged seemed to preclude judicial interference. Imagine that our statute now reads, if a minister *thinks* that an employee is injured at work then compensation may be granted, or it states explicitly that the minister's determination of the issue should be *conclusive*. If the courts are simply enforcing the boundaries of legislative intent through the *ultra vires* principle, then should not their role be limited or precluded in such instances? If the answer is no, then the traditional model would now have to be modified to accommodate the idea that the judiciary were not simply *implementing* legislative intent, but were also *supplementing* it, through the existence of certain judicially developed principles which would be implicitly read into any legislation. This idea has considerable historical lineage,[21] but the content of the resulting principles can, as we shall see, be problematic.

A *third* difficulty is more general and relates to the changing nature of the legislation which the courts have to interpret. We have already touched upon the way in which the development of the welfare state was integrally related to the growth of administrative law; many of the "jobs" within the welfare state were administered by tribunals or agencies. This growth of the welfare state has also led to the use of more open-textured legislation and the grant of wide discretionary powers. The task of interpreting legislative intent has become correspondingly more difficult in the following sense. The traditional model assumed that laws could be relatively general, in the sense of being applicable to a large number of like cases, and relatively autonomous in the sense that the legal decisions would be reached in a manner which is different from that used by, for example, economists or politicians. The use of broad, open-textured legislation places this idea under strain.[22] If statutes are vague, forcing the courts to interpret phrases such as "public interest" and "individual need", then it may not be possible to interpret these phrases in a generalised manner; a balancing of a wide range of considerations in each instance may be required. Autonomy may be sacrificed because the very range of facts which the court has to consider when undertaking this balancing may make its decisions closely resemble political acts of the government itself. Legislative intent may provide scant guidance as to how these broadly framed discretionary powers should be interpreted. The courts are forced to form their own view as to what considerations should be deemed to be relevant and what purposes can legitimately be pursued by the agency. Legislative intent becomes more indeterminate and its application in particular instances more contentious.

---

[20] *Ibid.* p. 67.
[21] *e.g.* the rationale for natural justice was sometimes expressed as the application of implied legislative intent, and sometimes as the courts supplying the omission of the legislature.
[22] Unger, *Law in Modern Society* (1976), pp. 192-203.

(4) THE AMBIT OF PUBLIC LAW: THE STRAINING OF THE ULTRA VIRES
PRINCIPLE

A further difficulty with the *ultra vires* principle concerns the range of
institutions and the type of subject matter which are susceptible to judicial
review. The problem can be presented as follows.

The *ultra vires* principle is most readily applicable to *statutory powers*
wielded by *traditional public bodies*. There are, as we have seen above, very
real problems with applying the doctrine even in this context, but at the
least it makes some intuitive sense to think of the courts confining such
bodies within the ambit laid down in the empowering legislation. The
courts have, however, as will be seen below,[23] expanded the scope of public
law in a number of ways, each of which places the *ultra vires* principle
under further strain.[24] Two can be identified here.

On the one hand, the courts have applied the principles of judicial review
to *non-statutory exercises of power by public bodies*. These principles have
been held to be applicable to the prerogative and to certain forms of common law contracting power exercised by such public bodies. The rationale
for doing so has normally been that the very degree of power warrants
judicial control, irrespective of the source of the power. This may well be
so. It is, however, difficult to give real meaning to the *ultra vires* principle
in these instances quite simply because the power under scrutiny is not
delineated in the same way as statutory grants of authority. It can of course
always be maintained that any species of power must be subject to some
outer limits, and that there must therefore be some designated area outside
which it cannot properly be exercised. Yet even though this may be so it is
considerably more difficult to characterise the courts' role in these cases as
delineating the ambit of parliamentary intent.

On the other hand, the courts have for some considerable time applied
principles of a public law nature to *exercises of power by institutions which
are not public bodies in the traditional sense, in circumstances where these
bodies do not derive their power from statute*. This trend has become more
marked of late because of the reforms in the law of remedies.[25] It would
nonetheless be wrong to regard this as a recent development. The courts
have applied these principles to such bodies ever since the time when it
became meaningful to speak of judicial review and public law principles
at all. Trade associations, trade unions and corporations with *de facto*
monopoly power have, for example, been subject to some of the same
principles as are applied to public bodies *stricto sensu*. There are sound
reasons for this stance, given that such bodies may often have the same
degree or type of power as that possessed by a public institution. Yet it is
difficult to apply the *ultra vires* concept to such bodies without substantially changing its meaning. These bodies do not derive their power
from statute and therefore judicial control cannot be rationalised through
the idea that the courts are delineating the ambit of Parliament's intent.
The language of *ultra vires* can only be preserved by transforming the

[23] See Chap. 15.
[24] Oliver, "Is the *Ultra Vires* Rule the Basis of Judicial Review?" [1987] P.L. 543.
[25] See Chap. 15.

concept in the following way: the principles of judicial review are regarded as of generalised application to many institutions which wield a certain degree of power and the principles are then, if circumstances permit, read into the articles of association or other governing document under which the body operates. This step can be taken in formal legal terms. It does, however, transform the *ultra vires* concept. No longer can it be regarded as the vehicle through which the courts effectuate the will of Parliament. It becomes rather a juristic device through which these private or quasi-public institutions are subject to controls which the courts believe should be imposed upon those who possess a certain type of power.

(5) THE DEFECTS IN THE PRIVATE RIGHTS THEME

We have already seen that one of the characteristics of the traditional model was that the gateways to administrative law were only to be open to those who possessed private rights in contract, tort, etc. This aspect of the traditional model has three related defects.

We have already touched on the first difficulty with this approach. If the private rights theme were to be taken literally it would mean that the courts could not police or monitor the boundaries of legislative intent in any area, unless such rights were present. There are many areas of administrative law where legislation is passed which does not accord rights in contract, tort, etc., to the affected parties. Much licensing and social welfare legislation falls into this category. Courts which have been faced with this legislation have often ignored the need for private rights, or have defined "rights" more expansively in their desire to exercise their policing role over such legislation.

The second difficulty with the private rights theme is more important. It can be expressed as follows: even if traditional private rights are indeed present in a particular case, it would be mistaken to suppose that the case can be regarded simply as a private dispute which an individual has with a defendant who happens to be a public body. An example will demonstrate this point. Let us imagine that the public body has made a compulsory purchase order on John's property. John believes that the order is invalid. If he is correct then he will have a trespass action in tort, his private rights will be affected and he comes happily within the gateways of administrative law. However, even in this instance it is clearly mistaken to say that the case is simply one which is "about" John's private rights. *If* John wins his private rights will be vindicated. *Whether* he wins will however be dependent upon the validity of the compulsory purchase order. When arguing on this issue John will not be voicing his own private interests as such, but those of the public at large. He will be concerned with the scope of the planning legislation, of which the order is but one part. The case is not just about John's private rights or a private dispute which he has with the public body. It is about the legitimate ambit of the regulatory legislation in that area.[26]

The third defect in the private rights theme is that we have come to realise that interests which do not assume the form of rights may nonetheless be extremely important and should properly be the subject of

---

[26] See pp. 499-502.

administrative law. Legislation on social welfare, race relations, sexual equality, licensing and trade regulation, may seriously affect people even if the legislation does not accord them rights. Whether people should, for example, be accorded a right to social welfare is much debated. However, even if such legislation does not do so, but remains in more open textured discretionary terms, administrative law should be concerned with such areas. The interests at stake may be as important to the individual as are the more traditional interests in property.

Section 3. Rights, Legality and Abuse of Power

1. *Basis of the Model*

The defects of the traditional model of public law have been presented above. What then is to replace it? Criticism of traditional orthodoxy is all very well, but we must have something to put in its place. An approach which is becoming more prevalent as of late is to argue for a rights-based conception of public law, which is openly and unashamedly concerned with the imposition of certain standards of legality and which is designed to prevent the abuse of power both by public bodies *stricto sensu*, and by a range of other quasi-public or private bodies which possess a certain degree of power. On this view judicial intervention is no longer premised on the idea that the courts are simply applying the legislative will. Their role is to articulate a number of principles which should guide the exercise of administrative action and to interpret legislation in the light of these principles.

But what more specifically do we mean by a rights-based approach, and what are the standards of legality which are to be applied? There are, as will be seen, a number of possible interpretations which can be given to these ideas and it is important at the outset to clear the ground by delineating some of the possible meanings. It will become apparent in the course of the analysis that the approach presently under consideration is not a substitute for considering some background ideas of justice and the like, but rather a general programme the more precise implications of which will in fact depend upon the theory which is poured into it.

2. *Interpretations of the Model*

The implications which flow from this approach to administrative law will, as indicated above, depend upon the more particular interpretation which is given to this set of related ideas. A number of such interpretations will be examined within this section.

(1) A RIGHTS-BASED APPROACH:
THE PROTECTION OF FUNDAMENTAL RIGHTS

One common element of a rights-based approach is that the courts should whenever possible be interpreting legislation and the exercise of administrative discretion to be in conformity with fundamental rights. It is accepted that the courts cannot at present actually invalidate primary legislation because of parliamentary sovereignty. Every attempt should, however, be made to construe such legislation and discretion exercised pursuant thereto to be in conformity with fundamental rights. This can be achieved through, for example, the creation of strong judicial presumptions that legislation is not intended to interfere with these rights, combined with a more intensive, searching scrutiny which demands greater justification of discretionary decisions impinging upon such important interests. The courts have, as will be seen below, begun to take important steps in this direction.[27] Precisely which rights should be held to fall within this protected sphere is, as will be seen, more controversial.

(2) A RIGHTS-BASED APPROACH: APPROACH (1) PLUS THE ARTICULATION OF PRINCIPLES OF GOOD ADMINISTRATION

A second interpretation of a rights-based approach builds upon the first in the following way. Fundamental rights are to be protected in the manner indicated above, but the courts should, in addition, openly articulate a number of procedural and substantive principles. The range of these principles varies, but normally includes ideas such as: legality, procedural propriety, participation, openness, rationality, relevancy, propriety of purpose, reasonableness, legitimate expectations, legal certainty and proportionality. The object is to render the holders of power accountable. These holders of power certainly include public bodies, and governmental agencies. Some would go further and apply the principles to private bodies which exercise a like degree of power. Two related comments upon this view are warranted at this juncture.

One is that many of these principles are of course similar to those which the courts have traditionally applied within the confines of the *ultra vires* principle, although it would under this newer model be easier to apply them to quasi-public bodies than it was hitherto.

The other is that we should not too readily assume that uncertainties which led to criticism of the *ultra vires* principle will necessarily be absent in this new order. An example will demonstrate this point quite simply. We have already seen how the indeterminacy of the *ultra vires* principle was one of the grounds on which it was criticised: the content of the principle could be interpreted in whichever way the court wished. It should not, however, be assumed that this type of problem will somehow magically disappear in the new order. Ideas such as legality are just as malleable as those which they replace. The presence of this type of control as one of the principles of good administration does not resolve any of the difficulties which surround the concept. Does, for example, this term mean that the courts should always substitute their view on the meaning of every condition which comprises the jurisdiction of the administrative body? Does it provide any clue as to which of the conditions making up a body's area of power are to be treated as matters of law? Does it tell us how intensively the court should be reviewing the way in which discretion is exercised? The

---

[27] See pp. 411-432.

answer to all these questions is no. The only way in which the mere invocation of a term such as legality could possibly provide such answers is if that term were somehow to be taken to incorporate in and of itself the answers to these difficult issues concerning the respective competence of agencies and courts. This would, however, simply conceal these issues or treat the resolution of them in a way which is thought to be self-evident even though it manifestly is not.

(3) A RIGHTS-BASED APPROACH: A PARTICULAR THEORY OF LAW AND ADJUDICATION

A third possible meaning which could be accorded to the idea of a rights-based approach to public law draws more specifically upon a particular theory of law and adjudication. The result may encompass the ideas mentioned in the previous two sections, but the approach is potentially more far-reaching.

A rights-based view of law and adjudication is commonly associated with the important work of Ronald Dworkin.[28] This is certainly not the place for any thorough examination of this theory of law, but the relevance of this work for our present purposes can be sketched quite briefly.

Dworkin's theory of adjudication is based on law as integrity. According to this theory, "propositions of law are true if they figure in or follow from the principles of justice, fairness and procedural due process that provide the best constructive interpretation of the community's legal practice."[29] Space precludes any detailed analysis of this theory, but it is integral to the Dworkinian approach that, subject to questions of fit, the court should choose between "eligible interpretations by asking which shows the community's structure of institutions as a whole in a better light from the stand-point of political morality".[30] On this view of law and adjudication an individual will have a right to the legal answer which is forthcoming from the application of the above test.

Any view of public law must be based upon some view, explicitly or implicitly, of law and the adjudicative process, and the view propounded by Dworkin has many attractions. It can and has been used as a means of justifying the existence of certain individual rights; as a way of giving a more particular interpretation to those rights; and as an interpretative device through which to decide which types of protections should be available even in cases where no fundamental rights are at stake at all. It is in this sense that a rights-based view of public law could be said to be one which draws upon the work of Dworkin.

3. *General Implications of the Model*

The general implications of the model must be carefully evaluated. It will be argued within this section that the nature of these implications can only

[28] *Taking Rights Seriously* (1977), and *Law's Empire* (1986).
[29] Dworkin, *Law's Empire* (1986), p. 225.
[30] *Ibid.* p. 256.

be assessed by looking behind the particular formulations in order to reveal the background ideas which serve to imbue the model with content. This can be demonstrated both as matter of first principle, by considering arguments derived from the rule of law and by reflecting upon more concrete experience overseas and at home.

(1) THE ARGUMENT FROM PRINCIPLE

Let us begin with the Dworkinian approach because the point being made here is of particular relevance to this approach. The matter can be stated quite shortly. Those who adopt this view are committed also to the view that law and adjudication necessitate some political theory or background set of ideas which will provide the criteria of justice and fairness which the theory requires in order to resolve questions in any particular case. It is, in this sense, simply not open to those who wish to adopt a Dworkinian methodology to deny this, since in doing so they would be contradicting the very theory which they purport to apply. That theory is based upon ideas of justice and fairness which will flesh out the results which should be arrived at in a particular case, and those ideas are themselves based upon a particular set of political principles which make the theory operative. Two related consequences follow from this.

On the one hand, it is not enough when applying this view simply to articulate some general concept of liberty or equality and then purport to derive particular legal conclusions therefrom. It is precisely because differing *concepts* of justice are themselves based upon differing *conceptions* of, for example, liberty and equality that application of this view requires the articulation and defence of one particular vision of these general ideas.

On the other hand, it is clear that those who subscribe to the Dworkinian view of law and adjudication may reach differing conclusions, not just in the sense that they differ as to what the implications of the same theory of justice should be in a particular case, but also because they may differ as to what the best theory of justice actually is. Thus while certain extreme political theories such as fascism might well not pass the threshold test of fit, Dworkin readily admits that theories other than liberalism, such as utilitarianism or communitarianism, could lay claim to be those which should be employed in applying the adjudicative technique described above.[31] It would then be a matter of deciding which of these contending theories really did provide the best conception of justice. Those who believe in other political theories have indeed drawn upon the Dworkinian methodology to support their own conclusions.[32]

Now it might be felt at this juncture that it would be better to adopt one of the other two interpretations of a rights-based model, and that this would obviate the difficulties which are presented by choosing the Dworkinian technique. Is this in fact so? Can versions 1 or 2 outlined above avoid these problems? They cannot in fact do so for the following reasons.

---

[31] *Ibid.* pp. 408-409.
[32] *e.g.* Michelman, "Foreword: Traces of Self-Government" 100 Harv. L. Rev. 4 (1986).

First, both versions require the courts to interpret and apply fundamental rights in the manner described above. The very choice as to what are to count as fundamental rights, *and* the more particular meaning ascribed to such rights, will reflect certain assumptions as to the importance of differing interests in society. This is unavoidable.

It may well be argued, by way of response, that we all broadly agree upon what are to count as fundamental rights within a liberal democracy, and that therefore the conundrums are not in reality as difficult as might have been thought.

This will not withstand examination. It is of course true that any democracy to be worthy of the name will have some attachment to particular liberty and equality interests. If, however, we delve beneath the surface of phrases such as liberty and equality then significant differences of view become apparent even amongst those who all subscribe to one version or another of liberal belief. This leaves entirely out of account the issue as to how far social and economic interests ought to be protected. It also fails to take account of other visions of democracy, of a communitarian rather than liberal nature, which might well interpret the civil/political rights and the social/economic rights differently.[33]

The difficulties can, therefore, only be avoided if we assume a particular model of democracy, which carries with it a certain conception of liberty and equality, and a given hierarchy between these rights and those of a social/economic nature. But this amounts to saying no more than that matters are rendered easier if we presume the answer to the question in issue.

The second reason why versions 1 and 2 of the rights-based approach will take on a different colour depending upon the more general background set of beliefs against which they are read relates to the elements other than fundamental rights. The point can be stated quite shortly and will be developed more fully below. Ideas such as rationality, participation, openness, proportionality, procedural fairness and the like can be given significantly different interpretations depending upon the more general scheme into which they are to fit.

A brief example will serve to demonstrate this. Should participation be limited to those who are party to a legal suit which specifically affects their rights as defined in a traditional sense? Should it be extended to cover situations in which no such rights are at stake, where an agency is making rules which affect the general interests of a particular group? Should we be aiming to foster participation by groups which are disadvantaged in the political "market place"? The scope of participation rights will differ markedly depending upon the answers to these questions, and these answers will themselves be reflective of more general background beliefs. Much the same can be said of many of the other principles included within option 2.

This does not mean that we should not strive to attain and apply these principles within our administrative law. It does mean that two systems of administrative law, each of which possessed such principles,

---

[33] See generally, Kymlicka, *Contemporary Political Philosophy* (1990); Plant, *Modern Political Thought* (1991).

could, nonetheless, be very different if the meaning ascribed to these terms varied significantly.

(2) THE RELEVANCE OF THE RULE OF LAW

Now it may be argued that one way of avoiding the difficulties identified above is to seek to base this newer view upon the rule of law. Let us consider whether this is plausible. Space precludes any detailed examination of the range of meanings which have been given to this concept, but two interpretations can be contrasted.

In one sense the rule of law is primarily a *formal* concept. It is a constitutional concept which demands that there should be lawful authority for the exercise of power, *and* that individuals should be able to plan their lives on the basis of clear, open and general laws. On this hypothesis the rule of law tells us little as to the *content* of the laws which should operate within society: the rule of law is not the rule of the good law, and the dictates of the principle can be met even by non-democratic societies.[34] On this view the rule of law cannot provide the foundation for any particular substantive rights as such.

The reason for restricting the concept in this way has been clearly articulated by Raz: if the rule of law is to be taken to demand certain substantive rights then it becomes tantamount to propounding a complete social and political philosophy and the concept would then no longer have a useful role independent of that political philosophy. Claims that a society did or did not adhere to the rule of law would simply become the mechanism for articulating these competing philosophies. It should be made clear that adherents of this formal model of the rule of law may well believe that a society ought to have certain substantive rights, and in that sense be just. The nature of these substantive rights, and their attainment, should, however, be argued out in their own terms: if you believe in justice and rights etc., then argue for such concepts, against the background of the wealth of literature which openly addresses these issues.

A second sense of the rule of law is more *substantive* in its orientation. Advocates of this view accept that the concept should have the formal connotation outlined above, but wish to move beyond this and to imbue it with a more substantive content. They are unhappy with the purely formal version of the rule of law, but they are also mindful of the dangers adverted to above of making the rule of law synonymous with some particular vision of substantive justice. They seek, therefore, to incorporate within the rule of law some substantive ideas, while at the same time trying to avoid tying these too closely to any specific substantive conception of justice.[35]

The principal problem with this second approach is precisely the difficulty of maintaining this line. The closer that one looks at certain formulations the more apparent does it become that the doctrines which are said to fall within the rule of law thus conceived are of two kinds. They are either in fact just recapitulations of the *formal* attributes of the rule of law, such as procedural due process, no retrospective punishment, and a formal

---

[34] Raz, "The Rule of Law and its Virtue" (1977) 93 L.Q.R. 195.
[35] e.g. Allan, *Law, Liberty and Justice* (1993), Chap. 2.

conception of equality, all of which are accepted by those who espouse the first sense of the rule of law. Or they stray into the adoption of a *particular substantive* view of a right, such as equality, which *is* reflective of one conception of justice.[36] We can then draw the following conclusions.

(a) If the rule of law is taken in its formal sense then it may well be capable of providing the foundation for some of the component parts of this theory, such as the desirability of reasoned decision-making, and the recognition of a concept of legal certainty. It cannot, however, provide the *complete* foundation for a theory of public law which has the protection of individual rights as one of its essential components.

(b) If the rule of law is taken to encompass certain well defined, specific substantive rights then it simply becomes a vehicle for propounding that particular political philosophy. It does not avoid the problems addressed in the previous section, but merely purports to answer them in one way.[37]

(c) If the rule of law is taken to include certain substantive as well as formal dictates, but without actually propounding one political view, then this leads to the difficulties set out above. Even if these difficulties are overcome this version of the rule of law cannot, in itself, resolve the problems mentioned in the previous section, precisely because any substantive right which is recognised, such as liberty or equality, will have to be left at a very general level in order to avoid this approach becoming the equivalent of (b). There will then be a number of competing conceptions of any such general concept of liberty or equality.

(3) THE ARGUMENT FROM EXPERIENCE OVERSEAS AND AT HOME

It might well be thought that the difficulties presented have been overplayed, and that we do not in reality have to take on board the kind of questions addressed above. This contention can be tested against experience overseas and at home.

If we consider other common law systems which possess constitutionally enshrined rights, such as the United States or Canada, then what do we find? Both systems are democratic and both evince an attachment to rights which are of relevance in constitutional and administrative law adjudication. How do writers in those systems conceptualise the subject? Do they espouse a rights-based view *without more*? The merest glance at the voluminous literature indicates that the answer is no. Some do not believe that a rights-based approach is proper at all. But even amongst those who do support such a general approach, there is considerable diversity of opinion as to whether this should be taken to mean some version of liberalism, a pluralist model, or a modified notion of republicanism. If one argued for a rights-based model without more in the United States, the

---

[36] These problems are not present in a version of the rule of law put forward by Raz which is more specifically oriented towards the situation in the UK, "The Politics of the Rule of Law" (1990) 3 Ratio Juris 331.

[37] A common, though not logically necessary, consequence of this approach is that the contentious nature of the particular substantive meaning which is given to these rights is hidden, or the arguments for any specific interpretation of the rights is oversimplified.

immediate response would be a demand for "further and better particulars" about exactly which of these contending theories one had in mind.[38]

Now of course it may be that we are different and that we really can do without this sort of theorising, trusting instead to good old domestic pragmatism. This is not plausible in part because pragmatic judgments simply tend to conceal the theoretical premises which are at stake, rather than avoid them. It is equally implausible because we in this country often do engage in just these sort of evaluative judgments. Take the recent debates about citizenship. The idea of citizenship has recently re-entered the political vocabulary with the publication of Citizen's Charters and the like by the major parties. The comments upon these documents are instructive. One prominent theme has been that the Conservatives' version of the Citizen's Charter is flawed both because it does not pay attention to the civil and political rights which are a necessary facet of citizenship, and because it conceives of citizenship too much in market-oriented terms.[39] There is much force in both of these criticisms which will be considered more fully below. What is of relevance for present purposes is that commentators have taken issue with the range and meaning of the political, civil, social and economic rights which ought to feature in any concept of citizenship. This is, of course, simply another way of articulating a background theory which one believes ought to underlie public law rights.

4. *Particular Implications of the Model: I – Traditional Pluralism*

It may be helpful to move beyond the general propositions discussed above, and to consider in more detail the differing implications which could flow from the adoption of divergent background conceptions of our subject. As we shall see this produces distinct interpretations of rights, and of many of the other ideas, such as participation, rationality, control of power, and the proper scope for judicial review. Two differing background conceptions will be considered within this section and the one which follows.

(1) INTELLECTUAL FOUNDATIONS

We have already seen that the traditional view of administrative law was itself premised upon a particular view as to how our democracy functioned. This was termed unitary democracy, to express the idea that all public power was and should be channelled through Parliament, which body possessed a legislative monopoly. When practical necessity required the delegation of power to a minister or agency the purpose of administrative law was to ensure that the agency remained within its assigned area and therefore did not trespass upon the legislative monopoly of Parliament by

---

[38] Craig, *Public Law and Democracy in the United Kingdom and the United States of America* (1990).
[39] Blackburn (ed.), *Rights of Citizenship* (1993).

exercising power outside of this sphere. This Diceyan view of administrative law (and indeed of constitutional law) was expressly challenged on the grounds that his vision of unitary democracy was both descriptively flawed and prescriptively questionable. Three strands of this challenge should be distinguished.

The *first strand* was composed of writers in the late nineteenth and early twentieth centuries who advanced an explicitly pluralist vision of democracy to replace the unitary view espoused by Dicey.[40] The views of the pluralists differed, but central themes within their argument can nonetheless be delineated.

They began by revealing the historical foundations of the unitary view of the state. The idea that sovereignty was indivisible appeared initially in the writings of, among others, Hobbes as a defence against anarchy. Only if the state was all powerful could a breakdown in society be prevented. If groups or associations were rivals to the state then chaos would ensue. This political justification for the unitary state was unsurprising given the turmoil that occurred in the English civil war. This reasoning was reinforced in the nineteenth century by jurists like Austin, who argued in a more analytical vein, that it was simply not possible to have a sovereign who was limited in any way. Dicey then built on Austin. In a democracy where the people elected MPs who represented their views and controlled the executive, it was "right" that this central power should be all embracing. The democratically elected Parliament did have and should have all public power.

Having revealed the foundations of the unitary view, the pluralists then proceeded to challenge them. They presented both descriptive and prescriptive arguments.

In *descriptive terms*, they contested the idea that all public power was in fact wielded by the state. They pointed to pressure groups which shaped and constrained state action. Religious, economic and social associations exercised authority, and took part in decisions of a public character. "Legislative" decisions would often be reached by the executive, after negotiation with such groups, and would then be forced through the actual legislature.

In *prescriptive terms*, group power was applauded rather than condemned. The all powerful unitary state was dangerous. Liberty was best preserved by the presence of groups within the state to which the individual could owe allegiance. Decentralisation and the preservation of group autonomy were to be valued.

This vision of political pluralism was complemented by a concern with the social and economic conditions which existed within the state. There was a strong belief that political liberty was closely linked with social and economic equality. This influenced the pluralists' approach to the emergent regulatory welfare legislation which was passed in the early decades of the twentieth century. Such legislation was viewed in a favourable light, being

---

[40] *e.g.* Laski, *Studies in the Problem of Sovereignty* (1917), *Authority in the Modern State* (1919), and *Foundations of Sovereignty* (1921); Figgis, *Churches in the Modern State* (1913); Barker, *Reflections on Government* (1942).

one step in the alleviation of social and economic hardship and therefore of
central importance to the effective operation of a pluralist democracy.

A *second strand* of the challenge to the unitary vision of democracy has
assumed a slightly different form. Its thrust is implicitly, rather than
explicitly, pluralist. The essence of this argument is as follows. The unitary
vision of democracy is flawed not just because public power is exercised by
groups outside of the parliamentary process. It is also misleading because
even those rules which are formally legitimated by Parliament are not really
properly scrutinised by them. Pressures of time, and executive dominance
of the legislature combine to ensure that legislative control over, for
example, secondary legislation is minimal. In addition, departmental policy
choices which are made pursuant to the implementation of legislation may
be inadequately thought through, with the consequence that there is no
proper consideration of differing ways to attain legislative goals. Accountability is reduced to a minimum because there is no realistic method of
testing the departmental policy choice, ministerial responsibility itself being
ineffective.[41]

How then does this type of argument have pluralist implications? The
answer, in outline at least, is simple. If Parliament cannot effectively control
such matters, and if the parliamentary legitimation is really just formal,
then we might need to think of other additional ways in which to legitimate
and control the use of public power in society. One such way is to think of
legitimation and control through citizen participation in the process of
making agency rules. Whereas the unitary vision of democracy sees all
public power as being legitimated through participation by MPs in Parliament, the pluralist vision carries the implication that power can be legitimated and constrained in more diverse ways, such as by citizen
participation. It is not therefore surprising that the provision of consultation rights was such an important part of the suggestions proffered by the
early pluralists.

A *third strand* in the challenge to the unitary state is that of
"corporatism." Now corporatism is one of those terms which has assumed
a wide variety of meanings, not all of which are mutually consistent. The
central thrust of this idea can nonetheless be conveyed in a straightforward
manner. Corporatism provides an explanation both of the form which
pressure group action will assume, and also the reasons for its existence.[42]

The *form* of interest group pressure under corporatist theory is best
viewed as a modification of pluralism. The latter depicts the political
process as one in which a relatively wide range of different groups will
affect political decision-making. Such groups will compete between
themselves for political influence and no particular group will enjoy a
monopoly of representational status with the government. Corporatist
theory depicts the form of interest group pressure differently. The principal

---

[41] *e.g.* Harden and Lewis, *The Noble Lie, The British Constitution and the Rule of Law*
(1986).
[42] *e.g.* Schmitter and Lehmbruch (eds.), *Trends Toward Corporatist Intermediation* (1979);
Cawson, *Corporatism and Welfare* (1982); Harrison (ed.), *Corporatism and the Welfare State*
(1984); Birkinshaw, Harden and Lewis, *Government by Moonlight: The Hybrid Parts of the
State* (1990).

distinction is that a particular group or groups will be accorded a privileged representational status with the government; that the government will "license" such a group to represent the interests of other less powerful groups within the same area; and that the privileged status accorded to the dominant group carries a "price", in the sense that such a group will then accept certain controls or constraints on the range of demands which it advances.

What then are the *reasons* for the existence of this type of pressure group action? The modern state is required to undertake a wide range of activities in order to correct defects in, or problems arising from, the capitalist system. Governments are forced to juggle with goals such as full employment, economic growth, the resolution of labour conflicts, inflation and the provision of protection for consumers and workers. The pursuit of these objectives necessitates discussion and collaboration with major interest groups. Such groups help to shape governmental policy and their own objectives are fashioned or constrained by the same process. Major power groups achieve their dominant representational status for a number of reasons. The government perceives obvious benefits in dealing with one bargaining agent. A relationship of trust can be built up, an understanding of the rules of the game and an assuredness that the organisation will promote an agreed policy among the relevant "constituency". Industrial concentration and economies of scale further the impetus towards the emergence of a particular interest group which will bargain and speak for the whole.

It is readily apparent from the preceding discussion that corporatist theory is to some extent at odds with classical pluralist doctrine, insofar as the latter assumes the existence of a more multiple, competitive structure amongst pressure groups. What is more relevant for our present purposes is the fundamental conflict between corporatism and the unitary view of the state which provided the basis of the traditional model. Corporatism undermines the unitary thesis in two complementary ways. On the one hand, it postulates the existence of groups which wield public power outside of the normal parliamentary process. On the other hand, it helps us to understand how the alliance between such groups and the executive can bypass Parliament. This can happen in a variety of ways. A policy may be agreed between a dominant group and the executive, which is then forced through Parliament with little opportunity for comment. Or the executive and the relevant group may simply arrive at an understanding which never sees the parliamentary light of day at all, but remains in a non-statutory form.

(2) IMPLICATIONS FOR ADMINISTRATIVE LAW

(a) Accountability and the scope of administrative law

The traditional model encapsulated a particular vision of the accountability of the administrative state. The premise behind this model which is explicit in Dicey's own work was that Parliament did control the executive, and was itself controlled by the electorate. Judicial control, based upon legislative intent and the application of the ordinary law which was designed to ensure that agencies remained within their designated area, was therefore all that was required to render the operation of the administrative state account-able. The pluralist model undermines this notion of accountability in two ways, which relate to the scope and sufficiency of intervention respectively.

First, a natural corollary of the traditional notion of accountability was that the *scope* of administrative law was essentially only concerned with those bodies to whom power had been given by statute or the prerogative. It was only where such bodies were exercising delegated power from Parlia-ment that there was a danger of encroachment on the legislative monopoly of Parliament by such an agency going outside its assigned sphere. This explains the insistence in the case law that administrative law would only regulate agencies whose power did derive from statute or the prerogative.[43] The pluralist model undermines this presupposition by its very insistence that other institutions can and do exercise public power. Any realistic vision of administrative law would therefore have to decide how to treat such institutions. The administrative state could not be rendered truly account-able unless and until this issue was resolved.

Secondly, the pluralist model also undermines the idea that the techniques of traditional theory are *sufficient* to ensure accountability even within those areas where an agency has received power under a statute. Traditional theory, with its assumptions of electoral control over the legislature and legislative control over the executive, could comfortably reach the conclusion that keeping an agency within the area designated by legislative intent would ensure that the will of the people expressed through their elected representatives would triumph. The administrative state would be tamed and accountable. This happy picture is upset by the pluralist model which recognises both the power which the executive wields over the legislature, and the fact that policy often emerges as a result of accom-modation between pressure groups and the executive. Even if we could accurately interpret legislative intent we could no longer assume that the administrative state had been rendered accountable, at least not in the sense presumed by the traditional model. We could no longer presuppose that the will of the people expressed through their elected representatives would be fulfilled. All that we could conclude would be that the will of the executive forced through the legislature was being implemented. To accept that this amounted to or could be equated with the accountability of the administrative state would be difficult.

The two ways in which the pluralist model have undermined the idea of accountability within the traditional theory provide the foundation for many of the suggestions which will be provided hereafter. All of these more detailed proposals are aimed, directly or indirectly, at rendering the notion of power within the pluralist administrative state more accountable. To talk of accountability in such broad terms does not however take one very far. Every view of administrative law is based upon some conception of accountability, including the traditional theory. It is only by exploring more specific proposals that content can be given to this idea.

---

[43] See Chaps. 14-15.

*(b) The gateways to administrative law: natural justice, standing
and intervention*

We have already seen why the traditional model tended to construe the
"gateways" to administrative law narrowly. What then are the possible
implications of the pluralist model for the breadth of these gateways?
Supporters of this model would argue both that the existing gateways
should be broadened, and that new types of gateway should be opened up.
Let us examine these ideas in turn.

Why does the pluralist model indicate that the existing gateways of
standing and natural justice should be *broadened*? The answer is not too
difficult. Let us take standing as an example. This doctrine, as we have seen,
determines the range of people who can seek judicial review of suspect
agency action. The traditional model contributed to a narrow construction
of standing. The public body exercised delegated power from Parliament
and was the arbiter of the public interest in that area. An individual could
only challenge such an agency decision, or so some cases held, where strict
private rights were at stake. In such cases the individual was simply settling
a private dispute in contract, tort, etc., which he had with the public body.

The pluralist model undermines this narrow construction. The public
body may still be conceived as the arbiter of the public interest. It is,
however, recognised that other private groups can wield "public" power
and exercise influence over the decisions which the agency reaches. The
thrust behind the pluralist argument is therefore that a third party should
be able to come to court, even if no traditional private rights are affected,
and ask the court to judge whether the result reached by the agency, in the
light of representations from a particular group, really is in accord with the
intent of the legislation. An example will make this clear. Let us imagine
that a particular agency is deciding whether to renew the franchise of a
television company. It has decided to do so after reviewing the record of the
company. A group expressing listener interests wishes to argue that the
agency has ignored certain evidence, or has not taken relevant considerations into account. It seeks standing to challenge the agency decision
before the ordinary courts. A court which accepts, even implicitly, the
premises behind the pluralist model is likely to accede to this request. The
fact that no private interests, in the traditional narrow sense of that term,
are at stake will not be conclusive. The listener group will be helping the
agency to determine the public interest; they would be regarded, in the
language of the United States' courts, as "private Attorney-Generals".

The pluralist model might also be taken to suggest that our other
principal gateway, that of natural justice, should be given a broader interpretation than it has received under the traditional model. There are two
reasons for such a development.

The first we will consider in detail below. The traditional model was, as
we have seen, reluctant to admit of procedural rights in legislative contexts.
A commitment to increased consultative rights would necessitate a reversal
of this idea. Such consultative or participatory rights are required principally in those contexts where an agency is making rules of a legislative
nature. If a statute does not accord procedural rights in such instances,

then, if we wish to develop the idea of participation, it will have to be through the ordinary courts supplying the omission of the legislature. The gateway of natural justice would have to be broadened to accommodate such a development.

The second reason why our natural justice gateway would be broadened is rather different. We have already seen that some cases held that only those with strict private rights should be afforded a hearing before an agency made its decision. The courts have, as we shall see in more detail later, moved away from this theme and have granted process rights even where no traditional substantive rights were present. The pluralist model would support this development for the following reason. We have seen that one thread in pluralist thought stresses the interconnection between economic and political liberty, and views the governmental provision of, for example social welfare benefit, as a step in this direction. Procedural protection should therefore apply before the distribution of such benefits is terminated.

We have thus far considered ways in which the existing gateways to administrative law might be broadened. What *new* gateways would be suggested by the pluralist model? The principal new gateway would take the form of a right to intervene. This could operate in two different situations.

First, there may be circumstances in which an interested group wishes to intervene in existing adjudicative proceedings before the agency itself. Our gateways do not provide much assistance. The law of standing tells us who can challenge the agency decision before the reviewing court. Natural justice indicates who should be heard by the agency before it makes a decision which relates to that individual in some fairly direct way. What one may require is an opportunity for an individual to intervene in proceedings before the agency itself even if he or she is not immediately concerned.

Why do we need such intervention rights? The answer is not difficult. Adjudication in public law areas may have far reaching implications, the effects of which are not confined to the nominal plaintiff and defendant in the actual case. A group may wish to intervene because it feels that the actual parties to the action are not putting all the arguments which are of relevance to this dispute, or that the parties have reached an accommodation with the agency which is resolving the dispute and that this does not reflect the public interest. The pluralist model which stresses the existence of group pressure on governmental agencies and accommodation between agency and group when they are making their decisions, recognises this problem. The provision of intervention rights is to help prevent such cosy accommodation. Thus in our example given above concerning the granting of television franchises, one could argue that there should be rights to intervene before the agency itself, and not simply rights to take the case on review to the ordinary courts.

Secondly, intervention rights may be required precisely because the agency has taken no action at all. An agency may well be misusing its powers by inaction, as well as by acting in an improper way. Let us suppose that it has decided not to pursue a certain issue. This decision may well have been influenced by a particular client group with which it has close relations. A dissatisfied individual may seek an order from the reviewing court to compel it to discharge its functions. Alternatively we could accord such an individual the right to bring his or her view to the agency itself, and impose an obligation on the agency to take such a view into account in deciding whether to proceed or not.

(c) Process rights: fostering participation

Consideration of the gateways through which individuals are admitted to administrative law leads naturally on to discussion of participation rights more generally.

One important implication from the pluralist model might be that we ought to foster participation in administrative decision-making to a greater extent than we do at present. The argument for enhanced participation rights, or what is sometimes termed interest representation, is in outline as follows.

Rules are often made by those who make administrative decisions. These rules can assume many different forms. Sometimes they take the form of secondary legislation; on other occasions such rules emerge naturally from the process of bureaucratic decision-making. Officials may not wish to rethink a problem on each and every occasion. The provision of a rule, guide-line or policy may save administrative time, make it easier to treat like cases alike, and allow people to plan their actions if such a rule is published. Anyway, let us assume that such a rule of a broadly legislative nature has indeed come into being for some such reason.

Now a key question is how do we legitimate and control the making of such rules? Our traditional theory tells us, as we have seen, that rules of a legislative nature should be legitimated by being passed through Parliament and subjected to scrutiny therein. However this type of control fails to achieve its goal for two related reasons: even those administrative rules which do assume the form of secondary legislation are not subject to effective parliamentary scrutiny; and there are many administrative rules which do not see the parliamentary light of day at all because they are not classified as statutory instruments.[44]

How then should we ensure the legitimacy of rules of a legislative nature in the light of these difficulties? The pluralist model suggests that participation in the making of such rules by interested parties can help to achieve this. The argument is that our democracy is representative primarily because problems of time and scale preclude any more direct form of democracy in the complex modern world. However even representative democracy may be unable, for the reasons given above, adequately to review and control all rules of a legislative nature. A direct form of input from the "bottom", in the form of citizen participation in the administrative process can therefore help in the sense of making rule-making more directly democratic and hence accountable.

The pluralist model provides support for this idea in a double sense. In *descriptive terms*, proponents of this model acknowledge that some participation from external pressure groups already exists. The degree of such participation may however be uneven, and the participatory process

---

[44] See pp. 270-277.

may be dominated by particular groups who are powerful and who have favoured relationships with the public body. Pluralists may well therefore advocate more formal participatory rights in order that a wider variety of groups can actively become involved in the administrative process. The development of such consultative rights can be viewed as a way of countering the corporatist tendencies within the modern state through which, as we have seen, a dominant group can attain "exclusive" representational status with a public body. In *prescriptive terms*, the pluralist model assumes that the decentralisation of public power which is fostered through the grant of such consultative rights is a "good thing". Liberty is best preserved by such dispersion of power. The state is rendered more accountable by allowing an element of direct democracy within the administrative process, and the problem of legitimating rules of a legislative nature which our normal organs of representative democracy cannot adequately control is alleviated.

A number of the more specific problems which will have to be addressed if we choose to enhance participation rights will be considered at a later stage.[45]

(d) The scope of judicial review

The pluralist model could affect the scope of judicial review in two ways. First, this model is more sympathetic to a functionalist approach towards such review. The generalist tendency of the traditional model has already been considered. Within this model the ordinary law is to be equally applicable to all, and the ordinary courts are superior to any other law-applying agency. There is a consequential reluctance to recognise the distinctive requirements of different subject-matter areas, and also a consequential tendency to prefer the judiciary's interpretation upon disputed questions of law or mixed fact and law which arise within the "X question". The pluralist model accepts neither of these assumptions. The idea that the meaning of legal terms should reflect and be shaped by the distinct needs of power structures within particular areas of society fits comfortably within pluralist thought; and the assumption that the interpretation of any of these terms by the ordinary courts should necessarily be preferred to that of the agency is felt to be unwarranted.

Secondly, the implications which the pluralist model has for judicial review of discretion are more controversial. Let us imagine that a discretionary decision has been made after consulting the relevant interests. How far should the court review this decision and what criterion should it use? This issue will be examined in detail later,[46] but a short "schematic" discussion is warranted here:

> (a) The basic premise should still be that the court should not simply substitute its view for that of the agency. This aspect of the traditional model has continuing validity even for those of a pluralist persuasion. Parliament has assigned the task to the agency, and the court should

---

[45] See pp. 258-262.
[46] See Chap. 11.

not overturn its decision simply because it would prefer a different decision. This much is relatively easy.

(b) It might be argued as a consequence of this that the courts should only intervene if the agency has made an arbitrary decision. Review should be very limited because any wider intervention will inevitably lead to the risk that the courts will substitute their view for that of the agency. This option is not open to the pluralist because one cannot realistically foster participation rights and countenance only such limited review. The reason is simple. We have to ensure that the agency does not just go through the motions of listening to people. If we wish seriously to enhance participation rights then we must be prepared to listen to arguments that the agency did not give adequate consideration to the views of interested parties. We cannot sanction judicial intervention only when the resultant agency decision is substantively arbitrary, because there may be many instances when it falls far short of this, but still wholly or partially ignores the views of concerned participants.

(c) It could therefore be argued that we need something "between" (a) and (b). One suggested option is that the court should take a "hard look" at the reasoning process by which the agency reached its decision and that this can be achieved without trespassing on the substance or merits of that decision.[47] The courts should play a role in forcing the agency to be more thorough in its reasoning process, and in ensuring that the views of interested parties are adequately considered. This sits comfortably with the pluralist thesis. Participatory rights which are important to the pluralist model are protected and the state is rendered more accountable because the scrutiny of its policy choices is now more thorough. The general merits and demerits of this approach will be considered below. For now one comment will suffice: the distinction between process and substance is not sustainable. A simple example will demonstrate this. Imagine that an agency with responsibility for electric power decides to build a dam in a certain way. This is opposed by environmental interests, and by property owners in the immediate vicinity. They offer evidence suggesting a better technique for dam construction which they claim is less damaging to the environment, equally efficient and causes less disruption to local property interests. The agency upholds the original scheme, and this is challenged before the courts. Under a hard look doctrine the court will require the agency to give its reasons, and will evaluate these reasons against the evidence presented by the parties. But the court cannot make any such evaluation without some prior idea as to the purposes of the statute, the relevance of both environmental and property interests in that scheme and the weight which these interests should have been given by the agency. The court is forced to consider "purpose" and "relevancy" because no decision can be reached without doing so. It is therefore not surprising that the test is framed in these terms. Nor is it surprising that the interpretation of these terms is contentious and that it involves

[47] See pp. 438-441.

some view as to the substance of the discretionary decision under review.

The pluralist model does not therefore provide an escape from the difficulties of interpreting legislative intent which beset the traditional model. Similar questions are posed albeit in a somewhat different way. Judicial intervention under the pluralist model may be premised on the more "honest" idea that the judiciary are complementing or supplementing the role of the legislature. This does not however make the answer to fundamental questions concerning the purpose of legislation and the range of interests which are entitled to be represented therein, any easier to resolve. We have no choice but to attempt to define the type of substantive considerations which the courts should be bringing to bear on this issue. This difficult question will be considered in more detail later.

(e) Remedies and the ambit of administrative law

In our earlier discussion we considered the impact which a pluralist model could have upon the "gateways" to administrative law, on those who could use the system. There is a reverse side to this same coin, which concerns the extent to which a pluralist model indicates those against whom public law principles should be applied.

The response of the traditional model has already been considered. Public law remedies applied to those whose power was derived from statute, or perhaps the prerogative. These were the agencies given power by Parliament. It followed naturally that only such bodies threatened the legislative monopoly of Parliament. Provided that these agencies were kept within the ambit of their power this monopoly would be preserved. Public law remedies, such as the prerogative orders, were therefore only applicable to such bodies.

The pluralist model undermines this complacency. Parliament is not seen as possessing a monopoly of public power. Such power is also exercised by others, including interest groups on both the capital and labour sides of the market. The consequences which follow from this realisation are less easy to predict. We may well drop the restrictive requirement that a body must derive its authority from statute before the public law remedies can "bite". Where we should go from there is less clear. It may be argued that any distinction between public and private law is impossible to draw, or more moderately, that which bodies should be subject to public law will have to be defined on an *ad hoc* basis. Which of these responses is correct will be contestable.

5. Particular Implications of the Model: II – Market-Oriented Pluralism

(1) INTELLECTUAL FOUNDATIONS

Pluralism has both descriptive and prescriptive elements. The descriptive aspect of pluralism helps us to understand how governmental decisions are made within society and the role which non-elected groups can and do play in this process. The prescriptive aspect of pluralism seeks to delineate an appropriate role for the state in the light of these "facts". Writers have drawn radically differing conclusions from these facts, and these differing conclusions have significant ramifications for administrative law. Two differing visions of pluralism have emerged.

On the one hand, there is the pluralism of those who in the early twentieth century reacted against the unitary state postulated by Dicey. These pluralists were generally left of centre politically, and this was reflected in the policies which they advocated. Their vision stressed the existence of group power, group rights and obligations, decentralisation, and the interconnection between economic and political liberty, the latter requiring governmental intervention in order to secure such liberties for the individual. This approach was always subject to an inner tension between the desire for decentralisation, and the existence of the requisite central authority to enable the desired economic objectives to be fulfilled.

On the other hand, there is a more market-based conception of pluralist democracy which is manifest in governmental policy within the late 1970s and 1980s, and which is closer to pluralism as understood in the United States.[48] This second species of pluralist democracy acknowledges the existence of group power which constrains and shapes governmental action and wishes to decentralise decision-making by devolving many spheres of governmental activity to the market. The prescriptive role for the state is conceived in different terms from that of the earlier pluralist model in part because the connection between economic and political liberty is seen from a different perspective. The market is viewed as the best "arbitrator" of economic issues, and direct governmental regulation thereof is perceived as necessary only when there is market failure, the existence of which is narrowly defined. The sphere of legitimate governmental action is therefore closely circumscribed. This second type of pluralism is also subject to inner tensions. The thesis may well be pluralist in admitting the existence of group power which constrains governmental action and albeit more controversially, by devolving decision-making in certain areas to the market. In certain respects it has, however, produced a more powerful centralised role for the government. The very fulfilment of the free market vision may, as we shall see later, require a strong central government. There is also a more overtly authoritarian element which is present within this philosophy which serves further to enhance the power of the centre.[49]

(2) IMPLICATIONS FOR ADMINISTRATIVE LAW

An understanding of these two very different pluralist visions has implications for administrative law. The full ramifications of these differences cannot be examined here. The object is to demonstrate how concepts such as rights, citizenship, participation, rationality, and the like which go to

---

[48] Craig, *Public Law and Democracy in the United Kingdom and the United States of America* (1990), Chaps. 3, 4.
[49] *e.g.* Levitas (ed.), *The Ideology of the New Right* (1986); Skidelsky (ed.), *Thatcherism* (1988); Jessop, Bonnett, Bromley and Ling, *Thatcherism* (1988).

make up the newer model of administrative law can assume very different meanings depending upon the background ideas against which they are read. Three examples will convey the differing conclusions which follow from the two visions.

(a) Rights, Citizenship and Society

The re-emergence of citizenship on the political agenda has been noted above. The term is open to a range of possible meanings and it may therefore be helpful to explain how the term will be used in this context.

Citizenship connotes the civil, political, social and economic rights which individuals presently possess, or ought to possess, within society. Which rights individuals do *presently have* will itself be affected by the particular theory of law and adjudication which is adopted. A positivist might give one answer to this question, based upon the existing corpus of statutory and common law materials. A follower of Dworkin might give a different answer if it is warranted by the application of that theory of law and adjudication. Which rights citizens *ought to have* has been one of the major preoccupations of political theory for at least two thousand years.

It is readily apparent that the conceptions of citizenship currently employed by the major political parties have differed significantly. The Conservatives' document did not deal with traditional civil and political rights at all, placing its emphasis upon the rights which consumers of services ought to have as against the service provider.[50] The documents produced by the Liberal Democrats[51] and the Labour party[52] addressed a wider range of issues which are political, social and economic in nature.

The differences which are evident in the conceptions of citizenship will therefore inevitably have an impact upon the interpretation accorded to a model of public law based upon rights, legality and the abuse of power. It will influence the particular construction given to a concept which all would agree should be part of the protected sphere of rights. It will also have a marked impact upon which rights are recognised at all. These points can be simply demonstrated.

All would agree that some concept of equality should feature within a list of protected rights, and that this should preclude differential treatment on the grounds of race, gender and the like. Disagreement normally centres upon the particular conception of equality which should be applied. Traditional pluralists tended to favour a conception of equality and distributive justice which entailed state intervention to promote greater equality in the resources held by individual citizens. The more market-based species of pluralism has a very different conception of distributive justice, which, on some versions at least, regards existing property rights as sacrosanct holdings which should not be redistributed by the state. These differences of view concerning equality and distributive justice can themselves have consequential implications for the legitimacy of state action which seeks, for example, to promote equality through affirmative action programmes.

---

[50] *The Citizen's Charter: Raising the Standard*, Cm. 1599 (1991).
[51] *Citizens' Britain: Liberal Democrat Policies for a People's Charter* (1991).
[52] *Citizen's Charter: Labour's Deal for Consumers and Citizens* (1991).

All would agree that speech rights ought to be among those which are safeguarded. Differences become apparent when we move to more specific applications of this right. Should, for example, we be attempting to protect not only these rights as such, but also the "worth" or "value" which they have? Would this serve to justify limits upon campaign expenditure?

The same theme is even more apparent when we consider which rights should fall within the protected sphere at all. Employment can be taken by way of example. Traditional pluralists, such as Laski, argued that society existed in order that citizens can realise their lives in the best possible manner. They saw a prominent connection between political and economic liberty,[53] and this provided the foundation for the analysis of the employment relationship: a citizen should have both the right to work, and certain rights while in work, including adequate wages and the ability to participate in the government of industry. Citizenship should not therefore stop at the factory gates, both because economic well-being was regarded as essential to political participation, and also because "ideas of political citizenship are as relevant in the economic as in the political arena",[54] in the sense that protection from arbitrary treatment is not something to be left at the beginning of work and "donned again at the end of a shift".[55] The market-oriented pluralist adopts a very different view of the employment relationship. Market forces should be left to govern the employment field with little in the way of rights to minimum terms or conditions of service; worker participation in the governance of the industry is not encouraged; and the collective rights of unions are closely circumscribed and subordinated in certain respects to the rights of the citizen as consumer.

The two models will therefore produce differing conclusions concerning the judicial review of discretion. The inevitability of the judiciary making some substantive judgments when evaluating agency discretion has been touched upon above and will be considered more fully later.[56] The two models embody distinct theories concerning rights and distributive justice. The results which flow from judicial review may therefore be very different depending upon which theory is adopted.

(b) Process rights and participation

The two models also produce differing conclusions concerning both the incidence and objective of participation in agency decision-making.

The *incidence* of participation is affected because both models find it necessary to place constraints on groups who are seen as opposed to the basic philosophy on which the model itself is based. The most obvious recent example of this is the constraint placed on local authorities who are opposed to the market-oriented philosophy of the Conservative government. The power of such groups is curbed and their participatory role is limited, because they are seen as jeopardising the political philosophy on

---

[53] Craig, *Public Law and Democracy in the United Kingdom and the United States of America* (1990), Chaps. 5, 6.
[54] Ewing, "Citizenship and Employment", *Rights of Citizenship* (Blackburn ed., 1993), p. 117.
[55] *Ibid.* p. 100.
[56] See pp. 433-446.

which the model is based. The earlier pluralist model also found it necessary to impose constraints, the difference being in the type of group whose power was thereby curbed, this being the power of private property. Such power had to be restrained and the participatory role of those with property rights had to be diminished, precisely because they jeopardised the philosophy which underpinned the model.[57]

The *objective* of granting participatory rights under the two models may also differ. The tendency of the market-oriented pluralist is to grant such rights to those involved in the economic activity in question, with the object of ensuring efficiency. Accountability is seen in market terms and granting participatory rights to "consumers" of the activity is justified in these terms. This theme is apparent in the Citizen's Charter, the aims of which are in part to make the service provider more accountable to the consumer. The early pluralists viewed the objective of such rights more broadly. They were to enable the individual to participate in the process of government, and to foster the full development of the individual within society.

(c) The ambit of public law

Different conclusions are also apparent concerning the type of bodies which should be run by the state. The earlier pluralist model required greater government intervention in order to secure the conditions of economic equality which were regarded as necessary for the attainment of political liberty. Nationalisation of industry, direct regulation of other aspects of economic life and economic redistribution of wealth were the consequences of this approach. The more recent market-oriented model views the meaning and connection between economic and political liberty very differently. Deregulation and privatisation are the consequences of this approach. Even where some continuing regulation of a privatised industry is felt to be required, the underlying aim of this regulation is coloured by the market-oriented vision. The purpose of such regulation is often to prevent an industry with monopolistic power from abusing its dominant position.

It is nonetheless evident that the scope of public law is a contestable issue even *within* this newer market-oriented vision. A significant body of case law has been generated on this topic, as will be seen below.[58] It is clear that the courts have moved away from the previous formalism which sought to limit the ambit of public law to those institutions which derived their power from statute or the prerogative. The tensions which this expansion has caused for the traditional *ultra vires* model of public law have been noted above. The precise metes and bounds of the wider application of public law principles are, however, still being worked out. Two separate, albeit related, questions must be distinguished when deciding upon these limits.

---

[57] One may well argue that curbing local democracy is "worse" than curbing private property. The argument in the text makes no judgment on this issue as such. Any answer itself presupposes a background political theory. The point is rather to stress that both pluralist models are forced to constrain the participatory rights of those who jeopardise the foundations on which that model is based.

[58] See Chap. 15.

The first concerns the *nature of the bodies* which should be subjected to public law principles at all. Some would restrict this to bodies which in one way or another have a connection with the state. Others would argue that principles of public law should apply to any institution which possesses power over the lives of others, irrespective of whether there is any formal connection with the state or not. Yet others adopt an intermediate position, the effect of which is that public law should be applied to bodies which possess some monopoly power over a sphere of activity, irrespective of whether the body with such power has any formal connection with the state.

The second question concerns the *nature of the principles* which should be applied to those bodies which are deemed to be part of public law. Now it might well be thought that the answer to this question is obvious: once a body is deemed to be subject to public law then public law principles should be applied to it. Matters are not so simple. The broader the answer given to the first question the more difficult does it become to assume that *all* public law principles should be deemed to be equally applicable. This can be simply demonstrated.

It might well be natural to think of *procedural* principles, such as those of fair hearings and the like, applying to bodies such as trade associations, or unions. These principles have been applied to such bodies for some considerable time. If however we think it appropriate to bring within the ambit of public law large corporate undertakings which exercise monopoly power over a particular sphere of life then matters become more difficult. Would this mean that *all substantive* public law principles would be equally applicable to such bodies? Would the exercise of corporate discretionary judgment be open to attack on the basis that relevant considerations had not been taken into account, or on the grounds of proportionality? If the answer is in the affirmative then this will have a marked impact upon the way in which our market economy operates. It is of course true that private law has placed constraints upon freedom of action in the market place. But this does not mean that public law principles can be neatly added to these, nor does it necessarily mean that the respective types of constraint operate in the same manner. If all species of power were to be regarded as public, with the consequence that procedural and substantive principles of public law became applicable, then the ramifications would be significant indeed.

6. Conclusion

It should be made clear that the particular interpretations of this second model of public law are not the only ones which are possible. It is perfectly feasible to extol different interpretations of a general approach based upon rights, legality and abuse of power. This should be apparent from the previous discussion. It may nonetheless be helpful to identify, albeit briefly, two other possible understandings of this general approach to public law.

One such interpretation has been developed more recently by Lewis.[59] He believes that public law should be based upon rights and accountability, and believes also that markets are a central part of this picture. However, this market-based perspective does not come with all the intellectual baggage of the New Right or the public choice theorists. Markets are felt to be desirable because they allow for human choice, autonomy and freedom, and government by contract can facilitate both choice and accountability. If this choice and freedom is being impaired then regulation is both necessary and desirable. Moreover certain social and economic rights are felt to be the necessary background within which the market-based perspective subsists. This approach also affords a significant place to pluralism within the political arena: there should be properly accountable institutions intermediate between citizen and state; local communities should have a real say in how they are run and there should be real opportunities for people to have an input into public decision-making.

Participatory democracy has also been suggested as a basis for administrative law doctrine.[60] The phrase participatory democracy can be employed in two very different senses.

On the one hand, it could be used in a "non-technical" general sense, to extol the benefits of participation as one goal for a political society. This first interpretation does not, however, take us very far since the extent to which a society fosters such participation will be but part of the broader political theory which it espouses. It is only by examining that broader theory that any answer concerning the nature and incidence of participation can be forthcoming.

On the other hand, the phrase could be used in a more "technical" sense, to refer to the democratic tradition reaching back to Athenian democracy, and stretching from there through the Italian republican tradition, Harrington and onwards to the American republicans of the revolutionary and independence period; or to some related variant on the communitarian theme. This *is* a specific democratic vision which entails a certain view of citizen and state. It has implications for rights, socio-economic conditions within society and for distributive justice. There is a large literature, both historical and philosophical, concerning the problems attendant upon the establishment of such a regime as well as the benefits which could ensue therefrom.[61] It is perfectly possible to suggest that society should be ordered in this way. It is not however possible for this species of democracy to exist and legitimate public power within a society which adopts a very different vision of democracy.

There are doubtless other readings which could be given to a model of public law based upon rights, legality and abuse of power. The more particular consequences of this model will, however, only become evident if we are willing to articulate the theory of justice which underpins it and which serves to give colour and meaning to its constituent elements.

---

[59] *How to Reinvent British Government* (European Policy Forum, 1993).
[60] *e.g.* Prosser, "Towards a Critical Public Law" (1982) 9 Jnl. of Law and Society 1.
[61] Craig, *Public Law and Democracy in the United Kingdom and the United States of America* (1990), Chaps. 10, 11.

2. THE ADMINISTRATIVE SYSTEM: AN HISTORICAL PERSPECTIVE

Section 1. Introduction

The type of institutions subject to administrative law include the Executive itself, fringe bodies or quangos, local authorities, tribunals, inquiries and inferior courts. This list is not exhaustive. It identifies only the main components of our administrative system.[1] Question marks as to the ambit of administrative law will recur throughout the course of this work. Nor does what follows purport to be an exhaustive historical analysis of each of those components. This would be worthy of a book in itself. What follows is a sketch of some of the main themes in the development of those institutions, together with an outline of the principal twentieth-century governmental investigations into the problems perceived to beset this developing system. Details as to the working and control of government, agencies, local authorities and the like will be considered in subsequent chapters. An understanding of the antecedents of our present set of administrative institutions is important. It enables us to comprehend how our present institutions have developed and acts as a counterweight to the often unspoken assumption that our current difficulties are generated by the present or immediate past. The twentieth century may well have produced some novel problems. Nevertheless, there is an underlying continuity in the difficulties of administrative organisation and allocation of power which can only be fully appreciated with the aid of an historical perspective. There is, moreover, something faintly absurd about discussing administrative law with only the vaguest idea of how its subject-matter has evolved.

Section 2. The Nineteenth Century

1. *General*

We have always had a somewhat messy system of administrative institutions. Bodies would be created to deal with particular problems as they arose with little thought being given to any rational allocation of

[1] This phrase is not intended to imply that the allocation of functions between institutions was guided by some rational plan.

41

decision-making. Many administrative functions were, and are, performed by the local justices of the peace, while others were undertaken by institutions such as the Commissioners of Sewers, or Turnpike Trustees. The limited size and scope of central government in the nineteenth century must be kept very much in the forefront of one's mind. In 1833 the central departments of government employed 21,305 civilian officials of which those who worked in the Revenue departments constituted the vast majority. The Home Office had a staff of 29, the Foreign Office 39, and the Board of Trade 25.[2] This is hardly the staff necessary for running a state which performs anything other than the minimum of governmental functions.

The size of central government in 1833 was not, however, simply a reflection of the more limited role played by the state in the nineteenth century. Political and pressure groups, albeit for differing and often contradictory reasons, favoured the limitation of central government.[3]

The Tories disliked expansion of central government, since this would often impinge upon the autonomy possessed by local squires and magistrates. Nor was this jealousy of local interests confined to the countryside. In areas controlled by Whigs there was a similar dislike of central influence encroaching upon local power. The Radicals had their own reasons for wishing the authority of central government to remain limited. Such expansion was seen too often to be the vehicle for the creation of new sinecures and monetary waste.

In addition there were those who were influenced by the writings of Ricardo and Adam Smith. These writers expounded the doctrines of *laissez-faire* economics in contrast to the mercantilism of the eighteenth century. The new industrialists saw in such theories a conceptual basis on which to resist governmental encroachment upon private property, whether in the form of projected factory legislation limiting hours and conditions of work or in schemes for improving health.

Private groups also resisted expansion of central authority in areas which would involve a correlative diminution of their own power. Thus voluntary institutions, schools and hospitals provided a further institutional pressure group opposed to the growth of central government.

Despite this opposition the period between 1830 and 1850 witnessed a considerable expansion in the functions performed by central government. Reform in four main areas provides the basis for this expansion: factory legislation, the Poor Law, railways and public health.[4] The advocates of these reforms had differing objectives. In the most general sense, however, the reforms were all the result of the growing industrialisation which was such a mark of the nineteenth century. For the administrative lawyer they are of particular interest because they gave rise to forms of administrative control, and debates over the appropriateness of public institutions, which

---

[2] Roberts, *Victorian Origins of the British Welfare State* (1960), pp. 14-16 (hereinafter cited as Roberts).

[3] *Ibid.* pp. 22-34. See also Lubenow, *The Politics of Government Growth* (1971) (hereinafter Lubenow), and Chester, *The English Administrative System 1780-1870* (1981).

[4] See Roberts, above n. 2, Chaps. 2-3; Lubenow, above n. 3, Chaps. 2-5; Fraser, *Evolution of the British Welfare State* (1973), Chaps. 1-4 (hereinafter Fraser).

are still very much current today. A word about the reforms themselves is, therefore, necessary in order that the institutional question can be better understood.

Factory reform was the result of the efforts of Oastler, Ashley and Sadler. Oastler was the agent for a landowner in Yorkshire whose humanitarian instincts were severely shocked after witnessing the conditions in Bradford's textile mills. This prompted him to write a letter to the *Leeds Mercury* comparing the lot of the textile worker with that of the negro slave. Oastler's tone is fierce.[5]

> "The very streets which receive droppings of an 'Anti-Slavery Society' are every morning wet by the tears of innocent victims of the accursed shrine of avarice, who are compelled (not by the coach-whip of the negro slave driver but) by the dread of the equally appalling throng or strap of the overlooker, to hasten, half-dressed, but not half-fed, to those magazines of British infantile slavery – the worsted mills in the town and neighbourhood of Bradford!!!"

Oastler was an Evangelical. So was Thomas Sadler, who took up Oastler's cry in the House. Opposition to the demand for legislation on children in factories came from a variety of sources. The factory owners were, not surprisingly, adverse to the scheme and sought support from the economic literature current at the time. Sadler was unmoved by such "scientific" reasoning, but his attempts to enact legislation were cut short by his defeat in a Leeds election in 1832. The banner of reform was taken up by Ashley. His own bill failed in 1832 but, largely as a consequence of a report produced by Sadler and the report of a subsequent commission headed by Edwin Chadwick, the Whig Government produced their own measure which was enacted as the Factory Act 1833.

While opposition to the passage of factory legislation had been strong, it did not quite equal the passions roused by the debate over the Poor Law. Prior to the nineteenth century the Poor Law was governed by the Poor Relief Act 1601. This legislation had been designed to deal differently with the aged or lunatic, the able-bodied unemployed and the able-bodied who had absconded from their own area. The idea was that the first group would be looked after, the second would be set to work and the third group would be punished. Administration was to be through the justices of the peace who were authorised to appoint overseers of the poor. The latter would levy a rate on property in their area, which fund would then be used to carry out the functions connected with the three different groups. Pressures on the system came from a variety of sources, the strongest of which was the increase in unemployment in the late eighteenth century combined with bad harvests and rising prices. Wages of those who were in employment became deficient to meet basic needs.

The early decades of the nineteenth century witnessed increasing dissatisfaction with the old Poor Law. Two general themes lay behind the disquiet. The first was the cost. In the years 1817 to 1819 the Poor Law cost £8 million, or 12s. per head of the population; by 1831 it was still

---

[5] Fraser, above n. 4, p. 233.

£7 million or in excess of 10s. per head. Moreover, the cost had not yielded the benefits of social stability.[6] The second pressure for reform came from those who believed that the old Poor Law was simply wrong, particularly the allowance system of which Speenhamland was an example. This was the age of Malthus and Ricardo. The former with his dire predictions about population growth exceeding food supplies provided ammunition for those who saw the Poor Law as encouraging hasty marriages and then providing support for the numerous offspring thereby produced. Ricardo authored the wage fund theory under which only a fixed percentage of the national wealth could be expended on wages. The reasoning step was straightforward: the sums expended on poor relief could not be spent on wages thereby creating an inexorable downward spiral in wages with more and more people being forced to become paupers.

The new Poor Law was born out of the Poor Law Report of 1834, the work of Edwin Chadwick and Nassau Senior. The workhouse test which emerged from the report was to provide much material for later Victorian literature. For Chadwick, however, the logic of the argument was unassailable. The old Poor Law, and particularly the allowance system, had simply encouraged idlers who could have worked. Poor relief had to be rendered less attractive than any other option; only in this way could the truly needy, the pauper be catered for. The workhouse test, *i.e.* the idea that relief would only be available in a workhouse, was simply an adjunct of this philosophy. The Poor Law should not be concerned with poverty as reflected in low wages, but with destitution;[7] it should be a deterrent to pauperism. The idea that there could be workers who through no fault of their own were rendered unemployed was recognised by the authors of the report but treated as an exception, an extreme to be dealt with by private charity and not by government intervention. The Poor Law Amendment Act was passed in 1834.

Health was a third area subject to governmental intervention. Growing industrialisation brought with it an increasing realisation of the health hazards that attend the presence of large groups of people with inadequate sanitary facilities. It was the organising genius of Chadwick which provided the main impetus towards reform. During his time as Secretary of the Poor Law Commission Chadwick became aware that a certain proportion of the expenditure on poor relief was being devoted to the widows and offspring of those struck down by disease. For Chadwick the realisation of this connection demanded prophylactic measures to stem the root cause of the disease.[8] His belief in the necessity for sanitary improvement grew and found its most complete expression in the 1842 Report on the Sanitary Condition of the Labouring Population of Great Britain. The report showed the clear correlation between living conditions and disease. The Chadwick Report was followed by the appointment in 1843 of a Royal Commission under the Duke of Buccleuch. The study undertaken by the Royal Commission confirmed many of the findings arrived at by the Chadwick Report,

---

[6] Fraser, above n. 4, p. 38.
[7] *Ibid.* pp. 41-42.
[8] Finer, *The Life and Times of Edwin Chadwick* (1952), p. 155.

but went further in detailed and systematic investigation than had its predecessor. Despite the weight of evidence indicating the need for reform opposition to change came from a number of sources, the combined effect of which was to render the 1848 Public Health Act a much less effective measure than its advocates had initially hoped. The rationale for the opposition varied. Some objected to the cost involved. Whereas the Poor Law reforms had resulted in cost savings compared with the allowance system, implementation of the public health programme would involve considerable expense. Expense moreover which would be borne in greater proportion by the wealthier inhabitants of an area. Arguments concerning interference with property rights thus became involved in the general debate. These concerns were overlaid by the continuing disagreement as to the correct division of function between central and local government. The spectre of a London based bureaucracy dictating how much expenditure local areas should incur was not pleasing to the bastions of the reformed municipal boroughs. As a result of these pressures the 1848 Public Health Act emerged as a shadow of the original proposals. The legislation suffered from being generally permissive rather than obligatory in character. It was to take another 30 years before the Public Health Acts 1872 and 1875 introduced obligations to be fulfilled by sanitary authorities across the nation.

Pressures for governmental action did not come solely from considerations of health or welfare. New technology produced novel problems, one of the most important of which was the development of railways. The motives for state intervention were eclectic.[9] One of the prime reasons for state action was the fear of monopoly and the ability to charge excessive prices which accompanied it. The competitive process would in its self-regulating manner normally be expected to break down monopolistic dominance and restore competitive equilibrium. In this, as in other areas, the magic wand of market forces appeared less than effective. This was partly due to the nature of the industry with only one company serving on one route. The edge of the competitive process was further blunted by the frequency of price fixing engaged in by rival companies, thereby providing an example of Adam Smith's belief as to what occurred when businessmen met together. Gladstone was certainly less than sanguine as to the efficacy of the competitive process,[10]

"It was said, let matters...be allowed to go on as at present, and let the country trust to the effects of competition. Now, for his part, he would rather give his confidence to a Gracchus, when speaking on the subject of sedition, than give his confidence to a Railway Director, when speaking to the public of the effects of competition."

Fear of monopoly was but one reason prompting state intervention. Safety was another. A number of the problems were purely technical, though of some concern to the ordinary traveller. Braking power, for

---

[9] Parris, *Government and the Railways in Nineteenth Century Britain* (1965), Lubenow, above n. 3, Chap. 4.
[10] Quoted in Lubenow, above n. 3, p. 129.

example, was not the strong point of early railway transportation. Nor were track or signalling anywhere near pristine condition. Such mechanical problems were compounded by managerial decisions the correctness of which was not always immediately self-evident. To the problems of monopoly and safety was added that of over-speculation. The railway mania of the 1840s brought forth a rash of projects and speculation. Companies were often under-funded and exceeded their statutory borrowing limit. The result was the passage of a series of Acts in the 1840s and thereafter regulating various aspects of railway development, some of the details of which will be elucidated below.

Factory legislation, health, the Poor Law and railways represent four of the main areas in which the nineteenth century state intervened. They do not in any sense represent the totality of legislative intervention. A glance through Holdsworth[11] indicates the range and diversity of enactments passed at various times during the nineteenth century which regulated directly or indirectly wide areas of economic and social activity. There was legislation on mining, chimney sweeps, contagious animals, and building to name but a few. Trades such as chemists, doctors, peddlers and public houses were subject to increasing regulation. Both sides of industry, capital and labour, were the subject of legislative intervention albeit in very different ways.

2. *The Machinery of Administration*

(1) THE BOARD SYSTEM

It is common at the present time to think of new governmental functions being assigned to existing ministries, or to ministries created specifically for that purpose. The term ministry is used here to denote a department of state where the power is vested in a single person who sits in one of the Houses of Parliament and is responsible to Parliament for every act undertaken by that department. However, ministerial government was not in the nineteenth century the standard procedure that it has become today. The more common form of administration in the eighteenth and nineteenth centuries was the Board system. The precise structure and powers of Boards differed from area to area as will be seen below. What they possessed in common was a degree of independence from direct parliamentary control, although a minister might be answerable for part of their business.[12]

The Board system was not an unusual form of administration in the eighteenth and early nineteenth centuries. It was an integral and accepted part of the machinery of government. A number of factors contributed towards its use.[13] For the Crown, the Board pattern possessed advantages over ministers. The latter could be too strong or too weak, either of which

---

[11] *A History of English Law* (1965), Vol. 15, pp. 6-93.

[12] I have taken this formulation from Willson, "Ministries and Boards: Some Aspects of Administrative Development since 1832" (1955) 33 Pub. Adm. 43, 44.

[13] See generally, Roberts, above n. 2, Chap. 4; Willson, above n. 12; Parris, *Constitutional Bureaucracy* (1968), Chap. 3.

could be disadvantageous. Positions on Boards could be a useful source of patronage. They allowed greater continuity of policy, being less affected by the ebbs and flows of political change. And they were more flexible to the particular needs of decentralised administration. Developments within the constitutional balance of power did, however, place stresses on this form of organisation. As Parris states,[14]

> "The system worked well so long as boards were responsible in fact as well as in name to the King. But once the executive became primarily responsible to parliament, the system came under strain. The result was a decline in the board pattern of administration and its supersession to a large degree by a ministerial pattern."

The reasons for the Boards' decline were part practical and part conceptual. Practical reasons for dissatisfaction arose from the inefficiency which could attend their business. Large numbers on Boards could produce ineffective management and waste. These practical problems were not, however, the prime cause for the decline in the use of Boards. Such difficulties could well be present if the administration were to be carried out by a ministry. The real cause of their decline was the altered constitutional position highlighted by the quotation from Parris. Parliament wished to control government action. At the least this required someone answerable in the House, a person responsible for the actions of the Board. This was particularly the case with those activities which were themselves controversial in nature. When the Poor Law Commission was created in 1834 none of the Board members could sit in Parliament. Communication was naturally extremely difficult. Parliament became frustrated due to the absence of a person who could be rendered directly answerable. The Commissioners themselves suffered through having no direct way of defending themselves against personal attack or vilification. As a result the Commission was replaced by a ministry in 1847. The experience of Poor Law administration sent shock waves through other areas.

One middle way which was tried was to have one or more members of the Board with a seat in Parliament. This was adopted for the Board of Woods, Forests and Land Revenues, to be followed in the case of the General Board of Health. The experiment was not a noted success, largely because the two crucial elements of the scheme were unclear: the relationship of the parliamentary member to the rest of the Board and the relationship with Parliament.

Dissatisfaction with this constitutional no man's land led to one of two results. The Board was either converted into a formal ministry, or a minister was made directly responsible for the activity of a Board. Gradually the paradigm of the modern ministry evolved: a minister running a department, being in charge of it and responsible to Parliament for it. The corollary was the development of civil service anonymity. This concept, with which we are now so familiar, only really developed in the mid-nineteenth century. Prior to that it was quite common for civil servants to voice their views, an

---

[14] *Constitutional Bureaucracy* (1968), p. 83. See Le May, *The Victorian Constitution* (1979), for a stimulating discussion of nineteenth century political development.

attitude not surprising when placed within the overall context of the Board system. It was with the growth of individual ministerial responsibility of and for departmental policy that the bureaucracy developed its protective cloak.

A glance at the type of powers possessed by some of the Boards is, however, instructive. The Board system has revived this century. The problems presented by the range and type of powers exercised by these modern quangos have attracted public attention. A brief review of the powers held by their nineteenth-century ancestors will help to place the modern problem in context. Reference will also be made to powers wielded by ministries where the comparison is apposite.

(2) POWERS OF BOARDS

Generalisation concerning the powers wielded by Boards is difficult. They were established to deal with diverse problems and the powers granted to them reflect that divergence. The difficulty is compounded by the need to distinguish between those powers granted to a Board and those which they actually exercised. The two could often differ substantially, with the Boards using powers which in a strict sense they did not possess. Given this diversity the type of powers exercised by Boards is best illustrated by way of example, with comparisons being made to other institutions where appropriate.

The Poor Law Commission established under the Poor Law Amendment Act 1834 established a three man Commission which was independent of Parliament. As an example of a nineteenth-century Board it is particularly interesting both in terms of the breadth of its powers and the limitations placed thereon. Its strengths lay in the fact that it could, in modern parlance, both make rules and adjudicate. It could make rules and regulations concerning the direction and management of the poor, the appointment of local officers and the government of workhouses. Breach of the rules could lead to a prosecution and an order of mandamus from the courts. General rules, defined as those applicable to more than one union at a time, had to be sanctioned by a Principal Secretary of State and by Parliament. However, as Roberts makes clear, the Commissioners adopted a technique which has been used by subsequent agencies in similar positions,[15]

> "Special orders to a single union needed no such confirmation, a fact which the hard pressed commissioners anxious to avoid delay, exploited to the fullest, issuing general regulations individually as special rules."

After 1844 the powers were augmented to include the appointment of auditors, the granting of money to school teachers and medical officers, and the establishment of schools for pauper children. The wide range of powers possessed by the Commission led Roberts to state that it was the "prototype for the administrative bureaus of the future", with discretionary power to legislate and grant aid.[16]

---

[15] Roberts, above n. 2, p. 110.
[16] *Ibid.* pp. 110-111.

Despite these extensive powers the Poor Law Commission's authority was limited in a number of ways. The legislation of 1834 reflected the Victorian balance between central and local government. The Commissioners could determine the qualification and duties of local Poor Law guardians, but the latter were elected by those eligible within that locality. The central Board could only alter the mode of appointment and order removal of the guardians with the consent of the rate-payers and property owners of a parish. And it was the local guardians who appointed the paid officers who would actually administer the relief, subject to confirmation by the Poor Law Commission. Practical difficulties of enforcement must be added to legislative restriction of the Commission's powers. The Commissioners were entitled to appoint assistants to aid in the implementation of the legislation, but all too often the numbers were insufficient for the area assigned to them. Visits to local guardians but once a year were little deterrent to those unions which treated their inmates badly.

While the precise ambit of a Board or department's powers differed they did nevertheless possess certain features in common. Speaking of the 16 new departments with nationwide responsibilities which existed in 1854 Roberts states,[17]

> "All...could inspect local authorities and publish reports on them. Most could order prosecutions if local officials or industrialists violated those laws established for their regulation. Three of the central agencies could draw up and enforce their own rules and regulations, and nine of them could confirm the rules and regulations drawn up by local officials...Ten of the departments could hold hearings and pass judgments on matters in dispute, and three could license or certify local institutions, such as hospitals for the insane and prison cells for the criminal. Only three agencies enjoyed the power of dispensing grants of money to local authorities. Six could insist that local authorities keep registers of pertinent information and almost all could demand that local authorities send in periodical releases on their activities."

Three more general points should be made to place matters in perspective. First, even where an addition to the administrative machinery was not a Board but a sub-department of for example the Home Office, there was often nonetheless a good deal of independence in the administration of the policy in that area. The classic example of this is indeed the working of the Home Office inspectorates. Factory, prison, mining and burial inspectors all came under the aegis of the Home Office.[18] Nineteenth-century papers of successive Home Secretaries are, however, replete with statements concerning the impossibility of the workload that this thereby

---

[17] Above n. 2, p. 106. The 16 departments of which Roberts speaks are the Prison Inspectorate, the Mining Inspectorate, the Factory Inspectorate, the Anatomy Inspectorate, the Burial Inspectorate, the Poor Law Board, the General Board of Health, the Charity Commission, the Lunacy Commission, the Railway Department, the Merchant Marine Department, the Emigration Office, the Tithe, Inclosure and Copyhold Commission, the Department of Science and Art, the Ecclesiastical Commission, and the Education Committee.

[18] See the useful diagrammatic representation in Roberts, above n. 2, pp. 93-95.

thrust upon them. Even the tireless Palmerston despaired of ever reading the prison inspectors' reports.

Secondly, whether one is talking about Boards *stricto sensu*, or whether one is including some ministries too, it is clear that merely looking at the relevant statute to determine the ambit of their powers can obviously be misleading. It is apparent, for example, that a number of both Boards and ministries made and applied rules in circumstances where their ability to do so in general terms was debatable, or where the particular rule which they sought to enforce may well have been outside the ambit of their powers. The evidence for such rule-making and its relevance for the modern debate over agencies will be considered later.[19]

Thirdly, while the precise reasons for the establishment of Boards in the nineteenth century and the expansion of agencies in the twentieth may differ, they do overlap in part and bear testimony to the continuing problems of administrative organisation in a state which undertakes an increasingly wide range of regulatory functions. To quote from Roberts once again,[20]

> "The Victorians' experiments in semi-independent, non political boards reflected their fear that administrative decision would be made the hand-maid of party bias or be caught in the maelstrom of factional politics. The Poor Law Commission was the classic and tragic example of such an attempt."

3. *The Rationale for Administrative Growth*

What were the main forces underlying the rapid administrative growth which characterised the nineteenth century? And how is this expansion to be squared with a view of that century as an age of *laissez-faire*? Opinions amongst historians continue to differ on this.

There are some for whom talk of an age of *laissez-faire* is in itself misleading. For Holdsworth it possessed only peripheral relevance in matters of trade,[21] and Kitson Clark believed that talk of a "period of *laissez-faire*" was unhelpful.[22] Whether it is meaningful to talk of an age of *laissez-faire* at all is something which continues to divide authorities on the subject.[23] Inextricably linked with this question is the relationship between Benthamite utilitarianism, *laissez-faire* and state intervention. For Dicey the utilitarian ideal of the greatest happiness of the greatest number was to be achieved by *laissez-faire* policies; the one implied the other. This verdict has been stood upon its head by subsequent authors, some of whom have gone so far as to see Benthamite theory as a direct cause or catalyst of state

---

[19] See below, pp. 270-276.
[20] Above n. 2, p. 133.
[21] *A History of English Law* (1965), Vol. 15, pp. 6-93.
[22] *An Expanding Society* (1967), p. 162.
[23] For a balanced account of the contending arguments see Taylor, *Laissez-faire and State Intervention in Nineteenth-Century Britain* (1972).

intervention.[24] Others have followed Halévy's[25] lead in distinguishing between economic affairs, in which Utilitarianism presupposed a *laissez-faire* ideology, and social policy in which state intervention was necessary to secure the requisite harmony of interests.

While this is not the place to enter into a full discussion of these contending views, each is in need of qualification. The Halévy approach presumes that one can see a reflection of his view in the type of reforms actually adopted in the mid-nineteenth century. Yet while the Poor Law, factory inspection and public health had clear social implications they had economic reverberations also, as the arguments of the advocates and opponents of these schemes make apparent. Maintenance of the social-economic dichotomy is even more problematic when viewed against the background of, for example, price regulation of common carriers and public utilities. The polar opposite conclusions reached by Dicey and Brebner also appear too extreme. While Bentham's economic writings may be based upon *laissez-faire* principles, he admits of exceptions, as indeed did the classical economists themselves. For Bentham while the basic premise might be that the greatest good of the greatest number could be best attained without legislative meddling, this was not in the nature of an *a priori* truth, but more in the form of an empirical hypothesis. With the growing evils of industrialisation state intervention could well be necessary to attain the utilitarian aim.

Underlying the discussion thus far is an unspoken premise. This is that utilitarian ideology did in fact play a significant role in the administrative growth which characterised the nineteenth century. This premise has in itself been challenged by two different views, each of which ascribes minimal importance to the emergent doctrines of utilitarianism.

MacDonagh[26] sees the expansion of government organs in much more functional and less ideological terms. He develops a model of governmental growth which has five stages. In the first some social evil was exposed. This could be by the adventitious discovery of factory conditions by Oastler, the outbreak of an epidemic, or a sudden tragedy such as the collapse of a mine. In some such way this brought the tragedy to the public attention, producing a demand in some quarters for change to end the intolerable situation. Support for legislative intervention was met by opposition, the result being a legislative measure much less efficacious than its original proponents had hoped. Stage two was a realisation that the original legislation, enacted as a result of this process of compromise, was indeed ineffective in its present form. The response was the grant of additional powers, the provision of summary legal procedures and most importantly, the development of an inspectorate to supervise the administration of the legislation. With the creation of an inspectorate (or some other form of executive enforcement) came stage three. Additional information

[24] Brebner, "Laissez-faire and State Intervention in Nineteenth-Century Britain", (1948) 8 Journal of Economic History 61.
[25] *The Growth of Philosophical Radicalism* (1929).
[26] "The Nineteenth-Century Revolution in Government: A Reappraisal" The Historical Journal I, 1 (1958) 52. See also MacDonagh's, *A Pattern of Government Growth: The Passenger Acts and Their Enforcement, 1800-60* (1961).

concerning the subject-matter involved became available as a result of inspectors' reports; an awareness of the problems at the grass roots evolved. This growing awareness was attended by demands for further legislation in order to close gaps that investigation had revealed, and also pressure towards a stronger, more centralised bureaucracy. The fourth stage witnessed a change of attitude by those who administered the system with the realisation that the "problems" with which they were dealing could not be solved once and for all. New legislation to plug loopholes in old was met by novel methods of circumventing the amended rules. Administration ceased to be a static concept and developed into a dynamic process. The final stage witnessed the further augmentation of the administration's powers, both in terms of the ability to impose penalties and to devise regulations. Investigation became more systematic and scientific, more professional.

The MacDonagh thesis has not gone unchallenged. Parris has questioned both strands of the argument.[27] He tests the MacDonagh thesis against various types of administrative growth which occurred in the nineteenth century and finds that the facts do not fit the model. He also disagrees with the role or lack of it that MacDonagh accords to Benthamite ideology. As Parris points out, it is indeed difficult to discern how many people knew or were influenced by utilitarian thought albeit in an indirect manner. And he argues that MacDonagh overstresses the anti-collective strain within Benthamism: the application of the principle of utility could lead to *laissez-faire* or state intervention depending upon the subject-matter. For Parris, therefore, nineteenth-century government development must be seen as a function both of organic change and contemporary political and ideological thought, one of the main currents of which was Benthamism.[28]

No doubt the debate over the nineteenth-century revolution in government will continue. As with most such revolutions the rationale for its occurrence was probably eclectic as both Parris[29] and Fraser assert.[30] Administrative momentum, political ideology, *laissez-faire* and utilitarianism all had their role to play, as did more fortuitous factors such as the political personalities comprising the government of the day and the presence of figures such as Chadwick and Simon.

4. *Local Government*

"A fundamental antithesis between centralisation and 'autonomous' decentralisation runs through the whole history of English government and its organisation. It is an antithesis that underlies every polity, but especially that of England, where the origin and building up of the

---

[27] "The Nineteenth-Century Revolution in Government: A Reappraisal Reappraised", The Historical Journal, III, 1 (1960) 17.
[28] For a different view, see Lubenow, *The Politics of Government Growth: Victorian Attitudes to State Intervention (1833-1848)* (1971).
[29] Above n. 27.
[30] *Evolution of the British Welfare State* (1973), Chap. 5.

nation give it an unparalleled importance. Indeed, among the primary causes which have governed the process of differentiating the early legal notions and institutions of the nation this conflict plays a leading part."[31]

We have already seen how the balance between central and local administration affected the shape and pattern of nineteenth-century reform. Thus far we have considered this development primarily from the perspective of the central government. The nineteenth century also witnessed fundamental reform in the character of local government. Many administrative functions have always and still are performed at the local level. A closer look at the transformation of local government is therefore integral to an understanding of the pattern of administration as a whole.

The balance between central and local administration runs throughout our history. It is evident far earlier than the nineteenth century. The centralising tendencies of the Norman administration were offset to some extent by the creation of the office of justice of the peace under Edward III. These were appointees of the Crown drawn from the county or town over which they had jurisdiction. Originally their main role was to preserve the peace, but this was augmented by the passage of later legislation. An increasing range of regulatory activities were committed to their charge, such as the statutes of labourers and the supervision of the Poor Law.

The precise degree of control exercised by the central authority varied. Powers of appointment and dismissal of justices of the peace could be used to exert Crown influence. It was, however, the Tudors who attempted to extend central influence most forcefully. There were a number of different aspects of this policy. Privy Council supervision over the justices was increased, particularly by the Star Chamber. The traditional machinery of local administration was threatened by the creation of new local machinery more directly under the aegis of the centre, such as the Councils of the North. And the grant of municipal charters of incorporation came to be used as a device through which the Crown exercised control over those sitting in Parliament. In the sixteenth century a large number of charters were granted to a narrow select body of the town. This was supposed to personify the burgesses, but in fact the main group of such burgesses was excluded from participation in government.[32] The select body could perpetuate itself by co-opting new members and thus began the reign of the narrow oligarchy in municipal life which was to persist until the nineteenth century. For the Crown the benefit resided in the greater ease with which the municipalities could be bribed or bullied into electing representatives to Parliament who would be subservient to the Crown.

Local autonomy increased in the eighteenth century. The events of the seventeenth century had profound effects upon the balance between central and local administration. The Star Chamber was abolished, the Bill of Rights (1689) was passed, parliamentary authority was increased and local

---

[31] Redlich and Hirst, *The History of Local Government in England* (2nd ed., 1970), p. 12. The book was originally printed in 1903. The second edition, with an introduction and epilogue by Keith-Lucas contains only Book I from the original work.
[32] *Ibid.* pp. 28-29.

power augmented. The legacy of earlier abuses however lived on. While the fate of Charles I, Charles II and James II added to the power of Parliament and reduced the central administration's hold on local authority, the corrupt nature of local politics continued unaltered. Nor is this surprising. As Redlich and Hirst observe,[33]

> "Town franchises were preserved with all their anomalies and confusion. After two centuries of growth Select Bodies received Parliamentary recognition, and the municipal was confirmed by the political oligarchy. The reason is not far to seek. The ruling classes having conquered, as they thought the King, had no wish to see the basis upon which their own rule rested extended, or the balance of constitutional power again altered. They had come into a King's inheritance and they intended to enjoy it."

It was to be over 100 years before they were forced to share their legacy. The catalyst to the reform of municipal government was the reform of the parliamentary franchise in the Reform Act 1832. That legislation was not radical in its immediate effects. Even after its passage less than 5 per cent of the populace could vote. Its main short term effect was to bring the better off within the towns under the parliamentary franchise, by allowing the vote to the £10 householder. In the long term its impact was far greater. The old system of parliamentary franchise may have been illogical and unjust, but it was at least strengthened by the very weight of history. The post 1832 system, whatever its framers felt, was based on no real principle at all. It was difficult to think of reasons of principle why the £5 householder should not be admitted to the vote too.

Extension of the franchise also produced ramifications in municipal government which came to fruition in the Municipal Corporations Act 1835. In 1833 a Royal Commission was appointed to investigate, *inter alia*, the defects in municipal corporations. The ills of municipal government were related with vigour. Specific examples of financial corruption were cited, as were the more general ills attendant upon a system in which power was concentrated in few hands and used for personal advantage. Inefficiency was added to peculation. Because so many municipal corporations were poorly administered, independent boards had developed to provide particular services. This produced divided authority, jealousy and squabbling between the different bodies. Inefficiency in the provision of services at a local level might at least have been tolerated by central government. Local disorder would not. Considerable disquiet was voiced at the inability of the local authorities to prevent riots and preserve the peace.

It would, however, be mistaken to see the passage of the 1835 Act as solely derived from Whig desires to end corruption. The Municipal Corporations Act 1835 was at least as much concerned with party advantage. As Fraser explains,[34]

---

[33] *Ibid.* p. 37.
[34] *Power and Authority in the Victorian City* (1979), p. 5.

"Since the freemen and other ancient rights voters were to retain the
Parliamentary vote for their lifetimes, and since the majority of
corporate towns were still to return MPs, this left in the hands of the
corporations considerable electoral power which, if past experience
was followed, they were likely to use extensively and in a corrupt
manner for the Tory interest in Parliamentary elections...The preservation of this electoral power would thus have frustrated the aims of the
1832 reform, and as *The Times* explained in 1833, 'the fact is that
Parliamentary reform, if it were not to include Corporation reform
likewise, would have been literally a dead letter.' "

The Municipal Corporations Act 1835 extended the vote to all those
who had resided and paid rates in the borough for three years. One quarter
of the council was comprised of aldermen who were elected by the council.
Towns which were not yet incorporated could petition the Crown for a
charter of incorporation. The effect of doing so was to render the 1835 Act
applicable. In conjunction with the Reform Act 1832, the Municipal Corporations Act 1835 laid the foundations for urban middle class involvement
in the political life of the country. For the Whigs there was the hope of
extending their power base, both through an alliance between the landed
gentry and urban middle class, and through the removal of the old
municipal corporations most of which were Tory. From the Tories there
was a mixed response. Peel in the Commons presented little opposition to
the 1835 Act. This was the Peel of the Tamworth manifesto, accepting the
need to reform flagrant abuses. Lord Lyndhurst, leading the Tories in the
House of Lords was more strident, fearing that the removal of the old
corporate bastions would herald the advent of democracy. For the Radicals
it was hoped that the 1835 Act would be but the first step. Joseph Parkes,
the Secretary to the Royal Commission, speaking of the recent reforms in
the parliamentary and municipal franchises, puts the matter in dramatic
apocalyptic terms.[35]

"The Tories are burked, no resurrection for them. The Whigs...are an
unnatural party standing between the People and the Tory aristocracy
chiefly for the pecuniary value of the offices and the vanity of power.
Their hearse is ordered...."

The limits of the 1835 reform must, however, be borne in mind. The
counties remained untouched, left to be ruled by the squirearchy for
another 50 years. Even after the reform of municipal corporations there
was still a considerable diversity in the type of body which would impinge
upon local life. Two reasons contributed towards this, both of which have
been mentioned in differing contexts. The first was that, because of the
previous inefficiency of the unreformed boroughs, municipal functions
from paving to lighting, and from cleaning to the supply of water, had been
undertaken by other bodies such as improvement commissioners. The 1835
Act did not unify these duties within the reformed corporations. It simply

---

[35] Quoted in Fraser, above n. 34, p. 16.

enabled the corporations to take over such jobs. Second, while the very reform of municipal government tended to bolster up, potentially at least, local as opposed to central power, other legislation produced the opposite effect. The Poor Law Amendment Act 1834 with its centralised administration provides an example of this.

Reform of the counties was longer in coming. Attempts at reform in the 1840s came to nothing. The justice of the peace continued as the main administrative and judicial organ. As the number of duties imposed upon the justices expanded, so also did the sphere of their summary jurisdiction. The counties could not, however, remain unreformed forever. Legislation in 1867 and 1884 had extended the parliamentary franchise. The former conferred household suffrage upon the inhabitants of parliamentary boroughs and rid the voting system of many anomalies; the latter broadened the borough franchise by the addition of a service vote and extended to the counties the household suffrage which already existed in the boroughs.

The Local Government Act 1888 was the early vehicle for county reform and by the turn of the century the pattern of local government had taken on the following form. The metropolis had a two-tier system with the London County Council at the top and metropolitan boroughs providing the second tier. County boroughs, the larger towns, were single purpose authorities. The counties were slightly more complex. The county council was the main authority for the area. Beneath it existed three types of institution: non-county boroughs; urban districts; and rural districts. The last of these could have parish councils within its area, thereby providing a third tier of authority. This system was to remain with little change until 1972.[36]

While the local franchise had been considerably widened the actual powers possessed by the local authorities were never clearly spelled out. We have already seen how the Municipal Corporations Act 1835 merely empowered the borough to take over functions performed by other institutions. As Fraser states,[37]

> "The lack of a clear legal prescription for corporate activity is the most important single factor to weigh against the Webbs' notion of a municipal revolution in 1835. Without adequate powers the councils were unable to fulfil the promise of municipal reform...."

Those powers were obtained either by use of the empowering provisions of general legislation or by obtaining the passage of local legislation. By the end of the nineteenth century Parliament was dealing with over 300 such Acts per year.[38] Underlying the vagueness as to the ambit of the local authorities' powers was the recurring theme of the balance between the centre and the parts. A desire to demonstrate that central control was not needed played a part in the welter of local Acts secured during this period.[39]

---

[36] For the present position, see below pp. 113-116.
[37] Above n. 34, p. 164.
[38] *Ibid.* p. 165.
[39] *Ibid.* pp. 165-166.

This tension between centralisation and decentralisation has not disappeared. It is endemic in our political and social system. The debate as to the precise balance is, as we shall see, a continuing one.[40]

5. *The Evolution of Statutory Inquiries*

While the emergence of statutory inquiries can be traced back earlier than the nineteenth century it is during that period that the inquiry procedure really developed. The agricultural and industrial revolutions increased the occasion for conflict between individual and individual, or individual and government, whether central or local. The inquiry procedure was one of the mechanisms for resolving this conflict.[41]

An early example of its use is to be found in relation to inclosures.[42] Inclosure of land was normally achieved by the passage of a private Act of Parliament. Inclosure Commissioners would be appointed to consider the facts of a particular scheme, and objections thereto. The Inclosure Act 1801 provided for the appointment of an *ad hoc* commission of inquiry. The meetings of the commission were to be advertised and the public could make objections to the scheme or parts of it. The normal private bill procedure was modified by the General Inclosure Act 1845. This provided for an expedited form of procedure. Normally a private bill would have to be considered by a Committee of each House. The provisional order procedure enshrined in the 1845 Act provided for an inquiry by a person who could investigate the matter at its actual physical location. The application for the provisional order was made to the appropriate government department which would appoint the inspector. Normally, a public inquiry would be held before a provisional order was made.[43] Much time could be saved by this procedure.

Inquiries were used in other areas besides that of inclosure. Local government was one of the main spheres. The Public Health Act 1875 empowered the Local Government Board to hold such inquiries as they thought fit in relation to any matters concerning the public health in any place or any matter in respect of which their sanction was required by the Act.[44] While the inquiry was utilised in the areas of inclosure and health to resolve conflicts between individual and individual, or individual and state, it was also used for other purposes. Accidents were investigated through the holding of an inquiry, when they occurred in areas such as railways, coal mining and factories, to name but three.

It has, however, been the expansion of governmental control over the use of land which has provided the main impetus for the expansion of inquiries

[40] See below, pp. 121-124.
[41] Wraith and Lamb, *Public Inquiries as an Instrument of Government* (1971), Chap. 2.
[42] *Ibid*. pp. 17-21.
[43] Under the General Inclosure Act 1845 the procedure was somewhat different. The Assistant Commissioner would hold a meeting to hear objections, the Provisional Order would be made, and then a second meeting would be held for considering objections.
[44] Wraith and Lamb, above n. 41, pp. 23-25.

in the twentieth century. The problems thereby created will be examined in due course.[45] The development of our administrative system in the present century must now be charted.

Section 3. The Twentieth Century

1. *From 1906 to the Present Day*

In 1906 the Liberal landslide produced a majority of 356. The next five years were to witness the introduction of a range of measures which have often been regarded as the basis for the Welfare State.[46] Protection of children was enshrined in the Children's Act 1908 to be followed closely by the introduction of old age pensions in the same year. It was, however, the gestation and ultimate passage of what became the National Insurance Act 1911 that was most significant in the long term.

It was through the combined energies of Lloyd George and Winston Churchill that this measure made its way onto the statute book. There was no shortage of ideas as to the path which reform ought to take. The Royal Commission on the Poor Law which had sat from 1905 to 1909 itself contained a plethora of opinion. Representatives of the Local Government Board wished for a reversion to the principles of 1834: relief had to be based upon less eligibility and there was alarm at the emergence of a variety of relief services outside of the provisions of the Poor Law. While the Majority Report of the Commission did not accept this draconian view, they did believe that a remodelled Poor Law could be the basis for future development. Although the terms "Poor Law" and "guardian" should be dropped for those of public assistance and public assistance committees, the essential idea that poverty was primarily a personal or moral, as opposed to a social or an economic problem, was still adhered to. Beatrice Webb's Minority Report advocated, by way of contrast, the scrapping of the Poor Law entirely and its replacement by a strong Ministry of Labour and the expenditure of public money in times of cyclical depression.

As it transpired neither view was adopted by Lloyd George who had strong ideas of his own. Insurance was to be the key to Lloyd George's scheme and to be the means of "dishing the Webbs". Like Bismarck before him, Lloyd George and the Liberals saw a social insurance scheme as the method of reducing the socialist threat. An insurance scheme possessed two other advantages. The first was a reduction in the financial burden placed upon the state as compared with a completely non-contributory plan. The second resided in the greater acceptability to the body populace of a scheme based upon contribution and hence entitlement. The moral stigma attached

---

[45] See Chap. 4.
[46] See generally, Hay, *The Origins of the Liberal Welfare Reforms 1906-1914* (1975); Fraser, above n. 30, Chap. 7.

to the reluctant grant of relief that characterised the Poor Law had become deeply etched upon the country's mentality. Part I of the National Insurance Act 1911 established the foundations of health insurance with contributions coming from the state, employer and employee.

While Lloyd George was piloting the passage of the health and sickness provisions Churchill and the young Beveridge were working on unemployment. The Labour Exchanges Act 1909 was intended as one half of a two-pronged attack upon the problem, the other part of which was once again insurance. This was encapsulated in Part II of the National Insurance Act 1911 which provided for tripartite contributions from employer, employee and the state. Little controversy attended the passage of this part of the Act as compared with the health provisions contained in Part I. This result is somewhat ironic given the benefit of hindsight, for it was the unemployment provisions which were to be placed under most strain in the ensuing years.

This new legislation required administration. It is in the Liberal enactments of this period that the modern tribunal system has its real roots. Individual tribunals do of course date back earlier than this. However, the reforms necessitated the development of an administrative and adjudicative mechanism on a scale different from that which had gone before.

A variety of machinery was established, the one constant theme being that the ordinary courts were kept in the background. A number of reasons contributed towards this. The cost of using the ordinary courts would often be disproportionate to the amounts involved and the number of potential disputes would simply overburden them. Added to these pragmatic reasons there was also the feeling that the courts were just not the appropriate mechanism.[47] Certain judicial decisions on the early factory legislation concerning hours of work for children had emasculated the legislative intent by upholding the legality of the relay system. The judiciary had not been happy with their role as arbiters of the reasonableness of railway charges, while experience of appellate involvement in the Workmen's Compensation Acts 1897 and 1906 had been far from successful. Trade union feeling that the ordinary courts were unsympathetic to their position, as evidenced by a series of decisions in the early 1900s, also militated against their use. The Liberal measures were therefore designed to avoid using the ordinary courts either for first instance adjudication or appeal.

Reforms continued during the inter-war years. The Ministry of Health was created in 1919 and extensions of state involvement in education were enshrined in the Education Act 1918. It was, however, with the problem of unemployment and depression that governments became increasingly concerned during the 1920s and 1930s. The theme which ran throughout these years was the *de facto* modification of the insurance principle which had underpinned the 1911 legislation. While this was extended in scope by the Unemployment Insurance Act 1920 the insurance principle came under strain. Rising unemployment caused the *quid pro quo* of contribution for entitlement to become warped. Increasingly the insurance fund came to

---

[47] Abel-Smith and Stevens, *Lawyers and the Courts* (1967), pp. 111-121.

bear the weight intended to be borne by the Poor Law. Further inroads into the insurance principle were made as a result of the Blanesburgh Report of 1927. The effect of its recommendations was to dilute the balance between contribution and entitlement. Benefits were no longer to be limited in time; they were no longer realistically seen as the equivalent of contributions. Provided some contributions had been made, benefits could be drawn on the basis of need.[48] The dichotomy between insurance based and non-insurance based assistance was however partially restored by the Unemployment Act 1934.

War brought further changes in its train, exemplified by the publication of the Beveridge Report in 1942. This report became a major document for social reform. Insurance was set in the wider context of the eradication of the five evils: Want, Disease, Ignorance, Squalor and Illness. To this end the idea was to have a single weekly contribution which would provide cover for sickness, medical, unemployment, widows, orphans, old-age, maternity, funeral benefits and industrial injury. Contributions and benefits were both to be flat rate and not earnings related. Subsistence was all that was to be guaranteed. Herein lay the seeds of future difficulty, since post-war Britain did not think simply of avoiding starvation, but of maintaining accustomed living standards when earnings were interrupted.[49]

What emerged from the post-war Labour Government was a scheme which reflected the essentials of the Beveridge proposals, although the details of contribution levels differed. Industrial injuries were treated separately in the National Insurance (Industrial Injuries) Act 1946, the main difference being that benefits were earnings related. Other benefits were dealt with in the National Insurance Act 1946. Contributions and benefits were both to be flat rate. Why on moral grounds work based injury should be treated differently from that resulting from other causes is something which has puzzled many for a long time. Alongside the insurance system was the National Assistance Board designed to provide a non-contributory sum for those who had used up their insurance entitlement or who had never qualified for any.

The emergence and generalisation of the social insurance and assistance principles brought with it a corresponding growth in the tribunal system, since it was by this mechanism that disputes concerning entitlement were to be resolved. It should not, however, be thought that developments in this type of welfare policy have constituted the only reasons for the growth of our administrative system. The government has implemented in an increasingly wide range of areas regulatory legislation which is often enforced outside the traditional court system. Rent and transport tribunals provide but two examples. Tribunals have also been established to provide protection for the citizen, such as the Mental Health Review Tribunal, while others enforce legislation affecting a specific, if large, group of people such as the industrial tribunals. Yet others are concerned with the competitive process such as the Monopolies and Mergers Commission. The list could be

---

[48] Fraser, above n. 30, pp. 171-174.
[49] *Ibid.* p. 202.

considerably extended. Indeed one of the difficulties of compiling such a list is that there is no accurate definition of what constitutes a tribunal, nor is there any hard and fast rule as to why decision-making should be allocated to a body called a tribunal, or for that matter a commission or an authority rather than somebody else.

What should be stressed is that the growth of tribunals has not been the only developing part of our administrative system. There has of course been the expansion of the inquiry procedure flowing largely from the increase in state control over land use, planning and development. But quite apart from this there has been a much less noticed but no less important increase in the rather grey area now variously characterised by the name of quangos or agencies. They have one thing in common with tribunals: no one can quite define what should be included within the labels and what should not. A realisation that we were reverting to something approximating to the Board system, in the sense of establishing institutions making policy decisions with only indirect control from Parliament, did not escape all commentators. Willson, writing in 1955, noted that many of the newer regulatory functions undertaken by the state were given to such bodies.[50]

An idea of the range and number of such institutions can be grasped by glancing through the appendices of the 1980 Report on Non-Departmental Public Bodies.[51] The report adopts a broad view of non-departmental public bodies, and provides a tripartite classification into executive bodies, advisory bodies, and tribunals. It is with the first two of these that we are primarily concerned at present and particularly with the category of executive bodies. The constitutional and administrative implications of the existence of such institutions will be considered later. For the present it is important simply to be aware of their presence and the significance of the functions which they perform. The report identifies 489 bodies in the executive group with an expenditure of £5,800 million and approximately 21,700 staff. Equally important is the fact that almost £5,000 million out of this sum was spent by what are called the top 20 executive bodies. These include regional water authorities, housing corporations, new town development corporations, the Manpower Services Commission, the Health and Safety Commission, the Civil Aviation Authority, the arts councils, research councils, and Industrial Training Boards. The size of the sums expended is not the only criterion of importance. There are a number of other such executive institutions whose expenditure may well be quite small, but which perform important social functions such as the Commission for Racial Equality or the Equal Opportunities Commission. Power may alternatively reside in the control over licensing such as that possessed by the Gaming Board or the Independent Broadcasting Authority.

The reasons for the growth of agencies, and the constitutional and administrative problems which attend their development, will be discussed below.[52] As a background to this discussion the reactions of government to the growth of administration will be considered through an examination

---

[50] Above, n. 12, p. 55.
[51] Cmnd. 7797.
[52] See pp. 81-86.

of four of the major studies completed this century. The details of these reports are not of direct relevance. The interest lies rather in their perception of the problems to be solved and the government's reaction thereto.

2. *Donoughmore, Franks, the 1980 Report and the 1988 Justice Report*

The Committee on Ministers' Powers,[53] known as the Donoughmore Committee, produced a report the contents of which not unnaturally reflected the rationale for its establishment. The Committee had been constituted to look at two specific, but important, areas both of which reflected the concern at the extent of ministerial power.[54] These were delegated legislation and the making of judicial or quasi-judicial decisions by a minister or those under his control. Increasing use of broad delegations of power resulted in the acquisition of both legislative and adjudicative functions by the Executive. A powerful Committee[55] produced a report which contained suggestions for reform in both areas of investigation.

Just over 30 years later there appeared the Report of the Committee on Administrative Tribunals and Enquiries,[56] known as the Franks Report. The terms of reference were drawn quite specifically. The Committee was to examine the areas of tribunals and inquiries. Aside from decisions made in the ordinary courts this also put beyond the Committee's purview the broad area of decision-making where no formal procedure had been prescribed, a fact emphasised by the Committee itself.[57] What emerged from the Committee's investigations was a series of recommendations as to the constitution and working of tribunals and inquiries, many of which were enacted in the Tribunals and Inquiries Act 1958.[58] Many worthwhile and valuable reforms passed on to the statute book. Of particular interest now, with the benefit of hindsight, are the more general premises from which the Committee reasoned. One of these was that tribunals should be seen as part of the machinery of adjudication.[59] This view has had an important indirect effect. It has for a number of years contributed to the administrative lawyer's blindness to agencies which simply are not and cannot be so regarded. The Franks Report is not to blame for this. It was speaking about tribunals against the background of its terms of reference. Many, though not all, of such institutions can properly be regarded as part of the machinery of adjudication: formal statutory procedures for the resolution of social welfare claims, or rent disputes, etc. However, an

---

[53] Cmd. 4060 (1932).
[54] See Lord Hewart, *The New Despotism* (1929).
[55] It contained Laski, Holdsworth, Scott and Anderson to name but a few.
[56] Cmnd. 218 (1957).
[57] *Ibid.* paras. 9-15.
[58] The reforms are considered in detail in Chap. 4.
[59] Cmnd. 218 (1957), para. 40.

indirect result of this categorisation has been the implicit assumption that all of our administrative institutions can be fitted into the pigeon holes "inquiry" or "tribunal" with those terms bearing their Franksian meaning.

Thus we come in a sense full circle back to the 1980 Report on Non-Departmental Public Bodies.[60] The report is useful for the factual information which it provides and for the short summary of the objections or difficulties which surround such bodies. The importance of this aspect of administrative law has been increased by recent developments in governmental policy. Privatisation and deregulation have indirectly augmented the number of such institutions, while the objective of reducing the size of the central civil service, and administering policy through a variety of executive agencies, has had an important impact in the same direction. These issues will be considered within the chapter which follows.

The most recent report[61] contains some useful recommendations on particular topics, such as the duty to give reasons and the operation of tribunals. It is, however, limited in its scope and in its approach. Thus, for example, the problems generated by agencies are barely touched on, there is no real discussion of how administrative agencies "operate", or of their relationship with government; the significance of participation within administrative decision-making is not appreciated, and the difficulties of determining the ambit of administrative law are not explored.

[60] Cmnd. 7797.
[61] *Administrative Justice, Some Necessary Reforms* (1988). Report of the Committee of the Justice – All Souls Review of Administrative Law in the United Kingdom.

3. INSTITUTIONS I: GOVERNMENT

Section 1. The Changing Pattern of Government

The definition of government has always been somewhat problematic, but
these problems have been increased by recent changes in the pattern of
administration. This is reflected in the title and content of this chapter. The
term government as used in this title is not a reference only to the executive
branch of the state, as represented by the major government departments.
The discussion will focus upon the whole range of institutions which make
up our government in the broader sense of the term. More specifically there
will be a consideration of the following issues:

(a) The executive and its relationship with Parliament.
(b) Agencies which operate at the central governmental level, the
rationale for their creation and the problems which they present.
(c) Contracting out by government to private bodies, the rationale for
this development and the problems which it has created.
(d) The increasingly complex administrative pattern of local government organisation and the impact upon local democracy.
(e) The extent to which changes should be introduced in order to
enhance open government.
(f) The control over the administration exercised by the Parliamentary
Commissioner for Administration.

It will become apparent from the subsequent discussion that the recent
developments which have occurred have thrown into sharp relief the whole
divide between the public and the private sphere. The difficulties which this
has produced will be addressed in the following pages, and at other
appropriate points in the book. The interpenetration of the public and
private spheres has, of course, not been a one way process. Private
institutions can come to exercise a degree of "public" power and this too
will be one of the issues to be faced within the following chapters.

The present discussion will be followed by an analysis of tribunals and
inquiries for which special statutory and non-statutory provision has been
made. The impact of the European Community will be considered within a
separate chapter. The focus will then shift to a case study of decision-
making within two particular areas: competition policy and the regulation
of market power.

Section 2. Regulatory Strategies

1. *"Whether," "How" and "Who"*

A crucial but oft neglected point on which it is necessary to be clear at the outset, is the distinction expressed in the title to this section: the whether, how and who of decision-making. Let me explain this rather cryptic heading. If a decision is made, whether it be by central government, an agency, a local authority, a tribunal or an inquiry, this necessarily implies a prior legislative choice to subject a particular area to some type of regulation. Planning legislation regulates the way in which a person can deal with land; health and safety legislation establishes legislative standards for those at work; social welfare legislation reflects a legislative intent to protect, *inter alia*, those with low incomes; and consumer protection legislation manifests a desire to intervene in the bargains struck between certain types of consumers and manufacturers.

Whether we decide to regulate at all, and if so *how*, is a question on which there can be considerable difference of opinion. Such divergence can be partly the result of differing political perspectives, and partly the consequence of varying beliefs as to the efficacy of the particular type of regulatory device which has been chosen. Two examples will make this clear. Nationalisation is a form of government regulation which has in the past deeply divided the main political parties. What are the alternatives? One would simply be not to regulate such activity at all: to allow the ordinary market mechanism to operate for utilities, in the same way in which it works for the remainder of the economy. Another would be to maintain some controls within these industries, but not to take them into public ownership. Clearly, which device is to be preferred will be dependent on a person's political perspective, on what is perceived to be the problem justifying intervention, and on judgments as to the relative efficacy of these devices.[1] A very different type of regulation is that which follows from the setting of standards, whether they be to control pollution, or to protect the consumer. Given an affirmative answer to the initial question as to whether we wish to have any regulation at all in these areas, the important subsidiary issue of *how* still remains. What is clear is that the ends being sought by the legislation in these areas could be attained by other means. The use of taxes to regulate pollution is but one example.

In some areas the *who* question will be automatically answered by the response to the *how* question. For example, if it is decided that certain environmental standards are best enforced through taxation then this automatically tells us who the enforcer will be. In other areas the answer is

---

[1] *e.g.* Breyer, "Analysing Regulatory Failure: Mismatches, Less Restrictive Alternatives, and Reform" 92 Harv. L.R. 549 (1979); Breyer, *Regulation and its Reform* (1982); Daintith, "Legal Analysis of Economic Policy" (1982) 9 Jnl. Law & Soc. 1991; Baldwin and McCrudden, *Regulation and Public Law* (1987); Kay, Mayer and Thompson, *Privatisation and Regulation – the UK Experience* (1986); Vickers and Yarrow, *Privatisation: An Economic Analysis* (1988); Foster, *Privatisation, Public Ownership and the Regulation of Natural Monopoly* (1992).

less clear cut. When we decide that provision should be made for greater sexual or racial equality this does not in and of itself tell us who the decision-maker should be. Should the function be preserved within central government? Should it be hived off to an agency? Should it be split between central and local authority? The substantive content of the legislation may provide some guide in this respect, but there is no reason why it must be determinative. Indeed as we shall see when we discuss agencies, one of the main causes for concern has been the haphazard allocation of decisions to one type of institution or another.

2. *Regulatory Strategy and Political Choice*

The very decisions of whether to regulate at all, who the regulator should be and how the regulation should be structured, may well therefore differ depending, *inter alia*, upon differences of political philosophy. This has been particularly evident in the policies of the Conservative government. Their regulatory strategy has been characterised by a preference for privatisation, deregulation, disburdenment and self-regulation.[2] This approach will determine the type of regulatory machinery which emerges, and the problems generated by these differing strategies will be considered below.

Privatisation entails a movement from public to private ownership, with the objective of increasing efficiency and limiting the appropriate sphere of state action. The primary mechanism for achieving these goals is the sale of the assets of previously nationalised industries such as British Telecom, British Gas and British Aerospace.

The object of *deregulation* is to reduce governmental control over an industry, and to allow ordinary market forces to operate to a greater degree. Thus, for example, financial services markets have been deregulated, as have domestic air tariffs.

Disburdenment aims to reduce the costs of complying with regulations and operates in two ways.[3] On the one hand, there is the desire to simplify wherever possible the regulatory requirements which business has to fulfil (e.g. filling in VAT forms). On the other hand, there is the objective of scrutinising existing and potential regulations more closely to determine whether they are worthwhile in cost-benefit terms. An Enterprise and Deregulation Unit has been established to administer this scheme.[4]

The Conservative government has also shown a preference for *self-regulation*, meaning that where regulation is felt to be necessary this is delegated to those participating in that activity. The recent developments in the market for financial services provide an important example of this strategy.[5]

---

[2] Baldwin and McCrudden, *Regulation and Public Law* (1987), pp. 23-26; Lewis and Harden, "Privatisation, De-Regulation and Constitutionality: Some Anglo-American Comparisons" (1983) N.I.L.Q. 207.

[3] *Lifting The Burden*, Cmnd. 9571 (1985).

[4] *Building Business...Not Barriers*, Cmnd. 9794 (1986)

[5] Page, "Self-Regulation: The Constitutional Dimension" (1986) 49 M.L.R. 141, and "Financial Services: The Self-Regulatory Alternative?", Baldwin and McCrudden, *Regulation and Public Law* (1987), Chap. 13.

Section 3.   Central Government

1. *Introduction*

What follows does not in any sense purport to be even a summary of central government. It does not attempt to set out in a systematic way the method by which legislation is enacted, the role of the civil service or the various ways in which the Prime Minister can impose his or her will. Detailed exposition of these and other matters would require a volume of its own. A knowledge of some of the realities of central government is however vital for an understanding of administrative law. There are a number of reasons why this is so.

First, ministerial decisions have often been challenged in the courts. An understanding of the relationship between the executive and the legislature is necessary in order to be able to comprehend how such decisions have been made.

Secondly, whether administrative functions should be performed within traditional departments of government, or whether they should be "hived off" to an agency, is the subject of much current debate. This debate has been fuelled by recent governmental initiatives to reduce radically the size of the central civil service, and to assign more tasks to agencies. Such allocation of decision-making raises, as we shall see, a number of problems concerning accountability. However, it should not be assumed that such problems are absent when decision-making is undertaken within traditional governmental departments. An understanding of the interrelationship of the executive and the legislature will enable us to comprehend the problems of accountability which exist even when decisions are made by "ordinary" governmental departments.

2. *The Power of the Executive*[6]

(1) GENERAL

"In the British Cabinet today is concentrated all political power, all initiative in legislation and administration, and finally all public authority for carrying out the laws in kingdom and empire. In the sixteenth century and down to the middle of the seventeenth this

---

[6] See generally, Norton, *The Commons in Perspective* (1981), *The Constitution in Flux* (1982) and *Does Parliament Matter?* (1993); Finer, *The Changing British Party System* (1980); Kavanagh, *British Politics: Continuities and Change* (1985) and *Thatcherism and British Politics* (1987); Mackintosh's, *The Government and Politics of Britain* (7th ed., 1988 by Richards); Adonis, *Parliament Today* (2nd ed., 1993); Birch, *The British System of Government* (8th ed., 1990); Rose, *Politics in England* (5th ed., 1989); Dunleavy, Gamble, Holliday, and Peele, *Developments in British Politics 4* (1993); Griffith and Ryle, *Parliament, Functions, Practice and Procedure* (1989); McDonald, *The Future of Whitehall* (1991); Punnett, *British Government and Politics* (5th ed., 1987).

wealth of authority was united in the hands of the Crown and its privy council; in the eighteenth century and the first half of the nineteenth Parliament was the dominant central organ from which proceeded the most powerful stimulus to action and all decisive acts of policy, legislation and administration; the second half of the last century saw the gradual transfer from Crown and Parliament into the hands of the Cabinet of one after another of the elements of authority and political power. This process took place side by side and in organic connection with the passing of political sovereignty into the hands of the House of Commons, supported as it now was by an electorate comprising all sections of the population."

This quotation, modern although it may sound, is taken from Josef Redlich writing in 1905.[7] What caused this shift in the constitutional balance of power?

The early part of the nineteenth century was a period in which the functions of the executive were more truly those of executing in the sense of carrying out. Maintenance of order, the raising of revenue and the conduct of foreign affairs were regarded as the main governmental functions. The idea that the government of the day had an obligation to carry out a set of domestic policies was not part of the accepted ordering of events. Domestic legislation would normally receive its stimulus, and sometimes its passage, from the efforts of private members. The government of the day might be persuaded to take up a particular measure, as with certain of the Factory Acts, but it was normally after a private member had provided the catalyst. As indicated previously, it was often the adventitious discovery of an "evil", shocking the nation, which produced the impetus for reform. This is not intended to imply acceptance of the Cleopatra's nose theory of history, rather that early nineteenth century legislation was not as a rule devised, piloted and controlled by the government.[8]

The flipside of this same coin was the relative weakness of the party system when it came to voting on such bills brought before the House. Divisions were not along rigid party lines. Labels such as Tory, Whig, Radical and Liberal contained a spectrum of divergent views within each grouping. Social and economic legislation of the early nineteenth century would, as seen, receive its support from those with widely differing views. The beliefs of those ranged in opposition were similarly broad. Measures could of course be promoted by the government which would naturally attempt to ensure the support necessary for their passage. Party based domestic legislation was not, however, the norm during this period.

---

[7] *The Procedure of the House of Commons* (1905), i, p. 20, quoted in *The House of Commons in the Twentieth Century* (Walkland ed., 1979), p. 247.
[8] A wider range of functions was undertaken by various commissions and boards, particularly at the local level. See above, pp. 52-57.

It was, as Redlich observed, the development of the suffrage which was a main cause of the altered constitutional balance of power. As the electorate increased in size so it became necessary for governments to be able to appeal to a wider cross-section of the population. The Liberal government's social welfare legislation of 1906 to 1911 was prompted in part at least by the perceived need to offer the "people" some tangible benefits. There were of course a number of other reasons leading to its passage – developing social ideas, the desire to cut the ground from under the feet of the Fabians, and a real wish to cope with the problems of sickness, old age and unemployment, to name but three. There was nonetheless an understandably distinct political motive, namely that many of those who would benefit could vote.

Herein lies the organic connection between the passing of political sovereignty into the hands of the House of Commons and the passing of real power into the hands of the executive, of which Redlich speaks. The legitimacy of the House of Commons had been strengthened by the extension of the suffrage. Somewhat paradoxically it was this very extension of the Commons' political base which proved to be one of the causes of the strengthening of the executive. The ever increasing need to appeal to the expanded electorate was to be one of the reasons leading the executive to bring within its own purview a much broader range of tasks than its predecessors had undertaken.

Political change is seldom a one-dimensional process. Factors affecting such development overlap and feed off each other. The fact that the government began to play an increasing role in the initiation, shaping and promulgation of domestic legislation helped to create, and was itself influenced by, a growing expectation that government could be looked on to remedy social and economic evils. The aspirations of the populace were continually increasing. Not only was government seen as having a social responsibility but the nature of that responsibility was altering. In the realm of social policy, for example, the idea that the government had fulfilled its obligations by providing subsistence benefits was, by the middle of this century, fast becoming outdated. As the fear of real destitution and starvation diminished, so the aim became one of preserving living standards in times of hardship caused by sickness, death or unemployment. A more positive social role for government manifested itself in other areas too. Increases in educational opportunity and improved health standards were but two outworkings of the same theme.

Juxtaposed to this alteration in the nature of the government's social responsibility, was the executive's increasing role in the management of the economy. The macro-economic theories of Keynes indicated a positive role for government to rectify imbalances in the economic system.

The increase in executive involvement in an ever broadening range of domestic policy was attended by changes in both the party system and the methods of legislation. If the government of the day was to be expected to secure the passage of its policies then it had both to control the reins of the legislative process and its own supporters more vigorously than it had done previously. It is to these developments that we should now turn.

(2) THE LEGISLATIVE PROCESS

Speaking of the change in the pattern of legislation during the late nineteenth and early twentieth centuries, Walkland states,[9]

"In the case of the legislative process, this period essentially saw a nationalisation and centralisation of legislative initiative in the hands of the government, a massive supplementation of Private Bill procedure by government-introduced Public General Acts, and a marked diminution in the opportunities for private Members to legislate."

Three of the main causes contributing towards this centralisation of legislative initiative have been the development of standing committees, the increasing discussion of legislation in cabinet committees, and the growth of delegated legislation.

Standing committees are not a development of this century. They were used on limited occasions in the late nineteenth century,[10] but were viewed with suspicion. It was felt that the government should defend its measures, even as to points of detail, in a Committee of the Whole House. This was indeed the norm. Attempts to take the committee stage in standing committee were regarded as devices by which the government sought to escape criticism. This dislike of standing committees was fuelled by the oft repeated sentiment that wholesale use of such committees would turn the Commons into a legislative machine, grinding out the maximum amount in the shortest possible time.[11] Despite these objections the use of standing committees has now become the normal way of considering the detail of legislation. Not surprisingly increase in their use corresponded with periods in which the government had a large legislative programme. The two key periods were 1906 and 1945.

In 1906 a procedure committee recommended that all bills – except finance, consolidated fund and appropriation bills, and bills for confirming provisional orders – should be sent to a standing committee after second reading unless the House otherwise ordered. The government supported these recommendations. Many backbenchers opposed them. It was to take four days of debate, during which the government stood out against demands for amendment, before the recommendations of the 1906 Committee were accepted. Despite assurances by the government that such committees would not be used for controversial measures, the ensuing years were to witness the sending of such minor matters as the National Insurance Act 1911 to a standing committee rather than a Committee of the Whole House.[12]

The use of standing committees received a significant boost as a result of the Select Committee on Procedure which was established in 1945. As in 1906, one of the principal reasons for wishing to expedite parliamentary

---

[9] "Government Legislation in the House of Commons", *The House of Commons in the Twentieth Century* (Walkland ed., 1979), p. 247.

[10] *Ibid.* p. 255.

[11] *Ibid.* p. 253.

[12] The existence of such committees did however benefit private Members' legislation, see Walkland, above n. 9, p. 259.

business was the size of the government's legislative programme. The Labour government, returned to power in 1945, wished to implement a number of measures the technical complexity of which exceeded that of normal legislation. If this were to be possible the flow of parliamentary business had to be speeded up. The Select Committee's main brief was to consider ways in which the passage of public bills could be accelerated. The Report of the Committee which was accepted by the government recommended the use of standing committees on all bills, except those of major constitutional importance, the increase in the number of such committees, and the utilisation of the guillotine within the Committees in order that the Government could be sure that its measures would not be unduly delayed.[13]

If the development of standing committees expedited the passage of business on the floor of the House, the centralisation of the legislative initiative within the executive was also affected by the increased sophistication of cabinet legislative planning. *Cabinet committees* were used by Liberal governments to settle on the details of legislative proposals.[14] It was, however, the Second World War and its aftermath which saw the growing systematisation of legislative planning at cabinet level. A distinct Legislative Committee of the Cabinet with responsibility for, *inter alia*, planning a legislative programme existed in 1940. This idea was built on by the post-war Labour government. The planning of the general legislative programme was assigned to a future legislation committee, with a distinct Legislation Committee which would advise on the more technical aspects concerning the form of the legislation.[15] Bills could well go through several drafts before even being presented to the House of Commons. Increased cabinet involvement in the drafting and planning of legislation has made the executive more certain as to the type of provision for which it seeks legislative approval. It is rare for an amendment to be forced on a government against its will, whether it be in committee or elsewhere.[16]

The growth of *delegated legislation* has centralised the legislative initiative within the executive in a way rather different from either the development of standing committees or cabinet oversight. Delegated legislation is not a new phenomenon. Various forms of rule-making have existed for many years.[17] The passage of a large volume of social and economic legislation has in its turn led to an increase in the quantum of delegated legislation. The crucial effect of an increase in such legislation is to centralise the legislative initiative within the executive as a whole. It is the government, albeit acting through individual ministers, who can decide when and whether to initiate such legislation. Most important is the fact that when such legislation is proposed the opportunity for effective

---

[13] *Ibid.* pp. 265-268.
[14] *Ibid.* pp. 251-252.
[15] *Ibid.* pp. 265-266.
[16] How rare is a matter of some debate; see Walkland, above n. 9, pp. 287-288; Griffith, *Parliamentary Scrutiny of Government Bills* (1975).
[17] See Chap. 7.

legislative control is beset by serious problems. As we shall see the organs for legislative scrutiny, although improved, labour under considerable difficulty.[18]

(3) THE PARTY SYSTEM

The power of the executive has also been markedly increased by the development of the party system and the consequential degree of control wielded by the government over its supporters in the House of Commons.

Parties are of course not a new phenomenon. They emerged in the late eighteenth and early nineteenth centuries. Even early parliamentary party organisation was designed to ensure that members adhered to the party line laid down by the party leaders.[19] The important point for present purposes is that the very existence of parties in themselves provided an avenue for the channelling of power from the legislature to the executive. It was, however, a combination of the extension of the suffrage and the expanded role of the state which were the seeds of the rigid party discipline to which we are so accustomed today.

The expansion of the franchise in 1832 and in 1867 changed the nature of politics. Voters could not simply be bought. There were too many. An organisation outside Parliament was required in order to persuade and cajole voters into using their newly acquired rights for the benefit of a particular party. Promises for reform provided the carrot. But promises have, in theory, to be kept. A necessary if not sufficient condition for doing so was greater executive control within Parliament to ensure the passage of the requisite legislation. The point is put neatly by Norton,[20]

> "Parties certainly had a profound impact upon Parliament: voters not only had to be contacted, they had to be promised something if their votes were to be forthcoming, and party promises could only be fulfilled if party nominees were returned in sufficient number to, and displayed voting cohesion in, the House of Commons; the consequence of this development was to be party government, with the parliamentary parties acting as a conduit for the transfer of power from Parliament to the executive."

The transition from the nineteenth to the twentieth century simply exacerbated the problem. The role of the state developed partly as we have seen because of the extension of the franchise itself. This broadened range of functions placed increasing strain upon parliamentary time. One response was reform of legislative procedures. Another was to tighten party discipline to ensure the passage of the expanded governmental programme. It should not be thought that backbench members are continually being harassed by harridans called Whips. This would be to misrepresent reality.

---

[18] See below, Chap. 7.
[19] Norton, "The Organisation of Parliamentary Parties", *The House of Commons in the Twentieth Century* (Walkland ed., 1979), p.9. See generally, Rose, *Do Parties Make a Difference?* (2nd ed., 1984); Norton, *Dissension in the House of Commons 1945-1974* (1975).
[20] *Ibid.* p. 8.

Whips perform valuable functions of communication and management as well as discipline. Nevertheless the government will maintain a carefully calculated legislative programme, the Whip system will be applied to standing committees, the guillotine will be used to maintain impetus, and there will be considerable pressure on a member not to vote against the government especially on an important issue where the difference in numbers between government and opposition is finely balanced.

The party system has not only centralised initiative and power in the executive as manifested in party voting cohesion, but also in the process of policy formation. As Johnson has noted,[21] policy is normally laid down by the executive when the party is in office, although on occasion the official leadership may defer to a particular powerful group because the executive fears to oppose them.

To this process of policy formulation may be added the impact of powerful interest groups outside Parliament. There is nothing wrong with extra-parliamentary groups having an effect on legislative programmes. It happens in all countries. What causes disquiet is the extent of this influence. This is not the time or place to enter into the debate concerning the influence of the trade unions within the Labour party, or for that matter of the pressure wielded by big business within the Conservative party. What is apposite here is the way in which this serves to weaken further the power of the legislature over legislation. It is to the implications of this executive dominance that we must now turn.

3. Two Views of the Legislature

Thus far we have described the fact of executive dominance over the legislature. Should we be dismayed by this? The answer must depend on what we believe the legislature's role to be. At least two views are tenable as to what this role is. One sees the legislature primarily as a critic, a body to scrutinise the government rather than one that has any real hand in the legislative process. The other perceives the House of Commons as still having a legislative responsibility which should be buttressed and strengthened at every opportunity. The two views are not antithetical. They do, however, judge the effectiveness of the House of Commons from different perspectives.

(1) THE COMMONS AND SCRUTINY

The picture of the Commons as critic is put forcefully by Ryle,[22]

"Thus much of the criticism of Parliament and particularly of the House of Commons today, flows, I believe, from this fundamental mistake in their perceived functions. Parliament is wrongly blamed for

---

[21] *In Search of the Constitution, Reflections on State and Society in Britain* (1977), p. 47. The extent to which this is so may differ as between the leading political parties.

[22] "The Commons in the Seventies – A General Survey", *The Commons in the Seventies* (Walkland and Ryle eds., 1977), p. 12.

bad government because Parliament does not govern. To put it baldly: the government governs; Parliament is the forum where the exercise of government is publicly displayed and is open to scrutiny and criticism. And the Commons does not control the executive – not in any real sense; rather the executive control the Commons through the exercise of their party majority power."

Control or influence over the substance of legislation is, says Ryle,[23] necessarily minimal; the government can always ensure that its policies become law in much the way that it desires.

This view of the House of Commons' role is essentially pragmatic: little control is possible over the content of legislation, therefore the value of the Commons must lie elsewhere. The Emperor cannot be naked. There is little doubt that scrutiny and criticism is a valuable function for a legislature to perform. Those who advocate that the House of Commons' legislative role should be enhanced would not thereby deny it a function of critical appraisal. What is questionable is not whether scrutiny is a viable function for a legislature, but whether our present system allows it to be undertaken effectively. If the mechanisms for performing this role prove to be ineffective to the task at hand we may yet find that the Emperor's new clothes provide no more than a shimmering transparent veil. Whether this is so is a matter on which opinions can differ. As Ryle himself observes,[24] the efficacy of scrutiny is dependent both upon the opportunities for raising matters and on adequate machinery for scrutinising government action.

Opportunities for raising matters do undoubtedly exist. The opposition has the supply days. Private members can, for example, table questions and utilise the debates on motions for the adjournment of the House to raise specific issues. Neither of these types of approach can be regarded as really satisfactory. The supply debates do not reveal any systematic opposition planning; parliamentary questions and the like, although capable of embarrassing the government, are inherently unsuited to the regular investigation of a broad area.

Not surprisingly most hopes for effective legislative control have been pinned on the development of *machinery for scrutinising government action*. Select committees are the main type of such machinery. They have been seen as the mechanism through which Parliament, as distinct from the government, could exercise a role even in the absence of any real legislative power. While this is the modern conception of the select committee they were not always utilised in this way.

Prior to 1914 such committees were used for a variety of purposes. Johnson lists four:[25] the investigation of alleged abuses, inquiries into areas of public policy on which action was demanded, consideration of actual bills, and the continuing scrutiny of financial rectitude provided through the Public Accounts Committee established in 1861. The use of such committees declined during the inter-war years, but they were utilised more

---

[23] *Ibid.* pp. 13-14.
[24] *Ibid.* pp. 15-16.
[25] "Select Committees and Administration", *The House of Commons in the Twentieth Century* (Walkland ed., 1979), p. 432.

often, albeit somewhat slowly at first, following the Second World War. Four main committees carried on investigative work: the Public Accounts Committee, the Estimates Committee,[26] the Select Committee on Nationalised Industry[27] and the Statutory Instruments Committee.

The development of select committees has received two further boosts, the first in the mid-1960s, the second in the late 1970s.

Partly as a result of the Report of the Procedure Committee of 1964-1965, and partly as a consequence of a more general feeling that the balance between the legislature and the executive needed redressing, a number of select committees were established in the late 1960s. The approach of the Government was, however, characterised by the *ad hoc*: no common theme runs through the committees which were established. Some could be best categorised as dealing with a particular subject-matter, others were based around the work of a department.

Dissatisfaction with the disorganised pattern of select committee structure, coupled with the belief that greater coverage was required, led the Select Committee on Procedure to recommend a reshaping and extension of select committees along departmental lines.[28] These recommendations were put into effect in 1979, the result being that such committees now cover all major aspects of government.

How effective have such committees been? Evaluation depends upon expectation. The strong argument for select committees was that the exercise of their investigative and critical functions would enable Parliament to reassert real control over the government. A less ambitious view saw select committees as relatively impartial generators of advice and information, hoping to influence government because of their non-partisan approach.[29] There is little evidence that the committees have played the stronger of these two roles. This is evident from research on their general work, the findings of which are reinforced by the limited impact of the committees in the area of financial scrutiny. Research on the new committees indicates a number of reasons for their relatively limited impact.[30]

First, the committees do not actually have a role in the process by which the government frames its legislation. In this sense they are ancillary to the principal work of the House, though some select committees have attempted to circumvent this limitation by examining matters which are likely to lead to legislation in the near future.[31] Secondly, the committees do not have adequate resources, and operate with minimal support staff and a small budget.[32] Thirdly, it is inappropriate to conceive of the new committees as a "system", since they have differing perceptions of their own

[26] Johnson, *Parliament and Administration: The Estimates Committee 1945-65* (1966).
[27] Coombes, *The Member of Parliament and the Administration: The Case of the Select Committee on Nationalised Industries* (1966).
[28] First Report from the Select Committee on Procedure (1977-78; H.C. 588).
[29] Johnson, "Select Committees as Tools of Parliamentary Reform: Some Further Reflections", *The Commons in the Seventies* (Walkland and Ryle eds., 1977), p. 195.
[30] Drewry (ed.), *The New Select Committees, A Study of the 1979 Reforms* (1985). See also Englefield (ed.), *Commons Select Committees: Catalysts for Progress?* (1984).
[31] Adonis, *Parliament Today* (2nd ed., 1993), p. 166.
[32] *Ibid.* p. 165.

function. As Giddings states, "they have defined their functions in ways which owe more to their own political chemistry than to any sustained analysis of their given task of examining expenditure, administration and policy."[33] Thus some committees have shied away from involvement with fundamental policy issues; others have acted as advocates for particular pressure groups; and yet others have engaged in more searching scrutiny of long-term governmental objectives. Fourthly, the Memorandum for Guidance of officials who are to appear before the committees limits the information which civil servants should provide. Thus officials are instructed not to meet requests for information irrespective of the cost; not to disclose advice given to Ministers, nor information concerning interdepartmental exchanges on policy issues; not to reveal discussions in Cabinet committees; and to confine their evidence, so far as possible, to questions of fact relating to existing governmental policy, and not to discuss alternative strategies.[34] Finally, the opportunities to debate the findings of select committees upon the floor of the House are limited. Between 1979 and 1988 only 25% of the reports were debated, and only 13 out of 500 reports were the subject of any substantive motion, although some form of government response will now normally be forthcoming.[35]

This general picture of the committees' limited effect is borne out by studies of their impact on financial matters. Scrutiny of expenditure on the floor of the House is severely limited. The details of the estimates cannot be altered, and members of Parliament have not sought to reject them for a long time. Exercise of any such control is made more difficult by the complexity of the financial issues, and the fact that expenditure and taxation are considered separately.[36]

The select committee structure has now replaced the Expenditure committee, the idea being that each committee will scrutinise expenditure within its subject-matter area. Robinson has argued that this has impeded the development of any systematic critical approach to the scrutiny of public expenditure, that each committee operates in its own discrete area, and that there has not been "much enthusiasm" for financial scrutiny.[37] Moreover, when select committees do focus upon financial matters the nature of their inquiry differs. Robinson posits three differing stances which the committees adopt in this area.[38] Some operate as balancing committees, scrutinising claims for extra spending against the costs which will be incurred; others function as spending committees, supporting the dominant

---

[33] "What Has Been Achieved", *The New Select Committees* (Drewry ed., 1985), p. 368. See also Wass, "Checks and Balances in Public Policy Making" [1987] P.L. 181, 183, 192-193.
[34] For more recent battles between select committees and the executive and civil servants over access to information see Drewry, "Parliament", *Developments in British Politics 4* (Dunleavy et al. eds., 1993), pp. 160-161.
[35] Adonis, *Parliament Today* (2nd ed., 1993), p. 167.
[36] Robinson, "The House of Commons and Public Expenditure", *The Commons in the Seventies* (Walkland and Ryle eds., 1977), pp. 129-130; Robinson, *Parliament and Public Spending* (1978).
[37] "The Financial Work of the Select Committees", *The New Select Committees* (Drewry ed., 1985), pp. 307-308.
[38] *Ibid.* pp. 309-318.

pressure groups and advocating higher expenditure in that area; yet other committees operate "non-financially", in the sense that they either devote little time to public expenditure or make no clear judgments either way on the financial implications of their reports. Drewry echoes these sentiments and finds that the record of departmental select committees in relation to financial scrutiny has been "decidedly patchy".[39]

Some increase in legislative control over money already expended has, however, been provided by the National Audit Act 1983. The Comptroller and Auditor-General is now formally regarded as an officer of the Commons, and can investigate the "economy, efficiency and effectiveness" with which departments and certain other public authorities discharge their functions.[40]

While there is therefore little evidence to support the strong role which it was hoped that select committees would play in reasserting parliamentary control over government, it would be mistaken to suppose that they have had no impact. Select committees have had an effect in a number of ways. They have been able to affect governmental policy on certain issues before it has become too fixed; their very existence has it seems led departments to be more rigorous in justifying their policy choices because these can now be probed by the committees;[41] civil servant anonymity has been "dented", notwithstanding the limitations on the advice which they are allowed to offer;[42] they have provided a forum for debate in which particular interest groups can offer their opinion on existing policies;[43] and there is some evidence that the committees are now willing to tackle more controversial issues, such as the future of the NHS and privatisation, than hitherto.[44]

That there are limitations on the scrutiny function of Parliament is not surprising.They should be seen in the context of a more general problem underlying the whole concept of an effective critical role for Parliament. Changes in procedure are often thought of as "technical" alterations, changes in mechanism, which do not have any wider significance. The corollary of this is the assumption that alterations can be made without any substantive modification in the balance of power existing between the parts which comprise our political system. A moment's reflection will show that this is not possible.[45] Our political system is characterised by two major themes: the dominance of the executive (this we have already commented upon), and the existence of an adversarial approach to politics. It is one in which government and opposition face each other in a partisan, gladiatorial combat, each backed by its own legions.

[39] "Parliament", *Developments in British Politics* 4 (Dunleavy, Gamble, Holliday and Peele eds., 1993), p. 158.

[40] Drewry, "The National Audit Act – Half a Loaf" [1983] P.L. 531.

[41] Giddings, "What Has Been Achieved", *The New Select Committees* (Drewry ed., 1985), pp. 370-371, 374, 377.

[42] Drewry, "The 1979 Reforms – New Labels On Old Bottles?", *The New Select Committees* (Drewry ed., 1985), pp. 388-389.

[43] Giddings, "What Has Been Achieved", pp. 378-379.

[44] Adonis, *Parliament Today* (2nd ed., 1993), p. 168.

[45] Johnson, "Select Committees and Administration", *The House of Commons in the Twentieth Century* (Walkland ed., 1979), pp. 444-445.

Select committees run counter to both of these tenets: they seek to strengthen the power of Parliament as against the executive, and to proceed by a more non-partisan approach. The fundamental point is that a strengthening of Parliament must imply a consequential weakening of the executive's power for relatively untrammelled action, and a less partisan approach to politics in committees presumes either a dichotomy between policy and administration which is so elusive, or a distinction between the approach to politics on the floor of the House and that in committee. Some commentators believe that such a distinction may be emerging, with the committees operating more by way of consensus, with the members not unthinkingly accepting the party Whips, and with the prime aim being the objective scrutiny of governmental action rather than "the knee-jerk reflexes of Government and Opposition."[46]

There is little doubt that the committees have increased the Commons' scrutiny of the executive as compared to that which existed prior to 1979. A survey of their work carried out by the Select Committee on Procedure[47] reached the conclusion that the system provided an improved framework for the sustained scrutiny of government departments. But if the select committees really are to have more than a limited impact then the executive will have to shed some of its powers, or to allow more than a symbolic genuflection to less partisan politics.

(2) THE COMMONS AND LEGISLATION

Not all commentators accept that the legislative role of Parliament should be consigned to history. While recognising that the golden age of Parliament cannot be recaptured, proposals have been forthcoming for ways in which the impact of Parliament on the legislative process could be strengthened. The advocates of such an approach are under no illusion that the legislature could take over the legislative process; the proposals are rather designed to allow more critical input from the floor of the House.

Griffith has proposed a modification of the standing committee procedure. Speaking of the existing procedure he says,[48]

"If the value of the proceedings in standing committee on Government bills is judged by the extent to which Members, other than ministers, successfully move amendments, then the value is small. It has been as rare for ministerial amendments to be rejected as for other Members' amendments to be successfully moved against government opposition."

Griffith acknowledges that the present procedure can put a minister on the spot as the committee proceeds through the legislation line by line. It is, however, time consuming, members are often ill informed, the real,

---

[46] Adonis, *Parliament Today* (2nd ed., 1993), p. 172.
[47] *The Working of the Select Committee System* (H.C. 19, 1989-90); Judge, "The Effectiveness of the Post-1979 Select Committee System: the Verdict of the 1990 Procedure Committee"(1992) 63 Pol. Q. 1.
[48] "Standing Committees in the House of Commons", *The Commons in the Seventies* (Walkland and Ryle ed., 1977), p. 107. See also, Wass, "Checks and Balances in Public Policy Making" [1987] P.L. 181, 193-194.

controversial issues can become buried in the detail, and the committee divides on formalistic party lines.

While the picture of the standing committee as an image of the House in miniature follows inevitably from the adversary nature of our political system, its effects could be reduced.[49] A number of inquiries have addressed this general issue,[50] the most recent of which is the Rippon Commission.[51]

The Rippon Commission has made a number of interesting proposals for improving Parliament's role in the legislative process. The initial assumption of this study is that Parliament does not "make the law" as such. This is done by the government, but Parliament must have proper facilities for scrutinising the proposed legislative changes, and determining the soundness of these alterations.[52] A number of more specific proposals were made which would enhance Parliament's role in this respect.

Pre-legislative proceedings could be improved by making use of departmental select committees which could comment upon White papers and other consultative documents. On other occasions when a fuller inquiry was merited into proposed legislation then a select committee could be appointed specially for this purpose.[53]

Scrutiny of the actual bill by the House should be divided into two stages. The first would be a *preliminary briefing stage*, which would operate after the bill's first reading and publication for more complex or important measures. This would be undertaken by a specially appointed select committee, "first reading committee", which should be free of ministers and opposition shadow ministers. It was hoped that such committees might be able to work by the more consensual approach which characterises departmental select committees. They would have the power to take evidence from civil servants, outside experts and the wider public. The committees would then produce a report which drew attention "to ambiguities in purpose or meaning, apparent problems in the application or implementation of the legislation, possible consequences of the proposed policies and other practical, technical or drafting points that have emerged."[54]

The second part of parliamentary scrutiny of a bill would be the *formal committee* stage and would continue to be undertaken by standing committees. The Rippon Commission noted the existing widespread dissatisfaction with the present standing committee procedures: many MPs regard the work of such committees to be a waste of time under the current arrangements; and the Opposition is frustrated because it can make so little

[49] Griffith's own suggestions for change are similar to those advanced by the Rippon Commission considered below.

[50] Second Report of the Select Committee on Procedure of 1984-85 (HC 49); Second Report of the Select Committee on Procedure of 1985-86 (HC 324); Second Report of the Select Committee on Procedure of 1989-90 (HC 19-I).

[51] *Making the Law, The Report of the Hansard Society Commission on the Legislative Process* (1992).

[52] *Ibid.* para. 310.

[53] *Ibid.* paras. 322-323.

[54] *Ibid.* para. 337.

real impact on the bill.[55] It suggests that the norm should be for bills to be referred to *special standing committees*, which would enable such "committees to examine witnesses and to publish their evidence at the beginning of their examination of a bill before turning to the more formal debates (and party disciplines) for the decision-taking processes on proposed amendments and on the clauses of the bill."[56] Membership should include, wherever possible, those who were on the first reading committee, and those who were on a relevant departmental select committee. As far as possible special standing committees should carry out detailed scrutiny of all parts of the bill, looking in particular at practical problems of implementation and at matters where the purpose or meaning of the bill was unclear.[57] It should not, by way of contrast, be the function of these committees to debate major issues of policy which had been dealt with on the floor of the House during the second reading, or could be raised during the report stage after the committee had done their work.

4. *Conclusion*

It is clear that there is an underlying connection between the recent developments and proposals which have been made concerning Parliament and scrutiny of government action on the one hand, and Parliament and the legislative process on the other: this is the desire to enhance Parliament's role in both these spheres *and* to reduce the extent to which the political system works in an adversarial manner dominated by the executive. The desire for some less party based, more objective, scrutiny of both governmental action and legislative proposals is a recurrent theme. This is a laudable objective. Whether it is realisable is another matter. Some would argue that in the absence of a major catalyst[58] prompting a realignment of power between the executive and the legislature any change is bound to be interstitial. What form such development should take is outside the scope of this book.

For our present purposes what the discussion of the balance of power at the centre highlights are some important factors which could influence the way in which we allocate decision-making as between different institutions. The most important of these is simply to ensure that when we compare alternative avenues we do so against a realistic rather than idealistic background. In the debate over agencies, their accountability must be juxtaposed to the constitutional reality, not some paradigm long since disappeared. Ministerial responsibility as a constitutional concept still holds sway but its emphasis has altered: its potency as a mechanism for bringing the executive to account has waned, but the other side of this Janus-like image still insists that power be vested in or through the minister.[59] The

---

[55] *Ibid.* para. 345. See also, Griffith and Ryle, *Parliament* (1989), pp. 315-317.
[56] *Ibid.* para. 349. Such a system was used on five occasions between 1980-84.
[57] *Ibid.* para. 351.
[58] The emergence of a third party which broke the traditional two-party dominance could be such a catalyst.

extent to which organisations have been established outside of the normal departmental structure must now be examined.

Section 4. Agencies

The increasingly complex nature of "government" was noted at the outset of this chapter. It is time now to investigate the causes of this complexity and the legal ramifications which flow there from. It should be emphasised that the term "agency" will not be used within this section as a term of art, but rather as an omnibus description of a number of institutions, the actual names of which may vary, which perform governmental functions albeit not within the traditional departmental framework.

1. *The Reasons for the Creation of Agencies*

(1) FULTON, HIVING OFF AND AGENCIES

Until recently the civil service was still cast in the mould set by the Northcote-Trevelyan reforms of the mid-nineteenth century. It was a unified and uniform service in theory at least, and in most instances in reality too. Governmental functions were organised in and through departments with new needs met by the creation of a new department or the partition of an existing department.

This was in contrast with the pattern of administration in the earlier part of the nineteenth century when, as we have seen,[60] public functions were often undertaken by boards which operated outside the confines of the now traditional departmental organisational norm. The latter part of the nineteenth century witnessed the decline in the use of such institutions and the emergence of the concept of ministerial responsibility, with the corollary of civil service anonymity.

By the 1960s strains had begun to appear in what had become the accepted organisational structure. These became apparent in the Report of the *Fulton Committee*.[61] Two major themes are evident in the Committee's Report. One was the need for improved efficiency within traditional departments, and this entailed a structure in which different units had clearly defined authority for which they could be held responsible. The other theme was that we should reassess precisely which activities required to be undertaken directly within the department at all. Many activities might work better if they were "hived off" and run by bodies which existed outside the departmental framework, albeit subject to overall ministerial guidance.

The proposals of the Fulton Committee had some effect and were one of the catalysts for the hiving off of a number of functions to newly created agencies: the Civil Aviation Authority was formed from the Department of

[59] Johnson, *In Search of the Constitution* (1977), pp. 83-84.
[60] See above, pp. 46-50.
[61] *Report of the Committee on the Civil Service 1966-68*, Cmnd. 3638 (1968).

Trade and Industry in 1971; the Manpower Services Commission, the Advisory and Conciliation and Arbitration Service (ACAS) and the Health and Safety Commission were split from the Department of Employment in 1974. These agencies were *regulatory* in nature, even though part of their brief might also include the giving of advice.

The general reasons for creating such agencies are neatly summarised in one study as follows:[62]

"First, there is the 'buffer' theory which sees them as a way of protecting certain activities from political interference. Second, there is the 'escape' theory which sees them as escaping known weaknesses of traditional government departments. Third, the 'Corson' theory, following Mr. John Corson sees them as used to 'put the activity where the talent was', which might be outside government departments. Fourth, there is the participation or 'pluralistic' theory which thinks it desirable to spread power. Fifth, there is the 'back double' theory. This is based on the analogy with a taxi-driver who finds the main streets too busy and therefore uses back streets – what are known to taxi drivers as 'back doubles.' The back double theory is that if governments, local authorities or other bodies find that they cannot do the things they want within the existing structure, they set up new organisations which make it possible to do them. Sixth, the 'too many bureaucrats' view, mainly an American one, suggests that if the public thinks a country has too many civil servants it can set up quasi-non-governmental organisations whose employees are not classified as civil servants."

(2) RAYNER, IBBS AND NEXT STEPS AGENCIES

Various other attempts at improving efficiency and effectiveness in the civil service were to follow the Fulton Committee Report, but it was the establishment of the *Rayner Unit* in 1979, (now known as the *Efficiency Unit*), by the Prime Minister after her election victory that was to sow the seeds for more major reform. Lord Rayner had run Marks & Spencer and was brought in by Mrs Thatcher to improve efficiency and reduce waste within the civil service. Rayner headed a small team which undertook a number of efficiency scrutinies of particular departmental activities. In this sense Rayner operated through the medium of the laser beam rather than the arc light.[63]

The scrutinies produced savings in their own right, and also acted as a catalyst for further change in the system. Thus it was a Rayner scrutiny of the Department of Employment which was the impetus for the

---

[62] Hague, Mackenzie and Barker (eds.), *Public Policy and Private Interests: The Institutions of Compromise* (1975), p. 362. See also, the *Report on Non-Departmental Public Bodies*, Cmnd. 7797 (1980), paras. 10-16 for a list of similar considerations; Baldwin and McCrudden, *Regulation and Public Law*, Chap. 1. An additional reason underlying the creation of some agencies is that government can immunise itself from criticism in certain politically sensitive areas. In the public mind it will often be the "X commission" or the "Y authority" which receives the brunt of public disquiet.

[63] Hennessy, *Whitehall* (1990), Chap. 14; McDonald, *The Future of Whitehall* (1991), Chap. 1.

establishment of MINIS or Management Information Systems, designed to enable the minister to explore "who does what, why and what does it cost?"[64] The Efficiency Unit under Rayner also conceived what is now known as FMI, Financial Management Initiative, although this was then put into operation by a different body, the Financial Management Unit.[65] As Hennessy notes[66] the FMI was meant to be "fast breeder reactor which would achieve a permanent self-sustaining reaction the length and breadth of every Civil Service chain of command." All managers were intended to have a clear view of their objectives, well defined responsibility for making the best use of their resources, and the information, training and expertise necessary to exercise their responsibilities effectively.

Sir Robin Ibbs succeeded Lord Rayner as head of the Efficiency Unit and began by undertaking an overview of the achievements of the Rayner scrutinies.[67] This was followed by a more radical study, which culminated in the "Next Steps" Report.[68] The radical nature of its proposals led to it being concealed until after the 1987 election. The object of the study was to discover what had been achieved by the scrutiny exercises and FMI, and what should be the next steps in civil service reform. The general conclusions of the study are aptly summarised by Hennessy.[69]

"Despite the real achievements of the Rayner years, it showed how little in the way of *real* financial and management responsibility had been devolved down the line; how meddlesome the Treasury and Cabinet Office remained; how dominant was the Whitehall culture of caution; how great was the premium on a safe pair of hands; and how rarely were proven managerial skills perceived as the way to reach the top of the bureaucratic tree."

The *Next Steps Report* proposed two fundamental changes:

(a) There should be a split between service delivery and the making of policy. As a consequence there should be a real devolution of power to executive agencies in the area of service delivery, which would cover approximately 95% of civil service activity.
(b) There should be an end to the fiction that the minister was responsible for everything done by officials in his or her own name.

After an initially shaky start the recommendations in the Report began to be acted upon in 1988-89. A project manager, Peter Kemp, was

---

[64] Drewry and Butcher, *The Civil Service Today* (2nd ed., 1991), pp. 203-206.
[65] *Financial Management in Government Departments*, Cmnd. 9058, (1983); Gray, Jenkins, Flynn and Rutherford, "The Management of Change in Whitehall: The Experience of the FMI" (1991) 69 Pub. Adm. 41.
[66] *Whitehall*, p. 606.
[67] *Making Things Happen: A Report on the Implication of Government Efficiency Scrutinies* (1985).
[68] *Improving Management in Government: The Next Steps* (1988); Goldsworthy, *Setting Up Next Steps: A Short Account of the Origins, Launch, and Implementation of the Next Steps Project in the British Civil Service* (1991); Lewis, "A New Way of Governing?" (1993) 64 Pol. Quarterly 316.
[69] *Whitehall* (1990), p. 620. Italics in the original.

appointed to carry forward the report's proposals, with reference to the creation of executive agencies responsible for service delivery. Government departments were required to review their activities and to consider five possibilities: abolition, privatisation, contracting out, creating an agency, and preservation of the status quo. If the agency route is chosen then the matter will be put into effect by a Project Executive made up of representatives from Kemp's Project Team, the Treasury, the Efficiency Unit and the sponsoring department itself.

Large parts of the civil service have been hived off and have agency status. As of October 1993 there were 92 agencies, including: the Passport Office; the Vehicle Inspectorate; the Social Security Benefits Agency; the Central Statistical Office; the Patent Office; the Occupational Health Service; the Driver and Vehicle Licensing Agency; HMSO; the Royal Mint; the Meteorological Office; the Insolvency Service; the Employment Service, the Medicines Control Agency and many others. Many, but not all, of the bodies which have been created are *service delivery agencies*.

(3) CONCLUSION

The developments from Fulton to Rayner to Ibbs do not follow in a series of logically inevitable steps. Few changes in the pattern of administration can be viewed in this manner. Yet they are not unconnected either. Once the drive for efficiency was on, and once the existing departmental structure had been challenged, it was natural to ask whether it really was desirable for activities to be performed in house. And once this question was posed it became natural also to ask whether the activity should continue to be performed by government at all, as opposed to being privatised; whether it should be undertaken by an executive agency, rather than in house; or whether it should be done outside the department on a contracting out basis, rather than by an executive agency. All three options have been employed in differing contexts, as will be seen below. It is for this reason that our administrative landscape has become more complex.

It should, moreover, be emphasised that there are connections between the administrative changes charted above and what has been termed the "New Public Management" (NPM). The doctrinal components of NPM include:[70] hands-on professional management in the public sector; standards of performance; output controls; the break-up of large bureaucratic structures; greater public sector competition; and greater discipline in resource use.

These new developments pose new challenges for public law, relating to accountability, susceptibility to judicial review, and the appropriate procedural and substantive norms to be applied to such bodies. It is to these issues which we must now turn.

---

[70] Hood, "A Public Management for All Seasons?" (1991) 69 Pub. Adm. 3, 4-5; see also, Lewis, "Reviewing Change in Government: New Public Management and Next Steps" [1994] P.L. 105.

2. Problems of Terminology and Scope

The *particular* names of the institutions which have been hived off, in one way or another, from central government vary enormously: commission, directorate, agency, inspectorate, authority, service and office are all to be found. Nothing technical normally turns upon these differences.

Various labels have been used to describe in more *general* terms the range of bodies discussed within this section. One such label which commonly appears is *quango*. This term is not the most useful general label that could be devised. The term originally connoted quasi-autonomous non-governmental organisation. As applied to a certain limited number of institutions this may be an informative label, but as a general term it is misleading for two reasons.

First, the special feature which is common to many of these bodies is that they are non-departmental, rather than non-governmental.[71] Secondly, it groups together institutions which although related are best kept separate. There is, on the one hand, the panoply of public institutions which are outside the ordinary departmental structures of government; on the other hand, there are a number of private institutions which subsist very largely as a result of government contracts. Usage of the general label "quango" clouds this fact by the very ambiguity inherent in the phrase "non-governmental". This can mean, *inter alia*, anything which is not a normal part of the departmental structure, or it could connote institutions which are private as opposed to public, but which rely very heavily upon government business.

The general term *agency* will, therefore, be employed. This is not, as stated at the outset of this section, intended to have a technical meaning. It is rather proposed as an omnibus label to describe the plethora of institutions which perform functions of a governmental nature and which exist outside the normal departmental framework.

It is possible to make a further division between *regulatory agencies* and *service delivery agencies*: the former being concerned with the regulation of a particular area, such as gaming, civil aviation, race relations and the like; the latter being primarily concerned with the provision of services, such as social welfare. This distinction must, however, be treated with caution since many agencies concerned with service delivery perform regulatory functions and vice versa.

3. Two Types of Agency: Organisational Framework

It *is*, however, important to draw a distinction between many of the agencies established independently of the Next Steps reforms, and those created pursuant thereto, quite simply because the organisational framework differs markedly in the two instances.

---

[71] *Report on Non-Departmental Public Bodies*, Cmnd. 7797 (1980), para. 17; Barker, "Quango: a Word and a Campaign", *Quangos in Britain* (Barker ed., 1982), pp. 219-225.

Agencies which have been established independently of the Next Steps initiative will almost always be based upon statute, or on occasion the prerogative. The empowering legislation for bodies such as the Civil Aviation Authority, the Monopolies and Mergers Commission, the Gaming Board, and the regulatory authorities created to oversee the privatised industries, will normally state in some detail the composition and powers of such bodies. This legislation will also indicate what role the minister is to have within that particular area. The minister may, for example, be able to give statutory directions to the agency, or ministerial approval may be required before certain courses of action can be taken. Any legal action for judicial review will normally be brought against the agency in its own name, unless the applicant is seeking to impugn a particular decision taken by the minister.

The position with respect to Next Steps agencies is markedly different. The powers of such agencies are defined not by statute, but through "framework agreements". These agreements will be made between the sponsoring department and the agency, and the Treasury will often be a party. The agreements cover a number of important topics: they set out a corporate plan defining current and future objectives; they dictate the financial arrangements for the agency, including accounting and auditing procedures; and they detail the agency's personnel and staffing policy. Once the agency is established the Chief Executive is responsible for its day to day running and he or she can be removed if goals are not met. While the agency is meant to be concerned with service delivery rather than policy the Chief Executive will inevitably have some input into the latter, if only to pass comment upon its workability. Framework agreements are reviewed on average every three years, but adjustments can be made within this period. The nature of the appropriate defendant in any legal action is more difficult with respect to these agencies, and this issue will be considered in more detail below.[72]

It should, however, be noted that there are some considerable differences *even within* the category of Next Steps Agencies: thus some of these agencies have a monopoly status over their activity while others do not; some agencies are self-funding while others rely upon departmental disbursement; and a number of the agencies perform regulatory roles, while others are primarily concerned with service delivery. These differences can have a marked impact upon the practical operation of the agencies.[73]

4. *Agencies: Problems and Concerns*

The existence of agencies outside the normal departmental framework gives rise to a number of problems which will be addressed within this section. The nature of these concerns can differ as between those agencies which

---

[72] See below, pp. 93-95.
[73] Greer, "The Next Steps Initiative: An Examination of the Agency Framework Documents" (1992) 70 Pub. Adm. 89.

were created pursuant to the Next Steps initiative and those which have been established for other reasons. Separate treatment of the two kinds of agency will, therefore, be necessary in relation to some of the issues which follow.

(1) PATRONAGE AND STAFFING

(a) *Patronage*

People are required to staff and run agencies. They must perforce be appointed. Who appoints? Well it depends upon the particular organisation in question. As they have been created in an *ad hoc* manner no fixed policy applies. Normally however it will be the minister of the department under whose aegis the organisation exists that will make the appointment. Therein lies the concern. A concern that the power will be used to achieve ends felt to be undesirable. One major department was responsible for nearly 1,000 appointments of which 30 carried a salary or entitlement to a fee, and the total annual payments on this account were approximately £200,000.

The whole question of appointments must, however, be kept within perspective. It is not left completely in the uncontrolled discretion of the relevant minister. The Public Appointments Unit of the Civil Service Department maintains a central list of potential members of public bodies. The minister is accountable to Parliament for the appointments which are made, and he or she will consult the Prime Minister on major posts. A Directory of Paid Public Appointments made by ministers is produced by the Civil Service Department, complemented by a periodical white paper which gives a list of Members of Public Boards of a Commercial Character containing the actual names of the appointees. Added to both of these sources are the annual reports produced by bodies in the executive group.

The idea that we are faced with a completely closed, concealed pattern of ministerial patronage is therefore misleading. More information could be made available concerning advisory bodies, but in general secrecy is not a major concern. It is no doubt true that parliamentary scrutiny of such appointments is of limited effectiveness. So also however is the party political benefit to be gained by having a say in the appointments thus made.[74] Moreover, as Johnson states, it may well be valuable to have opportunities for the public-minded citizen to engage in public service.[75]

The direction of reform or improvement in this area is not entirely clear, and the optimal membership may vary depending upon the type of agency. Serious thought should, however, be given to Davies' suggestion that real public representation should be increased and that more open competition for appointments should be allowed.[76]

---

[74] Johnson, "Editorial: Quangos and the Structure of British Government" (1979) 57 Pub. Adm. 379, 385.

[75] *Ibid.* pp. 385-386.

[76] "Patronage and Quasi-Government: Some Proposals for Reform", *Quangos in Britain* (Barker ed., 1982), Chap. 10.

(b) Staffing: Next Steps Agencies

The problems with respect to staffing and Next Steps Agencies are rather different in nature. These agencies are staffed by civil servants, although Chief Executives will be recruited through open competition and approximately one third have come from outside the civil service.

The question is how far the image of a uniform civil service can realistically be maintained, given the creation of these agencies. The official response has been to talk of a unified, but not uniform civil service, the message being that the structural diversity created by the existence of agencies is bound to have some ramifications for uniform conditions of pay, and conditions of service, which were the norm hitherto. HMSO has, for example, introduced a new pay and grading structure tailored to meet its business needs, and more flexibility in terms and conditions of service is very much the order of the day. Other agencies are also doing so. Bonus schemes are run by a number of agencies.[77] The passage of the Civil Service (Management Functions) Act 1992, discussed below, is designed to facilitate agency autonomy with respect to pay bargaining and conditions of service.

These ramifications may well be greater than initially envisaged: the more that Chief Executives are encouraged to develop pay structures which suit their own agency, the less easy will it be for there to be a regular interchange between the agency and the department itself, more particularly if agency pay is determined in part by commercial criteria, while that at the centre is held in check by political considerations.[78] Would we ever go as far as one agency in Spain which has responsibility for revenue collection, and can retain a certain percentage of whatever it collects? Incentive indeed.

(2) CONTROL AND ACCOUNTABILITY:
AGENCIES OTHER THAN NEXT STEPS AGENCIES

It is particularly important to distinguish control and accountability. Control refers to the way in which the parent department may influence or direct an agency. Accountability is concerned with the answerability of that institution to the public, either through Parliament or through some more direct means of public participation. Degrees of control and accountability need not necessarily go hand in hand. It may for example be desirable that the agency exercises a large degree of independence in the decisions which it makes; this may have been the chief reason for its establishment. While therefore this would indicate relatively little direct control, it would not necessarily follow that accountability should be similarly minimal.[79] It is not, however, difficult to perceive why the term accountability has been used in an omnibus sense to cover both control and the narrower sense of accountability mentioned here. Our traditional notions of ministerial responsibility see accountability in its narrow sense as existing by and through

---

[77] 14 as of October 1993.

[78] Drewry and Butcher, The Civil Service Today, pp. 234-237.

[79] Keeling, "Beyond Ministerial Departments: Mapping the Administrative Terrain 1. Quasi-Governmental Agencies" (1976) 54 Pub. Adm. 161, 169.

normal departmental mechanisms to the minister and hence to Parliament. It is presumed that what the minister is answerable for he or she also controls, or should do at least in theory. In the case of agencies this presumption cannot always be maintained.

Control can take two principal forms. Firstly, it may be *ex ante*. This will be a function of *the degree of precision laid down in the enabling legislation*, primary or secondary, as to what is to be done, how it is to be achieved,[80] and the type of relationship between the institution and the department responsible for it. Often a wide discretion will be accorded to the organisation. This may be because the problem itself is novel and requires to be worked out over a period of time. It may be because the subject-matter is of a type which renders it difficult to delegate anything other than a broad discretion. Or it may be that the very purpose of the agency's establishment is to provide an independent judgment. On the other hand the minister may well set limitations or guidelines indicating the general principles which the agency should employ.

Secondly, control may be exercised by *monitoring* the decisions reached by the institution. How closely departments exercise this type of control is difficult to assess and even more difficult to generalise about. The degree of monitoring will in itself be partly dependent upon the composition of the particular organisation and the type of subject-matter with which it is dealing. Johnson concludes that executive control is blurred and spasmodic.[81] He does, however, point out that this does not mean that diffuse control is necessarily a bad thing. Organisational theory indicates that there may well be certain institutions which function better where restraint is diffuse as opposed to a more rigid form of internal management control.[82]

It is in the realm of *traditional accountability* that most public disquiet has been focused. The discussion of the administrative machinery in the nineteenth century revealed the strains placed on the Board system by the growing desire of Parliament to have a person directly answerable in the House for its activities.[83] The resurgence and expansion of agencies has raised this same problem in a more acute form, since we are now accustomed to the idea of ministerial responsibility as the "constitutional norm". Accountability can assume three principal forms.

First, the organisation may be *accountable to the minister*, with the latter being responsible to Parliament. There are very real limits to the application of this concept in this area. The establishment of an agency means that, for one of the reasons given above, it has been decided to locate decision-making in an institution somewhat removed from the departmental norm. In a formal sense it could be said that the minister is still responsible for all acts of every agency irrespective of its status and the way in which it operates. The problem with doing this is that it would be wholly inconsistent with the legislative framework establishing certain bodies,

---

[80] Hague, Mackenzie and Barker (eds.), *Public Policy and Private Interests*, pp. 363-364.
[81] "Editorial: Quangos and the Structure of British Government" (1979) 57 Pub. Adm. 379, 388.
[82] *Ibid.* pp. 388-389.
[83] See above, pp. 46-48.

which openly grants them a measure of independence, or where such independence is the very rationale for their existence.[84]

Secondly, accountability may be secured through direct *parliamentary supervision* within the new regime of select committees.[85] The problem with the select committee as a mechanism for control in this area is but one aspect of the more general question as to their efficacy, which was considered above. Johnson has expressed significant reservations as to whether they are capable of comprehensive oversight of agencies, as opposed to having a more selective impact upon particular issues.[86] Recent research on the performance of select committees would appear to substantiate these reservations.[87] The possibility of devising some new parliamentary body to oversee agencies will be considered below.[88]

A third and less direct form of accountability would be to place greater reliance upon the *Parliamentary Commissioner for Administration* (PCA), who already exercises oversight over some agencies.[89] The Select Committee on the PCA recommended that the number of such bodies which are within the jurisdiction of the PCA should be increased, and this has now occurred.[90] While such a development is beneficial, it is difficult to see how it can provide any form of comprehensive oversight. The authority of the PCA is likely to be invoked when particular behaviour of an agency has burdensome consequences for individuals which may evidence maladministration by the institution. Systematic scrutiny of agencies would still be lacking.

There is therefore no simple solution to the problem of accountability. Two further comments are warranted. On the one hand, even if agencies were to be "reincorporated" into the normal departmental structure, very real problems would still remain, precisely because the accountability of departments is itself limited due to the executive's dominance of the legislature. On the other hand, given that there are serious obstacles to ensuring traditional accountability "to the top", we may wish to consider supplementing this with accountability "from the bottom" via participation in agency decision-making and the like.[91]

(3) ACCOUNTABILITY: NEXT STEPS AGENCIES

In general terms the same types of problems apply to executive agencies created pursuant to the Next Steps programme. These problems have, however, been felt particularly keenly, in part because the subject-matter

---

[84] *e.g.* the Arts Council, research councils, nationalised industries and the Civil Aviation Authority.

[85] Suggested by the *Report on Non-Departmental Public Bodies*, Cmnd. 7797 (1980), paras. 81-85.

[86] "Editorial" (1979) 57 Pub. Adm. 379, 390; Johnson, "Accountability, Control and Complexity; Moving Beyond Ministerial Responsibility", *Quangos in Britain* (Barker, ed., 1982), Chap. 12.

[87] See above, pp. 74-78.

[88] See below, pp. 105-107.

[89] *e.g.* Health and Safety Commission and Executive and the Office of Fair Trading.

[90] Parliamentary and Health Service Commissioners Act 1987.

[91] See below, Chap. 7.

dealt with by the agencies has been drawn so directly from that previously undertaken in-house by departments, and in part because the resolution of the problems in this area is especially problematic.

The degree of ministerial *control* will be largely dependent upon the specificity of the framework agreement, and this varies from area to area.[92]

The problems of *accountability* have occupied more attention. The issue is put succinctly by Drewry and Butcher.[93]

> "The basic problem is quite simply stated but not at all easily resolved. How can ministers credibly cling to their virtual monopoly of account-ability to Parliament, via traditional models of ministerial responsibility that (according to Mrs Thatcher) were to remain unaltered by the *Next Steps*, in respect of agencies whose chief executives are expected to take managerial initiatives at arm's length from ministerial control?"

Concerns of this nature have been expressed by the Treasury and Civil Service Committee,[94] but the government has indicated that no change in the basic constitutional arrangements is required.[95]

Having said this it is clear that some modification in the traditional conception of ministerial accountability has been accepted. Framework documents are normally to be published and the government appears to accept that MPs might prefer to deal with the Chief Executive on opera-tional matters. Moreover, the government also appears to accept that while Chief Executives will normally give evidence to a select committee on behalf of the minister, it will be the former who is the most appropriate person to respond when a select committee has day-to-day concerns about the agency's operation.

This "compromise", reflecting as it does traditional British pragmatism, may be no bad thing. The minister will still be there and responsible, in theory at least, for matters of principle or general policy. In addition to this the Chief Executive will, under the new regime, be visible and the objectives of the agency will be publicly known. In this sense there will be a new figure who can be called to account for operational agency failure and this is to be welcomed.

Moreover, in considering accountability it should be borne in mind that under the traditional regime prior to the Next Steps initiative it was often difficult to determine what the detailed departmental goals actually were, which rendered it difficult for accountability to be meaningful. The con-trast with the reformed institutional order is highlighted in a Briefing Note issued by the Next Steps team in 1992. Even if one may have doubts about the attainment of the enhanced sense of accountability mentioned in the following quotation one can see the force of the sentiments expressed. Having stated that agencies are accountable to Parliament through the relevant minister the Note continues in the following vein.[96]

---

[92] McDonald, *The Future of Whitehall* (1991), pp. 54-55.
[93] *The Civil Service Today* (2nd ed., 1991), p. 228.
[94] *e.g.* Eighth Report, 1987-88.
[95] *Government Reply*, Cm. 524 (1988).
[96] *Next Steps, Briefing Note* (1992), para. 20.

"Next Steps has enhanced accountability to Parliament through its requirements for Agencies to publish their framework documents, annual targets, annual reports and accounts and, where appropriate, their corporate and business plans. Agency Chief Executives are accounting officers and, as such, are answerable to the Public Accounts Committee for the use of the resources allocated to them."

What is perhaps of equal importance to our concerns about accountability is the extent to which the division between policy consideration, undertaken by the core department, and service delivery, done by the agency, is maintainable. It is not simply that these two activities can naturally overlap. It is also the case that past experience with nationalised industries, where a similar functional divide was meant to operate, has taught us both that governments often meddled with day-to-day operations, while staunchly resisting answering any questions on the topic by claiming that such matters were not within its purview; and also that governmental guidance on more general issues of policy was often not forthcoming or was subject to frequent revision.[97]

(4) THE CITIZEN'S CHARTER AND EFFECTIVENESS

Measuring the effectiveness of agencies has always been problematic, both in relation to those agencies established independently of the Next Steps initiative and with respect to Next Steps agencies themselves. Any such measurement requires two tools, statistical evidence of some type and criteria by which to use it. Both of these can involve problems.

Statistical evidence may be unreliable either because there is simply not enough data, or because the variables which have to be "computed" in the analysis are too speculative.[98]

The process of determining whether given objectives are being pursued effectively, is, if anything, even more difficult for a number of reasons: the enabling legislation may be unclear as to what those objectives are, or they may clash *inter se*; even where objectives are clear there may be a choice as to the means to achieve the given end and what the "best choice" is may not be readily apparent; and the area may be one in which it is inherently difficult to decide whether and how far the given end has in fact been successfully attained.[99] These difficulties of determining institutional effectiveness are not, however, limited to agencies. They would be equally problematic if such policies were pursued through the normal departmental structure.

Having said this it is clear that the government perceives a real link between Next Steps agencies and the attainment of the objectives in the Citizen's Charter. The Charter established a number of principles which should operate in the context of governmental service delivery:[100] the setting

---

[97] Prosser, *Nationalised Industries and Public Control* (1986).
[98] *e.g.* it may be unclear how those who are to be regulated will react to the proposed regulation and the costs of regulation may be affected by external factors (such as the costs of evasive techniques) which cannot be determined with accuracy.
[99] *e.g.* in the case of support for the Arts, or the prevention of sexual or racial discrimination.
[100] Cm. 1599 (1991).

of *standards* for service delivery and the assessment of actual performance against those standards; *openness* as to how the services are run; *consultation* with service users; *choice*, wherever possible, as to the services which are available; *value for money*; *remedies* when things go wrong. Charter Mark awards are made to those agencies that have provided services to the highest standards, taking account of the principles in the Citizen's Charter.

It is precisely because the Next Steps agencies are so often in the front line of service delivery that the government attaches considerable weight to the attainment of the Charter goals in this area. The official documents which periodically emerge bear testimony to the zeal for demonstrating cost savings and better delivery of services.[101] These documents are replete with instances where this has occurred, ranging from: increases in productivity by Companies House with consequential reduction in the time which it takes to place company documents on record; to the publication of more particular Charters in specific areas.[102] These views on efficiency and enhanced service delivery are from the "inside", and should be read in this light. They should not, however, be ignored.

The Citizen's Charter has, moreover, had an impact upon statutory agencies and other public bodies which exist independently of the Next Steps regime. The Charter has provided part of the stimulus for legislation which is designed to measure standards of performance of bodies such as utilities[103] and local government.[104]

One of the interesting effects of these developments has been to raise the public's expectations about the standards which public agencies should meet. This in turn has led to more complaints to the Parliamentary Commissioner for Administration. As the PCA has noted, individuals' hopes are whetted by the promises in the Citizen's Charter and other charters, of better governance, tighter targets and higher standards, and there may be a gap between these hopes and actual performance.[105]

5. *Agencies: Legal Status*

A range of technical legal questions are raised by the existence of agencies. Are they emanations of the Crown? What remedies will be available against them? Can they be proceeded against in their own name or must the sponsoring department be joined? The answer will vary depending upon the way in which the particular organisation was established. It is difficult to extrapolate from one organisation to another and it would be a Herculean labour to catalogue the answers to all such questions as they apply to all

---

[101] *Improving Management in Government – The Next Steps Agencies*, Cm. 1760 (1991); *Improving Management in Government – The Next Steps Agencies*, Cm. 2111 (1992); *Next Steps, Briefing Notes* (1992 and 1993).
[102] These include the Benefits Agency Customer Charter, the Employment Service Jobseeker's Charter, and the Taxpayer's Charter.
[103] Competition and Service (Utilities) Act 1992.
[104] Local Government Act 1992.
[105] Parliamentary Commissioner for Administration, Annual Report 1992, p. 1.

such organisations. There are, nonetheless, certain points of general importance which should be made, and these relate to the difference in the status of agencies created prior to, or independently of, the Next Steps initiative, and the Next Steps agencies themselves.

Agencies which have been created prior to, or independently of, the Next Steps initiative will, as noted above, almost always be founded upon statute. The relevant legislation will set out the agency's powers and responsibilities. Applications for judicial review can be brought against the agency itself in the normal way if an individual feels that the agency has exceeded its powers. Actions against bodies such as the Monopolies and Mergers Commission, the Commission for Racial Equality or the Gaming Board have been brought not infrequently. The relevant minister may also be a party to any such action if the applicant claims that ministerial powers granted under the legislation have been exceeded.[106]

The position with respect to Next Steps agencies is markedly different. They owe their existence to administrative reorganisation of the civil service.[107] The basis of their powers is laid down in the relevant framework documents, and they are clearly intended to operate as largely independent entities with the Chief Executives being responsible for the attainment of targets or corporate goals.

This sense of independence has been enhanced by statutory changes which have further emphasised the separateness of the agencies. One such change is that a number of these agencies are now financed as trading funds pursuant to the Government Trading Act 1990, which in essence allows certain activities to be run through moneys obtained from the provision of goods or services. Bodies such as HMSO, Companies House, the Patent Office, the Vehicle Inspectorate and the Land Registry are now run in this manner. This method of financing increases the autonomy of such institutions. The other important legislative innovation is the Civil Service (Management Functions) Act 1992. The effect of the statute is to increase agency autonomy in relation to the discharge of its functions, and to facilitate separate appointment and management practices by agencies. Earlier legislation had provided for the transfer of functions as between different Ministers of the Crown. These transfers were to be effectuated by a transfer of functions Order.[108] The 1992 legislation now provides that where such an Order has been made the Minister of the Crown in whom the function has been vested may delegate that function to any other Crown servant, subject to such conditions as he or she thinks fit.[109] The delegee may also authorise other Crown servants to carry out the relevant function.[110] Equally important are the provisions of the Act which relate to appointment and management of members of the civil service. Section 2 of

---

[106] Baldwin and McCrudden, *Regulation and Public Law* (1987).

[107] There may be statutes which are of relevance for a small number of Next Steps agencies in circumstances where the body which has now attained agency status was subject to some statutory provisions.

[108] Ministers of the Crown Act 1975, s.1.

[109] Civil Service (Management Functions) Act 1992, s.1(2).

[110] *Ibid.* s.1(4).

the Act states that any statutory powers concerning appointment and management which require ministerial sanction can, if the minister so wishes, be exercised without this sanction, or subject to such conditions as are thought fit.[111] Prior to the passage of this Act pay settlements had to be approved by the Treasury, and this was the case even where, as in the case of HMSO, a separate pay structure had been established. The effect of the 1992 legislation is to authorise agencies to settle pay conditions for themselves. This will become effective in April 1994 for agencies which have more than 2,000 employees.

Notwithstanding these factors which serve to emphasise the separateness of Next Steps agencies they do not have any formal legal status of their own.[112] Legal actions will in general have to be brought against the relevant minister under whose aegis the agency functions. This will have consequences for a number of possible legal types of action, but it is by no means clear that all such consequences have been fully thought through. Three principal types of legal challenge are of relevance here.

First, there is ordinary judicial review. If one of these agencies abuses its powers then it seems that it will be the minister who will appear in any such action. The agency will simply be regarded as part of the parent department.

Secondly, there are issues concerning both contractual liability and contractual authority. When a Next Steps agency makes a contract of some kind then who precisely is the private party making the contract with? There is little doubt that many private parties would imagine that they are making the contract with the agency itself. But the "logic" of the Next Steps agency relationship would seem to indicate that in law the contract is with the department, in the same way as if a civil servant who remains within the core department had entered a contract. In both instances the civil servant would be acting on behalf of the minister and the department itself. Moreover, although the general thrust of the Next Steps initiative would suggest that agencies should only have contractual authority within their own areas it is by no means clear how this fits with more general doctrines of contract as they apply to public bodies.[113]

Finally, there are matters relating to tortious liability. Once again the logic of the Next Steps scheme would indicate that the parent department remains responsible if there has, for example, been operational negligence by an agency, subject to the normal rules which apply in this area.

These and other matters of legal liability will have to be resolved in due course. They do, however, highlight a tension which is inherent in the whole Next Steps regime.[114]

On the one hand, there is the desire to foster the institutional autonomy and responsibility of these new agencies. Framework documents which set targets, corporate plans and the like are all designed to separate off service delivery from policy formation. The aim is to create institutions which will

---

[111] Subject to ss.2(3),(4).
[112] Harden, *The Contracting State* (1992), pp. 44, 46.
[113] See below, Chap. 19.
[114] Freedland, "Government by Contract and Public Law" [1994] P.L. 86, 88-89.

have responsibility for their particular area. Agency performance is then to be measured and evaluated. This theme is complemented by new arrangements for pay and conditions of service which are performance-related.

On the other hand, there is the continued legal responsibility of the department itself. This unchanging responsibility follows from the fact that the agencies have been granted no formal status as such. To be sure the framework document has the advantage for the department that it can be revised more easily than legislation. Yet it is this very basis for the agency-departmental relationship which means that departmental legal responsibility may well remain when something goes wrong. And the preservation of this legal liability detracts from the objective of creating agencies which really do bear the consequences of the choices which they make.

6. *Agencies: Institutional Design and Legal Principle*

A number of important issues of institutional design and legal principle are raised by the existence of agencies. These issues are connected and are best approached initially through the study of different agencies in order to determine the types of legal problem which they pose.[115] Some more general conclusions will be drawn thereafter.

(1) THE CIVIL AVIATION AUTHORITY

Baldwin shows how the CAA evolved as a result of dissatisfaction with its predecessor, the Air Transport Licensing Board.[116] The ATLB operated like a traditional tribunal and suffered from three related defects: it failed to develop a working relationship with the minister; it was unable to produce durable policies to guide its licensing decisions; and it lacked expertise. These criticisms and others were echoed by the Edwards' Committee on "Air transport in the seventies" which advocated the replacement of the ATLB by an agency which would combine economic and safety regulation,

---

[115] Hague, Mackenzie and Barker (eds.), *Public Policy and Private Interests: The Institutions of Compromise* (1975); Baldwin and McCrudden, *Regulation and Public Law* (1987); Lewis, "IBA Programme Contract Awards"[1975] P.L. 317; Bradley and Wilkie, "The Arts Council: The Case for an Organisational Enquiry" (1975) 53 Pub. Adm. 67; Giddings, "Parliament, Boards and Autonomy: The Case of Agricultural Marketing Boards" (1975) 53 Pub. Adm. 383; Baldwin, "A British Independent Regulatory Agency and the 'Skytrain' Decision" [1978] P.L. 57; Purdue, "The Implications of the Constitution and Function of Regional Water Authorities" [1979] P.L. 119; Baldwin, "A Quango Unleashed: The Abolition of Policy Guidance in Civil Aviation Licensing" (1980) 58 Pub. Adm. 287; Tyrrell, "The Politics of a Hived Off Board: The Advisory, Conciliation and Arbitration Service" (1980) 58 Pub. Adm. 225.

[116] Baldwin, *Regulating the Airlines, Administrative Justice and Agency Discretion* (1985) and "Civil Aviation Regulation: From Tribunal to Regulatory Agency", Baldwin and McCrudden, *Regulation and Public Law*, Chap. 8. See also the two articles by Baldwin, [1978] P.L. 57 and (1980) 58 Pub. Adm. 287.

air traffic control and the negotiation of traffic rights. Departmental licensing was rejected as an alternative because independent airline operators were unsure that they would obtain fair treatment from the government.[117] To circumvent the constitutional problems flowing from the creation of an independent agency to control air transport licensing, it was proposed that the CAA be subject to guidance by the minister by way of written policy statements.

With some modification what emerged as the Civil Aviation Act 1971 followed the main thrust of the Edwards' Committee Report.[118] The Secretary of State for Trade was empowered to give guidance on policy[119] and this he duly did when the CAA was established. The formation of these broad policies was not a one-way operation; the CAA itself had an impact on the resulting statement of government policy through reports and consultation. In addition to such policy guidance from the department, the CAA has itself structured its discretion through announcements and consultation.

While the CAA was not the first regulatory agency to be given broad powers, its scope of authority and degree of independence was more redolent of United States' administrative machinery than English. The Poor Law Commission possessed a broad spectrum of powers, but Parliament's desire for more direct control and the controversial nature of the subject-matter led to its downfall. What the establishment of the CAA represented was a realisation of the benefits to be gained from administration outside of the departmental norm plus an attempt to avoid a dual problem which has beset the United States' agencies: how to maintain some political control over the agency and how to give it a clearer idea as to the manner in which its broad discretion should be exercised.[120] The system of policy guidance was intended to achieve both of these ends.

One unfortunate result of the guidance indicating no competition on long haul routes was that the Laker "Skytrain" was told that it would not be allowed to operate. This was unfortunate because Laker had invested nearly £7 million on the strength of government representations that he should be granted the route. Nothing daunted, Laker took the government to court alleging that the policy guidance which resulted in the withdrawal of Laker Airways from the North American route was *ultra vires*. The Court of Appeal agreed.[121] The essence of their reasoning was that "guidance" had a limited role. The Secretary of State's power to give such guidance was contained in section 3(2) of the Civil Aviation Act 1971. The preceding subsection, 3(1), set out four basic objectives that the CAA was to pursue. Guidance given pursuant to section 3(2) could not reverse or contradict the general objectives of the statute as laid down in section

---

[117] "Civil Aviation Regulation: From Tribunal to Regulatory Agency", Baldwin and McCrudden, pp. 164-165.
[118] *e.g.* the negotiation of traffic rights was left to the Secretary of State.
[119] s.3(2).
[120] See, *e.g. Perspectives on the Administrative Process* (Rabin ed., 1979).
[121] *Laker Airways Ltd* v. *Department of Trade* [1977] Q.B. 643.

3(1).[122] The Secretary of State's policy guidance was, said the Court of Appeal, attempting to do just that. It was therefore *ultra vires*.

The case raises a number of important legal issues. The precise way in which the policy guidance contradicted the statutory objectives was, for example, never made quite clear.[123] It is however with the broader questions as to the relationship of the CAA and the Secretary of State that we are most concerned here. Baldwin argues persuasively that the court misconceived the role of the CAA.[124] They treated it as if it were a traditional body with quasi-judicial functions which should be "protected" from executive interference, failing to perceive that it was a multi-faceted agency which was not intended to be independent of government.

The aftermath of the *Laker* decision is of interest.[125] The limitations placed upon the ability of the Secretary of State to issue policy guidance has resulted in an increased structuring of discretion by the CAA itself. There seems no inherent reason why the CAA should not be able to structure its own discretion in this way. Strong arguments can be made that even if the Secretary of State's role had not been limited, the CAA should be encouraged to confine and structure its own powers.[126] This does not however touch the issue of principle which is whether it is preferable to have some broad political control exercised through the mechanism of policy guidance. The debates on the Civil Aviation Bill 1979 reflect the two opposing views. The government decided to drop the notion of policy guidance, the argument being that if an area was to be hived off it should be truly independent; "both hands should be taken off the wheel". Political control could, it was said, be maintained by alterations in the list of statutory criteria. The Opposition saw this as an abdication of legislative responsibility to a largely unaccountable body. Refining the list of statutory objectives would not solve the problem; such criteria were often in conflict and required balancing.[127]

What the foregoing discussion of the CAA demonstrates is that issues of legal principle concerning decision-making by agencies can come in many shapes and forms. They can involve questions as to the proper levels of procedural constraint, or the most appropriate scope for substantive review. Examples of both of these will be given hereafter. Attacks framed in terms of *ultra vires* can, however, also raise fundamental questions as to the very institutional structure established for a particular agency. While, as argued above, such organisations cannot by their very nature be forced into the traditional framework of ministerial responsibility for measures carried out within a department, this does not necessarily lead to a "both hands off

---

[122] The Court of Appeal was influenced in reaching this conclusion by the power to give directions contained in s.4 of the 1971 Act which would override the objectives set out in s.3(1).

[123] Baldwin, "A British Independent Regulatory Agency and the 'Skytrain' Decision" [1978] P.L. 57, 78-79.

[124] *Ibid.* p. 78.

[125] It is set out in Baldwin, "A Quango Unleashed: The Abolition of Policy Guidance in Civil Aviation Licensing" (1980) 58 Pub. Adm. 287.

[126] See below, pp. 396-400.

[127] (1980) 58 Pub.Adm. 287, pp. 293-294. See now the Civil Aviation Act 1980, ss.12, 13.

the wheel" approach. Given the initial decision that air transport licensing should be hived-off, it is arguable that the institutional balance secured by the Civil Aviation Act 1971 was a desirable one.[128] The system of policy guidance enshrined therein went some way at least to preserve account-ability and to provide a more detailed clarification of inherently vague statutory standards, two of the most pressing problems in this whole area.

(2) NATIONALISATION AND THE PUBLIC CORPORATION[129]

Public corporations have been the principal vehicle used in the national-isation of industry. The reasons for such nationalisation have varied, and have included the following: a belief that certain functions are vital to the nation and should not be left in the hands of private enterprise; a desire to provide services which the market mechanism would not generate or sustain; a belief that certain natural monopolies should be run by the state in order to prevent the accumulation of excessive profits were the industry to be left in private hands; and a political doctrine based on the idea that the people should own the industrial assets of the nation, or at least a proportion of them.

The principal institutional form utilised to realise these objectives was the establishment of a public corporation.[130] The precise details of nation-alisation statutes varied, but certain common features were evident.[131] The general theme was that the industry should be autonomous in its day-to-day administration, but that ministers should have power to determine overall policy. This theme manifested itself in a number of ways: ministers pos-sessed the power of appointment to the boards of the industries; they could issue general directions to these boards; ministerial sanction was required for major development programmes and ministers exercised certain specific powers over financial matters.

The ideal of day-to-day autonomy coupled with ministerial control over long term planning has proven unsuccessful. It has been undermined from both sides. On the one hand, successive governments have used nationalised industry to respond to short term pressures. Long term planning has been upset by ministerial pressure to buy British, to resist wage increases, or to curtail a capital investment programme. Such pressure has moreover been exerted covertly, rather than through the usage of the power to give directions. On the other hand, governments have been notably lacking in the type of broad policy directive envisioned by the enabling legislation.

Both of the preceding points are united by a single theme, uncertainty as to the role that such industries should play in the economy of the country.

---

[128] The CAA itself did, however, have reservations about the guidance system, Baldwin, "Civil Aviation Regulation: From Tribunal to Regulatory Agency", pp. 167-168.

[129] Robson, *Problems of Nationalised Industry* (1952); Friedmann and Garner (eds.), *Govern-ment Enterprise* (1970); Friedmann, *The State and the Rule of Law in a Mixed Economy* (1971); Friedmann (ed.), *Public and Private Enterprise in Mixed Economies* (1974); Coombes, *State Enterprise: Politics or Business?* (1971); Prosser, *Nationalised Industries and Public Control* (1986).

[130] Other techniques include the government taking a shareholding in an existing company.

[131] *e.g.* Coal Industry Nationalisation Act 1946; Civil Aviation Act 1946; Transport Act 1946; Gas Act 1948; Iron and Steel Act 1949.

Some have seen them as operating primarily as commercial enterprises, at least to the minimal extent that this enables the management to fulfil their obligations to balance revenue and expenditure. Others have perceived their commercial role as largely secondary to their function as an extended arm of government, whether this be in preventing regional unemployment, or in helping to implement the broad aims of the government's financial policy. This has not made life easy for those running the major corporations. Pushed from pillar to post they are lambasted for poor commercial returns, while being cajoled by government to achieve ends which ordinary commercial judgment would reject.

The preceding uncertainty as to the role of nationalised industries has enabled successive ministers to use the formal statutory scheme as both a sword and a shield: a sword in the way in which it allows the minister to exercise influence formally and informally over the industry; a shield in the protection it provides to the executive from embarrassing questions from the Commons. Such unwelcome interrogatories are often met by the response that the issue concerns day-to-day administration, and hence is outside the minister's responsibility.

The uncertainty as to the role which such industries should play and as to their objectives can be demonstrated "schematically" by considering in temporal sequence a range of proposed "answers" to this issue. The initial idea which permeated Labour thinking from 1945-1950 was that the change of ownership from private to public would remove the profit motive and enable nationalised industries to act as "high custodians of the public interest". The shift from private to public ownership does not however resolve, in and of itself, the task of defining the public interest, and the imprecision in this phrase could enable managers and politicians alike to pursue their own objectives under the guise of acting in the national interest; "wolfish self-interest is all too easily cloaked in the public interest sheepskin".[132]

A second approach to the problem is evident in the White Papers of 1961 and 1967,[133] the latter of which strove to bring greater clarity to the objectives of nationalised industries. It advocated, *inter alia*, marginal cost pricing, set criteria for investment decisions, and proposed that non-commercial activities should be accounted for separately, with the government deciding whether to support such activities on cost-benefit criteria. This approach while reflecting a coherent policy proved to be of little effect for two reasons. On the one hand, "there was no attempt to develop an adequate structure of incentives to encourage managers to act in the desired ways",[134] and consequently many ignored the pricing and investment guidelines. On the other hand, the problem of informal ministerial influence designed to attain goals other than those stipulated in

---

[132] Vickers and Yarrow, *Privatisation, An Economic Analysis* (1988), p. 130.

[133] *Financial and Economic Obligations of the Nationalised Industries*, Cmnd. 1337 (1961); *Nationalised Industries: A Review of Economic and Financial Objectives*, Cmnd. 3437 (1967).

[134] Vickers and Yarrow, *Privatisation*, p. 132.

the White Paper, was left unresolved. Not surprisingly ministers continued to exert such influence.

A third approach is apparent in the 1978 White Paper, and in Conservative policy subsequent thereto.[135] Financial target setting became the principal form of control, supplemented by performance indicators which each industry was required to publish in order that sponsoring departments could assess efficiency within the industry.[136] The post-1978 framework of control has relied most heavily upon external financing limits (EFL), which place constraints upon the annual change of the net indebtedness of public corporations to the government. This serves to restrict the difference between revenue and expenditure. The use of EFLs also serves to highlight the difficult situation of public corporations. EFLs were accorded such prominence principally because of governmental concern over macro-economic issues, such as the existence of fiscal deficit and the corresponding desire to control public sector borrowing. The tension between the exercise of commercial freedom, and the utilisation of public corporations as part of a broader governmental strategy is apparent once again.

(3) PRIVATISATION AND REGULATORY CONTROL

The way in which decisions as to *whether* to regulate, and if so *how*, are influenced by considerations of political choice has already been considered. The reasons for privatisation and the problems which this poses for public law, must now be considered in more detail. A fuller analysis of the problems of regulating market power will be considered in a subsequent chapter.[137]

The reasons for privatisation are, like those for nationalisation, eclectic.[138] They include the following: improving efficiency, reducing government involvement in industrial decision-making, widening share ownership, encouraging share ownership by employees, alleviating problems of public sector pay determination, reducing the public sector borrowing requirement and the enhancement of economic freedom.

The cogency of these reasons has been challenged.[139] For example, the argument that privatisation will enhance economic freedom has been criticised because it assumes that a private monopoly will be less threatening to such freedom than a statutory monopoly and because it defines "freedom" in a limited way to mean solely the absence of government intervention in the market, thereby foreclosing the viability of a more

---

[135] *The Nationalised Industries*, Cmnd. 7131 (1978). Vickers and Yarrow, *Privatisation*, pp. 133-135; Prosser, *Nationalised Industries*, pp. 44-47, 54-74.

[136] Compare these themes to the policy espoused by the NEDO study of 1976, Prosser, *Nationalised Industries*, pp. 41-43.

[137] See below, Chap. 6.

[138] Vickers and Yarrow, *Privatisation, An Economic Analysis* (1988), pp. 157-160; Kay, Mayer and Thompson (eds.), *Privatisation and Regulation– the UK Experience* (1986), Chaps. 3, 4; Foster, *Privatisation, Public Ownership and the Regulation of Natural Monopoly* (1992), Chap. 4.

[139] *e.g.* Heald and Steel, "Privatising Public Enterprises: An Analysis of the Government's Case", Kay, Mayer and Thompson (eds.), *Privatisation and Regulation*, Chap. 2.

active role for the state which might actually enhance economic liberty. Moreover the argument that privatisation augments economic freedom has to be qualified because, as we shall see, some privatised industries will require regulatory control.

The contention that privatisation will improve efficiency has also been questioned.[140] The "conclusion" that nationalised industry performed inefficiently is itself contested. Any such conclusion is dependent upon the analysis of complex performance data, which must then take account of the managerial difficulties experienced by public corporations stemming from the lack of clarity as to their objectives. Furthermore, even if one accepts that a change in ownership rights can have an effect upon incentives and behaviour and hence upon efficiency, by sharpening corporate incentives to cut costs and to fix prices in line with costs, the realisation of these benefits will "depend crucially upon the framework of competition and regulation in which the privatised firm is to operate."[141]

The problems which privatisation poses vary, but it is important to keep distinct two different situations. First, there has been the privatisation of companies which, although large, do not possess undue market power. Firms such as British Aerospace, Britoil, and Cable and Wireless, operate in reasonably competitive industries. Once privatised, these corporations should, on the face of it, cause no more (or less) concern to public law as such, than do the operations of other large companies which have never been within public ownership.[142] This proposition is true in the sense that such firms do not possess the requisite market power to make it necessary to devise any regulatory regime to control their prices, etc. Such privatised companies do, however, often possess "special features" which set them apart from the normal corporation. The government may possess shareholdings in the company, there may be government directors and the articles of association may be structured to allow the government to prevent undesirable takeovers or changes in control.[143]

The second situation is where the corporation which is privatised does possess significant market power, and this requires the establishment of some regulatory regime to oversee it. The end result is a privatised firm or firms which are then controlled by an agency. The telecommunications industry can be taken as an example.

The Telecommunications Act 1984 privatised the first major public utility in this country. From 1912 until 1981 telecommunications were the responsibility of the Post Office, a state-owned monopoly. Legislation in 1981 separated telecommunications from postal services and established British Telecom as a public corporation.[144] The 1981 Act also allowed some

---

[140] Kay, Mayer and Thompson, Chaps. 5 and 6.

[141] Vickers and Yarrow, *Privatisation*, pp. 7-44, 157-159.

[142] This leaves open the more general issue as to how far corporate power generally should be the concern of public law.

[143] Graham and Prosser, "Privatising Nationalised Industries: Constitutional Issues and New Legal Techniques" (1987) 50 M.L.R. 16; Graham and Prosser, *Privatising Public Enterprises, Constitutions, the State, and Regulation in Comparative Perspective* (1991).

[144] British Telecommunications Act 1981.

liberalisation in the industry by, for example, abolishing BT's exclusive privilege to supply customer equipment, and by allowing the Secretary of State to license other firms to run telecommunications systems. The 1984 Act privatised BT and created a regulatory framework to oversee the industry.

Section 1 of the 1984 Act created the Director General of Tele-communications (DGT) who is appointed by the Secretary of State and section 2 abolished BT's exclusive privilege of running telecommunications systems. The duties of the Secretary of State and the DGT are set out in section 3. They must act in the manner best calculated to secure the provision of telecommunications services, consonant with the demand for such services throughout the country. Eight broad guidelines are to guide the fulfilment of these duties. They include the promotion of: the interests of consumers, effective competition, efficiency and economy, research and development and the international competitiveness of United Kingdom firms supplying telecommunications services. Section 5 requires that operators of telecommunications systems possess a licence. These are granted by the DGT and the Secretary of State under section 7.[145] Under section 12 the DGT can modify licence conditions, and section 13 empowers him to refer a matter to the Monopolies and Mergers Commission (MMC), which can decide whether the matter referred to in the reference will operate against the public interest. Enforcement of licence conditions is provided for in section 16, which enables the DGT to make an order requiring compliance by the licensee. This can be enforced either by the DGT himself,[146] or by an action for breach of statutory duty.[147] The DGT also has other duties and powers which include:[148] the investigation of complaints, the publication of information to consumers, etc., and the DGT can exercise the powers of the Director General of Fair Trading to investigate possible anti-competitive practices or abuses of market power.[149] Three comments on this system are warranted.

First, removing a firm from public ownership does not provide the answer as to the type of new regime which is to be established. If a privatised firm has significant market power then this can be addressed either through a remedy which is primarily structural, or by one which is principally regulatory.[150] The former entails the breaking-up of the large firm, as has occurred in this context in the United States; the latter involves monitoring the conduct of the dominant firm, with the added theme of introducing new competitors via the issuing of new licences. The United Kingdom has adopted the latter approach, the effectiveness of which

---

[145] See also s.9, which creates the separate category of public telecommunications systems; such systems have the conditions of s.8 attached, which include a duty not to discriminate and require the operator of such a system to permit interconnection with other systems.
[146] s.18(8).
[147] s.18(6).
[148] Pt. III of the Act.
[149] s.50. These powers are contained in the Fair Trading Act 1973, and the Competition Act 1980.
[150] Vickers and Yarrow, *Privatisation*, p. 212.

depends upon two crucial issues, the criteria for regulation and the attitude of the regulator.

Secondly, the most important of the regulatory criteria relate to the price which the regulated industry can charge for its services. This will determine whether it is being "fair" to consumers. Deciding upon the correct formula is a complex issue.[151] Claims that privatisation will necessarily produce efficiency are crucially dependent upon the correct resolution of such issues.

Thirdly, the success of the scheme is also dependent upon the energy, attitude and resources of the DGT. The DGT runs an agency called the Office of Telecommunications (Oftel). The breadth of the main empowering provisions of the legislation and the guidelines contained therein, give the DGT considerable latitude. Evidence to date indicates that the DGT and Oftel have avoided the danger of being "captured" by the firms which they seek to regulate, and that they have pursued a fairly vigorous pro-competitive strategy.[152]

However, the effectiveness of Oftel was circumscribed by a number of factors.

(i) Regulatory control was dependent upon adequate information being available to the regulator, and the DGT has complained that this has not been forthcoming from BT on a regular basis.

(ii) It is not clear that Oftel possessed the requisite resources to discharge the range of its functions adequately.

(iii) Decisions by the MMC pursuant to a reference by the DGT have, for example, allowed BT to acquire other companies subject to conditions which are difficult to enforce.

(iv) There is more evidence that BT "captured" the government rather than Oftel.[153] The privatisation "package" was devised by government with the change from public to private ownership being of principal concern; the promotion of competition was a secondary objective. The government has made several policy decisions which favour BT, including the choice of the pricing formula, and the limit upon licensees.

It was partly in response to these problems, and partly because of the spirit of the Citizen's Charter, that the regulatory powers available to Oftel were increased by the Competition and Service (Utilities) Act 1992. The 1992 Act modifies section 27 of the Telecommunications Act 1984. It empowers the DGT to make regulations prescribing the standards of performance which ought to operate in individual cases, with provision for the award of compensation if these are not met.[154] The DGT can, moreover, determine standards of overall performance in connection with the provision of the relevant services.[155] The 1992 Act also contains additional

---

[151] *Ibid.* pp. 213-216.
[152] *Ibid.* pp. 217-241.
[153] *Ibid.* pp. 210-211, 235-236.
[154] Competition and Service (Utilities) Act 1992, s.1, adding a new s.27A to the Telecommunications Act 1984.
[155] Telecommunications Act 1984 s.27B.

powers with respect to the information which can be demanded by the DGT as to the levels of individual and overall performance.[156] Customers are themselves to be given information about overall performance,[157] and there are to be complaints procedures established by the telecommunications operators.[158] Specific provisions govern matters such as discriminatory pricing and billing disputes.[159]

7. *A Constitutional and Legal Framework for Agencies*

Discussion of different agencies gives one a sense of the type of problems which their existence poses. While the diversity in type of institution makes statements of principle difficult, consideration of constitutional and legal principle at a more general level is important. Problems of the same type do recur in differing organisations and this alone warrants broader treatment. This is not to say that such bodies should be forced into some administrative strait-jacket. There is, however, a significant spectrum running between the pure *ad hoc* and institutional rigidity.

The first issue which should be addressed concerns the divide between agencies created independently of, and those created pursuant to, the Next Steps initiative. The important differences between these two types of agency have been considered above. Now it may well be the case that we should simply accept these differences. They do, to some extent, reflect differing philosophies as to how far agencies should be independent from the traditional departmental structure: Next Steps agencies have no separate legal foundation or personality of their own, having been created by means of administrative reorganisation, unlike agencies established independently of this initiative. Having said that we have already seen the real tensions which exist within the Next Steps scheme, between the desire to foster agency autonomy and the preservation of departmental responsibility. This tension will not disappear and one might hazard the guess that we will see some of these agencies being accorded formal status in their own right. It is evident that current arrangements for any particular Next Steps agency are not regarded as writ in stone, as witnessed by the fact that other ways of providing the relevant service, such as privatisation or contracting-out, are kept continually under review by the Next Steps team. Given that this is so it would not be beyond the bounds of possibility for it to be decided that the optimum strategy would be to maintain an agency, but to accord it more formal status.

Secondly, it is important that there should be some general overseeing institution. Given that the divide between the two types of agency exists, this will have to be split between two institutions. Next Steps agencies are kept under review by the Next Steps team. There is no general oversight

---

[156] 1992 Act s.2, adding a new s.27C to the Telecommunications Act 1984.
[157] 1992 Act s.3, adding s.27D to the Telecommunications Act 1984.
[158] 1992 Act s.4, adding s.27E to the Telecommunications Act 1984.
[159] 1992 Act ss.5, 6.

over agencies which have been created independently of these reforms. This task could be assigned to the Council on Tribunals which could advise on the name, institutional form, personnel and structure of such agencies.

The third stage in our framework concerns the relationship which any such organisation should have with both the parent department and Parliament. It is necessary once again to make a distinction between Next Steps agencies and others. In the case of the former the relationship is defined by the framework document which establishes the agreement between agency and department. The degree of detail as to this relationship will vary with respect to different agencies, but the general aim is, as we have seen, to foster agency autonomy on matters of policy implementation. The question as to ministerial power over agencies is also present in relation to agencies established by statute independently of the Next Steps regime. The enabling legislation should make as clear as possible what degree of insulation or control the agency should have from the minister. The extent of any such control will obviously be dependent upon the nature of the area over which the agency exercises power: what is suitable for competition policy will not be the same as in the context of arts funding.

Having achieved greater clarity in the relationship between the institution, the minister and Parliament, the next stage in our framework would be to consider the procedures by which the institution reaches its decisions. In determining what procedural constraints should be imposed it is important to realise that the form such rules should take will directly reflect the purposes of any particular scheme.[160] If, for example, it is felt that a high premium should be placed upon public participation then this may be reflected in rules as to notice and standing, and produce a procedure more akin to consultation than the adversary process. Trade-offs will, however, have to be made between the degree of participation and the time that this involves. The Citizen's Charter has already had some impact on this issue with its emphasis upon consultation with users of services, and the impetus which it has given to the making of Charters which apply to particular substantive areas. The Citizen's Charter has also provided the conceptual foundation for statutory changes in certain areas which are designed, *inter alia*, to increase the openness of the process, to improve citizen access to information and to enhance reasoned decision-making.[161]

The last stage in our framework is control. This can have three meanings. The extent of *legislative* control should have been answered by the terms of reference on which the institution was first established.

Control may connote *judicial review*. Particular problems concerning review and Next Steps agencies have been considered above. The whole topic of judicial review will be discussed below.[162] More general arguments as to what the scope of review ought to be will be analysed at that stage. What is said now should be read in the light of the theoretical and policy arguments advanced hereafter. The central theme to emphasise is that

---

[160] See below, Chap. 8.
[161] *e.g.* Competition and Service (Utilities) Act 1992.
[162] See below, Chaps. 10-12.

judicial review, whether it be of procedure or substance, should be sensitive to the nature of the organisation in question. If, for example, the institutional form is one in which it is clear that the minister is intended to retain control over the general direction of policy then this should be respected; judicial decisions should not operate from an inarticulate premise of organisational "independence" and ministerial "interference" which does not reflect the true division of roles between them. Where procedures have been designed for a specific body they should not be struck down merely because they do not conform to the adversary model which characterises adjudication in the ordinary courts.

Control can also mean *quality* control, supervision over the effectiveness of the internal institutional structure and study as to how far the aims of the agency are being fulfilled. This has been considered above.[163]

The framework presented above is only a sketch. It does not purport to be an exhaustive analysis of the problems which agencies present. It is hoped that it may, however, provide a tool for further analysis. The limits of any such analysis must also be noted. Even if a framework of the above type were to be adopted there are limits as to what it can achieve. A prime example is provided by the question of the appropriate degree of executive and legislative control. Statutes can be passed which indicate that a minister should only, for example, give directions on matters of general policy. However, as we have seen in the context of public corporations, the reality is often different. Preventing the executive from using such a statutory framework as both shield and sword as it sees fit, and ensuring that legislative control is maintained over such organisations, cannot be solved by a constitutional and legal framework of the type under consideration here. Such problems can only be resolved by addressing them in the forum from which they arise, Parliament, and the balance between the executive and the legislature. The way in which the executive can manipulate a statutory scheme is only a reflection of its power; it can only be prevented by a change in the balance of power itself.

Section 5. Contract and Service Provision

The government has always had to make contracts in order to purchase the goods and services which it requires. Recent years have, however, witnessed increased use of contractual language over a broader area. We have already seen how contractual ideas have influenced the relationship between Next Steps Agencies and their sponsoring departments, even though there cannot be a real contract because the agency possesses no separate legal personality. Contractual themes have also had a marked impact upon other areas such as the Health Service.[164] What we will be principally concerned with

---

[163] See above, pp. 92-93.
[164] Longley, *Public Law and Health Service Accountability* (1992); Harden, *The Contracting State* (1992); Freedland, "Government by Contract and Public Law" [1994] P.L. 86.

in this section is the use of contracting-out as a method of providing public services, and the links between this and the Next Steps regime. This topic will become even more important when the Deregulation and Contracting Out Bill becomes law.[165]

1. *Contracting-Out*

A number of problems, both constitutional and legal, arise as a result of central government or public bodies contracting with a private individual or company. This issue is now of increased importance because of Conservative government policy. The connection between the present topic and the previous discussion should be made clear at the outset. We have already seen that when a department reviews its existing activities it considers five options. The activity can be abolished, privatised, contracted-out, given to a Next Steps agency or the status quo can be maintained. The previous section has considered the implications of choosing the agency route. This section will be concerned with the consequences of adopting the contracting-out option.

It should, however, be made clear that the contracting-out option can apply *both* to activities performed in-house and to those for which agencies are responsible. This requires a word by way of explanation in order to avoid confusion and error. The five choices mentioned above will apply to a *general* sphere of activity. It may, for example, be decided to create an agency for the payment of social welfare benefits, or for social welfare contributions. It may be decided to preserve some of the more general policy matters in the social welfare field in-house. Contracting-out as an option will be considered for more *particular* activities *irrespective* of whether they are currently done by the agency or the department itself. Thus, certain functions of the Social Security Benefits Agency, which is a Next Steps creation, were assessed in 1993 in order to decide if they should be contracted-out. These included: video production, archival storage, publishing, medical services, debt recovery and audit. However it is equally the case that particular activities performed in-house by the Department of Social Security itself will be similarly evaluated in order to determine if they would not be better done by contracting them out. In 1993 the provision of legal services and accommodation and office services were to be evaluated in this way.

The *reasons for* contracting-out are said to be that:[166] public sector "in-house" monopolies are inefficient and this is reflected in low productivity; there is "open-ended" financial commitment to public sector "in-house" units and such units do not take sufficient account of costs; competition

---

[165] The Bill is designed to facilitate contracting-out by central and local government, clauses 59-70. See below, Appendix.
[166] Hartley and Huby, "Contracting-Out Policy: Theory and Evidence", Kay, Mayer and Thompson, *Privatisation and Regulation*, p. 289.

generates new ideas, techniques, etc.; and contractors can be penalised for defective performance and late delivery.

The *reasons against* contracting-out are said to be that: private contractors are unreliable, and may well default; contractors use low bids to eliminate the in-house capacity, thereby making the public body dependent on a private monopoly; competitive tendering entails monitoring costs; and private contractors in areas such as the Health Service can place patients at risk.

We shall return to these arguments. Before doing so it is important to understand what the contracting-out process involves.

2. *Contracting-Out and Market Testing*[167]

Let us assume that the privatisation option has been ruled out, and that the activity will continue to be undertaken by the state in some way. How is the decision made as to whether it should be performed by the department/agency, or by a private firm to whom the work is contracted-out?

Market testing provides the key.[168] This works as follows. A department will establish a special project team to carry forward the market testing process. This will then decide which activities in a service area are appropriate for market testing and the way in which they can best be packaged to stimulate competitive bids. A detailed specification of the service required will be prepared, and bids will then be invited from in-house and selected external contractors. These bids will then be evaluated to assess the quality and cost of offers, and the contract will be awarded appropriately. If the external bid is successful then the in-house service will be closed down, or it may be transferred to the new contractor to manage.

Not surprisingly the whole process is taken very seriously by in-house teams whose activity is being market tested, since their jobs are often on the line. The Department of Social Security publishes a corporate newsletter devoted solely to market testing which is designed both to keep civil servants aware of the status of the market testing programme and to attempt to allay their fears about the outcomes in terms of job security.

One issue of this newsletter contains a graphic account of a successful bid by the in-house microfilming team within the Contributions Agency. The in-house unit established its own project team to orchestrate its bid. Their very first move was to realise that they needed assistance and in the best spirit of the market place they employed the management consultants Touche Ross. Various teams were then established to consider finance, business analysis and the like, and these worked within a more general overall strategy co-ordinated by a steering committee. The conclusion of the

---

[167] *The Government's Guide to Market Testing* (1993).
[168] *The Citizen's Charter, First Report*, Cm. 2101 (1992), pp. 60-64, contains a detailed breakdown of market testing being carried out by different government departments and agencies.

successful leader of the in-house team was that "you may not enjoy the process of market testing, but if you win, the taste of victory is very sweet." The key word in this sentence is "if": in-house teams have won approximately 55-60% of competitive bids and the established civil service is clearly still concerned about both job security and the implications of transferring functions to the private sector, as evidenced by the strike in November 1993.

3. *Contracting-Out: Problems and Concerns*

We have already noted that two of the principal reasons for choosing to contract-out the provision of a service are efficiency and the better provision of services. But we have also touched on the problems and concerns with the ever increasing use of this technique for service delivery. These will now be addressed in more detail.

An appropriate place to begin is with the *issue of principle*: are there types of activities which should not be contracted-out in this manner? Should certain types of service only be run by the state *stricto sensu*? If so which services would be placed within this category? The police, adjudication, prisons? The latter have in fact already been contracted-out to some degree. So too have some aspects of the court process such as the movement of prisoners, as witnessed by the continuing saga of Group 4 Security losing prisoners. What of services where confidentiality is at a premium, or does this not matter given that so much information is already available to private parties?

If an activity is contracted-out are there problems of *accountability*? The answer is both yes and no. Clearly the very fact that the activity has been contracted-out, rather than being privatised, means that the state has responsibility for its provision. This is particularly the case given that, as we have seen above, the types of activity which are contracted-out will often be integral to the service provided by the agency or the department. We should, moreover, be aware of the danger that a contractor who was intended only to "execute" a chosen policy, may come to have a real influence over the choice of policy itself. Furthermore, such contracts can be extremely valuable, and hence their disbursement can help to make or break fortunes and power in the corporate sector.[169]

Having said this it can be argued that these very contracts, like the framework documents used in agency creation, sharpen accountability by defining goals, setting targets and monitoring performance. In this way administrative discretion can be beneficially structured. As Harden states,[170]

"Although contract is not a panacea for the problem of discretion, it does offer an opportunity to make real progress towards greater accountability by clearly identifying who is responsible for a policy,

---

[169] Smith and Hague (eds.), *The Dilemma of Accountability in Modern Government* (1971).
[170] *The Contracting State* (1992), p. 71.

what it is, whether it is being carried out in practice and if not, why not."

This does not mean that we should be complacent about accountability in this context. Techniques may have to be fashioned to fit the new order. An interesting suggestion has been to distinguish between three senses of accountability: programme, process and fiscal.[171] Programme accountability is concerned with the quality of the work being undertaken and whether it has achieved the goals required of it. Process accountability asks whether the procedures used to perform the research were adequate, while fiscal accountability investigates whether the funds were expended as stated. These techniques of control are not, however, self-executing. They require positive input from the government side. In order that programmes can be made accountable, government must be as clear as is possible in the terms of the contract as to what it requires of the contractor. Clarity as to the initial objectives of a scheme is a necessary condition for programme accountability. It is not sufficient. Management within government must be capable of assessing the completed work. This requires personnel with the appropriate skills and also the existence of criteria by which performance can be judged.[172]

At a more practical level there are *organisational* concerns. Can contracting-out function with sufficient *flexibility*, given that the demand for certain public services may fluctuate either due to exogenous market factors, or because of more radical shifts in governmental policy? How far does contracting-out produce problems of *integration*: are there difficulties of ensuring a coherent, integrated service when some parts of the whole are operated by private undertakings, while others are performed in-house? As Harden notes,[173]

"The public interest – i.e. the overall functioning of the public service in question – is not the responsibility of a single unitary organization, but instead emerges from the process of agreement between separate organizations, none of which has responsibility for the public interest as a whole."

Closely related to the organisational concerns are those relating to *personnel*. There are a number of different dimensions to this problem. One concerns the complexities involved with the Transfer of Undertakings Regulations, and their relevance where employees are transferred to a private firm. Another is the less legalistic, but equally important issue concerning the morale of those within the department who fear the results of the market testing exercise will be that they will lose their jobs, especially in circumstances where the recession may tempt the private bidder to tender at a very low price. Yet another dimension to this problem is of a more

[171] Robinson, "Government Contracting for Academic Research: Accountability in the American Experience", Smith and Hague (eds.), *The Dilemma of Accountability in Modern Government* (1971), Chap. 3.
[172] Smith, "Accountability and Independence in the Contract State", *ibid.* pp. 34-35, 39-42.
[173] *Ibid.* p. 33.

general nature and relates to the broader work ethic which has characterised the public service. When work is contracted-out to private firms they will not normally have a "public service ethos", but will be principally concerned with the interests of their shareholders. How important will any such change of attitude be?

4. *Contracting-Out: Contract Formation and Legal Principle*

The agreements which are made as a result of the contracting-out process are legal contracts: contractual language as used here produces a legally binding obligation between two entities which have separate legal status. This raises a number of important issues of legal principle.

The first of these relates to the very *creation* of the contract. We have already seen in outline the process whereby the government decides to market test an activity and then to hold a competition between the in-house unit and selected outside contractors. This procedure will now be subject to the Community law regime on public procurement which has been extended to cover services.[174] This regime has important provisions as to the holding of the competitive process, and the criterion for choosing to whom the contract should be awarded. The transparency of the whole process is safeguarded by requirements as to publicity and reasoned decision-making. More detailed examination of these rules on procurement will be undertaken later.[175]

A second set of legal issues concerns the application of *public law principles* to contracted-out activities. The contract itself will obviously provide the basis for the legal rights and duties of the respective parties. But how far should these be supplemented by principles which have traditionally been applied to public bodies? How far should the private contracting party be subject to procedural and even substantive norms of a public law nature? These may or may not be needed, depending upon the type of activity which has been contracted-out, and the terms of that contractual relationship. Yet the more the contracting-out technique is employed the more likely will it be that this question will become a live one.

As a matter of principle the general approach should be as follows. If the department or agency is fulfilling a statutory function, whether this be framed as a duty or in discretionary terms, then it will be subject to the normal public law principles. If it chooses to fulfil part of that statutory remit by contracting-out to a private undertaking then it would be contrary to principle for the citizens' protections to be reduced as a result of this organisational choice. Given that this is so there are then two ways of proceeding. *Either* the parent department maintains a residual public law responsibility for the tasks which have been contracted-out. *Or* the private contracting party must itself be subject to the rigours of the public law controls where this is appropriate. There are, as will be seen, precedents for

---

[174] Council Directive 92/50.
[175] See below, Chap. 19.

this latter approach.[176] The courts have shown themselves willing to apply public law principles in circumstances where a private undertaking is performing a regulatory role with the backing, directly or indirectly, of the state. If this is so then it is difficult to see why these principles should not also be potentially applicable in the context of contracting-out. The fact that many of these contracts are concerned with service delivery rather than regulation as such should make no general difference, although it might affect the number of occasions when public law would be invoked.

The final interesting legal issue pertains to the ascription of *legal responsibility* for activities which have been contracted-out. Imagine that a tort is committed against an individual by a prison officer who works in a prison the running of which has been contracted-out to a private firm. Who can the individual sue? No doubt the prison officer would be individually liable and the private employer would be subject to the normal rules on vicarious liability. But could any action be maintained against the department which had contracted-out the work? Would it have any legal responsibility? This might well be of importance if the private firm turns out to be not too solvent. The answer should depend upon the nature of the statutory duty/discretion, the fulfilment of which has been contracted-out to the private firm. A court might well interpret the governing statute as imposing a duty, the legal responsibility for which could not ultimately be delegated to another. On this view it would be open to the department to contract-out the activity if it wished to do so as a matter of organisational choice, but this would not necessarily serve to divest it of legal responsibility.

5. Conclusion

Contracting-out has assumed greater prominence in the last few years and discussion of the topic serves to concentrate our minds on the whole public/private division: private institutions become involved in making decisions which have public impact, while the government both becomes more reliant upon a private enterprise to carry out its policies and also draws upon the lessons of the market even when it continues to be responsible for the task itself. We shall have occasion to return to this theme on other occasions throughout the book.

Section 6. Local Government

1. *The Changing Pattern of Local Government*

The development of local authorities in the nineteenth century has already been charted. No attempt will be made to provide any comprehensive legal

---

[176] See below, Chaps. 6 and 15. The Deregulation and Contracting Out Bill 1994 clause 62 appears to render the Minister responsible for the acts of the contractor, but clause 62(3) is ambiguous. See further below, Appendix.

guide to these authorities within the discussion which follows. This is a specialist field with a wealth of literature.[177]

Some understanding of local government is, however, essential, since such authorities are amongst the principal decision-makers in the public law sphere. Moreover, as we shall see, the very nature of their powers has recently been radically transformed. This transformation means that it is no longer possible to define *local government* merely by describing the present pattern of *local authorities* and their respective powers. This is because the powers of the elected local authorities have been diminished and many of their traditional responsibilities have been transferred to a variety of *agencies* which are often subject to central control, while others have been *contracted-out* to private contractors. It is this development which has led some commentators to distinguish between formal and informal local government.[178] This section will, therefore, chart the formal powers of local authorities themselves and then consider some of the other bodies which have responsibilities at the local level.

2. *Local Authorities: Present Organisation*

The pattern of local authorities which had been established by the end of the nineteenth century was to continue largely unchanged until 1972. In the period after the Second World War there was however increasing disquiet. The shape of local government was felt to be outdated and ill adapted to the demographic and technological development that occurred in the post-war period. This sentiment was voiced most strongly by Richard Crossman in 1965, who was then Minister of Housing and Local Government. In 1966 a Royal Commission was established under the chairmanship of Lord Redcliffe-Maud.[179] The Report of the Royal Commission identified a number of key problems in the existing system: the division between town and country, that between boroughs and counties, the allocation of responsibility within counties, the small size of some local authorities, and the relationships between local authority and public, and local authority and government.

---

[177] For a legal analysis see Cross, *Principles of Local Government Law* (7th ed., 1986); Davies, *Local Government Law* (1983). For a broader view see Griffith, *Central Departments and Local Authorities* (1966); Hill, *Democratic Theory and Local Government* (1974); Cockburn, *The Local State* (1977); Haynes, *Organisation Theory and Local Government* (1980); Alexander, *Local Government in Britain since Reorganisation* (1982); Elliott, *The Role of Law in Central-Local Relations* (1981); Jones (ed.), *New Approaches to the Study of Central-Local Government Relationships* (1980); Loughlin, Gelfand and Young (eds.), *Half a Century of Municipal Decline 1935-1985* (1985); Jones and Stewart, *The Case for Local Government* (2nd ed., 1985); Goldsmith, *New Research in Central-Local Relations* (1986); Loughlin, *Local Government in the Modern State* (1986); King and Pierre (eds.), *Challenges to Local Government* (1990).
[178] King, "Government Beyond Whitehall: Local Government and Urban Politics", Dunleavy, Gamble, Holliday and Peele (eds.), *Developments in British Politics 4* (1993).
[179] Cmnd. 4040 (1969).

The response of the Royal Commission to these perceived difficulties was, in short, to reverse conventional thinking about decision-making at the local level. The traditional pattern had had as its key the concept that single-tier authorities would be suited to the larger urban areas and that a two-tier structure was required in other contexts. This thinking was directly challenged. For the future the Redcliffe-Maud Report proposed that unitary authorities should be the norm. These would cover urban and rural areas, normally being focused around the main towns. The unitary principle would be departed from only in those large urban conurbations where to adhere rigidly to the single-tier principle would render the authority unwieldy and remote from the community. In such conurbations a two-tier structure was recommended.

The Labour government was largely in favour of the Royal Commission's proposals with some modifications. Certainly the unitary concept was accepted.[180] The Conservative party was, however, in favour of the two-tier principle. The return of that party to government in 1970 ensured the demise of the Redcliffe-Maud proposals. The Conservative party's proposals[181] represented a reversion to the two-tier principle, and their plan was enacted as the Local Government Act 1972.[182]

There were four different types of local government. The first was the metropolitan counties of which there were six, divided into 36 metropolitan districts. Second, there were 39 non-metropolitan counties with 296 districts. Both types of county can have parishes beneath the districts. Third, in London the top level authority was the Greater London Council, under which existed 32 London boroughs. Fourth, Wales had eight counties, 37 districts, and communities below these. Boundary Commissions, one for England and one for Wales, were constituted by the 1972 Act.[183] Both Commissions have the duty to review district and county areas within 10 to 15 years, or otherwise as the Secretary of State may direct.

This pattern of local authority organisation has undergone radical revision, with the abolition of the metropolitan county councils (MCCs) and the Greater London Council (GLC). The Conservative government argued that such authorities should be abolished because: they had limited operational responsibilities; their expenditure had been excessive; and because they had sought to establish a role which was not really required. It was argued that reform would "streamline" the cities, save money, and provide a simpler system. The cogency of these arguments is dubious, and was challenged by studies commissioned by the MCCs. Evidence as to likely cost savings was not readily apparent; and the argument concerning simplicity appeared to be undermined by the very institutional changes which were to replace the MCCs and the GLC. The Local Government Act 1985, abolished the MCCs and the GLC. Some of their functions have been transferred to district or borough councils.[184] Others have been assigned to

---

[180] *Reform of Local Government in England*, Cmnd. 4276 (1970).
[181] *Local Government in England*, Cmnd. 4584 (1971).
[182] It did not take effect until April 1, 1974.
[183] ss.46, 53.
[184] *e.g.* planning, highways and waste disposal.

new joint authorities composed primarily of members from the relevant district or borough councils.[185] The decision to abolish the MCCs and the GLC appears to have been motivated rather more by the desire to dismantle large authorities which had been predominantly Labour, rather than by the objective of improving local government in large conurbations.[186]

The present structure of local authorities is as follows. Unitary authorities operate in London, which has 32 boroughs, and in six other metropolitan areas, which have 36 district councils. Three tier authorities are the norm elsewhere. Thus England has 39 counties, 296 district councils and approximately 900 community and town councils which function as third tier authorities; Wales has 8 county councils, 37 district councils and approximately 800 community and town councils; in Scotland there are 9 regions, 53 district councils and roughly 1200 community and town councils.

3. Local Authorities: Functions and Powers

The functions of local government have altered considerably over the last 100 years. Three differing periods can be identified.

The modern role of local authorities has its origins in the problems attendant upon industrialisation and urbanisation in the nineteenth century. This necessitated collective action to provide a variety of goods and services, and local authorities were perceived as well placed to undertake this task.[187] Some of these services were "public goods", i.e. services which the market either would not provide at all or would do so only inefficiently; others were trading services, which the private market could provide, but only with the attendant risk of private monopoly profit; yet other services were redistributive, being designed to benefit certain groups within society, such as by the provision of social welfare.[188]

The second period is characterised by the relative decline in the importance of trading services, and the relative increase in the importance of providing redistributive services. In 1885 the latter accounted for only 23% of local authority expenditure, whereas by 1975 this had risen to 65%.[189]

Perceptions as to the proper functions of local authorities have recently altered more radically as a result of Conservative policy in the late 1970s and 1980s. The general theme which permeates this policy is that the functions of local authorities should be opened up to market forces, and should be judged by the criteria of market efficiency. Local authority services should be provided in accordance with what are essentially individualistic principles for action rather than any overriding conception of collective good.[190] A range of devices has been employed to this end

---

[185] e.g. police, fire and civil defence and passenger transport.
[186] Leach and Game, "English Metropolitan Government since Abolition: An Evaluation of the Abolition of the English Metropolitan County Councils" (1991) 69 Pub. Adm. 141.
[187] Loughlin, Local Government in the Modern State (1986), p. 4.
[188] Ibid. pp. 4-5.
[189] Ibid. p. 6.
[190] Ibid. p. 170.

including: direct competition with private industry for the provision of services; contracting-out service provision; the sale of local authority assets, and the encouragement of market accountability to consumers.[191]

Thus legislation such as the Local Government Act 1988[192] specified a number of services which local authorities were required to put out to competitive tendering; the Housing and Building Control Act 1984 extended the policy of selling off council houses to tenants; the Education Reform Act 1988 reduced local authority control over schooling; the Local Government Act 1992 empowers the Audit Commission and the Scottish Accounts Commission to require local authorities to supply information which will enable the Commission to make comparisons, based upon cost, economy, efficiency and effectiveness, between the standards of performance of different bodies; and recent legislative initiatives are aimed at forcing local authorities to privatise further areas, such as municipal airports, and to sell off other municipal property. The change in the role of local authorities is brought out by King.[193]

> "Instead of envisaging local government as an institution representing a local community and its local tradition, it is to be designed as an institution responsible for overseeing service provision. Local government is thought of as an enabling institution and not one of direct service delivery...This new role maximises efficiency and profit criteria in local government. It treats citizens as customers of government services. Furthermore, local authorities are viewed as purchasers rather than providers of services."

4. *Local Authorities and Central Government: A Changing Relationship*

Observing the purely legal instruments which exist within a given area can often be misleading. Statutes which gave power to local authorities were often phrased in broad, open-textured terms. These were supplemented by legislation which gave supervisory powers to a minister, and such statutes could vary in nature. They might impose an obligation upon a local authority to secure ministerial approval for action which was being planned; they might allow the minister to prescribe standards which local authorities should follow; or they could enforce central control through an inspectorate. A number of statutes also contained default powers which enabled a minister to takeover the functions of a local authority if he or she considered that it was failing to perform its duties.[194] The executive also

---

[191] *Ibid.* pp. 167-171.
[192] The list of services to which competitive tendering applies has been increased by the Local Government Act 1992, s.8.
[193] "Government Beyond Whitehall: Local Government and Urban Politics", Dunleavy, Gamble, Holliday and Peele (eds.), *Developments in British Politics 4* (1993), p. 204.
[194] Griffith, *Central Departments and Local Authorities* (1966).

possessed financial powers which it could utilise in order to constrain local authorities.

Notwithstanding this framework, central–local relations were, on the whole, governed by bargain, negotiation and administrative practice rather than resort to formal legal machinery. The latter provided the framework for the bargain rather than being determinative of the particular outcome.[195] This has however now changed. Legislation from the late 1970s onwards has placed an increasingly large number of more specific duties upon local authorities and has sought to curb expenditure by local government. Consensus has ended.[196] The result is that central-local relations have become more politicised, in the sense that a previous general mutuality as to objectives has been questioned and they have also become more juridified, in the sense that the law now assumes a more significant role in both defining the boundaries of central–local power, and in resolving conflicts between the two levels of government.[197] These features are evident in the financial and other controls contained in recent legislation.

5. Local Authorities: Finances[198]

(1) RESOURCES

Local authorities do not have their own source of revenue derived from any form of local income tax. The traditional basis of local authority revenue was the rates which were levied upon property owners,[199] combined with income from charges and fees. These sources of revenue were, as will be seen below, supplemented by grants from central government.

A radical change was brought about by the Local Government Finance Act 1988 which replaced the rating system with the community charge/poll tax. The object behind the new legislation was to increase the financial accountability of local authorities. The rating system imposed the financial burden upon property owners. It was argued that as a consequence many who lived in an area could happily support expensive local policies secure in the knowledge that they would not have to bear the financial burden if they were not liable to pay rates. The poll tax was to be levied on all those who lived in an area, subject to certain exceptions, at a flat rate.

The political debacle which the introduction of this tax caused is well known. The poll tax was finally replaced by the council tax in the Local Government Finance Act 1992. The new tax is made up of both a personal and a property element, although each household only receives one bill.

---

[195] Rhodes, *Control and Power in Central-Local Government Relations* (1981).

[196] Kavanagh, *Thatcherism and British Politics, The End of Consensus?* (1987).

[197] Loughlin, *Local Government in the Modern State* (1986), Chap. 9; Gyford, "The Politicization of Local Government", Loughlin, Gelfand and Young, *Half a Century of Municipal Decline 1935-1985* (1985), Chap. 4.

[198] The system of local authority finances is complex and only the most general outline can be provided here.

[199] Rating and Valuation Act 1925; Local Government Act 1948; Rating and Valuation Act 1961; Local Government Act 1966.

Properties are valued through a banding system so that houses in the same band should receive the same bill. One of the obvious problems of this, and indeed any, system which is based upon property values is that the financial returns are susceptible to fluctuations with movements in the value of property.

(2) GRANTS AND CURBS ON SPENDING

Local authorities have only ever derived part of their funds from rates, the poll tax or the council tax. Grants from central government provide a significant proportion of their funds. The basic grant was the Rate Support Grant (RSG),[200] the main objective of which was to provide some degree of equalisation between the financial resources and expenditure requirements of different local authorities.

The method of calculating the RSG was felt to be both complex and prone to encourage higher spending by local authorities. A new mechanism for calculating the grant was therefore introduced in 1980.[201] The technique for calculating the grant is complex, and cannot be examined here. The essential idea was, however, to provide a simpler, more equal system of grant allocation and one which would remove incentives for "excessive spending". Expenditure above the level of the grant would have to be funded from the rates (or the poll tax etc.), and it was argued that such expenditure would itself indicate that the local authority was seeking to provide a higher level of service than was necessary, or that it was being inefficient. These arguments are of questionable validity, as is the claim that the new method of calculation is simpler.[202]

This attempt to curb local expenditure also proved relatively ineffective because many local authorities chose not to cut the provision of services, but to raise the additional revenue from rates.[203] This led to the Rates Act 1984, which empowered the Secretary of State to limit the rating level of local authorities. The criteria which enable the government to intervene in this manner give broad discretionary power to the Secretary of State,[204] and this has been used to "rate-cap" a number of authorities.

Local authorities attempted to use certain creative accounting devices and schemes in order both to enhance local financial independence and to make ends meet when income fell short of expenditure. The best known of these devices was the "swaps" transaction which was held to be *ultra vires* by the House of Lords.[205]

The rationale for such controls over local authority current expenditure remains questionable. The principal plank of the government's argument is

---

[200] Local Government Act 1974.
[201] Local Government, Planning and Land Act 1980, ss.54-62; Local Government Finance Act 1987, ss.1-5.
[202] Loughlin, *Local Government in the Modern State* (1986), pp. 25-35, 38-39.
[203] *Ibid.* pp. 38-49.
[204] Rates Act 1984, s.2; Local Government Finance Act 1987, ss.6, 7, 8.
[205] *Hazell* v. *Hammersmith and Fulham London Borough Council* [1992] 2 A.C. 1; Loughlin, "Innovative Financing in Local Government: The Limits of Legal Instrumentalism" [1990] P.L. 372, [1991] P.L. 568.

that such control is necessary in order to enable its macro-economic strategy to be successful. One central aspect of this strategy is the control of public expenditure and this is said to necessitate control over local authority expenditure. Whether this justifies the measures which have been adopted is however contested.[206]

Government also exercises control over capital expenditure. Prior to 1980 local authorities required loan sanction from central government for specific projects. The present system is to exercise control over the programme for a financial year, rather than over particular schemes. The expenditure of money is sanctioned under five main blocks, but authorities can aggregate these sums and use them for purposes which fit their own priorities.[207] This does give local authorities some extra autonomy as to the choice of specific capital projects, but this flexibility can only be exercised within a total approved by central government.

The financial controls considered above, which aim to control and limit expenditure in advance, are supplemented by the existence of the audit which reviews past expenditure decisions. Local authority spending is overseen by the Audit Commission. The auditor appointed by the Commission will ensure that the authority's records are in order and that proper arrangements have been made for securing economy and efficiency in the use of resources.[208] There are also powers to surcharge and disqualify those who expend money in breach of the law.[209]

6. *Agencies and Service Delivery*

The statutory changes which have taken place have not only reduced the powers of local authorities, but have also led to the creation of a variety of agencies which are responsible for certain important functions which affect the local community. Two examples can be provided.

The Local Government, Planning and Land Act 1980 laid the foundation for urban development corporations. UDCs are intended to regenerate a particular urban environment. To this end they have powers to acquire land within their area, to build factories, housing and other infrastructure facilities. Funds are acquired in part from central government and in part from private sources. The boards of UDCs are nominated by the relevant minister.

UDCs have been subject to a number of criticisms: there is insufficient integration of their work with that of the local authority in whose area they function; it is unclear whether they are really accountable, since central government control over UDCs may constitute accountability only in a formal sense; and it is uncertain how successful they have actually been in their tasks since it is difficult to obtain reliable figures and equally difficult

---

[206] Loughlin, *Local Government*, pp. 20-22.
[207] Local Government, Planning and Land Act 1980, Pt. VIII.
[208] Local Government Finance Act 1982, s.15.
[209] *Ibid.* ss.19, 20. See also, Local Government Act 1988, s.30.

to assess the quality of the improvements to the area which are said to have been made.[210]

Developments in the educational sphere have been directed to reducing local authority control and increasing the influence of market-based principles. These changes were initiated by the Education Reform Act 1988 which lessened managerial and financial functions previously exercised by local authorities and transferred these to the schools themselves. Budgets are to be allocated to the school directly and the chain of responsibility will flow to the Department of Education and not to the local authority. Schools have the opportunity to opt-out of the control of the local education authority and to acquire grant-maintained status. More recent government initiatives in this area look toward the establishment of a Funding Agency for Schools (FAS), on the supposition that all schools will opt out. Judged by the rate at which schools have opted-out up until now this does, however, look to be an unlikely scenario. Notwithstanding this the government's policy in relation to education exemplifies its preference for taking matters out of local control, subjecting them to market principles and utilising centralised regulatory controls through agencies where this is felt to be necessary.

7. *Central–Local Relations and Democracy*

The previous discussion has indicated how much influence the central government wields over local authorities. How much influence it should wield is quite another matter. The whole debate on central–local relations can only be touched upon here. It involves a number of fundamental questions which have ramifications for the entire structure of government in our society. The balance between efficiency and democracy, between uniformity of standard and diversity, and the meaning to be attached to that most ambiguous of terms, participation, are but three such questions. While one cannot venture even a cursory glance at all of these issues, their importance warrants some consideration.

Whether it would be desirable to increase the power of local authorities, and if so how, is a matter which has been debated for a long time. It has found expression in two of the opposing views of central–local relations, that which sees the latter as a mere agent of the former, and that which accords the two a more equal or autonomous status.

The agency view was adopted by some at least of the utilitarians. For Chadwick the prime consideration was one of efficiency and a presumption of uniformity. This was reflected in the administrative structure of the Poor Law, and public health. A strong central authority was what was desired and concessions to local autonomy were grudgingly accepted. The utilitarian approach must also be seen in its temporal setting. Municipal corporations were only just being reformed. Little faith could be placed in the corrupt oligarchies who had not yet come to conceive of themselves as

---

[210] King, "Government Beyond Whitehall", Dunleavy et al, p. 208.

trustees of public funds. Most municipal functions were still performed independently of the municipal corporation by improvement commissioners and the like. Small wonder that Chadwick was chary of local power.

The modern heirs of the agency view add notions of equality and pragmatism to that of efficiency.[211] Divergent treatment of the same problem in different areas is regarded as unjust. Benefits and services should not depend upon the fortuitous circumstances of where one lives. This is especially so given the fact that the poorer areas will be those with greater needs and smaller sources of independent revenue from the rates etc. Pragmatism is used to buttress arguments from equality. The major sums involved in local authority financing, both in terms of revenue and from borrowing, necessitate centralised control in the form of loan sanctions, government grants and the like. A coherent economic policy would be impossible without such restraints.

The structural expression of the agency view has tended towards relatively large unitary authorities. Fewer authorities providing the combined services a local community requires, making the maximum use of economies of scale, has been thought to be the ideal. While admitting the benefits of local democracy and participation, the proposals of the Redcliffe-Maud Report[212] reflected a preference for the unitary model. More modern manifestations of the agency view have, however, to some extent moved away from the preference for large unitary authorities. This is in part because of the "dangers" which large power structures outside of central government were felt to pose, and in part because of the very desire to remove functions from local authorities and place them with a plethora of other institutions in either the public or private sector.

The agency concept also manifests itself in the type of powers that are left with local authorities. The totality of these may well be diminished if it can be shown to be preferable for functions to be administered from the centre or by an institution separate from the traditional local authority.

The agency view was vehemently opposed in the nineteenth century by Toulmin Smith for whom the parish was sacred. Opponents of the agency view do not, however, have to rely solely upon the Victorian sentimentality of a Toulmin Smith. The argument for more equal treatment between the centre and the local authorities can stand on stronger ground than that. This second view of central–local relations takes as one of its starting points disagreement with certain key tenets of the agency approach. The argument from equality is tendentious or at least founded upon a premise which can be disputed. At base whether one finds the equality argument convincing or not is dependent upon the definition of democracy taken as the yardstick. However, our notions of representative democracy provide no sure guide as to the degree of freedom to be accorded to different levels of administration both of which have been duly elected.[213] A response to the equality argument advanced above is that if a duly elected local authority chooses to administer benefits and services differently from some other authority that

---

[211] Hill, *Democratic Theory and Local Government* (1974), Chap. 5.
[212] Cmnd. 4040 (1969).
[213] Griffith, *Central Departments and Local Authorities* (1966), pp. 507-508.

choice should within bounds be respected. What those bounds are is the main focus of the debate. The agency view tends to set narrow limits reflecting a predisposition for centrally determined standards uniformly applied. The view of central–local relations which perceives of a more equal relationship between the two would allow greater latitude to the local body, although subject to some constraints. While central government would ensure that minimum standards for a particular service were adhered to, greater choice over and beyond this would remain with the local authority than that allowed by subscribers to the agency view.

Opponents of the agency model also adopt a different view both as to the structure of local authorities and the ambit of their powers. Large unitary authorities are opposed because of the distancing effect that this produces. People no longer perceive of such authorities as "local" in any real sense, but as simply another arm of government with its seat appearing remote from the community. Two-tier authorities are preferred. Greater community participation is advocated and finds expression in the addition of a further limb to the hierarchy, that of neighbourhood councils. Involvement of the local populace in community decision-making is encouraged. This may take the form of co-option of local people onto council committees dealing with particular matters; it may take a more radical appearance becoming allied with movements for tenants' rights and social welfare pressure groups.

The distinction between the two views of central–local relations has no doubt been presented in an overly black and white fashion. Shades of grey clearly exist. It should not, moreover, be thought that the two views discussed here represent the only perspectives on central local relations. Theories abound. Some argue that the relationship is more accurately characterised as one of exchange, in which the central and the local authorities bargain with each other to maximise their respective positions. Others articulate a more complex model which denies a straightforward dichotomy between central and local authorities. They emphasise the fact that the centre is itself a collection of different units, as are the local authorities. Each of these theories focuses upon distinct facts. They place varying weights on the sum total of facts which constitute the central–local relationship.[214]

It is, however, readily apparent from the preceding discussion of recent governmental policy that central control over local authorities has dramatically increased, and that this has changed the way in which the two spheres of government interrelate. Local authorities are perceived as agents of central government. Their expenditure is controlled by the executive; the manner in which they conduct their operations is imbued with the central government's market-based perspective; and the ambit of their powers has been curtailed as more of their functions are given to the private sector or agencies which operate at the local level. Participation in local authority decision-making is not perceived as being beneficial in the sense of facilitating the development of the individual, or as being an integral aspect

---

[214] See, e.g., Rhodes, *Beyond Westminster and Whitehall, The Sub-Central Governments of Britain* (1988).

of partaking in civic life. When people participate they do so in a "market-role" as "consumers" of local services.[215] Whether this is the type of democratic society which we wish to foster may well be doubted.[216] It may well be that the only way to ensure a protected sphere of autonomy for local authorities is through a written constitution.

Section 7. Freedom of Information

It is evident from the discussion within the previous sections that access to information and openness are of crucial importance in ensuring the accountability of government. It is also readily apparent that we do not have any general freedom of information legislation such as exists within many other countries.[217] It is important to consider both the reasons for such legislation, and its effectiveness.

The most prominent *reasons* for freedom of information legislation are as follows. First, and most fundamental, it is felt that access to information concerning governmental decision-making is central to the idea of a democratic society. Government and its agencies should be accountable for their actions, and this is rendered difficult if they have a "monopoly" over the available information. Secondly, individual citizens should be able to know the information which is held about them in order to check its correctness and the uses to which it is put. Thirdly, public disclosure of information will, it is hoped, improve agency decision-making because it will be easier to reveal the impact of powerful interest groups upon the agency.

The *effectiveness* of any such legislation is dependent upon three crucial variables. The first is the range of exceptions contained in the legislation, and the way in which these are interpreted. All statutes upon freedom of information contain exceptions, but the number and variety thereof vary considerably. For example, the United States' Freedom of Information Act 1966 has nine basic exceptions which include: national security; internal personnel rules; the private business information exception; agency memoranda; and an exception relating to personal privacy.

A second factor which is of importance in determining the effectiveness of such legislation is the manner in which it is administered. Thus the original American legislation was modified in 1974 to meet problems arising from agency delay in responding to requests for documents. The amended legislation set time limits within which the documents must be produced, and subjects those officials who arbitrarily withhold information to disciplinary proceedings.[218] Another important factor in the

---

[215] This is equally true of the participation which is fostered by the Citizen's Charter initiatives.
[216] *cf. The Conduct of Local Government Business*, Cmnd. 9797 (1986); McAuslan, "The Widdicombe Report: Local Government Business or Politics" [1987] P.L. 154.
[217] Birkinshaw, *Freedom of Information, The Law, the Practice and the Ideal* (1988).
[218] See also the difficulties experienced by Ombudsmen in monitoring the Canadian and Australian legislation, Birkinshaw, *ibid.*, pp. 51-56.

administration of such a scheme is the cost of using it. The general position in, for example, the United States is that requests for commercial purposes will be charged, but that search fees will be waived for many other organisations. The way in which the material is presented by the agency to the individual will also be important in determining the utility of the scheme.

The third factor which is of relevance in assessing the effect of such legislation is the use to which it is put. The legislation has not surprisingly been used by a variety of interest groups and individuals. However the American legislation has often been utilised by a corporation seeking to discover the trade secrets of a rival, or other competitively sensitive information.[219] This has prompted "reverse" freedom of action litigation by those who seek to protect themselves against such disclosure.[220]

Legislation to ensure freedom of information is long overdue in this country. Specific statutes have had some impact,[221] but these are not a substitute for more general legislation along the lines of that which exists in many other countries.[222]

Various arguments have been advanced against any such general Freedom of Information Act. They include the claim that such legislation is unnecessary; that it would interfere with the effectiveness of government; that it would somehow subvert the ordinary democratic process; and that it would prove to be too costly.[223] These arguments are unconvincing. For example, in relation to the contention that such legislation would interfere with the efficiency of government Birkinshaw states,[224]

> "Quite frankly, this argument has no support from the evidence of those countries where FOI operates. Organizing sections of the administration to facilitate responses to requests from citizens for information about their government and its operations is a small price to pay for treating citizens as citizens and not as subjects."

The Campaign for Freedom of Information published a draft bill designed to provide general access to information.[225] It would apply to all government departments, agencies of central government including Next Steps agencies, nationalised industries, NHS bodies and also those bodies which provided advice to government departments and agencies. There would be access to documentation irrespective of the form in which it was

---

[219] Breyer and Stewart, *Administrative Law and Regulatory Policy* (2nd ed., 1985), p. 1230.
[220] *Ibid.* pp. 1248-1253.
[221] Data Protection Act 1984, and see Austin "The Data Protection Act 1984: The Public Law Implications" [1984] P.L. 618; Local Government (Access to Information) Act 1985, and see Birkinshaw, *Open Government, Freedom of Information and Local Government* (1986); Access to Personal Files Act 1987.
[222] The related, but distinct, topic concerning the extent to which a government employee can reveal information obtained in confidence cannot be examined here. See Cripps, "Disclosure in the Public Interest; The Predicament of the Public Sector Employee" [1983] P.L. 600; *Att.-Gen. v. Guardian Newspapers Ltd. (No. 2)* [1990] 1 A.C. 109.
[223] Birkinshaw, "Citizenship and Privacy", *Rights of Citizenship* (Blackburn ed., 1993), pp. 43-47.
[224] *Ibid.* p. 46.
[225] Frankel, *A Freedom of Information Act for Britain* (1991).

held, whether this was on paper, disk, tape etc. The relevant authorities would be under a duty to assist those seeking information, and would normally have to respond to such a request within 30 days. Exemptions would apply to information relating to defence, security, international relations, law enforcement, legal professional privilege, and policy advice, though this would not cover factual information as such. Many of the exemptions would only apply where disclosure would be likely to cause some significant damage to the interest in question. Even if information was prima facie exempt there would be a defence where the disclosure of such information was in the public interest. This could operate where, for example, there was evidence of some real abuse of power or individual injustice. There would be a right of appeal to the Ombudsman who could examine all information including the exempt portion, and provision has been made for a further appeal to an Information Tribunal.

The present government has evinced some concern for greater openness and transparency and this has been mentioned within the Citizen's Charter which has openness as one of its central principles: there should be no secrecy about how public services are run, how much they cost and whether they are meeting their standards.[226] This theme has now been taken up in the White Paper on *Open Government*[227] which seeks to build upon the Charter initiatives. The major proposals in the White Paper are as follows.

There is to be a Code of Practice on Government Information which will allow access to facts and analysis relevant to major policy decisions or proposals. This access is qualified by a list of exceptions which include: defence and international security; internal policy discussion and advice; law enforcement; immigration and nationality; effective management of the economy; and effective management of the public service. The Parliamentary Commissioner will be able to consider any breach of the Code which has been referred by an MP. While any scheme for freedom of information will contain exceptions, those contained in the Code are particularly far-reaching. For example, the exclusion relating to internal policy discussion will make it impossible for individuals to have access to information on alternative policy proposals. Yet one of the common criticisms of any government's policy is that the issue could have been better dealt with in another way, but information which may be needed to test or verify such hypotheses will not be available.

The Code does not establish any general legal right to access to government information. The White Paper does, however, propose that there should be new statutory rights for access to personal information relating to individuals, and to health and safety information.

While any initiative which increases openness is to be welcomed, the exceptions to the Code give the impression that many requests for information will receive a negative response. The government does not appear to be willing to countenance freedom of information legislation as such, but legal rights may well be needed in order to safeguard citizen access to information adequately.

---

[226] *The Citizen's Charter, Raising the Standard*, Cm. 1599 (1991), p. 5.
[227] Cm. 2290 (1993).

Section 8. The Parliamentary Commissioner for Administration

1. General

In the late 1950s there was increasing concern over the operation of the administration. The Crichel Down affair, which was a catalyst for the establishment of the Franks Committee, proved to be outside the terms of reference of that Committee. In 1961, *Justice*[228] published a report which contained two broad suggestions. There were recommendations for the establishment of a General Tribunal to deal with a miscellaneous group of appeals against decisions alleged to be wrong. This suggestion was not adopted. The report also considered the possibility of machinery to deal with maladministration, that is, decisions taken with bias, negligently, unfairly, etc. While some of these could be tackled by the courts, others might not be reviewable or such control might be inappropriate. What provided the inspiration for the subsequent proposals was the existence of the Ombudsmen in Scandinavian countries. Originating in Sweden, and differing in the detail of their powers, the general nature of the office was to appoint an independent and impartial person who would investigate complaints of maladministration which were made by members of the public.

Largely as a result of those recommendations the Parliamentary Commissioner Act 1967 was passed, appointing a Parliamentary Commissioner for Administration,[229] (PCA). The PCA is appointed by the Crown and holds office during good behaviour. He or she may be removed from office as a result of an address from both Houses of Parliament.

2. Scope of the PCA's Powers

(1) WHO AND WHAT CAN BE INVESTIGATED?

The PCA is empowered to investigate complaints relating to any action, subject to the limitations mentioned below, which is taken by or on behalf of a government department or other authority to which the Act applies, where the action taken is in the exercise of administrative functions of that department or authority.[230] The departments and other authorities to which the Act applies are listed in Schedule 2 which can be altered by Order in Council. The list of bodies which are within the PCA's jurisdiction has been

---

[228] The Whyatt Report, *The Citizen and the Administration: the Redress of Grievances* (1961).
[229] See generally, Stacey, *The British Ombudsman* (1971); Gregory and Hutchesson, *The Parliamentary Ombudsman* (1975); Wheare, *Maladministration and its Remedies* (1973), Chap. 5; Stacey, *Ombudsmen Compared* (1978).
[230] Parliamentary Commissioner Act 1967, ss.4(1), 5(1).

expanded, and now includes many agencies.[231] Reference to a department or other authority is taken to include a reference also to the ministers, members or officers of the department.[232]

How far has the creation of agencies and how far has the process of contracting-out affected the range of institutions within the PCA's jurisdiction? Agencies which were created independently of the Next Steps initiative will normally have to be added to Schedule 2 to be within the PCA's remit. Next Steps agencies are, as we have seen, still part of the parent department and do not have any formal separate identity. Given that this is so they would be within the PCA's ambit of authority by virtue of his jurisdiction over the department itself. Somewhat more difficult is the position of firms to whom work has been contracted-out. The 1967 Act does, however, talk of administrative functions being carried out by or *on behalf of* departments.[233] Firms to whom work has been contracted-out are acting on behalf of the department and should therefore be regarded as within the 1967 Act. This is the view taken by the PCA, and it is surely correct as a matter of principle.[234]

Not only must the body against which the complaint is alleged be one to which the Act applies, it must also be a complaint which relates to action taken in the exercise of administrative functions of that department. This could be said to exclude judicial or legislative functions performed by such a body. Thus, the question arises as to whether, for example, the making of delegated legislation is within the PCA's jurisdiction. The Attorney-General, in evidence before the Select Committee,[235] has expressed the view that the making of a statutory instrument is a legislative process and hence outside the PCA's jurisdiction, and that this applied equally to the preliminary stages of the making of the instrument. Once the instrument has been made, the Attorney-General felt that the PCA could receive complaints about its operation and ensure that the relevant department was keeping the matter under review, but that the actual content of the rules could not be questioned. This appears to be the position adopted by the PCA. Where a statutory order is not a statutory instrument, the PCA's powers appear to be wider, allowing an investigation of maladministration in the administrative process leading to the actual making of the order.[236]

Judicial functions in the sense of the work of tribunals or courts are not in any event within the PCA's powers. But it should not be supposed that any matter which has any judicial flavour will be excluded. Public inquiries have, for example, been the subject of the PCA's attention.

---

[231] Parliamentary and Health Service Commissioners Act 1987, s.1, providing a new s.4 of the Parliamentary Commissioner Act 1967.

[232] Parliamentary Commissioner Act 1967, s.(8), as amended by the Parliamentary and Health Service Commissioners Act 1987, s.1.

[233] s.5(1).

[234] Parliamentary Commissioner for Administration, Annual Report 1992, p. 2.

[235] Report from the Select Committee on the Parliamentary Commissioner for Administration (1968-1969; H.C. 385).

[236] Given that the decision whether a rule becomes a statutory instrument is often fortuitous, the wisdom of this dichotomy is questionable. See further on this, Chap. 7 below.

Provided that the action is taken by a body listed in the Act, and the action is taken in the exercise of administrative functions, the PCA is empowered to investigate claims of injustice resulting from maladministration which have been referred by a Member of Parliament.[237] The requirement of the Member of Parliament filter will be considered later.[238]

What is the meaning of the term maladministration?[239] The term is nowhere defined in the Act. A sense of what the legislature intended is to be derived from the Crossman catalogue which included bias, neglect, inattention, delay, incompetence, ineptitude, arbitrariness and the like. In reality the types of defect most commonly found in the context of executive administrative action are: failing to provide information; misapplication of departmental rules; misleading advice; unjustifiable delay and inconsiderate behaviour. Discretionary administrative action is most often subject to criticism by the PCA because some relevant consideration has not been taken into account, or the evidence has not been properly collated prior to making the decision.

The PCA is not authorised to question the merits of a decision taken without maladministration by a government department or other authority in the exercise of a discretion vested in that department or authority.[240] The precise purpose of this provision is not entirely clear. On one view, it seems merely to restate the requirement from section 5(1), that maladministration is indeed a condition precedent to the exercise of jurisdiction by the PCA, without telling us anything further about what maladministration means. On another view, it indicates that the maladministration must reside in the procedure by which the decision itself was made. It was this latter interpretation which was adopted by the first PCA. He drew a distinction between the procedure leading up to a decision and the decision itself. The latter he regarded as outside his competence, even if it resulted in manifest hardship to the complainant. This interpretation was regarded as over-restrictive by the Select Committee[241] and the PCA has subsequently broadened his perspective. A similar caution initially constrained the PCA in relation to departmental rules and regulations. Again, the Select Committee encouraged a broader interpretation,[242] enabling the PCA to consider the effect of statutory instruments and the action taken to review their operation, with a wider jurisdiction in relation to rules which were not statutory instruments.

(2) MATTERS EXCLUDED FROM THE PCA's JURISDICTION

The PCA's jurisdiction is limited in two ways. First, there are the provisions of section 5(2). These prevent the PCA from investigating any action in

---

[237] 1967 Act, s.5(1).

[238] Cohen, "The Parliamentary Commissioner and the 'M.P. Filter'" [1972] P.L. 204.

[239] Marshall, "Maladministration" [1973] P.L. 32.

[240] s.12(3).

[241] Second Report from the Select Committee on the Parliamentary Commissioner for Administration (1967-1968; H.C. 350), para. 14.

[242] Report from the Select Committee on the Parliamentary Commissioner for Administration (1968-1969; H.C. 385), para. 11; First Report of Parliamentary Commissioner for Administration (1974-1975; H.C. 49), para. 63.

respect of which the person aggrieved has or had a right of appeal, reference, or review to, or before, a tribunal constituted by, or under, any enactment or by prerogative, and any action in respect of which the person aggrieved has or had a remedy by way of proceedings in any court of law. This prohibition is subject to an exception where the PCA is satisfied that it would not be reasonable to expect the claimant to resort to such a remedy.[243] The presence of section 5(2) raises issues of general interest as to the role which the PCA is and should be performing. These will be considered in the next section. For the present, it is sufficient to say that there has, despite section 5(2), been some overlap between the jurisdiction of the courts and that of the PCA. This is particularly so as the courts have expanded the ambit of judicial review.

The second type of exclusion is contained in section 5(3). This prevents the PCA from investigating any action or matter described in Schedule 3 of the Act. This Schedule covers: actions certified by a minister to affect relations between the United Kingdom government and any other government or international organisation; the commencement or conduct of civil or criminal proceedings before any court of law in the United Kingdom; any exercise of the prerogative of mercy; action taken on behalf of the minister by a regional health authority, an area health authority, and family practitioner committees;[244] action relating to contractual and commercial transactions, other than the acquisition of land whether compulsorily or by agreement, and the disposal of surplus land thus acquired. Personnel matters are also excluded, and this encompasses both civil and military services, and cases where the government has power to take, determine or approve action. The investigation of crime and the protection of state security, by or with the authority of the Secretary of State, is also outside the PCA's jurisdiction. This exception covers action taken with respect to passports. The grant of honours, awards or privileges by the Crown is also excluded.

The two areas where there has been most pressure for reform have been the exemptions of contractual/commercial matters and personnel. A number of arguments against any such change have been presented. The existence of other machinery for scrutiny of these areas, and the idea that the PCA's role is concerned with the relationship of the government and the governed and not with the government as employer or trader, provide the main arguments against reform. Neither of these reasons seems wholly convincing.[245]

(3) THE COMPLAINANT AND THE PROCEDURE

Section 6(1) spells out who can complain. In essence, it provides that complaints can be made by any individual or body of persons, whether incorporated or unincorporated; complaints cannot however be made by

---

[243] Foulkes, "Discretionary Provisions of the Parliamentary Commissioner Act" (1971) 34 M.L.R. 377.
[244] However, action taken by a minister in relation to such authorities is included. See also the discussion of the Health Service Commissioners, below pp. 134-135.
[245] Clothier, "The Value of an Ombudsman" [1986] P.L. 204, 210-211.

local authorities, nationalised industries, or other bodies appointed by a minister or by a government department. These exclusions are designed to emphasise the character of the PCA as someone who arbitrates between the government and the governed, but who does not hear complaints by one department against another. The complaint must be made by the person aggrieved, or a personal representative. It must be submitted to a Member of Parliament within 12 months from the date on which the person aggrieved first had notice of the matters alleged in the complaint; but the PCA has a discretion to allow a claim to proceed outside that time limit.[246] The complainant must either be resident in the United Kingdom or the complaint must relate to action taken while he or she was present in the United Kingdom.[247]

The complaint must be addressed initially to a Member of Parliament.[248] This is in contrast to the position in a number of other countries where the individual is allowed direct access to the Ombudsman. Such a position has always been rejected in the United Kingdom. The PCA is viewed as an adjunct to Parliament. He aids Parliament in the performance of its traditional function of protecting the citizen, but is not intended to be an independent citizen protector. The argument against allowing direct access has been bolstered by more practical considerations: in a country with a large population direct access would place an impossible burden upon the PCA. The disadvantages in not allowing direct access have partly been overcome by a system whereby the PCA passes on to the relevant Member of Parliament a complaint which he receives directly from the public, stating that he is willing to consider the case should the Member of Parliament wish him to do so. This allows the Member of Parliament to continue to function as a filter, but avoids the necessity of outright rejection of the claim by the PCA. It would nonetheless be preferable if individuals could have direct access to the PCA.

The PCA has considerable choice as to the method of investigation[249] and possesses wide powers in relation to the obtaining of evidence. Where the PCA proposes to conduct an investigation he must afford to the principal officer of the department or authority concerned, and to any other person who is alleged to have taken or authorised the action complained of, an opportunity to comment upon any of the allegations contained in the complaint. Investigations must be conducted in private, but the PCA has a broad discretion as to the type of information required, the persons who are questioned, and whether any person may be represented by counsel, solicitor or otherwise in the investigation.[250] Provision is made for the payment of expenses to the complainant, or to a person involved in the investigation.[251] An investigation by the PCA does not, however, invalidate or

---

[246] s.6(3).
[247] s.6(4). See also, Parliamentary Commissioner (Consular Complaints) Act 1981.
[248] Parliamentary Commissioner Act 1967, s.5(1).
[249] The PCA also has discretion as to whether to investigate or not, s.5(5); Re Fletcher's Application [1970] 2 All E.R. 527.
[250] s.7(1), (2).
[251] s.7(3).

suspend action taken by an authority.[252] The PCA can require that the minister or any other person who has information relevant to the investigation should furnish it to him; and the PCA has the same powers as a court with respect to the attendance of witnesses, including the administration of oaths, and the production of documents.[253] No obligation to maintain secrecy, whether derived from any enactment or any rule of law, applies to the disclosure of information for the purposes of an investigation under the Act, nor can the Crown claim Crown privilege in respect of such documents.[254] Information related to the Cabinet or Cabinet committees cannot, however, be furnished. A certificate issued by the Secretary of the Cabinet with the approval of the Prime Minister certifying that any document does so relate is conclusive of the matter.[255]

The PCA must furnish a number of reports at various stages of the investigatory procedure. A report must be sent to the Member of Parliament who requested the investigation stating the results of it, or the reasons why it cannot be undertaken.[256] Where an investigation is conducted a report shall also be sent to the principal officer of the department concerned.[257] If, having made a report finding maladministration, it appears to the PCA that the injustice will not be remedied, he may lay before each House of Parliament a special report on the case.[258] An annual general report must be laid before each House, and the PCA may submit other reports if he thinks fit.[259]

(4) REMEDIES

The PCA has no formal power to award a remedy. As seen, his investigation will in general not even have a suspensory effect upon the action under investigation.[260] If the recommendations are not complied with a special report can be submitted to Parliament,[261] but the PCA can do nothing formally beyond this.

This should not lead to the supposition that the investigations are fruitless. Nothing could be further from the truth. The reports of the PCA have resulted in a wide range of remedies. This is apparent from any of his annual reports. In 1992 out of 177 investigations which the PCA found to be wholly or partially justified he managed to secure some remedy over and

---

[252] s.7(4). Except in so far as the person aggrieved has been removed from the UK, he must, if the PCA so directs, be brought back to the UK, subject to such conditions as the Secretary of State may direct, for the purposes of the investigation.

[253] s.8(1), (2).

[254] s.8(3). There are however provisions to prevent the PCA disclosing information to any person where it would be contrary to interests of the state. This does not prevent the PCA himself from seeking such documents, s.11(3).

[255] s.8(4).

[256] s.10(1).

[257] s.10(2), and to any other person who is alleged to have taken or authorised the action complained of.

[258] s.10(3).

[259] s.10(4).

[260] s.7(4).

[261] s.10(4).

beyond a mere apology. In 92 of the cases a financial remedy was obtained, and in 30 of these cases the department changed some of its practices as a result of the investigation. A change of departmental practice also occurred in 25 other cases, although without any accompanying compensation. In a further 15 cases there was some other form of remedial redress.[262] In addition, he has in certain instances prevailed upon a department to abide by an assurance or representation that it has made to an individual which it now wishes to depart from.[263] Nor have the investigations led only to the correction of individual error. Departmental practices have been altered as a result of the injustice brought to light by his reports. For example, the rules concerning prisoners' access to legal advice have been liberalised, and certain welfare benefits duly backdated.

The PCA has also had an impact on certain more high profile cases. The Sachsenhausen case[264] concerned the distribution of money provided by the German government to compensate those who had been victims in the Sachsenhausen concentration camp. The sum was distributed by the UK government, but money was withheld from 12 people who claimed that they fell within the relevant criteria. The PCA investigated the matter and found that there had been maladministration and the government gave compensation to the complainants even though the original sum given by the German government had already been distributed.

A more recent example of the PCA's impact upon a high profile case is the Barlow Clowes affair.[265] The Barlow Clowes investment business collapsed in 1988 leaving many investors with substantial losses. The business had been licensed by the Department of Trade and Industry under the relevant legislation. The PCA found that there had been maladministration by the DTI and although the government did not accept these findings it did provide *ex gratia* compensation for up to 90% of the losses.

(5) WORKLOAD

In 1992 the PCA received 945 complaints, which was 144 more than in 1991. Of these 28% were accepted for investigation.[266] The PCA perceived a connection between the rise in complaints and the increased expectations generated by the Citizen's Charter and associated initiatives.[267] The main reasons for rejecting complaints were because they did not fall within the coverage of the 1967 Act. More specifically: 43% were rejected because they did concern administrative action as required by section 5(1); 24% were excluded because of section 5(2)(a) in that the applicants had rights of appeal to a tribunal; 10% of complaints failed because the authority was not within the scope of the PCA's jurisdiction, and interestingly the largest

---

[262] See, *e.g.*, Parliamentary Commissioner for Administration, Annual Report 1992, p. 41.
[263] *Ibid.* Appendix A; Mowbray, "The Parliamentary Commissioner and Administrative Guidance" [1987] P.L. 570.
[264] Third Report of the Parliamentary Commissioner for Administration (1967-68; HC 54).
[265] Gregory and Drewry, "Barlow Clowes and the Ombudsman-Part I" [1991] P.L. 192; "Barlow Clowes and the Ombudsman-Part II" [1991] P.L. 408.
[266] Annual Report 1992, pp. 38-41.
[267] *Ibid.* p. 1.

group within this category were complaints against the courts or other legal bodies; 6% were not proceeded with because they concerned personnel matters; and 6% were turned down in the exercise of the PCA's discretion.

In 103 (54%) of the completed cases the complaint was found to be wholly justified; it was held to be partially justified in 74 cases (39%); while in 13 cases (7%) there was found to be no justification for the allegation. The Department of Social Security and the Inland Revenue attracted between them nearly 50% of all complaints, although this is not surprising given the nature and volume of their work.

(6) THE SELECT COMMITTEE ON THE PCA

The Select Committee examines the PCA's reports which have been laid before the House. It provides a focal point for parliamentary attention upon the work of the PCA. It has also been of value in two more direct ways. The Select Committee has encouraged the PCA to adopt a broad view of his powers and it exerts political pressure to ensure departmental compliance with the PCA's recommendations.[268]

3. *The Health Service Commissioners*

The National Health Service Reorganisation Act 1973 created two Health Service Commissioners, one for England and the other for Wales. Scotland was provided with a Commissioner by the Health Service (Scotland) Act 1972. The principal governing statute for England is now the National Health Service Act 1977 and that for Scotland is the National Health Service (Scotland) Act 1978.[269] The PCA will normally hold these offices as well as the office created by the 1967 Act.

One difference between his jurisdiction under the 1967 Act and the legislation relating to health is that direct access is allowed under the latter legislation. The reason for allowing this is that Members of Parliament do not occupy the same constitutional position with respect to the health service as they do in connection with ordinary departments. A condition precedent to direct access is, however, that the complainant first brings the matter to the notice of the health authority who must be allowed a reasonable opportunity to respond to the complaint. The complainant must be the person aggrieved, but if that person is unable to present the complaint it may be advanced by a member of the family or by any body or individual suitable to represent the complainant.[270]

The Health Commissioner can investigate regional health authorities, area health authorities, designated special health authorities, family

---

[268] Gregory, "The Select Committee on the Parliamentary Commissioner for Administration 1967-1980" [1982] P.L. 49.

[269] National Health Service Act 1977, Pt. V and National Health Service (Scotland) Act 1978, Pt. VI, as amended by the Parliamentary and Health Service Commissioners Act 1987 and the National Health Service and Community Care Act 1990.

[270] National Health Service Act 1977, s.111.

practitioner committees, certain health boards[271] and now also NHS trusts.[272]

The matters which the Health Commissioner may investigate are an alleged failure in a service provided by the authority, an alleged failure by an authority to provide a service that it was meant to provide, and any other action taken by or on behalf of an authority. The complainant must allege that injustice or hardship has been suffered in consequence of the first two heads of failure, or that there has been maladministration in connection with the third type of matter referred to.[273]

The matters excluded from the jurisdiction of the Health Commissioner are similar to those excluded from the general jurisdiction of the PCA. Thus, he cannot investigate matters which are within the jurisdiction of the courts or a tribunal, subject to the same discretion to proceed as he ordinarily has.[274] Other matters which are outside the jurisdiction of the Health Commissioner relate more directly to the nature of his office. Thus, the exercise of clinical judgment is excluded from the Health Commissioner's jurisdiction.[275] This is one of the main reasons for the rejection of complaints.

4. Local Commissioners

(1) SCOPE OF AUTHORITY

The 1967 Act did not include within its ambit complaints against local authorities. This had long been a source of criticism which was remedied by the Local Government Act 1974. Two Commissions for local administration were established, one for England and one for Wales.[276] The PCA is a member of both. However, the work is performed by local commissioners who are appointed by the Crown and who, like the PCA, hold office during good behaviour.

The local commissioners can investigate complaints against any local authority except a parish council, and this includes committees, members and officers.[277] Joint boards are also covered, as are water and police authorities[278] other than the Secretary of State. Subsequent legislation has brought development corporations and the Commission for New Towns within the local commissioners' jurisdiction.[279]

---

[271] *Ibid.* s.109.
[272] National Health Service and Community Care Act 1990, Schedule 9, para.18(10).
[273] National Health Service Act 1977, s.115.
[274] *Ibid.* s.116. Other matters which are excluded are personnel matters relating to pay, discipline, etc., contractual or commercial transactions, except in relation to the provision of services for patients, disciplinary actions of an executive council or family practitioner committee.
[275] National Health Service Act 1977, Schedule 13, Pt.II.
[276] Scotland has its own system, Local Government (Scotland) Act 1975, Pt. II.
[277] Local Government Act 1974, ss.25, 34(1).
[278] s.25.
[279] Local Government Act 1988, s.29, Schedule 3.

Access to the local commissioner was originally indirect, the complaint being referred initially to a member of the local authority.[280] Since 1988 individuals have been given a right of direct access to the local commissioner.[281]

The complainant must allege that injustice has been suffered as a consequence of maladministration and, as in the case of health, allow the local authority a reasonable opportunity to investigate and reply to the complaint.[282] Exclusions exist similar to those governing the jurisdiction of the PCA. Thus, cases where there is a remedy before a court of law or a tribunal are excluded, as are cases which are subject to an appeal to a minister; there is a discretionary exception to this prohibition which is the same as that in the 1967 Act.[283] Other exclusions which are of importance are cases where the complaint affects all or most of the inhabitants of the authority's area.[284]

The procedure for investigation is similar in certain respects to that of the PCA.[285] Copies of the report must be sent to the complainant, the local authority and the member who originally referred it. The report must be made available for public inspection for a period of three weeks.[286] The procedural powers of the local commissioners were reinforced in 1989.[287] Once an adverse report has been made the local authority is under a duty to respond to it within three months. If no such action is forthcoming, or the commissioner is not satisfied with the proposed course of action, the local commissioner must make a further report setting out these facts and making further recommendations about remedying the injustice. If the local authority still proves recalcitrant, or has not taken the necessary action, then it can be forced to issue a statement in the press containing the local commissioner's proposals and any reasons why it has not taken action. A minister of the Crown or a local authority may by written notice prevent any disclosure of information or documents if such disclosure would be contrary to the public interest.[288]

---

[280] s.26(2), (3).

[281] Local Government Act 1988, s.29, Schedule 3, para 5.

[282] Local Government Act 1974, s.26(5); R. v. Local Commissioner for Administration, ex p. Bradford Metropolitan Council [1979] Q.B. 287; R. v. Commissioner for Local Administration, ex p. Eastleigh Borough Council [1988] Q.B. 855; Jones, "The Local Ombudsmen and Judicial Review" [1988] P.L. 608.

[283] s.26(6). See, R. v. Commissioner for Local Administration, ex. p. Croydon London Borough Council [1989] 1 All E.R. 1033.

[284] s.26(7). Other exclusions are investigation or prevention of crime, contractual or commercial transactions, personnel matters, educational matters.

[285] The decision in Re a Complaint against Liverpool City Council [1977] 1 W.L.R. 995 has been bypassed by the Local Government, Planning and Land Act 1980, s.184. This brings the provisions of the Local Government Act 1974, s.32(3) into line with those of the Parliamentary Commissioner Act 1967, s.11(3).

[286] s.30.

[287] Local Government and Housing Act 1989, s.26, amending s.31 of the Local Government Act 1974.

[288] Local Government Act 1974, s.32(3).

A local commissioner will make an annual report. There is, in addition, an obligation on each of the Commissions as a whole to report annually to the local authorities.[289]

(2) THE BROADER CONTEXT

A complainant will have only to resort to the local ombudsman if a grievance is not redressed by the local authority itself. This is an obvious proposition, but it is important nonetheless. Our focus should not therefore be exclusively upon the local commissioner, but also upon internal grievance procedures which are used by local authorities.

Valuable work on this has been done by Lewis and others at Sheffield.[290] They found that less than 50% of local authorities have general complaints procedures, that those which did possess such procedures did not advertise their existence and that few systematically monitored complaints with a view to checking on service quality. Their recommendations, which include a statutory duty to have a complaints procedure, the appointment of a complaints officer, and the adoption of a code of good administrative practice,[291] should be taken seriously.

The Sheffield study also contains interesting suggestions about the role of the local commissioners. Some of these, such as direct access, have been implemented. Other recommendations include: modification of the jurisdictional limits; allowing the local commissioners to investigate on their own initiative, rather than waiting for a complaint; enabling them to comment on issues where many people are affected; shifting away from the concern with maladministration as such, in part because the word carries an unfortunate connotation, and in part because it acts as a barrier to a more wide-ranging role which would allow the local ombudsmen to investigate more general failure in the administrative system.[292] The study did not, however, come out in favour of judicial enforcement in the event that a local authority did not comply with the commissioner's recommendations. Although this role for the courts has been advocated[293] such a change would be likely to render the investigative process more formal. If local authorities know that a report of the local commissioner could produce legal liability, even indirectly, they are likely to demand more extensive right to controvert his findings.[294]

---

[289] Local Government Act 1974, s.23 as amended by the Local Government and Housing Act 1989, s.25.

[290] Lewis, Seneviratne and Cracknell, *Complaints Procedures in Local Government*; Crawford, "Complaints, Codes and Ombudsmen in Local Government" [1988] P.L. 246.

[291] Local Government and Housing Act 1989, s.31 makes provision for a National Code of Local Government Conduct.

[292] Local Government and Housing Act 1989, s.23 modifies s.23 of the Local Government Act 1974, by allowing the local commissioners to give general advice to local authorities about good administrative practice.

[293] As recommended in *Administrative Justice, Some Necessary Reforms* (1988), pp. 128-129.

[294] See the comments by local authority officers reported in the Justice Study, *ibid.* pp. 127-128. See also, the Sheffield study, *Complaints Procedures*, p. 39; Himsworth, "Parliamentary Teeth for Local Government Ombudsmen" [1986] P.L. 546; Marshall, "Ombudsmanaging Local Government" [1990] P.L. 449.

5. *Northern Ireland*

The Parliamentary Commissioner Act 1967 was not applicable to Northern Ireland. This situation was remedied by the Parliamentary Commissioner (Northern Ireland) Act 1969 which is in substance the same as the 1967 Act except that allegations of maladministration relating to personnel matters in the Northern Ireland Office are also covered.

There is also a Commissioner of Complaints.[295] The jurisdiction covers action taken by any local body and by the public bodies listed. There is direct access to the Commissioner on payment of a small sum which can be refunded or waived. The most interesting provision is one whereby the complainant can apply to the county court after a finding of injustice caused by maladministration made by the Commissioner. The county court can award damages, an injunction or other specific relief. Where there is evidence of continuing maladministration, the Commissioner can request that the Attorney-General apply to the High Court for an injunction.

6. *The Role of the PCA*

The role of the ombudsman has developed considerably since the office was first introduced in this country. The scope of bodies which fall within the jurisdiction has been expanded, and we have seen the creation of commissioners for health and local government. The idea of an ombudsman has taken hold more generally and has been applied in areas such as banking and insurance.[296] An ombudsman has now also been created for Community law. But what of the role of the ombudsmen who operate in the context of public law? There are at least three ways in which the PCA can be viewed.

The first is to see the main task as the remedying of individual grievances caused by neglect, bias, or inattention within the administration. In performing this role, he or she operates as an adjunct to Parliament, aiding that body in the protection of the individual. The Member of Parliament filter, the absence of the power to award remedies, and the duty to report to Parliament, all reinforce this perspective. This picture of the PCA sees the job as essentially or primarily concerned with the avoidance of mistakes. The jurisdictional divide between the courts and the PCA only serves to emphasise this further: each is responsible for ensuring the avoidance of mistakes within their own sphere of responsibility, and this is so even accepting that there is some overlap in this respect. There is no doubt that correction of individual grievances constitutes an important aspect of the PCA's work, and that it might be facilitated by the adoption of a two track system which would entail a more and less intensive type of investigation

---

[295] Commissioner of Complaints Act (Northern Ireland) 1969; Poole, "The Northern Ireland Commissioner for Complaints" [1972] P.L. 131.

[296] Mowbray, "Ombudsmen: The Private Sector Dimension", *Edinburgh Essays in Public Law*, (Finnie, Himsworth and Walker eds., 1991), pp. 315-334.

depending upon the nature of the complaint. The existence of a fast track procedure could, moreover, serve to make the system more attractive to MPs who make the references.[297]

A second way in which the PCA could be viewed preserves the mistake avoidance approach, but seeks to expand the existing jurisdiction. Suggestions are made that citizens should have direct access to the PCA, and that the discretion to take cases even if they are within the jurisdiction of the ordinary courts should be generously exercised. Some advocate this as a means of obtaining the expeditious and cheap disposition of justice. Allied to such ideas are those that see the PCA armed with remedial power, directly or indirectly. That is, either to give remedies in his own capacity or to be able to apply to the court in order that the court will grant relief. The image of the PCA as a small claims administrative court emerges.

The attractions of this second approach are obvious. It does, however, have a number of disadvantages which are less obvious but very real. The most extreme form of this line of reasoning, which implicitly, if not explicitly, sees the PCA as a small claims court, would involve a fundamental re-orientation of the PCA's original role. This is of course not a logical bar to proceeding further, but is worth stating nonetheless. The effects of such a change need to be thought through. What is clear is that any move in this direction would entail an expansion in personnel and the transformation of the PCA into a judicial figure with a bureaucratic hierarchy of his or her own. Benefits of the present system, particularly those of informality of procedure and negotiated settlement, would be lost or placed in jeopardy; there would be a tendency, not inexorable but strong, for it to become adversarial in nature. Procedures would become more rigid. Many of these comments apply with equal force to suggestions that the PCA should have the power to award a remedy himself. Such a power is bound to carry with it demands for more formal hearings before being condemned, the right to representation, and other safeguards normally associated with judicial proceedings.[298]

The suggestion that the PCA should liberally exercise the discretion to hear complaints which the courts can hear[299] also has ramifications which may not be immediately self-evident. There is, of course, bound to be some overlap between the PCA and the courts. The nature of administrative law precludes rigid statements that a matter is or is not within the purview of the courts. The reason for caution is simple: the development of two views upon the same subject-matter which are inconsistent, or the application of the same view in an inconsistent manner.

There is a link between this point and the possibility of the PCA applying to a court for the award of a remedy. If the PCA did have this power and also liberally interpreted the discretion to take cases which could come

---

[297] Gregory and Pearson, "The Parliamentary Ombudsman after Twenty-Five Years" (1992) 70 Pub. Adm. 469, 492-496.

[298] And note the reservations about such a system expressed by Clothier, "The Value of an Ombudsman" [1986] P.L. 204, 210.

[299] Bradley, "The Role of the Ombudsman in Relation to the Protection of Citizen's Rights" (1980) 39 C.L.J. 304, 331-332.

before the court, we would be faced with the following conundrum. Let us assume that in some cases at least the PCA might reach a result inconsistent either with the judicial principle applied in an area or, while consistent with the principle, applied it in a way in which a court would not. The PCA approaches the court claiming maladministration. Either the court accepts the charge and simply hands out the remedy, in which case the dual system of jurisprudence spoken of above would be even more of a reality, or the court would look to the substance of the charge and reassess whether maladministration had taken place. If the court re-examined the matter and found that the action called maladministration could not be thus dubbed because, for example, estoppel should not bind the Crown, then the dual system of jurisprudence would be avoided, but a cumbersome and partial form of review would have taken its place.

It is no answer to the above example to suggest that the fears expressed are misconceived because the courts and the PCA are doing different things: the former being concerned with the limits of jurisdiction and the principles on which discretion should be exercised, while the latter is occupied with principles of good administration. We are in danger of allowing form to blind us from substance. Whether, for example, a representation should bind is the substantive question. The conclusion may be expressed in the affirmative or negative. To imagine that there is no conflict if the conclusions are reached under different labels called *ultra vires* or good administration is short-sighted. It may well be that the content expressed under the two labels differs in some degree. Yet, when the content expressed by those two names is analysed one would find the same types of value simply being weighted differently. We are back once again with a dual system of jurisprudence or, to put it more neutrally, a dual set of values being applied to the same problem.

If this second view of the PCA is indeed felt to have deficiencies, the office could still be expanded in a different direction. A third view would accept the more limited mistake avoidance role of the PCA, outlined as the first view, but would advocate an expansion of the jurisdiction in a different direction. This is to ask the PCA to draw attention to lessons which should be learned from individual cases in order to improve administrative practice generally.[300] This broader conception of effectiveness would not have to mean neglect of individual cases. It would be an additional task. The investigation of individual cases would be, as Harlow says,[301] a catalyst for discovering more general administrative deficiencies. An additional task of this kind could be particularly helpful given that MPs do not at present seem to pay undue regard to the PCA's role in addressing individual grievances.[302]

It is clear that the PCA already does fulfil this more general function to some degree, as a glance at any of the annual reports will confirm: problems

---

[300] Harlow, "Ombudsmen in Search of a Role" (1978) 41 M.L.R. 446.

[301] *Ibid.* p. 452.

[302] Drewry and Harlow, "A Cutting Edge? The Parliamentary Commissioner and M.P.s" (1990) 53 M.L.R. 745; Bradley, "Sachsenhausen, Barlow Clowes-And Then?" [1992] P.L. 353.

in individual cases do lead onto the discovery of a more general concern, and the result is often recommendations for changing the administrative practice which gave rise to the initial problem.[303] Statutory provisions serve to reinforce this aspect of the ombudsman's role, by encouraging the giving of general advice on good administrative practice.[304] Moreover, the Select Committee on the PCA has emphasised that the PCA may have a role in assessing whether an agency's performance has matched up to the standards laid down in the Citizen's Charter.[305]

While the PCA has, therefore, made contributions of this type, he should be encouraged to proceed further. He would still be able to operate so as to apply pressure in a Sachsenhausen type of case, but the remedying of more general administrative deficiencies would play a more prominent part than it does at present. Nor should the PCA have to be entirely reactive in this respect: investigations should be capable of being mounted on the PCA's own initiative.

---

[303] See also, Gregory and Pearson, "The Parliamentary Ombudsman after Twenty-Five Years" (1992) 70 Pub. Adm. 469, 480-484.
[304] Local Government and Housing Act 1989, s.23, amending s.23 of the Local Government Act 1974.
[305] The Implications of the Citizen's Charter for the Work of the PCA, 2nd Report of the Select Committee on the PCA, (1991-92; HC 158).

4. INSTITUTIONS II: TRIBUNALS AND INQUIRIES

Section 1. Statutory Tribunals[1]

1. *Reasons for their Creation*

The reasons for the creation of tribunals have been touched upon already when discussing the history of administrative institutions.[2] A word or two more on this is warranted at this juncture. It is important to realise that a number of differing types of argument have been used to justify creating tribunals and assigning tasks to them. Three such arguments can be distinguished here.

Firstly, tribunals are often preferred to courts because they are said to have the advantages of speed, cheapness, informality and expertise. These advantages are of particular importance in areas involving mass administrative justice, such as the distribution of social welfare benefits. It would, moreover, be extremely difficult for the ordinary courts to cope with the large increase in case load which would result if these matters were assigned to the ordinary judicial process.

Secondly, a rather different type of argument is that the ordinary courts might not be sympathetic to the protection of the substantive interests contained in some of the legislation which laid the foundation of the welfare state at the turn of the century, and that therefore the matter should be assigned to a tribunal instead.

A third and more radical argument sees the creation of some tribunals as a symbolic means of giving the appearance of legality in a particular area in order to render more palatable unpopular changes in the substantive benefits to which individuals were entitled.[3]

These differing reasons may well have force in different contexts. What is readily apparent is that tribunals have been set up in a great many areas. There are, for example, tribunals dealing with industrial matters, financial services, mental health, immigration, social security, vaccine damage, revenue and child support to name but a few, and new tribunals are often created. The creation of a tribunal system can, moreover, alleviate

---

[1] Wraith and Hutchesson, *Administrative Tribunals* (1973); Farmer, *Tribunals and Government* (1974); Birkinshaw, *Grievances, Remedies and the State* (1985); Rawlings, *Grievance Procedure and Administrative Justice. A Review of Socio-Legal Research* (1987).
[2] See above, pp. 58-61.
[3] Prosser, "Poverty, Ideology and Legality: Supplementary Benefit Appeal Tribunals and their Predecessors" (1977) British Jnl. of Law and Soc. 44.

problems for the courts which can become inundated by judicial review applications within a particular area.[4]

2. *The Nature of Tribunals*

What then is a tribunal? It is clear that the precise name of an institution is not determinative in this context. The institutions which are under the supervision of the Council on Tribunals include bodies called authorities, commissions, and committees, as well as tribunals. Given that this is so, it is clear that we must look beyond the label attached, and have regard to the substance or nature of the body in question. No easy answer is, however, forthcoming. One might proceed by articulating a number of properties which a tribunal should possess and then test to see how many do in fact possess them.[5] The properties enunciated could be: the ability to make final, legally enforceable decisions (subject to review and appeal); independence from any department of government; the holding of a public hearing judicial in nature, although more informal than that of the ordinary courts; the possession of expertise; a requirement to give reasons; and the provision of appeal to the High Court on points of law. However, very few of the tribunals listed in the Tribunals and Inquiries Act 1992 possess all of these features.[6] Recognition of this very diversity is important in two ways.

First, it may help us when we come to consider the appropriate scope of review. The realisation that there is not simply a distinction between tribunals and inquiries, but also a considerable divergence between those bodies which go by the name of tribunals may well act as a counterweight to the normal implicit assumption that the same types of principles should apply to all such institutions.[7] Secondly, not every institution which is called a tribunal can properly be regarded as part of the machinery of adjudication. Not all such authorities can be regarded as court-substitutes. There are, as we have seen, many agencies which, irrespective of their name, do not fit this model, and the problems generated by them are not identical to those of more traditional court-substitute tribunals.[8]

3. *The Franks Report*[9]

(1) GENERAL

The historical background to the development of our present tribunal system has already been related.[10] In the 1950s there was growing concern

---

[4] Sir Harry Woolf, "Judicial Review: A Possible Programme for Reform" [1992] P.L. 221, 228.
[5] Farmer, *Tribunals and Government* (1974), pp. 185-186.
[6] *Ibid.* pp. 186-187.
[7] See above, pp. 7-8.
[8] See above, pp. 81-86.
[9] *Report of the Committee on Administrative Tribunals and Enquiries*, Cmnd. 218 (1957).
[10] See above, pp. 58-61.

as to the range and diversity of such bodies, uncertainty as to the procedures they followed, and worry over their lack of cohesion and supervision. However, somewhat paradoxically the catalyst for the establishment of the Franks Committee was the Crichel Down affair.[11] This received wide publicity at the time, but as it was an example of *ad hoc* high-handed administrative behaviour it was not within the brief subsequently given to the Franks Committee.

This was limited in two important ways. The Committee was not to consider decisions made in the ordinary courts and, perhaps more importantly, it was only to discuss those areas in which a decision was reached after a formal statutory procedure had been followed. There were two aspects to this latter limitation. One was the type of case manifested by the Crichel Down affair itself, the "one-off" high-handed administrative action. Less attention has been paid to the fact that the terms of reference also excluded more informal varieties of decision-making. Decisions are made continually, in an informal manner, which may not in any sense be high-handed, but may well be dispositive for the individual concerned.

(2) THE RECOMMENDATIONS

The Franks Committee proceeded on the assumption that tribunals should be regarded as part of the machinery of adjudication and not as part of the machinery of the administration,[12] thereby rejecting the view of some of those within the bureaucracy who had advocated the latter position. Two comments are apposite on this important point of principle.

The first is that one can well accept that this should be so without necessarily accepting that it must entail all elements attendant upon the ordinary court procedures. This does not simply mean, as the Franks Committee itself acknowledged, that rules as to evidence and procedure should be modified in their application to tribunals. It also raises fundamental questions as to whether regarding tribunals as part of the machinery of adjudication necessitates acceptance of the normal adversary system as opposed to some more inquisitorial role for the tribunal. The second comment is a reiteration of a point made earlier.[13] While it may be correct to regard certain types of tribunals as part of the machinery of adjudication, those dubbed court-substitute tribunals, it is clear that other tribunals, authorities or commissions fit much less easily into this pigeonhole. They are institutions which, while making decisions, may lack the independence which must be an essential prerequisite of the Franks' view, and they subsist subject to a variety of controls imposed by the government.

The specific recommendations of the Franks Committee were framed against the background that tribunals should be seen as part of the machinery of adjudication, the correlative of which was that they should be open, fair and impartial. To quote from the Committee,[14]

---

[11] See below, p. 171.
[12] Cmnd. 218 (1957), para. 40.
[13] See above, p. 143.
[14] Cmnd. 218 (1957), para. 42.

"In the field of tribunals openness appears to us to require the publicity of proceedings and knowledge of the essential reasoning underlying the decisions; fairness to require the adoption of a clear procedure which enables parties to know their rights, to present their case fully and to know the case which they have to meet; and impartiality to require the freedom of tribunals from the influence, real or apparent, of Departments concerned with the subject-matter of their decisions."

The Franks Report contained a series of valuable general recommendations concerning the constitution and procedure of tribunals.[15]

As to *constitution*, the Committee stated that chairmen of tribunals should be appointed by the Lord Chancellor and wing members by the Council on Tribunals. Chairmen should normally have legal qualifications and should always do so in the case of appellate tribunals. Remuneration should be examined by the Council on Tribunals.

Detailed recommendations were made concerning *procedure*. The procedure for particular tribunals should be formulated by the Council on Tribunals in the light of the general principles of the report, the aim being to combine orderly procedure with an informal atmosphere. The citizen should be aware of the right to apply to a tribunal and should know in good time before the hearing the case that will have to be met. Tribunal hearings should be public except where there were considerations of public security, intimate personal or financial circumstances had to be disclosed, or the hearing was a preliminary investigation of a case involving professional reputation. Legal representation before tribunals should normally be allowed. Tribunals should be empowered to award costs, to take evidence on oath and to subpoena witnesses. Decisions should be as fully reasoned as possible and a written notice of the decision should be sent to the parties as soon as possible after the hearing. This should set out the decision itself, the findings of fact by the tribunal, the reasons for the decision and the right of appeal against the decision. Final appellate tribunals should publish selected decisions and circulate them to lower tribunals.

The report also contained recommendations on *appeal* and *judicial review*. As to the former, the Committee advocated an appeal on fact, law and merits from a first instance tribunal to an appellate tribunal except where the tribunal of first instance was particularly well qualified. On principle there should not be an appeal from a tribunal to a minister. As to review, the Committee recommended that no statute should contain words purporting to oust the remedies of certiorari, prohibition and mandamus.

In addition to traditional judicial control by way of review and appeal the Committee urged that bodies called the Council on Tribunals for England and Wales and the Scottish Council be established. Their main functions would be to advise on the detailed application to the various tribunals of the general principles contained in the Franks Report. As well as this implementary role the councils were envisaged to have a general co-ordinating role. Thus any proposal to establish a new tribunal should be

---

[15] The recommendations are summarised in Cmnd. 218 (1957), Chap. 31.

referred to the councils for their advice. Both councils should consist of lay and legally qualified members.

(3) IMPLEMENTATION

Many of the measures advocated by the Report of the Franks Committee were enacted in the Tribunals and Inquiries Act 1958, now replaced by the Tribunals and Inquiries Act 1992, a piece of consolidating legislation. Other recommendations were implemented by changes in administrative practice. An outline of the main provisions will be given here; particular aspects will be discussed in more detail below.

The Council on Tribunals was established with a membership of not more than 15 and not less than 10.[16] Its functions are advisory and it is instructed to keep under review the constitution and working of the tribunals listed in a schedule to the Act. In addition it must report on any matter referred to it by the government. It has power to make general recommendations concerning the membership of those tribunals listed in the schedule and it must be consulted prior to the enactment of any new procedural rules which pertain to them.[17] Lay members and lawyers are included within its membership, the former being in the majority as the Franks Report had urged.

Other provisions of importance were the right to a reasoned decision subject to the condition that it was requested on or before the giving or notification of the decision,[18] and the restrictive construction to be placed upon clauses which purported to exclude judicial review.[19] The list of tribunals which are subject to the legislation can be augmented by ministerial order, as has been done.

In some areas, however, less was achieved than that advocated by the Franks Committee. Appeals to the High Court were limited to questions of law, excluding questions of fact and the merits,[20] and the procedure for the appointment of chairmen and members of tribunals diverged from that recommended by the Franks Committee. The members of that Committee had felt that it was wrong for chairmen to be appointed by ministers within whose subject-matter area they fell. Hence the recommendation that they should in the future be appointed by the Lord Chancellor. Some were of the opinion that lay members should be appointed in the same way, but the framers of the report felt that this was impracticable. However, it was thought that public confidence in the impartiality of tribunals would be better preserved if these wing members were appointed by the Council on Tribunals rather than the minister. What emerged in the legislation did not reflect these views. Chairmen are appointed either by the Lord Chancellor directly or chosen by the minister concerned from a Lord Chancellor's

---

[16] Tribunals and Inquiries Act 1992, ss.1, 2. There is provision for a Scottish Committee of the Council.
[17] Tribunals and Inquiries Act 1992, s.8.
[18] *Ibid.* s.10.
[19] s.12. See generally below, Chap. 16.
[20] s.11.

panel.[21] Wing members are, in the main, selected by the minister, though in certain instances the Lord Chancellor himself appoints.

4. *The Tribunal System*

The statutory and administrative reforms which followed the Franks Report introduced a measure of rationality and cohesion into a system which had developed very largely in an *ad hoc* manner. It would, however, be mistaken to assume that uniformity has been produced, nor indeed that it was intended. The structuring of, for example, procedural rules to fit the particular tribunal in question is a theme which recurs throughout the Franks Committee's Report. It is necessary therefore to look more closely at the diversity which subsists beneath the umbrella of the 1958 reforms.

(1) STRUCTURE, COMPOSITION AND STAFF

Tribunals may be organised nationally, regionally or locally depending upon the type of subject-matter.[22] An important structural development which has taken place has been the spread of what is known as the Presidential system.[23] The essence of this organisational pattern is the existence of a president who is responsible for the general administration of tribunals within a particular area. The president will decide how many locally based tribunals are required and in what areas they should be established, a function particularly useful where there are a large number of similar claims across the nation. The system has a number of advantages.[24] Some of these are obvious but no less important for being so. Thus the Presidential system enhances the sense of tribunal independence from any department of government, a feeling augmented by the possession of separate premises. Flexibility is increased by the president's power to create tribunals in particular areas. Greater consistency in decision-making can be achieved, a problem always present where the same rules have to be applied by a large number of people in a wide range of locations. A less obvious advantage secured by the Presidential system is that it eases communication between a department and a tribunal. The Council of Tribunals has recommended greater use of the Presidential mode of organisation.[25] It is not uncommon for a judge to be the head or president of a system of tribunals and the extension of this pattern has been recommended.[26]

A number of tribunals will have lay members, as well as a chairman who is usually legally qualified. The Council of Tribunals can make recommendations to the appropriate minister as to membership of tribunals.[27]

---

[21] s.5.

[22] Wraith and Hutchesson, *Administrative Tribunals* (1973), Chap. 3.

[23] Important examples are the industrial tribunals, and the field of National Insurance.

[24] Wraith and Hutchesson, pp. 90-92.

[25] Annual Report 1982-83, para. 2.15.

[26] Sir Harry Woolf, *Protection of the Public – A New Challenge* (1990), p. 72.

[27] Tribunals and Inquiries Act 1992, s.5.

What type of people serve in such positions?[28] Research which has been completed tends to confirm what one might well have expected. The average age is relatively high, a reflection of the fact that it is often only such people who can afford the time to undertake the task. The social background tends to be middle class, with an under-representation of the less privileged or of ethnic groups. How far this actually influences decisions which are reached is difficult to measure. The platitude that we are all affected or "conditioned" by our social background is nonetheless an important one.

The diversity in the type of tribunals is reflected in a variety of staffing arrangements. Some institutions have staff which have no connection with the civil service at all, such as the clerk to local valuation courts. For the most part staff are appointed by, and are connected with, the government department most closely concerned with the subject-matter. Again the precise details of the staffing structure will vary from area to area.[29] One aspect of staffing which has given rise to particular difficulties is in relation to the position of the clerk at a hearing. Sometimes the clerk will retire with the tribunal as an adviser, but even when this does not occur questions have been raised as to the influence that can be exercised by the clerk over the tribunal. The whole question of staffing of the tribunal system is a difficult one. Thus many tribunals must accept the staff nominated by a department, and the staff themselves may feel in an ambivalent position having been "loaned" to the tribunal. Such arrangements can undermine the independence of tribunals.[30]

The suggestion that clerks should be appointed by the Lord Chancellor's Department rather than by the subject-matter department was rejected by the Franks Committee. While recognising the advantages of independence that this would entail it was felt to be impossible because there would be no real career structure that could be held out to such officers.[31] Whether this is indeed a convincing rationale now is debatable. Wraith and Hutchesson have argued that the expansion in the number of tribunals, combined with the changing nature of the Lord Chancellor's Department, has altered the position, and advocate the creation of a separate tribunal service,[32] a view worthy of further consideration.

(2) TRIBUNAL ORGANISATION: SOCIAL SECURITY

The structure and organisation of any tribunal system will be tailored to the needs of that particular area. It is, however, helpful to focus upon one such area in order to understand in more concrete terms how tribunals are organised. Social welfare can be taken by way of example.

The earlier discussion has described the genesis and evolution of the administrative system for distributing social welfare benefits. That system drew a sharp distinction between claims for contributory benefits under national insurance, and non-contributory benefits which were means tested.

---

[28] e.g. Adler and Bradley, *Justice, Discretion and Poverty* (1975), Chaps. 7-11.
[29] Wraith and Hutchesson, *Administrative Tribunals*, pp. 120-122.
[30] *Ibid.* p. 127.
[31] Cmnd. 218 (1957), paras. 59-61.
[32] *Administrative Tribunals*, pp. 127-128 and Chap. 13.

The former generated a right to the substantive benefit, whereas the latter did not.

The system is now governed by the Social Security Administration Act 1992. Claims for most types of social security benefit, including unemployment benefit, income support and pensions, are initially decided by adjudication officers, who are full-time civil servants working in local offices of the Social Security Benefits Agency, the largest of the Next Steps agencies. A Chief Adjudication Officer can give advice and guidance to individual officers.[33] An appeal lies from the adjudication officer to a social security appeal tribunal. The tribunal will have a lawyer chairman plus two other members drawn from a panel of those who have knowledge of the area. It will sit in the local area. The chairman of the tribunal will be chosen by the President of the Social Security Appeal Tribunals from a panel of lawyers appointed by the Lord Chancellor. There is an appeal on a point of law from the tribunal to the Social Security Commissioners, who are lawyers of 10 years standing. Leave is required for such an appeal, and the case will be heard in London, normally by a single Commissioner. A further appeal is possible on a point of law from the Commissioner to the Court of Appeal. Leave is once again required. A number of the decisions made by the Commissioners will be published, and will be binding upon those lower in the hierarchy.

Other procedures operate in certain instances. Thus, for example, medical questions will be determined by a medical practitioner employed by the Department of Social Security, and there will then be an appeal to a medical appeal tribunal. This will be staffed by a lawyer chairman, plus two independent doctors. There is an appeal, with leave, on a point of law to the Social Security Commissioners. A distinct system also operates in the context of claims to disability benefits. In this type of case the disability appeal tribunal will be staffed by a lawyer chairman, a doctor and a third person who has experience of dealing with the needs of the disabled.

Payments made from the Social Fund which are intended to provide a minimum protection from hardship are dealt with differently again. The initial decision will be made by a social fund officer, subject to review by another such officer and after that by the social fund inspector who will act under the general guidance of the Social Fund Commissioner. There is no appeal to a tribunal in most cases of this type.

The social security appeal tribunals have had a beneficial impact upon the administration of the social welfare system. The fact that adjudication officers have to appear before such tribunals in and of itself has an impact upon the making of the initial decision,[34] and Wikeley and Young have concluded that the appeal tribunals have had a real effect by providing a system of external scrutiny which helps to ensure the objective and impartial resolution of disputes.[35] The absence of any such appeal mechanism in

---

[33] Social Security Administration Act 1992, s.39.
[34] Wikeley and Young, "The Administration of Benefits in Britain: Adjudication Officers and the Influence of Social Security Appeal Tribunals" [1992] P.L. 238, 260-261.
[35] Ibid. pp. 260-262; Baldwin, Wikeley and Young, Judging Social Security: The Adjudication of Claims for Benefit in Britain (1992); Sainsbury, "Administrative Justice: Discretion and Procedure in Social Security Decision-making", The Uses of Discretion (Hawkins ed., 1992), Chap. 9.

the context of many decisions made under the Social Fund is to be regretted.[36]

(3) PROCEDURE: BEFORE, DURING AND AFTER THE HEARING

The recommendation of the Franks Committee had been that the Council on Tribunals should itself draft procedural rules. This was not implemented in the ensuing legislation which requires only that the Council be consulted.[37] Pursuant to this function the Council has considered a large variety of such rules. In fulfilling this role the Council has to balance two different sets of considerations, that between formality and informality, and that between uniformity and the need to design procedures to cope with the special problems attendant upon a particular tribunal. Uniformity here does not imply the idea that all tribunals could or should have the same procedural rules; rather that where the same point is being expressed in two different contexts it should be drafted in the same way, and that thought should be given as to whether it would not be desirable for each tribunal's rules to possess a similar ordering of materials, covering topics such as the right to apply, pleadings, notice of the hearing and so on. Indeed the breakdown contained in the Franks Report itself between procedure before, at and after the tribunal hearing, with suitable subdivisions, could be taken as a starting point. What is apparent is that simple, clear and uncomplicated procedural rules are vital if a citizen is not to be discouraged from utilising the tribunal system. Numerous examples of this proposition can be provided, in relation to aspects of procedure which operate before, during and after the hearing.

The most obvious procedural norm which applies *before the hearing* is that an individual must know of his or her right to apply to a tribunal, particularly where this constitutes the mechanism of appeal from an earlier official's decision. What seems relatively clear is that although the individual is normally informed of this, there is no uniform way in which it occurs; in some areas there is a statutory obligation to inform, in others it may be left to lie with established practice, while in yet other areas the individual is left to discover the appeal rights. The other factor which is crucial in order that tribunals can be truly accessible is that individuals have the means to utilise them. The present policy is that there is no general provision for legal aid to all tribunals, and that assistance by way of representation and financial aid are given "where it is shown to be necessary and resources allow". It seems clear that absence of the financial means to secure assistance does hamper individuals who appear before tribunals, and it is to be hoped that more generous provision may be forthcoming in the future.[38]

The importance of procedural rules can also be demonstrated by examples drawn from the *hearing process* itself. Whether an individual in

---

[36] Sainsbury and Eardley, "Housing Benefit Review Boards: A Case for Slum Clearance?" [1992] P.L. 551.

[37] Tribunals and Inquiries Act 1992, s.8.

[38] A valuable survey of this aspect of tribunals is to be found in, *Administrative Justice, Some Necessary Reforms* (1988), pp. 225-251.

fact has a right to a hearing and what this entails will be decided by a combination of statute and the common law principles of natural justice.[39] Particular aspects of the hearing process are likewise governed by one or both of these elements. The rules of evidence have, for example, been relaxed in their application,[40] and the tribunal is allowed to rely on its own knowledge in addition to the evidence tendered before it.[41] In most instances a party before a tribunal will be allowed to be represented by a lawyer if he or she so chooses, as was recommended by the Franks Report.[42]

A number of procedural principles are of relevance *after the hearing*. One of the most important procedural innovations introduced as a result of the Franks Report was the requirement that a tribunal provide reasons for its decision.[43] No such principle constrains the superior courts, and the obligation which rests on tribunals is itself limited in two important respects: it only applies to those institutions listed in the Act, and is only rendered operative when the individual requests a statement, which request must be tendered on or before the giving or notification of the decision. Once given the reasons are deemed to form part of the record.[44] Exceptions exist to these general provisions. Thus reasons need not be given where a decision is made in connection with a scheme or order of a legislative and not an executive character.[45] A statement of reasons can be withheld on the grounds of national security,[46] or if the request for reasons is from one who is not primarily concerned with the decision where to furnish those reasons would be contrary to the interests of the person who is primarily concerned.[47] The Lord Chancellor also possesses the power to dispense with the need for a tribunal to give reasons where he is of the opinion it would be impracticable or unnecessary for the tribunal to do so.[48] Certain tribunals are also exempted from any duty to give reasons in relation to decisions made in the exercise of their executive functions.[49]

Where the obligation to give reasons does apply the court has made it clear that the reasons must deal with the substantial points which have been raised and must not be too vague.[50] The legal consequence of failure to provide the required reasons is however not entirely clear. Some

---

[39] See below, Chaps. 8-9.
[40] R. v. *Deputy Industrial Injuries Commissioner, ex p. Moore* [1965] 1 Q.B. 456.
[41] R. v. *City of Westminster Assessment Committee, ex p. Grosvenor House (Park Lane) Ltd.* [1941] 1 K.B. 53; *Crofton Investment Trust Ltd.* v. *Greater London Rent Assessment Committee* [1967] 2 Q.B. 955; *Metropolitan Properties Ltd. (F.G.C.)* v. *Lannon* [1969] 1 Q.B. 577.
[42] Cmnd. 218 (1957), para. 87.
[43] Tribunals and Inquiries Act 1992, s.10.
[44] *Ibid.* s.10(6).
[45] *Ibid.* s.10(5)(b).
[46] *Ibid.* s.10(2).
[47] *Ibid.* s.10(3).
[48] *Ibid.* s.10(7).
[49] *Ibid.* s.14.
[50] *Re Poyser and Mills' Arbitration* [1964] 2 Q.B. 467. They can, however, be brief, *Westminster City Council* v. *Great Portland Estates* [1985] A.C. 661.

authorities have held that such a failure itself constitutes an error of law,[51] while others have held that inadequate reasons do not *per se* constitute an error of law, and will lead to invalidity only if they furnish evidence of such an error.[52] Further developments of the common law duty to provide reasons will be discussed below.[53]

(4) PROCEDURE: ADVERSARIAL v. INQUISITORIAL?

We are in this country strongly wedded to the adversary system. It is this ritualistic combat which forms the basis for adjudication in the superior courts, and it is this process of decision-making which is very much the norm for the tribunal system. The Council on Tribunals has generally adopted the same view and has, on occasion, come out against an inquisitorial procedure when this has been brought to its attention.[54] On a more general level the Council has disagreed with the Franks Committee's recommendations that tribunals should have the power to subpoena, feeling that this should continue to be exercised on the responsibility of the parties, not the tribunal.[55] Despite this attitude a number of tribunals do in fact have powers to require that witnesses attend or that documents be produced,[56] while others, particularly those dealing with land and property, have powers of inspection and examination. How often such powers are used is of course a different matter. Should we be setting our face so firmly against any inquisitorial element in a tribunal's procedure? Will it lead to the tribunal being accused of partiality?

The answers to these questions are not easy. Whether in fact the adversary procedure is the best method for eliciting the truth in the normal court system may itself be debatable, but in any event some of the fundamental premises underlying its use in that context may well be absent in certain types of tribunals. One of the implicit premises behind the adversary system is that the two opponents are equal, save for natural inequalities of intellect and experience. Battle is waged and the judge, in the position of umpire, will decide. This premise is not sustainable in the context of certain types of tribunals, such as those concerned with supplementary benefits and immigration. In these areas to imagine that the unrepresented claimant is in a position of parity with the public body is illusory. In addition to this the adversary system tends to see parties in the position of "plaintiff" and "defendant", which may very well be inappropriate in some areas. A second reason for distinction resides in the fact that the role of the decision-maker in the public law field should not

---

[51] *Re Poyser and Mills' Arbitration* [1964] 2 Q.B. 467; *Givaudan v. Minister of Housing and Local Government* [1967] 1 W.L.R. 250.
[52] *Mountview Court Properties Ltd. v. Devlin* (1970) 21 P. & C.R. 689; *Crake v. Supplementary Benefits Commission* [1982] 1 All E.R. .498; Richardson, "The Duty to Give Reasons: Potential and Practice" [1986] P.L. 437, 450-457.
[53] See below, pp. 310-316.
[54] Annual Report 1964, para. 67; Annual Report 1965, para 45.
[55] Annual Report 1960, paras. 76 et seq. The Council did give some reconsideration to the matter; Annual Report 1968, para. 88, Annual Report 1964, para. 28(8).
[56] Ganz, *Administrative Procedures* (1974), pp. 31-32; Wraith and Hutchesson, *Administrative Tribunals* (1973), pp. 146-147.

automatically be presumed to be the same as in the area of private law litigation. The adversary model fits the latter area so well[57] because it accords with a notion of two individuals disputing a piece of property in which the essential interests at stake are private, as reflected in the transfer of Blackacre from A to B. Public law litigation often contradicts the premises behind private law actions. There may be a wider public interest involved, over and beyond that of the particular parties before the tribunal, and whereas much private law litigation[58] is retrospective in the sense of concerning a completed set of past events, public law will often be concerned with the future, with the modification of the public body's conduct, and with a series of events which will continue to have ramifications outside of the present dispute.[59]

Both of the reasons set out in the preceding paragraph would demand of the court a more, to use a neutral word, active role. One would have to take care to ensure that this more active position did not develop into what one writer has termed accusatory inquisition,[60] in which the individual feels under attack from the tribunal itself, and hence comes away with a sense of partiality on the decision-maker's part. Granted that these difficulties exist, there is nonetheless an arrogance in the blanket rejection of anything that really savours of an inquisitorial role for any tribunal. The idea that better justice can never be achieved by a procedure adopted by a large number of civilised jurisdictions smacks of the parochial and insular.

(5) TRIBUNALS, DECISION-MAKING AND THE LIMITS OF INFORMALITY

How do tribunals operate in practice? How far do they depart from the procedure of the ordinary courts in the way in which they reason and use precedent?

Anyone seeking simple answers is advised to stop here; the multitude of differing types of institution which pass under the name tribunal, authority, or commission precludes any such neat response. It is indeed tempting to eschew any general reply to these first two questions, to respond instead by a series of individual examples demonstrating the way in which tribunals work. There is no doubt that detailed studies in the law and practice relating to various tribunals are extremely valuable.[61] Such works should be consulted for more specific information. What follows will perforce be in the form of generalisation, and, as we know, all generalisations are false.

A number of the facets of these first two questions have already been touched upon in the discussion above, including the rules of evidence, representation, and the giving of reasons for a decision. On a more general

---

[57] This does not of course mean that one could not have an inquisitorial system for adjudicating on private law disputes.
[58] cf. McNeil, "Contracts: Adjustment of Long-Term Economic Relations under Classical, Neo-Classical and Relational Contract Law" 72 Nw.U.L. Rev. 854 (1978).
[59] Chayes, "The Role of the Judge in Public Law Litigation" (1976) 89 Harv. L.R. 1281; cf. Fuller, "The Forms and Limits of Adjudication" (1978) 92 Harv. L.R. 353, 382-384.
[60] Ganz, Administrative Procedures, p. 35.
[61] See, e.g. Whitesides and Hawker, Industrial Tribunals (1975); Adler and Bradley, Justice, Discretion and Poverty (1975); Evans, Immigration Law (2nd ed., 1983); Dickens, Jones, Weekes and Hart, Dismissed (1985); Peay, Tribunals on Trial (1989).

level what can be said is that while tribunals may differ from the courts in the way in which they operate, the difference is one of degree rather than kind. Studies have shown[62] that, for example, while not bound by precedent in the same way as the superior courts, tribunals will often follow and build on past decisions. Nor is this necessarily something to be deprecated. Consistency of treatment and rational development of principles are important. That the differences between the courts and tribunals should, in the main, be ones of degree is not surprising; the chief factor limiting any tribunal from straying too far from the judicial fold is the basic model of the adversary system itself. This is of course capable of significant variation. While it is the norm the degree of disparity between the process of the ordinary courts and that of tribunals is necessarily constrained.

From the perspective of the individual before a tribunal or court, the main distinction that he or she is likely to perceive lies in the general atmosphere of the proceedings, rather than any of the more legal differences which permeate the two types of institution. The siting of the hearing, the absence of the accoutrements of judicial office, and the presence of lay members on the adjudicating panel, all tend to produce a less formal, more relaxed atmosphere. This is not meant to imply that appearance before a tribunal cannot be a harrowing experience for those concerned. It may well be so. The type of tribunal in question and the nature of the claimant will both be relevant factors. Nonetheless the more informal and relaxed atmosphere of a tribunal in comparison with most courts holds true if viewed as a generalisation as opposed to an inevitable truth.

This picture of tribunal informality should not, however, be taken too far. There are very real limits to informality as the valuable work of Genn has shown.[63] She identifies four factors which serve to constrain the degree of informality of the proceedings. First, the complexity of the subject-matter which many tribunals have to deal with militates against an approach which is too informal. The fact that the sums at stake are small does not render the case simple. Many issues which arise in, for example, social welfare cases are in fact very complex because of the statutory material and secondary legislation. Secondly, the fact that the procedure itself is informal may lead the claimant to believe that the substantive outcome itself is to be decided on a similarly informal basis, whereas in reality this is not the case since the statute will prescribe a set of criteria which must be satisfied if the claimant is to succeed. Thirdly, unrepresented applicants are often at a disadvantage in tribunal proceedings, notwithstanding the efforts of the tribunal itself to put the person at their ease. The disadvantage is often a consequence of the applicant believing that the whole matter could be dealt with by a quiet chat, tailoring any solution to the applicant's own personal circumstance, and not realising the constraints which the legislation place upon the tribunal's discretion. Finally, the tribunal itself may be less able to assist an unrepresented claimant than has been commonly thought in the past. The standard picture is of a tribunal

---

[62] Wraith and Hutchesson, *Administrative Tribunals* (1973), Chap. 10; Farmer, *Tribunals and Government* (1974), Chap. 7.
[63] "Tribunals and Informal Justice" (1993) M.L.R. 393.

composed of those with expertise in the area who are capable of aiding the individual, particularly if he or she is unrepresented. Such assistance may be less forthcoming, in part because of constraints of time, in part because the tribunal may not know what types of question would best help the applicant, and in part because the more adversarial are the proceedings the more reluctant are tribunal members to get involved on one side of the case.

(6) SUPERVISION: THE COUNCIL ON TRIBUNALS

The establishment of an institution to keep under permanent review the organisation and structure of the tribunal system developed out of evidence tendered to the Franks Committee by academics.[64] As seen, the Franks Committee agreed that such an institution should be established and in fact proposed the setting up of two councils, one for England and Wales, the other for Scotland.[65] Their functions reflected the views of those who had tendered evidence: they were to be concerned with the procedure, consti- tution, and organisation of tribunals, they should be consulted prior to the creation of any new tribunal, and should have responsibility for the appointment of lay members. What emerged in the subsequent legislation was rather different. In terms of organisation there was to be only one council, albeit with provision for a Scottish Committee, and appointment of lay members was to remain with departments. Most important of all, the role of the Council in the procedural area was reduced. Whereas it had been envisaged by the Franks Committee that the Council would actually formulate such rules, what emerged was a role in which it was to be consulted, but would not itself do the drafting. The Council was thus an advisory as opposed to executive body, although its advisory role did encompass the job of keeping under review the general constitution and working of the tribunals brought within the legislation.

How effective has the Council been? In terms of proposed procedural rules on which the Council has a right to be consulted, there is evidence that it has been able to make some real contribution towards simplification and clarity. The Council will work in collaboration with the department concerned and it would be wrong to picture this as a constant combat between the two. Collaboration does indeed appear to be the norm with open disagreement the exception. The real problem with respect to procedural rules appears to lie in the limitations placed upon the Council by the very legislative structure. As the Council itself has said,[66] the main problem is not that of serious disagreement with the department but of devising departmental machinery to produce better, simpler and clearer rules. Had the original proposal (to give the Council itself responsibility for formulating rules) been carried through this problem might well have been eased. The Council on Tribunals has now produced a valuable set of model procedural rules for tribunals.[67] The Council accepts that the compilation is not a code which can immediately be adopted without alteration by

---

[64] Professors W. A. Robson and H. W. R. Wade.
[65] Cmnd. 218 (1957), paras. 131-134.
[66] Annual Report 1964, para. 34.
[67] *Model Rules of Procedure for Tribunals*, Cm. 1434 (1991).

differing tribunals. It views the code rather as a store which will facilitate the compilation and revision of procedural rules by particular tribunals, and hopes that it will lead to some greater measure of uniformity than existed hitherto.[68]

Success in other fields has been more limited. The government is under no statutory obligation to consult the Council about proposed legislation creating or affecting tribunals,[69] and there is no guarantee that any consultation will take place in good time, before the legislative measure is too far advanced for the Council to have any real impact. Although there is a voluntary Code for Consultation[70] between the Council and the government, which is intended to ensure that the Council is consulted while proposals are in the formative stage, these arrangements do not in fact work well. The Council is often not consulted adequately or at all. Nor has the Council always been happy with the reaction to its suggestions. The standard ministerial reaction is to say that action was taken after consulting the Council, while omitting to mention that the Council disagreed with the department's suggestions. Dissatisfaction has been voiced by those who have worked on the Council such as Wade, who has noted the relatively weak position of the Council as compared to the Parliamentary Commissioner for Administration, and he has argued that its membership and resources do not equip it adequately to perform its tasks.[71] Similar sentiments have been expressed by Foulkes.[72] Moreover the government has not been supportive of the Council's suggestions that its powers should be extended to cover the whole area of administrative adjudication.[73]

A strong argument can be made that the Council's responsibilities should be increased. The powers given to the Council made some sense 30 years ago, although it is arguable that they were too limited even at that time. The changing pattern of administrative machinery has, however, increased the need for a body with more extensive responsibilities, both in terms of the authorities which it can consider, and in terms of the type of investigations which it can conduct. To extend the ambit of the Council's power to the whole area of administrative adjudication would be beneficial.[74] This should embrace regulatory agencies, as well as more traditional court-substitute tribunals. The former would benefit from such general oversight, and any attempt to establish separate overseeing bodies for such agencies and for tribunals would run into intractable definitional problems. Other

---

[68] Neville Brown, "Tribunal Adjudication in Britain: Model Rules of Procedure" (1993) Special Number E.R.P.L. 287.
[69] As opposed to the promulgation of procedural rules in relation to which there is such a duty.
[70] Annual Report 1986-87, Appendix C.
[71] *Administrative Law* (6th ed.,1988), pp. 919-920.
[72] *Administrative Law* (7th ed., 1990), pp. 164-168.
[73] *The Functions of the Council on Tribunals: Special Report by the Council*, Cmnd. 7805 (1980).
[74] cf. the recommendations in *Administrative Justice, Some Necessary Reforms* (1988), Chap. 4, where an Administrative Review Commission is proposed which would exist in addition to the Council on Tribunals. It would however seem preferable to have one such oversight agency, rather than a system of divided authority.

legal systems possess institutions which undertake this more extensive type of oversight,[75] and such a development would be beneficial in this country.[76]

(7) APPEALS

Under the Tribunal and Inquiries Act 1992, section 11, a right of appeal is granted to a party who is "dissatisfied in point of law" with the decision reached by certain tribunals specified in that section. The aggrieved individual may, according to rules of court, appeal to the High Court or require the tribunal to state a case for the opinion of the High Court. The Act provides that rules of court can be made which then empower the High Court to give any decision which could have been given by the tribunal, to remit the case to be reheard by the tribunal against the background of the court's opinion, and to give directions to the tribunal.[77] In addition to these rights of appeal granted to the individual, the tribunal itself is empowered to state a case to the High Court on any question of law which arises in the course of its proceedings.[78] The crucial issue is therefore, what is the meaning of question of law?

Generations of scholars and judges alike have spent much time in analytically dissecting statutory formulae, precedents, and delegated legislation, assigning various parts thereof into one category or another. There is no doubt that a certain amount can be achieved by this analytical approach. Distinctions can be made between primary facts, what people saw, heard, did, etc., and the application of some statutory term to these facts, which is a question of law. Numerous cases avowedly support this division.[79] This dichotomy immediately produces a fundamental difficulty. Is the meaning of any statutory term a question of law? Once the primary facts are established does the construction of any of the words in the statute become one which is susceptible to appeal? Not necessarily. Denning L.J., as he then was, drew a distinction between the case where the inferences from the primary facts could be declared by a layman, albeit one instructed on the relevant legal principles; the conclusion reached would be one of fact. Where, however, to reach a correct conclusion from the primary facts required a thoroughgoing legal knowledge, then that conclusion would be one of law.[80]

---

[75] e.g. Australia: Administrative Review Council established by the Administrative Appeals Tribunal Act 1975, s.48; USA: Administrative Conference of the United States, Administrative Conference Act 1964, s.51.

[76] Sir Harry Woolf, "Judicial Review: A Possible Programme for Reform" [1992] P.L. 221, 235-236.

[77] Tribunals and Inquiries Act 1992, s.11(4).

[78] Ibid. s.11(3).

[79] Farmer v. Cotton's Trustees [1915] A.C. 922, 932; British Launderers' Research Association v. Hendon Rating Authority [1949] 1 K.B. 462, 471; Woodhouse v. Peter Brotherhood Ltd. [1972] 2 Q.B. 520, 536; R. v. Barnet L.B.C., ex p. Nilish Shah [1983] 2 W.L.R. 16, 24; A.C.T. Construction Ltd. v. Customs and Excise Commissioners [1981] 1 W.L.R. 49.

[80] British Launderers' Research Association v. Hendon Rating Authority [1949] 1 K.B. 462, 471-472.

What is apparent is that in reality the division between law and fact will, in this as in other areas, be affected by an important factor which is not susceptible to such an analytical or linguistic approach: the desire of the court to intervene or not. The very difficulty of analytically separating law from fact, or vice versa, will allow the courts to apply the label which best fits their aim of intervention or not, as the case may be. This functional or pragmatic approach is the key to an understanding of a number of the cases within this area.

Judgments on the law/fact distinction for the purpose of appeal present the reader with another less well perceived difficulty. Two questions can arise which are not always properly distinguished. The first is whether the error alleged involves any question of law at all. Presuming an affirmative answer to this first question, the second is by what standard will the courts determine whether there has been an erroneous construction of this legal term? Will they simply substitute their view as to what the meaning ought to be or will they apply some less rigorous standard, which demands only that the construction was reasonable and based on some evidence?[81]

One of the leading and most oft-cited decisions on the meaning of law for the purposes of an appeal is *Edwards* v. *Bairstow*[82] and the judgment of Lord Radcliffe therein. Bairstow alleged that the General Commissioners for income tax had made an error of law in finding that a transaction to which he was a party was not "an adventure in the nature of trade" for tax purposes. His Lordship's opinion is more easily followed if broken down into stages.

Lord Radcliffe begins by stating unequivocally that the disputed phrase involves a question of law, the meaning of which had to be interpreted by the courts. But the law did not give a precise meaning to that phrase. Quite the contrary, it was clearly susceptible to a range of meanings.[83]

> "...the field so marked out is a wide one and there are many combinations of circumstances in which it could not be said to be wrong to arrive at a conclusion one way or the other. If the facts of any particular case are fairly capable of being so described, it seems to me that it necessarily follows that the determination of the Commissioners...to the effect that trade does or does not exist is not 'erroneous in point of law'."

Thus far Lord Radcliffe demonstrates clearly the distinction highlighted above. The meaning of trade is a legal question, but there may be no error of law given the standard applied by the above quotation. The role of the court was, in his Lordship's own terms, to lay down the limits within which it would be permissible to say that a trade existed within the meaning of the legislation.

What follows is somewhat more difficult, for Lord Radcliffe immediately labels cases in which the facts warrant a determination either way as questions of degree, and therefore as questions of fact. This appears to be a

---

[81] *Global Plant Ltd.* v. *Secretary of State for Social Services* [1972] 1 Q.B. 139.
[82] [1956] A.C. 14, 33-36.
[83] *Ibid.* p. 33.

reflection, or more accurately a corollary, of the view that there had been no error of law given the standard applied in the above quotation. It is, with respect, a confusing tag to apply. A legal issue does not cease to be such either because it is open to a range of possible meanings or, *a fortiori*, because there was no error. The reason for denying an appeal where these conditions are met is simply to say that there is a point of law, but that there has been no error in construction, and therefore the appeal fails.

Lord Radcliffe's judgment does, however, continue to reflect his view that the test to be applied does not necessarily entail substitution of judgment. The court would, said his Lordship, intervene if there was anything *ex facie* which was bad law and which affected the determination. There would also be an error of law if, in the absence of any misconception appearing *ex facie*, the facts found were such that no person acting judicially and properly instructed to the relevant law could have reached the determination under appeal. Such a case should best be described as one in which the true and only conclusion contradicted the determination actually made.[84] The decision arrived at by the Commissioners was overturned for this very reason. A number of other cases have followed this approach.[85]

In other decisions courts have adopted an approach closer to substitution of judgment. *Woodhouse* v. *Peter Brotherhood Ltd*[86] provides an example. The case involved calculation of continuity of employment for the purposes of redundancy payments, which in itself entailed questions as to the transfer of business assets. It was argued that the meaning of the latter term was one of fact and degree. Lord Denning M.R. disagreed.[87] The primary facts were not in dispute; the question was one as to the correct meaning of a statutory term. This was a question of law. But what was the test to determine whether there had been an error of law? Lord Denning M.R. cited the *Edwards* case, and Lord Radcliffe's formulation that if a tribunal reached a conclusion which could not reasonably be drawn then it would be wrong in law, but paraphrased this to mean something rather different: if the tribunal drew the wrong conclusion from the primary facts it would be wrong in law. The gentle sleight of linguistic formulation transforms the test to be applied.[88]

These examples demonstrate the pragmatic approach in operation. In operation moreover at both of the levels discussed above: as to whether the appeal raises a question of law at all, and as to the standard to be applied in determining whether there has been an error. The influences guiding the judicial choice with respect to both topics are not difficult to discern. Where

---

[84] *Ibid.* p. 36.
[85] e.g. *Marriott* v. *Oxford and District Co-operative Society Ltd. (No. 2)* [1969] 1 W.L.R. 254; *Global Plant Ltd.* v. *Secretary of State for Social Services* [1972] 1 Q.B. 139, 154-156; *Central Electricity Generating Board* v. *Clwyd County Council* [1976] 1 W.L.R. 151, 158, 160; *O'Kelly* v. *Trusthouse Forte plc* [1984] Q.B. 90.
[86] [1972] 2 Q.B. 520.
[87] *Ibid.* pp. 536-537.
[88] *Instrumatic Ltd.* v. *Supabrase Ltd.* [1969] 1 W.L.R. 519; *British Railways Board* v. *Customs and Excise Commissioners* [1977] 1 W.L.R. 588; *Farmer* [1915] A.C. 922; *A.C.T. Construction* [1981] 1 W.L.R. 49.

matters of real technical legality or broad principle[89] are involved the courts will veer towards substitution of judgment. They will be influenced in addition by the comparative qualifications of the courts and the particular decision-maker for resolving the type of question posed, and also by the need to provide a uniform answer in an area where a number of lower courts or tribunals are interpreting the same term differently. By way of contrast there may be a large area in between technical legality and broad principle in which the court is content to allow the decision-maker the degree of latitude provided by Lord Radcliffe's test in the *Edwards*[90] case. There is no reason why we should not continue to utilise both standards. Quite the opposite, the diversity of types of institutions to which a right of appeal on law is given would render any attempt to force them all under one standard rather than another inappropriate.

Section 2. Statutory Inquiries

1. *The Background*

The historical antecedents of the inquiry procedure have already been related.[91] It has, however, been the twentieth century which has witnessed the expansion in the use of inquiries, most particularly in the context of land and housing. A variety of purposes are served by the inquiry procedure, the two most important of which are as a mechanism of appeal and as a means for airing objections. An example of the former is the system of appeal against the refusal of planning permission by a local authority, while objections to the siting of a road or building provide an example of the latter. In addition to these two functions inquiries may also be used as a form of post-mortem to investigate an accident, or a breach of governmental secrecy, or as a method of preliminary investigation into the viability of a proposal.[92]

Why has the inquiry procedure become such a function of everyday life and is there any underlying theme common to the diverse areas in which the procedure is used? At the most general level inquiries are used to collect and collate information, or to serve as a vehicle for the resolution of conflicts. They may of course do both of these things. Insofar as they serve the latter function they are utilised for the most part in circumstances where it is felt desirable that political control be maintained by the ultimate decision vesting in a minister. Decisions concerning the siting of a new town, the approval of a slum clearance order, or the confirmation of a road building scheme, involve considerations of policy which should be decided by those who are politically accountable. It will not be the minister who makes the

---

[89] *e.g. Ransom* v. *Higgs* [1974] 1 W.L.R. 1594, 1610-1611.
[90] [1956] A.C. 14, 36.
[91] See above, pp. 57-58.
[92] Wraith and Lamb, *Public Inquiries as an Instrument of Government* (1971), pp. 14-15, 305-306.

initial decision and very often officials will render decisions in the minister's name. The process of government would grind to a halt were it to be otherwise. The minister will, however, make the final choice in circumstances which are especially contentious or important.

2. *The Franks Committee*

(1) THE RECOMMENDATIONS

Prior to 1957 there was increasing public disquiet not just with tribunals, but also with inquiries. Issues concerning cost and delay were overlaid by a sense of frustration at the secrecy surrounding the whole procedure. The report of the inspector who had held the inquiry would normally not be made public, and there was a feeling that the administration was very much just "going through the motions".

Witnesses who gave evidence before the Committee were divided as to what they perceived the role of inquiries to be. One group saw inquiries as part of the process of administration, as an extension of departmental decision-making in specific areas, which should be relatively free from controls other than those supplied by Parliament. A different view was expressed by those who saw the inquiry as akin to a judicial process in which the inspector who undertook the hearing was in the position of a judge. The corollary of this latter approach was that the procedures by which the inquiry was run should be modelled upon the judicial process, at least to the extent that this entailed the decision being taken directly on the evidence presented at the inquiry.[93] The Franks Committee rejected both positions.[94]

"Our general conclusion is that those procedures cannot be classified as purely administrative or purely judicial. They are not purely administrative because of the provision for a special procedure preliminary to the decision – a feature not to be found in the ordinary course of administration – and because this procedure, as we have shown, involves the testing of an issue, often partly in public. They are not on the other hand purely judicial, because the final decision cannot be reached by the application of rules and must allow the exercise of wide discretion in the balancing of public and private interest. Neither view at its extreme is tenable, nor should either be emphasized at the expense of the other."

Instead of attempting to model the inquiry procedures upon either of these two extremes the Franks Committee drew up a series of recommendations which attempted to balance the conflicting interests. What emerged were proposals concerning the pre-inquiry stage, the procedure at the inquiry, and post-inquiry practice.[95]

---

[93] Cmnd. 218 (1957), paras. 263-264.
[94] *Ibid.* para. 272.
[95] These are summarised at pp. 96-98 of the Franks Committee Report.

As to the practice *before the inquiry*, the Committee recommended that the public authority should be required to make available in good time a written statement giving full particulars of its case. The minister who had the ultimate power of decision should whenever possible provide a statement of the policy relevant to the particular case, but should be free to direct that the statements be wholly or partly excluded from discussion of the inquiry. Where this policy changed after the inquiry the letter which conveyed the ministerial decision should explain the change and its relation to the decision.

As to procedure *at the inquiry* it was recommended that the initiating authority should be required to explain its proposals fully and support them by oral evidence, and that in principle the procedure should be public. A code or codes of procedure should be formulated by the Council on Tribunals which should then be made statutory; rules of evidence should be relaxed; the inspector should have power to subpoena witnesses and should have a wide discretion in controlling the proceedings.

Post-inquiry procedure was mainly concerned with the inspector's report and the consequent ministerial decision. It was proposed that the inspector's report be divided into two parts comprising a summary of the evidence, finding of facts and inferences of fact on the one hand, and reasoning from those facts, including application of policy on the other. The whole report should then accompany the minister's letter of decision, and there should be provision for a person to suggest corrections of fact. When the minister made the final decision he or she should be required to submit to the parties concerned any factual evidence obtained after the inquiry, while the decision itself should set out in full the findings and inferences of fact and the reasons for the decision.

Apart from proposals concerning procedure there was also an important recommendation that the main body of inspectors should be placed under the control of the Lord Chancellor, while being allowed to be kept in contact with policy developments in the departments responsible for inquiries.

(2) IMPLEMENTATION

The Franks Committee Report was warmly received and justly so. A number of its proposals were taken up rapidly by the government and the Tribunal and Inquiries Bill duly appeared before Parliament. What however readily became apparent, at least at the Committee stage, was that the bill actually said very little about inquiries, being mainly concerned with tribunals. As a result of pressure in the House of Lords, the government introduced a new sub-paragraph, which became section 1(1)(c) of the Tribunals and Inquiries Act 1958, which provided that the Council on Tribunal was to consider and report on such matters as may be referred to it, or as the Council itself should determine to be of special importance with respect to administrative procedure involving an inquiry.[96] The Council's powers with respect to inquiries were therefore somewhat different to those concerning tribunals: while it had no power to keep such inquiries under

---

[96] See now Tribunals and Inquiries Act 1992, s.1(1)(c).

review, as it did with tribunals, it did have power to intervene on its own initiative in more specific terms than those used in connection with tribunals.[97] Again however, as with tribunals, the powers of the Council were advisory rather than executive.

Despite the extension of the Council's role in relation to inquiries as a result of the Committee stage of the bill, most of the changes advocated by the Franks Committee were implemented by administrative practice and not by statute. As will be seen, the substance of many of these recommendations has been thus put into effect, but two important proposals were rejected by the government: those relating to placing the inspectorate under the Lord Chancellor, and the requirement that the minister should make available a statement of policy prior to the inquiry. The type of procedure which now applies will be a result of a mixture of law and administrative practice. The precise details will differ in different areas, but the general principles are the same. It is to these that we must now turn.

3. *Inquiries: Practice and Procedure*

(1) PROCEDURE BEFORE THE INQUIRY

A number of statutory instruments have now been enacted, drafted by the Lord Chancellor's office pursuant to the Tribunals and Inquiries Act 1992, section 9. These will normally be drafted in conjunction with the appropriate department.[98] Others have emanated directly from, for example, the Ministry of Housing and Local Government. As stated, the details of these rules will differ but there are a large number of points of general importance which they have in common.

Thus there are provisions concerned with procedure prior to the inquiry covering both the length of notice that must be given of the holding of the inquiry, and also a statement of reasons of the case that has to be met. The precise length of notice varies; in some areas it is 21 days; in others 28 days; and in yet others 42 days. There will in addition be rules requiring, for example, an acquiring authority acting under compulsory purchase legislation to provide facilities for the inspection of relevant documents and plans.

(2) PROCEDURE AT THE INQUIRY

(a) General

The procedure at the inquiry is, as recommended by the Franks Committee, very much left in the hands of the inspector, subject to the rules of natural justice. Legal rules of evidence do not, for example, apply[99] and the inspector is often given power to enforce the attendance of persons and the production of documents. The inspector will also have the power to take

---

[97] A point made by Wraith and Lamb, *Public Inquiries*, p. 222.
[98] See, *e.g.* S.I. 1990 No. 512 dealing with compulsory purchase; S.I. 1988 Nos. 944 and 945 dealing with planning appeals and applications.
[99] *Miller (T.A.) Ltd.* v. *Minister of Housing and Local Government* [1968] 1 W.L.R. 992.

evidence on oath. The breadth of the discretion accorded to the decision-maker can be demonstrated by *Bushell* v. *Secretary of State for the Environment*.[100] A public local inquiry was held to consider objections to a road building scheme. At the time of the inquiry procedural rules concerning highway inquiries had not yet come into force. A key element in the department's case for the new motorways was projected traffic flow, the statistical basis of which was derived from a publication known as the "Red Book". Objectors at the inquiry sought to challenge the accuracy of the Red Book's predictions, but the inspector refused to allow them to cross-examine the department's witnesses as to the reliability of the Red Book. He did, however, allow the objectors to call their own evidence as to the need for motorways. The objectors sought to quash the decision of the minister confirming the scheme. There were two reasons, one being that the denial by the inspector of a right to cross-examine was in breach of natural justice and wrong in law. The House of Lords found for the minister.

The majority decided that in the absence of statutory rules prescribing the conduct of the inquiry the procedure to be followed was a matter for the discretion of the minister and inspector, subject to the general safeguard that the procedure be fair to all concerned, including the general public and supporters of the scheme. In deciding what was a fair procedure the court should not be tied to the ordinary model of civil litigation between private parties. Lord Diplock put this point most strongly.[101]

> "To 'over-judicialise' the inquiry by insisting on observance of the procedures of a court of justice which professional lawyers alone are competent to operate effectively in the interests of their clients would not be fair. It would, in my view, be quite fallacious to suppose that at an inquiry of this kind the only fair way of ascertaining matters of fact and expert opinion is by the oral testimony of witnesses who are subjected to cross-examination on behalf of parties who disagree with what they have said. Such procedure is peculiar to litigation conducted in courts that follow the common law system of procedure; it plays no part in the procedure of courts of justice under legal systems based upon the civil law...So refusal by an inspector to allow a party to cross-examine orally at a local inquiry a person who has made statements of facts or has expressed expert opinions is not unfair *per se*."

If refusal to allow cross-examination was not unfair *per se* how did one determine whether it was unfair? The answer depends upon all the circumstances of the case, including the nature of the topic on which the opinion was expressed, the forensic competence of the proposed cross-examiner, and the inspector's view as to whether the cross-examination would enable him to make a report more useful to the minister than it otherwise would be, and that this justified the extra cost in time thereby expended.

---

[100] [1981] A.C. 75.
[101] *Ibid.* p. 97.

As it transpired the most important of these factors for the majority was the nature of the topic itself. The majority distinguished between general government policy which would clearly not be suitable for discussion at a local inquiry, an example being the desirability of having a nationwide set of motorways, and a matter such as the exact line that a road should follow which would be amenable to local discussion.[102] Midway between these there was a "grey area" in which the suitability of a point for cross-examination could well be debatable. The validity of the Red Book's methodology was treated as akin to a matter of government policy and therefore not suitable for local discussion and cross-examination. It was not that the majority saw these technical matters as of the same order as the decision to have a nationwide set of motorways. Rather that the techniques for determining traffic need involved a wider range of issues than could appropriately be considered at a local inquiry.[103]

(b) Rights to participate

The rules governing procedure in any particular area will also delineate those who have a right to appear. In general such a right is only accorded to those who have some legal interest at stake, while allowing the inspector in his discretion to admit others. This discretion is normally exercised liberally, but such third parties may nevertheless be placed at a disadvantage as compared with those who do have a right to appear. They do not, for example, have a right to see a statement of the authority's case, nor does evidence obtained outside of the inquiry have to be disclosed to them. Whether the restrictions laid down in the rules as to who is entitled to be present would be upheld if challenged is unclear. There are certainly dicta in cases which take a broader view than the entitlement afforded by the regulations.[104] How wide the right to appear at inquiries ought to be will be considered within the more general context of third party rights below.

(3) PROCEDURE AFTER THE INQUIRY

(a) Inspectors' reports

Procedure consequent upon the inquiry itself raises a number of important issues, one of the most controversial of which has been the question of whether the inspector's report ought to be published or not. An inspector will be appointed to conduct a wide range of inquiries. Typically the

---

[102] *Ibid.* pp. 97-98, 108-109, 121-123. See also, R. v. *Secretary of State for Transport, ex p. Gwent County Council* [1987] 2 W.L.R. 961.

[103] *cf.* Lord Edmund-Davies, dissenting pp. 116-117, who felt that the Red Book was not a matter of government policy and should have been amenable to cross-examination.

[104] *Local Government Board* v. *Arlidge* [1915] A.C. 120, 147; *Wednesbury Corporation* v. *Ministry of Housing and Local Government (No. 2)* [1966] 2 Q.B. 275, 302. In the *Bushell* case there are statements that the procedure should be fair to all concerned including the general public, but it would be inappropriate to read this as an endorsement of any such general right to appear.

situation will be one in which a local authority proposes to acquire land, to clear an area of slums. Having passed a resolution to that effect it will have to advertise the matter in the local press, as well as informing those whose property rights are affected that they have an opportunity to object. If such objections are forthcoming then the appropriate minister will be obliged to establish an inquiry presided over by an inspector. It is this report which will then be confirmed or overturned by the minister.

The Franks Committee received much evidence and a diversity of opinion on the question of publication of these reports.[105] The arguments for publication were those primarily of fairness and acceptability. One of the main causes of public dissatisfaction had been a feeling of secrecy shrouding the whole inquiry procedure, a sense which publication of the reports would have done much to dispel. Greater knowledge would bring a greater acceptance, since the public would be more aware of the policies underlying the decisions being made. A number of arguments were put against publication. It was argued that the inspector's report was but one of the considerations which the minister should take into account, and that to publish it alone would be to accord it an unwarranted primacy, creating a misguided impression as to its relative importance. In addition, it was felt both that inspectors would be less frank if their reports were to be published and that there was not in fact a widespread demand to see the reports.

The Franks Committee came down firmly in favour of publication,[106] and this has been the general practice since 1958. In some instances the statutory instruments make provision for this, in others publication is dependent upon departmental practice. None of the fears voiced by those opposed to publication appears to have transpired and public confidence in the inquiry procedure has undoubtedly been augmented by this reform. The Franks Committee had also suggested that the early part of the report, dealing with findings of fact, should be disclosed so that the parties could suggest corrections prior to the decision being made, but this proposal has not been taken up.

(b) Extrinsic evidence

As noted above, one of the arguments used against publication of the inspector's reports was the fact that they were but one of the sources which would be relied on by the minister when reaching a decision. What types of extrinsic evidence the minister does and should be enabled to take into account is a difficult problem, an example of which is provided by the Essex Chalkpit case of 1961. A company had been refused planning permission to dig and work chalk, this decision being upheld by an inspector, on the basis that the proposed development would injuriously affect neighbouring landowners. The company appealed to the minister who consulted the

---

[105] Cmnd. 218 (1957), paras. 327–346. The hearing will normally be in public, Planning Inquiries (Attendance of Public) Act 1982.
[106] *Ibid.* para. 344.

Ministry of Agriculture, experts from which stated that the development of the land could take place without any injurious effect upon the neighbours provided that an appropriate process was used. On receipt of this evidence the minister upheld the appeal even though the objectors to the scheme had had no opportunity for comment on such new evidence. An appeal to the courts having failed,[107] the objectors complained to the Council on Tribunals. The Council criticised the way in which the case had been dealt with and recommended that if a minister differed from an inspector on a finding of fact or because of the receipt of fresh evidence, or because a fresh issue had arisen which was not one of government policy, then the parties should be notified and be allowed to comment thereon. This has become the established practice and is enshrined in some of the statutory instruments governing the procedure at inquiries. Difficulties can however still arise when distinguishing between findings of fact and matters of opinion.[108]

Natural justice will also impose limits upon the receipt of extrinsic evidence. Thus in the *Bushell*[109] case it was accepted that the minister could not, after the close of the inquiry, hear one side rather than the other, or receive evidence from third parties without allowing comments thereon. There is, however, a distinction between evidence from such sources and advice from within the department itself.

In the *Bushell* case a further ground of complaint was that after the close of the inquiry, but before the report was made, the department revised their methods of computing traffic needs, the result being a prediction of slower traffic growth than originally forecast. The objectors asked the minister to reopen the inquiry but he declined, saying that he would look at their representations as part of his continuous consideration of the department's proposals. In his decision the minister stated that despite the change in the criteria for traffic need he still felt that the inspector's recommendation should be upheld. The House of Lords rejected the argument that the minister had acted wrongfully by confirming the inspector's report without allowing the objectors an opportunity to comment on undisclosed information. The minister was, said Lord Diplock,[110] perfectly in order in consulting his own department for advice on whether to confirm the recommendations. He did not have to disclose this advice to objectors, nor to allow them to comment thereon. Viscount Dilhorne and Lord Lane placed the matter rather more generally on the ground that such consultation involved no breach of natural justice in the circumstances of the case.[111]

[107] *Buxton v. Minister of Housing and Local Government* [1961] 1 Q.B. 278.
[108] *Luke (Lord) v. Minister of Housing and Local Government* [1968] 1 Q.B. 172; *Murphy and Sons Ltd. v. Secretary of State for the Environment* [1973] 1 W.L.R. 560; *Darlassis v. Minister of Education* (1954) 52 L.G.R. 304.
[109] [1981] A.C. 75, 102.
[110] *Ibid.* pp. 102-103.
[111] *Ibid.* p. 110 and pp. 123-124. See also, *Steele v. Minister of Housing and Local Government* (1956) 6 P. & C.R. 386, 392.

(c) Reasons

An obligation to provide reasons is imposed by section 10(1)(b) of the Tribunals and Inquiries Act 1992. The section provides for the giving of reasons where the minister notifies any decision taken by him after the holding by him or on his behalf of a statutory inquiry, or taken by him in a case in which a person concerned could (whether by objecting or otherwise) have required the holding of such a statutory inquiry, where an individual requests the reasons for the decision, on or before the giving or notification of the decision.

The provisions of the Act operate in the same way and subject to the same qualifications as in the case of tribunals. A decision will be quashed if the reasons given are obscure, too vague, or confused.[112]

(d) Costs

In a number of areas ministers have power to award costs to cover expenses incurred in connection with an inquiry. The Council on Tribunals made a special report on the subject in 1964[113] recommending that this power be extended to cover all inquiries and hearings. In addition they proposed that the power be used more liberally, especially when a person had been vexatious or frivolous, that costs should normally be granted to a successful objector, that inspectors should always make recommendations as to costs in their reports, and that a stricter standard of behaviour should be demanded of a public authority than of an ordinary citizen. The proposal with respect to the successful objector was implemented administratively. No legislation has, however, been passed to apply the power to inquiries in general.

(4) INQUIRY RULES OF PROCEDURE: AN EXAMPLE

We have already seen that rules of procedure for tribunals can be enacted by the Lord Chancellor pursuant to section 9 of the Tribunals and Inquiries Act 1992. A number of the more specific aspects of these rules have been touched upon in the previous discussion. It may nonetheless be helpful to consider such rules as they have been made in a specific area. Planning appeals will be taken by way of example.[114]

The Secretary of State can cause a *pre-inquiry* meeting to be held in order to facilitate the efficient and expeditious resolution of the problem. The local planning authority and the appellant must provide an outline statement of the principal submissions which they intend to advance. The

---

[112] *Iveagh (Earl)* v. *Minister of Housing and Local Government* [1964] 1 Q.B. 395; *Givaudan & Co. Ltd.* v. *Minister of Housing and Local Government* [1967] 1 W.L.R 250; *French Kier Developments Ltd.* v. *Secretary of State for the Environment* [1977] 1 All E.R. 296; *Barnham* v. *Secretary of State for the Environment* (1985) 52 P. & C.R. 10; *Reading Borough Council* v. *Secretary of State for the Environment* (1985) 52 P. & C.R. 385.
[113] Cmnd. 2471 (1964).
[114] S.I. 1988 Nos. 944 and 945.

meeting will be presided over by an inspector. The parties must furnish a *statement of their case* to the other parties involved in the inquiry.

Those who are *entitled to appear* at the inquiry itself are: the appellant, the local planning authority, any other local authority in whose area the land is situated and any person who, in effect, claims proprietary rights over the land in question. Other parties are allowed to appear at the discretion of the inspector. Those who are entitled or permitted to appear can be represented by a lawyer.

The *procedure at the inquiry* is determined by the inspector. Those who are entitled to appear also have the right to call evidence and cross-examine those giving evidence. For other parties the calling of evidence is at the inspector's discretion. Written representations may be received by the inspector from any person before the inquiry, provided that disclosure is made at the inquiry itself.

The *procedure after the inquiry* is that the inspector will report to the Secretary of State. The minister may disagree with the inspector's report either because he takes a different view on a matter of fact, or because of fresh evidence which is not a matter of government policy. If the former occurs then those taking part in the inquiry are to be afforded an opportunity of making written representations within 21 days. If the latter takes place then those who participated in the inquiry can either make written representations or request that the inquiry should be re-opened within the 21 day period.

(5) LIMITATIONS: DISCRETIONARY INQUIRIES

One of the most important limitations upon the scope of the legislation on tribunals and inquiries is that the term statutory inquiry was originally defined to include only those inquiries held in pursuance of a statutory duty. This excluded the important class of inquiries the holding of which was at the discretion of the minister, such as inquiries held under the general powers of the Education Act 1944[115] and the Highways Act 1980.[116] The Tribunals and Inquiries Act 1966 dealt with this unsatisfactory situation by empowering the Lord Chancellor to make orders designating certain groups of inquiries as subject to the Tribunals and Inquiries Act 1958.[117] Designating orders have been made pursuant to this power.[118]

4. *Related Types of Decision-Making*

An inquiry conducted by an inspector who then sends proposals to the minister may well be the "standard" or "normal" method of proceeding.

---

[115] s.93.
[116] s.302
[117] Tribunals and Inquiries Act 1992, ss.16(1)(b), 16(2) makes the designated inquiries subject to the Act. The provisions concerning the giving of reasons do not, however, apply unless the designating order specifically so directs, s.10(4).
[118] *e.g.* S.I. 1967 No. 451; S.I. 1975 No. 1379; S.I. 1983 No. 1287.

There are, however, a number of related procedures all of which have in common the central theme of preserving decision-making in the hands of those who are politically accountable while allowing some degree of public participation.

(1) DECISIONS BY APPOINTED PERSONS AND WRITTEN REPRESENTATIONS

Both of these techniques are designed to expedite the process of reaching a decision as compared with the full panoply of an inquiry. Serious delays over planning appeals led to legislation empowering the Secretary of State to designate certain classes of appeal which could be decided by a person whom he had appointed. Flexibility in procedure was increased by making statutory provision for such appeals to be decided on written representations if both parties agreed.[119] Even within areas in which the final decision resides with the Secretary of State the parties may agree to have their case settled on the basis of purely written representations.[120] Pressures of time have rendered the written representation procedure an attractive one for the parties, and over half of all planning appeals are decided in this way. The main disadvantages of this procedure are that third parties have no opportunity to participate or air their views,[121] and that, while each side is enabled to see the submissions of the other, the report of the person who carries out the inspection is not shown to them.

(2) PLANNING INQUIRY COMMISSIONS

If the increase in the number of decisions reached by written representation reflects one development in the planning sphere, the planning inquiry commission reflects another. While the former is a response to the demand for quicker, and cheaper decisions, the latter demonstrates the need for planning machinery to consider problems on a level which the previous institutions did not allow.

Under the Town and Country Planning Act 1990, section 101, a planning inquiry commission can be established. It will be used in circumstances where there are considerations of regional or national importance demanding a special inquiry, or where novel technical or scientific questions are involved which cannot adequately be resolved without some such mechanism. The Commission will proceed in two stages, the first being a general investigation, the second a local inquiry conducted by one of the members of the Commission. The former will be in the nature of a roving, unrestricted investigation, comparable to a Royal Commission, to be used in circumstances such as the development of a new airport.[122]

---

[119] Town and Country Planning Act 1971, Sched. 9, para. 2(2); S.I. 1981 No. 804; Town and Country Planning Act 1990, Sched.6. The Tribunals and Inquiries Act 1992 still applies.
[120] Purdue, *Cases and Materials on Planning Law* (1973), pp. 218–221; Wraith and Lamb, *Public Inquiries*, pp. 198–200.
[121] Council on Tribunals, Annual Report 1966, paras. 89–91.
[122] Town and Country Planning Act 1990, Sched.8.

(3) NON-STATUTORY INQUIRIES

The use of procedures somewhat different from that of the ordinary inquiry is not confined to the field of planning. Inquiries which do not have a statutory base may be used for a variety of purposes,[123] such as the first inquiry into the expansion of Stansted airport.

One of the best known of such inquiries was that which investigated the Crichel Down affair. Crichel Down was a piece of land in Dorset which had been compulsorily acquired by the Air Ministry in 1937, later being transferred to the Ministry of Agriculture in 1944. The latter decided to sell the land as a single unit farm. Lieutenant-Commander Marten wished to acquire part of the land which had, prior to the compulsory acquisition, been in his wife's family. He felt that his offer to purchase was being neglected and with the help of his Member of Parliament applied pressure for a government inquiry. Although the inquiry[124] dispelled any notions of dishonesty, and although the decision to sell the farm as a single unit was reasonable, there emerged a feeling that certain civil servants had behaved somewhat high-handedly. This feeling of unease was one of the main catalysts behind the establishment of the Franks Committee, though paradoxically the type of behaviour evidenced by the Crichel Down affair was not within its terms of reference.

(4) TRIBUNALS OF INQUIRY

The Tribunals of Inquiry (Evidence) Act 1921 was passed to provide a procedure for investigating allegations of improper behaviour by certain officials in connection with armaments contracts.[125] It has since been used mainly to investigate similar allegations of misconduct by ministers, civil servants or other organs of government. Thus the leaking of budget secrets[126] and the bribing of a junior minister were both the subject of such an inquiry,[127] as were the circumstances surrounding the spying activities of Vassall.[128]

The powers possessed by such tribunals of inquiry came to the forefront of the public eye during the Vassall inquiry, the catalyst being the imprisoning of three journalists for contempt of court[129] after failing to disclose the sources of stories which they had written about the Vassall affair. In 1965 a Royal Commission was established to review the operation of such inquiries.[130] The Commission was in favour of the preservation of tribunals of inquiry, but made 50 recommendations designed to safeguard their operation. The absence of procedural checks was central to the Commission's Report, as is evident from the cardinal principles which they

---

[123] Wraith and Lamb, *Public Inquiries*, pp. 202-212.
[124] Report of the Inquiry by Sir Andrew Clarke Q.C., Cmd. 9176 (1954).
[125] Wraith and Lamb, *Public Inquiries*, pp. 212-217.
[126] Cmd. 5184 (1936).
[127] Cmd. 7616 (1948).
[128] Cmnd. 2009 (1962).
[129] The Tribunal of Inquiry could not itself punish for contempt, but it did certify the journalists before the High Court.
[130] *Report of the Royal Commission on Tribunals of Inquiry*, Cmnd. 3121 (1966).

said should be observed. These included the tribunal being satisfied that there were circumstances affecting a particular person which the tribunal proposes to investigate before that person becomes involved in an inquiry; adequate notice of the allegation to be made against the person; sufficient opportunity for the individual to prepare for the case with legal advice; and the opportunity for the individual's solicitor or counsel to cross-examine.[131] A later report dealt with the question of contempt of the tribunal resulting from prejudicial comment in the press.[132]

The government has expressed its agreement with many of these proposals,[133] other than those concerned with contempt, but the legislation necessary to put these changes into effect has not yet been implemented.

It should be noted that the government may well choose to establish an inquiry which is not within the ambit of the 1921 Act. The investigation into the collapse of BCCI, and that into the Matrix Churchill affair have both been presided over by judges, but are not tribunals of inquiry as such.

(5) PRIVATE BILLS

Private bills are still on occasion used to achieve ends of a type like those of a public inquiry. Large developments such as the building of a reservoir may be attained by these means.[134] The private bill procedure involves proceedings not very different from those of a public inquiry. It has however declined in importance this century. The government has itself taken over a large number of the functions which used to be fulfilled by statutory undertakers. And the private bill mechanism is a costly alternative to the normal process of public inquiry.

5. Supervision

(1) THE COUNCIL ON TRIBUNALS

The powers of the Council on Tribunals have already been touched upon. Section 1(1)(c) of the Tribunals and Inquiries Act 1992 gives the Council power to consider and report on such matters as may be referred to them, or as the Council may deem to be of special importance. The Council has in addition to be consulted by the Lord Chancellor when the latter is devising procedural rules for inquiries, an obligation which does not attach to procedural rules made by other ministers.

As in the case with tribunals, the Council's powers are therefore advisory and not executive. It has nonetheless been of value in a number of differing areas. In some ways it has been fulfilling an Ombudsman role, receiving

---

[131] The Commission also recommended that a person's legal expenses should normally be borne out of public funds, and that he should, provided it was practicable, be able to call his own witnesses.

[132] Cmnd. 4078 (1969). The main proposals were that while there should be no restriction of comment on the subject-matter of the inquiry at any time, once the tribunal had been established it should be contempt to suppress or pervert the evidence.

[133] Cmnd. 5313 (1973).

[134] Wraith and Lamb, *Public Inquiries*, pp. 217-218.

complaints from individuals concerning specific problems which they have encountered at inquiries. It has published a number of special reports, one of which grew out of the Essex Chalkpit case considered above, another out of the somewhat messy way in which the investigations into Stansted airport were conducted. There have also been reports on problems which are not limited to any single inquiry, such as the short report on third party rights.[135]

The government's rejection of the Franks Committee proposal that procedural rules for inquiries should be formulated by the Council has left it with a purely advisory role. Only the Lord Chancellor has an obligation even to consult. While it appears that consultation does nevertheless take place, this is unsatisfactory as compared to the position of having one body responsible for devising procedural rules. Moreover it can, obviously, only review the rules once it is consulted. It cannot itself insist that rules be devised for any area.

The Council has no statutory right to be consulted on matters pertaining to inquiries which emerge in proposed legislation. However it voiced the view in its Annual Report for 1963[136] that it would be valuable if such consultation on the allocation of decision-making between courts, tribunals and inquiries did take place. This does now occur, and the Council has made valuable suggestions for amendment in draft legislation.[137]

(2) THE PARLIAMENTARY COMMISSIONER FOR ADMINISTRATION

The Parliamentary Commissioner is an ex-officio member of the Council on Tribunals.[138] In his own capacity, when investigating complaints of maladministration, he has had occasion to examine matters arising from public inquiries such as delay and cost. This overlap between the Council and the Commissioner may not be neat, but it is beneficial given the more extensive powers of investigation possessed by the latter.

(3) JUDICIAL REVIEW

Principles of judicial review are applied to inquiries. The application of these principles will be considered below.

6. Planning Inquiries, the Government and the Public

Lawyers tend to have a limited interest in inquiries. They will be concerned to ensure that procedures are fair, but will often baulk at more penetrating questions. To some extent this is a result of the fact that the whole system of inquiries presents the lawyer with issues which are less familiar, as compared with those that arise within the context of tribunals. Our

---

[135] Cmnd. 1787 (1962). See also, *Report on the Award of Costs at Statutory Inquiries*, Cmnd. 2471 (1964).
[136] Para. 12.
[137] Wraith and Lamb, *Public Inquiries*, p. 236.
[138] Parliamentary Commissioner Act 1967, s.1(5).

uncertainties as to the nature of the inquiry procedure are reflected in the way in which we do or do not, as the case may be, consider some of the fundamental questions which arise for debate. What rights should third parties have at inquiries? How much time should be expended on consultation with interested parties? To what extent should we allow discussion of policy at inquiries? How costly are these procedures and what do we mean when we speak of an efficient process of decision-making? The central point to be aware of is one made at the inception of this section: the answers which we provide to these questions will, explicitly or implicitly, be based upon the perceived aim of the law in any particular substantive area. There is nothing surprising about this. Indeed it would be odd if the situation were otherwise. What is less immediately obvious is that, in determining what those purposes are, we may well be confronted by value judgments of a type the implications of which go over and beyond the particular area in question.

That this is so is well brought out by McAuslan's study of planning law.[139] The author identifies three different ideologies which have helped to shape the law in this area. The first sees the aim of the law as to protect private property, which is termed the traditional common law approach to the legal role. The second views the purpose of the law as to advance the public interest, even as against traditional property rights; this is called the orthodox public administration approach to the legal role. The third, that the function of the law is to aid the cause of public participation in decision-making, may be in opposition to both the traditional common law and the public interest approaches. This third ideology is labelled the populist approach.[140] Which of these approaches predominates will profoundly affect the answers to the central questions posed above, as well as influencing the formality and type of procedure which should be adopted.

That this is so can be seen by looking further at McAuslan's study. The essence of the argument he advanced is that the first two approaches towards planning are dominant, albeit in varying degrees, that participation is much genuflected to in theory but pushed very much into third place in practice. The author demonstrates this in a number of areas,[141] two of which may be taken as examples here.

The legislation on planning is now contained in the Town and Country Planning Act 1990 which imposes an obligation on the local planning authority to make a survey of its area, including size, composition and distribution of the population, and the principal physical and economic features of the area.[142] The survey is then forwarded to the Secretary of State together with what is known as a unitary development plan for metropolitan areas and a structure plan for non-metropolitan areas. These plans

---

[139] *The Ideologies of Planning Law* (1980). On planning law in general see Heap, *An Outline of Planning Law* (9th ed., 1987); McAuslan, *Land, Law and Planning* (1975); Purdue, *Cases and Materials on Planning Law* (1977); Grant, *Urban Planning Law* (1983).
[140] *The Ideologies of Planning Law* (1980), p. 2.
[141] *Ibid.* Chaps. 1-2. I am indebted to McAuslan's study for the material which appears in this example. See also, Harlow and Rawlings, *Law and Administration* (1984), Chaps. 14, 15.
[142] s.11 applies to metropolitan areas, s.30 to non-metropolitan areas.

consist of a written statement which formulates the local planning authority's policy and general proposals for development and other use of the land in that area, together with a statement as to how that development relates to development in neighbouring areas.[143] Local plans are designed to fill in the details of the wider ranging policies considered in the structure plan.[144] Public participation takes place both before and after submission of the plans to the Secretary of State.[145]

In 1966 the Skeffington Committee had been established specifically to consider and report on the best method of ensuring publicity for and public participation in the formative stages of drawing up plans for an area. The Committee reported in 1968.[146] It recommended that there should be pauses in the plan-making process to enable the public to comment, and that the local planning authority should arrange meetings for local groups to consider planning issues. Alternative choices should be put forward and community involvement with the project should be encouraged. These recommendations must, however, be seen in the light of the Committee's conclusion that responsibility for the making of the plan lay with the elected representatives and that their role should not be diminished.

It was three years before the government responded to the proposals of the Skeffington Committee. A circular was sent to the local authorities setting out the government's attitude.[147] The general impression that emerges from this document is to leave the discretion with the local authorities as to implementation of the Committee's proposals. Juxtaposed to this general theme are warnings concerning the time and cost that participation could entail, which are particularly evident in the way in which the circular addresses the Skeffington proposals concerning stages of participation. As McAuslan states,[148]

"The overall impression given by the circular is that the Skeffington Committee had been a little over enthusiastic...and that the hard headed realism and discipline of costs and time, very much administrative concerns, were to be determining factors in public participation in plan-making. Only by placing the organisation and implementation of participation firmly under the jurisdiction of local authorities and reminding them of their statutory obligations, as opposed to the Report's recommendations, were these overriding concerns likely to be met."

Consultation prior to the submission of the unitary development or structure plan to the minister is intended to be but part of the participation by the public. It is intended to be complemented by examination of the plan before it is approved by the Secretary of State.[149] The nature and degree of

---

[143] ss.12, 31.
[144] s.36.
[145] ss.13, 20, 33, 35, 39-42.
[146] *People and Planning, Report of the Committee on Public Participation in Planning* (1969).
[147] Department of the Environment, Circular No. 52/72.
[148] *The Ideologies of Planning Law* (1980), p. 23.
[149] *Ibid.* pp. 39-45.

any such participation is, however, firmly placed in the hands of the Secretary of State. The legislation leaves no doubt that the scope of any examination into the structure plan will be decided upon by the Secretary of State. There is no general duty to consult or to consider the views of interested parties.[150] This reflection of the public interest ideology of planning, with that interest being decided upon by the government of the day, is further reinforced by the non-statutory code of practice which has provided guidance as to the nature of the examination. The code makes clear that the conduct of the examination will be kept very firmly in the hands of the Secretary of State, who will choose which matters will be considered at the examination, and who will be entitled to take part in the discussion.

The second example of the conflicting ideologies underlying the planning sphere can be seen in the public local inquiry pursuant to a refusal of planning permission. The very idea of, or necessity for, an inquiry prior to the refusal of planning permission[151] is a natural outgrowth of the common law's protection of private property. If property belongs to you and someone wishes to prevent you using it as you choose an appeal should be provided.[152] Despite this the actual inquiry procedure prior to the Franks Committee reflected the predominance of the public interest perspective: the absence of procedural rules, the secrecy surrounding inspector's reports, and the closed nature of the government policy all contributed towards this. With the reforms of the Franks Committee came a shift in the ideology underlying the inquiry. The pendulum was realigned to take greater account of private property rights through the grant of procedural safeguards prior to, at, and after the inquiry. What is of interest is that, as commentators have observed, provisions originally enacted to protect the interests of property owners have been used by third parties to widen the scope of the inquiry. The "pure milk" of planning doctrine that the inquiry was limited to the appellant, the local authority and the minister has been rendered out of date by administrative practice. The inspector, having general discretion over the procedure at the inquiry, can and normally will admit those without a legal right to attend. Interest groups will use the inquiry to advance arguments over and beyond the facts of the particular case, and once admitted to the inquiry such third parties may for some purposes at least be in as good a position as those with legal rights.[153] Notwithstanding these advances of the public participation ideology, third parties still stand in a somewhat uneven position. They are not entitled to receive a statement of the initiating authority's case, nor are they beneficiaries of the rule concerning disclosure of evidence from sources other than the inquiry itself. Efforts by the Council on Tribunals[154] to increase the right of third parties have not met with success.

---

[150] 1990 Act, ss.20, 35.

[151] McAuslan, *Ideologies*, pp. 45-55; Wraith and Lamb, *Public Inquiries*, pp. 253-264.

[152] Town and Country Planning Act 1990, Pt. III.

[153] See, *e.g. Turner* v. *Secretary of State for the Environment* (1973) 28 P. & C.R. 123.

[154] *Report of the Council on Tribunals on the Position of Third Parties at Planning Appeal Inquiries*, Cmnd. 1787 (1962).

The preceding two examples may be supplemented by a third drawn from recent developments in planning. Two interrelated themes characterise much of this recent change. On the one hand, there has been the fostering of partnership between the public and the private sector in land development. On the other hand, there have been moves to expedite the planning process, to enable such joint schemes to proceed more rapidly.[155] Local authorities have been encouraged by central government to "play the roles of facilitator and underwriter of the profitability of private development proposals".[156] Bargains may be negotiated in secret to facilitate particular developments, with the consequence that "public participation is squeezed out, and policy conflict internalized within the local authority".[157]

What these examples show is that both the type of procedure we adopt at the inquiry, the very type of inquiry itself, and the substantive rights accorded to participants will depend directly on what the prevailing ideology in that particular area is. Questions as to third party rights, or the inquisitorial as opposed to adversarial method of investigation, cannot be resolved without implicitly if not explicitly adopting one of these perspectives.

Thus the private property approach to planning would tend to favour an adversarial procedure akin in broad nature to the common law model of adjudication with its rules of examination and cross-examination. Substantive rights would be restricted to the property owner being affected, and the issues that could be raised at an inquiry would be confined to the case at hand.

The public interest approach to planning would gravitate towards a less formal, more inquisitorial style of procedure. It sees the government of the day as the embodiment and guardian of the public interest which should be relatively free to pursue the procedures of its choosing, subject to certain elementary concepts of fairness. This view finds expression in the House of Lords decision in the *Bushell* case,[158] and especially in the judgment of Lord Diplock therein. The substantive rights accorded are limited, as the example of the structure plan shows. Policy is retained firmly in the hands of the government of the day, and the public interest as thereby defined takes prominence over private property and the view of those participating in the decision-making.

The public participation ideology of planning would bring in its wake more diverse types of institutional mechanism. An inquiry procedure would itself be modified to enable a wider variety of views to be taken into account at the formative stages of, for example, a structure plan or unitary development plan. Consultation would be a continuing process and would take place after the plan has been submitted to the Secretary of State. As

---

[155] *e.g.* enterprise zones, Local Government, Planning and Land Act 1980, s.179, and Town and Country Planning Act 1990, ss.88-90; simplified planning zones, Town and Country Planning Act 1990, ss.82-87.

[156] Loughlin, *Local Government in the Modern State* (1986), p. 157.

[157] Grant and Healey, "The Rise and Fall of Planning", *Half a Century of Municipal Decline 1935-1985* (Loughlin, Gelfand, Young eds., 1985), p. 185.

[158] [1981] A.C. 75, 92-104.

seen both pre- and post-submission consultation does indeed take place, but the reins are kept firmly in hand by the local and central government. A real commitment to the public participation ideology would entail an increase in the rights of the participator and a corresponding diminution in the control and discretion of the government. In some areas the procedure would cease to be either inquisitorial or adversarial, but be more in the nature of consultation and discussion, with broader community involvement.

The portrayal of these three different ideologies, and the implications of each, is of course somewhat stark and absolute. The edges of each become blurred and softer. And a system of planning may well be a balance between them. Yet this is not to deny the formative influence that each can have on the type of procedures adopted and the nature of the rights granted to those entitled to participate. It is not therefore surprising that lawyers find inquiries involving them in territory with which they are less familiar. Answers to apparently more straightforward issues such as those of costs and delay, let alone those of third party rights and the questioning of government policy, cannot however be formulated without addressing our minds to these complex problems.[159]

---

[159] Purdue, Kemp and O'Riordan, "The Government at the Sizewell B Inquiry" [1985] P.L. 475, and "The Layfield Report on the Sizewell B Inquiry" [1987] P.L. 162, for an interesting account of the problems presented by the large public inquiry.

5. INSTITUTIONS III: THE EC

The discussion thus far has focused upon the principal domestic institutions which are of relevance for administrative law. To stop there would, however, be to give a misleading picture, since many important "public" decisions are now made not in Whitehall, but in Brussels.[1] This chapter will therefore examine the European Community and its significance for administrative law. There will be a description of the main Community institutions, which will be followed by a discussion of the legislative process. There will then be an analysis of the main Community legal doctrines which are of relevance. Subsequent chapters of the book will include more detailed discussion of particular points of Community law doctrine and these will be integrated into the analysis of specific topics.

Section 1. The Institutions

There are five principal institutions mentioned in Article 4 of the EC Treaty, as amended by the Treaty on European Union (TEU), which are entrusted with carrying out the tasks of the Community: the European Parliament, the Council, the Commission, the Court of Auditors and the Court of Justice. The TEU is better known as the Maastricht Treaty and was signed on February 7, 1992. The difficulties of ratifying this latest modification of the original EC Treaty are well known, but ratification has now occurred. The structure and powers of the Council, the Commission, the European Parliament, the European Council and the European Court of Justice (ECJ) will be described here.

1. *The Council*

Article 146 of the EC Treaty, as amended by the TEU, states that the Council shall consist of a representative of each Member State at ministerial level who is authorised to commit the government of that state. The members of the Council are, therefore, politicians as opposed to civil servants, but the politician can be a member of a regional government where this is appropriate. It is common for meetings of the Council to be arranged

---

[1] Wyatt and Dashwood's, *European Community Law* (3rd ed., 1993); Weatherill and Beaumont, *EC Law* (1993); Hartley, *The Foundations of European Community Law* (2nd ed., 1988); Craig and de Burca, *Text, Cases and Materials on Community Law* (1995). See now, European Communities (Amendment) Act 1993.

by subject-matter. There can be a General Affairs Council, attended by foreign ministers, which deals with external relations. The Economic and Financial Affairs Council, by way of contrast, is concerned with the implementation of the programme for the completion of the single market.

Article 146 also provides for the Presidency of the Council to be held by each Member State in turn for six months. The position of President of the Council has assumed greater importance in recent years, as different states have "competed" with each other in order to see which country could achieve more within the designated period.

The work of the Council is prepared by the Committee of Permanent Representatives (COREPER), which is, after the TEU amendments, dealt with in Article 151 of the EC Treaty. COREPER is staffed by senior national officials and it operates at two levels. COREPER II consists of permanent representatives who are of ambassadorial rank, and deals with matters such as external relations. COREPER I is composed of deputy permanent representatives and is responsible for more technical issues. COREPER plays an important part in the decision-making within the EC, in part because it sets the agenda for Council meetings. The agenda is divided into Parts A and B: the former includes those items which COREPER has agreed can be adopted by the Council without discussion; the latter will cover topics which do require discussion.

The powers of the Council are described in Article 145, albeit in a rather vague manner. The Council is to: "ensure the co-ordination of the general economic policies of the Member States"; it is to "have power to take decisions"; it can delegate to the Commission powers to implement the rules which the Council has laid down.

2. The Commission

While the Council represents the interests of the Member States, the Commission is independent of any such national concerns. There are 17 Commissioners[2] and under Article 157 of the EC Treaty, as amended by the TEU, they are to be persons whose "independence is beyond doubt", and they "shall neither seek nor take instructions from any government or from any other body." There shall be at least one, and no more than two, Commissioners from each state, and they take decisions by majority vote.[3]

The method of choosing Commissioners has been altered by the TEU, with the consequence that, from 1995, the Parliament has more say in the process than hitherto. Under Article 158 the governments of the Member States, after consulting the European Parliament, nominate the person they intend to be President of the Commission. These governments, together with the nominee for President, then nominate those who are intended to serve as Commissioners. All such nominees are then subject to a vote of approval by the European Parliament, after which they are appointed by

---

[2] This number can be increased by the Council acting unanimously, Article 157(1).
[3] Article 163 EC Treaty, as amended by the TEU.

common accord of the Member State governments. Their term of office is five years, and this term can be renewed.

The permanent officials who work in the Commission, and who form the Brussels bureaucracy, are organised into Directorates General covering the major differing subject-matter areas, and these will normally be headed by a Commissioner. The Commissioners will, in addition, have their own personal staff (or *cabinet*), which consists partly of national and partly of Community officials.

The powers of the Commission are set out in Article 155 of the EC Treaty. In order to ensure the proper functioning of the Community the Commission is to: ensure that the Treaty and attendant measures are applied; formulate recommendations or deliver opinions on matters dealt with in the Treaty if requested to do so, or if the Commission thinks that it is necessary; have its own power of decision and take part in the shaping of measures taken by the Council and by the European Parliament in the manner provided for in the Treaty; exercise the powers conferred on it by the Council.

It is important to realise that the Commission has a whole array of powers, which are judicial, administrative, executive and legislative in nature. The Community institutional structure is not characterised by any rigid doctrine of separation of powers, and the Commission is at the heart of many Community initiatives.

One of the most important aspects of its powers concerns the legislative process itself. The common format in the Treaties is for the Council to act on a proposal from the Commission when making legislation which fills out the Treaty articles themselves. In this sense the Commission has a right of initiative, which places it in the forefront of the development of Community policy.[4]

3. The European Parliament

The European Parliament has been transformed since the inception of the Community. It was originally known as the Assembly, and the change of name was brought about by the Single European Act (SEA), which was signed in 1986, and ratified in 1987. The European Parliament was originally indirectly elected from the parliamentary institutions of the Member States, and direct elections occurred in 1979. The powers of the European Parliament have, moreover, been continually increased in subsequent revisions of the original Treaty, as will be seen below.

There are now 518 Members of the European Parliament (MEPs), and the number of seats varies roughly with the size of the country. MEPs sit in party-political groupings, rather than along national lines. These groupings correspond to those to be found within the states, including

---

[4] The major qualification to this right of initiative is to be found in the provisions dealing with foreign policy and cooperation in the fields of justice and home affairs to be found in the TEU, Titles V and VI.

Conservatives/Christian Democrats, Labour/Socialist and more centrist parties. This form of political organisation undoubtedly enhances the sense that there is a *European* Parliament. However, as the Parliament increases its power there can be expected to be greater pressure from particular national constituencies to represent their interests and these interests will not always be identical across the same political party.

The European Parliament has three different types of power: budgetary, legislative and supervisory.

The European Parliament plays an important role in the budgetary process within the Community, particularly with respect to non-compulsory expenditure. This process is complex and is dealt with in Article 203 of the Treaty.

The legislative powers of the European Parliament have been increased significantly over the last 30 years, and will be considered within the next section.

There are a number of ways in which the European Parliament exercises supervisory control, and these have been increased by amendments introduced by the TEU: it can establish a temporary Committee of Inquiry to consider alleged contraventions or maladministration in the administration of Community law, except where the matter is *sub judice*;[5] Community citizens can petition the Parliament on a matter which affects them directly;[6] and provision is made for an Ombudsman to investigate maladministration.[7]

4. *The European Council*

The European Council consists of the Heads of State or governments of the Member States, together with the President of the Commission. It came into existence in 1974, and regular meetings have been held ever since. Formal recognition was accorded by Article 2 of the SEA, and Article D of the TEU now states that the purpose of the European Council is to provide the necessary impetus for the development of the Union, and the definition of its guidelines.

The European Council emerged to deal with problems or issues which were of such importance that they could only be resolved at the highest governmental level. These might be concerned with intra-Community issues, such as crises over the level of budgetary contributions by the different states; the problems might involve foreign policy, such as the consequences of the collapse of Communism in Eastern Europe; or the European Council might set the timetable for the Community's development, such as the steps towards economic and monetary union. The decisions reached by the European Council will, therefore, be of considerable consequence for the speed and direction of Community change.

---

[5] Article 138c.
[6] Article 138d.
[7] Article 138d.

5. *The European Court of Justice*

The European Court of Justice (ECJ) has, as will be seen below, played a vital role in the development of the Community. There are 13 judges. Under Article 167 of the EC Treaty judges are appointed by common accord of the governments of the Member States for a period of six years which is renewable. One judge is appointed from each state, the 13th post being held by a judge from one of the five larger states in turn. A President of the ECJ will be elected by the judges for a period of three years, and the post is renewable. The ECJ can decide cases either in plenary session where the quorum is seven, or in Chambers of three or five. Article 165 of the EC Treaty, as amended by the TEU, now provides that the ECJ shall sit in plenary session when a Member State or a Community institution that is party to the proceedings so requests. Many other types of case can be heard by a Chamber, including references for preliminary rulings, damages actions and appeals from the Court of First Instance.

There are also six Advocates General, one from each of the four largest states; the fifth and sixth posts rotate among the other eight states.[8] The Advocate General has no real analogy within the common law system. After the parties have submitted their arguments, and before the Court delivers its judgment, the Advocate General will present an impartial Opinion on both fact and law to the Court. It is not formally binding on the Court, but will often be influential. It will normally be longer than the ECJ's own judgment, since the Opinion of the Advocate General will consider the existing precedents more explicitly than will the Court itself.

In addition to the ECJ there is now a Court of First Instance which was established pursuant to the SEA. Its existence is now regulated by Article 168a of the EC Treaty. The new court commenced business in October 1989. It was created both to relieve the ECJ of some of its case load, and also to facilitate detailed factual investigation in cases where this is required. There are certain classes of case which the Court is not competent to hear: actions brought by Member States, or Community institutions, or requests for preliminary rulings. The Court of First Instance has been given jurisdiction in three types of case: those concerned with staff; certain actions against the Commission brought under Articles 33 and 35 of the ECSC Treaty; and actions for annulment or failure to act brought by private persons under Articles 173 and 175 of the EC Treaty relating, for example, to the implementation of the competition rules.

Section 2. The Legislative Process

The legislative process which operates in the Community is complex, with different legislative procedures applicable in different contexts. Detailed

---

[8] Article 166.

examination of these procedures cannot be undertaken here. What follows is an outline of the relevant principles.[9]

1. *Democratic Legitimacy and Political Pragmatism*

Because of the complexity of the legislative procedures it is easy to lose sight of the very reasons for this intricacy. A word on this issue may well serve to render the procedures which will be outlined below more comprehensible.

The European Parliament is the Community institution with the greatest claim to political legitimacy because it is directly elected. The Council's democratic credentials are indirect: the Council representatives are, as we have seen, political appointees, but they are not directly elected at a European level. As for the Commission, it has no democratic legitimacy as such, since it is not elected at all.

The reasons for the complexity of the Community's legislative process have their roots in this simple fact: the body which has the greatest democratic claim to legislative power, the European Parliament, was given the smallest part to play in the legislative process in the original Rome Treaty. All of the subsequent Treaty modifications have been designed to increase the role of the European Parliament, but to do so in a way which is politically acceptable to the other players in the game. The ultimate goal from the European Parliament's perspective would be to have a right of legislative initiative itself, but this has not yet been attained.

Why then has there been opposition to according the European Parliament a greater say in the Community's legislative process? Why has it not been granted its own right of legislative initiative?

The answer to this is complex, but in essence it is because the other institutional players have differing reasons for being unenthusiastic about increasing the European Parliament's power in this way. National Parliaments fear that a fully empowered European Parliament would undermine their own authority, and give greater legitimacy to the Community. The Council is wary of the diminution in its own power if the European Parliament were to possess a right of legislative initiative, as is the Commission. It is doubtful whether the Commission's own independent right of legislative initiative could really survive were the European Parliament to be also granted this right. It would, at the very least, diminish the extent to which the Commission was in control of the development of policy.

The paradox is, of course, that the Community as a whole has to try to bolster its own democratic credentials, the more so as it covers an ever wider range of subject-matter. It is already susceptible to attack on the grounds that important policy matters are being made by a process which is, at best, only imperfectly democratic. It is for this reason, amongst others, that the European Parliament has been given greater powers than hitherto

---

[9] For detailed treatment see, *e.g.*, Wyatt and Dashwood, above n.1, Chap. 3.

in order to try to meet this critique. With these thoughts in mind we can now consider the various legislative procedures which exist.

2. *Five Procedures*

(1) COUNCIL AND COMMISSION ACTING ALONE

There are a number of areas where the Council and the Commission can take action without any intervention by the European Parliament at all. In these areas the Council will act on a proposal from the Commission and take the decision in accord with the voting requirement laid down in the relevant Treaty article.[10]

(2) COUNCIL, COMMISSION AND CONSULTATION WITH PARLIAMENT

The legislative process in the original Treaty concentrated power upon the Commission and the Council: the former would propose a measure, and the latter would vote upon it. The European Parliament might have to be consulted, if required by a specific provision of the Treaty, and failure to wait for its opinion could lead to the measure being annulled.[11] However, a bare requirement to consult with the European Parliament was all that was required, and the real legislative process was dominated by the Council and the Commission.

(3) COUNCIL, COMMISSION AND THE CO-OPERATION PROCEDURE WITH THE EUROPEAN PARLIAMENT

It was to be nearly 30 years before there was any real modification in this process. The change was brought about by the SEA, and the relevant provision is now Article 189c of the EC Treaty. This procedure applies whenever the Treaty provides that the adoption of an Act is to be in accordance with Article 189c.

> (a) The Council acting on a proposal from the Commission, and after obtaining an Opinion from the European Parliament, adopts a common position.
> (b) This is then communicated to the European Parliament, and if within three months it has either approved the common position or has not taken a decision then the Council shall definitively adopt the act in accord with the common position.
> (c) If the Parliament rejects the common position then the Council can only adopt the act by unanimity. The Parliament may, alternatively, propose amendments by an absolute majority of its members.
> (d) It is then for the Commission within one month to re-examine the original proposal in the light of the Parliament's amendments. The Commission then forwards the re-examined proposal to the Council, together with the amendments of the Parliament which it has not accepted. The Council can then adopt such amendments by unanimity.

---

[10] A list of such areas can be found in Weatherill and Beaumont, above n. 1, pp. 796-797.
[11] Case 138/79, *Roquette Frères* v. *Council* [1980] E.C.R. 3333.

(e) The Council, acting by qualified majority, shall then adopt the proposal as re-examined by the Commission. Unanimity is required in the Council to amend this proposal.

(f) The Council must act within three months in the situations covered by (c), (d), and (e) above. If no decision is made within this period then the Commission proposal will be deemed not to have been adopted.

The procedure described above clearly gives the European Parliament a greater role in the legislative process than hitherto. When it was originally introduced in the SEA it was used for many of the measures which were designed to implement the single market. The TEU has now changed this, and requires the stronger procedure of Article 189b described below. The Article 189c procedure will, however, be used in new areas such as transport[12], and vocational training.[13]

(4) COUNCIL, COMMISSION AND EUROPEAN PARLIAMENT: THE ARTICLE 189B PROCEDURE

The TEU has introduced yet another complex procedure which bolsters still further the powers of the European Parliament. This new procedure has been referred to as "co-decision", both because it is designed to prevent a measure being adopted without the approval of the Council and the European Parliament, and because the procedure within the Article places emphasis on the reaching of a jointly approved text. The procedure is contained in Article 189b of the EC Treaty, and it applies whenever the Treaty refers to it for the adoption of an Act.

(a) The process begins in the same way to that set out in Article 189c, with the qualification that the Commission's proposal is sent to both the Council and the European Parliament. The Council then, acting by qualified majority, adopts a common position after obtaining the Opinion of the Parliament.

(b) If the Parliament either accepts this, or does not take a decision within three months, then the Council adopts the Act in accord with the common position.

(c) If the Parliament indicates by an absolute majority of its members that it intends to reject the common position then it must inform the Council, which may convene a meeting of the Conciliation Committee to explain further its position. The Parliament can then either confirm its rejection of the common position, in which case the proposed Act shall be deemed not to have been adopted, or propose amendments by an absolute majority of the component members.

(d) If the Parliament does propose amendments then the amended text is to be forwarded to the Council and Commission, which shall deliver an opinion on the amendments.

(e) The Conciliation Committee is composed of equal numbers of the Council and the European Parliament. Its task is to try to reach

---

[12] Article 75(1).
[13] Article 127(4).

agreement on a joint text when there has been disagreement as to the original common position adopted by the Council.

(f) There are then complex provisions which indicate what is to happen if this Committee cannot agree upon a joint text.[14] In essence the proposed Act is deemed not to have been adopted: *unless* the Council by qualified majority reconfirms the original common position to which it agreed before the conciliation procedure was initiated, in which case the Act will be adopted; *unless* this is trumped by the Parliament rejecting the text by an absolute majority, in which case the proposed Act will be deemed not to have been adopted.

This legislative procedure will apply to a number of important areas including: provisions concerned with the completion of the internal market,[15] certain aspects of environmental policy,[16] and some measures relating to public health.[17]

(5) COUNCIL, COMMISSION AND THE EUROPEAN PARLIAMENT: ASSENT

The assent procedure is simplicity itself as compared to those considered above: the Council acts on a proposal by the Commission, after obtaining the assent of the European Parliament. This is a true form of co-decision, and the Act can only be adopted if it has been approved by both the Council and the European Parliament.

This procedure was introduced by the SEA for important matters such as the expansion of Community membership,[18] and association agreements.[19] It has, however, been extended to cover other high profile concerns by the TEU. For example, the provisions on citizenship and free movement are to be furthered by adopting measures through the assent procedure.[20]

(6) THE SEEDS OF LEGISLATIVE INITIATIVE: ARTICLE 138B

The procedures outlined above encapsulate the existing ways in which measures can be enacted in the Community. It should, however, be noted that the European Parliament can be the catalyst for the initiation of the legislative process by virtue of Article 138b. This provides that the European Parliament may, acting by a majority of its members, request the Commission to submit any appropriate proposal on matters on which it considers that a Community Act is required for the purpose of implementing the Treaty. The proposal will then take the legislative route which is appropriate for measures of that kind as identified in a particular Treaty article. While Article 138b does not vest the Parliament with any right of initiative as such, it does provide a means whereby it can be "proactive" rather than simply being "reactive".

---

[14] Article 189b(6).
[15] Article 100A.
[16] Article 130s(3).
[17] Article 129(4).
[18] Article 237.
[19] Article 238.
[20] Article 8a(2).

3. *The Voting Requirements*

The general principle is that voting in the Council is to be by majority voting,[21] with a qualified majority being 54 out of a possible 76 votes. Qualified majority voting has been the formal legal norm in many areas where the Community acts since the end of the second stage of the transitional period in 1965. The range of issues which can be decided in this way was extended by the SEA, particularly through the addition of Article 100A which allows many matters concerned with the completion of the internal market to be determined in this manner. A requirement of unanimity now only applies to politically sensitive topics, to decisions which are of particular importance for the character of the Community, or in circumstances where the Council is seeking to depart from a proposal from one of the other Community institutions as described above.

For some considerable time these formal legal powers were over-shadowed by the Luxembourg Compromise. This was the result of a political crisis in the Community in the mid-1960s, and coincided with the shift to qualified majority voting in the Council. In essence it provided that when majority voting applied to a topic which concerned the important interests of states, they should attempt to reach a solution acceptable to all, and France added the rider that discussion should continue until unanimity was attained. Suffice to say for the present that the impact of the Compromise was to foster a climate in which majority voting prejudicial to the interests of a particular state tended to be avoided, and consensus decision-making fostered instead. The "threat" that a Member State would exercise a *de facto* power of veto over proposals which it considered as threatening to its vital interests certainly did not enhance the speed of Community decision-making. While the Luxembourg Compromise has not been formally abolished, because it never formally existed in legal terms, the climate in the Community after the SEA and the TEU renders it less likely that states will attempt to use any explicit veto power.

Section 3. The Legal Order: Supremacy and Direct Effect

The ECJ has had a marked impact on the development of the Community as a whole and has been a major force in securing greater Community integration. Two of the most important contributions of the ECJ in this respect have been concerned with supremacy and direct effect. These will be examined in turn.

1. *Supremacy*

It is readily apparent that, even with the best will in the world, there will be clashes between Community law and national law. These will often be

---

[21] Article 148(1).

inadvertent, simply the result of an "absence of fit" between complex Community provisions on a topic and those subsisting within national law. More intentional recalcitrance on the part of the Member States will be less common, though it is not by any means unknown. In any event some rules must exist for such cases. Not surprisingly the ECJ has held that EC law must be supreme in the event of any such conflict. This principle was first enunciated in *Costa* v. *ENEL*[22] where the ECJ responded to an argument that its preliminary ruling would be of no relevance to the case at hand because the Italian courts would be bound to follow national law. It held,

> "By creating a Community of unlimited duration, having...powers stemming from a limitation of sovereignty, or a transfer of powers from the States to the Community, the Member States have limited their sovereign rights, albeit within limited fields, and thus have created a body of law which binds both their nationals and themselves."

The Community's supremacy was given added force by the ECJ's ruling in the *Simmenthal* case[23], where the Court made it clear that Community law would take precedence even over national legislation which was adopted after the passage of the relevant EC norms. The existence of Community rules rendered automatically inapplicable any contrary provision of national law, *and* precluded the valid adoption of any new national law which was in conflict with the Community provisions.

> "It follows from the foregoing that every national court must, in a case within its jurisdiction, apply Community law in its entirety and protect rights which the latter confers on individuals and must accordingly set aside any provision of national law which may conflict with it, whether prior or subsequent to the Community rule."

The supremacy of Community law poses particular problems for legal systems such as our own which are wedded to the idea of parliamentary sovereignty. The leading decision on this issue is now *R.* v. *Secretary of State for Transport, ex p. Factortame Ltd.*[24] The background to the case was as follows. The applicants were companies which were incorporated under UK law, but the majority of the directors and shareholders of these companies were in fact Spanish. The companies were in the business of sea fishing and their vessels were registered as British under the Merchant Shipping Act 1894. The statutory regime governing sea fishing was radically altered by the passage of the Merchant Shipping Act 1988 and the regulations made pursuant thereto. Vessels which had been registered under the 1894 Act now had to register once again under the new legislation. Ninety-five vessels failed to meet the criteria in the new legislation and they sought to argue that the relevant parts of the 1988 Act were incompatible with Articles 7, 52, 58, and 221 of the EC Treaty.

The UK government responded by advancing two arguments. First, it was argued that nothing in Community law prevented a Member State

---

[22] Case 6/64, [1964] E.C.R. 585, 593.
[23] Case 106/77, [1978] E.C.R. 629.
[24] [1990] 2 A.C. 85.

from defining for itself who was to be regarded as a national of that state, and that the relevant sections of the 1988 legislation under attack by the applicants were doing no more than that. Secondly, the government contended that the 1988 legislation was not in fact in breach of Community law and that it was consistent with the Community policy·on fisheries.

Whether the 1988 statute was in fact in breach of EC law was clearly a contentious question. All the UK courts involved in the case agreed that a reference should be made to the ECJ under Article 177. The question which remained for decision in the first *Factortame* case concerned the status of the 1988 Act pending the decision on the substance of the case by the ECJ. This decision might not be forthcoming for some time and if the applicants could not fish in this intervening period they might well go out of business. The applicants sought, therefore, either for the 1988 Act to be "disapplied" pending the outcome on the substance of the case before the ECJ, or, if this was not to be the case, and the Act remained in force to prevent them from fishing, then the government should have to give an undertaking to provide compensation should the ultimate decision given by the ECJ be in the applicants' favour. In other words, if the court did grant an interim injunction to the government to prevent the applicants from fishing, then the government should have to give a cross-undertaking to pay damages if they should lose in the main action before the ECJ. Lord Bridge gave the judgment of the House of Lords and reasoned as follows.

First, his Lordship rejected the applicants' argument that the 1988 Act should be disapplied pending the final determination of the matter by the ECJ. An Act of Parliament was presumptively valid and this presumption would only be displaced if a challenge to the Act was upheld. A court might exercise its discretion to refuse to grant an order to enforce a disputed legislative measure in circumstances where it was necessary to invoke the court's jurisdiction in order to secure the enforcement of the legislation. However, the position was different here since the government did not require the assistance of the court in this sense: the government was simply refusing to register the applicants under the 1988 Act.

Secondly, Lord Bridge decided that in any event there was no jurisdiction under English law to grant interim injunctions against the Crown, and that this provided an additional reason why the relief sought by the applicants could not be granted. This aspect of the case is considered in detail within the general framework of remedies against the Crown.[25]

Thirdly, Lord Bridge then considered the applicants' argument that the absence of any interim relief against the Crown was itself a violation of Community law. They argued more specifically that: there is an overriding principle of Community law which imposes an obligation on the national court to secure effective protection of rights having direct effect under Community law where a seriously arguable claim is advanced to be entitled to such rights and where the rights claimed will in substance be rendered nugatory or will be irremediably impaired if not effectively protected during any interim period which must elapse pending determination of a dispute as to the existence of those rights. Lord Bridge was unsure whether this was

---

[25] See below, Chap. 20.

indeed required by EC law, but since the point was clearly contentious and of importance a preliminary ruling was requested from the ECJ. The ECJ was therefore in effect being asked to rule on whether a "gap" in the availability of administrative law remedies in UK law was itself a breach of EC law, at least insofar as this "gap" affected actions which had an EC element to them.

The ECJ decided in favour of the applicants.[26] The reasoning was founded on the earlier judgment in the *Simmenthal* case.[27] In that case, as we have seen, the ECJ held that provisions of Community law rendered "automatically inapplicable" any conflicting provision of national law. The *Simmenthal* decision had given a broad construction to the idea of a "conflicting provision" of national law, interpreting it to cover any legislative, administrative or judicial practice which might impair the effectiveness of Community law.[28] With this foundation the ECJ in the *Factortame* case concluded that,[29]

> "...the full effectiveness of Community law would be just as much impaired if a rule of national law could prevent a court seised of a dispute governed by Community law from granting interim relief in order to ensure the full effectiveness of the judgment to be given on the existence of the rights claimed under Community law. It follows that a court which in those circumstances would grant interim relief, if it were not for a rule of national law is obliged to set aside that rule."

The case then returned to the House of Lords to be reconsidered in the light of the preliminary ruling given by the ECJ, *R. v. Secretary of State for Transport, ex p. Factortame Ltd (No.2)*.[30] A number of interesting issues emerge from their Lordships' decision, including the availability of interim relief against the Crown. This topic will be dealt with fully below.[31] Suffice to say for the present that their Lordships accepted that, at least in the area covered by EC law, such relief would be made available against the Crown. The present discussion will focus upon the approach taken by the House of Lords to the issue of sovereignty and the EC.

Factortame (No.2) contains dicta by their Lordships on the more general issue of sovereignty, and the reasons why these dicta are contained in the decision are not hard to find. The final decision on the substance of the case involved a potential clash between certain norms of the EC Treaty itself, combined with EC rules on the common fisheries policy, and a *later* Act of the UK Parliament, the Merchant Shipping Act 1988, combined with regulations made thereunder. One aspect of the traditional idea of sovereignty in the UK has been that if there is a clash between a later statutory norm and an earlier legal provision the former takes precedence. The strict

---

[26] Case C–213/89, *R. v. Secretary of State for Transport, ex p. Factortame Ltd.* [1990] E.C.R. I-2433.

[27] Case 106/77, *Amministrazione Delle Finanze Dello Stato v. Simmenthal SpA* [1978] E.C.R. 629.

[28] *Ibid.* paras. 22 and 23.

[29] [1990] E.C.R. I-2433, para. 21.

[30] [1991] 1 A.C. 603.

[31] See below, Chap. 20.

application of this idea in the context of the EC could obviously be problematic, since the ECJ has, as we have seen, repeatedly held that Community law must take precedence in the event of a clash with national law. Earlier UK cases had exemplified a variety of approaches to the issue of a potential clash between the two legal systems. Some authorities appeared to stick to the traditional orthodoxy of giving precedence to national law.[32] Others appeared to be more willing to apply a rule of construction, under which it would be assumed that Parliament had not intended there to be any inconsistency between UK law and EC law, unless Parliament had expressly stated its intent to derogate from the norms of EC law. The dicta of the House of Lords in *Factortame (No.2)* are therefore clearly of importance. Lord Bridge had this to say.[33]

"Some public comments on the decision of the Court of Justice, affirming the jurisdiction of the courts of the member states to override national legislation if necessary to enable interim relief to be granted in protection of rights under Community law, have suggested that this was a novel and dangerous invasion by a Community institution of the sovereignty of the United Kingdom Parliament. But such comments are based on a misconception. If the supremacy within the European Community of Community law over the national law of member states was not always inherent in the EEC Treaty it was certainly well established in the jurisprudence of the Court of Justice long before the United Kingdom joined the Community. Thus, whatever limitation of its sovereignty Parliament accepted when it enacted the European Communities Act 1972 was entirely voluntary. Under the terms of the 1972 Act it has always been clear that it was the duty of a United Kingdom court, when delivering final judgment, to override any rule of national law found to be in conflict with any directly enforceable rule of Community law. Similarly, when decisions of the Court of Justice have exposed areas of United Kingdom statute law which failed to implement Council directives, Parliament has always loyally accepted the obligation to make appropriate and prompt amendments. Thus there is nothing in any way novel in according supremacy to rules of Community law in areas to which they apply and to insist that, in the protection of rights under Community law, national courts must not be prohibited by rules of national law from granting interim relief in appropriate cases is no more than a logical recognition of that supremacy."

It is clear that Lord Bridge was speaking in broad terms about the general relationship between EC law and UK law. His dictum represents a general statement concerning the priority of Community law over national law in the event of a clash between the two. The foundation for this reasoning is essentially contractarian: the UK knew when it joined the EC that priority should be accorded to EC law, and it must be taken to have contracted on

---

[32] Craig, "Sovereignty of the United Kingdom Parliament after *Factortame*" (1991) 11 Y.B.E.L. 221, 240-243.
[33] [1991] 1 A.C. 603, 658-659.

those terms. If, therefore, "blame" was to be cast for a loss of sovereignty then this should be laid at the feet of Parliament and not the courts.

Lord Goff, who gave the leading judgment of the House of Lords, said less on this particular issue than did Lord Bridge. However, even Lord Goff did state, in the course of deciding whether to grant interim relief to the applicants, that the applicants had strong grounds for "challenging the validity" of the provisions relating to residence and domicile in the UK legislation.[34]

Space precludes a thorough analysis of the effects of the second *Factortame* decision on the traditional concept of sovereignty as it operates in the UK. This can be found elsewhere.[35] At the very least the decision means that the concept of implied repeal, under which inconsistencies between later and earlier norms were resolved in favour of the former, will no longer apply to clashes concerning Community and national law.[36] If Parliament ever does wish to derogate from its Community obligations then it will have to do so expressly and unequivocally. Whether our national courts would then choose to follow the latest will of Parliament, or whether they would argue that it is not open to our legislature to pick and choose which obligations to subscribe to while still remaining within the Community, remains to be seen.

2. *Direct Effect*

The doctrine of Community law supremacy has undoubtedly been one of the notable achievements of the ECJ and it has been a cornerstone in the building of a Community legal order. The other principal contribution which the Court has made in this respect has been through the development of the doctrine of direct effect. In order to appreciate the importance of this doctrine, it is necessary to understand why it was introduced.

(1) THE LIMITS OF PUBLIC ENFORCEMENT

The concept of direct effect allows individuals to bring actions in their own names within national courts in order to vindicate rights secured to them by the Treaty. It is in this sense a species of *private enforcement*. Whether the framers of the original EC Treaty intended individuals to be able to bring such actions is debatable. It is nonetheless clear that the obligations in the Treaty have to be enforced in some manner, and the principal mechanism for doing so was through *public enforcement* as provided for in Article 169 of the EC Treaty. One of the principal rationales for the introduction of direct effect was to supplement public enforcement of Community law with private enforcement, because of the weaknesses of the former. What then is the mechanism for public enforcement and what are its limitations?

---

[34] *Ibid.* p. 674.
[35] Craig, "Sovereignty of the United Kingdom Parliament after *Factortame*" (1991) 11 Y.B.E.L. 221, and "Administrative Law, Remedies and the EEC" (1991) 3 E.R.P.L. 521.
[36] See further the discussion on direct effect and indirect effect, below, pp. 195–208.

Under Article 169 it is the Commission which is charged with the responsibility of bringing Member States who have failed to comply with the Treaty before the ECJ. Article 170 allows a Member State to bring another Member State to the ECJ, provided that it first submits the issue to the Commission. There are six principal deficiencies with this manner of enforcing EC norms, each of which is cured, or at the least alleviated by, the development of direct effect.

The first, and most obvious, difficulty created by this approach is that it thereby effectively places the entire burden of policing EC law on the Commission. One Member State will rarely sue another, and even when this does occur under Article 170 the Commission is still involved in the action. Such a scheme of public enforcement therefore entails a considerable expenditure of *time* on the part of the Commission. This is of particular importance within a system such as the EC, in which the Commission has a plethora of other responsibilities quite separate from that of "prosecutor". If the burden of pursuing claims becomes too great then the Commission will have relatively less time to, for example, devise legislation, which is one of its main tasks under the Treaty. Private actions, rendered possible by the concept of direct effect, complement the enforcement role of the Commission by sanctioning claims brought by individuals in their own capacity.[37]

A second difficulty with public enforcement is closely related to the first. In order for such a system to be effective the Commission must be aware that a breach of the Treaty or legislation made pursuant thereto has occurred. *Knowledge* of the existence of a breach is clearly a condition precedent for enforcement action. Such knowledge could of course be acquired by the Commission itself, but this would be an extremely complex and protracted process given the size of the Treaty and the volume of regulations and directives which have been promulgated. This would be so even if, as is the case at present, individuals can inform the Commission of a possible Treaty violation. Direct effect alleviates this problem. An individual who believes that a wrong has been done by a Member State contrary to the EC Treaty is in the optimal position to know the facts to which the alleged violation relates, and has a strong incentive to take steps to have the matter tested.

The third limit of public enforcement is that it is only available against a Member State. While an individual may, on many occasions, wish to assert rights against the state, there may also be many instances where the appropriate defendant is another individual or a corporation. This will often be the case in actions involving, for example, competition law or discrimination. Direct effect imposes obligations on private parties, subject to the limits mentioned below, and allows such actions to be brought within the national courts.

---

[37] Another way of putting the same point is that direct effect creates a large number of "private attorney-generals", who operate not only to vindicate their own private rights, but also to ensure that the norms of the EC treaty are correctly applied by the Member States. Enforcement of the Treaty is thereby shared and the Commission is no longer solely responsible for this important task.

The fourth problem with relying on public enforcement *per se* is rather different in nature from the two which have already been considered. It can be termed the *conflict of interest* problem. There is an extensive literature within public law concerning agency capture, the situation in which an agency comes to associate with the interests of those which it was established to regulate. There is little evidence of this occurring within the EC, where the Commission has pursued the objectives of the Community vigorously, even where this has met with strenuous opposition from Member States. Notwithstanding this strident approach, the Commission may be vulnerable to a conflict of interest, and the result may be similar to, albeit less dramatic than, agency capture. The reason is as follows. The Commission, as we have seen, possesses a wide range of powers, including those of a legislative as well as a judicial nature. This can lead to tension which manifests itself in the exercise of prosecutorial discretion. An important legislative initiative may be under consideration in the Council, with the consequence that the Commission may be wary of pursuing an action against a Member State lest the latter should manifest its displeasure by rendering the passage of the legislation more protracted. If the legislation is of importance, and the wrongdoing is of less significance, the temptation to ignore the latter, or to pursue it less vigorously, may be great, even though the breach may be of import to the particular group affected by it. It would obviously be difficult to determine empirically how often the Commission had been placed in this conundrum, since the members thereof are unlikely ever to admit that their decision has been affected in this manner. At the very least it can be said that a system which relies exclusively on public enforcement, and in which the "prosecutor" also exercises legislative powers, will be prone to this type of tension. The introduction of direct effect eases this tension dramatically. It is now the individual who is bringing the action. The individual is not, and cannot be, subject to the same pressures as the Commission.

The fifth shortcoming with the regime of public enforcement which is enshrined in the Treaty concerns *remedies*. These have inherent limitations. Article 171 provided, until recently, that a Member State found to be in breach of the Treaty should take the necessary measures to comply with the judgment of the ECJ. This clearly imposes an obligation on the state, but it sounds principally as a breach of an international obligation derived from the Treaty. If the state should continue to prove recalcitrant there was, until, the modification of the EC Treaty by the TEU, little more that could realistically be done, short of bringing a further action. The ECJ now has the power to fine a Member State pursuant to the modified Article 171. Notwithstanding this, direct effect, and the private actions which are thereby countenanced, provide a particularly effective way to secure a remedy. In part this is because the action is begun and ended in the national courts, and national governments are more likely to adhere to a judgment given directly from within their own system. This much is well known. The impact of direct effect at the remedial level is, however, more significant than this. The ECJ, while leaving some choice of remedy to the national courts, has made it clear that the remedy must provide an effective protection for the right in question. The more precise implications of this will vary depending on the nature of the issue. At the most general level the ECJ has demanded that national courts should, in effect, treat as done what ought to be done. Thus if, for example, a state has imposed a tariff which is inconsistent with Community law and has levied money pursuant thereto, then the national court should treat the tariff as invalid and return the money which has been paid over. Whether this means formally invalidating the tariff, or whether it means disregarding it in this litigation, will depend upon the constitutional structure in the particular state.

The final stumbling block with the regime of public enforcement which operates under the Treaty is of a more symbolic nature. It has already been seen how such a system could be creative of tensions between Member States and the Commission in particular cases. At a more general level the approach in Article 169 produces a *public relations problem*. The preamble to the Treaty speaks of laying the foundations "of an ever closer union among the peoples of Europe". This theme has always been close to the heart of the federalist-minded Commission. Vigorous enforcement of existing Treaty norms against Member States is, of course, not formally inconsistent with this long-term goal. It does nonetheless not look "quite right" that a Community which is meant to be moving towards a closer social and political union should have countless cases in which one organ of the Community is continually suing its constituent members. Direct effect therefore possessed a significant symbolic advantage. EC norms could be enforced without there being endless cases in which the Commission was directly suing the states. The reality was, as reality is, unchanged. Actions brought by individuals were still about states whose compliance with EC law was imperfect. Yet, at the least, direct effect served to ensure that this did not appear as a direct confrontation between the Commission and the Member States.

(2) DIRECT EFFECT AND RIGHTS: THE EMPOWERMENT OF THE INDIVIDUAL

The discussion thus far has concentrated on the way in which direct effect has alleviated the problems attendant upon public enforcement of EC norms. The discussion would, however, be incomplete if it were to rest there. Direct effect has made a positive contribution to the development of EC law quite independently of its curative effect on the difficulties which beset public enforcement. Granting rights to individuals which they can enforce in their own name transformed the very nature of the EC treaty. No longer would the Treaty be viewed solely as the business of nation states in the manner of many other international treaties. It was to be a form of social ordering in which individuals were involved in their own capacity. They were no longer to be passive receptors who had to await action taken on their behalf by other organs of the Community. They were now accorded rights which they could enforce in their own name. This was a necessary step in the transformation of the Community from a compact between states which was principally economic in nature, to that vision glimpsed at in the preamble of the Treaty, "a closer union among the peoples of Europe". It represented the first step in the judicial contribution towards the building of a more federal Europe.

(3) VAN GEND EN LOOS

The seminal case in the development of the concept of direct effect was *Van Gend en Loos*.[38] Dutch importers challenged the rate of duty imposed on a chemical imported from Germany. They argued that a reclassification of the product under a different heading of the Dutch tariff legislation had led to an increase in the duty and that this was prohibited under Article 12 of the Treaty, which prohibits the imposition of any new customs duties on imports and also precludes any increase in existing rates. The Dutch court asked the ECJ whether Article 12 gave rise to rights which could be invoked by individuals before their national courts.

The details of the arguments advanced by Holland, Germany and Belgium differed, but their general tenor was the same. The major theme was that provisions already existed through which EC law could be enforced, and these were to be found in Articles 169 and 170. This theme was complemented by a second, the substance of which was that the Treaty was simply a compact between states, to be policed in the manner dictated by the Treaty itself. If a Member State was in breach of the Treaty then it should have to face the consequences at the hands of another state, or at the hands of the organ explicitly accorded the task of policing the Treaty, the Commission. To afford individuals the right to initiate actions within national courts would be to alter the nature of the obligations accepted by the signatories.

Three strands of reasoning are apparent in the judgment of the ECJ itself. The first demonstrates the use of a purposive and teleological approach which has become such a characteristic of the ECJ's jurisprudence. The core of the judgment opens with reference to the general aims and spirit of the Treaty, and the objective is to deny the very basis of the reasoning advanced by the states. The EC was *not* simply to be viewed as a compact between nations. The "interested parties" include the people, a fact which is affirmed by the preamble and by the existence of institutions charged with the duty of making provisions for those individuals. It is this crucial conceptual starting point which lays the foundation for the now famous passage from the judgment, depicting the Community as a new legal order for the benefit of which states have limited their sovereign rights, with the consequence that individuals have rights and can be regarded as subjects of the Community.

The second strand which is evident in the judgment of the ECJ is designed to buttress the first by drawing upon the Treaty itself to substantiate the conclusion that individuals can proceed before national courts. The ECJ utilises Article 177, which is concerned with the reference of questions on Community law by national courts to the ECJ. This provision is said to indicate that the states have acknowledged that Community law has an authority which can be invoked by their nationals before national courts.

The third, and final, aspect of the ECJ's reasoning focuses on the particular articles of the Treaty which were in contention in the case. The

---

[38] Case 26/62, *Van Gend en Loos* v. *Nederlandse Administratie der Belastingen* [1963] E.C.R. 1.

essence of the argument is to demonstrate that Article 12 is a natural candidate for enforcement in this manner. Thus the ECJ stresses the *negative* nature of the obligation, the fact that it is *unconditional*, and that its *implementation is not dependent on any further measures* before being effective under national law. It is thereby able to conclude that the very nature of this prohibition makes it ideally suited to produce direct effects in the legal relationship between Member States and their subjects.

(4) EXPANSION OF DIRECT EFFECT: TREATY ARTICLES

The years immediately following the decision in *Van Gend en Loos* witnessed the application of the concept to a growing range of Treaty articles, as individuals sought to utilise the power which had been given to them by the ECJ. The Court itself was keen to expand the concept given the advantages it possessed. In applying direct effect to other Treaty articles the ECJ began to relax the conditions for the application of the concept. Direct effect was applied in circumstances where it could not be said that the Treaty article in question created a negative obligation which was legally perfect, in the sense that no further action was required by the Community or the Member States, and no real residue of discretion existed. The concept was applied to Articles of the Treaty dealing with broad areas of regulatory policy which were as much social as economic.

The *Reyners* case[39] provides a simple example. The plaintiff was a Dutch national who had been educated in Belgium and who had obtained a Belgian legal qualification. He was, however, unable to practise because of a Belgian law which restricted this right to those of Belgian nationality. Dispensation from the nationality condition could be granted, but the plaintiff had been unsuccessful in such applications. He therefore sought to argue that the Belgian law was inconsistent with Article 52 on freedom of establishment.

A number of Member States contended that Article 52 could not have direct effect because it represented simply a statement of general principle which had not yet been fleshed out by the secondary legislation in the manner explicitly envisaged by the Treaty. Further action was required by the Community and the Member States before this part of the Treaty could fulfil the conditions for direct effect to operate. It was not therefore for "the courts to exercise a discretionary power reserved to the legislative institutions of the Community and the Member States".[40]

The ECJ did not accept this argument. Its reasoning is based upon an interpretation of the purpose of the relevant chapter taken as a whole. Viewed in this light primacy of position is accorded to the prohibition of discrimination contained in Article 52 itself. The further legislation is perceived as a way of effectuating this goal, but the absence thereof is not to be allowed to impede one of the fundamental legal provisions of the Community.

The ECJ may well have been correct in deciding that Article 52 should have direct effect even in the absence of these norms being promulgated, but

---

[39] Case 2/74, *Reyners* v. *Belgian State* [1974] E.C.R. 631.
[40] *Ibid.* pp. 648-49.

this should not blind us to the fact that the original conditions for direct effect were modified and that this was necessitated by the difference in the type of Treaty article in question. Article 52, when placed within the relevant chapter of the Treaty, cannot be regarded as complete and legally perfect in the same sense in which this phrase is used in relation to, for example, Article 12. This is so even if one accepts the analysis of the ECJ. Article 52, and the provisions on freedom of establishment, expressly contemplate further action by the legislative organs of the Community and by the Member States in order to effectuate the social and economic aims of this part of the Treaty. The very regime of freedom of establishment involves a complex array of legislative norms in order that these aims can be achieved.

The requisite Community legislation pursuant to Article 52 had not been enacted in large part because Member States were unwilling to make the sacrifices and compromises to allow this to happen. The choice was clear. Either these spheres of policy could be left unfulfilled, or the ECJ, through direct effect, could ensure that the basic principles within these areas should be enforced and developed through the judicial process.[41]

The same theme is evident in other important decisions of the ECJ on the direct effect of Treaty articles, such as in the seminal *Defrenne* case.[42] Defrenne was employed by Sabena as an air hostess. Her contract stated that she should retire at 40. She sought to argue that the conditions of her employment were discriminatory and contrary to Article 119, insofar as they were less favourable than those applicable to male cabin stewards who performed the same task. The fact that the tasks performed by female hostesses and male stewards were identical was not disputed.

The ECJ acknowledged the central importance of Article 119 from both an economic and a social perspective. It recognised that the complete implementation of the Article might well involve "the elaboration of criteria whose implementation necessitates the taking of appropriate measures at Community and national level".[43] This was not, however, to be a bar to giving direct effect to the Article. Direct and overt discrimination could be identified solely through Article 119 itself. Direct effect could operate in relation to such forms of discrimination, even if the proscription of more indirect and disguised forms of discrimination could only be identified by reference to explicit implementing provisions of a Community or national character.

Article 119, like Article 52, provides the general aim for a complex sphere of regulatory social and economic policy. It cannot be regarded as complete and legally perfect in the same manner as, for example, Article 12, without radically distorting the meaning of that phrase. It is clear that Article 119 requires, as the Court recognised, further measures at both Community and national level in order for the aims to be fulfilled. Not all the requisite

---

[41] Weiler, "The Community System: The Dual Character of Supranationalism" (1981) 1 Y.B.E.L. 267; Craig, "Once Upon a Time in the West: Direct Effect and the Federalization of EEC Law" (1992) 12 O.J.L.S. 453.
[42] Case 43/75, *Defrenne* v. *Sabena* [1976] E.C.R. 455.
[43] *Ibid.* p. 473.

measures had been promulgated in the stipulated time. As in the case of *Reyners*, the ECJ introduced direct effect to provide an alternative method through which the principles of equal pay could be furthered, at least in the area of direct discrimination.

(5) EXPANSION OF DIRECT EFFECT: REGULATIONS

The discussion thus far has concentrated on the application of direct effect to Treaty provisions. The ECJ has, however, also made it clear that the concept can apply to legislation enacted pursuant to the Treaty itself. One of the main species of legislation made pursuant to the Treaty is the regulation. This is defined in Article 189 of EC Treaty: "A regulation shall have general application. It shall be binding in its entirety and directly applicable in all Member States."

In *Leonosio* v. *Italian Ministry of Agriculture and Forestry*[44] (known affectionately as *Slaughtered Cow*), the applicant sought to rely on two Community regulations under which she was entitled to receive a premium if she slaughtered a dairy cow. The relevant Italian authority was awaiting the necessary allocation of funds before it could pay over the desired sums. The ECJ held that the regulation did confer rights on individuals which they could use in national courts, and that the absence of the requisite allocation of funds was no excuse.

It is, moreover, clear that the Member State cannot alter the content of the relevant Community norm. Thus in *Amsterdam Bulb*[45] the ECJ held that the direct application of a Community regulation meant that its entry into force was "independent of any measure of transformation into national law",[46] and that states were precluded from adopting "any measure which would conceal the Community nature and effects of any legal provision from the persons to whom it applies".[47]

(6) EXPANSION OF DIRECT EFFECT: DIRECTIVES

According to Article 189 of the EC Treaty, directives are binding as to the result to be achieved while leaving the choice of form and methods to the states to whom they are addressed. Moreover, while regulations are binding on all states, directives are only binding on the specific states to whom they are addressed.

Directives have proved to be a particularly useful device for legislating in an enlarged Community. Many areas of Community policy concern complex topics ranging from products liability to the environment, and from the harmonisation of company law to the free movement of capital. The "normal" methods of legislating are ill-suited to these spheres. Regulations, as noted above, are intended to be directly applicable in the Member States without even being transformed into national laws. This legislative technique therefore requires that the content of the legislation be written with sufficient clarity and specificity to pass into national systems without

---

[44] Case 93/71, [1973] C.M.L.R. 343.
[45] Case 50/76, *Amsterdam Bulb* v. *Produktschap voor Siergewassen* [1977] E.C.R. 137.
[46] *Ibid.* p. 146.
[47] *Loc. cit.*

more ado. It also requires that the norm be capable of so entering 12 different legal systems, some of which have a common law foundation, others of which have a civil law base, and where differences abound even within these two groupings. Now it may well be the case that some regulations are indeed written more loosely than indicated above, and that certain directives are imbued with considerable specificity. Notwithstanding this fact, directives are invaluable precisely because without this doctrinal form it would in a literal sense be difficult to legislate in many important areas.

The application of direct effect to directives has proven to be more controversial than in the context of regulations. This is in part because directives clearly do require further action on the part of the Member States, and because they leave the states with some measure of discretionary choice as to methods of implementation. The reluctance to admit that directives can have direct effect is also in part because of the wording of Article 189 which states that regulations are directly applicable, while not using this phraseology in relation to directives.

Notwithstanding these points the ECJ has held that directives are capable of having direct effect. The Court has used three arguments to justify this conclusion.

First, there is an argument from *general principle*, the essence of which is that it would be inconsistent with the binding effect of directives to exclude the possibility that they can confer rights. The mere fact that regulations are deemed to be directly applicable, and hence capable of conferring rights, should not be taken to mean that other Community norms can never have the same effect.[48]

The second argument is derived from *Article 177*. This Article allows questions concerning the interpretation and validity of Community law to be referred by national courts to the ECJ. From the generality of this provision the Court has concluded that questions relating to directives can be raised by individuals before national courts.[49]

The third reason for according direct effect to directives, in some instances at least, is the *estoppel* argument. Given that the peremptory force of directives would be weakened if individuals could not rely on them before national courts, a Member State which has not implemented the directive "may not rely, as against individuals, on its own failure to perform the obligations which the directive entails".[50]

Provided, therefore, that the directive is sufficiently precise, that the basic obligation is unconditional and that the period for implementation has passed, an individual can derive enforceable rights from a directive.

The decision in *Van Duyn*[51] provides an apt example. The applicant was a Dutch woman who wished to take up employment with the Church of Scientology. Article 48 of the EC Treaty protects the free movement of workers within the Community, subject to exceptions based upon public

[48] Case 41/74, *Van Duyn* v. *Home Office* [1974] E.C.R. 1337, para. 12.
[49] *Loc. cit.*
[50] Case 148/78, *Pubblico Ministero* v. *Ratti* [1979] E.C.R. 1629, para. 22.
[51] Case 41/74, [1974] E.C.R. 1337.

policy. The UK sought to exclude the applicant on the ground that it believed that the Church was socially undesirable, even though it did not prevent its own nationals from working there. One of the questions posed in the case was whether an individual could rely on Directive 64/221 which specified in greater detail the circumstances in which foreign nationals could be excluded on grounds of public policy, public security or public health. More specifically, the applicant sought an interpretation of Article 3(1) of the Directive which provided that exclusionary measures must be based solely on the personal conduct of the individual concerned.

(7) DIRECTIVES: HORIZONTAL AND VERTICAL DIRECT EFFECT

While the ECJ has been willing to give direct effect to directives it has, however, also held that they only have vertical as opposed to horizontal direct effect. Treaty articles and regulations give individuals rights which can be used both against the state, vertical direct effect, and against private parties, horizontal direct effect. Directives only have vertical direct effect.

The seminal case on this point is *Marshall*.[52] The Southampton Area Health Authority operated different retirement ages for men and women, and the applicant claimed that this was in breach of Directive 76/207 on Equal Treatment. The ECJ reiterated its previous holding that directives were capable of having direct effect, and that whether this was so would depend on the subject-matter of the provision: if it were sufficiently precise and unconditional it could be so relied on, if the state had not applied it within the requisite period. A directive could not, however, impose obligations on individuals, but only on the state, either *qua* state or *qua* employer. The reason proffered by the court for this limitation was the wording of Article 189 itself: the binding nature of the directive existed only in relation to "each Member State to which it is addressed".

Opinions have differed on the correctness of and rationale for this ruling. The arguments cannot be fully explored here.[53] Whether the actual argument advanced by the ECJ itself is self-evidently correct is doubtful. It is of course true that Article 189 talks of directives being binding on the state to which they are addressed. To infer from this that they cannot impose duties on individuals is more questionable. The relevant wording of Article 189 is simply expressive of the fact that states are the primary addressees of the obligation contained in the directive. It is they who have the correlative duty to take the required measures to effectuate the ends stipulated therein. This does not necessarily mean that individuals should not be under an obligation flowing from a directive. A similar argument was rejected in the *Defrenne* case.[54]

If there is a more meaningful argument against giving directives horizontal direct effect then it is based on legal certainty. The essence of the argument is that private individuals should not be placed in unreasonable

---

[52] Case 152/84, *Marshall* v. *Southampton & South West Hampshire Area Health Authority (Teaching)* [1986] 1 C.M.L.R. 688.
[53] See, *e.g.*, Advocate General Reischl in *Ratti* [1979] E.C.R. 1629, 1650; Advocate General Slynn in Case 8/81, *Becker* [1982] E.C.R. 53, 81.
[54] Case 43/75, [1976] E.C.R. 455.

doubt concerning the nature of their obligations. Given that directives require national implementing legislation this uncertainty might occur if individuals were required to scrutinise differing texts both at national and Community level in order to find out what the law was.[55] There are, however, two real limits to this argument.

On the one hand, it will not always have force even in its own terms. The articles of many directives may be suited to application between private parties, without encountering any problems of legal certainty. Directive 76/207 on equal treatment can be taken as an example. Article 3(1) of the Directive prohibits discrimination on grounds of sex in relation to access to employment, and Article 5 bans such discrimination in relation to working conditions. The state is then instructed to take a range of measures to implement the Directive. These include measures which will ensure that terms in contracts of employment which are contrary to the Directive will be declared null and void. Now even if the state has not taken these measures there would seem to be no reason not to impose duties on individuals. The obligations contained in the Directive are clear, and an employer who continues to discriminate on these grounds should not be allowed to shelter behind the fact that the state has been tardy in fulfilling its duties to implement the Directive.

On the other hand, it is not immediately obvious why the objection based upon legal certainty is thought to be relevant in the context of directives when no such objection is raised in the context of the primary Treaty provisions themselves. Many of these articles, such as Article 30, have been used expansively by the ECJ to cover a great variety of situations. These articles have horizontal direct effect and no one has raised the objection of legal certainty, even though there are often conflicting national norms on precisely the same issue, and even though it may not be easy for an individual to know in advance whether there will in fact be any clash between the requirements of Community law and national law.

Even though directives only have vertical direct effect the force of this limitation has been weakened in two ways: by an expansive definition of the state, and by the development of the doctrine of indirect effect. These will be examined in turn.

(8) DIRECTIVES: THE SCOPE OF VERTICAL DIRECT EFFECT

Given that directives only have vertical and not horizontal direct effect it is clearly important to know what the ambit of the state is to be for these purposes. The ECJ has given an expansive interpretation to this concept.

In *Foster*[56] the applicant wished to rely upon the Equal Treatment Directive 76/207 because she had been compulsorily retired earlier than male employees. The defendant was British Gas, and the question was whether it was to be treated as part of the state for these purposes. The ECJ held that the Directive could be relied upon against any body, whatever its legal form, which has been made responsible, pursuant to a measure adopted by the state, for providing a public service under the control of the

---

[55] Wyatt and Dashwood, above n. 1, p. 75.
[56] Case C-188/89, *Foster* v. *British Gas* [1990] E.C.R. I-3133.

state, and has for that purpose special powers over and beyond those which normally apply as between individuals.[57]

The correctness of this expansive definition may be questioned. It may well be accepted that bodies such as British Gas should be treated as part of the state for certain purposes, given the nature of its powers and the service which it is providing. What is less obvious is whether it should be so treated for this purpose, *given* the reasoning in *Marshall* itself. The premise in that case must be that the state as the addressee of the directive is meant to implement it. Yet bodies such as British Gas plainly have no powers in this respect, nor can estoppel type arguments apply against such institutions. It will often only be central government which has the authority to execute the directive. It is, of course, true that other bodies may well be in a position to abide by a directive or not as the case may be. But this is equally true for purely private parties as it is for bodies such as British Gas. There is no more or less reason to apply a directive against such bodies than against any other corporation. It is difficult to escape the conclusion that the expansive definition of the state given in *Foster* is an indirect way of circumventing the holding in *Marshall* itself.

(9) DIRECTIVES: INDIRECT EFFECT

The other way in which the force of the *Marshall* limitation has been blunted has been through the development of the doctrine which has become known as indirect effect.

The concept is associated with the important decision in *Von Colson*.[58] The applicants relied upon the provision of a directive in order to argue that the quantum of relief provided by German law in cases of discrimination was too small. The ECJ held that these provisions were not sufficiently precise to have direct effect. It went on, however, to hold that national courts had an obligation to interpret national law so as to be in conformity with the directive. The purpose of the directive was to provide an effective remedy in cases of discrimination, and if states chose to fulfil this aim through the provision of compensation then this should be adequate in relation to the damage which had been suffered. National courts should, therefore, construe their own national law with this in mind.

This principle of construction was applied and extended in *Marleasing*.[59] The case was concerned with Council Directive 68/151 which contained rules on safeguards for the establishment of companies within the Community. The plaintiff claimed that one of the defendant companies had been established "without cause" and that the purpose behind its establishment was to perpetrate a fraud. The plaintiff sought a declaration that the contract establishing this defendant corporation should be held to be void, and sought to found this claim on a provision of Spanish law. The defendant resisted the claim on the ground that Article 11 of Directive 68/151, which

---

[57] Curtin, "The Province of Government: Delimiting the Direct Effect of Directives in the Common Law Context" (1990) 15 E.L.Rev. 195.

[58] Case 14/83, *Von Colson and Kamann* v. *Land Nordrhein-Westfalen* [1984] E.C.R. 1891.

[59] Case C-106/89, *Marleasing S.A.* v. *La Commercial International De Alimentation S.A.* [1990] E.C.R. 4135; [1992] C.M.L.R. 305.

lists the grounds on which the nullity of a company may be ordered, did not include lack of cause amongst these grounds. The Directive had not yet been implemented in Spain, but the Spanish court nonetheless asked the European Court whether Article 11 could be said to be directly applicable, so as to preclude a declaration of nullity of a public company on a ground other than one set out in that Article.

The action was between private corporations, and the ECJ reiterated its holding that a directive could not, in itself, impose obligations on individuals, citing the *Marshall* case as authority.[60]

However, the ECJ qualified this by drawing on its ruling in *Von Colson*. The Court used the judgment in that case as the foundation for the argument that the authorities of the Member States have an obligation to effectuate the ends stipulated in a directive, and that this obligation is binding on all authorities in the state, including the courts. It followed that in applying national law, whether *passed before or after* the directive, a national court was required to interpret national law *in every way possible* so as to be in conformity with the directive. From this it followed that the Spanish court should interpret their national law so as not to order the nullity of a company on a ground not listed in Article 11 of the Directive.

While the ruling of the ECJ preserves its previous position, that there is no horizontal direct effect for directives, its findings on the interpretative duties of the national courts go a considerable way to according directives a measure of "indirect" direct effect. Thus, although an individual cannot, in a literal sense, derive rights from a directive in an action against another individual, it is possible to plead the directive in such an action, in the manner exemplified by the defendant in the present case. Once the directive has been placed before the national court in this way, then the interpretative obligation derived from *Von Colson*, and built upon in *Marleasing*, comes into operation. It has, moreover, been held that this interpretative obligation operates even before the time period for the implementation of the directive has expired.[61] Where the directive does encapsulate precise obligations, and where the national court is so minded to interpret national law in the required fashion, this "indirect" species of enforcement of a directive as between individuals will have the same results as if the directive had been accorded horizontal direct effect.

There is little doubt but that indirect effect does offer a way to circumvent the holding in *Marshall* itself, or at the least, to reach similar results in many instances, albeit by a different route. There is also little doubt that the interpretative obligation creates real problems of its own.[62] On the one hand, it places national courts in some difficulty in deciding how far they can go in reconciling national legislation with Community norms while still remaining within the realm of interpreting, as opposed to rewriting or overruling, national norms. On the other hand, it raises questions of legal certainty for individuals which are, paradoxically, more problematic than if directives had been given horizontal direct effect.

---

[60] *Ibid.* para. 6.
[61] Case 80/86, *Officier van Justitie* v. *Kolpinghuis Nijmegen* [1987] E.C.R. 3969.
[62] de Burca, "Giving Effect to European Community Directives", (1992) 55 M.L.R. 215.

Individuals will now have to decide or guess how far their national courts might feel able to go in reconciling national law with differently worded Community legislation. If directives did have horizontal direct effect then at least the individual would know that in the event of any inconsistency between the two norms Community law would trump national law.

Our own courts have, on the whole, shown themselves to be willing to construe national law in the light of the directive in the event of any inconsistency between the two, particularly where the national law was passed to realise the directive.[63] The courts have shown more ambivalence where the relevant national law was not promulgated to carry out the directive.[64]

3. Direct Effect: Rights and Remedies

The discussion thus far has focused upon the extent to which Community law creates rights which are enforceable by individuals in their own national courts. Rights demand remedies. How far does EC law have an impact upon the type of remedies which are available at the national level? The approach of the ECJ has become more interventionist as of late.

The early stance of the ECJ is exemplified by the decision in *Rewe* v. *Hauptzollamt Kiel*[65] where it was held that, while national courts were under an obligation to use all available national remedies to aid the enforcement of Community law, they were not bound to create new remedies for this purpose. However, in the *San Giorgio*[66] case the Court held that a Member State could not render claims for the repayment of charges, which were levied in breach of Community law, subject to procedural requirements which made that recovery virtually impossible.

The reconciliation of these two authorities was by no means easy. It was felt that a litigant could only claim a form of relief in aid of Community law rights if national law allowed that relief to be granted between the parties in proceedings before the court in question. If it did not do so then recourse was to be had to the legislature to fill the gap. However, if national law did allow the relief claimed to be granted between the parties by the court before which the proceedings were instituted, it was the duty of that court to make that relief available in aid of Community law, and "to disregard any substantive restrictions or procedural conditions of national law which are either discriminatory, or deprive the Community right of useful effect".[67]

Indications that Community law might well require greater modifications in the regime of remedies which existed at national level are to be found in the *Factortame* litigation. Prior to the House of Lords' decision in the second *Factortame* case[68] United Kingdom law did not allow interim

---

[63] *Litster* v. *Forth Dry Dock* [1990] 1 A.C. 546.
[64] *Duke* v. *G.E.C. Reliance* [1988] 1 A.C. 618.
[65] Case 158/80, [1981] E.C.R. 1805, 1838.
[66] Case 199/82, [1983] E.C.R. 3595.
[67] Wyatt and Dashwood, *The Substantive Law of the EEC* (2nd. ed., 1987), p. 56.
[68] R. v. *Secretary of State for Transport* , *ex p. Factortame Ltd. (No.2)* [1991] 1 A.C. 603.

injunctive relief against the Crown. It did not permit that relief to be granted between the parties in proceedings before the court in question. The decision of the ECJ in *Factortame*[69] had, nonetheless, held that such relief should be available in principle, and that the absence of any relief of this nature was itself a breach of Community law. The requirements of Community law as to the remedies which must exist in national law to protect Community rights might, therefore, be more stringent than had previously been thought. The principle underlying the *Factortame* litigation appears to be that provided the type of relief sought by the applicant is recognised by national law, in this instance in the form of the injunction, the fact that it was not previously available against the Crown will be regarded as an example of ineffective protection of Community rights, with the consequence that the national law must be changed, if possible by the courts in the case at hand.[70]

The *Francovich* case[71] represents a further development along the same lines. The applicant claimed damages from the Italian government for losses suffered as a result of the non-implementation of a directive which was designed to safeguard workers when a firm became insolvent. The issue of the Community's competence with respect to remedies was not considered by the ECJ itself, but it was addressed by Advocate General Mischo. The states contended that the previous case law of the ECJ had left to the national courts not only the methods by which possible damages actions should be governed, but also the principle according to which it should be determined whether such actions could lie at all. They relied on the jurisprudence of the court, arguing that it established that the Treaty was not intended to create *new* legal remedies in national legal systems where none had existed before. The response of the Advocate General was double-edged.

On the one hand, he made reference to decisions of the court which *had* indicated that liability in damages might be required in order to make good a breach of Community law by a Member State.[72] On the other hand, he addressed more generally the issue as to how far the Community could intrude upon the regimes of remedies which were available in Member

---

[69] Case C-213/89, *R. v. Secretary of State for Transport, ex p. Factortame Ltd.* [1990] E.C.R. I-2433. See also, Craig, "Administrative Law, Remedies and the EEC" (1991) 3 E.R.P.L. 521, 535.

[70] More recently the ECJ has held that interim measures should be available if the legality of Community law is questioned before national courts, and that the conditions for suspending Community norms may not vary from one Member State to another, Cases C-143/88 and C-92/89, *Zuckerfabrik Suderdithmaschen et Zuckerfabrik Soest v. Hauptzollamt Itzehoe* [1991] E.C.R. I-415. See also, Case C-208/90, *Emmott v. Minister for Social Welfare* [1991] 3 C.M.L.R. 894; Oliver, "Interim Measures: Some Recent Developments" (1992) 27 C.M.L.Rev. 7.

[71] Cases C-6 and 9/90, *Francovich v. Italian Republic, Bonifaci v. Italian Republic* [1992] I.R.L.R. 84. For comment see Ross, "Beyond *Francovich*" (1993) 56 M.L.R. 55; Lewis and Moore, "Duties, Directives and Damages in European Community Law" [1993] P.L. 151; Bebr, "*Francovich v.Italy, Boniface v. Italy*" (1992) 29 C.M.L.Rev. 559; Curtin, "State Liability under Private Law: a New Remedy for Private Parties" [1992] I.L.J. 74; Steiner, "From Direct Effects to *Francovich* (1993) 18 E.L.Rev. 3; Craig, "*Francovich*, Remedies and the Scope of Damages Liability" (1993) 109 L.Q.R. 595.

[72] Case 6/60, *Humblet* [1960] E.C.R. 559, 569; Case 60/75, *Russo* [1976] E.C.R. 45, 57.

States. On this point the Advocate General stated that "once the liability action exists as a type of action, the Member State can no longer rely on the status of the party alleged to be liable to prevent an individual bringing an action and therefore to question the effectiveness of Community law with direct effect".[73] The same point is further emphasised later in the opinion, where Advocate General Mischo stated that it cannot be deduced from the jurisprudence of the Court that "Community law can never oblige a Member State to provide parties with a remedy permitting them to rely effectively on their rights under Community law where similar remedies either do not exist or are not accessible on the same conditions on a national level."[74]

The language used by the Advocate General throws the issue of the impact of Community law on the remedies available under national law into sharp relief. On this view Community law might impose a duty on a Member State to construct a remedy *either* where similar remedies to that being claimed by the applicant do not exist at national level, *or* where the remedy is not accessible on the same conditions at the national level as the applicant is in fact seeking.

Now it may be contended that the most difficult aspect of this issue did not have to be faced squarely in *Francovich* itself, since the case was not concerned with the situation where the relevant national law had to create a wholly new type of remedy. After all the actual relief at stake was a damages remedy against the state, and most legal systems recognise an action of this kind.

This reasoning serves to conceal as much as it reveals. The crucial issue is the meaning to be accorded to phrases such as "type of action" used by Advocate General Mischo. It is readily apparent that the broader the construction given to these phrases, the less often will it appear to be the case that Community law is requiring the Member State to create a new remedy. Thus, while most, if not all, legal systems will recognise some species of damages action against the state, there will be significant differences as to the more precise conditions of that liability. These divergences will affect seminal matters such as the standard of liability, whether it is strict or fault based, and if the latter, the meaning which is ascribed to "fault" in this context. If Community law requires a Member State to provide, for example, a damages action which is subject to very different criteria from that which has previously existed, then in reality that state is being required to create what amounts to a new remedy.

This having been said, the obvious question is why not? Why should Community law not be able to direct Member States to develop new remedies, or new species of existing remedies, where these are needed to effectuate Community rights, *given* the textual foundation of Article 5 of the Treaty?[75] After all it is accepted that Community law can lead to the

---

[73] [1992] I.R.L.R. 84, para. 47.

[74] *Ibid.* para. 49.

[75] Article 5 provides that Member States are under an obligation to take all appropriate measures to ensure the fulfilment of obligations arising out of the Treaty. The ECJ in *Francovich* concluded from this provision that states had the duty to make good the unlawful consequences of a breach of Community law.

introduction of new rights which might not have previously existed in a Member State, so why not new remedies to give effect to those rights? To this two answers are possible.

One is that it might be said that this would impinge upon the division of competence between the ECJ and a national court. In Article 177 actions the former interprets Community law, while the latter applies that interpretation to the case at hand when it returns to the national forum. This objection is, however, misplaced. Insofar as the ECJ does indicate the type of remedies which are necessary to give effect to Community rights, it *is* interpreting Community law. The fact that this will have an impact at the national level is both obvious and intended, but it does not involve any transgression of function by the ECJ. It will continue to be for national law to determine the more precise conceptual label to be attached to this cause of action, and the procedural conditions under which the remedy can be sought.

The other objection to the Court demanding the establishment of new remedies within Member States is that this may necessitate domestic legislative action, if such new remedies cannot be developed by the national courts themselves. But this cannot, in reality, be an objection to ECJ rulings requiring such action. The method by which any particular Member State fulfils its Community law obligations is a purely contingent issue which is dependent on the detailed constitutional arrangements within that state. It cannot, of itself, affect the actual legitimacy of the ECJ ruling in this respect.

These developments are reflected in the current edition of Wyatt and Dashwood, where it is stated that "Community law, as well as defining rights, may in certain cases also determine the nature of the remedies provided by national courts."[76]

Section 4. The Impact of Community Law

It is clear that many public law cases will centre around the application of Community law principles at the national level. National agencies and institutions will be under a duty to apply the principles laid down in the Treaty and the norms made pursuant thereto. If they do not do so then an action can be brought. This will either be brought by way of the public law procedures, if the case is deemed to be of a type which demands the use of the application for judicial review;[77] or an ordinary action will be used.

In reading the materials in this book one should, moreover, be aware of the fact that Community law can have an impact in four different ways.

First, and most obviously, there are the instances in which EC law dictates the result in a particular area, and takes precedence over national law.

Secondly, there are those situations where the ECJ dictates a result which should be applied within the realm of Community law, but this has what might be termed a "spillover" effect for the resolution of analogous

---

[76] Wyatt and Dashwood's, *European Community Law* (3rd ed., 1993), p. 84.
[77] See below, Chap. 15.

210   ADMINISTRATIVE LAW

problems of a purely domestic character. For example, the acceptance by our courts that interim injunctive relief must be available against the Crown in the Community law context, operates as a catalyst for the rethinking of this issue within domestic law, in part at least because it looks, and is, odd for the remedy to be obtainable in the one context but not the other.

Thirdly, Community law acts as a spur for more general doctrinal development in our regime of public law. The fact that we are, for example, closer to developing a concept of proportionality as a ground for review is due, in no small measure, to the fact that it exists as such within Community law.

Finally, the existence of the Community has had the effect of bringing the public law systems of the differing European countries closer together. This is in part due to the fact that EC law itself draws its inspiration from the laws of the Member States. It is in part due also to the fact that the very existence of the Community has fostered a growing awareness of the mutual dependence of its component parts, and this has led to an increased interest in understanding the ways in which civilian and common law systems tackle the same problem.

6. A CASE STUDY: COMPETITION AND REGULATION

The institutions which are directly covered by administrative law have been considered in the previous chapters, and we have touched upon some of the more particular problems which surround these institutions. It is, however, helpful to consider the operation of the administrative process in more detail, and this chapter will be devoted to that task within the areas of competition policy and the regulation of market power. These areas are particularly well suited to such an analysis: they demonstrate how the choice of regulatory machinery has been affected by political considerations; they exemplify many of the procedural and substantive issues with which administrative law has to grapple; and they are areas which are of growing importance given the government's market-based approach to regulation.

Section 1. Competition: Whether to Regulate

Competition policy is in essence concerned with controlling and regulating firms within the market in order that they do not operate in such a way as to harm the competitive process. Central examples of such behaviour are cartels and monopolies. The former are agreements by rival companies to fix prices or divide the market between themselves with the consequence that fewer goods will be available to consumers at a higher price than if normal market conditions prevailed. Monopolies may require regulation because the market power possessed by a monopolist may enable that company to raise price and restrict output with the consequence that it can reap "abnormal" profits. The possession of monopoly power may also enable its holder to drive other firms from the market or prevent their initial entry.

The common law did exercise some control over these areas, but this was, by the end of the nineteenth century, almost wholly ineffectual in promoting competition. For example, the interpretation accorded to the restraint of trade doctrine meant that the preservation of competition was not to be the prime objective. Reluctance to interfere with a bargain even if the direct consequence was to injure the economic interest of another reached its high point in the case law on conspiracy. A price-fixing and market-allocation scheme, backed up by exclusionary tactics employed against those unwilling to submit, was held not to be an illegal conspiracy at common law.[1] The nineteenth century did, however, see some statutory regulation of monopoly power. Thus it was common for utility services to be regulated by the Board of Trade which would oversee the rates which could be charged.

---

[1] *Mogul S.S. Co. Ltd.* v. *McGregor Gow* [1892] A.C. 25; *Sorrell* v. *Smith* [1925] A.C. 700.

It was nonetheless to be some considerable time before Parliament attempted any more comprehensive control of market power.[2] The reasons for the absence of intervention were eclectic. Three may be mentioned here.

First, it was felt that there was in fact no urgent case for legislation dealing with market power.[3] Secondly, the First World War had fostered a climate of co-operation between firms which was regarded as beneficial.[4] Thirdly, the failure of post-war prosperity, the depression, business failure and unemployment, brought forth cries of "ruinous competition". This feeling that the market mechanism had failed, and that collusion was "good", was further fostered by the idea of rationalisation, one tenet of which was that large firms were more efficient and therefore should be encouraged.

The eventual passage of legislation after the Second World War owed its origins partly to a change in attitude towards competition, and partly to other governmental policies canvassed during this period. Thus, some within government began to feel that industry would have to become more efficient, and that cartels were an impediment to this development. This view was given added force by the White Paper on employment policy:[5] it was argued that the object of securing full employment could be jeopardised by monopoly power and cartels, both of which could lead to higher prices and restricted output, thereby hampering employment prospects.[6]

Section 2. Competition: Who Should Regulate

The first general, modern piece of legislation was passed in 1948, the Monopolies and Restrictive Practices (Inquiry and Control) Act. We have already seen in the previous chapters that the choice of regulatory institution, both its type and name, are often influenced as much by short-term political arguments as by any attempt to devise an optimum, rational administrative strategy. The choice of regulatory institutions for competition policy provides a perfect example of this. Four stages can be identified.

The initial allocation of regulatory power was to an agency, the Monopolies and Restrictive Practices Commission (MRPC). It was felt that a body outside of the normal departmental framework would be better suited to the investigatory nature of the work, and this institutional choice facilitated the involvement of non-civil servants who possessed specialist expertise. These are, as we have seen, both common reasons for establishing an agency.[7]

The second stage came in 1956. The Restrictive Trade Practices Act 1956 was passed to deal specifically with the problems of cartels, and the

---

[2] Some governmental initiatives occurred after the First World War, *e.g. Committee on Trusts*, Cmd. 9236 (1918).

[3] *Committee on Trade and Industry*, Cmd. 3282 (1929).

[4] Hannah, *The Rise of the Corporate Economy* (1976), pp. 32-33.

[5] Cmd. 6527 (1944).

[6] Allen, *Monopoly and Restrictive Practices* (1968), p. 62.

[7] See above, pp. 81-84.

Restrictive Practices Court (RPC) was established to adjudicate upon the area. The shift from a system of discretionary administration via an agency, to a judicial regime which purported to apply "black-letter" legal rules is particularly interesting. It was motivated principally because of industry's dissatisfaction with the operation of the MRPC. The selection of an industry for investigation was regarded as arbitrary, firms which appeared before the MRPC felt themselves to be on trial, and corporations said that they had little idea as to which types of behaviour were suspect. The legislators responded by enacting a statute framed in formalistic, legal terms, which purported to clarify the type of proscribed behaviour. A court was created to adjudicate upon the matter, as opposed to a court-substitute tribunal, because it was thought that such a body would gain the respect of industry more easily.

The third stage is characterised by the expansion of the functions of the Monopolies Commission. This body was retained to investigate issues concerning monopoly power after 1956. Its powers were augmented by two major legislative developments. The Monopolies and Mergers Act 1965 added merger regulation to its jurisdiction, and the body was henceforth to be called the Monopolies and Mergers Commission (MMC). The Competition Act 1980 has given the MMC power to investigate certain anti-competitive practices, which are defined in broad, open textured terms. In exercising its powers in relation to monopolies, mergers or anti-competitive practices, the MMC works with the Office of Fair Trading (OFT). It is the Director General of Fair Trading (DGFT) who will make[8] a monopoly reference to the MMC, or a reference concerning an anti-competitive practice.[9] Merger references are dealt with rather differently, and the DGFT will advise the Secretary of State as to whether a reference should be made to the MMC.[10] The OFT is itself an agency with responsibilities in the field of consumer protection as well as competition policy.[11]

The fourth stage in the choice of institutions to administer competition policy was the rejection of a composite, single authority which could oversee the area. The division between cartel policy, which is regulated by the OFT and the RPC, and the remainder of competition policy which is within the jurisdiction of the OFT and the MMC, has always been of doubtful validity. The inability of one authority to consider all anti-competitive aspects of a problem makes no sense given the underlying aims of competition policy. The division of authority has also produced a large volume of complex legislation dealing with these distinctive areas. The issue came to a head during the discussion which led to the Competition Act 1980. It was unclear whether this new area should be assigned to the MMC or the RPC, or whether there should be a new authority which would have jurisdiction over all areas of competition policy.[12] In the end the new powers were

---

[8] Fair Trading Act 1973, s.50. A government minister can also refer, s.51.
[9] Competition Act 1980, s.5.
[10] Fair Trading Act 1973, s.76.
[11] Ramsay, "The Office of Fair Trading: Policing the Consumer Market-Place", Baldwin and McCrudden, *Regulation and Public Law* (1987), Chap. 9.
[12] *Review of Restrictive Trade Practices Policy*, Cmnd. 7512 (1979).

assigned to the MMC, and plans for a single competition authority were not pursued. The reasons for rejecting this bolder option were not convincing,[13] and the result is the continuance of an administrative strategy which is over complex and outdated.

Section 3. Competition: How to Regulate

1. *Effectiveness and the Choice of the Legislative Criterion*

Any legal system which seeks to regulate competition will have to decide whether to frame its legislation in terms of legal form or economic effects. The essence of this choice is easily explained. Cartels can come in many shapes and forms. They can be agreements to fix price, divide the market, share information or boycott third parties; they can be contracts under which one party will accept a certain type of product, such as beer or petrol, only from a particular supplier, as in the case of contracts covered by the restraint of trade doctrine.[14]

An approach based upon legal form will attempt to set out in black-letter legal terms the types of agreement which it wishes to catch, and this has been the approach of the legislation upon cartels.[15] There are, however, two difficulties with this approach. One is that it was introduced, as we have seen, partly under pressure from industry which wished to have a more "certain" system than that which had preceded it. Legal form was intended to provide this. There are, however, certain key terms within any such legislation, such as whether activity "restricts" competition, which prove impossible to define purely "legally" without producing absurd results; an economic analysis is required. The other difficulty is that companies who are making agreements which they believe might fall foul of the legislation will not spell out their aims expressly. They will attempt to conceal the fact that they are dividing the market by, for example, an elaborate exchange of information about production. Legislation based on legal form encourages such "escape" devices.[16]

An approach based upon economic effects uses economic criteria to determine whether the legislation will "bite". Such legislation tends to be much shorter, and focuses upon the economic effects of an agreement irrespective of the way in which it is "dressed up" by the parties. This is the approach used in the EC and the United States, and it is exemplified by the Competition Act 1980 in this country.

---

[13] Craig, "The Monopolies and Mergers Commission: Competition and Administrative Rationality", Baldwin and McCrudden, above n. 11, Chap. 10. Later government reports are now more favourable to an effects based system: *Review of Restrictive Trade Practices Policy*, Cm. 331 (1988); *Opening Markets: New Policy on Restrictive Trade Practices*, Cm. 727 (1989).

[14] *e.g. Esso Petroleum Co. Ltd.* v. *Harper's Garage (Stourport) Ltd.* [1968] A.C. 269.

[15] Restrictive Trade Practices Act 1976.

[16] *e.g. Re Cadbury Schweppes Ltd. and J. Lyons & Co. Ltd.'s Agreement* [1975] 1 W.L.R. 1018. See generally, Whish, *Competition Law* (3rd ed., 1993), Chap. 5.

We have already seen that one of the issues of general concern when assessing regulatory agencies is their effectiveness. There is increasing consensus from those in the competition area that form-based legislation does not work;[17] and moreover that it is not sensible to base one part of the regulatory strategy upon a criterion of legal form, and another upon a test of economic effects. If the legislation is not enacted on the most appropriate criterion there is little hope that the regulatory scheme will be successful.

2. *Procedure and Procedural Rights*

The earlier discussion touched upon the choice between adversarial and inquisitorial procedures which an agency might adopt.[18] Competition policy provides an apt illustration of the usage of these differing approaches.

The procedure before the RPC is essentially adversarial. Cartels which are within the ambit of the legislation have to register, and the DGFT then has a duty to take proceedings before the RPC.[19] In the subsequent trial the RPC will hear arguments from the DGFT and the firms concerned as to whether the agreement should be allowed to stand because it is claimed to be beneficial to the public interest.[20]

The procedure before the MMC is more inquisitorial and investigative in nature. When the MMC receives a monopoly reference from the DGFT it will collect information concerning the industry. An oral hearing may be held to ascertain the facts. It will then consider the impact of the monopoly upon the public interest. The firms involved will be sent a "public interest letter", and they can make representations to the MMC about it. A public interest hearing will then be held at which the firms can present their arguments. It is clear that the MMC must comply with natural justice.[21] It is also clear that its procedure does not fit the traditional adversarial mould. The MMC does not sit as an "umpire" to hear the arguments from opposing sides. It carries out investigative work of its own, it possesses technical staff to assess financial evidence, it will have its own view as to what constitutes the public interest in a particular area, and it has considerable latitude in devising its own procedures.[22]

3. *Defining the Public Interest: Rule-making and Discretion*

The question of whether regulatory agencies should proceed through the application of rules/policy guidelines, or through the exercise of *ad hoc*

---

[17] Recent government reports show a remarkable change, now favouring an effects system: Review of Restrictive Trade Practices Policy, Cm. 331 (1988); *Opening Markets: New Policy on Restrictive Trade Practices*, Cm. 727 (1989).
[18] See above, pp. 152-153.
[19] Restrictive Trade Practices Act 1976, s.1(2)(c), subject to s.21.
[20] *Ibid.* ss.10, 19.
[21] *Hoffmann-La Roche & Co.* v. *Secretary of State for Trade and Industry* [1975] A.C. 295.
[22] Fair Trading Act 1973, s.81(2).

discretion is one which is of particular interest to administrative lawyers.[23] Competition policy provides an interesting example of this general problem. The legislation allows the MMC to take into account a wide variety of factors in determining the public interest including:[24] maintaining effective competition; promoting the interests of consumers; reducing costs; developing new products; maintaining the balanced distribution of industry and employment in the United Kingdom; and encouraging overseas competitiveness. This broad list would seem to dictate that the MMC should proceed by way of *ad hoc* discretion and this is indeed generally the case. It has, however, been argued that a more rule-based system should be applied in, for example, the area of mergers.

The essence of the argument can be conveyed quite simply.[25] Economic analysis might well indicate that mergers can produce welfare benefits in terms of economies of scale. These could in theory be balanced against the disadvantages which flow from having a larger firm as the result of the merger, which would then have more market power and therefore greater ability to raise price and restrict output. Such cost-benefit analysis is, however, extremely difficult and time-consuming, and the necessary data is often not available. It has been argued that the best approach is therefore to proceed by way of rules rather than through *ad hoc* discretion. A rule might, for example, prohibit all mergers leading to a market share in excess of 50 per cent.

The preceding argument is nevertheless based upon an important implicit premise. If the reduction of competition is regarded as the principal factor within the public interest analysis, then it might well be possible to devise rules accordingly. Where the range of factors felt to be of relevance is broader, then the problems of rule definition become more intractable. Thus, if the effects of a merger on unemployment, the balance of payments, regional policy and the like are felt to be of integral importance, then the possibility of formulating appropriate "rules" which take such factors into account, and yet still yield any real predictability of result is questionable.[26]

4. *Defining the Public Interest: Politics, Policy and Justiciability*

It is readily apparent that governments have differed on precisely the issue raised in the previous paragraph. They have had very different views as to the way in which the public interest "list" ought to be interpreted. These

---

[23] See below, pp. 391–400.

[24] Fair Trading Act 1973, s.84.

[25] Crew and Rowley, "Antitrust Policy: Economics versus Management Science" Moorgate and Wall Street, Autumn 1970; Howe, "Antitrust Policy: Rules or Discretionary Intervention" Moorgate and Wall Street, Spring 1971; Crew and Rowley, "Antitrust Policy: The Application of Rules" Moorgate and Wall Street, Autumn 1971.

[26] The 1969 and 1978 Merger Guidelines took a broad range of factors into account, but how much "guidance" they actually provided is debatable.

views can have a considerable impact upon the operation of the OFT and the MMC because the Secretary of State has power both in the initiation of references to the MMC, and at the remedial level. Two such views of the "public interest" can be contrasted.

The Labour party of the 1970s believed that, for example, merger policy should be based upon a relatively thorough consideration of the list of public interest factors mentioned in the legislation. The MMC should weigh the economic costs and benefits to competition, industrial efficiency, and the balance of payments, against the wider social costs and benefits to workers and consumers in each merger reference. Such an assessment had to be qualitative as well as quantitative, partly because of the difficulties of quantitative measurement, and partly to ensure that any benefits did not favour one particular interest group.

The Conservative party's attitude has, not surprisingly, differed. Their market-based philosophy has meant that they attach prime importance to competition within the public interest list. Other factors, such as the possible effects upon employment, are not regarded as the principal concerns of the OFT and MMC.[27] This approach has also favoured quicker investigative mechanisms in order to determine whether behaviour is in fact injurious to competition.[28]

It would be wrong to assume that the government can in a literal sense dictate to the MMC the type of view which it should adopt on the meaning of the "public interest". It would also be wrong to assume that the fact that the government does exercise some power in this respect is "wrong". The legislation upon competition is structured to leave discretion and ultimate control in the hands of the minister. Competition, like planning, is regarded as an area which cannot be completely divorced from political considerations, and one where some executive control is required. No conclusion can be reached about the effectiveness of a regulatory institution without some prior idea as to the purposes it should serve, and the purposes which competition policy should serve are crucially bound up with the political question concerning the meaning of the public interest. Indeed attempts to divorce such matters more thoroughly from the political arena have produced arguments that they are not readily justiciable. This has been a recurring theme in the operation of the RPC which has to consider whether a cartel should be exempted under one of a number of "gateways". These can be very broad. It can, for example, be argued that removal of the restrictive agreement would deny specific and substantial benefits to users of goods. It is doubtful whether a court is best suited to resolving such issues, and questionable whether they should be divorced from the political arena.[29]

---

[27] See, *Charter Consolidated Ltd., Anderson Strathclyde Ltd.* Cmnd. 8771 (1982); *R. v. Secretary of State for Trade, ex p. Anderson Strathclyde plc* [1983] 2 All E.R. 233.
[28] Competition Act 1980.
[29] *e.g.* Stevens and Yamey, *The Restrictive Practices Court* (1965); Hunter, *Competition and the Law* (1966).

5. *Enforcement*

If a regulatory strategy is to be successful then it must be enforced. The choice of enforcement mechanisms will often throw considerable light upon the regulatory regime itself, and this is certainly the case with competition policy. Two features characterise the enforcement process in this area: the emphasis upon negotiation, and upon public as opposed to private enforcement. These will be considered in turn.

Regulatory systems often have formal enforcement powers which mask a more informal process of negotiation between the parties. Competition policy places negotiation expressly at the forefront of its regulatory strategy. The DGFT is instructed to seek undertakings pursuant to an adverse report from the MMC under the Fair Trading Act 1973.[30] While under the Competition Act 1980, the whole emphasis is upon negotiation between the DGFT and the firm under investigation.[31] More formal powers exist should the negotiating strategy prove unsuccessful,[32] but they are regarded as a long stop. The importance given to the "negotiated solution" reflects the belief that this will be more effective than a formal legal sanction, and that the latter can be difficult to devise and enforce in this area.

Competition policy also evinces a strong preference for public as opposed to private enforcement. With few exceptions, the enforcement process is concentrated in the hands of the DGFT and the Secretary of State. Individuals have little role to play. They may serve as a catalyst for the initiation of an investigation, but they are not generally viewed as a separate means of enforcement in their own right. This stands in stark contrast to competition policy in, for example, the EC and the United States where private actions assume a far more prominent role.[33]

6. *Accountability and Control*

The general concern over the accountability and control of agencies has been considered above.[34] Two aspects of this general problem can be considered here: ministerial control and judicial control.

Ministerial control is evident at varying points within the system. The relevant minister possesses powers to initiate a reference to the MMC; such consent is necessary before any merger reference can take place at all; the minister can stop certain types of reference from being considered further; it is the minister who has the power to order formal sanctions where

---

[30] Fair Trading Act 1973, s.88.

[31] Competition Act 1980, ss.4, 8, 9, 10.

[32] *e.g.* Fair Trading Act 1973, ss.56, 73.

[33] Private enforcement and fines are both recommended in *Opening Markets: New Policy on Restrictive Trade Practices*, Cm. 727 (1989). Less change appears to be contemplated in relation to market power, *Abuse of Market Power*, Cm. 2100 (1992). See generally, Elzinga and Breit, *The Antitrust Penalties* (1976).

[34] See above, pp. 86-92.

negotiation has failed; and he or she can exert more general influence over the pattern of competition policy dependent upon the political party's interpretation of the public interest. How far such control is warranted is itself a contentious issue. The fact that decisions concerning the public interest may be felt to warrant some political oversight does not immunise particular ministerial decisions from criticism.

Judicial review has generally played a limited role in this area. This may seem surprising: given that companies have no continuing "client" relationship with the OFT and MMC, there would be no risk of upsetting future relations by seeking judicial review. The explanation lies principally in the broad discretion possessed by the OFT and the MMC both in the decision whether to investigate, and also in determining whether behaviour is in the public interest. There is, however, recent evidence of a greater willingness to challenge the actions of the MMC, OFT and the Secretary of State.[35] The best known example of this is one stage in the long running saga for the control of the House of Fraser, which has raised the important issue of the extent of the duty to give reasons under the competition legislation.[36]

7. The Importance of Competition Policy

The overall effectiveness of competition policy has become increasingly important as a result of the government's privatisation programme. The privatisation of utilities has led to the creation of new regulatory bodies to oversee such industries, as we have seen in the context of telecommunications. These new regulatory structures are, in general, run by a Director General, the Secretary of State and the MMC. Two important consequences flow from such developments.

First, the degree of prominence or importance given to the promotion of competition by the different Director Generals may well differ. They are given a duty framed in broad terms, which is then "guided" by a wide range of factors, including the promotion of consumer interests, effective competition, and the encouragement of research and development. The prominence which each Director General accords to the promotion of effective competition may therefore differ.

Secondly, the extra burdens which these legislative developments have placed upon the MMC means that there is an even greater need to ensure that the resources of the MMC are "properly" used. References have in the past been made to the MMC by the OFT which could, by no stretch of the imagination, be regarded as vital to the basic competitive structure of the industry concerned. If competition policy is to cope with the demands placed upon it by privatisation then a more sensitive use of the MMC may well be required.

---

[35] See, however, R. v. Monopolies and Mergers Commission, ex p. Elders IXL Ltd. [1987] 1 W.L.R. 1121; R. v. Monopolies and Mergers Commission, ex p. Mathew Brown plc [1987] 1 W.L.R. 1235.
[36] R. v. Secretary of State for Trade and Industry, ex p. Lonrho plc [1989] 1 W.L.R. 525.

Section 4. Market Power: Whether to Regulate

1. *The Basic Problem*

It is evident from the previous discussion that competition policy is itself concerned, *inter alia*, with the regulation of market power. Monopolies can infringe the rules on competition policy, and can be reprimanded accordingly under the relevant legislation. It is, however, also apparent from the earlier discussion on agencies that regulatory regimes can be established to control privatised firms which possess market power,[37] and that this type of regulatory control can subsist in addition to that provided under competition law. The rationale for this regulatory control which exists over and above that provided by competition law is as follows. When a firm possesses significant market power society may wish to regulate its behaviour to a greater extent than that which is practically possible under ordinary competition policy, particularly where there are barriers, natural or artificial, to the entry of new competitors. There may be a desire to regulate the detailed pricing policy of the monopolist and the terms on which it will deal with its customers; there may be concern over the way in which it can hinder new entry into the industry; and there may be fears over the quality of service provided by the dominant firm. As Breyer has stated,[38]

> "The most traditional and persistent rationale for governmental regulation of a firm's prices and profits is the existence of a 'natural monopoly'. Some industries, it is claimed, cannot efficiently support more than one firm. Electricity producers or local telephone companies find it progressively cheaper (up to a point) to supply extra units of electricity or telephone service. These 'economies of scale' are sufficiently great so that unit costs of service would rise significantly if more than one firm supplied service in a particular area. Rather than have three connecting phone companies laying separate cables where one would do, it may be more efficient to grant one firm a monopoly subject to governmental regulation of its prices and profits."

We have already seen that a monopolist will tend, left to itself, to set prices higher than those under normal competition, and also to restrict the amount which is produced. The objective of the regulator will therefore often be to set prices which are closer to those which would arise under more normal competitive conditions, in order to induce the firm to expand its output accordingly.[39] Two comments on the preceding analysis are relevant at this stage.

First, the validity of the traditional economic rationale for regulating such forms of monopoly power has been questioned.[40] Secondly, it should not be assumed that the privatised industries in the UK, such as British

---

[37] See above, pp. 101-105.
[38] Breyer, *Regulation and its Reform* (1982), p. 15.
[39] *Ibid.* p. 16.
[40] *Ibid.* pp. 16-19.

Telecom and Gas, were necessarily preserved as monopolies because of their potential for enhanced efficiency. When these public corporations were privatised it would have been possible to enhance competition by the "structural remedy" of breaking up, for example BT, rather than opting for the "regulatory remedy" which was chosen.[41] The preference for the latter appears to have had more to do with political strategy, than with alleged benefits of enhanced efficiency which might follow from the preservation of a monopoly. As Vickers and Yarrow state,[42]

> "The objective of promoting the well being of BT was favoured by those in Government wishing to maximise the proceeds from the sale of BT shares, their merchant bank advisers, and of course the management of BT. Especially in view of the Government's evident desire to privatise BT speedily, good relations with BT management were imperative, and they came to have considerable influence."

2. *Regulating Natural Monopoly: Aims and Objectives*

The above discussion has revealed why some form of regulation of natural monopoly has been felt to be necessary. But should we not be approaching the problem by breaking up the monopolies? If we choose not to do so what more specifically should the regulator be trying to do? How far should the regulator be attempting to enhance competition in other ways and what other objectives should be pursued? We will consider these issues in turn.

Let us begin with the argument that the monopolies should in fact be broken up, with a corresponding increase in competition. This is an option, but it is not always the most desirable one. Breaking up the monopoly may not in fact lead to greater efficiency for two reasons. On the one hand, the monopoly may possess economies of scale which would not be available to smaller units. On the other hand, it may be more efficient to organise a particular economic activity within one corporate unit rather than through a number of smaller firms.[43] Although it would be theoretically possible for all economic activity to be undertaken by individuals who contract with one another, this may not be efficient because the individuals may not have the knowledge through which to make the rational calculation as to the best course of action in all circumstances. As Foster notes,[44]

> "It is because of lack of information and bounded rationality – that is an inability to weigh all factors relevant to making a rational decision between all feasible alternatives – that firms develop as alternative ways of completing a set of transactions."

---

[41] Vickers and Yarrow, *Privatisation, An Economic Analysis* (1988), p. 121.

[42] *Ibid.* pp. 235-236.

[43] Williamson, *Markets and Hierarchies* (1975).

[44] *Privatisation, Public Ownership and the Regulation of Natural Monopoly* (1992), p. 147.

It is not therefore surprising that when a firm is experiencing difficulties in devising satisfactory contracts it may well take on the activity itself.[45] The reverse side of the same coin is the problem encountered if the monopoly is broken up: how far can the transactions which were previously internalised be undertaken "contractually between the divorced parties"?[46]

If the break-up of a monopoly is not always the most desirable solution what then should the regulator be trying to do when regulating the firm? Some economists would argue that regulation is in fact unnecessary even in the absence of competition: they contend that natural monopolies can be kept efficient by ensuring that there is free entry into the particular market, with the corollary either that there should be no licensing conditions at all, or that any firm which satisfies those conditions should be able to obtain such a licence. Others disagree. They believe that regulation of such markets is both necessary and desirable in order to attain a number of objectives. These include: the prevention of predatory behaviour by the monopolist which, in essence, is behaviour designed to drive would-be competitors out of the market in order to preserve the monopolist's power; the monitoring of prices charged by the monopolistic undertaking in order to prevent it reaping excess monopoly profits; the detection of organisational inefficiency which can be attendant upon firms which possess monopoly power; and the fostering of competition by allowing other firms to use the distribution network of the monopolist, or what is often known as competition through interconnection.[47] These rationales for regulatory intervention have been the subject of vigorous debate between economists,[48] but the existence of regulatory regimes to oversee the privatised industries is some evidence that the government in the UK has accepted some of these arguments.

Section 5. Market Power: Who Should Regulate

The choice of "regulator" for market power has undergone a number of transformations over the last two hundred years. Five differing institutions have undertaken the regulatory mantle.

1. *The Common Law and the Courts*

The common law has exercised considerable influence over corporations which possess monopoly power. Two areas are of principal interest, one of which is well known, the other almost completely unknown.

---

[45] *Ibid.* p. 148.
[46] *Ibid.* p. 150.
[47] Foster, *Privatisation*, pp. 1-13 and Chap. 5.
[48] *e.g.* there is considerable disagreement as to whether predation is in reality a problem at all, and as to whether the difficulties of defining it render regulatory cure worse than the disease. Compare, Bork, *The Antitrust Paradox* (1978), Chap. 7, with Foster, *Privatisation*, pp. 163-167.

The area which is relatively well publicised is the law of monopolies *stricto sensu*. Somewhat paradoxically this was the less important of the two areas in which the common law courts exercised control over market power. Such control was indeed used, but the leading cases had as much to do with other issues, as they did with the regulation of market power for the adverse economic effects which it could have. Thus in *Darcy* v. *Allen*[49] it was held that a royal grant of a patent to manufacture and import playing cards was void if it created a monopoly. Two main themes pervade the court's judgment: the desire to protect the right to work which would be weakened should the patent be allowed to stand, and the desire not to allow the Crown prerogative powers of this novel form. It would therefore be mistaken to allow such classic cases on the law of monopolies to create the impression that the common law courts were zealous in their control of market power *per se*. Nor should one believe that the right to work precluded the existence of any monopoly power. As Letwin states,[50]

> "The common-law right to work was predicated on an economic system that would protect the established trades from competition, whether from foreign workmen, improperly qualified English workmen, overly aggressive guilds, or domestic monopolists. The right to work was protected by giving each guild a monopoly, and Darcy's grant was condemned not because it was a monopoly and therefore necessarily bad, but because it was a bad monopoly."

The other area in which the common law courts exercised influence is, as stated, much less well known. It has indeed been almost forgotten, but it was and is of considerable importance. The courts held that the common law imposed an obligation on those who had market power to charge no more than a reasonable price for their goods. The courts in effect were imposing a common law based species of price regulation on those who wielded monopoly power. Not only did they take this step, but they reasoned through the rationale for doing so from first principles.

In *Allnutt* v. *Inglis*[51] the question arose as to whether the London Dock Company, which by licence from Parliament possessed a monopoly to receive certain wines, could lawfully exclude from the docks a cargo owner who had refused to pay their schedule of charges. Lord Ellenborough reasoned as follows.[52] While a man could fix his own price for the use of his property, he could not do so where the public have a right to resort to the premises and to make use of them. Where a person had the benefit of a monopoly this entailed a correlative responsibility, the consequence of which was that he could charge no more than a reasonable price for the service offered. The monopoly itself could be either "legal" or "factual": it could result from the grant of an exclusive licence from Parliament, or it

---

[49] (1602) 11 Co. Rep. 84, (*The Case of Monopolies*).

[50] Letwin, *Law and Economic Policy in America: The Evolution of the Sherman Antitrust Act* (1965), pp. 28-29. The court in *Darcy* v. *Allen* does, however, take note of the potential for monopoly power to lead to price increases.

[51] (1810) 12 East 527.

[52] *Ibid*. pp. 538-539. See also, *Bolt* v. *Stennett* (1800) 8 T.R. 606.

could exist because, on the facts, the provider of the service controlled the entirety of the space available for the warehousing of the goods. The statute which required that the goods be warehoused in the Dock Company's premises was not passed solely for the benefit of the Company, but also for the benefit of trade and the public. The latter two purposes could be defeated if the Dock Company was at liberty to charge any price which it chose.

Similar reasoning is evident in other areas where monopoly power existed. In *Corporation of Stamford* v. *Pawlett*[53] the corporation possessed the right to hold two fairs each year. It customarily received a "toll" of 2d on the sale of certain items at the fair. The defendant refused to pay the toll. The court held that where the word "toll" was found in a charter it should be taken to mean reasonable toll. It was not open to the King to allow a corporation to charge an unreasonable toll, and any such excess charge could be recovered in a legal action. The principle underlying such cases is the same as that expounded above: the grantee of rights to a market or fair becomes the holder of an exclusive privilege. The grant was not merely for his own benefit but for the benefit of the public and the trade. It could be defeated if any price whatsoever could be charged.[54]

The reasoning in the above areas receives further support from that which has been used in the context of common callings. There is abundant authority for the proposition that those who exercise a common calling can charge only a reasonable price for their services.[55] The history of common callings is complex and cannot be fully developed here. The relevance of the courts' jurisprudence in this area can, however, be conveyed at a general level. The origin of the term common calling was simply one that was available to the public generally, "a holding out". There could therefore be common carriers, common innkeepers, and common millers. Those who exercised a common calling had a duty to serve at a reasonable price. Historically this obligation appears to have evolved due to economic and social conditions. In times of social hardship, such as the period following the Black Death, it could be possible for surviving tradesmen to exact "any price they pleased".[56] The obligation to serve at reasonable rates was intended to counteract this potential for abuse of market power. As the law developed the types of industry which retained the label "common" tended to be those which possessed a monopoly character such as railways and public utilities.

---

[53] (1830) 1 C. & J. 57, 400.
[54] See also, *Gard* v. *Callard* (1817) 6 M. & S. 69; *Wright* v. *Bruister* (1832) 4 B. & Ald. 116; *Att. Gen.* v. *Horner* (1912) 107 L.T. 547; *Duke of Newcastle* v. *Worksop Urban District Council* [1902] 2 Ch. 145, 161; *Nyali* v. *Att. Gen.* [1955] 1 All E.R. 646, 651, [1956] 2 All E.R. 689, 694; McAllister, "Lord Hale and Business Affected with a Public Interest" Harv.L.R.Rev. 759 (1929-30); Craig, "Constitutions, Property and Regulation" [1991] P.L. 538.
[55] *Harris* v. *Packwood* (1810) 3 Taunt 263; *Thompson* v. *Lacy* (1820) 3 B. & Ald. 283; *Ashmole* v. *Wainwright* (1842) 2 Q.B. 837, 845; *Peek* v. *North Staffs. Ry. Co.* (1862) 11 H.L.C. 473; *Great Western Railway* v. *Sutton* (1869) L.R. 4 H.L. 226, 237-238.
[56] Arterburn "The Origin and First Test of Public Callings" 75 Univ. of Penn. L.Rev. 411, 421 (1926-27).

It would therefore be mistaken to regard the common law as having had no regulatory role within this area. There is moreover a link between common law regulation by the courts and departmental regulation: the two formed an intersecting web as will be apparent from the subsequent discussion.

2. *Departmental Regulation*

The pattern of administrative development within the nineteenth century has already been reviewed and one aspect is of particular relevance here.[57] Many administrative functions during this period were undertaken by neither central nor local government. They were often performed by corporations who were given special statutory authority insofar as this was necessary in order to enable them to carry out their tasks. The provision of most utilities, such as water and lighting, as well as the operation of canals, railways and roads, was carried on by these means even after the reform of the municipal corporations. Moreover such bodies normally possessed a large degree of market power. A considerable amount of time was spent in the Commons on the legislation which would empower the statutory undertakings to perform these tasks. For example, in 1844 there were 248 Railway Bills which necessitated a system of Commons' committees in order to oversee their passage. It also led to the introduction of certain "Model Bills" concerned with issues such as the compulsory purchase of land, and railway development, which were intended to ensure greater uniformity in the types of measures which emerged.[58] The growing need to pave roads in order to render them suitable for increased use by heavier wheeled traffic was the motivation behind the turnpike trusts, and by 1830 there were 1,100 in existence.[59] Once again each such turnpike trust derived its power from a local Act of Parliament, subject to supervision pursuant to more general Turnpike Acts. The provision of municipal lighting and cleansing was often undertaken by Improvement Commissioners, who also derived their authority from a local Act of Parliament.

The rates to be charged for services by those who possessed a degree of monopoly power granted to them by statute had to be regulated. One common technique was for direct departmental supervision of the "tariff" which the statutory undertaking proposed to charge. This was used in, for example, the areas of roads and canals. The relevant trustees or commissioners would forward to the Board of Trade a detailed list of the prices which they intended to levy, specifying, for example, that the toll to be charged for a wagon of certain size and weight which journeyed from Oxford to Woodstock would be xd. The Board of Trade would have to approve such charges before they could be lawfully levied. Direct departmental price regulation of areas in which there was market power was, therefore, quite common.

---

[57] Chap. 2.
[58] Chester, *The English Administrative System 1780-1870* (1981), pp. 118-119.
[59] *Ibid.* p. 326.

We can now understand the link between common law and departmental price regulation. The former was utilised particularly in those circumstances where direct departmental price regulation was absent. This could be for one of two reasons: either the area might be one over which no such departmental supervision had yet been established; or it might be an area where the type of supervision exercised by the department was difficult to operate. This latter point requires explanation. Departmental supervision normally operated through scrutiny of a relatively fixed series of possible charges: so much per mile, per weight, etc. There could be areas in which this type of advance delineation of charges might not be possible, principally because the area was one in which the range of subject-matter, and the variables which could affect the price thereof, were more complex. It was such areas in which the common law proscription that "unreasonable charges" should not be levied remained of particular relevance.[60]

3. *Regulation by Tribunal or Board*

The importance of Boards within the nineteenth-century administrative landscape has been considered above.[61] They provided a further institutional technique through which to regulate entrepreneurial behaviour. Railway regulation within the last century can be examined by way of a brief example.[62]

Prior to 1840 the main regulatory body was the Railway Commission. Although its formal powers were limited it did possess the authority to certify that a railway was "complete" before it could commence operations. It could attach conditions to its certificate, and was quite willing to use this as a mechanism for requiring minimum standards of service on the part of the railways. Failure to abide by the conditions of the certificate led to its revocation, and the commission published criteria by which applications would be judged.[63] From the 1840s significant responsibility was transferred to the railway department of the Board of Trade.[64] The department however suffered a political set-back in 1844-1845 and this, combined with

---

[60] The common law insistence upon the reasonableness of prices charged by public utilities has been of particular importance in the US, see McCurdy, "The Power of a Public Utility to Fix Its Rates in the Absence of Regulatory Legislation" 38 Harv. L. Rev. 202 (1924-25); *Smyth* v. *Ames* 169 U.S. 466 (1898); *Texas & Pacific Ry.* v. *Abilene Cotton Oil Co.* 204 U.S. 426 (1906). The common law authorities were also of seminal importance in determining the constitutionality of later attempts at statutory regulation of price, *Munn* v. *Illinois* 94 U.S. 113 (1877). See, Finkelstein, "From *Munn* v. *Illinois* to *Tyson* v. *Banton*, A Study in the Judicial Process" 27 Col. L. Rev. 769 (1927).

[61] Chap. 2.

[62] Parris, *Government and the Railways in Nineteenth Century Britain* (1965); Foster, *Privatisation, Public Ownership and the Regulation of Natural Monopoly* (1992), Chaps. 1, 2.

[63] Arthurs, '*Without the Law,*' *Administrative Justice and Legal Pluralism in Nineteenth Century England* (1985), pp. 120, 124.

[64] Railways Regulation Act 1840.

concern over railway speculation, led to the establishment of an independent Railway Commission in 1846.[65] This body was to be short-lived: the
railway boom collapsed, the Commission was dissolved and its powers
reassigned to the Board of Trade.

Experimentation with differing institutional devices to regulate railways
continued in the 1850s with the assignment of responsibility to the common
law courts, where "it languished for almost twenty years, hostage to the
notion that all adjudication is properly the business of the courts".[66] A
further turn of the institutional wheel occurred in 1873. A new Railway and
Canal Commission was established with a range of activities including the
fixing of tolls, fares and routes. The Commission was also meant to ensure
that the public could use the facilities with as much ease as was possible.[67]
The Commissioners had power to inspect property, require the production
of documents and the giving of testimony, and could use assessors who
had technical knowledge.[68] Notwithstanding these powers the Commission
established in 1873 was not deemed to be a noted success, with one critic
observing that it had "the power enough to annoy the railroads, and not
power enough to help the public efficiently".[69] A new Railway and Canal
Commission was set up in 1888, and although it enjoyed some early
success, it, like its predecessors, turned out to be an ineffective regulatory
mechanism. Control over the rates charged by railways was assigned to the
Railway Rates Tribunal in 1921, and in 1947 the railways were nationalised.

4. *Public Ownership*

The nationalisation of the railways provides a suitable point of transition
to the option of public ownership. Earlier discussion has revealed how the
choice of regulatory institution has been influenced by the political credo of
those who operate the system. This has been evident at varying points in the
preceding analysis. The very demise of the board system was caused by the
growing insistence that there should be a member of the executive directly
answerable in the Commons for major spheres of administrative activity.[70]
Certain of the changes in the institutions which were to regulate the
railways were motivated by the wish for more direct legislative control.

The shift towards public ownership provides a further exemplification of
this theme. While the reasons for nationalisation were eclectic,[71] one
prominent rationale was the sense that major repositories of market power
should be within state ownership in order that excess profits should not be
left in private hands, and in order to ensure that the industry operated in

---

[65] Commissioners of Railways Act 1846.
[66] Arthurs, *'Without the Law'*, p. 126.
[67] Regulation of Railways Act 1873.
[68] Arthurs, *'Without the Law'*, p. 128.
[69] *Ibid.* p. 129.
[70] See above, pp. 46-48.
[71] See above, pp. 99-101.

the public interest. The general difficulties which have beset the nationalised industries have been considered above.[72] What is particularly relevant at this juncture is the fact that public ownership of a firm which possesses market power does not, in and of itself, mean that the firm will necessarily be operated in such a way as to further the public interest.[73] The force of this point can be conveyed by considering certain aspects of the gas industry prior to privatisation.

The industry was nationalised by the Gas Act 1948, and there were 12 area boards which were largely autonomous as regards the manufacture and supply of gas. Operations were later centralised[74] with a single public corporation assuming responsibility for the activities covered by the 12 area boards. As Vickers and Yarrow state,[75]

"By the 1970s the policy framework for the industry had been brought into line with that pertaining in telecommunications and electricity generation: there was a single national firm, protected from competition by statutory entry barriers and regulated by a department of central government. The underlying rationale for this approach was the familiar argument that the core activities of gas transmission and distribution constituted a natural monopoly, and that the operation of more than one firm in the market would therefore lead to cost inefficiencies. To protect consumers from the effects of the resulting market power, it was considered desirable that the industry should be publicly owned and controlled."

The transfer of the industry to public ownership and control did not, however, necessarily serve to ensure that the consumers really were protected. Two important aspects of the operation of the British Gas Corporation were open to serious question.

First, British Gas was granted sole rights to purchase gas from other producers thereof. The ostensible reason for this was in order to prevent the accumulation of excessive profits by such producers, but it is highly questionable whether the award of this privileged position to British Gas was the optimum method of achieving this goal.[76] Secondly, research indicates that British Gas were in fact selling their product at too low a price.[77] Consumers can be harmed by paying too little as well as by being overcharged. If the former occurs the product is rendered "artificially" attractive as compared with other possible fuels. Too much is consumed at the inaccurate low price, with the consequence that resources within society are allocated inefficiently. Irrespective therefore of the problems caused by *ad hoc* governmental interference with public corporations, the retention of ownership in public hands did not always lead to the accrual of public benefit.

---

[72] See above, *loc. cit.*
[73] Foster, *Privatisation*, Chap. 3.
[74] Gas Act 1972.
[75] *Privatisation*, p. 255.
[76] This statutory privilege was terminated by the Oil and Gas (Enterprise) Act 1982.
[77] Vickers and Yarrow, *Privatisation*, pp. 256-257.

5. *Privatisation and Agencies*

If the move towards public ownership was motivated by the political beliefs of those who advocated this step, the shift away from nationalisation and towards privatisation has been equally prompted by the political beliefs of its protagonists. The general reasons for this shift have been considered above, as have some of the difficulties which face the regulatory organisations which must now oversee the monopolistic power wielded by the newly privatised corporations.[78] The decision as to "who" should regulate the use of market power has therefore, for the present, come down firmly in favour of using such agencies to control the firms which possess this monopolistic capacity. In a sense this strategy bears some analogy to the regimes which existed in the nineteenth century where a private firm with market power would be regulated by a commission or board.[79] Experience from this period also indicates that the efficacy of such regulatory devices will depend crucially both on the degree of market power wielded by the private firm, and the range of regulatory powers actually granted to the board or commission. These two factors will be central to the analysis which follows. This will be concerned with "how" market power is controlled under the present regime of privatised industry plus regulatory agency. This discussion will bring out the difficulties which beset the new programme, and will reveal the implications which this has for public law.

Section 6. Market Power: How to Regulate

1. *Selling State Assets: Constitutional Implications*

The privatisation programme entailed the sale of assets which had previously been within public ownership in the form of nationalised industries.[80] This is a trite proposition, but one which nonetheless has important implications which have been barely examined by public lawyers. The fact that the assets were public raises a legitimate public interest in seeing that they were disposed of on beneficial economic terms; or at the very least that the public coffers did not end up being under compensated on the sale of public property.

The government has employed two main methods for the sale of public assets, offers for sale and tender offers. The former involves offering shares to the public at a price which is fixed in advance of the sale; the latter entails inviting bids at or above a stated minimum price, with the final price being established once all the bids have been received. Offers for sale have

---

[78] See above, pp. 101-105.
[79] See above, pp. 46-50.
[80] See Daintith and Sah, "Privatisation and the Economic Neutrality of the Constitution" [1993] P.L. 465, for a discussion of constitutional constraints relevant to privatisation in a range of countries.

been used more widely than tender offers, largely because they were simpler to operate. The latter are, however, probably more accurate economically, since they do not require a precise estimate of the value of the firm to be made prior to the sale itself. This is advantageous because most assets which have been sold to the public have not had a previously quoted value. Given that this is so there has been a relative scarcity of information on which to base estimates of value. The tender offer procedure which "permits the market to establish the valuation therefore has substantial appeal".[81]

Whether the proceeds from the sales would have been significantly improved by greater reliance on tender offers may be debatable. However, few would argue that the public coffers received the real value of the assets sold. As Mayer and Meadowcroft state,[82]

"Whatever one's views about the desirability of a programme of privatisation, considerable concern must be felt about the techniques that have been employed in implementing the programme to date. As set out at the beginning of this article there are three primary considerations that may have influenced the form of the asset sales: extent of ownership, costs of sale, and disruption to markets. Certainly on the first two there is little evidence that objectives have been met: costs have been high, primarily as a consequence of underpricing of assets, and large personal shareholdings have only been maintained for very short periods. Furthermore, there would appear to be a simple way of avoiding high costs by staggering sales, which would also diminish financing disruptions to equity markets."

Now it might well be felt that this undervaluation of state assets was "unfortunate", but in what way can it be said to have constitutional or legal implications? The very form of this question bears testimony both to the way in which we think in "pigeon holes" and also to the limited nature of our constitutional constructs. These two connected issues are best addressed separately.

First, the question is indicative of the way in which we categorise legal issues. Let us imagine the converse type of situation in which the state is nationalising assets held by private individuals. If those assets were "forcibly" acquired at a value significantly less than that determined by the market, lawyers would immediately be aware of the appropriate legal rhetoric to employ. There would be talk of interference with private rights, expropriation without proper compensation and infringement of private autonomy. Whether an effective legal remedy could be provided would of course depend upon the form of the governmental action: the sovereignty of Parliament would serve to protect such governmental action if it was enshrined in a statute. Lawyers would nonetheless know the relevant legal discourse to utilise.

---

[81] Mayer and Meadowcroft, "Selling Public Assets: Techniques and Financial Implications", *Privatisation and Regulation – the UK Experience* (Kay, Mayer and Thompson eds., 1986), p. 325.
[82] *Ibid.* p. 339.

The situation in which the state decides to sell public property, and does so at a price which is too low, prompts no such automatic legal response. No conception of "public property rights" comes readily to hand. The distinctive manner in which we respond to these similar situations is an exemplification of the thesis advanced by Daintith concerning the exercise of dominium powers.[83] The legal response to situations in which the government can be said to "own" something, whether money or other assets, is far more muted than it is to situations where the government operates so as to command others to do something with property etc. of their own. In the former situation the government is implicitly treated like a private individual and can dispose of "its" property on the terms which it thinks best. If the bargain is bad so be it.

Secondly, the very fact that we draw a "legal blank" in the situation where the government undervalues state assets which are being sold is reflective of the limited nature of the constitutional concepts with which we operate. It is abundantly clear that such concepts can be utilised in the context of privatisation, as experience from France indicates. The Conseil Constitutionnel has applied constitutional provisions to the sale of state holdings. While it held that the basic law on privatisation did not infringe the Constitution it attached a number of important conditions to the privatisation process. As Prosser states,[84]

> "A central issue was the pricing of the enterprises to be privatised. The deputies had argued that it would be unconstitutional to sell enterprises below their true value as this would breach constitutional principles of equality and would give vendors an unfair advantage; indeed it was argued that the obligation to sell by 1991 could have precisely this effect, and could also lead to transfers to foreigners threatening national independence. The Conseil accepted that both the Constitutional principle of equality and the protection for rights of property in the Declaration of the Rights of Man prohibited the sale of public goods to private parties at a price below their value; these principles applied to the property of the state as well as to that of private individuals."

The French government in fact anticipated this response of the court and proposed that an independent body of experts should undertake the valuation work. A Privatisation Commission was established which values the assets to be sold. The actual price for sale is established by the minister, but it must not be below that recommended by the Commission.[85]

The absence of a written constitution, combined with the mode of thinking which regards public assets as property of the government which can be disposed of as if it were an ordinary private sale, renders it difficult to reach the same conclusion in this country. There are, however, threads

---

[83] "Legal Analysis of Economic Policy" (1982) 9 Jnl. Law & Soc. 191. See below, 697-698.
[84] *The Privatisation of Public Enterprises in France and Great Britain, The State, Constitutions and Public Policy*, EUI Working Paper No. 88/364 (1988), p. 37. See more generally, Graham and Prosser, *Privatising Public Enterprises, Constitutions, the State and Regulation in Comparative Perspective* (1991).
[85] *Ibid.* pp. 38-39.

of legal reasoning which point in a more interventionist direction. Thus the courts have, for example, held that local authorities owe a fiduciary duty towards their ratepayers in the way in which they manage local funds.[86] The application of this concept has been criticised. However if such a concept does exist it is difficult on principle to see why an analogous idea should not apply to central government's duties towards taxpayers. A sensible and sensitive use of such a concept could provide the basis for the development of public property rights which are better suited to the needs of the age.

2. *The Regulatory Regime: Legal Powers and Legal Constraints*

The law both empowers and constrains. This, like the proposition which began the previous section, is trite. It is also important, and particularly so in the context of new regulatory mechanisms. The success of any regulatory machinery will be crucially dependent upon the degree of monopoly power which still resides with the privatised firm and the type of powers accorded to the regulator. Other things being equal, the greater the degree of monopoly power statutorily preserved to the privatised company, the more necessary it is for the regulator to have effective supervisory powers since the firm will be relatively immune from the discipline of the market.

The legal structure within which the firm is privatised will therefore be of considerable importance. The legal rules will both empower and constrain the privatised corporation, and will also empower and constrain the regulatory agency. The effectiveness of the new scheme will be crucially dependent upon these respective powers. This is evident from the earlier discussion of the telecommunications industry,[87] but it can be demonstrated in more detail by considering the privatisation of the gas industry.

Historically the major activities of the gas industry have been as follows:[88] the production of natural gas, which was mostly from off-shore fields; transmissions of the gas to landing points; transmission of the gas to regional take-off points; local distribution of gas to customers' premises; the sale of gas; the sale and installation of gas appliances. Prior to privatisation the British Gas Corporation had a monopoly in the third, fourth and fifth of these tasks, and also enjoyed a statutory exclusive right to buy gas produced by other companies.

The industry was fully privatised by the Gas Act 1986, the principal provisions of which are as follows. Section 1 empowers the Secretary of State to appoint the Director General of Gas Supply, who will then appoint the staff of the Office of Gas Supply (Ofgas). The Gas Consumers' Council which is a watch-dog body for consumers is established by section 2. British Gas's monopoly privilege in relation to the supply of gas through pipes is abolished by section 3, and this opens the possibility for alternative

---

[86] See below, pp. 435-438.
[87] See above, pp. 101-105.
[88] Vickers and Yarrow, *Privatisation*, p. 248.

suppliers to sell their product to customers. Section 4 establishes guidelines for the DGGS and the Secretary of State in pursuit of their functions. These include: protecting the interests of consumers in relation to the prices charged and the other terms of supply; promoting efficiency by gas suppliers and users; preventing dangers which can arise from gas transmission; and enabling persons to compete effectively in the supply of gas which, in relation to any premises, exceeds 25,000 therms a year. Sections 7 and 8 must be read together. Section 7 empowers the Secretary of State to authorise a "public gas supplier" to supply the product to any premises within a designated area, but section 7(9) precludes such an authorisation in any area which is within 25 yards from the main of another public gas supplier. Given that British Gas is an authorised public gas supplier, this has the effect of preventing a new gas supplier from emerging to challenge British Gas in the ordinary domestic sales market. Section 8 does, however, allow the Secretary of State to authorise other persons to supply gas where, *inter alia*, the supply is expected to exceed 25,000 therms per annum. The effect of this is to allow competition in the provision of gas to large commercial customers. Subsequent legislation has now empowered the Secretary of State to modify or remove the 25,000 therm condition.[89] Section 19 empowers the DGGS to grant an applicant the right to use a pipeline owned by a public gas supplier.

The legal powers and constraints which the legislation applies to British Gas and the DGGS leave one in little doubt that the former has emerged in a strong position as a result of the original legislation. That this is so can be understood by reflecting on the respective powers and duties which each possesses. British Gas has been empowered in three important ways by the 1986 legislation.

First, the law sanctified the continued existence of British Gas as a single corporation post privatisation. The assets of the previously nationalised industry were transferred to a successor corporation.[90] The possibility of restructuring the industry prior to privatisation was therefore not pursued. Such a course would have been perfectly feasible, and could have been achieved by the creation of 12 separate regional gas companies together with an enterprise which would operate the transmission system.[91] Given that one of the major aims of privatisation has been said to be enhanced efficiency, such a restructuring would have increased the element of competition within the system. It would more particularly have had the following advantages.[92] It would have lowered the barriers to entry and facilitated the task of other producers of gas who wished to become direct sellers of gas to, for example, large industrial concerns; it would have reduced the exclusive purchasing power of British Gas since each of the regional companies would have had to compete in the purchase of supplies from other gas producers; and it would have improved the regulatory

---

[89] Competition and Service (Utilities) Act 1992, s. 37.
[90] Gas Act 1986, ss. 49-61.
[91] Hammond, Helm and Thompson, "British Gas: Options for Privatisation" (1985) 6(4) Fiscal Studies 1.
[92] Vickers and Yarrow, *Privatisation*, pp. 268 – 269.

control for, although each distribution company would still have monopoly power within its own region, Ofgas "would have been able to draw on information from several independent sources, opening up the possibility of yardstick competition".[93]

The failure to pursue such a policy of regionalisation despite the competitive advantages of doing so appears to have been the result of various intersecting political factors:[94] a restructuring of the industry would have slowed down the privatisation process with the consequence that the receipts from the sale would have accrued to the revenue authorities at a date which was less advantageous to the government, given its concerns over the public sector borrowing targets; the management of the British Gas Corporation were hostile to any such restructuring; and short term gas prices might have increased to the consumer, which was disadvantageous in electoral terms, even though restructuring the industry and installing greater competition would have yielded greater medium and long term efficiency. The decision not to reorganise the industry has been termed a response to interest group pressure from management and consumers in which short term electoral considerations assumed precedence over longer term considerations of economic efficiency.[95] There is no doubt that this decision has coloured the whole privatisation process within this area, and that the dominance of the privatised corporation has been augmented by the other legal powers which it has been accorded. It is to these that we should now turn.

Secondly, the original legal regime established by the Gas Act 1986 also served to insulate the dominant privatised firm from new competitors. As noted above, section 7(9) effectively precluded new entrants into the market for the domestic sale of gas, although, as seen, later legislation has modified this. There are, moreover, significant difficulties to be faced by the new entrant who attempts to supply to the larger industrial concerns. British Gas has access to low price gas and can probably undercut potential new entrants, or even engage in disguised "predatory pricing" to deter any such new competitor. Furthermore, control over the pipeline network provided British Gas with certain tactical advantages over new entrants who must negotiate for the transfer of their gas, "thus providing the incumbent with advance notice of its rival's intentions and giving the former time to offer more favourable terms to the targeted customer".[96] This was all the more important given that the proscriptions in the legislation on giving undue preference to any person do not it seems apply to sales to industrial concerns; British Gas could therefore price as it chose in relation to these concerns.[97]

---

[93] Ibid. p. 269
[94] Ibid. pp. 270-271.
[95] Ibid. p. 271.
[96] Ibid. p. 275.
[97] The obligation not to show undue preference is contained in Gas Act 1986, s.9(2), but only applies to the supply of gas "to persons entitled to a supply". The effect of s.10(5) is that a public gas supplier is under no obligation as such to supply gas to any premises in excess of 25,000 therms per year, which effectively removes the force of s.9(2) from sales to major gas users such as large industry. The only limit on this freedom would be the general provisions of competition law.

Thirdly, given that the privatised industry was not restructured, and given the difficulties faced by new entrants into the industry, the pricing formula for gas supplies to tariff customers[98] becomes of particular importance. The details of the formula are complex and cannot be examined here, but one detailed study has concluded that the "pricing constraints imposed on British Gas can hardly be described as stringent".[99]

The powers given to the DGGS and to Ofgas are not strong when juxtaposed to those possessed by British Gas. The DGGS can impose conditions upon the grant of authorisation to a public gas supplier;[100] these conditions can then be modified either by agreement with the supplier,[101] or the DGGS can make a reference to the Monopolies and Mergers Commission which can specify the ways in which modification of the authorisation can remedy any possible harmful effects on the public interest which are being caused by the gas supplier.[102] The DGGS also has power to secure compliance with the authorisation conditions,[103] and to investigate complaints made to him by the Gas Consumers' Council and certain interested parties.[104] He must keep under review the general provision of gas supplies and can publish information and advice to customers.[105] Moreover, as has been seen, the DGGS must exercise his functions in the manner best calculated to advance the interests mentioned in section 4.

Notwithstanding this array of legal powers the original regulatory mechanism is relatively weak for the following reasons. Firstly, the DGGS cannot alter the legal structure of the 1986 Act itself and this places British Gas in a strong monopolistic position which, for the reasons given above, it is difficult for competitors to assail. Secondly, an important factor in determining the effectiveness of the DGGS is the degree of access to information concerning costs etc. from British Gas. The DGGS does have statutory power to require information,[106] but the provisions of the authorisation granted to British Gas concerning its accounting do not place the DGGS in a strong position. The company has to prepare separate accounts for its gas supply business, but this is defined very broadly and covers the bulk of its activities. It will therefore "be difficult to assess whether or not British Gas is willing to make its transmission grid available to third party suppliers on reasonable terms, since there is no requirement to treat the transmission system as a separate cost centre";[107] and it will also be difficult more generally to monitor the efficiency of the firm. The conclusion reached by Vickers and Yarrow is not encouraging:[108]

---

[98] Tariff customers are, in essence, those within the market who receive less than 25,000 therms per year, Gas Act 1986, s.14. Large industrial concerns are therefore not included.
[99] Vickers and Yarrow, *Privatisation*, p. 265.
[100] Gas Act 1986, s.7(7).
[101] s.23.
[102] ss.24, 26.
[103] ss.28, 29, 30.
[104] s.31.
[105] ss. 34, 35.
[106] s.38.
[107] Vickers and Yarrow, *Privatisation*, p. 263.
[108] *Ibid.* p. 278.

"We conclude that the most fundamental weaknesses of UK regulatory policy are associated with an excessively short-term view of the underlying economic issues. The Government has been content to focus upon the initial post-privatisation period, leaving many fundamental issues unresolved...What has happened is that one of the major deficiencies of the UK control system for nationalised industries – preoccupation with short-term political issues – has been duplicated in the policy framework set for the regulated privately owned gas industry."

Two important developments have taken place since the passage of the 1986 legislation. One is the enactment of the Competition and Service (Utilities) Act 1992, to be considered below, which reinforces the regulatory powers possessed by the agency. The other is the Monopolies and Mergers Commission report which recommends a restructuring of British Gas, through divestment of its supply business. It remains to be seen how far these two developments will affect the overall balance of power between the regulator and the regulated industry.

3. *The Regulatory Regime: Institutional Design*

The previous discussion has focused upon the regulatory regime which has been established for the gas and the telecommunications industries.[109] It is now necessary to stand back from the detail of these two areas and consider some of the more general pre-conditions for effective regulatory control.

An appropriate starting point is the importance of *information*. As Foster notes, "a state of unbalanced or asymmetric information benefits the regulated by comparison with not only the regulator, but also actual and potential competitors and customers."[110] Regulated bodies will resort to one of a number of tactics in order to reduce the effectiveness of the regulatory machinery. They may produce too little information; they may give too much in a form which is unclear or opaque; or they may offer the desired information too slowly.[111] An effective regulatory scheme requires the production of relevant information on a periodic basis, set against the background of clear objectives as to why the information is needed.[112] The information should, moreover, be geared to the detection of the types of offences which the regulatory regime hopes to control.[113]

A second aspect of effective regulatory control concerns the *objectives* of the regulatory regime. It is evident from the preceding discussion that the powers of the regulatory authorities are set out in broad terms, coupled with the more specific proscription of certain types of activity, such as

---

[109] For telecommunications, see above, pp. 101-105.
[110] *Privatisation*, p. 226.
[111] *Ibid.* pp. 235-236.
[112] *Ibid.* pp. 236-238.
[113] *Ibid.* pp. 250-254.

discriminatory pricing. It is clear also that a significant part of the remit of the regulatory bodies is economic in nature, whether this be in the form of protecting consumers from excessive prices or potential competitors from predation. What is less apparent is how far non-economic considerations can or should feature as part of the regulator's objectives. Such considerations can be non-economic in the sense that the legislation may proscribe certain types of activity, such as discriminatory pricing, which may in fact enhance economic efficiency. Or the considerations may be of an explicitly political character, such as regulating pricing in a way which is geared towards those with low incomes. While some may feel that it is desirable to interpret the regulatory objectives to embrace issues such as these, there are complications and dangers in going down this path: it may be more difficult to monitor the data in relation to social offences; there may be a conflict between the pursuit of economic and non-economic goals; non-economic goals can themselves conflict; and the greater the number of divergent aims which are being pursued the more difficult might it be to develop a coherent overall strategy.[114]

A third aspect of the institutional design of a regulatory system is that it should minimise the possibility of *regulatory failure*. This term can cover a number of differing scenarios.

It may mean that the regulated industry itself is no longer capable of sustaining profitable trading because the regulatory controls do not, for example, allow it to adapt to new market circumstances such as inflation. It may mean that the regulator is no longer capable of properly fulfilling his or her remit because of governmental interference with the regime, or because there are inadequate powers in the original legislation.

One more general cause of regulatory failure is *regulatory capture*, in the sense that the regulator is captured by the very industries which are being regulated. There is a wealth of theoretical and empirical literature on this issue. One well known version of the causes of regulatory capture has been developed by the Chicago School.[115] The essence of the argument is that the monopolist in an industry about to be regulated has a great economic incentive to influence the content of the legislation since the regulatory regime will constrain what the monopolist can do with its monopoly profits. This same incentive will also lie behind attempts by the monopolist to influence the regulator once the regulatory regime has been established. In more formal terms what this means is that the monopolist will predictably be willing to expend a great amount of its monopoly profits upon influencing the regulator in order to retain at least some of these profits. A somewhat different account of regulatory capture, or bias, is provided by the Public Choice School.[116] One aspect of this theory is to

---

[114] *Ibid.* pp. 316-323.
[115] Stigler, "The Theory of Economic Regulation" (1971) 2 Bell Jnl. of Economics 3; Peltzmann, "Towards a More General Theory of Regulation" (1976) 19 Jnl. L. & Econ. 211; Posner, "Theories of Economic Regulation" (1974) 5 Bell Jnl. of Economics 335.
[116] Buchanan and Tullock, *The Calculus of Consent* (1962); Buchanan, *The Limits of Liberty: Between Anarchy and Leviathan* (1975); Becker, "A Theory of Competition among Pressure Groups for Political Influence" (1983) 98 Quarterly Jnl. of Econ. 371.

draw analogies between markets for ordinary goods and the making of legislation, which is conceived of as a political market. The content of any legislation will reflect the contesting pressures of the differing interest groups who are concerned with the topic. On this view "trade continues until the marginal value to the politicians and regulator of the obligation assumed by the regulated industry equals its marginal financial cost to the industry".[117]

The theoretical assumptions underlying both of these models have been contested, as have the empirical findings which are said to support the models.[118] This should not, however, be taken to mean that we should be unconcerned about the possibility of regulatory capture or bias. The regulatory regime should be so devised as to minimise the likelihood of this occurring. Foster has provided a number of helpful pointers in this regard.[119] There should be an independent regulator who retains discretion to interpret regulatory offences; formal court procedures should be avoided since these are likely to favour the regulated industry, but there should be appropriate procedural rights, discussed more fully below, which safeguard the interests of affected parties; appeals on the merits should be provided in some instances, but preferably to another regulatory agency which has appropriate expertise; the more firms within an industry the less likely will it be that the regulator will be captured by any one firm; it is equally the case that proper scope should be given to other interested parties, including consumers, who will act as some counterweight to the power of the regulated industry itself; and the scope of any ministerial power should be defined as clearly as possible, in order that the regulated industry is not tempted to by-pass the regulator and seek to capture the minister instead.

The final aspect of a coherent regulatory strategy is to ensure that the regulatory authority itself observes the requisite *procedural and substantive norms* which we expect of other public agencies.[120]

In procedural terms this means that the basic principles of fair procedure apply to decisions made by such bodies, whether in the setting of prices, the grant of licences or the adjudication of offences under the 1992 legislation to be discussed below. This does not mean that such agencies should necessarily have to operate in accordance with the full rigours of the ordinary adversarial/adjudicative conception of fair procedure, modelled as it is upon ordinary court processes.[121] Procedural justice is a more flexible concept which can be tailored to the needs of the particular area. It seems as if the regulatory agencies have sensibly adopted ideas of informal adjudication and rule-making commonly adopted by US agencies.[122] This is to

---

[117] Foster, *Privatisation*, p. 387.
[118] Foster, *Privatisation*, Chap. 11; Craig, *Public Law and Democracy in the United Kingdom and the United States of America* (1990), Chap. 4; Kelman, "On Democracy Bashing: A Skeptical Look at the Theoretical and Empirical Practice of the Public Choice Movement" 74 Virg. L.Rev. 199 (1988).
[119] *Privatisation*, p. 413.
[120] Graham and Prosser, *Privatising Public Enterprises* (1991), Chap. 7.
[121] See below, pp. 302-306.
[122] Foster, *Privatisation*, pp. 274-275.

be welcomed provided that our own agencies do apply these ideas with the necessary degree of procedural rectitude. This is particularly so where the nature of the issue affects a large number of parties. In such cases procedural norms should be devised so as to ensure that the material is produced in a way which is accessible to all those involved.

In substantive terms the agencies which oversee the regulated industries are subject to the ordinary principles of judicial review.[123] There is in addition a form of internal appeal to the Monopolies and Mergers Commission on a number of issues, such as when a licence condition is to be changed. It may well be that this should be extended to cover contested interpretations of a licence and other matters,[124] although whether the MMC could cope with this additional workload is questionable.

The relevance of the issues concerning institutional design considered within this section has been brought sharply into focus by recent calls from some parties that the powers of the regulators should be curbed, re-defined, or that there should be an appeal from the regulators to some other body. There is a concern that the regulators have changed the commercial conditions which were detailed in the privatisation prospectuses, and this has been further fuelled by British Gas' anger at the regulatory initiative which led to the Monopolies and Mergers Commission reference, the conclusion of which was the recommendation that British Gas should be restructured.

A number of the themes discussed above are immediately apparent in these developments. There is the concern over whether the procedures being utilised by the regulators are adequate, and the possibility of some new appellate machinery against decisions made by the agencies. There is the equally interesting spectacle of the regulated industry attempting to persuade government that the powers presently possessed by the regulators are too great, or that they are being misapplied. If capture of the regulatory agency fails, one can always revert to the political arena and capture the minister instead.

4. *The Regulatory Regime: The Limits of Public Law*

It is clear, as noted above, that the principles of administrative law can apply to the activities of the regulatory agencies themselves.[125] If therefore the DGGS was felt to be acting in excess of his powers, either procedurally or substantively, an appropriate action could be entertained under the public law procedures.[126]

---

[123] See below, Chaps. 10-12.
[124] Foster, *Privatisation*, pp. 284-285.
[125] For problems which can arise from the government's continued share holdings in some privatised corporations, Graham and Prosser, "Privatising Nationalised Industries: Constitutional Issues and New Legal Techniques" (1987) 50 M.L.R. 16.
[126] See below, Chap. 15.

It also seems clear that the exercise of monopoly powers by a local authority in administering an ancient market are susceptible to judicial review concerning the level of rents which can lawfully be charged. [127]

More interesting and controversial is the issue as to whether these procedures and principles could be used directly against bodies such as British Gas. This raises the vexed topic as to the scope of "public law" for the purposes of the remedial procedures which will be considered below.[128] More particularly it requires us to judge how far those procedures are appropriate to a corporation which is nominally private, with monopoly powers which are buttressed directly and indirectly by a statute. It is readily apparent from the earlier discussion that the courts have in the past found little difficulty in subjecting such institutions to rules which differ from those of the ordinary "private" corporation.[129] It might well be argued that any complainant would have to exhaust the "internal" remedial options before seeking judicial review.[130] The force of this argument would depend upon whether the complaint fell within the relevant internal procedures, and also upon the general law governing the relationship between the pursuit of judicial review and the availability of alternative remedies. Given the power possessed by the privatised industry, buttressed as it is by statute, the possibility of suits which can challenge, for example, British Gas directly by way of judicial review might be no bad thing.[131] This idea has been mooted by Sir Gordon Borrie who has had a wealth of experience as Director General of Fair Trading. He had this to say.[132]

> "Is it satisfactory...that neither private individuals or bodies nor (in many instances) public officials can bring to bear on private centres of power the kind of legal challenge in the courts that has been so effective as the challenges to the exercise of local government power by way of application for judicial review in recent decades? The lack of any possibility for the industrial customers of British Gas or even for a public official such as the Director General of Fair Trading to take British Gas to court to challenge their exercise of monopoly power meant that a reference to the Monopolies and Mergers Commission, which the customers had no right to initiate themselves and which could result only in recommendations for government action, was the only possible way of pursuing the matter."

---

[127] R. v. Birmingham City Council, ex p. Dredger and Paget [1993] C.O.D. 340.
[128] See below, Chap. 15.
[129] See above, pp. 222–225.
[130] See below, pp. 597–599.
[131] Although we have noted above the preference of some commentators for restricting the courts' role in these matters and opting for other "appeal" routes instead.
[132] "The Regulation of Public and Private Power" [1989] P.L. 552, 560–561.

5. The Regulatory Regime: The Citizen's Charter and the 1992 Legislation

Some at least of the force of Sir Gordon's complaint has now been addressed by legislation which is one application of the principles contained in the Citizen's Charter: the Competition and Service (Utilities) Act 1992.

Part I of this legislation amends the existing statutes through which utilities were privatised[133] and imposes standards of performance and service to customers. The details of the legislation vary with respect to telecommunications, gas, water and electricity. The description given below focuses principally upon telecommunications by way of example.

The Director of the agency is empowered to make regulations which prescribe standards of performance which ought to be achieved by designated operators in *individual* cases.[134] The regulations require the consent of the Secretary of State, and can only be made after consulting those operators and parties likely to be affected by the regulations. Compensation is to be payable to any person who is affected by failure to meet the specified standard. The Director will adjudicate on any dispute as to whether the standards have been met, and any order which is made takes effect as if it were a judgment of a county court. The Director is also empowered to determine *overall* standards of performance for the industry.

The Director is then instructed to collect *information* with respect to compensation paid by designated operators in individual cases, and with respect to overall levels of performance.[135] Failure to provide the information is punishable by a fine. The Director is then to publish the information provided at least once a year.

Other sections of the legislation deal with more particular issues such as discriminatory pricing, billing disputes and deposits.[136] Once again it will be the Director, or an arbitrator, who will adjudicate on these issues.

The 1992 Act has a number of other interesting features, one of which is that those operating within the industry have a duty to establish a *complaints procedure*. This must be publicised and a description of the procedure must be provided free of charge to any person who asks for it.[137] The Director is given power to order modifications to the procedure.

It might be felt that the penalties which the legislation imposes will be too small to have much deterrent effect upon the regulated industry, and this

---

[133] Telecommunications Act 1984; Gas Act 1986; Electricity Act 1989; Water Industry Act 1991.
[134] *e.g.* Competition and Service (Utilities) Act 1992, s.1, which modifies the Telecommunications Act 1984, s.27.
[135] *e.g.* with respect to telecommunications, see 1992 Act, s.2.
[136] *e.g.* ss.5-7 respectively.
[137] *e.g.* 1992 Act, s.4.

might well be so if the legislation went no further than described above. It does, however, have an added punch: adherence to the norms described above is made part of the *licence conditions* under which the firm operates.[138] This means that breach of these conditions can lead to an order for compliance by the Director, and a subsequent action brought either by the Director or by another for breach of statutory duty.

The link between these provisions and the general aims of the Citizen's Charter is readily apparent. The importance of the 1992 legislation in attaining these goals is brought out further in the First Report on the Citizen's Charter which identifies the progress which the utilities have made towards complying with the statutory requirements on performance and standards.[139] The regulatory agencies themselves have begun to apply their new powers. Oftel has, for example, initiated a consultative procedure seeking views as to what should be the standards of performance to be expected of designated operators.[140]

This statute is clearly aimed in the right direction, but it will be some time before we can determine the effectiveness of the changes brought about by the 1992 legislation.

Section 7. Conclusion

No attempt will be made to summarise the entirety of the preceding arguments. What this discussion demonstrates is that the administrative law principles which we utilise must be seen as but part of a larger picture concerned with the institutional design of administrative systems. The "whether", "who" and "how" questions which have formed the framework of this chapter could be applied to any of the substantive areas with which administrative law is concerned.

---

[138] *e.g.* s.9.
[139] Cm. 2101 (1992), pp. 20-23.
[140] *Oftel*, Annual Report (1992), p. 8.

7. RULE-MAKING

Section 1. Introduction

People may, as stated earlier,[1] be affected not only by a result reached through individualised adjudication or some other form of decision-making, but also through the application of pre-determined rules. While these rules will of course have to be applied to the case at hand they will often be determinative of the actual result, or will at least strongly influence the outcome. It is with the controls over the promulgation of such rules that we are now concerned.

The term rule-making is used here instead of the more customary appellation of delegated legislation. The reason is simple. The latter is but one species of the former. The test of whether a particular rule is to be subjected to our legislative checks is one of form. A particular piece of legislation which empowers a minister to make rules or regulations will specify whether those rules are to be regarded as statutory instruments for the purposes of the Statutory Instruments Act 1946. It is this Act which contains the provisions for publication and legislative scrutiny.[2]

There are, therefore, three areas not touched by our legislative controls. First, there are rules made by a minister or local authority or agency which are not expressed to be statutory instruments and are therefore outside of the 1946 legislation. Secondly, there are areas in which administrative institutions will develop rules or something closely akin to them, even if they are not expressly empowered to do so. This leads directly to the third area not covered by our existing controls. This is, ironically, that in which no rules are made. How can controls over rule-making apply to a situation in which no rules exist? This is not so absurd as it first appears. Although bureaucracies will often develop rules to guide the exercise of their discretion, there are still large areas in which they will not – areas in which decisions will be made by the informal exercise of discretion. Such decisions may be made against the background of an officially understood policy; or they may simply be the exercise of judgment by a particular hearing officer. The key question here is how far should we encourage the crystallisation of this informal discretion into a series of rules? How desirable is this?

---

[1] See above, pp. 48-49.
[2] See below, pp. 247-250.

What checks should the rules be subject to and what are the limits of such controls?

The types of control to which any rule-making can be subject are varied. Four broad mechanisms are available: consultation, publication, legislative scrutiny and judicial review. Consultation is designed to secure consideration of the rule by interested parties prior to its passage. Publication ensures knowledge of the rule. Legislative supervision takes the form of parliamentary scrutiny. What consultation and legislative scrutiny have in common is the way in which control is exercised: it is general in the sense that all rules subject to these procedures are thereby open to examination, and the focus will be upon the merits of the rule as well as its technical legality. Judicial supervision is in contrast to this by being *ex post facto*, particular, and focusing on the legality of the measure and not its merits. It will take place once the rule has been passed;[3] it is dependent upon an individual invoking the court's assistance and is in this sense particular, and because of the constitutional position of our courts they cannot, overtly at least, attack the merits of the rule. This is not to deny that judicial pronouncements may have an effect upon the making of future rules by prescribing procedural standards or by decisions upon aspects of legality. The nature of the judicial process is nonetheless unsuited to controlling the content of the rules. For this checks in the form of consultation, legislative supervision and publication must remain the chief weapons. Where the courts could be more adventurous is, as will be seen, in the standards imposed upon the bureaucracy with respect to the making of administrative rules.

One trite observation should be made before proceeding further. It is easy when discussing the plethora of forms of rule-making, and weighing varying options for control, to lose sight of why such constraints are required. This in turn can lead to conclusions being reached about the desirability of particular forms of control which are unwarranted or incomplete. We are concerned about rule-making, whatever form it takes, because our ideas of representative government tell us that legislative norms achieve validation and legitimacy through the expression of consent in the legislature itself. The existence of rules of a legislative character other than primary statutes poses the problem of how this validation and control is to be accomplished. That is the central concern of this chapter.

We will examine first the existing constraints upon delegated legislation and then take a closer look at the whole problem of administrative rule-making.

---

[3] Subject to the judicial role in enforcing compliance with the requirements of, for example, consultation. As to whether the courts would intervene by injunction to prevent the passage of delegated legislation, see below pp. 542-543.

Section 2. Delegated Legislation

1. *History*

Delegated legislation is not a new phenomenon.[4] While the Statute of Proclamations 1539, giving Henry VIII extensive powers to legislate by proclamation, proved to be a relatively shortlived measure, the Statute of Sewers 1531 was the harbinger of a more general trend. The latter vested the Commissioners of Sewers with full powers to make laws and decrees concerning drainage schemes and the levying of rates to pay for them.[5]

It was, however, the social and economic reforms of the nineteenth century that proved to be the origin of delegated legislation on the scale to which we have now become accustomed. We have already seen how the Poor Law Amendment Act 1834 vested the Poor Law Commissioners with power to make rules for the management of the poor.[6] Many other nineteenth century statutes contained power to make rules. After 1890 statutory rules and orders were published annually. Between 1901 and 1914 the average number of orders made was 1,349, which increased in the war years to 1,459.[7] The advent of war increased not only the amount, but also the complexity and generality of delegated legislation. The Defence of the Realm Act 1914 gave the government power to make regulations for securing the public safety and the defence of the realm, a power liberally used. Regulations were made on dog shows and the supply of cocaine to actresses, neither of which appears of prime concern to the war effort. While the generality of the empowering provisions diminished immediately after the First World War, it did not entirely wane. Thus the Emergency Powers Act 1920, which is still in force, gave the government extensive powers to deal with peace-time emergencies.[8] The advent of the Second World War found the draftsmen ready with the Emergency Powers (Defence) Acts 1939 and 1940, empowering the Crown to make regulations, *inter alia,* for public safety, the defence of the realm, the maintenance of order, the maintenance of supply and the detention of persons whose detention appeared to the Secretary of State to be expedient in the interests of public safety or the defence of the realm.

While wide delegated powers could be accepted during war or civil emergency, there was growing disquiet about their scope and number in peacetime. Some felt that the whole scale of delegated legislation was out of

---

[4] Allen, *Law and Order* (3rd ed., 1965), Chap. 2; Carr, *Delegated Legislation* (1921) and *Parliamentary Control of Delegated Legislation* (1956); Griffith and Street, *Principles of Administrative Law* (5th ed, 1973), Chaps. 2 and 3.

[5] The Commissioners of Sewers are also a good example of a body vested with administrative, judicial and executive powers.

[6] Above Chap. 2.

[7] Allen, above n. 4, p. 32.

[8] The Act was used in the General Strike 1926, the 1948 and 1949 dock strikes, the 1955 rail strike, the 1966 seamen's strike, the 1970 dock strike and the coal strike of 1973.

control raising fears that we were about to be ruled by the bureaucracy. These fears were voiced by Lord Hewart, the Chief Justice, who castigated the development in the *New Despotism* (1929). While controls over delegated legislation were desirable Lord Hewart's general attack upon such delegation was overplayed as was made apparent by the Committee on Ministers' Powers. The Committee was appointed to consider delegated legislation and the making of judicial or quasi-judicial decisions by ministers.[9] Its conclusions can be summarised briefly: delegated legislation is inevitable but could be improved by a clearer use of terminology; by defining the delegated powers as clearly as possible; and by adequate facilities for publication and legislative scrutiny.[10]

Few have doubted the continuing need for delegated legislation, although there is concern about control over its content. The exigencies of the modern state have increasingly led to the use of statutes containing delegated power. A number of reasons have contributed towards this. First, the area may be one which is technically complex, making it extremely difficult to set out all the permutations in the original statute. Second, the subject-matter may be novel. Time may be needed to experiment and to determine how the legislation is operating. Only then can all the details be filled in. This process may best be carried out over a period of time, making delegated legislation the most appropriate tool. Third, even where the area is well known, the executive may wish to implement the legislation at a later stage or to alter its detail. Delegated legislation is a useful mechanism for achieving these ends.

All these reasons have contributed towards the continued growth of delegated legislation. By themselves they do not, however, represent the whole picture. A fourth reason exists in the advantage which such legislation gives to the executive. For a government with an onerous legislative timetable, and/or only a small majority, there is always the temptation to pass skeleton legislation with the details being etched in by the minister. These details may in fact contain important aspects of the legislation, and although they are subject to legislative scrutiny this is not always effective.

2. *Form*

There is a bewildering variety of terminology through which to express delegated legislation. Orders in Council, rules, regulations, bylaws and directions all jostle one another upon the statute book. The key to sanity is the realisation that nothing turns upon the precise nomenclature.[11] A word about the differing devices is nonetheless necessary.

Orders in Council tend to be the more important pieces of subordinate legislation. The executive will draft the legislation, but it will be enacted as

---

[9] Cmd. 4060 (1932).
[10] For a complete list of the recommendations, *ibid.* pp. 64-70.
[11] The Donoughmore Committee did recommend that each of these terms should be used for a specific purpose, but their ideas were not implemented, *ibid.* p. 64.

an Order of the Privy Council. The authority to make such Orders will be derived from a statute.[12] *Regulations* and *rules* are used in a wide variety of situations to denote subordinate law-making power. The power will normally be conferred upon a minister of the Crown, but regulations, rules or orders may also be passed by agencies and local authorities. *Bylaws* are commonly promulgated by local authorities, but can also be made by agencies.[13] The reason why the precise name given to the delegated legislation is of such little relevance is because of the reforms brought about in 1946 which now govern much subordinate legislation.

3. *The Passage of Delegated Legislation*

(1) THE STATUTORY INSTRUMENTS ACT 1946

Section 1 of the 1946 Act states,

"1(1) Where by this Act or any Act passed after the commencement[14] of this Act power to make, confirm, or approve orders, rules, regulations or other subordinate legislation is conferred on His Majesty in Council or on any Minister of the Crown then, if the power is expressed –
(a) in the case of a power conferred on His Majesty, to be exercised by Order in Council;
(b) in the case of a power conferred on a Minister of the Crown, to be exercisable by statutory instrument,
any document by which that power is exercised shall be known as a "statutory instrument" and the provisions of this Act shall apply thereto accordingly."

The Act therefore provides for two different types of cases. First, all Orders in Council made in pursuance of a statutory power must be exercised by statutory instrument.[15] Secondly, other rules, regulations or orders must be exercised by statutory instrument only when the particular statute states that the power must be so exercised. The test is, as stated above, purely one of form. Moreover, section 1(1)(b) only applies when the power is conferred on a minister of the Crown. This is defined flexibly: if there is any question whether any board, commissioner or other body on whom any such power is conferred is a government department, or which minister of the Crown is in charge of them, the question is to be referred to the

---

[12] The Privy Council can, however, pass legislation which is not subordinate legislation at all on matters within the Royal Prerogative, provided that the power to do so has not been restricted by statute, *Att.-Gen.* v. *De Keyser's Royal Hotel* [1920] A.C. 508.
[13] For special problems concerning bylaws see Garner's *Administrative Law* (7th ed., 1989), pp. 74-80. There are also devices known as Provisional Orders and Special Procedure Orders (for the latter see the Statutory Orders (Special Procedure) Act 1945) which are intended to expedite the passage of private Acts, see Allen, above n. 4, pp. 76-82.
[14] January 1, 1948.
[15] Orders in Council made in pursuance of the Royal Prerogative are not covered.

K

Treasury.[16] As section 1 makes clear, it is sufficient if the minister of the Crown has power to make, confirm or approve the subordinate legislation.[17]

(2) PUBLICATION AND MAKING

(a) General

One of the principal purposes of the 1946 Act is to provide for the publication of statutory instruments. This is dealt with in section 2(1): immediately after the making of any statutory instrument it shall be sent to the King's printer of Acts of Parliament and numbered in accordance with regulations made under the 1946 Act. Copies shall be printed and sold as soon as possible, subject to any exceptions made by Acts passed after the 1946 Act or contained in any regulations made under the 1946 Act. It is further provided that statutory instruments must contain a statement on their face of the date at which they will become operative.[18]

The main exceptions from the requirement for publication are as follows: local instruments, which connote local and personal or private Acts;[19] and general instruments[20] certified by the responsible authority to be a class of documents which would otherwise be regularly printed.[21] The Reference Committee[22] may direct that such an instrument should be published. Exemptions from publication also exist for temporary instruments,[23] the publication of bulky schedules,[24] and for confidential instruments.[25]

What is the consequence of failure to publish? Does it affect the validity of the statutory instrument? It might be thought that the answer should be in the affirmative. After all, the public will not otherwise have had an opportunity to know the law which is being applied to them. This is not however the case. Primary statutes take effect as soon as they have received the Royal Assent. It was at one time thought that subordinate legislation required publication in order to be valid. There is some authority for this proposition,[26] but the weight of authority is against this view. In *R.* v. *Sheer Metalcraft Ltd.*,[27] a company was prosecuted for infringing an Iron and Steel Prices Order. The Order had been printed but certain schedules had

---

[16] s.11(2).

[17] A third type of case is dealt with in the Statutory Instruments Act 1946, s.1(2), which covers statutes passed before 1946, and provides the criterion as to when rules passed pursuant to such statutes after 1946 should count as statutory instruments. See further Statutory Instruments Regulations 1947, 1948 (No. 1).

[18] Statutory Instruments Act 1946, s.4(2).

[19] Statutory Instruments Regulations 1947, 1948 (No. 1), reg. 4(2).

[20] General instruments are those in the nature of a public general Act, *ibid.* reg. 4.

[21] *Ibid.* reg. 5.

[22] Two or more persons nominated by the Lord Chancellor and Speaker of the House of Commons, reg. 11(1).

[23] Reg. 6.

[24] Reg. 7.

[25] Reg. 8. This exception only applies so as to restrict publication before the instrument comes into operation.

[26] *Johnson* v. *Sargent* [1918] 1 K.B. 101.

[27] [1954] 1 Q.B. 586. See also, *Jones* v. *Robson* [1901] 1 Q.B. 673.

not, and no certificate of exemption had been obtained. Streatfield J. stressed the fact that the existence of section 3(2) of the 1946 Act indicated that the Order was valid despite failure to publish. That section provides a defence to an action for contravention of a statutory instrument where the instrument has not been issued at the date of the contravention unless it can be shown that reasonable steps were taken to bring it to the public's knowledge. If an Order was ineffective before publication then section 3(2) would be redundant, as there would be no law contravened and hence no offence. Streatfield J. stressed that the making of the instrument was one thing and the issue of it another. An instrument was valid once it was made by the minister and laid before Parliament.[28]

This still leaves open the question as to when the instrument is "made" by the minister. The enabling legislation may stipulate that an instrument shall not be made until it has been laid before Parliament. There may also be a provision stipulating when the instrument should come into operation. In the absence of such provisions the statutory instrument would appear to be made when either enacted by the Queen in Council, or signed by the competent authority who will normally be a minister or a civil servant with authority to sign for the minister.[29]

(b) Subordinate legislation not published

Whatever the deficiencies of the 1946 Act, that legislation does in general ensure the publication of statutory instruments. There are, however, five categories of case where there is no guarantee whatsoever of publication. One of these has already been mentioned: this is where statutory instruments are exempted from publication under regulations made pursuant to the 1946 Act. A second type of case where there is no provision for publication is where Orders in Council are made in exercise of the Prerogative, and a third where delegated legislation is passed in furtherance of a statute which does not deem that legislation to be a statutory instrument.

The fourth exception warrants more extensive treatment. While the point has not yet been fully argued it is doubtful whether sub-delegated legislation is covered by the 1946 Act: this is legislation made under a power conferred by a regulation or other legislative instrument not being itself an Act of Parliament. The 1946 Act requires that the delegated legislation be made under powers conferred by an Act of Parliament. Whether this does really exclude all sub-delegated legislation is questionable. The answer is ultimately dependent upon three questions. First, the meaning of "confer". If this word is interpreted so as to include "derive" then some, at least, sub-delegated legislation will be included. Such legislation can be traced back to the primary statute which originally conferred the power to make the rules

---

[28] There is some doubt whether validity requires the instrument even to be laid before Parliament, *Starey* v. *Graham* [1899] 1 Q.B. 406, 412, and in any event not all instruments are required to be laid. On the other hand, when a statute provides that a statutory instrument is to be laid before Parliament after being made the general rule is that it must be laid before coming into operation, Statutory Instruments Act 1946, s.4.

[29] Allen, above n. 4, p. 114.

from which the sub-delegated legislation originated. Secondly, it depends upon the breadth given to the term "minister of the Crown" which is left open-ended by section 11 of the 1946 Act. The third question is how much of the sub-delegated legislation is actually legislation, as opposed to administrative direction or executive order. While circulars and the like may be published by departments, if they are not the citizen will be faced with a mass of literature which may well be dispositive of the case, but the contents of which cannot be ascertained. As Streatfield J. has said, such a provision is four times cursed,[30]

> "First, it has seen neither House of Parliament; secondly, it is unpublished and is inaccessible even to those whose valuable rights of property may be affected; thirdly it is a jumble of provisions, legislative, administrative, or directive in character and sometimes difficult to disentangle one from the other; and, fourthly, it is expressed not in the precise language of an Act of Parliament or an Order in Council but in the more colloquial language of correspondence, which is not always susceptible of the ordinary canons of construction."

The fifth and last type of rule which is not published overlaps with the fourth, but is distinct from it. Administrators may, as said earlier, make rules to guide their discretion. What distinguishes these from sub-delegated legislation is that there may be no express power to make rules, whether derived from an Act of Parliament or other legislative instrument. This does not mean that administrative rule-making is either unlawful or something which is to be regretted. It is neither as we shall see below. What it may well be is unpublished and hence unknown. How we should tackle this problem will be considered in the general context of administrative rule-making.[31]

4. Control by Parliament

(1) SCRUTINY ON THE FLOOR OF THE HOUSE

There are numerous ways in which delegated legislation may come before the House.[32] Four principal methods can, however, be identified.

First, the empowering legislation may simply require the subordinate legislation to be laid before the House. If a document has been presented to the House it has been laid,[33] and the laying should take place before the instrument comes into force. Where it is vital that it should become

---

[30] *Patchett* v. *Leathem* (1949) 65 T.L.R. 69, 70. See also, *Blackpool Corporation* v. *Locker* [1948] 1 K.B. 349, 369. Allen, above n. 4, pp. 194-195, reaches no definite conclusion on the publication of sub-delegated legislation.

[31] See below, pp. 272-276.

[32] Allen, above n. 4, pp. 122-125.

[33] *R.* v. *Immigration Appeal Tribunal, ex p. Joyles* [1972] 1 W.L.R. 1390. The effect of the Laying of Documents before Parliament (Interpretation) Act 1948 is that each House is a master of the meaning of laying. The general rule is that the instruments will be laid at the Votes and Proceedings Office of the House of Commons, and at the Office of the Clerk of Parliaments for the House of Lords.

operational before being laid this can occur provided that notification is sent to the Lord Chancellor and the Speaker of the House of Commons.[34] Some statutes may simply require the subordinate legislation to be laid before the House. In such cases the laying is simply a mechanism to inform Parliament of the content of the legislation before it becomes operative. Questions may be asked, but no direct form of attack upon such delegated legislation is possible.

A second mechanism affords even less opportunity for scrutiny. In a number of areas there is not even a requirement that the subordinate legislation be laid before Parliament.[35]

The third mechanism does offer some measure of parliamentary control: this is the affirmative resolution procedure. This requires the subordinate legislation to be subject to an affirmative resolution of each House or the House of Commons alone. This procedure can operate somewhat differently in different areas. A statute may state that instruments made thereunder do not have any effect until parliamentary approval has been secured. If there is no such provision the instrument will have effect as soon as it is made, with a rider that if it is not approved within the requisite period it should not be invalidated retrospectively.[36] Relatively few instruments are subject to the affirmative procedure for the very reason that the government then has to find time to secure their passage. There are now nearly 3,000 statutory instruments each year and, on average, only 170 are subject to the affirmative procedure.[37]

The fourth principal way in which statutory instruments are processed through Parliament is by the negative resolution procedure. With this procedure it is the private member who must secure time to attack the delegated legislation. Where the negative resolution procedure operates, the instrument is open to a prayer for annulment within 40 days of being laid. Such instruments are as a general rule to be laid before becoming operative.[38] The prayer for annulment may be moved in either House but it is not easily secured. A member must ensure a quorum to retain the House in session; there is no provision for amendment, only outright rejection; debates on annulment resolutions are subject to time limits; and there is insufficient time provided for such debates, so that in, for example, 1990-91 78% of prayers for annulment were not debated.[39] Even if a prayer for annulment succeeds this does not of itself administer the death blow to the subordinate legislation. A successful prayer precludes further action from being taken under the instrument and empowers Her Majesty to pass an Order in Council revoking it. It does not invalidate anything done prior to the prayer, nor does it bar the making of a new statutory instrument.[40]

---

[34] Statutory Instruments Act 1946, s.4.

[35] Kersell, *Parliamentary Scrutiny of Delegated Legislation* (1960), p. 19.

[36] Allen, above n. 4, p. 123.

[37] Adonis, *Parliament Today* (2nd ed., 1993), p. 113.

[38] This is the effect of s.5 of the 1946 Act which applies s.4 to the negative resolution procedure.

[39] *Making the Law, The Report of the Hansard Society Commission on the Legislative Process* (1993), p. 93.

[40] Statutory Instruments Act 1946, s.5.

Approximately 900 statutory instruments are subject to this procedure each year.[41]

Many instruments are, therefore, subject to the negative resolution procedure,[42] but no real principle seems to guide the choice between the available options. On principle the most important types of instrument should be subject to the affirmative resolution procedure and only purely technical matters should be exempt from the need to be laid. While it is true that the affirmative procedure does seem to have been used for important matters such as those affecting statutes and the grant of very broad delegated powers, this practice is by no means uniform. It is common to find the affirmative and negative procedures used indiscriminately to implement the same statute. Moreover, while instruments not subject to the requirement of laying should be reserved for minor matters, subordinate legislation of such peripheral importance as the alteration of county council electoral boundaries and the constitution of Regional Hospital Boards has been passed in this manner.[43]

The effectiveness of control on the floor of the House is constrained by the shortage of time for debate and the difficulty of securing sufficient support to move a prayer for annulment. Some such prayers are moved after the period in which the instruments can be annulled, in which case they can only be discursive, while others are attended by relatively few members. Nor is there any requirement that there be consultation with Members of Parliament prior to the promulgation of the rules.[44] Sir Carleton Kemp Allen concludes that it is a constitutional fiction to say that Parliament exercises any real safeguards over delegated legislation.[45]

(2) SCRUTINY IN COMMITTEE

Control on the floor of Parliament is supplemented by scrutiny in committee. In 1944 a Scrutiny Committee was appointed and in 1973 a Joint Committee on Statutory Instruments was formed from the committees of the Commons and Lords. Its terms of reference require that it should examine every statutory instrument, rule, order or scheme laid or laid in draft before Parliament in order to determine whether the attention of the House should be drawn to an instrument for any of the following reasons: that it imposes a tax or charge; that it is made under a statute which prevents challenge in the courts; that it appears to make an unusual or unexpected use of powers conferred by the statute; that it purports to have retrospective effect without statutory authorisation; that there seemed

---

[41] Adonis, above n. 37, p. 113.

[42] A fifth mechanism is for laying the instrument in draft, see the 1946 Act, s.6.

[43] Allen, above n. 4, pp. 128-133. The Joint Committee on Delegated Legislation, Second Report, (1972-1973; H.L. 204), (1972-1973; H.C. 408) recommended that the affirmative procedure should be used for rules which substantially affect the provisions of primary legislation, impose or increase taxation, or otherwise involve special considerations.

[44] Beatson, "Legislative Control of Administrative Rulemaking: Lessons from the British Experience" 12 Corn. I.L.J. 199, 213-215 (1979).

[45] Allen, above n. 4, p. 136.

to be unwarranted delay in the publication or laying of the instrument; that the statutory instrument has not been laid and that notification to the Speaker has not been prompt; that it is unclear whether the instrument is *intra vires*; that for any special reason its form or purport requires elucidation; that the drafting appears to be defective.

In addition to the Joint Committee there is also a Merits Committee. The Joint Committee only considers the technical legality of a measure. Because of the pressure of time on the floor of the House, a standing committee was established in 1973 to consider the merits of the rules. However, only about 5% of statutory instruments are considered in this way.[46]

How effective are these controls? Scrutiny of both the technical legality and the merits has been of value. The attentions of the Joint Committee have improved drafting and increased the number of explanatory notes provided by departments. The very presence of the Committee sounds a warning to departments. Notwithstanding these positive features considerable obstacles lie in the path of effective control over technical legality.

The most important is the limited nature of the Committee's powers. It can refer an instrument to the House, but it has no means of ensuring that a prayer for annulment or debate will occur following its report. Nor can it even be sure that its report will reach the House before the period for annulment is over, and debate may well ensue on the merits of an instrument before technical scrutiny has occurred.[47] The Merits Committee is also limited in what it can achieve. It can only consider a rule and take note of it; it cannot take action or make recommendations. It has, moreover, proved a useful device for the executive: ministers faced with motions for annulment can refer the rules to the Merits Committee and once they have been thus perused they can be brought to a vote on the floor of the House without notice or debate.[48] The Select Committee on Procedure[49] has criticised the Merits Committee as unsatisfactory and suggested that its powers should be increased to include the power to make recommendations. Beatson concludes that,[50]

"The British system of legislative veto has proved less than satisfactory in rendering administrators accountable to their political superiors and protecting those affected by administrative rules. This limited success stems from many factors. These include *de facto* executive control of the legislature, the unavailability of information about the substance of a rule in the time available for control, the limited time available for debate, and the apparent unwillingness of Members of Parliament to take an interest in scrutiny, especially of technical infirmities."

---

[46] Punnett, *British Government and Politics* (5th ed., 1987), p. 370. Committee Scrutiny has now been reinforced to some extent; see, First Report of Select Committee on the Scrutiny of Delegated Powers (1992-93; H.L. 57).

[47] Beatson, above n. 44, pp. 215, 218. See also, Hayhurst and Wallington, "The Parliamentary Scrutiny of Delegated Legislation" [1989] P.L. 547.

[48] *Ibid.* p. 217.

[49] First Report, (1977-78; H.C. 588), Chap. 3.

[50] Above n. 44, p. 222.

These sentiments are echoed by Alan Beith MP[51] who emphasises the control wielded by government business managers over the existence and the reality of any scrutiny of delegated legislation, whether on the floor of the House or in committee. This is all the more important given the changing nature of delegated legislation which is often not only the detailed implementation of a "legislative mosaic", but also the level at which quite major issues of social policy will be worked out.[52]

(3) SCRUTINY OF EUROPEAN LEGISLATION

The United Kingdom's accession to the European Economic Community produced novel problems of supervision and control. European legislation, or at least some parts of it, is, as we have seen,[53] directly applicable within the Member States. This means that once passed by the organs of the Community it is automatically incorporated into municipal law without the normal requirements of adoption or transformation.[54]

Both Houses of Parliament have established committees which perform two functions. They consider delegated legislation in order to implement the provisions of a directive or regulation issued by the Community. The committees also scrutinise proposals which emerge from the Council, in order to provide Parliament with information about likely European legislation.

The committee system which exists to scrutinise legislation emanating from Europe has now been modified following recommendations from the House of Commons Procedure Committee. The changes were prompted by concern that such legislation was not receiving proper scrutiny. The Procedure Committee recommended the establishment of five standing committees, but only two have in fact been established, in part because of the difficulty of finding MPs willing to staff more committees. The new system has been in operation since 1991. It works in the following way. The Select Committee on European Legislation, which has been in existence for twenty years, refers legislation which it deems to merit further debate to one of these committees. The standing committee will then consider the merits of the issues, and has the power to question ministers and officials. It can also refer a matter for debate on the floor of the House with the agreement of the Leader of the House.

The new regime has undoubtedly had a positive impact. In the first ten months of its existence the Select Committee looked at 606 documents and

---

[51] "Prayers Unanswered: A Jaundiced View of the Parliamentary Scrutiny of Statutory Instruments" (1981) 34 Parliamentary Affairs 165, 170. The recommendations of the Select Committee on Procedure, (1977-1978; H.C. 588), which were designed to strengthen parliamentary control, have not been implemented. Even if they had been implemented, it is arguable that, particularly with respect to the negative procedure, they do not go far enough, see, Beith pp. 171-173.

[52] Hayhurst and Wallington, above n. 47, pp. 573-574.

[53] See above, Chap. 5.

[54] Orders or regulations passed to implement the European legislation must either be made in draft and be approved by both Houses, or be subject to the negative resolution procedure, European Communities Act 1972, Sched. 2, para. 2(2).

sent on 54 for further discussion in standing committee.[55] However, it is questionable how great this impact has been. As Adonis notes,[56]

"The saga of the setting up of the European Committees is a telling commentary on the unwillingness of individual MPs to take on the burden of detailed Parliamentary scrutiny yielding little media or party kudos, however great the clamour among MPs *collectively* as to the need for such work to be done. Equally telling is the fact that most of the MPs finally recruited to man the new committees are extreme partisans on one or other side of the European debate."

5. Control through Consultation

Consultation may be required by the terms of a particular statute, or there may, in certain instances, be a duty to consult imposed by the common law.[57]

(1) CONSULTATION RIGHTS AND STATUTE

It should be made clear at the outset that there is no *necessary* connection between the existence of a statutory obligation to consult about the making of an order or regulation and the characterisation of this order as a statutory instrument. It all depends upon the enabling legislation. It is therefore perfectly possible for there to be a statutory duty to consult, and for the resulting measure to be a statutory instrument.[58] It is equally possible for there to be such an obligation where the resultant order or regulation is not a statutory instrument at all.[59]

When consultation is specified by statute this may be a mandatory requirement or it may only be directory. Where the statute states that consultation shall take place the former construction is more common.[60] Such legislation may also differ as to who must be consulted before any rules are made. On some occasions a general discretion will be left with the relevant authority to consult such interests as appear to be appropriate; in other areas the statute may be more explicit as to which interests should be consulted.[61] Where a duty to consult exists it requires the authority to supply sufficient information to those being consulted to enable them to

---

[55] Adonis, *Parliament Today* (2nd ed., 1993), p. 156.
[56] *Loc.cit.* Italics in the original.
[57] Garner, "Consultation in Subordinate Legislation" [1964] P.L. 105; Jergesen, "The Legal Requirement of Consultation" [1978] P.L. 290.
[58] *e.g.* Local Government Act 1992, s.8(3)(4).
[59] *e.g.* Competition and Service (Utilities) Act 1992, s.1.
[60] *May v. Beattie* [1927] 3 K.B. 353; *Rollo v. Minister of Town and Country Planning* [1948] 1 All E.R. 13; *Re Union of Benefices of Whippingham and East Cowes, St. James's* [1954] A.C. 245; *Port Louis Corp. v. Att.-Gen. of Mauritius* [1965] A.C. 1111; *Sinfield v. London Transport Executive* [1970] Ch. 550, 558; *Agricultural, Horticultural and Forestry Industry Training Board v. Aylesbury Mushrooms Ltd.* [1972] 1 W.L.R. 190; *Powley v. ACAS* [1978] I.C.R. 123.
[61] Compare *Post Office v. Gallagher* [1970] 3 All E.R. 712 and *Rollo v. Minister of Town and Country Planning* [1948] 1 All E.R. 13.

tender advice, and a sufficient opportunity to tender that advice before the mind of the authority becomes unduly fixed.[62] Where the obligation to consult is mandatory, failure to comply with the duty will result in the order subsequently made being held to be void. The approach of the courts is captured by the following extract from *R. v. Brent London Borough Council, ex p. Gunning*:[63]

> "First, that consultation must be at a time when proposals are still at a formative stage. Second, that the proposer must give sufficient reasons for any proposal to permit intelligent consideration and response. Third, that adequate time must be given for consideration and response and finally, fourth, that the product of the consultation must be conscientiously taken into account in finalising statutory proposals."

Consultation may also take place on a more informal, non-statutory basis. Advisory committees abound and will commonly be brought into discussions concerning proposed rules,[64] as will other interest groups.

(2) CONSULTATION RIGHTS AND THE COMMON LAW

What is absent from English law is any general duty to consult, imposed either by common law or statute. At common law there is no duty to give a hearing where the order under attack is of a legislative nature;[65] the right to a reasoned decision does not apply where the order is of a legislative or executive character;[66] and question marks hang over the application of the prerogative orders to legislative instruments. The cogency of the reasoning underlying this attitude will be examined later.[67] The absence of any common law duty to consult is matched by the lack of any such general statutory duty.[68]

More recent common law authority has, however, increased the scope of consultative rights where an individual argues that an established policy should be applied to the particular case, in circumstances where a public body seeks to resile from it. This topic will be examined in detail below,[69] but the general position is as follows.

> (a) If a public body has made a representation to a specific individual or group of individuals that a particular policy will be followed, or that they will be informed before any such change in policy takes place, then the individual will be entitled to insist that this policy is pursued in

---

[62] See *Rollo, Port Louis* and *Sinfield*, above n. 60.

[63] (1985) 84 L.G.R. 168. See also, *R. v. Warwickshire District Council, ex p. Bailey* [1991] C.O.D. 284; *R. v. Secretary of State for Social Services, ex p. Association of Metropolitan Authorities* [1993] C.O.D. 54; *R. v. British Coal Corporation and Secretary of State for Trade and Industry, ex p. Price* [1993] C.O.D. 482.

[64] Garner, above n. 57.

[65] *Bates v. Lord Hailsham* [1972] 1 W.L.R. 1373, 1378. *cf. R. v. Liverpool Corporation, ex p. Liverpool Taxi Fleet Operators' Association* [1972] 2 Q.B. 299.

[66] Tribunals and Inquiries Act 1992, s.10(5)(b).

[67] See below, pp. 258-262.

[68] The Rules Publication Act 1893 was the nearest which we have ever come to providing any general duty to consult.

[69] See below, Chap. 18.

relation to the instant case, provided that the implementation does not conflict with the authority's statutory duty. Or at the least there should be an opportunity of commenting before any such change occurs, and this change will only be countenanced for the instant case if the public interest so demands.[70]

(b) If an individual has in the past enjoyed a benefit or advantage which could legitimately be expected to continue, that person may be entitled to a statement of reasons for the change of position, and an opportunity to be consulted thereon.[71]

(c) The existence of any such legitimate expectation, whether arising from a representation or past practice, will be a matter of construction. Thus in *ex p. Khan*[72] Parker L.J. was willing to hold that a Home Office circular concerning adoption procedures for foreign children generated a legitimate expectation that the procedures would be followed. The minister could not depart from them without affording the applicants a hearing and then only if the public interest demanded it. However, in *Re Findlay*[73] a change of policy concerning parole was not held to infringe the legitimate expectations of certain prisoners, notwithstanding the fact that they would, under the previous policy, have expected earlier release. The content of the prisoners' legitimate expectations was held to be that their cases would be individually considered under whatever policy the minister sought fit to adopt.

(d) The content of the duty to consult which is held to flow from the legitimate expectation may also depend upon the circumstances. The applicant may, as in *Khan*, be allowed to argue why the pre-existing policy should continue to be applied to the instant case. The duty may, however, be more extensive, and the applicant may be enabled to contest the soundness of the new policy itself. Thus, in *Dredger*[74] stall-holders were held to have a legitimate expectation of being consulted about a major change in rental policy for market stalls. This was held to entail consultation rights very similar to those set out in the *Gunning* case: the council had to provide details of its proposals; the applicants should be given sufficient time to respond; the council had to listen to the applicants' responses with an open mind; and these responses must be taken into account when reaching a final decision.

---

[70] e.g. *Att.-Gen. of Hong Kong v. Ng Yuen Shiu* [1983] 2 A.C. 629; *R. v. Liverpool Corporation, ex p. Liverpool Taxi Fleet Operators' Association* [1972] 2 Q.B. 299; *ex p. Khan*, below n. 71; *Council of Civil Service Unions v. Minister for the Civil Service* [1985] A.C. 374, 408-409; *R. v. Secretary of State for the Home Department, ex p. Ruddock* [1987] 1 W.L.R. 1482; cf. *R. v. Secretary of State for Transport, ex p. Richmond upon Thames London Borough Council* [1994] 1 All E.R. 577, 596-597. See below, pp. 673-675.

[71] e.g. *C.C.S.U.* [1985] A.C. 374, 408-409; *R. v. Secretary of State for the Home Department, ex p. Khan* [1985] 1 All E.R. 40; *ex p. Ruddock* [1987] 1 W.L.R. 1482; *R. v. Birmingham City Council, ex p. Dredger* [1993] C.O.D. 340. Cases may be difficult to classify as type (i) or (ii) particularly where, as in *Khan* or *Ruddock*, there is a circular in question. This could be regarded either as some type of representation or as the past practice justifying the legitimate expectation.

[72] [1985] 1 All E.R. 40.

[73] [1985] A.C. 318, 338.

[74] *R. v. Birmingham City Council, ex p. Dredger* [1993] C.O.D. 340.

(e) There may be a duty to consult, in addition to that mentioned above, which is derived from the duty to act fairly. The precise ambit of this duty to consult is unclear, but it may exist independently of any legitimate expectation based on a prior representation or a prior practice of consultation. There is, however, case law which appears to deny the existence of any such duty.[75]

(3) CONSULTATION RIGHTS: FUTURE PROSPECTS

A more general concept of prior consultation possesses a number of advantages.

First, it enables views to be taken into account before an administrative policy has hardened into a draft rule. Part of the problem with current attempts at legislative control is this very absence of input while the rule is being promulgated.

Secondly, it would relieve Parliament from some of the burden of technical scrutiny. This is not a job which is best performed by Members of Parliament, nor one which they are particularly interested in.

Thirdly, the duty to consult has a wider significance. It allows those outside government to play some role in the shaping of policy. In this sense it enhances participation. This theme will be developed further within the next section.

Fourthly, it is not immediately self-evident why a hearing should be thought natural when there is some form of individualised adjudication, but not where rules are being made. The unspoken presumption is that a "hearing" will be given to a rule indirectly through the operation of our principles of representative democracy, through scrutiny in Parliament. We have already seen how far reality falls short of this ideal. But even in principle the argument is assailable. What degree of representation of interests is warranted outside of the normal parliamentary channels is precisely the question in issue. It is one that cannot be solved through blank incantation of the term "representative democracy" as if that were capable of only one inexorable meaning. Moreover, many of the rules which we are concerned with in this section are not statutory instruments and have, therefore, never seen the parliamentary light of day at all.

This then is, in outline, the nature of the argument for increased participatory rights. Commentators within the United Kingdom who favour such a development tend to look approvingly at the position in the United States where such rights are indeed fostered to a greater extent than in the United Kingdom. There is, however, a danger of overlooking the problems which accompany any such development. These have been addressed by American writers, some of whom are ambivalent about the benefits to be

---

[75] Contrast the reasoning of the Court of Appeal in *R. v. Devon County Council, ex p. Baker* [1993] C.O.D. 253, in which it appears to be assumed that such a duty can exist, with that of Popplewell J. in the same case [1993] C.O.D. 138, who denied the existence of any such obligation. Hutchison J. in *R. v. Birmingham City Council, ex p. Dredger* [1993] C.O.D. 340 held that no duty to consult could be based on the duty to act fairly, in the absence of a legitimate expectation, but it is unclear whether this was meant as a comment related to the facts of the case, or as a statement of principle.

secured by the grant of such process rights. We may well feel that the field
is greener on the other side of the fence or ocean. We cannot however
ignore the experiences of those who are more familiar with their own
system.[76]

What then are the issues which must be addressed if we wish to develop
such rights? Two principal issues can be identified.

The *first* relates to the *type of consultative process* which is established,
and this can be broken down into three more specific problems. How
formal should the participatory process be? How do we define the nature
of an "interest" which is entitled to be represented? And how do we prevent
the more powerful groups dominating any such consultative process which
we have established? A brief word should be said about each of these issues
which will be considered in more detail later.

How formal should the participatory process be? Are we envisaging a
"trial" with the presentation of formal arguments for and against the
proposed rule, or should there be something less cumbersome than this? In
the United States there is an Administrative Procedure Act 1946, section 4
of which states that notice of any proposed rule-making is to be published
in the Federal Register and is to include a statement of the time and place
of the rule-making proceedings and the terms or substance of the proposed
rule.[77] After notice the agency is to afford interested persons an opportunity
to participate in the rule-making. There are, in essence, three differing
modes of participation which have varying degrees of formality. Many
administrative rules are subject to what is termed *notice and comment*,
whereby such proposed rules are published and written comments can be
proffered by interested parties. Other such rules are subject to a *full trial
type hearing*, which can include the provision of oral testimony and cross
examination.[78] Yet other rules are governed by an *intermediate* or *hybrid
process* which entails more formality than notice and comment, but
less than the trial type hearing.[79] If we are to develop more extensive
participatory rights in the United Kingdom we would therefore have to
decide initially upon which of these routes or combination of routes to
follow within any particular area. The suitability of any such technique
would moreover have to be judged against the constitutional and political
position of agencies or government departments in the United Kingdom
which is different from that in the United States.

---

[76] *e.g.* the important article by Stewart, "The Reformation of American Administrative Law"
88 Harv.L.Rev. 1667 (1975), is ambivalent about the value of such participatory rights and
addresses many of the problems produced by such an approach.

[77] Except where notice or hearing is required by statute, this does not apply to interpretative
rules, general statements of policy, rules of agency organisation, procedure or practice, or in
any situation in which the agency for good cause finds that notice and public procedures are
impracticable, unnecessary, or contrary to the public interest.

[78] s.7.

[79] *International Harvester Co.* v. *Ruckelshaus* 478 F. 2d 615 (D.C. Cir. 1973); *Portland
Cement Assn.* v. *Ruckelshaus* 486 F. 2d 375 (D.C. Cir. 1973). The development in this
direction was, however, checked by *Vermont Yankee Nuclear Power Corp.* v. *Natural
Resources Defence Council, Inc.* 435 US 519 (1978). See generally, Breyer and Stewart,
Administrative Law and Regulatory Policy (2nd ed., 1985), pp. 561-625.

How do we define the nature of an "interest" which is entitled to be represented? One easy response to this question would be that we simply do not do so. Any person or group which wishes to offer comments is allowed to do so. Their very eagerness to participate means that they are by definition entitled to be represented and have their views taken into account. The matter is not so easily resolved for a number of reasons. On the one hand, there may be an inter-relationship between the type of rule-making process which we choose to adopt, and the range of groups which we can regard as legitimately interested parties. Thus, to take a simple example, if we choose to have a formal trial type hearing on a proposed rule within a certain area it may not be feasible to allow any person who believes that they have something to say to take part. The hearing could become wholly unwieldy and protracted. On the other hand, there may be difficulties in not exercising any control over the range of interested parties even where the rule-making process is more informal. Let us imagine that we adopt a notice and comment type approach in the context of the making of a rule which relates to the grant of licences for taxis within Liverpool. Do we really mean that taxi drivers within other areas should be notified and could send in comments? If we allow them to do so, does the rule-making authority have to give them as much weight as the comments which it receives from those who are more directly affected?

How do we prevent the more dominant groups from exerting excessive pressure upon the rule-making authority? This is a real problem which must be addressed if the enterprise is to be worth embarking upon at all. The scale of this problem should be fully appreciated. Pluralist writers in the UK may have recognised the existence of groups which influenced the political process.[80] They did not however regard groups as equal in power, or the degree of access which they had to the public body. Corporatist arguments, which postulate the existence of a dominant group which can possess a "monopoly" of representational status, only serve to underline this point. Some theorists go even further and argue that certain agencies have in fact been "captured" by the group which they seek to regulate; the agency comes to protect the client group and its interests rather than advancing the public interest. It is therefore readily apparent that if we are seriously interested in advancing participatory rights we will have to address this problem.

How do we do so? This is a complex question, which may have to be tackled in a number of differing ways. One approach would be to use judicial review. The courts would insist that the agency give adequate consideration to the range of groups which offered evidence to it. This may be valuable, but such intervention may come "too late". Certain less organised and less powerful groups may simply not be in a very good position to advance their views before the agency at all. They may not possess the necessary financial means. If we are to take the problems of unequal group power seriously we may need to devise strategies which help such disadvantaged groups to put their case. This may entail direct financial aid, relief from costs and the provision of assistance in formulating and

---

[80] See above, pp. 24-27.

advancing their views. Experience in the United States has shown that these avenues can be explored, but that there are real difficulties in successfully implementing such approaches. While the problem of inequality of group power is a real one it must however be kept within perspective. Given that such inequality does exist, it is difficult to believe that the less advantaged groups will do better under a system which does not enshrine participatory rights than under one which does. The more powerful groups will exert influence upon a public body even where such formal rights are absent just through the very fact of their power. The introduction of a more structured system of participatory rights does at least give the less advantaged groups a chance to air their views which would otherwise not have been possible.

It is time now to consider the *second* difficulty with the grant of greater participatory rights, which is that certain disadvantageous consequences have been said to follow if such rights are granted. Two specific problems are relevant.

The first is the practical problem of *time, cost, and delay*. It may seem obvious that making decisions only after consulting what may be a wide range of affected interests will slow down decision-making, and will entail increased costs for the administration. There are, however, a number of responses to this argument. One would be to admit the substance of the argument, but to reply that such costs are worth bearing. If all decisions were made by an autocrat they would doubtless be made more speedily. A cost of democracy is precisely the cost of involving more people. Another type of response is less obvious. The argument for increased participatory rights is based, in part at least, upon the idea that the people who are consulted may have something to offer the administrator. The rule which emerges will, it is hoped, be better. Whether this is always so may be debatable, but there is little reason to suggest that the argument does not hold in certain instances. Where it does have validity, then it is far less clear that the granting of such rights will entail an overall increase in cost. If a less good rule emerges where there is no consultation then the total costs may be greater because, for example, the rule fails to achieve its objective. Clearly there will be areas within which decisions in a democratic society need to be made speedily, and where therefore, irrespective of issues of cost, consultation in rule-making is not feasible. If there is an outbreak of foot and mouth disease one cannot engage in a protracted consultative process before making the necessary rules.

The second type of problem which can ensue from the granting of participatory rights causes us more problems. The essence of the argument is that *there may be certain areas in which such participatory rights are not suitable*. This is not simply a generalisation from the preceding specific example (of foot and mouth disease), which shows the impracticability of affording consultative rights in cases where time is of the essence. The problem is more fundamental and can be expressed as follows. Participatory rights are simply one type of tool at our disposal through which to render the exercise of administrative discretion accountable. There are many others, including political checks, judicial review, internal organisational safeguards within the bureaucracy, the training of personnel and financial oversight.

Two important points follow from this realisation. One is that when we are advocating the use of one of these techniques we may need to be aware of the way in which this does or does not fit in with the other techniques at our disposal. The other is that any conclusion as to how these differing techniques should fit together can only be reached by having some clear understanding as to the principal purposes which regulation within a particular area is designed to serve.

A brief example will help to demonstrate this. Let us focus upon the administration of social welfare. What might be our underlying aim within this area and how does this affect the suitability of participatory rights? One type of goal would be to ensure "bureaucratic rationality", meaning that true claims should be distinguished from false claims in the most efficient manner.[81] If this were our underlying aim then we might well focus our attention upon improving organisational safeguards within the bureaucracy, thereby ensuring a minimum of error; the training of personnel; specialisation of function; and internal checks to test both the accuracy and efficiency of the decision-making. Extensive procedural rights for those concerned with the making of agency rules would not necessarily be of central importance, nor would they necessarily "sit" well with the other objectives mentioned. Let us assume that we change the basic goal of our social welfare system. People now believe that the principal objective should be one of fairly determining "rights" to social welfare in ways which are analogous to the common law's determination of rights in other areas. Given this background aim the way in which we use the different techniques at our disposal subtly alters. We would focus more attention upon procedural rights, both in the making of individual decisions, and in terms of the rules which guide the distribution of social welfare. Greater attention would be focused upon the ability of the individual to argue his or her case, and the ordinary courts would assume a more prominent role as arbiters of whether the conditions for the individual "entitlement" were fulfilled in a particular case.

The matters considered above do undoubtedly require resolution if we are to make progress in this area. These particular points should not, however, mask the general benefits which increased participatory rights can bring. The Rippon Commission, as we shall see below, rightly regards developments with respect to consultation as one important way of improving the overall quality of secondary legislation.

6. *Control through the Courts*

Subordinate legislation does not partake of the immunity from judicial control which applies to primary legislation. It can be attacked in any of the following ways.

---

[81] Mashaw, *Bureaucratic Justice* (1983), pp. 21-41; Craig, "Discretionary Power in Modern Administration", *Verwaltungsermessen im Modernen Staat* (Bullinger ed., 1986), pp. 79-112.

(1) PROCEDURAL ULTRA VIRES AND FORMAL INVALIDITY

As is apparent delegated legislation may be enacted by a variety of procedures. If the requisite procedure is not followed and that procedure is held to be mandatory rather than directory it will lead to the invalidation of the legislation. We have already come across one example of this in our discussion of the statutory requirement for consultation.

The secondary legislation will also be invalidated if it is formally outside the parent Act. In one case a notice requisitioning certain property was held to be void because the notice did not exclude furniture and the power to requisition did not extend to furniture.[82] In another, a bylaw restricting access to a military site was impugned because the enabling legislation only allowed such bylaws to be made on condition that they did not infringe upon any rights of common.[83] On some occasions it may be necessary to pass legislation to correct an earlier mistake, such as when it was realised that certain regulations concerning fire services had never been laid as required by the parent Act. An Act of Indemnity was passed to correct the error.[84]

(2) SUBSTANTIVE ULTRA VIRES

Delegated legislation may also be struck down because its substance infringes the parent Act or some other primary statute. This can occur in a number of ways.

For example, although we have no written constitution the courts do utilise certain *constitutional principles* when construing delegated legislation. An instrument which contravenes such principles will be declared void unless express statutory authority can be produced to justify the action. In *Attorney-General* v. *Wilts United Dairies Ltd*[85] the Food Controller was empowered to regulate the sale, purchase, etc., of food and to regulate price. A dairy company was granted a licence to trade in milk, but it had to pay a charge of 2d. per gallon. This condition was accepted by the company but it later resisted and refused to pay. Despite its express consent to the condition, the court held that its refusal to pay was justified. The charge infringed the fundamental provision contained in the Bill of Rights 1689 that no money should be levied to the use of the Crown without the consent of Parliament. A power to charge would not be implied from the general power to control that trade.

The use of constitutional presumptions is also apparent in the recent *Leech* case.[86] The court struck down a rule which authorised a prison governor to read every letter from a prisoner and stop any that were objectionable or of inordinate length. In reaching this conclusion the court reasoned on the basis that the more fundamental the right interfered with by a rule, and the more drastic the interference, the more difficult was it to

---

[82] *Patchett* v. *Leathem* (1949) 65 T.L.R. 69.
[83] *Director of Public Prosecutions* v. *Hutchinson* [1990] 2 A.C. 783.
[84] National Fire Service Regulations (Indemnity) Act 1944.
[85] (1921) 39 T.L.R. 781.
[86] R. v. *Secretary of State for the Home Department, ex p. Leech* [1993] 4 All E.R. 539.

imply a rule-making power of this kind. The fundamental right in question was the right of access to court and it was held that the contested rule could not be upheld because of the extent to which it impeded the exercise of that right.

While the courts have protected other interests by a reliance on constitutional presumptions,[87] they have on occasion, especially during wartime, liberally construed statutory instruments.[88]

Subordinate legislation will in addition be subject to many of the substantive checks which apply to administrative action in general. The courts will apply notions of *purpose, relevancy* and *reasonableness* to constrain the exercise of discretionary power.[89]

Powers are granted for certain purposes. If it can be shown that subordinate legislation is being used for an *improper purpose*, which is other than that intended by the parent Act, it will be declared void.[90]

The courts will also intervene if the exercise of the delegated power is held to be *unreasonable*. An instrument will not be held to be unreasonable merely because the particular judge disagrees with its content, or believes that it goes further than is prudent, necessary, or convenient. To be struck down on this ground the instrument must be manifestly unjust, involve the oppressive or gratuitous interference with the rights of those subject to it such as could find no justification in the minds of reasonable men, disclose bad faith, or be partial and unequal in its operation as between different classes.[91] An instrument may also be unreasonable if it is too vague, but the courts may well place a generous construction on statutory instruments in certain instances. In *McEldowney* v. *Forde*[92] a regulation was challenged which created a criminal offence of belonging to an organisation which described itself as a "republican club" or "any like organisation howsoever described". The person convicted belonged to such a club. His conviction was upheld by a majority despite the fact that no threat to public order was apparent, and notwithstanding that the wording of the regulation was vague to say the least. By way of contrast in *Bugg* v. *D.P.P.*[93] the court struck down a bylaw restricting access to a military base on the ground that the area covered by the bylaw was not delineated clearly enough.

The substantive controls which the courts impose can be applied with varying degrees of *intensity*. This will be discussed in more detail below,[94] and is apparent in the *McEldowney* case itself. The courts have, moreover, made this explicit. In *R.* v. *Secretary of State for the Environment, ex p.*

---

[87] *e.g. Chester* v. *Bateson* [1920] 1 K.B. 829.
[88] *e.g. R.* v. *Halliday* [1917] A.C. 260; *Liversidge* v. *Anderson* [1942] A.C. 206.
[89] See generally, Chap. 11.
[90] *Att.-Gen. for Canada* v. *Hallett & Carey Ltd.* [1952] A.C. 427; *R.* v. *H.M. Treasury, ex p. Smedley* [1985] Q.B. 657.
[91] *Kruse* v. *Johnson* [1898] 2 Q.B. 91. See also, *Monro* v. *Watson* (1887) 57 L.T. 366; *Repton School Governors* v. *Repton Rural District Council* [1918] 2 K.B. 133; *Sparks* v. *Edward Ash Ltd.* [1943] 2 K.B. 223.
[92] [1971] A.C. 632.
[93] [1993] 2 All E.R. 815.
[94] See below, Chap. 11.

Nottinghamshire County Council[95] the local authority challenged expenditure limits which had been imposed by the Secretary of State. Failure to comply with those limits would lead to a reduction in the rate support grant available to the local authority. The limits required the approval by resolution of the House of Commons before they could take effect. The local authority argued, *inter alia*, that these limits were unreasonable. Lord Scarman held that the courts should be reluctant to intervene on this ground. This was in part because the subject-matter, public financial administration, inevitably involved political judgment by the minister. It was also because approval of the House of Commons had been given. While the court would intervene if there had been a misconstruction of the statute, it would be constitutionally inappropriate for the court to interfere on the grounds of unreasonableness unless the minister had abused his power, in the sense of deceiving the House or producing expenditure limits which were so absurd that he must have taken leave of his senses.[96] This approach has been subsequently endorsed by the House of Lords.[97] While the subject-matter of such cases, being concerned as it was with economic regulation, may warrant less intensive review than in some other contexts, the relevance of a resolution by the Commons may be questioned. As we have seen, the passage of such a resolution does not indicate any meaningful parliamentary scrutiny, and hence the effect of this approval is largely symbolic.

(3) DELEGATION

The normal principles concerning delegation will apply. These are dealt with in detail later[98] and may be briefly summarised here. The general rule is that where a power is conferred upon one person it must be exercised by that person. A necessary qualification to this exists in the case of ministers where officials will exercise powers in the name of the minister. How far delegation will be allowed will depend upon the nature of the power in question and the general circumstances of the case. While the matter has not been firmly decided in the English courts, on principle legislative power should be exercised by those in whom it is vested.[99]

(4) REMEDIES

The invalidity of a statutory instrument may normally be raised collaterally or directly. There may, for example, be a collateral challenge by way of defence to an enforcement action, or as a defence to a contract suit. It has, however, been held that a bylaw can only be challenged collaterally in

---

[95] [1986] A.C. 240.
[96] *Ibid.* pp. 247, 250-251.
[97] *R.* v. *Secretary of State for the Environment, ex p. Hammersmith and Fulham London Borough Council* [1990] 1 A.C. 521.
[98] See below, Chap. 11.
[99] See *Hawke's Bay Raw Milk Products Co-operative Ltd.* v. *New Zealand Milk Board* [1961] N.Z.L.R. 218. In the First World War sub-delegation of legislative power was not expressly authorised, but the Emergency Powers (Defence) Act 1939 allowed further delegation. This could produce as many as five tiers of authority; a veritable wedding cake of regulations.

criminal proceedings where the invalidity alleged is substantive as opposed to procedural.[100] How far this will be taken to apply to other kinds of secondary legislation, and to other forms of collateral attack, is unclear.

A statutory instrument may also be attacked directly through the declaration. Subject to the doubts voiced below,[101] the direct action should be brought as an application for judicial review for a declaration or injunction.

The scope of *locus standi* to challenge secondary legislation is not entirely clear. It has traditionally been assumed to be quite wide. However, it has been held that individuals have no right to complain of procedural defects in delegated legislation unless they have been prejudiced by the default.[102]

The possibility of an injunction to prevent a minister from proceeding with making an instrument,[103] and the possible immunisation of delegated legislation from judicial control[104] are considered later.

The prerogative orders of certiorari and prohibition were traditionally regarded as applying only to judicial functions and hence as being inapplicable to delegated legislation. What inroads have been made on this principle are considered in the discussion of remedies.[105]

7. *Delegated Legislation: Possible Reforms*

There is no ready made solution which is capable, at the stroke of a pen, of solving the problems associated with delegated legislation. Improvements are, however, possible. The problems were highlighted by the Rippon Commission[106] whose recommendations for change in the primary legislative process have already been discussed. The Commission stated that "we consider the whole approach of Parliament to delegated legislation to be highly unsatisfactory",[107] and it recognised that much delegated legislation was of real importance.[108] It made a number of serious suggestions for improving the existing regime.

(1) PUBLICATION AND ACCESS TO THE LAW

The Commission made its views on the present arrangements for publication and access to the law very clear.[109]

---

[100] *Bugg v. Director of Public Prosecutions* [1993] 2 All E.R. 815.
[101] See below, pp. 558-559.
[102] *Bugg* [1993] 2 All E.R. 815, 827.
[103] See below, pp. 542-543.
[104] See below, Chap. 16.
[105] See below, Chap. 14. Mandamus seems to be subject to no such limitations and has been used in relation to bylaws, *R. v. Manchester Corporation* [1911] 1 K.B. 560.
[106] *Making the Law, The Report of the Hansard Society Commission on the Legislative Process* (1993).
[107] *Ibid.* pp. 89-90.
[108] *Ibid.* p. 89.
[109] *Ibid.* p. 108.

"At present the accessibility of statute law to users and the wider public is slow, inconvenient, complicated and subject to several impediments. To put it bluntly, it is often very difficult to find out what the text of the law is – let alone what it means. Something must be done."

It recommended that as far as possible new laws should not come into effect before they are published, and that the government should press ahead as fast as possible with a Statute Law Database which would facilitate the publication and updating of statute law.[110] There should, moreover, be financial assistance provided to those bodies, such as Citizens Advice Bureaus, in order to help them to explain the law to the public.[111]

The Commission also addressed the problems which can be present where a primary statute is to be implemented by delegated legislation. It suggested that the government should indicate the general nature of the regulations which it intended to introduce, and that this could be done by a White Paper or through an explanatory statement published with the bill.[112]

(2) THE SUBJECT-MATTER WHICH SHOULD BE SCRUTINISED BY PARLIAMENT

We have already seen that the definition of a statutory instrument is a purely formal one, with the consequence that many rules which may be legislative in nature are not open to scrutiny by Parliament at all. This matter was not considered by the Commission in any real depth, but it did touch on the issue in passing. The Commission noted that much sub-delegated legislation was not, and could not be, debated in Parliament. This was not, said the Commission, acceptable. It recommended that all Acts and delegated legislation should be drafted so that all important regulations and delegated legislation could be debated in Parliament.[113] The realisation of this particular recommendation is, as will be seen below, problematic.

(3) DEBATES ON STATUTORY INSTRUMENTS

The ineffectiveness of the present regime for debating statutory instruments on the floor of the House has been noted above. The Rippon Commission has proposed a number of significant alterations which centre on a greater use of standing committees.

For those statutory instruments which are subject to *affirmative resolution* the Commission suggests the following new procedure.[114] Unless the House otherwise ordered, all statutory instruments which require affirmative resolution should be automatically referred to standing committee for debate. Longer or more complex instruments could be referred to a special standing committee. Such standing committees should have the power to question ministers on the meaning, purpose and effect of the instrument. The minister responsible for the instrument would move a

---

[110] *Ibid.* p. 109.
[111] *Ibid.* p. 113.
[112] *Ibid.* p. 112.
[113] *Ibid.* p. 93.
[114] *Ibid.* pp. 91–93, 149.

motion recommending its approval, and members of the committee would then be able to move amendments recommending either that the instrument should not be approved, or that it should be approved subject to changes. There would, in general, be no time limit on debates. If the committee recommended approval of the instrument this should then be put to the House without debate. Where the committee recommended that the instrument should be rejected, or approved of it subject to amendments, there would then be a debate in the House which would be constrained by time limits.

For those statutory instruments which are subject to *negative resolution* then, unless the House otherwise ordered, all prayers for the annulment of such instruments should be referred to a standing committee. The procedure within the committee would be the same as for affirmative instruments except that the MP who tabled the prayer would either move a motion for annulment of the instrument concerned, or a motion recommending its amendment. The minister could then move amendments to such motions. If the MP's motion failed that would be an end of the matter. If this motion succeeded in committee then the MP who moved the motion should then have the right to move a formal motion in the House for the annulment of the instrument. Debates would be subject to time limits.

These suggestions are to be welcomed. The centralilty accorded to the standing committee as an initial vehicle for scrutiny is designed to alleviate the real difficulty of finding time to conduct the whole procedure on the floor of the House itself.

(4) SCRUTINY BY COMMITTEE

It may be thought that the recommendations of the Rippon Commission blur the divide between debates on statutory instruments and scrutiny by committee. This is in reality not so. The function of the standing committees described above is to render the debate by Parliament itself more workable and more thoroughgoing. There is still room for reform of the pre-existing committee regime. A number of such reforms are suggested by the Commission.

Some relate to the work of the *Joint Committee on Statutory Instruments*. It is proposed that, except in cases of emergency, no statutory instrument should be debated until the Joint Committee has reported. Furthermore, if that committee has reported that an instrument is *ultra vires* or otherwise defective, there should be no motion approving the instrument without a resolution to set aside the committee's findings.[115]

A further suggestion is for scrutiny of delegated legislation to be assigned to the *departmental select committee* which is responsible for that area, which would then report on those instruments that raise matters of public importance.[116] There is much to be said for this idea, and it may go some way to alleviating the present malaise.

---

[115] *Ibid.* p. 91.
[116] *Ibid.* p. 90.

The current committee system is beset by a number of difficulties, four of which are: the workload placed on the Joint Committee; its lack of expertise in many subject-matter areas; lack of interest among MPs in the work of the committee; and the hazy division between technical scrutiny and the merits. If statutory instruments were reviewed by departmental select committees then this would, at the least, meet some of these problems. The workload would be spread amongst a number of committees. The departmental select committees would be staffed by those who had some knowledge of, and interest in the area. Often it is, with the best will in the world, not easy for those who are unfamiliar with a topic to know whether a new piece of delegated legislation is sound either in technical terms, or in terms of its merits, without having some background expertise in that area. Members of select committees are more likely to possess the understanding which is a prerequisite for reasoned scrutiny. Given the evidence of the workings of the present system this idea must be worth a trial.

(5) CONSULTATION

The Commission prefaced its recommendations about consultation and delegated legislation with this observation.[117]

> "The importance of proper consultation on delegated legislation should not be underestimated. For many bodies its importance is equal to – or greater than – the importance of consultation on bills. And from the point of view of those directly affected, it is equally important to get delegated legislation right. Delegated legislation may be of secondary importance to Ministers and those in Parliament...but to those to whom the law applies or to the practitioners...who have to apply it, the method by which the law is made is of little significance. Primary and delegated legislation are equally the law of the land."

These observations are to be welcomed, as are the suggestions which flow from them. The Commission recommended that there should be consultation where appropriate at the formative stage of delegated legislation, and that wherever possible departments should consult outside experts and affected bodies on the drafts of instruments which they propose to submit to Parliament. Moreover, the guidelines for consultation on primary bills should be applied with suitable modification to delegated legislation.[118]

The problem with this proposal relates not to its substance, but to its application. The force of law may well be required in order to ensure that departments really do consult in the desired manner, rather than by "marking" certain groups which are regarded as acceptable with the consequence that others are unable to play any real part in this consultative process. It is for this reason, amongst others, that developments along the lines described in the United States would be desirable.

---

[117] *Ibid.* p. 42.
[118] *Loc.cit.*

Section 3. Rules Made by the Administration

1. *Type and Rationale*

There is a duality latent in the term legislative instrument. It has been touched on already, but it has not been directly faced. When we speak of delegated legislation we mean the grant of power by the parent legislature to a minister or other body to make rules or regulations. While the test of what is to count as a statutory instrument in the 1946 Act is primarily one of form,[119] the whole idea of publication and legislative scrutiny is premised upon the hypothesis that the rules thus made are themselves legislative in nature. Legislative in this sense signifies that the rule has a generality of application which distinguishes it from a mere executive order. Sub-delegated legislation poses problems at both levels. It may be unclear whether Parliament did delegate power to this particular person, and it may be questionable whether the rule that that person made really was legislative in character or not.

What is clear is that there exists an important category quite outside that of sub-delegated legislation. Its distinguishing hallmark is that there may be no legislative mandate to make any regulations at all, but it is clear that the administration has made rules which are legislative in character using that term in the second sense. They are of a generality of application such that if they were juxtaposed to real statutory instruments they would be indistinguishable in terms of the nature of their content. To use the language of the advertiser, if the labels were removed from both the experienced observer would be hard pressed to say why one was any more legislative than the other. Thus, although such rules may be made by the administration, they are not necessarily administrative rules. Some of them may be, but many are not.

There is a tremendous variety in the *types* of such rules. Codes of practice, circulars, directions, rules and regulations are all to be found within the administrative landscape. These labels are not, however, terms of art, and the precise label which is employed does not therefore "solve" the problem of classification. One suggested classification categorises administrative rules in the following manner:[120] procedural rules; interpretative guides; instructions to officials; prescriptive/evidential rules; commendatory codes; voluntary codes; rules of practice; management and operation; and administrative pronouncements.

There are not surprisingly a number of differing *rationales* for the existence of such rules, and for preferring them to more formal delegated legislation. Four such reasons can be distinguished.[121] First, even where no

---

[119] Except for rules made after the 1946 Act came into force under statutes existing prior to that date.

[120] Baldwin and Houghton, "Circular Arguments: The Status and Legitimacy of Administrative Rules" [1986] P.L. 239, 240-244.

[121] See generally, Ganz, *Quasi-Legislation: Recent Developments in Secondary Legislation* (1987), Chap. 6.

explicit power to make regulations is granted to an agency, it will often make such rules which indicate how it will exercise its discretion. This is a natural tendency for bureaucracies when faced with a recurring problem, and obviates the need to think out the problem afresh each time. The whole debate about rules versus discretion will be addressed in more detail later.[122] Secondly, non-legal rules facilitate the use of non-technical language, exemplified by the Highway Code, and the Health and Safety Codes. Thirdly, such rules may be preferred because they are more flexible than statutory instruments, and hence can be changed or modified more easily. Finally, these rules may be preferred to delegated legislation precisely because they are not legally binding; they enable policies to be developed voluntarily in the sense that "persuasion may be preferable to compulsion".[123] These reasons will be considered in the course of the ensuing analysis.

2. *Legal Status*

The precise legal status of these rules may well differ depending upon the type of rule in question. Three points of general importance can, however, be made.

First, the fact that an agency does not have express power to make rules does not, *per se*, render them invalid. The capacity to make such rules flows from the way in which agencies are allowed to exercise their discretion. The courts have held, as we shall see later,[124] that rules or policy guidelines are valid provided that they are not too rigidly applied, and provided that certain other conditions are met.

Secondly, the precise *legal status* of any particular rule can only be discerned by examining the relevant statutory provisions, and the judicial interpretation thereof, which operate within differing areas. Thus legislation may, for example, stipulate that a code, such as the Highway Code, should have a certain degree of legal force in legal proceedings, by identifying the weight to be given to a breach of the code in any such action.[125] Codes may also possess "indirect" legal effect.[126] Non-compliance with the provisions thereof may provide a reason why, for example, a television programme contractor should not have its franchise renewed.[127] Non-compliance with a code may also furnish the rationale for the passage of a statutory instrument, the object of which is to provide "full" legal force for the attainment of the objectives contained in the code itself.[128] Given that the precise legal status of rules can vary it is therefore not surprising

---

[122] See below, Chap. 11.
[123] Ganz, *Quasi-Legislation*, pp. 97-98.
[124] See below, Chap. 11.
[125] See, *e.g.* Transport Act 1982, s.60.
[126] Ganz, *Quasi-Legislation*, pp. 16-18.
[127] Independent Broadcasting Authority Act 1973, ss. 5, 9, 13.
[128] Local Government, Planning and Land Act 1980, ss. 2, 3.

that the judiciary can be divided as to what that status actually is, even within one particular area.[129]

Thirdly, even if a particular rule is not "related to" primary legislation in any of the ways considered above, it may still have *legal consequences* in a double sense. On the one hand, provided that such a rule is not too rigidly applied, it can be dispositive of a person's case.[130] On the other hand, the existence of such a rule may, as we have seen, generate consultation rights if the public body seeks to resile from the application of its rule.[131]

3. *Rules made by the Administration: Problems*

A number of problems are presented by the existence of the rules considered above. Four principal types of problem can be identified.

The first is that the promulgation of rules by the executive, together with the relevant interest group, may bypass the legislature and foreclose the possibility of parliamentary scrutiny. As Stewart states,[132]

"The ultimate problem is to control and validate the exercise of essentially legislative powers that do not enjoy the formal legitimation of one-person one-vote election."

A second problem follows from the first, in that particular pressure groups may exercise excessive influence over the content of the rules which emerge. The ability of the public more generally to have some input into the proposed rule may be absent, or vary in degree from area to area.

A third cause for concern centres upon the rule of law in the following sense. Many of the rules under consideration are unpublished, or not readily accessible; the intended and actual legal status of others is unclear. Yet other rules fit poorly with the relevant parent legislation, and appear to countenance action which is inconsistent with the enabling statute.

Finally, such rules have been used on issues of considerable political contention, thereby rendering the law "most vague at the points where it should be most clear".[133]

The resort to informal rules should not, however, always be deprecated. The reasons for utilising such rules rather than delegated legislation *stricto sensu* have been considered above. These reasons have force, and are strengthened by the difficulties which would be encountered were we to insist that all norms of a legislative character should be subjected to parliamentary scrutiny. The cogency of the particular arguments used in favour of informal rules must nonetheless be carefully analysed. For

---

[129] Compare R. v. *Heathrow Airport Immigration Officer, ex p. Bibi* [1976] 1 W.L.R. 979, R. v. *Home Secretary, ex p. Hosenball* [1977] 1 W.L.R. 766 and R. v. *Immigration Appeal Tribunal, ex p. Bakhtaur Singh* [1986] 1 W.L.R. 910, on the status of immigration rules.

[130] See below, pp. 391-393.

[131] See above, pp. 256-258.

[132] "The Reformation of American Administrative Law" 88 Harv.L.Rev. 1667, 1668 (1975). An excellent article which is to be recommended.

[133] Baldwin and Houghton, "Circular Arguments", p. 268.

example, the argument that informal rules are preferred because they reflect a voluntary approach whereby reliance is placed on co-operation and consent rather than the force of law, could mean three very different things.

(i) It could indicate that a policy which has been considered and approved by the legislature is then implemented by a code of some type rather than formal legislation because it is felt that this will be more efficacious.
(ii) It could exemplify a "corporatist strategy" whereby the executive and a major interest group bargain independently of the legislature to attain a goal which both seek, but which may be opposed by other less powerful interest groups, and/or the legislature.
(iii) It could mean that a powerful executive implements a code or rule which the relevant interest groups in that area oppose, but which they are powerless to fight. Legislative scrutiny can be avoided, and the minimum of legal formalism troubles the executive in pursuit of its aim. Not all informal rules are therefore necessarily more truly consensual in nature than those norms which emerge as legislation.

4. *Rules made by the Administration: Possible Solutions*

(1) DIRECT CONTROL

Direct control would require any rule of a legislative character to be subject to some form of parliamentary scrutiny. The effect would be to reverse the premise of the Statutory Instruments Act 1946. As we have seen that Act adopts a formalistic approach: delegated legislation will be subject to some form of parliamentary scrutiny and publication only where the instrument is described as a statutory instrument.[134] If we desire direct validation by Parliament the basic direction of the 1946 Act would, therefore, have to be altered. A general format would have to be devised which rendered any legislative rule formulated by a public body, whether under express delegation or not, subject to some form of parliamentary scrutiny, whether it be by the negative or affirmative procedures or by simply laying the instrument before Parliament. Exceptions could of course be made for certain types of rules. It might be felt for example that rules of internal organisation should not be subject to such scrutiny.[135] There are two immediate difficulties with this approach.

The *first problem* is inherent in any substantive definition of "legislative rule". The difficulties of applying this term are legendary, and administrative law is scattered with the remnants of such efforts, some of which have given up the ghost, others of which still, despite being much maligned, retain vitality. While this point has much force it should be kept within perspective. The criticism which has been voiced of the dichotomies between

---

[134] Although all Orders in Council made under statutory as opposed to prerogative power are automatically so regarded.
[135] Administrative Procedure Act 1946, s.4(a) (U.S.A.).

legislative and executive, or legislative and administrative, has force because it is felt not just that the distinction is difficult to draw, but more because it is irrelevant as a criterion for the solution of a problem, whether it be the application of natural justice or certiorari. The position is different here. Whatever are the very real difficulties of definition, the distinction *is* important and relevant in this context. It is rules of a legislative character which our views of political theory tell us ought to be controlled by the legislative organ of government. The 1946 Act with its formalistic approach simply ducks the whole matter. More precisely, it allows the decision to reside with the executive. Since it is the latter which will frame the legislation, it will decide whether the appellation statutory instrument should be applied to delegated powers contained therein.

Whether an attempt at substantive definition is worth the candle depends ultimately on the *second problem*. How efficacious would be such control? The answer to this must be a repeat of arguments made earlier about the constraints on effective legislative scrutiny. The addition of extra weight upon an already overburdened system of legislative control, both on the floor of the House and in committee, will give cause for hope only to the most sanguine. While such scrutiny would constitute validation it is unclear that this would be anything more than a formal obeisance to democratic control.[136]

Both of these problems should, therefore, be borne in mind when assessing the proposal from the Rippon Commission noted above, that Acts and delegated legislation should be drafted to ensure that all important regulations can be debated in Parliament.[137] This recommendation was framed with the problem of sub-delegated legislation in mind. Even if the 1946 legislation were amended to accommodate this suggestion this would still leave many rules outside the realm of parliamentary scrutiny. Many agencies make rules which are of a legislative character, even though those rules would not be classified as sub-delegated legislation.

(2) INDIRECT CONTROLS

Indirect controls could take a number of forms. The first, and in a sense the closest to direct parliamentary control, would be for Parliament in its initial grant of authority to *specify the standards* which it wishes the public body to apply as clearly as possible. Or, it could empower the relevant minister to supply guidelines or directions to the body in the course of its operations. This is a device already used in relation to nationalised industries and some other agencies. There is no doubt that it could, as argued above, be used to a greater extent and more effectively than at present.[138]

There are, however, two limits to this device. In so far as specification of standards is to stem from the legislature itself this may be of limited utility in an area where the problem is a novel one, in which the precise interests to be weighed are unclear at the outset. Legislative specification of

---

[136] Certain pieces of quasi-legislation are subject to legislative oversight, and scrutiny by select committee, Ganz, *Quasi-Legislation*, pp. 26-32.
[137] *Making the Law*, p. 93, para. 382.
[138] See above, pp. 105-106.

standards must perforce be at a relatively high level of generality. This problem can be partially circumvented by granting power to the minister to give directions after consultation with the public body. This is in itself constrained by the type of public institution in question. If it is one which warrants a high degree of autonomy from party political pressures then ministerial directives will be inappropriate.[139]

We are brought therefore to the second method of indirect control, that of *consultation* in the rule-making process. The merits of rule-making by public bodies have been extensively discussed by a number of writers. The general theme is that while discretion is inherent in any administrative system, such institutions should be encouraged to develop rules which will confine, structure and limit the way in which this discretion is used.[140] Discretion cannot and should not be eradicated. The aim is rather to secure the optimum balance between rules and discretion in any particular area. Rule-making of this type enhances justice in that it allows interference with private interests only on the condition that the individual knows of the rule in advance and can plan his or her actions accordingly. There are significant limitations to this device. While these limitations must be borne firmly in mind, they must be kept within perspective. What we are concerned with here is not so much the outer limits of rule-making, but with more specific questions. Given that administrators *do* in fact make rules which may be of a legislative character, should we approve of this or not, and what procedures if any should they be subject to? The answer to the first part of this question should be in the affirmative. When such rules are made they should, subject to certain limits, be regarded as legitimate. The nature of those limits will be considered more fully hereafter.[141] It is the second part of the question that concerns us more directly now.

The extent to which statutes and the common law at present provide consultation rights has been considered above. The key question is, therefore, whether we should develop some more general obligation to consult before a rule is made. The option of control through consultation is even more central here than it is in the context of delegated legislation. The latter will at least see the light of day through publication and will be subject to some legislative scrutiny. If we decide that other forms of rule-making are not suited to legislative scrutiny for one of the reasons given above, then validation and control by a different method becomes more important. Consultation through the representation of interested parties can go some way to achieving this. The conceptual and practical problems raised by the development of such consultation rights should not be underestimated. It should, moreover, be recognised that any such development raises broader issues concerning the nature of the democratic society within which we live. These issues have been considered above and reference should be made to that discussion.[142]

---

[139] See the analogous problems with the non-delegation doctrine in the US, Breyer and Stewart, *Administrative Law and Regulatory Policy*, pp. 68-95.
[140] Davis, *Discretionary Justice, A Preliminary Inquiry* (1969) and *Discretionary Justice in Europe and America* (1976).
[141] See below, pp. 391-400.
[142] See above, pp. 37-38.

(3) JUDICIAL CONTROL

There is clearly an overlap between judicial control and consultation rights, since it is the judiciary who will interpret (or develop) the ambit of these rights. However the judiciary have a role to play in this area which is independent of the issue of consultation. The role of the courts can be presented as follows.[143]

First, the court will decide whether the code or circular is susceptible to judicial review at all. For example, in the *Gillick* case[144] Lord Bridge stated that the general rule was that the reasonableness of advice contained in non-statutory guidance could not be subject to judicial review, but that there was an exception to this general rule: if a government department promulgates advice in a public document which is erroneous in law the court can correct this.

Second, in so far as codes, circulars etc. are given certain evidentiary or substantive force within legal proceedings, it is the judiciary who will interpret the meaning which they should bear.[145] They will also review the interpretation of such a code where it has been applied by an administrative agency.[146] The intensity of any such review may vary from area to area, and courts may well disagree upon the appropriate intensity of review which should operate even within a particular area.[147]

Thirdly, the courts can apply the tests of purpose, relevancy, reasonableness and fettering of discretion to determine whether a particular rule, etc., is within the ambit of the relevant empowering legislation. These tests are normally applied to the individual exercise of discretionary decision-making. It is, however, clear on principle that agency choices should not be immune from such oversight merely because they assume the form of a rule.[148] The courts' willingness to invalidate a particular rule itself on the grounds of, for example, unreasonableness may well differ from area to area. It appears that the courts are more willing to consider this where the rule is made in the context of a relatively clear statutory framework, against which its *vires* and reasonableness can be judged.[149] Where this is present the court will pronounce upon the legality of the rule, even if it is in non-statutory form.

---

[143] Ganz, *Quasi-Legislation*, pp. 41-46.
[144] *Gillick* v. *West Norfolk and Wisbech Area Health Authority* [1986] A.C. 112; *R.* v. *Secretary of State for the Home Department, ex p. Westminster Press Ltd.* [1992] C.O.D. 303.
[145] *R.* v. *Secretary of State for the Home Department, ex p. Lancashire Police Authority* [1992] C.O.D. 161.
[146] *H.T.V.* v. *Price Commission* [1976] I.C.R. 170.
[147] See, *e.g., R.* v. *Criminal Injuries Compensation Board, ex p. Schofield* [1971] 1 W.L.R. 926; *R.* v. *Criminal Injuries Compensation Board, ex p. Thompstone* [1984] 1 W.L.R. 1234.
[148] The precise degree of substantive oversight is itself a complex question which is considered below, Chap. 11.
[149] *Gillick* v. *West Norfolk and Wisbech Area Health Authority* [1986] A.C. 112; *Royal College of Nursing of the UK* v. *Department of Health and Social Security* [1981] A.C. 800.

(4) CONCLUSION

Quasi-legislation in one form or another has been present for a considerable time. The term was already current in the nineteenth century,[150] and concern over its existence was expressed 45 years ago.[151] Renewed interest in the topic is timely,[152] and reflects the importance of the issue addressed. No single, simple solution is likely to be forthcoming. A range of options lies at our disposal, none of which is free from difficulty. At the very least such quasi-legislation should be published, and rendered accessible to those affected by it.

---

[150] Todd, *On Parliamentary Government in England* (1867-1869), Vol. I, p. 288; Parris, *Constitutional Bureaucracy* (1969), pp. 193-194.
[151] Megarry, "Administrative Quasi-Legislation" (1944) 60 L.Q.R. 125.
[152] Baldwin and Houghton, "Circular Arguments" [1986] P.L. 239; Ganz, *Quasi-Legislation*.

PART 2

JUDICIAL REVIEW

8. NATURAL JUSTICE: HEARINGS

Section 1. Introduction

1. *Historical Development*

If an individual is aggrieved by the actions of government, a public body, or certain domestic tribunals or associations, he or she may claim that there has been a breach of natural justice. The phrase natural justice encapsulates two ideas: that the individual be given adequate notice of the charge and an adequate hearing (*audi alteram partem*), and that the adjudicator be unbiased (*nemo judex in causa sua*).[1] The former will be dealt with in this chapter; the latter in that which follows.

The development of the *audi alteram partem* principle has, like many other legal concepts, been eclectic. An early group of cases was concerned with deprivation of offices,[2] requiring notice and a hearing prior to the deprivation. Another somewhat later group involved the clergy: penalties or disciplinary measures to which the clergy were subjected had to be preceded by notice and a hearing.[3]

In the nineteenth century the *audi alteram partem* principle was applied to a wide variety of bodies, private as well as public. Clubs,[4] associations[5] and trade unions[6] were included within its ambit. The increase in the regulatory role of public authorities provided further opportunity for the generalised application of the maxim. Thus in *Cooper* v. *Wandsworth Board of Works*[7] it was held that demolition powers vested in the defendant Board were to be subject to notice and hearing requirements. The omission of positive words in the statute requiring a hearing was held to be no bar since the justice of the common law would supply the omission of the legislature.[8] The generality of application of the *audi alteram partem* maxim, and its flexibility in operation, were brought out by Lord Loreburn L.C.,[9] who stated that the maxim applied to "everyone who decides

---

[1] See generally, Jackson, *Natural Justice* (2nd ed., 1979); Flick, *Natural Justice: Principles and Practical Application* (1979).
[2] *Bagg's Case* (1615) 11 Co. Rep. 93b; *R.* v. *Chancellor of the University of Cambridge* (1723) 1 Str. 557; *Osgood* v. *Nelson* (1872) L.R. 5 H.L. 636; *Fisher* v. *Jackson* (1891) 2 Ch. 824.
[3] *Capel* v. *Child* (1832) 2 Cr. & J. 588; *Bonaker* v. *Evans* (1850) 16 Q.B. 163; *R.* v. *North, ex p. Oakey* [1927] 1 K.B. 491; *cf. R.* v. *Canterbury (Archbishop), ex p. Morant* [1944] K.B. 282.
[4] *Dawkins* v. *Antrobus* (1881) 17 Ch.D. 615; *Fisher* v. *Keane* (1878) 11 Ch.D. 353.
[5] *Wood* v. *Woad* (1874) L.R. 9 Ex. 190; *Lapointe* v. *L'Association de Bienfaisance et de Retraite de la Police de Montréal* [1906] A.C. 435.
[6] *Abbott* v. *Sullivan* [1952] 1 K.B. 189; *Lawlor* v. *Union of Post Office Workers* [1965] Ch. 712.
[7] (1863) 14 C.B.(N.S.) 180.
[8] *Ibid.* p. 194; *Hopkins* v. *Smethwick Local Board of Health* (1890) 24 Q.B.D. 713.
[9] *Board of Education* v. *Rice* [1911] A.C. 179, 182.

anything", while recognising also that the manner in which a person's case was heard did not necessarily have to be the same as an ordinary trial.

2. *The Rationale for Procedural Rights*

Before examining the subsequent development of natural justice, some examination of the background theory which justifies procedural rights is warranted. Justifications for process rights in adjudication vary. One rationale emphasises the connection between procedural due process and the substantive justice of the final outcome. All rules are designed to achieve a particular goal, for example that liquor licences should only be granted to those of good character. Giving a person a hearing before deciding to refuse such a licence application can help to ensure that this goal is correctly applied in a particular instance. Procedural rights perform an *instrumental* role in the sense of helping to attain an accurate decision on the substance of the case.[10] Other rationales focus upon *non-instrumental* justifications for procedural rights. Formal justice and the rule of law are enhanced, in the sense that the principles of natural justice help to guarantee objectivity and impartiality.[11] Procedural rights are also seen as protecting human dignity by ensuring that the individual is told why he is being treated unfavourably, and by enabling him to take part in that decision.[12]

These twin rationales for the existence of procedural rights have been recognised by the judiciary. Thus, in R. v. *Secretary of State for the Home Department, ex p. Doody,*[13] which was concerned with whether prisoners given a life sentence for murder should be told the reasons relating to the length of their imprisonment, Lord Mustill stated that a prisoner would wish to know why the particular term was selected, "partly from an obvious human desire to be told the reason for a decision so gravely affecting his future, and partly because he hopes that once the information is obtained he may be able to point out errors of fact or reasoning and thereby persuade the Secretary of State to change his mind, or if he fails in this to challenge the decision in the courts." The non-instrumental and instrumental justifications for procedural protection are readily apparent in this quotation.

In reading the material which follows two important points should be borne in mind. First, the content of natural justice which should be applicable in any particular instance may well vary depending upon whether one accords primacy to instrumental or non-instrumental considerations.[14] Secondly, the traditional approach has been to model procedural rights by

---

[10] *e.g.* Resnick, "Due Process and Procedural Justice", *Due Process* (Pennock and Chapman, eds., 1977), p. 217.

[11] Hart, *Concept of Law* (1961), pp. 156, 202. See also Rawls, *A Theory of Justice* (1973, Oxford edition), p. 235.

[12] *e.g.* Michelman, "Formal and Associational Aims in Procedural Due Process", *Due Process,* above n. 10, Chap. 4; Mashaw, *Due Process in the Administrative State* (1985), Chaps. 4-7.

[13] [1993] 3 All E.R. 92, 98.

[14] See below, pp. 296-300.

analogy to ordinary court procedure; the principles of natural justice reflect an adversarial-adjudicative conception of process rights. Process rights can however, as we shall see,[15] be fashioned in other ways which may be both better suited to the needs of particular areas, and also better attain the instrumental and non-instrumental values which process rights are designed to serve.

Section 2. Limitation of the Principle

The breadth of the *audi alteram partem* principle was limited in the first half of this century. This occurred in a number of ways, some of which overlap.

1. *Administrative v. Judicial*

It is evident from the nineteenth-century cases on the right to a hearing that the principle was invoked in a number of areas which could properly be called administrative. In so far as the term judicial was used it was automatically implied whenever a decision was made which affected a person's rights in a broad sense.[16] Despite this the courts began to draw a dichotomy between administrative and judicial decisions, to take a narrow view of what constituted a judicial or quasi-judicial decision and to require this as a condition precedent for the application of a right to a hearing. For example in *Errington v. Minister of Health*[17] it was argued that the minister was in breach of natural justice by conferring with the local authority and receiving further evidence from it after the close of a public inquiry. The Court of Appeal found that there had been a breach, but the phrasing of the judgment was nonetheless restrictive. Maugham L.J. stated that if the minister were acting administratively natural justice would not apply, that the minister was in fact acting quasi-judicially but only because the situation was "triangular" in that the minister was deciding a *lis inter partes* between the local authority and objectors.[18] In cases where the *lis* had not yet been joined the applicant was less successful.[19]

---

[15] See below, pp. 302-306.
[16] *e.g. Hopkins v. Smethwick Local Board of Health* (1890) 24 Q.B.D. 713. The courts did not define precisely what type of right would have to be affected before natural justice could apply. The case law indicates that it was not confined to Hohfeldian rights, above nn. 2-6. See below, p. 284, for the way in which the courts have interpreted rights more narrowly.
[17] [1935] 1 K.B. 249.
[18] *Ibid.* pp. 270-273. See also, *Local Government Board v. Arlidge* [1915] A.C. 120.
[19] *Offer v. Minister of Health* [1936] 1 K.B. 40; *Frost v. Minister of Health* [1935] 1 K.B. 286. Further examples of similar restrictive reasoning can be found in *R. v. Metropolitan Police Commissioner, ex p. Parker* [1953] 1 W.L.R. 1150, 1153-1154; *Nakkuda Ali v. Jayaratne* [1951] A.C. 66.

2. Rights and Remedies

The detailed study waits to be written on the way in which developments
in the law of certiorari affected the law on natural justice. The problem can
be briefly stated as follows; it was thought that for certiorari to be available
there would have to be not just a determination affecting the rights of
individuals, but also a superadded duty to act judicially.[20] This view has
now been overturned.[21] However, while it held sway it was interpreted on
occasion to mean not just that there had been a breach of natural justice
with no remedy available. The courts went further and said that natural
justice itself was not applicable.[22] Indeed one of the reasons given in *Ridge*
v. *Baldwin* by Lord Reid for the demise of natural justice was the mis-
understanding over the scope of certiorari.[23]

3. Rights v. Privileges

Closely allied to the previous reasons for the limitation of natural justice
was the distinction drawn between rights and privileges. In *Nakkuda Ali*
one of the reasons why the Privy Council denied the application of natural
justice was because the cancellation of a licence was characterised as the
withdrawal of a privilege and not the determination of a right,[24] and in *ex
p. Parker*[25] the cab licence which was withdrawn was just a "permission".
How far the distinction does still exist, and how far it should do so, will be
considered below.

4. Statutory Hearings and Inquiries

The application of natural justice in the context of inquiries has already
been touched upon in discussing the administrative-judicial dichotomy.
A further example of the limited application of natural justice in this
area may be given. In *Local Government Board* v. *Arlidge*[26] the House of
Lords considered whether an individual should have an oral hearing before

---

[20] R. v. *Legislative Committee of the Church Assembly, ex p. Haynes-Smith* [1928] 1 K.B. 411,
415 interpreting R. v. *Electricity Commissioners, ex p. London Electricity Joint Committees
Co. (1920) Ltd.* [1924] 1 K.B. 171, 205.
[21] *Ridge* v. *Baldwin* [1964] A.C. 40, 72-76.
[22] The clearest example of this reasoning is to be found in *Nakkuda Ali* v. *Jayaratne* [1951]
A.C. 66, 75-77. See also R. v. *Metropolitan Police Commissioner, ex p. Parker* [1953] 1
W.L.R. 1150, 1153; R. v. *St. Lawrence's Hospital Statutory Visitors, ex p. Pritchard* [1953]
1 W.L.R. 1158.
[23] [1964] A.C. 40, 72-76.
[24] [1951] A.C. 66, 77-78.
[25] [1953] 1 W.L.R. 1150, 1153. See also, R. v. *Leman Street Police Inspector, ex p. Venicoff*
[1920] 3 K.B. 72.
[26] [1915] A.C. 120.

the Board itself and whether the person should be entitled to see the report of the hearing inspector in the context of a statutory scheme to determine whether a closing order on a house should be rescinded. Lord Haldane L.C. upheld the general principles in the *Rice* case, but refused access to the housing inspector's report or to the Board itself: when a matter is entrusted to a department of state or similar body, Parliament should be taken, subject to contrary intent, to have meant that it could follow its own procedure which would enable it to work with efficiency. When, therefore, the Board was entrusted with appeals this did not mean that any particular official should undertake the task, nor was the Board bound to disclose the report any more than minutes made on the paper before a decision was arrived at.[27] Much of this is uncontroversial in principle, but the failure to disclose the report was a severe set-back in the evolution of inquiry procedures which has taken long to heal.[28]

Section 3. The Principle Revived

1. *Ridge v. Baldwin*

While the combined effect of a number of cases had been to limit the *audi alteram partem* principle,[29] it would be misleading to say that it had been wholly forgotten. There were indications in England,[30] Australia,[31] Canada[32] and New Zealand[33] of a less rigid application of the principle.

However it would be correct to say that the application of natural justice was at a low ebb prior to the decision of the House of Lords in *Ridge v. Baldwin*.[34] Their Lordships held that a chief constable who was dismissable only for cause was entitled to notice of the charge and an opportunity to be heard before being dismissed. The importance of the case lies in the general discussion of the principles of natural justice, especially that given by Lord Reid.

His Lordship reviewed the nineteenth-century case law which evidenced the broad application of natural justice and then proceeded to consider

---

[27] *Ibid.* pp. 132-134.

[28] For the position now, see Chap. 4.

[29] A further reason for the non-applicability of the rules of natural justice was said to be if the decision-maker was acting in a disciplinary manner, *Ex p. Fry* [1954] 1 W.L.R. 730, 733 though *cf.* the reasoning of the appeal court, p. 736. See now *Buckoke* v. *Greater London Council* [1971] 1 Ch. 655, 669; *R.* v. *Board of Visitors of Hull Prison, ex p. St. Germain* [1979] Q.B. 425, 445, 455.

[30] *e.g. Hoggard* v. *Worsborough Urban District Council* [1962] 2 Q.B. 93.

[31] *e.g. Delta Properties Pty. Ltd.* v. *Brisbane City Council* (1956) 95 C.L.R. 11, 18-19.

[32] *e.g. Alliance des Professeurs Catholiques de Montréal* v. *Labour Relations Board of Quebec* [1953] 2 S.C.R. 140.

[33] *e.g. New Zealand Licensed Victuallers' Association of Employers* v. *Price Tribunal* [1957] N.Z.L.R. 167, 203-205.

[34] [1964] A.C. 40.

why, given these authorities, the law had become confused. He gave three reasons. The first was that natural justice could have only a limited application in the context of the wider duties or discretion imposed upon a minister; unfortunately the courts had applied those limited notions of natural justice to other areas where the constraints were unnecessary.[35] The second reason was that the principle had received only limited application during the war. Again, special considerations which might be pertinent during wartime should not affect the ambit of natural justice now. The third was the confusion between rights and remedies evident in the alleged requirement of a superadded duty to act judicially as a requirement of certiorari, and the way that this had stilted the development of natural justice.[36] The judicial element should be inferred from the nature of the power and its effect on the individual.

Lord Morris of Borth-y-Gest also based his judgment on the nineteenth-century jurisprudence.[37] For Lord Hodson[38] the absence of a *lis inter partes* was not decisive, nor was the characterisation of the act as judicial, administrative or executive.[39]

2. *The Importance of Ridge v. Baldwin*

It is necessary to place *Ridge* in its context to understand its importance. Their Lordships revived the principles of natural justice in two connected ways. On the one hand, they rediscovered the nineteenth-century jurisprudence which had applied the principle to a broad spectrum of interests and a wide variety of decision-makers. On the other, they disapproved of some of the impediments which had been erected in the twentieth century: the requirements of a *lis inter partes* and a superadded duty to act judicially were said to be false constraints.

However, little positive guidance is to be found in the case as to when natural justice should apply. The closest to any general formulation emerges in the idea that the applicability of natural justice will be dependent on the nature of the power exercised and its effect upon the individual concerned. This is not a criticism of the decision. As will be seen, it is notoriously difficult to lay down what the boundaries of natural justice should be. It is rather by way of explanation for what followed *Ridge*. The subsequent years were characterised by a host of cases on natural justice in which the courts were concerned not just with the content of those rules,

---

[35] *Ibid.* pp. 71-72.
[36] *Ibid.* pp. 72-78. His Lordship expressly disapproved Lord Hewart C.J.'s requirement of a superadded duty to act judicially which had been developed in the *Church Assembly* case and disapproved also of *Nakkuda Ali* in so far as that case supported the requirement.
[37] *Ibid.* pp. 120-121.
[38] *Ibid.* pp. 127-132.
[39] Lord Devlin based his judgment primarily upon the application of the police regulations, *ibid.* pp. 137-141; Lord Evershed dissented, *ibid.* pp. 82-100. His Lordship's judgment will be considered in Chap. 12.

but with the criterion for their applicability. The following two sections will deal with these two issues respectively.

Section 4. Applicability of Procedural Protection[40]

The case law subsequent to *Ridge* v. *Baldwin* has used a variety of criteria to determine whether natural justice should be applied.

1. *Categorisation: Administrative v. Judicial v. Legislative*

Legal history has a tendency to repeat itself. Put more accurately, conceptual doctrines thought to have expired often have a vitality which can surprise. Nothing provides a better demonstration of this than the continued usage of the administrative-judicial dichotomy as a basis for determining the applicability of natural justice. In *Pearlberg* v. *Varty*[41] the House of Lords considered whether a taxpayer should have the right to make written representations or have a hearing before a single commissioner prior to his granting leave to raise assessments for years beyond the normal time limit. Their Lordships rejected the claim saying that the statutory scheme showed that leave was to be *ex parte*. Viscount Dilhorne would also have dismissed the case because the function of granting leave was administrative and not judicial.[42]

Categorisation of this type has been disapproved of explicitly,[43] and has not been adopted by the majority of cases which have eschewed such pigeonholing. The nature of the decision may well be taken into account in determining what the *content* of natural justice should be in a particular instance, but the utility of the administrative, judicial, executive, legislative distinctions over and beyond this is difficult to perceive. Since such divisions held sway prior to *Ridge*, and have on occasion reappeared, it is worthwhile examining the value of such criteria.

To render the applicability of natural justice dependent upon a prior classification of the above type would have its utility in greater certainty and predictability: if a case fell within one category certain results would follow; if it fell in a different category differing results would ensue. There are however two difficulties which render this advantage hypothetical rather than real. First, there is the notorious difficulty of deciding whether a case should be categorised as judicial, administrative, executive, etc. Secondly, the presumption behind such an approach is that once the

---

[40] The phrase procedural protection is used instead of natural justice because this section will be examining types of procedural checks in addition to those of traditional natural justice.
[41] [1972] 1 W.L.R. 534.
[42] *Ibid.* p. 544.
[43] *e.g.* R. v. *Gaming Board for Great Britain, ex p. Benaim and Khaida* [1970] 2 Q.B. 417, 430; *O'Reilly* v. *Mackman* [1983] 2 A.C. 237, 279.

characterisation has been made the content of natural justice is fixed and certain: all administrative matters would be subject to the same rules, as would all judicial or quasi-judicial. If they were not the point behind the initial categorisation would be nullified, or at least seriously qualified; the certainty and predictability would be minimal. Yet the variety of matters comprehended within the terms "administrative", "quasi-judicial", or "executive" is vast, however sensitively they are defined. To presuppose, for example, that all "quasi-judicial" matters could be dealt with in the same way is to risk forcing cases into a strait-jacket that will be too big for some and too small for others.[44]

The above discussion has concentrated upon the distinction drawn between administrative and judicial decisions. The courts have also addressed themselves to the question of whether natural justice or fairness applies to matters of a legislative nature. Whether such protection should apply raises broader questions concerning the way in which delegated legislation and rules of a legislative nature are made, and also the type of remedy which should be available. At present rules of a legislative nature are not generally subject to natural justice.[45] The exceptions to this rule have been addressed above and will be considered further below.[46]

2. *Categorisation: Rights, Privileges and Legitimate Expectations*

Resurrected legal doctrine does not always assume the same form that it possessed before. This should not, however, blind us to its reappearance. The dichotomy between rights and privileges provides a clear example of this. We have already seen how that distinction was used prior to *Ridge* v. *Baldwin*. Lord Denning M.R. has subsequently held[47] that licences are subject to natural justice, and that *Nakkuda Ali*[48] and *ex p. Parker*[49] are no longer authority to the contrary. It was, however, Lord Denning M.R. himself in *Schmidt* v. *Secretary of State for Home Affairs*[50] who stated that while natural justice could apply to an administrative act, it would depend upon whether the individual had some right, interest or legitimate expectation, such that it would not be fair to deprive him of it without a hearing. While in *Cinnamond* v. *British Airports Authority*[51] his Lordship invoked

---

[44] See the similar point made by Lord Wilberforce in *Wiseman* v. *Borneman* [1971] A.C. 297, 317.

[45] *Bates* v. *Lord Hailsham* [1972] 1 W.L.R. 1373; *R.* v. *Devon County Council, ex p. Baker* [1993] C.O.D. 138. *cf. R.* v. *Liverpool Corporation, ex p. Liverpool Taxi Fleet Operators' Association* [1972] 2 Q.B. 299.

[46] See above, pp. 256-258, and below pp. 293-296.

[47] *R.* v. *Gaming Board for Great Britain, ex p. Benaim and Khaida* [1970] 2 Q.B. 417, 430.

[48] [1951] A.C. 66.

[49] [1953] 1 W.L.R. 1150.

[50] [1969] 2 Ch. 149, 168-170. Thus an alien had no right to enter the country and could be refused an extension of his stay without reasons and without a hearing.

[51] [1980] 1 W.L.R. 582.

the same type of reasoning, stating that operators of cabs at an airport had no legitimate expectation which would warrant granting them a hearing.

It seems clear on principle that the technical distinction between rights and privileges should not be determinative of the applicability of procedural protection. Many interests may be extremely important to an individual even though they would not warrant the label "right" or "Hohfeldian right".[52] The absence of a substantive right to a particular benefit should not lead to the conclusion that procedural rights are inapplicable, and the term legitimate expectation should not be manipulated to reach this end.

It is, however, also clear that the concept of legitimate expectation, like many legal concepts, can be used in more than one way. It does not have to be given a restrictive interpretation. Thus, a number of later cases have given a broader meaning to that term, utilising it as the foundation for procedural rights for immigrants, workers and local authorities. A more detailed examination of the role played by legitimate expectation will be provided below.[53]

3. Natural Justice and Fairness

The years since Ridge v. Baldwin have not, however, been wholly marked by atavistic reasoning. Those years have also witnessed the development of new terminology. The case law is replete with mention of "fairness", or a "duty to act fairly". These terms made their initial appearance in the judgment of Lord Parker C.J. in Re HK.[54] Since then their use has varied. Some courts treat these terms in an omnibus fashion: natural justice is said to be but a manifestation of fairness.[55] In other cases the courts will apply natural justice to judicial decisions, and reserve a duty to act fairly for administrative or executive determinations.[56] It is not uncommon for different members of the same court to be in agreement as to the contents of the procedural duty, but to differ as to whether they describe this as resulting from natural justice or fairness.[57]

How significant is the development of fairness, whether it be seen as synonymous with natural justice, or in juxtaposition thereto? One view sees the development of fairness as a corollary of the expansion of procedural rights post Ridge v. Baldwin. The judgment of Megarry V.C. in McInnes v. Onslow-Fane[58] is illuminating in this respect. He states that natural justice, being a flexible term which imposes distinct requirements in different cases,

---

[52] See further, Reich, "The New Property" 73 Yale L.J. 733 (1964).
[53] See below, pp. 293-296.
[54] [1967] 2 Q.B. 617, 630.
[55] e.g. Wiseman v. Borneman [1971] A.C. 297, 308-309; McInnes v. Onslow-Fane [1978] 1 W.L.R. 1520, 1530; O'Reilly v. Mackman [1983] 2 A.C. 237, 276.
[56] e.g. Re HK (an infant) [1967] 2 Q.B. 617, 630; Pearlberg v. Varty [1972] 1 W.L.R. 534, 547, 550; Bates v. Lord Hailsham [1972] 1 W.L.R. 1373, 1378.
[57] e.g. Re Pergamon Press Ltd. [1971] Ch. 388, 399-400 (Lord Denning M.R., "fairly"), 402-403 (Sachs L.J., "natural justice"), 407 (Buckley L.J., "not a judicial function").
[58] [1978] 1 W.L.R. 1520.

is capable of applying to the whole range of situations encapsulated by the terms "judicial", "quasi-judicial", "administrative", or "executive". However, the further that one moves away from anything resembling a "judicial" or "quasi-judicial" situation, the more appropriate it becomes to use the term fairness rather than natural justice. On this view the distinction between the application of the terms natural justice and fairness is linguistic rather than substantive. The former could cover all cases, but it is felt to be more appropriate to use the term fairness in the context of, for example, company inspectors or immigration officers.[59] The significant point about this view is that whichever label is used, the expansion in procedural rights is not regarded as involving any fundamental change in the nature of natural justice. As discredited limitations have generally been discarded, and natural justice has expanded to new fields, fairness is seen by some as a more appropriate tag.

Some commentators take a different view, seeing a broader significance in the shift from natural justice to fairness.[60] It is argued that the basis of natural justice was the desire of the ordinary courts to maintain control over adjudication, and to impose their own types of procedures on those subject to judicial control. The necessity for the function to be characterised as "judicial" before procedural constraints would be imposed is said to be integral to this approach, because only bodies exercising such functions would be suited to adjudicative procedures. A corollary of this view was that the content of the rules of natural justice could be relatively fixed and certain. The shift to a broader notion of fairness is said to alter fundamentally the basis of procedural intervention: it can no longer be restricted to adjudicative settings, and there can no longer be fixed standards for determining whether there has been a breach of procedural fairness. The courts are forced to engage in a difficult balancing operation, taking into account the nature of the individual's interest and the effect of increased procedural protection upon the administration.

That the development of procedural fairness does involve the court in a balancing function is undeniable. How significant are the *changes* brought about by the introduction of this concept is more contentious. The starkness of the contrast between the premises and application of traditional natural justice, and those of fairness, is open to a number of objections.

First, the *premise* is that natural justice stemmed from a judicial desire to maintain control over adjudication and to impose its own procedures on those subject to its control. While this may have formed part of the rationale for natural justice, the major reason for the development of the doctrine was the protection of property rights and interests akin thereto.[61]

---

[59] de Smith, *Judicial Review of Administrative Action* (4th ed., 1980), p. 239, makes a similar point.
[60] Loughlin, "Procedural Fairness: A Study in Crisis in Administrative Law Theory" (1978) 28 U.Tor.L.J. 215; Macdonald, "Judicial Review and Procedural Fairness in Administrative Law" (1979-1980) 25 McGill L.J. 520, (1980-1981) 26 McGill L.J. 1.
[61] See the cases on officers and the clergy above nn. 2-3 which were particularly influenced by this consideration.

Secondly, the argument that the term "judicial" was used to ensure that only those bodies suited to adjudicative procedures should be subjected to natural justice is not sound. That term was automatically held to be satisfied when the effects on the interests of the individual were felt to be serious enough to warrant procedural protection, and this was so whether the context was deprivation of an office, expulsion from a trade association, the destruction of one's property, or the loss of something which would juridically be termed a privilege.[62] Indeed, in cases where the remedy sought was not certiorari there was often no mention of the "judicial" requirement at all. It is, moreover, mistaken to view the twentieth-century cases which limited natural justice through manipulation of the judicial-administrative dichotomy as doing so primarily because of a feeling that those categorised as administrative would be unsuited to adjudicative procedures. This may have been a factor, but the authorities dealing with aliens, licensing and discipline[63] reflect much more a judicial conclusion that the substantive interests at stake were not worthy of judicial protection.[64]

Thirdly, the *application* of the rules of natural justice, prior to the introduction of the term fairness, was not and never has been uniform in its operation. Courts have often explicitly or implicitly balanced the interests of the individual with the effects on the administration in deciding where the line should be drawn on many issues which comprise the content of natural justice.[65]

What is undoubtedly true is that the imposition of natural justice has resulted in adjudicative types of procedural constraints. Process rights are modelled on those of the ordinary courts, and any balancing is undertaken within this context.[66] Whether the introduction of the term fairness causes any modification in this stance depends upon which of the two following meanings is accorded to that term.[67]

One interpretation would see fairness as simply fitting into an adjudicative framework, and not necessitating the development of non-adjudicative procedures. On this view the courts would determine what adjudicative procedures are required in particular areas. In some it may approximate to the full panoply of procedural safeguards including: notice, oral hearing, representation, discovery, cross-examination, and reasoned decisions. In others it may connote considerably less. There will be a broad spectrum in between. This is indeed how the system generally works at present. The

---

[62] See cases above ns.1-8.

[63] See below, pp. 320-322, 323-324.

[64] The thesis under consideration holds up best in the context of statutory inquiries, where the nature of the subject-matter did influence the courts in reaching the conclusion that it was not suitable for fully adjudicative procedures, and in the unwillingness to accord procedural rights in "legislative" contexts.

[65] See, *e.g. Board of Education* v. *Rice* [1911] A.C. 179, 182, where Lord Loreburn L.C. openly acknowledges the necessity for flexibility in the operation of the procedural safeguards; *Russell* v. *Duke of Norfolk* [1949] 1 All E.R. 109, 118. And see the cases on, *e.g.* notice, hearing and representation, below pp. 306-310.

[66] See above, pp. 280-281, and below, pp. 296-300, for further consideration of this point.

[67] The shift in terminology from natural justice to fairness does not, of itself, demand any particular one of these meanings.

term fairness can be used to cover all such instances, or differing labels can be used in differing circumstances. If one prefers the latter option then the term natural justice can be used for that part of the spectrum which requires a relatively wide range of procedural checks, while fairness can be used in those areas where either the nature of the decision-maker renders the term natural justice inappropriate, or the set of safeguards tends towards the lower end of the spectrum. In so far as fairness is used within the traditional adjudicative framework the balancing involved therein may be different in degree, but not in kind from that which has always been undertaken within natural justice itself. Lord Loreburn L.C. might well question whether there is really a difference in degree.

The *other interpretation* would see the emergence of fairness as having a broader implication. Adjudication is only one form of procedure. Mediation, managerial direction, and procedural controls internal to the institution itself, are but some of the other forms which decision-making could take. A general concept of procedural fairness could, therefore, lead the courts into developing procedural forms other than classical adjudication. If this transpires then the emergence of fairness really will have a substantial effect on the whole area of procedural due process. Whether this should take place, and the implications of any such development, will be considered below.

The following sections will be concerned with these two ways in which natural justice and fairness could operate. We will consider how the term fairness is presently used in an adjudicative context. This will be followed by a look at some of the broader possible implications of fairness, and the way in which that term might aid in the development of procedural forms other than classical adjudication.

4. *Fairness: Balancing in an Adjudicative Context*

(1) GENERAL

One of the most oft-cited statements in cases after 1964 has in fact been a dictum of Tucker L.J. given some years earlier,

> "The requirements of natural justice must depend on the circumstances of the case, the nature of the inquiry, the rules under which the tribunal is acting, the subject-matter that is being dealt with, and so forth."[68]

Although, as seen above, some courts have persisted in a form of prior categorisation to decide whether natural justice should be applicable, many courts have eschewed such labels. They have exercised control over procedural rights not by rigid prior classification, but rather by admitting that natural justice or fairness applies and varying the content of those rules

---

[68] *Russell* v. *Duke of Norfolk* [1949] 1 All E.R. 109, 118; *Lloyd* v. *McMahon* [1987] A.C. 625, 702.

according to the facts of the case.[69] In a number of cases the courts have, as said, simply treated natural justice and fairness as synonymous; the former is regarded as the latter writ large, the content of which will vary in different areas.[70] But how more precisely will the court fix the procedural requirements and what concept of fairness is thereby entailed?

The court will take account of a wide variety of factors: the nature of the individual's interest; the type of decision being given; whether it is final or preliminary; the type of subject-matter; and how far it is felt necessary to supplement statutory procedures, to name but a few. None of these will be determinative alone. The result is arrived at after balancing three different types of factor: the individual interest at issue; the benefits to be derived from added procedural safeguards; and the costs to the administration, both direct and indirect, of complying with these procedural safeguards. Closer examination of these factors is warranted. Let us begin by examining the nature of the individual's interest.

(2) THE NATURE OF THE INDIVIDUAL'S INTEREST: RIGHTS, INTERESTS AND LEGITIMATE EXPECTATIONS

We have already seen that the courts will regard procedural rights as applicable if the applicant has some right, interest or legitimate expectation which has been affected by the decision being challenged.[71] What then do these terms connote?

The term *right* in this context will clearly cover instances in which the challenged action affects a recognised proprietary or personal right of the applicant. Thus, if, for example, the public body's action threatens to impinge upon a person's actual real property, then this will certainly require some form of process rights before the action will be deemed legal.[72] This has been equally the case in respect of personal property, and process rights will be deemed applicable where a job is regarded as an office and a species of personal property.[73] Some form of hearing right will also be demanded if the action actually affects the personal liberty of the individual, more particularly if that action entails some actual loss of liberty.[74]

The term *interest* is looser than that of right, and has been used as the basis for the application of some type of hearing even where the individual would not be regarded in law as having any actual substantive entitlement or right on the facts of the case.[75] Many of the cases concerning the application of natural justice in the context of clubs, unions and trade associations provide examples of the courts demanding that process rights

---

[69] e.g. *Wiseman* v. *Borneman* [1971] A.C. 297; *Maxwell* v. *Department of Trade and Industry* [1974] Q.B. 523; *R.* v. *Race Relations Board, ex p. Selvarajan* [1975] 1 W.L.R. 1686.
[70] e.g. *Wiseman* v. *Borneman* [1971] A.C. 297, 308-309; *Re Pergamon Press Ltd.* [1971] Ch. 388, 402; *McInnes* v. *Onslow-Fane* [1978] 1 W.L.R. 1520, 1530.
[71] See, *e.g.*, *Schmidt* [1969] 2 Ch. 149.
[72] As in the situation exemplified by *Cooper* v. *Wandsworth Board of Works* (1863) 14 C.B. (N.S.) 180.
[73] See the cases above n.2.
[74] See, *e.g.*, *R.* v. *Parole Board, ex p. Wilson* [1992] 1 Q.B. 740.
[75] The dividing line between rights and interests can be problematic precisely because the definition of what constitutes a right is itself contentious.

be accorded in circumstances where the applicant has an interest as such, rather than any substantive entitlement.[76] The application of natural justice or fairness in the context of, for example, licensing and aliens is also based upon the individual possessing an interest as opposed to a right *stricto sensu*.[77]

What then is the role played by the concept of *legitimate expectations* in this context? What does that term add to the concepts of right and interest?[78] The concept of legitimate expectation adds to the concepts of right and interest in three different ways.

First, the court may decide that the interest, although not presently held, is important enough that an applicant should not be refused it without having some procedural rights. In this sense the courts are protecting *future interests*. In such instances the courts are making a normative judgment to the effect that one consequence of applying for a substantive interest is that some of the requisites of procedural protection are warranted. Thus, in *McInnes* v. *Onslow-Fane*[79] Megarry V.C. held that there was a class of case in which the applicant could be said to have a legitimate expectation that an interest would be granted: where the applicant was a licence holder who was seeking the renewal of a licence, or where a person was already elected to a position and was seeking confirmation of the appointment from a different body. Precisely which future interests should be deserving of this procedural protection will obviously be contestable, as will the level of procedural rights thereby afforded.[80]

A second way in which the concept of legitimate expectation adds to the ideas of right and interest is where there is a representation. There will be detailed discussion of the problems concerning representations later.[81] For the present let us consider their importance as the foundation of procedural rights. A representation can generate a legitimate expectation in two types of case.

On the one hand, there may be cases in which the representation provides the foundation for the procedural rights, even though in the absence of the representation it is unlikely that the substantive interest would, in itself, entitle the applicant to natural justice or fairness. In this type of case the *interest* of the applicant, by itself, would not warrant procedural protection. It is the *conduct* of the public body, through its representation, which provides the foundation for the procedural protection. This is exemplified by *A.G. of Hong Kong* v. *Ng Yuen Shiu*.[82]

---

[76] See cases above nn.4-6.

[77] See below, pp. 320-321, 323-324.

[78] For discussion, see Forsyth, "The Provenance and Protection of Legitimate Expectations" (1988) 47 C.L.J. 238; Elias, "Legitimate Expectation and Judicial Review", *New Directions in Judicial Review*, (Jowell and Oliver, eds., 1988), pp. 37-50; Craig, "Legitimate Expectations: A Conceptual Analysis" (1992) 108 L.Q.R. 79 R. v. *Devon County Council, ex p. Baker* [1994] 6 Admin. L.R. 113, 130-132.

[79] [1978] 1 W.L.R. 1520.

[80] Megarry V.C., in *McInnes*, held that even a pure applicant would be entitled to a measure of procedural protection, in that the deciding authority should reach its decision without bias and without pursuing a capricious policy.

[81] See below, Chap.18.

[82] [1983] 2 A.C. 629.

In that case it was held that although the rules of natural justice or fairness might not generally be applicable to an alien who had entered the territory illegally, a person could claim some of the elements of a fair hearing if he had a legitimate expectation of being accorded such a hearing. Such an expectation could arise if, as was the case, the government had announced that illegal immigrants would be interviewed with each case being treated on its merits, albeit there was no guarantee that such immigrants would be allowed to remain in the territory. The point is well captured by Elias, who states that,

> "...it was only the legitimate expectation arising from the assurance given by the Government that enabled the court to intervene on behalf of the illegal immigrant: his status as an illegal immigrant would not of itself have created any entitlement to a hearing."[83]

On the other hand, the *conduct* of the defendant in the form of a representation, and the consequential legitimate expectation which flows from it, may serve to *augment* the extent of procedural rights granted to the applicant. The decision in *R. v. Liverpool Corporation, ex p. Liverpool Taxi Fleet Operators' Association*[84] provides a suitable example. In that case the council had pursued a policy of limiting the number of licensed taxis to 300. The applicants were assured on a variety of occasions that the figure would not be increased without consultation with them. This position was reinforced by an undertaking given by the relevant committee chairman that the figure of 300 would not be exceeded until certain relevant legislation on the matter had been passed. Notwithstanding this sequence of events the committee resolved to increase the number of taxis without any further opportunity for consultation by the applicants.

It is unclear whether the court believed that the applicants would have had any procedural rights in the absence of the initial assurances given on behalf of the council.[85] It is, however, clear that the scope or content of the applicants' procedural rights were enhanced by the existence of the representations which had been made. Thus, Lord Denning M.R. stated that the council ought not to depart from the undertaking, "except after the most serious consideration and hearing what the other party has to say: and then only if they are satisfied that the overriding public interest requires it."[86] Roskill L.J. formulated the applicants' rights in somewhat different terms, but he too held that the council could not resile from their undertaking, "without notice to and representations from the applicants", and only after "due and proper consideration of the representations of all those interested".[87]

---

[83] "Legitimate Expectation and Judicial Review", p. 41.
[84] [1972] 2 Q.B. 299.
[85] Lord Denning M.R. believed that they would have some such rights, *ibid.* pp. 307-308, Roskill L.J. left the matter open, *ibid.* p. 311.
[86] *Ibid.* p. 308.
[87] *Ibid.* p. 311. See also, *R. v. Secretary of State for Health, ex p. United States Tobacco International Ltd.* [1992] Q.B. 353, 370; *cf. R. v. Devon County Council, ex p. Baker* [1994] 6 Admin. L.R. 113.

The third and final way in which legitimate expectations can arise is closely related to, but distinct from, the second. This is where the defendant institution has established criteria for the application of policy in a certain area, an applicant has relied on these criteria, and the defendant then seeks to apply different criteria. In *R. v. Secretary of State for the Home Department, ex p. Asif Mahmood Khan*[88] the applicant sought to adopt his brother's child from Pakistan. The Home Office, while stating that there was no formal provision for this in the immigration rules, did provide a circular stating the criteria which the Home Secretary would use in such cases. The applicant sought entry clearance for the child on the basis of these criteria, but was refused, and the Home Office indicated that different tests had in fact been used. The court found for the applicant. Parker L.J. developed the reasoning which had been used in the *Liverpool Taxi* case. He reasoned as follows. While it was true that there was no *specific* undertaking in this case, the principle from *Liverpool Taxi* was nonetheless applicable: thus if the Home Secretary stipulated certain *general* entry conditions he should not be allowed to depart from them "without affording interested persons a hearing and then only if the overriding public interest demands it".[89] A new policy could be implemented, but the recipient of the letter which set out the previous policy must be given the opportunity to argue that the "old" policy be applied to the particular case.

(3) THE BALANCING PROCESS

In deciding upon the application of natural justice or fairness the court will, as noted above, balance between, on the one hand, the nature of the individual's interest, and on the other, the likely benefit to be gained from an increase in procedural rights and the costs to the administration of having to comply with such process rights. An example of this is to be found in *Re Pergamon Press Ltd.*[90] Inspectors had been appointed to investigate two companies under the control of Robert Maxwell. The directors were unwilling to respond to questions unless given a number of assurances, and on condition that a judicial type inquiry was conducted. When the inspectors refused to give all the detailed assurances the directors claimed a breach of natural justice. The Court of Appeal found for the inspectors. Although they were under a duty to act fairly, they had not broken this duty. While the potentially serious effect of the report required some procedural protection, this was weighed against the interest of the administration in ensuring confidentiality, added to which were the factors of speed and the preliminary nature of the proceedings. The *G.C.H.Q.*[91] case exemplifies judicial "balancing" within a very different context. Their

---

[88] [1984] 1 W.L.R. 1337.
[89] *Ibid.* p. 1344. See also, *R. v. Rochdale Metropolitan Borough Council, ex p. Schemet* [1993] C.O.D. 113. Reliance is required to sustain an action of this nature, *R. v. Lloyd's of London, ex p. Briggs* [1993] C.O.D. 66.
[90] [1971] Ch. 388. And see the "sequel", *Maxwell v. Department of Trade* [1974] Q.B. 523.
[91] *Council of Civil Service Unions v. Minister for the Civil Service* [1985] A.C. 74. G.C.H.Q. is the Governmental Communications Headquarters responsible for the security of military and official communications and the provision of signals intelligence to the government.

Lordships decided that past practice in the operation of G.C.H.Q. generated a legitimate expectation that those who worked there would be consulted before any important changes were made in the terms and conditions of their employment. The government decision that workers at G.C.H.Q. could no longer belong to national trade unions, which was reached without prior consultation, was prima facie in breach of natural justice. Considerations of national security were, however, held to outweigh those of procedural fairness. The court accepted the view of the executive that to give prior notice of their intentions would run the risk of actions which would disrupt the intelligence services. Whether this approach to considerations of national security was too deferential will be considered in more detail below. A number of comments upon the balancing process are warranted.

First, it is clear that balancing necessitates not only an identification of the individual's interest, but also some judgment about how much we *value* it, or the *weight* which we accord to it. Some such judgment is necessary to proceed at all. For example, to take some position, as Megarry V.C. did in *McInnes*,[92] as to whether the renewal of a licence is a "higher" interest than an initial application, is not to engage in rigid conceptualism, but is rather a necessary step in reaching any decision. Provided that we do not assume that all renewal cases warrant more protection than all initial application cases, irrespective of the nature of the substantive area under scrutiny, then such ranking is both necessary and helpful.

This point is also exemplified by later cases. For example in R. v. *Parole Board, ex p. Wilson*[93] the court was concerned with whether the applicant who was given a discretionary life sentence should be told of the reasons why the Parole Board had refused to recommend his release on licence. In deciding that the applicant should be entitled to information of this kind the court was strongly influenced by the fact that the liberty of the subject was involved, and that this justified departure from previous authorities which had held that information of this kind did not have to be disclosed.

The *Lautro* case furnishes a further example derived from a different context.[94] The case was concerned with the exercise of powers by Lautro, which was a self-regulatory organisation for life insurance and unit trusts. The applicant was a director of WG Ltd, which in effect solicited for business on behalf of life insurance societies and unit trusts. Lautro decided that WG Ltd should no longer be able to solicit for such business, because of concerns as to the financial probity of its past dealings. WG Ltd was not itself a member of Lautro, and thus the decision barring WG Ltd was served on the life insurance societies, with copies going to WG Ltd itself. The latter held that there had been a breach of natural justice, because it had been unable to make representations prior to the decision. The court reasoned as

---

[92] *McInnes* v. *Onslow-Fane* [1978] 1 WL.R. 1520. See also, Friendly, "Some Kind of Hearing" 123 U.Pa.L.Rev. 1267 (1975).
[93] [1992] 1 Q.B. 740.
[94] R. v. *Life Assurance and Unit Trust Regulatory Organisation Ltd., ex p. Ross* [1993] 1 Q.B. 17. See also, R. v. *Secretary of State for Health, ex p. United States Tobacco International Ltd.* [1992] Q.B. 353, 370.

follows. A body such as Lautro was under a duty to act fairly, but this duty could not be owed literally to every person who might be affected by the decision. However, some elements of fairness might be owed to such a third party, where, as here, the decision addressed to the life insurance society would necessarily have a direct impact on the applicant. The applicant should then have some ability to make representations, *particularly when the person's livelihood was at stake*. The importance of the interest was, therefore, of central importance in determining whether this third party applicant should have any hearing rights.[95]

Secondly, valuing the other elements in the balancing process, the social benefits and costs of the procedural safeguards, may be equally problematic. This is not simply a "mathematical" calculus. Resolving the question as to what are to be perceived as such costs and benefits is itself a hard task.[96]

Thirdly, the existence of judicial balancing should not lead us to conclude that all such balancing is necessarily premised on the same assumptions. The premises which underpin an essentially law and economics approach to natural justice or fairness, may be far removed from those which underly a more rights-based approach to process considerations. A proponent of the latter philosophy may well accept the need for some balancing, but the reasoning involved therein and the results achieved, can be very different.[97] This is a point of some importance and it is, therefore, worthwhile dwelling on it a little longer.

A law and economics approach to judicial balancing in order to determine the appropriate level of procedural protection is exemplified by the following extract from Posner.[98]

> "...while most lawyers consider that the question whether there is a right to a trial-type hearing in various administrative contexts, such as the exclusion of aliens..., turns on some irreducible concept of "fairness", the economic approach enables the question to be broken down into objectively analysable, although not simple, inquiries. We begin by asking, what is the cost of withholding a trial-type hearing in a particular type of case? This inquiry has two branches: first, how is the probability of an error likely to be affected by a trial-type hearing?...Second, what is the cost of an error if one occurs?...Having established the costs of error, we then inquire into the costs of the measures – a trial type hearing or whatever – that would reduce the

---

[95] The court did, however, hold that the necessity for Lautro to act with speed could mean that there was no right to make representations before the notice to terminate dealing was actually issued.

[96] *e.g.* Mashaw, "The Supreme Court's Due Process Calculus for Administrative Adjudication in *Mathews* v. *Eldridge*: Three Factors in Search of a Theory of Value" 44 U.Chic.L.R. 28, 47-48 (1976).

[97] Compare, *e.g.*, Posner, "An Economic Approach to Legal Procedure and Judicial Administration" 2 J. Legal Studies 399 (1973), and Mashaw, *Due Process in the Administrative State* (1985).

[98] *Economic Analysis of Law* (2nd ed., 1972), p. 430. See also, Posner, 2 J. Legal Studies 399 (1973).

error costs. If those direct costs are low...then adoption can be expected to reduce the sum of error and direct costs and thus increase efficiency."

This particular species of balancing focuses principally upon an instrumental connection between the presence of process rights and the correct determination on the substance of the case. The process rights are accorded insofar as they constitute an efficient mechanism for ensuring the correctness of the substantive outcome. There are connections between this mode of thought and utilitarianism which can be traced back to Bentham.[99]

This approach to judicial balancing has, however, been criticised. On the one hand, there are problems of implementing a calculus of this kind. Thus, Mashaw has pointed out that balancing of this kind "has an enormous appetite for data that is disputable, unknown, and, sometimes, unknowable",[100] and that "the accounting task that a thorough analysis of social costs and benefits would impose on the Court is simply too formidable".[101] Moreover, the "dynamic effects of procedural change are unpredictable".[102] On the other hand, the approach risks undervaluing concerns relating to process rights which are not directly related to the accuracy of the decision-making.[103] It is also inconsistent to test procedural rules by some pure utilitarian calculus in circumstances where one believes that a person has a substantive entitlement of some kind.[104]

Having said this by way of criticism of the law and economics perspective, it seems that some species of balancing must, nonetheless, be undertaken. To denominate certain interests as rights for the purposes of procedural protection, and to take no account of other factors in determining the nature of this protection, is implausible given that the costs of such protection have to be borne by society. As Mashaw states,[105]

"...we cannot sustain a vision of the world in which rights ring out true and clear, unencumbered by the consideration of conflicting claims of others to scarce resources. It is the fundamentally compromised nature of social life that interest balancing recognizes and confronts."

This same point has been recognised by Dworkin, who notes that in both the criminal and civil process the individual is provided with less than the optimum guarantee of accuracy, and that "the savings so achieved are justified by considerations of the general public welfare".[106]

What species of judicial balancing *would* then be countenanced by those who disapprove of some "pure" cost-benefit analysis, and yet at the same time recognise that society cannot provide some absolute level of procedural protection which pays no heed to cost considerations? One such

---

[99] Mashaw, *Due Process in the Administrative State* (1985), pp. 104-108.
[100] *Ibid.* p. 115.
[101] *Ibid.* p. 127.
[102] *Loc.cit.*
[103] *Ibid.* p. 113. See also, the literature above nn.11-12.
[104] Dworkin, *A Matter of Principle* (1985), pp. 79-84.
[105] *Due Process*, pp. 154-155.
[106] *A Matter of Principle* (1985), p. 74.

approach is provided by Dworkin[107] who argues as follows. He draws the distinction between the bare harm inflicted on an individual who suffers punishment, and the further injury suffered when the punishment is unjust, simply by virtue of that injustice. This injustice factor is termed moral harm.[108] The importance of this element is brought out in the following extract.[109]

> "People are entitled that the injustice factor in any decision that deprives them of what they are entitled to have be taken into account, and properly weighted, in any procedures designed to test their substantive rights. But it does not automatically follow either that they do or do not have a right to a hearing of any particular scope or structure. That depends on a variety of factors, conspicuously including those the Court mentioned in *Mathews*.[110] The Court was wrong, not in thinking those factors relevant, but in supposing that the claimant's side of the scales contained only the bare harm he would suffer if payments were cut off...The claimant's side must reflect the proper weighting of the risk of moral harm, though it may well be that the balance will nevertheless tip in the direction of denying a full adjudicative hearing anyway."

Now of course it may well be a contentious issue as to whether a court has weighted the injustice factor appropriately. But this should not lead one to doubt the importance of the line of inquiry being pursued by Dworkin. It *is* very difficult to reconcile a view of the law as comprising, in part at least, substantive rights or entitlements, while at the same time being contented with a view of procedure in some pure utilitarian cost-benefit terms. There can, moreover, be a sense that the courts, on occasion, undervalue the importance of the individual's interest when balancing the factors which are taken into account. The recognition that there is an injustice factor of the kind mentioned above, and according it due weight, will do much to ensure that the balancing, necessary though it may be, does not undervalue the nature of the individual's interest.[111] It can in fact be argued that the Dworkinian approach does not go far enough, because Dworkin restricts its use to those cases where the individual possesses a substantive right, and as Galligan has persuasively argued this restriction is unwarranted.[112]

---

[107] *Ibid.* Chap. 3.
[108] *Ibid.* p. 80.
[109] *Ibid.* pp. 100-101.
[110] The case is *Mathews* v. *Eldridge* 424 U.S. 319 (1976), in which the Supreme Court of the United States held that the availability of procedural rights would depend upon the following factors: the interest of the individual; the risk of any erroneous deprivation of that interest through the procedures actually used, and the probable value of additional procedural safeguards; and the governmental interest, including the costs imposed by the additional procedural requirement.
[111] See also, Mashaw, *Due Process*, Chaps. 4-7.
[112] "Rights, Discretion and Procedures", *Law, Rights and the Welfare State* (Sampford and Galligan eds., 1986), pp. 139-141.

(4) FORM OR SUBSTANCE

Does fairness relate to form or substance? Can the applicability of procedural protection be affected by the likelihood that the hearing would make a difference to the result reached in this particular instance? There are a number of authorities holding that this should be irrelevant.[113] This is surely correct. The path of the law is, as Megarry J. stated,[114] strewn with examples of unanswerable charges which were completely answered. The objections to assessing whether the hearing would have made a difference are not confined to those expressed by Megarry J. A superior court in the context of review is not in a good position to calculate whether a hearing would have made a difference, and to do so could well leave the individual with the feeling that she has not been afforded any opportunity of controverting the public body's view.[115] Recent authority has come out strongly against the reviewing court taking into account whether the hearing would have made any difference, and this decision is to be welcomed.[116]

Some courts have, however, looked to the causal link between the existence of a hearing and the final outcome. This has manifested itself in three ways.

First, a court may regard the likelihood of the hearing making a difference as a reason for denying the existence of natural justice or fairness. In *Cinnamond* v. *British Airports Authority*[117] a number of minicab drivers had been repeatedly prosecuted by the BAA for touting for passengers at the airport. The BAA prohibited the drivers from entering the airport except as bona fide passengers. The drivers sought a declaration that the ban was invalid arguing, *inter alia*, that the ban was in breach of natural justice, since they had not been given an opportunity to make representations before the ban was imposed. Lord Denning M.R. stated that where there was no legitimate expectation of being heard there was no requirement for a hearing. Because the drivers had a long record of bad behaviour and convictions no such expectations were held to exist here.

Secondly, the likelihood of the hearing making a difference may influence the discretionary power to grant a remedy. In *Glynn* v. *Keele University*[118] the court found that there had been a breach of natural justice by the failure to give a hearing to a student who had been disciplined. A remedy was refused, the court holding that nothing the student could have said could have affected the decision reached.

---

[113] *General Medical Council* v. *Spackman* [1943] A.C. 627, 644; *Annamunthodo* v. *Oilfield Workers' Trade Union* [1961] A.C. 945, 956; *Ridge* v. *Baldwin* [1964] A.C. 40; *R.* v. *Thames Magistrates' Court, ex p. Polemis* [1974] 1 W.L.R. 1371, 1375; *R.* v. *Board of Visitors of Hull Prison, ex p. St. Germain (No. 2)* [1979] 1 W.L.R. 1401, 1411-1412.

[114] *John* v. *Rees* [1970] Ch. 345, 402.

[115] The point is put powerfully by Lord Morris of Borth-y-Gest in *Ridge* [1964] A.C. 40, 127; Clark, "Natural Justice: Substance or Shadow" [1975] P.L. 27.

[116] *R.* v. *Chief Constable of the Thames Valley Police Forces, ex p. Cotton* [1990] I.R.L.R. 344. See also, Sir Thomas Bingham, "Should Public Law Remedies be Discretionary?" [1991] P.L. 64, 72-73.

[117] [1980] 1 W.L.R. 582; *Malloch* v. *Aberdeen Corporation* [1971] 1 W.L.R. 1578, 1595, 1600.

[118] [1971] 1 W.L.R. 487.

A third way in which the courts have moved from considerations of procedural form to substance, is by interpreting the concept of fairness as allowing them to consider, in a general sense, whether the decision reached was fair and reasonable. This issue arose indirectly in *Chief Constable of North Wales Police* v. *Evans*.[119] The decision is discussed more fully below,[120] but it is of importance in the present context because the House of Lords explicitly disapproved of statements made in the Court of Appeal that a court could exercise a general power to consider whether the decision reached was fair and reasonable. It was firmly stated that where review was based upon breach of natural justice, the court should only be concerned with the manner in which the decision was reached, and not with the correctness of the decision itself.[121]

Where review is based upon procedural grounds the applicability of such protection should not be placed in jeopardy by the court second guessing whether a hearing would have made a difference. The weight of authority is firmly against such an approach, and arguments of principle firmly support the predominant approach of the case law.

5. *Fairness: Non-Adjudicative Procedures*

"This whole analysis will derive from one simple proposition, namely that the distinguishing characteristic of adjudication lies in the fact that it confers on the affected party a peculiar form of participation in the decision, that of presenting proofs and reasoned arguments for a decision in his favour. Whatever heightens the significance of this participation lifts adjudication towards its optimum expression. Whatever destroys the meaning of that participation destroys the integrity of adjudication itself."

Thus wrote Fuller[122] in a paper published after his death, on which he had worked for over 20 years. Fuller proceeds to lay down what he conceives the forms and limits of adjudication to be. The precise nature of these need not be rehearsed here, although they will be touched upon in the course of discussion. What is of immediate importance is the realisation, often lost sight of when discussing procedure, that adjudication is but one form of decision-making. As has been evident, our procedural rules are sown in an adjudicative framework.[123] All those rules which constitute natural justice are related directly or indirectly to the idea of presenting

---

[119] [1982] 1 W.L.R. 1155; in *R.* v. *Secretary of State for the Environment, ex p. Brent London Borough Council* [1982] Q.B. 593, 645-646 the argument that the hearing would make no difference and therefore should not be required was expressly rejected. Ackner L.J. quoted the passage from *John* v. *Rees* [1970] Ch. 345, 402 with approval.

[120] See, p. 317.

[121] [1982] 1 W.L.R. 1155, 1160-1161, 1174-1175. *cf.* the reasoning in *Cheall* v. *APEX* [1983] 2 A.C. 180, 190.

[122] "The Forms and Limits of Adjudication" 92 Harv.L.R. 353, 364 (1978).

[123] This does not mean that the principal aim of natural justice was to impose uniform adjudicative procedures. On this see above, pp. 290-292.

proofs and reasoned argument. Thus, to give an obvious example drawn from Fuller,[124] participation through reasoned argument loses its meaning if the arbiter of the dispute is insane or is hopelessly prejudiced. Similar connections clearly exist in relation to matters such as notice. The development of fairness within our jurisprudence has not, as yet, caused us to depart from the adjudicative framework within which we operate.

While attention has been paid to the modification of adjudicative procedures to meet the requirements of a particular area, there has been little thought directed to the broader question of whether adjudication is the correct decision-making process on which to be fashioning procedures. The vital point, brought out forcefully by Fuller, is that just as adjudication is distinguished by the form of participation that it confers so are other types of decision-making, and just as the nature of adjudication shapes the procedures relevant to its decisional form, so do other species of decision-making. Nine categories are listed by Fuller: mediation; property; voting; custom; law officially declared; adjudication; contract; managerial direction; and resort to chance. In each of these instances the relationship between the type of decision-making, and the procedural rules which are attendant thereon, can be presented in the following manner. The procedural rules will be *generated* by, and will *protect* the integrity of, the type of decision-making which is in issue. For example, adjudication is one species of decision-making. The rule against bias is generated by this type of decision-making. It would be inconsistent with our idea of what judging means to allow the decision to be made by one who was biased. In this sense, the procedural rule is there to protect the integrity of what we mean by adjudication.

What relevance has all of this? The answer, at least in outline, is simple. There may well be situations when the procedures modelled on adjudication are not the most effective or appropriate. Areas where safeguards developed against the backdrop of a different type of decision-making may be more efficacious and apposite. The emergence of fairness may help us towards a realisation of this. The point is well put by Macdonald,[125]

> "Rather than ask what aspects of adjudicative procedures can be grafted onto this decisional process reviewing tribunals must ask: what is the nature of the process here undertaken, what mode of participation by affected parties is envisioned by such a decisional process, and what specific procedural guidelines are necessary to ensure the efficacy of that participation and the integrity of the process under review?"

It may well be the case that the very concept of adjudication as applied to disputes between private individuals will have to be modified in its

---

[124] 92 Harv.L.Rev. 353, 364 (1978).

[125] "Judicial Review and Procedural Fairness in Administrative Law: II" (1980-1981) 26 MGill L.J. 1, 19. As is evident, I disagree with some of MacDonald's assumptions about the basis of natural justice but agree with the author on the important general point under discussion. The piece as a whole is stimulating and to be recommended.

application to litigation involving public bodies. It can be argued that the types of participation involved in the latter will not necessarily be the same as the former. This does not negate the point being made by Fuller and MacDonald: it may still be the case that a different decisional form is more appropriate in a particular area.[126] Two brief examples of this idea may be given.

Let us take first statutory inquiries. They have always presented a problem for the application of natural justice.[127] The courts have been troubled by the very nature of the decision-making process, bifurcated as it is between the inspector and the minister. By their nature such inquiries do not fit one of the requisites of classical adjudication, which has been termed strong responsiveness.[128] This expresses nothing more than the notion that the decision should proceed from the proofs and arguments advanced by the parties. The position of the minister, and the broad range of policy considerations that he must take into account, precludes this. This same fact prevents the minister from being an impartial adjudicator. Despite this lack of harmony between the facts and the ideal, the courts have traditionally seen the procedures for such inquiries against an adjudicative backdrop. It is true that they have recognised that the minister cannot be impartial in the way that a judge would be. It is true also that judicial statements afford considerable latitude to the public authority in devising its own procedures.[129] Nevertheless, these are seen as modifications within the traditional adjudicatory framework. What these modifications indicate, however, is that this decisional paradigm may not be the most appropriate. As the quotation from Fuller makes clear, whatever destroys the meaning of participation which characterises adjudication destroys the integrity of adjudication itself. The modifications which adjudication has been subjected to in the realm of statutory inquiries come close to doing just this. Moreover, it is arguable that classical adjudication is in general unsuited to the resolution of what are termed polycentric problems,[130] which may form the subject-matter of statutory inquiries. Judicial realisation that the full

---

[126] Chayes, "The Role of the Judge in Public Law Litigation" 89 Harv.L.Rev. 1281 (1976); Eisenberg, "Participation, Responsiveness and the Consultative Process" 92 Harv.L.Rev. 400, 426-431 (1978); Fuller, "Mediation: Its Forms and Functions" 44 S.Cal.L.Rev. 305 (1971). Not all private law transactions are necessarily far removed from those of a public law nature, MacNeil, "Contracts: Adjustment of Long Term Economic Relations Under Classical, Neo-Classical, and Relational Contract Law" 72 N.W.U.L.Rev. 854 (1977).

[127] e.g. Errington v. Minister of Health [1935] 1 K.B. 249; Offer v. Minister of Health [1936] 1 K.B. 40; Franklin v. Minister of Town and Country Planning [1948] A.C. 87.

[128] Eisenberg, "Participation, Responsiveness and the Consultative Process" 92 Harv.L.Rev. 400, 411-412 (1978).

[129] Bushell v. Secretary of State for Environment [1981] A.C. 75; R. v. Secretary of State for Transport, ex p. Gwent County Council [1987] 2 W.L.R. 961.

[130] Put simply, this is a problem in which one part interacts with a number of others so that a change in any one will produce ramifications in the whole: the decision of the team captain to move X from centre-back to half-back may necessitate alteration in the whole team. See Polanyi, The Logic of Liberty (1951), 171; Fuller, 92 Harv.L.Rev. 353, 384-405. Compare Chayes, "The Role of the Judge in Public Law Litigation" 89 Harv.L.Rev. 1281 (1976) and Eisenberg, 92 Harv.L.Rev. 400, 426-431 (1978).

implications of the adjudicative model cannot be applied in this area is, of course, beneficial. A broad notion of procedural fairness may, however, demand more. It may require us to rethink the type of decision-making process from which we are deriving our procedures. Statutory inquiries may be better seen as a form of mediation or consultation. Some of the legislation in the planning sphere reflects such an approach.[131] If inquiries, or some of them,[132] were to be viewed in this light then the courts could help to devise procedural rules to fit *this* type of decision-making. What those rules are would be derived from the type of participation demanded by that decisional process. Some of these may overlap with characteristics found in adjudication, others may not.[133]

The field of social welfare provides a second example of the theme under discussion. Claimants for social welfare provisions have not always been in a good position so far as procedural protection is concerned. There has been a tendency to regard such provisions as government largesse to be dispensed at the unfettered will of the public body. This view has been more manifest in the United States[134] than in this country, although we have not entirely escaped the same phenomenon. The response has been to bolster up the procedural checks attendant upon the disbursement of such benefits. These safeguards are framed in an adjudicative fashion, albeit one which is significantly modified to take account of the circumstances. It may however be that this type of procedural check is not the most effective in this area. A number of reasons contribute towards this.

First, giving claimants appeal rights with a hearing before a higher tribunal ignores the factual background from which such cases spring. There will often be a continuing relationship between the claimant and the original officer which the former is unlikely to want to sully by taking appellate action. To this must be added the nature of the claimants themselves, who may not fully comprehend the mechanics of such an appeal process.[135] Secondly, the adversary nature of the adjudicative process may not be well suited to this area. The idea of "opponents" and the "winner take-all" attitude inherent in it is not necessarily the best form of decision-making for social welfare cases.[136] What this suggests is that a different type of decision-making with correspondingly different procedures

---

[131] See above pp. 175-180.

[132] In particular those dealing with more major schemes.

[133] Fuller, "Mediation: Its Forms and Functions" 44 S. Cal.L.Rev. 305 (1971); Eisenberg, "Private Ordering Through Negotiation, Dispute Settlement and Rule-Making" 89 Harv.L.Rev. 637 (1976). See generally, McAuslan, *The Ideologies of Planning Law* (1980).

[134] Reich, "The New Property" 73 Yale L.J. 773 (1964); "Midnight Welfare Searches and the Social Security Act" 72 Yale L.J. 1347 (1963); "Individual Rights and Social Welfare: The Emerging Issues" 74 Yale L.J. 1245 (1965); "The Law of the Planned Society" 75 Yale L.J. 1227 (1966). The Supreme Court has now strengthened the procedural rights of such claimants in the seminal case of *Goldberg* v. *Kelly* 397 U.S. 254 (1970). The case appears, however, to have been distinguished more than it has been followed, Breyer and Stewart, *Administrative Law and Regulatory Policy* (2nd ed., 1985), Chap. 7.

[135] Handler, "Controlling Official Behaviour in Welfare Administration" 54 Cal.L.Rev. 479 (1966); Adler and Bradley, *Justice, Discretion and Poverty* (1975).

[136] Ganz, *Administrative Procedures* (1974), p. 35.

may be more relevant. A mixture of consultation and internal management control might well prove a better starting point.[137] It should, however, be noted that other commentators have expressed reservations about the extent to which informal procedures can be successful, and have also pointed to the benefits of a broadly adjudicative appeal regime.[138]

One of the most important questions facing us in the field of procedural protection is whether we are prepared to think more broadly about what procedural protection connotes. Procedures developed against a backdrop of adjudication may well be the most appropriate in certain areas. They may not however be equally suited to all the institutions that comprise administrative law. What is equally important is that other types of procedural norms may, in certain circumstances, better effectuate the twin rationales which were identified above for the existence of process rights generally. Procedures which are developed in the context of consultation may, for example, better attain the instrumental and non-instrumental aims which underly process rights.[139] For the present we must return to the adjudicative context within which natural justice and fairness operate.

Section 5. Content of Natural Justice: General

1. *Notice*

As Lord Denning has said,[140]

> "If the right to be heard is to be a real right which is worth anything, it must carry with it a right in the accused man to know the case which is made against him."

The right to notice manifests itself in a number of ways. Thus, it is contrary to natural justice to inform an individual of only one complaint if there are two,[141] or to find the person guilty of a different offence from the one that she was actually charged with.[142] Similarly, it was held to be contrary to natural justice to confirm an order on facts which the individual had no opportunity to show to be erroneous.[143] The right to notice extends

---

[137] Mashaw, *Bureaucratic Justice* (1983).
[138] Wikeley and Young, "The Administration of Benefits in Britain: Adjudication Officers and the Influence of Social Security Appeal Tribunals" [1992] P.L. 238.
[139] See above, pp. 282-283.
[140] *Kanda* v. *Government of Malaya* [1962] A.C. 322, 337. See also, *Att.-Gen.* v. *Ryan* [1980] A.C. 718; *Hadmor Productions Ltd.* v. *Hamilton* [1982] 2 W.L.R. 322. *cf. R.* v. *Secretary of State for the Home Department, ex p. Santillo* [1981] Q.B. 778.
[141] *Board of Trustees of the Maradana Mosque* v. *Mahmud* [1967] 1 A.C. 13, 24-25.
[142] *Lau Luit Meng* v. *Disciplinary Committee* [1968] A.C. 391.
[143] *Fairmount Investments Ltd.* v. *Secretary of State for the Environment* [1976] 1 W.L.R. 1255, 1260, 1265-1266. See also, *R.* v. *Deputy Industrial Injuries Commissioner, ex p. Jones* [1962] 2 Q.B. 677, 685; *Sabey & Co. Ltd.* v. *Secretary of State for the Environment* [1978] 1 All E.R. 586; *R.* v. *Secretary of State for the Environment, ex p. Norwich City Council* [1982] Q.B. 808; *Mahon* v. *Air New Zealand Ltd.* [1984] A.C. 808.

also to giving the individual a reasonable amount of time in which to prepare the case.[144]

While the courts have jealously protected an individual's right to
notice,[145] they have imposed limitations upon it. In the *Gaming Board*[146]
case B and K had applied for a certificate of consent from the Gaming
Board to entitle them to apply for a gaming licence. The Board asked the
applicants questions arising from information possessed by the Board, but
did not disclose the source of the information. B and K claimed that the
Board should give them sufficient information to enable them to answer the
case against them. The Board declined to reveal their source claiming that
it would be contrary to the public interest. The Court of Appeal stated that
the Board did have a duty to act fairly which entailed granting B and K the
opportunity to satisfy them of matters in the statute, and to let B and K
know the impressions of the Board so that they might be dispelled; but the
Board did not have to quote "chapter and verse", nor did it have to disclose
the source of its information if it would be contrary to the public interest,
nor did the reasons for the refusal have to be given.[147]

An even more limited approach has been adopted in some other cases. In
Breen v. *Amalgamated Engineering Union*[148] a majority of the Court of
Appeal held that a disciplinary committee of a trade union did not have to
tell a shop steward why they had refused to endorse his election, and in
McInnes v. *Onslow-Fane*[149] it was held that the council of the Boxing Board
of Control did not have to give an applicant for a manager's licence an
outline of their objections to him. The test adopted in both cases was that
the decision-maker should not capriciously withhold approval.[150]

Underlying these decisions there has been a tension between two
principles operating within this area, the right to notice and the absence of
any general duty to give reasons. In the context of, for example, an
application for a licence, there is no "charge". Where the applicant has
made repeated unsuccessful requests the person may wish to know why a
licence is not being granted. This is, however, tantamount to requiring the

---

[144] R. v. *Thames Magistrates' Court, ex p. Polemis* [1974] 1 W.L.R. 1371, 1375. And see,
R. v. *Grays Justices, ex p. Graham* [1982] Q.B. 1239 for when delay in bringing a criminal
prosecution could be an abuse of process.
[145] *In re Hamilton* [1981] A.C. 1038; R. v. *Chichester Justices, ex p. Collins* [1982] 1 W.L.R.
334; R. v. *Diggines, ex p. Rahmani* [1985] Q.B. 1109; R. v. *Secretary of State for the Home
Department, ex p. Al-Mehdawi* [1990] 1 A.C.876; R. v. *Bolton Justices, ex p. Scally* [1990] 1
Q.B. 537.
[146] [1970] 2 Q.B. 417, 430-432.
[147] cf. R. v. *Kent Police Authority, ex p. Godden* [1971] 2 Q.B. 662; *Denton* v. *Auckland City*
[1969] N.Z.L.R. 256.
[148] [1971] 2 Q.B. 175, 195, 200.
[149] [1978] 1 W.L.R. 1520
[150] There is some indication that more would have to be disclosed to the applicant if a charge
was made against the person, *Breen* [1971] 2 Q.B. 175, 200; *McInnes* [1978] 1 W.L.R. 1520,
1534, or if the refusal constituted a slur against the applicant or deprived the individual of a
statutory right, *McInnes*, p. 1535.

giving of reasons, a point made explicitly by Megarry V.C. in *McInnes*.[151] Whether reasons should be given will be considered below.[152]

2. The Hearing

Two of the most important aspects of the hearing are the type of hearing required and the rules of evidence that will apply.

While hearings will normally be oral, there is no fixed rule that this must be so.[153] The courts will, however, avoid construing a statute so as to dispense with a hearing completely. A statute empowering a public body to dispense with a hearing will, for example, be interpreted to allow oral hearings to be omitted; courts will lean against allowing a tribunal to decide a matter without giving the individual a chance to see the opposing case and have his own considered.[154] Furthermore, while an individual can waive the right to a hearing,[155] this will not always be an option which is open. Thus, in *Hanson* v. *Church Commissioners*[156] it was held that where the matter was one in which there was a wider public interest it may not be possible for one party to withdraw without the assent of the other once the proceedings were begun. Even if both agreed the issue might not be withdrawn if the tribunal objected. However, where an individual has lost the opportunity to present the case through the fault of her own advisers this could not constitute a breach of natural justice.[157]

There are some cases which appear to hold that natural justice may not require a hearing.[158] These statements must be treated with great reserve. While the type of hearing may differ within different areas, and while it might vary depending upon, for example, the stage which the proceedings have reached or the nature of the interest being asserted, to go further than this would be contrary to principle. To assert that, quite apart from the above factors, natural justice could be satisfied even though there was nothing in the nature of a hearing at all would be to denude the concept of all content.

---

[151] [1978] 1 W.L.R. 1520, 1532.
[152] How much the applicant is entitled to know may also depend upon what stage the proceedings are at: *Maxwell* v. *Department of Trade* [1974] Q.B. 523. On the requirement of reasons, see pp. 310-316.
[153] *e.g. R.* v. *Amphlett (Judge)* [1915] 2 K.B. 223; *Kavanagh* v. *Chief Constable of Devon and Cornwall* [1974] Q.B. 24; *Att.-Gen.* v. *Ryan* [1980] A.C. 718.
[154] *R.* v. *Housing Appeal Tribunal* [1920] 3 K.B. 334; *Re Wilson* [1985] A.C. 750. See also, *R.* v. *Birmingham JJ, ex p. Lamb* [1983] 1 W.L.R. 339; *R.* v. *Central Criminal Court, ex p. Boulding* [1984] Q.B. 813.
[155] *R.* v. *Deputy Industrial Injuries Commissioner, ex p. Moore* [1965] 1 Q.B. 456, 489-490. The onus placed on the individual to request a hearing may well be inappropriate.
[156] [1978] Q.B. 823.
[157] *R.* v. *Secretary of State for the Home Department, ex p. Al-Mehdawi* [1990] 1 A.C. 876.
[158] *R.* v. *Aston University Senate, ex p. Roffey* [1969] 2 Q.B. 538, 552, 556; *Breen* v. *Amalgamated Engineering Union* [1971] 2 Q.B. 175. The requirement that a party must have an opportunity to present her case will not apply with full force if the public body has to act in an emergency, *R.* v. *Secretary of State for Transport, ex p. Pegasus Holdings (London) Ltd.* [1988] 1 W.L.R. 990.

The strict rules of evidence do not have to be followed.[159] Diplock L.J. (as he then was) set out the following general principles. The tribunal is not restricted to evidence acceptable in a court of law; provided that it has some probative value the court will not reassess its weight. Where there is an oral hearing, written evidence submitted by the applicant must be considered, but the tribunal may take account of any evidence[160] of probative value from another source provided that the applicant is informed and allowed to comment on it. An applicant must also be allowed to address argument on the whole of the case.[161] These general principles are, however, subject to the following reservation. The overriding obligation is to provide the applicant with a fair hearing and a fair opportunity to controvert the charge.[162] This may in certain cases require not only that the applicant be informed of the evidence, but that the individual should be given a sufficient opportunity to deal with it. This may involve the cross-examination of the witnesses whose evidence is before the hearing authority in the form of hearsay. Where there are insuperable difficulties in arranging for that evidence to be questioned it should not be admitted in evidence, or the hearing authority should exclude it from their consideration.

3. Representation

The position as to whether an individual can choose a representative, including a lawyer, is as follows.[163]

First, there appears to be no absolute right to such representation.[164] Legal representation may be counterproductive, unnecessary or overcumbersome

---

[159] Ex p. Moore, [1965] 1 Q.B. 456, 476-477, 486-490; Mahon v. Air New Zealand Ltd. [1984] A.C. 808, 820-821.

[160] For the extent to which personal knowledge and impression can be used, R. v. City of Westminster Assessment Committee, ex p. Grosvenor House (Park Lane) Ltd. [1941] 1 K.B. 53; Crofton Investment Trust Ltd. v. Greater London Rent Assessment Committee [1967] Q.B. 955, 967; Wetherall v. Harrison [1976] Q.B. 773. See generally, de Smith, Judicial Review of Administrative Action (4th ed., 1980), pp. 204-206; Smillie, "The Problem of Official Notice" [1975] P.L. 164.

[161] Mahon [1984] A.C. 808, 820-821. cf. R. v. Monopolies and Mergers Commission, ex p. Mathew Brown plc [1987] 1 W.L.R. 1235. It is doubtful whether there is a right to cross-examination in all cases, Kavanagh v. Chief Constable of Devon and Cornwall [1974] Q.B. 624; Bushell v. Secretary of State for the Environment [1981] A.C. 5; R. v. Commission for Racial Equality, ex p. Cottrell and Rothon [1980] 1 W.L.R. 1580; Chilton v. Saga Holidays plc [1986] 1 All E.R. 841; R. v. Secretary of State for the Home Department, ex p. Tarrant [1985] Q.B. 251, 288-289; Public Disclosure Commission v. Isaacs [1989] 1 All E.R. 137.

[162] R. v. Board of Visitors of Hull Prison, ex p. St. Germain (No. 2) [1979] 1 W.L.R. 1401, 1408-1412.

[163] Alder, "Representation Before Tribunals" [1972] P.L. 278.

[164] Enderby Town Football Club Ltd. v. Football Association Ltd. [1971] Ch. 591, 605; Fraser v. Mudge [1975] 1 W.L.R. 1132, 1133, 1134; R. v. Secretary of State for the Home Department, ex p. Tarrant [1985] Q.B. 251, 270-272, 295-296; R. v. Board of Visitors of H.M. Prison, The Maze, ex p. Hone [1988] 1 A.C. 379. Earlier dicta in Pett v. Greyhound Racing Association Ltd. [1969] 1 Q.B. 125, 132, gave the impression that there was a right to such legal representation when livelihood or reputation were at stake, see however Pett v. Greyhound Racing Association (No. 2) [1970] 1 Q.B. 46.

in cases where a matter must be speedily resolved, and hence the courts have resisted claims that there should be a *right* to such representation.[165]

Secondly, the courts have, however, emphasised that tribunals possess a *discretion* as to whether to allow such representation, and are willing to review the manner in which the discretion is exercised. A tribunal is master of its own procedure, and this provides the foundation from which it can permit such representation.[166] Consideration of the statutory scheme within a particular area may convince the court that representation by a lawyer should on construction be excluded.[167] However, the courts are in general reluctant to exclude the possibility of such legal representation *in toto* within a particular area.[168] In exercising their discretion whether to permit such representation, tribunals should take the following factors into account:[169] the seriousness of the charge or penalty; whether any points of law are likely to arise; the capacity of a person to present their own case; procedural difficulties; the need for speed in reaching a decision; and the need for fairness as between the individual and the officers concerned.

Thirdly, there does not appear to be any general right to attend a hearing as the friend or adviser of the individual directly concerned; whether such a right exists depends on the nature of the tribunal in question. Any such tribunal does, however, possess the discretion to allow the individual to be assisted by such an adviser.[170]

4. Reasons

The general importance of reasoned decisions has been considered above, and the topic will be returned to below.[171] The present discussion will focus on reasons and natural justice.

There are a number of advantages to be secured by insisting upon reasons for decisions.[172] Firstly, reasons can assist the courts in performing their supervisory function. This supervisory function is often based on criteria such as whether the agency took account of relevant considerations or acted for improper purposes, and these criteria are much easier to apply

---

[165] See the reasoning in the authorities cited above n.164.

[166] *ex p. Tarrant* [1985] Q.B. 251, 273.

[167] *Maynard* v. *Osmond* [1977] Q.B. 240, 253, 255.

[168] In *Enderby Town* [1971] Ch. 591, Lord Denning M.R. thought that a rule which sought to exclude the possibility of legal representation might be an unlawful fetter on discretion. See also, p. 609, *per* Fenton Atkinson L.J.

[169] *ex p. Tarrant* [1985] Q.B. 251, pp. 284-286; *R.* v. *Secretary of State for the Home Department, ex p. Anderson* [1984] Q.B. 778; *ex p. Hone* [1988] 1 A.C. 379.

[170] *ex p. Tarrant* [1985] Q.B. 251, pp. 282-283, 298.

[171] See, pp. 438-441.

[172] See generally, Akehurst, "Statements of Reasons for Judicial and Administrative Decisions" (1970) 33 M.L.R. 154; Flick, "Administrative Adjudications and the Duty to Give Reasons – A Search for Criteria" [1978] P.L. 16; Richardson, "The Duty to Give Reasons: Potential and Practice" [1986] P.L. 437. See also, Galligan, "Judicial Review and the Textbook Writers" (1982) 2 O.J.L.S. 257.

if the agency's reasons are actually made evident. Secondly, an obligation to provide reasons will often help to ensure that the decision has been thought through by the agency. This is particularly so where the agency in question deals with a large number of applications, or where the decision in question is of generalised importance for the functioning of that administrative system. Thirdly, the provision of reasons can have real significance in ensuring that other objectives of administrative law are not frustrated. If, for example, we decide to grant consultation rights in certain areas, then a duty to furnish reasons will make it more difficult for the decision-maker merely to go through the motions of hearing interested parties without actually taking their views into account. Finally, a duty to give reasons can also perform a more general function. As Rabin[173] has stated, the "very essence of arbitrariness is to have one's status redefined by the state without an adequate explanation of its reasons for doing so". By way of contrast the provision of reasons can increase public confidence in, and the legitimacy of, the administrative process. A duty to provide reasons can, therefore, help to attain both the instrumental and non-instrumental objectives which underly process rights more generally.

The disadvantages which are said to be attendant upon a duty to provide reasons are that it can stifle the exercise of discretion and overburden the administration. How cogent these arguments are is questionable. While English law has gone some way to providing a reasons requirement there are still significant gaps. Such a requirement may be imposed by statute or the common law, and these will be considered in turn.

Statutory intervention owes much to the Franks Committee which recommended the giving of reasons.[174] This has been enacted in the Tribunals and Inquiries Act 1958,[175] which requires those tribunals listed in the Act to give a statement, written or oral, of the reasons for a decision, if requested by the individual. The statute also applies to ministerial decisions subsequent to statutory inquiries. In addition, legislation both primary and secondary, has imposed a duty to give reasons in specific situations.[176] The stringency of the duty to provide reasons will depend to some extent upon the language of the particular statute and the context. The reasons which are given must be adequate, intelligible and deal with the substantial points which have been raised; and they must enable the individual to assess

---

[173] "Job Security and Due Process: Monitoring Administrative Discretion Through a Reasons Requirement" 44 U.Chi.L.Rev. 60, 77-78 (1976).
[174] Cmnd. 218 (1957), paras. 98, 351.
[175] s.12(1). Now replaced by the Tribunals and Inquiries Act 1992, s.10(1). The section is considered in more detail above pp. 151-152.
[176] e.g. R. v. *Minister of Housing and Local Government, ex p. Chichester R.D.C.* [1960] 1 W.L.R. 587; *Givaudan & Co. Ltd.* v. *Minister of Housing and Local Government* [1967] 1 W.L.R. 250; *Brayhead (Ascot) Ltd.* v. *Berkshire County Council* [1964] 2 Q.B. 303; *French Kier Developments Ltd.* v. *Secretary of State for Environment* [1977] 1 All E.R. 296; R. v. *Secretary of State for the Home Department, ex p. Dannenberg* [1984] Q.B. 766; *Bone* v. *Mental Health Review Tribunal* [1985] 3 All E.R. 330; R. v. *Mental Health Review Tribunal, ex p. Pickering* [1986] 1 All E.R. 99; *Westminster City Council* v. *Great Portland Estates plc* [1985] A.C. 661.

whether the decision can be challenged.[177] Yet the courts have also held that an alleged deficiency in the provision of reasons will only lead to the decision being quashed if the applicant has been substantially prejudiced.[178] Moreover, the preponderant view appears to be that a mere failure to comply with the duty to provide reasons does not, of itself, provide grounds for appeal on a point of law; the decision will only be quashed if the reasons as stated actually furnish evidence of such an error.[179]

The *common law* has failed to develop any general duty to provide a reasoned decision.[180] There are a number of exceptions to this general principle.

One method of indirectly requiring reasons is illustrated by *Minister of National Revenue* v. *Wrights' Canadian Ropes Ltd.*[181] Wrights' Canadian Ropes Limited complained that the minister should have allowed claims for expenses to be set off against tax. The Privy Council held that although the minister was not bound to disclose his reasons, he could not thereby render the company's right of appeal nugatory. The Court could look at the facts before the minister, and if those were insufficient in law to support his determination then the Court would deem that it must have been arbitrary. The same approach has been adopted in later cases.[182] It will be of interest to see whether the reasoning is applied to the courts' powers of review; if this occurred a general right to reasoned decisions would have evolved.[183] The exception would have devoured the principle. Some indications of such a development are apparent. *R.* v. *Secretary of State for the Home Department, ex p. Doody*[184] was concerned with life sentences for murder, and whether the Secretary of State should tell the prisoner the reasons why he was deciding on a certain period of time for imprisonment. Lord Mustill, giving the judgment of the court, reiterated the orthodoxy that there was no general duty to provide reasons. However, he also found that there was a

---

[177] *Re Poyser and Mills's Arbitration* [1964] 2 Q.B. 467, 478; *Westminster City Council* v. *Great Portland Estates plc* [1985] A.C. 661, 673.

[178] *Save Britain's Heritage* v. *Secretary of State for the Environment* [1991] 1 W.L.R. 153. It is not clear whether this was intended as a general proposition, or as one which was restricted to the planning context which was in issue in the case.

[179] *Mountview Court Properties Ltd.* v. *Devlin* (1970) 21 P.&C.R. 689; *Crake* v. *Supplementary Benefits Commission* [1982] 1 All E.R. 498; *R.* v. *Legal Aid Area No.8 (Northern) Appeal Committee, ex p. Angell* [1990] C.O.D. 355. See generally, Richardson, [1986] P.L. 437, 450-457.

[180] *Minister of National Revenue* v. *Wrights' Canadian Ropes Ltd.* [1947] A.C. 109, 123; *R.* v. *Gaming Board for Great Britain, ex p. Benaim and Khaida* [1970] 2 Q.B. 417, 431; *McInnes* v. *Onslow-Fane* [1978] 1 W.L.R. 1520, 1532; *R.* v. *Civil Service Appeal Board, ex p. Cunningham* [1991] 4 All E.R. 310. *cf. R.* v. *Wear Valley District Council, ex p. Binks* [1985] 2 All E.R. 699.

[181] [1947] A.C. 109. If there were sufficient material to support the determination the court would not interfere merely because it would have reached a different conclusion, *ibid.* p. 123.

[182] *Norton Tool Co. Ltd.* v. *Tewson* [1973] 1 W.L.R. 45, 49; *Alexander Machinery (Dudley) Ltd.* v. *Crabtree* [1974] I.C.R. 120, 122; *Bone* [1985] 3 All E.R. 330; *ex p. Dannenberg* [1984] Q.B. 766, 775-776; *R.* v. *Crown Court at Harrow, ex p. Dave* [1994] 1 All E.R. 315.

[183] *R.* v. *Knightsbridge Crown Court, ex p. International Sporting Club (London) Ltd.* [1982] 2 Q.B. 304, 314-315; *R.* v. *Immigration Appeal Tribunal, ex p. Khan* [1983] Q.B. 790.

[184] [1993] 3 All E.R. 92, 111.

duty to give reasons in this instance, and one rationale for this conclusion was that the reasons would facilitate any judicial review challenge by the prisoner, who might wish to argue that the Secretary of State had erred in departing from the sentence originally recommended by the judges. Similarly in *R. v. Commissioners of Customs and Excise, ex p. Tsahl*[185] Nolan J. held that if, under a particular statute it was clear that the authority should act in a rational and consistent manner, then it must follow that it should have a duty to provide some explanation for its action, since it would otherwise be impossible for the applicant to determine whether it had behaved capriciously.

A *second way* in which the courts have indirectly imposed a requirement to state reasons is by labelling the result reached in their absence as arbitrary. This approach was adopted in the *Padfield* case,[186] but the scope of this exception to the general rule must now be read in the light of the House of Lords' decision in *Lonrho*.[187] The case is one in a long saga for the control of the House of Fraser waged by Tiny Rowlands and Lonrho. In this action it was claimed, *inter alia*, that the Secretary of State should have referred a merger between AIT (Lonrho's rivals) and the House of Fraser to the Monopolies and Mergers Commission; and that in the absence of convincing reasons for not doing so, the decision not to refer should be regarded as irrational. Their Lordships disagreed and held as follows. If there was no duty to provide reasons in a particular instance, then their absence could not, of itself, provide any support for the suggested irrationality of the decision. The only significance of the absence of reasons was that if all known facts appeared to point overwhelmingly in favour of a decision other than the one reached, then the decision-maker could not complain if the court drew the inference that there was no rational reason for the decision actually taken.

A *third way* in which the courts can indirectly inquire into the reasoning process is by examining the evidence which the decision-maker used to arrive at the jurisdictional findings; the court can then assess whether that evidence justified the findings which were made.[188]

A *fourth exception* to the general rule that there is no duty to provide reasons has been touched upon already: if a public body has created a legitimate expectation that it will act in a certain manner then this may lead to the imposition of a duty to provide reasons as to why it has departed from the course of action which was expected of it.[189]

Community law constitutes the *fifth exception* to the generality of the rule that reasons are not required. Under Community law there is a duty to furnish reasons imposed by Article 190 of the Treaty. The extent of this duty will depend upon the nature of the relevant act and the context

---

[185] [1990] C.O.D. 230, 231.
[186] *Padfield v. Minister of Agriculture, Fisheries and Food* [1968] A.C. 997.
[187] *R. v. Secretary of State for Trade and Industry, ex p. Lonhro plc* [1989] 1 W.L.R. 525.
[188] *Secretary of State for Education and Science v. Tameside Metropolitan Borough Council* [1977] A.C. 1014; *Mahon v. Air New Zealand Ltd.* [1984] A.C. 808, 832-833. See also, *R. v. Sykes* (1875) 1 Q.B. 52; *R. v. Thomas* [1892] 1 Q.B. 426.
[189] See above, pp. 294-296.

within which it was made.[190] The duty is principally imposed upon the Community organs themselves, but it is not inconceivable that it could apply to national authorities which are themselves applying relevant Community norms.[191]

The *final technique* which the courts employ when deciding whether to impose a duty to provide reasons is potentially the most far reaching. They consider the nature of the decision-maker, the context in which it operates and whether the provision of reasons is required for the attainment of fairness. This was the approach of Lord Donaldson M.R. in R. v. *Civil Service Appeal Board, ex p. Cunningham*.[192] The Master of the Rolls re-affirmed previous orthodoxy by making it quite clear that there was no general duty to provide reasons. However, he did impose such a duty on the CSAB, which had given the applicant far less compensation for unfair dismissal than he would have received under the normal employment protection legislation. The duty was imposed in these circumstances because the CSAB was held to be a judicial body performing functions analogous to those of an industrial tribunal. The latter would have to provide reasons, and fairness demanded that so too should the CSAB.

The approach adopted in this case may turn out to be of greater importance than is apparent at first sight. This is because, although the court continues to state that there is no general duty to provide reasons, it does base its decision that some reasons should be provided in this instance on the general principles of natural justice and fairness. The very fact that the court founds its judgment on this ground will render it easier for applicants in other cases to contend that they too should be granted some reasons in the context of their particular cases.

The same type of approach is evident in later cases. Thus, in R. v. *Parole Board, ex p. Wilson*[193] Taylor L.J. based his decision that the applicant should be entitled to know the reasons why the Parole Board was not recommending him for release, on the general ground of natural justice. This method is also apparent in *Doody*.[194] Lord Mustill noted the recent tendency to greater transparency and openness in the making of administrative decisions, and gave an alternative rationale for his judgment to that considered above. His Lordship stated that the statutory scheme should be operated as fairly as possible in the circumstances, and that one should ask whether the refusal to give reasons was fair. On the facts of the case he thought not, since the prisoner had a real interest in understanding how long might be the term of imprisonment and why this particular period was imposed.[195]

---

[190] Case 5/67, *Beus* [1968] E.C.R. 83; Case 24/62; *Germany* v. *Commission* [1963] E.C.R. 63; Case 9/56, *Meroni* v. *High Authority* [1958] E.C.R. 133.
[191] Hartley, *The Foundations of European Community Law* (2nd ed., 1988), pp. 119-126.
[192] [1991] 4 All E.R. 310.
[193] [1992] 1 Q.B. 740.
[194] [1993] 3 All E.R. 92, 105-110.
[195] See also, R. v. *Dairy Produce Quota Tribunal and Minister for Agriculture, Fisheries and Food, ex p. Cooper* [1993] C.O.D. 277.

Cases decided after *Doody* have confirmed the trend of basing the duty to give reasons on fairness itself. Thus in *Walters*[196] Sir Louis Blom-Cooper Q.C. held that, although there was no general duty to give reasons, fairness in the circumstances of the case demanded that a council should give reasons as to why it believed that a flat was suitable for the applicant, when the latter, because of the medical condition of her son, thought that it was not. Similarly in *Standish*[197] Potts J. held that in the absence of written reasons the Secretary of State should, when exercising powers to debar a teacher, provide the court with a short written statement which set out factual findings and conclusions.

Even in cases where the court has denied that any such duty exists the judgment bears testimony to the common law developments which have occurred in this area. This is exemplified by the *Institute of Dental Surgery* case.[198] The applicants sought judicial review of the decision by the Higher Education Funding Council which rated the Institute for research purposes at a level which was lower than the Institute believed was correct. The Institute sought to challenge the rating on the grounds that reasons for the assessment were not provided and that this was unfair. Sedley J. rejected the application, on the grounds, *inter alia*, that where what was sought to be impugned was *no more* than an exercise of informed academic judgment, fairness alone would not require reasons to be given. Notwithstanding this decision on the facts of the case, the judgment as a whole contains many indications of the strides which the common law has made in relation to the duty to provide reasons. The judgment accepts that reasons should be given either when the interest at stake is so important that fairness demands the provision of reasoned explanation, or where the decision appears to be aberrant. Of particular importance is Sedley J.'s view that where reasons ought to have been given, but have not been forthcoming, this in itself constitutes a breach of an independent legal obligation with the consequence that the impugned decision is a nullity: it was not necessary to establish that the failure to provide the reasons established some other head of review, such as irrationality or irrelevancy.

While the statutory and common law rules referred to do impose a duty to provide reasons in certain circumstances, the absence of any general duty is still a significant gap in our procedural protection.[199] The historical origins of the rule that there is no general duty to provide reasons are obscure.[200] In so far as they are based upon analogy with the position of courts of law which are not under any such general duty, this reasoning is being undermined as the judiciary increasingly require some statement of reasons within judgments.[201]

---

[196] R. v. *London Borough of Lambeth, ex p. Walters*, The Times, 6 October 1993.

[197] R. v. *Secretary of State for Education, ex p. Standish*, The Times, 15 November 1993.

[198] R. v. *Higher Education Funding Council, ex p. Institute of Dental Surgery* [1994] 1 All E.R. 651.

[199] For a survey of the practice in other countries, see *Administrative Justice, Some Necessary Reforms*, pp. 46-68. And see R. v. *Secretary of State for the Home Dept., ex p. Harrison* [1988] 3 All E.R. 86; R. v. *Civil Service Appeal Board, ex p. Bruce* [1989] I.C.R. 171.

[200] *Administrative Justice, Some Necessary Reforms*, pp. 29-32.

[201] *e.g. Eagil Trust Co. Ltd.* v. *Piggott-Brown* [1985] 3 All E.R. 119.

While there may be justifications for withholding reasons in certain circumstances, it is surely time, at the very least, to reverse the current position so that the general rule stipulates that reasons should be accorded, with exceptions being made to this proposition where warranted.

5. Appeals and Rehearing

How far can a defect of natural justice be cured by an appeal within the administrative hierarchy or by a rehearing by the original body? The authorities have been reviewed by the Privy Council in *Calvin* v. *Carr*.[202] It was argued that a breach of natural justice at the original hearing conducted by racing stewards could not be cured by an appeal to a committee of the Australian Jockey Club since there would be nothing to appeal against, the first decision being a nullity.[203]

Lord Wilberforce reviewed the authorities and adopted a tripartite distinction. First, where the rehearing was by the same body or some more complete form of it the general rule was that defects at the original hearing could be cured.[204] Secondly, there were cases where after considering the whole hearing structure in its particular context a fair hearing might be required at the original stage and on appeal.[205] This second proposition was not however an absolute one. His Lordship posited a third situation where, looking again at the whole context, it could be seen whether the end result was fair despite some initial defect. This would depend *inter alia* on the type of appeal process: for example, if the appeal body was only entitled to a transcript from the original decision then the later hearing would probably be inadequate.[206] The facts of *Calvin* itself were said to fall into category three. The stewards inquiry had to make a quick decision; any defect in natural justice at that stage would be cured by the hearing before the full committee of the Jockey Club.

---

[202] [1980] A.C. 574.

[203] For the importance of the case in the void-voidable debate, see below p. 463.

[204] [1980] A.C. 574, 592. *De Verteuil* v. *Knaggs* [1918] A.C. 557; *Ridge* v. *Baldwin* [1964] A.C. 40, 79. Presumably this would be subject to a caveat to cover cases where failure to give an initially fair hearing prejudiced the individual in a way that could not be cured by the later rehearing.

[205] [1980] A.C. 574, 592-593. An example of this is *Leary* v. *National Union of Vehicle Builders* [1971] Ch. 34, otherwise the individual could be deprived of "two cracks of the whip" since the appeal would be the first fair hearing, *per* Megarry J., 48-58. See also, *R.* v. *Aston University Senate, ex p. Roffey* [1969] 2 Q.B. 538.

[206] [1980] A.C. 574, 593. *Annamunthodo* v. *Oilfields Workers' Trade Union* [1961] A.C. 945 and *Pillai* v. *Singapore City Council* [1968] 1 W.L.R. 1278 were treated as contrasting examples of a case where a defect was not cured on appeal and one where it was.

6. *Deciding Without Hearing*

How far is the decision-maker allowed to determine a matter without a hearing? The answer depends upon the enabling legislation, the type of function being performed, and the nature of the decision-maker. Thus, it is accepted that if a minister is made the deciding authority the decision will often have to be made through officers, who will collect the material and the officer may even make the decision in the minister's name.[207]

In other areas the general principle is that the greater the judicial element involved, the more likely it is that the decision-maker must also hear.[208] Investigation may well be undertaken by a sub-committee, but the deciding authority must then be apprised of that material. Whether the material thus collected can be summarised, and whether all those on the deciding authority must possess all the papers[209] will depend on the nature of the function being performed and the language of the enabling statute. The decision in *Chief Constable of the North Wales Police* v. *Evans*[210] provides an example of what may be required. A probationer constable sought, *inter alia*, an order of certiorari to quash the decision of the Chief Constable that he should resign or be discharged. The Chief Constable had decided to dispense with his services because of a report made on the probationer constable which led the Chief Constable to believe that he was not fitted to be a member of the police force. The investigation had been conducted by the deputy Chief Constable. Delegation of the inquiry was allowed provided that a number of conditions were met. The ultimate decision must be made by the Chief Constable. The delegate must tell the constable the nature of the complaint against him and allow him an opportunity to comment upon it before the final decision was taken by the Chief Constable. It seems that the Chief Constable must also show the report to the constable and invite his comments before reaching his final decision. On the facts of the case the rules of natural justice had been broken because the constable had had no opportunity to comment upon the allegations made against him.

Section 6. Content of Natural Justice: Specific Areas

Given that the content of procedural protection will vary from area to area it is important to look at specific topics. Only by doing so can one judge whether the amount of procedural protection is being pitched at the correct level.

---

[207] *Local Government Board* v. *Arlidge* [1915] A.C. 120. See, pp. 390-391.
[208] *Barnard* v. *National Dock Labour Board* [1953] 2 Q.B. 18; *Vine* v. *National Dock Labour Board* [1957] A.C. 488; *Jeffs* v. *New Zealand Dairy Board* [1967] 1 A.C. 551, 568, 569; *R.* v. *Race Relations Board, ex p. Selvarajan* [1975] 1 W.L.R. 1686.
[209] *Ex p. Selvarajan* [1975] 1 W.L.R. 1686, 1695-1696, 1698; *R.* v. *Commission for Racial Equality, ex p. Cottrell and Rothon* [1980] 1 W.L.R. 1580, 1589.
[210] [1982] 1 W.L.R. 1155, 1161, 1165. This particular matter was only considered by Lord Hailsham and Lord Bridge.

1. *Employment*

Traditionally, the availability of natural justice in the area of employment has depended upon the nature of the employment relationship. If there is what is regarded by the law as an office then public law remedies are available to protect its holder who is entitled to natural justice; the individual can thus regain the office if dismissed without a hearing.[211] The position of the office-holder should be juxtaposed both to ordinary master-servant relationships and offices held at pleasure.

The courts will not, in general, specifically enforce an ordinary master-servant relationship.[212] From this the courts have inferred that, except where the employer is under a statutory duty or there is some other restriction as to the type of contract that it can make with its servants or the grounds on which it can dismiss them, the servant has no procedural protection.[213] Where an office-holder can be removed at pleasure, as opposed to for cause, the same connection has been forged between the absence of substantive rights and the lack of procedural protection; the latter has been treated as a natural corollary of the former.[214] The incidence of procedural protection in this area has been less than satisfactory. Distinctions have been drawn which when examined have little to recommend them.

First, the line between what is regarded as an office and what is construed as a pure master-servant relationship can be very fine, thereby rendering the applicability of natural justice difficult to predict and producing divisions which are capricious.[215]

Secondly, the line between officers dismissable for cause and those dismissable at pleasure can also be hard to draw.[216] For example, an office held at pleasure might nevertheless be subject to procedural fairness where the statutory scheme would be less effective if the right to be heard were not implied.[217]

---

[211] See, *Bagg's Case* (1615) 11 Co.Rep. 93b; *R. v. Chancellor of the University of Cambridge* (1723) 1 Str. 557; *Fisher* v. *Jackson* (1891) 2 Ch. 824; *Ridge* v. *Baldwin* [1964] A.C. 40, 66; *Chief Constable of the North Wales Police* v. *Evans* [1982] 1 W.L.R. 1155; *R. v. East Berkshire Health Authority, ex p. Walsh* [1985] Q.B. 152; *R. v. Secretary of State for the Home Department, ex p. Benwell* [1985] Q.B. 554.

[212] *cf. Hill* v. *C.A. Parsons & Co. Ltd.* [1972] Ch. 305.

[213] *Ridge* v. *Baldwin* [1964] A.C. 40, 66; *Evans* [1982] 1 W.L.R. 1155; *Walsh* [1985] Q.B. 152, 164-165.

[214] *Ridge* v. *Baldwin* [1964] A.C. 40.

[215] Contrast *Cooper* v. *Wilson* [1937] 2 K.B. 309 and *Ridge* v. *Baldwin* [1964] A.C. 40 (police are office-holders) with *Barber* v. *Manchester Regional Hospital Board* [1958] 1 W.L.R. 181 (consultant surgeon) and *Vidyodaya University Council* v. *Silva* [1965] 1 W.L.R. 77 (university teacher, not office holders). Compare further *Walsh* [1985] Q.B. 152 and *Benwell* [1985] Q.B. 554.

[216] For an early example of the absence of procedural protection where offices are held at pleasure, see *R. v. Darlington School Governors* (1844) 6 Q.B. 682, though the courts often evaded the rule *Willis* v. *Childe* (1851) 13 Beav. 117.

[217] *Malloch* v. *Aberdeen Corporation* [1971] 1 W.L.R. 1578.

Thirdly, and perhaps most importantly, the logic of the equation – no substantive rights to the job itself, therefore no procedural protection – which permeates the jurisprudence on both master-servant and offices held at pleasure is false. The absence of substantive protection renders the presence of procedural rights even more important, a point made cogently by Lord Wilberforce in *Malloch* v. *Aberdeen Corporation*. His Lordship would confine the absence of procedural protection in the pure master-servant area to cases where there was no element of public employment, no service, no statutory support, and nothing in the nature of an office.[218] Moreover, as Woolf J. has observed, the enactment of employment protection legislation has blurred the line between office holders and ordinary servants.[219]

Finally, the existence of the preceding distinctions between differing types of employment relationship has caused considerable difficulty in determining whether an employee can use the new procedures for remedies.[220]

The common law rules have now been overlaid by statute.[221] The statutory protection covers both public and private employees (subject to exceptions). A dismissal may be unfair either because it was procedurally arbitrary or because it lacked good cause. The remedies are compensation and recommendations for reinstatement, although the latter are not specifically enforceable. While this legislative protection is beneficial, a reform of the common law position would be most welcome.[222]

2. *Students*

Students are regarded as having contracts with their institution, one of the implied terms of which will be that the institution will act in accordance with natural justice. Thus, natural justice has been held to be applicable to cases of disciplinary action within a university[223] and to expulsion for failure in examinations,[224] although in the latter case the examiners had based their decision on the personal attributes of the candidate as well as exam marks. In both cases however the remedy was withheld.[225] In other cases where the matter has arisen the court has found either that natural

---

[218] [1971] 1 W.L.R. 1578, 1595–1598. See also, *Stevenson* v. *United Road Transport Union* [1977] I.C.R. 893.

[219] *R.* v. *British Broadcasting Corporation, ex p. Lavelle* [1983] 1 W.L.R. 23.

[220] See below, Chap. 15.

[221] See the Employment Protection (Consolidation) Act 1978, Pt. V; Employment Act 1980, s.6. See below, pp. 710–711.

[222] Moreover, while the areas covered by common law and statute overlap they are not identical: there may, for example, be individuals who are not employees for the purposes of the legislation, but who could come within the common law concept of an office.

[223] *Glynn* v. *Keele University* [1971] 1 W.L.R. 487.

[224] *R.* v. *Aston University Senate, ex p. Roffey* [1969] 2 Q.B. 538.

[225] For the dangers of witholding remedies for causal reasons, see above, pp. 301–302; for a discussion of the extent of discretion in granting remedies, see below pp. 596–597.

justice has been complied with,[226] or that the matter was within the jurisdiction of the Visitor.[227] The jurisdiction of the Visitor is exclusive, and covers all matters relating to the internal or domestic laws of the foundation, irrespective of whether a particular claim could, for example, be formulated as one involving a breach of contract.[228] However, the courts still retain a supervisory jurisdiction over the Visitor, which can be exercised if the Visitor acts *ultra vires* (in a narrow sense), in abuse of power or contrary to natural justice.[229]

3. Licensing

The number of activities for which a person requires a licence are legion.[230] Prior to *Ridge* v. *Baldwin*[231] the combined effect of the administrative-judicial dichotomy and that drawn between rights and privileges, resulted in the rules of procedural fairness having only a limited application in this area. The liberalisation of those rules since *Ridge* has affected procedures attendant upon the grant of a licence. Some elements of natural justice or fairness will normally be required,[232] although precisely which will be dependent upon the nature of the issuing authority and whether the case is concerned with the application, renewal, or revocation of the licence.

In *McInnes* v. *Onslow-Fane*,[233] Megarry V.C. held that in the case of forfeiture the individual was entitled to an unbiased tribunal, notice and a hearing, whereas in the case of an application less was required. Since nothing had been taken away the duty in such a case was to reach an honest conclusion without bias and not in pursuance of a capricious policy.[234] Renewal of a licence fell into an intermediate category. Here the individual might have a legitimate expectation that the licence would be renewed. These cases were, said Megarry V.C., to be treated as closer to forfeiture than to those of initial application.[235] The distinctions drawn by Megarry V.C.

---

[226] *Herring* v. *Templeman* [1973] 3 All E.R. 569.
[227] *Thorne* v. *University of London* [1966] 2 Q.B. 237; *Patel* v. *University of Bradford* [1978] 1 W.L.R. 1488, affirmed [1979] 1 W.L.R. 1066.
[228] *Thomas* v. *University of Bradford* [1987] A.C. 795. See also, *Hines* v. *Birkbeck College* [1986] Ch. 524; *Oakes* v. *Sidney Sussex College, Cambridge* [1988] 1 W.L.R. 431. See generally, Bridge, "Keeping the Peace in the Universities: The Role of the Visitor" (1970) 86 L.Q.R. 531; Smith, "The Exclusive Jurisdiction of the University Visitor" (1981) 97 L.Q.R. 610.
[229] *Page* v. *Hull University Visitor* [1993] 1 All E.R. 97.
[230] See generally, Williams, "Control by Licensing" [1967] C.L.P. 81; Street, *Justice in the Welfare State* (2nd ed., 1975), Chap. 4.
[231] [1964] A.C. 40.
[232] *R.* v. *Gaming Board for Great Britain, ex p. Benaim and Khaida* [1970] 2 Q.B. 417; *R.* v. *Liverpool Corporation, ex p. Liverpool Taxi Fleet Operators' Association* [1972] 2 Q.B. 299; *McInnes* v. *Onslow-Fane* [1978] 1 W.L.R. 1520.
[233] [1978] 1 W.L.R. 1520.
[234] *Ibid.* pp. 1532-1535.
[235] *Ibid.* pp. 1520, 1529. See also, *R.* v. *Calgary, ex p. Sanderson* (1966) 53 D.L.R. (2d) 477; *R.* v. *Secretary of State for the Environment, ex p. Brent London Borough Council* [1982] Q.B. 593, 642-643.

should not be allowed to become over-rigid. There may well be an area where the interest at stake in an application for a licence is considerably more important than that involved in a forfeiture or failure to renew in a different context. Moreover, the duty owed to the applicant may well be higher in certain areas than that indicated by Megarry V.C.

While the application of procedural checks to licensing activities has, therefore, increased it would be mistaken to say that it is now accepted that any licensing function should be subjected to such safeguards. We have already seen how the courts still, on occasion, interpret the notion of privilege or legitimate expectation to deny or curtail procedural rights.[236] In addition, there are for example licensing functions performed by the executive in respect of which the traditional view has been that procedural safeguards do not apply.[237] There are probably also many minor licensing decisions where no element of fairness is accorded, particularly with respect to licences granted by local authorities.[238] The last 20 years have witnessed the increase in procedural rights for licence holders or applicants, but the disbursement of such benefits is still subject to irrational distinctions. It is not that varying degrees of procedural protection should not exist: the range of licences demands this diversity. It is rather that little rationality is evident in the decision whether to accord any procedural protection at all and as to how much protection should be given.

4. Discipline

The application of natural justice in the context of discipline suffered, like the case of licensing, from the administrative-judicial distinction; disciplinary measures were deemed not to be judicial with the correlative inapplicability of natural justice.[239] As with licensing, the position has now altered, though the content and indeed application of natural justice or fairness will vary as between areas. It has been seen that academic institutions have to abide by procedural fairness when applying disciplinary measures,[240] as do trade unions,[241] and it has now been held that prison visitors and governors exercising their disciplinary functions are subject to certiorari for breach of natural justice.[242] An example of the application of

---

[236] Schmidt v. Secretary of State for Home Affairs [1969] 2 Ch. 149, 170, 173; Cinnamond v. British Airports Authority [1980] 1 W.L.R. 582.

[237] In Cinnamond Lord Denning M.R. stated that there was no legitimate expectation to justify a hearing for a person seeking an industrial development certificate, [1980] 1 W.L.R. 582, 590.

[238] But see, R. v. Barnsley Metropolitan Borough Council, ex p. Hook [1976] 1 W.L.R. 1052.

[239] R. v. Metropolitan Police Commissioner, ex p. Parker [1953] 1 W.L.R. 1150; ex p. Fry [1954] 1 W.L.R. 730.

[240] Glynn v. Keele University [1971] 1 W.L.R. 487. cf. Ward v. Bradford Corporation (1971) 70 L.G.R. 27.

[241] e.g. Taylor v. National Union of Seamen [1967] 1 W.L.R. 532.

[242] R. v. Board of Visitors of Hull Prison, ex p. St. Germain [1979] Q.B. 425; Leech v. Parkhurst Prison Deputy Governor [1988] A.C. 533.

the principles of natural justice in this area is provided by *R. v. Board of Visitors of Hull Prison, ex p. St. Germain (No. 2)*.[243] After a riot in a prison, offences against prison discipline were alleged against a number of prisoners, including the applicants. The charges were heard by the prison's board of visitors. The chairman of the board ruled that certain witnesses which a prisoner had requested to attend should not be called. It was held that, while the chairman possessed a discretion to disallow witnesses to be called, that discretion had to be exercised reasonably and in good faith. To exclude witnesses because there was ample evidence against a prisoner, or on a mistaken understanding of the prisoner's defence, or on the basis of administrative inconvenience, would be an improper exercise of that discretion. This was particularly so where, as here, the applicant had been charged with serious disciplinary offences which would result in a loss of liberty. Recent authority, extending natural justice to prison governors, has emphasised that natural justice ought to apply when the rights or legitimate expectations of an individual are affected.[244]

5. *Preliminary Hearings*

The application of natural justice to preliminary hearings or investigations has tended to produce polarised arguments: the public body arguing that procedural rules have no place in the context of such hearings or investigations, and the individual asserting that they should apply with their full vigour.[245] The courts, not surprisingly, have eschewed both such philosophies preferring an intermediate ground where some element of fairness is required, but not the full rigour of natural justice. As Lord Wilberforce stated, there are many types of prima facie or preliminary determination and the requirements of fairness in one area may be unsuited to another.[246] The actual content given to natural justice or fairness will depend upon a range of factors: the proximity between the initial investigation and the final decision; the construction of the statute; the importance of the subject matter for the individual; and the need for administrative efficiency.

Thus, in *Wiseman v. Borneman*[247] the Inland Revenue Commissioners believed that section 28 of the Finance Act 1960 concerning share transactions was applicable to the case before them; the taxpayer objected and entered a statutory declaration setting out his reasons. The Commissioners still believed that the Act applied and referred the statutory declaration, a certificate and counter-statement setting out their views on the taxpayer's statutory declaration, to a tribunal which would decide whether there was a prima facie case for proceeding. The taxpayer claimed

---

[243] [1979] 1 W.L.R. 1401.
[244] *Leech* [1988] A.C. 533.
[245] *Wiseman v. Borneman* [1971] A.C. 297.
[246] *Ibid.* p. 317.
[247] [1971] A.C. 297.

that he should be entitled to see the counter-statement. The House of Lords, while accepting that some elements of natural justice could apply to investigations and preliminary determinations, held that an opportunity to see the counter-statement was not required: no final decision was being made and if the taxpayer could comment on the counter-statement the Commissioners would wish to comment on those comments, thereby producing an endless succession of exchanges, bringing the administration to a standstill.[248]

6. Aliens

The common law has not proved a great source of procedural protection for aliens.[249] Most of the conceptual distinctions which have been used to narrow the scope of such protection have been applied to them. Thus, in *R. v. Leman Street Police Station Inspector, ex p. Venicoff*[250] it was held that when the Secretary of State was deporting a person where he deemed it to be conducive to the public good, he was acting in an executive and not in a judicial capacity. He was therefore not bound to hold an inquiry or grant a hearing prior to making the deportation order.[251] Nearly 50 years later the language has altered, but the substance looks strikingly familiar. In *Schmidt v. Secretary of State for Home Affairs*[252] the plaintiffs were scientology students who had been given a limited leave to enter the country. Lord Denning M.R. held that whether a hearing was required before the request that their stay be extended was rejected depended on whether the individual had a right, interest or legitimate expectation. Applied here, the plaintiffs had no right to stay one day beyond their allowed period, and therefore they had no right to a hearing.[253]

While the nature of the plaintiff's interest may, as argued above,[254] affect the content of natural justice or fairness, the argument from *Schmidt*, which equates the absence of procedural protection with the absence of a right to stay, is subject to all the criticism of such reasoning outlined in the discussion of employment relationships.[255] It may well be accepted that a

---

[248] *Ibid.* pp. 308, 310, 315, 319-320; *Pearlberg v. Varty* [1972] 1 W.L.R. 534. See also, the reasoning in *Re Pergamon Press Ltd.* [1971] Ch. 388, 399-400, and *Maxwell v. Department of Trade and Industry* [1974] Q.B. 523, 534.

[249] Legomsky, *Immigration and the Judiciary* (1987), pp. 38-46.

[250] [1920] 3 K.B. 72.

[251] In *R. v. Governor of Brixton Prison, ex p. Soblen* [1963] 2 Q.B. 243, 298-299, Lord Denning M.R. stated that while there was no right to be heard before the deportation order was made, there may be circumstances where a hearing was required after the making of the order and prior to its execution.

[252] [1969] 2 Ch. 149.

[253] It would be different if the permit had been revoked before the time limit had expired. In such a case there would be a legitimate expectation and a right to make representations. See also, *Re H.K. (An Infant)* [1967] 2 Q.B. 617; *Att.-Gen. of Hong Kong v. Ng Yuen Shiu* [1983] 2 A.C. 629.

[254] See pp. 293-300.

[255] See pp. 318-319.

person who is deported should have greater protection than one who is refused entry, or that a person whose permit has expired has a lesser interest than one whose permit is revoked. These are relevant factors to take into account. The language of rights, legitimate expectations or privileges should not be elevated to any higher status.[256] It should not be determinative in itself.

Aliens are not entirely without protection. Statute provides an appeals procedure against deportation, the non renewal of residence permits and other types of restrictions.[257] Appeals are excluded, however, where the Secretary of State certifies that the refusal of leave to enter or a refusal of entry clearance is conducive to the public good.[258] Similar provisions exclude appeals in relation to deportation.[259] Conducive to the public good covers the interests of national security, reasons of a political nature, and the relations between the United Kingdom and any other country. Moreover, it has been held that when the Home Secretary deports a person "for reasons of national security" a statement to that effect was sufficient and no further specification of reasons was required.[260] A practice developed of allowing the individual to make representations and call witnesses before a panel of three people who would advise the Secretary of State. While the panel is under a duty to act fairly the content of that duty will be limited by the nature of the case. Thus requests for further particulars of allegations against an individual may be denied where the information received by the Secretary of State is of a highly confidential nature and relates to national security.[261]

Section 7. Conclusion

The courts have not been idle since the landmark decision in *Ridge* v. *Baldwin*.[262] While many of the subsequent developments are to be welcomed, certain cautionary notes should be sounded. First, while the

---

[256] Greater procedural rights have been granted when the applicant has a statutory right to enter on proof of specified conditions, *Shareef* v. *Commissioner for Registration of Indian and Pakistani Residents* [1965] 3 W.L.R. 704; *Att.-Gen.* v. *Ryan* [1980] A.C. 718. The content of the duty to act fairly in *Re H.K.* [1967] 2 Q.B. 617 was, however, narrowly drawn.

[257] Immigration Act 1971, Pt. II. Under European Community law nationals of Member States have the same remedies against administrative action as do our own nationals, Council Directive 64/221, Art. 8. This provision has direct effect, Case 41/74, *Van Duyn* v. *Home Office* [1974] E.C.R. 1337.

[258] ss.13(5), 14(3).

[259] s.15(3).

[260] *R.* v. *Secretary of State for the Home Department, ex p. Cheblak* [1991] 1 W.L.R. 890.

[261] *R.* v. *Secretary of State for the Home Department, ex p. Hosenball* [1977] 1 W.L.R. 766; *ex p. Cheblak* [1991] 1 W.L.R. 890. Compare, however, the greater willingness to enforce a reasons requirement in *R.* v. *Immigration Appeal Tribunal, ex p. Khan (Mahmud)* [1983] Q.B. 790, and *R.* v. *Secretary of State for the Home Department, ex p. Dannenberg* [1984] Q.B. 766.

[262] [1964] A.C. 40.

courts have generally avoided rigid classifications in deciding on the applicability of natural justice, they have not discarded such tools altogether. Objections to such forms of pigeon-holing have been given above.[263] Secondly, continuing analysis is required to determine whether the content of the rules in general, and their application to particular areas, is being pitched at the "right" level. Recognition of a general duty to provide reasons furnishes an example of a central aspect of natural justice which could well be improved, while the application of procedural rights in the context of employment relationships and aliens exemplifies particular areas where significant change should be made. Thirdly, more thought should be given to understanding the general nature of the balancing process which operates within fairness. The extent to which this should be viewed as a utilitarian calculus of some kind, or whether a more dignitarian approach should be pursued is of considerable importance.

The concluding comments thus far have been directed towards the application and content of natural justice and fairness seeing both of these terms against an adjudicative framework. This is how they operate at present. Procedures derived from a backdrop of adjudication may not, however, be the most appropriate or effective in particular areas. Other decisional forms, whether they be mediation or managerial direction, may be better in certain contexts. The recognition and development of other types of decision-making, with the procedures necessarily consequent upon them, is one of the important tasks for the administrative lawyer, just as important as the workings of fairness within the traditional adjudicative context.

---

[263] See pp. 287-288.

9. NATURAL JUSTICE: BIAS

The second limb of natural justice is that decisions should be made free from bias or partiality.[1] The issue can arise in two main contexts. First, the decision-maker might have some interest of a pecuniary or personal nature in the outcome of the proceedings. Secondly, there are problems where the decision-maker is interested in the result of an inquiry or investigation, not in any personal sense, but because the institution which he or she represents is desirous of attaining a certain objective. Discussion of these two types of problems will be followed by consideration of what the test for establishing bias actually is.

Section 1. Personal Interest

1. *Pecuniary Interest*

The courts have long insisted that any pecuniary interest disqualifies the decision-maker be he high or low. Thus, in *Dimes* v. *Grand Junction Canal Co. Proprietors*[2] the House of Lords reversed a decision made by the Lord Chancellor, Lord Cottenham, when the latter had affirmed decrees by the Vice-Chancellor in relation to a company in which the Lord Chancellor held some shares. No imputation of any actual bias was made against Lord Cottenham, but their Lordships held that the principle that no man can be a judge in his own cause must be sacred.[3] The courts have consistently held that if a pecuniary interest exists it is not necessary to go on to consider reasonable suspicion or real likelihood of bias.[4] It is therefore of importance to establish what will constitute a pecuniary interest.

Blackburn J. has held that any pecuniary interest, however small, will be sufficient.[5] Some qualification is however required to the breadth of these

---

[1] See generally Jackson, *Natural Justice* (2nd ed., 1979), Chap. 2; Flick, *Natural Justice* (1979), Chap. 6.
[2] (1852) 3 H.L.C. 759.
[3] *Ibid.* pp. 793-794.
[4] *e.g. R.* v. *Rand* (1866) L.R. 1 Q.B. 230; *Leeson* v. *General Council of Medical Education and Registration* [1889] 43 Ch.D. 366.
[5] *R.* v. *Hammond* (1863) 9 L.T.(N.S.) 423; *R.* v. *Rand* (1866) L.R. 1 Q.B. 230, 232.

statements. If the pecuniary interest is not personal to the decision-maker then the matter will fall to be considered as a challenge on the grounds of favour.[6] Moreover, if the alleged pecuniary interest is extremely remote[7] or based upon contingencies which are unlikely to materialise,[8] then the matter will similarly be treated as a challenge on the grounds of favour. Subject to these qualifications, the prohibition of pecuniary interest seems to be an absolute one and is not further qualified by any requirement that the interest be substantial.[9]

2. *Other Personal Interests*

Other types of personal interest may disqualify the decision-maker if the courts find that the interest gave rise to a reasonable suspicion or real likelihood of bias.[10] In this area much will be dependent upon the factual nexus between the decision-maker and one of the other parties involved in the dispute. Family relationship,[11] business connections, and commercial ties,[12] are examples of the interests which can disqualify the decision-maker, as is membership of an organisation interested in the dispute.[13] On occasion it may be someone other than the actual adjudicator who has been involved. Nevertheless, provided that he or she has, or may appear to have, an influence on the decision given, then that will be sufficient to render the determination invalid.[14]

---

[6] In the *Rand* case those challenged were two justices who were trustees for a hospital and friendly society, respectively, which bodies had funds invested in a corporation which had applied to the justices.

[7] *R. v. McKenzie* [1892] 2 Q.B. 519.

[8] *R. v. Burton, ex p. Young* [1897] 2 Q.B. 468.

[9] *e.g. R. v. Gaisford* [1892] 1 Q.B. 381, the interest of a ratepayer was held to be a pecuniary interest.

[10] The relationship between these tests will be considered below, pp. 330-333.

[11] *e.g. Metropolitan Properties (F.G.C.) Ltd. v. Lannon* [1969] 1 Q.B. 577.

[12] *e.g. R. v. Barnsley Licensing JJ., ex p. Barnsley and District Licensed Victuallers' Association* [1960] 2 Q.B. 167; *R. v. Hendon Rural District Council, ex p. Chorley* [1933] 2 K.B. 696; *R. v. Chesterfield Borough Council, ex p. Darker Enterprises Ltd.* [1992] C.O.D. 466.

[13] *Leeson's* case, above n.4; *Allinson v. General Council of Medical Education and Registration* [1894] 1 Q.B. 750.

[14] *e.g. R. v. Sussex Justices, ex p. McCarthy* [1924] 1 K.B. 256 (clerk to the justices was member of a solicitor's firm acting for one of the parties in a collision out of which the prosecution of the other party arose); *Cooper v. Wilson* [1937] 2 K.B. 309 (chief constable who had purported to dismiss a policeman sits with the Watch Committee when they hear the policeman's case); *R. v. Kent Police Authority, ex p. Godden* [1971] 2 Q.B. 662 (in deciding whether a policeman should be compulsorily retired a report should not be sought from a psychiatrist who had already formed an adverse view of the person); *R. v. Barnsley Metropolitan Borough Council, ex p. Hook* [1976] 1 W.L.R. 1052 (market manager in the position of a prosecutor should not give evidence to a committee in the absence of the accused). *cf. R. v. Frankland Prison Board of Visitors, ex p. Lewis* [1986] 3 W.L.R. 61.

Section 2. Institutional

1. *Prosecutor and Judge*

A somewhat different way in which the issue of bias can manifest itself is when the prosecutor of an offence is also the judge. This may happen *directly* as in *R. v. Lee, ex p. Shaw*[15] where the sanitary committee of a town council instructed the town clerk to prosecute a person and one of the justices before whom he was prosecuted was a member of that committee. The court held that the decision could not stand.[16] The matter may also arise *indirectly* in situations in which the decision-maker belongs to an organisation which initiated the proceeding, but where he himself has taken no part in the decision to prosecute. In *Leeson's* case[17] the General Medical Council had disqualified a doctor for infamous misconduct in a prosecution brought by the Medical Defence Union, an organisation designed to uphold the character of doctors and to suppress unauthorised practitioners. Two of the 29 who held the inquiry were members of the Medical Defence Union, but not of its managing body. The court found that, looked at in substance and fact, the two Medical Defence Union members on the General Council were not accusers as well as judges and that they could not reasonably be suspected of bias.[18] The court may also overturn a decision if it is felt that, for example, a justice has pre-judged the matter before hearing the full case.[19]

The difficulty presented here is more acute in the context of governmental agencies who have responsibility both for adjudication and prosecution, a combination more normal in the United States than in this country. In response to this problem the 1946 Federal Administrative Procedure Act section 5(c) established an internal separation of function between decider and prosecutor.[20]

---

[15] (1882) 9 Q.B.D. 394.

[16] See also, *R. v. Gaisford* [1892] 1 Q.B. 381; *R. v. Pwllheli JJ., ex p. Soane* [1948] 2 All E.R. 815; *Frome United Breweries Co. Ltd. v. Bath Justices* [1926] A.C. 586; *Roebuck v. National Union of Mineworkers (Yorkshire Area) (No. 2)* [1978] I.C.R. 676.

[17] [1889] 43 Ch.D. 366. And see *Re S (A Barrister)* [1981] Q.B. 683.

[18] See also, *Allinson v. General Council of Medical Education and Registration* [1894] 1 Q.B. 750; *R. v. Burton, ex p. Young* [1897] 2 Q.B. 468, (Incorporated Law Society initiates prosecution against a person falsely pretending to be a solicitor. One of the magistrates was a practising solicitor. This did not prevent him sitting since membership of the society gave no control over prosecutions brought by it.) *cf. Law v. Chartered Institute of Patent Agents* [1919] 2 Ch. 276.

[19] *R. v. Romsey JJ., ex p. Gale* [1992] C.O.D. 323.

[20] For a discussion of the application and limits of this provision, Davis, *Administrative Law Text* (3rd ed., 1972), Chap. 13; Breyer and Stewart, *Administrative Law and Regulatory Policy* (2nd ed., 1985), pp. 859-870.

2. *Institutional Opinion*

Overlapping with, but nevertheless separate from the mixture of function between prosecutor and judge, is the difficulty that administrators of a particular scheme may well have "strong views" or "preconceived ideas" concerning the subject-matter before them.[21] The subject-matter may be of a discretionary or regulatory nature and while these elements should not exclude proscriptions against bias they are likely to modify their application. Administrators may have guidelines to help them to interpret a broadly worded statute, the application of which should not in itself constitute bias. Clear prejudgment of a case is to be disapproved of, but the success of a piece of legislation may well be dependent upon the administrator enforcing the institution's policies with some rigour; indifference to the end in view, even if it were possible, might well be undesirable.[22]

Seen against this background the decision in *Franklin* v. *Minister of Town and Country Planning*,[23] although undoubtedly influenced by the judicial conservatism of the time, would probably not be decided differently today. In that case the House of Lords stated that the minister had a duty to give genuine consideration to a report of an inspector concerning the siting of a new town at Stevenage and to consider objections to that position. It was held that reference to bias was out of place in this context. However, while the result might well be the same, the reasoning of the Court of Appeal is to be preferred; complete impartiality could not be expected and the term impartiality when used in the context of a minister making a decision such as the siting of a new town, would not necessarily be the same as when applied to a magistrate deciding a case of nuisance. While complete impartiality cannot always be expected in such a case, the obligations of natural justice or fairness may still require that a minister hear representations. In *R.* v. *Secretary of State for the Environment, ex p. Brent London Borough Council*[24] the applicant local authorities claimed that they should be entitled to make representations to the minister as to the way in which he should exercise his powers concerning local authority grants. Representations had been made prior to the passage of the legislation, but the court held that the minister was still under a duty to act fairly in the way in which he exercised his discretion under the legislation. He should, therefore, have listened to representations made after the Act received the Royal Assent, but before he actually exercised his discretion. The court accepted that the minister would not be expected to hear such representations as if he were a judge. The minister would not be expected to approach the matter with an empty mind, but his mind should, in the words of the court, at least be ajar.

---

[21] A valuable discussion of this can be found in Flick, above n.1, pp. 122-129.
[22] See the Committee on Ministers' Powers, Cmd. 4060 (1932), p. 78.
[23] [1948] A.C. 87; *Turner* v. *Allison* [1971] N.Z.L.R. 833. An expression of opinion by the adjudicator will not constitute bias, *R.* v. *London County Council, Re The Empire Theatre* (1894) 71 L.T. 638; *R.* v. *Nailsworth Licensing Justices, ex p. Bird* [1953] 1 W.L.R. 1046.
[24] [1982] Q.B. 593.

The problem adverted to above can also manifest itself at local as well as at central level. Thus, it has been held that licensing justices are not precluded from hearing an appeal for a licence, even though some of them had been concerned with an earlier application: the nature of the licensing function required those with local knowledge to form a policy for their area which they could have regard to when hearing individual applications, and the limited number of licensing justices meant that they might, on occasion, hear an appeal when they had been concerned with an earlier application.[25]

Section 3. The Test for Bias

1. *General*

The test for determining bias in cases other than those concerning pecuniary interest is, in short, in a state of confusion. Two tests have been espoused by the courts, that of "real likelihood of bias", and that of "reasonable suspicion of bias".[26] In the nineteenth-century cases the former test held sway: if there was no pecuniary interest the court inquired whether there was a real likelihood of bias.[27] However in *R. v. Sussex Justices, ex p. McCarthy*,[28] Lord Hewart C.J. said that a reasonable suspicion of bias was sufficient to quash the determination.

Later cases witnessed the "competitive invocation" of the two tests, the authority whose decision was to be impugned claiming that the applicant still had to satisfy the higher hurdle of real likelihood of bias. The tide appeared to be shifting back to this higher test for in two cases (at least) the courts expressly adopted that criterion and disapproved of Lord Hewart C.J.'s formulation.[29] Certainty was not however to last for in *Metropolitan Properties (F.G.C.) Ltd.* v. *Lannon* Lord Denning M.R. "rescued" Lord Hewart's reasonable suspicion test.[30] Later cases have not thrown much light on these muddied waters.[31] To understand why the confusion has been generated it is necessary to separate two different issues, the first of which is particularly important.

---

[25] *R. v. Crown Court at Bristol, ex p. Cooper* [1990] 2 All E.R. 193. See also, *Darker Enterprises Ltd.* v. *Dacorum Borough Council* [1992] C.O.D. 465.
[26] Alexis, "Reasonableness in the Establishing of Bias" [1979] P.L. 143; Cranston, "Disqualification of Judges for Interest, Association or Opinion" [1979] P.L. 237; Rawlings, "The Test for the Nemo Judex Rule" [1980] P.L. 122.
[27] e.g. *R. v. Rand* (1866) L.R. 1 Q.B. 230, 232; *R. v. Sunderland JJ.* [1901] 2 K.B. 357.
[28] [1924] 1 K.B. 256, 259.
[29] *R. v. Camborne JJ., ex p. Pearce* [1955] 1 Q.B. 41; *R. v. Barnsley Licensing JJ., ex p. Barnsley and District Licensed Victuallers' Association* [1960] 2 Q.B. 167.
[30] [1969] 1 Q.B. 577, 598-600, 606.
[31] In *Hannam* v. *Bradford Corporation* [1970] 1 W.L.R. 937, Sachs L.J. doubted if there was a difference between the two tests but if there was would agree with *Lannon*, 941, Widgery L.J. applied a real likelihood test which he took to be the ratio of *Lannon*, 946, Cross L.J. thought there was no difference, 949; in *R. v. Altrincham JJ., ex p. Pennington* [1975] Q.B. 549 Lord Widgery C.J. felt that it was unclear from *Lannon which* test was to apply.

2. Bias for Whom?

From which or whose perspective is the court viewing the issue of bias? There are in logic four possibilities: the mind of the justice (or other challenged individual); the reasonable person; the individual affected; or *ex post facto* by the reviewing court. It is clear from the judgments in the *Camborne* and *Barnsley* cases that the disapproval of the reasonable suspicion test is because the court believes that it will have to view the answer from the perspective of the applicant himself or the public generally. Both Slade J. and Devlin J., respectively, felt that this would be setting the hurdle too low, and certainly Devlin J. in the *Barnsley* case wanted the court *ex post facto* to be the yardstick by which to determine whether bias was likely to arise.

In the *Lannon* case Lord Denning M.R. was clear that the bias issue was *not* to be considered from the perspective of the person impugned, who was unlikely to be biased. The criterion was our ever-present reasonable man. If a reasonable man would believe that there was a real likelihood of bias then the decision should be overturned; surmise or conjecture was insufficient.[32]

Thus far we have seen that the perspective from which Lord Denning chose to view bias was to be that of the reasonable man; it was not to be the individual affected himself (because the person may be perverse, over-sensitive, etc.), nor was it to be the *ex post facto* detachment of the reviewing court (which was the disagreement with the *Barnsley* formulation). The next issue concerns the degree of possibility of bias which must exist.

3. The Question of Degree

What must the reasonable man be perceiving? Is it sufficient that he perceives a suspicion of bias, or must he perceive the higher hurdle of likelihood? For Lord Denning M.R. in *Lannon* it is clearly the latter. Similarly in *Hannam,* although the court is unclear which of the tests is the "law", they actually apply the Denning version of the likelihood test: would a reasonable man say that a real danger of bias exists?[33] However, a number of cases have framed the test in terms of reasonable suspicion.[34]

---

[32] The root of the confusion for later cases is that Lord Denning M.R. begins by approving of the Lord Hewart C.J. test and ends by talking of real likelihood.

[33] [1970] 1 W.L.R. 937, 941, 945, *cf.* 949. And see R. v. *Colchester Stipendiary Magistrate, ex p. Beck* [1979] 2 W.L.R. 637.

[34] R. v. *Liverpool City Justices, ex p. Topping* [1983] 1 W.L.R. 119; R. v. *Crown Court at Bristol, ex p. Cooper* [1990] 2 All E.R. 193; R. v. *Governor of HM Prison Pentonville, ex p. Watkins* [1992] C.O.D. 329; R. v. *Romsey JJ., ex p. Gale* [1992] C.O.D. 322.

4. *The Law Clarified*

The law on this issue has now been clarified by the decision of the House of Lords in *R. v. Gough*.[35] In that case their Lordships reviewed the confused state of the existing case law and came to the following conclusion. The same test should be applied in all cases of apparent bias, whether concerned with justices, members of inferior tribunals, jurors or arbitrators.

In terms of the *degree of bias*, the test should be whether there was a real danger of bias on the part of the relevant member of the tribunal etc., in the sense that he might unfairly regard with favour, or disfavour, the case of a party to the issue under consideration by him; though in a case concerned with bias on the part of the justices' clerk, the court should go on to consider whether the clerk had been invited to give the justices advice, and if so whether it should infer that there was a real danger of the clerk's bias having infected the views of the justices adversely to the applicant. The phrase "real danger" as opposed to "real likelihood" was used to convey the idea that a possibility rather than a probability of bias would suffice.

In terms of the *perspective from which bias should be viewed*, it was not necessary, said Lord Goff, who gave the leading judgment, to formulate the test in terms of the reasonable man, both because the court personified the reasonable man; and because the court had to ascertain the relevant circumstances from the evidence which might not be available to an ordinary observer.

This clarification of the law is to be welcomed. What is still somewhat unclear is whether a different test should apply when bias is alleged against a body other than one in the above list. The authorities supporting the different formulation were not considered in *Gough*.[36] It has been suggested that administrative decisions should only be overturned if the higher hurdle of real likelihood of bias could be overcome.[37] Moreover, it has been held that the test should be further modified when the administrative body, such as a local authority, necessarily has an interest in the outcome of a decision. In such situations its decision should only be overturned for bias when it acted in such a way prior to its decision that it could not properly have exercised its discretion, taking due account of its interest in the proceedings.[38]

---

[35] [1993] 2 W.L.R. 883, 904, 905.

[36] *Loc. cit.*

[37] *Steeples* v. *Derbyshire County Council* [1985] 1 W.L.R. 256, 287-288. *cf. R.* v. *Liverpool City Justices, ex p. Topping* [1983] 1 W.L.R. 119.

[38] *R.* v. *St. Edmundsbury Borough Council, ex p. Investors in Industry Commercial Properties Ltd.* [1985] 1 W.L.R. 1157; *R.* v. *Sevenoaks District Council, ex p. Terry* [1985] 3 All E.R. 226; *Darker Enterprises Ltd.* v. *Dacorum Borough Council* [1992] C.O.D. 465; *R.* v. *Chesterfield Borough Council, ex p. Darker Enterprises* [1992] C.O.D. 466.

Section 4. Exceptions

1. Necessity

The normal rules against bias will be displaced in circumstances where the individual whose impartiality is called in question is the only person empowered to act. Thus in the *Dimes*[39] case it was held that the Lord Chancellor's signature on an enrolment order which was necessary in order for the case to proceed to the House of Lords, was unaffected by his shareholding in the company because no other person was given the power to so sign. Similarly, in *Phillips* v. *Eyre*[40] it was held that the Governor of a colony could validly assent to an Act of Indemnity which protected, *inter alia*, his own actions because the relevant Act had to receive this signature.

2. Statute

Parliament has at differing times made statutory exceptions to the rule against bias, allowing justices to sit who have some type of interest in the subject-matter of the action.[41] The courts have construed such statutory provisions strictly.[42] Thus in *R.* v. *Lee, ex p. Shaw*[43] section 258 of the Public Health Act 1872, which enabled a justice of the peace to sit even though a member of a local authority, was held not to protect him where he acted in a prosecutorial and adjudicatory capacity. In other areas statute may create an offence, for example, to take part in a decision on a matter in relation to which a person has a pecuniary interest, and yet it will allow acts thus made to remain valid.[44]

3. Waiver

It is permissible for an individual to waive the interests of an adjudicator,[45] and the courts were quick to infer such a waiver.[46] Later courts have been

---

[39] (1852) 3 H.L.C. 759,787.
[40] (1870) L.R. 6 Q.B. 1. See also *Re Manchester (Ringway Airport) Compulsory Purchase Order* (1935) 153 L.T. 219; *Jeffs* v. *New Zealand Dairy Production and Marketing Board* [1967] 1 A.C. 551; *cf. Wilkinson* v. *Barking Corporation* [1948] 1 K.B. 721.
[41] See, *e.g.* Justices Jurisdiction Act 1742.
[42] *Frome United Breweries Co. Ltd.* v. *Bath Justices* [1926] A.C. 586.
[43] (1882) 9 Q.B.D. 394; *cf. R.* v. *Pwllheli Justices, ex p. Soane* [1948] 2 All E.R. 815.
[44] Local Government Act 1972, ss.82, 94, 97. Similar provisions in licensing legislation have been strictly construed, *R.* v. *Barnsley Licensing Justices, ex p. Barnsley and District Licensed Victuallers' Association* [1960] 2 Q.B. 167. It is unclear whether actual bias would have to be shown in order to circumvent the statutory provisions, see Rawlings, above, n. 26, pp. 125-126.
[45] *R.* v. *Nailsworth Licensing Justices, ex p. Bird* [1953] 1 W.L.R. 1046.
[46] *R.* v. *Williams, ex p. Phillips* [1914] 1 K.B. 608.

more reluctant to so infer, particularly where the applicant did not know of the right to object at that stage.[47] This restriction on waiver is to be welcomed; such a surrender of rights should not be inferred lightly. It is in fact open to question whether it should be allowed at all, at least in certain types of cases. The premise behind the ability to waive is that it is only the individual who is concerned, and thus if that person "chooses" to ignore the fact that the adjudicator is an interested party then so much the worse for the applicant. However there may well be a wider interest at issue, in that it may be contrary to the public interest for decisions to be made where there may be a likelihood of favour to another influencing the determination.[48]

Section 5. Conclusion

The rules against bias work reasonably well apart from confusion over the test for establishing bias, and happily there are few reported cases upon the subject and most of these are not "heinous". The wider issue of the extent to which the judiciary may naturally favour certain types of values is outside the scope of this book.[49]

---

[47] R. v. *Essex Justices, ex p. Perkins* [1917] 2 K.B. 475.
[48] And see below, pp. 523-525, for a fuller discussion of the concept of waiver.
[49] See, *e.g.* Griffith, *Politics of the Judiciary* (3rd ed., 1985); Lord Devlin, "Judges, Government and Politics" (1978) 41 M.L.R. 501.

10. JURISDICTION

Section 1. Introduction

1. *Introduction*

The problem that concerns us now can be expressed as follows. A tribunal is given authority to decide upon a particular issue. If a furnished tenancy exists the tribunal may adjudicate on the rent. If a person is unfairly dismissed he or she may be awarded compensation. All such grants of authority may be expressed in the following manner: if X exists the tribunal may or shall do Y. X may consist of a number of different elements, factual, legal and discretionary. An individual wishes to complain of the tribunal's findings. In what circumstances should the court say that the tribunal has exceeded the power given to it?

It should be made clear that judicial review has traditionally dealt not with the correctness of the findings as such, but with their legality. For a full rehearing of the merits, appeal, a creature of statute, is required. The inherent power of the courts to review the findings of a tribunal has, by way of contrast, been concerned with ensuring that the decision-maker remains within the jurisdiction granted to him. Whether in fact the distinction between review and appeal is sustainable will be one of the issues to be discussed.

In resolving the question of what matters will be held to go to jurisdiction the following point should be borne in mind. If review is drawn too *narrowly* then the spectre is raised of the tribunal becoming a power unto itself, of it adjudicating upon matters widely different from those that the legislature intended, and yet being free from control. The Albert Hall is deemed to be a furnished tenancy and a rent set for it. However, if review is drawn too *broadly* it will approximate to appeal on the merits. Almost every finding made by the tribunal would be reassessed in the superior courts and be binding if right, but would not be binding if judged by the superior court to be wrong. The grant of jurisdiction to a tribunal or other decision-maker has, in the past, been thought to involve a power to come to a decision which in the opinion of a reviewing court may well be wrong. If the scope of review becomes too broad this is effectively destroyed. How far any such latitude still exists will be considered in due course.

The conceptual basis for judicial review over the conditions of jurisdiction has already been examined,[1] and reference should be made to

---

[1] See pp. 5-9.

335

that discussion when reading what follows. In essence the courts' control over the conditions of jurisdiction was premised upon the assumption that they were thereby effectuating the will of Parliament; they were ensuring that the tribunal or authority remained within the boundaries of what Parliament intended it to examine by ensuring that those conditions were present. However, while this may have provided the conceptual basis for judicial intervention, it is beset by two problems.

First, it furnished little in the way of guidance as to the *extent* of control over the conditions of jurisdiction. The dilemma is evident from the example given in the preceding paragraph. On the one hand, in a certain sense, all the elements which comprise X condition the tribunal's power to decide upon Y. The statute says, explicitly or implicitly, if X you may or shall do Y. On the other hand, to accept that the reviewing courts should be the ultimate arbiters of the meaning of all the elements comprising the X factor would cause review to become very like appeal. Such an approach is, moreover, open to a more potent objection. It presumes that the meaning to be ascribed to any of the elements which comprise the X factor is to be that determined by the reviewing court in preference to that decided on by the tribunal. As we shall see there are objections to accepting that this should always be so.

The second problem with the traditional conceptual basis of review is, as we shall see, that it is no longer self-evident that the courts are basing themselves upon it when exercising their powers within this area. Error of law is the organising principle which is evident in the more recent case law.

2. *Structure of the Chapter*

First, the theories which have purported to provide an answer to the question of which issues go to jurisdiction will be examined. It will become clear from the subsequent analysis that the more recent decisions of the courts have, to some extent, eradicated the divide between jurisdictional and non-jurisdictional issues. This more modern approach is itself premised upon certain theoretical assumptions, and these are often unstated and hence untested. It is only by bringing them into the light of day that we can assess their cogency.

Moreover, an analysis of theories which *have* rested more heavily upon the jurisdictional/non-jurisdictional distinction is of importance, since it is impossible to understand the current law without some understanding of the case law which preceded it, and of the theories upon which that case law was based.

It should be made clear that this analysis is not predicated upon the assumption that the courts which *did* employ the jurisdictional/non-jurisdictional distinction always used it in a purely logical manner. It is readily apparent that some courts, and some judges, have used the very ambiguity inherent in that dichotomy in an instrumental fashion; the decision whether to label a part of the X factor as jurisdictional or non-jurisdictional was influenced by a judicial desire to intervene or not as the case may be. Examination of the theories which purported to provide an answer to this question is nonetheless important. It would be wrong to assume that all or even most judges viewed the distinction in a purely instrumental fashion. It is manifestly clear from a reading of the case law that many believed that a real division could be drawn in analytical terms.

Secondly, after a consideration of the theories, the case law from both the nineteenth and twentieth centuries will be examined.

The final part of the chapter will consider some of the broader policy arguments concerning the scope of review.

Section 2. Theories of Jurisdiction

A number of theories of jurisdiction will be analysed which adopt differing views as to which matters should be held to go to jurisdiction. A general word concerning these theories will be helpful in understanding what follows.

The first two theories attempt to draw the following distinction. Errors which relate to the type or kind or scope of case into which a tribunal can inquire are regarded as jurisdictional; errors which relate to the truth or detail of the findings that it makes are categorised as non-jurisdictional. The line between the two is said to provide the justification for judicial review. The court only intervenes when the tribunal is outside the "scope" which has been assigned to it by the legislature; the judiciary will not intervene if the tribunal has simply made an error within its assigned area since this would eradicate the distinction between review of legality and appeal. The first two theories draw this distinction in different ways, and, as we shall see, the dichotomy may not be capable of being drawn satisfactorily at all.

The more recent approaches, by way of contrast, largely ignore any distinction between scope and truth or detail. Judicial intervention is based on error of law as the organising principle. While this approach, by rejecting any distinction between jurisdictional and non-jurisdictional errors of law, avoids the difficulties created by the earlier theories it is not unproblematic. Thus, as we shall see, there are crucial issues of classification to be resolved, such as the division between law and fact. There are also important policy issues which require discussion, such as whether the courts are always better suited to resolve issues of law than are the tribunals which they are reviewing.

1. *Collateral Fact Doctrine*

Until relatively recently the most widely accepted theoretical explanation of which issues should be held to go to jurisdiction was the collateral or preliminary or jurisdictional fact doctrine. It has a long historical lineage, but the most sophisticated explanation was that given by Diplock L.J.,[2] as

---

[2] *Anisminic Ltd.* v. *Foreign Compensation Commission* [1968] 2 Q.B. 862, 887-905. *cf.* Lord Diplock's view in *Re Racal Communications Ltd.* [1981] A.C. 374.

he then was. The exposition is more easily understood if broken down into a number of stages.

(1) PRELIMINARY QUESTIONS AND MERITS

A decision is "correct" if it is made by that person within the legal system to whose opinion on the existence of fact or law effect will be given by the executive. A tribunal is given power on the existence of certain conditions; there are certain preliminary questions that it must decide before it can proceed to the merits. These include matters such as whether the tribunal was properly constituted and whether the case was of a kind referred to in the statute. The tribunal must make an initial determination on such matters, but its decision is not conclusive. If the court on review believes that the requisite situation spoken of in the statute did not exist then the conclusion reached by the tribunal will be a nullity. Such preliminary questions can involve *fact, law or discretion.*

(2) THE AMBIT OF THE PRELIMINARY QUESTION

The crucial point is therefore the ambit of the preliminary or collateral question. The nature of this dilemma can best be described as follows. Let us revert to the example used before of a tribunal having power to decide whether a furnished tenancy exists. The existence of a furnished tenancy may be expressed as follows.

$$f\ (a,\ b,\ c,\ d\ \ldots\ n) = \text{furnished tenancy.}$$

Do not be alarmed by the equation. Its form is merely a useful shorthand. The elements within the bracket constitute the furnished tenancy; or, conversely, the term furnished tenancy is a shorthand description of the presence of those elements. Thus, here a would represent the need for time certain in a lease, b the intent of the parties, c the fixtures and fittings required to render the tenancy furnished. These factors can be law, fact, mixed fact and law or discretion. The letter f is simply a shorthand for indicating that a furnished tenancy will be determined by the elements within the bracket. Moreover, the above picture is a simplified one. The position will often be more complex. It is very common for a statute to say if X1, X2, X3 exist the tribunal may or shall do Y. X2 and X3 would, like X1, be shorthand descriptions presuming the existence of elements within the bracket.

What the preliminary or collateral fact doctrine seeks to do is to distinguish those elements within the bracket which can be regarded as conditioning the power of the tribunal to go on and consider the merits from the merits themselves. The word merits requires further explanation. As used within the collateral fact doctrine this does not and never has meant only what I have termed the Y question, the question of what is, in fact, a fair rent given the existence of a furnished tenancy. Courts which have employed the doctrine have accepted that there can be matters on the X level which are not jurisdictional and the term merits includes these items. The fundamental problem faced by the preliminary fact doctrine is that in an everyday sense all the elements relating to X, or, to X1, X2, X3, could be said to condition jurisdiction. The enabling statute always, explicitly or implicitly, states, if X1, X2, X3 exist you may or shall do Y. Yet, if X1, X2, and X3, and all the elements constituting them, were always held to be jurisdictional in a legal sense, the dividing line between review and appeal would be emasculated: the tribunal would have power to give only the right answer, this meaning the answer which accords with the view of the reviewing court.

Diplock L.J. attempts to solve this conundrum by drawing the following distinction: a misconstruction of the enabling statute describing the *kind* of case into which the tribunal is meant to inquire will go to jurisdiction, but misconstruing a statutory description of the *situation* that the tribunal has to determine will, at most, be an error within jurisdiction.

The problem is that this line is impossible to draw with any certainty or accuracy, because the definition of kind or type is *inevitably* comprised of descriptions within the statute of the situation which the tribunal has to determine. The former represents the sum, the latter the parts. This is simply demonstrated. If one was asked to produce a summary of the *kind* of case into which the tribunal was intended to inquire one would do so by looking at the *situations* which the tribunal has to determine which are mentioned in the statute. These situations are composed of the statutory terms in the enabling legislation. Thus, in a case such as *Anisminic* one would say, *inter alia*, that if there is property in Egypt, which belongs to a British national or successor in title at the relevant dates, which has been seized, the FCC shall award compensation. The kind of case is comprised of the situations described in the statute which the tribunal has to determine.[3]

One can make the distinction between *kind* or *type* on the one hand, and *truth* or *detail* or *situation* on the other, and one can apportion cases to one category or another. However, not only is there no predictability as to how a case will be categorised, there is also no *ex post facto* rationality that can be achieved by juxtaposing a series of cases and asking why one case went one way and another was decided differently.[4]

---

[3] The distinction may be capable of being drawn at a more philosophical, abstract level, but it does not provide any workable criterion for judicial intervention. See further, *Blanchard* v. *Control Data Canada Ltée* [1984] 2 S.C.R. 476, 14 D.L.R. (4th) 289, 300.

[4] In *Anisminic* [1968] 2 Q.B. 862, 904-905, Diplock L.J. found that the error was, at most, one within jurisdiction. It did not relate to the "kind" of case into which the FCC could inquire. No real indication is given as to why the error was categorised in this way. See, further, the examples given in Gordon, "The Relation of Facts to Jurisdiction" (1929) 45 L.Q.R. 458.

2. *Limited Review*

With these difficulties in mind let us approach a second theory of review put forward by Gordon.[5] Again, for didactic ease, the argument is best broken down into its component parts.

(1) RELATIVE RATHER THAN ABSOLUTE FACTS

If a tribunal is given jurisdiction over a certain topic the question is whether the facts relating to that topic exist in the opinion of the tribunal. Thus, if a tribunal is given jurisdiction over assault the question is whether an assault exists in the opinion of that tribunal.

Any tribunal might err in a finding that it makes: no tribunal is infallible. But so long as the tribunal decides the question assigned to it by the law, its relative opinion will bind, subject to appeal. Jurisdiction must involve the power to make a wrong as well as a correct decision.

(2) THE LIMITS

There must be a limit to a tribunal's jurisdiction, but that limit is determined *not* by the truth or falsehood of its findings, but by their scope or nature. Provided that the charge is laid in the correct form, that is sufficient. Thus, jurisdiction is determined at the commencement, not at the conclusion of the inquiry.

Gordon is scathing of the collateral fact doctrine for three reasons. First, every Act of Parliament, in effect, says that if a certain state of facts exists the tribunal may do a certain thing; those facts are always for the relative decision of the tribunal.[6] Secondly, it is unrealistic to divide the matters which a tribunal has to decide into preliminary and essential: all elements within the statement, "if X", in some way condition the jurisdiction to proceed to do Y. Thirdly, it is impossible to reconcile the cases which have used the collateral fact doctrine. No rhyme or reason can be found as to why the courts have called a fact preliminary in one case but not in another.

(3) CRITICISM OF THE GORDON THEORY

There are a number of difficulties with the Gordon theory. It may, for example, be hard to decide when an inquiry commences, particularly when it is the less formal variety of administrative action which is in question. It may also be that the limited review which the theory allows is unacceptable on policy grounds. The policy issues will be discussed in detail later. For the

---

[5] "The Relation of Facts to Jurisdiction" (1929) 45 L.Q.R. 458; "Observance of Law as a Condition of Jurisdiction" (1931) 47 L.Q.R. 386, 557; Conditional or Contingent Jurisdiction of Tribunals" (1959-1963) 1 U.B.C.L.R. 185; "Jurisdictional Fact: An Answer" (1966) 82 L.Q.R. 515; "What did the Anisminic case decide?" (1971) 34 M.L.R. 1. See also Hogg, "The Jurisdictional Fact Doctrine in the Supreme Court of Canada; *Bell* v. *Ontario Human Rights Commission*" (1971) 9 Osgoode Hall L.J. 203.

[6] This was made in response to the statement by Farwell L.J. in *R.* v. *Shoreditch Assessment Committee, ex p. Morgan* [1910] 2 K.B. 859, 880 that no tribunal of limited jurisdiction can have unlimited power to determine the extent of those limits.

present, attention will be focused on the most crucial part of the theory, the distinction between scope and truth.

For Gordon it is fallacious to say that if a tribunal blunders in its estimation of the factors involved in a subject-matter properly before it, and thereby misconceives the questions that it should consider, that it thereby exceeds its jurisdiction. The subject-matter of the tribunal's inquiry may involve decisions on a number of issues, but each of these is not a subject-matter by itself. Any error is only an error within jurisdiction.

This can best be understood by reverting to our previous example concerning a furnished tenancy. It was argued then that the term furnished tenancy could be expressed as:

$$f (a, b, c, d \ldots n) = \text{furnished tenancy.}$$

The elements in the bracket represent the need for time certain, intent of the parties, amount of fixture and fittings, etc. The premise underlying Gordon's argument is that scope or subject-matter means simply the assertion of the existence of a furnished tenancy by the tribunal. Any blunder concerning a, b, c, etc., would, at most, be an error within jurisdiction. What Gordon seeks to do, therefore, is to avoid the pitfalls of the collateral fact doctrine by, in effect, erecting a brick wall between the words furnished tenancy and the bracket. The court is not allowed to peer inside at the meanings assigned to those elements, except to find a non-jurisdictional error. Does this work?

There is clearly an element of circularity in the argument in that it presumes that the subject-matter is properly before the tribunal, a presumption which can only be made if subject-matter is defined purely in terms of furnished tenancy itself. Whether this assumption is properly made depends ultimately upon one's conception of meaning and on questionable premises concerning legislative intent.

The conception of meaning is raised in that the Gordon argument envisages a formal separation between the term furnished tenancy, which goes to scope, and the elements within the bracket which constitute it. An error relating to scope will be jurisdictional and thus, if the wrong term is used instead of furnished tenancy, a court should intervene. Mistakes concerning elements within the bracket are however regarded differently, being non-jurisdictional at most. Since however the words furnished tenancy are only a shorthand description of the presence of the elements, factual and legal, within the bracket, to regard an error relating to these words as jurisdictional, but mistakes concerning a, b, c or d as not, appears devoid of sense.

Gordon might well reply in two different ways. First, he could argue that because opinions are relative not absolute, therefore the equation drawn between the term furnished tenancy and the elements within the bracket is flawed. This proves too much. People may well disagree as to whether, for example, an assault has in fact occurred. But to argue from this that we can divorce the term furnished tenancy or assault[7] from the elements within the bracket is a *non sequitur*. It would mean accepting that an assault could

---

[7] The point being made could apply to any term.

exist without any of the elements which comprise that term; no one would, for example, have to be placed in fear for their bodily safety. One cannot, in other words, argue from the premise that people may disagree as to whether a person was in fact placed in fear for their bodily safety, to the conclusion that a decision-maker can have untrammelled power to decide whether such an apprehension is indeed a constituent part of the offence at all. To do so would have quite fundamental consequences for the way in which we use language. The words furnished tenancy would be empty vessels into which anything could be poured. The formal incantation of such words would suffice for the tribunal to remain within the scope of its authority. They could be applied to anything regardless of whether it was an Oxford College, or for that matter an oak tree or my dog.

A second argument which Gordon might use would be to say that the content of the bracket constituting the term furnished tenancy or employee or assault should, itself, be for the relative opinion of the tribunal. This goes one stage further than the contention considered above.[8] The argument is flawed in two respects. One is that it is doubtful in the extreme whether one can assume that the legislature *always* intended the tribunal to be the arbiter as to what the contents of the bracket ought to be. This, of course, could happen in a particular area. There is nothing to prevent the legislature preferring a tribunal's interpretation of the term, for example, employee, to that of the reviewing court. Greater recognition of this would be valuable.[9] The argument postulated above is, however, dependent upon showing not just that this may happen, but that it *must* happen. There is no reason why this should be so. The other problem with this second argument is that even if the tribunal's view of the meaning of a particular term were to be preferred, the formal separation of the term furnished tenancy from the contents of the bracket would still be unwarranted.[10]

3. *Extensive Review: The Academic Argument*

A theory of more extensive review has been advanced by Gould.[11] A similar approach is evident in some of the courts' more recent jurisprudence, and appears to represent the current tendency of the case law. The argument of Gould will be considered within this section, while the related ideas which are present in the courts' more recent case law will be analysed in the section which follows.

---

[8] It is in fact unclear whether Gordon would put this type of argument.

[9] See below, pp. 375-383, for consideration of this theme.

[10] Imagine that the content of such a term is assigned to the tribunal. Once the tribunal has decided that the bracket should contain certain elements, then everything said earlier would still apply. The only way out of this conundrum would be to argue, not only that the contents of the bracket are for the tribunal, but that it can alter these at will, and put any other contents in their place at any time. We are however in danger of losing all touch with reality by postulating such a scenario.

[11] Gould, "Anisminic and Jurisdictional Review" [1970] P.L. 358. See also, Rawlings, "Jurisdictional Review after Pearlman" [1979] P.L. 404.

(1) PRELIMINARY QUESTIONS AND SUBSTANCE

Gould's argument is as follows. Any tribunal will have two questions which it has to answer. First, it will have a preliminary question to decide, which is whether the question it is asked to answer is a question it is empowered to answer. This cannot be decided finally by the tribunal itself. A decision that jurisdiction exists is always a logically necessary precondition to the exercise of jurisdiction: because it is logically prior to the exercise of jurisdiction, it cannot in itself be part of the exercise of jurisdiction. It is not therefore a question on which the tribunal may go right or wrong. Secondly, the substance of the matter or the merits will be for the tribunal itself. Using our terminology, that would mean the remainder of the "if X" section as well as the consideration of the Y question.

Thus far, Gould has provided a restatement of the collateral or preliminary fact doctrine. The contribution made by his analysis is that he seeks to provide a logical answer to the question which had previously been unsolved: which matters *are* collateral or preliminary?

(2) THE CONTENT OF THE PRELIMINARY QUESTION

The factors which come within the first category are those which must exist independently of the substance to be decided. These factors are given: their meaning cannot be altered by the tribunal itself. It is not that they are facts in the absolute. Gould, like Gordon, agrees that they are relative. However, they are for the relative opinion of the reviewing courts, *not* the tribunal. But what are these factors? They are all legal rules and concepts because such rules must have a given meaning which is established by the courts. A coherent theory of jurisdiction is produced. The basis for judicial intervention becomes clear and worrisome problems of jurisdictional versus non-jurisdictional errors of law are left behind. All legal terms within our bracket would go to jurisdiction.

(3) CRITICISMS OF THE GOULD THEORY

The key to the theory is obviously the cogency of the argument that all issues of law are "given", to be determined by the courts. Why is this so? Three reasons can be extracted.

(a) Parliamentary intent

Legal issues are "given", Gould argues, because Parliament intends them to be decided by the ordinary courts. This argument could be regarded as a *rebuttable* presumption, but then the inexorable logic of the theory breaks down; it could not be said that legal rules were always to be determined by the ordinary courts. The argument must therefore be based upon an *irrebuttable* presumption as to parliamentary intent. Is there warrant for this in constitutional theory or judicial practice?

Constitutional theory would indicate the opposite conclusion. Parliament is sovereign and in theory it can give the task of determining the legal meaning of whatsoever it chooses to whomsoever it likes. It manifests an explicit intent to do so when it places a privative clause in a statute empowering a tribunal. The courts, it is true, will interpret these clauses and have construed them to mean that jurisdictional errors are not protected.[12] It is equally true that Lord Diplock has stated[13] that the normal presumption is that Parliament intends questions of law to be decided by the courts, but his Lordship did not state that this was an irrebuttable presumption. This presumption has been repeated by the House of Lords in the *Page* case, but their Lordships were equally clear that this was not, in all cases, to be viewed as an irrebuttable presumption.[14]

If constitutional theory does not provide positive support for the Gould thesis, what of judicial practice? It could be argued that Gould's irrebuttable presumption finds its support in the fact that the judiciary has arrogated to itself the ultimate decision on all questions of law. However the facts are that the courts have not for the last 300 years recognised, nor have they acted upon, a logic which renders all questions of law jurisdictional. Quite the contrary,[15] degrees of review may have differed over time, but it is indisputable that the judiciary accepted that non-jurisdictional errors of law could exist. A number of courts gave substantial latitude to the decision-maker. The attitude of the courts has altered, becoming more activist in recent years thereby demonstrating an increased desire to be the determinants of legal questions; but to build an *irrebuttable* presumption upon less than 25 years equivocal judicial practice is not meaningful.[16]

As noted above, there is some indication of the development of a rebuttable presumption that all questions of law should be for the ordinary courts. The authority supporting this view will be examined below. Whether that view should be sustained will, however, be dependent upon a value judgment as to whose opinion on the meaning of a term should be preferred. It is not to be derived from an allegedly logical *a priori* argument that all legal questions are "given".

(b) The impossibility argument

It would not be possible to talk of error of law at all unless such elements did have a "given" meaning because, says Gould, such language implies a departure from a criterion laid down by the courts. This is to confuse cause and effect. When the legal meaning of a term is given to, or arrogated by, the courts, then of course the phrase error of law implies a deviation from that standard. It cannot provide the *reason why* all matters of law should have an interpretation provided by the ordinary courts. If the interpretation of the point is not given to the ordinary courts then the error will not be an

---

[12] See generally, Chap. 16.
[13] *Re Racal Communications Ltd.* [1981] A.C. 374; *O'Reilly* v. *Mackman* [1983] 2 A.C. 237.
[14] For a discussion of this case see below, pp. 360-361.
[15] See below, pp. 350-362.
[16] The argument presented within this section assumes a variety of guises. It should not, however, be confused with the principle that the courts always have jurisdiction to declare the law unless that jurisdiction is specifically excluded by Parliament. This principle finds its application in the construction of privative clauses and alternative remedies, and is designed to preserve the *possibility* of judicial review. It says nothing as to the *scope* of review.

error of law at all; the criterion laid down by the tribunal will be the accepted standard.

The possibility of the latter occurring is neither absurd nor contrary to the rule of law. Many legal terms could have one of a number of possible meanings, each of which is reasonable. Words or phrases such as "furnished tenancy", "successor in title", "course of employment", "trade dispute", "boat" and "resources", all words appearing in various statutes, are open to a spectrum of possible meanings, a number of which may be reasonable. The statement that the tribunal has made an "error of law" means that the construction placed upon the term by the court is preferred to that of the tribunal. It would not be absurd, nor contrary to the rule of law, for Parliament to prefer the precise construction adopted by the tribunal to that given by the courts. Furthermore, it is quite possible to maintain control in such situations without the judiciary substituting their view for that of the tribunal. This point will be returned to.

(c) The uniformity argument

A third argument which has been put is as follows. It is only by giving the legal meaning of a term to the courts that uniformity can be achieved, as opposed to a number of inferior bodies giving diverse interpretations to the same term.

The limits of this argument should be noted. It will not apply to tribunals which have an internal hierarchy, the top of which can impose a uniform meaning, nor will it necessarily apply where there is only one tribunal in an area. The need for uniformity is greatest where there are a number of parallel tribunals deciding the same point. Uniformity should be achieved by providing an appeal rather than by distorting review to become appeal, or by insisting that the particular meaning adopted by one of the set of tribunals should be applied consistently by those in a similar position.

4. Extensive Review: The Judicial Argument

As indicated above, arguments for more extensive review have recently been forthcoming from the courts themselves. The detail of this case law will be examined below, but it is important to assess the arguments underlying the courts' jurisprudence at this juncture.

(1) REVIEW FOR ERROR OF LAW

Judicial indications that the courts would no longer follow the collateral fact doctrine have been apparent for some time.[17] These indications have been confirmed by the House of Lords in the Page case.[18] A detailed

---

[17] Indications of this kind are apparent in Anisminic [1969] 2 A.C. 147, Re Racal Communications Ltd. [1981] A.C. 374, and O'Reilly v. Mackman [1983] 2 A.C. 237. The cases are discussed below, pp. 353-362.

[18] [1993] 1 All E.R. 97.

analysis of the case will be provided below.[19] The present discussion will be confined to the more general assumptions which underlie the decision.

Lord Browne-Wilkinson gave the leading judgment, and reasoned as follows.[20] He held that the effect of the *Anisminic* case was to render obsolete the distinction between errors of law on the face of the record, and other errors of law, by extending the doctrine of *ultra vires*. Thenceforward it was to be taken that Parliament had only conferred a decision-making power on the basis that it was to be exercised on the correct legal basis: a misdirection in law when making the decision rendered it *ultra vires*. The general rule was that any (relevant) error of law could be quashed. The constitutional basis of the court's power was that the unlawful decision of the tribunal was *ultra vires*. In general, the law applicable to an administrative institution was the ordinary law of the land. Therefore, "a tribunal or inferior court acts *ultra vires* if it reaches its conclusion on a basis erroneous under the general law".[21] It is clear from the judgment that the presumption (that any error of law is open to review) is rebuttable, and it also appears to be the case that the strength of this presumption might vary depending upon the nature of the institution being reviewed.[22]

(2) AN ASSESSMENT

Any assessment of the *Page* case must distinguish between three different aspects of the reasoning used therein.

First, there is the disapproval cast upon the approach of the collateral fact doctrine. This is to be welcomed. The difficulties with that doctrine have already been discussed, and it is high time that it was discarded.

Secondly, there is the replacement of that doctrine with the idea that all errors of law are open to scrutiny. The similarities between this approach and that advanced by Gould are readily apparent. It is not surprising, therefore, that some of the concerns expressed in the context of the Gould theory should be equally relevant here. If the reasoning in *Page* is to be taken to mean that *any* of the X factors which involves *any* element of law will lead to the court substituting its view for that of the tribunal on that issue, then this is open to two objections. *One* is that it will embroil the courts in the minutiae of disputed interpretations as to what many, or all, of the X conditions mean in any particular context. The *other* is that such an approach is based upon the presumption that the courts' particular interpretation of phrases such as "employee", "course of employment", "boat" or "resources" is necessarily to be preferred to that of the agency; *and* that such substitution of judgment is the only way to exercise control over such agency interpretations. Neither of these assumptions is well founded. The courts' particular interpretation of such terms may not

---

[19] See, pp. 360-362.
[20] Lord Slynn and Lord Mustill dissented on other grounds, but agreed with the majority on this general issue, *ibid.* p. 111.
[21] *Ibid.* p. 108.
[22] *Ibid.* pp. 108-109. And see the discussion, below, pp. 360-361.

necessarily be better than that of the agency, *and* adequate control may be maintained through a different standard of review.[23]

Thirdly, although Lord Browne-Wilkinson bases judicial intervention upon the *ultra vires* principle, this should not serve to conceal the fact that the principle has now acquired a different meaning than previously. When that principle was invoked as the basis for intervention, for example under the collateral fact doctrine, the assumption was that there was a distinction to be drawn between jurisdictional and non-jurisdictional errors. Only the former would result in the decision being regarded as *ultra vires* and void, because the tribunal had acted *outside* its jurisdiction. The latter were errors *within* jurisdiction and would only be open to attack if the error was one of law on the face of the record, and then the decision would only be regarded as voidable. However, the *ultra vires* principle as used in *Page* bears a different meaning. Any error of law may lead to the decision being regarded as *ultra vires*, because the tribunal has reached its conclusion on a basis which is erroneous under the general law.

It has been argued by Sir John Laws that once the distinction between jurisdictional and non-jurisdictional errors is discarded, as it has now been, there is no longer any need or purpose for the *ultra vires* principle as such, since the courts are in reality simply intervening to correct errors of law.[24] So why do the courts persist, as in *Page*, in employing the principle? On one view it provides a legitimating device for the exercise of the courts' power. Rather intervene by saying that the tribunal has acted *ultra vires*, than on the simple ground of error of law *per se*. Sir John Laws captures this idea.[25]

> "'Ultra vires' is, in truth, a fig-leaf; it has enabled the courts to inter-
> vene in decisions without an assertion of judicial power which too
> nakedly confronts the established authority of the Executive or other
> public bodies...The fig-leaf was very important in *Anisminic*; but fig-
> leaf it was. And it has produced the historical irony that *Anisminic*,
> with all its emphasis on nullity, nevertheless erected the legal milestone
> which pointed towards a public law jurisprudence in which the concept
> of voidness and the ultra vires doctrine have become redundant."[26]

Precisely *how* extensive the *Page* test of review proves to be will depend upon the meaning accorded to the phrase "error of law", and it is to this that we should now turn.

(3) THE DISTINCTION BETWEEN LAW AND FACT

The case law on judicial review provides little in the way of guidance on the question of whether a certain issue is one of law or fact. The reasons for this are not hard to find. First, as we shall see, the judicial attitude towards the scope of review was, until recently, premised upon either the collateral fact

---

[23] Fuller discussion of this issue can be found below, pp. 375-383.

[24] "Illegality: The Problem of Jurisdiction", in *Judicial Review* (Supperstone and Goudie eds., 1992), Chap. 4.

[25] *Ibid.* p. 67.

[26] By laying the foundation for the idea that all errors of law can be reviewed.

doctrine or the theory of limited review. Neither of these approaches necessitated the drawing of precise lines between legal and factual questions. Both theories applied equally to issues of law and fact. Thus, provided that the court categorised the issue as a collateral question it would substitute judgment on the point, whether that was one of fact or law.[27] Provided that the court felt that the issue was collateral, then intervention was justified.[28]

A second and related reason why there is little discussion of the law/fact distinction is because the characteristic type of question which is the subject-matter of jurisdictional disputes is the construction or interpretation of one of the constituent elements of the "if X" question. The cases are commonly concerned with the interpretation and application of terms such as boat, resources, employee, successor in title, furnished tenancy, structural alteration, and the like. As we shall see, the decision whether to categorise such questions as ones of law or fact is a matter on which opinion, both judicial and academic, differs.

More recent developments do, however, render it necessary to consider the law/fact dichotomy. The case law which states that all errors of law are jurisdictional means that the distinction between law and fact will be vital. How is the line between law and fact to be drawn for these purposes? Much of the literature on this topic has been generated by cases concerned with appeal and not review. Appeal will often only be allowed on questions of law, and not on questions of fact. The case law upon this point has already been examined and should be referred to for the purposes of the discussion which follows.[29] A useful starting point is to realise that there are three themes which run through the literature upon the law/fact distinction, which are often not distinguished.

The first is that there may well be disagreement as to whether, on analytical grounds, a question should be deemed to be one of law or fact. Thus both the case law and the academic commentary display considerable diversity of opinion as to whether, for example, the application of statutory terms to facts always involves a question of law or not. Should the meaning to be ascribed to a statutory term such as employee, trade, boat or successor in title always be regarded, in analytical terms, as a question of law? On *analytical* grounds the answer is probably in the affirmative.[30]

---

[27] It may well be the case that the courts felt less inclined to intervene in relation to matters which were purely factual, but the juridical basis of intervention was never premised upon the need to distinguish between law and fact.

[28] The only real occasion for distinguishing between law and fact was when the court intervened to quash an error of law on the face of the record.

[29] See pp. 157-160. For detailed discussion see, Wilson, "A Note on Fact and Law" (1963) 26 M.L.R. 609; "Questions of Degree" (1969) 32 M.L.R. 361; Mureinik, "The Application of Rules; Law or Fact?" (1982) 98 L.Q.R. 587; Beatson, "The Scope of Judicial Review for Error of Law" (1984) 4 O.J.L.S. 22. For discussion in the US context, see Jaffe, "Judicial Review: Question of Law" 69 Harv.L.Rev. 239 (1955); "Judicial Review: Question of Fact" 69 Harv.L.Rev. 1020 (1955).

[30] See the articles by Wilson and Mureinik, above n. 29; *R. v. Barnet London Borough Council, ex p. Nilish Shah* [1983] 2 A.C. 309; *A.C.T. Construction Ltd v. Customs and Excise Commissioners* [1981] 1 W.L.R. 49, aff'd [1981] 1 W.L.R. 1542.

Secondly, it is, however, quite clear that the courts have not always adopted this approach. The labels law and fact have been attached depending upon whether the courts wish to intervene or not. They have not, therefore, always reached their conclusion on analytical grounds; often these conclusions are expressive of a pragmatic desire not to intervene in a particular case.

Thirdly, in deciding which label to attach the courts have often been acting upon questionable assumptions as to the conclusions which follow from the attachment of one label or the other. Thus some courts have reasoned on the hypothesis that if an issue is deemed to be one of law then this must *inevitably* involve substitution of judgment on their part. Conversely where a statutory term is open to a spectrum of reasonable interpretations then it must be a question of fact.[31] This conclusion is controversial; a legal issue does not cease to be such simply because the term in question is open to a range of possible meanings.

The effect of the general adoption of the thesis that all errors of law are jurisdictional will, therefore, be crucially dependent upon which approach the courts adopt. If they pursue a rigid *analytical* approach then it is likely to result in many, if not all, of the constituent elements which comprise the "if X" question being labelled as questions of law. It may lead to the situation in which all inferences drawn from certain *primary facts*, whether something existed, was present etc., will be deemed to be questions of law. This would mean that the construction of most statutory terms would be characterised as a question of law. If, in addition, the judiciary then substitute their opinion as to the precise meaning that each of these terms should bear for that of the initial decision-maker, the result will be an extensive form of review.

This is not the only possible approach for the courts to adopt. They could interpret the word law in a more *pragmatic* or *policy oriented* sense. This could manifest itself in two ways. The application of certain statutory terms might be deemed questions of fact. Or the courts could call the application of a statutory term a question of law, but accept that it does not have to have only the one meaning which the court itself would accord to it. Provided that the authority adopts a meaning which is reasonable or has a rational basis the courts could accept that interpretation, even if it did not accord with the precise meaning which they would have ascribed. We will return to this matter after considering the case law on the scope of review.[32]

5. *Conclusion*

What conclusions can be drawn from all this, apart from the obvious one that simple questions do not always have straightforward answers? Two points should be emphasised. The first is that the line between scope and truth or detail is not capable of furnishing a satisfactory guide as to what

---

[31] See *Edwards* v. *Bairstow* [1956] A.C. 14, 33-36.
[32] See below, pp. 372-383.

should, and what should not, be regarded as jurisdictional. The second point is equally important. The scope of jurisdictional review is not self-defining. It is not capable of being answered by linguistic or textual analysis of the statute alone, however assiduously that is performed. The critical question, the answer to which underlies any statement concerning jurisdictional limits, is whose relative opinion on which matters should be held to be authoritative? All of the theories have a view upon this, although it is often not openly expressed. The answer to this decisive question resides not in a logic which compels, for example, all questions of law always to be for the courts or the tribunal. Such logic is flawed. A response must ultimately be based upon a value judgment, the precise content of which will not necessarily always be the same. My own views as to the proper limits of jurisdictional control will be spelt out after a consideration of the case law.

Section 3. Case Law History

The present attitude of the courts towards judicial review cannot be adequately understood unless some idea is conveyed of eighteenth- and nineteenth-century case law. There are two reasons for this. First, it demonstrates the continuity of approach in terms of the concepts being used: much of the language and many of the ideas utilised in modern cases stem directly from such nineteenth-century antecedents. Secondly, it shows the diversity of approach taken by the courts. While, as stated, some of the concepts used now have their origins in the nineteenth century and earlier, there were nevertheless different views taken of how far the courts ought to be reviewing tribunals and other inferior bodies. This debate conducted in the case law is instructive when viewing the present position of the courts. A division will be made between those authorities advocating limited and those advocating more extensive review. What follows does not pretend to be an exhaustive summary. The myriad of case law precludes this. It is intended to convey an impression of the main themes at work.

1. *Limited Intervention*

A number of leading authorities supported only limited review. To revert to our example of the equation, they were saying that if the subject-matter lies within the tribunal's jurisdiction, the factors within the bracket constituting that subject-matter will not be reassessed. In *R. v. Bolton*[33] magistrates having found that the plaintiff had occupied a parish house as a pauper and that a formal notice to quit had been served on him, directed constables to

---

[33] (1841) 1 Q.B. 66, 72-74. See also, *Brittain* v. *Kinnaird* (1819) 1 B. & B. 432, 442; *Ackerley* v. *Parkinson* (1815) 3 M. & S. 411; *Wilson* v. *Weller* (1819) 1 B. & B. 57; *Fawcett* v. *Fowlis* (1827) 7 B. & C. 396; *R.* v. *Justices of Cheshire* (1838) 8 Ad. & E. 398; *Re Baines* (1840) Cr. & Ph. 31; *Cave* v. *Mountain* (1840) 1 M. & G. 257.

enforce the notice. The applicant sought certiorari. He wished to be able to show by affidavit evidence that he had not occupied the house *qua* pauper but had paid rates and carried out repairs, and that he had not therefore been chargeable on the parish during the period of his occupation; the magistrate could not give himself jurisdiction by his own affirmation of it.

Lord Denman C.J. made the following distinction. Where the charge laid before the magistrate did not constitute the offence over which the statute gave him jurisdiction, affidavit evidence could be introduced. So too could it where the charge was insufficient, but had been mis-stated. In both cases, extrinsic evidence could be introduced to show a want of jurisdiction. However, where the charge had been well laid before the magistrate, on its face bringing itself within his jurisdiction, any error would be only an error within jurisdiction. The question of jurisdiction depended not on the truth or falsehood of the charge, but upon its nature and was determinable at the commencement not at the conclusion of the inquiry. The limit of the inquiry must be whether the magistrates have jurisdiction, supposing the facts alleged in the information to be true. The magistrates' return contained all that was needed to give them jurisdiction over the subject-matter: occupation of a parish house belonging to the hamlet and service of a notice to quit. The application for certiorari was therefore rejected. Examples of the same approach could be multiplied.[34]

2. *Collateral or Preliminary Fact Cases*

There were also a number of cases which advocated more extensive review through the mechanism, explicitly or implicitly, of the collateral fact doctrine. Certain facts were required to be proven to the satisfaction of the reviewing court before the magistrate or tribunal could go right or wrong.

An early example of this can be seen in *Nichols* v. *Walker*.[35] The plaintiff lived in Totteridge and was evaluated for the poor rates by the assessors for Hatfield. In a trespass action the plaintiff's case was upheld. Hatfield and Totteridge were separate places and the one could not levy rates for the other. A number of similar cases concerned with the Poor Laws followed.[36]

What had been implicit in the above cases was made explicit in *Bunbury* v. *Fuller*. The plaintiff brought an action in debt against the defendant owner of the land, claiming the amount due as being for tithes. The defendant

---

[34] See cases above n.33. See also *Mould* v. *Williams* (1844) 5 Q.B. 469; *Allen* v. *Sharp* (1848) 2 Ex. 352; *R.* v. *Buckinghamshire JJ.* (1843) 3 Q.B. 800; *R.* v. *Wilson* (1844) 6 Q.B. 620; *R.* v. *Wood* (1855) 5 El. & Bl. 49; *Revell* v. *Blake* (1872) 7 C.P. 300; *Usill* v. *Hales* (1878) 3 C.P.D. 319; *R.* v. *Whitfield* (1885) 15 Q.B.D. 122; *R.* v. *Justices of the Central Criminal Court* (1886) 17 Q.B.D. 598.

[35] (1632-1633) Cro. Car. 394.

[36] *Milward* v. *Caffin* (1778) 2 Black. W. 1330; *Lord Amherst* v. *Lord Somers* (1788) 2 T.R. 372; *Weaver* v. *Price* (1832) 3 B. & Ad. 409; *Governors of Bristol Poor* v. *Wait* (1834) 1 A. & E. 264; *Fernley* v. *Worthington* (1840) 1 Man. & G. 491. See also, cases on title, *Thompson* v. *Ingham* (1850) 14 Q.B. 710, 718; *Dale* v. *Pollard* (1847) 10 Q.B. 505; *Chew* v. *Holroyd* (1852) 8 Ex. 249.

had argued that part of the land was exempt from tithes, but an assistant tithe commissioner had denied this; the defendant now asserted that the determination was an excess of jurisdiction. Coleridge J. found for the defendant, his reasoning being as follows,

> "Now it is a general rule, that no court of limited jurisdiction can give itself jurisdiction by a wrong decision on a point collateral to the merits of the case upon which the limit to its jurisdiction depends; and however its decision may be final on all particulars, making up together that subject-matter which, if true, is within its jurisdiction, and, however necessary in many cases it may be for it to make a preliminary inquiry, whether some collateral matter be or be not within the limits, yet, upon this preliminary question, its decision must always be open to inquiry in the superior Court."[37]

The existence of land subject to a tithe was a point collateral to the decision of the assistant tithe commissioner. A number of similar cases could be cited.[38]

3. *Reconciliation?*

How can the cases discussed above be reconciled? One matter is clear. Any reconciliation cannot be achieved upon the basis that some judges preferred more limited and some more extensive review.[39] The most popular way to regard the cases is to say that both groups are equally valid and that differences turn on the legislative instrument.[40] In *R. v. Commissioners for Special Purposes of Income Tax*[41] Lord Esher M.R. distinguished between two types of tribunal. There were tribunals which had jurisdiction if a certain state of facts existed but not otherwise; it was not then for the inferior tribunal to determine conclusively upon the existence of such facts. There could, however, be a tribunal which had jurisdiction to determine whether the preliminary state of facts existed; here it would be for the inferior tribunal to decide upon all the facts.

The reconciliation is, with respect, not so straightforward. It is one of form rather than substance. It is impossible by juxtaposing the legislative instruments in these cases to determine why one case should fall within one category rather than the other. All statutes giving power in effect say

---

[37] (1853) 9 Ex. 111, 140.

[38] *e.g. R. v. Badger* (1856) 6 El. & Bl. 138; *R. v. Stimpson* (1863) 4 B. & S. 301; *Ex p. Vaughan* (1866) L.R. 2 Q.B. 114; *Elston v. Rose* (1868) L.R. 4 Q.B. 4; *Ex p. Bradlaugh* (1878) 3 Q.B.D. 509.

[39] *e.g.* Lord Denman C.J. decided *R. v. Bolton* (1841) 1 Q.B. 66 and *Governors of Bristol Poor v. Wait* (1834) 1 A. & E. 264; Coleridge J. decided *R. v. Buckinghamshire JJ.* (1843) 3 Q.B. 800 and *Bunbury v. Fuller* (1853) 9 Ex. 111: and see Coleridge J. *arguendo* in *Thompson v. Ingham* (1850) 14 Q.B. 710, 713.

[40] For a different, and unsuccessful, attempt at reconciliation, see *Thompson v. Ingham* (1850) 14 Q.B. 710, 718.

[41] (1888) 21 Q.B.D. 313. See also, *Colonial Bank of Australasia v. Willan* (1874) L.R. 5 P.C. 417.

if X exists, you may or shall do Y. The answer as to who is to determine X
(and the factors constituting X) is dependent upon which theory of
jurisdiction is accepted. The two groups of cases discussed above reflect
different answers to that question, and Lord Esher's analysis simply
reiterates *ex post facto* that divergence; the analysis does not provide us
with an *ex ante* tool to determine which group a case should fall into. This
is not to say that a statute might not assign the relative meaning of "if X",
as between courts and tribunals, differently in diverse areas. It is to say that
whether it has done so cannot be determined by asking whether the statute
requires a certain state of facts to exist before a decision is reached: all
statutes always do this.

4. *The Current Case Law*

(1) THE IMPACT OF ANISMINIC

The passing of the Victorian age, significant in so many spheres, brought no
great change in this area; there is no magic in the divide between the
nineteenth and twentieth centuries so far as the scope of judicial review is
concerned. There were still cases advocating only limited review.[42] These
were the heirs of *Brittain* and *Bolton*. There were also decisions which
adopted a more interventionist attitude.[43] The collateral or preliminary fact
doctrine was used as their mechanism. These were the descendants of
Bunbury. The nature of matters which would be characterised as collateral
or preliminary was still difficult to determine, and it was admitted that
there could be errors of law within jurisdiction which, if they appeared on
the face of the record, would be quashed.[44]

The scope of review must now be seen in the light of the decision in
Anisminic Ltd. v. Foreign Compensation Commission.[45] The plaintiff was
an English company which owned property in Egypt prior to 1956. In
November 1956 the property was sequestrated by the Egyptian authorities
and in April 1957 the sequestrator sold the property to TEDO, an Egyptian
organisation. Anisminic Ltd put pressure on their customers not to buy ore
from TEDO, as a result of which an agreement was reached in November
1957 whereby the plaintiff sold the mining business to TEDO for
£500,000. In February 1959 a treaty was made between the United
Kingdom and the United Arab Republic which provided for the return of
sequestrated property, except property sold between October 1956 and
August 1958. A sum of £27,500,000 was paid by the United Arab Republic

---

[42] *e.g. R. v. Mahony* [1910] 2 I.R. 695; *R. v. Bloomsbury Income Tax Commissioners* [1915]
3 K.B. 768; *R. v. Nat Bell Liquors Ltd.* [1922] 2 A.C. 128; *R. v. Swansea Income Tax
Commissioners* [1925] 2 K.B. 250; *R. v. Minister of Health* [1939] 1 K.B. 232; *Tithe
Redemption Commission v. Wynne* [1943] K.B. 756.
[43] *e.g. R. v. Fulham, Hammersmith and Kensington Rent Tribunal, ex p. Zerek* [1951] 2 K.B.
1; *R. v. Fulham, Hammersmith and Kensington Rent Tribunal, ex p. Hierowski* [1953] 2 K.B.
147.
[44] *R. v. Paddington North and St. Marylebone Rent Tribunal, ex p. Perry* [1956] 1 Q.B. 229.
[45] [1969] 2 A.C. 147.

in final settlement of claims to property which was not being returned. Orders in Council were then passed setting out the conditions for participation in the fund. The Foreign Compensation Commission, (hereafter the FCC), found that Anisminic Ltd did not qualify. The Foreign Compensation (Egypt) (Determination and Registration of Claims) Order 1962[46] stated in article 4(1)(b)(ii) that the applicant and the successor in title should be British nationals on October 31, 1956 and February 28, 1959. The FCC interpreted this to mean that they had to inquire whether there was a successor in title and, if so, whether the person qualified under article 4(1)(b)(ii). TEDO was a successor in title according to the FCC and was not a British national at the relevant dates, therefore the plaintiff failed. The plaintiff claimed that the nationality of the successor in title was irrelevant where the claimant was the original owner. Anisminic Ltd therefore sought a declaration that the determination was a nullity.

The House of Lords[47] found for the plaintiffs. Lord Reid stated that jurisdiction in a narrow sense meant only that the tribunal be entitled to enter upon the inquiry. There were, however, a number of ways in which, having correctly begun the inquiry, the tribunal could do something which rendered its decision a nullity. Misconstruction of the enabling statute so that the tribunal fails to deal with the question remitted to it, failure to take account of relevant considerations, and asking the wrong question were, said Lord Reid, examples of this.[48] The appellant's construction of successor in title was the correct one and the decision by the FCC was a nullity. Lord Reid's judgment significantly broadens the potential scope of review. A court, if it wishes to interfere, can always characterise an alleged error as having resulted from asking the wrong question, or having taken account of irrelevant considerations. Three observations are warranted.

The first is as follows. "Asking the wrong question" or "irrelevancy" tell one that an error has been made, but they do not tell one whether the error was jurisdictional.[49] The step from "asking the wrong question", to the error being regarded as jurisdictional, is only made on the presupposition that any matter which is in any sense a "condition" to the exercise of jurisdiction becomes jurisdictional. The implicit assumption as to why this should be so is that questions of law are for the ordinary courts. Hence the tribunal must give what the reviewing court regards as the correct meaning to the statutory terms, *before* the tribunal can be properly within the sphere of its jurisdiction; mistakes as to the meaning of these terms become jurisdictional errors. Concepts such as "asking the wrong question" then simply function as the vehicle through which the court can substitute its views on the meaning of such phrases for that of the tribunal. The premises

---

[46] S.I. 2187.
[47] [1969] 2 A.C. 147. The case was also concerned with privative clauses. This problem is considered in Chap. 16.
[48] [1969] 2 A.C. 147, 171.
[49] A point made by Diplock L.J. in the Court of Appeal [1968] 2 Q.B. 862, 904-905. See also R. v. *Furnished Houses Rent Tribunal for Paddington and St. Marylebone, ex p. Kendal Hotels Ltd.* [1947] 1 All E.R. 448, 449; R. v. *Paddington North and St. Marylebone Rent Tribunal, ex p. Perry* [1956] 1 Q.B. 229, 237-238.

which underpin the cogency of such an assumption have already been considered.[50] Applying such reasoning in its full rigour reduces the division between jurisdictional and non-jurisdictional error to vanishing point. To revert to our earlier terminology: given that all tribunals are delegated power in the form of if X1, X2, X3, you may or shall do Y, everything relating to X becomes potentially jurisdictional. Where the enabling legislation is complex this means that a large number of matters must be "got right" in the opinion of the reviewing court before the tribunal can go right or wrong.

The second point to note is that the language of judicial intervention should not serve to conceal the "basic" nature of the issue which is at stake in cases such as *Anisminic*. This issue is the meaning to be ascribed to one of the X conditions. The language of "asking the wrong question" and the like is simply an indirect way for the court to express the conclusion that it believes that a different construction of the term in question should be substituted for that adopted by the agency.

The third point concerns the scope of the decision. Notwithstanding the broad potential for jurisdictional error, Lord Reid reaffirmed the continued existence of errors of law within jurisdiction. For example, if the existence of successor in title had been relevant, the FCC's determination would, said Lord Reid, have been binding whether right or wrong.[51] This is difficult to understand. Let us take an example. On the actual facts of the case, the term "British national" clearly was relevant. Who is a British national is a complex issue involving questions of law and fact. Did his Lordship mean that the court would not have inquired into any alleged misconstruction of that term? This seems extremely unlikely. Such a mistake could certainly come within Lord Reid's list of errors going to jurisdiction, and the cases cited by his Lordship and the other Law Lords support such a view. If this is so, why would a misconstruction over the term successor in title, where that term is relevant, not also be a jurisdictional error?[52] As we shall see, recent case law has in fact drawn out the implications of *Anisminic* more fully, and held that the case does indeed eradicate the distinction between jurisdictional and non-jurisdictional error, at least in the context of findings of law.[53]

Lord Pearce and Lord Wilberforce both reach their conclusions in similar ways.[54] The tribunal has a limited authority, the correlative of which is the power of the court, on review, to keep that tribunal within the area or field given to it. It is for the court to determine the true construction of a statute delineating that area. Lack of jurisdiction could arise in various ways, *inter alia*, absence of a condition precedent to the tribunal's jurisdiction, irrelevancy, and asking the wrong question. Lord Pearson

---

[50] See pp. 342-349.
[51] [1969] 2 A.C. 147, 174.
[52] A refusal so to inquire would in fact mean that far from providing extensive review, the House of Lords was countenancing only very limited review. Mere invocation of a relevant term would suffice to preclude any review.
[53] See below, pp. 360-361.
[54] [1969] 2 A.C. 147, 194-195, 207-210.

agreed that if there had been an error it would have been jurisdictional, but found no such mistake.[55] Lord Morris of Borth-y-Gest dissented. His Lordship realised the implications of the majority judgments and pointed out that the Order bristled with words requiring statutory construction. It could not be the case that any misconstruction of any of these terms would involve a jurisdictional error.[56]

(2) FROM ANISMINIC TO RACAL

It was to be over a decade before the House of Lords was to engage in any detailed scrutiny of this area, which it did in the *Racal* case considered below. In the meantime the decision of the House of Lords in *Anisminic* provided a broad armoury for any later court. If a court wished to categorise an error as jurisdictional it could do so by using the "wrong question" or "irrelevant consideration" formula. However, the courts possess considerable discretion as to whether to utilise this armoury. If the court did not wish to intervene it could achieve this result by saying that there was no error at all, by characterising the error as one within jurisdiction, or by defining jurisdiction itself more narrowly than in *Anisminic*. Two cases may be contrasted by way of example.

In *R. v. Preston Supplementary Benefits Appeal Tribunal, ex p. Moore*,[57] Moore had applied for supplementary benefits during the university vacation. In working out Moore's resources for the purpose of calculating his benefit, the Commission took into account £1.90 per week which was the weekly equivalent of that part of the grant made to Moore as his vacation allowance. Moore sought certiorari on the basis that resources in the legislation meant actual resources and that, as he had spent his grant, the sum should not have been subtracted.

Lord Denning M.R. found that the interpretation of the Supplementary Benefits Commission was correct. He went on to enunciate the principles for review of the supplementary benefits system. On the one hand, the legislation should not become a hunting ground for lawyers whereby the court, on review, would have to interpret every minute point of law. On the other, like cases should be treated alike and there should be control over important points of principle. Further, the court would interfere if the tribunal exceeded its jurisdiction. Despite this last reference to excess of jurisdiction, it seems that Lord Denning M.R. was anxious to prevent every point of construction in the statute from becoming jurisdictional.

Lord Denning M.R.'s decision in *Pearlman* v. *Keepers and Governors of Harrow School*[58] may be contrasted with this. The question was whether the installation of central heating was "an improvement made by the execution of works amounting to a structural alteration" within the

---

[55] *Ibid.* pp. 220-222.
[56] *Ibid.* pp. 182-190.
[57] [1975] 1 W.L.R. 624; *R.* v. *Industrial Injuries Commissioner, ex p. Amalgamated Engineering Union (No. 2)* [1966] 2 Q.B. 31; *Re Allen and Mathews Arbitration* [1971] 2 Q.B. 518.
[58] [1979] Q.B. 56; *A.C.T. Construction Ltd.* v. *Customs and Excise Commissioners* [1981] 1 W.L.R. 49, the point was not touched on in the House of Lords [1982] 1 All E.R. 84.

Housing Act 1974. The county court said that it was not, this interpretation being opposite to that reached by a different county court.

The Court of Appeal said that there had been a jurisdictional error. The Master of the Rolls held that the words in the statute should receive a uniform interpretation. The error was an error of law. The line between such errors which went to jurisdiction and those within jurisdiction was a fine one, and the characterisation would often be dependent upon whether the court wished to intervene. Distinctions between errors within and errors going to jurisdiction should be discarded; any error of law should be held to be jurisdictional if the case depended upon it.[59] Eveleigh L.J. was more conventional in the form of his approach.[60] The meaning of the statutory term was a collateral matter within the principle in *Bunbury* v. *Fuller*.[61] Geoffrey Lane L.J. dissented. He also purported to apply the conventional collateral fact doctrine, but reached a different conclusion from that of his brethren. The error was at most an error within jurisdiction.[62]

(3) THE UNCERTAINTY OF RACAL

Despite the observations of the Master of the Rolls, it was too early yet to build a pyre on which to consign conventional doctrine to its timely or untimely end. The courts continued to equivocate as to whether the traditional approach should be maintained. Put more accurately, individual judges may have been clear as to their preferences, but those preferences did not always coincide. The decision in *Pearlman* must now be seen in the light of *Re Racal Communications Ltd.*[63] The Director of Public Prosecutions had made an application to a judge in chambers under section 411 of the Companies Act 1948 in order to obtain books and papers relevant to showing that an offence in connection with the management of the company had taken place. The application was refused, Vinelott J. holding that the alleged offence was not one in connection with the management of the company's affairs. The D.P.P. appealed and this appeal was allowed despite the express words of section 441(3) which provided that the decision of the judge in chambers should not be appealable. Lord Denning M.R.[64] circumvented section 441(3) by finding that the judge had misconstrued the words in section 411, had thereby made a jurisdictional error, and therefore, relying on *Anisminic* and *Pearlman*, the "no appeal" clause was ineffective.

This decision was overturned by the House of Lords, but the reasoning of their Lordships was not uniform. Lord Diplock, with whom Lord Keith of Kinkel agreed, reasoned as follows.[65] The decision of the Court of Appeal overturning that of Vinelott J. could be seen as appeal or review. It could not however be appeal since section 441(3) precluded appeal and such a

---

[59] [1979] Q.B. 56, 69-70.
[60] *Ibid.* pp. 76-80.
[61] (1853) 9 Ex. 111.
[62] [1979] Q.B. 56, 76.
[63] [1981] A.C. 374. On appeal from *Re A Company* [1980] Ch. 138.
[64] [1980] Ch. 138, 143.
[65] [1981] A.C. 374, 381-382.

limit was expressly authorised.[66] His Lordship then considered whether the decision of the Court of Appeal could be justified as an exercise of review rather than appeal. A tripartite distinction was drawn as to the scope of review. First, administrative tribunals or authorities were subject to the full rigours of the *Anisminic* judgment: the parliamentary intent was presumed, subject to a clear contrary indication, to be that questions of law were to be decided by the courts; the distinction between errors within jurisdiction and errors going to jurisdiction was, for practical purposes, abolished, and any error of law would automatically result in the tribunal having asked itself the wrong question. The resultant decision would be a nullity. Secondly, inferior courts were, however, subject to a different test. It would depend upon the construction of the statute whether Parliament intended questions of law to be left to an inferior court. There was no presumption that it did not so intend. *Pearlman* was wrong because in that case the county court did have the ability to determine conclusively interrelated questions of law and fact. The third category for the purposes of review was the High Court. These courts were not subject to judicial review at all which only applied to administrative authorities and inferior courts. Appeal was the only corrective for a mistake by a High Court judge, and that had been removed by statute.[67] The cogency of this distinction will be considered later. Suffice it to say for now that the premises underlying *Anisminic* are made explicit, at least for those institutions within Lord Diplock's first category.

Lord Salmon, Lord Edmund-Davies and Lord Scarman reached the same conclusion as Lord Diplock on the effect of section 441(3). Appeal was excluded.[68] No such uniformity existed in relation to review. To put the matter more precisely, there was little support in the judgments either for Lord Diplock's tripartite standard of review, or for as extensive a review as his Lordship advocates for administrative institutions. Lord Salmon confined himself to saying that *Anisminic* was of no relevance to the High Court: it was apposite only for tribunals, commissioners and inferior courts of law.[69] His Lordship drew no distinction as to the scope of review for inferior courts and administrative institutions. Nor did Lord Salmon follow through the reasoning from *Anisminic* to reach the conclusions arrived at by Lord Diplock. Lord Edmund-Davies similarly arrived at a narrower conclusion than Lord Diplock. The reasoning of Lord Denning M.R. in *Pearlman*[70] which had purported to destroy the distinction between jurisdictional and non-jurisdictional error was, said Lord Edmund-Davies, wrong. The dissenting judgment of Geoffrey Lane L.J.,[71] which had applied the traditional collateral fact doctrine, was approved.[72] Nor did his Lordship draw any demarcation between administrative institutions and inferior courts for the purposes of review. Lord Scarman disposed of the

---

[66] Supreme Court of Judicature (Consolidation) Act 1925, s.31(1).
[67] [1981] A.C. 374, 382-384.
[68] *Ibid.* pp. 385, 388-389, 393.
[69] *Ibid.* p. 386.
[70] [1979] Q.B. 56, 69-70.
[71] *Ibid.* p. 76.
[72] [1981] A.C. 374, 389-390.

appeal succinctly. The cases on ouster clauses and tribunals were irrelevant to clauses excluding appeal from the High Court. Judicial review had no place in relation to the High Court.[73] Nothing more was said about what the scope of review for administrative institutions and inferior courts actually was and no dichotomy was drawn between them.[74]

(4) FROM RACAL TO PAGE: UNCERTAINTY PERSISTS

It was to be over a decade before the House of Lords, (though not the Privy Council), had another detailed look at the issue. Decisions in the period between *Racal* and *Page* did little to establish a uniform judicial approach to the scope of review. Three such approaches could in fact be identified during this period.

First, some decisions, notably that in the *South East Asia Fire* case,[75] persisted with the traditional collateral fact doctrine, rejecting arguments that the distinction between jurisdictional and non-jurisdictional error had been discarded.

The second approach is exemplified by *O'Reilly* v. *Mackman*.[76] The case was primarily concerned with the new procedure for remedies.[77] However in the course of giving the judgment, with which all their Lordships concurred, Lord Diplock stated once again that the result of the *Anisminic* decision was to render unnecessary the continued distinction between errors of law going to jurisdiction, and errors of law within jurisdiction. Any mistake of law would mean that the authority had asked itself the wrong question, which would result in a jurisdictional error. It is unclear whether his Lordship still believed that there should be a different standard of review for inferior courts and for other administrative institutions, but other decisions made during this period interpreted the combined effect of *Anisminic* and *O'Reilly* to mean that the same broad standard of review should, in principle, apply to both.[78]

A third approach is evident in cases which accept in principle extensive review for error of law which flows from *Anisminic* and *O'Reilly*, but which then qualify it in varying ways. Thus, in *Tal*, Goff L.J., while accepting that the distinction between jurisdictional and non-jurisdictional error of law was obsolete, did not believe that the *Anisminic* principle should apply "with full force"[79] to every inferior court, and emphasised that

---

[73] *Ibid.* pp. 392-393.

[74] The headnote in the Official Law Reports is misleading. The second part gives the impression that a majority of their Lordships accepted Lord Diplock's view as to the scope of review for inferior courts. This is not borne out by the passages referred to in the decisions of Lord Salmon or Lord Edmund-Davies.

[75] *South East Asia Fire Bricks Sdn. Bhd.* v. *Non-Metallic Mineral Products Manufacturing Employees Union* [1981] A.C. 363, disapproving of Lord Denning M.R.'s dictum in *Pearlman* [1979] Q.B. 56, 69-70, and approving of the dissenting judgment of Geoffrey Lane L.J., [1979] Q.B. 56, 76.

[76] [1983] 2 A.C. 237. See also *Council of Civil Service Unions* v. *Minister for the Civil Service* [1985] A.C. 374, 410-411.

[77] See below, Chap. 15.

[78] *R.* v. *Greater Manchester Coroner, ex p. Tal* [1985] Q.B. 67, 82-83.

[79] *Ibid.* p. 82 G-H.

the reviewing court should not intervene "merely because some error of law has been committed during an inquest".[80] Similarly, in *ex p. Central Bank of India*[81] Slade L.J., while accepting in principle the extensive review propounded by Lord Diplock in *Racal*, emphasised that Lord Diplock himself had only cast this as a presumption even in relation to administrative institutions. The language of the statute in the *Central Bank* case led the court to rebut this presumption and to conclude that the Registrar of Companies could make certain binding decisions on issues of mixed fact and law.

(5) THE IMPACT OF PAGE

The decision of the House of Lords in *Page v. Hull University Visitor*[82] is the latest pronouncement upon this issue. Page was a lecturer at Hull University who was made redundant. He argued that the terms of his appointment did not allow termination of his employment on this ground. The University Visitor dismissed the argument, and Page then sought judicial review of the Visitor's decision. Much of the case turned upon particular issues concerning the nature of the Visitor's powers, and the extent to which these were susceptible to review. However, there are also more general observations concerning the scope of jurisdictional review. These observations can be summarised in the following manner.

First, Lord Browne-Wilkinson, who gave the leading judgment, held that *Anisminic,* combined with Lord Diplock's dictum in *O'Reilly,* had indeed rendered obsolete the distinction between errors of law on the face of the record and other errors of law, and had done so by extending the *ultra vires* doctrine. Thenceforward, it was to be taken "that Parliament had only conferred the decision-making power on the basis that it was to be exercised on the correct legal basis: a misdirection in law in making the decision therefore rendered the decision *ultra vires.*"[83] In general therefore, "any error of law made by an administrative tribunal or inferior court in reaching its decision can be quashed for error of law."[84]

Secondly, the constitutional foundation for the court's power was, said his Lordship, the *ultra vires* doctrine. This was so for the following reason. In an ordinary case,[85] the law applicable to a decision made by such a body was the general law of the land. A tribunal or inferior court would, therefore, be acting *ultra vires* if it reached a decision which was erroneous under the general law.[86]

---

[80] *Ibid.* p. 83 B.
[81] *R. v. Registrar of Companies, ex p. Central Bank of India* [1986] Q.B. 1114, 1175-1176.
[82] [1993] 1 All E.R. 97.
[83] *Ibid.* p. 107. Lord Slynn and Lord Mustill dissented in relation to certain aspects of the case concerning the Visitor. However, on the general point concerning the scope of review for error of law they were of the same view as the majority, *ibid.* p. 111.
[84] *Loc.cit.*
[85] The Visitor was regarded as being in a special position in this respect, since he was not applying the general law, but a special domestic legal regime, *ibid.* p. 108.
[86] *Ibid.* p. 108.

Thirdly, it was, however, only *relevant* errors of law which would lead to the decision being quashed or declared null. The error had to be one which affected the actual making of the decision and affected the decision itself. The mere existence of an error of law at some earlier stage of the proceedings would not vitiate the decision itself.[87]

Finally, the case is unclear as to whether varying presumptions still exist for administrative bodies on the one hand, and for inferior courts on the other. A distinction does still appear to exist. Lord Browne-Wilkinson cited the relevant dicta from Lord Diplock in the *Racal* case, and then reasoned on the assumption that differing presumptions did still exist in the two situations.[88] Moreover, the reasoning of Lord Griffiths also appears to be based upon the continued vitality of the distinction.[89]

(6) THE IMPACT OF THE SOUTH YORKSHIRE TRANSPORT CASE

Before drawing any more general conclusions about the impact of the *Page* case it is necessary to consider another important decision of the House of Lords, *R. v. Monopolies and Mergers Commission, ex p. South Yorkshire Transport Ltd.*[90]

The Secretary of State has power under the Fair Trading Act 1973, section 64(1)(a), to refer a merger to the Monopolies and Mergers Commission (MMC) where it appears to him that the two or more enterprises have ceased to be distinct and that as a result the supply of over 25% of the services of any description "in a substantial part of the United Kingdom" would be carried on by one person. The MMC investigated a merger between two companies which operated bus services within an area which was 1.65% of the total UK area, and which contained only 3.2% of the total population of the UK. The companies claimed that the investigation should be set aside because the jurisdictional condition relating to a substantial part of the UK had not been fulfilled. Lord Mustill gave judgment for the MMC. He reasoned as follows.

First, the term "substantial" was open to a range of possible meanings, ranging from "not trifling" to "nearly complete". In between these two senses of the term there were many others which drew colour from the statutory context in which they were found.[91]

Secondly, it was up to the court to decide where along the "spectrum of possible meanings"[92] the term was to be placed. Once the court had pronounced upon this matter the fact that the chosen meaning was formerly

---

[87] *Ibid.* pp. 107-108, explaining *R. v. Independent Television Commission, ex p. TSW Broadcasting Ltd* (1992) *Independent*, 27 March.
[88] *Ibid.* pp. 108-109. *cf. R. v. Greater Manchester Coroner, ex p. Tal* [1985] Q.B. 67, 82-83, where Goff L.J. assumed that differential tests for review would not operate depending upon the nature of the decision-maker.
[89] *Ibid.* p. 100.
[90] [1993] 1 All E.R. 289.
[91] *Ibid.* pp. 294-295.
[92] *Ibid.* p. 296.

part of a range of possible meanings on which opinions might legitimately differ became simply a matter of history.[93]

Thirdly, the criterion which was chosen might, however, itself be so imprecise that different decision-makers, each acting rationally, might reach different conclusions when applying it to the facts of a given case.

> "In such a case the court is entitled to substitute its opinion for that of the person to whom the decision has been entrusted only if the decision is so aberrant that it cannot be classed as rational: *Edwards* v. *Bairstow*...The present is such a case. Even after eliminating inappropriate senses of 'substantial' one is still left with a meaning broad enough to call for the exercise of judgment rather than an exact quantitative measurement."[94]

(7) SUMMARY

The present law may be summarised as follows. How satisfactory this position is will be examined below.[95]

(a) The courts will exercise review over any error of law, and will, in general, no longer employ distinctions between jurisdictional and non-jurisdictional error. When an error has been made the court will normally substitute its view for that of the body subject to review. There appear to be three qualifications to this basic proposition.

(b)(i) The error of law must be relevant in the sense discussed above.

(ii) The varying presumption as to legislative intent does still appear to operate depending upon the type of institution being reviewed. If the institution before the court is a tribunal or other administrative body, then the presumption will be that Parliament did not intend that body to be the final arbiter on issues of law. If, however, the institution subject to review is an inferior court then there is no presumption that Parliament did not intend questions of law to be left to that court.[96]

(iii) The court will not necessarily substitute its judgment for that of the agency in circumstances like those in the *South Yorkshire Transport* case. In such a case the reviewing court will define the actual meaning that the statutory term is to have, but where that particular meaning is itself inherently imprecise the court will only intervene if the application of the term is so aberrant as to be irrational.

---

[93] *Ibid.* p. 298.
[94] *Loc.cit.*
[95] See below, pp. 372–383.
[96] However, even in this latter instance it appears to be the case that, for example, a legislative finality clause, which purports to render a decision of an inferior court final and conclusive, will only be interpreted to protect that body from errors of law within jurisdiction, [1993] 1 All E.R. 97, p. 109.

5. *Error of Law Within Jurisdiction*

(1) HISTORY AND SCOPE

In addition to review for jurisdictional error, the courts have, in the past, maintained control over errors of law within jurisdiction if they appeared on the face of the record. Indeed certiorari appears to have developed to control this very type of error.[97] Control over such errors declined during the latter half of the nineteenth century,[98] and was only "rediscovered" 100 years later.[99]

This form of control could only be exercised if the defect existed on the face of the record. The courts construed this broadly to include the documents which initiated the proceedings, the pleadings and the adjudication.[100] The reasons for the decision might also be held to be part of the record.[101] Statute has also played a part in broadening the ambit of the record. The Tribunals and Inquiries Act 1958, section 12 initiated a right to reasoned decisions which were to be treated as part of the record,[102] but only in the sphere covered by the Act.

(2) DOES THE CONCEPT STILL SURVIVE?

There has, for some time, been an air of unreality when talking of errors of law within jurisdiction. The revival of this head of review was greeted enthusiastically. Whether it continued to survive was simply another way of asking whether the traditional collateral fact doctrine would continue to be used by the courts. This question has just been considered. Although the House of Lords in *Anisminic*[103] affirmed the continued existence of non-jurisdictional errors of law, we have seen that certain other judges were in favour of pushing the *Anisminic* reasoning to its limit and discarding the dichotomy. This has now been confirmed by the decision in the *Page* case. A separate category of error of law within jurisdiction will, therefore, very largely become redundant.[104]

---

[97] Rubinstein, *Jurisdiction and Illegality* (1965), Chap. 4.
[98] The primary reason was the passage of the Summary Jurisdiction Act 1848 which authorised a truncated form of record in which the charge, evidence and reasoning to support it were no longer required to be set out in criminal convictions, *R. v. Nat Bell Liquors Ltd.* [1922] 2 A.C. 128, 159.
[99] *R. v. Northumberland Compensation Appeal Tribunal, ex p. Shaw* [1951] 1 K.B. 711, [1952] 1 K.B. 338.
[100] *ex p. Shaw* [1952] 1 K.B. 338, 352.
[101] *R. v. Medical Appeal Tribunal, ex p. Gilmore* [1957] 1 Q.B. 574; *Baldwin and Francis Ltd. v. Patents Appeal Tribunal* [1959] A.C. 663. See also *R. v. Knightsbridge Crown Court, ex p. International Sporting Club (London) Ltd.* [1982] Q.B. 304; *R. v. Chertsey JJ., ex p. Franks* [1961] 2 Q.B. 152.
[102] Replaced by Tribunals and Inquiries Act 1971, s.12.
[103] [1969] 2 A.C. 147.
[104] The only instance where it might still remain relevant is where there is a finality clause *and* the court believes that Parliament might have intended that the decision-maker should be the final arbiter on questions of law. In such circumstances the finality clause might well immunise the decision from attack if there is an error of law within jurisdiction, see *Page* [1993] 1 All E.R. 97, 109.

6. *Statutory Review*

A number of statutes contain provisions allowing review only within a limited period, this commonly being six weeks. The effect of the six weeks time limit will be considered within the general context of exclusion of remedies.[105] What falls to be considered now is the effect of a specific statutory formula which allows challenge within the six week period on certain grounds.[106] The statute will normally establish two grounds of review. These are that the order impugned is not within the powers of the Act or that any requirement of the Act has not been complied with. If the latter is the ground of attack, there is the additional requirement that the interests of the applicant have been substantially prejudiced.

Construction of these clauses has produced considerable differences in judicial opinion. Part of the difficulty lies in the developments which have taken place in the ordinary common law of judicial review. If such statutory clauses were ever intended to reflect the common law (and this is not clear), the dichotomy drawn within them between the two heads of review makes little sense in light of the expansion of non-statutory review. Moreover, the very existence of the two heads of control has, in itself, exacerbated the confusion as judges have strived to find a function for each of the terms. This diversity of view is manifested in *Smith* v. *East Elloe Rural District Council*[107] in which their Lordships adopted a variety of views as to the meaning of "not within the powers of this Act". Lord Reid[108] held that bad faith and unreasonableness were outside the statute completely and therefore could be impugned even after six weeks. A similar result was reached by Lord Somervell[109] who was of the opinion that fraud did not go to jurisdiction and could be challenged at any time. The majority decided that challenge for fraud was precluded after six weeks. Lord Morton went on to construe the statutory terms extremely narrowly as permitting challenge only if express statutory requirements were violated.[110] The sensible interpretation would be to read the phrase, "not within the powers of this Act" so as to include any of the traditional heads of *ultra vires*, and there is authority for this position.[111] Later courts have given the formula a broad interpretation. It has been held to encompass not only traditional forms of jurisdictional error, but also no evidence, and any error of law.[112] The puzzles of *East Elloe* will therefore probably be quietly forgotten.

---

[105] See Chap. 16.
[106] This formula is common in legislation on housing and land use.
[107] [1956] A.C. 736.
[108] *Ibid.* p. 763.
[109] *Ibid.* p. 772.
[110] *Ibid.* p. 755.
[111] *Webb* v. *Minister of Housing and Local Government* [1965] 1 W.L.R. 755, 770 (Lord Denning M.R.). See cases, below n. 112.
[112] *Ashbridge Investments Ltd.* v. *Minister of Housing and Local Government* [1965] 1 W.L.R. 1320; *Coleen Properties Ltd.* v. *Minister of Housing and Local Government* [1971] 1 W.L.R. 433; *Gordondale Investments Ltd.* v. *Secretary of State for the Environment* (1971) 70 L.G.R. 158; *Peak Park Planning Board* v. *Secretary of State for the Environment* (1980) 39 P. & C.R. 361.

Despite this broad formulation, the courts still continue to use the second limb of the formula, that a requirement of the Act has not been complied with.[113] It may well be best, as Wade[114] suggests, that this limb be confined to the challenge of directory provisions, allowing a court to quash an order if non-compliance with such provisions has caused substantial prejudice to the applicant.

7. *Review of Fact and Evidence*

It is necessary to keep distinct a number of different issues which can arise under the general rubric of review of findings of fact and evidence.[115]

(1) REVIEW OF JURISDICTIONAL FACT

The *first* of these concerns the review of jurisdictional fact *stricto sensu*. As we have seen, the courts have considerable choice as to whether to categorise an issue as one of law or fact. Jurisdictional questions can be either. The current trend is to regard many issues of statutory interpretation as questions of law, or mixed law and fact. The courts will ascribe what they conceive to be the correct meaning to that term. However, even if the court calls one of the "if X" conditions a question of fact, it will substitute its view as to the meaning of that term if it conceives the fact to be jurisdictional. In this sense all that review over findings of fact means is that the court will decide what meaning the particular statutory provision should bear. For example, if a court decides that the meaning of the word "repair" is a question of fact, but that it is, in the context of the particular legislation, a jurisdictional fact, the court will then lay down the interpretation that should be given to such a term.

(2) REVIEW OF EVIDENTIARY FINDINGS

The *second* issue is the extent to which the courts will inquire whether the meaning of a term is satisfied by the evidence before the decision-maker. The answer to this second question is integrally related to the first. If the courts regard the allegation as relating to a statutory condition which is itself jurisdictional, then they will receive affidavit evidence to show that the condition is not met. Findings will be reassessed on these grounds. An understanding of this renders it much easier to comprehend the no evidence doctrine and the reasons for the exceptions made to it in more recent years.

The no evidence doctrine was commonly taken to mean that a decision will not be regarded as outside of the jurisdiction of the decision-maker even if the decision was reached on no evidence. The leading authority for

---

[113] *Gordondale Investments Ltd.* (1971) 70 L.G.R. 158; *Miller v. Weymouth Corporation* (1974) 27 P. & C.R. 468.
[114] *Administrative Law* (6th ed., 1988), p. 741.
[115] Jones, "Mistake of Fact in Administrative Law" [1990] P.L. 507.

this proposition has always been *R.* v. *Nat Bell Liquors Ltd.*[116] However, it is clear from a reading of the decision that the no evidence principle was itself simply a natural correlative of the limited theory of jurisdiction which was accepted by Lord Sumner. His Lordship reached the conclusion that no evidence was not a jurisdictional defect because he expressly adopted the limited concept of review adumbrated above. *Bolton, Brittain* and *Mahony* formed the cornerstone of his Lordship's reasoning. Under the commencement theory of jurisdiction propounded in those cases the reviewing court would not reassess whether the elements within the bracket constituting the statutory conditions were met or not. The conclusion that no evidence was not a jurisdictional defect was simply a natural result of this reasoning.[117] Thus, a conviction, regular on its face, was conclusive of all the facts stated in it, including those necessary to give the justices jurisdiction. On this hypothesis there was clearly no place for review of findings of fact, in the sense of determining whether the evidence justified the application of a statutory term to particular facts. This too was for the magistrates.

What is more surprising is that the *Nat Bell* case has exercised such a mesmeric hold over our jurisprudence, even though the premises leading to the conclusion have been rejected. Put simply, once we move away from the commencement theory of jurisdiction then the rationale for saying that absence of evidence does not constitute a jurisdictional defect simply disappears. Once the courts moved towards applying the collateral fact doctrine, and to that extent re-determining the constituent elements of certain of the conditions of jurisdiction, it became natural also to consider whether the evidence supported the existence of those collateral facts. Thus in *Eshugbayi Eleko* v. *Government of Nigeria*,[118] Lord Atkin treated the Governor of Nigeria's power to deport E as being dependent upon certain collateral facts, including whether E was a native chief or not. Evidence was therefore admitted and examined to determine whether the collateral facts existed in the actual case.

What can be concluded from the discussion thus far is that the approach to findings of evidence is integrally related to the view of jurisdiction adopted. The ratio of *Nat Bell*, that no evidence does not constitute a jurisdictional error, was simply the natural consequence of a conception of jurisdiction under which the courts would not reassess the meaning ascribed to the constituent elements of jurisdiction. Not only would the courts leave the *meaning* of the term to the magistrates; they would also accept the magistrates' view as to whether the *evidence* justified applying that term to the case. However, once the courts began to be willing to reassess the constituent elements of jurisdiction, under the collateral fact doctrine, then it was natural also to require some proof that the meaning of the term was indeed justified by the evidence on the facts of the particular

---

[116] [1922] 2 A.C. 128, 151–154.
[117] *Ibid.* pp. 152–153.
[118] [1931] A.C. 662, 670–672.

case.[119] How much proof should be required will be examined in the next section.

What we have witnessed in recent years is a subtle change whereby the courts, often without alluding to the authorities mentioned, have reviewed decisions to test their evidentiary basis. The most interesting development pointing in this general direction is to be found in the field of statutory as opposed to common law review. In *Ashbridge Investments Ltd* v. *Minister of Housing and Local Government*[120] the minister had power to modify a clearance order if he was of the opinion that land should not have been included in it. Lord Denning M.R. stated that the court could intervene if the minister acted on no evidence, or reached a decision to which on the evidence he could not reasonably have come, equating the case to one where a court interfered with a decision of a tribunal which had erred in law. The precise status of this case, and those which have followed it, is unclear. They are concerned with a statutory form of control rather than the common law, and did not mention the House of Lords' decisions which are to the contrary.

A related development is to be seen in *Secretary of State for Education and Science* v. *Tameside Metropolitan Borough Council*.[121] In that case the Secretary of State was empowered to give directions if he was satisfied that the local education authority was acting unreasonably. Lord Wilberforce stated that,[122]

"If a judgment requires, before it can be made, the existence of some facts then, although the evaluation of those facts is for the Secretary of State alone, the court must inquire whether those facts exist, and have been taken into account, whether the judgment has been made upon a proper self-direction as to those facts, whether the judgment has not been made upon other facts which ought not to have been taken into account. If those requirements are not met, then the exercise of judgment, however bona fide it may be, becomes capable of challenge."

These developments are not surprising. The conceptual basis underlying the *Nat Bell* decision has been removed as the courts have rejected the limited theory of jurisdiction, and have moved through the

---

[119] The above analysis is not vitiated by the fact that *Nat Bell* has been cited with approval in later cases, *e.g. R.* v. *Ludlow, ex p. Barnsley Corporation* [1947] K.B. 634, 637; *R.* v. *Governor of Brixton Prison, ex p. Armah* [1968] A.C.192, 234; *R.* v. *Governor of Pentonville Prison, ex p. Sotiriadis* [1975] A.C. 1, 30. These cases are explicable either because they adopted the same limited theory of review as *Nat Bell* itself, or because they adopted the collateral fact theory, but did not treat the particular condition in issue as collateral. On either hypothesis the conclusion that no evidence does not vitiate the decision is a natural conclusion for exactly the reasons given above.

[120] [1965] 1 W.L.R. 1320, 1326; *Coleen Properties Ltd.* v. *Minister of Housing and Local Government* [1971] 1 W.L.R. 433; *General Electric Co. Ltd.* v. *Price Commission* [1975] I.C.R. 1; *R.* v. *Secretary of State for the Environment, ex p. Ostler* [1977] Q.B. 122, 123. See also, *Allinson* v. *General Medical Council* [1894] 1 Q.B. 750, 760; *Lee* v. *Showmen's Guild of Great Britain* [1952] 2 Q.B. 329, 345.

[121] [1977] A.C. 1014.

[122] *Ibid.* p. 1047. See also, *Mahon* v. *Air New Zealand Ltd.* [1984] A.C. 808, 832-833.

collateral fact doctrine towards the theory of extensive review. Even if the courts do not wholly embrace the theory of extensive review, the way is now open for review of the evidence supporting the decision-maker's findings. The conceptual block of the *Nat Bell* case is circumvented by regarding a component of the X question as jurisdictional. Evidence can thereby be admitted to prove or disprove the existence of the element which has been deemed jurisdictional. How much evidence should be required will be discussed shortly. In this sense the increase in judicial review over whether the evidence warrants the application of a certain statutory condition is itself a correlative of the widening of the concept of jurisdiction.

(3) REVIEW OVER OPEN-TEXTURED AND SUBJECTIVELY PHRASED JURISDICTIONAL ISSUES

The *third* aspect of review over findings of fact and evidence is related to the second. It concerns the review of open-textured and subjective conditions of jurisdiction. If the X question states that the "Minister may intervene if he thinks it necessary or desirable", then the only way in which the courts can maintain control is to require the minister to provide some evidence to justify his action. In such cases there is no term, such as successor in title, or resources, which the courts can insist should bear a certain meaning. All they can do is to ensure that the decision-maker did have some reasonable grounds for his action. This necessarily leads, as in *Tameside*, to the courts reviewing the evidence on which the minister acted. This has arisen in two kinds of case.

(a) An express requirement of reasonableness

An empowering statute will often frame the jurisdictional requirement in the following terms: if the Secretary of State has *reasonable* cause to believe, for example, a person to be of hostile origin, he may imprison him. In general such areas give rise to little difficulty. The jurisdictional fact contains the requirement of reasonable cause to believe and this would be a condition precedent to the exercise of a power to imprison. A court would interpret such words in their natural manner which is objective, *i.e.* the Secretary of State could not simply rely upon his own subjective beliefs, but would have to point to some evidence from which it could reasonably be inferred that, for example, Napoleon was a person of hostile origin. Provided that the inference could reasonably be drawn from the evidence, the fact that the court itself might not have done so would be irrelevant.

Despite the seemingly uncontroversial nature of the above, statutes expressed in such terms have occasionally been the subject of a *cause célèbre*. The best known example of this is *Liversidge* v. *Anderson*[123] in which the majority of the House of Lords found that the phrase "reasonable cause to believe" in wartime emergency legislation would be complied with provided that the Secretary of State acted on what he thought to be such a reasonable cause, and that it was not necessary for

---

[123] [1942] A.C. 206. Defence (General) Regulations 1939, 18B, para. 1.

there to be objective facts to support this. Lord Atkin, in one of the century's most powerful dissents, adopted the opposing view.[124] The case produced a significant impact at the time,[125] and has been restrictively construed. It has been confined to an interpretation of the specific regulations.[126] The House of Lords has stated that *Liversidge* need no longer haunt the law,[127] and it can be confidently predicted that the more natural objective meaning will henceforth be ascribed to such words.

(b) No express requirement as to reasonableness

More difficulty has been encountered when the jurisdictional requirements are phrased subjectively, with no requirement as to reasonableness, such as "if the Minister thinks fit, necessary, he may...". Viewed historically, the courts' attitude towards such grants of power has varied.

There are instances in both the nineteenth and twentieth centuries in which the courts have, despite such subjective wording, overturned decisions by finding that the power was being used for an improper purpose,[128] or that the public body had applied the wrong test[129] when construing legislative criteria. Control in such instances was facilitated by the statute containing criteria which the courts felt capable of construing.[130]

The war years were, however, characterised by a period of judicial restraint. Subjectively worded regulations were treated literally, and the courts eschewed any attempt to persuade them to judge the necessity or reasonableness of such regulations. This was undoubtedly due partly to the war, and partly because the statutes contained criteria which were felt to be less justiciable: if the minister stated that a regulation concerning trademarks was necessary for securing the safety of the realm the court would not adjudicate upon this.[131] Judicial restraint or inactivity continued after hostilities had ceased.[132]

However, in a number of cases the courts began to indicate that some control over subjective discretion might be attained. The methods varied. In some instances constraints would be imposed indirectly through the

---

[124] *Ibid.* pp. 226-246.
[125] Heuston, "Liversidge v. Anderson in Retrospect" (1970) 86 L.Q.R. 33.
[126] *Nakkuda Ali* v. *Jayaratne* [1951] A.C. 66, 76-77.
[127] *R.* v. *Inland Revenue Commissioners, ex p. Rossminster Ltd.* [1980] A.C. 952, 1011.
[128] *Lynch* v. *Commissioners of Sewers of the City of London* (1886) 32 Ch. D. 72.
[129] *Estate and Trust Agencies (1927) Ltd.* v. *Singapore Improvements Trust* [1937] A.C. 898.
[130] In the above cases the grant of power concerned street widening and insanitary housing, respectively, *i.e.* the grant of power was "if Z thinks houses prevent the widening of a street, Z may acquire them."
[131] *R.* v. *Comptroller General of Patents, ex p. Bayer Products Ltd.* [1941] 2 K.B. 306. See also, *Carltona Ltd.* v. *Commissioners of Works* [1943] 2 All E.R. 560; *Point of Ayr Collieries Ltd.* v. *Lloyd-George* [1943] 1 All E.R. 546; *Progressive Supply Co. Ltd.* v. *Dalton* [1943] Ch. 54.
[132] *Robinson* v. *Minister of Town and Country Planning* [1947] K.B. 702; *Land Realisation Co. Ltd.* v. *Postmaster-General* [1950] Ch. 435; *Re Beck and Pollitzer's Application* [1948] 2 K.B. 339.

imposition of a duty to provide reasons;[133] in other cases the courts hinted at the limits they would set, such as if the decision was perverse or made in bad faith.[134] Indirect limitations gave way to direct in *Commissioners of Customs and Excise* v. *Cure and Deeley Ltd*[135] in which Sachs J. found that legislation empowering tax commissioners to make regulations as they deemed necessary did not always make the commissioners the sole judge of the extent of their powers. The nature and object of the statute had to be considered to determine the area of power possessed.

This approach was adopted in the important case of *Padfield* v. *Minister of Agriculture*.[136] The minister was empowered, under section 19 of the Agricultural Marketing Act 1958, to direct a committee to investigate the operation of a milk marketing scheme; if the committee reported to the minister that the scheme was having an effect contrary to the interest of consumers and was not in the public interest, the minister could, if he thought fit, amend the scheme. The minister refused to refer a complaint to the committee and the complainant sought mandamus. It was argued on behalf of the minister that the legislation gave him an unfettered discretion as to whether to refer or not. This was firmly rejected by the House of Lords: discretion was vested in the minister to further the policy of the legislation and could not be thwarted by ministerial misconstruction of the legislation.[137] The form of control was to be through the concepts of purpose and relevancy, and each of the alleged reasons put forward by the minister for not referring was subjected to them. Short shrift was given to the argument that the minister could escape control by not giving reasons. Their Lordships accepted that there was no general duty to provide reasons, but attached a caveat, that if the preponderance of reasons pointed in favour of taking action and the minister gave no explanation for taking a different course, the court would infer that he had no good reason and that he was misusing his authority.[138]

The general approach now is for the courts to require that a minister produce reasonable grounds for his action, even where the jurisdictional fact is subjectively framed.[139]

---

[133] *Minister of National Revenue* v. *Wrights' Canadian Ropes Ltd.* [1947] A.C. 109.
[134] *Demetriades* v. *Glasgow Corporation* [1951] 1 All E.R. 457, 463; *Att.-Gen. for Canada* v. *Hallett and Carey Ltd.* [1952] A.C. 427.
[135] [1962] 1 Q.B. 340.
[136] [1968] A.C. 997. And see *Secretary of State for Education and Science* v. *Tameside Metropolitan Borough Council* [1977] A.C. 1014.
[137] [1968] A.C. 997, 1030, 1053, 1059-1060.
[138] *Ibid.* pp. 1032-1033, 1049, 1053-1054, 1059, 1061-1062. See generally, *Secretary of State for Employment* v. *ASLEF (No. 2)* [1972] 2 Q.B. 455, where the Court of Appeal found that it was sufficient if reasons were put forward which might have guided the minister's conduct; *Wilover Nominees Ltd.* v. *Inland Revenue Commissioners* [1974] 1 W.L.R. 1342. *Cf. Dowty Boulton Paul* v. *Wolverhampton Corporation (No. 2)* [1976] Ch. 13. For a more general discussion of the duty to give reasons, see pp. 310-316.
[139] See *Tameside* [1977] A.C. 1014; *Mahon* v. *Air New Zealand Ltd.* [1984] A.C. 808, 832-833.

(4) THE SCOPE OF REVIEW

A *fourth* aspect of the review of fact and evidentiary findings concerns the scope or intensity of such review.

We have already seen that when the courts deem a statutory term to be jurisdictional, whether it be a question of law or fact, they will substitute their view as to the meaning of the term for that of the decision-maker. They will decide what the term employee, resources or successor in title should mean. This approach has been criticised and an alternative will be considered below.

What we are, however, concerned with now is the standard of review which should apply to determine whether the meaning of that term is satisfied by the evidence before the decision-maker. Given a certain meaning which the courts *have* ascribed to the term employee, how closely should they supervise the application of that term to the facts of a particular case?

The distinction between the two issues posed above is neatly demonstrated by *R. v. Secretary of State for the Home Department, ex p. Khawaja*.[140] The House of Lords considered certain provisions of the Immigration Act 1971. One question which was raised was whether the term illegal entrant could cover a person who had obtained leave to enter by deception or fraud, as well as a person who had entered by clandestine means. Their Lordships answered this question in the affirmative. A second question was as to the standard of proof to be required of the immigration officer. Given that a person could be an illegal entrant through deception, what standard of proof was to be applied when reviewing the immigration officer's decision that a person had entered by deception? Their Lordships held that it was insufficient for the immigration officer to show that he had some reasonable grounds for his action. The standard should be higher when a power to affect liberty was in issue. An immigration officer would have to satisfy a civil standard of proof to a high degree of probability that the entrant had practised such deception. The court would determine whether that standard of proof had been met.

While one can accept that a high standard of proof is apposite in cases affecting liberty it is doubtful whether it should apply outside of this area. The question as to the sufficiency of evidence will normally arise in one of two contexts. A public body may be applying a statutory term which has been defined by the courts, and the question is whether the facts justify the application. Or it may be a situation in which the conditions of jurisdiction are open-textured or subjective, in the sense described above, and the courts wish to know whether there was evidence to justify the action taken.

In both instances the general test should be whether there was some reasonable or sufficient evidence to justify the action. To require more runs the risk of the courts substituting their view for that of the authority.

---

[140] [1984] A.C. 74, overruling, in this respect, *R. v. Secretary of State for the Home Department, ex p. Zamir* [1980] A.C. 930. *cf. R. v. Secretary of State for the Home Department, ex p. Bugdaycay* [1987] A.C. 514. See also, *R. v. Immigration Appeal Tribunal, ex p. Khan* [1983] Q.B. 790; *Ali v. Secretary of State for the Home Department* [1984] 1 W.L.R. 663; *R. v. Hampshire County Council, ex p. Ellerton* [1985] 1 W.L.R. 749.

Lord Wilberforce's statement in *Tameside*,[141] that the decision-maker should properly direct himself to the facts, provides a good example of one aspect of factual review which would allow the courts great latitude for substituting their view for that of the decision-maker. Moreover, a point to be considered later is particularly relevant here. We shall see that decision-makers tend to reach decisions on the basis of bounded rationality.[142] They do not have and cannot have all the possibly relevant materials and evidence before them. No decisions would ever be made if this were to be demanded. While this may provide some justification for ensuring that the decision-maker indicates what was the factual basis for his action, we should be wary of developing review of facts upon the premise that all such material could or should be considered.

(5) CONCLUSION

There is no doubt that we can fit rules concerning evidentiary findings into our traditional terminology. The lawyer's talisman, the implied condition, can be wheeled out to perform its trusty service: a grant of power to a public body is subject to the implied condition that the findings it makes be supported by some evidence. If they are not the determination is *ultra vires*. The fabric of jurisdiction is infinitely flexible. While we can thus remain within conventional discourse our very desire to review findings of evidence is indicative of the weakness of the jurisdictional strait-jacket in which we operate. The whole spirit of a no evidence, or reasonable evidence, doctrine is contrary to the split in the "if X" question between those elements which are jurisdictional and those which are not, and provided a further strain upon the now discredited collateral fact doctrine. It is now time to investigate further as to what, generally, should be the test for judicial review of jurisdictional issues.

Section 4. What Should the Test for Review Be?

1. *The Existing Approaches*

(1) THE COLLATERAL FACT DOCTRINE

The collateral fact doctrine has, as we have seen, now been disapproved of. This is to be welcomed since it has always been beset by two principal flaws. The first, is the arbitrariness and uncertainty of its application. The difficulty of distinguishing between the *kind* of case which a tribunal has to determine and the statutory description of the *situation* which the tribunal must decide is the root cause of the problem.[143] We cannot predict

---

[141] [1977] A.C. 1014, 1047.
[142] Below pp. 445-446.
[143] See above, pp. 337-339.

in advance the way in which a case will be decided, nor can we find any *ex post facto* rationality to explain why cases were categorised in different ways.

The second flaw is that the doctrine simply has never achieved its desired goal. The object was to steer a middle course by maintaining control over administrative institutions, while not making review the same as appeal, which would be the result if the judiciary substituted their views on every contested issue. What the doctrine actually achieved was a middle way of a rather different type to that which may have originally been conceived. The median was attained by total control over the topics dubbed collateral; the judiciary substituted their judgment on those aspects of the "if X" question which were deemed jurisdictional. No control was exercised over other issues,[144] and the line betwixt the two was arbitrary in the sense described above.

(2) LIMITED REVIEW

The Gordon thesis is also beset by two difficulties. The first is that it is analytically flawed in the sense considered above.[145] The second is that it does not appear satisfactory on policy grounds. While the spectre of the Albert Hall being deemed a furnished tenancy, like that of the vexatious litigant in the law of standing, haunts the annals of legal literature rather than the real world, we do nonetheless require more control than that allowed by Gordon's commencement theory. It may be extremely difficult to discern when a decision-maker has "commenced" his inquiry, and to prevent the courts from ever looking beyond the formal invocation of the finding "furnished tenancy" is too limited.

(3) REVIEW FOR ERRORS OF LAW

The Gould theory reaches a polar opposite conclusion to that advanced by Gordon. The effect of *Anisminic*, as interpreted in *Racal*, *O'Reilly* and *Page*, has been that the courts have accepted a similar view to that of Gould, whereby all errors of law become open to review. It would, in a paradoxical way, be reassuring if we lived in a world of extremes. If the modern educational system was administered by a Dickensian Squeers constantly flagellating discalced pupils, theory could be neatly shelved and a pragmatic response could be given to the perceived problem. In the real world things are more complex. While the demise of the collateral fact doctrine is to be welcomed, four comments on its "replacement" are warranted.

First, the attempt to suggest that this scope of review is logically demanded is not convincing.[146] There is no *a priori* reasoning process which indicates that the courts' view on the meaning of one of the "if X" issues should necessarily and always be preferred to that of the agency. The answer resides not in some logically compelled statement as to whose

---

[144] Unless the error was one of law on the face of the record.

[145] See above, pp. 340-342.

[146] See above, pp. 342-343.

opinion should count, but in a normative judgment as to whose relative opinion on a particular matter we wish to adopt.

Secondly, if we adopt the view that all errors of law are reviewable, in the sense that the court will substitute its view for that of the decision-maker, *and* we interpret the idea of error of law in the analytical sense discussed above,[147] there is a real danger that a valuable aspect of administrative autonomy will be eliminated. The standard problem of judicial review arises over a contested interpretation given to one of the statutory terms which the tribunal has to interpret. The tendency of the courts, and the thrust of Gould's argument, is to regard misconstruction of many of these terms as errors of law, the effect being that the court will substitute its view of that term for that of the tribunal. Yet terms such as "resources", "employee", or "structural alteration" may be capable of having a spectrum of possible meanings depending upon the overall scope and policy of the legislation. It is difficult to believe that the ordinary courts' particular interpretation of all of these terms will necessarily be better than that of the tribunal. The latter is established partly because of the expertise it can develop, and this expertise is not related solely to fact finding. Whether "course of employment" in a particular statute should include a tea break or the trip to work may be better decided by a tribunal staffed with a lawyer chairman and "wing" members representing the interests of trade unionists and employers rather than the ordinary courts.[148]

Thirdly, the problems outlined above would be mitigated if the courts were to interpret the term law in a more pragmatic, functional or policy-oriented way, taking into account the desirability of interfering with the agency decision, and the relative abilities of the court and the agency for deciding the question in issue. Whether this path is taken by the courts remains to be seen. One thing is however clear. If the courts did give this construction to the term law they would be applying a very different thesis from that originally conceived by Gould and applied more recently by the courts. As Beatson has stated,[149] "a system that uses the pragmatic approach is not using the concept of error of law as an organizing principle" as such, but rather as a facade behind which to weigh the relative competence of court and agency. They would in fact be applying a test for review not dissimilar to the one to be examined within the next section. The decision in the *South Yorkshire Transport* case[150] goes some way in this direction, but only to a limited extent. Their Lordships made it clear that they would decide upon the meaning of the open textured statutory term, while accepting that if that meaning was itself imprecise then the court would only intervene if the agency's decision was so aberrant as to be irrational.

The final comment concerns the issue of how far the nature of the decision-maker should affect the scope of review that we should adopt. As

---

[147] See above, pp. 348–349.

[148] See the similar point made by Beatson, "The Scope of Judicial Review For Error of Law" (1984) 4 O.J.L.S. 22, 40–42.

[149] *Ibid.* p. 43. *cf.* Emery and Smythe, "Error of Law in Administrative Law" (1984) 100 L.Q.R. 612.

[150] [1993] 1 All E.R. 289.

we have seen, Lord Diplock in *Racal*[151] drew a distinction between the scope of review for tribunals and inferior courts. The latter would be subject to less extensive review than would tribunals and other administrative institutions. Although the continued vitality of this distinction was doubted in *Tal*,[152] it appears to have been accepted by the House of Lords in *Page*.[153] There are real difficulties with any such dichotomy. It is often fortuitous whether a new institution is called a "court" or a "tribunal". The types of functions allocated between them may be equally haphazard. Moreover, while it is possible to give undue weight to expertise, it is also possible to underrate its significance. Many administrative institutions possess qualifications which render them just as capable of giving conclusive judgments on legal issues, or issues of mixed fact and law, as are the inferior courts. This is more particularly so given that tribunals are very likely to have a specialised, as opposed to a general jurisdiction. This enables them to develop expertise within their own area in a way which is more difficult for a generalist inferior court.

2. *A Middle Way: Rightness and Rational Basis*

(1) A RATIONAL BASIS TEST

If the above arguments possess cogency, how can control be achieved without the court automatically substituting judgment for that of the tribunal, and without allowing the tribunal to have unlimited power? A way forward would be to adopt a test of reasonableness or rational basis. The role of the court would be to establish the limits to the spectrum of meanings that a term could bear; the awesome visage of the Albert Hall would disappear. Substitution of judgment would also be avoided because the tribunal would determine which precise meaning should be adopted. The breadth of the spectrum would be dependent upon the type of tribunal and the content of the enabling legislation. This approach has been used in the United States and Canada. While by no means all cases have been decided in this way, the doctrine is nevertheless well established particularly in the United States. The very demarcation between those types of cases where it has been and where it has not been utilised is, in itself, informative.

A seminal case illustrating the theory in operation is *National Labour Relations Board* v. *Hearst Publications, Inc.*[154] Hearst published a number of newspapers and had refused to bargain collectively with a union representing newsboys who distributed the papers on the streets. The newspaper proprietors argued that the newsboys were not "employees" within the relevant legislation; the Board claimed that they were. Justice Rutledge delivered the opinion of the Supreme Court. Hearst argued that the ordinary common law meaning of the term employee, in contra-distinction

---

[151] [1981] A.C. 374, 382-383.
[152] [1985] Q.B. 67, 82-83.
[153] See above, pp. 360-361.
[154] 322 US 111, 64 S. Ct. 851, 88 L.Ed. 1170 (1944).

to independent contractor, should be used. The court disagreed. The common law standard was itself subject to differing interpretations in different States and, more important, even within any one particular State a person might be an independent contractor for the purposes of vicarious liability while being an employee for the purposes of unemployment compensation. Justice Rutledge proceeded to examine the evil which the statute was designed to cure and decided that it encompassed people outside the traditional common law classification of an employee. Clearly, the precise types of workers who could or should be termed "employees" for the purpose of the statute was a matter on which opinion could differ. There were "myriad forms of service relationship" within the economy.[155] The Board's determination would, said the court, be accepted if it had warrant in the record and a reasonable basis in law. Given the spectrum of possible interpretations to be accorded to the term employee, the Board's choice would be accepted provided that it was an interpretation which the reviewing court believed, in the light of the overall statutory objective, to be one which had a rational basis. The court did not simply substitute its own view because Congress had assigned the task primarily to the agency which, because of its greater experience, placed it in a better position to resolve the matter than the Court. Other cases have adopted the same approach.[156]

An important more recent example of this approach is to be found in *Chevron U.S.A.* v. *NRDC.*[157] In that case the Supreme Court drew the following distinction. *If* a court reviewing an agency's construction of a statute decided that Congress did have a specific intention on the precise question in issue then that intention should be given effect to. *If*, however, the reviewing court decided that Congress had not directly addressed the point of statutory construction, the court did *not* simply impose its own construction on the statute. Rather, if the statute was silent or ambiguous with respect to the specific issue, the question for the court was whether the agency's answer was based on a permissible construction of the statute. In answering this question the reviewing court might uphold the agency finding even though it was not the interpretation which the court itself would have adopted, and even though it was only one of a range of permissible such findings that could be made.[158] Moreover, the Supreme Court also held that the delegation to an agency of the determination of a particular issue may well be implicit rather than explicit, and that in such

---

[155] *Ibid.* p. 126.
[156] *Rochester Tel. Corp.* v. *United States* 307 US 125, 59 S. Ct. 754, 83 L.Ed. 1147 (1939); *Gray* v. *Powell* 314 US 402, 62 S. Ct. 326, 86 L.Ed. 301 (1941); *S.E.C* v. *Chenery Corp.* 332 US 194, 67 S. Ct. 1575, 91 L.Ed. 1995 (1947); *Ford Motor Co.* v. *N.L.R.B.* 441 US 488 (1979); *Ford Motor Credit Co.* v. *Milhollin* 444 US 555 (1980); *FEC* v. *Democratic Senatorial Campaign Committee* 454 US 27 (1981); *Mississippi Power and Light Company* v. *Mississippi, ex rel. Moore* 108 S.Ct. 2428, 2442-2444 (1988).
[157] 467 US 837 (1984) 84.
[158] *Ibid.* pp. 842-3.

instances "a court may not substitute its own construction of a statutory provision for a reasonable interpretation made by the administrator of an agency."[159]

It would, however, be misleading to say that the United States' courts have always utilised the rational basis test. As Davis has pointed out,[160] the Supreme Court has in a number of decisions simply substituted judgment without reference to the reasonableness or rational basis test. How far they will continue to do so in the light of the *Chevron* decision is another matter. However, it is clear that even *Chevron* allows a court to be more interventionist should it wish to be so. The court can clearly categorise the case as one in which Congress demands a specific interpretation of the particular statutory provision, or as one where the construction of the statute by the agency was not reasonable.[161]

Some evidence of a similar development is apparent in the Canadian jurisprudence. The decision of Reid J. in *Re Hughes Boat Works Incorporated and United Automobile Etc. Workers of America, Local 1620*[162] provides a good example. The applicant challenged a decision by the Ontario Labour Relations Board that the applicant was a purchaser of a business. If he was he would be bound by a pre-existing collective agreement that had been made between the union and North Star Yachts Ltd. The legislation contained a clause rendering the decision of the Board final and conclusive on the question of whether a business had been sold by one person to another. There was also a no certiorari clause which applied to all decisions of the Board. The applicant argued, not surprisingly, that the question as to whether he was a purchaser of the business was a collateral question, and that the privative clauses provided no bar to the court investigating such issues.

Reid J. reasoned as follows. He accepted that the distinction between jurisdictional and non-jurisdictional issues was difficult, if not impossible, to draw. It would be more profitable to concentrate on deciding what

---

[159] *Ibid.* p. 844. See also, *NLRB* v. *United Food and Commercial Workers Union, Local 23, AFL-CIO* 484 US 112, 123 (1987); *Mississippi Power* v. *Moore* 487 US 354, 380-382 (1988); *Sullivan* v. *Everhart* 494 US 83, 89 (1990), *Pension Benefit Guaranty Corporation* v. *LTV Corporation* 496 US 633, 648 (1990); *Department of the Treasury, Internal Revenue Service* v. *Federal Labour Relations Authority* 494 US 922, 928 (1990); *Armstrong World Industries, Inc.,* v. *Commissioner of Internal Revenue* 974 F.2d 422, 430 (3rd Cir. 1992); *West* v. *Sullivan* 973 F.2d 179, 185 (3rd Cir. 1992).

[160] *Administrative Law Text* (1972), Chap. 30. See, *e.g.*, *Davies Warehouse Co.* v. *Bowles* 321 US 144, 64 S. Ct. 474, 88 L.Ed. 635 (1944); *National Labor Relations Board* v. *Bell Aerospace Co.* 416 US 267, 40 L.Ed. 2d 134, 94 S.Ct. 1757 (1974).

[161] Gellhorn and Levin, *Administrative Law and Process* (3rd ed., 1990), pp. 83-92. See also, *Etsi Pipeline Project* v. *Missouri* 484 US 495, 517 (1988); *Pittston Coal Group* v. *Sebben* 488 US 105, 113 (1988); *Bowen* v. *Georgetown University Hospital* 488 US 204, 212 (1988); *Adams Fruit Company, Inc.,* v. *Ramsford Barrett* 494 US 638, 649 (1990); *Department of the Treasury* 494 US 922 (1990); *Dole* v. *United Steelworkers of America* 494 US 26, 43 (1990); *NRDC* v. *Defense Nuclear Facilities Safety Board* 969 F.2d 1248, 1250-1251 (D.C.Cir. 1992).

[162] (1980) 102 D.L.R. (3d) 661.

factors should lead the courts to intervene in any particular case. Reid J. referred to previous authority in the area of labour relations,[163] and concluded that the court should only intervene if the Board's decision could not be rationally supported on a reasonable construction of the legislation.[164] The court[165] should use "reasonableness" rather than "correctness" as the criterion of judicial intervention because the tribunal had acquired expertise and sensitivity to the needs of the particular area.[166]

More recent jurisprudence of the Canadian courts has cast some doubt on the continuance of this approach,[167] and the Supreme Court has drawn the following distinction. If the issue is jurisdictional then the court will substitute judgment and intervene if the agency finding is wrong; deference to the agency's interpretation is said not to be warranted in this context. If the issue is non-jurisdictional then deference to agency expertise can be taken into account, as reflected in a standard of review framed in terms of reasonableness. However, it also appears to be the case that in deciding what issues are to be regarded as jurisdictional the court can take account of functional considerations, such as the expertise of the tribunal, and the rationale for its existence.[168] Notwithstanding this case law, the Supreme Court has also continued to apply general criteria of reasonableness to test agency interpretations, shorn of any harkings back to the language of jurisdictional error.[169]

---

[163] *Service Employees' International Union, Local No. 33* v. *Nipawin District Staff Nurses' Association* [1975] 1 S.C.R. 382, 41 D.L.R. (3d) 6; *Canadian Union of Public Employees, Local 963* v. *New Brunswick Liquor Corporation* [1979] 2 S.C.R. 227, 97 D.L.R. (3d) 417.

[164] (1980) 102 D.L.R. (3d) 661, 671.

[165] See further, *Re Liquor Control Board of Ontario and Ontario Liquor Board Employees' Union* [1981] 114 D.L.R. (3d) 715; *Re Att.-Gen. for Ontario and Keeling* [1981] 117 D.L.R. (3d) 165; *Re MacFarlane and Anchor Gap and Closure Corporation of Canada Ltd.* [1981] 124 D.L.R. (3d) 303.

[166] See generally Evans, Janisch, Mullan, Risk, *Administrative Law, Cases, Texts and Materials* (3rd ed., 1989).

[167] See *Syndicat des Employés de Production du Quebec et de L'Acadie* v. *Canada Labour Relations Board* [1984] 2 S.C.R. 412, 14 D.L.R. (4th) 457. For comment, see Evans, "Developments in Administrative Law: The 1984-1985 Term" (1986) 8 Supr. Ct. Rev. 1, 26-41; Evans "Developments in Administrative Law: The 1985-1986 Term" (1987) 9 Supr. Ct. Rev. 1, 50-56.

[168] *Union des Employés de Service, Local 298* v. *Bibeault* [1988] 2 S.C.R. 1048; *Public Service Alliance of Canada* v. *Attorney General of Canada* [1991] 1 S.C.R. 614. For critical appraisal of this approach see, Evans, "Developments in Administrative Law: The 1988-1989 Term" (1990) 1 Supr.Ct.L.R. (2nd.Series) 1, 9-24.

[169] *CAIMAW* v. *Paccar of Canada Ltd.* [1989] 2 S.C.R. 983. For a powerful reiteration of the rationale behind the courts' less interventionist approach, see the judgment of Wilson J. in *National Corn Growers' Assn.* v. *Canada Import Tribunal* [1990] 2 S.C.R. 1324, 1353, and in *Lester (1978) Ltd.* v. *U.A.J.A.P.P.I., Local 740* [1990] 3 S.C.R. 644, 650-656. For comment see, MacLauchlan, "Developments in Administrative Law: The 1989-1990 Term" (1991) 2 Supr.Ct.L.R. (2nd.Series) 1, 45-52.

(2) THE RATIONAL BASIS TEST AND THE APPROACH IN THE SOUTH YORKSHIRE CASE

The differences and similarities between the rational basis test and that in the *South Yorkshire Transport* case[170] should be made clear.

The important *difference* between the two is that under the rational basis test as applied in cases such as *Hearst* and *Chevron* it will be the agency's interpretation of the statutory term which is accepted if it is within the spectrum of possible rational interpretations which such a term could bear. By way of contrast the *South Yorkshire* case leaves this choice with the court itself which will determine the meaning which the statutory term should bear.

The *similarity* between the two formulations is that both allow some scope for agency evaluation. The *South Yorkshire* case, however, restricts this to the level of evaluating whether the reviewing court's criterion was established on the facts or not: if the term, even as defined by the reviewing court, is inherently imprecise, then the agency's application of it will not be overturned unless it was so aberrant as to be irrational.

(3) RATIONAL BASIS v. RIGHTNESS

What has influenced the courts in choosing between the rational basis test and that of rightness or substitution of judgment? Which test ought to be the standard for judicial review? These are two of the central questions which require consideration. Although separate, the questions are interrelated.

The courts in the United States normally do not articulate the reasons why they are using one approach rather than another. Unspoken premises guide the judicial hand. Nevertheless, as Davis points out,[171] a number of factors have influenced the judicial choice. The extent to which the court sympathises with the agency's result will be one factor tending towards use of the rational basis or reasonableness test. Other considerations will include the type of agency under review and the nature of the invalidity alleged. If, for example, the alleged error relates to the construction of a term with which the courts are familiar then this will tend towards substitution of judgment, whereas more specific or technical matters will normally lead to a greater degree of discretion being granted to the agency, the legal conclusion being expressed in the form of the rational basis test.

At this stage a cynic might well say that even if we adopted a United States' type of approach the courts would simply manipulate the labels. The label rational basis would simply be reflective of a conclusion already reached that the court does not wish to intervene. A test of rightness would indicate the opposite conclusion. How, our cynic might well ask, would this differ from the present position? The courts can express the same feeling by the creative choice as to whether an alleged defect should be characterised

---

[170] [1993] 1 All E.R. 289.
[171] *Administrative Law Text* (1972), Chap. 30. See also Davis, *Administrative Law of the Seventies* (1976), Chap. 30.

as an error of law. There is undoubtedly some truth in such observations. However, like many cynical statements, the point can be overplayed. The crux of the matter is that while one can accept the proposition that judicial labels often express a conclusion already reached, rather than dictate the result which should be arrived at, to infer that therefore the type of labels that we use are irrelevant is a *non sequitur*. For example, the extensive theory of review holds that all errors of law are jurisdictional. Intervention could be limited by defining an issue as one of fact and not law. Yet, the very thesis that all questions of law should be for the ordinary courts itself fashions the result that the court believes to be correct. Compare this to the labels used in the United States. Obviously the courts can and will choose as between rational basis and rightness depending, *inter alia*, on whether they are in accord with the interpretation reached by the agency. However, the labels used in the United States also react with and influence the result which the court believes to be correct. The premise underlying them expresses an unwillingness to be drawn into any alleged dichotomy between jurisdictional and non-jurisdictional fact.[172] The labels also tell us that the United States' courts see nothing absurd in admitting the multiplicity of meanings that a statutory term can have, nor in accepting that the agency's choice as to the precise meaning should govern. They also indicate that, despite this, the courts will often just substitute their own opinion.

The American approach will not offer some easy solution, let alone a panacea. By avoiding the insoluble problems surrounding jurisdictional terminology it does however focus on the relevant issues directly: whose opinion on the existence and meaning of a statutory term should be accepted, that of the agency or that of the courts? Once we can rid ourselves of the dual notions that some magic divides jurisdictional and non-jurisdictional questions and that all matters of law have one inexorably correct meaning which must *always* be supplied by the courts, we are in a position to make a reasoned choice. This choice allows us to accord primacy to the authority's interpretation, while still preserving judicial control. Given the diversity of tribunals, commissions, authorities, ministers and inquiries which constitute our administrative system, it would be surprising if we did not conclude that in some instances the rational basis test was the correct stance and in others a test of substitution of judgment.

Whether the diversity depicted above is reflected in the presence of two tests, rational basis and rightness, or whether we should simply work through the former, is largely a matter of semantics. If we preserve both standards of review we then have to assign different subject-matter areas to each test. If we work through the former alone the range of choice or the breadth of the spectrum will vary from area to area. Not only will it alter, but the spectrum might be reduced to one; a court could say that although hypothetically varying interpretations of a term are possible, they are convinced that their view is the correct one.

---

[172] The US courts have tangled with the jurisdiction test, but it is not now widely used as a device for determining judicial review: Gellhorn, Byse and Strauss, *Administrative Law* (7th ed., 1979) pp. 277-297.

(4) OBJECTIONS

(a) Certainty

One objection is that the proposed approach would produce uncertainty. The objection based upon uncertainty can be raised in a number of different forms, and it is important to distinguish between them.

First, it might be argued that to adopt a rational basis/rightness approach would create more uncertainty than if we proceeded on the hypothesis that all errors of law are jurisdictional. Uncertainty as used here relates to the difficulty which an applicant might have of *predicting* which test for review, rational basis or rightness, would be adopted in any particular case. This objection can, in one sense, be conceded. If the courts were to develop the idea that all errors of law are jurisdictional, defined the word law in a purely analytical way so that it embraced any, or almost any, application of a statutory term and substituted judgment on the meaning of that term, then a prospective applicant would be clear that the courts would intervene using that standard. But this is to say no more than that the presence of only one arbiter on the meaning of any of the conditions of jurisdiction produces more certainty than a division of responsibility. The courts would decide all questions of law using that word in the sense described above. Yet the price of certainty in this sense would be to reduce the competence of the initial decision-maker to a mere fact-finder, to deny any weight to its opinion on the interpretation of the constituent parts of the X question, and to embroil the courts in the minutiae of all the elements which comprise the conditions of jurisdiction. This is extremely difficult to justify either in terms of legislative intent, or in terms of the relative competence of the two institutions.

A second meaning of the term certainty relates to the *probability* that the court would *uphold* the finding of the initial decision-maker. This, after all, is the question of most practical concern to the applicant. In this respect the proposed test is, if anything, clearer than the two rivals. It will be extremely difficult for even the most experienced adviser to predict whether the reviewing court will accept that the interpretation of a term adopted by the initial decision-maker was right, in the sense of what the reviewing court believes to be the correct interpretation. Contrast this with the position under the proposed test. Within those areas covered by the rational basis part of the test there would be greater certainty. A criterion of reasonableness or rational basis is obviously a narrower standard of review. Other things being equal, there is a greater chance that the original decision will be upheld as having a rational basis, even if the interpretation is not the precise one which the court itself would have chosen.

If objections based on uncertainty have any validity, then that word must be being used in a third sense. It could mean that a claimant would be uncertain as to whether, on a rational basis test, an administrative authority would apply the *same meaning* to a term that it had used previously, or whether it would adopt a different interpretation. This is a problem from which the ordinary courts are not immune, but it is true that this type of uncertainty is absent from the rival schemes because there the courts lay down the precise meaning which a term should bear. To what extent this represents a significant quantitative problem is unclear. In any event, it is not insoluble. Principles of consistency could be developed under which an authority should not change the interpretation accorded to a term, even if the second interpretation was reasonable, without due notice. Indeed, this represents part of the larger problem of ensuring that administrative authorities accord due facilities for representation before the promulgation of rules.[173]

(b) Constitutional principle

A second possible objection to the rational basis/rightness approach is that it would be somehow inconsistent with the juridical basis on which judicial review has been built in this country. The inherent power of the courts to ensure that inferior jurisdictions remain within their assigned ambit has always, it may be argued, related to the legality of the findings that can be made and not their correctness. To adopt an approach akin to that used in the United States would be fundamentally to alter the rationale for judicial review.

There is undoubtedly truth in this argument, but it must be placed in perspective. The original conception of review is indeed that set out above. It has however always been fraught with difficulty; the line between legality and correctness has always been hard to define. The distinction appeared to be maintainable while the courts applied a very limited form of review. Once they moved towards the collateral fact doctrine the line became hazy at best. Any attempt at continued demarcation is impossible once the courts moved to a theory of extensive review for error of law. We can of course continue to talk in jurisdictional terminology; we can say that a tribunal's jurisdiction is conditional on it making no errors of law. It is, however, this very flexibility of the jurisdiction concept which, if pushed too far, contains the seeds of its own destruction, or at least redundancy. To regard the jurisdictional cloak as a vital precondition justifying judicial intervention, while allowing the categories of jurisdictional error to multiply, simply conceals reality. It provides a fragile mask for avoiding awkward questions. The conceptual basis of judicial review, that the courts are thereby enforcing the legislative will by ensuring that the authority remains within the limits of its assigned area, has never provided any sure guide as to the appropriate scope for review. Almost any answer that we give to this question can, if we so wish, be formally accommodated within the language of jurisdiction. It is high time that we assessed the desirability of judicial intervention in its own terms.

---

[173] A related problem arises where there is no formal administrative hierarchy, and hence different tribunals could give different meanings to the same term. In the absence of such hierarchies one should insist that all such tribunals apply the interpretation presently held by the courts to be reasonable.

(c) Which types of error?

A third objection which could be raised is that it would be undesirable if the suggested approach were to be applied to certain types of jurisdictional error. The twin foundations for the standard advocated were that in choosing between a range of possible reasonable interpretations of statutory terms the precise meaning attached by the tribunal may be preferable to that of the court, and that this approach can serve to maintain the appropriate control of administrative authorities without the necessity for wholesale substitution of judgment. This has no application when the type of substantive error is that the tribunal was improperly constituted, or that it made an order which it was not empowered to make. Where the statute simply states that a fine of £50 is the maximum that can be imposed, arguments concerning rational basis are irrelevant.[174]

---

[174] Nor is there any suggestion that the test should be applied in the context of procedural error, *i.e.* if the rules of natural justice have been breached, the decision should not be upheld on the basis that the substantive decision has some rational basis.

11. DISCRETION

Section 1. Introduction

1. *Discretion: Types of Constraint*

At the inception of the previous chapter it was said that all grants of power to public bodies could be broken into two parts: if X exists, you may or shall do Y. This chapter will be principally concerned with the judicial constraints imposed upon the Y level. Discretion may well also exist on the X level, in the conditions which determine the scope of the tribunal's jurisdiction. The cases which are illustrative of this have already been considered within the general discussion of jurisdiction,[1] but will be referred to in the course of the following analysis where they are of relevance.

This is not the place for a jurisprudential analysis on the nature of discretion.[2] Discretion for the purposes of this chapter will be defined as existing where there is power to make choices between courses of action or where, even though the end is specified, a choice exists as to how that end should be reached.

There are three principal ways in which such discretion can be controlled. First, the courts can impose controls on the *way in which* the discretion is exercised. The objective is to ensure that there is no *failure* to exercise the discretion which has been vested in the decision-maker. Limitations on delegation, and on the extent to which an authority can proceed through policies or rules, provide the two main limbs of this type of constraint.

Secondly, the judiciary can impose limits on *whose* views should be taken into account when discretion is exercised. Such constraints are in principle related to the process by which the discretion is exercised. However, as we shall see, the line between substantive and procedural oversight of discretion is difficult to maintain.

Thirdly, constraints can be placed upon the *means* which an authority can adopt and the *ends* which it can pursue in order to ensure that there is no *misuse of power*. The concepts of relevancy, purpose and reasonableness have traditionally provided the main mechanisms through which this type of control is expressed, although concepts such as proportionality, fundamental rights and legitimate expectations are now playing an increasing

---

[1] See above, pp. 368-370.
[2] See generally, Galligan, *Discretionary Powers, A Legal Study of Official Discretion* (1986); Hawkins (ed.) *The Uses of Discretion* (1992).

role in this area. Substantive limits are placed on the power of the public body, and the appropriate test for such limits is a topic of much contention.

2. *Discretion: The Rationale for Intervention*

The conceptual rationale for judicial intervention in this area is, as will be seen, in a state of flux.

The *traditional rationale* has already been examined.[3] When the courts intervene to control the X factor they do so in purported fulfilment of the legislative will, by delineating the boundaries of one institution's powers from that of another: a public body adjudicating on furnished tenancies cannot trespass on the territory of a different body dealing with unfurnished tenancies. The rationale for judicial intervention on the Y level has always been more indirect. The authority is within its assigned area, in the sense that it is, for example, properly adjudicating on furnished premises. The issue now is as to the rationale for judicial control over, for example, the fair rent which should be charged for such premises. Traditional theory posited the link with sovereignty and with the *ultra vires* doctrine in the following manner: Parliament only intended that such discretion should be exercised on relevant and not irrelevant considerations, or to achieve proper and not improper purposes. Any exercise of discretion which contravened these limits was *ultra vires*. The ease with which the judicial approach can be reconciled with sovereignty demonstrates the limits of that concept as an organising principle for administrative law. Almost any such controls can be formally squared with legislative intent.

It is in part because of this that the more *modern conceptual rationale* bases judicial intervention on rather different grounds. Legislative intent and the will of Parliament are still regarded as of relevance, but the judicial controls are seen as being as much concerned with *supplementing* legislative intent as with *implementing* it. On this view the judicial role is to fashion and enforce *principles of fair administration* in accordance with the rule of law.[4] The implications of this will become apparent in the discussion which follows.

3. *Structure of the Chapter*

The discussion within this chapter will focus on the main themes which arise in this area. The first part of the analysis will examine the constraints relating to the *way in which* the discretion is exercised. How far can the decision-maker delegate to another? How far can it proceed by way of

---

[3] See above, pp. 4–9.
[4] See above, pp. 17–19. Sir Harry Woolf, *Protection of the Public – A New Challenge* (1990), pp. 122–124.

policies rather than through giving individualised consideration to each and every case?

Later sections of this chapter will be concerned with the substantive controls which are placed upon *means* and *ends*. The present law will be considered, to be followed by a discussion of other principles which are becoming of relevance within this area. The possible tests for substantive control will be evaluated as part of this analysis.

Section 2. Failure to Exercise Discretion

A decision may be attacked because the court may feel that the *means* whereby the decision has been reached amount to a *failure* to exercise the discretion which has been granted to the primary decision-maker. This can occur in four different ways. First, the public body in whom the discretion is vested may have unlawfully delegated the decision-making to another. Secondly, the body may have bound itself by a predetermined policy, which the courts feel has precluded that body from exercising its discretion in a particular case. Thirdly, the body in whom the discretion is vested may be bound by a contract which prevents it from exercising its discretion. Fourthly, the public body itself, or one of its officials, may have made a representation as to how its discretion would be exercised, and the representee seeks to keep the authority to its representation through the medium of estoppel. The first and second of these problems will be considered here. Those relating to contracts and estoppel will be dealt with later; they raise wider issues which it is more appropriate to discuss separately.

1. *Delegation*

(1) GENERAL PRINCIPLES

The general starting point is that if discretion is vested in a certain person it must be exercised by that person. This principle finds its expression in the maxim *delegatus non potest delegare*. It is important, however, to bear in mind that the maxim is expressive of a principle and not a rigid rule. Whether a person other than that named in the empowering statute is allowed to act will be dependent upon the entire statutory context, taking into account the nature of the subject-matter, the degree of control retained by the person delegating, and the type of person or body to whom the power is delegated.[5]

Thus, in *Allingham* v. *Minister of Agriculture*[6] the court held that it was unlawful for a wartime agricultural committee, to which powers concerning cultivation of land had been delegated by the Minister of Agriculture, to

---

[5] Willis, "Delegatus non Potest Delegare" (1943) 21 Can. B.R. 257.
[6] [1948] 1 All E.R. 780.

delegate to an executive officer the choice of which particular fields should be subject to a certain type of cultivation. In *Ellis* v. *Dubowski*[7] a condition imposed by the licensing committee of a county council that it would not allow films to be shown unless certified for public exhibition by the Board of Film Censors, was held invalid as involving a transfer of power to the latter.[8] Numerous other instances exist in which the courts have found that an unlawful delegation has occurred.[9]

The type of power which is to be delegated will be of importance, though not conclusive. Thus, the courts are reluctant to allow further delegation of delegated legislative power.[10] Similarly, the courts are reluctant to sanction the delegation of judicial power. In *Barnard* v. *National Dock Labour Board*,[11] the National Dock Labour Board had lawfully delegated powers, including those over discipline, to the local Boards. The latter purported to delegate these to the port manager who suspended the plaintiff from work. This was held to be unlawful, the court stressing that a judicial function could rarely be delegated. In a subsequent case the House of Lords reached the same conclusion, though emphasising that there was no absolute rule that judicial or quasi-judicial functions could never be delegated; the golden rule was always to consider the entire statutory context.[12]

(2) AGENCY AND DELEGATION

The relationship between agency and delegation is difficult and the case law is often contradictory. It is best therefore to approach the matter by considering first principles and juxtaposing these to the decided cases.

(a) The creation of agency and delegation

Both delegation and agency involve an authorisation that someone may act on behalf of another. The types of things which may be delegated are limited, as indicated above. A glance at the leading treatise on agency indicates that limits also exist on the capacity of an agent. An agent can perform any act on behalf of a principal which the principal could execute, except for the purpose of executing a right, or power, or performing a

---

[7] [1921] 3 K.B. 621.

[8] See *Mills* v. *London County Council* [1925] 1 K.B. 213 where the opposite result was reached because the county council retained the power to review the decision made by the Film Censors; *R.* v. *Greater London Council, ex p. Blackburn* [1976] 1 W.L.R. 550; *R.* v. *Police Complaints Board, ex p. Madden* [1983] 1 W.L.R. 447.

[9] *e.g. Jackson, Stansfield & Sons* v. *Butterworth* [1948] 2 All E.R. 558; *Lavender H. & Son Ltd.* v. *Minister of Housing and Local Government* [1970] 1 W.L.R. 1231; *Ratnagopal* v. *Attorney General* [1970] A.C. 974.

[10] *King-Emperor* v. *Benoari Lal Sarma* [1945] A.C. 14; Aikman, "Sub-delegation of the Legislative Power" (1960) 3 Victoria Univ. of Wellington L.R. 69; Thorp, "The Key to the Application of the Maxim 'Delegatus non Potest Delegare'" (1972-1975) 2 Auck. U.L.J. 85.

[11] [1953] 2 Q.B. 18.

[12] *Vine* v. *National Dock Labour Board* [1957] A.C. 488. Terminology or "categories" can, however, still be important. The questionable decision in *R.* v. *Race Relations Board, ex p. Selvarajan* [1975] 1 W.L.R. 1686 was influenced by labelling the proceedings administrative.

duty imposed on the principal personally, the exercise of which requires discretion or skill, or where the principal is required by statute to do the act personally.[13] Although the ability both to delegate and to appoint an agent are limited, there is a difference as to presumption. Where public bodies possess powers the presumption is that the power should be exercised by the person named in the statute, though this is of course rebuttable; where private parties are concerned the norm is that a principal should be able to appoint an agent subject to the limits mentioned above.

This difference in presumption is, however, of importance and failure to comprehend it has led the courts into error. The error is the belief that principles of agency can "cure" an unlawful delegation. In the *Lever Finance*[14] case a planning officer represented to a developer that minor changes in a building plan were not material. The developer proceeded to build the houses, the residents complained, the developer applied for planning permission for the modifications and his application was rejected by the planning committee, the body duly authorised to make the decision. Lord Denning M.R. held that the public body was estopped from contesting the representation made by their planning officer who had acted within the scope of his ostensible authority. The result may well have been a just one and will be considered in more detail in the context of estoppel.[15] The importance of the case for present purposes is that it was clear from the statutory context that any delegation to the planning officer would have been *ultra vires*.[16] This cannot somehow magically be circumscribed by calling the officer an agent who acts within his ostensible authority. If the initial delegation to the officer would have been unlawful that is an end to the matter. A cure is not effected by saying that the officer possessed apparent authority, since one of the necessary conditions to make the parent responsible for the acts of its agent is that the parent was not deprived, *inter alia*, of the capacity to delegate authority of that kind to the agent.[17]

The correct position was stated by Denning L.J. (as he then was) in the *Barnard* case. It was argued that the unlawful delegation to the port manager could be cured by ratification of the Labour Board. Denning L.J. rejected this, stating that the effect of ratification is to make the action equal to a prior command. However, since a prior command in the form of delegation would be unlawful, so also would ratification.[18]

A second example may be taken from cases concerning local authorities. A number of cases have raised the problem of a delegate who takes certain action, for example, to institute legal proceedings, without prior approval; the authority whose approval is required then purports to ratify the action

---

[13] *Bowstead on Agency* (15th ed., 1985), p. 36.
[14] *Lever Finance Ltd.* v. *Westminster (City) London Borough Council* [1971] 1 Q.B. 222.
[15] See below, Chap. 18.
[16] Craig, "Representations By Public Bodies" (1977) 93 L.Q.R. 398, 404-408.
[17] *Freeman & Lockyer* v. *Buckhurst Park Properties (Mangal) Ltd.* [1964] 2 Q.B. 480, 506.
[18] [1953] 2 Q.B. 18, 39-40. See also, *Western Fish Products Ltd.* v. *Penwith District Council* [1981] 2 All E.R. 204, discussed below pp. 657-658.

already undertaken.[19] Two issues become intertwined and have not always been distinguished. One is whether ratification could occur at the stage the proceedings had reached. The other is whether the officer instituting the proceedings was capable of doing so at all, i.e. whether that task could ever be validly delegated to that person.

(b) The characteristics of agency and delegation

A question that has also produced contradictory answers from the courts is the extent to which a lawful delegation of authority partakes of the attributes of a normal principal/agent relationship. Two aspects of that relationship are of particular importance.

The first is that an agent acts on behalf of and in the name of the principal. Acts carried out by the agent within the scope of the agent's authority become those of the principal. The same is in general true with delegation. Indeed one of the factors likely to invalidate any delegation would be an attempt to render the delegate "independent" from the delegating authority, in the sense of giving authority to exercise power in the delegate's own name. However, as has been pointed out,[20] the delegation of legislative power by Parliament, or the valid sub-delegation thereof, does not fit so easily into the above framework; here the delegate or sub-delegate would normally exercise power in her own name.

A second issue is whether the person delegating retains power concurrently with the delegate in the way that a principal retains power with an agent. On principle there is no reason why this should not be so and there is authority supporting this view.[21] However Scott L.J. in *Blackpool Corporation* v. *Locker*[22] reached the opposite conclusion. The Minister of Health had delegated power to the Corporation or its town clerk to requisition property subject to certain conditions, which conditions were not complied with on the facts of the case, thereby rendering the requisition by the Corporation inoperative. Scott L.J. stated that the relationship between the minister and Corporation or town clerk was not one of principal/agent, that there had been a sub-delegation of legislative power and that this divested the minister of any concurrent power unless he had expressly reserved such power to himself.[23] In the absence of any such reservation a later attempt by the minister himself to requisition the property was inoperative.

---

[19] *Firth* v. *Staines* [1897] 2 Q.B. 70; *R.* v. *Chapman, ex p. Arlidge* [1918] 2 K.B. 298; *Bowyer, Philpott & Payne Ltd.* v. *Mather* [1919] 1 K.B. 419; *Warwick Rural District Council* v. *Miller-Mead* [1962] Ch. 441.

[20] de Smith, *Judicial Review of Administrative Action* (4th ed., 1980), p. 301.

[21] *Huth* v. *Clark* (1890) 25 Q.B.D. 391; *Gordon Dadds & Co.* v. *Morris* [1945] 2 All E.R. 616, 621. *cf. Battelley* v. *Finsbury Borough Council* (1958) 56 L.G.R. 165.

[22] [1948] 1 K.B. 349, Asquith L.J. agreed with Scott L.J.

[23] *Ibid.* pp. 365, 367-368, 377.

The case has been criticised by writers[24] and doubted in the courts. In *Lewisham Borough Council* v. *Roberts*,[25] Denning L.J., on similar facts, stated that the town clerk was an agent of the Ministry, that the delegation, whether general or specific, was not a legislative act, and that it did not divest the government of its powers. The *Locker* case was said to turn on the inability of the minister to ratify the acts of an agent who had exceeded the assigned authority.

On the facts of the *Locker* and *Roberts* cases the opinion of Denning L.J. is to be preferred: the relationship resulting from the lawful delegation was analogous to one of principal/agent, with the former possessing power concurrently with the latter. However, the essence of what Scott L.J. was saying in *Locker* should not be dismissed so easily. We saw that the ordinary model of the agent acting on behalf of the principal did not fit easily into a delegation or sub-delegation of legislative power, where the delegate or sub-delegate would normally exercise power in his or her own name. By extension of the same reasoning, where the power delegated or sub-delegated *is* legislative then it makes sense that the delegator should not have concurrent powers.

(3) GOVERNMENT DEPARTMENTS

It is accepted that where powers are granted to a minister they can be exercised by the department. This is clearly sensible since it would be impossible for the minister personally to give consideration to each case. The authority for the official to act need not be conferred by the minister personally. It may be granted in accordance with departmental practice,[26] but it is unclear whether it is necessary for the officer to act explicitly on behalf of the minister.[27] The ability to delegate may be limited where the empowering statute explicitly states that certain functions must be performed by the minister in person.[28]

It is uncertain whether, apart from this, there is a class of case in which the minister must personally direct his or her mind to the issue. It has been stated that such a distinction would be impossible to apply and that it is not established by the case law.[29] Some other cases dealing with personal liberty such as deportation[30] and fugitive offenders[31] left the matter more open.

---

[24] Jackson, "County Agricultural Executive Committees" (1952) 68 L.Q.R. 363, 375-376.
[25] [1949] 2 K.B. 608, 621-622.
[26] *Carltona Ltd.* v. *Commissioner of Works* [1943] 2 All E.R. 560; *Lewisham Borough Council* v. *Roberts* [1949] 2 K.B. 608; *R.* v. *Skinner* [1968] 2 Q.B. 700; *Re Golden Chemical Products Ltd.* [1976] Ch. 300; *Bushell* v. *Secretary of State for the Environment* [1981] A.C. 75; *R.* v. *Secretary of State for the Home Department, ex p. Oladehinde* [1991] 1 A.C. 254. See generally, Lanham, "Delegation and the Alter Ego Principle" (1984) 100 L.Q.R. 587.
[27] *Woollett* v. *Minister of Agriculture and Fisheries* [1955] 1 Q.B. 103, 120-121.
[28] *R.* v. *Secretary of State for the Home Department, ex p. Oladehinde* [1991] 1 A.C. 254, 303.
[29] *Re Golden Chemical Products Ltd.* [1976] Ch. 300, 309-310.
[30] *R.* v. *Superintendent of Chiswick Police Station, ex p. Sacksteder* [1918] 1 K.B. 578, 585-586, 591-592.
[31] *R.* v. *Governor of Brixton Prison, ex p. Enahoro* [1963] 2 Q.B. 455, 466.

However, it has now been held by the House of Lords in the *Oladehinde* case[32] that the power to deport can be delegated to immigration inspectors who were of a suitable grade and experience, provided that this did not conflict with the officers' own statutory duties.

In the above cases concerning officers acting on behalf of ministers the better view is that there is no delegation as such at all; the responsible officers are the *alter ego* of the minister who maintains responsibility before Parliament.[33] It is doubtful whether this principle can apply outside the sphere of government departments. If action taken by an individual is to be regarded as lawful, it must be by showing that a delegation or sub-delegation, express or implied, was allowed by the legislation.[34]

(4) STATUTORY POWER

Power to delegate will often be granted by statute, a prominent example of this being the Local Government Act 1972 authorising local authorities to discharge any of their functions by committees, officers, or acting jointly with other local authorities.[35] Similar powers exist in other areas such as planning.

2. *Rules/Policies and Discretion*

Unlawful delegation is one way in which a public body may be held to have failed to exercise its discretion. A second is where the public body adopts a policy which precludes it from considering the merits of a particular case. Two related, but distinctive issues, will be separated in the discussion which follows. First, given that a public authority does have a policy or rule, what test should the courts apply in determining whether such a general policy should be allowed to stand; and if it does uphold the rule, what further consequences should ensue, in terms of, for example, allowing participation in the rule-making process? Secondly, if a public body does not have a rule or policy, how far can and should the courts go in actually encouraging the agency to make such rules? The words policy and rule will be used interchangeably for the present.

(1) AN EXISTING RULE OR POLICY: THE PRESENT LAW

(a) *General principles*

A public body endowed with discretionary powers is not entitled to adopt a policy or rule which allows it to dispose of a case without any consideration of the merits of the individual applicant who is before it. In *R. v. London County Council, ex p. Corrie*[36] the court quashed a decision

---

[32] [1991] 1 A.C. 254.
[33] *e.g. R. v. Skinner* [1968] 2 Q.B. 700, 707; *Nelms* v. *Roe* [1970] 1 W.L.R. 4, 8.
[34] *Nelms* v. *Roe* [1970] 1 W.L.R. 4.
[35] ss.101, 102; *R. v. Secretary of State for the Environment, ex p. Hillingdon London Borough Council* [1986] 1 W.L.R. 192, affirmed [1986] 1 W.L.R. 807.
[36] [1918] 1 K.B. 68.

refusing the applicant permission to sell pamphlets at certain meetings. The decision had been taken in reliance upon a council bylaw that nothing was to be sold in parks. Darling J. stated that each application must be heard on its merits; there could not be a general resolution to refuse permission to all.[37] This did not mean that a public body is precluded from having any general policy/rule at all. A general policy is allowed provided that due consideration of the merits of an individual case takes place, and provided that the content of the policy is regarded as *intra vires*.[38]

(b) The weight to be given to the policy/rule

As has been pointed out,[39] the weight which the courts allow a public body to accord to its policy or rule has differed. The stronger line of authority allows the body to apply its rule provided only that the individual is granted the opportunity to contest its application to the particular case.

Thus, in *ex p. Kynoch,* Bankes L.J.[40] contrasts two situations, the former being permissible, the latter not. It is lawful for an authority to adopt a policy, to intimate to the applicant what that policy is, and to tell that person that it will apply the policy after a hearing, unless there is something exceptional in the case. It is, however, not permissible for the authority to make a determination not to hear any application of a particular character. A similar approach was adopted in *British Oxygen Co. Ltd* v. *Board of Trade.*[41] The Board of Trade exercised the discretion that it was given under the Industrial Development Act 1966 in deciding not to give grants towards expenditure of less than £25. BOC had spent a large sum on gas cylinders, the individual cost of which was however only £20, and it sought a declaration that the Board of Trade's practice was unlawful. Lord Reid disagreed. His Lordship stated that while anyone possessing a discretion could not shut his ears to an application, and while there may be cases where it should listen to arguments that its "rules" should be changed, an authority was entitled to have a policy. This policy would have evolved over a multitude of similar cases and might well have become so precise that it

---

[37] *Ibid.* p. 73; *R.* v. *Flintshire County Council Licensing (Stage Plays) Committee, ex p. Barrett* [1957] 1 Q.B. 350; *Att.-Gen., ex rel. Tilley* v. *London Borough of Wandsworth* [1981] 1 W.L.R. 854.
[38] Numerous cases could be cited. See, *e.g. Boyle* v. *Wilson* [1907] A.C. 45; *R.* v. *Torquay Licensing Justices, ex p. Brockman* [1951] 2 K.B. 784; *Merchandise Transport Ltd.* v. *British Transport Commission* [1962] 2 Q.B. 173, 186, 193; *R.* v. *Commissioner of Police of the Metropolis, ex p. Blackburn* [1968] 2 Q.B. 118, 136, 139; *R.* v. *Commissioner of Police of the Metropolis, ex p. Blackburn (No. 3)* [1973] Q.B. 241; *R.* v. *Tower Hamlets London Borough Council, ex p. Kayne-Levenson* [1975] 1 Q.B. 431, 440, 453.
[39] Galligan, "The Nature and Function of Policy within Discretionary Power" [1976] P.L. 332, 346-355. The article contains a valuable analysis.
[40] *R.* v. *Port of London Authority, ex p. Kynoch Ltd.* [1919] 1 K.B. 176, 184; *Boyle* v. *Wilson* [1907] A.C. 45, 57.
[41] [1971] A.C. 610.

could be called a rule. That was acceptable provided that the authority was willing to listen to anyone who had something new to say.[42]

There are, however, some cases which allow only a more minor role to be played by the policy. It is allowed to be but one relevant factor used by the public body in arriving at its determinations. Thus in *Stringer* v. *Minister of Housing and Local Government*[43] Cooke J. reviewed the legality of a policy which restricted planning permission for developments which could interfere with the Jodrell Bank telescope. He held that the general policy could stand provided that it did not inhibit the taking account of all issues relevant to each individual case which came up for determination.[44]

The difference between the two approaches is brought out well by Galligan.[45]

"The implications of this more restrictive approach are that not only must an authority (a) direct itself to whether in the light of the particular situation a predetermined policy ought to be altered, but also (b) must refrain from regarding a policy as anything more than one factor amongst others to take into account. In other words a policy may not become a norm which, subject only to (a) determines the outcome of particular decisions."

Recent authority has endorsed the less restrictive approach,[46] and the reasons for preferring this will be examined below.

(c) Control over the substance of the policy

It is clear on authority[47] and on principle that the policy must be one which is legitimate given the statutory framework in which the discretion is granted. It must be based upon relevant considerations and must not be attempting to achieve improper purposes.[48] These controls are necessary

---

[42] *Ibid.* p. 625; *Cumings* v. *Birkenhead Corporation* [1972] 1 Ch. 12; *R.* v. *Tower Hamlets London Borough Council, ex p. Kayne-Levenson* [1975] 1 Q.B. 431; *Kilmarnock Magistrates* v. *Secretary of State for Scotland* (1961) S.C. 350; *R.* v. *Secretary of State for the Environment, ex p. Brent London Borough Council* [1982] Q.B. 593, 640-642.

[43] [1970] 1 W.L.R. 1281, 1297-1298.

[44] See also, *H. Lavender & Son Ltd.* v. *Minister of Housing and Local Government* [1970] 1 W.L.R. 1231, 1240-1241; *Sagnata Investments Ltd.* v. *Norwich Corporation* [1971] 2 Q.B. 614.

[45] [1976] P.L. 332, 349.

[46] *e.g. R.* v. *Rochdale Metropolitan Borough Council, ex p. Cromer Ring Mill Ltd.* [1982] 3 All E.R. 761; *R.* v. *Eastleigh Borough Council, ex p. Betts* [1983] 2 A.C. 613, 627-628; *Re Findlay* [1985] A.C. 318, 334-336. *cf. R.* v. *Windsor Licensing Justices, ex p. Hodes* [1983] 1 W.L.R. 685; *R.* v. *Secretary of State for the Environment, ex p. Brent London Borough Council* [1982] Q.B. 593, 640-642.

[47] *e.g. British Oxygen Co. Ltd.* v. *Board of Trade* [1971] A.C. 610, 623-624; *Cumings* v. *Birkenhead Corporation* [1972] 1 Ch. 12, 37-38; *R.* v. *London Borough of Lambeth, ex p. Ghous* [1993] C.O.D. 302.

[48] For a consideration of these concepts, see pp. 405-409.

since otherwise a public authority could escape the normal constraints upon the exercise of discretion by framing general policies.

However, the extent of control that the courts should be exercising is more questionable, in particular when the courts demand evidence and facts for hypotheses which are not susceptible to such clear-cut analysis. Thus, while it may be the case that one could test factually whether the Jodrell Bank telescope would function less efficiently if planning permission were granted for houses, it is much less easy to test assumptions such as whether amusement arcades have a socially deleterious effect upon young people. Yet the courts have struck down decisions in pursuance of policies of the latter type for just this reason.[49] To insist on the type of factual "back-up" which the majority demanded in the *Sagnata* case appears excessive.[50]

(d) Rules and process rights

The existence of a rule or policy which is upheld by the courts under the preceding tests raises important questions concerning process rights. Three such questions must be distinguished.

First, the individual may wish to argue that the policy *should not be* applied to the particular case. There is authority for the view that such an applicant should be informed of what the policy entails, this being necessary if there is to be any effective right to challenge it.[51] The extent of this right is unclear. There may, depending on the circumstances, be a right to a hearing of some type. It is, however, unclear whether the individual would be entitled to an oral hearing,[52] although the answer would be in the affirmative if the applicant were normally entitled to this degree of protection. Equally it is not certain whether the individual can only challenge the application of the policy to the instant case, or whether the substance of the policy itself can be questioned. The latter issue can clearly be raised at the stage of judicial review, the question being whether the individual can raise the matter before the authority itself.[53]

---

[49] *Sagnata Investments Ltd.* v. *Norwich Corporation* [1971] 2 Q.B. 614. There is a marked difference in approach between Lord Denning M.R. (dissenting) and Edmund Davies and Phillimore L.JJ.

[50] It should be borne in mind that the test should be not what evidence a social scientist with full research grant and expertise, etc., could produce, but what evidence would be available to the Corporation, apart from the general feeling that such places were a bad influence on the young.

[51] e.g. *ex p. Kynoch* [1919] 1 K.B. 176, 184; *R.* v. *Torquay Licensing Justices, ex p. Brockman* [1951] 2 K.B. 748, 788; *R.* v. *Criminal Injuries Compensation Board, ex p. Ince* [1973] 1 W.L.R. 1334, 1344-1345.

[52] In the *British Oxygen* case Lord Reid stated that the hearing did not have to be oral, [1971] A.C. 610, 625.

[53] Contrast *Boyle* v. *Wilson* [1907] A.C. 45, 57, where the court doubted whether the applicant could challenge the policy itself, with *British Oxygen*, where Lord Reid thought that there were instances where this was possible, [1971] A.C. 610, 625. The latter view is supported by *R.* v. *Criminal Injuries Compensation Board, ex p. Ince* [1973] 1 W.L.R. 1334, 1344.

The second situation is the converse of the first. The individual may wish to argue that an established policy *should be* applied to the particular case, while the public body may wish to change its policy or resile from it. Consideration of this issue overlaps with that of representations and estoppel.[54] The law in this area is still developing, and frequent use has been made of the concept of legitimate expectations, which has already been considered in the context of natural justice.[55] The general position would appear to be as follows.

(i) If a public body has made a representation to a specific individual or group of individuals that a particular policy will be followed, or that they will be informed before any such change in policy takes place, then the individual will be entitled to insist that this policy is pursued in relation to the instant case, provided that the implementation does not conflict with the authority's statutory duty; or at least there should be an opportunity of commenting before any such change occurs.[56]

(ii) If an individual has in the past enjoyed a benefit or advantage which could legitimately be expected to continue, that person may be entitled to a statement of reasons for the change of position, and an opportunity to be consulted thereon.[57]

(iii) The existence and content of any such expectation, whether arising from a representation or past practice, may well be contentious. Thus in *ex p. Khan*[58] Parker L.J. was willing to hold that a Home Office circular concerning adoption procedures for foreign children generated a legitimate expectation that the procedures therein would be followed. The minister could not depart from them without affording the applicants a hearing and then only if the public interest demanded it. However, in *Re Findlay*[59] a change of policy concerning parole was not held to infringe the legitimate expectations of certain prisoners, notwithstanding the fact that they would, under the previous policy, have expected earlier release. The content of the prisoners' legitimate expectation was only that their cases would be individually considered under whatever policy the minister sought fit to adopt.[60]

---

[54] See below, Chap. 18.
[55] See above, pp. 294-296.
[56] *e.g. Att.-Gen. of Hong Kong v. Ng Yuen Shiu* [1983] 2 A.C. 629; *R. v. Liverpool Corporation, ex p. Liverpool Taxi Fleet Operators' Association* [1972] 2 Q.B. 299; *ex p. Khan* [1985] 1 All E.R. 40; *Council of Civil Service Unions v. Minister for the Civil Service* [1985] A.C. 374, 408-409; *R. v. Secretary of State for the Home Department, ex p. Ruddock* [1987] 1 W.L.R. 1482.
[57] *e.g. C.C.S.U.* [1985] A.C. 374, 408-409; *R. v. Secretary of State for the Home Department, ex p. Khan* [1985] 1 All E.R. 40; *ex p. Ruddock* [1987] 1 W.L.R. 1482. Cases may be difficult to classify as type (i) or (ii) particularly where, as in *Khan* or *Ruddock*, there is a circular in question. This could be regarded either as a type of representation or as the past practice justifying the legitimate expectation. See also, *R. v. Secretary of State for Transport, ex p. Greater London Council* [1986] Q.B. 556.
[58] [1985] 1 All E.R. 40.
[59] [1985] A.C. 318.
[60] *Ibid.* p. 338 See also, *Re Westminster City Council* [1986] A.C. 668, 692-693, 716.

The third aspect of process rights and rules is the most general. As we have seen, the traditional position has been that the courts do not in general apply the principles of natural justice or fairness to legislative proceedings: there is no general right to participate in rule-making.[61] How far such a right should be developed, and how far it can be derived from the authorities concerned with legitimate expectations, has been considered above.[62]

(2) NO EXISTING RULE OR "INSUFFICIENT" RULES

(a) The debate over rules v. discretion

The discussion thus far has focused upon the appropriate judicial response to a situation where an agency has made rules. There is, however, an important literature concerning the extent to which an agency should actually be encouraged to make rules rather than proceeding by way of individual discretionary decisions. Davis was responsible for much of the early work in this area.[63]

He begins by making clear the importance of discretionary action: while informal adjudication may be more important than formal adjudication, the former is only one part of discretionary action taken as a whole. Discretion is a vital tool in society aiding the individualisation of justice, and no society has existed in which discretion has been absent. Writers and theorists[64] who have expressed a yearning for a purely rule-based government from which discretion has been expunged (what Davis terms the extravagant version of the rule of law), were postulating an ideal which has and could never be attained by any country. Although Davis therefore rejects the extravagant rule of law doctrine, the purpose of the book is to argue that, while discretion may be indispensable, there is "too much of it".[65] He suggests two principal ways in which unnecessary discretion can be curtailed.

The first is to eliminate unnecessary discretionary power or *confine* it within necessary bounds.[66] This can be achieved by encouraging administrators to make standards and rules which will clarify vague legislative criteria. Courts should require an administrative agency to achieve this within a reasonable time. The agency should not feel hesitant about making rules for fear that they will involve too broad a generalisation, for Davis argues that such rules may be limited to the resolution of a narrow spectrum of cases. Development of agency policy through rule-making is felt to be preferable to such development being brought about through adjudication because it allows more consultation and participation by interested parties.

---

[61] See above, pp. 255-258.
[62] See above, pp. 255-262.
[63] *Discretionary Justice, A Preliminary Inquiry* (1969); *Discretionary Justice in Europe and America* (1976).
[64] Hayek, *The Road to Serfdom* (1944) and *The Constitution of Liberty* (1960).
[65] Davis, *Discretionary Justice, A Preliminary Inquiry* (1969), Chaps. 1-2.
[66] *Ibid.* Chap. 3.

The second method of controlling discretion is to ensure that it is *structured*.[67] Whereas the confining of discretion seeks to keep it within certain boundaries, structuring discretion is aimed at controlling the way in which that discretionary power is exercised within those boundaries. Davis suggests a number of ways in which this can be achieved: open plans, open policy statements and rules, open findings, open reasons, open precedents and fair procedure. The overall aim is not to exterminate discretion as if it were some wicked pariah. It is to find the optimum degree of structuring in respect of each discretionary power.

Structuring of discretion is not the only technique of control that is advocated. Discretion should also be *checked*. A variety of such checks can be used, supervision by superiors, administrative appeals and judicial review being just three.

A number of other writers have pursued similar themes, albeit with modifications. For example, Jowell[68] tabulates the merits and demerits of rules. The former include the clarification of organisational aims, thereby rendering it less likely that an official will take a decision based upon improper criteria, and that rules will be more exposed to public scrutiny, thereby rendering the administration more accountable. There are, moreover, the benefits of like cases being treated alike and the possibility of greater public participation in the formulation of goals. The defects of rules are familiar including in particular the legalism and rigidity that can be attendant upon them.[69] Despite such disadvantages other writers have joined in the call for more structuring of discretion.[70]

Reservations have, however, been expressed. It has been argued that where the issue is inherently subjective, such as that of "need" within social welfare, rules are unsuitable for resolution of the question. Another area where rules are said to be of limited value is that in which the problem is polycentric with a number of interacting points of influence such that alteration of one variable produces an effect on all the others.[71] A similar point is made by others who argue that agencies may not make rules because the issues are highly complex or controversial and the agency does not yet feel capable of committing itself, or wishes to gain more experience before doing so.[72]

---

[67] *Ibid.* Chap. 4.

[68] *Law and Bureaucracy* (1975), Chap. 1.

[69] *Ibid.* p. 22; "For example, a parking meter will not show understanding or mercy to the person who was one minute over the limit because he was helping a blind man across the street." See also Jowell, "Legal Control of Administrative Discretion" [1973] P.L. 178.

[70] *e.g.* Reich, "The New Property" 73 Yale L.J. 733 (1964); Molot, "The Self-Created Rule of Policy and Other Ways of Exercising Administrative Discretion" (1972) 18 McGill L.J. 310.

[71] Jowell, *Law and Bureaucracy*, Chap. 5.

[72] Bernstein, "The Regulatory Process: A Framework for Analysis" (1961) 26 L.C.P. 329; Shapiro, "The Choice of Rulemaking or Adjudication in the Development of Administrative Policy" 78 Harv.L.Rev. 921 (1965); Robinson, "The Making of Administrative Policy: Another Look at Rule-Making and Adjudication and Administrative Procedures Reform" 118 U.Pa.L.Rev. (1970); Baldwin and Hawkins, "Discretionary Justice: Davis Reconsidered" [1984] P.L. 570.

(b) Organisations, the decision-making process, rules and discretion

Any assessment of the relative merits of rules and discretion will often be based, implicitly or explicitly, upon assumptions as to how bureaucracies are structured, how they operate, and the decision-making process which operates therein. Some understanding of the literature within this area will therefore be of help in the debate about rules and discretion.

Interest in organisational structure emerged earlier this century with the work of the "classical" school of scientific management, the object being to discover the most efficient method of performing an assigned task, and the type of command structure most likely to effectuate the purposes of the organisation.[73] The work of the scientific school was directed initially at private industry, but was viewed with increasing interest by governments who sought to apply such ideas to public functions.[74]

Weber focused more directly upon the public sector when constructing his "ideal-type" bureaucracy.[75] The main attributes of a Weberian bureaucracy were that:[76] duties should be distributed in a fixed way as official duties; officers should be hierarchically ordered, being responsible to the person above, and responsible for those below; the institution should apply abstract rules to particular cases; the official should operate "without hatred or passion", neutrally applying the given rules; and advancement and dismissal should be objectively assessed. All aspects of the Weberian scheme are designed to ensure the objective, efficient pursuit of the task assigned to the agency.[77] Whether they do in fact achieve this is more debatable. For example, reserved detachment could hinder the development of *esprit de corps*, while the insistence on conformity could engender rigidity and inhibit the rational exercise of judgment.[78]

More modern theory has reacted against the "mechanistic" aspects of earlier analysis. One strand has emphasised the role of more complex motivational considerations which operate on the individual.[79] Another, more promising strand, has been the development of systems theory as a response to the perceived limitations of the earlier approaches. Drawing analogies from the biological sciences, organisations are perceived as

---

[73] *e.g.* Fayol, *Industrial and General Administration* (1930); Taylor, *Scientific Management* (1947).

[74] Brown and Steel, *The Administrative Process in Britain* (2nd ed., 1979), pp. 156-157.

[75] *The Theory of Social and Economic Organisation*, transl. by Henderson and Talcott Parsons (1947), pp. 302-313; Max Weber, *Essays in Sociology* (1946), pp. 196-245.

[76] For a succinct summary, see Blau and Meyer, *Bureaucracy in Modern Society* (2nd ed., 1971), pp. 18-23.

[77] *e.g.* the application of rules "without passion or hatred" is aimed at the exclusion of favouritism or bias.

[78] Blau and Meyer, *Bureaucracy in Modern Society*, pp. 23-24. See also, the criticisms and qualifications of the Weberian approach in Crozier, *The Bureaucratic Phenomenon* (1964); Burns and Stalker, *The Management of Innovation* (2nd ed., 1966); Meyer, *Change in Public Bureaucracies* (1979).

[79] *e.g.* March and Simon, *Organisations* (1958), Chap. 3; Argyris, *Personality and Organisation* (1957).

systems which have inputs, process those inputs and produce outputs.[80] The processing of inputs will have technical, social and structural aspects, all of which will combine to determine the shape which the organisation takes. Structural influences would, for example, be whether work was organised in terms of specific client groups or on geographical criteria. Social influences would include the organisation's own perception of the primary goals which it was seeking to pursue. The outputs would encompass the rules and regulations, etc., produced by the organisation. These will have to satisfy the demands placed upon the organisation by government, client groups, and affected parties. If they do not the institution will become endangered.

Systems theory has important ramifications for the rules/discretion debate. Lawyers tend to view decisions as relatively simple and discrete.[81] A more realistic picture would view them as "complex, subtle and woven into a broader process":[82] they result from a variety of intersecting inputs each of which may itself be a complex variable. This more realistic depiction of decision-making has three important consequences for the debate on rules and discretion.

First, if we decide that a certain administrative area should be more "rule-based", then we must be aware that this can lead to problems of displacement. An attempt to limit discretion in one part of the system can lead to its re-emergence elsewhere; "squeeze in one place, and, like tooth-paste, discretion will emerge at another".[83] Rendering sentencing more rule-based may, for example, increase the pre-trial discretion exercised by prosecutors since a person knows that if there is a guilty plea on a certain charge, there will necessarily be a particular sentence.[84]

Secondly, the Davis thesis emphasises what may be termed the external aspect of discretion: the potential for arbitrary action if agencies possess broad, unstructured discretionary power. However, organisational theory would also emphasise the internal aspect of discretion: systems theory would stress that the execution of a programme may be materially affected by the "managerial structures which are built and sustained in connection with it".[85] If discretion is permitted in the building of such an organisation, this may well affect the shape of the policy which emerges. To enshrine the external aspect of discretion, through its formulation into rules, without any regard for the internal aspect could simply reinforce existing imbalances. Thus if the internal organisational structure of an agency has been so constructed that the inputs and outputs favour particular interests,

---

[80] *e.g.* Bourn, *Management in Central and Local Government* (1979). See also, Brown and Steel, *The Administrative Process in Britain*, pp. 167-169; Self, *Administrative Theories and Politics* (1972), pp. 48-50; Evan, *Organisation Theory* (1976).
[81] Baldwin and Hawkins [1984] P.L. 570, 580-586.
[82] *Ibid.* p. 580.
[83] *Ibid.* p. 582.
[84] *Ibid.* pp. 582-583. See also, pp. 576-577.
[85] Selznick, *T.V.A. and the Grass Roots* (1949), p. 67; Brown and Steel, *The Administrative Process*, pp. 193-194.

a requirement that the agency should make rules to confine the external aspect of its discretion could simply reinforce these existing imbalances.[86]

Thirdly, and perhaps most fundamentally, attention to organisational structure is vital because the nature of this structure will necessarily be dependent upon the purpose which regulation is designed to serve in that area; and the choice of purpose will directly affect the balance between rules and discretion. This can be simply demonstrated. The structure of an organisation distributing benefits for disability will depend upon the objective behind such a scheme. One such objective has been termed "professional treatment", the idea being that decisions which are made should provide support or therapy viewed from the perspective of a particular professional culture.[87] Given this model, "the incompleteness of facts, the singularity of individual context, and the ultimately intuitive nature of judgment are recognised, if not exalted."[88] In such a system considerations of hierarchy and rules would have little role to play. To insist upon the structuring of discretion could undermine the very purpose of regulation.

(c) Conclusion

It is readily apparent that the optimum balance between rules and discretion will vary from area to area. Only careful analysis of particular regulatory contexts can reveal that balance. Given that this is so, one should treat with reserve suggestions that the courts should force or persuade agencies to develop more rules than they presently possess. The judiciary are not in a good position to assess whether the complex arguments for and against rule-making should lead to an increase in the prevalence of such rules within a particular area.

Section 3. Misuse of Power: I

The courts have, ever since the origins of judicial review, exerted control over the discretion exercised by tribunals, agencies and the like, in order to prevent that power from being misused or abused. Thus in *Rooke's Case*[89] Commissioners of Sewers had repaired a river bank and taxed R for the whole amount despite the fact that other landowners had benefited

---

[86] Such rules might make existing biases more overt and hence more open to attack. It is more likely that they would be built into the system and become the accepted way of administering it, but not be apparent on the face of the rules. Such rules need not appear absurd or even openly biased, see, *e.g.* the subtle but real prejudices at work within the T.V.A. in favour of wealthier farming interests, Selznick, Chaps. 3-5.

[87] Mashaw, *Bureaucratic Justice* (1983), pp. 25-27.

[88] *Ibid.* pp. 27-28. See generally, Craig, "Discretionary Power in Modern Administration", *Verwaltungsermessen im modernen Staat* (M. Bullinger ed., 1986), pp. 79-111.

[89] (1598) 5 Co. Rep. 99b. See also, *Hetley v. Boyer* (1614) Cro. Jac. 336; *R. v. Askew* (1768) 4 Burr. 218; *Leader v. Moxon* (1773) 2 W.B1. 924.

from the work. The Commissioners had a discretion as to the levying of the money, but the court struck their decision down: the discretion was to be exercised according to reason and law and it was unreasonable for R to bear the whole burden. The judiciary have, as will be seen, monitored the ends which such bodies have pursued in order to ensure, *inter alia*, that these ends are consonant with the empowering legislation. Discussion of this topic will be divided into two sections. The present law, including emerging concepts, will be considered within this section. The subsequent section will consider some of the broader issues which underly this topic, and place these newer trends in the case law within a broader frame.

1. *The Types of Power which Can be Controlled*

Before examining the types of controls which the courts impose it is important to understand the types of power which are subject to these controls. Certain points are clear.

First, *statutory discretionary power* is subject to the controls which are discussed below. Indeed, the majority of cases deal with just such discretionary powers which have been granted pursuant to a statute.

Secondly, it is now clear that *prerogative powers* are also subject to judicial review. The traditional position was, in the past, that the courts would control the existence and extent of prerogative power, but not the manner of exercise thereof.[90] There were, however, some dicta supporting a wider review power.[91] The traditional position has now been modified by the decision in the *G.C.H.Q.*[92] case. Their Lordships emphasised that the reviewability of discretionary power should be dependent upon the subject-matter thereof, and not whether its source was statute or the prerogative. Certain exercises of prerogative power would, because of their subject-matter, be less justiciable, and Lord Roskill compiled the broadest list of such forbidden territory.[93] Thus, in the actual case their Lordships held that although the minister had to adduce evidence that the decision to ban national unions at G.C.H.Q. was based on considerations of national security, the question of whether such considerations outweighed the prima

---

[90] *Case of Monopolies* (1602) 11 Co.Rep. 84b; *Prohibitions del Roy* (1607) 12 Co.Rep. 63; *Burmah Oil Co. Ltd.* v. *Lord Advocate* [1965] A.C. 75; *Att.-Gen.* v. *De Keyser's Royal Hotel Ltd.* [1920] A.C. 508; *Chandler* v. *D.P.P.* [1964] A.C. 763.
[91] *Chandler* [1964] A.C. 763, 809-810 (Lord Devlin); *Laker Airways Ltd.* v. *Department of Trade* [1977] Q.B. 643 (Lord Denning M.R.).
[92] *Council of Civil Service Unions* v. *Minister for the Civil Service* [1985] A.C. 374, 407, 411, 417-418.
[93] *Ibid.* p. 418. The making of treaties, the defence of the realm, the dissolution of Parliament, the appointment of ministers, as well as other areas where the subject-matter was not justiciable.

facie duty of fairness was for the minister himself to decide.[94] Subject to this important caveat, their Lordships were willing, albeit in varying degrees,[95] to consider the manner of exercise of prerogative power as well as adjudicating on its existence and extent. The success of such a challenge could also be affected by the ground of attack,[96] as well as the nature of the subject-matter. The ambit of the court's role in this area is exemplified by the decision in *Bentley*,[97] where it was held that the prerogative of mercy was subject to judicial review, and the court could stipulate the types of consideration which could be taken into account when exercising this power.

Thirdly, there is some debate as to whether public bodies possess discretionary powers which are neither statutory nor prerogative in nature, but which are more properly to be classified as common law discretionary powers.[98] For example, the power to contract can be regarded as an inherent common law power of this nature. Insofar as there is this further type of power the trend of the case law is, as seen above in the context of the prerogative, to base reviewability upon the subject-matter of the power and not its source.

Finally, the courts have imposed controls on the way in which discretion is exercised by bodies which are not themselves the creature of statute. The law in this area has been driven principally by developments relating to remedies, and its precise metes and bounds are still being worked out. There will be a detailed consideration of this issue within the chapter on remedies.[99]

2. *Levels of Review and Intensity of Review*

Before examining the actual case law in this area it may be of help in understanding this material to make some more general observations about both the *levels* at which review can operate, and the *intensity* of this review.

It is important to realise that there are essentially two differing *levels* at which the judicial controls can operate. On the one hand, the courts can act

---

[94] *Ibid.* pp. 402-403, 406-407, 412-413, 420-421, unless *semble* the minister's decision was one which no reasonable minister could make, p. 406. See also, *R. v. Secretary of State for the Home Department, ex p. Ruddock* [1987] 1 W.L.R. 1482, where the court emphasised that the evidence concerning national security must be cogent and that the court could, if necessary, hear such evidence in camera; *R. v. Secretary of State for Foreign and Commonwealth Affairs, ex p. Everett* [1989] 2 W.L.R. 224.
[95] Thus Lord Fraser and Lord Brightman reserved the question, not directly raised by the case, of whether the direct exercise of prerogative power would be subject to review, [1985] A.C. 374, 398 423-424.
[96] *e.g.* Lord Diplock stated that an applicant would be more likely to succeed if alleging illegality or procedural impropriety, as opposed to irrationality, *ibid.* p. 411. See generally, Walker, "Review of the Prerogative: The Remaining Issues" [1987] P.L. 62.
[97] *R. v. Secretary of State for the Home Department, ex p. Bentley* [1993] 4 All E.R. 442.
[98] Harris, "The 'Third Source' of Authority for Government Action" (1992) 109 L.Q.R. 626.
[99] See below, Chap. 15.

because the tribunal has, for example, used its discretionary power for a purpose not allowed by the legislation at all. On the other hand, judicial intervention may occur because the tribunal, while able in principle to use its power to reach a certain end, has done so in a manner which is felt to be unreasonable, irrational, or disproportionate. Lord Diplock's distinction in the G.C.H.Q.[100] case between review based upon illegality and that based upon irrationality captures the idea being presented here. Having said this it should be acknowledged that it may not always be easy to distinguish between the two levels, and that courts and commentators may differ as to whether a particular case should be placed within one or the other of these divisions. The reason is that statutes conferring broad discretionary powers do not have neat corners, nor is the process of statutory construction self-executing. Challenges which allege that an authority used its power illegally, may, therefore, not be easy to distinguish from those based upon irrationality. Moreover, the court may, in determining the permitted ambit of a broad discretionary power utilise substantive principles. These points should be noted, but they do not undermine the separate existence of the two levels of challenge.

This distinction is not merely a point of formal intellectual nicety. It has important substantive ramifications in both practical and conceptual terms. In practical terms much of the current debate has focused upon the type and degree of judicial control which should exist within the second category, and there have been calls for extending the scope of the substantive principles which operate at this level. This has, as will be seen, broader conceptual ramifications. While the main focus of control was at the first level the impression could be maintained that the courts were applying parliamentary intent, in the sense of delineating the purposes for which such discretionary power could legitimately be used. If the controls at the second level are expanded then it becomes much more difficult to preserve this rationale for judicial intervention. The courts' role shifts inevitably towards ensuring principles of fair administration.

This naturally leads us to a consideration of the *intensity* of judicial review. One facet of review which is becoming increasingly prominent is for the courts to adopt a variable standard of review, the intensity of which alters depending upon the subject-matter of the action. Terms such as irrationality or proportionality can be applied with differing degrees of rigour or intensity. This feature has become more marked as the courts have shown a greater willingness to protect individual rights, employing more intensive review in such instances. This can be briefly demonstrated by contrasting two recent decisions. In the *Brind* case,[101] to be considered fully below, a number of their Lordships made it clear that if the exercise of discretionary power impinged upon a fundamental right then the courts would require an important competing public interest to be shown in order to justify this intrusion. By way of contrast in the *Hammersmith* case[102] the

---

[100] [1985] A.C. 374, 410-411.

[101] R. v. *Secretary of State for the Home Department, ex p. Brind* [1991] 1 A.C. 696.

[102] R. v. *Secretary of State for the Environment, ex p. Hammersmith and Fulham London Borough Council* [1991] 1 A.C. 521.

House of Lords reviewed charge capping by the Secretary of State which the applicant local authorities claimed was in breach of the relevant statute. In the course of reaching his decision Lord Bridge, giving the judgment of the court, held that while the court could intervene if the Secretary of State had acted illegally (for improper purposes, or on irrelevant considerations), it should, in this sphere of economic policy, be very wary of review based upon irrationality unless there was some manifest absurdity or bad faith. When reading the material which follows one should, therefore, consider not simply whether we should or should not utilise a particular concept, such as proportionality, in our armoury of judicial review, but also the intensity with which this tool should be applied in differing contexts.

3. Reasonableness: the Two Meanings

The distinction drawn above concerning the levels of review is apparent in the two senses of unreasonableness which are to be found in the oft cited judgment of Lord Greene M.R. in the *Wednesbury Corporation*[103] case. The corporation was empowered to grant licences for Sunday entertainment subject to such conditions as it thought fit. A picture house was licensed subject to the condition that no children under 15 be admitted. It was this condition which was challenged as unreasonable and *ultra vires*. Lord Greene M.R. stressed that the court should not substitute its view for that of the corporation, and then proceeded to examine what the term unreasonable meant in this context. What emerged from his judgment are two meanings of the term unreasonable.

The first can be called the "umbrella sense": unreasonable is used here simply as a synonym for a host of more specific grounds of attack, such as taking account of irrelevant considerations, acting for improper purposes and acting *mala fide*, which, as Lord Greene M.R. himself said, tend to run into one another. The second meaning may be termed the "substantive sense" of unreasonableness: a decision may be attacked if it is so unreasonable that no reasonable public body could have made it. To prove this would require something quite extreme. Lord Greene M.R. gave the example of a teacher being dismissed because of red hair.

The role of unreasonableness in its substantive sense is conceived of as a safety net to be used after tests such as relevancy or purpose.[104] One looks first to see whether, for example, the body has acted for improper purposes. If it has not the decision may still be struck down if it is unreasonable in the substantive sense. The two senses of the term unreasonable reflect, therefore, the two levels at which judicial control can take place which were mentioned above.

It is evident that neither of Lord Greene M.R.'s constructions of the term reasonable accord with the dictionary meaning of that word. The special interpretation of the term reasonableness is warranted by the constitutional

---

[103] *Associated Picture Houses Ltd.* v. *Wednesbury Corporation* [1948] 1 K.B. 223, 228-230.
[104] *Ibid.* pp. 233-234.

position of the courts.[105] They cannot intervene simply because they believe that a different way of exercising discretionary power would be more reasonable than that chosen by the public body. This would be to substitute a judicial view as to, for example, the most appropriate way in which to allocate aid, or to disburse licences, for that of the public body. Hence the controls over the substantive ends which can be pursued by an administrative authority are expressed in terms of relevancy, purpose or unreasonableness in its substantive sense. By phrasing control in these terms, the courts can preserve the impression that they are thereby only fulfilling the legislative will. They will not dictate which result should be reached, but they will impose limits on which ends cannot be pursued. However, what are relevant considerations or proper purposes will often not be self evident. Decisions about these factors will themselves involve social and political value judgments. Moreover the boundary line between intervention in this way, and a more direct substitution of opinion by the judiciary may well become blurred.

The subsequent discussion will focus upon the way in which the courts exercise controls at the two levels described above. Following Lord Diplock in the *G.C.H.Q.* case[106] the first level will be termed control for illegality, and the second will be labelled control for irrationality.

4. *Control at the First Level: Illegality*

(1) IMPROPER PURPOSES

The law reports abound with examples of the courts striking down discretionary decisions where the discretion has been used for an improper purpose: a public body which had power to construct lavatories could not use that power in order to build a subway under a street;[107] deportation could not be used to achieve extradition;[108] the Home Secretary could not use his powers to revoke television licences where people had bought a new licence early in order to avoid a price increase;[109] and a local authority had no power to enter into speculative financial swap transactions.[110]

What the purpose of a particular statute is will normally be determined by the courts as a matter of construction, and it is interesting what influences judicial thinking in this respect. While the courts continue to insist that they are only keeping the authority within the boundaries of its power and not substituting their view, the dividing line can be a thin one. For example, planning authorities may grant planning permission

---

[105] This point is brought out forcefully in, *e.g. Pickwell* v. *Camden London Borough Council* [1983] Q.B. 962. See also, *Council of Civil Service Unions* v. *Minister for the Civil Service* [1985] A.C. 374, 410-411.

[106] [1985] A.C. 374.

[107] *Westminster Corporation* v. *L. & N.W. Ry.* [1905] A.C. 426; *Galloway* v. *London Corporation* (1866) L.R. 1 H.L. 34.

[108] *R.* v. *Governor of Brixton Prison, ex p. Soblen* [1963] 2 Q.B. 243.

[109] *Congreve* v. *Home Office* [1976] Q.B. 629.

[110] *Hazell* v. *Hammersmith and Fulham London Borough Council* [1992] 2 A.C. 1.

unconditionally or subject to such conditions as they think fit. A number of cases have turned on the legality of such conditions. The general position adopted has been that the conditions must fairly and reasonably relate to the permitted development.[111] In applying this test the courts have upheld fairly broad conditions,[112] but they have also struck down a number by using concepts which are open to debate. Thus, the court held to be invalid conditions attached to the grant of a caravan site licence which required, *inter alia,* site rents to be agreed with the council and security of tenure to be provided for caravan owners.[113] The House of Lords found that the legislation only allowed terms to be attached which related to the use of the site and not to the types of contract the site owner could make with the caravan owners. In reaching this conclusion the court argued that freedom of contract was a fundamental right, and that if Parliament intended to empower a third party to make conditions which affected the provisions of a contract between others then this should be expressed in clear terms.[114] In other cases the courts have relied on the principle that private rights of property should not be taken without compensation unless there exists clear authority in the statute.[115]

This is not to say that either of the above decisions was necessarily wrong. The balance between, on the one hand, presumptions as to freedom of contract and the protection of private property rights unless due compensation is paid, and the overall direction of the planning system is a complex one on which opinions may differ.[116] There is, however, no doubt that the denomination of a purpose as proper or improper in such circumstances raises issues of political and social choice which do not cease to be so by being expressed in the language of *vires.* More recent[117] authority has held that planning law is of a "public character", and that the courts should not introduce private law principles unless these are expressly authorised by Parliament or are necessary to give effect to the legislative purpose.

Cases raising such issues are not restricted to the planning field. In *Roberts* v. *Hopwood*[118] Poplar Council had decided to pay their low grade

---

[111] *Pyx Granite Co. Ltd.* v. *Ministry of Housing and Local Government* [1958] 1 Q.B. 544, 572, affirm'd [1960] A.C. 260; *Newbury District Council* v. *Secretary of State for the Environment* [1981] A.C. 578.

[112] *e.g. Fawcett Properties Ltd.* v. *Buckingham County Council* [1961] A.C. 636.

[113] *Chertsey Urban District Council* v. *Mixnam Properties Ltd.* [1965] A.C. 735.

[114] *Ibid.* pp. 763-764.

[115] *Minister of Housing and Local Government* v. *Hartnell* [1965] A.C. 1134. But *cf. Kingston London Borough Council* v. *Secretary of State for the Environment* [1973] 1 W.L.R. 1549.

[116] *e.g.* there are indeed instances where the law deprives a person of a right or interest without compensation, even in the case of traditional property rights, without raising the broader question of how far interests which are not traditional property interests should be protected, see Chap. 17.

[117] *Pioneer Aggregates (UK) Ltd.* v. *Secretary of State for the Environment* [1985] A.C. 132, 140-141. See also, *R.* v. *St. Edmunsbury Borough Council, ex p. Investors in Industry Commercial Properties Ltd.* [1985] 1 W.L.R. 1157.

[118] [1925] A.C. 579. But see now, *Pickwell* v. *Camden London Borough Council* [1983] Q.B. 962.

workers £4 per week. The relevant statute[119]empowered the council to pay such wages as it thought fit. Despite this the House of Lords found that the payment was excessive: the statute was to be read subject to an implied condition that the wages should be reasonable, which was to be judged by the current rates payable in the industry. Anything above this was a gratuity, and a social purpose, such as payment of a minimum wage, was unlawful.[120]

It would of course be a simple world in which an authority always acted for one purpose only. Complex problems can arise where one of the purposes is lawful and one is regarded as unlawful. De Smith has noted four different tests which the courts have at one time or another used.[121] First, what was the true purpose for which the power was exercised? Provided that the legitimate statutory purpose was achieved it is irrelevant that a subsidiary object was also attained.[122] Secondly, what was the dominant purpose for which the power was exercised?[123] Thirdly, were any of the purposes authorised? This has less support in the case law than the previous two tests. Fourthly, if any of the purposes was unauthorised and this had an effect upon the decision taken, that decision will be overturned as being one based upon irrelevant considerations.[124]

(2) RELEVANCY

The second main method of controlling the exercise of discretion is relevancy: a decision will be declared *ultra vires* if it is based upon irrelevant considerations or if relevant considerations are not taken into account. Relevancy overlaps with control maintained through improper purposes and a number of the cases could be classified under one section or the other.[125]

In exercising control based upon relevancy, the courts have, for example, defined the types of considerations which licensing justices can take into account. These might include the character and needs of an area,[126] but could not encapsulate the terms on which an applicant would conduct the

---

[119] Metropolis Management Act 1855, s.62.
[120] See also, *Prescott* v. *Birmingham Corporation* [1955] Ch. 210; *Taylor* v. *Munrow* [1960] 1 W.L.R. 151; *Bromley London Borough Council* v. *Greater London Council* [1983] 1 A.C. 768.
[121] *Judicial Review of Administrative Action* (4th ed., 1980), pp. 329-333.
[122] *Westminster Corporation* v. *L. & N.W. Ry.* [1905] A.C. 426; *R.* v. *Brixton Prison Governor, ex p. Soblen* [1963] 2 Q.B. 243.
[123] e.g. *R.* v. *Immigration Appeals Adjudicator, ex p. Khan* [1972] 1 W.L.R. 1058; *R.* v. *Greenwich London Borough Council, ex p. Lovelace* [1991] 1 W.L.R. 506.
[124] *Hanks* v. *Minister of Housing and Local Government* [1963] 1 Q.B. 999, 1016, 1020, 1037; *R.* v. *Inner London Education Authority, ex p. Westminster City Council* [1986] 1 W.L.R. 28; *R.* v. *Broadcasting Complaints Commission, ex p. Owen* [1985] Q.B. 1153. A fifth test which has been used in Australia is whether the power would still have been exercised if the public body had not wished to achieve an unlawful aim.
[125] *cf.* Taylor, "Judicial Review of Improper Purposes and Irrelevant Considerations" (1976) 35 C.L.J. 272.
[126] *Sharp* v. *Wakefield* [1891] A.C. 173.

business if those terms did not affect the applicant's fitness to hold the licence.[127] Control of a like kind is maintained over other areas such as education,[128] housing,[129] the police,[130] the mentally disordered,[131] and aspects of nationalised industry.[132]

The stringency with which the courts have applied the criterion of relevancy has varied in different areas[133] and there has been an unwillingness to declare invalid administrative decisions simply because the applicant could point to one "relevant" factor which the authority did not take into account. This is particularly so where it is felt that the consideration did not have a causative effect upon the authority's determination and where the decision being impugned is not determinative of rights, such as a decision by a local authority to refer a landlord to a rent tribunal.[134]

As in the context of improper purposes, the denomination of a consideration as relevant or irrelevant may involve the court in substituting its own views for those of the administration, a danger appreciated by Diplock L.J. (as he then was) in *Luby* v. *Newcastle-under-Lyme Corporation*.[135] The Housing Act 1957, section 111, vested the management of local authority houses in the Corporation and gave it power to charge reasonable rents. The policy of the defendant was to fix rents for the houses as a whole at an aggregate sum necessary to balance the cost of the loan capital and repairs. There was no differential applied whereby tenants paid rent according to their means. After a series of rent increases L complained that the basis of assessment was invalid as it did not take account of his personal circumstances, and resulted in him having to pay an unreasonable rent. Diplock L.J. rejected the claim. The court should not, he said, substitute its view for that of the Corporation. The latter was applying a social policy on which reasonable men could differ: it had decided against differential rating and this was not a decision so unreasonable that no reasonable corporation could come to it. Any deficit in housing revenue would have to be made good from the general rate fund. The choice of rent

---

[127] R. v. Hyde [1912] 1 K.B. 645; R. v. Bowman [1898] 1 Q.B. 663; R. v. Wandsworth Licensing JJ., ex p. Whitbread and Co. Ltd. [1921] 3 K.B. 487; R. v. Birmingham Licensing Planning Committee, ex p. Kennedy [1972] 2 Q.B. 140.
[128] Sadler v. Sheffield Corporation [1924] 1 Ch. 483; Short v. Poole Corporation [1926] Ch. 66.
[129] Bristol District Council v. Clark [1975] 1 W.L.R. 1443; Cannock Chase District Council v. Kelly [1978] 1 W.L.R. 1; Victoria Square Property Co. Ltd. v. Southwark London Borough Council [1978] 1 W.L.R. 463.
[130] R. v. Commissioner of Police of the Metropolis, ex p. Blackburn [1968] 2 Q.B. 118; ibid. (No. 3) [1973] Q.B. 241.
[131] Retarded Children's Aid Society Ltd. v. Barnet London Borough Council [1969] 2 Q.B. 22.
[132] South of Scotland Electricity Board v. British Oxygen Co. Ltd. [1956] 1 W.L.R. 1069, [1959] 1 W.L.R. 587.
[133] Re Fletcher's Application [1970] 2 All E.R. 527 n.
[134] R. v. Barnet and Camden Rent Tribunal, ex p. Frey Investments Ltd. [1972] 2 Q.B. 342; R. v. Secretary of State for Social Services, ex p. Wellcome Foundation Ltd. [1987] 1 W.L.R. 1166.
[135] [1964] 2 Q.B. 64.

structures involved, therefore, a weighing of the interests of tenants as a whole (including impoverished tenants) with those of the general body of ratepayers.

(3) BAD FAITH

The concept of bad faith has remained either largely in the region of hypothetical cases,[136] or has been treated as synonymous with improper purposes or relevancy.[137] It is indeed difficult to conceive of bad faith which would not automatically render applicable one of the two traditional control mechanisms. This is not to say that spite, malice or dishonesty may not exist. They clearly can.[138] It is to question the necessity of this being a separate method of control.[139]

5. Control at the Second Level: Irrationality and Substantive Principles

Assuming that the public body has passed the hurdles of purpose and relevancy, and is in that sense allowed to exercise its discretion in the general manner which was intended, the court may still intervene if the decision is irrational. The meaning to be ascribed to this term is, as will be seen, in a state of flux. It clearly covers *Wednesbury* unreasonableness. Precisely what other substantive constraints are and should be imposed upon the exercise of discretion is a more open question. The discussion within this section will begin with an analysis of substantive unreasonableness, and will then move on to consider the status of other principles which should constrain the use of discretionary power.

(1) UNREASONABLENESS: THE SUBSTANTIVE MEANING

As seen, Lord Greene M.R. in the *Wednesbury* case conceived of unreasonableness in its substantive sense as a long stop and a fairly extreme one at that:[140] if an exercise of discretion successfully negotiated the hurdles of improper purpose and relevancy it could still be invalidated on the altar of substantive unreasonableness if it was so unreasonable that no reasonable body could reach such a decision. It may well be that arguments could be made that this sense of unreasonableness should be the only mechanism for controlling discretion. Such arguments will be considered later. Our

---

[136] *Smith* v. *East Elloe Rural District Council* [1956] A.C. 736, 770.
[137] *e.g. Westminster Corporation* v. *L. & N.W. Ry.* [1905] A.C. 426; *Webb* v. *Minister of Housing and Local Government* [1965] 1 W.L.R. 755, 784.
[138] *Roncarelli* v. *Duplessis* (1959) 16 D.L.R. (2d) 689.
[139] It may be easier to evade a clause excluding judicial review if the allegation is of bad faith, *Lazarus Estates Ltd.* v. *Beasley* [1956] 1 Q.B. 702, 712-713, 722. *cf. R.* v. *Secretary of State for the Environment, ex p. Ostler* [1977] Q.B. 122, 138-139.
[140] [1948] 1 K.B. 223, 233-234.

concern here is to understand how the concept is used by the courts now, in conjunction with purpose and relevancy.

It was noted earlier that there are indeed two levels upon which judicial control can operate, the first of which relates to whether the decision was of a type which could be made at all, the second of which concerns decisions which are in principle of the kind which can be made, but which are deemed to be unreasonable, irrational or disproportionate. Viewed in this way Lord Greene's substantive sense of unreasonableness is a clear example of this latter mode of control.

However, somewhat paradoxically, if this is indeed the *only* component of control exercised at the second level then it is questionable whether it is in fact needed. The simple reason is that the safety net function it performs is only rendered necessary by a semantic sleight of hand: we think we need the net because our original conceptions of propriety of purpose or relevancy are drawn unrealistically wide, thus allowing cases to "tumble through". Let us take the classic example of the unreasonable decision, dismissal of a teacher because of the colour of her hair.[141] If the considerations relevant to dismissal of a teacher are broadly defined as "any physical characteristic" then of course dismissal on the above ground is relevant. However, common sense dictates that this is not the way that we would approach the matter. The question would be posed more specifically, distinguishing between the types of physical characteristics that were felt to be relevant to teaching and those, such as hair colour, which were not. Other decisions which are said to be examples of the substantive meaning of unreasonable could equally be resolved through the more traditional conceptions of purpose and relevancy.[142]

This does not mean that *all* controls which operate at the second level are similarly to be regarded as redundant, or capable of incorporation within the first level. It does mean that the cases intended to be dealt with by the substantive sense of unreasonableness can quite easily be resolved at the first level.

A sacrifice of analytical rigour may not be that important if the concept which has been thereby given life is never used, and it is clear from Lord Greene M.R.'s judgment in the *Wednesbury* case that he conceived of it being utilised only in the extreme (and hypothetical) instance of "dismissal for red hair type of case". However, in the same way that nature abhors a vacuum, so also concepts demand a function and the concept of unreasonableness in its substantive sense is no exception to this. It has developed in two ways.

First, it has been applied to discretionary decisions which could not, whether right or wrong, be classified as of the "red hair type". In the planning sphere it has been used to invalidate conditions attached to planning permission, such as that the developer should construct an ancillary road over the frontage of the site at his own expense to which

---

[141] *Short* v. *Poole Corporation* [1926] Ch. 66.
[142] e.g. *Williams* v. *Giddy* [1911] A.C. 381; *UKAPE* v. *ACAS* [1981] A.C. 424. I am not arguing that logically one could never conceive of a situation in which the safety net was needed. I have, however, yet to see one.

rights of passage should be given to others,[143] and that a property developer should allow those on a council housing list to occupy the houses with security of tenure for 10 years.[144] The test has also been adopted in the context of industrial relations,[145] though in this instance the decision attacked was upheld. As stated, these cases may have been correctly decided. The point is that it is hard to see the subject-matter under attack as determinations which are so unreasonable that no reasonable authority could come to them, at least not when viewed as Lord Greene M.R. visualised the notion. The criterion moves closer to asking whether the courts believe that the exercise of discretion was reasonable. This latter formulation would give the courts a greater scope for substitution of judgment, with the additional risk that they would not have to articulate their rationale as clearly as under the heads of purpose and relevancy.

The second development has been the assumption that the meaning of the term unreasonable used by Lord Greene M.R. should govern whenever that word appears within a statute. It will be argued below that there are strong reasons why this should not be so.[146]

(2) PROPORTIONALITY

The status of the concept of proportionality as a head of review is more uncertain. The discussion will begin with the present status of this concept within our law, to be followed by a more general consideration of the desirability of developing this head of review.

(a) Proportionality: legal status

The leading authority on the status of proportionality is the decision of the House of Lords in R. v. Secretary of State for the Home Department, ex p. Brind.[147] The Home Secretary issued directives under the Broadcasting Act 1981 requiring the BBC and the IBA to refrain from broadcasting certain matters by persons who represented organisations which were proscribed under legislation concerning the prevention of terrorism. The ambit of this proscription was limited to direct statements made by the members of the organisations. It did not, for example, prevent the broadcasting of such persons on film, provided that there was a voice-over account paraphrasing what had been said. The applicants sought judicial review on a number of grounds. The arguments which related to a breach of the European Convention will be considered below. The present analysis will be directed towards the other main ground of challenge, which was that the directives

---

[143] Hall & Co. Ltd. v. Shoreham-by-Sea Urban District Council [1964] 1 W.L.R. 240.
[144] R. v. Hillingdon London Borough Council, ex p. Royco Homes Ltd. [1974] Q.B. 720; noted in (1974) J.P.L. 507.
[145] UKAPE v. ACAS [1981] A.C. 424; Note, Elliott (1980) 43 M.L.R. 580. See also, R. v. Boundary Commission for England, ex p. Foot [1983] Q.B. 600; R. v. Crown Court of St. Albans, ex p. Cinnamond [1981] Q.B. 480.
[146] See below, pp. 434-435.
[147] [1991] 1 A.C. 696.

were disproportionate to the end sought to be attained. This objective was both to deny such organisations any appearance of political legitimacy, and also to prevent intimidation.

Their Lordships denied that proportionality was a separate ground of review, but accepted that it could be of relevance in establishing *Wednesbury* unreasonableness. Lord Bridge held that the restrictions on freedom of speech were not unreasonable in scope, and did not believe that the applicants' case could be improved by invoking the idea of proportionality.[148] Lord Bridge did, however, agree with Lord Roskill that proportionality might at some time be incorporated within our law. Lord Roskill himself acknowledged that Lord Diplock had, in the *G.C.H.Q.* case,[149] held this open as a possible future development, but Lord Roskill did not believe that this was an appropriate case for such a development, believing that this would lead the courts into substituting their view for that of the Home Secretary on the particular issue before the court.[150] Similar concerns are apparent in the judgments of Lord Ackner and Lord Lowry. Thus Lord Ackner[151] reasoned that if proportionality was to add something to our existing law, then it would be imposing a more intensive standard of review than traditional *Wednesbury* unreasonableness. This would mean that an "inquiry into and a decision upon the merits cannot be avoided", in the sense that the court would have to balance the pros and cons of the decision which was being challenged.[152] Lord Lowry was equally wary of overstepping the boundary between a supervisory and an appellate jurisdiction. He felt that the judges are not well equipped by training or experience to "decide the answer to an administrative problem where the scales are evenly balanced".[153] His Lordship also feared that stability would be jeopardised because "there is nearly always something to be said against any administrative decision", and that recognition of proportionality would, therefore, lead to an increase in the number of applications for judicial review.[154]

The cogency of these objections will be considered in due course, but before doing so it should be recognised that the courts have in the past applied a concept of proportionality, or something closely analogous thereto, whether as an independent concept or as part of a finding of *Wednesbury* unreasonableness. Precisely *which* cases should be regarded in this light is, however, a more controversial question. Advocates of the recognition of proportionality within our law wish, not surprisingly, to categorise a large number of cases in this manner.[155] Others disagree, arguing that many of the cases placed within this category would not be

---

[148] *Ibid.* pp. 748-749.
[149] [1985] A.C. 374, 410.
[150] [1991] 1 A.C. 696, 749-750.
[151] *Ibid.* pp. 762-763.
[152] *Ibid.* p. 762.
[153] *Ibid.* p. 767.
[154] *Loc.cit.*
[155] Jowell and Lester, "Proportionality: Neither Novel nor Dangerous", *New Directions in Judicial Review* (Jowell and Oliver eds., 1988), pp. 51-73.

classified in this way in, for example, France.[156] Three types of case can be distinguished.

First, there are those decisions which do unequivocally make reference to proportionality. A clear example of this is to be found in R. v. *Barnsley M.B.C., ex p. Hook*[157] where a stallholder had his licence revoked for urinating in the street and using offensive language. Lord Denning M.R. struck down the decision in part because the penalty was excessive and out of proportion to the offence.

Secondly, there are decisions which make no explicit reference to proportionality as such, but which are said to reflect that concept.[158] *Wheeler* v. *Leicester City Council*[159] is said to be one such case. The Council had withdrawn the rugby club's licence because the club had not taken sufficient action to press certain of its members not to tour South Africa. It did so in pursuance of its statutory powers to license its own land, and relied also on its duty under the Race Relations Act 1976, section 71, to promote good race relations. The House of Lords held that this was a misuse of power because, *inter alia*, the club was being punished where it had done no wrong.

Thirdly, there are cases which are said to provide some support for proportionality, which do not mention that concept and where one has to dig considerably deeper to find any implicit presence of the idea. The *Fares Fair* case,[160] considered in detail below, which concerned the legality of a scheme to provide subsidised bus fares, is said to furnish some support for the concept. The scheme was struck down in part by reliance upon the idea of a fiduciary duty which the G.L.C. owed to ratepayers, and it has been argued that underlying the fiduciary duty "there is surely a hidden notion of proportionality – requiring a rational balancing of the benefits to transport users against the burdens to ratepayers".[161] Whether cases of this kind really should be regarded as involving proportionality, and the consequences of doing so, will be examined below.

More recently it was held in the *NALGO*[162] case that while proportionality could be applied by our courts when deciding a case concerning Community law, or when deciding upon the appropriateness of a particular penalty, or it seems the exercise of a judicial discretion, it was not, in the light of the *Brind* case, open to a court below the House of Lords to depart from the traditional grounds of *Wednesbury* unreasonableness when reviewing the exercise of ministerial discretion. The court did, however, state that there was much to be said for the view that all courts in the Community should apply common standards in the field of administrative law.

---

[156] Boyron, "Proportionality in English Administrative Law: A Faulty Translation" (1992) 12 O.J.L.S. 237.
[157] [1976] 1 W.L.R. 1052, 1057.
[158] Jowell and Lester, "Proportionality: Neither Novel nor Dangerous", p. 61.
[159] [1985] A.C. 1054.
[160] [1983] 1 A.C. 768.
[161] Jowell and Lester, "Proportionality: Neither Novel nor Dangerous", p. 62.
[162] *National and Local Government Officers Association* v. *Secretary of State for the Environment* (1992) Times Law Reports 576.

(b) Proportionality: place and meaning

Notwithstanding the decision in *Brind* it is important to investigate the concept of proportionality further in order to understand both its place within the more general scheme of review, and also to assess what the concept actually means.

It is important at the outset to be clear about the *place* of proportionality within the more general scheme of review, and its relationship with other existing methods of control. As a matter of principle it is clear that to talk of proportionality at all assumes that the public body was entitled to pursue its desired objective. The presumption is, therefore, that this general objective was a legitimate one, and that the public body was not seeking to achieve an improper purpose. If the purpose was improper then the exercise of discretion should be struck down upon this ground, without any investigation as to whether it was disproportionate. Proportionality should then only be considered once the controls which operate at the first level have been passed.

Now this may sound obvious, and so it is. It is important nonetheless. Proportionality is perceived to be a valuable extra safeguard for the individual, over and above our traditional methods of control. It will not, however, serve this function if the zeal to find authority for the concept leads to cases being treated as examples of proportionality when, in reality, they would be better classified as instances where the public body was acting for an improper purpose: it was doing something which it should simply not have been doing at all. If we bypass this level of control then the danger is that the courts will assume that the public body *was* able to use its discretion for the purpose in question, the only live issue being whether it did so proportionately.[163]

Let us turn now to the *meaning* of the concept itself. It is obvious that at a general level proportionality involves some idea of balance between competing interests or objectives, and that it embodies some sense of an appropriate relationship between means and ends. We can, however, go beyond this. There are five steps in any application of proportionality.

(i) The relevant interests must be identified.

(ii) There must be some ascription of weight or value to those interests, since this is a necessary condition precedent to any balancing operation.

(iii) Some view must be taken as to whether certain interests can be traded off to achieve other goals at all. Should we, for example, trade off a fundamental right in order to enhance the general economic good? Certain respected theories would answer no.[164]

(iv) A decision must be made as to whether the public body's decision was indeed proportionate or not on the facts of the case in the light of

---

[163] This is a danger consequent upon the analysis of Jowell and Lester, "Proportionality: Neither Novel nor Dangerous". Contrast the treatment of many of Jowell and Lester's examples with that given by Boyron, (1992) 12 O.J.L.S. 237.

[164] *e.g.* modern theories of liberalism espoused by writers such as Rawls and Dworkin.

the above considerations. Differing criteria can be used when answering this question. The test could be formulated in a number of ways:

Is the disputed measure the least restrictive which could be adopted in the circumstances?
Do the means adopted to achieve the aim correspond to the importance of the aim, and are they necessary for its achievement?[165]
Is the challenged act suitable and necessary for the achievement of its objective, and one which does not impose excessive burdens on the individual?[166]
What are the relative costs and benefits of the disputed measure?

As will be seen different formulations tend to be used in the context of different types of case. For example, the first version will commonly be used in cases where the disputed measure is in conflict with a fundamental right.
(v) The court will have to decide how intensively it is going to apply any one of the tests mentioned above. It is important to realise that all of these tests can be applied more or less intensively, as will become apparent.

(c) Proportionality: application

It is readily apparent that the application of the five steps mentioned above might well produce differing results depending upon the circumstances of the case. That much is obvious. We can, however, go further in providing some guidance as to how proportionality will be applied in differing *types* of case. Three such types of case can be differentiated for present purposes. As will be seen the application of a notion of proportionality is easier in the first two situations than it is in the third.

The *first type of situation* is one in which the exercise of discretion impinges upon, or clashes with, a recognised civil liberty or fundamental right. The precise role of fundamental rights within our law will be examined below, but the point to be made here can be understood in advance of any such discussion. It can be explained quite simply. If we do recognise certain interests as being of particular importance, and are willing to categorise them as fundamental rights or something akin thereto, then this renders the application of proportionality more likely and easier.

Proportionality is *more likely* to be applied because the very denomination of those interests as fundamental rights means that any invasion of them should be kept to the minimum. Society may well accept that these rights cannot be regarded as absolute and that some limitations may be warranted in certain circumstances. Nonetheless there is a presumption that any inroad should interfere with the right as little as

---

[165] Case 66/82, *Fromancais* [1983] E.C.R. 395.
[166] This is very close to the test used in Germany, Schwarze, *European Administrative Law* (1992), p. 687.

possible, and no more than is merited by the occasion. In this sense the recognition of some idea of proportionality is a *natural* and *necessary* adjunct to the regard for fundamental rights.

Proportionality is also *easier* to apply in conditions such as these. The reason why this is so is that in such cases a difficult aspect of the proportionality calculus has already been resolved: one of the interests, such as freedom of speech, has been identified *and* it has been weighted or valued. We do not have to fathom out this matter afresh on each and every occasion, precisely because the fundamental nature of the right has been acknowledged. Now to be sure we will still have to decide whether the invasion of the right was proportionate, and this may well be controversial. But, as will be seen, this is much less problematic than in cases of the third type considered below.

It is natural in cases concerning rights to apply proportionality in the sense of asking whether the interference with the fundamental right was the least restrictive possible in the circumstances.

The *second type of case* is that in which it is the punishment or penalty which is deemed to be disproportionate to the offence which has been committed. Once again people may well disagree as to the precise penalty which is appropriate for a particular offence. Yet here too, as in the first type of case, proportionality is less problematic than it is in the third type of situation. We know the penalty which has been imposed; we know the offence; and we know also the interest which is being affected by the penalty. This interest may be personal liberty in the case of imprisonment, or it may be loss of livelihood as in *Hook*. It *is* a recognised principle of justice that penalties should not be excessive, as acknowledged in the Bill of Rights 1689. A court is unlikely to intervene unless the disproportionality is reasonably evident,[167] and judicial review of this kind is to be welcomed. A recent recognition of the importance of proportionality in this type of case is to be found in *Uchendu*[168] where Laws J. held that when justices decided what sentence to impose upon a person who had failed to pay rates they should have regard to the principle of proportionality.

The *third type of case* is harder. This category includes those situations not dealt with by the previous two. There are no fundamental rights at stake, and no excessive penalties. The paradigm of this third category is the case where the public body decides to exercise its discretion in a particular manner, this necessitates the balancing of various interests, and a person affected argues that the balancing was disproportionate in some way. There are two reasons why these cases present particular difficulties.

On the one hand, there is the fact that it may be harder to apply the steps required by a proportionality inquiry. How do we, for example, weight the respective values of ratepayers and transport users in a *Fares Fair*[169] type of case? What precisely would a balancing or cost-benefit analysis entail in such circumstances?

---

[167] *Commissioners of Customs and Excise* v. *P & O Steam Navigation Co.* [1993] C.O.D. 164. See also, *Bolton* v. *Law Society* [1994] 2 All E.R. 486.
[168] *R.* v. *Highbury Corner Justices, ex p. Uchendu, The Times*, 28 January 1994.
[169] [1983] 1 A.C. 768.

On the other hand, there is the problem of the division of function as between the administration and the judiciary. Many decisions involve just the sort of balancing described above. It is of the very essence of political determinations and also of many administrative choices. Given that this is so it cannot be right for the judiciary to overturn such a decision merely because the court would have balanced the conflicting interests differently. This would amount to substitution of judgment by any other name. So we are then faced with three consequential problems.

One relates to the *intensity* of such review. How far can the administration depart from the result which the court itself might have deemed to be appropriate in the circumstances before the court should label the decision disproportionate?

A second problem concerns the *adjudicative difficulties* which this task presents for the courts. These complications have been recognised by academics and judges alike. Thus as Mashaw has pointed out,[170] the process of social cost accounting which would be required if the balancing task were to be performed adequately would impose considerable burdens on the judiciary. Similarly Lord Lowry in *Brind*[171] questioned whether the courts are well placed, by training, experience and knowledge, to provide an answer where the scales are fairly evenly balanced.

A third problem, closely related to the second, concerns the *scope* of any such inquiry. Are the courts to perform a cost-benefit analysis which is confined to the particular administrative decision under attack? Or are they also to consider alternative policy strategies? Consideration of the former may in any event push the analysis in the direction of the wider ranging inquiry. If this does occur then the adjudicative problems outlined above will be rendered more difficult. Such an inquiry would, moreover, not fit well with the current strategies for remedies, since the courts have made it very clear that they are not keen on engaging in detailed factual inquiry, at least not within the confines of the public law procedures for remedies.[172] Some detailed factual investigation would be required if any thoroughgoing cost-benefit analysis were to be attempted. Furthermore, if any such thorough analysis were to be undertaken, which looked at alternative policy strategies, then both the parties and the courts might be impeded by the lack of necessary information on these alternatives. The recent government White Paper on *Open Government* states that such information is not to be made readily available.

It is clear that these problems will be exacerbated the more intensive review of this kind becomes. It will bring the judiciary closer to substitution of judgment; it will make the adjudicative conundrums more apparent; and

---

[170] *Due Process in the Administrative State* (1985), Chap. 3. Mashaw was writing in the context of process rights, but the points which he makes are if anything even stronger in this context.
[171] [1991] 1 A.C. 696, 767.
[172] See below, Chap. 15.

it will also reduce certainty and stability, in the sense that, as Lord Lowry indicated in *Brind*,[173] those disappointed with the determination would always be tempted to challenge it in court, given that there "is nearly always something to be said against any administrative decision".

Now this should not be taken to mean that proportionality has no role to play in this third type of case, and it may well be advantageous for administrative policy choices to be susceptible to scrutiny in the courts.[174] It could be argued that the problems identified above would be alleviated if we were to break down this third category into at least two more discrete sections: those areas where the court did not feel able or suited to scrutinise the administration's choice could be subject to a less intensive form of proportionality review, while those in which it felt competent to consider the administration's discretionary choice would be subject to a more searching inquiry, albeit not substitution of judgment. Such a division could be made, although the difficulty of assigning cases to particular categories should not be underestimated.

What it does mean is that if scrutiny is to be via proportionality then we have some further choices to make. We must decide upon the sense of proportionality which is to be used, *and* the intensity with which it will be applied. In those cases where the courts wish to engage in searching review under the guise of a cost-benefit analysis or one of the other tests which have been set out, we must be willing to confront the problems outlined above. Alternatively a less intensive form of review can be utilised for some of the cases which arise in this area. Precisely what this means can be appreciated by considering proportionality within the EC.

(d) Proportionality: the EC dimension

Proportionality is one of the General Principles of Community law, and therefore our courts are obliged to have regard to it in those cases which have a Community law dimension.[175] These general principles have been developed by the ECJ and draw their inspiration from the laws of the Member States. They can be relied upon in actions to contest the legality of Community measures, or national measures designed to implement Community law. The concept of proportionality has been applied in all three types of case described above.

There have been a number of cases falling within the *first category*, which deal with proportionality in the context of *rights* granted by the Community Treaties. One common scenario is where the Member State seeks to take advantage of a public policy exception to, for example, the free movement of workers. The right to free movement is guaranteed by Article 48 of the Treaty, and the public policy exception finds expression in Article 48(3). The ECJ has, however, insisted that derogation from the fundamental principle of Article 48 can only be sanctioned in cases which

---

173 [1991] 1 A.C. 696, 767.
174 Harden and Lewis, *The Noble Lie* (1986).
175 Hartley, *The Foundations of European Community Law* (2nd ed., 1988), Chap. 5; Wyatt and Dashwood's, *European Community Law* (3rd ed., 1992), pp. 88-103.

pose a genuine and serious threat to public policy, and then only if the measure is the least restrictive possible in the circumstances.[176] The same principle is evident in cases upon freedom to provide services which is a protected right under Article 59 of the Treaty. In *Van Binsbergen*[177] the Court held that residence requirements limiting this freedom may be justified, but only where they were strictly necessary to prevent the evasion, by those resident outside the territory, of professional rules which were applicable to the activity in question. A similar approach is evident in cases concerning the right to free movement of goods. Thus in the famous *Cassis de Dijon* case[178] the ECJ considered whether a German rule which prescribed a minimum alcohol content for a certain alcoholic beverage constituted an impediment to the free movement of goods under Article 30 of the EC Treaty. Having decided that the rule could constitute such an impediment the Court assessed the defence that the rule was necessary in order to protect consumers from being misled. The Court rejected the defence, because the interests of the consumers could be safeguarded in other less restrictive ways, by displaying the alcohol content on the packaging of the drinks.

Application of proportionality can also be seen in cases where individuals claim that Community regulations infringe their fundamental rights. Thus in the *Hauer* case[179] the ECJ held that the validity of a regulation which restricted the areas in which wine could be grown, and thus limited the applicant's property rights, must not constitute a disproportionate and excessive interference with the rights of the owner.

The principle has been often applied in the *second category* of case, where the applicant claims that the *penalty* which has been imposed is disproportionate to the offence which has been committed.[180] This is exemplified by *R. v. Intervention Board, ex p. Man (Sugar) Ltd.*[181] The applicant was required to give a security deposit to the Board when seeking a licence to export sugar outside the Community. The applicant was then late, but only by four hours, in completing the relevant paperwork. The Board, acting pursuant to a Community regulation, declared the entire deposit of £1,670,370 to be forfeit. Not surprisingly the company was aggrieved. The ECJ held that the automatic forfeiture of the entire deposit in the event of any failure to fulfil the time requirement was too drastic given the function performed by the system of export licences.[182] In addition to cases dealing with penalties *stricto sensu* the ECJ has applied proportionality in the field of economic regulation, scrutinising the level of charges which have been imposed by the Community institutions. Thus in *Bela-Muhle*[183] the Court held that a scheme whereby producers of animal

---

[176] Case 36/75, *Rutili* [1975] E.C.R. 1219; Case 30/77, *Bouchereau* [1977] E.C.R. 1999.
[177] Case 33/74, [1974] E.C.R. 1299; Case 39/75, *Coenen* [1975] E.C.R. 1547.
[178] Case 120/78, [1979] E.C.R. 649; 178/84, *Commission v. Germany* [1987] E.C.R. 1227; Case 40/82, *Commission v. United Kingdom* [1984] E.C.R. 2793.
[179] Case 44/79, [1979] E.C.R. 3727.
[180] Schwarze, *European Administrative Law* (1992), pp. 729-746.
[181] Case 181/84, [1985] E.C.R. 2889.
[182] *Ibid.* para. 29; Case 240/78, *Atalanta* [1979] E.C.R. 2137; Case 122/78, *Buitoni* [1979] E.C.R. 677.
[183] Case 114/76, *Bela-Muhle Josef Bergman v. Grows-Farm* [1977] E.C.R. 1211.

feed were forced to use skimmed milk in their product, in order to reduce a surplus, rather than soya, was unlawful because, *inter alia*, skimmed milk was three times more expensive than soya: the obligation to purchase the milk, therefore, imposed a disproportionate burden on the animal feed producers.

Proportionality has likewise been applied in cases of the *third type* described in the previous section. What is of particular interest is the meaning given to the concept in many of the cases which are of this kind. *Fedesa*[184] provides a good example. The applicants challenged the legality of a Council directive which prohibited the use of certain substances which had a hormonal action in livestock farming. The challenge was based on a number of grounds including proportionality. The ECJ stressed that the Community institutions must indeed pursue their policy by the least onerous means, and that the disadvantages must not be disproportionate to the aims of the measure. It then continued as follows.[185]

"However, with regard to judicial review of compliance with those conditions it must be stated that in matters concerning the common agricultural policy the Community legislature has a discretionary power which corresponds to the political responsibilities given to it by Articles 40 and 43 of the Treaty. Consequently, the legality of a measure adopted in that sphere can be affected only if the measure is manifestly inappropriate having regard to the objective which the competent institution is seeking to pursue."

What is readily apparent is that if the ECJ wishes to adopt a standard of review which is less intensive in a particular area then this will carry across to proportionality, as well as to other grounds of illegality. A decision will only be overturned if it is "manifestly inappropriate" to the objective which the institution is seeking to pursue. When proportionality is given this meaning then there will be little difference between it and review for *Wednesbury* unreasonableness.

The case law furnishes, moreover, interesting insights into why the ECJ has adopted this more limited form of review. Space precludes any detailed consideration of this issue, but in essence it is because it does not wish to be continually faced with challenges to Community norms in an area where the Community institutions possessed of discretionary power have to balance a number of variables which can often conflict among themselves. If the ECJ countenanced a more intensive review for proportionality in this sphere then it would be continually faced with challenges by groups which believed that the variables should have been balanced in some other way. It is the classic realm in which, as Lord Lowry stated in *Brind*,[186] "there is nearly always something to be said against any administrative decision". The Court would be in danger of second guessing the policy choice made by the Community institutions. Evidence of this reluctance to overturn the

---

[184] Case C-331/88, R. v. *The Minister of Agriculture, Fisheries and Food and the Secretary of State for Health, ex p. Fedesa* [1990] E.C.R. I-4023.
[185] *Ibid.* p. 4063; Case 265/87, *Schrader* [1989] E.C.R. 2237.
[186] [1991] 1 A.C. 696, 737.

Community's choices in relation to agriculture is evident in other similar cases,[187] and in the secondary literature.[188]

The relative intensity with which proportionality is applied in the agricultural sphere may not necessarily be indicative of how the concept will be used in other cases which come within this third category. There may, as noted above, be other areas where the ECJ is willing to intervene with a more searching form of inquiry, particularly where the area is one in which the administrative authorities possess a narrower discretionary power or one which is more clearly circumscribed. This third category of cases may, therefore, have to be broken down into more discrete categories to reflect this fact.

(e) Proportionality: conclusion

It is highly likely that proportionality will be recognised as an independent ground of review within domestic law. This is in part because the possibility was left open in *Brind* itself, and a number of the judiciary are in favour of taking this step. In part it is because the developments within the EC and the European Convention will acclimatise our judiciary to the concept and require them to apply it when applying EC law. And in part because the concept is accepted in a number of civil law countries, and one indirect consequence of the EC has been greater interpenetration of the domestic laws of the differing Member States.[189] Like many new developments this should neither be regarded as some panacea which will serve to cure all ills, real and imaginary, within our existing regime of review; nor should it be perceived as something entirely dangerous or alien. Two general points may be made by way of conclusion on this topic.

One is that the application of the concept may have differing implications in the three (or more) types of case described above.

The other is that if proportionality really is to provide a more intellectually honest species of review than unreasonableness then we must be prepared to do the job properly. We must be willing to provide a reasoned argument as to why a certain decision was indeed disproportionate, making clear both the particular meaning of the concept which is being applied and the intensity with which it is being used.

(3) FUNDAMENTAL RIGHTS

It may appear odd to have a section with this title in a work based on UK law. After all, on the traditional theory of sovereignty Parliament is omnipotent and capable of passing any law whatsoever. This constitutional

---

[187] See among many, Case 5/73, *Balkan Import-Export* [1973] E.C.R. 1091; Case 138/78, *Stolting* [1979] E.C.R. 713; Cases 197-200, 243, 245, 247/80, *Walzmuhle* [1981] E.C.R. 3211; Case C-8/89, *Zardi* [1990] E.C.R. I-2515, 2532-2533; Case 98/78, *Racke* [1979] E.C.R. 69.

[188] Vajda, "Some Aspects of Judicial Review within the Common Agricultural Policy – Part II" (1979) E.L.Rev. 341, 347-348.

[189] Schwarze, *European Administrative Law* (1992), Chap. 5.

orthodoxy has, moreover, been taken to mean that talk of fundamental rights within our system is simply a misnomer: what we have are residual liberties. This may well represent the traditional position. It does not, however, accurately reflect present reality, nor does it capture the emerging trends within our jurisprudence.

The very doctrine of sovereignty has undergone transformation as a result of our membership of the EC.[190] There have been judicial decisions which, at the very least, place those interests which would normally be denominated as fundamental rights in a stronger position than hitherto thought. And there have been a number of extra judicial statements by members of the judiciary which are indicative of a more secure foundation for such rights.

These developments will be charted within this section, and their relevance for the control of administrative discretion will be assessed. The analysis will begin with consideration of the three grounds which can be used by an individual in order to give a special status to rights: the European Convention, the common law and Community law. This will be followed by an overview of the secondary literature. The word "right" rather than "liberty" will be used throughout for reasons which will become apparent in the course of the discussion.

(a) The legal status of rights: the relevance of the European Convention

The leading authority on the role of the European Convention for the Protection of Human Rights and Fundamental Freedoms is the *Brind* case,[191] the facts of which have been set out above. One of the main grounds of challenge was that the restrictions which were imposed on the BBC and the IBA were contrary to Article 10 of the European Convention which safeguards freedom of speech. The Convention has not been incorporated into domestic law, and therefore individuals cannot directly enforce the rights contained therein. The applicants contended that, notwithstanding this fact, recourse could be had to the Convention. They argued that it was established law that resort could be had to the Convention if there was ambiguity in a statute: it would be presumed that Parliament had intended to legislate in conformity with the Convention and not contrary to it.[192] From this it was argued that it should therefore follow that when a statute confers a discretion upon an administrative authority it should be similarly presumed that this discretion should be used in conformity with the Convention. Their Lordships rejected the argument.

Lord Bridge found the argument initially persuasive, but ultimately flawed.[193] The presumption which applied to statutes was said to be a mere

---

[190] Craig, "Sovereignty of the United Kingdom Parliament after *Factortame*" (1991) 11 Y.B.E.L. 221.
[191] [1991] 1 A.C. 696.
[192] *Garland* v. *British Rail Engineering Ltd.* [1983] 2 A.C. 751, 771; *R.* v. *Chief Immigration Officer, Heathrow Airport, ex p. Bibi* [1976] 1 W.L.R. 979, 984, 988.
[193] [1991] 1 A.C. 696, 748.

canon of construction and did not involve the importation of international law into domestic law. The presumption which the applicants argued should apply to the exercise of discretion would go beyond the resolution of ambiguity. It would be to impute to Parliament the intention not only that the executive should exercise its discretion in conformity with the Convention, but also that our courts should enforce this conformity by importing the Convention into domestic administrative law. This would be to usurp the legislative function, since it was for Parliament to decide whether to incorporate the Convention or not. Similar reasoning can be found in the other judgments. Thus Lord Ackner held that the applicants' contention would lead to incorporation by the back door, with the result that the courts would have to police the operation of it in each and every case concerning discretion.[194]

(b) The legal status of rights: the common law jurisprudence

Although the decision in *Brind* places limits on the extent to which the Convention can be used in the absence of incorporation, it does contain interesting dicta on the relevance of rights within the common law itself. Lord Bridge, having noted the absence of any code of rights in domestic law, then had this to say.[195]

> "But...this surely does not mean that in deciding whether the Secretary of State, in the exercise of his discretion, could reasonably impose the restriction he has imposed on the broadcasting organisations, we are not perfectly entitled to start from the premise that any restriction of the right to freedom of expression requires to be justified and nothing less than an important competing public interest will be sufficient to justify it."

Lord Bridge went on to say that while the primary judgment as to whether the public interest warranted the restriction which had been imposed rested with the minister, the court could exercise a secondary judgment by asking whether a reasonable minister could reasonably make that judgment on the material before him.[196] Lord Templeman reasoned in a similar manner. He held that freedom of expression is a principle of every written and unwritten democratic constitution; that the court must inquire whether a reasonable minister could reasonably have concluded that the interference with this freedom was justifiable; and that "in terms of the Convention" any such interference must be both necessary and proportionate.[197]

The decision in *Brind* is by no means the only authority to advert to the relevance of rights for the purposes of public law adjudication. Other cases which are concerned with freedom of speech demonstrate a similar

---

[194] *Ibid.* pp. 761-762.
[195] *Ibid.* pp. 748-749.
[196] *Ibid.* p. 749.
[197] *Ibid.* pp. 750-751.

approach. In the *Spycatcher* case[198] Lord Goff, in delineating the ambit of the duty of confidentiality, and the exceptions thereto, stated that he saw no inconsistency between the position under the Convention, and that at common law. This was further emphasised in *Derbyshire County Council v. Times Newspapers Ltd.*[199] Their Lordships held that, as a matter of principle, a local authority should not be able to maintain an action in its own name for defamation, since this would place an unwarranted and undesirable limitation upon freedom of speech. Lord Keith, giving judgment for the House, reached this conclusion on the basis of the common law itself and echoed Lord Goff's satisfaction that there was no difference in principle between the common law and the Convention.[200] The importance of rights was also underlined in *Leech*.[201] In that case the court when construing the validity of a rule which allowed a prison governor to read letters from prisoners and stop those which were inordinately long or objectionable, adopted the principle of interpretation that the more fundamental the right which had been interfered with, the more difficult was it to imply any rule-making power in the primary legislation. The same concern for fundamental rights is apparent in other cases. Thus in *NALGO*,[202] which involved a challenge to regulations restricting the political activities of local authority officers who held politically restricted posts, the Court of Appeal accepted that while an applicant could not rely directly on the European Convention in national courts, none the less if the exercise of ministerial discretion interfered with a fundamental right the minister would need to show that there was an important competing public interest to justify the restriction. The same theme is apparent in the reasoning of Sedley J. in *R. v. Canons Park Mental Health Review Tribunal, ex p. A.*[203] The case concerned the construction of the Mental Health Act 1983, and the provisions therein relating to the discharge of patients who suffered from problems of mental health. Sedley J. interpreted the legislation against the background principle that clear justification had to exist for depriving citizens of their freedom when they had committed no crime, and that the statute should be interpreted to be in conformity with the European Convention which it was designed to implement.

Lord Browne-Wilkinson, writing extra-judicially, has endorsed such developments and would go further.[204] He accepts that there are limits as to how far the Convention can be relied upon in our courts. But he raises the question as to whether there is not a more general presumption against interference with human rights which is grounded in the common law.[205] This presumption should apply when there is ambiguity in the domestic

---

[198] *Att.-Gen. v. Guardian Newspapers (No.2)* [1990] 1 A.C. 109, 283–284.

[199] [1993] 1 All E.R. 1011.

[200] *Ibid.* p. 1021.

[201] *R. v. Secretary of State for the Home Department, ex p. Leech* [1993] 4 All E.R. 539.

[202] *National and Local Government Officers Association v. Secretary of State for the Environment* (1992) Times Law Reports 576. The court did, however, state that when reviewing the minister's decision it should only be overturned on grounds of unreasonableness.

[203] [1994] 1 All E.R. 481.

[204] "The Infiltration of a Bill of Rights" [1992] P.L. 397.

[205] *Ibid.* p. 404.

provisions. It should, he argues, also be utilised where there is no ambiguity as such, but just general statutory language.[206]

> "There is respectable authority for the proposition that such general words, even though unambiguous, are not to be construed as to authorise interference with individual freedom unless Parliament has made its intention so to do clear by express provision or necessary implication."[207]

The potential inherent within the common law itself is the subject of a similar piece by Sir John Laws.[208] He draws a distinction between reliance upon the European Convention as a legal instrument *stricto sensu*, and reliance upon the contents of the Convention as a series of propositions which are either already inherent in our law, or can be integrated into it by the judiciary through the normal process of common law adjudication. He maintains that it is not for the courts themselves to incorporate the Convention, since that would be to trespass upon the legislature's sphere. But the courts could legitimately pursue the latter approach. They could, argues Sir John Laws, consider the Convention jurisprudence as one source for charting the development of the common law, in the same way that the courts not infrequently make reference to decisions from foreign jurisdictions. One consequence of this would be a variable standard of review.[209]

> "...the greater the intrusion proposed by a body possessing public power over the citizen in an area where his fundamental rights are at stake, the greater must be the justification which the public authority must demonstrate ...It means that the principles [of review] are neither unitary nor static; it means that the standard by which the court reviews administrative action is a variable one. It means, for example, that while the Secretary of State will largely be left to his own devices in promulgating national economic policy...the court will scrutinise the merits of his decisions much more closely when they concern refugees or free speech."

(c) The legal status of rights at common law: an evaluation

Is it then correct to talk of fundamental rights within our law at all? Is the label "right" which has been used throughout this discussion, as opposed to "liberty" or some other term, really warranted? This is not the place for a complex jurisprudential inquiry into the distinction between rights and

---

[206] *Ibid.* p. 406.

[207] The authorities cited by Lord Browne-Wilkinson include, *R. and W. Paul* v. *The Wheat Commission* [1937] A.C. 139; *Morris* v. *Beardmore* [1981] A.C. 446, 463; *Raymond* v. *Honey* [1983] 1 A.C. 1; *Marcel* v. *Commissioner of Police of the Metropolis* [1992] 2 W.L.R. 50, approving [1991] 2 W.L.R. 1118, 1124.

[208] "Is the High Court the Guardian of Fundamental Constitutional Rights?" [1993] P.L. 59.

[209] *Ibid.* p. 69. See also, Sir Stephen Sedley, "The Sound of Silence: Constitutional Law without a Constitution" (1994) 110 L.Q.R. 270.

liberties. Some consideration of this point is, however, necessary in order to justify the usage of the word "right" here.

At one level the use of this term can be defended simply because the judiciary have expressed themselves in this manner on an increasing number of occasions. In addition to those cited above one can point to other well known instances where this has been the chosen mode of expression.[210] This does not, of course, conclude the matter, but it does provide some defence against the argument that usage of the term "right" is simply an academic's view of how the matter ought to be stated.

The usage of this term can in addition be defended as a matter of principle. Let us begin by disposing of one argument to the contrary which is frequently put: we do not have any constitutional or fundamental rights in this country because it is always ultimately open to Parliament to limit or even abrogate such interests, and therefore the individual only possesses these interests in the residual area left open after the sum of all legal limits have been taken into account. Leaving aside the question as to whether the courts would in fact stand idle, mesmerised by sovereignty, if Parliament did attempt a sweeping limitation of rights,[211] this proposition is still flawed because it elides two separate issues: one is whether it is meaningful to denominate an interest as a right at all, the other is the degree of protection afforded to that interest if it is deemed to be a right. It is clear, on principle, that the existence or not of constitutional entrenchment for rights, or a Bill of Rights, goes to the second issue and not to the first. Legal theory does not regard the existence of this degree of protection as a necessary condition before the term right can be applied.[212] Thus one prominent definition states that a right can exist when a person has an interest which can be regarded as a sufficient reason for holding another person to be under a duty.[213] If considerations which conflict with the interest of the "would-be right-holder" altogether defeat that interest, so that no one could ever meaningfully be said to be under a duty, then there will be no right. Where these "considerations override those on which the right is based on some but not all occasions" then the core right can still exist, albeit in a narrower range.[214]

It is evident that many of the interests commonly regarded as traditional civil liberties are of sufficient importance to be termed rights and do impose duties on others, and that judicial practice, described above, recognises this. It is, furthermore, apparent that, notwithstanding the absence of entrenchment, the courts ascribe these interests with a real *weight*: if the infringement of a speech interest is to be upheld then the executive must provide *reasons* why this is necessary and justifiable. Now one may believe

---

[210] See, *e.g.*, *Raymond* v. *Honey* [1983] 1 A.C. 1, 10, 14; *R.* v. *Secretary of State for the Home Department, ex p. Anderson* [1984] Q.B. 778; *R.* v. *Secretary of State for the Home Department, ex p. Wynne* [1992] Q.B. 406.

[211] Craig, "Sovereignty" (1991) 11 Y.B.E.L. 221.

[212] MacCormick, "Rights in Legislation", in *Law, Morality and Society* (Hacker and Raz eds., 1977), Chap.11; Raz, *The Morality of Freedom* (1986), Chaps. 7 and 10.

[213] Raz, *The Morality of Freedom* (1986), pp. 166, 180-183.

[214] *Ibid.* pp. 183-184.

that the courts should be even more forthright in this respect, but the presence of such a potential infringement does now signal a *more intensive review* than would commonly occur in the context of other types of interests.

(d) The legal status of rights: the EC dimension

An individual may also derive rights from Community law and these rights will be capable of being used, *inter alia*, to challenge discretionary decisions or governmental action which is inconsistent with them. Individuals may obtain rights from Community law in two different ways.

On the one hand, individuals can gain rights from the provisions of the Treaty or norms made thereunder via the concept of direct effect. This concept has been described above,[215] and has been applied to an increasing number of Community norms. Certain provisions of the Treaty which are directly effective deal with subject-matter which would undoubtedly merit inclusion in any list of constitutional or fundamental rights. One obvious example is to be found in Article 119 of the Treaty which is concerned with equal pay and gender discrimination. This was held to be directly effective in the seminal case of *Defrenne*.[216] Defrenne was employed as an air hostess with Sabena. She argued that her conditions of service were discriminatory as compared with those of male cabin stewards who performed the same tasks. The ECJ held that Article 119 was directly effective, in some cases at least, that Defrenne therefore derived rights from the Treaty and that these were enforceable against the airline. Many other cases have followed. For example, in *Johnston*[217] a provision in a UK statutory instrument which, in effect, differentiated between men and women as to the nature of the judicial remedies which they possessed was held to be in breach of Article 6 of Directive 76/207 on Equal Treatment.[218]

On the other hand, there is the Community concept of fundamental rights which has been developed by the ECJ.[219] The EC Treaty contains no list of traditional fundamental rights as such, in large part because the original rationale for the Treaty was principally economic. The catalyst for the creation of such rights was the threat of revolt by the courts of some Member States. Individuals who were dissatisfied with the provisions of, for example, a regulation would challenge it before their national court and contend that it was inconsistent with rights in their own national constitutions, and moreover that these rights could not have been given away by the state when acceding to the Community. An argument of just this kind was made before the German courts in *Internationale*

---

[215] See above, Chap. 5.
[216] Case 43/75, *Defrenne* v. *Sabena* [1976] E.C.R. 455.
[217] Case 222/84, *Johnston* v. *Chief Constable of the Royal Ulster Constabulary* [1986] E.C.R. 1651.
[218] Wyatt and Dashwood's, *European Community Law* (3rd ed., 1993), Chap. 21.
[219] *Ibid.* pp. 98-102.

Handelsgesellschaft.[220] The threat which this posed to the supremacy of Community law was not lost on the ECJ, and it stated that Community norms could not be challenged in this manner. However, in order to stem any possible national rebellion the ECJ declared that fundamental rights were indeed part of the general principles of Community law, and that the compatibility of a Community norm with such rights would be tested by the ECJ itself.[221] Three points concerning the fundamental rights doctrine are of particular relevance here.

First, although the EC is not formally bound by the decisions of the European Court of Human Rights, the ECJ has referred to specific provisions of the Convention on a number of occasions.[222] Insofar as it does so this provides the Convention with a peremptory force in national courts which it would otherwise lack.[223]

Secondly, fundamental rights have been used principally to attack Community norms, such as regulations or decisions. However, if a national provision is based upon a Community norm then the former may not survive a challenge to the latter. Thus in *Kirk*[224] the ECJ held that the retroactivity of a Community regulation could not validate *ex post facto* national measures which were penal in nature, where these measures imposed penalties for an act which was not punishable at the time that it was committed.

The third point is the most important, and is potentially of far reaching significance. While, as noted above, the principal thrust of the fundamental rights doctrine has been to attack Community norms it may not prove to be so limited in the future. In many ways the logic of the doctrine would dictate that it can apply against national action too, provided that this action can in some way be connected with Community law. This logic can be simply stated: fundamental rights are part of Community law, and therefore they should be capable of being used not only when the Community authorities act in contravention of these rights, but also when it is a Member State which has done so in an area covered by the Treaties. The impact of this expansion of the doctrine would be far reaching. It would mean that individuals would, in this area, possess protected rights, and that the ultimate arbiter of the meaning of such rights would be the ECJ and not national courts.

This may seem fanciful, but the decision in the *Grogan* case[225] indicates otherwise. The Irish constitution prohibited the dissemination of information about abortion. An association of Irish students sought to provide such information about abortion services in the UK, and claimed that the prohibition was contrary to Community law. Their argument was,

---

[220] Case 11/70, [1970] E.C.R. 1125.

[221] *Ibid.* p. 1134.

[222] See, *e.g.*, Case 136/79, *National Panasonic* [1980] E.C.R. 2033, 2057.

[223] Grief, "The Domestic Impact of the European Convention on Human Rights as Mediated through Community Law" [1991] P.L. 555.

[224] Case 63/83, [1984] E.C.R. 2689.

[225] Case C-159/90, *Society for the Protection of Unborn Children Ireland Ltd.* v. *Grogan* [1991] 3 C.M.L.R. 849.

in essence, that the provision and receipt of services are protected by Articles 59 and 60 of the Treaty, and legislation made thereunder; that freedom of speech is one of the recognised fundamental rights under Community law; and that therefore an Irish rule which prohibited the dissemination of information, and in that sense impeded free speech, in an area covered by the Treaty, freedom to provide and receive services, must be struck down. The subject-matter could hardly have been more controversial. This undoubtedly influenced the ECJ which avoided the issue by deciding that there was no formal link between the student associations and the clinics in the UK, and that therefore the prohibition on the dissemination of information was not a restriction for the purposes of Article 59 of the Treaty. The Court did, however, lay down a marker for the future.[226]

> "...where national legislation falls within the field of application of Community law the Court, when requested to give a preliminary ruling, must provide the national court with all the elements of interpretation which are necessary in order to enable it to assess the compatibility of that legislation with the fundamental rights – as laid down in particular in the European Convention on Human Rights – the observance of which the Court ensures."

It would not have taken very much to bring the facts of *Grogan* itself within this field. If, for example, there had been some more formal link between the student organisations and a clinic this may well have sufficed.

Given that the area of application of Community law is already broad, and still expanding, then the potential impact of the Community's concept of fundamental rights on national legislation or action will be far reaching.

(4) EQUALITY

The relevance of equality in cases of judicial review has already been touched upon in the previous section dealing with fundamental rights: insofar as such rights are recognised then some conception of equality would almost certainly feature within any such list. It may nonetheless be helpful to give separate consideration to equality and judicial review.

(a) Domestic law

Even though we do not have any written Bill of Rights equality features at a number of different levels within our own domestic jurisprudence.

First, there is the *formal* concept of equality to be found in Dicey's conception of the rule of law: that all should be subject to the same law in the sense that officials should not be afforded any special privileges by the laws of the country. This particular statement concerning equality has long been subjected to criticisms by those who have pointed out that it is both acceptable for there to be differences in the laws which apply to different

---

[226] *Ibid.* p. 892.

groups within society, and that the laws which are applicable to public bodies may have to differ in certain respects from those which apply to private individuals.

Secondly, there is the related but more sophisticated concept of equality which demands both that like groups be treated in a like manner, and that different groups should be treated differently. These dictates can be taken into account under our existing heads of review, such as improper purpose or relevancy, but it would be beneficial to decide such cases more openly upon the basis of equality as such. Thus in *Kruse* v. *Johnson*[227] the court held that a bylaw could not be partial or unequal in its operation as between different classes.

It can obviously be contentious as to whether two groups should or should not be treated as like groups for these purposes. Some guidance in this respect is provided by legislation which prohibits discrimination upon the grounds of, for example, race or gender. The very existence of these prohibitions on discrimination means that groups cannot be validly distinguished merely because of their respective ethnic backgrounds: disadvantageous treatment of one such group cannot be defended by claiming that they are different groups merely because of racial origin.

This second connotation inevitably crosses the boundaries between a *formal* and a *substantive* sense of equality. The very decision as to whether a certain group should or should not be regarded as the same or different from another inevitably requires the making of value judgments. Administrative action which is felt to draw the distinction at the wrong point may well be overturned on one of the traditional grounds of review, or more openly upon equality itself.

A third sense of equality is closely related to the second: this would demand that there should be substantive equality before the law. This meaning of equality is undoubtedly *substantive*, and will be determined by the "political, social and ethical ideas of the time".[228] Any substantive conception of equality will itself be premised upon, and reflect, a certain vision of distributive justice: the desired pattern of ownership of goods, wealth etc. within society. There is, not surprisingly, sharp disagreement among varying schools of thought as to what is the proper theory of distributive justice. Now it might be thought that this is of no concern to lawyers as such. There are two types of reason why this is not so.

On the one hand, differing conceptions of distributive justice markedly affect arguments concerning: the legitimacy of affirmative action programmes to benefit the disadvantaged;[229] the legitimacy of state action to redistribute wealth;[230] and the extent to which we should be attempting

---

[227] [1898] 2 Q.B. 91.
[228] Schwarze, *European Administrative Law* (1992), p. 546.
[229] Dworkin, *Taking Rights Seriously* (1977) and "What Is Equality? Part 2. Equality of Resources" (1981) 10 Phil. & Pub. Affairs 283.
[230] Buchanan, *Freedom in Constitutional Contract* (1978); Brennan and Buchanan, *The Reason of Rules* (1985).

to protect the value of some political liberties, such as speech or voting rights, by placing limits upon expenditure by political parties.[231]

On the other hand, the very conception of distributive justice may well be integrally connected to the fact that civil rights are recognised as an independent species of interests to which the law should accord privileged status. Individuals may only agree to this protected status *if* society is to be ordered in a certain socio-economic manner.[232]

The controversial nature of these questions often means that they are ignored or the answer is presumed to be self-evident. Neither of these sentiments is warranted. They cannot be ignored because the issues do arise before the courts. The answer cannot be regarded as self-evident when it is clearly controversial.

(b) Community law

The influence of Community law will most certainly be felt in this area, both directly and indirectly.

The *direct* impact of Community law on equality is to be found in the proscription of any discrimination on the grounds of nationality. This is a central feature of Community law and is enshrined in general terms in Article 7 of the Treaty, while finding more specific recognition in, for example, Articles 48, 52 and 59 which prohibit discriminatory treatment in relation to free movement of workers, freedom of establishment and freedom to provide services in another Member State. These provisions have direct effect, both vertical and horizontal, and thus can be relied upon in national courts against either the state or a private individual. Other articles of the Treaty prohibit discrimination on other grounds, such as Article 119 which proscribes discrimination on grounds of gender. Action by the state or a private company which infringes this Article will be open to attack via Article 177 in the national courts, as exemplified by the well known *Defrenne* case,[233] in which a Belgian air hostess successfully argued that the terms and conditions of her contract were discriminatory as compared to those of her male colleagues who were doing the same job.

Community law also has an *indirect* impact in relation to equality in the sense that it provides a fertile source of information about how decisions are made in cases where an individual argues that like cases are not being treated alike, or that groups which are different are being treated in the same manner. One of the main areas in which this issue arises is under the Common Agricultural Policy. An individual may challenge such a Community regulation on the ground that it was discriminatory under Article 40(3) of the Treaty. It has therefore been necessary for the ECJ to articulate a test to apply in such cases. This test combines two complementary ideas: one is that there should be similar treatment of

---

[231] Rawls, "The Basic Liberties and their Priority", *Liberty, Equality and Law* (McMurrin ed., 1987), pp. 1-87.
[232] *e.g.* Rawls, *A Theory of Justice* (1973).
[233] Case 43/75, *Defrenne* v. *Sabena* [1976] E.C.R. 455.

comparable situations; the other is that it may only be possible to decide whether situations really are comparable by considering the background policy aims of the area in question.[234]

(5) LEGITIMATE EXPECTATIONS, LEGAL CERTAINTY AND LEGALITY

The role of legitimate expectations at the procedural level has been discussed earlier.[235] This concept may also have a more substantive role to play. The law on this topic is complex and is treated in depth below.[236] It is important, however, to make clear the relevance of this issue within the general context of the control of discretionary power.

A public body may have made a representation that it would exercise its discretion in a particular manner which has been reasonably and detrimentally relied on by the individual. This representation may be said to generate a legitimate expectation that the power would indeed be exercised in this way. In this sense the *principle of legal certainty* would indicate that the individual ought to be able to plan his or her action on that basis.[237] There can, however, be a clash between this principle and the *principle of legality*. This can occur in one of two ways.

First, the representation may have been outside the power of the public body or the officer who made it. The principle of legality manifests itself here in the simple form that the representation was *ultra vires*.

Secondly, the principle of legality has been an impediment to the individual even where the representation itself was not outside the public body's power. In this second situation the public body may have made a representation which is *intra vires*, but later seeks to depart from it. Or it may have published policy criteria for dealing with a particular issue, which criteria are *intra vires*, but it may now wish to adopt new tests for dealing with the same topic, these new criteria also being lawful. The individual then seeks to rely on the initial representation or original statement of policy. A traditional objection to the individual being able to do so is that this would be a fetter on the discretion of the public body, which should be able to develop policy in the manner which it believes to be best in the public interest. In this type of case the principle of legality is apparent in the doctrine that such a fetter on discretion would itself be *ultra vires*.

The way in which we should balance the competing principles of legal certainty and legality will be considered in detail below. It will suffice to say for the present that the very recognition that there are competing principles at play in this area is itself an important precondition for resolution of the problem.

---

[234] Case 6/71, *Rheinmullen* [1971] E.C.R. 823; Case 79/77, *Firma Kulhaus Zentrum AG* [1978] E.C.R. 611; Case 8/82, *Wagner* [1983] E.C.R. 371; Case 230/78, *Eridania* [1979] E.C.R. 2749; Case 139/77, *Denkavit* [1978] E.C.R. 1317.

[235] See above, pp. 293-296.

[236] See below, Chap. 18.

[237] For a detailed consideration of the problem in other European systems see, Schwarze, *European Administrative Law* (1992), pp. 874-1173.

Section 4. Misuse of Power: II

Having examined the principles which the courts apply in this area it may be helpful to stand back and consider, in more general terms, the options which are at our disposal for deciding how far the courts should impose substantive constraints on those who are subject to review.

1. *Five Options for Judicial Review*

(1) SUBSTITUTION OF JUDGMENT

The courts could systematically substitute their choice as to how the discretion ought to have been exercised for that of the administrative authority; they would in other words reassess the matter afresh and decide, for example, whether funds ought to be allocated in one way rather than another. Our basic conceptions of political theory and the allocation of governmental functions are against this approach. Decisions as to political and social choice are made by the legislature, or by a person assigned the task by the legislature. To sanction general judicial intervention simply because the court would prefer a different choice to that of the administrator runs counter to this fundamental assumption, and would entail a re-allocation of power from the legislature and bureaucracy to the courts.

(2) "DRAWING THE BOUNDARIES" THROUGH TRADITIONAL TECHNIQUES OF PURPOSE, RELEVANCY AND REASONABLENESS

A less extreme form of control would be one in which the courts do not impose a particular conclusion by way of substitution for that of the administrator, but rather draw the boundaries for the legitimate exercise of discretion. This would involve judicial intervention on both of the levels mentioned above.[238] The courts would use the first level of control via purpose and relevancy to decide what ends the authority should and should not be entitled to pursue, or what considerations must or must not be taken into account. They would also intervene using the second level of control, but only if the decision was manifestly unreasonable. This is the approach manifest in the *Wednesbury* case: the concepts of purpose, relevancy and reasonableness provide the principal judicial tools through which option two is attained.

While the courts have refrained from explicit substitution of judgment (option one), the line between this mode of control and the second can be perilously thin. The underlying reason for this is that statutes do not really have "corners" in the neat way postulated by theory. The language is often elliptical, ambiguous and inherently open-textured. What the legitimate ambit of a certain power actually is will necessarily be a value judgment. It is relatively easy for a court using the formal language of keeping a body within the four corners of its powers to impose its own view as to what the authority should have done. It is only by examining particular cases closely that we can determine whether this has occurred.

---

[238] See above, pp. 402-403.

The decision in *Secretary of State for Education and Science* v. *Tameside Metropolitan Borough Council*[239] is worthy of such consideration. A local authority scheme which included plans for the abolition of certain grammar schools was altered following a local election at which the party in power changed from Labour to Conservative. The Secretary of State, acting under section 68 of the Education Act 1944, purported to give directions to the council for the implementation of the original Labour scheme. Section 68 states, in essence, that if the Secretary of State is satisfied that any local education authority is acting unreasonably in relation to any power conferred on it, the Secretary may give directions as to the exercise of that power. The Secretary of State argued, *inter alia*, that the selection process necessary now that the grammar schools were to be retained could not be adequately organised within the available time, and that this was unreasonable behaviour within section 68. The House of Lords disagreed. The judgment can be analysed in stages.

First, the subjective formulation of section 68 is made objective so as to read, "if the Secretary of State has reasonable grounds to believe". This is most apparent from the judgment of Lord Wilberforce[240] who makes clearer than their remaining Lordships that the case is one about jurisdictional fact. All however concurred in this alteration.[241] The standard meaning to be attributed to "reasonable grounds for belief" is that if the decision-maker has some such grounds the decision will be upheld even though a court might differ.[242] However, the objectivity infused into section 68 is found by their Lordships to connote more than this. Thus, it was held that if certain facts must exist before the exercise of judgment then the court will examine whether those facts exist, whether the decision was made upon a proper self direction as to those facts, and whether irrelevant facts were taken into account.[243] The novel concept of "proper self direction" as to the facts which was mentioned by Lord Wilberforce is particularly open-ended. Thus, the Secretary of State has to show reasonable grounds for believing (in this broadened sense) that the local authority was acting unreasonably.

The second question therefore is, what is meant by the term unreasonable? With the exception of Lord Wilberforce,[244] their Lordships adopt the *Wednesbury* meaning. Applied here the Secretary of State would have to show some reasonable grounds in the above sense, that the local authority was proposing action so unreasonable that no reasonable authority would countenance it. Not surprisingly he failed. Little if any consideration was given as to whether unreasonable in the statute should bear this very narrow meaning. Good reasons can be given why it should not.

As we have seen, Lord Greene M.R.'s meaning of unreasonable was developed for the judicial review of discretionary power. It was not the

---

[239] [1977] A.C. 1014.
[240] *Ibid.* pp. 1047-1048.
[241] *Ibid.* pp. 1054, 1065, 1072, 1074.
[242] *e.g. Liversidge* v. *Anderson* [1942] A.C. 206, 239; *Re W. (An Infant)* [1971] A.C. 682, 699-700.
[243] *Tameside* [1977] A.C. 1014, 1047-1048, 1065, 1072.
[244] *Ibid.* p. 1048.

construction of a statutory term, but a judicially imposed limit on discretion. It was drawn narrowly because of the constitutional position of the courts. They cannot intervene unless the decision-maker steps outside the boundaries of what the legislature was believed to have allowed. The artificial meaning of unreasonable developed by Lord Greene M.R. must be seen in this light. That construction was intended to ensure that the courts do not substitute their view for that of the administrator just because they believe that a different conclusion would have been more reasonable. Compare this to the position of the Secretary of State. He does not have review powers because he is not a court. He possesses one form of statutory control, *i.e.* unreasonableness. None of the legitimate reasons for the artificial *Wednesbury* sense of the term apply here. The minister does not sit over the local authority, in the way that a court supervises administrative authorities, including the executive. His constitutional position is entirely different. Parliament has expressly given him power to intervene when the local authority is acting unreasonably. The natural meaning of that term is "not acting as a reasonable local authority would act", as opposed to "behaviour so unreasonable that no reasonable authority would countenance it". There is no reason why the natural meaning should not apply. None of the constitutional reasons which are the basis for the artificial *Wednesbury* meaning are relevant. If the interpretation given to the term unreasonable in *Tameside* is to mean that the Secretary of State must find behaviour akin to the "red haired school teacher case", then this emasculates the one control mechanism which he possesses.

Now all of this may well have made no difference to the final result; the court's reading of the facts may have led them to the same conclusion whatever the meanings given to reasonable and unreasonable. Yet those meanings matter: given the breadth of what the courts required of the Secretary of State as reasonable grounds for the action, and the narrowness of what would be regarded as unreasonable local authority action, it is hard to visualise a different result.

A second case which is worthy of analysis is the decision in *Bromley London Borough Council* v. *Greater London Council*.[245] Section 1 of the Transport (London) Act 1969, imposed upon the GLC a duty to develop policies which promoted the provision of integrated, efficient and economic transport facilities for Greater London. The London Transport Executive (LTE) was to implement these policies. Under the Act the LTE was required, so far as was practicable, to make up any deficit incurred in one accounting period within the next such period.[246] The legislation empowered the GLC to take such action as was necessary and appropriate in order to enable the LTE to comply with this obligation;[247] the GLC also had power to make grants to the LTE for any purpose.[248]

---

[245] [1983] 1 A.C. 768. See now, *R.* v. *London Transport Executive, ex p. Greater London Council* [1983] Q.B. 484, in which a revised fares reduction scheme was held to be lawful.
[246] s.7(3)(b).
[247] s.7(6).
[248] s.3(1).

The GLC decided to implement a resolution, which had been included by the majority group in their manifesto, to reduce fares by 25 per cent. To this end, the GLC issued a supplementary precept for rates to all London boroughs. The money thereby obtained would be paid by the GLC to the LTE as a grant, in order to enable the latter to balance its accounts. An indirect result of the reduction of the fares was that the GLC would lose approximately £50 million of the rate support grant. Bromley London Borough Council sought certiorari to quash the supplementary rate, arguing that it was either beyond the powers of the GLC under the 1969 Act, or that it was an invalid exercise of discretion under that legislation.

The House of Lords upheld this claim. Their Lordships recognised that the power to make grants contained within section 3 conferred a wide discretion, and that such grants could be made to supplement the revenue received by the LTE from fares. This discretion was, however, limited. The LTE's basic obligation was to run its operations on ordinary business principles, which the fare reduction contravened. The GLC could not use its grant-making powers to achieve a social policy which was inconsistent with these obligations. Reduction of the fares was also invalid because it involved a breach of the fiduciary duty owed by the GLC to the ratepayers. The effect of the 25 per cent reduction in fares would be to place an inordinate burden on the ratepayers, particularly because this would be accompanied by a known loss of rate support grant. Nor could the GLC defend its policy on the basis that it possessed a mandate to lower fares. Those who were elected were representatives and not delegates. They could not regard themselves as irrevocably bound by their manifesto.

The case is interesting in many respects.[249] As Lord Diplock said,[250] the statutory language was sometimes opaque and elliptical, and this is reflected in the fact that although the House of Lords reached a unanimous conclusion, their Lordships differed in their interpretation of the legislation. Because of the intricacy and ambiguity of the statute, all of their Lordships, explicitly or implicitly, adopted a purposive approach to the construction of the legislation. Two aspects of that approach will be examined here, the fiduciary duty owed to the ratepayers, and the argument based upon the election manifesto.

The idea that a local authority owes a fiduciary duty to its ratepayers is by no means new,[251] but it has never been subjected to a thorough judicial investigation. The idea seems self-evident: a local authority occupies a position of trust, or a fiduciary duty, in relation to the ratepayers whose money it is using, and who are the beneficiaries of the services being provided. Closer analysis reveals a shakier foundation.[252] First, ratepayers do not provide all, or even the major proportion of, local authority revenue. Central government grants furnish the main source of such funds. Secondly,

[249] Dignan, "Policy-Making, Local Authorities and the Courts: the 'GLC Fares' Case" (1983) L.Q.R. 605; Loughlin, *Local Government in the Modern State* (1986), Chap. 3
[250] [1983] 1 A.C. 768, 822-823.
[251] *Roberts* v. *Hopwood* [1925] A.C. 578; *Prescott* v. *Birmingham Corporation* [1955] Ch. 210.
[252] Note, Griffiths (1982) 41 C.L.J. 216.

control through the imposition of this fiduciary duty operates in an asymmetrical fashion. It serves to quash expenditure which is deemed to be in breach of this duty, but does not impose any obligation to spend money which is being unreasonably withheld.[253] This is a reflection of a more general characteristic of review, which is that it is geared towards the avoidance of mistakes. Effectiveness and mistake avoidance are treated as synonymous, which is often overly simplistic. Thirdly, the invocation of the fiduciary duty concept does not, of itself, provide the courts with the answer, but rather forces them to answer an extremely difficult question. Given that ratepayers are, as their Lordships admitted, only one part of those to whom the local authority owes duties, how does one determine where the correct balance lies between their interests and those of other sections of local society? The answer must lie ultimately in the perceptions of those making the decisions, in this instance the court. It is arguable that such determinations are best left to the elected representatives. How one balances the interests of property, in the guise of ratepayers, and other interests is a classic political choice. If that choice is not to the liking of those with voting power, many of whom will be ratepayers, they can make their views evident through the ballot box. This leads us directly onto the argument based on the manifesto.

The response of the House of Lords to the argument based upon the election manifesto is, in many ways, incontrovertible. A person who is elected is not a delegate of those who voted. He or she is a representative who must act in the best interests of all the constituents. The representative cannot be irrevocably bound to fulfil election promises. This is unexceptionable in itself, but it does not sit easily with the views expressed by the House of Lords in the *Tameside*[254] case. In that case their Lordships placed much emphasis upon the fact that the local authority had a virtual mandate to retain certain grammar schools in the area. It was a significant factor to be taken into account when assessing the reasonableness of the local authority's conduct in attempting to allocate children to the correct school.

It seems clear that if we pursue the present forms of control the judiciary will inevitably continue to be embroiled in decision-making which is of a broadly political nature in a double sense. First, the discernment of what are legitimate purposes, and what are relevant considerations, within particular cases can never be value-free. This is evident from the preceding discussion. Secondly, and of equal importance, is the fact that, as we have seen, the courts possess creative choice as to the general intensity of review which should operate within a particular area. The concepts of purpose, relevancy and reasonableness can be used in an intensive or less intensive fashion. Thus the courts have, for example, limited their intervention in cases concerning homeless persons,[255] using arguments concerning the subjectivity of administrative discretion which found little favour in cases such as *Tameside* considered above; and they have counselled restraint in

---

[253] Williams, "The Control of Local Authorities", *Welsh Studies in Public Law* (Andrews ed., 1970), pp. 132-133.
[254] [1977] A.C. 1014.
[255] *Puhlhofer* v. *Hillingdon London Borough Council* [1986] A.C. 484, 510-511, 518.

circumstances where propositions of law are interwoven with issues of social and ethical controversy concerning the scope of parental rights,[256] while being more willing to intervene where legal issues are intertwined with questions of social and economic choice, as in the *Bromley* case.

(3) HARD LOOK

A third option which has been advocated is that we should draw upon American experience and adopt a "hard look" standard of review for discretionary decisions.[257] This suggestion is based upon the difficulties and defects of other attempts to ensure the rational consideration of policy alternatives within government. The hard look doctrine is espoused as a corrective, albeit partial, for these difficulties, and as a method for reinforcing governmental accountability. The objective is to ensure that policy alternatives are adequately considered, that reasons are proffered for agency decisions, and that differing interests can present their views to the agency and have those views adequately discussed. There is much force in the general direction of this suggestion. How far we require a new "doctrine" to achieve such ends is more questionable. Three comments on this suggestion are warranted.

First, the "hard look" test is contrasted with the "kid glove" standard of review within the United Kingdom under the *Wednesbury* test which is said to demand no more than that a decision be not so unreasonable that no reasonable body could make it. Lord Greene M.R.'s substantive sense of unreasonableness was, however, only ever one aspect of review. Purpose and relevancy furnished the other two aspects, and all three have been and can be used in an expansive fashion which renders the label "kid glove" inappropriate.

Secondly, the difference between the standard of review under hard look and that presently employed by our own courts can only be assessed by understanding the *evolution* and *meaning* of hard look in the United States.

The term hard look *evolved* by way of contrast with the previous standard of review generally employed by United States' courts which was narrow. Agency findings could be set aside if they were found to be "arbitrary, capricious or an abuse of discretion".[258] This criterion was strictly interpreted: litigants would have to persuade the court that the decision had "no rational basis whatsoever",[259] and not surprisingly few managed to do so.[260] In short, the United States' standard of review was akin to having Lord Greene M.R.'s narrow sense of unreasonableness as the only basis for attack; it was the United States' courts who adopted a "kid glove" approach compared to their United Kingdom counterparts. The label "hard look" developed in essence because the United States' courts

---

[256] *Gillick* v. *West Norfolk and Wisbech Area Health Authority* [1986] A.C. 112, 193-194, 206. See further, *e.g. British Airways Board* v. *Laker Airways Ltd.* [1985] A.C. 58.

[257] Harden and Lewis, *The Noble Lie, The British Constitution and the Rule of Law* (1986).

[258] Administrative Procedure Act 1946, s.706(2)(a).

[259] Breyer and Stewart, *Administrative Law and Regulatory Policy* (2nd ed., 1985), p. 337.

[260] *Ibid.* p. 336.

began to desire more control[261] than allowed by this limited test. Has this development now led to the United States having more intensive review than the United Kingdom?

This can only be assessed by examining the *meaning* of hard look more closely. A leading United States' authority[262] describes the newer test as the "adequate consideration or hard look" approach to the review of discretion. This nomenclature is revealing, as is the meaning ascribed to such review in a leading decision. In the *State Farm*[263] case the Supreme Court founded its intervention on the arbitrary and capricious test, but then gave a broader reading to that phrase than that provided in earlier cases. The court accepted that it should not substitute its judgment for that of the agency. It could, however, intervene if any of the following defects were present: if the agency relied on factors which Congress had not intended it to consider; failed to consider an important aspect of the problem; offered an explanation which ran counter to the evidence before the agency; was so implausible that it could not be sustained; or failed to provide a record which substantiated its findings. Commentators in the United Kingdom will no doubt perceive the doctrinal analogy with the fluid *Wednesbury* principle. The hard look doctrine therefore represents a shift from a previously more minimal standard of review, where judicial intervention would occur only if there was irrationality, to one where the courts will interfere where the broader list of defects set out above are present. That list is clearly analogous to the totality of Lord Greene M.R.'s own list (purpose, relevancy and reasonableness). Viewed in this light hard look appears as a movement away from the earlier "kid glove" approach of the American courts to the tougher standard which we have had in the United Kingdom for over 100 years.[264] Moreover, in the same way that the United Kingdom tests can be used more or less intensively, similar flexibility resides in the analogous American doctrines. There are indications that hard look is being applied less intensively than hitherto.[265]

Thirdly, it has been suggested that by focusing upon the hard look doctrine issues concerning the merits can be more readily avoided.[266] This is doubtful for precisely the same reasons we considered when discussing option two.

---

[261] See, *Greater Boston Television Corp.* v. *Federal Communications Comm.* 444 F.2d 841, 850-853 (D.C.Cir. 1970), cert. denied 403 US 923 (1971); *Environmental Defense Fund Inc.* v. *Ruckelshaus* 439 F.2d 584 (D.C.Cir. 1971); Leventhal, "Environmental Decision-making and the Role of the Courts" 122 U.Pa.L.Rev. 509 (1974); Stewart, "The Development of Administrative and Quasi-Constitutional Law in Judicial Review of Environmental Decision-making; Lessons From the Clean Air Act" 62 Iowa L.Rev. 713 (1977).

[262] Breyer and Stewart, *Administrative Law*, p. 341.

[263] *Motor Vehicle Manufacturers Assn.* v. *State Farm Mutual Automobile Insurance Co.* 463 US 29, 42-43 (1983). The case was concerned with the adequacy of an agency's explanation for rescinding a regulation concerned with passive restraints in motor vehicles.

[264] The *Wednesbury* decision did not create, but merely synthesised, what the UK courts had been doing for considerable time. Many important decisions on purpose and relevancy pre-date Lord Greene M.R.'s decision, see above, pp. 405-409.

[265] e.g. *Chevron, U.S.A. Inc.* v. *Natural Resources Defense Council, Inc.*, 467 US 837, 81 L.Ed. 694, 104 S.Ct. 2778 (1984).

[266] Harden and Lewis, *The Noble Lie*, pp. 205-206, 234, 263.

On the one hand, it may well be true that neither option two nor option three entail direct substitution of judgment by the court. However, deciding whether a particular consideration is relevant, whether a particular object is within the allowable range, whether an adequate hearing has been given to interested parties, and whether the reasons ultimately provided are sufficient, are all factors which can encroach indirectly on the merits. The court may not be stipulating a particular substantive conclusion. It may however be explicitly or implicitly ruling out certain options by the way in which it addresses and answers the preceding issues. If a particular interest group challenges an agency decision, claiming that the rights of property owners were not adequately considered, or that the interests of the environment were improperly excluded, the subsequent judicial review will inevitably entail some vision concerning the nature of such interests within the overall constitutional structure, the relevance of such interests in this statutory scheme, and their relationship with other statutory goals. Such issues which touch upon the merits can no more be avoided under option three than under option two; both options address many of the same issues, and face the same problems.[267]

On the other hand, the assumption underlying this third argument is that by concentrating, in so far as the court can, upon "process" rather than the "merits", judicial review will be less controversial. It has, however, been convincingly demonstrated that complex substantive value judgments underlie the determination of many ostensibly process-related issues. Whose views should be taken into account, and what type of process rights an individual should be given, both entail substantive judgments of considerable complexity.[268]

The American doctrine is worthy of consideration nonetheless for a number of related reasons. One is that the United States' courts have put more teeth into the *State Farm* "list" through their greater concern for the provision of reasons and a fully developed record. This is a point of importance. However, the United Kingdom courts have recently insisted upon more evidentiary support for discretionary decisions, and exhibited a greater willingness to assess the cogency of the reasoning therein.[269] A second reason for the focus upon American doctrine is that United States' law has generally evinced a greater concern for allowing interested parties to express their views, than has UK law.[270] Expanded review under the hard look doctrine can serve to reinforce such ideas, by ensuring that adequate consideration is accorded to the differing views presented to the agency.

---

[267] See, Breyer, "Vermont Yankee and the Courts' Role in the Nuclear Energy Controversy" 91 Harv.L.Rev. 1833 (1978); Wright, "The Courts and the Rulemaking Process: The Limits of Judicial Review" 59 Cornell L.Rev. 375 (1974).

[268] *e.g.* Tribe, "The Puzzling Persistence of Process Based Constitutional Theories" 89 Yale L.J. 1063 (1980); Brest, "The Substance of Process" 42 Ohio St. L.J. 131 (1981); Dworkin, "The Forum of Principle" 56 N.Y.U.L. Rev. 469 (1981).

[269] See above, pp. 310-316.

[270] Stewart, "The Reformation of American Administrative Law" 88 Harv.L.Rev. 1667 (1975).

There is much to be said for such increased participatory rights.[271] Should we decide to develop our law more fully in this direction this can be accommodated within the idea that all relevant considerations should be taken into account by the decision-maker.[272]

(4) DRAWING THE BOUNDARIES AND APPLYING PRINCIPLES OF SUBSTANTIVE REVIEW

A fourth option can be presented as follows. The courts continue to intervene if the authority exceeds the ambit of its power by acting *illegally*, in the sense of using that power for an improper purpose, or taking an irrelevant consideration into account. This option, therefore, builds upon the mode of review described in option two. It does, however, go beyond this by expanding the range of principles which are embraced by the idea of *irrationality*. Whereas option two includes only unreasonableness in its substantive *Wednesbury* sense, advocates of option four argue that other matters such as proportionality and concern for fundamental rights should be regarded as controls on the exercise of discretion, either instead of *Wednesbury* unreasonableness or in addition thereto. The exercise of administrative discretion is thus subjected to a set of more specific substantive principles. This would have the benefit of forcing the courts to articulate more openly the premises on which they are reasoning. An argument along these lines has been developed,[273] drawing upon the reasoning used by Lord Diplock in the *G.C.H.Q.*[274] case. His Lordship articulated three grounds for judicial review: illegality, irrationality and procedural impropriety. Illegality meant that the decision-maker must understand correctly the law that regulates the power and must give effect to it; irrationality connoted *Wednesbury* unreasonableness, but could be expanded to cover other grounds of challenge; and procedural impropriety covered a breach of natural justice or failure to comply with the procedural rules in the enabling legislation.

The extent to which the courts are moving in this direction has been charted above,[275] and there is much to be said in favour of the clearer and more specific articulation of substantive principles to guide the exercise of administrative discretion. We have already seen how the courts have used the *Wednesbury* sense of unreasonableness to invalidate exercises of discretionary power which could not realistically be regarded as absurd, or manifestly irrational. As Jowell and Lester argue, "intellectual honesty requires a further and better explanation as to why the act is

---

[271] See above, pp. 258-262.

[272] See the developments concerning consultation rights and legitimate expectations, pp. 256-258.

[273] Jowell and Lester, "Beyond Wednesbury: Substantive Principles of Administrative Law" [1987] P.L. 368. See also Allan, "Pragmatism and Theory in Public Law" (1988) 104 L.Q.R. 422; Bell, "The Expansion of Judicial Review Over Discretionary Power in France" [1986] P.L. 99. *cf.* Hutchinson, "The Rise and Ruse of Administrative Law and Scholarship" (1985) 48 M.L.R. 193.

[274] *Council of Civil Service Unions* v. *Minister for the Civil Service* [1985] A.C. 374, 410-411.

[275] Jowell and Lester, "Proportionality", p. 62.

unreasonable".[276] The justification for the clearer articulation of substantive principles can be reinforced by the type of thesis advanced by Reich.[277] He argues that the role of government in distributing "largesse" (in the form of licences, social welfare, subsidies, government contracts and the like), has increased government power over the individual. Benefits are withheld for reasons indirectly related at best to the activity in question. The judiciary should employ substantive review as one method of ensuring that the grant of such largesse does not become a mechanism for illegitimately regulating a large number of peripherally related activities. The development of substantive principles *supplements* and not merely *implements* legislative intent, by furnishing more specific criteria for "*good administration*". A number of features of this approach should be noted.

First, the difficulties which beset the process of statutory construction, discussed in the context of option two, in order to determine the purposes etc. for which the discretionary power can be used, will continue to be present within option four. This is not a critique as such, since these problems are inherent within almost any species of substantive review.

Secondly, there is no doubt, as we have seen, that a number of existing cases can be regarded as examples of proportionality. However, in seeking to prove the existence of "authority" for such an idea the argument has been made that proportionality underlies decisions as diverse as those relating to the legitimacy of planning conditions or local transport policy, disciplinary actions or sex discrimination.[278] There are two problems with this argument. On the one hand, it may indirectly serve to reduce the protection for the individual. As noted above proportionality should be considered only when it has been decided that the authority had the power to use its discretion in the way that it did. If it was seeking to use its power for an improper purpose then it should be struck down at the first level without any discussion of proportionality.[279] To seek to explain so many cases on the grounds of proportionality runs the risk that the courts will assume that the authority did have the power to act in the way in which it did, the first level hurdle will be forgotten and the only relevant inquiry will then be as to whether the exercise of discretion was proportionate or not. On the other hand, if the concept is viewed in this broad way, then its application to some of the diverse areas mentioned above is scarcely more self-executing or clear-cut than usage of terms, such as reasonableness, which it seeks to replace. For example, to categorise the *Bromley* decision as one which has a "hidden notion of proportionality",[280] requiring a balance between the benefits to transport users against the burdens to ratepayers, does not resolve any of the crucially difficult issues in the case. Any answer requires evaluation of the purpose of the legislation; a

---

[276] "Beyond *Wednesbury*" [1987] P.L. 368, 371.
[277] "The New Property" 73 Yale L.J. 733 (1964).
[278] Jowell and Lester, "Proportionality: Neither Novel Nor Dangerous", *New Directions in Judicial Review*, (Jowell and Oliver eds., 1988), pp. 51-72.
[279] Boyron, "Proportionality in English Administrative Law: A Faulty Translation" (1992) 12 O.J.L.S. 237.
[280] Jowell and Lester, "Proportionality", p. 62.

normative judgment on the strength of property interests and user interests; and some criterion as to what balance between them "means".

Thirdly, as we have seen above,[281] the concept of proportionality does not resolve in and of itself the actual standard of review. That concept can, like any of the others within our armoury of review, be used more or less intensively. The courts are more likely to apply intensive review when fundamental rights are at stake than when confronted with a discretionary choice involving economic regulation. Thus, when the above questions concerning the *Bromley* case have been answered there is still the further crucial question as to how far the authority can deviate from what the court believes to be the correct proportionate balance between the respective interests.[282]

Fourthly, the existence and application of the substantive principles which option four adds to option two can, of course, be contentious. They can be used to mask more controversial issues in the same way as usage of the labels purpose or reasonableness. An example will demonstrate this. In *Wheeler*[283] it was held that while section 71 of the Race Relations Act 1976 allowed the council to consider the best interests of race relations when exercising its discretion in the management of a recreation ground, it could not, in the absence of any infringement of the law or improper conduct, penalise a rugby club for failure to support the council's policy of condemning a tour of South Africa. The council had acted unfairly. It has been suggested[284] that the decision would have been more convincing had the court focused directly upon the principles of proportionality and legal certainty: the withdrawal of the licence was a disproportionate method of achieving the council's aims, coupled with the idea that there should be no punishment without breach of an established law. However, to state that the council's response was disproportionate is to state a conclusion, and more detailed reasoning is required to sustain it. Such reasoning would have to explore, *inter alia*, the nature of the council's duties and powers in relation to race, the conduct of the club, and the possible clash between policies concerned with racial harmony and speech rights. The analysis might lead to the conclusion that the council was in the wrong. This reasoning process must, however, be fully explicated. The argument from a principle of legal certainty is equally problematic. It appears to be that an agency which has an explicit power or duty to achieve a certain end (e.g. good race relations) cannot exercise it in such a way as to disadvantage a person, unless that person has committed an independent breach of the common law or statute. Such a conclusion could emasculate the exercise of many discretionary powers.[285]

---

[281] See, pp. 411-421.

[282] If the answer were to be "not at all" then we would in reality be close to option one and substitution of judgment.

[283] *Wheeler* v. *Leicester City Council* [1985] A.C. 1054. See also, *R.* v. *Lewisham London Borough Council, ex p. Shell UK Ltd.* [1988] 1 All E.R. 938.

[284] Jowell and Lester, "Beyond *Wednesbury*", pp. 376-377.

[285] If an agency has the power or duty to foster ties with Europe pursuant to 1992, and has the power to award licences or grants, would a refusal to renew such a licence or award a grant to a firm with anti-European sympathies be an infringement of the principle of legal certainty?

The final aspect to note concerning option four is more general, and is a corollary of the preceding points: the application of substantive principles will require the proper articulation of some background theory which will serve to explain why a particular principle is said to produce or demand a particular result in a given case. This point requires brief exposition. Intellectual honesty may well require a better explanation as to why an act is unreasonable than that which has been provided by the courts using traditional techniques of review. Concepts such as fundamental rights, proportionality or legal certainty may be able to provide a more finely tuned approach. But these concepts are not self-executing. That much is readily apparent from the previous analysis. If the call for the development of substantive principles is to be pursued, then the scale of the undertaking must be fully appreciated.

It requires, in all but the most self-evident cases, the recognition that the content which is given to concepts such as rights or proportionality will be dependent upon the identification of the particular theory which is said to warrant the conclusion which is being drawn.[286] Those who have differing political philosophies may readily accept and utilise concepts such as fundamental rights or proportionality. Their content may, however, differ radically depending on the way in which the precise subject-matter is viewed by those theories. For example, various background theories may well recognise the same general right, such as freedom of speech or equality, but the more particular *conception* of that right may be markedly different. This is equally true in the context of proportionality. Thus, assuming for the present that some such notion does underlie discrimination cases, the content that should be given to this will differ depending on whether the commentator is a utilitarian, a Rawlsian liberal, or a modern communitarian. Legal labels will not in this instance provide a ready-made answer; they can only serve as the repository for the conclusion reached from a particular system of political thought. The task will not therefore be an easy one, but intellectual honesty will not be served by assuming that there is any easier route.[287]

This does not mean that option four is misguided. It represents the best way forward in the modern day. Fundamental rights should be protected. Proportionality is, as seen above,[288] a natural adjunct of this protection. The comments made above are designed to work out some of the implications of this development, and should be read in this light.

(5) LIMITED REVIEW FOR ARBITRARINESS

The preceding discussion may lead some to believe that the appropriate standard of review should be more limited than that advanced by advocates of options two, three or four. The test under option five would, therefore, be that the court should intervene *only* if there is unreasonableness in

---

[286] Dworkin, *Law's Empire* (1986).
[287] Craig, *Public Law and Democracy in the U.K. and the U.S.A.* (1990); Loughlin, *Public Law and Political Theory* (1992).
[288] See above, pp. 411-421.

Lord Greene M.R.'s narrow sense of that term, or *only* if there is manifest irrationality in the sense that preceded the development of the hard look doctrine in the United States. Two comments on this proposal are warranted, one of which is obvious, the other less so.

First, the very fact that this standard of review is so limited means that it will only serve as a long stop to catch extreme examples of aberrant administrative behaviour. Secondly, one cannot, in practical terms, advocate option five if one believes in the expansion of participatory rights before the agency. More intense review than that provided by a test of arbitrariness will be necessary in order to ensure that the agency does not just go through the motions of listening to people. If we wish seriously to enhance such process rights, then we must be prepared to listen to claims that the agency did not give adequate consideration to certain views. Judicial intervention which occurs only when the resultant agency decision is substantively arbitrary will be insufficient, because there may be many instances when it falls short of this, but still wholly or partially ignores the views of interested parties.

2. *Decision-making, Discretion and Substantive Review*

Many of the preceding options are based implicitly or explicitly upon ideas as to how administrators make decisions. Some understanding of the literature upon decision-making may therefore facilitate evaluation of the options considered above. Two well known "models" can be identified.

One of the best known approaches as to how decisions ought to be made is that of Simon, who developed the behaviour alternative model.[289] An administrator faced with a problem should, initially, examine all possible courses of action, consider the consequences of pursuing each of these strategies and then comparatively evaluate these consequences. The difficulties of pursuing such a methodology are immediately evident. No administrator possesses the material, time or vision to operate in the way postulated by Simon. There is moreover a further difficulty with the thesis which is that it is based upon a dichotomy between fact and value which is hard to sustain.

In contrast to Simon's conception of rationality is the view of Lindblom.[290] The thesis has both descriptive and prescriptive connotations. In descriptive terms the argument is that decision-making is always incremental. Officials never have or can have the full range of choices displayed before them. Policy choices will always be made within a relatively narrow spectrum of possible options. Marginal alteration in policy is the norm, reflecting the limited information which is available, the cost of extensive analysis, the interdependence of fact and value, and the diversity of forms in which policy problems actually arise. In prescriptive terms this method of decision-making is viewed as desirable. "Better" results will ensue from a "contest" between partisan advocates, than would

---

[289] *Administrative Behaviour* (2nd ed., 1957). For general discussion, see McGrew and Wilson (eds.), *Decision-making Approaches and Analysis* (1982).
[290] "The Science of Muddling Through" 19 Pub.Adm.Rev. 79 (1959); Braybrooke and Lindblom, *A Strategy of Decision* (1963).

follow if the decision were to be reached by an allegedly unbiased administrator completing a comprehensive survey.

The cogency of this prescriptive analysis is highly questionable.[291] The descriptive aspect of the analysis does, however, appear to reflect administrative practice more accurately than the ideal of rational decision-making. Subsequent study, while not necessarily endorsing all of the "incremental thesis", has been directed towards understanding which factors an official will take into account. Thus March and Simon[292] accept that bureaucrats will not necessarily seek the optimal solution, but that which satisfies. Rationality will be bounded. The administrator will have certain material to hand; if this is felt to be inadequate there will be a further search. How much further will depend upon pressures of time and cost. Two immediate points of contact can be perceived between the differing options for substantive review, and the literature on decision-making.

On the one hand, it reinforces the argument that officials should have a general duty to provide reasons for decisions.[293] Since they will not be viewing the whole picture comprehensively, since they will perforce be selectively choosing values and acting on limited information, it is all the more important that the reasons why they have chosen a particular course of conduct should be articulated

On the other hand, it serves to place in perspective the idea, found in options two, three and four, that the official must base the decision on all relevant considerations, and exclude all irrelevant considerations. The literature on decision-making shows that this does not represent actual practice. Now it could well be argued that the very object of judicial scrutiny is to force the bureaucracy to consider a broader range of policy choices; that the courts' role is precisely to "redress" the tendency of officials to adopt a very narrow bounded rationality which thereby forecloses policy choices.[294] This may well be a laudable objective. How effective the judiciary can be in fulfilling such a role is another matter. The fact that review may occur relatively rarely for any one agency, the fact that the agency may still be subject to pressures of time and cost which incline it towards a narrow bounded rationality, the relative strength of different interest groups pressing upon the agency, and the competence of the court to assess whether such an authority has improperly excluded a particular policy option, can all combine to limit the effectiveness of this aspect of judicial scrutiny.[295]

---

[291] See, e.g., Dror, *Public Policy Making Re-examined* (1965); Self, *Administrative Theories and Politics* (1972).

[292] *Organisations* (1958), Chap. 6.

[293] See above, pp. 310–316.

[294] This is part of the claim advanced by proponents of option three.

[295] Compare, e.g. Sax, "The (Unhappy) Truth About NEPA" 26 Okla. L.Rev. 239 (1973), and Pedersen "Formal Records and Informal Rulemaking" 85 Yale L.J. 38 (1975).

12. INVALIDITY

Section 1. Direct and Collateral Attack

1. *General*

In the previous chapters the extent of the *ultra vires* doctrine and the concept of error of law within jurisdiction were discussed. What must be considered now is the result of a finding that the decision is *ultra vires*, or that there is an error of law on the face of the record, and with the status of the decision pending such a finding. However, before concerning ourselves with these thorny problems it is necessary to consider the different methods of attack available to an aggrieved individual.

A person who wishes to challenge a decision may do so directly or collaterally. The dividing line between the two is not entirely clear and is to some extent dependent upon terminology. There are two ways of looking at the matter, neither of which is entirely satisfactory.

Direct and collateral attack may be taken to refer to the form of remedy sought. Thus, direct attack would cover the prerogative orders, injunction, declaration and possibly habeas corpus. The individual here is seeking a remedy which directly impugns the administrative order. The problem with this classification is that it groups together remedies which go only to the validity of the challenged finding with those which pertain to the merits. Examples of the latter are certiorari when used to challenge an error within jurisdiction and appeal. On this hypothesis collateral attack would cover the manifold ways in which a decision can be challenged indirectly, such as by way of defence to enforcement proceedings or in a tort action. The link between the forms of collateral attack is that they challenge the decision incidentally.

Alternatively, the distinction between direct and collateral methods of attack may be determined by the scope of review given by the remedy and not by its form. Collateral proceedings would be those in which only the nullity of the decision is at issue, and direct proceedings would cover challenges to the merits.[1] The difficulty with this classification is that a remedy such as declaration, which is traditionally regarded as available only for jurisdictional defects, would be regarded as a collateral challenge while having little connection with an incidental form of attack by way of a tort action.

---

[1] Rubinstein, *Jurisdiction and Illegality* (1965), pp. 37-39, prefers this view.

One matter may, however, be regarded as clear: collateral attack covers many forms of incidental challenge and has been recognised for over 300 years. It constituted the early method of attacking decisions and pre-dated the general development of the prerogative writs.[2] For example, in the *Case of the Marshalsea*[3] the plaintiff brought an action for trespass and false imprisonment, claiming that the Marshalsea Court possessed no jurisdiction over him as he was not of the King's House. The Court held that an action would lie where the challenged authority had no jurisdiction over the case, the entire proceedings being *coram non judice*; no such action would lie where the error was one within jurisdiction.

In this type of case the plaintiff brings an action in tort, the defendant relies upon, for example, a warrant from a magistrate and the plaintiff then rebuts that defence by proving a jurisdictional defect in the warrant. There are many other ways in which collateral attack can occur.[4] An accused's guilt may be dependent upon the validity of an administrative or ministerial order. If the order is *ultra vires* then the accused will be exonerated.[5] A ratepayer can resist a demand for rates or charges by claiming that the demand is invalid.[6]

2. *Limitations on Collateral Attack*

(1) JURISDICTIONAL DEFECTS

It is evident from the above cases that collateral attack will only be an option where the defect alleged is jurisdictional.[7] Errors of law on the face of the record could thus not be impeached collaterally, but only by way of certiorari. The rationale for this was that the court in a collateral action could take account of the invalidity of a challenged order; it was acting in a "declaratory" role. If, however, the decision was valid, albeit tainted with some error, it could only be challenged by appeal, or by certiorari where the error was one of law and was on the face of the record. A court not possessed of appellate jurisdiction could not obliquely assume such.[8] This limitation on the scope of collateral attack is, however, of less importance than previously given the expansion in the scope of jurisdictional error and the consequential demise of error of law within jurisdiction.

---

[2] *Ibid.* Chap. 4.
[3] (1612) 10 Co. Rep. 68b; *Terry* v. *Huntington* (1668) Hard. 480. See also, *Fuller* v. *Fotch* (1695) Carth. 346; *Doswell* v. *Impey* (1823) 1 B. & C. 163.
[4] Rubinstein, above n. 1, pp. 39-46.
[5] *DPP* v. *Head* [1959] A.C. 83. Whether the validity of the act should always be relevant will be considered below.
[6] *Daymond* v. *Plymouth City Council* [1976] A.C. 609.
[7] See further, *Groenvelt* v. *Burwell* (1700) 3 Salk. 354; *Gahan* v. *Maingay* (1793) Ridg. L. & S. 20.
[8] *Gahan* v. *Maingay*, above n. 7.

(2) POLICY REASONS FOR LIMITING COLLATERAL ATTACK

It might be thought that any defect which would be treated as jurisdictional in the context of direct proceedings should be equally available in a collateral action. In many instances this is so. Thus in *Foster*[9] it was held that Social Security Commissioners hearing appeals under the Social Security Act 1975 had jurisdiction to determine any challenge to the *vires* of a provision in regulations made by the Secretary of State on the ground that it was beyond the scope of the enabling power whenever this was necessary in order to decide whether a decision under appeal was erroneous in point of law. Matters are not always so simple for a number of reasons.

First, while a direct action is concerned with the citizen's rights against the state a collateral action may, but need not necessarily, involve this. Merely because one individual might have a direct action should not necessarily mean that a different individual should be able to use this invalidity in a collateral action.[10]

Secondly, the suitability of, for example, enforcement proceedings or a criminal trial as a forum for discussion of what the relevant considerations under a statutory order were, or what was a proper or improper purpose, may well be questioned.

Thirdly, and perhaps most importantly, the recent reforms of the law of remedies have raised important questions as to how far an individual should be able to challenge a decision collaterally. These difficult issues are best considered within the discussion of remedies more generally.[11]

The second and third of these considerations are exemplified by the decision in *Bugg* v. *DPP*[12] where it was held that in the context of criminal proceedings for breach of a bylaw a magistrate could entertain a challenge to the bylaw on the grounds that it was substantively invalid, but not on the ground of procedural invalidity. The rationale for this distinction was that substantive invalidity could be determined on the face of the bylaw, in the sense that this would suffice to show whether it was beyond the powers of the parent legislation. Procedural invalidity was, by way of contrast, said to be different: proof of such invalidity would require evidence which would not be readily available within the confines of a criminal proceeding, nor would the party who was interested in upholding the validity of the bylaw necessarily be a party to the action.[13]

While one can appreciate the difficulties of adjudicating upon validity in the context of a criminal trial before magistrates, the distinction drawn

---

[9] *Chief Adjudication Officer* v. *Foster* [1993] 1 All E.R. 705.

[10] See, *e.g.* Rubinstein's cogent critique of *DPP* v. *Head* [1959] A.C. 83, above n.1, p. 47.

[11] See below, Chap. 15, for discussion as to when an individual can and cannot proceed to challenge a decision collaterally.

[12] [1993] 2 All E.R. 815, distinguishing *R.* v. *Crown Court at Reading, ex p. Hutchinson* [1988] Q.B. 384.

[13] *Ibid.* pp. 823–827; in *Foster* [1993] 1 All E.R. 705 Lord Bridge left open the question whether a similar dichotomy would operate in the context of cases coming before the Social Security Commissioners.

between substantive and procedural invalidity is, nonetheless, questionable.[14] There are a number of aspects of substantive invalidity which would not be apparent upon the face of the disputed order, and this might well be so if the challenge was based upon relevancy or propriety of purpose. Moreover, the argument that the person most concerned with the bylaw might not be a party to the proceedings could apply just as much in a case of substantive as procedural invalidity.

(3) POSITIVE AND NEGATIVE DECISIONS

Collateral attack will by its nature not normally be available to challenge decisions denying an individual something which the person desires.[15] If a public body refuses a licence or a supplementary benefit then if the applicant does nothing no licence will be granted or no benefit will be paid. Attack by prerogative order or declaration is the only recourse available to the aggrieved individual. This may be contrasted with a demand by the public body for rates or duties. The individual can wait to be sued and then assert the invalidity of the order.

(4) INTERPRETATION OF THE STATUTE

A court may interpret a statute to preclude collateral attack. This may be because there is provision in the statute for appeal which the court interprets as preventing any other form of attack, direct or collateral; or it may be that the court feels that the scheme of the legislation would be defeated by allowing collateral challenge.[16] More generally, recent reforms of the law of remedies have restricted the circumstances in which an order can be challenged other than by an application for judicial review.[17]

(5) DE FACTO JUDGES AND OFFICERS

A long standing exception to the possibility of collateral attack is to be found in the context of judges or public officers whose appointment is defective. The courts have not allowed collateral challenge where the judge or officer was acting *de facto* as such even though his appointment was *de jure* invalid.[18] The rationale for this limitation is essentially practical: annulment of all the officer's subsequent acts because the appointment was invalid could have serious consequences.[19] The protection accorded to *de facto* officers appears to have its origin in connection with officers or judges whose appointment was valid when made, but where the appointment was subsequently rendered invalid.[20] The doctrine has, however, been

---

[14] Feldman, "Collateral Challenge and Judicial Review: The Boundary Dispute Continues" [1993] P.L. 37.
[15] Collateral attack will, however, be available if the individual can assert a common law or statutory right to the benefit in question.
[16] R. v. Davey [1899] 2 Q.B. 301.
[17] See below, Chap. 15.
[18] Rubinstein, above n.1, pp. 205-208.
[19] Crew v. Vernon (1627) Cro. Car. 97.
[20] See the discussion in Re Aldridge (1893) 15 N.Z.L.R. 361, 369-370

extended beyond this to encompass appointments which were invalid at their inception. Thus, a justice who had not taken the requisite oath was still to be regarded as a *de facto* justice;[21] the acts of assessors and collectors of taxes who did not fulfil residency requirements were treated as valid,[22] and a rate levied by vestrymen, one of whom was not duly elected, was not annulled.[23]

It is not entirely clear whether the doctrine of *de facto* officers operates only where there is some "colour of authority". There are certainly indications that this is so,[24] and it would make sense if part of the rationale for the doctrine is that a person is entitled to rely on the actions of a judge or public officer provided that there is no reason to doubt the validity of the appointment.

Section 2. Void and Voidable

1. *Void and Voidable: Correct and Incorrect Uses*

If a public body makes a decision which is *ultra vires* this means that it had no power to make such a decision. The layman might be forgiven for thinking that the effect of such a decision should be quite simply no effect. Leaving aside arcane legal language, if a public body has exceeded its power in reaching a decision then that decision should have no legal effect. The classic harmony of this reasoning is, however, disturbed by two related factors. First, the theory is not quite as simple as it appears at first sight. Secondly, even when we have worked out the theory satisfactorily we find that it must be compromised in certain types of case owing to the unacceptable consequences of its draconian application.

(1) VOID: A RELATIVE NOT ABSOLUTE CONCEPT

The effect of finding that a decision is *ultra vires* is, like many other matters, best approached from first principles. Looked at in this way our intelligent layman's reaction has cogency and value at least as a starting point: if you, the decision-maker, had no power then your decision should have no effect whatsoever. Translated into the lingua franca of our profession, we would say that such an administrative finding was void *ab initio*, retrospectively

---

[21] *Margate Pier Company* v. *Hannam* (1819) 3 B. & Ald. 266.

[22] *Waterloo Bridge Company* v. *Cull* (1858) 1 El. & El. 213, affirmed (1859) 1 El. & El. 245.

[23] *Scadding* v. *Lorant* (1851) 3 H.L.C. 418.

[24] In *Crew* v. *Vernon* (1627) Cro.Car. 97 the commissioners' acts seemed only to be valid until they received notice of the death of James I. In *R.* v. *Bedford Level Corporation* (1805) 6 East 356 the officer in question was a deputy whose principal had died. It was held that once the principal dies and this becomes known the *de facto* authority of the deputy ceases. In *Adams* v. *Adams* [1971] P. 188 the court rejected the argument that a Rhodesian judge held office *de facto* if not *de jure*, one reason being that the illegality of the Rhodesian regime was widely known. The court in *Re Aldridge* (1893) 15 N.Z.L.R. 361 was more divided on this question.

null. Matters become more complex when we ask who is entitled to take advantage of, or who can invoke, the ineffectiveness of the administrative decision? Our informed lawyer would reply by telling us that void is a relative not an absolute concept. What does this mean?[25]

In our system of administrative law there are rules of *locus standi*, time limits, and other reasons for refusing a remedy such as acquiescence. It is only if an applicant for relief surmounts these hurdles that he will be able to obtain a remedy. The sequence of events would therefore be as follows. An administrative decision takes place. An individual feels aggrieved and challenges the decision. If the court finds that the individual has standing, is within the time limits, and that there is no reason to deny a remedy the decision will be found to be void *ab initio*. It is descriptive of the conclusion reached that an *ultra vires* act has occurred and that it is being challenged by the right person in the correct proceedings. As Lord Diplock[26] has said, it is confusing to speak of the terms void or voidable before the validity of an order has been pronounced on by a court of competent jurisdiction.

What would the difference be if void were to be used in an absolute as opposed to a relative sense? The short answer is that the word void would be moved to earlier in the sentence. This would now read: if there is an *ultra vires* act, the finding thus made is void *ab initio* and therefore any person can take advantage of it. Applied literally there could be no limits of standing and no discretion in granting the remedy.

Two examples of the use of void or nullity in this absolute sense may be given. In *Ridge* v. *Baldwin* Lord Evershed stated that because the declaration is a discretionary remedy, therefore the result of a breach of natural justice must be to render the decision voidable and not void. Why? Because his Lordship felt that if the decision was a complete nullity the court would have to say so in some form or another.[27] A similar usage occurs in *Durayappah* v. *Fernando*.[28] The Jaffna city council was dissolved by a minister after a report had been made to him by a commissioner. The commissioner had inquired into the council's activities, but had not given a hearing to any member of it. The mayor sought certiorari, claiming that the dissolution was in breach of natural justice. Lord Upjohn, giving the decision of the Privy Council, found that there had been a breach of natural justice and then proceeded to consider whether the mayor could complain of this. His Lordship stated that this depended upon whether the decision

---

[25] See Wade, "Unlawful Administrative Action: Void or Voidable?" (1967) 83 L.Q.R. 499, (1968) 84 L.Q.R. 95; Akehust, "Void or Voidable? Natural Justice and Unnatural Meanings" (1968) 31 M.L.R. 2, 138; Peiris, "Natural Justice and Degrees of Invalidity of Administrative Action" [1983] P.L. 634; Taggart, "Rival Theories of Invalidity in Administrative Law: Some Practical and Theoretical Consequences", *Judicial Review of Administrative Action in the 1980s* (Taggart ed., 1986), pp. 70-103. As to whether the courts act in a constitutive or declaratory role, and the relevance of this dichotomy, see Cane, "A Fresh Look at Punton's Case" (1980) 43 M.L.R. 266.

[26] *Hoffmann-La Roche & Co. A.G.* v. *Secretary of State for Trade and Industry* [1975] A.C. 295, 366; *Isaacs* v. *Robertson* [1985] A.C. 97; *Bugg* v. *DPP* [1993] 2 All E.R. 815, 821; *R.* v. *Hendon Justices, ex p. DPP* [1993] C.O.D. 61.

[27] [1964] A.C. 40, 87-88, 91-92.

[28] [1967] 2 A.C. 337.

was a complete nullity, of which any person having a legitimate interest could complain, or whether it was voidable only at the instance of the party affected.[29] Lord Upjohn found that it was the latter and therefore that it could not be attacked by the mayor when the council had chosen not to challenge it.[30]

Both Lord Evershed in *Ridge* and the Privy Council in *Durayappah* are using void or nullity in the absolute sense described above. An *ultra vires* act is found, and it is said not to be void because that would leave the court no discretion in granting the remedy and no, or reduced, control over standing. Juxtapose this to the relative meaning of the term void. In this latter sense it is only if, in addition to finding an *ultra vires* act, the person possesses standing and there are no other reasons to refuse the remedy that the decision would be held to be void *ab initio*. This relative concept of void was endorsed by Lord Diplock in the *Hoffmann-La Roche*[31] case, where his Lordship stated that the *Durayappah* decision was best explained as a case relating to standing. A correlative of this is that there is nothing odd in a decision being capable of being rendered void by one person but not another, or in a decision which would be void if challenged within the correct time, being valid if not so challenged.[32] When a successful challenge is made by the right person in the correct proceedings the decision is retrospectively null.

It should not, however, be thought that an aggrieved individual must always challenge an action directly via the prerogative orders in order to prevent its application to him. If the decision requires, for example, a payment by the individual to a public body then the individual could resist the demand, wait to be sued, and then attack the decision collaterally. In this limited sense statements by Lord Denning M.R. that there is no need for an order to quash a nullity are correct:[33] the individual does not need to seek a prerogative order or declaration as a mechanism of direct attack, but can impugn the decision collaterally. If the finding is not attacked directly or collaterally it will, however, remain valid irrespective of whether, if it had been challenged, it would have been deemed to be *ultra vires*. It will not in some Houdini sense disappear.

(2) VOIDABLE: DIFFERENT USES.

The term voidable has not been used in a uniform sense within the case law. At least four distinct meanings have been attributed to the term.

---

[29] *Ibid.* pp. 353-354. Lord Upjohn stated that in *Ridge* Lord Reid and Lord Hodson had used the word void in the sense that Lord Upjohn is using the word nullity here. There is, with respect, no evidence for this.

[30] *Ibid.* pp. 354-355. Lord Upjohn went on to say that if it was challenged by the right person then the decision would be void *ab initio*.

[31] *Hoffmann-La Roche & Co. A.G.* v. *Secretary of State for Trade and Industry* [1975] A.C. 295, 366. See also, Lord Wilberforce, p. 358.

[32] *Smith* v. *East Elloe Rural District Council* [1956] A.C. 736, 769, *per* Lord Radcliffe.

[33] *DPP* v. *Head* [1959] A.C. 83, 111-112; *R.* v. *Paddington Valuation Officer, ex p. Peachey Property Corporation Ltd.* [1966] 1 Q.B. 380, 402. Reference should, however, be made to the discussion of the presumptive exclusivity of s.31 of the Supreme Court Act 1981, below, Chap. 15.

(a) Indicative of the need to challenge

Lord Morris of Borth-y-Gest uses the term voidable in this sense in *Ridge* v. *Baldwin*.[34] In this context voidable is simply descriptive of the need for the chief constable to challenge his dismissal. Unless he did so the decision of the Watch Committee would prevail. In this sense all decisions are voidable. His Lordship went on to say that if and when the court found for the individual the decision would be null and void.[35]

(b) As an alternative to locus standi

This connotation of the term voidable is demonstrated by *Durayappah* v. *Fernando*[36] and is the flip side of the reasoning concerning absolute nullity considered above. It is nevertheless worth making this part of the reasoning explicit. The Privy Council clearly does not wish the mayor to be able to challenge the dissolution of the City Council. To arrive at this end the Privy Council draw a dichotomy between defects which any person having a legitimate interest can take advantage of, which are nullities, and those defects which only the person affected could raise. The term voidable was used to describe errors of the latter type, and the Court held that the facts of the case fell within this category. Thus, the distinction between acts which are null and those which are merely voidable manifests itself in the class of claimant who can raise the invalidity. It has, in other words, an impact upon those who will be accorded standing. Precisely why the Privy Council did not wish the mayor to succeed is an interesting question which will be reverted to later.

(c) The gravity of the error

In some cases the term voidable has been used to indicate the relative gravity of the defect. An example of this is the reasoning of Lord Denning M.R. in *R.* v. *Paddington Valuation Officer, ex p. Peachey Property Corporation Ltd.*[37] The basis on which a rating list had been compiled was challenged in the courts. One objection made by the rating authority was that if the list was struck down there would be widespread administrative upheaval, particularly if the invalidity meant that the list was retrospectively null. To circumvent this problem Lord Denning M.R. said that a grave invalidity would render the list a nullity. There would be no need for

---

[34] [1964] A.C. 40, 125.
[35] In *Durayappah* [1967] 2 A.C. 337, 354 Lord Upjohn stated that Lord Morris of Borth-y-Gest had agreed with Lord Evershed and Lord Devlin in *Ridge* in holding that a breach of the *audi alteram partem* rule only made the decision voidable. This is, with respect, not so. Lord Morris was not using voidable in the same sense as Lord Evershed and Lord Devlin. See, *Hounslow London Borough Council* v. *Twickenham Garden Developments* [1971] Ch. 233, 258.
[36] [1967] 2 A.C. 337.
[37] [1966] 1 Q.B. 380, 401-402. *cf.* Lord Denning M.R.'s statement in *Lovelock* v. *Minister of Transport* (1980) 40 P. & C.R. 336, 345.

an order to quash a list tainted by such a defect. Less serious defects would only render the list voidable. One result of this would be that any invalidity would only be prospective, not retrospective. The rating assessments could remain valid until replaced by a new list.

Both parts of this formulation are open to question. The concept of a grave defect producing a nullity which need not be challenged either directly or collaterally, and yet can still be ignored without ill effects to the individual, is difficult to comprehend. As stated above,[38] the offending order will not somehow disappear of its own accord. The formulation of the term voidable is equally questionable. On traditional theory, as it stood at that time, an error which was not jurisdictional could only be struck down if it was an error of law on the face of the record. Given the facts of the *Paddington* case it is hard to discern such a patent error. These criticisms are important, but in and of themselves they do not provide the whole answer. His Lordship utilised the somewhat unnatural meanings of void and voidable to avoid a conclusion which he found to be inconvenient: the retrospective nullity of the challenged list and the administrative consequences that this would produce.[39] This aspect of the topic will be considered more fully below.

(d) Errors of law within jurisdiction

The one context within which commentators agreed that it was legitimate to use the term voidable was as descriptive of an error of law within jurisdiction. Such errors are not, by definition, jurisdictional. They indicate that the tribunal has made a mistake, not that it never possessed the power to act. Such mistakes are valid until quashed, and actions taken in pursuance of an order tainted by a patent non-jurisdictional error remained valid even when the order had been quashed. Thus, in *DPP* v. *Head*[40] a man was convicted of carnal knowledge with a mental defective. He argued by way of defence that he could not be guilty since the medical certificates did not contain any evidence showing the woman to be a moral defective. The majority of the House of Lords upheld this argument and set the conviction aside. Lord Denning concurred in this result, but his reasoning differed from that of the other Law Lords. He stated that the defect in the detention order only rendered the order voidable and not void. A voidable order would remain good until set aside. Thus at the time of the offence the detention order was still good, the woman was legally held, and the accused could be guilty of the crime charged. The expansion in the scope of jurisdictional error and the corresponding demise of the category of error of law within jurisdiction does, however, mean that voidable will no longer have a role to play as descriptive of the latter kind of error.

---

[38] See p. 453.
[39] A similar theme underlies *Durayappah* [1967] 2 A.C. 337.
[40] [1959] A.C. 83. Moral defective was one category of mental defective under the Mental Deficiency Act 1913, s.1.

2. Judicial Discretion: Theory and Reality

It might well be thought that we have come to the end of our inquiry. We have revealed the differing reasons why the courts have used the term voidable; we have found that the only justifiable use of that term was in the context of errors of law within jurisdiction; and we know that this category of error no longer exists. This all seems to point to the conclusion that we can in fact discard the language of void and voidable. This is, in one sense, obviously true, since it is no longer needed to describe the differing effects of jurisdictional and non-jurisdictional errors.[41] There are, however, two related reasons for pressing the inquiry further.

On the one hand, the expanded scope of error of law still requires us to consider the consequences of such an error. The error may still mean that the decision-maker had no power to make that decision and that, prima facie, it should be devoid of any effect from the date on which it was made. One can then choose to use the language of nullity, voidness or invalidity to describe those consequences. On the other hand, it is evident that the courts have not always used the term voidable to signify non-jurisdictional errors. They have employed it for other reasons. Now one can, of course, lament this and hope that they will not do so in the future, but it is necessary to understand *why* they have done so in the past.

The root cause of the problem is, as will be seen, that the courts have sometimes sought to escape from the conclusions that will follow if they find that the contested decision was made outside jurisdiction. As we have seen, this means that the decision-maker never had the power to make the decision, and that, therefore, the decision could have no effect at all. This is encapsulated by the idea that decisions made outside jurisdiction are retrospectively null or invalid. In their desire to avoid this conclusion the courts have on occasion used the term voidable instead, in order to express the conclusion that the contested order should only be ineffective from the date when it was found to be invalid by the court, and not from the date when it was first made.

The general argument which will be made within this and the following section is that the concept of retrospective invalidity, in the relative sense considered above, is the correct starting point in principle and we are in danger of losing sight of this. Cases will indeed arise in which the full effects of retrospective invalidity will be unacceptable, and where the principle will, therefore, have to be modified. The most appropriate manner in which to express these modifications is through discretion exercised at the remedial level, *not* by manipulating the concepts of void or voidable. The problem will be approached in four stages.

First, we must take a closer look at the reasons why the courts have departed from the conventional meanings of these terms. Secondly, we must be aware of other stages in the judicial process within which similar types of reasoning appear. Thirdly, it will be necessary to consider whether the

---

[41] Sir John Laws, "Illegality: The Problem of Jurisdiction", *Judicial Review* (Supperstone and Goudie eds., 1992), Chap. 4.

discretion is needed and what the effects of the removal of the judicial discretion would be. Fourthly, we will have to inquire whether the present manipulation of the concepts void and voidable is the best way to achieve our desired solution.

(1) THE REASONS FOR JUDICIAL DEPARTURE FROM THE TRADITIONAL MEANINGS OF VOID AND VOIDABLE

(a) Administrative convenience and justice

Traditional theory, derived from first principles, tells us that a decision which is *ultra vires* should be void, using that term in its relative sense. The voidness will be retrospective, invalidating action taken in the period between the making of the order and the court decision. Voidable decisions involve only prospective and not retrospective invalidity. The error does not take the tribunal outside the ambit of its power. It remains within its jurisdiction but simply makes a mistake. Action taken in reliance upon the order until the time at which it is struck down will be upheld; the invalidity will be only prospective. On traditional theory the only type of defect which should be termed voidable is the error of law on the face of the record. Other non-patent errors of law within jurisdiction would also be voidable, but could only be subject to appeal and not review. It is apparent by now that not all courts have used the terms void and voidable in this way. The meanings that they have ascribed to these concepts are not uniform, but they do possess a common characteristic, a desire for greater flexibility than the traditional interpretation will allow. To be more specific, the common denominator is a dislike of the results produced by the concept of retrospective nullity.

We have come across evidence of this already. In the *Paddington*[42] case one of the reasons why Lord Denning M.R. wished to characterise the error as voidable was in order that the challenged rating list could remain in existence until a new list was prepared. If the error made the list retrospectively void then it (and possibly many other such lists) would never have existed and there would have been a gargantuan unravelling task for the rating authorities to perform.

Considerations of administrative convenience have not been the only factors at work. Notions of the "just" result have also affected the judiciary. In *DPP v. Hoad*[43] Lord Denning was reluctant to allow an accused to escape a criminal charge by relying upon a defect in the certificate. Hence his Lordship's characterisation of the defect as making the certificate only voidable; the woman was therefore lawfully detained at the time of the offence charged, and the accused could be found guilty.[44]

---

[42] [1966] 1 Q.B. 380. Similar fears appear to underlie the *Durayappah* decision [1967] 2 A.C. 337.

[43] [1959] A.C. 83, 111-112. Lord Denning did not in the end dissent, pp. 113, 114.

[44] See also, *Ridge* v. *Baldwin* [1964] A.C. 40, 87-92, where Lord Evershed appeared to believe that it was only by terming a breach of natural justice "voidable" that the court could prevent undeserving applicants from seizing upon a technical breach of these rules. This is a *non-sequitur* even in its own terms.

(b) Frontal assault and rigidity

While the courts in the above cases have sought to manipulate the meanings of void and voidable to reach their desired conclusion, certain more recent authorities have expressed general dissatisfaction with what is seen as the rigid results flowing from the use of those terms. In *London and Clydeside Estates Ltd* v. *Aberdeen District Council*[45] Lord Hailsham was particularly critical of conventional rhetoric. His Lordship felt that terms such as mandatory and directory, void and voidable, and nullity could often be expressive of over-rigid classification. When a public body failed to comply with a statutory requirement it could produce three differing types of result. At one end of the spectrum, there would be instances of egregious breach of a fundamental obligation. In such cases, if the authority sought to rely on its action the individual could simply use that defect as a defence without having to take positive action. At the other end of the spectrum there could be trivial defects which would probably be ignored by the courts. In the middle, however, there was a large group of cases in which it would be wise for the individual to challenge the public action and where the effect of the breach would be dependent upon the circumstances. Terms such as void and voidable should not cramp the exercise of judicial discretion in determining what consequences should flow from the breach.[46] Whether concepts such as void and voidable do entail unwarranted rigidity, and whether they should be replaced by broader judicial discretion will be examined later.

(2) THE LEVELS ON WHICH DISCRETION OPERATES

Before making a value judgment about the reasoning and results used in the cases considered above it is necessary to place the issue in a broader context. This in itself involves two parts. It is necessary, first, to realise that there are other stages in the judicial process within which the type of discretion discussed above can manifest itself. The second is to bring into focus certain rules which at present limit the operation of retrospective nullity.

(a) Where discretion operates

Judicial discretion is evident primarily at two stages of the judicial process, quite apart from the manipulation of the concepts of void and voidable.

The first is the very step of categorising a decision as *ultra vires* or illegal. The courts, in deciding whether to label an error as jurisdictional, exercise discretion. Our expanded scope of judicial review has rendered life more perilous for administrators. Yet, in a paradoxical way, the correlative of this is a broadening of judicial discretion, allowing the courts to categorise an error with one eye upon the likely effects of the label which is being

---

[45] [1980] 1 W.L.R. 182.
[46] *Ibid.* p. 190. See also, Lord Keith of Kinkel, p. 203. See further, Lord Hailsham's comments in *Chief Constable of the North Wales Police* v. *Evans* [1982] 1 W.L.R. 1155, 1162-1163; *Bugg* v. *DPP* [1993] 2 All E.R. 815, 820-821.

attached. Concepts such as improper purposes or irrelevancy are inherently malleable. So also are the terms mandatory and directory. The *Aberdeen*[47] case is indicative of the way in which the latter terms can be used to reflect the seriousness of the defect, or the administrative consequence of striking down a public body's determination.

Discretion is also evident at the remedial level itself. Statements are commonly found to the effect that the grant of the prerogative orders or declaration or injunction are at the discretion of the court. The precise breadth of this discretion has never been clearly delineated by the courts. It encapsulates requirements of standing, but statements concerning the discretionary nature of the remedies are not normally made exclusively with this in mind. What other factors a court will take into account is a more open question. It is, however, clear that concepts such as waiver, acquiescence, the existence of alternative remedies, and time limits do and have provided gateways through which to deny a remedy for reasons which are similar to those expressed in the manipulation of the terms void and voidable.[48] Two specific examples may be given here which evidence the type of discretion which can be exercised under the guise of time limits. The decisions of the courts which have upheld clauses which restrict challenge to a six week period, despite high-handed behaviour by the administration, are explicable in part at least by the administrative inconvenience which would ensue if the contrary result had been reached. In both cases much demolition and building work had been carried out.[49] Similarly, the provisions on time limits which are contained in the new procedure for remedies,[50] allow the courts to take into account, *inter alia*, the possible detrimental effects upon the administration as a ground for refusing relief.

(b) Other limits to the concept of retrospective invalidity

Apart from the discretion inherent in the very categorisation of a defect, or that exercised on the remedial level, there are other limits to the concept of retrospective nullity. One such direct limitation is to be found in the concept of *de facto* officers discussed above. In theory, if a determination is retrospectively invalidated then all acts done in reliance upon its being valid would themselves be invalidated, thereby making those concerned with the enforcement of the decision liable in damages in certain instances. The

---

[47] [1980] 1 W.L.R. 182.

[48] See amongst many, *e.g. R. v. Herrod, ex p. Leeds City Council* [1976] Q.B. 540; *R. v. Mayor of Peterborough* (1875) 44 L.J.Q.B. 85; *R. v. Hampstead Borough Council, ex p. Woodward* (1917) 116 L.T. 213; *Re Bristol and North Somerset Railway Co.* (1877) 3 Q.B.D. 10, 12; *R. v. Bristol Corporation, ex p. Hendy* [1974] 1 W.L.R. 498, 503. For detailed consideration of the factors which the courts will regard as precluding relief, see below, Chap. 14.

[49] *Smith v. East Elloe Rural District Council* [1956] A.C. 736, 756; *R. v. Secretary of State for the Environment, ex p. Ostler* [1977] Q.B. 122, 133, 136. See Chap. 16 for a detailed consideration of ouster clauses and time limits.

[50] See pp. 585-586.

doctrine of *de facto* officers denies this logical consequence for pragmatic reasons. As Wade has said,

> "In many legal situations it is a mistake to suppose that the consequences of invalidity should be worked out with rigid logic and without regard to the facts."[51]

The concept of *de facto* officer has most commonly been used to "cure" a defect in the election or qualifications of the officer, but it has also been utilised to "cure" defects flowing from the invalidity of someone else's appointment.[52] Despite this, the doctrine provides only a limited exception to the general concept of retrospective nullity; it will not provide a cloak if the decisions made by the officers are themselves *ultra vires*.[53]

Another type of limitation on retrospective nullity is to be found in the common law and statutory immunities to actions in tort given to courts and enforcing officers in varying degrees.[54]

(3) IS THE DISCRETION NEEDED?

This is a complex question, but it is not the type of question to which a simple yes or no answer can be given. The response will no doubt depend upon the values and perspectives of the individual answering. Quite apart from this inherent subjective element, the question – should discretion exist? – has a number of facets.

(a) Discretion and compensation

Whether the discretion that we have seen the courts using is needed is itself a value judgment. This does not, however, prevent us from considering some of the issues relating to it. For example, one type of argument that has been put forward is that manipulation of the terms void and voidable is often a mask to avoid having to pay damages. Thus if English law developed a more general compensatory remedy for harm caused by *ultra vires* acts many of the problems concerned with void and voidable would disappear. Lord Wilberforce has expressed powerful arguments along these lines.[55]

There is no doubt an argument in favour of developing a remedy for loss caused by *ultra vires* administrative action. The factors involved in developing such an action will be considered below.[56] The relevance of such a remedy to the general debate on void and voidable should, however, be kept within perspective. It is not a panacea which will solve all the

---

[51] Wade, *Administrative Law* (6th ed., 1988), p. 338.
[52] *Crew* v. *Vernon* (1627) Cro.Car. 97.
[53] It is also not entirely clear what type of action is prevented by the doctrine of *de facto* officers, *Re Aldridge* [1893] 15 N.Z.L.R. 361, 368, 377, 380.
[54] See pp. 635-636.
[55] *Hoffmann-La Roche* [1975] A.C. 295, 358-359.
[56] See pp. 646-651. Craig, "Compensation in Public Law" (1980) 96 L.Q.R. 413.

complexities attendant upon those terms. Such a remedy does not render the need for discretion otiose. The common type of case is where the individual asserts the invalidity of an administrative act and the public body raises the argument that this could have drastic administrative consequences. A developed system of damages could be highly useful. Presuming that the public body's fears are well founded, a court could say that the action was void, but that the only remedy was compensation and not an order to quash the act or declare it to be null. This could well be the most equitable solution.

What is important for present purposes is to realise that the addition of the damages remedy does not dispel the need for judicial discretion. Rather, it shifts the terminology within which the discretion is exercised. Instead of juggling with void and voidable, to prevent administrative upheaval, the court would use its discretion to restrict the results of the label void. The, as it were, physical manifestations of the illegal action would remain: they would not be laid to waste or torn down. The retrospective invalidity would show only in the legal liability of the public body to pay compensation for losses incurred prior to the action as well as for any such prospective loss. This may, of course, be a preferable way for discretion to manifest itself. At present, faced with pleas of administrative chaos, the court either rejects them totally, or manipulates void and voidable, or the grant of the remedy, to give effect to such arguments. The ability to give compensation would provide added flexibility in the manner demonstrated above. The presence of such a remedy would not, however, be testimony to the workability of retrospective invalidity or to the absence of a need for discretion. On the contrary, it would provide a more convenient and equitable framework within which to exercise that discretion.

(b) Discretion and Parliament

All this is, however, at present conjecture. We do not have such a monetary remedy. How should we approach the question of discretion leaving this factor aside? How should we assess whether the flexibility that the courts desire is needed? One way to approach the matter would be to consider what would happen if we insisted on carrying through the logic of retrospective nullity. What if we were to insist that *ultra vires* decisions became void retrospectively, that this should not be mitigated by playing with the meanings of void and voidable, and that discretion to refuse a remedy should be severely limited? Provided that the correct person is challenging the decision in the correct proceedings, within the time limits and has not acquiesced, then a remedy must be granted. What would happen? We are of course within the realm of fiction, but some guess as to how our *dramatis personae* might behave can be chanced.

One effect might be that the courts would simply reach the desired conclusion through the inherent flexibility of jurisdiction itself. Faced by undesirable administrative results which would flow inexorably from finding a decision to be void, a court could deny the existence of any jurisdictional error. Denial of discretion could, therefore, reduce the protection afforded to the citizen.

Alternatively, the courts could embrace the new order, turning a deaf ear to pleas of injustice or administrative chaos. What would the result of this be? The traditional response is that it would be for Parliament to redress the resulting confusion. This solution suffers from both practical and conceptual difficulties. In *practical* terms, the possibility that Parliament could pass a series of one-off pieces of legislation to remedy the effects of retrospective nullity is distinctly unlikely. The *conceptual* or *constitutional* problems are more severe. Let us make the sequence of events clear. The courts state that administrative action is retrospectively void and this produces problems because, for example, it would involve the expenditure of vast sums of money, or would involve losses in terms of destruction of half finished buildings. Parliament is pressed to intervene. The problem with any such intervention is that it would constitute retrospective legislation which takes away people's rights, those having been given by the court's judgment. Such legislation has always been frowned upon, and correctly so.[57]

(c) Discretion and the case law

The preceding analysis should not be taken to imply that every exercise of judicial discretion which departs from the concept of retrospective nullity is to be applauded. Moreover, even where such a departure is warranted, the language of void and voidable may not be the best way of expressing this conclusion; this will be considered in the following section. Whether such a departure is in fact warranted, or is even necessary, can only be determined in the light of the facts within the particular case or type of case, as the following contrast will make clear.

Certain authorities have manipulated void and voidable for reasons of administrative convenience. The *Paddington*[58] case provides a good example of this, and such considerations will and should play a role in order to prevent the unmitigated application of the *ultra vires* principle from wreaking administrative havoc.

Other authorities have departed from the conventional meaning of void influenced by feelings of justice in the particular case. This is clearly a highly sensitive area, but certain cases could have been legitimately solved without becoming embroiled in the debate over void and voidable. Thus in *DPP* v. *Head*[59] the whole case proceeded on the assumption that the accused should be able to take advantage of the defect within the certificate. Yet, as Rubinstein has pointed out,[60] there is no necessary reason why the conditions for detention which could have been legitimately raised by the detainee should have been available for the benefit of the accused.

---

[57] *Burmah Oil Co. Ltd.* v. *Lord Advocate* [1965] A.C. 75 and the subsequent War Damage Act 1965.
[58] [1966] 1 Q.B. 380.
[59] [1959] A.C. 83.
[60] Above, n. 1, p. 47.

Yet other cases could have been happily resolved without any modification in the traditional meaning of void. Problems only arose because of spurious interpretations of that term advanced in argument. Thus in *Calvin* v. *Carr*[61] the plaintiff had been found guilty of an offence connected with horse racing, and his conviction upheld on appeal to the Jockey Club. He argued that since the original hearing was a nullity owing to a procedural defect, therefore the internal appeal body could not cure any defect in the original hearing. This view was rejected by the court. It should, however, be made clear that nothing within the traditional idea of void justifies the plaintiff's argument. Until the original decision was challenged it remained valid. If it was never challenged at all it would always be valid. If and when it was challenged it would be void *if* there was a breach of natural justice. *Whether* there had been such a breach depended on whether the internal appellate proceeding could cure any defect in the original hearing, the very question before the court. The traditional concept of void tells us nothing about this one way or the other.

(4) THE MEDIUM THROUGH WHICH DISCRETION SHOULD OPERATE

In so far as discretion is to be exercised, how should we express this in legal language? We have three options. The language of jurisdiction can be used to arrive at the desired conclusion; the terms void and voidable can be manipulated; or the discretion can appear at the remedial level. It will be argued that the last of these is most apt and convenient on most occasions. This can best be demonstrated by examining in greater detail the opinion of Lord Hailsham of St. Marylebone in the *Aberdeen*[62] case.

His Lordship favours the exercise of a broad discretion, a spectrum of possibilities, as opposed to what he sees as the stark categorisation of mandatory versus directory, or void versus voidable. The different points which can exist within the spectrum are set out in the discussion of his Lordship's judgment given above.[63] Lord Hailsham would, therefore, use discretion at all of the three levels.

This is with respect an over-reaction against our traditional terminology. The difficulty with the argument is that it reasons from the particular to an implicit conclusion about the general which is unwarranted.

The *particular problem* prompting Lord Hailsham's exegesis is what he views as the rigidity imposed by the terms mandatory, directory, void and voidable. Wherein lies this rigidity? The answer given is that failure to comply with a statutory provision might be easily categorised if that provision is of a fundamental nature, so that the individual could simply disregard the order and attack it collaterally.[64] Equally, a defect may be so trivial or nugatory that the authority could proceed without remedial action

---

[61] [1980] A.C. 574.

[62] [1980] 1 W.L.R. 182, 189.

[63] See p. 458.

[64] Collateral attack would only in fact be possible if the case was one in which the public body was demanding something from the individual. If the individual were seeking a benefit from the public body then direct attack would be the only recourse no matter how serious the defect was.

confident that the courts would decline to listen to the complaint. There is, however, said Lord Hailsham, a wide group of cases in the middle in which it is necessary for the individual to bring an action. In such a case the court should not feel bound to reach a certain result by the use of the labels mandatory, directory, void or voidable. The discretion of the court would determine the result.

Is this *particular problem* a real one and should it lead to the general conclusion posed by his Lordship? The particular difficulty resides in the over-rigid results produced by the mandatory versus directory distinction. Lord Hailsham is quite correct in pointing out that there may be some statutory provisions disregard of which cannot always be categorised one way or another, that a middle ground exists in which the consequences of the breach will have to be taken into account to determine what the remedy should be. There are obvious analogies here with the condition-warranty distinction in the law of contract and the development of innominate terms. But a recognition that such a middle ground should exist has nothing to do with void and voidable. If such a middle ground were to be openly developed and recognised all that we would say is that with respect to certain terms which fall within its ambit the consequences of the breach will have to be looked to in order to determine the result. If those consequences are serious enough then the decision is and should be void. Nothing concerning the existence of this middle ground tells us why, if the consequences *are* serious enough, the result should not be retrospective nullity. If the existence of this middle ground is to have an effect on our traditional void-voidable dichotomy it must, therefore, be because the consequences of breach of such a term may not be thought serious enough to warrant the decision being void *ab initio*, but are of sufficient importance that the court would want to say that the decision was, for example, prospectively null. Prospective nullity only applied to those defects which had been categorised as errors of law on the face of the record, although, as we shall see, there have been developments in relation to this form of nullity.

It is at this point that we move from the particular to the *general*. Let us presume that there are terms breach of which are not regarded as sufficiently serious to justify invocation of retrospective, but only of prospective nullity. Even if this is so, to discard the entirety of our reasoning based upon void and voidable, to say that all depends upon a broad discretion is open to question. It runs the risk of throwing the baby out with the bath water. Why is this so? The reason resides in the fact that in the great majority of cases retrospective nullity gives rise to no problems in practice and is the correct starting point in theory. We are in serious danger of losing sight of this important point of principle if we follow the reasoning of Lord Hailsham. It is common to see statements which regard the terms void and voidable as unnatural inhabitants of the administrative law world, as aliens somehow engrafted onto public law cases from the world of contract and status.[65] A convincing explanation as to how this unnatural grafting process is meant to have come about has not, however, been presented. In any event if those terms did originate within private law

---

[65] *e.g. Isaacs v. Robertson* [1985] A.C. 97, 102-103.

it would be a mistake to regard them as recent interlopers. They have been in administrative law cases since the beginning of the time at which it was reasonable to talk of an administrative law jurisprudence at all, for over 300 years.[66] Nor does the traditional term void in the sense of retrospective nullity express an unnatural meaning. Quite the contrary, it expresses the natural, simple conclusion that if a decision-maker had no power to act then the act should be of no consequence. As Lord Diplock has stated,

> "It would, however, be inconsistent with the doctrine of *ultra vires* as it has been developed in English law as a means of controlling abuse of power by the executive arm of government if the judgment of a court in proceedings properly constituted that a statutory instrument was *ultra vires* were to have any lesser consequence in law than to render the instrument incapable of ever having had any legal effect upon the rights or duties of the parties to the proceedings...."[67]

That the concept of retrospective invalidity can give rise to awkward problems is no doubt true. But to infer that therefore it ought to be totally discarded is a *non sequitur*. The problems are the exceptions. Retrospective nullity is and should be the rule. The danger of reasoning such as Lord Hailsham's is that the important point of principle contained in the traditional meaning of the term void, set out by Lord Diplock, will be lost sight of. If we need to depart from the principle so be it, but let us at least be clear that we are departing from the norm, and let us at least provide cogent explanations of why we are doing so. It is for this reason, amongst others, that the exception should operate via the discretion to refuse or limit the remedy, rather than in the juggling of jurisdictional criteria, or in a sleight of hand over the meanings of void and voidable. Both of these latter avenues suffer from three related defects.

First, they conceal what is taking place. They provide a convenient mask of legal form to hide reality. Instead of saying that an applicant cannot be granted the remedy desired, because of the administrative results that would be entailed, the applicant is placated by being told that the nature of the defect unfortunately only renders the decision voidable. Secondly, use of either of these avenues produces confusion by ascribing a welter of meanings to the same terms, meanings which when analysed make little sense. Thirdly, if the discretion is exercised via either of these routes there is a danger that what may have been intended as only an *ad hoc* exception to the norm of retrospective nullity, an exception justified by the facts of the particular case, will become unintentionally generalised. A certain type of defect will henceforth be regarded as non-jurisdictional, even though the special problems leading to that appellation in the original case are entirely absent in a later case. The terminology takes on a life of its own, a result easily arrived at when the original rationale for using that language is concealed. Legal form, like Frankenstein's creation, becomes unresponsive to the commands of its creator.

---

[66] See Rubinstein, above n.1, particularly Chaps. 1-4.
[67] *Hoffmann-La Roche & Co. A.G.* v. *Secretary of State for Trade And Industry* [1975] A.C. 295, 365.

Discretion will no doubt continue to exist and be used in deciding whether a defect should be regarded as jurisdictional or not. This is inevitable. However, wherever possible a clear and open recognition that we are departing from principle is to be preferred. The most appropriate place for this to operate is at the level of discretion in refusing a remedy, or limiting the application of the remedy so that it only operates prospectively. This is not intended to imply that we should play fast and loose with discretion to refuse a remedy. Rather that if it is felt that a departure from the norm of retrospective nullity is warranted the most appropriate medium through which to express this is by saying that a decision is void, but that for reasons of, for example, practicality the effects of this must be confined to the future, or that the only remedy can be a monetary order rather than a physical undoing of what has transpired. There is some indication that our own courts are developing the idea of prospective rulings,[68] and it is one which the ECJ has employed on a number of occasions.[69]

3. *Natural Justice*

The problem of whether decisions are void or voidable has been particularly prevalent in the context of natural justice.

(1) HEARINGS

The view taken by the majority in *Ridge* v. *Baldwin*,[70] that failure to comply with the rules as to hearings makes a decision void, accords with precedent and principle. The rationale for regarding such a failure as leading to a decision which is void is expressed by Lord Selbourne L.C.,

"There would be no decision within the meaning of the statute if there were anything of that sort done contrary to the essence of justice."[71]

There have been many other cases where the courts have stated that a failure to hear renders the decision void or a nullity. Thus, the action of a committee which purported to expel a person from a club without a hearing was held to be null and void, as was the refusal of a pension to a policeman who had resigned from the force.[72] Cases of collateral attack are also

---

[68] Lewis, "Retrospective and Prospective Rulings in Administrative Law" [1988] P.L. 78; Sir Harry Woolf, *Protection of the Public – A New Challenge* (1990), pp. 53-56.
[69] Case 43/75, *Defrenne* v. *Sabena* [1976] E.C.R. 471; Case 24/86, *Blaizot* v. *University of Liege* [1989] 1 C.M.L.R. 57.
[70] [1964] A.C. 40, 80, *per* Lord Reid, 125-126, *per* Lord Morris of Borth-y-Gest, 135-136, *per* Lord Hodson.
[71] *Spackman* v. *Plumstead District Board of Works* (1885) 10 App.Cas. 229, 240.
[72] *Fisher* v. *Keane* (1878) 11 Ch.D. 353; *Lapointe* v. *L'Association de Bienfaisance et de Retraite de la Police de Montréal* [1906] A.C. 535. See also, *e.g. R.* v. *North, ex p. Oakey* [1927] 1 K.B. 491; *R.* v. *Huntingdon Confirming Authority, ex p. George and Stanford Hotels Ltd.* [1929] 1 K.B. 698; *Abbott* v. *Sullivan* [1952] 1 K.B. 189; *Disher* v. *Disher* [1965] P. 31; *Hounslow London Borough Council* v. *Twickenham Garden Developments Ltd.* [1971] Ch. 233; *Firman* v. *Ellis* [1978] Q.B. 886.

instructive.[73] A number of these cases explicitly state that a failure to hear renders the decision void.[74] Even where this is not so stated it is implicit in the ability to attack the decision collaterally; if a failure to hear constituted only an error within jurisdiction the decision could not be attacked collaterally.

Despite this long line of authority Lord Evershed in *Ridge* v. *Baldwin*[75] decided that failure to hear only made the decision voidable. His Lordship did not find the above cases convincing and preferred to rely upon *Osgood* v. *Nelson*[76] as support for the proposition that the court should only interfere if there had been a real and substantial miscarriage of justice. This, said Lord Evershed, must mean that the decision would be voidable and not void.[77] Three comments can be made upon this. First, his Lordship's reasons for distinguishing those cases which have held that a failure to hear makes the decision void are unconvincing. Secondly, the *Osgood* case does not in reality support Lord Evershed's argument.[78] Thirdly, even if the *Osgood* case did provide support for the idea that a finding should only be quashed if there had been a substantial miscarriage of justice, the conclusion that therefore this means that the decision must be voidable rather than void does not follow. It is, like his Lordship's reasoning concerning the declaration, based upon an absolute rather than relative meaning of the term void. Lord Diplock has stated[79] that a breach of the rules of natural justice should render the decision void. One can only hope that this will lay the argument to rest.

(2) BIAS

There are also several authorities supporting the proposition that bias results in a decision being void; a biased judge ceases to be a judge at all.[80] Further, if bias only made a finding voidable then declaration would not on traditional theory have been available, nor could the court have quashed in

---

[73] *Cooper* v. *Wandsworth Board of Works* (1863) 14 C.B. (N.S.) 182; *Hopkins* v. *Smethwick Local Board of Health* (1890) 24 Q.B.D. 712; *Capel* v. *Child* (1832) 2 C. & J. 558. See also, *Innes* v. *Wylie* (1844) 1 Car. & K. 257; *Bonaker* v. *Evans* (1850) 16 Q.B. 162; *Wood* v. *Woad* (1874) L.R. 9 Ex. 190.

[74] As in *Capel, Innes, Bonaker* and *Wood*.

[75] [1964] A.C. 40, 87-92.

[76] (1872) L.R. 5 H.L. 636.

[77] [1964] A.C. 40, 91-92.

[78] There is no reference in the *Osgood* case to void or voidable. The notion of substantial miscarriage of justice appears in the judgment of Martin B. (1872) L.R. 5 H.L. 636, 646. However, there is no indication that Martin B. intended to use the notion in the sense used by Lord Evershed.

[79] *O'Reilly* v. *Mackman* [1983] 2 A.C. 237. The remainder of their Lordships concurred. *cf.* *R.* v. *Dorking JJ., ex p. Harrington* [1983] Q.B. 1076, 1082.

[80] *Serjeant* v. *Dale* (1877) 2 Q.B.D. 558, 566, 568; *Allinson* v. *General Council of Medical Education and Registration* [1894] 1 Q.B. 750, 757; *R.* v. *Furnished Houses Rent Tribunal for Paddington and St. Marylebone, ex p. Kendal Hotels Ltd.* [1947] 1 All E.R. 448, 449; *R.* v. *Paddington North and St. Marylebone Rent Tribunal, ex p. Perry* [1956] 1 Q.B. 229, 237; *Anisminic Ltd.* v. *Foreign Compensation Commission* [1969] 2 A.C. 147, 171.

the presence of a no certiorari clause. Both have, however, occurred.[81] Despite these arguments some maintain that bias only renders a decision voidable.[82] This view is based upon *Dimes* v. *Grand Junction Canal Co. Proprietors*.[83] A decision of the Lord Chancellor in the Court of Chancery was challenged on appeal on the basis that the Lord Chancellor possessed a financial interest in the company which was the subject of the litigation. Parke B., in giving advice to the House of Lords, stated that such bias only resulted in the decision being voidable and not void. There are, however, a number of points to notice about the case.[84] First, it was concerned with an appeal from one superior court to another and not with review. Appeal is the classic instance of a voidable act,[85] whereas for review to be applicable the act must be void (or voidable in the area which used to be covered by patent errors of law within jurisdiction). Secondly, the authorities cited by Parke B. do not support his proposition.[86]

(3) WAIVER

An argument which has been used to support the proposition that a breach of the rules of natural justice only makes a decision voidable and not void is that such rules can be waived.[87] The argument is as follows: jurisdictional defects cannot be waived[88] and therefore if the rules of natural justice can be waived this is indicative that the defect is not jurisdictional. It is true that there are cases which indicate that a plaintiff can be barred from obtaining a remedy by waiver.[89] These cases will be discussed in detail later.[90] However, although the premise is to some extent correct, the conclusion that, therefore, a defect of natural justice only renders a determination voidable is open to question.

The whole discussion of waiver and natural justice has an air of circularity about it. A neat syllogism is set up. Jurisdictional defects cannot be waived, defects relating to natural justice can be waived, therefore,

---

[81] *Cooper* v. *Wilson* [1937] 2 K.B. 309 (declaration); *R.* v. *Cheltenham Commissioners* (1841) 1 Q.B. 467 and *R.* v. *Hertfordshire JJ.* (1845) 6 Q.B. 753 (no *certiorari* clauses).

[82] Rubinstein, *Jurisdiction and Illegality* (1965), p. 203.

[83] (1852) 3 H.L.C. 759, 785-786. See also, *Wildes* v. *Russell* (1866) L.R. 1 C.P. 722, 741-742; *Phillips* v. *Eyre* (1870) L.R. 6 Q.B. 1, 22.

[84] The case is cogently criticised in Wade, "Unlawful Administrative Action: Void or Voidable?" (1968) 84 L.Q.R. 95, 106-108.

[85] Rubinstein, *Jurisdiction and Illegality*, pp. 5-6.

[86] *Brookes* v. *Earl Rivers* (1668) Hardr. 503; *Company of Mercers and Ironmongers of Chester* v. *Bowker* (1726) 1 Stra. 639.

[87] *e.g.* Rubinstein, *Jurisdiction and Illegality*, p. 221.

[88] *e.g. Essex Incorporated Congregational Church Union* v. *Essex County Council* [1963] A.C. 808, 820-821.

[89] *e.g. R.* v. *Salop JJ.* (1859) 2 El. & El. 386, 391; *Mayor and Aldermen of City of London* v. *Cox* (1867) L.R. 2 H.L. 239, 279-283; *Farquharson* v. *Morgan* [1894] 1 Q.B. 552, 559; *R.* v. *Williams, ex p. Phillips* [1914] 1 K.B. 608, 613-614; *R.* v. *Comptroller-General of Patents and Designs, ex p. Parke Davis* [1953] 2 W.L.R. 760; *R.* v. *British Broadcasting Corporation, ex p. Lavelle* [1983] 1 W.L.R. 23, 39.

[90] See below, pp. 523-525.

breach of natural justice cannot be a jurisdictional defect. The neatness of this conceptual reasoning belies its difficulties. One difficulty is the very fact that a number of cases do not fit into it; they see no inconsistency with waiver and voidness. A second objection is more important. Why do we say as a matter of principle that jurisdictional defects cannot be waived? The answer is that the limits to an administrator's jurisdiction are imposed by the statutory grant of authority and by common law principles. These limits at one and the same time establish and reflect a public interest in maintaining the public body within its sphere. It should not, therefore, be open to the whim of an individual alone, or in collaboration with the authority, to disregard those boundaries. Those boundaries are not established solely or primarily for the individual's benefit but for the general public interest; they cannot therefore be waived at the instance of an individual.

Now as a starting point this may well be correct. It is, however, modified or compromised already in a number of respects.[91] Leaving aside the general question of how far this balancing operation should be taken, a strong argument can be made that defects of natural justice should be susceptible to waiver without this involving any allegedly logical conclusion that such defects are only voidable and not void. The reasoning is quite simply this: if the purpose of natural justice is conceived as primarily for the protection of the individual there is no reason in principle why such a defect should not be waivable. If, in other words, an individual is fully aware that the rules of natural justice are not being obeyed to the letter, but is content to proceed, then this should be possible, and the applicant should not be able to raise the defect thereafter. This is in fact the result which the cases allowing waiver of procedural rules reflect. The premise underlying the aphorism that jurisdictional defects cannot be waived is, therefore, inapplicable here. There is nothing inconsistent in admitting a doctrine of waiver and still regarding a procedural defect if not waived as producing a void decision. It would of course be open to society to say that there is a wider public interest underlying the procedural rules over and beyond that of the particular individual. The result of saying this would be that procedural defects could not be waived. However, the current case law does not in general adopt this attitude. While it continues to regard the procedural rules as imposed primarily for the benefit of the individual, there is no conceptual inconsistency in admitting that such rules can be waived and yet denominating a breach of those rules as jurisdictional and one which produces a void decision.[92] It is to be hoped that the remarks of Lord Diplock mentioned above will be taken to have settled the law in this area.

---

[91] The sanctity of the *ultra vires* principle is compromised by the balancing process inherent within the time limits for remedies, and in the rules concerning delay, acquiescence and the effect of alternative remedies, see Chaps. 14, 15. See also, the discussion of representations, Chap. 18.

[92] Akehurst, [1968] 31 M.L.R. 138, 149, and Wade (1968) 84 L.Q.R. 95, 109 express a similar idea.

Section 3. Problems of Proof

1. *General*

The question of who has the burden of proof when the validity of administrative action is challenged appears to be as follows.

As a general rule the complainant wishing to assert the invalidity of administrative action must produce some evidence which throws doubt upon the apparent validity of that action before the burden shifts to the public body. The presumption is that the actions of the public body are lawful, and it is for the complainant to lead evidence to the contrary. In *Minister of National Revenue* v. *Wrights' Canadian Ropes Ltd*[93] the minister had power to disallow any expense which he felt to be in excess of what was normal or reasonable for the business carried on by the taxpayer. The court held that it was for WCR Ltd to show that there was some ground for interfering with the minister's determination. A number of other cases support the same proposition.[94] In *R.* v. *Inland Revenue Commissioners, ex p. Rossminster Ltd*[95] revenue officers seized documents under certain tax legislation which empowered them to do so where they had reasonable cause to believe that they would be required as evidence of tax fraud. Lord Diplock[96] stated that the court must generally proceed on the presumption that the officers acted *intra vires* until that presumption had been displaced by the applicant for review.

How much evidence will be required in order to shift the burden of proof will depend upon the type of case. If the defect is one which is apparent on the face of the decision this burden will not be a heavy one. Equally, where the applicant is claiming that the decision-maker has misconstrued a condition of jurisdiction, there is unlikely to be a difficulty. A reasoned assertion that the tribunal has misinterpreted, for example, the term employee, would normally suffice in order to force the tribunal to defend its interpretation. The position will, however, be different where the ground of attack is that of unreasonableness or bad faith. The applicant will also have a heavier task where the statute requires the decision-maker to be satisfied of some matter, or where it is required to form some opinion.[97]

This general rule is subject to two qualifications. First, where the applicant alleges something which would, in the absence of statutory authority, be a tort, it seems that the claimant only has to prove the facts

---

[93] [1947] A.C. 10, 122.
[94] *Point of Ayr Collieries Ltd.* v. *Lloyd-George* [1943] 2 All E.R. 546, 547; *Potato Marketing Board* v. *Merricks* [1958] 2 Q.B. 316; *Wilover Nominees Ltd.* v. *Inland Revenue Commissioners* [1973] 1 W.L.R. 1393, 1396, 1399, affirmed [1974] 1 W.L.R. 1342, 1347; *Fawcett Properties Ltd.* v. *Buckingham County Council* [1959] Ch. 543, 575, affirmed [1961] A.C. 636; *Bugg* v. *DPP* [1993] 2 All E.R. 815, 828.
[95] [1980] A.C. 952.
[96] *Ibid.* p. 1013. See also, Viscount Dilhorne, pp. 1006-1007. The case was complicated by the fact that the revenue officers claimed public interest immunity for not disclosing the grounds of their belief.
[97] See cases, above nn. 93 and 94.

which would constitute the wrong. The burden of proof is then on the public body to show justification. Thus, in the *Rossminster*[98] case Lord Diplock stated that, since the handling of a man's property without his permission was prima facie tortious, then in a civil action for trespass to goods based on the seizure and removal of the things, the onus would be on the officer to satisfy the court that there did in fact exist reasonable grounds for believing that the documents were evidence of a tax fraud.[99] It seems that this qualification will only apply where the allegation is that a statutory condition has not been complied with, and not where the allegation is, for example, one of bad faith.[100]

The second possible qualification arises from the law on habeas corpus. The law in this area is, however, unclear. In one case the courts held that the public body must show that it has complied with the statutory conditions. It was insufficient for a detaining authority to make a return which was valid on its face. A detainee could be put to proof of an allegation of bad faith, but it was otherwise where the allegation related to compliance with the statutory conditions.[101] This case has been distinguished, the court holding that where the return was good on its face it was for the detainee to show that the detention was illegal.[102] The present position does, nonetheless, seem to be that the burden of proof rests upon the detaining authority. In *R. v. Secretary of State for the Home Department, ex p. Khawaja*[103] Lord Scarman stated that the initial burden was on the applicant, but that this was transferred to the detaining authority once the applicant had shown that there was a prima facie case that liberty or property were being interfered with. The burden of proof would then be on the detaining authority to justify the detention. Thus, on the facts of that case, once the applicant had shown that he had entered the United Kingdom with the leave of the immigration officer the burden of proving that he had obtained leave by deception was on the executive.

The question which is under consideration within this section should not be confused with a separate, albeit connected one. We have been considering the status of an order or decision once made, and the question of who has the initial onus of proving a defect. The general answer is that the onus is initially on the person alleging the invalidity. A related but separate question is what will the court demand of the public body if it is to justify its action? In other words if the individual does shift the burden of proof to the public body what will that body have to prove and what will be the

---

[98] [1980] A.C. 952, 1011. See also, *R. v. Secretary of State for the Home Department, ex p. Khawaja* [1984] A.C. 74.

[99] This was not relevant in the actual case which was concerned with an application for judicial review, and return of the documents. See also, *St. Pancras Borough Council v. Frey* [1963] 2 Q.B. 586, 592; *Harpin v. St. Albans Corporation* (1969) 67 L.G.R. 479. But see, *Bristol District Council v. Clark* [1975] 1 W.L.R. 1443, 1448 where doubt was cast upon these cases.

[100] *R. v. Governor of Brixton Prison, ex p. Ahsan* [1969] 2 Q.B. 222, explaining *Greene v. Secretary of State for Home Affairs* [1942] A.C. 284.

[101] *R. v. Governor of Brixton Prison, ex p. Ahsan*, above n. 100; *Eshugbayi Eleko v. Government of Nigeria* [1931] A.C. 662.

[102] *R. v. Governor of Risley Remand Centre, ex p. Hassan* [1976] 1 W.L.R. 971, 976-979.

[103] [1984] A.C. 74, 111-112.

standard of review? This will depend upon the statutory context. Normally, as we have already seen, if the allegation relates to a jurisdictional fact the court will substitute its judgment for that of the public body. Where the question is whether the evidence justifies the application of a certain statutory term the standard of proof will differ depending upon the area in question.[104]

2. *Validity Pending Determination*

A corollary of the basic principle enunciated in the previous section is that an administrative order will be presumed to be valid unless and until successfully challenged. That this is indeed so was confirmed by the decision of the House of Lords in *Hoffmann-La Roche & Co. A.G.* v. *Secretary of State for Trade and Industry*.[105] Pursuant to an inquiry and report made by the Monopolies Commission on the profit levels attained by Hoffmann-La Roche on the sale of certain drugs, the Secretary of State laid before Parliament statutory orders directing the company to reduce the price on its drugs. The third of such orders was approved by both Houses of Parliament. The company informed the Secretary of State that it would not obey the Order. It claimed that the procedures of the Monopolies Commission contravened the rules of natural justice and that the order was *ultra vires*. The Secretary of State responded by claiming an interim injunction to restrain the company from charging prices in excess of those specified in the Order. As the case progressed the main argument became whether the interim injunction should be conditional on the Crown giving an undertaking to pay damages should the company prove successful in the main action. The Secretary of State had refused to give any such undertaking. Their Lordships found against the company. Their reasoning may be summarised as follows.

The statutory instrument is, unless and until successfully challenged, the law of the land. It has a presumption of validity. If and when it is successfully impugned it will be retrospectively null. The normal practice of the courts is to condition the grant of an interim injunction upon an undertaking in damages given by the person in whose favour the injunction issues. This is to safeguard the position of the party against whom the injunction issues should this party prove to be successful in the main action, and has suffered loss in the period between the interim injunction and the final decision. It was at one time maintained that the Crown would never be required to give such an undertaking, but this rule had been rendered out of date by the passage of the Crown Proceedings Act 1947. In principle, therefore, such an undertaking could be extracted from the Crown and would be normally required where the Crown was asserting its purely private law rights of a proprietary or contractual nature. The position was, however, different where the Crown was enforcing the law of the land. In

---

[104] See above pp. 371-372 for a consideration of this point.
[105] [1975] A.C. 295.

such cases, although an undertaking in damages could be required as a condition for the grant of an injunction, the private party would have to show a strong case for imposing this condition. The factors which the court would take into account in deciding whether to impose the undertaking in damages included the strength of the company's prima facie case of invalidity, the financial interest possessed by the Crown in the form of the National Health Service being the main buyer of the drugs, the viability of a plan proposed by the company under which it would charge the higher prices but recompense buyers of the drugs should the Order be upheld, and the effect upon members of the public who were not parties to the action.[106]

Lord Wilberforce dissented.[107] The Statutory Order could not, said his Lordship, have any presumption of validity since it was now being challenged by the right person in the correct proceedings. The optimum position would be to be able to issue the interim injunction since the only loss to be suffered would be pecuniary, but to require the Crown to provide compensation should the final decision be in favour of the company.

The difficulty with the decision is that the issues involved therein, the status of the Order and the undertaking in damages, were linked both in the majority and dissenting judgments, in a way which is apt to mislead. These issues will be considered in turn.

The majority judgment should be accepted in relation to the status of the Order. It is and should be regarded as presumptively valid. The argument to the contrary put by Lord Wilberforce is, with respect, flawed. The Order must be presumptively something: it must be either presumptively valid or invalid. A neutral stance is not possible. How would one even begin to assess the demands for injunctive relief if the order was neutral and who would have the burden of proof? Moreover, Lord Wilberforce's assertion that no such presumption of validity should exist because the correct person was challenging the order in the correct proceedings leaves out of account two crucial connected factors: the time scale and the normal burden of proof. The time scale problems are simply a reflection of the fact that the claim was for interim relief. The presumption of validity voiced by the majority is a presumption which applies unless and until the order is challenged in the final action. This is reflected by the fact that at the trial of the main action the general principle is that the burden of proof will rest initially on the person disputing the validity of the decision or order.

There is, however, no logical connection between regarding the order as presumptively valid and the question of the undertaking in damages. It was the latter that Lord Wilberforce was most concerned with and in this respect his opinion is to be preferred to that of the majority. The fact that the statutory order is presumptively valid does not, in and of itself, tell us anything concerning the basis on which it should be enforced in interim proceedings. The link between presumptive validity and the undertaking in damages seen by the majority is part conceptual and part practical. The *conceptual* connection is said to be that because the Order is at present the

---

[106] *Ibid.* pp. 341-342, *per* Lord Reid, pp. 351-354, *per* Lord Morris of Borth-y-Gest, pp. 361-370, *per* Lord Diplock, pp. 370-372, *per* Lord Cross of Chelsea.
[107] *Ibid.* pp. 354-360.

law of the land, and because the Crown has a duty to enforce it, by way
of contrast to a private individual who has no such duty and who will
normally only bring an action if there is a private interest at stake,
therefore, the Crown should not always be fettered by the requirement of a
damages undertaking.[108] This is overlaid by the *pragmatic* consideration
that such a requirement could be a deterrent to the Crown bringing an
action at all.[109]

Neither of these reasons is convincing. Let us consider the *conceptual*
argument first. True, the Crown may have a duty to enforce the law, but
this premise does not warrant the conclusion extracted from it. The whole
point about the presumption of validity is that it is just that, a presumption.
It can be rebutted. The crucial point is that when losses result from an
invalid statutory order, who should bear that loss? Where, in other words,
the presumption is rebutted, who should shoulder the responsibility? This
takes us into the more general question of compensation in administrative
law which will be considered below.[110]

At this juncture it is, however, sufficient to point out that the equation
of a duty to enforce the presumptive law with the absence of responsibility
if that presumption proves unwarranted at the end of the day, is open
to serious question. The Crown or a public body is generally given
responsibility for law enforcement because it represents the public interest,
even if the Crown or the public body itself does not have a financial
stake.[111] The body populace or a section of it is benefited by ensuring that
the law is enforced through this medium. If it transpires that the public
body was wrong then the public generally should equally shoulder the
burden, through the losses being placed upon it via taxation. Any
distributive windfall gain or loss to a section of society[112] is minimal
compared to the burden placed on the private party if no undertaking in
damages is required.

The *pragmatic* argument concerning deterrence is equally suspect. A
public body could of course be deterred from bringing an action if there
was the possibility that it could be liable to pay substantial sums in
compensation should it prove to be unsuccessful. But this amounts to no
more than saying that doing something with no risk of financial liability is
less risky than doing something with some such risk. It begs the whole
question of where losses from invalid governmental action ought to lie. In
any event, the chief deterrence to the public body is likely to be the breadth
and vagaries of jurisdictional attack itself.

The availability of interim relief against the Crown will be considered
more fully below.[113] The House of Lords has had occasion to consider the

---

[108] See, *e.g.* [1975] A.C. 295, 364, 367, *per* Lord Diplock.
[109] *Ibid.* p. 371, *per* Lord Cross of Chelsea.
[110] See pp. 646-651.
[111] *Gouriet* v. *Union of Post Office Workers* [1978] A.C. 435.
[112] *Hoffmann-La Roche* [1975] A.C. 295, 367. See also, *Rochdale Borough Council* v. *Anders*
[1988] 3 All E.R. 490, holding that a local authority should have to give a cross undertaking
in damages. *cf. Director General of Fair Trading* v. *Tobyward Ltd.* [1989] 1 W.L.R. 517.
[113] See below, pp. 726-729.

validity of laws pending their final determination in *Factortame(No.2)*.[114] In that case the plaintiffs sought interim relief against the Crown to prevent it from applying a national law which they argued was in breach of Community law. It was held that there was no *rule* that a party challenging the validity of a law must show a strong prima facie case that the law was invalid. The court had a *discretion* in the matter. However, their Lordships also held that the court should not restrain a public authority by interim injunction from enforcing an apparently valid law unless it was satisfied that, in all the circumstances, the challenge to the validity of the law was, prima facie, so firmly based as to justify this exceptional course of action being taken.[115]

3. *Partial Invalidity*

A court may, under certain conditions, hold that the invalid part of an order can be severed while holding that the remainder thereof is still valid. The court will not, however, "rewrite" such an order or decision, and the invalid part must not be inextricably interwoven with the whole order.[116]

The leading decision on this point is now *DPP v. Hutchinson*.[117] The appellants were convicted of offences under the Greenham Common Bylaws, in that they entered a protected area as defined by the bylaw. They contended by way of defence that the bylaw was invalid, because it was in breach of the enabling legislation. The parent statute had stated that bylaws could be made provided that they did not interfere with rights of common, and the appellants claimed that these bylaws did interfere with such rights. The issue for the House of Lords was, therefore, whether the invalid part of the bylaw could be severed.

Their Lordships distinguished between two situations. The first was one in which textual severance was possible. In this instance a test of substantial severability was to be applied, which would be satisfied when the valid text was unaffected by, and independent of, the invalid. The second situation was one in which textual severance was not possible. In this case the test which should be applied was whether the legislative instrument with the parts omitted would be a substantially different law in its effect from what it would be if the omitted parts were included.

---

[114] R. v. *Secretary of State for Transport, ex p. Factortame Ltd. (No.2)* [1991] 1 A.C. 603.
[115] *Ibid.* p. 674; R. v. *H.M. Treasury, ex p. British Telecommunications plc* [1994] 1 C.M.L.R. 621.
[116] *Potato Marketing Board* v. *Merricks* [1958] 2 Q.B. 316; *Kingsway Investments (Kent) Ltd.* v. *Kent County Council* [1971] A.C. 72; *Dunkley* v. *Evans* [1981] 1 W.L.R. 1522; *Thames Water Authority* v. *Elmbridge Borough Council* [1983] Q.B. 570; R. v. *Secretary of State for Transport, ex p. Greater London Council* [1986] Q.B. 556; R. v. *North Hertfordshire District Council, ex p. Cobbold* [1985] 3 All E.R. 487.
[117] [1990] 2 A.C. 783; Bradley, "Judicial Enforcement of *Ultra Vires* Byelaws: The Proper Scope of Severance" [1990] P.L. 293.

PART 3

REMEDIES
I

13. REMEDIES: STANDING

Section 1. Introduction

Locus standi is concerned with whether this particular plaintiff is entitled to invoke the jurisdiction of the court. This question must be distinguished from that of justiciability which asks whether the judicial process is suitable for the resolution of this type of dispute at all, whoever may bring it to the courts. It is also distinct from the issue known in the United States as ripeness,[1] under which abstract or hypothetical questions are not adjudicated upon. Neither the concepts of justiciability nor ripeness exist here in the developed form which they possess in the United States, but the case law contains evidence of both doctrines, albeit in a fledgling state. Although different, the issues of standing, justiciability and ripeness can be confused. As will be seen some of the reasons given for a restrictive view of standing would be better dealt with under expanded notions of justiciability or ripeness.

The issue of who should be enabled to invoke the judicial process is a fundamental one that has given rise to much debate[2] and controversy.[3] Implicit in the answer given will be something more than the fact that X, a taxpayer, can or cannot seek an application for review. Assumptions about the nature of administrative law and the role of the courts are inherent in the response which is elicited.

The law will be examined both prior to and consequent upon the recent reform of administrative law remedies.[4] A brief historical perspective is necessary for a proper understanding of the present law. Following this, some of the broader questions about the scope of standing will be examined.

Section 2. The Position Before 1978[5]

The case law on standing displays considerable diversity both within each particular remedy and as between them. Even when the same words such

---

[1] Jaffe, *Judicial Control of Administrative Action* (1965), Chap. 10; Davis, *Administrative Law Text* (3rd ed., 1972), Chap. 21.
[2] See on standing generally, Thio, *Locus Standi and Judicial Review* (1971); Vining, *Legal Identity* (1978); *Locus Standi* (ed. Stein, 1979); Van Dijk, *Judicial Review of Governmental Action and the Requirement of an Interest to Sue* (1980).
[3] The secondary literature will be reviewed below pp. 499-513.
[4] S.I. 1977 No. 1955; S.I. 1980 No. 2000; Supreme Court Act 1981, s.31.
[5] S.I. 1977 No. 1955 came into effect on January 11, 1978.

as "private right", "special damage", "person aggrieved" or "sufficient interest" are used it cannot be assumed that they bear the same meaning. This multiplicity of meaning is evident not only when these phrases appear in the different remedies, but also when cases concerning the same remedy are juxtaposed. The main cause of this confusion resides in a failure to adopt a clear view as to what the remedies as a whole are trying to achieve, which reflects at one stage removed a lack of clarity as to what administrative law is about. The law prior to 1978 will be sketched briefly, in order to understand the present law and in order to comprehend the more general policy reasons which underly standing.

1. Certiorari

There are at least two views as to standing requirements for certiorari. The first view is that certiorari has no standing limits as such. Any person can apply for an order, and his standing will only be of relevance to the granting of the remedy. If the application is made by a person aggrieved, then the court will intervene *ex debito justitiae*, in justice to the applicant; where the applicant is a stranger, the court considers whether the public interest demands intervention.[6] A second view is that an applicant must show some interest before being accorded standing.[7] The position is "clearly unclear", but the weight of authority appears to be in favour of the former view.[8] The degree of practical difference between the two views should not however be over-emphasised. If a court does not wish to grant an applicant standing, it can reach that conclusion either by adopting the first view, but refusing in its discretion to admit the applicant, or by deeming him not to be an interested party. Whether theoretical distinctions inhere in the two formulations will be considered later.

2. Prohibition

The case law on standing to seek prohibition makes that on certiorari appear simple.[9] One line of authority does however stand out for the clarity

---

[6] R. v. *Surrey JJ.* (1870) L.R. 5 Q.B. 466, 473; R. v. *Butt, ex p. Brooke* (1922) 38 T.L.R. 537; R. v. *Stafford JJ., ex p. Stafford Corporation* [1940] 2 K.B. 33; R. v. *Brighton Borough JJ., ex p. Jarvis* [1954] 1 W.L.R. 203; R. v. *Thames Magistrates' Court, ex p. Greenbaum* (1957) 55 L.G.R. 129.

[7] See, *e.g.* Thio, above n. 2, Chap. 5; Gordon, "*Certiorari* and the Problem of Locus Standi" (1955) 71 L.Q.R. 483, 485. Certain cases are said to support this view, *e.g.* R. v. *Bradford-on-Avon Urban District Council, ex p. Boulton* [1964] 1 W.L.R. 1136; R. v. *Paddington Valuation Officer, ex p. Peachey Property Corporation* [1966] 1 Q.B. 380; R. v. *Russell, ex p. Beaverbrook Newspapers Ltd.* [1969] 1 Q.B. 342.

[8] Cases cited for the second view appear to be either *obiter dictum*, *e.g. ex p. Boulton,* above n. 7, or ambiguous, *e.g.* the *Paddington* case, where Lord Denning M.R. purported to apply the *Greenbaum* case, above n. 6, which is supportive of the first view.

[9] See, *e.g.* the lamentation in Shortt, *Informations, Mandamus and Prohibitions* (1887), p. 441.

of both the result and the reasoning. The cases held that prohibition must be granted whoever the applicant is, the reason being that an excess of jurisdiction by an inferior court was a contempt against the Crown, in the sense of being an infringement of the royal prerogative.[10] The applicant was therefore approaching the court to represent the public interest. This reasoning which is indicative of a citizen action[11] approach towards standing, was however rendered more uncertain by cases which sought to view the grant of standing from a perspective of the private rights of the individual affected. Thus some authorities appeared to require a specific interest in the applicant,[12] while others sought to sidestep the reasoning in the first line of authority by arguing that it applied only to patent and not to latent jurisdictional defects.[13] The tension between these two approaches to standing recurs within other remedies, and reflects an important divergence of opinion as to the role of the individual within administrative law.[14]

3. *Mandamus*

The diversity of approach towards standing is clearly exemplified in the confused case law on mandamus. Two approaches can be discerned. *One* line of cases appears to require the applicant to show infringement of a legal right in the traditional private law sense such that he would be able to maintain a cause of action in contract, or tort, etc., against the public body.[15] Other cases which have employed the terminology of private right have however given the term "right" a broader meaning by granting standing even where no contractual or tortious right has been affected.[16] *Another* line of authority has explicitly regarded a sufficient or special interest as satisfying the requirements for standing. Thus in *R. v. Paddington Valuation Officer, ex p. Peachey Property Corporation Ltd.,*[17] a company was allowed to challenge a valuation list for rating purposes without showing that it was more aggrieved than any other ratepayer, Lord Denning M.R. stating that the court would listen to anyone whose interests were affected, but not to a mere busybody interfering in things which did not concern him.

---

[10] *De Huber v. Queen of Portugal* (1851) 17 Q.B. 171; *Worthington v. Jeffries* (1875) L.R. 10 C.P. 379. See also, the way in which *Forster v. Forster and Berridge* (1863) 4 B. & S. 187 was distinguished in *Worthington*.

[11] See below, pp. 504-511 for a discussion of this idea.

[12] See, *e.g. Forster*, above n. 10; *R. v. Twiss* (1869) L.R. 4 Q.B. 407, 413-414.

[13] *Mayor and Aldermen of City of London v. Cox* (1867) L.R. 2 H.L. 239; *Farquharson v. Morgan* [1894] 1 Q.B. 552.

[14] See below, pp. 497-513.

[15] *R. v. Lewisham Union* [1897] 1 Q.B. 498, 500; *R. v. Industrial Court, ex p. A.S.S.E.T.* [1965] 1 Q.B. 377.

[16] *R. v. Hereford Corporation, ex p. Harrower* [1970] 1 W.L.R. 1424. See also *R. v. Commissioners of Customs and Excise, ex p. Cook* [1970] 1 W.L.R. 450.

[17] [1966] 1 Q.B. 380, 401. See also, *R. v. Commissioners for Special Purposes of Income Tax* (1888) 21 Q.B.D. 313; *R. v. Manchester Corporation* [1911] 1 K.B. 560; *R. v. Commissioner of Police of the Metropolis, ex p. Blackburn* [1968] 2 Q.B. 118.

More recently the House of Lords in the *IRC*[18] case has disapproved of the very restrictive private right test applied within mandamus. The nature of the test which should be employed within this area will be considered below.

4. *Injunction and Declaration*[19]

Declarations and injunctions were until recently available through Order 15, rule 16 or by way of application to the High Court respectively. They may now also be claimed by way of application for judicial review under section 31 of the Supreme Court Act 1981. Two related reasons have reduced the importance of the restrictive rules described below. First, the test for standing under section 31 appears to be more liberal than that which existed previously. Secondly, the courts have emphasised that public law cases should be brought under the new procedure. The criteria for standing outside of section 31 are still important for a number of reasons. On the one hand, there will still be some cases in which a declaration or injunction can be sought by the previous route. On the other hand, the *locus standi* rules for these remedies cast interesting light on the purpose behind such rules. What follows is an analysis of the tests for standing outside section 31. The effect of the new procedure will be considered thereafter.

The circumstances in which an individual can seek an injunction or declaration have, in general, been narrowly construed. In *Boyce* v. *Paddington Borough Council*[20] Buckley J. held that an action for an injunction could only be maintained without joining the Attorney-General in two types of case: either the plaintiff had to show that the interference with the public right constituted also an infringement of a private right, or in a case where no private rights of the plaintiff were interfered with, there had to be special damage. This criterion has been endorsed by the House of Lords,[21] and later cases on declaration have adopted the same reasoning. Thus in *Gregory* v. *Camden London Borough Council*[22] the plaintiff was denied standing to challenge a grant of planning permission. Paull J. reasoned directly by analogy with private law, and concluded that the plaintiff could not succeed unless he could show either that the statute had

---

[18] R. v. *Inland Revenue Commissioners, ex p. National Federation of Self-Employed and Small Business Ltd.* [1982] A.C. 617.

[19] Any differences between the two remedies for the purposes of standing will be specifically mentioned.

[20] [1903] 1 Ch. 109, 114. See also, *Stockport District Waterworks Co.* v. *Manchester Corporation* (1863) 9 Jur.(N.S.) 266; *Pudsey Coal Gas Co.* v. *Corporation of Bradford* (1872) L.R. 15 Eq. 167.

[21] *London Passenger Transport Board* v. *Moscrop* [1942] A.C. 332, 342.

[22] [1966] 1 W.L.R. 899. See also, *Anisminic* v. *Foreign Compensation Commission* [1968] 2 Q.B. 862, 910-911; *Wilson, Walton International (Offshore Services) Ltd.* v. *Tees and Hartlepool Port Authority* [1969] 1 Lloyd's Rep. 120; *Booth and Co. (International) Ltd.* v. *National Enterprise Board* [1978] 3 All E.R. 624.

been passed to benefit a class of people including himself, or that other private law rights had been infringed.

Why have the courts embraced such narrow rules for standing? Two reasons can be perceived, neither of which is convincing. First, the test established in *Boyce* is based upon the criteria for actionability for public nuisance, as is made clear by the authorities cited therein.[23] This argument from public nuisance proves nothing. In private law there is no separation of standing and the merits. Who can sue is not treated as a distinct issue, but is part of the definition of the cause of action. Thus, for example, those placed in fear of their bodily safety can claim in assault, or those whose reputation is injured can claim in defamation. The argument from public nuisance therefore tells us who should be able to sue in that action. To infer from this that the same test should apply generally within public law is a complete *non sequitur*.[24]

A second argument flows from the wording of Order 15, rule 16 under which declarations were sought prior to 1978.[25] Something akin to a private law right is said to be required because the Order speaks of "declarations of rights". This argument is equally unconvincing. Declarations fulfil both an original and a supervisory role. In the former sense they are used in many circumstances which may have nothing to do with public law, for example, to declare the parties' respective rights under a contract. Within this context it will obviously be apposite to know what rights X and Y have so that declarations can be made about them. Where, however, the declaration is being used in its supervisory role, to control excess of power by public bodies, it is unwarranted to assume that such a remedy can only be granted where a private law right is present.

Not all cases have required a private law right in the sense of a cause of action in contract or tort before the plaintiff can proceed.[26] The prospect of utilising these cases to broaden the standing requirement in this area was however curtailed by the decision in *Gouriet* v. *Union of Post Office Workers*.[27] The Post Office Act 1953, sections 58 and 68, makes it an offence to interfere with the mail. The Union of Post Office Workers (U.P.W.) had called on their members not to handle letters being sent to

---

[23] *Winterbottom* v. *Lord Derby* (1867) L.R. 2 Ex. 316; *Benjamin* v. *Storr* (1874) L.R. 9 C.P. 400.

[24] Cane, "The Function of Standing Rules in Administrative Law" [1980] P.L. 303, 305.

[25] Declarations can still be sought under this Order, but the courts have held that public law cases must generally be brought within the new procedure save in exceptional cases, see below, Chap. 15.

[26] *(a)* e.g. on declaration: *Nicholls* v. *Tavistock Urban District Council* [1923] 2 Ch. 18; *Prescott* v. *Birmingham Corporation* [1955] Ch. 210; *Brownsea Haven Properties* v. *Poole Corporation* [1958] Ch. 574; *Eastham* v. *Newcastle United Football Club* [1964] Ch. 413; *Thorne Rural District Council* v. *Bunting* [1972] Ch. 470; *Tito* v. *Waddell (No. 2)* [1977] Ch. 106, 260; *R.* v. *Greater London Council, ex p. Blackburn* [1976] 1 W.L.R. 550. *(b)* e.g. on injunction: *Chamberlaine* v. *Chester and Birkenhead Ry. Co.* (1848) 1 Ex. 870; *Bradbury* v. *Enfield London Borough Council* [1967] 1 W.L.R. 1311. *cf. R.C.A. Corporation* v. *Pollard* [1982] 3 W.L.R. 1007 and *Lonrho Ltd.* v. *Shell Petroleum (No. 2)* [1982] A.C. 173, restrictively interpreting *Ex p. Island Records Ltd.* [1978] Ch. 122; and *Barrs* v. *Bethell* [1981] 3 W.L.R. 874 not following *Prescott*, or *R.* v. *Greater London Council, ex p. Blackburn*.

[27] [1978] A.C. 435.

South Africa. Gouriet sought the consent of the Attorney-General to a relator action, but this consent was not forthcoming. By the time that the case went to the House of Lords the plaintiff was no longer asserting that this refusal of consent could be reviewed, rather that the failure to secure his approval was not fatal to the claim. Their Lordships rejected this argument. A number of themes recur in their Lordships' opinions, two of which are especially important, one particular, the other general.

The former arose because the case concerned a relator action "in support" of the criminal law: the injunction was being sought to prevent the commission of a criminal offence. Although the Attorney-General had been granted injunctive relief in this context before,[28] their Lordships felt that the power should be utilised with caution.[29]

It is however with the more general themes of the case that we are most concerned. The court's reasoning is permeated by a conception of the role of the citizen in public law. Put shortly, the citizen has no such role. In the absence of the Attorney-General a citizen could enforce his private rights, but public rights could be asserted only through the Attorney-General as representative of the public interest. It therefore followed that consent to a relator action was not something fictitious or nominal, to be circumvented at will; it was the substantive manifestation of the fact that public rights were to be represented by the Attorney-General.[30] The precise ambit of the term private right is not clear,[31] and some uncertainty hangs over the question whether special damage is still an alternative basis on which to claim declaratory or injunctive relief[32] in one's own name.

The decision illustrates a conception of standing which in itself reflects a view of administrative law: the vindication of private rights. The general difficulties of such an approach will be considered below,[33] but this approach is subject to a more particular difficulty which should be mentioned here. When an applicant seeks a prerogative order he is not tied to the enforcement of private law rights; he is in effect vindicating the public interest in some degree, subject to a judicial discretion to preclude the phantom busybody or ghostly inter-meddler. Given that this is so, the

---

[28] e.g. Att.-Gen. v. Smith [1958] 2 Q.B. 173; Att.-Gen. v. Chaudry [1971] 1 W.L.R. 1614.

[29] Because, e.g., sanctions and methods of proof could differ between prosecution for a crime, and the grant of injunctive relief; problems of double jeopardy also worried their Lordships. See generally, Feldman, "Injunctions and the Criminal Law" (1979) 42 M.L.R. 369.

[30] [1978] A.C. 435, 477-480, 483, 495, 498-499, 508. cf. the view in the Court of Appeal [1977] 1 Q.B. 729, 768-772, 773-779.

[31] e.g. Lord Wilberforce states that a plaintiff can seek a declaration in his own name whenever a plaintiff asserts a legal right which is being denied, or threatened, or claims an immunity, [1978] A.C. 435, 483-484; Lord Diplock states that an existing cause of action is not required, but does seem to require that such an action could eventuate, ibid. pp. 501-502; Viscount Dilhorne speaks of the need for a personal right or interest without further elucidation, ibid. p. 495; Lord Edmund-Davies states that a private right is necessary, but that a cause of action in contract or tort is not, ibid. pp. 514-515.

[32] Lord Wilberforce is the only one of their Lordships to mention special damage, but this may be because special damage was not pleaded. In Barrs v. Bethell [1981] 3 W.L.R. 874 it was held that an individual could proceed in his own name if he could prove such damage; and see below, pp. 498-499.

[33] See below, pp. 499-502.

statement underpinning *Gouriet*, to the effect that individuals enforce private rights and the Attorney-General enforces public rights, cannot be unqualifiedly accepted as an accurate description of what the courts themselves have been doing.[34] *Gouriet* did in fact argue that, given the broader notion of interest which suffices for standing within the prerogative orders, a similar concept should apply in injunction/declaration cases. Their Lordships rejected this argument, and the cogency of their reasons will be examined when the general conceptual basis of standing is explored.[35]

Section 3. The Present Position: The Attorney-General, Public Authorities and Statutory Appeals

The standing of the Attorney-General and of public authorities require separate treatment, as does the issue of who is entitled to utilise certain statutory appeal formula. These areas will be examined before considering the general rules on standing which operate in ordinary judicial review actions.

1. *Attorney-General*

The Attorney-General as the legal representative of the Crown represents the interests of the Crown *qua* Sovereign and also *qua parens patriae*. The areas in which the jurisdictions were first invoked were public nuisance and the administration of charitable and public trusts. It is of interest that even here the initial impetus seemed to be one stemming from private law proprietary interests, the Crown possessing a *jus publicum* for the use of highways and rivers, coupled with the desire to prevent multiplicity of litigation.

As seen above, the Attorney-General may proceed at the relation of an individual complainant. He may, however, act on his own initiative. As guardian of the public interest, he can restrain public nuisances and prevent excess of power by public bodies.[36]

One area which gives rise to particular problems is that in which the Attorney-General seeks to buttress the criminal law. In *Att.-Gen.* v. *Smith*[37] an injunction was granted to prevent S. from making repeated applications for planning permission for a caravan site despite the presence of penalties in the relevant legislation, and in *Att.-Gen.* v. *Harris*[38] a flower vendor who contravened police regulations many times was prevented from continuing to do so by the award of an injunction. The problems of using the civil law

---

[34] See also Wade, Note (1978) 94 L.Q.R. 4.

[35] See below, pp. 501-502.

[36] *e.g Att.-Gen.* v. *PYA Quarries Ltd.* [1957] 2 Q.B. 169; *Att.-Gen.* v. *Manchester Corporation* [1906] 1 Ch. 643; *Att.-Gen.* v. *Fulham Corporation* [1921] 1 Ch. 440.

[37] [1978] 2 Q.B. 173, 185.

[38] [1961] 1 Q.B. 74; *Att.-Gen.* v. *Premier Line Ltd.* [1932] 1 Ch. 303.

in support of the criminal were considered above and their Lordships in the *Gouriet*[39] case felt that this power should be used sparingly, and should be reserved for cases where continued breaches of the law existed or serious injury was threatened.[40] It is not entirely clear whether the Attorney-General seeking an injunction is in an especially privileged position. The law appears to be as follows. It is at the discretion of the Attorney-General to decide whether to bring an action or not.[41] If an action is brought and the breach proven the court is not bound to issue an injunction in the Attorney-General's favour, but exceptional circumstances would have to exist before the claim was refused. It will be regarded as a wrong in itself for the law to be flouted.[42] In circumstances where a plaintiff does not possess the requisite interest to bring a case in his own name, the consent of the Attorney-General is necessary, the procedure being known as a relator action. We have already seen that the failure to secure this consent cannot be sidestepped or circumvented.[43] When the action brought is a relator action the Attorney-General is the plaintiff, but in practice the private litigant will instruct counsel, and will remain liable for costs.[44]

2. Public Authorities

The *locus standi* of public authorities has been restrictively construed by the courts, the general principles being the same as those for individuals. Interference with proprietary rights, special damage, or a showing that the public authority is the beneficiary of a statutory duty have generally been required in order that the action can be maintained without the Attorney-General. Thus, in *Devonport Corporation* v. *Tozer*[45] the plaintiff corporation failed to obtain an injunction when complaining that the defendant's building had constituted the laying out of a new street in contravention of the bylaws. No proprietary interest of the plaintiff was affected and the courts deprecated the bringing of such actions in the absence of the Attorney-General. Even where standing seemed to be accorded by a specific statute the courts have tended to construe such provisions restrictively,[46] as they have done with more general statutory terms.[47]

The legislature has responded to the restrictive attitude adopted by the courts through the enactment of section 222 of the Local Government Act 1972

---

[39] [1978] A.C. 435. See also, the restrictive observations in *Stoke-on-Trent City Council* v. *B. & Q. (Retail) Ltd.* [1984] A.C. 754; *Att.-Gen.* v. *Able* [1984] Q.B. 975.

[40] *e.g. Att.-Gen.* v. *Chaudry* [1971] 1 W.L.R. 1614.

[41] *London County Council* v. *Att.-Gen.* [1902] A.C. 165, 169; *Gouriet* [1978] A.C. 435.

[42] *Att.-Gen.* v. *Bastow* [1957] 1 Q.B. 514; *Att.-Gen.* v. *Harris* [1961] 1 Q.B. 74.

[43] See above, pp. 483-484.

[44] The relator may be joined as co-plaintiff, Thio, above n. 2, pp. 157-159.

[45] [1903] 1 Ch. 759; *Att.-Gen.* v. *Pontypridd Waterworks Co.* [1909] 1 Ch. 388.

[46] *Wallasey Local Board* v. *Gracey* (1887) 36 Ch. D. 593; *cf. London City Council* v. *South Metropolitan Gas Company* [1904] 1 Ch. 76.

[47] See, *Prestatyn Urban District Council* v. *Prestatyn Raceway Ltd.* [1970] 1 W.L.R. 33, disapproving a more liberal approach by Lord Denning M.R. in *Warwickshire County Council* v. *British Railways Board* [1969] 1 W.L.R. 1117 concerning the construction of the Local Government Act 1933, s.276.

which allows a local authority to maintain an action in its own name where the authority considers it expedient for the promotion and protection of the interests of the inhabitants of its area. This has been held to entitle the local authority to sue without joining the Attorney-General and has been liberally interpreted.[48]

3. *Statutory Appeals*

The question of who has standing arises not only in the context of the prerogative orders, declarations and injunctions, but also where a statute allows a "person aggrieved" to challenge a decision.

The case law on this topic has considerable similarities with the areas discussed above, not in precise detail but in approach. Thus one line of cases has adopted a narrow, restrictive meaning of the term person aggrieved, requiring the infringement of a private right or something closely akin thereto. The more modern case law has, however, embraced a more liberal philosophy.

A leading example of the former group is *Ex p. Sidebotham.*[49] S. had been declared bankrupt. It was alleged that the trustee in bankruptcy had not been performing his duties properly, an allegation verified by the Comptroller in Bankruptcy who recommended that the trustee make good certain losses. The latter did not do so and was taken to the County Court which made no order compelling the trustee to make good the deficiency. The Comptroller did not appeal on this decision, but S. attempted to do so as a person aggrieved. He was unsuccessful, the Court interpreting a person aggrieved to require something more than one who was disappointed in a benefit which he might have received. There had to be a legal grievance, a wrongful deprivation of something to which the appellant was entitled. There is, of course, no necessary reason why the interpretation of bankruptcy legislation should carry analytical weight in other areas, and ample reasons can be found for distinguishing the decision.[50] The decision nevertheless became the *locus classicus* on the subject and was often applied.[51] One of the best known of such applications was *Buxton* v. *Minister of Housing and Local Government*[52] in which B., an owner of land adjacent to a chalk pit, was held not to be a person aggrieved so as to be able to challenge the grant of planning permission for the quarrying, even

---

[48] See generally, *Solihull Metropolitan Borough Council* v. *Maxfern Ltd.* [1977] 1 W.L.R. 127; *Stafford Borough Council* v. *Elkenford Ltd.* [1977] W.L.R. 324; *Thanet District Council* v. *Ninedrive Ltd.* [1978] 1 All E.R. 703; *Kent County Council* v. *Batchelor (No. 2)* [1979] 1 W.L.R. 213; *Stoke-on-Trent City Council* v. *B. & Q. (Retail) Ltd.* [1984] A.C. 754.

[49] (1880) 14 Ch. D. 458.

[50] The court in *Sidebotham* was influenced by the structure of the relevant legislation and the fact that the debtor had an independent cause of action against the trustee, (1880) 14 Ch.D. 458, 466.

[51] *e.g. R.* v. *London Quarter Sessions, ex p. Westminster Corporation* [1951] 2 K.B. 508; *Ealing Corporation* v. *Jones* [1959] 1 Q.B. 384.

[52] [1961] 1 Q.B. 278.

though his pedigree pigs and landscape garden would be affected by the dust. He had no legal rights affected by the decision to grant planning permission and thus could not complain.

The courts did recognise that some types of financial burden could qualify one as a person aggrieved,[53] thereby indirectly broadening the limited interpretation given above. Direct attack on this limited formulation came from Lord Denning.[54] The *Sidebotham-Buxton* interpretation was held to be too narrow. While busybodies should, of course, be excluded, any person with a genuine grievance whose interests were affected should be admitted. The more liberal philosophy has since been applied by the House of Lords in *Arsenal Football Club Ltd* v. *Ende*.[55] Their Lordships held that a ratepayer living in the same borough or even in the same precepting area could qualify as a person aggrieved so as to be able to challenge the assessment of another's rates as too low. The applicant did not have to show financial detriment, and *a fortiori* the infringement of a legal right was not a necessary prerequisite in order to be able to maintain a claim.[56] One can hope that this more liberal line of reasoning will become the general rule.

The law in this area has now been clarified by the decision in *Cook* v. *Southend Borough Council*.[57] Woolf L.J. undertook an extensive review of the authorities in this area. He recognised that some of these earlier decisions had taken a restrictive view of the term "person aggrieved", but he pointed to the more liberal approach adopted in more recent jurisprudence, and held that some of the foundational cases supporting the restrictive view should no longer be treated as good law.[58] Henceforth the following principles should apply whenever the phrase "person aggrieved" appeared in any statute concerning appeal rights, subject to a clear contrary intent in the particular statute.[59] First, a body corporate, including a local authority, was just as capable of being a person aggrieved as an individual. Secondly, any person who had a decision made against him, particularly in adversarial proceedings, would be a person aggrieved for the purposes of appealing against that decision, unless the decision amounted to an acquittal of a purely criminal case. Thirdly, the fact that the decision against which the person wished to appeal reversed a decision which was originally taken by that person, and did not otherwise adversely affect him, did not prevent that person being a person aggrieved. Quite the contrary, it indicated that he was a person aggrieved who could use his appeal rights to have the original decision restored.

---

[53] R. v. *Quarter Sessions, ex p. Lilley* [1951] 2 K.B. 749; *Phillips* v. *Berkshire County Council* [1967] 2 Q.B. 991.
[54] *Att. Gen. of the Gambia* v. *N'Jie* [1961] A.C. 617, 634; *Maurice* v. *London County Council* [1964] 2 Q.B. 362, 378. See also, *Turner* v. *Secretary of State for the Environment* (1973) 28 P. & C.R. 123, 134, 139.
[55] [1979] A.C. 1.
[56] Being a taxpayer was not, however, sufficient. *Cf.* the *IRC* case [1982] A.C. 617.
[57] [1990] 2 W.L.R. 61.
[58] R. v. *London Quarter Sessions, ex p. Westminster Corporation* [1951] 2 K.B. 508, was overruled.
[59] [1990] 2 W.L.R. 61, 64-65.

Section 4. The Present Position

1. *Introduction*

To describe the common law position as unnecessarily confused would be to pay it a compliment. Although the general trend was towards liberalisation of the standing requirement, particularly in the context of the prerogative orders, the dichotomy between those orders and injunctions or declarations was still maintained. Even within the prerogative remedies themselves differences of formulation persisted, particularly between certiorari and mandamus.

The Law Commission when examining remedies in administrative law disapproved both of the restrictive formulations of legal right and of the different standing requirements which governed each of the remedies. It recommended that any person adversely affected by a decision should possess *locus standi*.[60] In its subsequent report the Law Commission adopted the general flexible approach favoured by the earlier Working Paper and proposed that a person should possess standing when he has sufficient interest in the matter to which the application relates. This was felt to represent the existing position with regard to the prerogative orders; the position in relation to declarations and injunctions was to be liberalised and the sufficiency of interest test applied in these areas also.[61]

The test proposed by the Law Commission was adopted in Order 53, rule 3(7). This has now been incorporated in the Supreme Court Act 1981, s.31(3), which states,

> "No application for judicial review shall be made unless the leave of the High Court has been obtained in accordance with rules of court; and the court shall not grant leave to make such an application unless it considers that the applicant has a sufficient interest in the matter to which the application relates."

It would be good if one could say that this now represented a uniform test of standing to be applied to all the remedies. Unfortunately, the precise ambit of the reform is not entirely clear. To understand the problems surrounding the present law reference must be made to the first important decision by the House of Lords on this topic.

2. *The IRC Case*

The facts of *R. v. Inland Revenue Commissioners, ex p. National Federation of Self-Employed and Small Businesses Ltd*[62] were as follows. Casual labour was common on Fleet Street newspapers, the workers often

---

[60] Working Paper No. 40 (1970), pp. 125–132.
[61] *Report on Remedies in Administrative Law*, Law Com. No. 73, Cmnd. 6407, pp. 22, 33.
[62] [1982] A.C. 617; Cane, "Standing, Legality and the Limits of Public Law" [1981] P.L. 322.

adopting fictitious names and paying no taxes. The IRC made a deal with the relevant unions, workers and employers whereby if the casuals would fill in tax returns for the previous two years then the period prior to that would be forgotten. The National Federation argued that this bargain was *ultra vires* the IRC and sought a declaration to that effect plus mandamus to compel the IRC to collect the back taxes. The IRC defended by arguing that the National Federation had no standing. Their Lordships found for the IRC but it would be misleading to say that they upheld the IRC's claim. The case is best analysed in stages.

(1) STANDING: SUBSTANCE OR PROCEDURE

When the *IRC* case was decided the test for standing was still to be found in Order 53, rule 3(7). It had not yet been incorporated within a statute. This was important because the Rules of the Supreme Court can only alter matters of procedure and not substance. If standing were to be regarded as substantive then no change could be effectuated through rule 3(7). This question is now of historical interest because rule 3(7) has been enacted in section 31(3) of the Supreme Court Act 1981.

Even if all of their Lordships had unequivocally stated that standing was a matter of substance, which they did not,[63] this would only have led to the conclusion that it could not be altered by the Rules of the Supreme Court. It could however be reformed by the courts themselves. The rules of standing were made by the judges and can be altered by them. The courts could therefore simply have used Order 53 as a catalyst for rethinking standing, in which the substantive change was brought about by the judiciary. The vital question is therefore, what test or tests of standing did the *IRC* case adopt?

(2) THE APPROACH IN THE IRC CASE

Two issues require to be separated. First, did their Lordships say that sufficient interest should bear the same meaning whichever remedy was being applied for? Secondly, given a meaning or meanings ascribed to sufficiency of interest, how should the test or tests be applied in any particular case?

(a) A uniform test?

On the former issue their Lordships differed. Interpretation is rendered more difficult because two matters became interwoven: whether there should be a uniform test for the prerogative orders and whether there should be a uniform test for all the remedies. Lord Diplock answered both questions affirmatively.[64] The other judgments are less clear. Lord Fraser of Tullybelton felt that the differences between the prerogative orders had been eradicated, but that not all the older law had been overthrown.[65] Lord Scarman held that there should be no difference in standing for the

---

[63] *e.g.* [1982] A.C. 617, 638.
[64] *Ibid.* pp. 638, 640.
[65] *Ibid.* pp. 645-646.

prerogative orders, and, it seems, that that should be the same test when a declaration or injunction was sought in a public law context.[66] Lord Roskill was clear that many of the old technical distinctions between the remedies, particularly the prerogative orders, should be swept away. The inference was certainly that there should be a uniform test for all the remedies but this was never made absolutely clear.[67] Lord Wilberforce was, by way of contrast, of the opinion that there should be a distinction even between the prerogative orders, with certiorari being subject to a less strict test than mandamus.[68]

Part of the difficulty in interpreting their Lordships' judgments on this point arose from the way in which the issue was presented. In the lower courts the IRC had placed reliance on the *Gouriet* decision, arguing that the National Federation lacked standing to apply for a declaration because no legal right of its own had been affected. This rendered it necessary for the House of Lords both to interpret the *Gouriet* decision and to consider the general place of declaration and injunction within Order 53.

The *Gouriet*[69] decision was treated as referring only to *locus standi* for declaration and injunction in their private law roles, and as having nothing to say about the standing for those remedies in public law. Rule 1(2) was interpreted to allow an applicant to claim a declaration or injunction instead of a prerogative order, but only in those areas or circumstances where a prerogative order would itself have been available. If an applicant would have had standing to seek a prerogative order then a declaration or injunction could be granted instead even though the standing requirements for declaration or injunction would not have been met. Both parts of this argument require analysis.

To regard the *Gouriet* case as one involving only standing in private law is to allow form to blind one to substance. It may well be the case that different people could take divergent views as to the limits of "public law" litigation. On one level, the parties in *Gouriet* appear "private": a trade union and a private citizen, albeit involving a breach of the criminal law. But the real argument in that case was as to whether a private citizen should be able to vindicate the public interest without joining the Attorney-General. This was how the case was argued, and this was how their Lordships responded to the argument. The judgments and the authorities relied on, disapproved and upheld only make sense in that light.[70]

---

[66] *Ibid.* pp. 649-653.
[67] *Ibid.* pp. 656-658.
[68] *Ibid* p. 631.
[69] [1978] A.C. 435. Ord. 53, r. 1(2) allows a declaration or injunction to be claimed via an application for judicial review in certain circumstances. See pp. 550-551 for a full discussion.
[70] Insofar as this was the real question at stake in *Gouriet*, it clearly was "about" public law, and this is nonetheless true even though the issue of whether a citizen should be able to vindicate the public interest can arise in a non-public law case. This view is reinforced by the fact that both older and more recent authority, in what were indubitably public law cases, have expressed the test for standing in terms of private rights and special damage, where a declaration is being sought outside of section 31. See, *e.g. Gregory* v. *Camden London Borough Council* [1966] 1 W.L.R. 899; *Barrs* v. *Bethell* [1982] Ch. 294; *Stoke-on-Trent*, above n. 48.

Gouriet and *IRC* in fact reflect different philosophies. The former conceives the private citizen as having no role in enforcing the public interest as such, and thus preserves the dichotomy in standing criteria for the prerogative orders and declaration and injunction, ignoring the fact that the private citizen is doing this when seeking prerogative relief. The *IRC* case eschews the historical distinction between the remedies, and takes as its touchstone the more liberal rules for prerogative relief to which standing for declaration and injunction are then assimilated.

The *IRC* decision reflects the continuing interplay between rights and remedies within administrative law, and displays a strange duality. On the remedial level, the constraints of *Gouriet* are shed as that case is labelled private law. The declaration and injunction appear to adopt the criteria for standing of the prerogative orders, thereby recognising that private citizens do vindicate public rights to some extent. This is accompanied by laudable statements that archaic limitations on standing should be discarded in order that public law can meet the new challenges of a developing society. In this respect the decision looks forward. However, juxtaposed to such statements are others which appear to confine the scope of public law to the areas where the prerogative orders will issue.[71] This restrictive view of public law seems to have been influenced by the fear that, to do otherwise, would be to condemn Order 53 as *ultra vires*.[72] Later cases[73] have however taken a more expansive view of public law. This particular matter will be returned to.[74]

Notwithstanding the above uncertainties, a spirit does emerge from the case and one might hazard a guess that this will mould the pattern for the future. The spirit is a willingness to develop standing to meet new problems, not to become embroiled in endless discussion of previous authority and, perhaps most important of all, even subject to the limitations mentioned above, the change of philosophy reflected in the court's handling of standing for declaration and injunction. The sum effect of these elements will be a tendency towards a unified conception of standing based upon sufficiency of interest.[75] Arguments that the test for standing should differ depending upon which particular remedy was being sought have been generally absent from the subsequent case law.

A warning note is however in order. Even if the courts do adopt a uniform test this does not mean that individual judges share the same view as to what should count as a sufficient interest. Diversity of opinion upon this matter is evident within the *IRC* case itself.[76] This leads us to the second half of the question, which is how one determines whether an applicant possesses such an interest.

---

[71] [1982] A.C. 617, 639, 648.

[72] *Ibid.* p. 648.

[73] *e.g. O'Reilly* v. *Mackman* [1982] 3 W.L.R. 604; *R.* v. *B.B.C., ex p. Lavelle* [1983] 1 W.L.R. 23.

[74] Below Chap. 15.

[75] Lord Denning M.R. in *O'Reilly* v. *Mackman* [1982] 3 W.L.R. 604 stated that there was a uniform test.

[76] Compare, *e.g.* [1982] A.C. 617, 644 Lord Diplock, 661 Lord Roskill.

(b) The fusion of standing and merits?

The approach of the House of Lords to the question of how one determines whether an applicant has sufficient interest or not is one of the most interesting in the whole case. It was stated at the outset that in private law the merits and standing were not regarded as distinct; who could sue was automatically answered by the definition of the cause of action. In public law, by way of contrast, standing was one matter, the merits another. This may have to be radically revised in the light of the *IRC* case.

The one matter on which their Lordships agree, albeit with differing degrees of emphasis, is that standing and the merits often cannot be separated in this way. While it may be possible to do so in relatively straightforward cases, in those which are more complex it will be necessary to consider the whole legal and factual context to determine whether an applicant possesses a sufficient interest in the matter. This will include: *the nature of the power or duties involved; the breach which has allegedly been committed; and the subject-matter of the claim.* The term merits here is not being used in the sense of a value judgment as to whether the applicant's claim is meritorious or good. It means that the court will look to the substance of the allegation in order to determine whether the applicant has standing.

The term *fusion* will be used to refer to the process whereby the court will consider the above list of factors in order to determine whether the applicant has standing in this particular case.

To appreciate fully how this operates the place of rule 3(7)[77] should be explained further. That rule requires the court to consider sufficiency of interest at the application for leave stage. This will often be *ex parte* and thus the court may only be possessed of evidence from one side. A court may feel at this stage that the applicant has demonstrated a sufficient interest. The second stage is the hearing of the application itself, at which point the court will consider affidavit evidence from both parties. At this second stage the court might well form the view that, on consideration of fuller evidence, the applicant does not in fact possess the interest which he claims. This conclusion will be reached from an appraisal of the nature of the duty cast upon the public body, the nature of the breach, and the position of the applicants. Thus, in the *IRC* case itself the only evidence at the *ex parte* stage was from the National Federation. By the time that the hearing came on the revenue authorities had prepared affidavits giving their view of the case. This caused the House of Lords to dismiss the case, but the reasoning is subtly different. Some of their Lordships[78] rely most heavily on the statutory framework and background to reach the conclusion that the applicant possesses no sufficient interest. A qualification is added that such a person or group might possess sufficient interest if the illegality were sufficiently grave. Other Law Lords, while referring to the statutory context, place more emphasis on the absence of illegality. If at the hearing

---

[77] See now Supreme Court Act 1981, s.31(3).

[78] [1982] A.C. 617, 632-633, *per* Lord Wilberforce, 646, *per* Lord Fraser, 662-663, *per* Lord Roskill.

of the application itself the applicant had established (or prima facie established?) the allegations made at the application for leave then the case would have proceeded.[79]

(c) Summary

One can summarise the impact of the *IRC* case in the following manner. First, the general message which emerges is that there will be a unified test of standing based upon sufficiency of interest, shorn of archaic limitations, which will probably operate in the same way irrespective of which particular remedy is being sought. In this sense the *formal test* for standing will be uniform. Secondly, this formal sense of uniformity must, however, be qualified. The fusion technique will mean that who is actually entitled to standing will in substance vary from area to area. This will depend upon the nature of the statutory power or duty in issue, the subject-matter of the claim and the type of illegality which is being asserted. Thirdly, the application of these criteria may, however, well be unclear or uncertain. Where this is so, the determination of standing will depend upon certain more general assumptions of the judge as to the role which individuals should generally have in public law. This will be exemplified by the subsequent discussion, but is also apparent in the *IRC* case itself. Thus, Lord Diplock approached the process of statutory construction with the explicit assumption that it would be a grave lacuna in our law if an interest group such as that in the case, or indeed a private citizen, could not "vindicate the rule of law and get the unlawful action stopped".[80] This is close to a citizen action view of standing,[81] and it was with this background assumption that his Lordship engaged in the process of statutory construction. This assumption was not shared by all of their Lordships, and differences of this kind can have a significant impact on the outcome of the interpretative process.

3. *Interpretation of the Test*

How then have later cases interpreted the *IRC* decision? These cases may be categorised in the following manner.

(1) INDIVIDUAL CHALLENGES: A LIBERAL APPROACH, BUT NO REAL FUSION

There are a number of cases in which the courts have treated the *IRC* decision as a liberalisation of the pre-existing standing rules. However, it is also to be noted that the cases mentioned within this section do *not* evidence a particular attachment to the fusion technique. In reaching the decision to accord the applicant standing the courts did not undertake any *detailed* analysis of the nature of the statutory powers or provisions which were in question, apart from adverting to the seriousness of the alleged

---

[79] *Ibid.* pp. 637, 644, *per* Lord Diplock, 654, *per* Lord Scarman.
[80] [1982] A.C. 617, 644.
[81] See below, pp. 504-511.

illegality. Thus a taxpayer who raised a serious question concerning the legality of governmental action in connection with the EC was accorded standing;[82] a journalist as a "guardian of the public interest" in open justice was held to have a sufficient interest to obtain a declaration that justices could not refuse to reveal their identity;[83] and the head of a set of chambers was accorded standing to contest a decision by the Bar Council that another barrister should be charged with a more serious, rather than a less serious, charge.[84] Attempts to argue that an applicant must possess something akin to a narrow legal right before being accorded standing have not been successful.[85] This more liberal approach has also been endorsed extrajudicially.[86]

(2) INDIVIDUAL CHALLENGES: A MORE RESTRICTIVE APPROACH, AND THE USE OF THE FUSION TECHNIQUE

The fusion technique is dependent upon statutory construction. It is evident, therefore, that results will differ from area to area. It is also evident that the application of the test can lead to broad or narrow categories of applicant being afforded standing. Some decisions on standing concerning individual applicants *have* adopted the fusion approach, but the result which has been reached has been relatively restrictive. Thus, in R. v. *Legal Aid Board, ex p. Bateman*[87] it was held, on construction of the relevant statutory provisions, that a legally-aided client did not have standing to contest an order made as to the taxation of her solicitor's costs, since she was not affected by the result of the taxation. The action could only be brought by the solicitor, and the fact that the applicant was genuinely concerned to see that her solicitor was properly remunerated did not suffice to afford her a sufficient interest for the purposes of judicial review.[88] Similarly in *Johnson*[89] it was held that the applicant did not have standing to question the validity of a notice served on his wife obliging her to answer inquiries into a fraud investigation currently under way against her husband.

---

[82] R. v. *Her Majesty's Treasury, ex p. Smedley* [1985] Q.B. 657, 667, 669-670.
[83] R. v. *Felixstowe JJ., ex p. Leigh* [1987] Q.B. 582, 595-598.
[84] R. v. *General Council of the Bar, ex p. Percival* [1990] 3 All E.R. 137.
[85] R. v. *Secretary of Companies, ex p. Central Bank of India* [1986] Q.B. 1114, 1161-1163. See also, R. v. *Secretary of State for Social Services, ex p. Child Poverty Action Group* [1990] 2 Q.B. 540; R. v. *International Stock Exchange of the United Kingdom and the Republic of Ireland, ex p. Else (1982) Ltd.* [1993] 1 All E.R. 420, 432; R. v. *London Borough of Haringey, ex p. Secretary of State for the Environment* [1991] C.O.D. 135.
[86] The Rt. Hon. Sir Harry Woolf, "Public Law – Private Law: Why the Divide? A Personal View" [1986] P.L. 220, 231.
[87] [1992] 3 All E.R. 490.
[88] Nolan L.J. accepted that, in cases where it was appropriate, a member of the public could represent the public interest, but regarded the applicant's behaviour here as "at best quixotic", *ibid.* p. 496. See also, R. v. *Lautro, ex p. Tee* [1993] C.O.D. 362; R. v. *Secretary of State for Defence, ex p. Sancto* [1993] C.O.D. 144.
[89] R. v. *Director of the Serious Fraud Office, ex p. Johnson* [1993] C.O.D. 58.

(3) GROUP CHALLENGES AND THE FUSION APPROACH

Group challenges can arise in various situations. One is where there is a group consisting of persons who are directly affected by the disputed decision; standing has been accorded in such circumstances.[90] Another is where the impugned action is challenged by a pressure group concerned with the subject-matter of that action, such as when the Child Poverty Action Group challenged decisions concerning social security which affected claimants.[91] Yet another type of group claim can arise in situations where the decision affects the public generally, or a section thereof, but no one particular individual has any more immediate interest than any other, and a group seeks to contest the matter before the courts, as exemplified by the *Rose Theatre* case discussed below.

The fusion approach has been used particularly commonly in the context of group challenges, as opposed to those made by specific individuals. Two points are apparent from the courts' more recent jurisprudence.

On the one hand, there is the obvious point that the process of statutory construction demanded by the *IRC* methodology can itself produce differences of opinion from members of the same court. This is exemplified by the decision in *R. v. Secretary of State for Employment, ex p. Equal Opportunities Commission.*[92] In that case the EOC sought *locus standi* to argue that certain of the rules concerning entitlement to redundancy pay and protection from unfair dismissal were discriminatory and in breach of EC law.[93] The Court of Appeal engaged in a detailed analysis of the Sex Discrimination Act 1975 in order to determine whether the EOC should be said to have standing to advance this type of argument. Section 53(1) of the Act provided that the duties of the EOC were to include, working towards the elimination of discrimination, and promoting equality of opportunity between men and women generally. Three differing views emerged from the process of statutory construction. Dillon L.J., dissenting on this point, concluded that the EOC should have standing, on the basis that the statute indicated that it could apply for judicial review whenever this would work towards the elimination of some aspect of discrimination.[94] The majority came to the opposite conclusion, but there are interesting differences in the reasoning. Kennedy L.J. did not believe that the *nature of the EOC's duties* under the statute were such as to accord it standing: the EOC's role was that of adviser to the Secretary of State, but the latter was under no obligation to heed that advice.[95] Hirst L.J. also found against the EOC, but for different reasons. In his view, the EOC *would* have been granted standing if one considered the *nature of its duties* under the statute, and he dismissed out of hand suggestions to the contrary. However, for Hirst L.J.

---

[90] *Royal College of Nursing of the UK v. DHSS* [1981] 1 All E.R. 545, 551; *R. v. Chief Adjudication Officer, ex p. Bland, The Times,* 6 February 1985.

[91] *R. v. Secretary of State for Social Services, ex p. Child Poverty Action Group* [1990] 2 Q.B. 540. Detailed argument on the standing issue was not heard by the court, p. 556.

[92] [1993] 1 All E.R. 1022.

[93] Article 119 of the Treaty and Directives 75/117 and 76/207.

[94] [1993] 1 All E.R. 1022, 1030-1032.

[95] *Ibid.* pp. 1039-1041.

it was the other element of the fusion "test", the *subject-matter* of the application, which served to rule out the EOC: it was not appropriate for the EOC to raise this type of challenge, involving as it did allegations that the UK was in breach of its Treaty obligations.[96] The decision of the Court of Appeal was reversed by the House of Lords which held that the EOC did have standing.[97] Lord Keith, giving the majority judgment, reasoned that if the contested provisions were discriminatory and could not be justified then steps taken by the EOC to change the offending provisions could reasonably be regarded as working towards the elimination of discrimination. It would, said his Lordship, be a retrograde step to hold that the EOC did not have standing to "agitate in judicial review proceedings questions related to sex discrimination which are of public importance and affect a large section of the population".[98] Differences over statutory construction did, however, persist even in the House of Lords: Lord Jauncey felt constrained to dissent on this point, arguing that the legislation made the EOC answerable to the minister, and not vice versa.[99]

On the other hand, there is the less obvious, but more interesting point, that the very process of statutory construction demanded by the *IRC* case will itself often turn upon more general views concerning the theory and purpose of standing. A moment's reflection will indicate that this is unsurprising for the following reason. The very process of statutory construction, looking to the nature of the duties therein and the subject-matter of the claim, will often not be self-executing: the answer will not leap out from the relevant materials, as exemplified by the differences in the *EOC* case. In reaching a conclusion on this issue the court will, therefore, have to fall back on certain more general beliefs about the role which standing should perform. This is demonstrated by the decision in *R. v. Secretary of State for the Environment, ex p. Rose Theatre Trust Co.*[100] Developers, who had planning permission for an office block, came upon the remains of an important Elizabethan theatre. A number of people formed a company seeking to preserve the remains. They sought to persuade the Secretary of State to include the site in the list of monuments under the Ancient Monuments and Archeological Areas Act 1979. The Secretary of State could do so if the site appeared to him to be of national importance. If the site was thus designated no work could be done without his consent. Although the Secretary of State agreed that the site was of national importance he declined to include it within the relevant legislation. Schiemann J. found that there had in fact been no illegality, but he also held that the applicants had no *locus standi*. He accepted that a direct financial or legal interest was not necessary in order for an applicant to have standing, and that it was necessary to consider the statute to determine

---

[96] *Ibid.* pp. 1048-1051.
[97] *R. v. Secretary of State for Employment, ex p. Equal Opportunities Commission* [1994] 1 All E.R. 910.
[98] *Ibid.* p. 919.
[99] *Ibid.* p. 925.
[100] [1990] 1 Q.B. 504. See also, Sir Konrad Schiemann, "Locus Standi" [1990] P.L. 342; Cane, "Statutes, Standing and Representation" [1990] P.L. 307.

whether it afforded standing to these individuals in this instance. However, he also approached the matter with the express view that not every person will always have sufficient interest to bring a case; that the assertion of an interest by many people did not mean that they actually possessed one; *and* that there might be certain types of governmental action which no-one could challenge. On the facts of the case he held that no individual could point to anything in the statute which would serve to give him or her a greater right or interest than any other that the decision would be taken lawfully; *and* that while in a broad sense we could all expect that decisions be made lawfully that was insufficient in itself to give the applicants standing.

The judgment bears testimony to the point made above: statutory interpretation is not value free or self-executing, and the result of this process will depend upon an underlying view as to the object of standing itself. The judgment in the *Rose Theatre* case is infused with the view that a citizen action perspective on standing is not to be accepted, in this area at least. The idea underpinning the citizen action,[101] that citizens generally should be able to vindicate the public interest without showing any individual harm over and above that of the general community, particularly in cases where this would be difficult to substantiate, was rejected. The fact that this results in an area of governmental activity being outside judicial control was acknowledged.

The same point is apparent in the *EOC* case. The differences of view as to the standing of the EOC as between the Court of Appeal and the House of Lords are not explicable solely on the basis of differences as to statutory interpretation. It is clear that Lord Keith disagreed with the majority in the Court of Appeal in part because he took a different view as to the role which the EOC should have in the regime of sex discrimination. His Lordship *approached* the process of statutory interpretation with the view that it was right and proper that the EOC *should* be able to raise questions concerning such discrimination which were of public importance and which affected large sections of the population.

The approach adopted by the House of Lords in the *IRC* case, and its interpretation in later cases, raises fundamental questions about the role of standing, and the importance of fusion therein, which are best considered in the next section.[102]

4. *Locus Standi Outside Section 31*

The passage of the revised Order 53 did not abrogate the previous methods of seeking a declaration or injunction. A plaintiff can still pursue his claim under Order 15, rule 16. What rules of standing will apply in such a case? The problem is unlikely to arise very often because the House of Lords has

---

[101] For a discussion of the citizen action, see below, pp. 504–511.
[102] See below, pp. 499–513.

held in *O'Reilly* v. *Mackman*[103] that the general rule is that public law cases should be channelled through section 31. It is clear that there are exceptions to this rule, and the problems produced by the rule and its exceptions will be considered below.[104]

The obvious answer is that the rules would be what they were previously. But what were they? It was thought to be the *Gouriet*[105] test of private rights and special damage, but the *IRC*[106] case restricted this to the private law role of declaration and injunction. The difficulty of regarding *Gouriet* as a purely private law case, and hence the artificiality of the way in which the case was distinguished, have already been mentioned.[107] The answer to the preceding question appears to be that *Gouriet* nonetheless "lives", and that the test for standing outside of section 31 is still private rights and special damage.[108] The rationale for a continued distinction in the standing rules, such that cases brought outside of section 31 are subject to stricter rules, will be considered below.

Section 5. The Function of Standing

Judicial pronouncements as to the breadth of standing necessarily reflect value judgments as to the purposes it will be serving, purposes which have been commented upon in the preceding pages. It is time now to stand back from the detail of the case law and to look more generally at the role of *locus standi*. This is particularly important at the present because, as we have seen, the courts are in the process of deciding what the test under section 31 of the Supreme Court Act should be. Even if a uniform test of sufficiency of interest does apply to all the remedies that still leaves open the all important question of what should count as a sufficient interest. An adequate answer to that question cannot be given without some understanding of the broader issues underlying *locus standi*. Indeed any answer which is given will implicitly, if not explicitly, presuppose a particular view of the function to be performed by standing.[109]

1. *Vindication of Private Rights*

It is interesting the way in which legal systems, for all their diversity, nevertheless display interesting points of contact. The theoretical foundation of

---

[103] [1983] 2 A.C. 237.
[104] See below, Chap. 15.
[105] [1978] A.C. 435.
[106] [1982] A.C. 617.
[107] Above pp. 491-492.
[108] *Barrs* v. *Bethell* [1982] Ch. 294; *Ashby* v. *Ebdon* [1985] Ch. 394; *Stoke-on-Trent City Council* v. *B & Q. (Retail) Ltd.* [1984] A.C. 754, 766-767, 769-771. See also, *Steeples* v. *Derbyshire City Council* [1985] 1 W.L.R. 256, 290-298, decided in 1981 but only reported later.
[109] Use will be made of literature from the USA. This does not of course necessarily mean that we should adopt the same view of standing here.

standing is one such instance. The most general theme which has characterised developments in this area has been the early insistence on the presence of a legal right, in the sense of a private cause of action, and a gradual movement away from that criterion.[110]

The reasons why the legal right test assumed such a central role are eclectic but overlapping. Two can be identified, and have been touched on above.[111] On the one hand, there has been the unthinking adoption of rules from private law causes of action into the realm of challenges against public bodies. The formulation in *Boyce*[112] is, for example, not attended by any evidence that the court perceived any distinction between a cause of action in public nuisance and a challenge to the legality of public action. On the other hand, there has been the more abstract argument which reaches its apotheosis in *Gouriet*.[113] A role for the individual is specifically etched out and that role is the vindication of private rights with the public interest being protected by the Attorney-General. This function of the individual mirrors that of the courts which is one of private dispute settling: the courts will adjudicate on a matter of public law at the instance of an individual, provided that it is settling the rights of the latter and because it is doing so.

This perspective on the role of the individual and the court has come under a number of strains. First, as argued above, it became clear that this presented a distorted picture of what the courts themselves *had* been doing. The approach within the prerogative orders, although not uniform, was certainly more liberal than that within the declaration and the injunction and could not be fitted into a conceptual strait-jacket called private dispute settling. Individuals were to a greater or lesser degree vindicating the public interest. This tension between the prerogative orders on the one hand, and declaration and injunction on the other, was largely ignored and *de facto* resolved in favour of the latter in the *Gouriet* case, whereas in the *IRC* decision it was faced more openly, inadequately explained, and resolved in favour of the prerogative orders.

A second reason why the private right model of standing has proved inadequate is that new values have developed which people feel are worthy of protection, but which cannot be accommodated by the traditional restrictive standing criteria. Broader social, economic, religious and non-economic values outside established property criteria are justly prized and protection sought against their infringement. Traditional legal rights in such values do not exist; no established cause of action arises if they are infringed, and thus if standing were limited to situations in which such a cause of action arose no person could invoke the protection of the court.

An objection to this second reason might be raised of the following type. It could be argued that the law could simply develop new "rights" or new concepts of "property" to provide protection for these emerging values and that to some extent they have done so. It is of course true that the courts can and have developed such new property rights; however, if the concept

---

[110] The test has been relaxed in, *e.g.*, the USA, Canada, and Australia.
[111] See above, pp. 482-485.
[112] [1903] 1 Ch. 109.
[113] [1978] A.C. 435.

of property or legal right is rendered too broad it contains the seeds of its own destruction and should be discarded since it no longer bears any relation to a private dispute settling function. The point has been well put by Vining.

> "The effect of a finding of legal interest may be to get to the merits, but such a finding tells one nothing about the merits or, for that matter, the litigating qualifications of the challenger. The purpose of the exercise is simply to determine whether a bow to the private-dispute-settling function of the courts can be made. If the definition of 'property' is pushed too far, by recognising, for instance, individual or organisational interests in non-economic public values as property interests, the exercise loses its point. It is better to give it up entirely."[114]

A third strain upon the legal right test is also well put by Vining and is contained in the first half of the above quotation. The premise behind the legal right test is that the individual is approaching the court to vindicate his private rights and the court will consider matters of public law only in so far as they form a necessary step in reaching the conclusion that the private right is infringed or not. Thus, to take a simple example, X claims that a public body has trespassed upon his property. The defence is raised that the taking of the property is justified by a compulsory purchase order. X will have standing to challenge the legality of the order because his private rights are at stake. The crucial point is that in the determination of the vital question, the legality of the order, X's status as an injured property owner is irrelevant as such. It will not be the determinant of the issue. When arguing as to the legality of the order X will not be voicing his own private interests, but those of the public at large. As Vining correctly observes, the *effect* of a finding of a legal right will tell one that the order was invalid and hence a trespass action lies. But that finding is not the merits itself. It is only a conclusion which follows from a finding that the order was illegal.[115]

Given that the legal right test has been effectively rejected *within* section 31, why should it continue to furnish the criterion in actions for a declaration or injunction brought *outside* that section? Two reasons can be identified, neither of which is convincing.

One argument is that removal of the Attorney-General would mean unrestricted access for individuals wishing to assert a public right.[116] This does not follow. The vital question is *who* is to decide the limitations upon standing, the courts as in section 31 cases, or the Attorney-General for cases outside that section? There are a number of reasons for preferring the courts. The Attorney-General is a quasi-political figure, and the day-to-day process of political responsibility may not be the most appropriate backdrop from which to make decisions about whether a case should proceed.

---

[114] *Legal Identity* (1978), p. 25; Cane, "The Function of Standing Rules in Administrative Law" [1980] P.L. 303.

[115] Vining, *Legal Identity*, p. 20.

[116] *Gouriet* [1978] A.C. 435, 483, 501–502.

The public interest is not, as counsel for Gouriet perspicuously observed,[117] one and indivisible; it is often an amalgam of intersecting and conflicting interests. A balancing process is entailed and the Attorney-General may not, for the above reason, be best placed to make this determination.

The other argument[118] for treating standing outside section 31 more restrictively is that by having a two-stage procedure frivolous applications will normally be weeded out without troubling the public body since the application will be *ex parte*; given that there is no such procedure in an ordinary action the public body will have to appear and argue that the plaintiff has no standing. There are three difficulties with this argument. First, it has never been made before even though it would have been equally relevant prior to the reform of remedies since the prerogative orders have had a two-stage procedure for some time. Secondly, if people who do not have private rights and have not suffered special damage are not regarded as vexatious in proceedings under section 31, why should they suddenly become so when the procedure alters? Thirdly, we have already seen that the *IRC*[119] case decided that, even under section 31, it would normally not be possible to treat standing as a preliminary issue divorced from the facts of the case. Given this interpretation it is difficult to see how the two-stage procedure would allow the courts to dispose of any but the most frivolous cases without troubling the public body.

The requirement of finding a strict legal right has nonetheless been weakened since the majority of cases will come under the more liberal rules of section 31. The key question now is what should replace the legal right test. A number of approaches are possible, the following two of which both destroy standing as a separate requirement, but for very different reasons.

2. *Fusion of Standing and Merits*

One way in which standing would cease to exist as a separate concept is if it were not regarded as a preliminary question, but as flowing from a consideration of the merits. It has been argued in the United States that the courts are to some extent looking at the merits in the way in which they frame the standing test, and that this should be developed to the point at which standing ceases to exist as an independent preliminary question.[120] Thus, it is said that when the courts look, on the *locus standi* level, to the amount or type of injury, the aims of the legislation, and the type of interest affected, this is not very different from the way in which such factors are used in private law to determine the existence of a cause of action. Advocates of this approach argue that it is only by looking at such matters as these

---

[117] *Ibid.* p. 461.

[118] *Barrs* v. *Bethell* [1982] Ch. 294. This point is not developed at all in *Gouriet* [1978] A.C. 435.

[119] [1982] A.C. 617.

[120] Albert, "Standing to Challenge Administrative Action: An Inadequate Surrogate for Claims to Relief" 83 Yale L.J. 425 (1973-1974); "Justiciability and Theories of Judicial Review: A Remote Relationship" 50 So. Calif. L.Rev. 1139 (1976-1977).

that any realistic determination can be made as to who should be able to claim; that attempts to decide such matters in the abstract are productive of misleading and unhelpful generalisation.[121] These sentiments clearly permeate the *IRC*[122] decision, evidenced by the House of Lords' insistence that sufficiency of interest should be seen against the subject-matter of the application, including the nature of the duty and the nature of the breach.[123] This thesis merits attention both in general and in regard to the particular way in which it was applied in the *IRC* case.

(1) THE FEASIBILITY OF FUSION

The advantage of the above thesis is that it provides a more accurate answer as to who should be able to maintain an action in a particular context by focusing in upon the aims of the legislation, the scope of the duty, etc. In doing so, what is achieved is a series of "causes of action", broadly or narrowly defined, in the sense that who can be an applicant will be intimately related to the particular subject-matter. The closest analogy is to the rules for determining whether an action lies at the suit of an individual for breach of statutory duty: who is enabled to sue will be dependent upon construction of the particular statute.

The analogy with breach of statutory duty is however also suggestive of the problems that such an approach can entail. Statutory construction is a notoriously difficult operation quite simply because the legislature has often given no thought as to who should be able to claim. Search for actual legislative intent becomes impossible. This leads the courts to infer intent from such matters as the nature of the duty and subject-matter of the claim. It is interesting that in cases on breach of statutory duty the courts' inference is not in fact drawn from a detailed consideration of all points relevant to the statute. Rather, the judicial process abstracts certain matters and regards these as central or strongly presumptive, such as whether a penalty exists, and the class of persons affected by the statute. Inferences are then drawn as to civil actionability from the answers given to these questions.[124] The very process of abstracting such criteria recreates standing as a preliminary issue. Moreover, because who can sue is meant to be a result of detailed consideration of the individual statute, and because in many cases it is palpably not,[125] a judicial disenchantment with the whole process is produced, manifesting itself in a refusal to be led through the

---

[121] *e.g.* it may be the case that the courts' continued use of the private right test for standing was rendered easier by seeing standing as a separate preliminary question.

[122] [1982] A.C. 617.

[123] Their Lordships framed their judgments as if the fusion technique was and had been an accepted part of the legal vocabulary. With respect, this was not so. It is of course true that one can point to cases in which the courts have considered the ambit and purposes of a statutory scheme in order to determine standing. However, these are far outweighed by the number of cases in which the issue of *locus standi* has been decided by abstracted categories, such as ratepayers or competitors, without any detailed analysis of the scope of the duty or nature of the breach, see above pp. 479-485.

[124] See generally, *Winfield and Jolowicz on Tort* (13th ed., 1989), Chap. 7.

[125] *e.g. Booth & Co. (International) Ltd.* v. *National Enterprise Board* [1978] 3 All E.R. 624.

competing lines of cases, and to the position which is at one and the same time both the ultimate generalisation and the ultimate in the *ad hoc*: we, the courts, will allow a person to be a beneficiary of the statute if we think it right that he should be.[126]

It is not being suggested that a court should decide standing completely independent of the merits. All that is being argued is that to believe that standing will disappear as an independent issue, to be swallowed up by the merits and re-emerge as a number of distinct "causes of action" in which those who can sue will depend entirely on the subject-matter area, is unlikely.[127] Even if this aim could be realised it would have serious disadvantages. As has been pointed out, access to the courts should, on principle, be as clear as possible and this would certainly not be the case under the fusion doctrine.

(2) THE APPLICATION IN THE IRC CASE AND LATER DECISIONS

Only time will tell how far the courts will press the fusion concept. It is apparent from their Lordships' judgments in the *IRC* case that they do not conceive of having to look to the merits on every occasion. It seems clear that a busybody could be excluded, or an applicant with a strong interest could be admitted without venturing into any detailed consideration of the merits. Three general observations are warranted.

First, as seen above, not all later cases have engaged in a detailed analysis of the nature of the statutory power, or subject-matter of the claim, in determining who has standing. Secondly, when the fusion technique has been applied in detail it has often generated significant differences of opinion as between the members of the same court as to whether this particular applicant was intended to have standing. Thirdly, because the statute will often provide no certain answer on this issue, even when examined in detail, the court's judgment will be influenced by more general perceptions as to the role which the individual should have in public law. This is exemplified by the *Rose Theatre* case considered above, and also by the decision in the *IRC* case itself.[128]

3. *Citizen Action*

(1) THE ARGUMENTS FOR SUCH AN ACTION

A second and very different way in which standing could cease to exist is through the development of a citizen action or *actio popularis*. Such a concept views the prime aim of public law as the keeping of public bodies within their powers, and to this end the presumption should be that citizens

---

[126] *e.g. Ex p. Island Records Ltd.* [1978] Ch. 122, 134. The case has been limited by *R.C.A. Corporation Ltd.* v. *Pollard* [1983] Ch. 135, but this does not affect the general point being made in the text.
[127] [1982] A.C. 617.
[128] See above, pp. 496-498.

generally should be enabled to vindicate the public interest without show-ing any individual harm over and above that of the general community. The general arguments in favour of such an approach are as follows.[129]

The first is succinctly put by Lord Diplock in the *IRC* case.[130]

> "It would, in my view, be a grave lacuna in our system of public law if a pressure group, like the federation, or even a single public-spirited taxpayer, were prevented by outdated technical rules of *locus standi* from bringing the matter to the attention of the court to vindicate the rule of law and get the unlawful action stopped."

Secondly, there be many instances of unlawful conduct which affect the public at large on matters of importance, but which do not in any real sense affect the interests of one individual more than another. Such illegalities should be capable of being challenged in our society.

Thirdly, even if the interests of more specific individuals are affected by the disputed governmental action, there may be reasons why such individuals have not directly raised the point and could not be expected to do so. This was acknowledged by Woolf L.J. in the *C.P.A.G.* case, when he recognised that the Child Poverty Action Group, which gives advice to social security claimants, might well contest general matters of importance which individual claimants for social welfare would not be expected to raise.[131]

A number of objections have been voiced against the adoption of such an approach. They can be broadly divided into the practical and the conceptual.

(2) PRACTICAL OBJECTIONS

There are a number of different types of practical objection which have been raised against the citizen action, the most oft repeated being that it would open the courthouse doors to vexatious litigants and busybodies. Scott has provided the most succinct response to this criticism:

> "The idle and whimsical plaintiff, a dilettante who litigates for a lark, is a spectre which haunts the legal literature, not the courtroom."[132]

A second practical objection is that an applicant who has no interest of his own at stake will not be the most effective advocate or presenter of the issue. This is simply a *non sequitur*. No one has demonstrated any correlation between the degree of interest that an applicant has and the effectiveness of the advocacy, and there is no reason to suspect that any such correlation exists. Indeed the public-spirited citizen who challenges

---

[129] See also, Sir Konrad Schiemann, "Locus Standi" [1990] P.L. 342, 346.

[130] [1982] A.C. 617, 644.

[131] [1990] 2 Q.B. 540, 546-547.

[132] "Standing in the Supreme Court – A Functional Analysis" 86 Harv. L.Rev. 645 (1973). If this spectre were ever to be a problem it is one which could be solved through provisions as to costs. Such provisions already exist, see below, pp. 578-579. See also, Jolowicz, "Protection of Diffuse, Fragmented and Collective Interests in Civil Litigation: English Law" (1983) C.L.J. 222.

governmental action even though he has no personal stake in the outcome may well be a more effective litigant simply because he will normally feel particularly strongly about the matter before bothering to bring a claim.

A final practical objection is that the greater number of suits against government which would be possible under a citizen action would distract those who are in the business of governing from their primary task by taking up their time in defending legal actions. Moreover, such challenges would take up court time, the costs of which are borne by the public purse, with the consequence that there would be less money available for other matters, such as legal aid.[133]

Both aspects of this argument are open to question. It is, of course, true that the primary task of those who govern or administer is to do just that. But it is equally true that they should administer or govern according to the law. The key issue is, therefore, *who* should be able to bring any potential illegality before the court. Why should it be thought that an action which affects the public at large, in which no individual is necessarily affected more than any other, is a less deserving distraction from the primary task of governing, or a less deserving use of court time,[134] than an action in which the applicant has some more particularised interest? This is particularly so given that the subject-matter in the former type of case may well be more important than in the latter.

(3) CONCEPTUAL OBJECTIONS

Aside from the practical objections, certain writers have seen more conceptual objections to the citizen action, arguing that such an action would run counter to the traditional role of the courts or, going even further, asserting that such an approach would be contrary to the judicial process as we know it.

(a) The need for a person

Vining puts an argument of the latter type.[135] He posits a situation in which the courts have discarded the legal rights test and put nothing in its place, and asks whether that would be possible, answering that it would not. His reasoning is as follows. People possess a number of different identities such as father, businessman, sports player, etc. When a person comes to the court he comes not as a "natural person" but in one of the more particularised guises set out above.

The problem with the above argument is that the conclusions follow inevitably from the premise, but it is the premise which is in issue. *If* the courts continue to require some harm personalised to the applicant then it will follow that the applicant will fail if he does not fall into the category, such as fathers, which the courts regard as harmed by the activity

---

[133] Sir Konrad Schiemann, "Locus Standi" [1990] P.L. 342, 348.
[134] For a more extensive discussion of this aspect of the matter from an economic perspective, see below, pp. 512-513.
[135] *Legal Identity* (1978), Chap. 4.

impugned. However, nothing in the argument demonstrates that the courts have to require such harm. It would be possible for a court faced with the above example to say that whether the applicant is or is not a father is not conclusive and that he possesses a citizen's interest in preventing such invalid regulations being promulgated. The only identity that the court would be concerned with is not any specialised identity or guise but the applicant's position as a citizen. The possibility of citizen actions cannot be rejected on the basis that they would somehow be logically inconsistent with the way in which courts "see" people who come before them.

(b) Inconsistent with the traditional judicial role

A more complex objection to the citizen action is that it would be inconsistent with the traditional judicial role, or at least place it under severe strain. The argument is as follows.[136]

The common law case method serves, *inter alia*, to prevent the use of the judicial process for the articulation of abstract principles of law, as opposed to the settlement of concrete disputes. To this end ripeness focuses on the temporal immediacy of the harm, justiciability on the suitability of the subject-matter for judicial resolution, and standing on the nature of the interest that a person has. As the connection between the interest asserted and the type of judicial intervention requested becomes more attenuated, so the possibility of broadly framed challenges increases.[137] Two consequences ensue: the focus of the courts shifts from the remedying of private wrongs to the making of abstract determinations of legal principle; and any interest asserted becomes simply an excuse for engaging a court in a discussion of administrative practice that the applicant does not like.[138] Moreover, one of the bases of our legal system is *stare decisis* and the more broadly framed the initial challenge becomes the more likely it will be that the initial applicant may fail adequately to represent future applicants who will be affected by the outcome of the first dispute. Narrower standing criteria, by way of contrast, implicitly look to the scope of those affected if the applicant wins or loses, and determine whether the harm alleged by the applicant is proximate enough to that suffered by other possible challengers in order that the former may "represent" the latter.

This argument is difficult to interpret because of ambiguity as to what the words "abstract" or "broadly framed" mean. Three interpretations are possible, none of which in fact supports the argument advanced.

The first sees "abstract" or "broadly framed" as meaning that the principles which the courts will propound will be vague or unripe, in the sense of premature, this being juxtaposed to the settlement of "concrete" disputes. This does not follow from the existence of a citizen action. Allowing a broad range of persons to challenge administrative action does not mean that the principles thereby propounded will be vague or untimely;

---

[136] *e.g.* Brilmayer, "Judicial Review, Justiciability and the Limits of the Common Law Method" 57 Boston U.L.R. 807 (1977).
[137] See, *e.g. Gouriet* [1978] A.C. 435, 501–502.
[138] See also, Schiemann, [1990] P.L. 342, 348–349.

limits of ripeness *and* justiciability would still exist. In the *IRC* case the illegality asserted by the National Federation was not abstract in the sense of vague or hypothetical at all; nor was it unripe in the sense of being premature; nor was the issue unsuited for legal resolution. The issue was sharply defined and current, albeit in the end unproven.

A second meaning of "abstract" and "broadly framed" would be to say that a decision will not be concrete, and thus will be abstract, if no person is individually affected. But this proves too much for it is a tautology. It amounts to saying no more than that abstract determinations are bad and are determinations not affecting a specific person more than others; therefore, a citizen action is bad because abstract. Now a person may take such a view and defend it, but it has nothing to do with the traditional role of the courts or any such thing; it is simply a value judgment. Moreover, such a meaning of abstract would automatically preclude any challenge to important areas of governmental activity which did not affect any person more than another.

A third interpretation of the phrases "abstract" and "broadly framed" is more complex and would be as follows. The premise behind the argument is that the traditional common law model of adjudication can be applied to public law provided that we observe certain limits in terms of justiciability, ripeness, and standing. Although I am oversimplifying the traditional model, it is one in which the contest is between two individuals, is retrospective in the sense of concerning a completed set of past events, and one in which right and remedy are interdependent, the defendant compensating the plaintiff for some breach of duty committed by him. Further, the judge will be a neutral umpire and the court's involvement will end with the conclusion of the case.[139] However, as we shall see, whether the traditional model of adjudication can be applied to public law has very little if anything to do with standing, be it broad or narrow, and much to do with the subject-matter of public law.

Public law litigation often contradicts the criteria which identify the traditional model. There may be a wide range of persons affected by the case and the judicial focus may be more prospective than retrospective, being concerned with the modification of a public body's conduct in the future. These differences are reflected in the decree which will be formed *ad hoc*, be forward looking, and one which the judge takes an active role in formulating. All of these distinctions rest ultimately upon the fact that the subject-matter in a public law case will often involve broad issues of social and political choice. The more "abstract" or "general" nature of the issues presented for judicial determination is *not* a correlative of who has standing but of the *subject-matter* itself.

An example may help to make this clearer. Let us take the facts of the *Prescott* case in which the challenge was to the provision of free bus rides for old age pensioners.[140] Imagine first that only those with private rights in

---

[139] Chayes, "The Role of the Judge in Public Litigation" 89 Harv. L.Rev. 1281 (1976); *cf.* MacNeil, "Contracts: Adjustment of Long Term Economic Relations Under Classical, Neo Classical, and Relational Contract Law" 72 Nw. U.L.Rev. 854 (1978).
[140] [1955] Ch. 210.

the strict sense are accorded standing and that such a person impugns the decision. Now the range of issues that the court will have to consider in determining the legality of the scheme will involve a broad inquiry as to the way local authorities hold their funds and the scope of uses to which they can be put. Alter the hypothesis so that any person is accorded standing. The nature of the inquiry would not be altered one wit by having the broadest imaginable standing rules. The root cause of this lies ultimately in the point made in an earlier section. Even when *locus standi* is restricted to those possessing private rights, although the result may have been the vindication of those rights, the substance of the case was, and always has been, the broader public interest as reflected in the *vires* issue. The bow to private rights was always one of form.

What *is* undeniably true is that because public law issues do have this broad reach there is a problem of interest representation, of ensuring both that those interested in the suit do have a chance to make representations, and that the "person" presenting the case adequately represents future interests. But this again is a result of the subject-matter at stake, not of the rules of standing. Narrow rules of *locus standi* do not solve this problem, they brush it under the carpet. In the example drawn from *Prescott*, if society only allowed those with private rights to argue the public interest about the legality of free bus rides for pensioners this would not somehow magically mean that others were not very concerned with the issue, nor would it ensure that the applicant who did possess the private rights would do the job of arguing the public interest adequately.

(c) The relativity of ultra vires

Perhaps the most cogent of objections to the citizen action has been voiced by one of its main proponents. Jaffe has long advocated broad rules of standing to allow the "private attorney-general" or "non-Hohfeldian plaintiff" to vindicate the public interest.[141] However, Jaffe favours a bipartite test of standing in which those with some interest would have standing as of right, whereas the standing of the citizen applicant would be at the discretion of the court. The reasoning underlying this dichotomy is as follows: there may well be cases in which the interests which the law chooses to protect are content with the situation. If this is so a stranger should not be allowed to raise a possible cause of invalidity. For example, if a restaurant is placed in an area where it should not have been allowed, but the residents are content with it, why should a stranger be allowed to complain? Any test of standing should therefore include a concept of the zone of interests which the legislation is intended to protect, since this

---

[141] "Standing to Secure Judicial Review: Public Actions" 74 Harv. L.Rev. 1265 (1960-1961); "Standing to Secure Judicial Review: Private Actions" 75 Harv. L.Rev. 255 (1961-1962); "The Citizen and Litigant in Public Actions: The Non-Hohfeldian or Ideological Plaintiff" 116 U. of Penn. L.Rev. 1033 (1967-1968); "Standing Again" 84 Harv. L.Rev. 633 (1970-1971). See also, Stewart, "The Reformation of American Administrative Law" 88 Harv. L.Rev. 1667, 1735-1737 (1975).

places control of the situation in the hands of those most immediately concerned. Where however the court feels that those possessing a defined legal interest do not adequately represent all interests intended to be protected by the legislation, and if there are no other devices for public control, or if those devices are unresponsive to unrepresented interests, then the court in its discretion can take jurisdiction at the instance of a private attorney-general.

Leaving aside for the present the difficulties of defining who should be regarded as having a protected legal interest and who should be a stranger, Jaffe performs a valuable service by, in effect, pointing out an aspect of the standing argument not often addressed. The existence or not of a citizen action is normally considered against the backdrop of public activity which affects all or a very large number of people, but no one person in particular. A number of people, including myself, feel that this should not preclude a challenge. The difficulty is in formulating a rule which will allow this to happen and yet not to encroach on the type of case that Jaffe has in mind. The essence of his argument is that invalidity is relative and that those who come within the "protected ambit" will differ depending upon the nature of the legislation involved. Thus, there are many cases where, if those affected do not complain, why should others be able to do so? In *Ridge* v. *Baldwin*,[142] if the chief constable had decided not to challenge his dismissal, should any one else have been able to do so? This is the key question.

The answer to it will of course be a value judgment. The most extreme view would be to say that any citizen has an interest in any government wrong-doing and therefore should have standing. And yet the reaction of many would be that that is wrong. If the Chief Constable does not wish to challenge the decision, that is his affair and his life should not be upset by someone else doing so. The example from *Ridge* v. *Baldwin* is of course capable of extension. What if two, three, 20 people are affected; what then?[143]

The resolution of this quandary prompts the answer that Jaffe is correct and not at all inconsistent. His advocacy of the citizen action is premised upon the sound reasoning that just because a very large number of people are equally affected this does not mean that no-one should have standing if the subject-matter of the dispute is otherwise capable of judicial resolution. This does not logically or inexorably mean that any person must always be accorded standing. That would be a *non sequitur* for it would amount to saying: "because X can have standing even though he is not specifically affected, therefore he must always be given a platform". There will be many cases which are of the *Ridge* v. *Baldwin* type where none but the person or persons concerned will be granted *locus standi*. If they choose not to complain, so be it. Nor should this be feared as a return to the times when dispensing powers were exercised. It is nothing of the sort and adequate safeguards are provided by the qualifications which Jaffe sets out.

---

[142] [1964] A.C. 40.
[143] The difficulties are well exemplified by the reasoning in *R.* v. *Secretary of State for the Home Department, ex p. Ruddock* [1987] 2 All E.R. 518, 521.

(d) The relationship between standing and representation

An interesting argument has been made by Stewart which is as follows.[144] He argues that standing should not be broader than the right to intervene in the agency proceeding itself. The basis of the argument is that the judicial role is confined to ensuring that the agency adequately considered affected interests. Therefore those accorded standing must also have participated in the agency process and have had an opportunity to give their views before a decision is reached.

This argument is important in indicating the real connection which exists between standing and an opportunity to be heard. It is however of limited application in this country. As we have seen,[145] we do not have a developed concept of interest representation, and the judiciary do not conceive their role in the way articulated by Stewart. Moreover, even if we did develop such a concept more fully, and it is arguable that we should,[146] it is by no means clear that the relationship between standing and hearing requirements would be the same as that conceived by Stewart. The political structure and the types of decision-maker are different in this country. For example, if a body like the Inland Revenue Commissioners makes a deal with certain taxpayers it is by no means self-evident that, even if we had a more developed concept of interest representation, taxpayers could or should be consulted. It does not follow from this that no person should be able to challenge the resultant deal, even if they are simply ordinary taxpayers.

4. Injury in Fact

Davis has for some time strongly favoured a test based purely upon injury in fact.[147] He has castigated the other part of the test established by the Supreme Court, the zone of interests test, as unworkable, conceptually unsound, and historically unnecessary. Davis is undoubtedly correct in pointing out the dangers and pitfalls in attempting to define legislative intent, but his insistence that injury in fact can provide the sole requirement for standing is open to objection.

For Davis, such injury is both a necessary and a sufficient test of standing. The effect of regarding such injury as a necessary test for *locus standi* is the outright rejection of the citizen action in so far as that allows a citizen who can demonstrate no such injury, apart from a citizen's concern for legality, to impugn governmental action. The objection to this, in its own terms, is that it leads to fortuitous distinctions being made which

---

[144] "The Reformation of American Administrative Law" 88 Harv.L.Rev. 1667, 1749-1751 (1975). *cf.* Jaffe, *Judicial Control of Administrative Action* (1965), pp. 524-526.

[145] See above, pp. 255-258.

[146] See above, pp. 258-262.

[147] "Standing: Taxpayers and Others" 35 U. Chic. L.Rev. 601 (1967-1968); "The Liberalised Law of Standing" 37 U. Chic. L.Rev. 450 (1969-1970). See also Davis, "Judicial Control of Administrative Action: A Review" 66 Col. L.Rev. 635, 659-669 (1966).

reflect little credit on legal reasoning. Cases in which the most ephemeral and indirect injury is found are applauded, even if this reaches the extreme of finding one applicant who has used a park area and allowing him to dispute proposed action in relation to that area, but to deprecate the attempt by an environmental group to do the same.

Treating injury in fact as a sufficient requirement for standing is also open to objections of a more conceptual nature. Such injury is not, in many instances, self-defining. What constitutes such injury is itself a normative value judgment, not simply an empirical observation. How is this value judgment to be made? It cannot be made in a vacuum and must in fact be decided against the legislative or constitutional background in question. The essence of the zone of interests test, rejected by the front door, re-appears in a veiled form by the side entrance.

5. *Costs of Litigation*

Scott has suggested a rather different type of analysis to solve the problem of standing.[148] His argument is as follows. Normally the market mechanism will operate to determine the quantum and price at which a good or service is offered; this does not operate within the context of the judicial system, the size of which is determined by legislative choice and financed in part by general taxation. Choice, therefore, has to be exercised as to precisely how the limited judicial services should be allocated and access standing can play a role in this. "Access standing" is a judicial determination as to whether the nature and extent of alleged harm to an applicant are such as to warrant the use of judicial resources to decide his case. Litigation will, however, also involve significant private costs, especially when the suit is brought against an organ of government. Since significant private costs do exist, what other extra barriers should be imposed or, put conversely, if the applicant is willing to bear the costs of the action why should he not be admitted to the court? Scott considers what other factors over and above willingness to bear litigation costs might be considered as relevant. These include whether the applicant is an appropriate person to represent the interests of his group, the possible "second order" effects of a decision on others affected by the relevant government programme, and the extent of the applicant's personal stake in the outcome of the decision. All are rejected primarily because the courts are not seen as capable of giving answers to such questions. If the legislature wishes to make social choices as to who should be awarded subsidised access to the courts then of course it can do so but, in the absence of such a choice, then willingness to bear the costs of litigation should remain the only standard.

Scott's view is of interest and cogently argued but rests ultimately on two linked conceptions. One is that, in the absence of other identifiable, work-able, limits, the role of standing is to ration judicial resources and that willing-ness to pay should be the criterion through which this occurs. The problem

---

[148] "Standing in the Supreme Court – A Functional Analysis" 86 Harv.L.Rev. 645 (1973).

with this is that the courts have never regarded willingness to bear the costs as a sufficient condition for standing and they have always looked to other factors of the type that Scott mentions, such as the degree of personal stake that X has, or how adequately X represents the interests of other Xs. Scott's objection to this is that the courts are not adequately placed or informed to make such decisions which should be left to the legislature. But is it really conceivable that a legislative body would sit down, charge for judicial services at their marginal costs, use any excess revenue to increase judicial capacity, and then make a decision as to which categories of litigants should have subsidised access? Empirical evidence indicates that this is unlikely to happen. Even though the court's determination of whether X has sufficient personal stake or adequately represents his group are difficult questions for a court to answer, they are no more so than many other issues which the court decides every day.

Even if this did take place, it still leaves unsolved the other side of the coin, the *Ridge* v. *Baldwin* type of case. A group of publicly-minded citizens gather funds to fight actions on behalf of any dismissed public employee whether the latter wishes to contest the matter or not. The fact is that in dismissing such claims for lack of standing the courts do and will continue to look to the extent of the applicant's stake even though they may not be in a "perfect" position from which to do this. In such instances there is no real alternative legislative guidance at all. The presence of legislation has certain inherent limits, one of which would be the impossibility of including in each piece of legislation comprehensive criteria as to who, despite their willingness to pay, should not be entitled to standing.

Section 6. Conclusion

Locus standi has given rise to case law which is complex and often conflicting. It will continue to be so until the courts develop a clearer idea as to what they believe the purposes to be served by standing actually are. The choices are clear even if the solutions are not.

The rigid reliance on the private right conception of standing is on the wane both in this country and elsewhere, and the key question is where we go from here. The polar extreme from the private right formulation is the destruction of standing through the acceptance of the citizen action in any and every case. For the reasons given above it is unlikely that this will prove to be acceptable or desirable. Nor is it likely that we will witness the complete submergence of standing within the merits and the surfacing of a number of distinct "causes of action" tailor-made to each particular area.

The optimal solution would be an approach akin to that propounded by Jaffe. This involves an acceptance of the fact that citizen actions can exist, particularly in those areas where a large number of people are equally affected by governmental irregularity, but in which no person is particularly singled out. To deny any access in such a case seems indefensible. If the subject-matter of the case is otherwise appropriate for judicial resolution, and the application is timely or ripe, to erect a barrier of "no standing" would be to render many important areas of governmental activity immune from censure for no better reason than that they do affect a large number of people. One might be forgiven for thinking that the common sense of the reasonable man would indicate the opposite conclusion; that the wide range of people affected is a positive reason for allowing a challenge by someone.[149]

At the same time this does not mean that any person should be allowed to raise any issue of invalidity. There will be many of what have been labelled *Ridge* v. *Baldwin* types of case, where one's reaction is naturally that if the person directly affected does not challenge the act then no-one should be able to do so. The precise dividing line between this type of case and that in which any person should be able to claim will not easily be drawn, and will necessarily involve a view of the merits to determine the ambit of those primarily entitled to invoke the illegality. But difficult borderlines will always have to be encountered unless one adopts one of the polar extremes indicated above. To adopt a middle position and yet to seek absolute certainty is not possible.

Academics are justly criticised for being negative, for destroying and not proposing. Thus, the following formulation is suggested: a citizen should be entitled at the discretion of the court to bring any action alleging invalid public activity, except where it can be shown from a consideration of the statutory framework that the range of persons with standing was intended to be narrower than this. In this latter instance standing should be as of right and limited to the protected class, with the qualification that there may be cases where those with a protected legal interest do not adequately represent a wider group affected by the legislation; this wider group should be admitted at the discretion of the court. The presumption is therefore that citizens simply *qua* citizens have a sufficient interest in governmental legality. All else should be seen as a qualification of this.

This formulation may be juxtaposed to that proposed by Lord Woolf who advocates a two track test for standing, similar to that adopted in Canada, and similar also to the old test for standing and certiorari: the applicant will have a sufficient interest in cases where he or she has been personally adversely affected by the challenged decision; in other cases standing will be at the discretion of the court, which will take into account matters such as the allocation of scarce resources, the relationship between courts and Parliament, and the screening out of busybodies.[150] How far this formulation differs from that presented above depends upon the construction of the term "personal adverse effect"; and upon how a court exercises its discretion to admit applicants who come within the second category. The broader the construction of the term personal adverse effect and the more liberally the court interprets the discretion to admit a case which comes within the second category, then the closer will this formulation be to that proposed above.

---

[149] And see the observations of Lord Diplock to this effect in the *IRC* case [1982] A.C. 617, 644.

[150] "Judicial Review: A Possible Programme for Reform" [1992] P.L. 221, 232-233.

The provisional view of the Law Commission is that a "broad test of standing to raise an issue of public law should be maintained."[151] Such a test is felt to be appropriate because it recognises that certain decisions which affect the public in general should be capable of being challenged.

Liberalisation of standing has in varying degrees been proceeding or proposed in other common law jurisdictions. The general theme in the *IRC* case and those which have followed is indeed towards a liberalisation of our standing rules, and this is to be welcomed. Lurking in the background is however the view that the private rights test is still the general "common law" rule for standing, to which section 31 actions and other statutory provisions are to be treated as exceptions.[152] The purported justifications for this view have been criticised above, but old habits of thought are hard to dispel.

---

[151] *Administrative Law: Judicial Review and Statutory Appeals*, Consultation Paper No. 126 (1993), p. 64.
[152] *Stoke-on-Trent City Council* v. *B & Q (Retail) Ltd.* [1984] A.C. 754, 769–771. See, however, Zamir and Woolf, *The Declaratory Judgment* (2nd ed., 1993), pp. 297–298.

14. THE JUDICIAL REMEDIES

A citizen who is aggrieved by a decision of a public body has a variety of remedies available. There are the prerogative orders of certiorari, prohibition and mandamus. In addition both the declaration and the injunction have been applied to public bodies. These are the main remedies, although reference will also be made to others. The law of remedies was until recently highly complex, with differing procedures applying to the prerogative orders and to declaration and injunction. Each remedy was subject to a number of advantages and disadvantages. Some of this disorder has been swept away by the reform which is now encapsulated in section 31 of the Supreme Court Act 1981, but this has also brought new complexities into the law. The reform is, moreover, principally one of form or procedure. It is for this reason that each of the remedies will be examined in turn, making reference to the reforms where appropriate. In the following chapter there will be a more detailed look at the procedural reforms, including a discussion as to how far they have provided us with a rational system of remedies.

Section 1. Certiorari and Prohibition

1. *Introduction*

Certiorari and prohibition have long been remedies for the control of administrative action. The former had its origins as a royal demand for information. The exact history of the development of the writ is complex, but Rubinstein[1] argues convincingly that certiorari was originally developed to fill a gap left by collateral attack and the writ of error. Collateral attack, in the form of an action for assault, trespass, etc., lay only for jurisdictional defects, while the writ of error was restricted to some courts of record.[2] Certiorari developed to fill a gap that might arise. What form did this gap take? The area left unfilled was an error within jurisdiction by an institution not amenable to the writ of error; the remedy

---

[1] *Jurisdiction and Illegality* (1965), Chap. 4. See also de Smith, *Judicial Review of Administrative Action* (4th ed., 1980), App. 1; Henderson, *Foundations of English Administrative Law* (1963); Jaffe and Henderson, "Judicial Review and The Rule of Law: Historical Origins" (1956) 72 L.Q.R. 345.

[2] Such courts had power to fine and imprison or had jurisdiction to try civil causes according to common law where the sum involved exceeded 40 shillings, Rubinstein, above n. 1, p. 57.

was thus initially aimed at errors within, as opposed to errors going to jurisdiction.[3]

It was in response to the development of finality clauses that certiorari began to be used more generally for jurisdictional defects. The courts restrictively construed such clauses to render them applicable only for non-jurisdictional error; where the error went to jurisdiction certiorari was held to be still available. The power of certiorari was augmented further by the acceptance of affidavit evidence to prove that a jurisdictional defect existed.[4]

Whereas certiorari operated retrospectively to quash a decision already made, prohibition was more prospective in its impact, enjoining the addressee from continuing with something which would be an excess of jurisdiction. It was a particularly useful weapon wielded by the King's Bench Division in the internecine struggles between it and the more specialised or ecclesiastical courts. The law reports are replete with judges of the King's Bench castigating such assumptions of authority.[5] Prohibition was, however, used more generally, like certiorari, to control a wide spectrum of inferior bodies both before and after the reforms in municipal government of 1835, and statements approbating its liberal usage were not uncommon.[6]

2. The Scope of Certiorari and Prohibition

In 1924 Atkin L.J. produced what has proved to be the most frequently quoted dictum as to the scope of certiorari,[7]

> "Whenever any body of persons having legal authority to determine questions affecting the rights of subjects, and having the duty to act judicially, act in excess of their legal authority, they are subject to the controlling jurisdiction of the King's Bench Division exercised in these writs."

Prohibition is in general subject to the same rules as certiorari; any points of distinction will be mentioned.[8] While not a statutory definition, the dictum of Atkin L.J. does provide a useful starting point in considering the scope of the remedies.

---

[3] *Groenvelt* v. *Burwell* (1700) 1 Ld. Raym. 454. See also, the reports in (1700) 1 Comyns 76; (1700) 12 Mod. 386. Other important early decisions were *Commins* v. *Massam* (1643) March N.C. 196, 197; *R.* v. *Hide* (1647) Style 60; *R.* v. *Plowright* (1686) 3 Mod. 94.

[4] Rubinstein, above n. 1, pp. 71-80. And the original basis of certiorari, for the control of errors within jurisdiction, was forgotten until *R.* v. *Northumberland Compensation Appeal Tribunal, ex p. Shaw* [1952] 1 K.B. 338.

[5] *e.g. Mayor and Aldermen of City of London* v. *Cox* (1867) L.R. 2 H.L. 239.

[6] *e.g. R.* v. *Local Government Board* (1882) 10 Q.B.D. 309.

[7] *R.* v. *Electricity Commissioners, ex p. London Electricity Joint Committee Co. (1920) Ltd.* [1924] 1 K.B. 171, 205.

[8] In the *Electricity Commissioners* case Atkin L.J. explicitly ties the two remedies together, [1924] 1 K.B. 171, 194.

(1) WHICH PERSONS AND WHAT TYPE OF AUTHORITY?

The general starting point is that certiorari and prohibition will apply to quash any decision which is deemed to be of a public law nature.[9] The scope of public law for these purposes will be considered in detail within the following chapter, and the material within this section should be read in the light of that discussion.[10]

Certiorari and prohibition will issue to any body which exercises statutory authority, including departments of state,[11] local authorities,[12] individual ministers,[13] and public bodies.[14] It is assumed that they will not be available against the Crown itself, the reason being that the orders are punishable by contempt, being commands from the court. This is, as de Smith points out, unsatisfactory and anachronistic: the existence of a potentially coercive remedy against the Crown as an institution does not necessarily imply that such measures would or could be taken against Her Majesty in person.[15] However, other provisions are based upon similar reasoning.[16] The availability of the prerogative orders against the Crown itself will be considered in more detail below.[17]

It would, however, be mistaken to assume that the remedies can only issue to those whose authority is based strictly upon statute. The prerogative orders are available to protect common law rights of a public nature,[18] and also to prevent institutions or persons acting under prerogative powers from exceeding their authority.[19]

It is unclear how far these decisions will be taken. The traditional assumption has been that certiorari will not be available where a body is exercising powers which may be of a public nature if the derivation of that power is contractual.[20] Certain more recent statements suggest that the

---

[9] Neither certiorari nor prohibition will lie against decisions of superior courts. Certiorari will not it seems lie against ecclesiastical courts, but as noted above, prohibition will issue to prevent excess of power by such courts.

[10] See below, Chap. 15.

[11] Board of Education v. Rice [1911] A.C. 179.

[12] R. v. London County Council, ex p. The Entertainments Protection Association Ltd. [1931] 2 K.B. 215.

[13] R. v. Minister of Health, ex p. Yaffe [1930] 2 K.B. 98.

[14] R. v. Milk Marketing Board, ex p. North (1934) 50 T.L.R. 559. And see R. v. Blundeston Prison Board of Visitors, ex p. Fox-Taylor [1982] 1 All E.R. 646, where it was held that certiorari could issue to the prison board, even though the breach of natural justice had been caused by the prison authorities. See also, R. v. Leyland Magistrates, ex p. Hawthorn [1979] 1 All E.R. 209. cf. Cheall v. APEX [1983] A.C. 180.

[15] Judicial Review of Administrative Action (4th ed., 1980), p.385.

[16] Crown Proceedings Act 1947, s.21.

[17] See below, pp. 725-732.

[18] R. v. Barnsley Metropolitan Borough Council, ex p. Hook [1976] 1 W.L.R. 1052, 1057, 1060.

[19] R. v. Criminal Injuries Compensation Board, ex p. Lain [1967] 2 Q.B. 864, 880-881, 884; Council of Civil Service Unions v. Minister for the Civil Service [1985] A.C. 374.

[20] e.g. R. v. National Joint Council for the Craft of Dental Technicians (Disputes Committee), ex p. Neate [1953] 1 Q.B. 704; Vidyodaya University Council v. Silva [1965] 1 W.L.R. 77. See also, Herring v. Templeman [1973] 3 All E.R. 569, 585, and R. v. Post Office, ex p. Byrne [1975] I.C.R. 221, 226, disapproving of the contrary assumption made in R. v. Aston University Senate, ex p. Roffey [1969] 2 Q.B. 538.

prerogative orders could, however, be available even if the source of the power was contractual.[21] It is, nonetheless, still doubtful whether an institution which derives its powers solely from contract will be amenable to the prerogative orders.[22] The case law on this particular aspect of the topic will be discussed in more detail in the following chapter.[23] The argument underlying such cases does not, however, appear to be that there is some "analytical" reason which precludes the application of the prerogative orders to bodies which derive their power from contract. It is rather that the facts of these cases disclosed no "public" law issue, but simply one of a private or domestic character.[24] The courts have, moreover, clearly shown themselves willing to look beyond the source of a body's power, and to inquire into its nature, in order to determine whether that body was susceptible to judicial review.[25]

(2) THE DETERMINATION OF RIGHTS

Two separate problems are involved here. First, what does determination mean? Secondly, what is encompassed by the term rights?

On the meaning of determination, it is clear that the decision challenged need not be absolutely final. In the *Electricity Commissioners*[26] case itself, the commissioners had to report their findings to the minister who would confirm them or not, and if the former he would then lay them before Parliament. Nevertheless, the court held that this did not preclude certiorari. A number of other authorities explicitly[27] or implicitly[28] affirm the same point. However, there are other cases which regard the necessity for approval or confirmation by another as preventing the orders from issuing.[29] The Supreme Court Act 1981, s.31(2) is likely to reduce the importance of this question: if the decision is felt not to be final enough for certiorari then declaratory or injunctive relief may be claimed instead.

The word "rights" has been broadly interpreted. It clearly includes personal security,[30] traditional property interests[31] and a person's interest in

---

[21] *O'Reilly* v. *Mackman* [1982] 3 W.L.R. 604 (Lord Denning M.R.), [1983] 2 A.C. 237, 279 (Lord Diplock).
[22] *R.* v. *B.B.C., ex p. Lavelle* [1983] 1 W.L.R. 23, 31; *Law* v. *National Greyhound Racing Club Ltd.* [1983] 3 All E.R. 300; *R.* v. *Panel on Take-overs and Mergers, ex p. Datafin plc* [1987] Q.B. 815, 847, approving *ex p. Neate* [1953] 1 Q.B. 704.
[23] See below, pp. 570–573.
[24] This appears to be the reasoning in *ex p. Lavelle* [1983] 1 W.L.R. 23, 31, and in *ex p. Datafin* [1987] Q.B. 815, 834–837, 847–849.
[25] See below, pp. 562–577.
[26] [1924] 1 K.B. 171, 192, 208. See also, *Church* v. *Inclosure Commissioners* (1862) 11 C.B. (N.S.) 664.
[27] *Estate and Trust Agencies (1927) Ltd.* v. *Singapore Investment Trust* [1937] A.C. 898, 917.
[28] *R.* v. *Kent Police Authority, ex p. Godden* [1971] 2 Q.B. 662; *R.* v. *Board of Visitors of Hull Prison, ex p. St. Germain* [1979] Q.B. 425.
[29] *R.* v. *St. Lawrence's Hospital Statutory Visitors, ex p. Pritchard* [1953] 1 W.L.R. 1158.
[30] *R.* v. *Boycott, ex p. Keasley* [1939] 2 K.B. 651.
[31] *R.* v. *Agricultural Land Tribunal for the Wales and Monmouth Area, ex p. Davies* [1953] 1 W.L.R. 722.

continued membership of a profession.[32] It is not, however, restricted to these categories and includes many interests which would, in Hohfeldian terms, be described as privileges.[33] Two cases illustrate how liberally the courts will interpret this requirement.

In *R. v. Criminal Injuries Compensation Board, ex p. Lain*[34] the applicant sought certiorari to quash a decision made by the Board. One objection raised was that the Board made purely *ex gratia* payments and therefore did not determine any rights at all. This contention was rejected by the court. It was not necessary that the Board should make decisions creating or affecting rights in a narrow sense. Although the precise formulations given by the members of the Divisional Court differed, they all concurred in holding the Board amenable to certiorari. In *R. v. Board of Visitors of Hull Prison, ex p. St. Germain*[35] disciplinary proceedings before a prison visitor consequent upon a prison riot were challenged. One defence raised was that the visitor's decision did not interfere with any of the prisoners' rights but only affected their expectations of having a privilege conferred on them, the privilege in question being remission for good behaviour. Counsel's endeavour to convince the court of the need for accurate Hohfeldian categorisation was to no avail; it was, said the court, irrelevant whether a privilege or right was at stake. This is obviously correct. Administrative law has been plagued for long enough by distinctions based upon rights versus privileges. One shudders to think of the jurisprudential intricacies that lie enmeshed in "expectation of having a privilege conferred", and can only be thankful that the court dismissed the argument so conclusively.

(3) A DUTY TO ACT JUDICIALLY

If the dichotomy between rights and privileges has been one plague visited upon administrative law, a second has been that between administrative and judicial functions. The history of the rise and fall of this confusion can be traced as follows.

In the early years of the development of certiorari and prohibition those remedies were used partly to control inferior courts, and hence bodies exercising judicial functions. However, even in their early infancy the writs

---

[32] *General Medical Council* v. *Spackman* [1943] A.C. 627, provided that the body has the necessary statutory authority and that the relationship is not deemed to be one of master-servant, *Vidyodaya University Council* v. *Silva* [1965] 1 W.L.R. 77.

[33] *e.g.* R. v. *Woodhouse* [1906] 2 K.B. 501; R. v. *Gaming Board for Great Britain, ex p. Benaim and Khaida* [1970] 2 Q.B. 417; R. v. *Liverpool Corporation, ex p. Liverpool Taxi Fleet Operators' Association* [1972] 2 Q.B. 299.

[34] [1967] 2 Q.B. 864. Lord Parker C.J. was content that the Board was a body of a public as opposed to private character and affected subjects, *ibid.* p. 882; Diplock L.J. doubted if certiorari could go to a body which did not have any effect on legal rights in any circumstances, but was content that the determination made by the Board rendered lawful a payment which would otherwise be unlawful, pp. 884, 889; Ashworth L.J. thought it sufficient if subjects were affected and believed that the word rights could be omitted, p. 892.

[35] [1979] Q.B. 425. See also, *O'Reilly* v. *Mackman* [1983] 2 A.C. 237, where Lord Diplock talks of common law or statutory rights and obligations.

were used to control a wide variety of activities which, if labels must be attached, could only be called administrative: commissioners of sewers, or of tithes were regarded as natural defendants in a certiorari action.[36] As both remedies developed they encompassed a whole spectrum of activities which although they might be termed "judicial" bore little relationship to a formal trial: governmental departments, individual ministers and quasi-governmental undertakings were all brought within their purview. Defences to the application of certiorari or prohibition based upon the non-judicial nature of the proceedings were treated dismissively by the courts.[37]

Unfortunately, some later cases placed emphasis on the fact that Atkin L.J. spoke of certiorari applying where the rights of subjects were affected and where the body had the duty to act judicially.[38] Now, it was clear from the context of his judgment that Atkin L.J. saw the judicial element being inferred from the nature of the power and its consequential effects on individuals. Nonetheless, in certain subsequent decisions courts held that apart from an effect on the rights of individuals there must be a superadded duty to act judicially. Some, but not all such cases, concerned natural justice and are the reverse side of the coin concerning the interaction between rights and remedies discussed above:[39] the requirement that proceedings be judicial before natural justice applied appeared in tandem with the judicial requirement in certiorari. Sometimes the substantive right took the driving seat, infecting the remedy with the same condition. On other occasions the fertilisation process was reversed with the remedy leading the right.[40] This conceptual confusion was bound to lead to bad decisions and did so by, for example, holding that disciplinary proceedings, not being judicial, were not susceptible to certiorari.[41]

All was not, however, darkness in these years, but the occasional ray of clarity was the more apparent for being exceptional.[42] It was clear that it would require a decision by the House of Lords to restore rationality. This came in 1964 in *Ridge* v. *Baldwin*.[43] The interaction between rights and remedies is again evident. One of the reasons given by Lord Reid for natural justice becoming unduly restricted was the confusion introduced by the requirement of a superadded duty to act judicially as a condition for certiorari which was adopted in certain natural justice cases. The judicial

---

[36] *e.g. Commins* v. *Massam* (1643) March N.C. 196; *R.* v. *Hide* (1647) Style 60.

[37] *e.g. R.* v. *Woodhouse* [1906] 2 K.B. 501, 534–535; *Electricity Commissioners* [1924] 1 K.B. 171, 198.

[38] *Electricity Commissioners* [1924] 1 K.B. 171, 205.

[39] See above, pp. 283–285.

[40] An early clear example of the requirement of a superadded duty to act judicially appears in *R.* v. *Legislative Committee of the Church Assembly, ex p. Haynes-Smith* [1928] 1 K.B. 411. This case had nothing to do with natural justice, but was clearly influential in *Nakkuda Ali* v. *Jayaratne* [1951] A.C. 66, 77–78, a case about natural justice and certiorari: the remedy thus infects the right. In *R.* v. *Metropolitan Police Commissioner, ex p. Parker* [1953] 1 W.L.R. 1150 the same type of process is evident.

[41] *e.g. ex p. Parker* [1953] 1 W.L.R. 1150.

[42] *R.* v. *Manchester Legal Aid Committee, ex p. R.A. Brand and Co. Ltd.* [1952] 2 Q.B. 413, 425–431.

[43] [1964] A.C. 40.

element was, said Lord Reid, simply to be inferred from the nature of the power;[44] 40 years on the stance adopted by Atkin L.J. in the *Electricity Commissioners* case was restored both for remedies and natural justice.

The extent to which categorisation of a function as judicial does still play a role in natural justice was considered in the chapter on that topic.[45] The law on remedies has been relatively free of such shackles and there are statements that it is no longer relevant how the function is described in determining the applicability of certiorari.[46] Moreover, decisions have been reached which, if the facts had arisen prior to *Ridge*, would almost certainly have been decided the other way. Certiorari has thus been held applicable to cases of discipline by a prison visitor,[47] and to decisions by a local planning authority.[48] Although, in both instances, the court imposed qualifications these related to factors other than the necessity of finding a judicial function as such. The argument that the judicial or administrative nature of the proceedings should not be relevant for the purposes of certiorari has now been confirmed by *O'Reilly* v. *Mackman*.[49] Lord Diplock, giving the unanimous decision of the court, stated that there is no longer a requirement of a superadded duty to act judicially before the prerogative orders can apply. It was, said his Lordship, no longer necessary to distinguish between judicial and administrative acts.

(4) CERTIORARI AND SUBORDINATE LEGISLATION

Although the tyranny of conceptual classification has been weakened, it would be premature to say that it has been overthrown. It is, for example, still generally accepted that certiorari should not apply to legislative functions. In *Ridge*, Lord Reid, while disapproving of the superadded duty requirement, agreed with the result in the *Church Assembly*[50] case because the process involved was legislative.

That this should be so is by no means self-evident. The prerogative orders cannot of course be used to challenge primary legislation, but the reason for this resides in the sovereignty of Parliament. Why should other "legislation" be immune from the prerogative orders, more particularly given that the declaration will issue against such secondary legislation? On authority it is in fact clear that those orders have issued to stages in the legislative process. This was the case in the *Electricity Commissioners*[51] decision itself, and in other cases the courts have expressed a willingness to award certiorari where the function has been delineated as legislative.[52] On

---

[44] *Ibid.* pp. 74-78.
[45] See above, pp. 287-288.
[46] *e.g. R.* v. *Barnsley Metropolitan Borough Council, ex p. Hook* [1976] 1 W.L.R. 1052, 1058; *cf. Jayawardane* v. *Silva* [1970] 1 W.L.R. 1365.
[47] *R.* v. *Board of Visitors of Hull Prison, ex p. St. Germain* [1979] Q.B. 425.
[48] *R.* v. *Hillingdon London Borough Council, ex p. Royco Homes Ltd.* [1974] Q.B. 720. See, however, the earlier decision in *R.* v. *Hendon Rural District Council, ex p. Chorley* [1933] 2 K.B. 696 decided by Lord Hewart C.J.
[49] [1983] 2 A.C. 237.
[50] [1928] 1 K.B. 411. See *Ridge* [1964] A.C. 40, 72.
[51] [1924] 1 K.B. 171; *Church* v. *Inclosure Commissioners* (1862) 11 C.B. (N.S.) 664.
[52] *e.g. Minister of Health* v. *R., ex p. Yaffe* [1931] A.C. 494, 532, 533.

principle there seems no reason why the prerogative orders should not be available against secondary legislation *stricto sensu* and to impugn rules of a legislative character made by a public body.[53] Insofar as the scope of the prerogative orders is meant to reflect the ambit of "public law", they will be defective in not covering an important area which, judged by any substantive criterion, is indeed public. The line between decisions made individually or *ad hoc*, and those institutionalised into rules, may be fine and fortuitous. The more one looks at the early development of the prerogative orders, the greater is the impression that these remedies were interpreted flexibly to meet the new types of institutions developing at that time. Real conceptual restrictions appear later. Is it an inevitable development that, once flexible, tools become, like equity has on occasion, ossified and confined?

The tendency in more recent authority is in fact to consider applying the prerogative orders to secondary legislation. Thus in one case it was assumed that certiorari was available to quash a statutory instrument which set out regulations on housing benefits, even though the court ultimately decided not to order the remedy as a matter of discretion.[54] A similar assumption underlies other decisions.[55]

3. *Grounds for the Award of Certiorari and Prohibition*

The grounds on which certiorari and prohibition will issue are those set out in Part II: jurisdictional defects including natural justice, and excess, abuse, or failure to exercise a discretionary power. Errors of law on the face of the record were also susceptible to certiorari, but as seen earlier this concept is now redundant. This is of course subject to the proviso that the above conditions are met and that none of the limitations detailed below are present.

4. *Limitations on the Grant of the Remedies*

(1) CONDUCT OF THE APPLICANT

(a) *Waiver*

Unless there is a statutory exception the general rule is that jurisdiction cannot be conferred upon a public body by acquiescence.[56] A decision made without jurisdiction is void. However, this general statement does not in fact accurately reflect all the case law, which is somewhat confused. What

---

[53] See, *Att.-Gen. of Hong Kong* v. *Ng Yuen-Shiu* [1983] 2 A.C. 629, and *R.* v. *Secretary of State for the Home Department, ex p. Khan* [1985] 1 All E.R. 40, in both of which certiorari was granted to prevent the public body from altering rules of a legislative character.
[54] *R.* v. *Secretary of State for Social Services, ex p. Association of Metropolitan Authorities* [1986] 1 W.L.R. 1.
[55] *R.* v. *Secretary of State for Health, ex p. United States Tobacco International Inc.* [1992] Q.B. 353.
[56] *Essex Incorporated Congregational Church Union* v. *Essex C.C.* [1963] A.C. 308.

exceptions exist in the case law and what exceptions should exist in principle must now be examined.

The most problematic part of the case law concerns prohibition and the problem is exacerbated both by the overlap between standing and waiver, and by the confusing welter of terminology used. Light may be shed by attempting to cut through to the core of the difficulty. As was seen when discussing standing, some nineteenth-century courts took the view that any person could have standing to seek prohibition on the dual hypotheses that for an inferior court to exceed its jurisdiction was an infringement of the royal prerogative (all courts deriving their authority from the Crown), and because to allow a patent defect to stand could establish a bad precedent.[57] Neither lateness of application nor triviality of sum was a bar since the essence of the action was not the vindication of a personal right, but of the royal prerogative. Logically this reasoning would admit no conception of waiver at all.

However, certain other cases reflect a different attitude, a willingness to accept the basic premises of the above argument and yet a desire to prevent an unworthy applicant from securing prohibition. A line was drawn or, as it might be more accurately put, etched. If the want of jurisdiction is patent, *i.e.* appears on the face of the proceedings, then acquiescence or waiver is irrelevant: the protection of the royal prerogative and preventing the establishment of a bad precedent hold supreme. Where, however, the defect is latent, not patent, and particularly where the defect lies within the knowledge of the applicant who neglects to bring it forward in the lower courts, then the court in its discretion could refuse to issue the writ or order. Here the fault or tardiness of the applicant is allowed to outweigh the public interest represented in the royal prerogative.[58] The distinction between patent and latent defects is overlaid by that between total and partial want of jurisdiction. Some cases are explained on the hypothesis that a total want of jurisdiction cannot be cured, but a partial one can.[59] It is by no means clear whether the pairings patent/latent and total/partial are treated as synonymous and it is clear that in principle they need not be. In any event, the leading authorities use the former terminology more consistently.

In addition to the above case law, authority exists from the area of natural justice to show that defects can be waived.[60]

What should the position be on principle? The basic proposition should be as stated at the outset of this section: a defect should not be curable by acquiescence or waiver, the rationale for this being that limits upon a tribunal, etc., are imposed for the public interest. An individual should not be able to extend that tribunal's jurisdiction by waiving limits to its

---

[57] *De Haber* v. *Queen of Portugal* (1851) 17 Q.B. 171; *Worthington* v. *Jeffries* (1875) L.R. 10 C.P. 379.

[58] *Mayor and Aldermen of City of London* v. *Cox* (1867) L.R. 2 H.L. 239; *Farquharson* v. *Morgan* [1894] 1 Q.B. 552; *R.* v. *Comptroller-General of Patents and Designs, ex p. Parke Davis* [1953] 2 W.L.R. 760.

[59] *Jones* v. *Owen* (1845) 5 D. & L. 669; *Moore* v. *Gamgee* (1890) 25 Q.B.D. 244.

[60] *R.* v. *Williams, ex p. Phillips* [1914] 1 K.B. 608, 613-614; *R.* v. *Comptroller-General of Patents and Designs, ex p. Parke Davis* [1953] 2 W.L.R. 760. See pp. 468-469.

authority. In this sense the *ultra vires* principle holds supreme and a void act cannot be validated by the individual. The defect itself cannot be cured.

However, unmitigated application of this general rule would lead to harsh results. The mendacious or crafty could, knowing of a defect, seemingly acquiesce in it in the hope of gaining a profit of some type and then, if it did not eventuate, seek a prerogative order. One's sense of justice is liable to be touched in such instances if the general rule were to be applied remorselessly. Surely a way to vindicate the *ultra vires* principle, and yet not to allow the above scenario, would be to state that in principle the action of the public body was *ultra vires*, but that the waiver or acquiescence will affect the discretion to grant a remedy. This is, in effect, what was happening in the leading nineteenth-century authorities. The precise dividing line as to when the courts would accord primacy to the *ultra vires* principle, and when they would feel that the individual should be rapped over the knuckles, may not be identical in the twentieth century, but the essence of the approach should be the same: the actions of the individual place a remedy out of his or her reach, rather than curing the defect itself.[61] Waiver, in this sense of precluding a remedy rather than curing the defect, should in principle be possible whatever the type of defect. Clearly, however, the importance of the *ultra vires* activity, the knowledge of the defect possessed by the applicant, and the extent to which the defect is personal to the applicant or could have wider ramifications, will be relevant factors to be taken into account.

(b) Delay

An applicant may also be denied relief because of undue delay in seeking relief. The relevant rules will be considered in the light of the new procedure for remedies.[62]

(2) ALTERNATIVE REMEDIES

Whether the existence of an alternative remedy precludes the application of any of the prerogative orders will be considered within a separate section.[63]

5. *The Effect of an Award of Certiorari*

When certiorari is issued it will serve to quash the offending decision and render it retrospectively null. The meaning of retrospective nullity has been considered above.[64]

---

[61] *Cf.* de Smith, *Judicial Review of Administrative Action* (4th ed., 1980), pp. 422-423 suggests that the nineteenth-century authorities talk in terms of curing the defect itself. In the leading authorities the only evidence of this is the way in which Davey L.J. in *Farquharson v. Morgan* [1894] 1 Q.B. 552, 563 distinguishes *Jones v. James* (1850) 19 L.J.Q.B. 257. See also, *R. v. Knightsbridge Crown Court, ex p. International Sporting Club (London) Ltd.* [1982] Q.B. 304; *cf. R. v. Knightsbridge Crown Court, ex p. Marcrest Properties Ltd.* [1983] 1 W.L.R. 300.

[62] See below, pp. 585-586.

[63] See below, pp. 597-599.

[64] See above, Chap. 12.

The reviewing courts now possess a further useful power. In circumstances where there are grounds for quashing the decision the court can remit the case to the original decision-maker with a direction to reconsider the matter and reach a decision in accord with the judgment of the court.[65] Thus instead of merely quashing the original decision and leaving the applicant to make a fresh application, the court can now, for example, quash the refusal to grant a benefit to the applicant, and remit the matter for reconsideration by the decision-maker in the light of the court's judgment.

Section 2. Mandamus

1. *Introduction*

The early history of the writ of mandamus is by no means clear. Commands from the King were, as de Smith points out, a common feature amongst the early writs, but he proceeds to show that it is doubtful whether any real connection existed between these early writs and what we now know as mandamus.[66] The seminal case for the emergence of the writ is *Bagg's Case*[67] and few legal rules can be said to have had so colourful a birth. Bagg was a chief burgess of Plymouth who had been removed from office for unseemly conduct, consisting *inter alia* of calling the mayor "a cozening knave", threatening to make his "neck crack" as well as other offensive gestures. Despite this behaviour a mandamus was issued against Plymouth because Bagg had been disenfranchised without a hearing. Similar cases of deprivation of office or position were to follow.[68] It was however Lord Mansfield who fully exploited the potential in mandamus stating that,[69]

> "It was introduced to prevent disorder from a failure of justice, and defect of police. Therefore it ought to be used upon all occasions where the law established no specific remedy, and where in justice and good government there ought to be one."

From these beginnings a vast body of jurisprudence developed which compelled Tapping[70] to undertake the herculean task of categorising the case law by subject-matter. A glance through the treatise reveals the diversity of this subject-matter, including Abbots and Yeoman. The reform of local government in the nineteenth century diminished the need for mandamus, as did the gradual disappearance of the freehold office, the

---

[65] Supreme Court Act 1981, s.31(5); Order 53, r.9(4).
[66] de Smith, *Judicial Review of Administrative Action* (4th ed., 1980), App. I, pp. 591–592; Henderson, *Foundations of English Administrative Law* (1963), pp. 45–65.
[67] (1615) 11 Co.Rep. 93b.
[68] *e.g. R. v. Chancellor of the University of Cambridge* (1723) 1 Str. 557.
[69] *R. v. Barker* (1762) 3 Burr. 1265, 1267. See also, *R. v. Askew* (1768) 4 Burr. 2186.
[70] Tapping, *The Law and Practice of the High Prerogative Writ of Mandamus, as it obtains both in England and Ireland* (1848).

existence of which had provided the factual basis for the early important mandamus decisions. This diminution in the need for mandamus was also a result of the extension of alternative remedies such as appeal.

2. *The Ambit of Mandamus*

(1) TYPE OF DUTY

For mandamus to lie there must be a public duty owed to the applicant. This involves two distinct requirements.

First, the duty must be of a public as opposed to a private character. The remedy was therefore held to be inappropriate when requested against a private arbitral tribunal, and when sought in relation to reinstatement in a trade union.[71] Whether these duties would still be characterised as private as opposed to public is now more questionable. Provided that the duty is public, it may flow from statute, prerogative, common law, charter, custom, or even contract.[72]

Secondly, even if the duty is of a public character it must be a duty owed to this individual or type of individual. In *R. v. Secretary of State for War*[73] an officer sought mandamus to compel the Secretary of State to upgrade the amount of compensation which he had received upon his retirement. He failed. The duty incumbent upon the Secretary of State was held to be owed to the Crown alone. This clearly need not be so, as was admitted in the case itself. Whether it is or not will be a matter of construction. In the modern day the general rule of construction will be that duties which are imposed upon ministers are owed to the public, or a section thereof, rather than to the Crown alone.

A different type of situation in which the courts might decline mandamus is where, although the duty is of a public character, its terms are so open textured as to indicate that the statute is not enforceable by individuals at all. The courts might reach this conclusion by saying that the issue is not justiciable. It is, however, more likely that the courts will retain control in principle. They will assert that mandamus could issue, but will find that on the facts of the case there is no cause. This approach will be considered in more detail in the following section.

(2) TYPE OF DEFECT

Mandamus will issue where the tribunal has made a jurisdictional error, and has thereby declined to exercise a power which it ought to have exercised.

---

[71] *R. v. Industrial Court, ex p. ASSET* [1965] 1 Q.B. 377. See however, *Imperial Metal Industries (Kynoch) Ltd. v. AUEW (Technical, Administrative and Supervisory Section)* [1979] I.C.R. 23, 33 where the court approved of the principle but disapproved of its application in the *ASSET* case; *Armstrong v. Kane* [1964] N.Z.L.R. 369.

[72] *ex p. Napier* (1852) 18 Q.B. 692, 695; *R. v. Secretary of State for War* [1891] 2 Q.B. 326, 335; *R. v. Criminal Injuries Compensation Board, ex p. Clowes* [1977] 1 W.L.R. 1353. *cf. ex p. Mann* (1916) 32 T.L.R. 479.

[73] [1891] 2 Q.B. 326; *ex p. Napier* (1852) 18 Q.B. 692.

Older cases have tended to distinguish between two situations: those in which the tribunal reached an erroneous decision on the merits, and those in which it refused to consider the merits at all, because it felt that they were outside its power. Mandamus would issue in the latter, but not in the former situation.

This traditional approach to mandamus is of questionable validity in the present day. The case law which drew this distinction was based upon the narrow commencement theory of jurisdiction, under which very few defects would be categorised as jurisdictional. The necessary corollary was that no remedy would be available. For example in *R. v. Dayman*[74] the applicant claimed that expenses he had incurred for paving a new street had not been met. The magistrate decided after hearing the parties that the street was not a new street, and the applicant sought mandamus. His application failed. The magistrate had, said the court, heard and determined the matter. That was all that was required of him. It was irrelevant that the court might believe that his view of "new street" was mistaken. The expansion in the concept of jurisdictional error considered above[75] would be likely to produce a different result. The reviewing court would reassess for itself the meaning of "new street", the magistrate would be held to have made a jurisdictional error, and mandamus would issue.

Mandamus can also be used to correct a mistaken exercise of discretion. Thus, the remedy is available if a decision is reached on the basis of irrelevant considerations or improper purposes,[76] if a pre-determined policy is applied too rigidly,[77] if the wrong question is answered,[78] if the body has not properly considered whether to exercise its discretion[79] or for other misuses of power.[80] Where, however, the duties are broadly framed and involve competing claims upon limited resources the court is less likely to find any *ultra vires* behaviour or, even if it does, it may in its discretion refuse the remedy.[81]

(3) DEMAND AND REFUSAL

The traditional approach was that before seeking mandamus the applicant must have conveyed a specific demand to the respondent that the latter perform the duty in question. In exceptional circumstances this requirement could be dispensed with.[82] It is doubtful whether this formalistic requirement

---

[74] (1857) 7 El. & Bl. 672, 676, 677, 679; *R. v. Cheshire JJ., ex p. Heaver* (1913) 108 L.T 374.
[75] See above, Chap. 10.
[76] *R. v. Birmingham Licensing Planning Committee, ex p. Kennedy* [1972] 2 Q.B. 140.
[77] *R. v. Port of London Authority, ex p. Kynoch Ltd.* [1919] 1 K.B. 176.
[78] *Board of Education v. Rice* [1911] A.C. 179.
[79] *R. v. Tower Hamlets London Borough Council, ex p. Chetnik Developments* [1988] A.C. 858.
[80] *Padfield v. Minister of Agriculture, Fisheries and Food* [1968] A.C. 997.
[81] *e.g. R. v. Commissioner of Police of the Metropolis, ex p. Blackburn* [1968] 2 Q.B. 118, 136, 148-149; *R. v. Commissioner of Police of the Metropolis, ex p. Blackburn (No. 3)* [1973] Q.B. 241, 254; *R. v. Bristol Corporation, ex p. Hendy* [1974] 1 W.L.R. 498; *R. v. Kensington and Chelsea (Royal) London Borough Council, ex p. Birdwood* (1976) 74 L.G.R. 424.
[82] For more detail on this see de Smith, *Judicial Review of Administrative Action* (4th ed., 1980), pp. 556-557.

will be insisted upon in the modern day, as it may be unrealistic in most instances to expect an individual to make a formal demand that the duty should be performed.

3. *Limits on the Availability of Mandamus*

(1) GENERAL

Even if the requirements set out above have been met, it is generally accepted that mandamus is a discretionary remedy.[83]

A variety of factors have influenced the court in deciding how the discretion should be exercised. The need for constant supervision has been one factor taken into account in refusing the award of the order,[84] as has been the willingness of the public body to comply voluntarily.[85] Public inconvenience or chaos has received varying treatment, some courts viewing this as an improper consideration in deciding whether to issue the order,[86] others taking more account of it.[87]

The applicant's motives will normally not be relevant in deciding whether an order should be issued. However, in some instances the courts have stated that a particular statutory provision can only be enforced by one who is advancing the general interests of the community, as opposed to his or her own private concerns.[88]

The court will not normally order a respondent to undertake the impossible,[89] nor will it make orders which cannot be fulfilled for other practical or legal reasons.[90] Moreover, as has already been seen, if a public body has a wide discretion and limited resources this will enter into the court's decision as to whether a remedy should be given.[91]

---

[83] e.g. R. v. *Churchwardens of All Saints Wigan* (1876) 1 App.Cas. 611, 620; *Chief Constable of the North Wales Police* v. *Evans* [1982] 1 W.L.R. 1155.

[84] R. v. *Peak Park Joint Planning Board, ex p. Jackson* (1976) 74 L.G.R. 376, 380; *Chief Constable of the North Wales Police* v. *Evans* [1982] 1 W.L.R. 1155.

[85] R. v. *Northumberland Compensation Appeal Tribunal, ex p. Shaw* [1952] 1 K.B. 338, 357; *Peak* (1976) 74 L.G.R. 376.

[86] e.g. R. v. *Kerrier District Council, ex p. Guppys (Bridport) Ltd.* (1976) 32 P. & C.R. 411, 418.

[87] e.g. R. v. *Paddington Valuation Officer, ex p. Peachey Property Corporation Ltd.* [1966] 1 Q.B. 380, 402, 416, but cf. p. 419, per Salmon L.J.

[88] R. v. *Mayor of Peterborough* (1875) 44 L.J.Q.B. 85; R. v. *Hampstead Borough Council, ex p. Woodward* (1917) 116 L.T. 213.

[89] Re *Bristol and North Somerset Railway Co.* (1877) 3 Q.B.D. 10, 12; cf. R. v. *Birmingham and Gloucester Ry.* (1841) 2 Q.B. 47.

[90] R. v. *Pembrokeshire JJ.* (1831) 2 B. & Ad. 391; R. v. *National Dock Labour Board, ex p. National Amalgamated Stevedores and Dockers* [1964] 2 Lloyd's L.R. 420, 429; *Evans* [1982] 1 W.L.R. 1155.

[91] e.g. R. v. *Bristol Corporation, ex p. Hendy* [1974] 1 W.L.R. 498, 503; R. v. *Inner London Education Authority, ex p. Ali* [1990] C.O.D. 317; R. v. *Lancashire County Council, ex p. Guyer* [1980] 1 W.L.R. 1024.

(2) ALTERNATIVE REMEDIES

The relevance of an alternative remedy for the grant of mandamus will be considered below.[92]

Section 3. Declaration

1. *Introduction*

The introduction and development of declaration in English law provides an interesting history largely because the main catalysts in its early development were not the courts themselves. Indeed, it might well be said that, with some exceptions, declaration flowered despite opposition from the judiciary.

Declaratory judgments, as opposed to purely declaratory orders, appear to be a relatively novel development.[93] A wealth of dicta can be found in the mid-nineteenth century asserting that the courts should not give a declaration of rights *per se*.[94] Moreover, as de Smith observes,[95] Lord Brougham's campaign advocating the introduction of the declaration only makes sense against such a background. Certain limited exceptions existed in which the courts could grant some declaratory relief.[96] There was, however, judicial reluctance to make use of declaratory relief and this is nowhere more clearly manifested than in the courts' treatment of the Court of Chancery Procedure Act 1852, section 50. This stated that no suit should be open to objection on the ground that a merely declaratory decree or order was being claimed, and that the courts could make binding declarations of right without granting consequential relief. The possibilities inherent within this legislation were largely nullified by judicial interpretation: declaratory relief was held to be available unaccompanied by any consequential relief, but only in those instances in which the plaintiff would have been entitled to other relief if it had been sought.[97]

In 1883, consequent upon powers conferred by the Judicature Acts, the Rule Committee passed Order 25, rule 5. This repeated the substance of the 1852 legislation with the important alteration that a declaration could be made whether any consequential relief "is or could be claimed, or not".

---

[92] See below, pp. 597-599.

[93] See, generally, Zamir and Woolf, *The Declaratory Judgment* (2nd ed., 1993).

[94] *e.g. Elliotson* v. *Knowles* (1842) 11 L.J. Ch. 399, 400; *Clough* v. *Ratcliffe* (1847) 1 De G. and S. 164, 178-179; *Barraclough* v. *Brown* [1897] A.C. 615, 623.

[95] *Judicial Review of Administrative Action* (4th ed., 1980), p. 477.

[96] *e.g.* the practice of the old Court of Exchequer which awarded relief against the Crown. The latter was represented by the Attorney-General and the power to grant the relief had its origins in the Crown Debts Act 1541. Its relevance here is that the judgments were normally declaratory in form. It is unclear whether this jurisdiction passed to the Court of Chancery, but in any event the jurisdiction does not seem to have been exercised after 1841; it was rediscovered in *Dyson* v. *Att.-Gen.* [1911] 1 K.B. 410.

[97] *Jackson* v. *Turnley* (1853) 1 Dr. 617, 628.

This was intended to circumvent the restrictive interpretation given to the legislation of 1852, but it was to be nearly 30 years before the courts were to exploit this new potential fully.

The occasion for the breakthrough came in *Dyson* v. *Attorney-General*.[98] Dyson was served with a notice by the Inland Revenue Commissioners which required him to supply certain particulars under pain of a penalty if he did not comply. Dyson refused. He sought declarations that the demand was unauthorised and was *ultra vires* the Finance Act. For authority he relied both upon Order 25, rule 5, and upon the Exchequer precedents prior to 1842. The Court of Appeal accepted that his method of proceeding was a proper one. The importance of the case lies in the fact that the court not only upheld this method of proceeding, but regarded it as a convenient and beneficial way through which to test the legality of government action. Moreover, the availability of collateral attack, of declining to furnish the particulars, being sued for the penalty, and raising the invalidity of the demand by way of defence, was not regarded as a bar to the more direct approach of the declaration. Whether any form of consequential relief would have been available in such a case is questionable.[99] Despite certain infelicities in the court's reasoning,[100] the *Dyson* case represented a landmark in the development of the declaration.[101]

2. *The Scope of Declaration*

(1) THE BROAD REACH OF DECLARATION

The period following the *Dyson* case was still characterised by judicial restraint. Statements are to be found that the declaration should be used with caution or sparingly.[102] However, as time progressed the courts became more used to the remedy and more aware of its flexibility, especially when contrasted with the limitations surrounding the prerogative orders. Judicial statements appeared which countenanced the broad spectrum of the declaration and the freedom from constraint provided by the "new" remedy.[103]

---

[98] [1911] 1 K.B. 410. See also, [1912] 1 Ch. 159.

[99] In *Gouriet* v. *Union of Post Office Workers* [1978] A.C. 435, 502, Lord Diplock stated that if Dyson had paid the penalty he could have recovered it in an action for money had and received. It is in fact unclear whether this restitutionary claim would have succeeded, Craig, "Compensation in Public Law" (1980) 96 L.Q.R. 413. But see now, pp. 638-642.

[100] The court mistakenly assumed that Exchequer precedents were equally relevant in the Court of Chancery and did not avert to the question of whether Ord. 25, r. 5 bound the Crown.

[101] In *Guaranty Trust Co. of New York* v. *Hannay and Co.* [1915] 2 K.B. 536, the court rejected the argument that Ord. 25, r. 5 was itself *ultra vires*.

[102] e.g. *Smeeton* v. *Att.-Gen.* [1920] 1 Ch. 85, 97; *Russian Commercial and Industrial Bank* v. *British Bank of Foreign Trade Ltd.* [1921] 2 A.C. 438, 445.

[103] e.g. *Pyx Granite Co. Ltd.* v. *Ministry of Housing and Local Government* [1958] 1 Q.B. 554, 571; *Ibeneweka* v. *Egbuna* [1964] 1 W.L.R. 219, 224.

No finite list of areas to which the declaration applies can be provided. All that can be done is to indicate the broad context within which the remedy operates. It should be made clear at the outset that the declaration can operate both as an original remedy, and as one which is supervisory. In the former instance a court will be declaring what rights the parties have, for example, under a contract or over land. In the latter case, the remedy will be controlling acts or decisions made by other bodies, such as declaring the attachment of certain planning conditions to be invalid. Indeed this duality of role is one of the strengths of the declaration. It allows a court to declare invalid certain action by a public body (the supervisory role) and then, if appropriate, to pronounce on the rights which the parties actually have (the original role).

The types of subject-matter to which the declaration has applied include administrative decisions or orders,[104] and subordinate legislation.[105] Rights to pursue a trade[106] and issues of status[107] are also subject to the declaration. In addition, the scope of a person's financial obligations is subject to the declaratory procedure,[108] as are questions relating to the scope of obligations imposed upon a public body,[109] and the construction of contracts with public authorities.[110]

The reforms of the administrative law remedies introduced in 1977 allow the declaration to be obtained as one of the more particular remedies to be sought in an application for judicial review. These reforms will be considered in detail in the following chapter. One matter should, however, be addressed at this stage. It is now clear that a declaration can be sought as part of the public law procedures even if one of the prerogative orders was not available in the circumstances. Thus a declaration can be granted to the effect that UK primary legislation is in breach of Community law, even though the prerogative orders would not issue in such a case.[111]

(2) TYPES OF DEFECT

While the subject-matter covered by the declaration is therefore broad, the type of defects which it will operate against remain questionable. It is clearly available against jurisdictional defects, but it was doubtful whether

---

[104] e.g. Hall & Co. Ltd. v. Shoreham-by-Sea Urban District Council [1964] 1 W.L.R. 240; Congreve v. Home Office [1976] Q.B. 629.

[105] e.g. Nicholls v. Tavistock Urban District Council [1923] 2 Ch. 18; Brownsea Haven Properties Ltd. v. Poole Corporation [1958] Ch. 574. cf. the criticism of London Association of Shipowners and Brokers v. London and India Docks Joint Committee [1892] 3 Ch. 242 in Gouriet v. Union of Post Office Workers [1978] A.C. 435, 480, 493.

[106] e.g. Eastham v. Newcastle United Football Club Ltd. [1964] Ch. 413; Nagle v. Feilden [1966] 2 Q.B. 633; Bucknell & Son Ltd. v. Croydon London Borough Council [1973] 1 W.L.R. 534; Racal Communications Ltd. v. Pay Board [1974] 1 W.L.R. 1149.

[107] e.g. Sadler v. Sheffield Corporation [1924] 1 Ch. 483; Ridge v. Baldwin [1964] A.C. 40.

[108] e.g. Nyali v. Att.-Gen. [1957] A.C. 253;

[109] e.g. Att.-Gen. v. St. Ives Rural District Council [1961] 1 Q.B. 366.

[110] e.g. Staffordshire Area Health Authority v. South Staffordshire Waterworks Co. [1978] 1 W.L.R. 1387. For more detail on the types of subject-matter covered by the declaration see Zamir and Woolf, The Declaratory Judgment (2nd ed., 1993).

[111] R. v. Secretary of State for Employment, ex p. Equal Opportunities Commission [1994] 1 All E.R. 910, 919-920, 925, 927-928.

it would issue to control an error of law on the face of the record. The rationale for this limitation was that such an error only rendered the decision of the tribunal voidable and not void. The original decision would stand and therefore if the plaintiff were to seek a declaration of her rights she would be faced with the problem that the tribunal had already determined what those rights were, and that the court could not assume an appellate jurisdiction for itself to make a second decision different from the one still extant made by the tribunal. Such a declaration would be of no effect unless the tribunal had power to rescind its original finding, or unless the declaration prevented the tribunal from acting on the decision.[112]

It is doubtful whether this reasoning is correct in its own terms,[113] but in any event the courts have now rendered the concept of error of law within jurisdiction redundant and the problem outlined above is, therefore, no longer a real one. The defect would in future be regarded as jurisdictional.

3. *Limits on the Availability of Declaration*

(1) EXCLUSION OF ORIGINAL JURISDICTION

As stated above, the declaration may be used in both an original and a supervisory role. Both of these roles may, however, be excluded.

The possibility of the original jurisdiction being excluded operates in the following manner. Parliament will often assign a certain topic to a particular tribunal, minister or other public authority. When it does so the question arises as to whether an individual can nevertheless have the same matter adjudicated upon by the High Court in the exercise of its original jurisdiction to grant a declaration. If the determination made by the tribunal is *ultra vires* for some reason then this will of course be subject to the court's supervisory jurisdiction (subject to any possible exclusion of this role). But the question posed above must be answered first: will the grant of power to a designated public body exclude the original jurisdiction of the court?

In answering this question two principles have to be reconciled. One is the presumption that when the legislature has created new rights and obligations and has empowered a specific tribunal to adjudicate upon them then recourse must be had to that body. The other principle is the courts' dislike of anything which takes away their jurisdiction. The outcome of particular cases has depended upon which of these principles has been accorded greater weight.

A number of cases can be cited which have held that the jurisdiction of the High Court has been excluded, one of the best known of which is *Barraclough* v. *Brown*.[114] The plaintiff was empowered to remove boats

---

[112] *Punton* v. *Ministry of Pensions and National Insurance* [1963] 1 W.L.R. 186; *Punton* v. *Ministry of Pensions and National Insurance (No. 2)* [1964] 1 W.L.R. 226.
[113] Cane, "A Fresh Look at Punton's Case" (1980) 43 M.L.R. 266.
[114] [1897] A.C 615.

which had sunk in a river if the owner did not do so. Expenses of the operation were recoverable from the owner in a court of summary jurisdiction. The plaintiff sought a declaration in the High Court that he was thus entitled to these expenses. His action failed despite the permissible words of the statute. The plaintiff could not at one and the same time claim to recover by virtue of the statute and insist on doing so by means other than those prescribed by that statute.[115] Other authorities have reached the same conclusion, holding that exclusive jurisdiction resided in a minister or some other type of public body.[116]

There are, however, cases which deny exclusive jurisdiction to the appointed public body, one of the best known of which is the *Pyx Granite* case.[117] The plaintiffs carried on the business of quarrying and claimed that they should be able to pursue this without recourse to planning permission.[118] This was denied by the defendants, who further argued that under the relevant legislation there was a specified procedure for determining whether planning permission was required or not,[119] which procedure was exclusive and prevented an application for a declaration. The House of Lords distinguished the *Barraclough* decision. Whereas in that case the statute had created new rights to be recovered by a certain procedure, in the *Pyx* case the plaintiff was simply relying on his own common law rights, the only question being how far they had been removed.[120]

The distinction drawn between common law and statutory rights is questionable both in its application to the facts of the case[121] and on principle. Whether an original jurisdiction granted to a public body should be taken to be exclusive or not should be determined by a consideration of the entire subject-matter and not by whether the rights owe their derivation to common law or statute. The ability to sidestep the enacted procedure should be dependent upon the type of procedure and its suitability for resolving the kind of question being postulated. If there is little dispute as to the facts, and a point of general legal importance is at stake, then a declaration may well be more appropriate.[122]

---

[115] Ibid. pp. 619-620.

[116] *Baron Reitzes de Marienwert* v. *Administrator of Austrian Property* [1924] 2 Ch. 282; *Wilkinson* v. *Barking Corporation* [1948] 1 K.B. 721; *Gillingham Corporation* v. *Kent County Council* [1953] Ch. 37; *Healey* v. *Minister of Health* [1955] 1 Q.B. 221; *Square Meals Frozen Foods Ltd.* v. *Dunstable Corporation* [1974] 1 W.L.R. 59.

[117] *Pyx Granite Co. Ltd.* v. *Ministry of Housing and Local Government* [1958] 1. Q.B. 554, [1960] A.C. 260.

[118] The reason being that they claimed entitlement to do so under a private Act of Parliament, and further argued that such statutes were exempt from the requirement of planning permission.

[119] Town and Country Planning Act 1947, s.17(1).

[120] [1960] A.C. 260, 286-287, 290, 302, 304.

[121] Borrie, Note [1960] P.L. 14-17.

[122] These factors did influence the court in the *Pyx Granite* case [1960] A.C. 260. See also, *Ealing London Borough Council* v. *Race Relations Board* [1972] A.C. 342.

(2) EXCLUSION OF SUPERVISORY JURISDICTION

Whether the supervisory jurisdiction of the High Court has been excluded will be considered as a separate topic.[123] The difference between exclusion of original and supervisory jurisdiction is brought out lucidly in *Fullbrook v. Berkshire Magistrates' Courts Committee*.[124] Section 35 of the Local Government Superannuation Act 1937 provided that any question concerning the rights and liabilities of an employee should be determined initially by the local authority and then, if the employee was dissatisfied, by the minister whose decision would be final. The plaintiff was deprived of his superannuation benefits. He challenged this by a declaration claiming that he had been denied a hearing. The defendants relied on section 35 and on analogous cases mentioned in the previous section which had interpreted similar provisions as vesting exclusive jurisdiction in the original decision-makers. This argument failed. While section 35 might well exclude the original jurisdiction to grant a declaration, the essence of the plaintiff's claim was the invocation of the supervisory jurisdiction of the courts, a power to declare void action which was *ultra vires*. This survived and could not be abrogated by the finality clause within section 35.

(3) HYPOTHETICAL QUESTIONS: RIPENESS AND MOOTNESS

Declaration by its nature offers a greater possibility of raising hypothetical questions than do the other remedies.[125] The problems surrounding such declarations are closely linked with those concerning future rights, and to questions of how far utility should play a role in deciding whether the remedy should be granted. Some of the cases within this section involve public authorities, others do not. Even the latter are however instructive. As will be argued later, questions of ripeness and mootness are integral to a rational system of remedies. Some examples drawn from private disputes are useful in examining how such concepts could operate.

Our courts have long set themselves against deciding hypothetical questions. A number of reasons have contributed to this, one of which is historical. The dislike of such hypothetical, abstract or academic questions stems from the close association between them and advisory opinions. Such opinions were once commonly asked for and given but, like much else, this practice was abused by the Stuarts. Since the judges could be dismissed by the Crown, the responses to these royal interrogatives were not always accompanied by Olympian detachment on the part of the judiciary. A recognition of judicial independence from the executive had yet to be accepted. Even in the rather different climate of the twentieth century reversion to the practice of giving advisory opinions has raised strong passions. Thus, the proposed inclusion of such a power in the Rating and Valuation Bill 1928, hardly the most explosive piece of legislation, was attacked as redolent of the power wielded by the Stuart monarchs.[126]

---

[123] See Chap. 16.
[124] (1970) 69 L.G.R. 75.
[125] See generally on hypothetical questions, Jaconelli, "Hypothetical Disputes, Moot Points of Law and Advisory Opinions" (1985) 101 L.Q.R. 587.
[126] Lord Hewart, *The New Despotism* (1929), p. 119.

A number of other reasons have at one time or another been advanced as to why hypothetical questions should not be answered. There is the endemic fear of a flood of litigation,[127] and the worry that a court, having given its opinion on an abstract matter, might be embarrassed when the case came up again in a more concrete form. More realistic than either of the two preceding arguments is that the parties most primarily interested in the dispute might not be before the court to argue the matter, placing the court in the invidious position of having to make a decision when it has not heard full argument from all sides.[128] The dislike of abstract determinations has been fuelled by the fact that if the event upon which the litigation rests never comes to fruition the judicial time and energy expended upon it will have been wasted. Even if the event does materialise the facts may have altered somewhat, thereby casting doubt upon the probative value of anything said in the earlier judgment. If advice on obscure or difficult points is required then provision already exists within the Judicial Committee Act 1833, section 4 of which empowers the Crown to seek legal advice from the Privy Council.

There is little doubt that some of the above reasons have some cogency, in particular those concerned with interest representation, wastage of judicial resources, and alteration of the facts after the advisory opinion has been given. To be counter-balanced against these is the important argument that a legal system should enable people to operate their lives with as much certainty as is feasible. We all make decisions for the future, and what those decisions are will more and more be influenced by the legal rights and obligations which are entailed. If the concept of abstract or hypothetical question is drawn too broadly it will prevent this function of a legal system from being performed. Moreover, as Lord Woolf has noted, it may be advantageous for a public body to be able to obtain an anticipatory ruling particularly in circumstances where there is doubt as to the legality of its proposed course of action.[129]

The courts have treated as hypothetical, questions which either come too early and are thus unripe, or which come too late and are therefore moot. An example of the former is *Draper* v. *British Optical Association*.[130] The defendant association informed the plaintiff that they believed him to be in breach of their code of ethics and that a meeting would be held to determine whether his name should be removed from the list of members. In advance of this the plaintiff sought a declaration that the association could not enforce the code against him or remove him from the list of members. Farwell J. held the application premature; the association had not yet done anything to the plaintiff and the meeting had not yet been held. The court

---

[127] *Re Clay* [1919] 1 Ch. 66, 78-79.

[128] *Maerkle* v. *British Continental Fur Co. Ltd.* [1954] 1 W.L.R. 1242, 1248.

[129] *Protection of the Public – A New Challenge* (1990), p. 47; Zamir and Woolf, *The Declaratory Judgment* (2nd ed., 1993), pp. 298-299.

[130] [1938] 1 All E.R. 115. See also, *Re Carnavon Harbour Acts* [1937] Ch. 72; *Re Barnato* [1949] Ch. 258; *Lever Brothers & Unilever Ltd.* v. *Manchester Ship Canal Co.* (1945) 78 Ll.L.R. 507.

is more likely to take jurisdiction over a particular case when it feels that a legal decision will prevent possible disruptive action. In *Ruislip-Northwood Urban District Council v. Lee*[131] the plaintiff council asked for a declaration that the defendant's caravans were temporary buildings and thereby liable to be removed. The defendant argued, *inter alia*, that no dispute existed. In rejecting this argument the court was influenced by the possibility of a fight or riot if the local authority attempted to remove the caravans without having first clarified the legal position.

Disputes may also be held to be hypothetical when they come too late and are in this sense moot.[132] However, where the courts feel an important point of legal principle is involved they may proceed and give judgment even though the matter has ceased to have practical import for the parties.[133]

Closely allied to, but distinct from, the cases discussed in the last paragraph are those in which a declaration is refused because of the practical impossibility of its terms being fulfilled, or because the inconvenience caused by issuing the remedy would be great compared with the benefits to be obtained. *Coney v. Choyce*[134] provides an example of the latter. A school reorganisation scheme was challenged for failure to comply with minor requirements concerning the posting of notices. The court characterised the requirements as directory rather than mandatory, but it made clear that it would in any event have exercised its discretion to refuse relief. Granting the remedy would at most have postponed the whole scheme for a year.

(4) JUSTICIABILITY

Justiciability is a word not frequently used in our jurisprudence. To ask whether a dispute is justiciable or not is to ask whether the type of dispute is suitable for resolution by the judicial process, irrespective of who is bringing the action. Although the term itself appears relatively rarely in judicial dialogue, it underlies or has influenced a number of different decisions, some of which concern the declaration.

For example, in reaching the conclusion that broadly framed duties under the Education Act 1944 were to be enforced through the minister, the courts were clearly influenced by the difficulties of adjudicating upon such subject-matter. While the possibility of judicial intervention was not totally excluded, it was restricted to the more extreme and obvious forms of unlawful behaviour.[135] In more recent cases the courts appear

---

[131] (1931) 145 L.T. 208, 214, 215.
[132] *Everett v. Ryder* (1926) 135 L.T. 302. See also, *Whyte, Ridsdale & Co. Ltd. v. Att.-Gen.* [1927] 1 Ch. 548; *Harrison v. Croydon London Borough Council* [1968] Ch. 479; *Howard v. Pickford Tool Co.* [1951] K.B. 417.
[133] *Eastham v. Newcastle United Football Club Ltd.* [1964] Ch. 413; *West Ham Corporation v. Sharp* [1907] 1 K.B. 445.
[134] [1975] 1 W.L.R. 422, 436-437; *Maerkle v. British and Continental Fur Co. Ltd.* [1954] 1 W.L.R. 1242; *Att.-Gen. v. Colchester Corporation* [1955] 2 Q.B. 207.
[135] *Watt v. Kesteven County Council* [1955] 1 Q.B. 408; *Bradbury v. Enfield London Borough Council* [1967] 1 W.L.R. 1311; *Cumings v. Birkenhead Corporation* [1972] Ch. 12.

to be displaying a greater readiness to tackle such issues, but in both instances the judicial expression of willingness to intervene must be read against the background of the type of illegality being asserted.[136]

The nature of the subject-matter has influenced the courts in other areas, aside from education. The effect has been either to eschew judicial intervention totally or to intervene on narrower grounds given the broad discretion granted to the public body. Alleged breaches of duty by university examiners provide an example of the former,[137] and the provision of accommodation by a local authority an example of the latter.[138] Categorisation of treaties as giving rise to no legally enforceable obligations until they have been incorporated into municipal law has also been partially influenced by the concept of justiciability,[139] as was the related decision that no declaration will be granted to preclude the Crown from undertaking an international obligation.[140]

The area is which justiciability has been most explicitly recognised is that of tort actions against public authorities.[141] This is important not simply for the conceptual clarity which it produces, but also because failure to recognise the problem can lead to the misapplication of other legal tools.[142]

(5) ALTERNATIVE REMEDIES

The effect of alternative remedies upon the availability of the declaration will be considered in a later section.[143]

4. *The Impact of the Declaration*

The normal impact of a declaration is to render the decision which has been impugned retrospectively invalid or void *ab initio*. There may, however, be instances in which the impact of the court order is prospective rather than retrospective in its operation. The court may in effect refuse to grant relief

---

[136] In *Meade* v. *Haringey London Borough Council* [1979] 1 W.L.R. 637 the Court of Appeal was clearly strongly influenced by what it felt was closure of the schools for non-educational reasons. See also, *Thornton* v. *Kirklees Metropolitan Borough Council* [1979] 3 W.L.R. 1.

[137] *Thorne* v. *University of London* [1966] 2 Q.B. 237.

[138] *R.* v. *Bristol Corporation ex p. Hendy* [1974] 1 W.L.R. 498 (mandamus).

[139] *e.g. Buck* v. *Att.-Gen.* [1965] Ch. 745.

[140] *Blackburn* v. *Att.-Gen.* [1971] 1 W.L.R. 1037.

[141] *Anns* v. *Merton London Borough Council* [1978] A.C. 728; *Rowling* v. *Takaro Properties Ltd.* [1988] A.C. 473.

[142] *e.g.* in *Gouriet* [1978] A.C. 435 the House of Lords appeared worried about the suitability of the legal process for resolving the type of dispute before it. If this was the case, the issue should have been deemed non-justiciable, rather than seeking the same end by limiting *locus standi*.

[143] See below, pp. 597-599.

in the instant case, but nonetheless proceed to give a declaration on the general point of law which is at stake.[144] The reasons for employing this technique are similar to those which we have already encountered when discussing invalidity.[145] To render the contested decision retrospectively null may have a profound effect on that area of the administration, or may adversely effect the rights of third parties. The court may decide to refuse to give relief in the instant case,[146] or it may, while declining relief in the instant case, take the opportunity to clarify the law in that area.[147] The desirability of modifying the impact of the concept of retrospective nullity in this fashion, and the implications of doing so, have been considered in the earlier discussion of invalidity.

5. Practice and Procedure

Declarations are available either under Order 15, rule 16 (the successor to Order 25, rule 5) or via an application for judicial review under section 31 of the Supreme Court Act 1981. It has been stated that the normal avenue for public law cases should be section 31,[148] but there are a number of exceptions to this basic proposition. The problems that this produces will be examined later, as will the nature of the possible exceptions to the general rule. What follows is a brief description of the type of procedure under Order 15, rule 16.

The power to make declarations is available in any Division of the High Court before a single judge. Which division a case goes to will be a function of the subject-matter. One possible gap in the courts' jurisdiction was the inability to grant an interim declaration of rights. This was particularly important when claims were brought against the Crown since injunctive relief was not at that time available.[149]

Order 5, rule 4 has broadened the ability of plaintiffs to proceed by way of originating summons. This procedure is acceptable where the sole or main question is, or appears to be, one concerning the construction of an Act or an instrument made thereunder, or of any deed, will, contract, or other document, or another question of law, or cases in which a substantial dispute as to the facts is unlikely.

---

[144] Lewis, "Retrospective and Prospective Rulings in Administrative Law" [1988] P.L. 78; Sir Harry Woolf, *Protection of the Public – A New Challenge* (1990), pp. 53-54.
[145] See Chap. 12.
[146] *R.* v. *Monopolies and Mergers Commission, ex p. Argyll Group plc* [1986] 1 W.L.R. 763.
[147] As indicated by Lord Donaldson M.R. in the *Datafin* case [1987] Q.B. 815.
[148] *O'Reilly* v. *Mackman* [1983] 2 A.C. 237.
[149] *Underhill* v. *Ministry of Food* [1950] 1 All E.R. 591; *International General Electric Co. of New York Ltd.* v. *Customs and Excise Commissioners* [1962] Ch. 784; *R.* v. *Inland Revenue Commissioners, ex p. Rossminster Ltd.* [1980] A.C. 952; *Clarke* v. *Chadburn* [1985] 1 W.L.R. 78. For more detailed discussion of this issue see below, pp. 726-731.

Section 4. Injunction

1. *Introduction*

The injunction has for many years had an effect on subject-matter within public law.[150] Two of the most common areas were within the realms of public nuisance and the administration of charitable or public trusts. As de Smith points out,[151] the latter was of particular importance. The Attorney-General's intervention was founded upon the position of the Crown as *parens patriae*. This role existed not only for charities, infants, and those infirm in mind, but also included a visitatorial authority over those charitable (and ecclesiastical) corporations which lacked visitors of their own. Proceedings by the Attorney-General often arose out of defaults by such bodies in the performance of their functions and took the form of actions to ensure that they observed their duties. The general right of the Attorney-General to prevent *ultra vires* action grew out of a broad conception of the prerogative of protection.[152]

Despite the respectability of its historical lineage, the injunction has remained largely on the periphery of public law compared to the position in the United States where it has developed into an all purpose public law remedy. A variety of reasons have contributed towards this. The established presence of the prerogative orders as the main method of maintaining control over invalid public action has undoubtedly been a factor. More important is the fact that it has remained shackled by its own history. The criteria for individual standing were derived from those of public nuisance;[153] if these were not satisfied the Attorney-General had to bring the action. The reasoning underpinning these rules has already been criticised in the discussion of standing. Those rules were, however, reaffirmed in the *Gouriet*[154] case. Not only have they been upheld but the fetters binding the injunction have been tightened. Whereas the old rules from public nuisance could have been shed or liberalised, the reasoning behind their vindication in the *Gouriet* case renders this much less likely. Those rules were buttressed because they reflected a view of the role of the individual in public law: the citizen could not protect the public interest unless he or she was also settling a private dispute (or one in which he or she had a special interest). With this limitation placed upon the injunction it will be impossible for it to fulfil its potential within public law.

The main hope for the future lies in section 31 of the Supreme Court Act 1981, through which declarations and injunctions can be obtained if the subject-matter concerns public law. As the discussion of standing has shown,[155] the courts may be taking a more liberal attitude than that which

---

[150] Many of the cases brought against local authorities were injunction cases.
[151] de Smith, *Judicial Review of Administrative Action* (4th ed., 1980), pp. 432-433.
[152] *Ibid.* p. 433.
[153] *Boyce v. Paddington Borough Council* [1903] 1 Ch. 109.
[154] [1978] A.C. 435; *Barrs v. Bethell* [1982] Ch. 294.
[155] Chap. 13.

they have adopted at common law. The general rules concerning injunctions will be considered here; problems arising from the interpretation of section 31 will be considered later.

2. *The Scope of Injunctive Relief*

(1) THE TYPES OF INJUNCTION

Injunctions can be negative or positive, prohibiting certain action from being done or commanding the performance of certain action.

In addition, an injunction can be perpetual or interlocutory. The former is granted at the end of the action and conclusively determines the respective rights and liabilities of the parties. How long the injunction is awarded for will be dependent upon the type of dispute. Interlocutory injunctions are designed to preserve the *status quo* pending trial of the main action.[156] The plaintiff must show that there is some arguable point of law and that the balance of convenience indicates that relief should be granted pending trial of the main action.[157] It has, however, been held by Lord Goff that a public authority should not normally be restrained from enforcing an apparently valid law unless the court is satisfied that the challenge to the validity of the law is prima facie so firmly based as to justify "so exceptional a course being taken".[158] It remains to be seen whether this approach will also be used when the contested measure is an administrative decision as opposed to a law or some other form of legal instrument. It may be particularly difficult to assess the balance of convenience in public law cases precisely because the public body will be representing a wider public interest when it is making the decision which is being challenged. It is, therefore, unsurprising that the courts are likely to take into account the strength of the applicant's case in challenging the administrative act when deciding where the balance of convenience actually lies.[159] The party in whose favour the interim relief is granted will normally have to give an undertaking in damages lest he or she proves to be unsuccessful and the defendant suffers loss.

(2) AREAS WITHIN WHICH INJUNCTIONS WILL ISSUE

(a) General

Injunctions can be issued in a whole range of situations: to prevent a public body from committing what would be a private wrong such as a trespass[160]

---

[156] Interim injunctive relief is available in judicial review proceedings by virtue of Ord. 53, r. 3(10)(b).

[157] This is, in brief, the two stage test established by the House of Lords in *American Cyanamid Co. v. Ethicon Ltd.* [1975] A.C. 396; *R. v. Secretary of State for Transport, ex p. Factortame (No.2)* [1991] 1 A.C. 603. See generally, Martin, "Interlocutory Injunctions: *American Cyanamid* Comes of Age" (1993-94) King's Coll. L.J. 52.

[158] *Factortame (No.2)* [1991] 1 A.C. 603.

[159] *Loc. cit.*

[160] *e.g. Broadbent v. Rotherham Corporation* [1917] 2 Ch. 31.

or a nuisance;[161] to restrain a public body from acting unlawfully;[162] to restrain the implementation of an unlawful decision;[163] and to enforce public duties, provided that they are not too vague.[164]

The remedy can also be used by the Attorney-General who can seek an injunction to prevent a public body from acting *ultra vires*.[165] The Attorney-General has also used the injunction to prevent repeated breaches of the criminal law, or in circumstances where injury to the person is threatened.[166]

Two more specific uses of the injunction should be mentioned here.

(b) Injunctions and Parliament

Possible challenge to the legality of ordinary public statutes immediately enmeshes one in debates on sovereignty, and the efficacy or otherwise of rules requiring special majorities. This is not the place to consider this debate.[167] Even before a measure has received the Royal Assent it is dubious whether it could be successfully challenged in the courts.[168]

The courts have, however, asserted that, in principle, they would be willing to issue an injunction to prevent a breach of contract where that breach consists of a promise not to oppose a private bill. The key word in the above sentence is "principle", since the courts have in fact declined to intervene even in what appears to be a strong case. Thus in *Bilston Corporation* v. *Wolverhampton Corporation*[169] the latter had contracted with Bilston Corporation that it would not oppose any application to Parliament by Bilston whereby Bilston sought a local Act of Parliament for the securing of a water supply. Despite this promise and the fact that it had been enshrined in an earlier local Act, the court declined to issue the injunction, the reasoning being that Parliament should have the opportunity to hear the argument of both parties in order to decide whether Wolverhampton Corporation should be released from its obligations by statute.

Challenge to subordinate legislation is subject to different considerations. Once such legislation has been passed it is open to attack as being *ultra vires*, and a declaration or injunction can be granted to a plaintiff. If a person wishes to bring an action prior to the final enactment of the order

---

[161] e.g. *Pride of Derby and Derbyshire Angling Association Ltd.* v. *British Celanese Ltd.* [1953] Ch. 149.

[162] *Bradbury* v. *Enfield London Borough Council* [1967] 1 W.L.R. 1311.

[163] *R.* v. *North Yorkshire County Council, ex p. M* [1989] Q.B. 411.

[164] *R.* v. *Kensington and Chelsea London Borough Council, ex p. Hammell* [1989] Q.B. 518.

[165] e.g. *Att.-Gen.* v. *Manchester Corporation* [1906] 1 Ch. 643; *Att.-Gen.* v. *Fulham Corporation* [1921] 1 Ch. 440.

[166] *Att.-Gen.* v. *Smith* [1958] 2 Q.B. 173; *Att.-Gen.* v. *Chaudry* [1971] 1 W.L.R. 1614. For more detailed consideration of these authorities and for the qualifications imposed on them in *Gouriet* [1978] A.C. 435, see above, pp. 485-486.

[167] See generally, Craig, "Parliamentary Sovereignty after *Factortame*" (1991) 11 Y.B.E.L. 221.

[168] de Smith, *Judicial Review of Administrative Action* (4th ed., 1980), pp. 465-466.

[169] [1942] Ch. 391. *cf. Att.-Gen.* v. *London and Home Counties Joint Electricity Authority* [1929] 1 Ch. 513, in which it was accepted that the Attorney-General could have an injunction to prevent unauthorised expenditure of corporate funds to promote a bill.

the issue is more problematic. The prerogative orders do not it seems run against legislative proceedings, although as noted above the position in this respect appears to be changing. An injunction will not issue against Her Majesty in Council, nor it seems against a minister of the Crown who is making a statutory instrument. A declaration might be possible if an appropriate defendant could be found. Where an order has been laid before Parliament, and has been approved by both Houses of Parliament, the courts are likely to feel reluctant to intervene.[170]

Even where the legislative process is not involved, the courts will not award an injunction where to do so would be an interference with the right of the House to regulate its own internal proceedings.[171]

The position with respect to Community law and the legislative process is, however, different. We have already seen that our courts have accepted that Community law must take supremacy in the event of a clash between it and domestic law. This was the essence of the holding in *Factortame (No.2)*.[172] In that case the House of Lords held that an interim injunction could be granted under section 37 of the Supreme Court Act 1981 preventing the enforcement of the domestic legislation, pending the final resolution of the disputed matter before the ECJ itself. It remains to be seen what attitude the courts would adopt if it were to be alleged that the domestic legislature were about to enact legislation which was felt to be in breach of Community law. It is clear that, as a matter of Community law, our Parliament is under an obligation not to pass legislation which is contrary to our Community obligations. However, it is likely that our courts would require strong evidence before accepting that such domestic legislation which was about to be enacted was in breach of Community law. If such evidence were forthcoming then it is not inconceivable that an interim injunction could be issued pending the final resolution of the substantive issue by the ECJ. In the event that the ECJ found that the proposed legislation was contrary to Community law then a final order could be addressed to the relevant minister. This could be in the form of prohibition, or it now seems in the form of an injunction.[173]

(c) Injunctions and public offices

An information in the nature of *quo warranto* was, until 1938, the procedure by which challenges to the usurpation of a public office were made. In 1938 the information in the nature of *quo warranto* was abolished and replaced by the injunction.[174] The substance of the action however remained the same, with the old rules still governing; only the form of the remedy was altered.

---

[170] *Harper* v. *Home Secretary* [1955] Ch. 238; *Nottinghamshire County Council* v. *Secretary of State for the Environment* [1986] A.C. 240. See, however, *Hoffmann-La Roche & Co. A.G.* v. *Secretary of State for Trade and Industry* [1975] A.C. 295.

[171] *Bradlaugh* v. *Gossett* (1884) 12 Q.B.D. 271.

[172] [1991] 1 A.C. 603; *R.* v. *H.M. Treasury, ex p. British Telecommunications plc* [1994] 1 C.M.L.R. 621.

[173] See below, pp. 726–732.

[174] Administration of Justice (Miscellaneous Provisions) Act 1938, s.9. See now, Supreme Court Act 1981, s.30.

Thus, the office must be public in character, and the usurper must have actually acted in pursuance of it; a claim *per se* was insufficient. The office itself had to be not only public but "substantive", as distinct from mere employment at the will of others. Standing to secure the remedy was broadly construed[175] but acquiescence or undue delay would operate to defeat the plaintiff.

Specific statutory provisions govern challenges to particular types of office.[176]

3. *Limits to Injunctive Relief*

(1) GENERAL

The injunction is an equitable remedy and equitable principles will influence the way in which it is applied by the courts. Undue delay or acquiescence will bar the plaintiff. The adequacy of a monetary remedy will also influence the court.

Considerations of practicality have been treated differently by the courts. They will not, on the one hand, order a defendant to do the impossible[177] and they will weigh the inconvenience caused by the public body's defective action with the cost of requiring it to comply with the statutory procedure to the letter;[178] on the other hand, general pleas by a public institution of the disruptive effects or difficulty of complying with a court order will not, in general, be effective.[179]

(2) INJUNCTIONS AND THE CROWN

Particular problems have surrounded the award of injunctive relief against the Crown. This topic is dealt with separately below.[180]

(3) THE EFFECT OF ALTERNATIVE REMEDIES

The availability of a different remedy, and the effect which this has upon the ability to claim injunctive relief, will be considered below.[181]

4. *Practice and Procedure*

Injunctions, like declarations, can be claimed both under section 31 of the Supreme Court Act 1981, and outside of it. Public law cases will, however,

---

[175] *R. v. Speyer* [1916] 1 K.B. 595, (affirmed [1916] 2 K.B. 858).
[176] *e.g.* Local Government Act 1972, s.92 applies to challenges to the qualifications of members of a local authority.
[177] *Att.-Gen.* v. *Colchester Corporation* [1955] 2 Q.B. 207.
[178] *Coney* v. *Choyce* [1975] 1 W.L.R. 422.
[179] *Pride of Derby* [1953] Ch. 149; *Bradbury* v. *Enfield London Borough Council* [1967] 1 W.L.R. 1311.
[180] See below, pp. 726-732.
[181] See below, pp. 597-599.

normally have to be brought under section 31. The exceptions to this presumption will be considered below. The procedure for obtaining an injunction outside of section 31 will be considered here. In 1875 the power to grant an injunction, which had previously resided solely within courts of equity, was made available to all divisions of the High Court where the award of the remedy appeared to be just and convenient.[182] The effect of the provision was to allow the High Court to grant an injunction where it would previously have granted a common law remedy; where no remedy would have been available at common law or equity an injunction could not be given.[183]

Section 5. Other Remedies

1. *Habeas Corpus*

Habeas corpus affects public law in an indirect way. If an individual is detained, the writ of habeas corpus may be sought to challenge the legality of the administrative order on which the detention was based.[184] A brief outline of this remedy will be provided here. Fuller treatment may be found elsewhere.[185]

The immediate progenitor of the present writ was the writ of habeas corpus *cum causa* which developed in the fourteenth century as a mechanism for testing the legality of detention. Reforms expediting the procedure were introduced by the Habeas Corpus Act 1679 which also contained financial penalties for those, whether they were judges or jailers, who refused service of the writ or impeded its effective execution. The application will normally be made by the detainee unless the circumstances of the imprisonment preclude this and the writ will be served on the person who has the applicant in custody.

The cases on scope of review in a habeas corpus action are a minefield, evidencing a bewildering variety of terminology. Starting from first principles, it seems clear that the writ cannot be used to challenge the correctness of the detention, but only its validity. Correctness can only be challenged on appeal.[186] This is simply an application of the traditional principles of judicial review, but it remains to be seen how far the expansion of jurisdictional error permeates this area so as to render the above distinction redundant. Errors which are jurisdictional provide a clear reason for awarding the writ.[187] It is less clear whether habeas corpus can

---

[182] Supreme Court of Judicature Act 1873, s.25(8). See now, Supreme Court Act 1981, s.37.
[183] *North London Ry.* v. *Great Northern Ry.* (1883) 11 Q.B.D. 30.
[184] For related challenges based on collateral attack, see above Chap. 12.
[185] Sharpe, *The Law of Habeas Corpus* (2nd ed., 1989); de Smith, *Judicial Review of Administrative Action* (4th ed., 1980), App. 2.
[186] *ex p. Hinds* [1961] 1 W.L.R. 325.
[187] *Eshugbayi Eleko* v. *Government of Nigeria* [1931] A.C. 662.

issue for an error on the face of the record, but the answer appears to be in the affirmative,[188] and the courts also seem to apply the no evidence rule as a ground for releasing the detainee.[189] In general, while the courts may insist that they are looking at validity rather than correctness, they will not normally be prevented from releasing a detainee who they feel ought to be released by inquiry into the jurisprudential niceties of errors going to and errors within jurisdiction.[190] Such distinctions are, in any event, now of historical interest only given the courts' recent expansion of the concept of jurisdictional error. A purely technical flaw in the process leading to detention may lead the court to decline to issue the writ.[191]

While the courts will normally apply the general principles of administrative law in order to determine whether the detention itself was valid,[192] they will not it seems do so where an applicant seeks to use habeas corpus to attack the underlying administrative decision which was the cause of the detention. Judicial review should be used in such circumstances.[193]

Applications for habeas corpus must be made to a Divisional Court of the Queen's Bench Division. If no such court is sitting at that time then the application can be made to a single judge of any Division.[194] Applications are normally made *ex parte*. Rules as to appeals were altered in 1960. An appeal now lies against any decision on a habeas corpus application except a decision made by a single judge to award the writ in a criminal matter.[195] There are territorial limits to the writ.[196]

2. *Private Law Remedies*

A person aggrieved with action taken by a public body may be able to bring a civil claim in tort or contract. The scope of these causes of action will be considered in Part IV.

3. *Criminal Prosecution*

Bringing a criminal prosecution was a common method of enforcing public duties in the nineteenth century. Any person can bring an indictment

---

[188] R. v. *Governor of Brixton Prison, ex p. Armah* [1968] A.C. 192.

[189] *ex p. Armah* [1968] A.C. 192; R. v. *Board of Control, ex p. Rutty* [1956] 2 Q.B. 109.

[190] Rubinstein, *Jurisdiction and Illegality* (1965), p. 115.

[191] R. v. *Governor of Pentonville Prison, ex p. Osman (No.3)* [1990] 1 W.L.R. 878.

[192] R. v. *Governor of Pentonville Prison, ex p. Osman* [1990] 1 W.L.R. 277.

[193] R. v. *Secretary of State for the Home Department, ex p. Muboyayi* [1992] 1 Q.B. 244.

[194] The theory that an applicant could make a fresh application to each superior judge was refuted in *Re Hastings (No. 2)* [1959] 1 Q.B. 358; *Re Hastings (No. 3)* [1959] Ch. 368. See now Administration of Justice Act 1960, s.14(2) which allows a fresh application only where there is fresh evidence, on the meaning of which see R. v. *Pentonville Prison Governor, ex p. Tarling* [1979] 1 W.L.R. 1417.

[195] Administration of Justice Act 1960, s.15.

[196] Sharpe, *The Law of Habeas Corpus*, Chap. 8.

against another where the latter has been guilty of a common law mis-demeanour. The courts held that it was such a misdemeanour to disobey the provisions of an Act of Parliament where no penalty was imposed and where the statute prohibited some public grievance or commanded some public convenience.[197] The action is however little used and the Law Commission has recommended that it be abolished.[198]

4. Default Powers

As a final sanction many statutes contain provisions which enable a more senior body in the administrative hierarchy or the minister to exercise powers where it is felt that the original grantee has failed to do so. Nor-mally the defaulting authority will be warned and given time within which to fulfil its duties. Failing this, the duties will be transferred to the minister, to an independent body, or new members may be appointed to replace those in default.

On some occasions the courts have treated the existence of such powers as excluding other remedies. Thus in *Pasmore* v. *Oswaldtwistle Urban District Council*[199] the existence of default powers in the Public Health Act 1875 was held to prevent a private person from obtaining mandamus to enforce a duty to provide such sewers as might be necessary for draining a district. In other cases the courts have not adopted this construction. Other remedies have been available despite the presence of default powers in cases involving, for example, education,[200] and television.[201] It is somewhat odd to regard default powers as an alternative remedy which is equally bene-ficial as a declaration or mandamus. In some ways it is not a legal remedy at all.[202] The cases which regard the presence of default powers as excluding other remedies should therefore be narrowly construed. Those cases where such powers have been regarded as exclusive are perhaps better explained as ones in which the nature of the duty rendered it unsuited to enforcement by individuals. There are indications in the case law that the courts have had this factor in mind when construing the relevant statute.[203]

Although default powers will only be used as a last resort they are a potent threat, particularly in times when the relationship between central

---

[197] *R.* v. *Hall* [1891] 1 Q.B. 747. This presumption could be rebutted if the statute contained provision for a penalty recoverable as a debt, provided for summary criminal proceedings, or if it contained its own enforcement mechanism.

[198] *Report on Conspiracy and Criminal Law Reform*, Law Comm. No. 76, (1976), paras. 6.1-6.5, and see *R.* v. *Horseferry Road Justices, ex p. Independent Broadcasting Authority* [1987] Q.B. 54.

[199] [1898] A.C. 387, applying *Doe d. Bishop of Rochester* v. *Bridges* (1831) 1 B. & Ad. 847. See also, *Bradbury* v. *Enfield L.B.C.* [1967] 1 W.L.R. 1311; *Wood* v. *Ealing L.B.C.* [1967] Ch. 364; *Southwark L.B.C.* v. *Williams* [1971] Ch. 734.

[200] *Meade* v. *Haringey L.B.C.* [1979] 1 W.L.R. 637.

[201] *Att.-Gen., ex rel. McWhirter* v. *Independent Broadcasting Authority* [1973] Q.B. 629.

[202] *R.* v. *Leicester Guardians* [1899] 2 Q.B. 632, 639.

[203] See, *e.g. Southwark L.B.C.* v. *Williams* [1971] Ch. 734, 743.

and local government is under strain.[204] The exercise of such powers will itself be subject to judicial review. If the minister acts on irrelevant considerations or misdirects himself in fact or law, then the intervention will be *ultra vires*. The court should not interfere simply because it takes a different view from that of the minister.[205]

---

[204] For an example of the use of such powers, *Asher* v. *Secretary of State for the Environment* [1974] Ch. 208.
[205] *R.* v. *Secretary of State for the Environment, ex p. Norwich City Council* [1982] Q.B. 808. Lord Denning M.R. also suggests that the minister has a procedural duty to hear the local authority's view before exercising his powers.

15. REMEDIES AND REFORM

Section 1. The Impetus for Reform

1. *General*

The range of remedies available to a potential claimant has always been a mixed blessing. Two types of problem can be immediately identified. First, there were uncertainties about the scope of the individual remedies or aspects of them. The reader of the previous pages will bear testimony to this without having to have specific instances spelt out. Secondly, what was clear was that the remedies possessed both advantages and disadvantages when compared with each other. This is evident by standing back from the two mainline remedies, certiorari and declaration. The former could apply to all types of error, including non-jurisdictional error while that concept still existed, the standing rules were relatively wide, and interim relief was available. Its disadvantages included the impossibility of combining a claim for certiorari with a damages action, a relatively short time limit, and the difficulty of adjudicating upon contested questions of fact. In addition, the problems caused by the judicial, administrative, legislative distinctions, and the dichotomy between rights and privileges never quite seemed to die: just when they had been expunged from one area they had a tendency to reappear in another.

The declaration was meant, by way of contrast, to be the shining white charger cutting through outmoded limitations encrusted upon the pick and shovel prerogative orders,[1] and so it might have been. It is unencumbered by the limitations mentioned above and its dual capacity as supervisory and original remedy gives it an added flexibility. It can, moreover, be combined with other claims for relief, is not subject to a short time limit, and can be attended by full discovery. The promise that declaration might bloom into a general, all purpose remedy, with the prerogative orders being left to atrophy from lack of use has not however come to pass. Three reasons have contributed to this. The fact that it was thought that no interim declaration could be granted, and the question mark surrounding the availability of declaration for non-jurisdictional error of law are two of the reasons. Yet by themselves these do not constitute an insurmountable hurdle, particularly given the expansion in the concept of jurisdictional error. The third reason why declaration has not fulfilled its youthful promise is that the

---

[1] *Barnard v. National Dock Labour Board* [1953] 2 Q.B. 18.

549

standing criteria have been restrictively interpreted in the *Gouriet* case.[2] This has been the major confining influence, not simply because it concerns something central and important, but because of the reasoning leading to the adoption of those rules. The portrayal of the minor role that the citizen is to play in public law stands in stark contrast to the principle propounded by the Law Commission,[3]

> "The remedies' primary object is not to assert private rights, but to have illegal public action and orders controlled by the courts."

2. *The New Procedure: General Approach*

Given that neither the effluxion of time nor the application of Darwinian principles had produced a single, strong remedy, reform was clearly required. The Law Commission's Report No. 73 was the culmination of earlier studies,[4] the most wide ranging of which had been the second. By the time that Report No. 73 was published the Law Commission felt that it must confine itself more narrowly to questions of procedure. The earlier Working Paper had undertaken a wider ranging study encompassing, *inter alia*, time limits, ouster clauses, and damages. These were felt to be outside the scope of the Law Commission's brief.

What emerged was a revised Order 53,[5] a number of the points of which have been touched upon already. Order 53 has itself been affected partly by changes in a later statutory instrument, and partly by some of its provisions being incorporated into a statute.[6]

The basis of the reform is the concept of application for judicial review.[7] The prerogative orders and declaration and injunction are subject to this mechanism, and the remedies may be sought in the alternative or cumulatively depending upon the type of case.[8] When revised Order 53 was first passed it was thought that declaration and injunction would still be obtainable under their pre-existing procedures. It would, however, be inappropriate for those remedies to be claimed under the new procedure unless the case was of a public law nature. Order 53, rule 1(2), which is now incorporated within section 31(2) of the Supreme Court Act 1981, defines when cases will be of this kind. Declarations and injunctions can be granted pursuant to an application for judicial review if the court considers, having regard to the nature of the matters and the nature of the persons or bodies against whom relief may be granted by the prerogative orders, and all the circumstances of the case, that it would be just and convenient for the

---

[2] [1978] A.C. 435.
[3] *Remedies in Administrative Law*, Working Paper No. 40 (1971), p. 56.
[4] Law Comm. No. 20, Cmnd. 4059 (1969); Law Comm. Working Paper No. 40 (1971); Law Comm. No. 73, Cmnd. 6407 (1976).
[5] S.I. 1977 No. 1955.
[6] S.I. 1980 No. 2000; Supreme Court Act 1981, s.31.
[7] See generally, Lewis, *Judicial Remedies in Public Law* (1992).
[8] *Ibid.* s.31(1); Ord. 53, r. 2.

declaration to be made or for the injunction to be granted. The test is therefore both functional and institutional with the tail piece being all the circumstances of the case. It is now clear that a declaration (and presumably an injunction) can be obtained under this procedure even though the prerogative orders would not themselves be available.[9]

How this provision is to be interpreted is obviously of importance. The importance has been increased by the decision of the House of Lords in O'Reilly v. Mackman,[10] which has limited the circumstances in which a declaration or an injunction in a public law case can be sought outside of section 31. Lord Diplock, giving the judgment of a unanimous House of Lords, reasoned as follows.

The prerogative orders had, prior to the reforms, been subject to a number of limitations. There was no right to discovery, damages could not be claimed in conjunction with one of the orders and cross-examination upon affidavits occurred very rarely if at all. These limitations justified the use of the declaration under Order 15, rule 16. However, the reformed Order 53 had removed the above defects by providing for discovery, allowing damages to be claimed, and making provision for cross-examination. The reformed procedure also provided important safeguards for the public body, including the requirement of leave to bring the case and a time limit short enough so that the public body would not be kept unduly in suspense as to whether its actions were valid or not. In the light of these changes it would normally be an abuse of process to seek a declaration outside of section 31. Two exceptions were mentioned: certain types of collateral attack and cases where none of the parties object to a remedy being sought outside section 31. The possibility that other exceptions might exist was left open to be decided on a case by case basis.

The approach of regarding the new procedure as mandatory is carried one stage further. Not only should the section 31 procedure be the norm, but within section 31 the prerogative orders should be the main remedies. The declaration is seen as having been of use, while the prerogative orders were unduly limited. Now that the latter had been liberated from their constraints, they should assume pride of place within section 31. When the sole aim was to quash a decision, certiorari and not declaration should be used.

The decision in O'Reilly raises a number of important questions. Four will be examined here. The case law since O'Reilly has centred upon two such questions which must be distinguished. First, what are the exceptions to the O'Reilly decision, i.e. how do you "get out" of section 31? Secondly, how public must a case be to be brought within section 31, i.e. how do you "get into" section 31? These questions will be followed by two of a more general nature. Thirdly, what tests could be used to distinguish a public from a private law case? Finally, is the whole approach in O'Reilly correct or not?

---

[9] R. v. Secretary of State for Employment, ex p. Equal Opportunities Commission [1994] 1 All E.R. 910, 919-920, 925, 927-928.

[10] [1983] 2 A.C. 237; Cocks v. Thanet District Council [1983] 2 A.C. 286.

Section 2. The Exceptions: "Getting out" of Section 31

1. *The Reasons for Seeking to Proceed Outside Section 31*

Lord Diplock in *O'Reilly* mentioned two types of exception. First, Order 15, rule 16 could be used where none of the parties objected. Secondly, a person could proceed outside of section 31 where the claim arose as a collateral issue in an action for infringement of a right of the plaintiff arising under private law. Attention has not surprisingly been focused upon the second of these exceptions.

In reading the materials which follow it is important to understand why applicants have sought to proceed with their actions outside section 31.

The *principal reason* is that if they were forced to bring their cases within section 31 they would be outside the short time limit for such actions and hence their claims would fail. This problem can be particularly acute, as will be seen below, when the person seeking to raise the public law issue is in fact the defendant in the action, and is, therefore, not in control of the time within which it has been brought.

A *secondary reason* for seeking to bring the claim outside section 31 is that the applicant may well wish to engage in extensive investigation of factual issues relating to the case, and to have the possibility of cross-examining those on the other side. While it is possible for this to be done within section 31 proceedings it is not normal. This point requires a brief explanation.

Prior to 1977 grant of leave to cross-examine under the prerogative orders was very rare. This was one of the main reasons why people preferred to use the declaration or the injunction: unless one could cross-examine it might be impossible to prove the error being alleged. The new procedure makes provision for discovery and cross-examination. Notwithstanding these provisions there were early indications that the ability to cross-examine should be used sparingly, and that the ordinary trial procedure was preferable for complex factual questions.[11] Later judicial[12] and extra-judicial[13] statements appear to confirm the reluctance to

---

[11] R. v. *Inland Revenue Commissioners, ex p. Rossminster Ltd.* [1980] A.C. 952, 1027. Provision for cross-examination is to be found in Ord. 53, r. 8.

[12] See *O'Reilly* [1983] 2 A.C. 237 itself, where Lord Diplock, having stated that cross-examination will be allowed whenever the justice of the case so requires, then stated that it will normally only be so required when there is a case of natural justice; R. v. *Secretary of State for the Home Department, ex p. Khawaja* [1984] A.C. 74 where their Lordships intimated that cross-examination should be used sparingly; *Air Canada* v. *Secretary of State for Trade (No. 2)* [1983] 2 A.C. 394, where Lord Denning M.R. stated that discovery will only be allowed in exceptional cases; *Lonrho plc* v. *Tebbit* [1992] 4 All E.R. 280, where one of the reasons for allowing the case to proceed outside section 31 was the complex nature of the factual issues involved. More recent cases which indicate the limited availability of discovery include, R. v. *Inland Revenue Commissioners, ex p. Taylor* [1989] 1 All E.R. 906; R. v. *Secretary of State for the Environment, ex p. Doncaster Borough Council* [1990] C.O.D. 441; R. v. *Secretary of State for the Home Department, ex p. B.H.* [1990] C.O.D. 445; R. v. *Secretary of State for Education, ex p. J* [1993] C.O.D. 146; R. v. *Secretary of State for Transport, ex p. APH Road Safety Ltd.* [1993] C.O.D. 150.

[13] Woolf [1986] P.L. 220, 229, 231.

allow discovery and cross-examination within section 31, because of the delays and extra costs generated by such concessions to the individual. This is somewhat paradoxical. One of the very reasons for making the new procedure exclusive was, as we have seen, that the reforms had removed defects in the previous law, including the inability to cross-examine and seek discovery. This justified confining the individual to section 31 with its various protections for the public body. If however the individual applicant is rarely allowed to use these procedural aids, the applicant may be unable to prove the invalidity which is the basis of the action. More recent authority has, as will be seen below, sometimes allowed a case to proceed outside section 31 because of the complex nature of the factual issues which are involved.

It will become apparent from reading the materials within this section that the interpretation which has been accorded to the private rights exception has altered over the last few years. It is for this reason that the analysis will consider the approach to this exception in the period immediately after *O'Reilly*, and then focus upon the interpretation given to it in the more recent case law.

2. *Collateral Attack and Private Rights: The Initial Approach*

The inherent difficulty of applying this exception can be exemplified by contrasting three of the leading cases decided in the years shortly after *O'Reilly*.

In *Cocks* v. *Thanet District Council*[14] the plaintiff claimed a declaration and damages alleging a breach by the defendant council of their duties under the Housing (Homeless Persons) Act 1977. The House of Lords insisted that the action should be brought under section 31 for the following reason. The existence of a duty to inquire whether the applicant might be made homeless, and the questions whether the applicant might be entitled to temporary or permanent housing, were public law questions. The determination of these issues in the applicant's favour was a condition precedent to the establishment of a private law right. Such issues must therefore be brought within section 31, because at that stage the applicant did not yet have private law rights allowing him to proceed outside section 31 by way of an ordinary action.

The decision in *Cocks* can be contrasted with that in *Davy* v. *Spelthorne Borough Council*.[15] The plaintiff was the owner of premises making precast concrete who made an agreement with the council in 1979 that he would not oppose an enforcement notice terminating his right to use the premises provided that the council did not enforce this notice for three years. In 1982 the plaintiff brought a damages action claiming that he had been negligently advised of his rights under the planning legislation, and that the

---

[14] [1983] 2 A.C. 286.
[15] [1984] A.C. 262.

1979 agreement was *ultra vires* and void. The council argued, *inter alia*, that the action should be brought under section 31 since any defence which Davy had to the enforcement notice was a right to which he was entitled to protection under public law. The House of Lords rejected this argument. Lord Fraser[16] regarded the negligence claim as "simply" an ordinary tort action, which did not raise any matter of public law as a "live issue".[17] *Cocks* was distinguished.[18] In that case the plaintiff had to impugn the defendant's decision that he was intentionally homeless (the "public law" issue), as a condition precedent to the establishment of a private law right. In *Davy* the plaintiff's private right did not depend upon the enforcement notice. The plaintiff was not challenging the enforcement order, but rather claiming damages because he had lost his chance to impugn it. The council would not, therefore, be kept "in suspense" as to the validity of its enforcement notice.[19]

Wandsworth London Borough Council v. *Winder*[20] exemplifies a further dimension in the complexity of the private rights exception to *O'Reilly*. The plaintiff council had raised the rent of Winder's flat; Winder refused to pay the increase, paying only such an amount as he considered to be reasonable; the council sued for arrears of rent and possession of the flat; Winder argued in defence that the council had acted *ultra vires* by charging excessive rents; the council contended that the legality of the rent could only be tested under section 31. The House of Lords found for Winder. *O'Reilly* and *Cocks* were distinguished for two reasons. First, the plaintiffs therein did not have private rights, whereas Winder complained of "the infringement of a contractual right in private law". Secondly, the individual had initiated the action in the earlier cases, whereas Winder was the defendant "who did not select the procedure to be adopted".

It was unclear whether this second factor would be sufficient by itself to allow an individual to raise the validity of a statutory exercise of power by way of defence to an action brought against him or her outside of section 31. Some cases emphasised the second of these factors, without inquiring too closely whether the individual had private rights which were affected, or what the precise nature of these rights were.[21] However, the weight of authority suggested the contrary. An individual should have some private right in order to be able to raise the invalidity of a public body's action by way of defence in an ordinary action outside section 31. If no such right existed the defendant would have to apply for a stay of proceedings in

---

[16] Lord Roskill, Lord Brandon and Lord Brightman agreed with Lord Fraser.
[17] [1984] A.C. 262, 273.
[18] *Ibid.* pp. 273-274.
[19] *Ibid.* p. 274 F.
[20] [1985] A.C. 461.
[21] *West Glamorgan County Council* v. *Rafferty* [1987] 1 W.L.R. 457; *R.* v. *Crown Court at Reading, ex p. Hutchinson* [1987] 3 W.L.R. 1062 (a defendant is entitled to challenge the validity of a bylaw under which he is charged, or a decision of a local authority which is an essential element in the proof of the crime alleged, in a magistrates' court and does not have to proceed by way of section 31), distinguishing *Plymouth City Council* v. *Quietlynn Ltd.* [1988] Q.B. 114.

order to be able to challenge the public body's decision by way of judicial review.[22]

3. Collateral Attack and Private Rights: The Emerging Doctrine

The cases decided in the immediate aftermath of O'Reilly demonstrate the twin difficulties in applying the private rights exception. On the one hand, it was often unclear whether a particular interest should be characterised as a private right or not. On the other hand, the precise effect of this characterisation was itself unclear. Did the presence of a private right mean that the principle in O'Reilly should be deemed no longer applicable at all, so that an applicant could proceed outside section 31 wholly unencumbered? Or was the existence of such a right merely an important element which would lead the reviewing court to make a discretionary exception to the O'Reilly principle, provided that the private right was the principal part of the action and the public law issue was only incidental thereto?

This ambiguity was brought to the fore in the important decision of the House of Lords Roy v. Kensington and Chelsea and Westminster Family Practitioner Committee.[23] The facts were as follows. The applicant was a doctor who was paid certain sums under the relevant National Health Service regulations for treating patients. The relevant regulations provided, however, that the doctor would only be paid the full basic rate if he was devoting a substantial part of his time to treating patients on the National Health Service, as opposed to private practice. The Kensington Committee decided that the applicant was not complying with this condition and therefore reduced his allowance by 20%. The applicant claimed that this was a breach of contract by the Committee. The Committee counterclaimed, inter alia, that the action should have been brought under section 31 by way of judicial review. If this counterclaim was upheld then the applicant would have failed since he would have been outside the time limit for actions under section 31.[24] The House of Lords found for the applicant. The judgments were given by Lord Bridge and Lord Lowry.

Lord Bridge reasoned as follows.[25] His Lordship accepted that the principle in O'Reilly had been subject to much academic criticism, but was not persuaded that it should be overruled or even significantly modified. He did, however, believe that the principle in that case should be kept within proper bounds, and the limits to that principle should be properly preserved. What then were the correct limits to the principle? For Lord Bridge the correct position was as follows. If the case turned exclusively on a purely public law right, then the only remedy was by way

---

[22] Waverley Borough Council v. Hilden [1988] 1 W.L.R. 246; Avon County Council v. Buscott [1988] 2 W.L.R. 788.

[23] [1992] 1 A.C. 624.

[24] The Committee's original decision was in October 1984. This was not legally challenged by the applicant until July 1986.

[25] [1992] 1 A.C. 624, 628-630.

of judicial review under section 31, with its attendant constraints of leave and strict time limits. *If*, by way of contrast, the case involved the assertion of a private law right, whether by way of defence or by way of claim, the fact that the existence of the private law right might incidentally involve the examination of a public law issue did not prevent the applicant proceeding by way of an ordinary action outside section 31. On the facts of the present case the applicant came within the latter category. It did not matter whether one regarded the applicant as asserting private law rights based on contract, or as asserting private law rights derived from the relevant statute. The result was the same: the applicant could proceed outside section 31 by way of ordinary action.

Lord Lowry gave the other judgment of their Lordships. His reasoning throws into sharp relief the difficulties generated by the decision in *O'Reilly*. In his Lordship's judgment he drew upon argument from counsel and proffered two possible interpretations of the exception in *O'Reilly* v. *Mackman*.[26]

> "The 'broad approach' was that the 'rule in *O'Reilly* v. *Mackman*' did not apply generally against bringing actions to vindicate private rights in all circumstances in which those actions involved a challenge to a public law act or decision, but that it merely required the aggrieved person to proceed by judicial review only when private rights were not at stake. The 'narrow approach' assumed that the rule applied generally to *all* proceedings in which public law acts or decisions were challenged, subject to some exceptions when private law rights were involved. There was no need in *O'Reilly* v. *Mackman* to choose between these approaches, but it seems clear that Lord Diplock considered himself to be stating a general rule with exceptions. For my part, I much prefer the broad approach, which is both traditionally orthodox and consistent with the *Pyx Granite* principle...It would also, if adopted, have the practical merit of getting rid of a procedural minefield. I shall, however, be content for the purpose of this appeal to adopt the narrow approach, which avoids the need to discuss the proper scope of the rule, a point which has not been argued before your Lordships and has hitherto been seriously discussed only by the academic writers."

In deciding the case in favour of the applicant, Lord Lowry took account of the following factors. First, Roy, the applicant, had a bundle of rights derived from statute, even if they were not actually regarded as contract rights. When individual rights were claimed there should be no need for leave or a special time limit and the relief should not be discretionary. Secondly, although Roy was seeking to enforce performance of a public duty under the relevant National Health Service regulations his private rights dominated the action. Thirdly, this was a case in which the facts were in dispute. Although factual matters could be adjudicated under section 31, this was better done under an ordinary action. Fourthly, Roy was seeking the payment of a specific sum by way of a remedy, as opposed to damages.

---

[26] *Ibid.* p. 653.

An ordinary action was, therefore, better, since orders for specific sums could not be made in judicial review actions. Finally, procedural barriers to claims are not desirable and should be interpreted liberally.

It is readily apparent from this list of factors that Lord Lowry is willing to construe the qualification to presumptive exclusivity broadly. It is also clear from the judgment that Lord Lowry prefers the broad view of the private rights exception, the effect of which is to render the rule in *O'Reilly* inapplicable when cases involve private rights: applicants can proceed unencumbered outside section 31. The implications of this construction will be considered below. A similarly liberal interpretation of the exception is to be found in other recent decisions.

Lonrho plc v. *Tebbit*[27] provides a good example. The case represented another stage in the long running saga waged by Tiny Rowlands for the control of Harrods. It is clear that hell hath no fury like a businessman spurned, and Tiny Rowlands has spared none of his shareholders' money in pursuit of his lost prize. The facts were as follows. In 1979 Lonrho (L) owned 29.9% of the House of Fraser (HF). A proposed merger between L and HF was referred to the Monopolies and Mergers Commission, which reported that any such merger would be likely to operate against the public interest. In 1981 L then gave an undertaking to the Secretary of State that it would not acquire more than 30% of HF. A further reference was made to the MMC in 1984, and on this occasion the MMC stated that a merger between L and HF would not operate against the public interest. This report was not, however, received by L until February 1985, and in November 1984 L sold its shares in HF to a company controlled by the AL-Fayed brothers. In the light of the second report from the MMC Lonrho requested that the Secretary of State release it from its undertaking given in 1981 not to acquire more than 30% of the shares in HF. Unfortunately for L this release was not given until 14 March 1985, which was too late, because on 11 March the company controlled by the AL-Fayed brothers had already acquired a majority holding in HF.

Lonrho does not like being beaten in contests of this kind, and set about using the courts to retrieve what it had lost in the market place. The claim was that the Secretary of State had been negligent in failing to release L from its undertaking until it was too late, and that this constituted a negligent exercise of a discretionary power which caused it economic loss. The Secretary of State contended that the matter should have been brought by way of judicial review under section 31, and that the time for such an action had already run out. The case was initially heard by Browne-Wilkinson V.C.

Counsel for the defendant Secretary of State argued the point neatly. He accepted that there was an exception to *O'Reilly*, but contended that this only operated where the private law claim arose collaterally to the public law issue. In a negligence action against a public body, however, it was necessary for the plaintiff to show that the action of the public body was *ultra vires*,[28] and that this public law issue was not collateral to the main action, but a central part of L's cause of action.

---

[27] [1991] 4 All E.R. 973.
[28] See, *Dorset Yacht* [1970] A.C. 1004.

Browne-Wilkinson V.C. disagreed. He did not believe that the exception to *O'Reilly* was that narrow. The judgment in that case did "not establish that in every action where the validity of the exercise of the statutory power is challenged it is an abuse of the process of the court not to proceed by way of judicial review".[29] Four reasons are given as to why the plaintiff should be able to proceed by way of ordinary action.

First, Browne-Wilkinson V.C. accepted that the *ultra vires* issue was not purely collateral, but he did think that it was only one ingredient in the cause of action for negligence and that this was the essence of the plaintiff's case. Secondly, the case was thought to be more appropriate to be heard in the ordinary courts, rather than through the procedure for cases on judicial review. Thirdly, if the defendant's acts were held to be *ultra vires* this would not have any great deleterious effect on the administration. And finally, Lonrho would be out of time for section 31 proceedings, which would be unfair since L did not know of the facts on which to base the claim till long after the time limit for judicial review proceedings had passed.

The judgment of Browne-Wilkinson V.C. was upheld on appeal to the Court of Appeal,[30] by which time the decision in the *Roy* case had been handed down. Counsel for the defendant again argued that the plaintiff had to show that the behaviour of the Secretary of State was *ultra vires* as a condition precedent to founding a claim in private law for negligence, and that this meant that the case had to be brought within section 31 proceedings for judicial review. The Court of Appeal disagreed, drawing upon the House of Lords' decision in the *Roy* case discussed above. Dillon L.J. stated that the plaintiff's action was based on the assertion of a private law right, "albeit arising out of a background of public law".[31] He continued as follows.[32]

> "That can be asserted in an action by writ as in *Roy*...If the plaintiff fails to establish the private law right claimed, the action will fail. But it is not necessary to apply for judicial review before bringing the action."

Although the courts' general tendency has, therefore, been to interpret the exception for collateral attack and private rights liberally, some cases have adopted a more qualified approach. In *Bugg* v. *DPP*[33] it was held that a bylaw could only be challenged in the course of a criminal proceeding for breaking it if the ground of challenge was for substantive as opposed to procedural invalidity. Woolf L.J. drew this dichotomy for two principal reasons: substantive invalidity could be established by looking at the

---

[29] [1991] 4 All E.R. 973, 987.
[30] [1992] 4 All E.R. 280.
[31] *Ibid.* p. 288.
[32] *Loc.cit.*
[33] [1993] 2 All E.R. 815, distinguishing *R.* v. *Crown Court at Reading, ex p. Hutchinson* [1988] Q.B. 384. See Emery, "Collateral Attack – Attacking *Ultra Vires* Action Indirectly in Courts and Tribunals" (1993) 56 M.L.R. 643.

enabling legislation without recourse to further evidence, by way of contrast to instances of procedural invalidity which would require such evidentiary material; and the appropriate defendant who might wish to argue for the upholding of the bylaw might not be present in a criminal action. These reasons are, with respect, unconvincing. Substantive invalidity may not be apparent without recourse to evidence and further inquiry, and the problem of the appropriate defendant not being a party to the action can be just as problematic in the case of a challenge upon substantive grounds. Insofar as the problem in a case such as this is that the court may not be well placed to consider the legality of the bylaw then it may be resolved by creating a reference procedure whereby the public law issue could be referred to the Crown Office list.[34]

4. *Collateral Attack and Private Rights: An Assessment*

The "message" which emerges from the *Roy* case is that the private rights exception to the need to proceed by way of section 31 *will* be treated very liberally. If private rights do emerge in a case, whether by way of defence, or as part of the claim itself, then the court will not insist that the applicant uses the judicial review procedure laid down in section 31. This will be so even if proof of a public law matter is an integral part of the action as a whole. Thus, although Lord Lowry does not formally decide as between the broad and the narrow approach, he does express a preference for the former, and this sentiment shapes the entirety of his reasoning. On this broad approach the need to proceed by way of section 31 would simply *not apply* in a case where private rights were at stake. Protections for the public body, in terms of narrow time limits and the requirement of leave, would, as a consequence, be irrelevant in such instances. What then are the implications of this approach, and what conclusions can be drawn about the principle in *O'Reilly* itself?[35]

(1) THE UNDERMINING OF O'REILLY

It is clear that the very approach adopted by the House of Lords in the *Roy* case serves to cast doubt on the principle in *O'Reilly* itself. The principle of presumptive exclusivity developed in the latter case was based on the assumption that public bodies warranted the protections of narrow time limits and the leave requirement, *and* that these protections should not be circumvented by allowing applicants to proceed through a different type of action. The reasoning in the *Roy* case indirectly undermines this in two ways, one practical, the other conceptual.

It undermines that principle in *practical* terms simply because there will be fewer cases to which the protections afforded to the public body apply. Those protections will not apply in cases concerning private rights. This

---

[34] Emery, "Collateral Attack" (1993) 56 M.L.R. 643.
[35] See also, Alder, "Hunting the Chimera – The End of *O'Reilly* v. *Mackman*" [1993] 13 L.S. 183.

aspect of the matter is exacerbated by the fact that the term "private right" is a malleable one open to a variety of interpretations. This is exemplified by the *Roy* case itself, in which the House of Lords was willing to give a broad construction to the idea of private rights, and to do so without too much nice inquiry as to the real nature of the rights possessed by the applicant. If statutory payments to individuals, which payments are themselves subject to a plethora of evaluative criteria, are always to be treated as private law rights, then the number of instances in which litigants will be able to choose to bring their actions outside of section 31 will be broad indeed.

The decision of the House of Lords in the *Roy* case also indirectly casts *conceptual* doubt on the reasoning in *O'Reilly* v. *Mackman*. The explicit assumption in the *Roy* case is that protections for the public body, in terms of time limits and leave requirements, are not warranted, or are overridden, when an individual asserts private rights against a public body; *and* that this is so even if the case undoubtedly involves matters which are of a public law nature. Yet this begs more questions than it answers. It is based on two complementary contestable assumptions. One is that litigants who come with no species of private law right are somehow necessarily to be subjected to different, and more disadvantageous, procedural norms than those who do have such rights. This is by no means an obvious proposition.[36] The other assumption is that insofar as one believes that public bodies do warrant certain procedural protections, then these can nonetheless be "sacrificed" in cases which entail some element of private right, even though, as noted above, the public law element will often be central to the dispute. This assumption is no more self-evident than the former.

(2) ARE THE CASES "ABOUT" PRIVATE RIGHTS?

Now it might well be argued that the approach in *Roy* is defensible precisely because cases which are "about" private rights do not need to be brought within the *O'Reilly* principle. Public bodies do not need any of the special protections associated with leave or time limits in such instances, because such cases are not really "about" public law at all. They are simply private law disputes where one party happens to be a public body. This will not withstand examination for two reasons, one of which is obvious, the other of which is not.

First, the very determination of whether a right should be characterised as a private, as opposed to a public right, *and* whether it can be viewed as distinct from a "public law" issue which the case raises is not solvable by some readily applicable mechanical formula.[37]

Secondly, even if a case does undeniably involve private rights it would be quite mistaken to believe that the action is therefore principally

---

[36] Craig, "Procedures, Rights and Remedies" (1990) 2 E.R.P.L. 425.

[37] See, *e.g.* (a) the criticism of the *Winder* case by the Rt. Hon. Sir H. Woolf, "Public Law–Private Law: Why the Divide? A Personal View" [1986] P.L. 220, 233-236. *cf.* Beatson, "'Public' and 'Private' in English Administrative Law" (1987) 103 L.Q.R. 34, 59-61; (b) the reasoning in *Gillick* v. *West Norfolk and Wisbech Area Health Authority* [1986] A.C. 112, 163, 177-178.

"about" private rights as opposed to public law. This can be easily demonstrated. Take a simple fact situation such as that in a case like *Cooper* v. *Wandsworth Board of Works*:[38] a public body makes a demolition order on the plaintiff's property which is said to be *ultra vires*. The plaintiff brings an action in trespass. Now this action clearly involves a private right, but it is equally clear that the action is not solely "about" private rights. *Whether* the plaintiff wins or not in the trespass action will be dependent upon the validity of the demolition order. This will be *the* issue in the case, and this is manifestly a public law matter the resolution of which will be dependent upon the construction of the relevant legislation. The same point can be exemplified by the *Lonrho* case. The decisions by Browne-Wilkinson V.C. and the Court of Appeal recognise that the public law issue was not purely collateral to the private rights aspect of the case. It was indeed central to the litigation. *Whether* Lonrho finally wins on the substance of the case depends upon whether the court ultimately finds that the Secretary of State did exercise his power to release Lonrho from its undertaking too slowly, and in that sense misused his statutory discretionary power. This can only be determined by an analysis of the relevant statutory framework and this public law issue will lie at the heart of the main litigation. The *consequence* of this finding will determine whether Lonrho can succeed in the tort claim, and in that sense vindicate its private rights. But this does not mean that the case is solely or principally one about private rights as such. The point being made in this paragraph applies equally to the *Roy* case itself. To be sure the case could be said to involve some issues concerning private rights, arising from Roy's relationship with Family Practitioner Committee and the fact that he was seeking a contract type remedy. However, the case also raised certain more general public law matters, flowing from the fact that the committee was a statutory committee which administered public funds pursuant to statutory powers to allocate fees. *Whether* Roy wins on the substance of the case will depend in large part on the construction of the relevant statutory norms in order to determine the import of the contested concept: what does it mean to say that a doctor must devote a substantial amount of his time to NHS work?

(3) CONCLUSION

It is readily apparent that the more recent jurisprudence of the courts in this area evidences a subtle, but real shift away from the prior understanding of the "rule" in *O'Reilly* v. *Mackman*. The ambit of the exception to the presumptive exclusivity of the public law procedure laid down in *O'Reilly* has been expanded. Courts now appear to be more willing than previously to rule that any case in which a private law right is asserted can proceed by way of ordinary action, as opposed to being forced into the framework of section 31. This aspect of the current jurisprudence of the courts has been furthered by taking a broad conception of private rights, or private law claims. The willingness of the courts to allow such cases to be litigated by way of ordinary action is, moreover, not diminished even where the facts

---

[38] (1863) 14 C.B. (N.S.) 180.

clearly do raise an issue of public law to be decided as part of the substance of the dispute.

Underlying this shift in the recent attitude of the courts one can detect an ambivalence as to the very principle in *O'Reilly* itself. On the one hand, there is a recognition that the protections for public bodies, which are enshrined in the short time limits and the need for leave, are important, and are to be preserved. This accounts, for example, for the approach in the *Roy* case, where the House of Lords refused to question directly the basis of the *O'Reilly* decision, notwithstanding the significant criticism to which it has been subjected. On the other hand, there is a sense, which comes through increasingly strongly in the recent case law, that the hurdles which are created by *O'Reilly* are merely technical and legalistic, using those terms in a pejorative sense. Thus, for example, one sees Henry J. in the *Doyle* case regretting that the complexity of the law in this area was coming to reflect the forms of action of the nineteenth century, which would rule us once again from the grave.[39] The corollary of this type of thought process is that it really does *not* matter too much whether individuals are allowed to proceed by a different route to that contained in section 31.

The point is, of course, that one cannot have it both ways. *If* one believes that the protections for public bodies which are enshrined in the section 31 procedure really are important, then the wider the exceptions which are created the less will those protections really apply. *If*, by way of contrast, one feels that they are expressive of technical and legalistic distinctions, then it is not clear why they are worth bothering with. The position to which we have now moved is based on two assumptions. One is that public bodies really do require the protections enshrined in the section 31 procedure. The other is that, notwithstanding the first assumption, these protections can be jettisoned if the claimant has, or plausibly asserts, some species of private law right. The views of the Law Commission on this issue will be considered below.[40]

Section 3. Public Law Cases: "Getting Into" Section 31

1. *The Reasons for Wishing to Use the Section 31 Procedure*

The preceding discussion has concentrated upon those cases where individuals wish to proceed outside section 31. The traffic has not, however, been purely "one way". There have been many cases where individuals have sought to argue their way into section 31, what one judge[41] has termed the "obverse" of the situation in *O'Reilly*. Why then have individuals sought to bring their actions within the section 31 procedure? The aims differ depending upon the type of case, but there are three principal

---

[39] *Doyle v. Northumbria Probation Committee* [1991] 4 All E.R. 294, 300.
[40] See below, pp. 590–593.
[41] R. v. *East Berkshire Health Authority, ex p. Walsh* [1985] Q.B. 152.

reasons why litigants have been anxious to avail themselves of the application for judicial review.

The first and most obvious reason for wishing to use section 31 is that the applicant may have *no other cause of action* which is readily identifiable. In the *Datafin* case, considered in detail below, the applicants could not frame a convincing cause of action in contract or tort against the Take-Overs Panel, and this was a factor which predisposed the court in their favour.[42] Some employment cases are also explicable on this ground. Thus in *Benwell* a prison officer was dismissable at pleasure. He could not use the employment protection legislation, and this inclined the court to admitting him into section 31.[43]

A second reason prompting applicants to seek to use the public law procedures is because they believe that the *remedy will be more effective*. The desire for a more effective remedy, provides the explanation for some of the other employment cases which will be considered below.[44] The reasons why the public law remedy appears to be more attractive than that outside section 31 can only be touched upon here.[45] The core of this reasoning is as follows. An employee will be entitled to certain procedural hearing rights as part of the general law on unfair dismissal. Breach of these rights will give the employee a damages action, compensation for unfair dismissal and a possible order for reinstatement. The public law remedy may nonetheless be preferred because the applicant perceives that it will afford him or her more chance of getting the job back. Certiorari will quash the dismissal, and leave the applicant in "possession" of the job. This result reflects the historical status of employment in a public office, in the sense that the office was regarded as akin to a property right which the applicant was entitled to have restored if he or she was improperly deprived of it. The whole question of whether employees should have job security rights is a complex one,[46] and the rationale for differential treatment between public and private employment may well be historically outdated. Whatever answer is given to these questions it is doubtful whether the general issue should be indirectly decided in cases on judicial review. What is clear, as will be seen below, is that the courts are wary of expanding indirect job security rights by allowing potentially large categories of employees into section 31. Cases are likely therefore to turn upon the court's perception of whether a type of individual should have such security. The statutory material will then be interpreted so as to be consonant with this conclusion.

The third reason why applicants are keen to use the application for judicial review is related to the second. Such applicants may wish to be admitted into section 31 because the *scope of the obligations* which are thereby imposed upon the defendant body exceeds those which might be imposed in any private law cause of action. The most recent in the saga of cases involving the Jockey Club, discussed in detail below, exemplifies

---

[42] R. v. *Panel on Take-Overs and Mergers, ex p. Datafin plc* [1987] Q.B. 815.
[43] R. v. *Secretary of State for the Home Department, ex p. Benwell* [1985] Q.B. 554, 571, 572.
[44] *e.g.* the *Walsh* case [1985] Q.B. 152.
[45] See Davies and Freedland, *Labour Law, Text and Materials* (2nd ed., 1984).
[46] *Ibid.* pp. 428-432.

this.[47] In this case the principal reason why the Aga Khan sought to utilise the public law procedures was not because he had no remedy in private law, but because he sought to test the legality of the Club's actions against the panoply of substantive and procedural norms which are used to test the validity of a public body's behaviour.

2. *Public Law: Possible Tests*

The meaning of public law for the purposes of section 31 is obviously crucial in a double sense: only public law cases are subject to the presumptive exclusivity of the *O'Reilly* decision, and have therefore to be brought within section 31, and only cases which are about public law are allowed into section 31. Unfortunately no simple test exists to determine the meaning of public law for these purposes. Three possibilities can be briefly reviewed.[48]

(1) THE SOURCE OF THE POWER

The most obvious test is to consider the source of the authority's power: if that power is derived from statute then the body is presumptively public. There are two fundamental difficulties with this test. First, applied literally it would bring within public law the activities of any body regulated by statute, even if that body generally operated within the private commercial sphere. The second problem is a converse of the first. A body may owe the source of its public authority to statute, but not all of its operations should nonetheless be regarded as raising public law issues. Local authorities and other public bodies operate in an ordinary commercial capacity on many occasions.[49]

(2) THE SCOPE OF THE PREROGATIVE REMEDIES

Closely related to the preceding criterion is that of the scope of the prerogative orders. If we are to have a separate set of remedies for public law, then to regard the scope of the prerogative orders as prima facie evidence of the scope of public law might be reasonable, particularly given the centrality of position accorded to such orders within the scheme of section 31.

The objection to this criterion is that there is a tendency to see the ambit of such orders as fixed. There is little justification for this. Historically those

---

[47] R. v. *Disciplinary Committee of the Jockey Club, ex p. Aga Khan* [1993] 2 All E.R. 853.

[48] See generally, Beatson, "'Public' and 'Private' in English Administrative Law" (1987) 103 L.Q.R. 34; Cane, "Public Law and Private Law: A Study of the Analysis of and Use of a Legal Concept", *Oxford Essays in Jurisprudence, 3rd Series*, (Eekelaar and Bell, eds., 1987), Chap. 3.

[49] Lloyd L.J. in *Datafin* [1987] Q.B. 815, 847 implied that if the source of the power was statutory then the body would be subject to judicial review. For the reasons given in the text I doubt, with respect, whether the source test can be taken so generally.

orders were used flexibly to provide a remedy against institutions not covered by existing forms of redress.[50] There are indications that they could be used to cover any duty of a public nature, whether it be derived from statute, custom, prerogative or contract, a view echoed by Lord Diplock himself.[51] The tendency to ossify them, to regard their boundaries as immutable, is a more recent phenomenon. There is no reason why a duty may not be of a public law nature, whatever its derivation.[52]

To focus upon the scope of the prerogative orders as the criterion for the meaning of public law does however lead to the following conundrum. On the one hand, if their scope is interpreted flexibly in the above manner they cease to furnish a ready criterion, or certainly not one which is distinguishable from the third test to be considered below. The nature of a "public" as opposed to a "private" duty still has to be determined, and if the ambit of the prerogative orders simply covers any "public law" obligation we are no further forward in our determination of whether such an obligation is present in any particular case.[53] On the other hand, if a narrow definition of the prerogative orders is adopted, so that they apply only to bodies created by statute, or pursuant to the prerogative, then we are faced with a formalistic criterion. This makes the applicability of different procedures turn upon the often fortuitous incident of whether a particular authority's powers were derived from a particular source, irrespective of the real power wielded by such a body.[54]

(3) THE "NATURE" OF THE POWER

The difficulties of a formalistic test have inclined the courts towards a more open-textured criterion which requires them to consider the nature of the power wielded by the particular body. The formulation of this criterion has varied. For example Lloyd L.J. in the *Datafin* case[55] stated that if the source of the power was statutory then the body would be subject to judicial review, but would not if the source of power were contractual. However, in between these "extremes" one would have to look at the nature of the power. Thus if the body was exercising public law functions, or such functions had public law consequences, then section 31 would be applicable. This formulation appears to beg the question,[56] as do such statements that if a duty is a public duty then the body is subject to public law. Lord Donaldson M.R., by way of contrast, seemed only to be concerned with the source of a body's power in order to exclude those institutions whose power was based upon contract or consent.[57] Any other body could be subject to review if there was a sufficiently public element. How far power

---

[50] See above, pp. 520-523. *Groenvelt* v. *Burwell* (1700) 1 Ld.Raym. 454 is particularly instructive.
[51] *O'Reilly* [1983] 2 A.C. 237, 279.
[52] Nor are there convincing reasons why rules of a legislative character, or duties imposed upon the Crown should not be subject to the prerogative orders, above pp. 522-523.
[53] See the observations of Lord Donaldson M.R. in *Walsh* [1985] Q.B. 152, 162.
[54] See also Wade, "Procedure and Prerogative in Public Law" (1985) 101 L.Q.R. 180.
[55] [1987] Q.B. 815, 846-869.
[56] As admitted by Lloyd L.J., *ibid.* p. 847, who nonetheless denied the circularity.
[57] *Ibid.* pp. 838-839.

which is based upon contract or consent is subject to judicial review will be considered more fully below.

The uncertainty which this third test generates is to be expected. It is the price to be paid for moving away from formalistic tests based upon the source of power or upon the narrow definition of the prerogative given above. Statements that a body must have a sufficiently "public element" or must be exercising a public duty cannot function as anything other than conclusory labels for whatever we choose to pour into them. They cannot guide our reasoning in advance. In *Datafin* itself the court was, as will be seen, influenced by a number of such factors including: the undoubted power wielded by the Panel, the statutory cognisance given to its existence, the penalties, direct and indirect, which could follow from non-compliance with its rules, and the absence of any other redress available to the applicants.

For the sake of clarity a further word should be said as to the technique for applying the nature of the power test. Two options are open to the courts. First, they could adopt a broad view as to the ambit of the prerogative orders. This is, as we have seen, tantamount to a test based upon the nature of the power. The prerogative orders would, on this view, apply when the power or duty is in the nature of a public power or duty. Secondly, the courts could adopt a more limited view of the scope of the prerogative orders, but allow an applicant to seek relief within section 31 by a declaration or injunction when the duty is sufficiently public in nature to warrant review. The judiciary appear to favour the former approach at present. The prerogative orders themselves are felt to be capable of embracing many types of public power.[58]

It is now time to consider more closely which types of institution have been deemed to be susceptible to judicial review under the new procedures.

3. *The Boundaries of Public Law*

It is clear that traditional public bodies will be able to use the application for judicial review, and that they can be subjected to such actions. What concerns us now are "other" types of case in which applicants have, for one of the above reasons, sought to bring their claims within section 31. The courts have been inundated with such cases in recent years. Placing these decisions into various categories is no easy task. It is, however, necessary in order to understand the differing types of claim which have been brought.

(1) PUBLIC BODIES, NEXT STEPS AGENCIES AND CONTRACTING-OUT

The applicability of public law principles to Next Steps Agencies and contracting-out by government departments or agencies themselves has been considered above.[59]

---

[58] *Ibid.* pp. 837-839, 848-849.
[59] See above, pp. 93-96, 112-113.

In principle it is clear that Next Steps Agencies must be subject to the section 31 procedure, given that they are not formally separate from their sponsoring department, and given also that most of these agencies are engaged in public service delivery.

It is equally clear that firms to whom business is contracted-out must also be susceptible to the public law procedures. The relevant statutory powers or duties are imposed upon the government department or agency. The fact that it chooses to fulfil those functions by contracting-out some of the work to private firms cannot, as a matter of principle, alter the fact that it is a statutory power or duty which is being exercised. It remains to be seen whether the appropriate respondent in any such case is the private firm, the government department, or both. There does not seem to be any reason in principle why the private firm should not be proceeded against by itself where this is appropriate given the nature of the allegation being made against it.

(2) PUBLIC AUTHORITIES AND CONTRACTING POWER: THE NEED FOR A "PUBLIC LAW ELEMENT"

It is clear that if a public body acts pursuant to statutory or prerogative powers then its decisions will be subject to judicial review. What then is the position when a *public body* exercises a *contractual form of power*? Is this also subject to judicial review?[60] The traditional tendency was to see contracts, even those made by public bodies, as essentially private matters. The courts have now moved away from this stance, but their attitude towards such contracts is still somewhat ambivalent. The preponderant approach has been to regard contracts made by public authorities as subject to judicial review if there is a sufficiently "public law element" to the case. This phrase can, however, be subject to different interpretations.

In the *Hook* case[61] the cancellation of a trader's licence was held to be susceptible to review because the council's powers affected a pre-existing common law right to trade in the market. The courts have also held that a public body's powers as a landlord are subject to review.[62] There is, moreover, authority that procurement decisions are capable of being judicially reviewed. In one such case the court reviewed a local authority decision not to deal with Shell because other companies in the same corporate group had contacts with South Africa.[63] Which procurement decisions will be subject to judicial review is, however, unclear. In *R. v. Lord Chancellor's Department, ex p. Hibbit and Saunders*[64] the Lord Chancellor's department invited tenders for court reporting services. The applicant, who was unsuccessful,

---

[60] Arrowsmith, "Judicial Review and the Contractual Powers of Public Authorities" (1990) 106 L.Q.R. 277.

[61] *R. v. Barnsley Metropolitan Borough Council, ex p. Hook* [1976] 1 W.L.R. 1052; *R. v. Birmingham City Council, ex p. Dredger and Paget* [1993] C.O.D. 340.

[62] *Cannock Chase District Council v. Kelly* [1978] 1 W.L.R. 1; *Sevenoaks District Council v. Emmett* (1979) 79 L.G.R. 346.

[63] *R. v. Lewisham Borough Council, ex p. Shell UK Ltd.* [1988] 1 All E.R. 938; *R. v. Enfield London Borough Council, ex p. Unwin* [1989] C.O.D. 466.

[64] [1993] C.O.D. 326.

sought judicial review on the ground that it had a legitimate expectation that discussions would not be held with some of the tenderers to enable them to submit lower bids. The court, while sympathetic to this claim, held that the decision itself was not amenable to review, because it lacked a sufficiently public law element. It was not sufficient to create a public law obligation that the respondent was a public body carrying out governmental functions: if such a body enters a contract with a third party then the contract will define the nature of the parties' obligations, unless there is some additional element giving rise to a public law obligation. A public law element might be found in cases where either there was some special aim being pursued by the government through the tendering process which set it apart from ordinary commercial tenders; or where there was some statutory underpinning, such as where there was a statutory obligation to negotiate the contract in a particular way, and with particular terms.

Is the idea of a "public law element", which serves to distinguish those contracts which are subject to review, really needed? It is clear that, as a matter of principle, *some* contracts made by public authorities ought to be susceptible to judicial review. It may be entirely fortuitous whether the government chooses to advance its policy objectives through a regulatory scheme involving statutory discretionary power, or whether it seeks to attain the same regulatory end through the use of a contractual relationship. The choice of method should not affect the application of public law principles to the case at hand.[65] The argument that *all*, or virtually all, contract type relationships made by public bodies should be subject to public law principles is said to be justified because of the public nature of the body.[66] It is, however, somewhat odd to suggest that *all* contracts entered into by public bodies should be subject to judicial review. Would this mean that in all such cases the substantive and procedural principles of public law should be applied? Are these really appropriate when a public body, for example, makes an ordinary commercial contract for furniture, a lease or the like? It is not self-evident that a private contractor who makes such a contract with a public body should have greater substantive and procedural rights than any other contracting party. Given that this is so it seems that it *is* necessary to retain the idea of a "public law element" in order to distinguish between the two types of case.

Having said this the question which of course remains is as to the meaning to be attributed to the phrase "public law element"? This is obviously not capable of precise definition. The ascription, or not, of this label will depend upon whether one believes that the task being performed by the public body when it makes the contract really partakes in some manner of "governing" or "public regulation" as opposed to private contracting.

---

[65] See above, pp. 93-96, 112-113, for further discussion.
[66] Arrowsmith, "Judicial Review and the Contractual Powers of Public Authorities" (1990) 106 L.Q.R. 277, 291, but it is accepted that there may be reasons for limiting the operation of review in specific areas for particular reasons.

(3) REGULATORY BODIES: THE "PRIVATISATION OF THE BUSINESS OF GOVERNMENT"

Hoffmann L.J. coined this phrase in the *Aga Khan* case,[67] and it provides an apt description of one important category of case which has been admitted into the public law procedures. These cases concern regulatory bodies which are private, but which have been integrated, directly or indirectly, into a system of statutory regulation. *Datafin* is the seminal decision in this category.[68]

In that case the applicants complained that the Panel on Take-Overs and Mergers (the Panel) had incorrectly applied their takeover rules, and had thereby allowed an advantage to be gained by the applicant's rivals who were bidding for the same company as the applicants. The Panel was a self-regulating body which had no direct statutory, prerogative or common law powers, but it was supported by certain statutory powers which pre-supposed its existence, and its decisions could result in the imposition of penalties. The Panel opposed judicial review, arguing that it was not amenable to the prerogative orders which had been restricted to bodies exercising powers derived from the prerogative or statute. The court rejected this view. The "source" of a body's powers was not the only criterion for judging whether a body was amenable to public law. The absence of a statutory or prerogative base for such powers did not exclude section 31 if the "nature" of the power being exercised rendered the body suitable for judicial review. The nature of the Panel's powers was held to satisfy this alternative criterion for a number of reasons.

First, the Panel although self-regulating did not operate consensually or voluntarily, but rather imposed a collective code on those within its ambit.[69] Secondly, the Panel was performing a public duty as manifested by the government's willingness to limit legislation in this area, and to use the Panel as part of its regulatory machinery.[70] There had been an "implied devolution of power"[71] by the government to the Panel, and certain legislation presupposed its existence. Thirdly, its source of power was only partly moral persuasion, this being reinforced by statutory powers exercisable by the government and the Bank of England.[72] Finally, the applicants did not appear to have any cause of action in contract or tort against the Panel.[73]

Similar reasoning can be found in other cases, such as *R. v. Advertising Standards Authority, ex p. The Insurance Services plc.*[74] The applicant

---

[67] [1993] 2 All E.R. 853, 874.
[68] [1987] Q.B. 815.
[69] *Ibid.* pp. 825-826, 845-846.
[70] *Ibid.* pp. 838-839, 848-849, 850-851.
[71] *Ibid.* p. 849.
[72] *Ibid.* pp. 838-839, 851-852.
[73] *Ibid.* pp. 838-839. See also, *R. v. Panel on Take-Overs and Mergers, ex p. Guiness plc* [1990] 1 Q.B. 146; *R. v. Civil Service Appeal Board, ex p. Bruce* [1988] I.C.R. 649, [1989] I.C.R. 171.
[74] [1990] C.O.D. 42. See also, *Bank of Scotland v. Investment Management Regulatory Organisation Ltd.* (1989) S.L.T. 432; *R. v. Financial Intermediaries Managers and Brokers Regulatory Association, ex p. Cochrane* [1990] C.O.D. 33; *R. v. Code of Practice Committee of the Association of the British Pharmaceutical Industry, ex p. Professional Counselling Aids Ltd.* [1991] C.O.D. 228; *R. v. Visitors to the Inns of Court, ex p. Calder* [1993] 2 All E.R. 876. Compare *R. v. Fernhill Manor School, ex p. Brown* [1992] C.O.D. 446.

complained that an adverse report on it made by the ASA was procedurally irregular. The initial question was whether the ASA was susceptible to judicial review. The court held that it was, following the *Datafin* case. The ASA had no powers granted to it by statute, and had no contractual relationship with the advertisers whom it controlled. It was, however, part of a scheme of government regulation of the industry in the following sense. A Community directive required Member States to make provision for the control of misleading advertising. This was implemented in the UK by regulations which gave the Director General of Fair Trading powers to investigate complaints of misleading advertising. The essence of this regulatory scheme was that the Director General would only take legal proceedings against a firm if the matter had not been satisfactorily resolved through the ASA. The court held that in these circumstances the ASA was susceptible to control through judicial review.

(4) REGULATORY BODIES: CONTRACT, POWER AND CONTROL

The courts have experienced rather more difficulty in determining the boundaries of judicial review in a group of cases which are not far removed from those in the preceding section. These cases also concern regulatory bodies which have control over a particular industry, and in that sense exercise a degree of real power over those who are subject to their remit. However, what serves to distinguish these cases from those considered above is that there is no governmental involvement in these areas as such. These regulatory institutions are not part of a schema of statutory regulation. Whether this should make a difference will be considered in due course. The courts have on the whole been unwilling to extend judicial review to cover such instances.

The story begins with the decision in *Law v. National Greyhound Racing Club Ltd.*[75] In that case the plaintiff was a trainer whose licence was suspended and he sought a declaration outside section 31 that the decision was *ultra vires*. The NGRC argued that the case should have been brought within section 31. This was rejected by the court. It held that the power which the NGRC exercised over those engaged in greyhound racing was derived from contract, and was of concern only to those who took part in this sport. While the exercise of this power could have benefits for the public by, for example, stamping out malpractices, this was true for many other domestic tribunals which were also not subject to judicial review.

The force of the ruling in *Law* was felt in relation to other such regulatory authorities. A number of actions arose concerning the Jockey Club in which the court reluctantly declined to admit the case into the section 31 jurisdiction because of the holding in the greyhound case.[76]

An opportunity to reconsider the point arose in yet another Jockey Club case, *R. v. Disciplinary Committee of the Jockey Club, ex p. Aga Khan.*[77]

---

[75] [1983] 1 W.L.R. 1302.
[76] Both of these cases were decided in 1989, but were only fully reported later, *R. v. Disciplinary Committee of the Jockey Club, ex p. Massingberd-Mundy* [1993] 2 All E.R. 207; *R. v. Jockey Club, ex p. RAM Racecourses Ltd.* [1993] 2 All E.R. 225.
[77] [1993] 2 All E.R. 853.

The applicant was an owner of racehorses and was therefore bound to register with the Jockey Club and to enter a contractual relationship whereby he adhered to the rules of racing established by it. One of the applicant's horses was disqualified after winning a major race, and he sought judicial review of this decision. The Court of Appeal found that in general the Club was not susceptible to judicial review, and it did not accept the argument that the decision in *Law* had been overtaken by that in *Datafin*. The court acknowledged that the Club regulated a national activity and Bingham M.R. accepted that if it did not regulate the sport then the government would in all probability be bound to do so. Notwithstanding this the court reached its conclusion because the Club was not in its origin, constitution, membership or history a public body, and its powers were not governmental. Moreover, the applicant in this particular case would have a remedy outside section 31 because he had a contract with the Jockey Club. The court did, however, leave open the possibility that some cases concerning bodies like the Jockey Club might be brought within the public law procedures, particularly where the applicant or plaintiff had no contractual relationship with the Club, or where the Club made rules which were discriminatory in nature.[78]

A similar reluctance to subject the governing authorities of sporting associations to judicial review is also apparent in the *Football Association* case.[79] The FA was the governing authority for football and all clubs who wished to play had to be affiliated to the FA. The FA sanctioned various competitions, the most important of which was the Football League (FL). The FL ran the four divisions comprising the league and had a contractual relationship with the FA. The dispute arose from the decision by the FA to establish the Premier League which would be run by it and not by the FL. In order to facilitate the top clubs breaking away from the FL and forming the Premier League, the FA declared void certain rules of the FL which rendered it difficult for clubs to terminate their relationship with the FL. The FL then sought judicial review of this decision, arguing that the FA had a monopoly control over the game, and that although there was a contract between the FA and the FL the rules of the FA were, in reality, a legislative code which regulated an important aspect of national life in the absence of which there would have to be a public body to perform the same function. Rose J. rejected the application for judicial review. He held that the FA was not susceptible to judicial review, notwithstanding its monopolistic powers. It was not underpinned in any way by any state agency, nor was there any real governmental interest in its functions, nor was there any evidence that if the FA did not exist a public body would have to be created in its place.

The disinclination to intervene via judicial review with such bodies is not restricted to those which operate in the sporting arena. In *R. v. Lloyd's of London, ex p. Briggs*[80] it was held that Lloyd's of London was not amenable

---

[78] *Ibid.* pp. 867, 873. In neither the *RAM* case [1993] 2 All E.R. 225 nor *Massingberd-Mundy* [1993] 2 All E.R. 207 did the applicant have a contractual relationship with the Club.
[79] *R. v. Football Association Ltd., ex p. Football League Ltd.* [1993] 2 All E.R. 833; *R. v. Football Association of Wales, ex p. Flint Town United Football Club* [1991] C.O.D. 44.
[80] [1993] C.O.D. 66.

to judicial review in an action brought by "names" who had lost money in insurance syndicates which had covered asbestosis and pollution claims. The court held that Lloyd's was not a public body regulating the insurance market, but rather a body which ran one part of the market pursuant to a private Act of Parliament. The case was concerned solely with the contracts between the names and their managing agents.

It is interesting to reflect a little further on the cases discussed within this section precisely because they do raise in stark form the question as to the boundary of public law. If one stands back from the individual decisions one can perceive three principal strands in the courts' reasoning.

The first is that *not all power is public power*. The courts undoubtedly recognise that these regulatory authorities exercise power over their area, but they do not necessarily accept that this should be characterised as a species of public power. Thus in the *Aga Khan* case Hoffmann L.J. had this to say about the Jockey Club:[81]

> "But the mere fact of power, even over a substantial area of economic activity, is not enough. In a mixed economy, power may be private as well as public. Private power may affect the public interest and the livelihoods of many individuals. But that does not subject it to the rules of public law. If control is needed it must be found in the law of contract, the doctrine of restraint of trade, the Restrictive Trade Practices Act 1976, Arts 85 and 86 of the EEC Treaty and all the other instruments available for curbing the excesses of private power."

A second strand in the courts' reasoning is related to the first. It concerns the *suitability of the public law controls* for the types of body under discussion. This is an important point. The volume of case law which is concerned with the public/private divide can all too easily lead us to forget that there are *consequences*, in terms of the procedural and substantive norms which are held to be applicable to such bodies, as a result of attributing the label "public" to them. The concern as to whether such norms are always well suited to the bodies considered within this section finds expression in the judgment of Rose J. in the *Football Association* case:[82]

> "...for my part, to apply to the governing body of football, on the basis that it is a public body, principles honed for the control of the abuse of power by government and its creatures would involve what, in today's fashionable parlance, would be called a quantum leap."

A third factor which has clearly influenced the court is more pragmatic in nature: if these bodies are deemed to fall within public law then *where should we stop?* Rose J. has this in mind when reflecting that if the FA is sufficiently public for the purposes of section 31 then presumably so too would the governing authorities of virtually all other sports, from tennis to motor racing and from golf to cricket.[83] And if this were so then why should not the exercise of power by private corporate undertakings which have a

---

[81] [1993] 2 All E.R. 853, 875.
[82] [1993] 2 All E.R. 833, 849.
[83] *Ibid.* p. 849.

monopolistic position be subject to the strictures of public law?[84] This then raises consequential practical concerns about the capacity of the courts to deal with this breadth and volume of material without becoming "even more swamped with applications than they are already."[85]

There is no doubt that people will differ as to the cogency of these reasons. For some all species of power are "public", and nominally private exercises of power *should* be subject to equally rigorous controls as when such power is exercised by a public body *stricto sensu*. We will return to these issues later. For the present it will suffice to say that these are endemic problems about the scope of public law which would be present even if the whole section 31 procedure had never been invented.

(5) EMPLOYMENT RELATIONSHIPS: THE STRAINING OF THE PUBLIC/PRIVATE DIVIDE

Numerous cases have come before the courts concerning employment relationships, with employees seeking to argue that the case has a sufficiently public component to warrant use of the section 31 procedure, while employers have on the whole sought to resist this type of argument. The applicant employees have had mixed success in their attempts to use the application for judicial review.

In *Lavelle*[86] the applicant claimed that she had been dismissed by the BBC in breach of natural justice, and sought judicial review. Woolf J. decided that this claim could not proceed under section 31. Although that section was not wholly confined to cases where relief could previously have been granted by prerogative order, it was restricted to matters of a public as opposed to a private or domestic nature. On the facts, the relationship between Lavelle and the BBC was private in nature and therefore judicial review was inappropriate.[87] The same result was reached in *Walsh*[88] where a senior nursing officer was dismissed and sought relief by way of judicial review for a breach of natural justice. The defendant contested the suitability of section 31 proceedings, and this challenge was upheld. The court reasoned as follows. Judicial review is only available for issues of public law. Ordinary master-servant relationships did not involve any such issue, the only remedy being a damages action, or relief under the relevant employment legislation. A public law issue could arise if Walsh could be said to hold an office where the employer was operating under a statutory restriction as to the grounds of dismissal.[89] However employment by a public authority did not *per se* "inject" a public law element; nor did the seniority of the employee; nor did the fact that the employer was required

---

[84] Borrie, "The Regulation of Public and Private Power" [1989] P.L. 552. See above, Chap. 6.
[85] *Football Association* [1993] 2 All E.R. 833, 849.
[86] *R. v. British Broadcasting Corporation, ex p. Lavelle* [1983] 1 W.L.R. 23.
[87] Woolf J. did, however, go on to say that an action for an injunction outside of section 31 could be pursued, and that the BBC was the type of employer which did have the duty to comply with natural justice. See above, pp. 318–319 for discussion of this aspect of the case.
[88] *R. v. East Berkshire Health Authority, ex p. Walsh* [1985] Q.B. 152. See also, *R. v. Derbyshire County Council, ex p. Noble* [1990] I.C.R. 808.
[89] Following *Ridge* v. *Baldwin* [1964] A.C. 40, 65, and *Malloch* v. *Aberdeen Corporation* [1971] 1 W.L.R. 1578, 1582, 1595. See above, pp. 318–319.

to contract with its employees on special terms. An employee could, however, be a "potential candidate" for administrative law remedies where Parliament "underpinned" the employee's position by "directly restricting the freedom of the public authority to dismiss".

The preceding cases can be contrasted with *Benwell*,[90] where a prison officer was allowed to seek judicial review, the court holding that there was a sufficient statutory underpinning to inject the requisite public law element. It is, however, now clear that a prison officer is not compelled to use the section 31 procedure. In the *McLaren* case[91] a prison officer who sought to argue that new working practices were in breach of a collective agreement known as Fresh Start was allowed to bring his action by way of ordinary writ.

In the *McLaren* case[92] Woolf L.J. distilled some of the more general principles which should apply in employment cases.

(a) The starting point, said Woolf L.J., was that employees of public bodies should pursue their cases in the normal way *outside* section 31, by way of ordinary action for a declaration, damages and the like. This was so even if the particular employee held an office from the Crown which was dismissable at pleasure: "whatever rights the employee has will be enforceable normally by an ordinary action".[93] Judicial review was therefore neither necessary, nor appropriate in normal cases.

(b) Judicial review could, however, be sought if the public employee was affected by a disciplinary body established under statute or the prerogative to which the employer or employee was required or entitled to refer disputes affecting their relationship. Provided that the tribunal had a sufficiently public law element then section 31 could be used.

(c) Judicial review could also be sought by a public employee if he or she was attacking a decision of *general* application and doing so on *Wednesbury* grounds. The *GCHQ*[94] case was regarded as an example of this.

(d) Even where review was not available because the disciplinary procedures were purely domestic in nature, it might still be possible for the employee to seek a declaration outside section 31 to ensure that the proceedings were conducted fairly.[95]

The guidelines in *McLaren* will hopefully render matters clearer for litigants and their advisers than has been the case in the past. Having said this the current position is still open to question for a number of reasons.

First, the whole issue of how employment cases are to be tried, whether within section 31 or by ordinary writ, has generated a complex body of case

---

[90] R. v. *Secretary of State for the Home Dept., ex p. Benwell* [1985] Q.B. 554.
[91] *McLaren* v. *Home Office* [1990] I.C.R. 824.
[92] *Ibid.* pp. 836-837.
[93] *Ibid.* p. 836.
[94] [1985] A.C. 374.
[95] As in *Lavelle* [1983] 1 W.L.R. 23.

law which has been difficult to interpret for all concerned.[96] The matter has been exacerbated by the fact that public bodies have played the procedural complexities from both sides: when civil servants have attempted to use the public procedures the Crown has argued that the issue was private and unsuited to review;[97] when the action has been begun by way of ordinary writ the public body has contended that it should have been brought within section 31.[98]

Secondly, it is evident that changes in the pattern of governance over the last few years have rendered it more difficult to distinguish between public and private employment.[99] This does not mean that the distinction between the two spheres has been entirely eroded, but it does mean that the "appropriate question is not whether employment is or is not 'public'...but rather ...whether an individual provision should be applicable to particular employment in light of the purpose which it is designed to serve."[100]

Thirdly, whether the approach adopted in *McLaren* achieves the correct balance is itself open to question. The starting assumption is that all employment actions should be brought outside section 31 on the hypothesis that the basic employment relationship is intrinsically private, whether the employer operates in the public or private sector. One consequence of this will be to relieve the court of such actions under the section 31 procedure, thereby reducing the workload and foreclosing attempts to secure job security rights indirectly through the use of the public law remedies. The starting proposition is then qualified in the manner described above, and what unites these exceptions is the idea that there is something more general or widespread at stake than in the normal run of the mill employment dispute. However, as Fredman and Morris point out, the exceptions could prove to have a wider application than might have been thought. Referring to the exception mentioned in (c) above they state,[101]

"The problem is that this exception could easily engulf the rule. Not only do decisions respecting public employees affect a large number of employees, but they also frequently concern issues which are of public interest and in respect of which the public has the right to expect responsible and accountable behaviour. This is well illustrated by *McLaren*: although McLaren appeared to be an individual litigating an individual point, in fact, he was testing the applicability of a collective agreement to all the prison officers at his establishment; and more fundamentally was pursuing a general public policy issue about the

---

[96] See Fredman and Morris, "Public or Private: State Employees and Judicial Review" (1991) 107 L.Q.R. 298, and "A Snake or a Ladder: *O'Reilly* v. *Mackman* Reconsidered" (1992) 108 L.Q.R. 353.
[97] *e.g. R.* v. *Civil Service Appeal Board, ex p. Bruce* [1988] I.C.R. 649, [1989] I.C.R. 171.
[98] *e.g. McLaren* [1990] I.C.R. 824.
[99] See above, Chap. 3.
[100] Morris and Fredman, "Is There a Public/Private Labour Law Divide?" (1993) 14 Comparative Labor Law Jnl. 115, 123.
[101] "The Costs of Exclusivity: the Case of Public Employees", paper delivered to Cambridge Conference on the Law Commission's proposals, 1993, pp. 5-6; "Public or Private" (1991) 107 L.Q.R. 298, 307; "The Costs of Exclusivity: Public and Private Re-examined" [1994] P.L. 69.

administration of the Prison Service and the Fresh Start agreement. It is difficult to argue that this latter point is not one that affects the public."

It remains to be seen how often employees will seek to avail themselves of the "*McLaren* exceptions" and how often the courts will accede to such requests.

Finally, there is, moreover, a latent tension between *McLaren* and *Roy*. The former sees "ordinary" employment disputes being litigated by writ outside section 31, with matters of more general importance which raise *Wednesbury* type issues being brought by way of review. *Roy*, as we have seen, countenances actions outside section 31 when private rights are involved *and* their Lordships appeared to be willing to answer public law issues which might arise within the ordinary action begun by writ. This latent strain will doubtless be resolved, but there is a real issue dividing the courts. The approach in *McLaren* is based on the idea that while pure private rights cases should be tried outside section 31, the protections of *O'Reilly* should avail public bodies when public law issues are involved. In *Roy*, by way of contrast, while the court is mindful of the protections afforded to public bodies by the requirement of leave and time limits, it appears to be more willing to allow a case to proceed by way of ordinary action if private rights are involved notwithstanding the fact that the action might also entail a consideration of public law issues.

(6) ACTIVITIES WHICH ARE "INHERENTLY PRIVATE"

Some activities are regarded as inherently private, or not public, and in that sense unsuited to the judicial review procedure. The *Wachmann*[102] case provides an example of this. The applicant sought judicial review of a disciplinary decision which removed him as a Rabbi because of conduct which rendered him morally unfit to continue in the position. Simon Brown J. refused the application, holding that the jurisdiction of the Chief Rabbi was not susceptible to judicial review. He held that the section 31 procedure could only be used when there was not merely a public, but a governmental interest in the decision-making power in question. The Chief Rabbi's functions were said to be essentially intimate, spiritual and religious, and the government could not and would not seek to discharge them if he were to abdicate his regulatory responsibility, nor would Parliament contemplate legislating to regulate the discharge of these functions. Moreover, the reviewing court was not in a position to regulate what was essentially a religious function, i.e. whether a person was morally fit to carry out his or her spiritual responsibilities.

(7) FUTURE PROSPECTS

It remains to be seen how far the courts will be willing to take the scope of judicial review. The reservations of many among the judiciary at the prospect of extending review to the exercise of private power have been

---

[102] R. v. *Chief Rabbi of the United Congregations of Great Britain and the Commonwealth, ex p. Wachmann* [1993] 2 All E.R. 249; R. v. *Iman of Bury Park Jame Masjid Luton, ex p. Sulaiman Ali* [1992] C.O.D. 132.

noted above. Some advocate a broader approach. Thus Lord Woolf would, it seems, be in favour of extending review to cover all bodies which exercise authority over another person or body in such a manner as to cause material prejudice to that person or body. These controls could, on principle, apply to bodies exercising power over sport and religion.[103]

If the scope of review is extended thus far then careful attention will have to be given to the question raised in a number of the cases considered above: how far should the procedural and substantive norms which are applied against traditional public bodies also be applied against private bodies? Many of the cases within this section are concerned with the application of procedural norms. If we were to follow Lord Woolf's suggestion then would we also think it appropriate to apply substantive norms? For example, would we insist that large private companies take account of all relevant considerations before deciding upon a course of action? Would we demand that their actions should be subject to a principle of proportionality, assuming that this becomes an accepted part of our substantive control? If there is an affirmative answer to these and other such questions then the change would be significant to say the very least. It would have ramifications for many other subjects, such as company law, commercial law and contract; it would radically increase the courts' case load under the section 31 procedure;[104] and it would involve difficult questions as to how such substantive public law principles fit with previously accepted doctrines of private law. How would these substantive controls interact with previously accepted notions of how those with power should conduct their operations in a market economy, given that private law has developed its own constraints upon such enterprises? What would, for example, we mean by the application of a principle of proportionality in such circumstances? Would the courts test the means-end relationship of a corporate plan, or of a scheme devised by the Football Association?

Section 4. The Rationale for Exclusivity

We have touched on the arguments for the presumptive exclusivity of the section 31 procedure in the preceding discussion. It is now time to consider these arguments in more detail. The main reason for this presumptive exclusivity of section 31 which is found in *O'Reilly* is that the requirement of leave and the limited time within which applications can be brought under section 31 both express policy judgments as to the conditions under which a remedy may be obtained. To allow these to be circumvented by sanctioning an ordinary action requires strong justification. Let us consider leave and time limits separately.

---

[103] "Judicial Review: A Possible Programme for Reform" [1992] P.L. 221, 235.
[104] This would surely be so notwithstanding Lord Woolf's caveat that review would only be available if there was no suitable alternative remedy, *ibid.* p. 235.

1. *Protecting Public Bodies: Leave*

(1) THE NATURE OF THE PROTECTION PROVIDED BY LEAVE

The reasons for requiring leave are mixed. Historically there is the idea that the action is being brought in the name of the Crown; in the case of certiorari, a royal demand for information. Leave has, however, only been required since 1933. Modern reasons focus upon the protection which the leave requirement provides for the public body. What then does "protection" mean? Two senses of this term can be distinguished.

On the one hand, it could be argued that public bodies must be protected from vexatious litigants and that leave achieves this. This argument is highly suspect. The vexatious litigant appears to be a hypothetical rather than a real problem. In so far as this spectre assumes a solid form the problem can be solved by adequate provisions as to costs.[105] The case law and literature on the declaration and injunction prior to 1977 contains no evidence that this was a problem even though there was no leave requirement, and evidence under the new procedure indicates that the frivolous nature of the application is a very rare ground for refusing leave.[106]

On the other hand, it could be argued that public bodies must be protected using that term in a less obvious, broader sense. The argument is as follows. Public bodies exist to perform public duties, which are for the benefit of the public as a whole. In deciding whether an action should proceed this wider public interest must be taken into account, as well as that of the applicant, because the public have an interest in seeing that litigation does not unduly hamper the governmental process. This type of reasoning is present in *O'Reilly* itself, and in the arguments of those who support the decision.[107] A corollary of this argument is that the leave requirement exists to protect public bodies from applicants who do not really have a chance of winning their case: it is a screening mechanism to prevent the public body from being troubled by cases which are likely to be unsuccessful. A crucial question concerns the *test* which is to be applied when striking out cases at the leave stage. What criterion is the court to use when deciding whether a case should proceed? This question was addressed by Lord Donaldson M.R. in *R. v. Secretary of State for the Home Department, ex p. Doorga*.[108] His Lordship gave directions to judges hearing applications for leave, and said that they should distinguish between three categories of case.

"The first is the case where there are, prima facie, reasons for granting judicial review. In such a case leave shall duly be granted. There are

---

[105] The court has, in any event, an inherent jurisdiction to strike out vexatious claims. In addition there are statutory powers to strike out vexatious claims, Supreme Court Act 1981, s.42, and there are Rules of the Supreme Court which enable provision to be made as to costs.
[106] Le Sueur and Sunkin, "Applications for Judicial Review: the Requirement of Leave" [1992] P.L. 102, 120.
[107] *e.g.* The Rt. Hon. Sir H. Woolf, "Public Law-Private Law: Why the Divide? A Personal View" [1986] P.L. 220, 230; Sir H. Woolf, *Protecting the Public – A New Challenge* (1990).
[108] [1990] C.O.D. 109, 110. See also, *R. v. Secretary of State for the Home Department, ex p. Begum* [1990] C.O.D. 107, 108.

other cases in which the application for judicial review is wholly unarguable, in which case, quite clearly leave should be refused. However, there is an intermediate category – not very frequent but it does occur – in which the judge may say, 'Well, there is no prima facie case on the applicant's evidence but, nevertheless, the applicant's evidence leaves me with an uneasy feeling and I should like to know more about this.' Alternatively he may say, 'The applicant's case looks strong but I nevertheless have an uneasy feeling that there may be some very quick and easy explanation for this.' In either case it would be quite proper, and, indeed, reasonable for him to adjourn the application for leave in order that it may be further heard *inter partes*. At such a hearing it is not for the respondent to deploy his full case, but he simply has to put forward, if he can, some totally knock-out point which makes it clear that there is no basis for the application at all."

(2) THE NEED FOR THE PROTECTION OF LEAVE: AN EVALUATION

The argument presented above is an essentially pragmatic one about the need to protect public bodies against cases which do not have the requisite chance of success to warrant proceeding to a full hearing. This practical justification is given added force by the rise in the number of applications for judicial review which has served to convince many within the judiciary that some filter mechanism is essential. Further reflection upon the criterion set out by Lord Donaldson M.R. may nonetheless cast some doubt upon the necessity for such a test. There are two possible interpretations of the above criterion.

One interpretation would take the language used by the court seriously. A case should only be refused leave if it is indeed "unarguable" or "wholly unarguable".[109] Now such language is strong and it would seem prima facie unlikely that there would be floods of cases being brought before the courts which really were unarguable in this extreme sense. If there are a large number of such cases then there must be something very wrong further back in the system. Public or private money would be being wasted by lawyers encouraging claimants to pursue cases which really were unarguable in this sense. At the least it can be said that the rational individual is unlikely to wish to press a case if he or she were advised by a lawyer that the action was wholly unarguable.

The other possible interpretation of Lord Donaldson's language would be as follows. It might be contended that this language should be construed more liberally than its literal meaning would suggest, and that a judge should refuse leave where he believes that there is no reasonable chance of success in the main action, or some other similar criterion. There are serious objections to this contention. It does not fit with the actual wording used by Lord Donaldson, and is also inconsistent with the third intermediate category set out by his Lordship. The purpose of this third category is not

---

[109] In *Doorga* [1990] C.O.D. 109, 110, Lord Donaldson M.R. used the language "wholly unarguable", whereas in *Begum* [1990] C.O.D. 107, 108, his Lordship stated that if there was no arguable case leave should be refused.

to refuse leave on the basis that the judge decides that the applicant will have little chance of success. It is rather to invite the respondent to a form of mini-hearing to consider whether the case should in fact proceed. Moreover, to advocate a judicial power to refuse leave because the judge decides that the applicant does not have a reasonable chance of success, or some similar test, is open to an equally important objection of principle. The judge at the leave stage would be playing a dangerous guessing game on fact and law, the outcome of which might well be based upon purely written documentation and reached under fairly severe time constraints. As Megarry J. has stated, albeit in a different context, the law is full of cases which appear to be open and shut, but which turn out not to be so straightforward.[110]

Those who advocate the leave requirement as a protection for public bodies are, therefore, faced with a choice. They can interpret Lord Donaldson M.R.'s words in their true spirit and only refuse leave where the case really is unarguable. Relatively few such cases are likely to exist, and one may well wonder whether the whole edifice erected to protect public bodies is worth the effort. They could, in the alternative, interpret his Lordship's words more liberally so as to exclude cases which do not have some reasonable chance of success at the substantive hearing. This hurdle would be more difficult to surmount at the leave stage, and in this sense would give more protection to public bodies who are being sued. However, this interpretation is open to the objections mentioned above.

(3) THE NEED FOR THE PROTECTION OF LEAVE: EMPIRICAL EVIDENCE

Two pieces of valuable empirical work have now been done on the leave requirement. One is by Le Sueur and Sunkin.[111] Their findings were as follows.

(a) Approximately 37% of applications for leave were refused. It is possible, as will be seen below, to make a renewed application before a different judge and roughly 40% of such renewed applications were successful. This demonstrates the significant rate of error at the initial application stage.

(b) Leave may be decided by way of written application, or by an oral procedure which tends to be more formal particularly when Lord Donaldson's mini-hearing is used. Even within the category of oral hearings the authors distinguished between "quick look" cases where the judge decided the leave issue in 40 minutes or less; and "good look" cases which took longer than this. The majority of oral applications were decided on the basis of the quick look approach and the leave procedure worked best in such cases. (It is now the norm for *ex parte* applications to be listed for 20 minutes.)[112]

---

[110] *John v. Rees* [1970] Ch. 345, 402.
[111] "Applications for Judicial Review: The Requirement of Leave" [1992] P.L. 102; Sunkin, "What is Happening to Applications for Judicial Review?" (1987) 54 M.L.R. 432.
[112] Practice Note [1991] 1 All E.R. 1055.

(c) The reasons given for refusing leave varied. Lack of sufficient interest was only rarely the reason why the applicant failed. The most important grounds for applications failing were: delay; the inappropriateness of the public law procedure; and the fact that the case was held to be unarguable. The last of these three reasons accounted for the great majority of unsuccessful applications, and the study makes two interesting points about the criterion of arguability. On the one hand, the authors found that it was difficult to differentiate the three categories of case identified by Lord Donaldson M.R. On the other hand, even where a judge did express himself in forthright language and declare a case to be unarguable such cases have proven to be far from clear: "cases characterised as wholly unarguable at the leave stage have gone on to win on the merits at the full hearing".[113] Many cases were found to be neither wholly unarguable nor patently arguable with the consequence that the judge was forced into playing a dangerous guessing game on fact and law.[114] Moreover, the largest category of cases deemed to be unarguable were those in which it was said that the facts or evidence did not sustain the applicant's claim. Yet this demonstrates the need for applicants to be able to present the factual basis of their claim as fully as possible, with consequential ramifications for discovery and the like.

(d) The authors argue that there should at the very least be more structuring of the judicial discretion at the leave stage, in order to imbue the vague term "arguability" with greater precision, or to replace it with some other related concept such as "serious issue to be tried". There should then be a presumption that leave should be granted unless one of a number of grounds for refusing relief are present, including: there is no serious issue to be tried; the application is premature; the applicant does not have standing; delay.

(e) Insofar as the judges in deciding upon questions of leave have been motivated by concerns over managing the overall case load the authors rightly point out the dangers which this entails. There is, as they say, "something profoundly ambiguous in giving to the judiciary 'administrative' powers to allocate scarce court resources in a context where the courts are required to supervise the 'administrative' decisions of government," more particularly so where the criteria for decision-making are unclear.[115]

The other important piece of empirical work which has been done on the application for judicial review is by Sunkin, Bridges and Meszaros.[116] Their main findings can be summarised as follows.

(a) The authors challenge the orthodoxy that judicial review applications have exploded, or at least place this in perspective. They point

---

[113] "Applications for Judicial Review" [1992] P.L. 102, 122.
[114] *Loc. cit.*, referring to Craig, "Procedures, Rights and Remedies" (1990) 2 E.R.P.L. 425, 436.
[115] *Ibid.* p. 126.
[116] *Judicial Review in Perspective: An Investigation of Trends in the Use and Operation of the Judicial Review Procedure in England and Wales*, Public Law Project, 1993.

out that while the number of review applications has increased fourfold since 1981 two main areas account for a very large number of such cases: nearly half of all applications relate to immigration and home-lessness.

(b) While most applications are brought by individuals many are targeted at local rather than central government.

(c) The authors point out that the criteria for refusing leave are not fixed and they find that the leave hurdle has become a rather more substantial hurdle for applicants in recent years. Whereas leave was granted in 73% of cases in the early 1980s, this figure fell to between 56% and 61% between 1987-1989. The study also found that an applicant's likelihood of success could vary dramatically depending upon the judge hearing the application: some were conservative in this respect, granting leave in only 25% of cases; others were more liberal, allowing 82% to proceed; yet others were in the middle of this range, giving leave in 40-60% of cases. Not surprisingly this rendered the application process something of a lottery for individuals.

(d) Many cases are withdrawn (between 31-42%), the majority of these being after leave *has* been given. One implication of this is that respondents may well be sheltering behind the leave requirement, and only considering a negotiated settlement once leave has been obtained.

Two general conclusions can be drawn from these informative studies.

(a) The first concerns the leave requirement itself. We come back to a point made earlier in the discussion: the actual test being applied at the leave stage. Even when the courts are purportedly applying the criterion of arguability they have been refusing roughly 40% of cases. This could mean that, contrary to what was suggested above, there really are this high number of wholly unarguable cases. The figures of failed appli-cations could, alternatively, mean that the courts are in reality applying a more stringent test, and only allowing cases to proceed if there is some reasonable chance of success, or if the case really appears to be arguable on the merits. This certainly appears to be so with respect to some judges who have a very low rate of allowing leave. The dangers of explicitly adopting any such test have been adverted to above, and are reinforced by the empirical studies in the following sense. Even where the courts have been applying the test of arguability, some at least of the cases deemed initially to be wholly unarguable have gone on to win on the merits at the full hearing, or have been granted leave on a renewed application. Given that this is so, the "error rating" on leave applications is likely to be even higher should the courts explicitly adopt the more stringent test, quite simply because there is more room for differences of opinion when a test is framed in terms of "reasonable chance of success" as compared with "wholly unarguable". There is clearly a need for more structuring of judicial discretion in this area of the kind described above.

(b) The second general conclusion concerns the overall number of applications for review. The studies show clearly that these figures must be kept in perspective because they are "bunched" around certain specific subject-matter areas. Equally important is the fact that the short time limits may be a factor in the increase in review applications. The detailed rules on time limits will be considered below. It will be seen that these limits often preclude any effective negotiated settlement of a case *prior* to resort to the courts. There are indeed explicit dicta that an aggrieved citizen will have to make a choice between political and legal resolution of a grievance, and that resort to the former will not be held to be a good reason for extending the time limit for review applications.[117] This is borne out by the second study, which highlights the way in which the grant of leave may be the catalyst to the initiation of a negotiated solution, and hence the withdrawal of the case from the court. Yet, as the authors of the second study indicate, this may not be the most rational way for disputes to be resolved. They argue that a somewhat longer time limit before applications have to be lodged, combined with fuller information on the reasons for the disputed decision, may facilitate pre-leave settlement and hence reduce the workload of the courts.

(4) THE NEED FOR THE PROTECTION OF LEAVE: BROADER ISSUES

The discussion thus far has concentrated upon the arguments advanced in favour of leave and an evaluation of those arguments. Two broader issues should not, however, be forgotten.

Firstly, the private rights exception to *O'Reilly*, whereby an individual can proceed outside of section 31 if he or she can assert the infringement of a private law right, indirectly undermines the argument that leave is required to protect public bodies. If one accepts that such protection is required, why should this be jettisoned merely because the applicant happens to possess or assert a private law right? The possession of such a right does not mean that public law issues are irrelevant, as we have seen above.[118] The *Davy* decision provides a further simple example. The damages claim was that the council had negligently advised the plaintiff of his rights under the planning legislation. This was regarded as a simple tort action which did not involve any matter of public law as a "live issue".[119] The plaintiff could, therefore, proceed outside of section 31 to vindicate his private rights. However the central point of any such case will be the proper construction of the relevant planning legislation, and hence whether the defendant council carelessly advised the plaintiff. If the plaintiff wins the effect will be to vindicate his private rights. But, *whether* he wins will depend upon the construction of this legislation. If the public interest requires that litigation should not unduly hamper the governmental process, why is this less relevant when there is a tort claim the central focus of which

---

[117] See below, pp. 586-587.
[118] See above, pp. 560-561.
[119] [1984] A.C. 262.

will be the ambit of a public body's powers, rather than a direct challenge to the validity of the authority's action?[120]

Secondly, if one accepts the preceding arguments about the need for public bodies to be protected by the leave requirement then one is implicitly making certain judgments about public and private law which should be made apparent. Public law applicants are not entitled to pursue a case of their own accord. They must argue their way into court. Moreover the fact that leave is intended to be *ex parte* strengthens this theme: the proposed respondent may be represented, but the onus is on the individual to argue him or herself into a full hearing. Contrast this with a normal private law case. The individual decides to bring a claim and provided that a cause of action asserting a breach of contract, tort, etc., can be framed the plaintiff is entitled to proceed with no requirement of leave. The onus is on the defendant to argue that the case should be struck out. It is questionable whether this dichotomy is justifiable.[121] We should, at the very least, be aware that we are drawing it and evaluate whether it really is defensible.

(5) LEAVE AND BENEFIT TO THE INDIVIDUAL: ADVICE, SPEED AND COST

The benefits of a presumptively exclusive procedure for public law cases are said not to reside solely in the protection thereby afforded to public bodies. Individuals are said to benefit from such a procedure. The leave requirement is said to enable the individual to ascertain at small cost and expeditiously whether there is a real legal case or not.[122]

This benefit of the leave requirement does, however, raise broader questions. A plaintiff in a private action bears the risks of the action, unless legal aid can be obtained. It is the individual's rights which are at stake, and the plaintiff must pay the going rate for a full adjudication which will provide an answer. In a public law case the applicant is not entitled to come to court as of right. But because this is the position we do not, it seems, feel that the applicant must necessarily bear all the costs. The leave requirement can provide a "remarkably quick, cheap and easy method of obtaining the view of an experienced High Court judge as to whether the application has any merit".[123]

This reasoning is, with respect, questionable. Cheap legal aid is of course beneficial. However, can it really be the case that the most cost effective way to provide such advice is through using the time of a judge? Moreover, given the strains placed upon the general legal aid budget, is it correct to assume that public law applicants should be placed in this privileged position in the allocation of such scarce "legal aid" services? It would,

---

[120] Lord Fraser stated that the council's interest in not being kept in suspense as to the validity of the enforcement notice did not apply, because the notice itself was not being challenged, [1984] A.C. 262, 274. However, the council would almost certainly be more concerned about whether their *general* interpretation of the planning legislation was correct, and it was this which the plaintiff would have to impugn to succeed in his negligence action.
[121] Craig, "Procedures, Rights and Remedies" (1990) 2 E.R.P.L. 425, 437-440.
[122] Law Comm. No. 73, Cmnd. 6407 (1973), para. 38; Woolf, "Public Law-Private Law" [1986] P.L. 220, 230-231.
[123] Woolf, "Public Law–Private Law" [1986] P.L. 220, 230.

moreover, be mistaken to assume that the new procedure always does possess the advantage of cheapness to the individual. One of the principal arguments used by an individual to allow her to raise the invalidity of a bylaw by way of defence in a magistrates' court was the relatively low cost of this when compared to bringing an action under section 31.[124]

2. *Protecting Public Bodies: Time Limits*

(1) THE RULES ON TIME LIMITS

The rules on time limits and delay are complicated. Before 1977 only certiorari was subject to an established time limit, which was six months, albeit with a discretion to extend beyond this period which was rarely exercised. Declarations and injunctions were not subject to formal limitation periods, but delay could be a factor in the court deciding whether in its discretion to refuse relief.

The rules concerning delay have now been altered. Order 53, rule 4 contained the new provisions for delay. This was ambiguous[125] and was replaced in 1980.[126] The amended rule states that an application for leave to apply for judicial review shall be made promptly and in any event within three months from the date when grounds for the application first arose, unless the court considers that there is good reason for extending the period within which the application shall be made. Where the relief sought is an order of certiorari in respect of any judgment, order, conviction or other proceeding, the date when grounds for the application first arose shall be taken to be the date of that judgment, order, conviction or proceeding. The general rule on prompt applications and the three months time limit are without prejudice to any statutory provision which has the effect of limiting the time within which an application for judicial review may be made.

The Supreme Court Act 1981, section 31(6) also contains provisions on delay, but is framed in somewhat different terms. This states that where the High Court considers that there has been undue delay in making an application for judicial review, the court may refuse to grant leave for making the application or any relief sought on the application if it considers that the granting of the relief sought would be likely to cause substantial hardship to, or substantially prejudice the rights of, any person, or would be detrimental to good administration.

There are four key differences between the two formulations. First, section 31(6) expresses no actual time limit at all, whereas the 1980 amendment to rule 4 sets a general limit of three months. Secondly, section 31(6) mentions the detriment to good administration and prejudice to a party's rights as factors to be taken into account. These factors were present in the original Order 53, rule 4, but were left out of the 1980 amendment.

---

[124] R. v. *Crown Court at Reading, ex p. Hutchinson* [1987] 3 W.L.R. 1062.

[125] Beatson and Matthews, "Reform of Administrative Law Remedies: The First Step" (1978) 41 M.L.R. 437, 442-444.

[126] S.I. 1980 No. 2000, r. 3, amending Order 53, r. 4.

Thirdly, section 31(6) contains no reference to the date from which time begins to run, not surprisingly since it contains no actual time limit. The 1980 amendment does at least provide guidance on this in relation to certiorari. This is a point of considerable practical importance given the brevity of the time period. What, for example, would be the appropriate point from which to start the clock where the order sought to be impugned was delegated legislation, or some other form of rule-making? Would it be the date on which the rule was made, which may in itself be unclear, the date when the applicant knows or ought to know about it, or some other time?[127] The final difference is that Order 53 applies at the leave stage,[128] whereas section 31(6) applies both at the leave stage and at the substantive hearing.

The leading decision on the issue is that of the House of Lords in *Caswell*.[129] Lord Goff accepted that the relevant provisions on delay were not easy to reconcile, but held that they interrelated in the following manner.

(a) When an application for leave is not made promptly, and in any event within three months, the court can refuse leave on the grounds of delay unless it considers that there is good reason for extending the period. This is derived from Order 53, rule 4.

(b) However, even if the court believes that there is good reason for extending the time, the applicant will still be held to have "unduly delayed" in bringing the case. This phrase is the condition precedent for invoking section 31(6). The court may, therefore, still refuse leave to apply for relief, or decline to grant the substantive relief itself, if it considers that the granting of such relief would be likely to cause substantial hardship to, or detrimentally prejudice the rights of, any person, or if it would be detrimental to good administration.

It is clear that the courts may hold that an application was not made promptly even if it was made within three months,[130] and moreover that the court at the substantive hearing may decide that there has been undue delay even where the issue of promptness has been argued at the leave stage.[131]

(2) JUSTIFICATION FOR THE PRESENT RULES

The reasoning here is more straightforward than in the context of leave. Shorter time limits are said to be required in public law cases because of the greater need for certainty than in private law. There is a wider public

---

[127] In *R. v. London Borough of Redbridge, ex p. G* [1991] C.O.D. 398, it was assumed that time ran from when a policy was actually made, but that the fact that the applicant had no knowledge of the policy until it was published later was regarded as a good reason for extending the time limit.

[128] *R. v. Stratford-on-Avon D.C., ex p. Jackson* [1985] 1 W.L.R. 1319.

[129] *R. v. Dairy Produce Quota Tribunal, ex p. Caswell* [1990] 2 A.C. 738.

[130] *Hilditch* v. *Westminster City Council* [1990] C.O.D. 434.

[131] *R. v. Swale Borough Council, ex p. Royal Society for the Protection of Birds* [1990] C.O.D. 263.

interest involved in ensuring that the public service knows whether its actions will be valid or not.[132] There are a number of objections to this reasoning.

First, there does not appear to be any evidence that the longer limitation periods in the declaration and injunction cases decided prior to 1977 caused problems.

Secondly, if such problems were to arise they could be dealt with by a number of techniques. In areas where there is a high premium on certainty, specific statutory provision could be made to ensure that the challenge was brought within a certain defined period. Such provisions are already common in legislation concerning planning. The exercise of discretion in granting particular types of relief, and the development of prospective as opposed to retrospective invalidity, could also be employed to resolve problems in particular cases.

Thirdly, in so far as there is a need for short time limits, this is, once again, undermined by allowing applicants with private rights to proceed outside section 31.[133]

The final comment on time limits is different in nature. We have already seen that the increase in the volume of applications for judicial review has been one of the reasons fuelling the demand for protection for public bodies in terms of the leave requirement. The short time limits may, in a paradoxical sense, increase the amount of litigation against the administration. An individual who believes that the public body has acted *ultra vires* now has the strongest incentive to seek a *judicial resolution* of the matter immediately, as opposed to attempting a *negotiated solution*, quite simply because if the individual forbears from suing he or she may be deemed not to have applied promptly or within the three month time limit. This has been acknowledged by the courts.[134]

> "...any citizen who had a problem with local government, or with any other bureaucracy, was faced with a choice: he could either seek by political means to influence the decision, or could consider whether he had any legal remedy. If he elected to adopt the first course, and achieved nothing, he could not rely on that as a ground for extending time."

Legal advisers must therefore tell their clients that an application for judicial review should be made at once, rather than attempting to negotiate a solution first. Negotiated solutions are of course possible once litigation has begun. However, the existence of a formal suit can polarise existing positions, rendering each party more intransigent. In any event the increase in the number of applications for judicial review may be partly explicable on this basis.

---

[132] *O'Reilly* v. *Mackman* [1983] 2 A.C. 237, 249.
[133] See also, Beatson, (1987) 103 L.Q.R. 34, 44-45.
[134] *R.* v. *London Borough of Redbridge, ex p. G* [1991] C.O.D. 398, 400.

3. A Specialist Court

A further possible reason for making the section 31 procedure exclusive might be that it thereby creates a specialist administrative law court, and that this is beneficial because the judges who staff such a court will develop expertise in this area. Such reasoning has influenced the judiciary,[135] although it is not specifically mentioned by Lord Diplock in *O'Reilly*. There are two difficulties with this rationale for exclusivity.

First, if this reasoning does have force then it should apply to all cases brought by or against public authorities, and not simply to those involving a direct challenge to the validity of administrative action. The private rights exception would not exist if this rationale were to be taken seriously. Secondly, as Beatson notes,[136] subject-matter specialisation may be a better way to promote expertise, rather than specialisation at the procedural level.

Section 5. Reform of the Reforms

The reforms introduced in the late 1970s have clearly not succeeded in rendering the law of remedies simpler, which was one of their principal objectives. The passage of time has witnessed the creation of an ever more complex tapestry of case law, and this has led to calls for further reform in the law of remedies. It is the direction of such reform which will be considered within this section.

1. Two Central Propositions

Before examining the reform proposals it is necessary to be clear about two central propositions, since confusion on these issues will cloud our thinking on detailed proposals for the future.

The first of these propositions is that "fault" concerning the idea of presumptive exclusivity should *not* be laid at the door of *O'Reilly* itself, *nor* is the idea of presumptive exclusivity necessarily illogical. Now this may seem to be an odd proposition given that it was that seminal case which gave birth to this idea, and given also the complex case law which has been generated by it. Notwithstanding this the seeds of future discord were in fact sown earlier by the Law Commission for the following reason. The Law Commission did not intend the new procedure to be exclusive,[137] but they failed fully to reason through the implications of their own reforms. It was the Law Commission which proposed the new procedure, complete

---

[135] *e.g. O'Reilly* v. *Mackman* [1983] 2 A.C. 237, 259, *per* Lord Denning M.R.; *Heywood* v. *Hull Prison Board of Visitors* [1980] 3 All E.R. 594, 598, 601.

[136] "'Public' and 'Private'" (1987) 103 L.Q.R. 34, 43, *e.g.* industrial tribunals may possess more expertise in employment cases than judges who hear judicial review applications.

[137] Law Comm. No. 73, Cmnd. 6407 (1976), para. 34.

with leave requirements and time limits in order to protect public bodies. Given this initial choice the courts were placed in a dilemma. They could treat the procedure as *non-exclusive*. The consequences would, however, be odd. Precisely the same factual situations would be treated in radically different ways depending on which remedial route the applicant chose. How could it be sensibly maintained that, on the same facts, one applicant could proceed without leave and with no formal time limit, while another applicant would be subject to leave proceedings and a very much shorter time period? As Lord Woolf has said,[138] it seems "to be illogical to have a procedure which is designed to protect the public from unnecessary interference with administrative action, and then allow the protection which is provided to be by-passed". The courts could alternatively insist, as they have done, that section 31 *is presumptively exclusive* for public law cases with all the attendant problems which this has entailed.

The important point which emerges from this is quite simple. Do public bodies really require the protections considered above? If the answer is yes then some species of exclusivity will have to follow in order to prevent these protections from being by-passed. The only way to avoid this conclusion, while still believing that public bodies merit some special protections, would be to move to a unified system based on the ordinary writ procedure, but to modify this procedure to accommodate the particular needs of public bodies. This would, however, still necessitate some procedural division which corresponded to those cases where it was felt that these special needs were present and those where they were not.

The second proposition is that the problem of deciding what is a public body, or which bodies should be amenable to public law principles, would be present even if we had a radically different system of remedies. This requires a brief explanation. It is common to hear people argue that if we did not have the present regime then the problems discussed in section 3 above, concerning the scope of public law, would disappear. This is quite mistaken. These problems are endemic. This can be simply demonstrated. Let us imagine that we do reform remedies; that we scrap the present system; that we assimilate the prerogative orders to declaration and injunction; and that we allow any action to be begun by ordinary writ. It would *still* be necessary to decide which bodies are sufficiently public for public law principles to be applied to them. The difference between such a new regime and the present is that at present the resolution of these questions one way or another leads to different procedural routes being deemed appropriate, whereas this would not be so under the new regime which was posited. The substantive questions themselves would not, however, disappear, and it would be idle to pretend otherwise. These questions were present long before the reforms in remedies introduced in the late 1970s, as witnessed by the fact that the courts had to decide whether to apply principles of procedural fairness to bodies such as trade associations, unions and the like. Put shortly, the substantive issues presented by cases such as *Aga Khan* and the like are here to stay.

---

[138] "Judicial Review: A Possible Programme for Reform" [1992] P.L. 221, 231.

2. Reform Options

(1) THE EXCLUSIVITY PRINCIPLE AND LEAVE

The choices for dealing with the exclusivity principle were neatly summarised by the Law Commission:[139]

> (a) the principle could be abolished, with the consequence that there would be no special rules for dealing with public law cases and public bodies would be exposed to the same liability to declaratory and injunctive relief as respondents in civil litigation;
> (b) the principle could be extended to all proceedings for declarations and injunctions against public authorities, with the consequence that the current exceptions to the principle would cease to operate;
> (c) the boundaries of application of the principle could be delineated more clearly, bearing in mind the competing policy interests of legality and certainty.

Time will tell which option is chosen. One might, nonetheless, make some estimation as to which route will be selected.

Option (a). It is unlikely that (a) will prove to be acceptable. While this choice might well be favoured by many academics who are sceptical of the need for leave and short time limits, many amongst the judiciary remain convinced that these protections are both warranted and necessary, particularly in the light of the increase in the number of applications for judicial review. The government itself is unlikely to be willing to accede to a change which would remove many of the existing procedural protections. It should nonetheless be remembered that a large percentage of the total number of review applications are in fact drawn from two areas, immigration and homelessness. If special provision could be made for these areas then the problem of the courts' case load would be correspondingly diminished. Lord Woolf has in fact made suggestions to deal with these areas, which would allow powers of review to be exercised by bodies other than the High Court itself.[140]

It is important to understand that under this option the prerogative orders would be assimilated to ordinary actions rather than vice versa. There would be no leave requirement, and the defendant would take the initiative to strike out the claim.[141] Suitable techniques for protecting public bodies in these actions could be devised when such protection was really warranted. They could take the form of expedited procedures, and dismissal of cases on grounds of delay.[142] While option (a) might prove to be more palatable if it were accompanied by such increased provision for

---

[139] Law Commission Consultation Paper No. 126, *Administrative Law and Statutory Appeals* (1993), pp. 18-19, hereafter LCCP.

[140] "Judicial Review: A Possible Programme for Reform" [1992] P.L. 221, 236-238.

[141] This idea had considerable support from amongst those who had supplied information to the Law Commission prior to the 1977 reforms. It was rejected because it was felt that it would present opportunities for delay, be more costly and slower.

[142] Wade, *Administrative Law* (6th ed., 1988), pp. 680-681.

striking out of claims,[143] in circumstances where there would, for example, be excessive administrative inconvenience, this option is still unlikely to be accepted. It is felt by some that the ordinary writ procedures, even as amended in the above fashion, would be too cumbersome for the multitude of judicial review applications, and that it would require the public body to enter a defence and plead that one of the special provisions should be applied to the instant case.[144]

Option (b). This will also probably be rejected. While the government might be in favour of extending *O'Reilly* in this manner, the experience of the last decade has shown that cases involving public law issues can arise in a number of ways. To impose requirements of leave *and* short time limits in all instances could well cause hardship to many litigants who are, for example, defendants in actions, such as in *Winder*, and therefore have no control over timing, or who did not know of the facts giving rise to the cause of action within the relevant time, such as in *Lonrho*.

Option (c). It is likely, therefore, that some version of option (c) will be adopted. Precisely what form remains to be seen, but it will probably be along the lines indicated in *Roy*.[145] Cases involving private rights[146] will most likely be allowed to be brought by ordinary writ outside section 31, especially if there are complex factual issues involved. Certainty for litigants would be increased if the "broad approach" identified by Lord Lowry in *Roy* were to be accepted,[147] with the consequence that cases concerned with private rights were regarded as outside the exclusivity principle altogether, with the section 31 procedure being insisted upon only in purely public law cases. The Law Commission provisionally supports this view.[148] This "result" would be open to the objections made above, to the effect that the protections for a public body would be sacrificed merely because some private right was at stake even though the public law issue was central to the case.[149] However, given that exclusivity is unlikely to be abolished, or extended to all proceedings, some form of option (c) is inevitable, and in this sense the clearer that it is the better. A consequential reform to allow cases to transfer into the public law procedure where, for example, it was found that the private right really did depend upon the exercise of administrative discretion, would be helpful.[150]

(2) THE LEAVE PROCEDURE ITSELF

The leave procedure itself will almost certainly remain for the reasons identified above: both the judiciary and the government believe that it is

---

[143] Wade, "Procedure and Prerogative in Public Law" (1985) 101 L.Q.R. 180.
[144] LCCP para. 5.8; Sir John Laws, "Procedural Exclusivity", paper delivered at Robinson College, Cambridge, 15 May, 1993.
[145] [1992] 1 A.C. 624.
[146] At least where those rights are not dependent upon the exercise of a public body's discretion, as in *Cocks* [1983] 2 A.C. 286.
[147] [1992] 1 A.C. 624, 653.
[148] LCCP para. 3.23.
[149] See above, pp. 559-562.
[150] LCCP, p. 20.

necessary for the protection of public bodies, and the Law Commission's provisional view is the same.[151] Assuming that this is so there are nonetheless beneficial changes which could be made.

The test for when leave is to be given or refused could be structured in the manner suggested by Le Sueur and Sunkin above.[152] The criterion of "arguability" could, in particular, be clarified in order that the threshold level for a case to proceed or not could become clearer. Whether cases should only be refused leave if they are wholly unarguable, or whether some more rigorous test is to be applied, which requires the applicant to demonstrate a reasonable chance of success or the like, is clearly of importance, both practically and conceptually.[153]

(3) TIME LIMITS

The present rules on time limits were considered above. It is clear that there should be some rules which recognise the need for legal certainty on the part of the administration and in that sense some time limits are inevitable. The real question is whether the current rules are set at the correct level. Practice in other countries varies, but relatively short time limits are not uncommon.[154]

The provisional view of the Law Commission is against abandoning specific time limits for public law proceedings and against relying on the ordinary limitation periods for civil actions. It believes that a period between three and six months is desirable, with the caveat that if the shorter of these is adopted then delay within the given period should be ignored.[155]

For the reasons given above[156] it is thought that anything less than six months would be too short, and even then delay in bringing the application within this time should only rarely be regarded as undue delay. The date from which the time begins to run will be particularly important. It should, moreover, be recognised that if time limits of this brevity are retained then, as noted earlier, this will fuel the number of applications for judicial review: applicants will not have the time to engage in any negotiated solution prior to seeking judicial relief.

(4) DISCOVERY

We have already seen the role played by discovery in the reforms: how these reforms made improved provision for discovery; how this was regarded in O'Reilly as part of the justification for procedural exclusivity; and how in reality the courts have in fact restricted discovery so that it is rarely awarded in judicial review proceedings, because of the costs and time implications of being more liberal in this respect.[157] The normal criterion is

---

[151] LCCP para. 5.14.
[152] See above, pp. 580-581.
[153] See above, pp. 578-580.
[154] LCCP pp. 26-29.
[155] *Ibid.* pp. 30-31.
[156] See above, pp. 586-587.
[157] See above, pp. 552-553.

that discovery will be allowed when it is necessary either for disposing fairly of the cause or for saving costs.[158]

The problem which this presents to the individual can be formidable. It can be extremely difficult to sustain certain types of challenge without discovery, and cross-examination. Allegations that an administrator has taken irrelevant considerations into account, or has acted for improper purposes are but two such instances. The need for discovery will, moreover, be needed if the courts are to develop emerging doctrines such as proportionality. As the Law Commission point out, if the present restrictive regime is not relaxed then it will be said that the revised Order 53 has not remedied the problems in this area, thereby fuelling the demand that applicants should be allowed to proceed by ordinary writ when discovery is required.

(5) STATUTORY APPEALS

The discussion thus far has concentrated upon the possibilities of reform to the procedures for judicial review. The need for reform of statutory appeals should not, however, be forgotten. The complexity of the existing appeal procedures has been brought out by the Law Commission.[159] Reform in this area is clearly desirable and the Law Commission has focused attention upon a number of ways in which the present procedures could be simplified.[160]

Section 6. Procedure

1. *The Application*

Applications for judicial review are, as we have seen, subject to a two-stage procedure.[161] The first stage is application for leave which is made *ex parte* to a single judge. Applications for leave used to be made to a Divisional Court of the Queen's Bench Division, except in vacation when they could be made to a judge in Chambers. This approach was preserved in the revised Order 53, rule 3(2). The modification whereby applications for leave should be made to a single judge was introduced at the beginning of 1981,[162] largely because of pressures of work and because of the establishment of a cadre of administrative judges. This latter point will be explained more fully below.[163] An application for leave must be made by filing in the Crown Office a notice containing a statement of the name and description of the applicant, the relief sought and the grounds on which it is sought, the

---

[158] R.S.C. Order 24, r. 13(1).
[159] LCCP pp. 95-106.
[160] *Ibid.* pp. 107-115.
[161] See generally, Supperstone and Goudie (eds.), *Judicial Review* (1992), Chaps. 16-17.
[162] S.I. 1980 No. 2000, r. 2, amending Order 53, r. 3.
[163] Blom-Cooper, "The New Face of Judicial Review: Administrative Changes in Order 53" [1982] P.L. 250.

name and address of the applicant's solicitors (if any), and the applicant's address for service. An affidavit verifying the facts relied on must also be filed.[164] The judge can determine the application without a hearing, unless a hearing is requested in the notice of application, and need not sit in open court; in any case, the Crown Office shall serve a copy of the judge's order on the applicant.[165] Where the application for leave is refused by the judge, or is granted on terms, the applicant may renew it by applying in any criminal cause or matter to a Divisional Court of the Queen's Bench Division, and in any other case, to a single judge sitting in open court, or if the court so directs, to a Divisional Court of the Queen's Bench Division; provided that no application for leave may be renewed in a non-criminal cause or matter in which the judge has refused leave after a hearing.[166]

The court hearing an application can allow the applicant's statement to be amended on such terms, if any, as it thinks fit.[167] Leave shall not be granted unless the court considers that the applicant has a sufficient interest in the matter to which the application relates.[168] The meaning of this term has already been considered.[169] Where leave to apply for judicial review is granted then, if the relief sought is an order of certiorari or prohibition and the court so directs, the grant shall operate as a stay of the proceedings to which the application relates until the determination of the application, or until the court otherwise orders; if any other relief is sought the court may at any time in the proceedings grant such interim relief as could be granted in an action begun by writ.[170] Applications for leave are also subject to rules on delay. The ambiguity in these provisions has been considered above.[171]

An application can be made to set aside leave. This will, however, only be successful in clear cases where the respondent can point to some evident "knock out" point,[172] such as material non-disclosure of facts by the applicant, the existence of a precedent which shows that the initial leave was given *per incuriam*, or a jurisdictional bar to review.[173]

From April 1991 applications for leave to apply for judicial review were to be listed on the basis that they would take only 20 minutes, with a further 10 minutes for a reply by any respondent who attended. If counsel

---

[164] S.I. 1980 No. 2000, r. 2, amending Order 53, r. 3. It is possible for cases to be expedited, Practice Note [1987] 1 W.L.R. 232.

[165] Order 53, r. 3(3), as revised by S.I. 1980 No. 2000, r. 2(1).

[166] Order 53, r. 3(4), as revised by S.I. 1980 No. 2000, r. 2(1); *Re Poh* [1983] 1 W.L.R. 2; *R. v. Commissioner for the Special Purposes of the Income Tax Acts, ex p. Stipplechoice Ltd.* [1985] 2 All E.R. 465.

[167] Order 53, r. 3(6). The subparagraphs of r. 3 have been renumbered in the lights of the changes introduced by S.I. 1980 No. 2000, r. 2(2).

[168] Order 53, r. 3(7); Supreme Court Act 1981, s.31(3).

[169] See above, Chap. 13.

[170] Order 53, r. 3(10). See below, p. 731., for the effect of these provisions on the availability of relief against the Crown.

[171] See above, pp. 585-586.

[172] *R. v. Secretary of State for the Home Department, ex p. Sholola* [1992] C.O.D. 226, 227.

[173] *R. v. Secretary of State for the Home Department, ex p. Khalid Al-Nafeesi* [1990] C.O.D. 106; *R. v. Jockey Club Licensing Committee, ex p. Wright* [1991] C.O.D. 306; *R. v. Secretary of State for the Home Department, ex p. Nazir Chinoy* [1991] C.O.D. 381; *R. v. Bromsgrove District Council, ex p. Kennedy* [1992] C.O.D. 129.

believe that a longer period is required then a special fixture must be arranged.[174]

If the applicant wishes the leave application to be expedited this should be mentioned on the notice of application, and it will then be for the judge who is deciding the leave application to determine whether it is placed on the expedited list.[175]

2. The Hearing

The second stage is the hearing itself. For a criminal cause or matter this is before a Divisional Court of the Queen's Bench Division. In any other matter the application shall be made by originating motion to a judge sitting in open court, unless the court directs that it shall be made by originating summons to a judge in chambers, or by originating motion to a Divisional Court of the Queen's Bench Division.[176] Most civil cases are heard by a single judge. The notice of the motion must be served on all persons directly affected.[177] The court also has power to admit a person not served who desires to be heard in opposition to the motion or summons, and who appears to be a proper person to be heard.[178] There are provisions allowing the applicant to amend his or her statements and to use further affidavits, provided that the court agrees.[179] Provision is made for discovery, interrogatories and cross-examination.[180] Damages can now be claimed in conjunction with the other remedies. It had previously not been possible to combine damages with a claim for prerogative relief. The provision does not, however, create a new damages remedy where none existed before: the court must be satisfied that if the claim had been made in an ordinary action the applicant would have been awarded damages.[181] There is a useful provision which applies to certiorari, whereby a court can, in addition to quashing the decision, remit the matter to the court, tribunal or authority concerned, with a direction to reconsider it and reach a decision in accordance with the finding of the court.[182]

The procedure for applications for judicial review has been overlaid with certain administrative modifications. The change whereby applications for leave are in general heard by a single judge has produced what is, in effect, an administrative list, based on the model of the Commercial List.

---

[174] Practice Note [1991] 1 All E.R. 1055.

[175] Practice Direction [1981] 1 W.L.R. 1296.

[176] S.I. 1980 No. 2000, r. 4, amending Order 53, r. 5(1), (2).

[177] Order 53, r. 5(3). And see r. 5(4), (8).

[178] Order 53, r. 9(1).

[179] Ibid. r. 6.

[180] Ibid. r. 8. But see above pp. for the discussion of how often cross-examination will be used. An appeal against discovery cannot be used to challenge the initial leave to apply for judicial review, R. v. Secretary of State for the Home Department, ex p. Herbage (No. 2) [1987] Q.B. 1077.

[181] Order 53, r. 7; Supreme Court Act 1981, s.31(4).

[182] Order 53, r. 9(4).

Judges with special expertise in administrative law have been assigned to operate the new Order 53. This process has been furthered by the Practice Direction referred to above,[183] which provides for the transfer of non-jury actions with an administrative flavour onto the Crown Office list. Further provisions bring in appeals to the High Court from tribunals and the like, and appeals under planning, and social welfare legislation.

3. *Discretion to Refuse Relief*

We have already seen that the courts exercise discretion in deciding whether to grant a remedy or not, and that they take into account a variety of factors, including: waiver, bad faith, the premature nature of the application, the absence of any injustice, the impact on third parties and the administration, and whether the decision would have been the same irrespective of the error.[184]

Whether they ought to do so is a matter on which opinions could well differ. Sir Thomas Bingham has expressed the view that such discretion is acceptable provided that it is strictly limited and the rules for its exercise are clearly understood.[185] There is much to be said for this view. Two further comments are in order.

The first is that, as Sir Thomas Bingham clearly accepts, differing considerations should apply to the various grounds for refusing relief. Commentators have, for example, been critical of decisions which have held that a failure to comply with the rules on natural justice and hearings can lead to a remedy being denied because the court believes that the outcome would have been no different anyway.[186] It is doubtful whether this should ever be a ground for refusing relief, and the strong judgment by Sir Thomas Bingham pointing out the dangers of denying relief on this ground is, therefore, to be welcomed.[187] This ground for withholding relief may be contrasted with the situation where the court decides not to award a remedy in the form of a coercive order because the respondent authority is doing all that it can to comply with its statutory duty,[188] where the error has been substantially cured,[189] where the problem is now moot,[190] or where there would be serious public inconvenience in upsetting the impugned order.[191]

---

[183] [1981] 1 W.L.R. 1296. See also, the Practice Direction [1982] 3 All E.R. 704 aimed at expediting decisions.

[184] See above, Chap. 14.

[185] "Should Public Law Remedies be Discretionary?" [1991] P.L. 64.

[186] See above, pp. 301–302.

[187] R. v. *Chief Constable of the Thames Valley Police Forces, ex p. Cotton* [1990] I.R.L.R. 344. Courts have, however, held that in cases of failure to comply with the rules on bias because of a pecuniary interest the court may in its discretion refuse relief, R. v. *Governors of Bacon's School, ex p. Inner London Education Authority* [1990] C.O.D. 414.

[188] R. v. *Bristol Corporation, ex p. Hendy* [1974] 1 W.L.R. 498.

[189] R. v. *Secretary of State for Social Services, ex p. A.M.A.* [1986] 1 W.L.R. 1.

[190] See above, pp. 535–537.

[191] R. v. *Secretary of State for Social Services, ex p. A.M.A.* [1993] C.O.D. 54.

The second comment is as follows. The discretion to refuse relief operates *against* the individual when the public body has prima facie committed an *ultra vires* act. This is so whether the discretion assumes the form of denying the remedy entirely or rendering the relief only prospectively rather than retrospectively applicable. Either way the *ultra vires* principle is being qualified for good reason. If we are willing to do this then we should also be willing to qualify the *ultra vires* principle *in favour* of the individual in circumstances where, for example, a person has relied upon an *ultra vires* representation and has suffered loss, provided that there are no dire consequences for the public interest.[192]

Section 7. The Effect of Alternative Remedies

1. *Choice of Remedies within Section 31*

The traditional view was that the availability of prerogative relief did not operate as a bar to seeking a declaration.[193] The position may now have changed. The removal of many of the restrictions upon the prerogative orders, and the availability of all the remedies under a unified procedure, has inclined some courts to the view that the prerogative orders should be used whenever the validity of a decision is attacked.[194]

2. *Alternative Statutory Remedies*[195]

The effect of statutory appeal procedures upon the availability of judicial review raises two issues which, although linked, should be distinguished.

First, while it is clear that the existence of such a procedure does not operate as a jurisdictional bar to judicial review, it is less clear how far such a procedure creates a presumption that resort should be had to that procedure rather than judicial review. In *Preston*[196] the House of Lords stated that judicial review should only rarely be available if an appellate procedure existed. This may be contrasted with the rather more liberal approach of

---

[192] See below, Chap. 18.
[193] *Pyx Granite Co. Ltd.* v. *Ministry of Housing and Local Government* [1960] A.C. 260, 290.
[194] *Cocks* v. *Thanet District Council* [1983] 2 A.C. 286.
[195] Lewis, "The Exhaustion of Alternative Remedies" [1992] C.L.J. 138.
[196] *R.* v. *Inland Revenue Commissioners, ex p. Preston* [1985] A.C. 835, 852, 862. See also, *R.* v. *Epping and Harlow General Commissioners, ex p. Goldstraw* [1983] 3 All E.R. 257, 262; *R.* v. *Chief Constable of the Merseyside Police, ex p. Calveley* [1986] Q.B. 424, 433-434; *Pasmore* v. *Oswaldtwistle Urban District Council* [1898] A.C. 387, 394; *R.* v. *Poplar Borough Council (No. 1), ex p. London County Council* [1922] 1 K.B. 72, 84-85, 88, 94; *R.* v. *Panel on Take-Overs and Mergers, ex p. Guinness plc.* [1990] 1 Q.B. 146; *R.* v. *Police Complaints Authority, ex p. Wells* [1991] C.O.D. 95.

Lord Denning M.R. in the *Paddington Valuation* case,[197] where his Lordship stated that review would be available where the alternative appellate procedure was "nowhere near so convenient, beneficial and effectual". The courts have on the whole adopted the approach in *Preston*,[198] but they have also been willing to recognise exceptions and allow the judicial review application.

Secondly, what factors will the courts take into account in deciding whether to allow an application for judicial review, even though an alternative appellate structure exists? A number of such factors can be identified.

(a) Judicial review is unlikely to be ousted where doubt exists as to whether a right of appeal exists,[199] or whether such an appellate right covers the circumstances of the case.[200]

(b) Review is also likely to be available where the alleged error is one of law. Thus in the *Paddington Valuation* case[201] Lord Denning M.R. stated that while the statutory appeal procedures might be suitable for individual challenges to the rating list, review was more appropriate where the legality of the whole rating list was impugned; similarly in the *Royco Homes* case,[202] Lord Widgery C.J. clearly felt that review was particularly well suited to errors of law; and in *Wells*[203] it was held that while an applicant should normally be left to pursue the statutory remedy, judicial review would be available if the tribunal had plainly misdirected itself on a matter of law. An applicant is, by way of contrast, likely to be restricted to the statutory appeal procedure where the case turns on mixed questions of law and fact,[204] disputed questions of fact, and/or the appeal tribunal possesses expertise.[205]

(c) An applicant will also be allowed to seek judicial review where the statutory appeal mechanism is felt to provide a remedy which is inadequate when compared to judicial review. Thus in *Leech* v. *Deputy Governor of Parkhurst Prison*[206] a prisoner was allowed to seek judicial review of a disciplinary decision reached by a prison

---

[197] [1966] 1 Q.B. 380, 400. See also, *R.* v. *Leicester Guardians* [1899] 2 Q.B. 632, 638-639; *R.* v. *North, ex p. Oakey* [1927] 1 K.B. 491; *Stepney Borough Council* v. *John Walker and Sons Ltd.* [1934] A.C. 365; *ex p. Jarrett* (1946) 52 T.L.R. 230.

[198] Lord Woolf is of the view that judicial review should normally be a matter of last resort, "Judicial Review: A Possible Programme for Reform" [1992] P.L. 221, 235.

[199] *R.* v. *Hounslow London Borough Council, ex p. Pizzey* [1977] 1 W.L.R. 58, 62; *R.* v. *Board of Visitors of Hull Prison, ex p. St. Germain* [1979] Q.B. 425, 456, 465.

[200] *Preston* [1985] A.C. 835, 862.

[201] [1966] 1 Q.B. 380.

[202] *R.* v. *Hillingdon London Borough Council, ex p. Royco Homes Ltd.* [1974] Q.B. 720. See also, *Pyx Granite Co. Ltd.* v. *Ministry of Housing and Local Government* [1960] A.C. 260.

[203] *R.* v. *Police Complaints Authority, ex p. Wells* [1991] C.O.D. 95; *R.* v. *Devon County Council, ex p. Baker* [1993] C.O.D. 253, 255.

[204] *R.* v. *Epping Forest District Council, ex p. Green* [1993] C.O.D. 81.

[205] *Clark* v. *Epsom Rural District Council* [1929] 1 Ch. 287; *Preston* [1985] A.C. 835; *Smeeton* v. *Att.-Gen.* [1920] 1 Ch. 85; *Coney* v. *Choyce* [1975] 1 W.L.R. 422, 434; *Hilditch* v. *Westminster City Council* [1990] C.O.D. 434.

[206] [1988] A.C. 533.

governor, notwithstanding the existence of a petition procedure to the Secretary of State. Their Lordships were influenced by the fact that the Secretary of State did not have the formal power to quash the disciplinary decision reached by the governor, but merely the power to remit the punishment inflicted on the prisoner.

(d) In deciding whether to allow an applicant to utilise judicial review the courts will also take into account more general factors concerning the nature of the appellate procedure, and consider how onerous it is for the individual to be restricted to the statutory mechanism. This is clearly sensible, although the results of this analysis may appear unjust. Thus in *Calveley*[207] the court took account of the fact that the alternative procedure was likely to be slow, and thus allowed police officers to seek judicial review. However, in *Swati*[208] an immigrant was restricted to the statutory appeals procedure, save in exceptional circumstances, notwithstanding the fact that this entailed leaving the United Kingdom in order to avail himself of that right.

3. *Conclusion*

It is clear that a number of factors have influenced the case law on the relationship between review and alternative grounds for relief. The courts have been mindful not to usurp Parliament's choice where the legislature has established a special statutory mechanism to adjudicate on a particular topic. The assumption that litigants must use available statutory machinery has also been influenced by the desire of the courts not to allow the already lengthy list of applications for judicial review to become even longer. Specialised statutory appeal mechanisms may, in addition, be better suited to resolving complex issues of fact, and possess expertise in the relevant area.

These are sensible considerations for the courts to take into account, given that they can and do make exceptions so as to allow a case to proceed by way of judicial review. However, as the Law Commission states,[209] there may well be advantages in determining the issue of the effect of alternative remedies at the leave stage, in order to save the costs of deferring consideration until the main hearing.

---

[207] [1986] Q.B. 424, 434, 440.
[208] R. v. *Secretary of State for the Home Department, ex p. Swati* [1986] 1 W.L.R. 477; R. v. *Secretary of State for the Home Department, ex p. Doorga* [1990] C.O.D. 109, 111.
[209] LCCP 14.14.

16. REMEDIES: EXCLUSION

Section 1. Complete Exclusion

Ever since Coke, Holt and Mansfield laid the first foundations for judicial review the legislature has attempted to prevent those principles from being applied. Various formulae have been inserted into legislation with the intent of precluding judicial intervention. Little success has attended these efforts as the courts have time and again restrictively construed the legislation. The interpretation given to these ouster clauses will be considered in this section, to be followed by discussion of clauses which limit rather than exclude the courts totally.

1. *Finality Clauses*

Finality clauses attempt to achieve just that. They are statutory terms which purport to render the decision of a particular justice or tribunal unassailable. The courts have given them short shrift, holding that they only protect decisions made on facts and not law.[1] Jurisdictional defects are not rendered immune from judicial scrutiny by such a clause,[2] nor were errors on the face of the record. Thus, in *R. v. Medical Appeal Tribunal, ex p. Gilmore*[3] it was held that the decision of the Tribunal was open to attack despite the existence of a finality clause. Denning L.J., as he then was, reviewed the authorities and concluded that the only effect of the clause was to prevent an appeal; judicial review, whether for jurisdictional error or error on the face of the record, remained unimpaired.[4]

Even this limited effect has been subsequently diminished. While high authority has stated that a finality clause can prevent an appeal,[5] that authority has been circumvented and characterised as out of date. The Court of Appeal has held that, notwithstanding the existence of finality

---

[1] *R. v. Plowright* (1686) 3 Mod. 94.
[2] *R. v. Moreley* (1760) 2 Burr. 1040; *R. v. Jukes* (1800) 8 T.R. 542. cf. where certiorari is the creature of statute, *R. v. Hunt* (1856) 6 El. & Bl. 409.
[3] [1957] 1 Q.B. 574.
[4] *Ibid.* pp. 583-585. See also, *R. v. Nat Bell Liquors Ltd.* [1922] 2 A.C. 128, 159-160.
[5] *Kydd v. Liverpool Watch Committee* [1908] A.C. 327; *Piper v. St. Marylebone Licensing JJ.* [1928] 2 K.B. 221.

provisions, it was still possible to state a case, at least where declaration or certiorari would themselves have been available.[6]

2. "No Certiorari" Clauses

Part of the reason for the legislative dislike of judicial review was that the courts would overturn decisions for reasons redolent of a Dickensian caricature. Technical error was seized upon and verdicts quashed with an excess of vigour that bordered upon the pedantic. The legislature responded in a number of ways, one of which was the insertion of no certiorari clauses within statutes. Judicial response to such terms was not wholly aggressive: the courts acknowledged that they had been over-technical.[7] Jurisdictional defects continued, however, to remain unaffected by no certiorari clauses; the courts still struck them down.[8] In R. v. Wood[9] a bylaw compelling home owners to remove snow from in front of their houses was attacked as ultra vires the parent legislation. The statute concerned the removal of dirt, manure, dung and soil. Lord Campbell C.J. rejected any generic identity between these substances and snow in the following firm terms,[10]

> "It might possibly have been advisable to extend the power to the case of all snow; but that is not done: the words of the section cannot, by any strain of construction, be extended to untrodden and unsunned snow, which is proverbially pure...."

The no certiorari clause was held ineffective; the Secretary of State could only give authority to bylaws which were in conformity with the parent legislation.[11]

Such clauses, while ineffective to insulate jurisdictional error, could exclude review for error on the face of the record, while this latter concept still had currency within our legal vocabulary. If the clause is contained in a statute enacted prior to August 1958 it will be subject to the Tribunals and Inquiries Act which will be discussed below. Where, however, the preclusive clause is contained in a statute passed after that date, it could be effective. This is demonstrated by the South East Asia Fire[12] case. The Malaysian Industrial Relations Act 1967, s.29(3)(a) contained an "omnibus" exclusion clause. Parliamentary draftsmen had obviously decided that, ceteris paribus, the more types of exclusion provisions the better. Thus,

---

[6] Tehrani v. Rostron [1972] 1 Q.B. 182, 187-188, 192. See also, Pearlman v. Keepers and Governors of Harrow School [1979] Q.B. 56, 68-69, 79, cf. 74.

[7] R. v. Ruyton (Inhabitants) (1861) 1 B. & S. 534, 545; R. v. Medical Appeal Tribunal, ex p. Gilmore [1957] 1 Q.B. 574, 586.

[8] R. v. Cheltenham Commissioners (1841) 1 Q.B. 467; R. v. Somersetshire JJ. (1826) 5 B. & C. 816.

[9] (1855) 5 El. & Bl. 49.

[10] Ibid. p. 55.

[11] See also, ex p. Bradlaugh (1878) 3 Q.B.D. 509, 512-513.

[12] South East Asia Fire Bricks Sdn. Bhd. v. Non-Metallic Mineral Products Manufacturing Employees Union [1981] A.C. 363.

section 29(3)(a) contained a finality clause, a shall not be challenged or questioned section, and a term providing that awards of the industrial court should not be quashed.[13] A dispute between a company and a union was referred to the industrial court which made a finding in favour of the union. The company sought to have this quashed for error of law on the face of the record. On appeal from the Malaysian courts, the Privy Council declined to interfere. Lord Fraser of Tullybelton, giving the judgment of their Lordships, agreed with the company's argument that the finality provision did not protect the industrial court.[14] The provision within section 29(3)(a) that an award should not be quashed was however sufficient to achieve this end; if it would not suffice by itself, the addition of the words "shall not be called in question in any court of law" were wide enough to cover certiorari. Only errors of law within jurisdiction were rendered immune from attack.[15] A jurisdictional error could still be impugned. The Privy Council rejected the argument that any error of law was now to be regarded as jurisdictional, but, as we have seen, later developments have effectively spelt the end for the concept of error of law within jurisdiction.[16] The expansion of jurisdictional error means that it will be difficult for the legislature to employ this type of clause in order to exclude the courts.

3. "Shall not be Questioned" Clauses

Another formula which has been used by the legislature to exclude the courts has been the "shall not be questioned clause". As has been seen from the *South East Asia Fire*[17] case, this may be used in conjunction with a no certiorari clause. Any hope that persevering parliamentary draftsmen might have had that this formula would work where all else had failed was to prove unfounded.

In the *Anisminic*[18] case, section 4(4) of the Foreign Compensation Act 1950 stated that a determination of the Commission should not be called in question in any court of law. Their Lordships unanimously held that this only protected determinations which were *intra vires*; *ultra vires* determinations were not really determinations at all. They were nullities which could be of no effect. Section 4(4), or any equivalent provision, could,

---

[13] The section states: "Subject to this Act, an award of the [Industrial] Court shall be final and conclusive, and no award shall be challenged, appealed against, reviewed, quashed or called in question in any court of law."

[14] [1981] A.C. 363, 369-370 following *ex p. Gilmore* [1957] 1 Q.B. 574. The court left open the question whether the addition of the words "conclusive" and of the phrase that no award shall be "challenged, appealed against or reviewed" would exclude certiorari. See also, *Re Waldron* [1986] Q.B. 824.

[15] *Ibid.* p. 370.

[16] See above, Chap. 10.

[17] [1981] A.C. 363.

[18] *Anisminic Ltd.* v. *Foreign Compensation Commission* [1969] 2 A.C. 147, 170-171, 181, 200-201, 210; *R.* v. *Secretary of State for the Home Department, ex p. Mehta* [1992] C.O.D. 484.

therefore, only immunise from attack errors of law within jurisdiction and this concept has itself now ceased to exist.

4. *"As if Enacted" and "Conclusive Evidence"*

A protective technique has been used to insulate subordinate legislation which differs from those discussed above. This is to provide that a statutory order shall have effect "as if enacted in this Act", or that confirmation by a designated minister "shall be conclusive evidence that the requirements of this Act have been complied with, and that the order has been duly made and is within the powers of this Act".

Such clauses have been condemned by the Committee on Ministers' Powers[19] which doubted whether such devices would safeguard an order which was flagrantly *ultra vires* from judicial censure. Other preclusive clauses have not proven effective even where the invalidity was not extreme.[20] Despite this, both formulations have been successful in excluding review. The authorities upholding the efficacy of the "conclusive evidence" formula date mainly from the earlier part of this century.[21] However recent authority has continued to uphold the effectiveness of such clauses.[22]

The current status of the "as if" formula is that two decisions of the House of Lords indicate opposite conclusions and are difficult to reconcile. In the earlier decision their Lordships interpreted the effect of the clause as being to render secondary legislation as immune from censure as if it were part of the parent legislation, the cloak of sovereignty protecting all.[23] If this ruling had been taken literally then the executive could have governed the country *de jure* as well as *de facto*. Its scope has, however, been limited. The House of Lords has subsequently held that the "as if" formula does not provide protection for secondary legislation which conflicts with the parent Act.[24] This latter statement appears not simply to limit the former but to contradict it, and indeed there are judgments in the second House of Lords' decision which are difficult to reconcile at all with the earlier authority. As stated above, the two decisions are difficult to interpret together. It may be that the clause will be effective if the statutory order in dispute does relate generally to the statutory scheme, even though it may be subject to relatively minor errors which would nevertheless, in the absence of the clause, render the decision *ultra vires*.[25]

---

[19] Cmd. 4060 (1932), p. 41.

[20] See *R. v. Wood* (1855) 5 El. & Bl. 49.

[21] *Ex p. Ringer* (1909) 73 J.P. 436; *Reddaway v. Lancs County Council* (1925) 41 T.L.R. 422; *Minister of Health v. R., ex p. Yaffe* [1931] A.C. 494, 520, 532-533, but see also *Graddage v. Haringey London Borough Council* [1975] 1 W.L.R. 241; *County and Nimbus Estates Ltd. v. Ealing London Borough Council* (1978) 76 L.G.R. 624.

[22] *R. v. Registrar of Companies, ex p. Central Bank of India* [1986] Q.B. 1114, distinguishing such clauses from the type used in the *Anisminic* case.

[23] *Institute of Patent Agents v. Lockwood* [1894] A.C. 347.

[24] *Minister of Health v. R., ex p. Yaffe* [1931] A.C. 494.

[25] This is the view adopted by de Smith, *Judicial Review of Administrative Action* (4th ed., 1980), pp. 375-376. See also, *Foster v. Aloni* [1951] V.L.R. 481.

The difficulty of interpreting the case law is compounded by uncertainty and disagreement as to what the purpose and effect of the clause originally was. One argument is that the formula had and was intended to have a substantive impact, giving subordinate legislation the same standing as a primary Act; the other is that the magic words were a survival from medieval times and possess now a formal function only. According to this latter view, the clause was used to indicate that the authority for the creation of secondary legislation was based upon Parliament.[26] In any event, this particular preclusive clause has passed out of fashion and, thus, the question is unlikely to arise.[27]

5. *Statutory Intervention*

In 1958 parliamentary intervention took a different form. Criticism about the use of exclusion clauses had been voiced from many differing quarters. The Franks Committee advocated the removal of clauses which purported to oust the prerogative orders.[28] The Tribunals and Inquiries Act 1958 implemented a number of the proposals of the Franks Committee. That Act was replaced by the Tribunals and Inquiries Act 1971, which has itself now been replaced by the Tribunals and Inquiries Act 1992, section 12(1) of which provides that,[29]

> (a) any provision in an Act passed before 1st August 1958 that any order or determination shall not be called into question in any court, or
> (b) any provision in such an Act which by similar words excludes any of the powers of the High Court,
> shall not have effect so as to prevent the removal of the proceedings into the High Court by order of certiorari or to prejudice the powers of the High Court to make orders of mandamus.

Three important limitations upon the scope of the section should be noted. First, the section is subject to two exceptions which are set out in section 12(3), the effect of which is that section 12(1) does not apply to orders or determinations made by courts of law, or to clauses which exclude the courts after a limited period of time. Secondly, the section only applies to certiorari and mandamus. The remedy of declaration is not included within the section. There appears to be no rational reason why this should be so.[30] Thirdly, section 12 has been held not to apply to "conclusive evidence" clauses.[31]

---

[26] Graham-Harrison, *Notes on the Delegation by Parliament of Legislative Powers*, pp. 26-68; Willis, *The Parliamentary Powers of English Government Departments* (1933), pp. 62-101.
[27] It still survives in some legislation, e.g. Emergency Powers Act 1920, s.2(4). *Quaere* whether this type of formula is caught by the Tribunals and Inquiries Act 1992?
[28] Cmnd. 218 (1958), para. 117.
[29] s.12(1) applies to England and Wales. s.12(2) makes similar provision for Scotland.
[30] In *Ridge* v. *Baldwin* [1964] A.C. 40, 120-121, Lord Morris of Borth-y-Gest was of the view that the Act did cover the declaration. But in *O'Reilly* v. *Mackman* [1983] 2 A.C. 237 it was said that this limit showed a preference for the prerogative orders.
[31] R. v. *Registrar of Companies, ex p. Central Bank of India* [1986] Q.B. 1114, 1170, 1178, 1182.

Section 2. Time Limits

In a number of different contexts it may be particularly important to know whether a decision can safely be acted upon. This is particularly so within the realm of regulatory legislation concerning planning, compulsory acquisition and the like. Statutes in such areas normally provide a cut-off period of six weeks after which the decision shall not be called in question in any legal proceedings whatsoever. Within the allowed time there are statutory grounds on which an order can be attacked. Two problems require consideration. First, what is the effect of the expiry of the six weeks? Secondly, what is the scope of review within that period? The first question will be considered in this section, the second has already been considered in the earlier discussion.[32]

The starting point for discussion is the rather confusing case of *Smith* v. *East Elloe Rural District Council*.[33] Smith alleged that a local authority had compulsorily acquired her property in bad faith. Despite the possible presence of fraud their Lordships held that the clause protected the local authority after the expiry of the six weeks.[34] It was unclear how far this decision had been affected by *Anisminic*.[35] The latter also involved a shall not be questioned clause, the difference being that the provision in the Foreign Compensation Act 1950 purported to exclude the courts altogether, whereas in the *Smith* case there was a six weeks time limit within which an order could be challenged. In the *Anisminic* case little favour was shown to the *Smith* decision. It was not expressly overruled, but it was distinguished upon a variety of grounds; the distinction between complete ouster of jurisdiction and time limitations was not, however, foremost in their Lordships' reasoning.[36]

Smith has survived despite this censure. In *R.* v. *Secretary of State for the Environment, ex p. Ostler*[37] the applicant sought to quash a road scheme and compulsory purchase order, alleging breach of natural justice and bad faith. The facts of the case were particularly strong. Ostler argued that he was only applying outside the six-week time limit because a covert agreement between a departmental officer and a local merchant had been hidden from him and had changed the whole complexion of the scheme. If the full facts had been revealed at the appropriate time he would have objected and been within the time limits.

The six-week time limit was, nonetheless, upheld. *Anisminic* was distinguished for a number of reasons. The distinction between a complete ouster clause and a time limit;[38] the administrative nature of the proceedings in the *Smith* case as compared with the more judicial nature of the

---

[32] See above, pp. 364-365.

[33] [1956] A.C. 736.

[34] See also, *Woollett* v. *Minister of Agriculture and Fisheries* [1955] 1 Q.B. 103. *cf. Webb* v. *Minister of Housing and Local Government* [1965] 1 W.L.R. 755.

[35] [1969] 2 A.C. 147.

[36] *Ibid.* pp. 170-171, 200-201, 210.

[37] [1977] Q.B. 122.

[38] *Ibid.* p. 135 (Lord Denning M.R.); *cf.* at p. 138 (Goff L.J.).

Foreign Compensation Commission;[39] and the allegedly differing degrees of nullity ensuing from the defects in the two cases[40] were advanced to uphold the clause. The Court of Appeal was undoubtedly also influenced by the fact that a significant part of the scheme had been begun. To apply a theory of retrospective nullity with remorseless logic would have resulted in considerable disruption and expense.[41]

The decisions in *Smith* and *Ostler* have been followed on a number of occasions. Thus in *R. v. Cornwall County Council, ex p. Huntington*[42] it was held that an order which was subject to a six-week time limit clause could only be challenged within that period, and by the method stipulated in the statute. An applicant could not choose to use the ordinary judicial review procedure instead. It made no difference whether the body whose decision was being challenged was quasi-judicial or administrative; and it was irrelevant whether the invalidity was fundamental or not.

The problem considered within this section is now of considerably greater importance given that the time limits for seeking judicial review within section 31 proceedings are short, and given also that the judiciary have insisted that many cases can only be brought by this route. While these provisions on time limits do not contain any explicit shall not be challenged clause the courts have not, on the whole, been willing to allow actions outside this period.[43]

Section 3. Conclusion

1. *Complete Ouster Clauses*

Whether it would be possible to devise an ouster clause which succeeded in excluding review is less a matter of semantics than of judicial attitude and legislative response. The courts have always been in the position to interpret the words in an Act of Parliament and, thus, they could, if they chose, construe them as only applying to errors within jurisdiction, or, going further, as precluding only appeal. Short of provoking a constitutional clash by rejecting this judicial interpretation, there is nothing that Parliament could do. Clearly the determination of the courts to preserve judicial review in the face of ouster clauses raises issues of sovereignty. Whatever the courts' interpretation of these clauses has been, the parliamentary intent was clear: to limit or remove the courts from the particular area in

---

[39] *Ibid.* p. 135 (Lord Denning M.R.), p. 138 (Goff L.J.).
[40] *Ibid.* pp. 135, 139, 140.
[41] See also, *Jeary v. Chailey Rural District Council* (1973) 26 P. & C.R. 280; *Routh v. Reading Corporation* (1971) 217 E.G. 1337.
[42] [1994] 1 All E.R. 694; *R. v. Secretary of State for the Environment, ex p. Kent* [1990] J.P.L. 124; *R. v. Secretary of State for the Environment, ex p. Upton Brickworks Ltd.* [1992] C.O.D. 301; *R. v. London Borough of Camden, ex p. Woolf* [1992] C.O.D. 456.
[43] See above, pp. 585–586.

question.[44] Until recently the courts could, in formal terms, continue to accept parliamentary authority, even when restrictively construing an ouster clause, by according such clauses some impact, in the sense of protecting errors of law within jurisdiction from attack. The expansion of jurisdictional control, and the corresponding demise of error within jurisdiction, means that this route is no longer open to the judiciary. Ouster clauses will in future have to be treated in one of two ways. Either the court restrictively interprets the clause and robs it of any effect, except perhaps in preventing an appeal. Or it can give the clause some effect by stating that the presumption that all errors of law are open to review has been displaced in a particular area. Even if it chooses this latter approach some judicial control can still be maintained, as experience in other jurisdictions demonstrates.[45]

What does one make of all this? It depends upon one's perspective. It can be seen as a triumph for the rule of law, an open recognition by Parliament that in fact the judicial insistence upon control was correct all along. It is doubtless true that an extensive and unthinking use of ouster clauses to insulate decision-makers from review would be open to abuse.

Yet, given the present judicial attitude, how does the legislature indicate that it believes that a particular area would be better left free from the ordinary judicial process? How does it signal that it might well prefer the view of the original decision-maker to that of the courts? To say that the rule of law will automatically be infringed if the courts' view on the construction of a term in a statute cannot be substituted for that of the decision-maker, is implicitly to presume the answer to the question at stake. *Whose* opinion the legislature regards as correct is the very question before us. We have seen that the answer to this vital question is not to be found in logic, or for that matter in labels.[46] There is a choice to be made; the presence of an ouster clause provides a good indication as to how the legislature would wish that choice to be resolved.

Arguments derived from legislative practice which are used to buttress the present judicial approach are also open to question. How a legislature reacts to the whole problem of ouster clauses depends partly on how the problem is presented to it. This is particularly the case given that the bulk of the legislature are laymen. If the issue is posed in terms of tribunals and commissions extending their powers untrammelled and uncontrolled, while sheltering behind an ouster clause, the legislative response is not difficult to conceive. Equally, one is likely to receive a different reception if one asked the average backbench Member of Parliament whose opinion is to be preferred on the meaning of the words "disablement", "lockout", or "resources", that of the specialist tribunal or that of the ordinary courts.

---

[44] This statement must be qualified in two ways: (a) Parliament has enacted the Tribunals and Inquiries Act 1992, s.12; (b) it has acquiesced, in the sense of continuing to use certain terms even after the legal effect ascribed to them by the courts has become clear.

[45] The Australian courts have retained power in the face of such terms if there is a clear excess of power, while not interfering if the agency has made a bona fide attempt to exercise its authority in a matter relating to the subject with which the legislation deals, Aronson and Franklin, *Review of Administrative Action* (1987), pp. 695-701.

[46] See above, Chap. 10. See also, the observations in *ex p. Central Bank* [1986] Q.B. 1114, 1176.

Both of the above scenarios are of course extremes, but it is important that in our concern for understanding how administrators reach decisions and the influences acting upon them, we do not forget to inquire how the parent legislature works.

As will be clear from the above, the question of when, if ever, ouster clauses should be allowed to stand raises many of the same problems that we considered within our discussion of jurisdiction. A discerning and sensitive use of such terms could, however, be a useful indicator of legislative preference. Nor, as noted above, does the presence of such a clause necessarily have to imply a total absence of judicial control.

Given the present attitude of the courts to clauses which seek to oust the jurisdiction of the courts completely a legislature which is minded to limit judicial intervention might, however, do better by introducing a time limit clause. As we have seen the courts have accepted that such clauses do prevent challenges outside the stipulated period, and that any action brought within that time must be by the procedure laid down in the enabling statute.

2. Time Limits

Statutes containing time limit clauses raise somewhat different problems. In the modern state with its panoply of controls and regulatory machinery, there will necessarily be a trade off between the need for administrative certainty, on the one hand, and justice for the individual and administrative legality on the other. The balancing operation thereby involved appears in varying guises throughout administrative law. It arises in the creative decision as to how to categorise an alleged error, as jurisdictional or not, or as law or fact. It rears its head in the way in which we deal with waiver, delay, and representations. It lies behind some of the judicial manipulation of void and voidable.

The effect to be given to time limits is just another manifestation of this problem. If the *Ostler*[47] decision had gone the other way then some other device, judicial or legislative, would have been required. Where an expensive planning and building project is undertaken then the traditional response of retrospective nullity will be difficult to apply. The method of distinguishing *Anisminic* may or may not have been convincing,[48] but the result does accord with common sense.

This does not mean that we can be complacent, or that there is no room for improvement. Two matters require especial attention. The first is a reconsideration of whether the length of the time limit is adequate. Six

---

[47] [1977] Q.B. 122.
[48] Alder, "Time Limit Clauses and Judicial Review" (1975) 38 M.L.R. 274; Gravells, "Time Limit Clauses and Judicial Review – The Relevance of Context" (1978) 41 M.L.R. 383; Gravells, "Time Limit Clauses and Judicial Review – Some Second Thoughts" (1980) 43 M.L.R. 173; Alder, "Time Limit Clauses and Conceptualism – A Reply" (1980) 43 M.L.R. 670.

weeks is short and thought needs to be given as to what would be the appropriate balance between the needs of the individual and the requirements of the administration. Second, the provision of a compensatory remedy for those unable to complain needs to be thought through. This is particularly important where the individual's recourse to the statutory machinery is effectively foreclosed by bad faith or fraud. The possibility of such a remedy will be considered below.[49]

---

[49] See below, pp. 646-651.

PART 4

REMEDIES
II

17. TORT AND RESTITUTION

Public authorities can, like other corporations, cause loss to individuals by their acts or omissions. The present chapter will examine five issues. First, we will consider the ordinary principles of tortious liability to determine how far individuals who have suffered loss can gain redress. This discussion will also address the difficulties of using these principles against public bodies.[1] Secondly, we will see how far the case law provides support for a special tort referable to public bodies, and the present ambit of such a cause of action. Thirdly, the application of the law of restitution to public bodies will be reviewed. This is a neglected area, but one which is important in principle. Fourthly, the relevance of Community law principles will be analysed, with consideration being given to the possible extension of those principles to situations which do not themselves possess a Community law component. The final part of the chapter will discuss proposals for reform of the law, and the difficulties which will be encountered if the scope of liability for public bodies is extended.

Section 1. Tortious Liability: General Principles

As a general principle a public body which acts *ultra vires* is liable in tort if a cause of action is established, just like any private individual would be.[2] There is no general cloak of immunity. This principle is, however, subject to both limitation and exception.

1. *Statutory Authority and Nuisance*

It is inherent within the above principle that if the loss is caused in pursuance of the lawful exercise of statutory authority no action will lie.

---

[1] See generally, Robinson, *Public Authorities and Legal Liability* (1923), Chaps. 4 and 5; Street, *Governmental Liability* (1953), Chap. 2; Hogg, *Liability of the Crown* (1971), Chap. 4. Harlow, *Compensation and Government Torts* (1982); Arrowsmith, *Civil Liability and Public Authorities* (1992).

[2] *Entick* v. *Carrington* (1765) 19 St. Tr. 1030; *Leach* v. *Money* (1765) 19 St. Tr. 2002; *Cooper* v. *Wandsworth Board of Works* (1863) 14 C.B. (N.S.) 180; *Pride of Derby and Derbyshire Angling Association Ltd.* v. *British Celanese Ltd.* [1953] Ch. 149. See generally, Craig, "Compensation in Public Law" (1980) 96 L.Q.R. 413. On the availability of exemplary damages see *AB* v. *South West Water Services Ltd.* [1993] 1 All E.R. 609.

If the loss is the inevitable result of the exercise of the statutory power or duty there will be no action.[3]

The difficulty is to determine what "inevitable" means. Where the statute prescribes that the public body should act within defined limits and it is obvious that a nuisance must result no action will lie. Similarly, where the statute confers a power to, for example, build for a particular purpose on a particular site and an individual complains of a nuisance flowing from the normal use of the building for that purpose the action will fail,[4] unless it can be proven that the public body did not use all reasonable diligence to prevent the nuisance from occurring.[5] Thus, actions brought for nuisance from the running of trains have failed where the above criteria have been met,[6] and restrictive covenants have been held to be unenforceable in so far as they clash with the exercise of statutory powers.[7]

Conversely, if the statute is permissive and allows a wide choice of site, area, and method, it has been held that the discretion must be exercised in conformity with private rights. A decision to site a smallpox hospital in Hampstead in pursuance of a general power to provide such hospitals was held to be an actionable nuisance unprotected by the statute, *Metropolitan Asylum District* v. *Hill*.[8]

These principles were reaffirmed by the House of Lords in *Allen* v. *Gulf Oil Refining Ltd*:[9] where Parliament, by express direction or by necessary implication, has authorised the construction and use of an undertaking, that carries with it the authority to do what is authorised with immunity from any nuisance action, provided only that there is no negligence.[10] On

---

[3] R. v. *Pease* (1832) 4 B. & Ad. 30; *Vaughan* v. *Taff Vale Ry. Co.* (1860) 5 H. & N. 679; *Hammersmith Ry. Co.* v. *Brand* (1869) L.R. 4 H.L. 171; *London and Brighton Ry. Co.* v. *Truman* (1886) 11 App. Cas. 45; *Manchester Corporation* v. *Farnworth* [1930] A.C. 171; *Dept. of Transport* v. *North West Water Authority* [1984] A.C. 336, 359. See generally, Linden, "Strict Liability, Nuisance and Legislative Authorization" (1966) Osgoode Hall L.J. 196.

[4] See the authorities above n. 3; and *Metropolitan Asylum District* v. *Hill* (1881) 6 App. Cas. 193, 212.

[5] *Manchester Corporation* v. *Farnworth* [1930] A.C. 171; *Tate & Lyle Industries Ltd.* v. *Greater London Council* [1983] 2 A.C. 509.

[6] *Hammersmith Ry. Co.* v. *Brand*, above n. 3.

[7] *Re Simeon and Isle of Wight Rural District Council* [1937] Ch. 525; *Marten* v. *Flight Refuelling* [1962] Ch. 115.

[8] (1881) 6 App. Cas. 193; *Vernon* v. *Vestry of St. James Westminster* (1880) 16 Ch. D. 449. Where an actionable nuisance has been committed it is no defence that the public authority did what was reasonable in the public interest, *Pride of Derby and Derbyshire Angling Association Ltd.* v. *British Celanese Ltd.* [1953] Ch. 149; *cf. Smeaton* v. *Ilford Corporation* [1954] Ch. 450.

[9] [1981] A.C. 1001. The principle also applies where the authorisation is given pursuant to planning permission, *Gillingham Borough Council* v. *Medway (Chatham) Dock Co. Ltd.* [1992] 3 W.L.R. 449.

[10] [1981] A.C. 1001, 1014, 1016, 1023-1024. There is an exception to take account of the *Hill* case, above n. 8. In the *Allen* case this exception is expressed by Lord Wilberforce as applying where the statute is permissive in form [1981] A.C. 1001, 1011: in such circumstances a nuisance action will still lie. It would seem that more is required to reconcile *Brand* and *Hill*, or *Hill* and *Allen*: the statute must not only be permissive, but also allow a wide choice of site or area. This view is supported by Lord Diplock, p. 1014, and by the fact that there was no real choice of site in the *Allen* case itself. The illogicality of this criterion is examined below.

the construction of the statute it was held that, despite the absence of detailed specification as to the building of the refinery, its building and operation were contemplated by the Act, and no nuisance action would lie unless there was negligence.

Despite this recent reaffirmation of established authority, the above analysis is open to challenge on four grounds. First, it cannot reconcile all the cases. For example, *London and Brighton Railway Co.* v. *Truman*,[11] decided by the House of Lords only five years after *Hill*, concerned a claim in nuisance for the noise resulting from cattle kept in a yard. The defendant railway company had power to acquire land for the yard, but no particular site was specified. The action nevertheless failed, their Lordships deciding that it was the intent of the legislature to authorise interference with private rights.[12]

The second problem is that the test of inevitability set out above may be inappropriate in the context of statutory powers which require a public body to do a variety of work in a given area as and when the body deems it expedient to do so.[13]

The third difficulty is more important. Whether the test of inevitability set out above is satisfied can be fortuitous, being dependent upon the wording of the enabling statute. Whether the statute is framed in terms of a duty, or a power, or within the latter category a power which specifies a site and method, is often dependent upon factors which should not be determinative of whether an action for nuisance survives or not. Many modern statutes are framed in permissive form for administrative reasons and contain no indication of site or method because the matter is too complex or best decided upon by the public body; this tells us nothing about whether a private law action should be sustainable or not.

The final problem is that it was presumed in certain of the leading cases that a nuisance had in fact occurred.[14] The essence of the tort is to balance the activities of neighbouring landowners to determine whether such use is a reasonable user of land. How exactly should this be applied when one of the parties is a public body which represents a wider public interest in the provision of, for example, a hospital?[15]

Underlying the above difficulties is a basic conflict that permeates this whole particular area. On the one hand, it is harsh to make the individual whose land is not taken, but who suffers inconvenience and diminution in value, bear the loss arising from new socially beneficial activities.[16] On the other hand, it is not at all clear that, whatever definition of inevitability is adopted, nuisance is the most appropriate medium whereby compensation should be granted. The criteria for whether private rights of action

---

[11] (1886) 11 App. Cas. 45.

[12] *Ibid.* pp. 53, 57-58, 63-65.

[13] *Marriage* v. *East Norfolk Catchment Board* [1950] 1 K.B. 284, 308, 309. See also, *Hawley* v. *Steele* (1877) 6 Ch. D. 521, 528, 530.

[14] See *Brand* above n. 3, and *Hill*, above n. 8.

[15] See *Hill*, above n. 8, pp. 207-208.

[16] This has been recognised judicially in *Manchester Corporation* v. *Farnworth* [1930] A.C. 171, 203-204, *per* Lord Blanesburgh who advocated placing the "true cost" of owning the power station on the defendant, including the cost of the loss in value of the plaintiff's land.

survive derived from the above authorities seem ill-fitted to much modern legislative activity.[17]

This area seems to be one where it is necessary to break away from the confines of "normal" legal reasoning which requires an actionable legal wrong as a precondition for the payment of compensation. It may be an area in which to consider the idea that the public body's action is lawful, but that compensation should be paid.[18]

To some extent this has been achieved by the Land Compensation Act 1973 which provides compensation where the value of an interest in land is depreciated by physical factors caused by the use of public works, whether highways, aerodromes, or other works on land provided or used under statutory powers.[19] Physical factors are defined as noise, smell, smoke, fumes, artificial lighting, and the discharge of any substance onto the land.[20] Interest in land is defined to cover a freeholder, or a leaseholder, with three years of the term unexpired; there is a maximum rateable value where the land is not a dwelling.[21] The Act applies to any nuisance which occurred on or after October 17, 1969.[22] The compensation is assessed at prices current on the first day when a claim could be made.[23] Cases where compensation could be obtained through an action in nuisance are excluded from the Act.[24]

The desirability of such legislation can, however, only be judged against the more general background of the area in which it subsists. Thus, the statute has been criticised on the ground that, although it appears to safeguard private rights, its primary object is to expedite planning and development. The provision of compensation is, moreover, viewed as an attempt to diminish the extent to which the public wish to participate in the planning process.[25]

The problem which has been discussed within this section should also be viewed within the context of more general reforms which might be introduced. Thus, as will be seen below, one such idea is to introduce a more general principle which would make public bodies bear the burden of losses which have been caused through the pursuit of *lawful* governmental activity.[26]

---

[17] The view of the House of Lords in the *Allen* case should be compared in this respect to that of Lord Denning M.R. in the Court of Appeal, [1980] Q.B. 156, 168-169. While the Master of the Rolls may have somewhat twisted the authorities, the result he reached may accord better with underlying policy considerations: that the general principle should be that Parliament did not intend to damage innocent people without redress.

[18] *cf. Burmah Oil Co. Ltd.* v. *Lord Advocate* [1965] A.C. 75.

[19] s.1; Davies, "'Injurious Affection' and Compensation" (1974) 90 L.Q.R. 361.

[20] s.1(2).

[21] s.2.

[22] s.1(8).

[23] s.4; see also ss. 5-6.

[24] s.1(6). On the problems surrounding the statute see Davies, above n. 19, pp. 372-377. See also, Local Government, Planning and Land Act 1980, ss. 112-113.

[25] McAuslan, *The Ideologies of Planning Law* (1980), pp. 106-117. See also, Harlow and Rawlings, *Law and Administration* (1984), pp. 353-370. See above, pp. 173-178, for consideration of the differing ideologies underlying planning law.

[26] See below, pp. 646-651.

2. *Statutory Authority and Rylands v. Fletcher*

Attempts to apply the principle in *Rylands* v. *Fletcher*[27] against public bodies have not on the whole succeeded. The courts have only applied the doctrine to bodies exercising statutory powers where there is a clause imposing liability in nuisance.[28] Where there is a statutory power, but there is no section expressly preserving liability for nuisance, no action will lie.[29] If the public body acts under a statutory duty rather than a power, there is no liability whether a nuisance section exists or not if what was done was expressly required by statute, or was reasonably incidental to that requirement, and was done without negligence.[30] Even where the statutory duty does not lead inevitably to the loss which occurred, there will still be no liability if a nuisance clause is present in the statute.[31]

The justification for this exemption from liability is questionable in terms of principle. Two arguments seem to be interwoven in the judgments which have exonerated bodies exercising statutory duties and powers from liability.

One is the general "inevitability" argument analogous to that found in the nuisance cases discussed above: if the body is required to act and by implication, or even expressly, cause loss thereby, it should not be liable.[32] The *other* related argument has its roots in the requirements of the *Rylands* v. *Fletcher* doctrine itself: should a body which acts not for its own purposes, but for the benefit of the community be liable? The courts have not been uniform in their response.[33] Both of these arguments can be answered.

The *inevitability argument* should receive the same response as in the case of nuisance and statutory authority. The activity, even if it is not to be characterised as tortious, and is regarded as lawful, should compensate a person who has suffered loss as a result.

Benefit to the community as a basis for excluding the principle reflects mistaken assumptions underlying strict liability, assumptions which have stultified the potential development of that tort into a socially useful instrument by which loss can be spread. Strict liability has no limit of moral censure, nor should it be restricted to socially unusual or abnormal activities. Liability without fault has one of its most important roles to play

---

[27] (1866) L.R. 1. Ex. 265, 279-280; (1868) L.R. 3 H.L.330.

[28] *Charing Cross Electricity Supply Company* v. *Hydraulic Power Company* [1914] 3 K.B. 772; *Midwood* v. *Manchester Corporation* [1905] 2 K.B. 597. A nuisance clause is simply a specific section in the enabling statute preserving liability in nuisance. Such a clause which *preserves* liability in nuisance has been construed to *exclude* liability unless the public body has been negligent, *Hammond* v. *Vestry of St. Pancras* (1874) L.R. 9 C.P. 316, 322. Not perhaps the most natural construction of such a clause.

[29] *Dunne* v. *North Western Gas Board* [1964] 2 Q.B. 806, 837-838 (the liability of Liverpool Corporation acting under statutory powers: no nuisance section, no liability).

[30] *Smeaton* v. *Ilford Corporation* [1954] Ch. 450, 476-477; *Dunne* v. *North Western Gas Board* [1964] 2 Q.B. 806, 834-835; *Department of Transport* v. *North West Water Authority* [1984] A.C. 336, 359.

[31] *Smeaton* v. *Ilford Corporation* [1954] Ch. 450, 477-478.

[32] *Smeaton* v. *Ilford Corporation*; *Dunne* v. *North Western Gas Board*.

[33] Compare the view of Sellers L.J. in *Dunne* [1964] 2 Q.B. 806, 832, with Upjohn J. in *Smeaton* [1954] Ch. 450, 468-470, 477-478.

in relation to normal activities which benefit the community and which involve a relatively high risk of loss or damage. It is *because* they benefit the community that it is unfair to leave the result of a non-negligent accident to lie fortuitously on a particular individual rather than to spread it among the community generally; those who take the benefit should bear the burden.[34]

The same general considerations affect this area as affect the relationship of statutory authority and nuisance: loss caused to innocent individuals as a result of the exercise of statutory powers and duties.

Some piecemeal reform has taken place by statute as, for example, in the Nuclear Installations Act 1965,[35] and the Deposit of Poisonous Waste Act 1972;[36] and the Land Compensation Act 1973 will cover some cases where recovery is presently denied at common law.[37] It can only be hoped that further such reform will follow.

It now appears to be unlikely that any further such reform will come through the common law in the light of the House of Lords decision in *Cambridge Water Co. Ltd* v. *Eastern Counties Leather plc.*[38] The case cannot be considered in detail here, but it is of relevance because their Lordships explicitly considered the possibility that the *Rylands* v. *Fletcher* action could be used as the foundation for the development of a modern notion of strict liability which would apply in the case of ultra-hazardous activities. This possibility was rejected by the court for a number of reasons including, that it would involve a departure from previous House of Lords' authority; that there would be uncertainties in the application of any such principle; and that any such development would be better dealt with through Parliament rather than the courts.

3. *Negligence*[39]

(1) THE EXISTENCE OF THE DUTY OF CARE: GENERAL

Negligence is, not surprisingly, one of the most common actions against a public body. After some initial doubts[40] it was established in *Mersey Docks*

---

[34] Law Commission Report No. 32 (1970), pp. 20-21.

[35] s.12.

[36] s.2.

[37] *e.g. Smeaton* [1954] Ch. 450 would be covered, but *Dunne* [1964] 2 Q.B. 806 would not, since the Act is not concerned with physical injury, but with depreciation in the value of land.

[38] [1994] 1 All E.R. 53, 75-76.

[39] For discussion of this topic see, Street, *Governmental Liability* (1953), pp. 40, 56-80; Hogg, *Liability of the Crown* (1971), pp. 85-91; Harlow, *Compensation and Government Torts* (1982); Arrowsmith, *Civil Liability and Public Authorities* (1992), Chap. 6; Friedmann, "Statutory Powers and Legal Duties of Local Authorities" (1944) 8 M.L.R. 31; Hamson, "Escaping Borstal Boys and the Immunity of the Home Office" (1969) C.L.J. 273; Ganz, "Compensation for Negligent Administrative Action" [1973] P.L. 84; Harlow, "Fault Liability in French and English Public Law" (1976) 39 M.L.R. 516; Craig, "Negligence in the Exercise of a Statutory Power" (1978) 94 L.Q.R. 428; Bowman and Bailey, "Negligence in the Realms of Public Law – A Positive Obligation to Rescue" [1984] P.L. 277; Weir, "Governmental Liability" [1989] P.L. 40.

[40] The doubts were raised by a misinterpretation of earlier cases such as *Sutton* v. *Clarke* (1815) 6 Taunt 29, and due to an *obiter dictum* of Lord Cottenham L.C. in *Duncan* v. *Findlater* (1839) Macl. & R. 911. See, *Mersey Docks and Harbour Board Trustees* v. *Gibbs* (1864-1866) 11 H.L.C. 686, 719-721.

and Harbour Board Trustees v. *Gibbs*[41] that a public body could be liable in negligence when exercising a statutory power. Blackburn J. disagreed with the defendant's contention that when a statute authorises a thing to be done compensation must be found under the statute or not at all, and held that there was nothing illogical in imposing upon a public body exercising a statutory power, a duty to take reasonable care.[42] His decision was affirmed by the House of Lords,[43] and applied in a number of later cases.[44] Many such decisions will turn on the rules of breach, causation and remoteness;[45] others will be more complex for reasons to be addressed in the ensuing sections.

(2) THE EXISTENCE AND AMBIT OF THE DUTY OF CARE: STATUTORY INTERPRETATION

The decision in *Gibbs* established that as a matter of principle a public body could owe a duty of care pursuant to the exercise of a statutory power. This is clearly correct. More recent cases have emphasised that whether a particular plaintiff can claim in negligence depends upon construction of the particular statutory power in order to determine the scope of any such duty of care. This technique is common in cases of statutory duties,[46] and it must be equally correct to apply it to statutory powers.

Thus in the *Peabody*[47] case it was held that a local authority was not liable in negligence to building developers because the purpose of the relevant statutory powers was not to safeguard such developers against economic loss, but rather to safeguard occupiers of houses and the public generally against dangers to health and safety flowing from defective drainage installations. In *Curran*[48] a statutory authority which provided funds for accommodation and home improvement was held not liable in negligence to a purchaser to whom they had provided a mortgage when the extension to the house which he had purchased proved to be seriously defective. The statutory authority had furnished funds for the extension to the previous owner, but it was held that since the relevant provisions gave the authority no power to control the actual building operation itself, it could not be sued in negligence for the defects to the property.

In addition to the exercise of statutory interpretation *stricto sensu* the courts will also take into account other factors in determining whether

---

[41] (1864-1866) 11 H.L.C. 686.

[42] *Ibid.* pp. 719-721.

[43] *Ibid.* pp. 725-734.

[44] *e.g.* Geddis v. *Proprietors of Bann Reservoir* (1878) 3 App. Cas. 430, 438, 452, 455-456; *East Fremantle Corporation* v. *Annois* [1902] A.C. 213, 217-219; *Great Central Ry. Co.* v. *Hewlett* [1916] 2 A.C. 511, 519, 525; *Fisher* v. *Ruislip-Northwood Urban District Council and Middlesex County Council* [1945] K.B. 584.

[45] *e.g.* Carmarthenshire County Council v. *Lewis* [1955] A.C. 549; *Hughes* v. *Lord Advocate* [1963] A.C. 837.

[46] *Winfield and Jolowicz on Tort* (13th ed., 1989), Chap. 7.

[47] *Governors of the Peabody Donation Fund* v. *Sir Lindsay Parkinson and Co. Ltd.* [1985] A.C. 210, 241, 245; *Investors in Industry Commercial Properties Ltd.* v. *South Bedfordshire District Council* [1986] Q.B. 1034; *Murphy* v. *Brentwood District Council* [1991] 1 A.C. 398.

[48] *Curran* v. *Northern Ireland Co-Ownership Housing Association Ltd.* [1987] A.C. 718, 728. The power to withhold the improvement grant was designed to protect the public purse and not a subsequent purchaser, pp. 727-728.

a duty of care exists. This is in line with the recent judicial approach to the duty of care in which a range of factors, in addition to foreseeability, will be considered in order to determine whether the requisite proximity exists for a duty of care to be owed.[49] Thus in the *Takaro*[50] case one of the arguments addressed by their Lordships was that the minister had been negligent in reaching a decision without first seeking legal advice on the matter. Their Lordships rejected the argument. A duty to seek such advice could lead to excessive caution by civil servants who would become wary of taking any action unless they first secured such advice. This would lead to unnecessary delay, and increase the costs of administration. There was, moreover, no readily applicable criterion on which to determine those areas in which this might be appropriate from those in which it would be otiose. A number of claims against the police have also been dismissed because of the consequences of imposing, for example, a duty to take care to prevent harm or loss caused by a criminal.[51]

(3) THE EXISTENCE AND AMBIT OF THE DUTY OF CARE: JUSTICIABILITY

(a) The nature of the problem

Let us assume that the type of loss caused by the alleged negligence of the defendants is not ruled out for the reasons given in the preceding section. A plaintiff may nonetheless have difficulties in sustaining an action against a defendant who is a public body. The following example which is drawn from *East Suffolk Rivers Catchment Board* v. *Kent*[52] will illustrate the nature of the problem. The plaintiff's land had become flooded when a wall protecting against inundation by a river had collapsed. Let us, however, vary the facts and suppose hypothetically that four different fields have been flooded, A, B, C and D. Field A is flooded first and work begins to drain this area. B, C and D are subsequently also flooded, and B and C are more valuable than A or D. The public body will have to decide how to utilise its limited resources. It might resolve initially to drain area A, but then feel that its resources ought to be transferred to B and C, or that part of them should be so moved. The owner of A complains of negligence due to the incomplete drainage of the land. How is the court to answer the question of whether the public body is liable in negligence?

The court has no ready criterion by which to decide whether the public body took reasonable care in choosing to drain B and C, rather than A or D. The issue has been left to the public body to determine how its scarce resources might be used, and that body might be affected by a number of

---

[49] See *Peabody* [1985] A.C. 210; *Curran* [1987] A.C. 718; *Yuen Kun-Yeu* v. *Att.-Gen. of Hong Kong* [1988] A.C. 175, 193; *Hill* v. *Chief Constable of West Yorkshire* [1989] A.C. 53; *Calveley* v. *Chief Constable of the Merseyside Police* [1989] A.C. 1228; *Clough* v. *Bussan* [1990] 1 All E.R. 431; *Richardson* v. *West Lindsey District Council* [1990] 1 W.L.R. 522; *Kirkham* v. *Chief Constable of the Greater Manchester Police* [1990] 2 Q.B. 283; *Davis* v. *Radcliffe* [1990] 1 W.L.R. 821; *Welsh* v. *Chief Constable of the Merseyside Police* [1993] 1 All E.R. 692.
[50] *Rowling* v. *Takaro Properties Ltd.* [1988] A.C. 473.
[51] *Hill* [1989] A.C. 53; *Alexandrou* v. *Oxford* [1993] 4 All E.R. 328; *Ancell* v. *McDermott* [1993] 4 All E.R. 355.
[52] [1940] 1 K.B. 319 (C.A.), [1941] A.C. 74 (H.L.).

factors such as the value of the property, other likely calls upon machinery and manpower, and the availability of alternative aid. The court is not in a good position to reassess or second guess whether the choice so made was negligent or not.

This is a corollary of a point considered earlier when discussing discretion. We have already seen that the courts should not invalidate a decision made by a public body just because they believe that a different way of performing the task would have been more reasonable. It is this realisation which provides the explicit rationale for the judgment of Lord Greene M.R. in the *Wednesbury*[53] case. The decision has been assigned to the public body and should not be reassigned to the judiciary, which would be the result were the latter to intervene simply because they believed that a more reasonable method of allocating the resources could be found. This would be undesirable if it were to happen within the context of a decision concerning the validity of public action, and it would be no less undesirable if it were to occur in a damages action.

(b) The appropriate legal label

How should we express the preceding conclusion in legal terms? There are three options. *One option*, which our courts have sometimes employed, is to distinguish between the planning and operational aspects of a decision. This division is not self-executing, and the best way to view these terms is to see them in a conclusory role. A court faced with an allegation of negligence will consider the substance of the complaint, what the individual claims the lack of reasonable care to be, and will decide whether the allegation is suitable for judicial resolution. When the court feels that the allegation of negligence is unsuited for judicial resolution it will apply the label planning decision to express that conclusion. In one sense any claim can be judicially resolved. Justiciability, however, expresses the suitability of the judicial process for resolving certain types of dispute. The essence of an operational decision is that it asks, "given the planning decision, has the public body taken reasonable care?" For example, given that the authority could only devote a limited number of men to area A, has it taken reasonable care? The Privy Council has recently accepted that justiciability underlies the planning-operational distinction.[54]

A *second option* would be to drop the planning-operational dichotomy and to focus directly upon justiciability. If justiciability is the real issue underlying these terms then this should be faced directly. Any possible confusion caused by misinterpretation of the terms planning and operational can thereby be avoided. There is much to be said for this idea. If, however, we do drop these terms they are likely to guide our thinking indirectly if not directly for the following reason. The types of decisions which are normally felt to be non-justiciable are those which entail the allocation of scarce resources, as in the preceding example, or the allocation of risk, exemplified by an allegation that the establishment of open borstal systems as opposed to closed, high security institutions, was negligent.

---

[53] *Associated Picture Houses Ltd.* v. *Wednesbury Corporation* [1948] 1 K.B. 223.
[54] *Rowling* v. *Takaro Properties Ltd.* [1988] A.C. 473.

Phrases such as allocation of scarce resources or distribution of risk can, however, only serve as general guides. Not all of these will necessarily warrant the conclusory label "non-justiciable". It is only those decisions which allocate scarce resources or distribute risk which the court feels unsuited to reassessing that justify the nomenclature "non-justiciable". These will tend to be determinations made at the more general level of policy formulation. Thus even if we do abandon the terms policy and operational, they are likely to guide indirectly the application of the criterion of justiciability.

It might be felt that the uncertainty inherent in the concept of justiciability is a serious disadvantage to its use. That uncertainty is, however, only reflective of the broader, unavoidable issue of what questions are suited to judicial resolution. If we choose certainty, that is only available at a price. In this context the price is a high one.

Either the courts would simply adjudicate on any negligence claim brought before them. They would reassess or second guess every administrative policy choice brought before them regardless of the factors involved therein.[55] Or, if this is felt to be beyond the legitimate judicial role, but certainty is still desired, then it must be sought in some other way. Some magic formula must be devised, the application of which will be determinative of whether a negligence action should proceed or not. The problem is that this produces only the illusion of certainty. For example, in the United States, it was once argued that the existence of discretion rendered the decision immune from negligence. As one court scathingly said of such an argument, there can be discretion even in the hammering of a nail.[56] The attempt to elevate any other element to be the sole criterion is doomed to similar failure. A magic formula once suggested in this country[57] was that a public body should always and only be responsible for the creation of fresh damage or a new source of danger. The problem with this criterion is that it goes both too far, and not far enough. It goes too far because if a decision is non-justiciable then immunity should be accorded whether it creates a fresh source of danger or not. The establishment of an open borstal system indubitably creates such a danger for those in the vicinity. It does not mean that the decision whether to establish such a borstal is justiciable. The test does not go far enough because there may be many instances where no fresh damage is created, but where there is no reason to grant immunity to the decision.

The *third option* which has been suggested is that the ordinary principles of negligence can be perfectly well applied to public bodies, and can cope with the types of problem outlined above.[58] Two separate, but related, points should be made concerning this argument.

---

[55] *e.g.* they would determine whether young offenders should be dealt with by open reformatories or closed prison systems.
[56] See *Johnson* v. *State of California* 447 P. 2d 352 (1968).
[57] For disapproval of the test see *Fellowes* v. *Rother District Council* [1983] 1 All E.R. 513.
[58] See the articles by Harlow, and Bowman and Bailey, above n. 39. See also, Harlow "'Public' and 'Private' Law: Definition Without Distinction" (1980) 43 M.L.R. 241.

First, those who have argued that problems of justiciability can be present when applying negligence to public bodies have generally accepted that such considerations can be accommodated within the framework of negligence. The recognition of this factor does not necessitate any "separate" tort for public bodies, and justiciability may well be of relevance in cases where no public body is involved. In cases where justiciability is of relevance it will be one type of factor which the court will consider in determining whether a duty of care should be excluded.[59] This analysis will take place within the reformulated concept of duty which is evident in recent cases, under which the court will consider a range of factors, in addition to foreseeability, in order to determine whether the requisite proximity exists for a duty of care to be owed.[60] This very reformulation does in fact encourage one to think of negligence as a series of more nominate torts, in the sense that differing considerations may well shape the type of duty owed in different circumstances.

Secondly, there is nothing in the analysis of those who favour option one or option two to suggest that more general issues which pervade the law of negligence, such as the division between misfeasance and nonfeasance, should not be of relevance when considering the liability of public bodies. How such issues should be resolved is of course a different matter. Nor is there anything in these options which precludes the normal rules on breach of duty applying. The relevance of justiciability at the duty level in certain cases concerning public bodies is perfectly consistent with the application of the normal rules on breach in other cases, or even to other issues in the same case.[61]

(c) The case law: from East Suffolk to Takaro

The cases in this area have recognised the difficulty of adjudicating upon negligence, but the response has not always been uniform. In the *East Suffolk* case the nature of the problem was understood,[62] and the example set out above of having to choose which area of land to drain is drawn from one given by Lord Porter. The resolution of the difficulty was, with respect, less satisfactory. Their Lordships stated that the defendant could only be liable for the creation of fresh damage, and not for causing loss by

---

[59] See *Rowling v. Takaro Properties Ltd.* [1988] A.C. 473.

[60] See *Peabody* [1985] A.C. 210; *Curran* [1987] A.C. 718; *Yuen Kun-Yeu v. Att.-Gen. of Hong Kong* [1988] A.C. 175.

[61] *Rigby v. Chief Constable of Northamptonshire* [1985] 1 W.L.R. 1242 is a good example of two different allegations of negligence, one of which was excluded at the duty level because the issue was non-justiciable, the other of which was determined by the normal rules of breach. People may of course disagree as to whether a particular issue should be regarded as non-justiciable, with the consequential exclusion of the duty of care, or whether the same issue should be considered at the breach level. This is not surprising. There are numerous areas in the law of negligence in which there is disagreement as to the correct "pigeon-hole", either generally or in a particular case. The law relating to misstatements, economic loss and nervous shock all exemplify the use of varying conceptual techniques (duty, breach and remoteness) to determine the limits of liability.

[62] [1940] 1 K.B. 319, 336-340, *per* du Parcq L.J., [1941] A.C. 74, 86, 104-107. An interesting background to the case is found in Bowman and Bailey, above n. 39, pp. 296-299.

undertaking work in an inefficient manner. The reason for limiting liability was in part due to the distinction between misfeasance and nonfeasance; this aspect of the case will be examined below.[63] It was also, for Lord Porter and Lord Romer,[64] in part due to the fear of being forced to adjudicate on the type of example given above which they did not believe to be justiciable. The fear is justified, but the unfortunate result of the fresh damage test is both that it can apply to preclude liability even when the issue is justiciable, and can lead to the imposition of liability where it is not justiciable. Moreover, the line between causing fresh damage, and causing loss by inefficient working, can be very difficult to draw.[65]

In *Dorset Yacht Co. Ltd* v. *Home Office*[66] borstal boys had been working on an island under the supervision of officers. They escaped and damaged the plaintiff's yacht. The claim in negligence was against the Home Office for the careless supervision of the boys. The defendant argued that immunity of suit should be given on grounds of public policy. Emphasis within the prison system had been placed upon reform and training which could be better achieved through open rather than closed institutions. If liability were to be imposed it would produce stricter discipline and the curtailment of outside activities. This wide claim for immunity was rejected. It would, nevertheless, be mistaken to suggest that their Lordships rejected the claim *in toto*. The Home Office had decided to institute a system of open rather than closed borstal institutions, which necessarily involved a higher risk of escape, and therefore a correlative increase of damage to property. To ask whether it had been negligent in adopting this choice would be to ask the court to balance society's interest in the reform of the offender, the interest of the offender, and the danger to private property. Their Lordships were clear that this was something that a court should not do.[67] The decision was, using our previous terminology, one of policy and was non-justiciable. Liability could, however, still exist at the operational level. *Given* that the authorities had chosen a more open prison system, had there been negligence within that framework?[68]

The planning-operational dichotomy was made explicit in *Anns* v. *London Borough of Merton*.[69] The plaintiffs alleged that the council had been negligent in their inspection of foundations, causing cracks in their maisonettes. On the hypothesis that there had been a careless inspection, Lord Wilberforce[70] held that it would be easier to impose a duty of care

---

[63] See below, pp. 627-629.
[64] [1941] A.C. 74, 86, 106-107. See also, [1940] 1 K.B 319, 338, *per* du Parcq. L.J. Viscount Simon L.C. and Lord Thankerton both decided the case primarily upon causation, but were also influenced by the arguments advanced by du Parcq L.J., [1941] A.C. 74, 86, 96.
[65] See further, *Fellowes* [1983] 1 All E.R. 513.
[66] [1970] A.C. 1004.
[67] This is most explicit in the judgment of Lord Diplock, *ibid.* pp. 1066-1068, but it is also evident in the judgments of Lord Reid, pp. 1031-1032, Lord Morris of Borth-y-Gest, pp. 1036-1037, and Lord Pearson, pp. 1055-1056.
[68] For an interesting comparison see, *Evangelical United Brethren Church of Adna v. State* 407 P. 2d 440 (1965) (Sup. Ct. Washington).
[69] [1978] A.C. 728.
[70] Lord Diplock, Lord Simon of Glaisdale and Lord Russell of Killowen concurred.

on the operational rather than the planning level. The latter would encompass the scale of the resources that should be made available to carry out the powers, the number of inspectors, and the type of inspections to be made.[71] Therefore, if the defendants had decided that their inspectors could only carry out limited tests, the costs of more extensive checks being prohibitive, an individual could not claim in negligence merely because a further test would have revealed the defect. Where the inspector was simply careless in performing the tests prescribed liability would ensue, since this would be purely operational negligence. On the alternative hypothesis that the defendant had not exercised the power, Lord Wilberforce held that although the defendant was under no duty to inspect it was under a duty to consider whether it should inspect or not. Negligence liability would ensue if the defendant failed to take reasonable care in its acts or omissions to secure compliance with the bylaws.[72]

Later authority has focused directly on the issue of justiciability which underlies the policy-operational dichotomy. In *Rowling* v. *Takaro Properties Ltd*[73] their Lordships held that this distinction does not itself provide a touchstone of liability, but rather is expressive of the need to exclude altogether those cases in which the decision under attack is unsuitable for judicial resolution, as in cases concerning the discretionary allocation of scarce resources or distribution of risks. Classification of a decision as a policy or planning decision may, therefore, exclude liability.

A public authority will not, however, simply be able to *assert* that it, for example, balanced thrift and efficiency in order to evade liability. It will have to *show* that it reached its decision in this manner, and it will then be for the court to decide whether the issue is non-justiciable. However, even if the case does not fall within this category a duty of care may be excluded for the reasons given in the previous section.[74]

(d) The case law: the impact of Murphy

The decision in *Anns* has now been departed from by the House of Lords in *Murphy* v. *Brentwood District Council*.[75] In the latter case the council, acting upon the advice of engineers who were independent contractors, approved plans for a house. The plans were in fact defective and the house was built with defective foundations. As a consequence there was extensive damage to the fabric of the property. The plaintiff sold it for considerably less than he would have received had the house been undamaged and claimed damages from the council.

The precise impact of *Murphy* on that part of *Anns* which was considered above is, however, not entirely clear. There were three principal reasons for the change of view in *Murphy* which led to the departure from *Anns*. One was dissatisfaction with the two part test for determining liability in negligence which Lord Wilberforce had laid down in *Anns*.

---

[71] [1978] A.C. 728, 754.
[72] *Ibid.* p. 755.
[73] [1988] A.C. 473 approving the analysis in the first edition of this book, pp. 534-538.
[74] See above, pp. 619-620.
[75] [1991] 1 A.C. 398.

A second reason concerned reluctance to award damages for pure economic loss, and the court in *Murphy* correctly characterised losses flowing from the defective state of the property itself as pure economic loss. The third reason for the change of view was that their Lordships held that a local authority which had the responsibility for ensuring compliance with building regulations should not be held to owe a common law duty of care to avoid losses of the type which the plaintiff had incurred. Two conclusions can be drawn from this.

On the one hand, there is nothing in the reasoning in *Murphy* which touches upon the approach in *Anns* towards the liability of public bodies in negligence insofar as this relates to the policy-operational distinction. The judgment in *Murphy* does not cast doubt upon the difficulties of adjudicating upon negligence claims made against such bodies. As we have seen, *Anns* itself was simply one in a series of cases which recognised this problem, and there is no hint that the court in *Murphy* intended to call into question the public law aspects of cases such as *East Suffolk, Dorset Yacht, Rowling*, to name but a few. Whether later courts choose to use the labels planning and operational, or to focus directly upon justiciability, will be largely a matter of choice. In any event we have already seen that the trend was to place justiciability in the forefront of the inquiry.

On the other hand, it is clear that *Murphy* has had a series of more particular effects on the scope of liability of public bodies. Two can be mentioned here.

Firstly, it is clear that the court is not willing for councils to become *de facto* insurers for those who suffer losses of the kind which occurred in *Murphy*.[76] In this sense the decision can be regarded as one in the line of cases which have looked more closely at the relevant statutory materials to see whether the public body should owe common law duties of care, and if so of what kind.[77]

Secondly, the decision in *Murphy* will undoubtedly have an impact on the extent to which economic loss is recoverable in tort. It is clear that such loss will not in general be held to be recoverable unless it is the result of a negligent misstatement, or is immediately consequential upon some personal injury or property damage. The ramifications of this for the general law of tort cannot be examined here. What is still somewhat unclear is the effect that this will have on actions against public bodies. Two views are possible. On one view, public bodies will never be liable for pure economic loss unless the plaintiff can fit the claim within one of the limited categories, such as misstatement, in which the general law allows recovery for this type of loss. On another view, the determining factor will be the construction of the statute under which the public body acts. On this view

---

[76] Their Lordships left open the question of whether the council would ever owe any duty to those who might suffer injury to person or health (or possibly damage to property other than the defective building) through a failure to take care to ensure compliance with the building regulations. For other cases which demonstrate reluctance to hold a public body liable when the primary wrong is that of a third party see, *Yuen Kun-Yeu* [1988] A.C. 175; *Davis* v. *Radcliffe* [1990] 1 W.L.R. 821.

[77] See above, pp. 619-620.

it would be perfectly possible for such a statute to be construed so as to render a public body liable for pure economic loss, even though there would be no analogous private law liability.[78] The latter view must, in principle, be correct, in the sense that it must always be open to Parliament to impose liability for economic loss upon a public body, even though this does not come within the accepted categories in which private individuals would be liable for such loss at common law. The reluctance of the courts to impose liability for pure economic loss may, however, affect how they interpret any such statute.

(4) THE EXISTENCE AND AMBIT OF THE DUTY OF CARE: MISFEASANCE v. NONFEASANCE

The preceding discussion has touched upon the problem of misfeasance versus nonfeasance, and the impact of this distinction in cases concerning public bodies. It is now time to address this problem a little more closely.

The general rule is that a person is not liable for a negligent omission: a person owes no general duty to assist another. A corollary of this proposition is that the law will often only award compensation to the person who does intervene, but does so carelessly, if the intervention has actually made the position of the injured party worse than it would otherwise have been.[79] Indeed one important reason for the decision in *East Suffolk* was that the defendant was not bound to take any action, and therefore could only be made liable if it had made the plaintiff's position worse than it would otherwise have been.[80]

This general proposition is subject to a number of well recognised exceptions, even if the application of them to the facts of particular cases may be contested. Thus, it is clear that a case will be regarded as one of misfeasance rather than nonfeasance if the defendant was already under some pre-existing duty, such as in the instance of the driver who fails to apply the brakes. It is equally well established that there may be duties to act affirmatively for the assistance of others in certain situations because of the relationship between the parties.[81] There are, in addition, circumstances in which the courts will impose a duty on the defendant to take care that a third party does not act to the detriment of the plaintiff, as exemplified by *Dorset Yacht*.[82]

Notwithstanding these exceptions, part of the disquiet caused by *Anns* was because of Lord Wilberforce's willingness to impose liability even on the assumption that the council had not inspected the building at all. His Lordship stated that a public body did not have an unfettered discretion as to whether to exercise its powers, since this discretion could be subject to

---

[78] In *Murphy* the discussion of the scope of liability for pure economic loss focused both upon the general reasons for denying such recovery, and also on the fact that the particular statute was not intended to protect against this type of loss, [1991] 1 A.C. 398, 468, 480-482, 490. See *Lonhro plc* v. *Tebbit* [1992] 4 All E.R. 280, where the claim was for an economic loss pursuant to the allegedly negligent exercise of a discretionary power.

[79] *Winfield and Jolowicz on Tort* (13th ed., 1989), pp. 91-98.

[80] [1941] A.C. 74.

[81] Markesinis, "Negligence, Nuisance and Affirmative Duties of Action" (1989) 105 L.Q.R. 104.

[82] [1970] A.C. 1004.

judicial review. Given that this was so then the force of the argument that if there was no duty to inspect, there was no duty to take care in inspection, no longer followed.[83]

Later authorities have not, on the whole, endorsed this reasoning. Thus, the link between a public law duty concerning the control of discretion, and the imposition of a duty of care, has been contested.[84] And Lord Bridge in *Curran*[85] was critical of *Anns* for extending the circumstances in which a public body might be under a duty to control the actions of a third party, and for blurring the distinction between misfeasance and nonfeasance. Some commentators have been critical of *Anns* for similar reasons.[86] While there is some force in these arguments there are a number of considerations which point in the other direction.

First, the position of a public body vested with a discretionary power is not the same as that of a private individual who simply "happens" upon some accident. The reasons for the reluctance to impose liability in cases of pure omission concerning private individuals, which are questionable in themselves,[87] are not necessarily transferable to public bodies which are granted discretionary powers. As Arrowsmith notes, [88]

"...one of the main policy reasons for the reluctance to develop duties in private law is that it would impose an unfair burden, and constitute an excessive interference with private autonomy, to require positive action. This argument has no application where there is a public duty to consider whether and how to exercise a particular power."

Secondly, it is overly formalistic to draw a radical division between those instances in which a public body is granted a statutory discretionary power (with the implication of no liability for omissions), and those areas where it is vested with a statutory duty (with the contrary implication). There are a number of reasons for being wary of such formalism: the very distinction may be difficult to draw as a matter of statutory interpretation; the legislature will often not have given any great thought as to whether the statute is framed in one form rather than the other; and many statutory duties contain discretionary elements. Perhaps most important is the fact that the general assumption underlying the grant of discretionary powers is that they *will* be exercised in some shape, manner or form. The reason for casting the statute in discretionary rather than mandatory terms, when parliamentary thought has actually been given to the matter, is normally reflective of the fact that the problem requires choices to be made by the public body as to how it carries out the statutory remit.

Any possible extension of liability for cases of omission would, in any event, be circumscribed in two ways. On the one hand, there is the case where the omission is simply the consequence of a legitimate planning

---

[83] [1978] A.C. 728, 755.

[84] *Sutherland Shire Council* v. *Heyman* (1985) A.L.R. 1, 31.

[85] [1987] A.C. 718, 724, 726.

[86] Smith and Burns, "Donoghue v. Stevenson – The Not So Golden Anniversary" (1983) 46 M.L.R. 147, and Bowman and Bailey, above n. 39.

[87] Atiyah's *Accidents, Compensation and the Law* (4th ed., 1987 by Cane), pp. 80-93.

[88] *Civil Liability and Public Authorities* (1992), pp. 183-184.

decision. A public body may make a planning decision to exercise its powers in a certain manner, with the inevitable consequence that it chooses not to act in particular circumstances. However, this species of "omission" is simply the necessary consequence of a policy decision to exercise the powers in one way. Any extension of liability would not lead to liability in this type of case, since the planning decision to use the power in the chosen manner would almost certainly be regarded as non-justiciable. On the other hand, it may well be the case, as we have already noted,[89] that the interpretation of the relevant statute leads to the conclusion that the public body should not be liable for the type of loss which has been suffered, no matter how this has been brought about.

What is readily apparent is that the continued preservation of the distinction between misfeasance and nonfeasance will inevitably prompt disagreement as to which side of the line any particular case falls.[90]

(5) ULTRA VIRES AND NEGLIGENCE[91]

(a) Planning decisions

The immunity from a negligence action is predicated upon the public body acting *intra vires*. It can be accepted that a planning decision which has been made *intra vires* cannot produce liability in negligence. The effect of a finding of *ultra vires* must, however, be considered more closely both at the planning and operational levels.

The short answer is that a finding of *ultra vires* will not, in itself, have an effect upon a subsequent negligence action. Let us imagine that a policy decision has been made pursuant to a statutory power that the limited funds at the disposal of the public body should be used to inspect all buildings or machinery within a certain class by tests one and two, rather than half of them by tests one to four. More extensive testing would have revealed problems in the building or machinery, and these problems have led to the plaintiff being injured. The policy decision is found to be *ultra vires* because it was based upon irrelevant considerations and the plaintiff then brings an action in negligence for the loss that has been suffered. The finding of *ultra vires* only tells us that the public body *in fact* took irrelevant considerations into account. A subsequent claim in negligence might seek to establish the carelessness in one of two ways.

One method would be to allege that the policy was unreasonable, in the sense that it was reasonably foreseeable that pursuit of such a policy would cause loss to one such as the plaintiff. There is an obvious difficulty in this argument. The finding of *ultra vires* has, as said, only shown that irrelevant considerations were *in fact* taken into account. Negligence requires fault. The response of the public body would be to admit that it was indeed

---

[89] See above, pp. 619-620.

[90] *e.g.* I have difficulty with the analysis in Bowman and Bailey, above n. 39, both in the categorisation of cases (*e.g. Dorset Yacht* is treated as a case of nonfeasance p. 284), and in the meaning ascribed to failure to confer a benefit as opposed to causing a loss (*e.g. Anns* is treated as a case where the council did not cause harm, irrespective of whether they negligently inspected or did not inspect at all, p. 293).

[91] Craig (1978) 94 L.Q.R. 428, 447-454.

reasonably foreseeable that their policy choice could cause loss to one such as the plaintiff, but that the choice they made was not negligent. Negligence requires not only reasonably foreseeable loss, but for that loss to be brought about by a failure to take reasonable care. For the court to find that the policy choice was negligent would require it to reassess the way in which the local authority utilised its limited resources. The finding of *ultra vires* does not render this any more or less justiciable than it had been before such a finding had been made. If the plaintiff were to succeed in negligence simply upon proof that the policy decision was *ultra vires* this would involve the conclusion that a finding of *ultra vires* automatically entailed a finding of negligence, a somewhat revolutionary and illogical proposition. Even where invalidity exists and relates to the policy determination, the difficulties of adjudicating upon negligence remain.

The *other form* that a claim in negligence could take would be one in which the plaintiff seeks to say not that the policy decision itself is unreasonable, but rather that it was arrived at by a failure to take reasonable care. While such a claim would be possible in theory, there is no necessary link between *ultra vires* and negligence in this second sense, and there are dangers in making any such connection too readily. *Dunlop* v. *Woollahra Municipal Council*[92] provides an apt illustration. The defendant council had passed two resolutions fixing a building line for the plaintiff's land and imposing a three storey height restriction. Both resolutions were passed upon the advice of the council's solicitor. As a result, the plaintiff refrained from developing his land, having been advised that it was not worthwhile doing so with the existing restrictions in force. The plaintiff challenged both resolutions and was successful: that concerning the building line was procedurally *ultra vires* for failure to comply with natural justice, while the height limit was substantively *ultra vires* given the relevant legislation. The basis of the claim in negligence was that the council had failed to take reasonable care to ensure that the resolution was within their statutory powers. The Privy Council rejected the claim. The municipal council had acted on the advice of their solicitors in fixing the maximum height for building. They had taken reasonable advice.

This was clearly correct as will be readily apparent if the sequence of events is made clear. A policy choice is made by a public body, which is declared invalid. A negligence action is then brought alleging a failure to take care by the public body to ensure that it did not exceed its statutory powers. What the limits of those statutory powers are may well be a complex question and even relatively clear legislative provisions can be subject to differing reasonable interpretations: the uncertainties inherent in the *ultra vires* doctrine have already been examined. To reason from a now established decision of invalidity, to the conclusion that the policy choice when made prior to that decision was made without reasonable care as to the limits of the public body's statutory powers, will only be possible in rare cases where those statutory limits are laid down in clear unambiguous terms. This is not often the case. To make the connection in any other

---

[92] [1982] A.C. 158.

instance would be to render meaningless the whole notion of reasonable care.[93]

A finding of *ultra vires* might, however, be of more help in subsequently alleging negligence in two types of case. The first is where the planning decision is so unreasonable that no reasonable authority would make it. Logically this does not mean that the council was necessarily negligent, but in practice the court might forgo logic and reassess a planning decision only to inspect houses painted red. Second, a court might feel capable of concluding that a policy decision reached on no evidence was indicative of a failure to take reasonable care.

Everything said above applies equally where the finding of *ultra vires* relates to an omission. In fact the very word omission is misleading. As applied at the policy level it is nothing more than a decision not to do something; not to inspect at all, or not to inspect a certain type of building. This is the natural correlative of a policy decision to exercise the powers in a particular way.

(b) Operational level

In *Dorset Yacht*[94] the court required proof that the officer acted outside the ambit of the power. The relationship of *ultra vires* and negligence at the operational level can arise in two ways.

The first does not in reality concern the operational level at all. The House of Lords is concerned to prevent the policy determination from being attacked indirectly. The plaintiff, in the above example, might argue that the officer has been careless in not carrying out tests three and four. However, while the officer is carrying out the agreed policy then this action is *intra vires* and any attempt to characterise the action as negligence would simply be challenging the policy determination itself. It is only where the officer exceeds the powers which have been given that there can be a negligence action.

The second way in which the issue might arise would be where the claimant asserts that the officer was simply careless in performing the tests which were within the council policy. The normal rules of negligence should apply here. The requirement of *ultra vires* is not a difficult hurdle to surmount. The discussion of *ultra vires* and negligence in the planning context has shown that a finding of *ultra vires* is not equivalent to a finding of negligence. However, principle and authority do provide support for the converse proposition, that a proven lack of care at the operational level involves a finding of *ultra vires*.

On principle, a power can be granted subject to three possible standards of liability: strict; fault; or a duty of honesty. Total immunity is possible but rare. Few statutory powers have been held to impose only a requirement of honesty.[95] Whether public bodies should be subject to strict or fault liability

---

[93] The factual situation in *Rowling* v. *Takaro Properties Ltd.* [1988] A.C. 473 provides a further example of the same sequence of events.

[94] [1970] A.C. 1004. This was also the case in *Anns* [1978] A.C. 728.

[95] See, *e.g. Partridge* v. *General Council of Medical Education* (1890) 25 Q.B.D. 90; *Everett* v. *Griffiths* [1921] 1 A.C. 631.

is not relevant here; what is apposite is that normally they are subject at least to fault liability. Therefore, one of the terms on which a power is given is that it will be exercised with reasonable care. If such care is not taken the public body will have exceeded its powers. This also seems correct in terms of public policy and fairness: it would be strange if a public body could be negligent at the operational level and remain *intra vires*. Both case[96] and text authorities[97] are based upon the premise that it is the negligent exercise of the power which takes the body *ultra vires*.[98]

4. *Breach of Statutory Duty*[99]

Until the nineteenth century the courts did not inquire closely whether the breach of a statute was intended to give a cause of action to individuals or whether it was only to be enforced by a penalty provided within the statute. A number of eighteenth- and early nineteenth-century authorities, some of which dealt with public officers or public bodies, expressed the liability in very general terms: when a public body has a duty imposed upon it an action lies at the suit of anyone injured by the neglect or refusal to perform it.[100]

However, by the latter part of the nineteenth century the courts had begun to restrict the action.[101] Whether an action will lie at the suit of

---

[96] *e.g. Sutton* v. *Clarke* (1815) 6 Taunt 29; *Whitehouse* v. *Fellowes* (1861) 10 C.B.(N.S.) 765; *Mersey Docks and Harbour Board Trustees* v. *Gibbs* (1864-1866) 11 H.L.C. 686; *Geddis* v. *Proprietors of Bann Reservoir* (1878) 3 App. Cas. 430; *Fisher* v. *Ruislip-Northwood Urban District Council and Middlesex County Council* [1945] K.B. 584.

[97] de Smith, *Judicial Review of Administrative Action* (4th ed., 1980), pp. 350-352.

[98] *Parnaby* v. *Lancaster Canal Company* (1839) 11 Ad. & E. 223; *Gilbert* v. *Corporation of Trinity House* (1886) 17 Q.B.D. 795; *Morrison* v. *Sheffield Corporation* [1917] 2 K.B. 866; *R.* v. *H.M. Treasury, ex p. Petch* [1990] C.O.D. 19, provide further examples of what would now be termed operational negligence.

[99] For detailed treatment see, *Winfield and Jolowicz on Tort* (13th ed., 1989), Chap. 7; Stanton, *Breach of Statutory Duty in Tort* (1986); Buckley, "Liability in Tort for Breach of Statutory Duty" (1984) 100 L.Q.R. 204.

[100] Com. Dig. tit. "Action Upon Statute," F; *Sterling* v. *Turner* (1672) 1 Ventris 206; *Rowning* v. *Goodchild* (1772) 2 W. Black 906; *Schinotti* v. *Bumsted* (1796) 6 T.R. 646; *Barry* v. *Arnaud* (1839) 10 Ad. & E. 646; *Ferguson* v. *Kinnoull* (1842) 9 Cl. & F. 251; *Pickering* v. *James* (1873) L.R. 8 C.P. 489.

[101] *Atkinson* v. *Newcastle Waterworks Co.* (1877) 2 Ex.D. 441 restricting the broad approach in *Couch* v. *Steel* (1854) 3 E. & B. 402. *cf.* Wade, *Administrative Law* (6th ed., 1988), pp. 773-774 who argues that the limits imposed upon the action for breach of statutory duty do not apply to public bodies which are still governed by the broad approach epitomised in *Ferguson* v. *Kinnoull* (1842) 9 Cl. & F. 251. This is not supported by the cases. Despite occasional reference to the broad view as in *Dawson* v. *Bingley Urban District Council* [1911] 2 K.B. 149, 159, the courts have in the main applied the criteria which govern breach of statutory duty generally, *e.g. Pasmore* v. *Oswaldtwistle Urban District Council* [1898] A.C. 387; *Read* v. *Croydon Corporation* [1938] 4 All E.R. 631; *Reffell* v. *Surrey County Council* [1964] 1 W.L.R. 358; *Thornton* v. *Kirklees Metropolitan Borough Council* [1979] Q.B. 626; *De Falco* v. *Crawley Borough Council* [1980] Q.B. 460; *Booth* v. *N.E.B.* [1978] 3 All E.R. 624; *Lonrho Ltd.* v. *Shell Petroleum (No. 2)* [1982] A.C. 173. See, moreover, the cases on statutory powers which use analogous reasoning: *Peabody* [1985] A.C. 210; *Curran* [1987] A.C. 718; *Yuen Kun-Yeu* [1988] A.C. 175; *Murphy* [1991] 1 A.C. 398.

an individual will be dependent upon a number of factors. The prime consideration is to look to the intent of the legislation.[102] When determining whether the statute was intended to give a cause of action the courts will consider, among other factors, whether the existing law of torts provides adequate compensation. If it does it will usually mean that no action under the statute will lie.[103] Conversely, where a statute simply enacts a pre-existing common law duty this will give rise to an action under the statute.[104] The mere fact that the statute is for the benefit of the public at large will not in itself preclude an action for breach of statutory duty,[105] although it might be easier to prove such an action where the statute protects a particular class of which the plaintiff is a member.[106] Another factor which the court will consider will be whether the statute provides a penalty for breach. If it does then it may be more difficult to establish a cause of action for an individual, though it is not an impossible hurdle to overcome.[107] In addition, the harm suffered must be within the risk which the statute was designed to prevent.[108] The standard of duty imposed will depend upon the construction of the legislation; the duty may be strict, or it may simply be one of reasonable care.[109]

The nature of the obligations imposed upon public bodies can give rise to a number of difficulties in applying these principles. First, certain duties may contain discretion as to how they should be carried out,[110] or they may entail difficult points of statutory construction.[111] Fault is probably the most appropriate standard of liability in such instances, and many of the issues considered above will be relevant here also. Secondly, the courts may regard alternative remedies laid down in the statute, such as default powers, as precluding a civil action.[112] The nature of the duty allegedly broken, and

---

[102] e.g. Atkinson v. Newcastle Waterworks Co. (1877) 2 Ex.D. 441, 448; R. v. Deputy Governor of Parkhurst Prison, ex p. Hague [1992] 1 A.C. 58.

[103] Phillips v. Britannia Hygienic Laundry Co. Ltd. [1923] 2 K.B. 832.

[104] e.g. Ashby v. White (1703) 2 Ld. Raym. 938, 954.

[105] Phillips [1923] 2 K.B. 832; Lonrho Ltd. v. Shell Petroleum (No. 2) [1982] A.C. 173.

[106] Evidence that the plaintiff is a member of a class covered by the statute will not, however, serve to prove that the plaintiff has a private law right flowing from the statute. It will still have to be shown that the legislature intended to confer such rights, ex p. Hague [1992] 1 A.C. 58.

[107] Atkinson v. Newcastle Waterworks Co. (1877) 2 Ex.D. 441; Groves v. Lord Wimborne [1898] 2 Q.B. 402; Cutler v. Wandsworth Stadium Ltd. [1949] A.C. 398.

[108] Gorris v. Scott (1875) L.R. 9 Ex. 125. See also, Peabody [1985] A.C. 210; Curran [1987] A.C. 718.

[109] Winfield and Jolowicz on Tort (13th ed., 1989), pp. 179-180; Buckley, above n.99, pp. 222-225.

[110] Haydon v. Kent County Council [1978] Q.B. 343 provides a good example of a statutory duty which entails many of the discretionary choices in deciding how to fulfil that duty which are regularly present in cases of statutory powers.

[111] See also, Lord Keith of Kinkel's observations on statutory misconstruction in Rowling v. Takaro Properties Ltd. [1988] A.C. 473, albeit made in the context of statutory powers.

[112] Watt v. Kesteven County Council [1955] 1 Q.B. 408; Wood v. Ealing London Borough Council [1967] Ch. 364; Cumings v. Birkenhead Corporation [1972] Ch. 12. cf. Meade v. Haringey London Borough Council [1979] 1 W.L.R. 637; Att.-Gen. ex rel. McWhirter v. Independent Broadcasting Authority [1973] Q.B. 626, 649. Cane, "Ultra Vires Breach of Statutory Duty" [1981] P.L. 11.

the extent to which the court regards this as justiciable, will influence its decision as to whether to restrict the plaintiff to the pursuit of a statutory remedy.[113] Thirdly, in certain instances a plaintiff who wishes to assert a breach of statutory duty will have to proceed initially by way of application for judicial review.[114]

5. The Crown

Until 1947 a citizen's redress against the Crown for tortious conduct committed by its servants was at best indirect. The Petition of Right had developed as a means of securing redress against the Crown. In effect what took place was that the Crown voluntarily referred the content of a Petition by a subject to a court of law, thereby overcoming the objection that the Crown could not be made a defendant in its own courts. By the nineteenth century it was accepted that the Petition of Right lay for breach of contract or recovery of property, but not for an action which sounded in tort. Such actions were doomed to failure by a combination of the maxim "the king can do no wrong" and a particular conception of vicarious liability. The former embraced the idea that the king has no legal power to do wrong. His powers were derived from the law and the law did not allow him to exceed them. The difficulty of rendering the Crown liable for the torts of its servants was exacerbated by the master's tort theory, which based vicarious liability upon the employer's fault. Neither the illogicality of allowing the Crown to be liable in contract but not in tort, nor the injustice of the immunity in tort impressed the nineteenth-century judiciary.

The servant could still be sued in person and a practice developed whereby the Crown would stand behind actions brought against their servants. Damages would be paid out of public funds and, if it was unclear who should be sued, a defendant would be nominated by the government department. This very English state of informal patching was subject to two flaws. Some torts only make the employer, not the employee, liable, and the House of Lords came out against the use of nominated defendants.[115] Various reforms were posited before 1947, but these were frustrated by opposition from powerful government departments.[116]

The old rules were swept away by section 2(1) of the Crown Proceedings Act 1947, which subjects the Crown to the same general principles of tortious liability as if it were a private person of full age and capacity. The Crown is thus rendered liable for torts committed by its servants or agents,[117] and has the duties commonly associated with ownership,

---

[113] Compare Ching v. Surrey County Council [1910] 1 K.B. 736 and Reffell v. Surrey County Council [1964] 1 W.L.R. 358, with Watt [1955] 1 Q.B. 408 and Wood [1967] Ch. 364.

[114] See above, Chap. 15.

[115] Adams v. Naylor [1946] A.C. 543.

[116] Jacob, "The Debates behind an Act: Crown Proceedings Reform, 1920-1947" [1992] P.L. 452.

[117] Except where the servant himself would not have been liable. There is no liability outside of the Act, Trawnik v. Lennox [1985] 1 W.L.R. 532.

occupation, possession and control of property. The Crown also owes the normal duties of an employer to its servants. Liability will attach to the Crown even where statute or common law impose the duty directly upon a minister or other servant; the Crown is held liable as if the minister or servant were acting on instructions from the Crown.[118] Although the Act leaves unaltered the presumption that the Crown is not bound by statute unless an intent to be so bound is expressed or can be implied,[119] the Crown can, subject to the above proviso, be held liable for breach of statutory duty.[120]

The Crown is made responsible for its servants and agents to the same extent as a private person. The term agent includes an independent contractor.[121] For the Crown to be liable for a servant or agent it is not sufficient that the person would have fallen within the common law definitions. The Crown will only be liable if the particular officer[122] was appointed directly or indirectly by the Crown and was at the material time paid wholly out of money provided by Parliament, or out of certain funds certified by the Treasury, or would normally have been so paid.[123] This has the effect of excluding from Crown liability action taken by servants of some statutory corporations and, most importantly, the police who are paid out of local funds.[124] Aside from these specialised provisions, the normal principles will operate to determine whether particular bodies are servants of the Crown.[125] Special rules apply to those discharging responsibilities of a judicial nature,[126] and separate rules used to apply to the armed forces.[127]

6. Judicial Immunity

The law draws a distinction between liability for *intra vires* and *ultra vires* acts, and between different types of courts. The precise metes and bounds of liability are not entirely clear, but would appear to be as follows.

> (a) No judge, whether of a superior or inferior court, is liable if acting within jurisdiction, even if this is done maliciously.[128] This immunity would appear to apply to justices of the peace.[129]

---

[118] s.2(3).

[119] s.40(2)(f).

[120] s.2(2), the duty must be one which is binding on persons other than the Crown or Crown officers alone, and the normal prerequisites for an action in tort must be present.

[121] s.38(2).

[122] Defined in s.38(2).

[123] s.2(6).

[124] The chief constable is rendered the person to sue by the Police Act 1964, s.48.

[125] *Tamlin* v. *Hannaford* [1950] 1 K.B. 18.

[126] s.2(5).

[127] s.10. Hardship could result, *Adams* v. *War Office* [1955] 1 W.L.R. 1116. See, however, the restrictive construction in *Pearce* v. *Secretary of State for Defence* [1988] A.C. 755. The Crown Proceedings (Armed Forces) Act 1987, s.1 has repealed s.10 of the 1947 Act, subject to s.2 of the 1987 Act which allows for the revival of s.10 in certain circumstances.

[128] *Sirros* v. *Moore* [1975] Q.B. 118, 132-133; *Re McC (A Minor)* [1985] A.C. 528, 540-541.

[129] *Re McC (A Minor)* [1985] A.C. 528, 533, 541, 559.

(b) No judge of a superior court is liable in damages for an act done outside jurisdiction, provided that this was done by the judge in the honest belief that the act was within jurisdiction.[130] Liability will only attach for knowingly acting outside jurisdiction.[131]

(c) An inferior court is one which is subject to the control of the prerogative orders. It is now clear that justices of the peace can be liable for acts done outside their jurisdiction,[132] and it appears that this liability attaches to other inferior courts.[133] It is, however, also clear that the phrase acting without or in excess of jurisdiction will be interpreted far more narrowly here than in the context of an ordinary action for judicial review which seeks to quash the finding of a public body.[134]

Section 2. Tortious Liability: A Remedy Specific to Public Bodies

The actions discussed above all involve application of ordinary tort law to public bodies. It is apparent from the preceding discussion that there are limits on these actions, some of which have been judicially engrafted, others of which are inherent in the nature of the tort, such as the need to prove fault in a negligence action, with the correlative difficulty of the court adjudicating on discretionary policy decisions. The fact remains that individuals will often suffer loss as the result of invalid administrative action in circumstances where no cause of action can be established. It is necessary, therefore, to examine the authority, such as it exists, for a tort which relates specifically to public bodies. The tort in question is misfeasance in a public office. The potential development of such a tort, and the difficulties that it could give rise to, will be considered later.

Authority does exist for a tort of maliciously or knowingly exceeding one's power.[135] Malicious excess of power has its origin in *Ashby* v. *White*[136] and the dissent by Holt C.J. The plaintiff was wrongfully prevented from voting and he brought an action on the case against the returning officer. He failed in the Kings Bench where the majority produced a variety of reasons for rejecting the claim.[137] But Holt C.J.'s spirited dissent was upheld by the House of Lords. The plaintiff had a right to vote and must have a remedy to vindicate that right. It was questionable whether

---

[130] *Sirros* [1975] Q.B. 118, 134-135; *Re McC (A Minor)* [1985] A.C. 528, 541, 550.

[131] *Sirros* [1975] Q.B. 118, 136, 149; *Re McC (A Minor)* [1985] A.C. 528, 540 G-H.

[132] *Re McC (A Minor)* [1985] A.C. 528, 541, 550, disapproving in this respect of the decision in *Sirros*. See also, *R.* v. *Manchester City Magistrates' Court, ex p. Davies* [1989] Q.B. 631.

[133] *Re McC (A Minor)* [1985] A.C. 528, 541, 550. *cf. Everett* v. *Griffiths* [1921] 1 A.C. 631.

[134] [1985] A.C. 528, 542G, 543B, 544E, 546. The precise breadth of this phrase is, however, unclear, *ibid.* pp. 546-547.

[135] See generally, Gould, "Damages as a Remedy in Administrative Law" (1972) 5 N.Z.U.L.R 105; Harlow, "Fault Liability in French and English Public Law" (1976) 39 M.L.R. 516.

[136] (1703) 2 Ld. Raym. 938; 3 Ld. Raym. 320.

[137] The matter was judicial; that it was for Parliament; multiplicity of similar actions, see (1703) 2 Ld. Raym. 938, 941-942, 943, 947; *cf.* Holt C.J., 950-954.

Holt C.J. required malice or not.[138] However, later cases held that malice was the essence of the action.[139]

A number of other authorities provide some support for a tort based upon malicious excess of power. In *Smith* v. *East Elloe Rural District Council*[140] the plaintiff could not set aside a compulsory purchase order because she was outside the six weeks time limit; the House of Lords did, however, believe that she could seek damages against the clerk for knowingly, and in bad faith, procuring the confirmation of the order. In *David* v. *Abdul Cader*[141] the plaintiff alleged that he had been wrongfully and maliciously refused a licence. On the basis that the applicant had done all that was necessary to be granted a licence, the defendant owed some duty to him when exercising the statutory power. If the licence had been maliciously refused an action in damages might lie.[142]

There is also a group of cases which either deny the need for malice entirely, requiring only a knowing excess of power, or so define malice as to make it equivalent to knowledge. *Farrington* v. *Thomson*[143] concerned the withdrawal of the plaintiff's liquor licence as a result of which he had to close his hotel. Smith J. said that the tort of misfeasance in a public office was constituted by a public officer doing an act which to his knowledge is an abuse of his office and thereby causing damage to another. The defendant had withdrawn the licence knowing that he did not have power to do so. Malice was not needed. In *Roncarelli* v. *Duplessis*[144] the plaintiff claimed that his liquor licence had been withdrawn arbitrarily to punish him for his support of the Jehovah's Witnesses. Rand J., in delivering one of the judgments against the defendant, the Prime Minister of Quebec, described the cancellation of the licence on this ground as malicious, but then proceeded to define malice as acting for a reason and purpose knowingly foreign to the administration.[145]

More recent authority has confirmed this line of reasoning. Thus in *Bourgoin*[146] it was held that there could be an action where the public body exceeded its powers either knowingly or maliciously.

It has, moreover, been established in *Racz* v. *Home Office*[147] that it is possible for a public body to be vicariously liable for the acts of its officers

---

[138] His dissent in the King's Bench did not require malice but, *cf. Tozer* v. *Child* (1857) 7 E. & B. 377, 381, (*arguendo* Shee Serjt).

[139] *Drewe* v. *Coulton* (1787) 1 East 563n.; *Harman* v. *Tappenden* (1802) 1 East 555; *Cullen* v. *Morris* (1821) 2 Stark 577; *Tozer* v. *Child* (1857) 7 E. & B. 377.

[140] [1956] A.C. 736, 752, 753.

[141] [1963] 1 W.L.R. 835; Bradley, "Liability for Malicious Refusal of a Licence" [1964] C.L.J. 4.

[142] [1963] 1 W.L.R. 835, 839-840. See also, *Jones* v. *Swansea City Council* [1990] 1 W.L.R. 1453.

[143] [1959] V.R. 286. See also, *Brayser* v. *Maclean* (1875) L.R. 6 P.C. 398, 405-406; *Whitelegg* v. *Richards* (1823) 2 B. & C. 45.

[144] [1959] 16 D.L.R. (2d) 689.

[145] *Ibid.* p. 706. See also the definiton of malice in *Ferguson* v. *Kinnoull* (1842) 9 Cl. & F. 251, 303.

[146] *Bourgoin S.A.* v. *Ministry of Agriculture, Fisheries and Food* [1986] Q.B. 716, 775-778, 788. See also, *Dunlop* v. *Woollahra Municipal Council* [1982] A.C. 158; *Calveley* v. *Chief Constable of the Merseyside Police* [1989] A.C. 1228.

[147] [1994] 1 All E.R. 97.

for the tort of misfeasance in a public office. Whether the public body would be so liable would depend upon whether the officers were engaged in a misguided and unauthorised method of performing their authorised duties or whether the unauthorised acts of the officers were so unconnected with their authorised duties as to be quite independent of and outside those duties.

The courts have, however, disapproved of suggestions for a very much broader cause of action.[148] Whether the present scope of liability should be extended, and if so in what manner, will be discussed below.[149]

Section 3. Restitution

Before considering any more general issues concerning reform in this area it is important to be clear upon the scope of restitutionary relief which is available to an aggrieved party. An individual may wish to claim the return of money that has been paid over to a public body rather than damages. Such restitutionary claims present a strong case for relief.[150] The law in this area must now be read in the light of the important decision of the House of Lords in the *Woolwich* case.[151] In order to appreciate the impact of this decision it is necessary to understand the state of the law which existed hitherto. It was generally accepted that in order to recover money which had been demanded without authority an individual would have to bring the case within one of the recognised categories in which such recovery was allowed under private law.[152] Duress and mistake were the two principal foundations for a claim to restitution.

1. *Duress*

The classic situation is that of money paid to obtain fulfilment of a duty which the payee is not entitled to charge for at all, or for which a lesser amount should be charged.[153] This is an established category within

---

[148] See the disapproval of the potentially broad application of *Beaudesert Shire Council* v. *Smith* (1966) 120 C.L.R. 145, in *Dunlop* [1982] A.C. 158, 170-171, and in *Lonrho Ltd.* v. *Shell Petroleum (No. 2)* [1982] A.C. 173, 188.

[149] See below, pp. 646-651.

[150] Fuller and Perdue, "The Reliance Interest in Contract Damages" 46 Yale L.J. 52, 373 (1936).

[151] *Woolwich Equitable Building Society* v. *Inland Revenue Commissioners (No. 2)* [1992] 3 W.L.R. 366.

[152] Craig, "Compensation in Public Law" (1980) 96 L.Q.R. 413, 428-435; Birks, "Restitution from Public Authorities" (1980) C.L.P. 191.

[153] See generally, Goff and Jones, *The Law of Restitution* (4th ed., 1993), Chap. 9; Birks, *An Introduction to the Law of Restitution* (1985), pp. 294-299; Dawson, "Economic Duress – An Essay in Perspective" 45 Michigan L.R. 253 (1947); Beatson, "Duress as a Vitiating Factor in Contract" (1974) 33 C.L.J. 97; Burrows, "Restitution, Public Authorities and Ultra Vires", *Essays on the Law of Restitution* (Burrows ed., 1991), p. 39.

duress.[154] The utility of the action for money had and received depends upon the meaning given to "compulsion". The broader that the idea of compulsion becomes, the more closely it will approximate a restitutionary claim with a finding of *ultra vires*. In *Steele* v. *Williams*[155] the plaintiff applied to the defendant, a parish clerk, for authorisation to search the parish register. The charge was not levied until the search had been completed and there was no right to make the charge at all. Martin B.[156] based his decision on a broad ground. The defendant had a duty to receive only what the Act of Parliament allowed him to take and nothing more. It was irrelevant whether the actual payment took place before or after the search had been made. To call such a payment a voluntary payment would be an abuse of language.

Qualified support for treating demands by a public body differently from those made by an individual exists in the Commonwealth[157] and in cases concerning public utilities.[158] In the latter the courts have allowed recovery because of the wrongful demand *per se*. The compulsion flows from the excess charge; the plaintiff does not have to prove any express threat to withhold the service. The statutes in question are often either technically complex, or contain criteria such as "undue discrimination" which may well be difficult for either party to interpret. In this context, to require overt threats by the public body or even protest by the individual is unrealistic.[159] The force implicit in a demand from a public body should suffice. A problem that follows if a wide construction is given to the term compulsion is that it comes close to granting compensation for pure mistake of law.

2. *Mistake*

The general principle is that money which has been paid under mistake of fact is recoverable, but that money paid under mistake of law is not.[160] The inability to recover for mistake of law has been criticised both judicially[161] and academically,[162] and it has been argued that restitution should only

---

[154] See, *e.g. Irving* v. *Wilson* (1791) 4 T.R. 485; *Lovell* v. *Simpson* (1800) 3 Esp. 153.
[155] (1853) 8 Ex. 625.
[156] *Ibid.* pp. 632-633. *cf.* the somewhat narrower reasoning of Parke B., pp. 630-631. See also, *Morgan* v. *Palmer* (1824) 2 B. & C. 729.
[157] See esp. *Mason* v. *State of New South Wales* (1958-1959) 102 C.L.R. 108.
[158] *e.g. Great Western Railway* v. *Sutton* (1869) L.R. 4 H.L. 226; *South of Scotland Electricity Board* v. *British Oxygen Co. Ltd. (No. 2)* [1959] 1 W.L.R. 587.
[159] The courts have not always been so willing to imply a threat, *Twyford* v. *Manchester Corporation* [1946] Ch. 236.
[160] *Bilbie* v. *Lumley* (1802) 2 East 469. Goff and Jones, *The Law of Restitution*, Chap. 4. The reasons given are that: there must be an end to litigation, multiplicity of litigation, and the fact that everyone is presumed to know the law.
[161] *e.g. Martindale* v. *Falkner* (1846) 2 C.B. 706, 718-720; *R.* v. *Mayor of Tewkesbury* (1868) L.R. 3 Q.B. 629, 635-638; *Kiriri Cotton Co. Ltd.* v. *Dewani* [1960] A.C. 192, 203-205; *Nepean Hydro Electric Commission* v. *Ontario Hydro* (1982) 132 D.L.R. (3d) 193, Dickson J.
[162] *e.g.* Winfield, "Mistake of Law" (1943) 59 L.Q.R. 327; *Restitution of Payments made under Mistake of Law*, Law Com. No. 120 (1991).

be precluded where there is bona fide submission to an honest claim. The problem in the past for those seeking recovery has been that the wider recovery for duress becomes, the finer is the dividing line between cases characterised as involving duress and those classified as simple mistake of law cases.[163]

The typical fact situation that has been dealt with until now has been one where the plaintiff has paid over money for a service which the public body should provide for less, or for no charge at all.

Where, however, the public body simply demanded money which it believed that it was entitled to, but the claim was misconceived because of a misconstruction of a statute, the position of the private party was even more difficult. One of two things might occur. The private party might simply pay, discover the error and attempt to reclaim the money. This would normally fail because the payment would be made on a mistake of law. Alternatively, the private party might resist the claim. This would be met by an express threat by the public body. The threat would, however, normally be a threat to litigate and such threats have been held not to be actionable. This was a development of the principle that a judgment is binding between the parties to it.[164]

There are a number of exceptions to the rule that money paid under a mistake of law is not recoverable. The most apposite is that which emerges from *Kiriri Cotton Co. Ltd* v. *Dewani*,[165] where Lord Denning stated that money paid under a mistake of law could not without more be recovered back. It could be different, however, where the duty of observing the law was placed upon one party rather than the other. Given the complexity of much modern legislation and the greater ability of the public body to interpret and understand it, a strong argument can be made that in certain areas at least the "risk" of misconstruction should be with the public body.

3. *Recovery for Ultra Vires Demands*

The state of the law prior to the decision in the *Woolwich*[166] case left many possible claimants in an unenviable position. If they were unable to prove duress or some form of compulsion then it was difficult to sustain an action. This difficulty was compounded by the possibility that the action would be denied because of the problems surrounding recovery for mistake of law. Legislation does make provision for recovery in certain circumstances, but the scope of any such rights varies from area to area.[167] The decision in the *Woolwich* case now places litigants in a stronger position.

---

[163] Compare *Morgan* v. *Palmer* (1824) 2 B. & C. 729, and *Steele* v. *Williams* (1853) 8 Exch. 625, with *Slater* v. *Mayor of Burnley* (1888) 59 L.T. 636.

[164] Beatson (1974) 33 C.L.J. 97; *W. Whiteley Ltd.* v. *King* (1909) 101 L.T. 741.

[165] [1960] A.C. 192.

[166] [1992] 3 W.L.R. 366. Birks, "'When Money is Paid in Pursuance of a Void Authority...' – A Duty to Repay?" [1992] P.L. 580.

[167] *Restitution of Payments made under Mistake of Law*, Law Com. No. 120 (1991), pp. 74-84.

The facts were as follows. The plaintiff building society had paid over money to the Inland Revenue on the basis of certain regulations. These were challenged by the Woolwich in judicial review proceedings and held to be *ultra vires*.[168] The money was repaid to the Woolwich with interest dated from the judgment in the judicial review action. The Woolwich then began a second action, seeking further payment of interest, covering the period from when the money was first paid over to the date of the judicial review proceedings. Such an action would only be sustainable if there was a restitutionary right to recover the capital sum itself. The defendant argued that none of the traditional grounds for restitutionary recovery existed in this case, since there was nothing which could be termed compulsion and no mistake of fact.

It was held by a majority of their Lordships that such a right did indeed exist. Money paid by a subject pursuant to an *ultra vires* demand was prima facie recoverable as of right at common law together with interest. This was regardless of the circumstances in which the tax was paid, since common justice required that any tax or duty paid by the citizen pursuant to an unlawful demand should be repaid, unless some special circumstances or some policy consideration required otherwise. This result was strongly influenced by the provision in the Bill of Rights that taxes should not be levied without the authority of Parliament: a restitutionary right to claim the return of taxes unlawfully levied was seen as a necessary adjunct of this constitutional principle. The right to repayment vested from the moment when the sums were handed over pursuant to the unauthorised demand and therefore interest could be claimed from the date of the original payment. Moreover, it was made clear that whatever the fate of the old rule that money paid under mistake of law was not recoverable should prove to be, that rule was no bar to an action of this kind based, as it was, upon the unlawful nature of the public demand.

The result in the *Woolwich* case is to be welcomed, and academic commentators had been pressing for reform along these lines for some time.[169] Difficulties of both a practical and a conceptual nature will, however, have to be resolved.

In *practical* terms there may be circumstances in which a restitutionary right of the kind which has been recognised could be problematic if it could be brought within a six year period by large numbers of claimants. The effects upon the finances of public authorities could be significant. This fact was recognised by their Lordships, and there were hints that shorter time limits might have to be set for actions of this kind. In *conceptual* terms other aspects of the action may also have to be worked out, in order to decide, for example, how to deal with the situation where the invalidity was only technical, or the circumstance where the plaintiff has not actually suffered any loss because the tax or levy has been passed on to another.[170]

---

[168] R. v. *Inland Revenue Commissioners, ex p. Woolwich Equitable Building Society* [1990] 1 W.L.R. 1400.

[169] Birks, "Restitution from the Executive: A Tercentary Footnote to the Bill of Rights", *Essays on Restitution* (Finn ed., 1990), p. 164; Cornish, "'Colour of Office': Restitutionary Redress against Public Authority" [1987] J. Malaysian and Comparative Law 41; Arrowsmith, "Ineffective Transactions, Unjust Enrichment and Problems of Policy" [1989] L.S. 307.

[170] See Arrowsmith, *Civil Liability and Public Authorities* (1992), pp. 273-275.

4. *Discretionary Payments*

Even if a claimant cannot sustain a right to repayment of sums which have been paid over to a public body an action may still be brought challenging the discretionary refusal to reimburse such money. Thus in *R. v. Tower Hamlets London Borough Council, ex p. Chetnik Developments Ltd*[171] the local authority possessed a statutory discretion to refund rates which had been overpaid, but refused to reimburse the applicant on the grounds, *inter alia*, that the payments had been made under a mistake of law which would not be recoverable at common law. The House of Lords held that the discretion was not unfettered, and struck down the refusal to reimburse the applicant. It held that such sums paid under a mistake of law or erroneous valuation should not in general be retained unless there were special circumstances warranting the retention. The financial position of the applicant, and the general finances of the local authority should not be relevant considerations for the purposes of the exercise of this discretionary decision.

5. *Restitution from the Individual*

The discussion until now has focused upon the ability of the individual to recover money paid over to the public body where the demand was unlawful. Restitutionary claims can arise in the converse situation, where the public body seeks to claim back money paid over to an individual in circumstances where the payment was *ultra vires*. It is clear on authority that restitutionary relief is available in this situation.[172] There is some doubt as to whether such a claim applies in the context of any *ultra vires* payment, but the better view on principle is that it should; and also that it should apply irrespective of whether the money is traceable in a technical proprietary sense.[173] The only defence for the individual should be if there has been a change of position in reliance upon the payment.

Section 4. Community Law

1. *Liability in Damages*

(1) THE FRANCOVICH CASE

The discussion until now has focused upon the application of domestic law. However, an individual may also be able to claim redress by relying upon principles of Community law. In order to understand the present law it is

---

[171] [1988] A.C. 858.
[172] *Auckland Harbour Board* v. *R* [1924] A.C. 318.
[173] Birks, "A Duty to Repay" [1992] P.L. 580, 588-589.

necessary to review some of the ECJ's earlier jurisprudence which is of relevance to this topic.

An initial question is how far Community law can specify the remedies which must be available for the enforcement of Community law rights, given that the Treaty itself contains no detailed provisions on this topic. It has never been easy to answer this question, in part because the ECJ's own case law on this issue has not been entirely clear. In the *Rewe* case the ECJ stated that while national courts were under an obligation to use all available remedies to aid the enforcement of Community law, they were not bound to create new remedies for this purpose.[174] However, in the *San Giorgio* case the Court held that a Member State could not render the repayment of charges which had been levied in breach of Community law subject to procedural requirements which made that recovery virtually impossible.[175]

More recent case law has indicated that the Court is moving away from the position as stated in the *Rewe* case, and is now willing to play a greater role in specifying the remedies which should be available to protect Community rights. Thus, for example, in the *Factortame* litigation the ECJ held that the absence of interim relief against the Crown was itself a breach of Community law.[176] Evidence of the Court's greater willingness to play a role in this area is also evident in *Marshall (No. 2)*.[177] In that case the ECJ decided that if a state implemented a directive through the provision of compensation, in this instance as a remedy for discriminatory dismissal on gender grounds, then the compensation must be adequate and therefore national rules which set upper limits to the amount claimable were invalid.

The decision of the ECJ in the *Francovich* case[178] marks a further move in this same direction. Italy had failed to pass the laws necessary to implement Directive 80/987, which was concerned with the protection of employees in the event of the insolvency of their employers. As a result the applicants were left with substantial arrears of salary unpaid, and sought damages for the losses which they had suffered from the Italian government. The ECJ held that, in principle, such an action was sustainable.

It held that the provisions of this directive did not have direct effect as such, but that nonetheless the action could be maintained. It reached this result by using arguments of principle, and by drawing upon more general provisions of the Treaty. The argument of *principle* was that the full effectiveness of Community law would be called into question, and the protection of the EC law rights would be weakened, if the individuals could not obtain compensation where their rights were infringed by a breach of

---

[174] Case 158/80, *Rewe v. Hauptzollamt Kiel* [1981] E.C.R. 1805.

[175] Case 199/82, [1983] E.C.R. 3595.

[176] Case C-213/89, *R. v. Secretary of State for Transport, ex p. Factortame Ltd. (No.2)* [1991] 1 A.C. 603.

[177] Case C-271/91, *Marshall v. Southampton and South West Hampshire Area Health Authority* [1993] 3 C.M.L.R. 293. The House of Lords has accepted the ruling of the ECJ in the *Marshall* case, *Marshall v. Southampton and South West Hampshire Area Health Authority (No. 2)* [1994] 1 All E.R. 736.

[178] Cases C-6 and 9/90, *Francovich v. Italian Republic, Bonifaci v. Italian Republic* [1992] I.R.L.R. 84.

Community law for which a state was responsible. This reasoning was reinforced by *textual foundation* drawn from Article 5 of the Treaty, which provides that states are under an obligation to take all appropriate measures to ensure the fulfilment of Treaty obligations. From this the ECJ concluded that states had the duty to make good the unlawful consequences of a breach of Community law.

The precise *conditions* for liability were said to depend upon the nature of the infringement which gave rise to the damage. In cases of non-implementation of a directive three such conditions had to be satisfied. The directive, if applied, must confer rights on individuals; the content of those rights must be apparent from the directive; and there had to be a causal link between the failure to implement the directive and the loss suffered by the individual.

The decision in *Francovich* raises many interesting and important questions as to the scope of the state's liability in damages for a breach of Community law, not all of which can be touched upon here.[179] Some of the consequences of the decision must, however, be addressed.

(2) THE IMPLICATIONS OF FRANCOVICH FOR DOMESTIC LAW: THE "CLEAR" CASE

UK courts are bound by the ECJ's ruling in *Francovich*, and a damages remedy will, therefore, have to be provided at least in the clear case of loss caused by non-implementation of a directive.

The provision of a domestic remedy will necessitate some revision of the holding in the *Bourgoin* case.[180] In that case it was held that a breach of Article 30 of the Treaty did not, without more, suffice for a damages action where the defendant was a public body rather than a private individual. There had to be something more, such as a proven abuse of power, or other recognised tort, before a damages action could proceed. This reasoning will have to be modified in order to allow damages for non-implementation of a directive to sound in UK law. There are two ways in which this could be accomplished.

One approach would be to argue that failure to implement a directive should itself be regarded as an abuse of power, or misfeasance in public office, consistently with the reasoning in *Bourgoin*. Given that the tort of misfeasance can, as held in *Bourgoin* itself, be based upon knowing excess of power then this would fit well with the type of case under consideration, since the government knows that it is meant to comply with the Community obligation within the requisite period.

---

[179] See Ross, "Beyond *Francovich*" (1993) 56 M.L.R. 55; Lewis and Moore, "Duties, Directives and Damages in European Community Law" [1993] P.L. 151; Curtin, "State Liability under Private Law: a New Remedy for Private Parties" [1992] I.L.J. 74; Steiner, "From Direct Effects to *Francovich*" (1993) 18 E.L.Rev. 3; Craig, "*Francovich*, Remedies and the Scope of Damages Liability" (1993) 109 L.Q.R. 595.
[180] [1986] Q.B. 716.

The *other approach* would be to argue that *Bourgoin* must be overruled for this type of case.[181] On this view an action could be brought for breach of statutory duty, since in the *Garden Cottage Foods* case[182] it was held that this should be regarded as the conceptual foundation for a damages action in UK law based upon a breach of the Treaty.

(3) THE IMPLICATIONS OF FRANCOVICH FOR DOMESTIC LAW: OTHER BREACHES OF COMMUNITY LAW

It is clear that individuals may suffer loss as a result of a breach of Community law by their own state in a whole variety of situations other than non-implementation of a directive. Incorrect implementation of a directive, misconstruction of the Treaty or a regulation or directive made thereunder, and misapplication of a provision such as Article 36, which is an exception to one of the principles laid down in the Treaty, are but a few of the instances in which such losses may be incurred.

Whether the state should incur damages liability in such instances, and if so on what conditions, will only become clear in the light of future jurisprudence from the ECJ. It is apparent from the decision in *Francovich* itself that the conditions for liability can vary depending upon the type of norm which has been breached.

The policy considerations involved in resolving future cases of the kind mentioned above are complex, and cannot be fully examined here.[183] Two of these considerations can, however, be touched upon. The first is that the ECJ has restrictively interpreted the Community's own liability when the Community's action has caused loss to individuals.[184] It was this fact which strongly influenced the court in *Bourgoin* not to subject the states to a wider liability than the Community itself. The second consideration is that many of the other breaches of Community law differ markedly from that of non-implementation of a directive. In this latter instance the state knows that it is meant to implement the directive within a certain time. Losses caused by, for example, misconstruction of the Treaty may be very different, in that the provision may be complex and the state may have been making a bona fide construction of it, even if ultimately this proves to be mistaken. To impose liability in such circumstances for invalidity *per se* would make the business of government risky indeed.

2. Recovery of Money

Community law will also be of assistance to an individual who has paid over money which has been levied by Member States contrary to Community law, and who seeks relief of a restitutionary nature.[185]

---

181 In *Kirklees Borough Council* v. *Wickes Building Supplies Ltd.* [1993] A.C. 227, it was suggested that *Bourgoin* might have to be overruled in the light of *Francovich*.
182 *Garden Cottage Foods Ltd.* v. *Milk Marketing Board* [1984] A.C. 130.
183 See Craig, (1993) 109 L.Q.R. 595. See also, *R.* v. *H.M. Treasury, ex p. British Telecommunications plc* [1994] 1 C.M.L.R. 621.
184 Wyatt and Dashwood, *European Community Law* (3rd ed., 1992), pp. 156-62.
185 Wyatt and Dashwood, pp. 80-82.

In *San Giorgio*[186] the ECJ considered a national rule which prevented the recovery of taxes which had been unduly levied where these had been passed on to third parties. Under the relevant national rule it was presumed, in the absence of contrary evidence, that the charge had been passed on whenever the goods to which the charge related had been transferred. The ECJ held that the passing on of a charge was a factor which could be properly considered by the national courts, but that a burden of proof which rendered recovery excessively difficult or virtually impossible would be contrary to Community law. This was so even if the same rule operated in the context of purely domestic cases. National rules can, subject to this stricture, still govern certain aspects of such restitutionary type claims.[187]

Section 5. Reform

1. *Options for Reform*

It is apparent from the preceding discussion that public bodies can cause loss to individuals in situations where there is at present no redress.[188] This may be for one of two reasons. First, there are the difficulties of applying established tortious principles to public bodies which we have considered above. Secondly, independently of this, public action may cause loss to an individual in circumstances which simply do not fit any of our recognised heads of liability. If a person is refused a licence loss may well result, but that loss may not have been occasioned by an established tort. There may simply have been a misconstruction of the legislation, in the sense that a court, on review or appeal, may have taken a different view of the law or its factual application to this individual. If we wish to develop the law beyond the established heads of civil liability there are three ways in which this could be done. Compensation could be given on the basis of a risk theory, for invalidity, or on an *ex gratia* basis. Whether the courts or some other agency should administer such a scheme is a separate question.

The *risk theory* expresses a conclusion, which is that certain interests in society should be protected against *lawful* or *unlawful* interference by government. It does not, however, provide a criterion as to which interests should be thus protected. This will be a value judgment for society to make. The conclusion expressed by the risk theory is that the burden of certain public activities should be borne by the whole community rather than

---

[186] Case 199/82, [1983] E.C.R. 3595.
[187] See, *e.g.*, Case 45/76, *Comet* [1976] E.C.R. 2043; Case 61/79, *Denkavit Italiana* [1980] E.C.R. 1205.
[188] Craig, "Compensation in Public Law" (1980) 96 L.Q.R. 413, 435-455. See also, McBride, "Damages as a Remedy for Unlawful Administrative Action" (1979) 38 C.L.J. 323; Harlow, *Compensation and Government Torts* (1982).

placed on an individual who has been harmed, but cannot prove an established tort.

Such an argument might be made in a *Dorset Yacht* type of situation.[189] Society hopefully benefits from the greater reformative effect of open borstals on offenders as compared to closed, high security prisons. The increased risk of individual escape may be an inevitable consequence of such borstals. The cost should be borne by society as a whole, and not by the individual who can prove no fault.[190]

Which interests do in fact receive statutory protection on the basis of a risk theory will depend upon the strength of the relevant pressure groups,[191] or the degree of public sympathy aroused for the plight of injured individuals,[192] rather than any "objective" assessment of the importance of that interest when compared to the plight of others who remain unprotected.[193]

Compensation upon the basis of a risk theory, or something closely analogous thereto, is far more developed in some other countries, such as France,[194] than it is in the UK.

Compensation for *invalidity*, like the risk theory, also expresses a conclusion: certain activities in society which cause loss should only give rise to liability if at all, when they are invalidly performed. Invalidity becomes a necessary condition of liability. The type of subject-matter which would commonly come within this area would be losses arising from modern regulatory legislation such as social welfare or licensing. For example, in *R. v. Metropolitan Borough of Knowsley, ex p. Maguire*[195] the applicants, who had been refused cab licences by the local authority, succeeded in having the refusal quashed, and then sought damages for the losses suffered in the interim. They based their claim upon a variety of grounds, including breach of statutory duty, negligence and breach of contract. These arguments failed on the facts, and Schiemann J. noted that there was no right to damages for breach of administrative law as such. There are two reasons why invalidity is seen as a necessary condition of liability, one practical, the other conceptual.

The *practical* reason is as follows. Legislation is constantly being passed which is explicitly or implicitly aimed at benefiting one section of the population at the expense of another. This may be in the form of tax changes, or a decision to grant selective assistance to industry. If a firm is

---

[189] [1970] A.C. 1004.

[190] The Home Office has accepted some responsibility in such instances, see Harlow and Rawlings, *Law and Administration* (1984), pp. 409-411.

[191] As in the case of the Land Compensation Act 1973, which protects property owners on the basis of a risk theory. Note, however, that there may also be a governmental interest in "buying off" oppositions to development in this way, McAuslan, *Ideologies of Planning Law* (1980), pp. 106-117.

[192] As in the case of the Vaccine Damage Payment Act 1979, on which see Harlow and Rawlings, *Law and Administration*, pp. 398-409.

[193] Fleming, "Drug Injury Compensation Plans" (1982) 30 Am.J.Comp. Law 297.

[194] Brown and Bell, *French Administrative Law* (4th ed., 1993), pp. 183-192.

[195] [1992] C.O.D. 499.

refused such assistance *intra vires* there can be no reason even in principle to grant compensation; to do so would defeat the object of the legislation.[196]

The *conceptual* reason is more contestable. The natural tendency is to assign cases which have some private law analogy to the risk theory, whereas losses arising from more modern regulatory legislation are held to require proof of invalidity.[197] We differentiate in this way because of a feeling that the establishment of a borstal or the building of roads affects "rights" in a way which a statute altering the conditions of manufacturing does not. This achieves plausibility because the loss from the public works has a private law analogy, which "strengthens" the call for sharing the cost among taxpayers when that loss is caused by lawful governmental action. By way of contrast, the passage of a statute which detrimentally affects a section of industry, by altering the conditions of business through restrictions on exports, produces no private law analogy. No private law rights strengthen the call for cost sharing among the public here. The absence of any such common law background does not, however, automatically settle a hierarchy of values or interests. It is, for example, not immediately self-evident that property interests are more precious than livelihood.

Quite apart from the question of which interests should be protected by the respective theories, there are a number of problems that will have to be resolved if reform is to proceed.[198]

In cases where compensation might be given for invalidity the most serious problem is the breadth of the *ultra vires* doctrine. To render public bodies liable in damages whenever *any* of the various heads of *ultra vires* behaviour can be found would be to impose a very extensive liability. A public body may be found to have acted *ultra vires* for one of a number of reasons including: procedural impropriety in the sense of breach of natural justice, breach of other mandatory procedural conditions, misconstruction of the enabling statute, or violation of one of the principles governing the exercise of discretion, such as irrelevancy, propriety of purpose, unreasonableness and perhaps proportionality. The consequences of rendering public bodies liable for any species of invalidity *per se* can be appreciated by focusing upon jurisdictional error and excess of discretion.

Cases involving allegations of jurisdictional error, such as *Dunlop*[199] and *Takaro*,[200] clearly demonstrate that the ambit of statutory provisions will often involve complex and contestable issues of statutory construction, and as Lord Keith has stated, even judges can misconstrue legislation.[201] Indeed

---

[196] There may, however, be cases where the disadvantage to the individual is not the object of the legislation, but only an incident of it. This is a difficult line to draw. In France there is a limited principle allowing recovery for losses caused by legislation, Brown and Bell, *French Administrative Law*, pp. 189-191.

[197] *e.g.* a case in which public works affects property values is regarded as a prime candidate for a risk theory, while one in which public action affects the livelihood of a particular manufacturer is regarded as a candidate for compensation only if there is invalidity.

[198] Craig, "Compensation in Public Law" (1980) 96 L.Q.R. 413, 438-443.

[199] [1982] A.C. 158.

[200] [1988] A.C. 473.

[201] *Takaro* [1988] A.C. 473.

the "correct" interpretation of the enabling legislation may be a matter on which the judges themselves disagree: for example in *Anisminic*[202] four out of the nine judges involved in the case from the High Court to the House of Lords believed that the FCC's construction of the term successor in title was in fact correct. These problems are often also present when the challenge is to the manner in which the public body has exercised its discretion. There are, to be sure, examples of *ultra vires* discretionary behaviour where the public body really has abused its power and behaved in an overbearing manner. There are, however, also many instances in which the discretionary decision of the body may be overturned when there is nothing of this sort present upon the facts of the case. Whether a particular consideration is deemed to be "relevant" or "irrelevant" will be a matter on which the judiciary can disagree amongst themselves,[203] as will the result of the balancing process which is required in the context of proportionality. It is for reasons of this kind that the ECJ has declined to impose liability in damages upon the Community where a regulation made pursuant to a discretionary power has caused loss, unless the applicant can show that there has been a manifest and flagrant breach of a superior rule of law to protect the individual; invalidity *per se* will not suffice for liability in damages.[204] This does not necessarily mean that liability should be construed as restrictively as has been done by the ECJ, but it does show the need for wariness about imposing any general liability for invalidity *per se*.

The recent reform proposed by the Justice study, which would impose damages liability upon proof of a wide category of wrongful behaviour, should, therefore, be treated with caution,[205] and the need for such caution has been stressed by Lord Woolf.[206] If damages for invalidity were to be granted then the term *ultra vires* should be more narrowly construed;[207] or there should be some qualification as to the manner in which the particular *ultra vires* act occurred, requiring the error to be manifest; or there should be proven reliance losses which have been incurred, as in *ex p. Maguire*,[208] as a result of a legitimate expectation generated by the defendant's representation.

In addition to the problems outlined above difficult questions of causation, remoteness and the quantum of recovery would also have to be resolved if any such reform were to be seriously considered.[209]

---

[202] [1969] 2 A.C. 147.

[203] As in the *Takaro* case [1988] A.C. 473 and many others.

[204] Hartley, *Foundations of European Community Law* (2nd ed., 1988), Chap. 17.

[205] *Administrative Justice, Some Necessary Reforms*, Report of the Committee of the Justice – All Souls Review of Administrative Law in the United Kingdom (1988), pp. 362-364. The breadth of the word "wrongful" is conveyed on p. 333. In so far as the report considered these problems they were unmoved by them, p. 364.

[206] *Protection of the Public – A New Challenge* (1990), pp. 56-62.

[207] There is indeed warrant for this in the case law on the liability of courts which exceed their jurisdiction, see above, pp. 635-636.

[208] [1992] C.O.D. 499.

[209] Craig, (1980) 96 L.Q.R. 413, 437-443. The response by the Justice study, pp. 362-363, to these problems is unsatisfactory. It is true that the law copes with issues of causation in other areas, but the particular way in which the problem arises here is certainly distinctive and problematic, Craig, *ibid.*, pp. 438-439.

The third direction which reform could take would be to grant compensation upon an *ex gratia* basis.[210] As with the criteria of risk and invalidity, this third standard expresses a conclusion, but does not tell us when it should be applied. The conclusion which is thereby expressed is that compensation should be granted even though there may be no formal legal entitlement to it as such. A person who is injured by the action of a public body may not be able to recover because no established tort has been committed, and because no statute gives any legal entitlement in addition thereto. The public body may nonetheless decide to grant compensation without formally admitting any legal liability, as has occurred in the context of damage caused by those who escape from borstal.[211] The reasons given for preferring *ex gratia* payments to one of the other grounds for giving compensation vary, but include: the difficulty of devising an adequate principle of liability; flexibility; and an unwillingness to accept that the individual has an entitlement to monetary recovery. The fact that the payment is *ex gratia* should not lead one to conclude either that decisions are wholly "open textured", or that the courts play no role in the process. Guidelines of some specificity will often exist, as in the case of the Criminal Injuries Compensation scheme administered by the CICB,[212] and the courts have applied principles of judicial review to its decisions.[213]

2. *The Impact of Community Law*

The direct impact of Community law upon liability in damages and restitutionary relief has already been considered. EC law may also have an indirect "spillover" effect on cases which do not themselves possess any Community component. This has already occurred in the *Woolwich* case,[214] where one of the reasons given for extending restitutionary relief was that EC law demanded the presence of such relief in cases which did possess a Community element. It was clearly felt that the existence of differing rules to govern situations in which there was or was not a Community law issue would be unsatisfactory. One can imagine that our rules on liability in damages might be similarly driven by developments post-*Francovich*, if later decisions by the ECJ do in fact demand liability for invalidity *per se* for certain breaches of Community law other than non-implementation of a directive. Such findings would undoubtedly lend support to the argument that such a cause of action should exist in purely domestic cases.

Two cautionary notes are, however, warranted in this respect. First, as noted above, the ECJ has clearly not imposed strict liability in damages on the Community under Article 215 of the Treaty when individuals have

---

[210] For a valuable account, see Harlow, *Compensation and Government Torts* (1982), Pt. 4.
[211] Harlow and Rawlings, *Law and Administration* (1984), pp. 409-411.
[212] *Ibid.* pp. 388-398. The scheme now has a statutory base, Criminal Justice Act 1988, Pt. VII.
[213] R. v. *Criminal Injuries Compensation Board, ex p. Lain* [1967] 2 Q.B. 864; R. v. *Criminal Injuries Compensation Board, ex p. Schofield* [1971] 1 W.L.R. 926.
[214] [1992] 3 W.L.R. 366.

suffered loss as a result of invalid regulations which involve discretionary choices by the Commission and Council. Secondly, the ECJ has also held that illegality which consists of the misconstruction of relevant regulations by the Commission will not of itself constitute a wrongful act for the purposes of the Community's liability in damages.[215]

Some may well believe that this jurisprudence is distinguishable, and that the considerations underlying it are not applicable to Member States which should be subject to a much more extensive liability. These arguments are often assumed rather than reasoned through, and they are by no means self-evidently correct.[216] Those who quite properly look to Community law as an indirect catalyst for change in domestic law must, therefore, consider the entirety of the relevant material, and not just assume that those parts which do not fit the desired end can be distinguished.

3. Conclusion

On one level the general conclusions to be drawn about tort liability and public bodies are deceptively simple: we either live with what we have or we create something new. Living with what we have possesses certain disadvantages. The existing torts have inherent restrictions which render them of limited value. The choice between piecemeal and general reform is a personal one. The very real practical and conceptual difficulties of general reform might indicate that piecemeal reform should be preferred, in the sense that particular areas should be considered at different times. However, any decisions made about one particular area will have broader ramifications. First, in relation to any such area, the choice will have to be made as to whether risk, invalidity or *ex gratia* payment is to be the basis of compensation.[217] Secondly, the decision to grant a novel form of compensation in one area necessarily causes one to consider whether it is fair or just that it should be absent in a different context. Thirdly, the effect of such compensation upon the operation of a particular area will have to be considered. Would there, for example, be a tendency for the administrator to play safe by granting the benefit sought on the hypothesis that less actions would be brought as there would be fewer disgruntled applicants? Reform may be piecemeal in practice, but the broader issues outlined above cannot be ignored.

---

[215] Cases 19, 20, 25, 30/69, *Richez-Parise* v. *Commission* [1970] E.C.R. 325.
[216] Craig, "*Francovich*, Remedies and the Scope of Damages Liability" (1993) 109 L.Q.R. 595.
[217] This will often be contentious. Should, *e.g.* victims of crime be treated in the same formal way as other welfare recipients rather than being given compensation on a nominally *ex gratia* basis?

18. REPRESENTATIONS BY PUBLIC BODIES

Public bodies often make representations concerning, for example, the interpretation of a statute or the application of legislation to a particular fact situation.[1] Two principles come into conflict in this area, that of legality and legal certainty.

The *principle of legality* is apparent in differing arguments which have served to prevent the application of estoppel to public bodies.

On the one hand, there are reasons which have been given as to why a representation which is itself *ultra vires*, in the sense that it is outside the power of the public body, or the officer who made it, should not be binding on that body. There is the fear that if estoppel were allowed to apply it would threaten the whole *ultra vires* doctrine, by enabling public bodies to extend their powers by making a representation outside their lawful authority, which would then be binding upon them through the medium of estoppel; there is the related concern that public bodies should simply not be estopped from performing their public duties;[2] and there is the argument that to allow estoppel to bind could prejudice third parties, who would have had no opportunity to present their views. For the sake of clarity the situation outlined in this paragraph will be referred to as the problem of *ultra vires* representations.

On the other hand, the principle of legality has been an impediment to the application of estoppel against public bodies even where the representation itself is *not* outside the agency's power. This second situation is exemplified by the case where a public body makes a representation which is *intra vires*, but later seeks to resile from it. Or the public body may have publicised policy criteria for dealing with a particular area, which criteria are *intra vires*, but it may now wish to adopt new tests for dealing with the same area, these new criteria also being lawful. The individual then seeks to rely on the representation or original statement of policy. The traditional

---

[1] Street, *Governmental Liability* (1953), pp. 156-159; Treitel, "Crown Proceedings: Some Recent Developments" [1957] P.L. 321, 335-339; Ganz, "Estoppel and Res Judicata in Administrative Law" [1965] P.L. 237; Fazal, "Reliability of Official Acts and Advice" [1972] P.L. 43; Gould, Note (1971) 87 L.Q.R. 15; Craig, "Representations By Public Bodies" (1977) 93 L.Q.R. 398; Bradley, "Administrative Justice and the Binding Effect of Official Acts" (1981) C.L.P. 1.

[2] *Minister of Agriculture and Fisheries* v. *Hulkin,* unreported but cited in *Minister of Agriculture and Fisheries* v. *Mathews* [1950] 1 K.B. 148. See also, *Maritime Electric Company Ltd.* v. *General Dairies Ltd.* [1937] A.C. 610, 620; *Commissioners of Inland Revenue* v. *Brooks* [1915] A.C. 478, 491; *Thrasyvoulou* v. *Secretary of State for the Environment* [1990] 2 A.C. 273, 289; *R.* v. *Inland Revenue Commissioners, ex p. M.F.K. Underwriting Agents Ltd.* [1990] 1 W.L.R. 1545, 1568.

objection to allowing this to happen is that it would be a fetter on the discretion of the public body, which should be able to develop policy in the manner it deems to be best in the public interest. In this type of case the principle of legality manifests itself in the doctrine that such a fetter on discretion would itself be *ultra vires*. For the sake of clarity this type of problem will be referred to as that of fettering of discretion. It should, however, be noted that there may be difficulties in deciding whether a case falls within this category, or that described above, the reason being that the court will not always make it clear whether it believes that the initial representation was in fact *intra* or *ultra vires*.

The *principle of legal certainty* is raised by cases involving representations in that hardship can clearly result from not allowing individuals to rely on representations made to them by public bodies, which have generated legitimate expectations on which they have based their conduct. This problem can be particularly acute since the individual will not normally be in a good position to know whether the public body is within the bounds of its permitted authority. Nor will the individual have any control over the general direction of agency policy. The tension between the principles of legality and legal certainty will be apparent in the discussion which follows.

The topic will be analysed in the following way. First, the present law concerning *ultra vires* representations will be examined. The law in this area has been based on the jurisdictional principle, and this principle has traditionally been taken to mean that representations made by an agent who lacks authority, or representations leading to decisions which are *ultra vires* the public body itself, cannot be binding. Secondly, the jurisdictional principle will be re-assessed. It will be argued that there are circumstances in which it is possible to allow even an *ultra vires* assurance to bind without the dire results predicted by traditional theory. Thirdly, alternative criteria upon which to base the application of estoppel[3] in cases of *ultra vires* representations will be suggested. Fourthly, the problems presented by cases concerned with the fettering of discretion will be considered. The final section will deal with the related issue known as estoppel by record.

Section 1. Ultra Vires Representations: The Present Law

1. *The Relationship of Ultra Vires, Agency and Delegation*

The starting point for any discussion is to distinguish two questions that may arise when a public body makes a representation. The first is whether

---

[3] In the first three sections the terms "common law", "equitable" or "promissory" estoppel will not be used. While the term equitable estoppel has been used in relation to public bodies, the terminology may not be entirely appropriate. It may be best to regard estoppel as applied to public bodies as *sui generis*: it may refer to fact or intent, and may be suspensory or extinguish the right, depending upon the circumstances. The one constant is that there would be no reason to apply the doctrine unless the representee suffered detriment.

the agent acting for the public body had authority, actual or apparent, to make the representation in question. This is dependent upon the law of agency. The second is whether the decision resulting from the representation made by the public body or agent is *intra vires* or *ultra vires*. This is dependent upon the extent of the powers given to that body.

Even if the decision itself is *intra vires*, the representation will not bind if the agent had no authority, actual or apparent, to make the representation. More important in the present context is the converse situation: for the jurisdictional principle to be effective a limit must be imposed upon the apparent authority of the agent. This is found in the principle that the agent's authority cannot extend to a matter which is *ultra vires* in either of two senses. The decision resulting from the representation may be outside the powers of the public body itself, or within its power but incapable of being made by that public officer. Thus, in theory at least, it can be said that whenever a public official has apparent authority the decision itself must be *intra vires*, otherwise the agent would not have had the authority in question.

This is not an exceptional position. Company law has had to face the problem of the relationship of *ultra vires* and agency arising from the limitations on the corporation imposed by its memorandum and articles of association.[4] The similarity between the formulation laid down above and that of Diplock L.J. in *Freeman and Lockyer* v. *Buckhurst Park Properties (Mangal) Ltd*[5] is due to the conceptual identity of the problem in public law and company law.[6] Public law has not yet produced a case which has set out the theory as clearly as Diplock L.J. did in the *Freeman* case.

However, application of the theory can be seen in the Privy Council decision in *Attorney-General for Ceylon* v. *A.D. Silva*.[7] The Collector of Customs in Ceylon advertised certain property for sale by auction in March 1947. He was mistaken in treating this as saleable, for in November 1946 an officer of the Ministry of Supply had taken over the goods and had contracted to sell them to a Ceylon firm in January 1947. The plaintiff was the buyer at the sale organised by the Collector of Customs. The Collector, having become aware of the earlier sale, refused to deliver the goods to the plaintiff who brought an action for breach of contract. The case turned upon whether the Collector had any authority to make the sale. The Privy Council considered the case in two stages.

First, did the Collector have actual authority to make the sale? Such authority could be derived from the Customs Ordinance, or, arguably, independently of it. The Court rejected the argument on both grounds. As to the former, the argument was dismissed because the Court found that the Customs Ordinance did not, on construction, bind the Crown.[8] As to the

---

[4] Sealy, *Cases and Materials in Company Law* (5th ed., 1992), Chap. 3.
[5] [1964] 2 Q.B. 480. See generally, *Bowstead on Agency* (15th ed., 1985), Arts. 5, 23, 76, 79.
[6] In company law the problem has been affected by the European Communities Act 1972, s.9(1). Prentice, "Section 9(1) of the European Communities Act" (1973) 89 L.Q.R. 518. See now Companies Act 1985, s.35(1).
[7] [1953] A.C. 461.
[8] *Ibid*. pp. 473–478.

latter, it was said that the mere fact that the Collector was a public officer did not give him the right to act on behalf of the Crown in all matters concerning the Crown. The right to do so must be established by reference to statute or otherwise.[9] This is an application of part of the theory stated above: even if the act of selling was *intra vires*, the contract could not be upheld if the agent had no authority to make it.

Secondly, did the Collector have apparent authority to sell the goods? The answer again was in the negative.[10] Such authority involved a representation by the principal as to the extent of the agent's authority; no representation by the agent could amount to a holding out by the principal.[11]

The Court went on to consider whether the defendant was bound because the Collector had authority, simply from his position *qua* Collector, to represent that the goods delivered were saleable even though they were not. The argument was rejected.[12] The Collector might have authority to do acts of a particular class, namely to enter on behalf of the Crown into sales of certain goods. Such authority was, however, limited to those areas actually covered by the Ordinance. Thus, although the Collector had authority derived from his position as Collector this would not extend beyond the limits of the Ordinance: he could not have authority to commit an *ultra vires* act.

2. *Applications of the Principle*

While the principles are clear, they have not always been applied. Confusion has been compounded by the vague use of the terms delegation and agency. The strain placed upon legal language stems partly from the hardship that can be produced by the unwillingness to allow estoppel to be applied, and the consequential desire to avoid such a conclusion. As one writer has stated, the reasoning denying estoppel has all the beauty of logic

---

[9] *Ibid.* p. 479.

[10] *Ibid.* pp. 479-480.

[11] *Freeman and Lockyer v. Buckhurst Park Properties (Mangal) Ltd.* [1964] 2 Q.B. 480, 506. Diplock L.J. stated four conditions to be fulfilled before a contractor could enforce a contract against a company entered into on behalf of the company by an agent who had no actual authority to do so.

"(1) that a representation that the agent had authority to enter on behalf of the company into a contract of the kind sought to be enforced was made to the contractor;

(2) that such a representation was made by a person or persons who had 'actual' authority to manage the business of the company either generally or in respect of those matters to which the contract relates;

(3) that he (the contractor) was induced by such representation to enter into the contract, that is, that he in fact relied upon it; and

(4) that under its memorandum or articles of association the company was not deprived of the capacity either to enter into a contract of the kind sought to be enforced or to delegate authority to enter into a contract of that kind to the agent."

[12] [1953] A.C. 461, 480-481.

and the ugliness of injustice.[13] How this injustice can be averted will be discussed later. It is, however, necessary to understand the "beauty" of the logic first. Covert distortions of this symmetry may achieve justice in a particular case, but they also serve to conceal the more general problem and thereby prevent consideration of a more overall solution.

One method of avoiding the undesirable conclusions of the traditional logic was to sidestep the problem by allowing estoppel to operate on the assumption that the decision was *intra vires*, even though it was extremely dubious whether the decision could be so regarded. *Lever Finance Ltd* v. *Westminster (City) London Borough Council*[14] is one such case. Developers had obtained planning permission in March 1969. They later made a slight alteration in their plans. The local authority planning officer said no further consent was required. The developers went ahead with their altered plans and the local residents objected. The planning authority then told the developers that they would require planning permission for the variation. It was shown in evidence that it was the practice of planning authorities to allow their planning officers to decide whether any proposed minor changes were material or not and, if not, for the developer to continue without any further planning permission. Lord Denning M.R., with whom Megaw L.J. agreed, referred to the many statements[15] that public authorities cannot be estopped from performing their public duty, but said that these statements must be taken with reserve. He propounded the following principle:[16]

> "There are many matters which public authorities can now delegate to officers. If an officer acting within the scope of his ostensible authority makes a representation on which another acts, then the public authority may be bound by it, just as much as a private concern would be."

We have seen that a decision may be *ultra vires* in one of two senses: the decision resulting from the representation may be outside the powers of the public body itself, or within their power but incapable of being made by that public officer. The decision in *Lever* was clearly not *ultra vires* in the former sense, but it appears that it was in the latter sense. When the statutory powers at issue in the *Lever* case are examined it is evident that there was no power to delegate to the officer.[17] Once that is made clear it matters not at all whether the language of the officer's power is expressed in terms of delegation or ostensible authority as an agent. If delegation is forbidden by a statute expressly or impliedly then a purported delegation will be *ultra vires*. That is obvious. That cannot be converted into an *intra vires* act by saying that what the officer does with ostensible authority will bind the principal. As stated above, there cannot be ostensible or apparent

---

[13] Schwartz, *Administrative Law* (1976), p. 134. This hardship was acknowledged in the *Silva* case, [1953] A.C. 461, 480-481.

[14] [1971] 1 Q.B. 222.

[15] Above n. 2, and *Howell* v. *Falmouth Boat Construction Co. Ltd.* [1951] A.C. 837.

[16] [1971] 1 Q.B. 222, 230. See also, *Robertson* v. *Minister of Pensions* [1949] 1 K.B. 227 in which Denning J. (as he then was) used estoppel against a public authority. The case was criticised in *Howell* [1951] A.C. 837.

[17] See Craig, above n. 1, pp. 405-406.

authority which binds the principal where the act committed is *ultra vires* in either sense identified above.[18] While we still accept the jurisdictional principle any other conclusion is not possible.[19] Even if the delegation had been permissible in the *Lever* case, Lord Denning M.R.'s words are clearly broad enough to allow estoppel to validate *ultra vires* decisions. This is inconsistent with higher authority.[20]

Orthodoxy has, however, returned with the decision in *Western Fish Products Ltd* v. *Penwith District Council*.[21] The plaintiff company purchased an industrial site which had previously been used for the production of fertiliser from fish and fishmeal. The company intended to make animal fertiliser from fishmeal and also to pack fish for human consumption. It alleged that it had an established user right which would entitle it to carry on business without the need for planning permission. The planning officer wrote a letter which, the plaintiff claimed, represented that the officer had accepted the established user right.[22] Work on renovating the factories was begun even though no planning permission had yet been obtained. This permission was subsequently refused by the full council and enforcement notices were served on the plaintiff. The latter sought a variety of relief. One allegation was that the statements of the planning officer estopped the council from refusing planning permission. This was rejected by the Court of Appeal.

Megaw L.J., giving judgment, stated that the planning officer, even acting within his apparent authority, could not do what the Town and Country Planning Act 1971 required the council itself to do. That Act imposed the decision concerning planning permission on the council, not the officer.[23] No representation by the planning officer could inhibit the discharge of these statutory duties. While specific functions could be delegated to the officer, the determination of planning permission had not been thus delegated.[24]

The traditional view was, therefore, reaffirmed. Apparent authority could not allow an officer to do that which was assigned to the council. If the representation is *ultra vires* either because it is outside the powers of that body, or because, although within its powers, it cannot be delegated to this officer, then it cannot operate as an estoppel. There are two exceptions to this principle.

---

[18] *Southend-on-Sea Corporation* v. *Hodgson (Wickford) Ltd.* [1962] 1 Q.B. 416; Craig, above n. 1, p. 406.

[19] Another example of a case where estoppel appears to have cured an *ultra vires* act is *Wells* v. *Minister of Housing and Local Government* [1967] 1 W.L.R. 1000; *cf. R.* v. *Yeovil Corporation, ex p. Elim Pentecostal Church Trustees* (1971) 70 L.G.R. 142.

[20] See above, nn. 2 and 15.

[21] [1981] 2 All E.R. 204. See also, *Brooks and Burton Ltd.* v. *Secretary of State for the Environment* (1976) 75 L.G.R. 285, 296; *Rootkin* v. *Kent County Council* [1981] 1 W.L.R. 1186.

[22] The planning officer also said that the application for an established user right was a pure formality.

[23] s.29.

[24] [1981] 2 All E.R. 204, 219. Compare the more liberal approach to delegation in *R.* v. *Southwark London Borough Council, ex p. Bannerman* [1990] C.O.D. 115.

First, a procedural irregularity *may* be subject to estoppel. Whether it in fact is depends upon the construction of the statutory provision setting out the procedure.[25]

The second exception may be slightly more problematic. It was said that where a power is delegated to an officer to determine specific questions any decision made cannot be revoked. How wide an exception this proves to be depends upon the way in which two variables are construed. These are the legality of the delegation, *i.e.* whether the statute allows the powers in question to be delegated, and whether they have in fact been delegated.

Presumably the first condition is an absolute one. If it is not then the whole force of the basic proposition, that estoppel cannot validate an *ultra vires* act, is negated. The *Lever* case was regarded, by the court in *Western Fish*, as an example of this exception in operation. While, as has been argued above, it is dubious whether the delegation was in fact lawful there, the case can be reconciled with basic principle by assuming that it was. The development of case law often exhibits such strained interpretation.

This still leaves open the latitude to be given to the second variable. Presuming that delegation is lawful under the statute, how far can the individual assume that it has taken place? The answer from *Western Fish* seems to be that it depends.[26] The individual cannot assume that any resolution necessary to delegate authority has been passed, nor is the seniority of the officer conclusive. If, however, there is some further evidence that the officer regularly deals with cases of a type which the individual might expect that official to be able to determine, this might be sufficient to entitle the individual to presume that delegation has occurred even if in fact it has not. In this residual area apparent authority can, therefore, have a validating effect in the following sense. Delegation may be lawful, but only when certain formalities have been complied with. It seems that, in certain circumstances, a decision made by an officer, even where those formalities of appointment have not occurred, may still be irrevocable. Whether this actually validates an *ultra vires* act or not depends upon whether the conditions setting out the conditions for delegation are mandatory or only directory.

So much for the beauty of logic; now for the ugliness of injustice.[27] The conclusions in a case such as *Western Fish* do possess a pristine symmetry. The logic of the jurisdictional principle is followed through to its inexorable end. A moment's reflection will, however, make evident the hardship to the individual. The person who reasonably relies upon a representation made by a public body will be left without any remedy. It may be possible in theory for the individual to ascertain the limits of the public officer's power, but theory does not always accord with practical reality. The cogency of the traditional theory must now be examined.

---

[25] [1981] 2 All E.R. 204, 221 referring to *Wells* [1967] 1 W.L.R. 1000. See also, *Re L. (A.C.) (an infant)* [1971] 3 All E.R. 743, 752.

[26] [1981] 2 All E.R. 204, 221-222.

[27] For consideration of analogous problems in the United States, see Craig, above n. 1.

Section 2. Ultra Vires Representations: A Re-Assessment of the Jurisdictional Principle

1. *The Policy behind the Jurisdictional Principle*

Various reasons have been suggested as the basis for the present rule. One is derived from sovereign immunity. It has however been demonstrated that this immunity did not prevent estoppel applying against the Crown.[28]

The most oft-repeated rationale for the rule, both here and in the United States, is that stated by Lord Greene M.R. in *Minister of Agriculture and Fisheries* v. *Hulkin*: if estoppel were to be allowed to run against the government the donee of a statutory power could make an *ultra vires* representation and then be bound by it through the medium of estoppel. This would lead to the collapse of the *ultra vires* doctrine with public officers being enabled to extend their powers at will.[29]

If one goes further and asks who is being protected by invocation of the jurisdictional principle, the answer given, again both here and in the United States, is the public or that section of it to which the duty relates.[30]

As stated earlier, two other themes recur in the case law. There is the argument that estoppel cannot be applied to a public body so as to prevent it from exercising its statutory powers. There is also the argument that to allow an *ultra vires* representation to bind a public body would be to prejudice third parties who might be affected, and who would have no opportunity of putting forward their views.

The rationale for the present rule suggested by Lord Greene M.R. will be considered first. It will be argued that this rationale is unconvincing, and that a better way of dealing with the problem can be found which can accommodate both of the other objections mentioned above.

2. *Intentional and Inadvertent Extension of Power*

The validity of the reasoning used by Lord Greene M.R. must be judged against the two ways in which a public body might extend its powers: intentionally or inadvertently.

---

[28] Farrer, "A Prerogative Fallacy – 'That the King is not Bound by Estoppel'" (1933) 49 L.Q.R. 511; Street, *Governmental Liability* (1953), p. 157.

[29] Above n. 2. Examples of similar reasoning appear in the US both at Federal and State level. *Utah Power and Light Company* v. *United States* 243 US 389 (1916); *San Diego County* v. *California Water and Telephone Co.* 186 P.2d 124 (1947); *Boren* v. *State Personnel Board* 234 P.2d 981 (1951); *Bride* v. *City of Slater* 263 SW. 2d 22 (1953); *Fulton* v. *City of Lockwood* 269 SW. 2d 1 (1954).

[30] *Att.-Gen. for Ceylon* v. *A.D. Silva* [1953] A.C. 461, 481; *Federal Crop Insurance Corporation* v. *Merrill* 332 US 380 (1947); *Bride* v. *City of Slater*, *Fulton* v. *City of Lockwood*, above n. 29.

(1) INTENTIONAL EXTENSION OF POWER

The cases on representations by public officers do not, on their facts, contain any examples of intentional extension of power, but let us presume that this has taken place. The jurisdictional principle deals with this by preventing the representee from raising an estoppel. To prevent intentional extension of power the "burden" is imposed upon the innocent representee. The question that is not answered is whether this is the most effective way to approach the problem. For these rare cases of intentional excess of power the appropriate person to penalise would be the public officer involved, not an indirect sanction on the representee by denying the use of estoppel. Interesting analogies already exist in related areas, which deal with intentional excess of power by penalising the public officer involved.[31]

There may be other factors which exist in certain areas which militate against allowing estoppel to be pleaded. At this point it is simply being suggested that the argument of Lord Greene M.R. for disallowing estoppel to be pleaded in the context of intentional extension of power is not convincing. The thesis that the innocent representee should bear the burden when the aim is to deter the extension of power by the public officer makes little sense.

(2) INADVERTENT EXTENSION OF POWER

In practical terms it is the inadvertent extension of power by a representation that forms the typical situation. A public officer will place a particular construction on a statute which is later overturned by a higher officer in the same department.[32] A practice will have developed that a particular individual should undertake a certain task when the statute places the duty on a different body.[33]

Any deterrence that the reasoning of Lord Greene M.R. is intended to have in this area will be of very limited effect. It may be possible to deter negligent conduct by making the actor more careful. However, in the present context the officer has often taken all due care. The official will normally be acting in the bona fide belief that the construction of the statute is correct, or that the representation is within the area of that officer's authority. Moreover, even where there has been carelessness there is little in the present system to deter the officer. The sole effect of a careless representation which turns out to be *ultra vires* is that the representee cannot rely.

The corollary of this is why should the loss be borne by the representee? The answer must be that it is still, in fact, an extension of statutory powers and that this outweighs any harm that may befall the representee, and therefore justifies the jurisdictional principle.

A rule of such generality cannot be presumed, without more, to be correct. It must be subjected to closer analysis in the diverse areas that combine to make up administrative law. The validity of the presumption

---

[31] See, *e.g.* Local Government Act 1972, s.161, and *Dickson* v. *Hurle-Hobbs* [1947] K.B. 879. See also, Local Government Finance Act 1982, s.19.
[32] *Clairborne Sales Co.* v. *Collector of Revenue* 99 So. 2d 345 (1957).
[33] *Lever Finance Ltd.* [1971] 1 Q.B. 222.

that the detriment to the public, who are the beneficiaries of the *ultra vires* doctrine, will always outweigh the harsh effect upon the individual, may be tested against the facts of *Robertson* v. *Minister of Pensions*.[34] The plaintiff had relied upon a representation given by the wrong body that his injury was attributable to military service, as a result of which he had not obtained an independent medical opinion to confirm this. It may be presumed for the sake of argument that the representation was *ultra vires*.[35] The immediate effect of allowing the *ultra vires* assurance to bind would be a loss to the department concerned. The loss would be in the form of having to pay a pension that could have been withheld. In any system there is bound to be a certain percentage of such mistakes. The question is who should bear the loss? The alternatives are either to leave the loss with the representee by not allowing estoppel to be pleaded, or to bind the department by permitting the defence. The effect of choosing the latter would be to spread the loss in minute proportions through those who benefit from performance of the public duty. The inadvertent misrepresentation could have happened to any of the taxpayers; it was quite fortuitous that it befell this individual. The effect of allowing estoppel to operate would be to impose the loss upon those who take the benefit. It does not seem at all self-evident that the detriment to the public interest would outweigh the harm to the individual.[36]

There are of course many situations where the loss to the public will outweigh that of the individual. This will be dependent upon the context, planning, social security or tax, in which the representation occurs. Simply to repeat Lord Greene M.R.'s dictum is not, however, sufficient. It is certainly not clear that the harm to the public will be greater than that of the individual in all areas. Three possible approaches to the problem of representations, apart from that of the jurisdictional principle, will now be considered.

Section 3. Ultra Vires Representations: Rethinking the Jurisdictional Principle

1. *Government-Proprietary Distinction*

The distinction between governmental and proprietary functions is not in fact a test separate from the jurisdictional principle. It has been developed in some of the United States' jurisdictions as an exception to the general

---

[34] [1949] 1 K.B. 227.
[35] The representation in *Robertson* is usually regarded as *intra vires*. It is far from clear whether this was so, see Ganz, "Estoppel and *Res Judicata* in Administrative Law" [1965] P.L. 237, 244-245. It is, however, the factual situation presented by *Robertson* that is of interest.
[36] This would also be so in cases of the *Clairborne* type, 99 So. 2d 345 (1957).

rule that estoppel should not bind a public body. It permits the application of the doctrine when the body is acting in a proprietary rather than governmental capacity, and where the agent making the representation had authority to do so. In *Branch Banking and Trust Company* v. *United States*[37] the Court of Claims allowed the defendants to be bound by a representation of one of its agents who had purported to waive a breach of contract by the plaintiff. This approach does, however, have serious limitations. The distinction between what is a governmental and what is a proprietary function is difficult to draw.[38] More important is that it is based upon the premise that estoppel should not apply to governmental matters which the law "does not sanction or permit". This takes us back to the jurisdictional principle itself, and to the criticism of such a theory given above.

2. *Internal Dealing*

A second approach is to allow estoppel to apply so far as the internal management of the public body is concerned, but not to those matters which are substantively *ultra vires*. The idea has obvious analogies with the rules of company law.[39] In the public law context it would operate to validate certain types of representation.[40] It would apply to situations where the subject-matter of the representation was within the power of the public body itself, and the officer who gave the assurance was not prohibited, expressly or impliedly, from doing so. For example, if a public body has power to delegate certain functions to an officer, the representee would be entitled to assume that the appropriate procedure had been followed and that the delegation had taken place, provided that there was nothing in the surrounding circumstances to put the individual on inquiry. As we have seen, a limited exception of this nature is allowed by the *Western Fish*[41] case.

Although the analogy has some attractions and affords the representee some protection, this approach does have serious limitations. In many of the cases which have arisen the problem has not been that the power to delegate was present, albeit not operated in the proper manner, but that it was not present at all.[42] Similarly, it would not provide protection in those cases where the construction placed upon a statute by an officer was later deemed to be *ultra vires*.

---

[37] 98 F.Supp. 757 (1951) (US Court of Claims). See also, *United States* v. *Georgia–Pacific Company* 421 F.2d 92 (1970) (US Court of Appeals, Ninth Circuit).
[38] As was admitted in the *Georgia–Pacific* case, 421 F.2d 92, 100 (1970).
[39] See above, n. 4.
[40] Lord Denning M.R. drew the analogy with company law in *Lever Finance Ltd.* v. *Westminster (City) London Borough Council* [1971] 1 Q.B. 222, 230-231.
[41] [1981] 2 All E.R. 204.
[42] e.g. *Southend-on-Sea Corporation* v. *Hodgson (Wickford) Ltd.* [1962] 1 Q.B. 416.

3. Balancing the Public and Individual Interest

It has been argued above that the traditional reason for denying the application of estoppel is unconvincing. The *ultra vires* principle is not an abstract notion. It has a definite purpose to fulfil in ensuring that public bodies remain *intra vires*, with the consequence that it protects the public from any unlawful extension of those powers. In this sense the *ultra vires* concept is the embodiment of the *principle of legality*.

This principle can, however, clash with the *principle of legal certainty*, and does so when an individual has detrimentally relied upon an *ultra vires* representation. Yet if the harm to the public would be minimal compared to that of the individual, there would seem to be good reason to consider the application of estoppel. This would be to recognise that the principle of legality might, on occasion, be trumped or outweighed by that of legal certainty.

There will be many situations where the public interest must take precedence over that of the individual. Examples of this will be considered below. The contexts in which representations are made can be as different as planning decisions are from tax assessments, and social security benefits are from licensing applications. The balance between the public interest and that of the individual may be completely different in each of these areas. It would be more realistic to recognise these distinctions, and the differing policies that may underlie each area, than to continue repeating the dictum of Lord Greene M.R. without thought for its application to the particular problem before the court. There are two ways in which such a solution could be effected, through the courts, or through the legislature.

(1) THE COURTS

An attempt to apply a more flexible rule has been made in some American jurisdictions. The attitude of both Federal and State courts has been to adopt one of two approaches to the problem. Many Federal decisions and most State jurisdictions have followed the Supreme Court in the *Federal Crop*[43] case, denying estoppel where it would validate an *ultra vires* decision. Other Federal[44] and State decisions have, however, departed from, or qualified, the Supreme Court's ruling.

The State which has developed a flexible rule most fully is California. In *City of Long Beach* v. *Mansell*[45] the Supreme Court of California acknowledged the existence of two competing lines of authority, one of

---

[43] 332 US 380 (1947). See also, *United States* v. *Certain Parcels of Land* 131 F. Supp. 65, 73-74 (1955) (US District Court); *Montilla* v. *United States* 457 F.2d 978, 985-987 (1972) (US Court of Claims).

[44] *United States* v. *Lazy F.C. Ranch* 481 F.2d 98 (1973) (US Court of Appeals, Ninth Circuit). See also, *Moser* v. *United States* 341 US 41 (1951); *Vestal* v. *Commissioner of Internal Revenue* 152 F.2d 132 (1945) (US Court of Appeals District of Columbia); *California Pacific Bank* v. *Small Business Administration* 557 F.2d 218 (1977) (US Court of Appeals, Ninth Circuit); *United States* v. *Ruby Company* 588 F.2d 697 (1978) (US Court of Appeals, Ninth Circuit). *cf. Scweiker* v. *Hansen* 450 US 785 (1981).

[45] 476 P.2d 423 (1970).

which applied estoppel where justice and right required it, the other which denied estoppel where the representation was beyond the power of the public body and where it would defeat a policy adopted to protect the public. The court propounded the following principle.[46]

> "The government may be bound by an equitable estoppel in the same manner as a private party where the elements requisite for such an estoppel against a private party are present, and in the considered view of a court of equity the injustice which would result from a failure to uphold an estoppel is of sufficient dimension to justify any effect upon public interests or policy which would result from the raising of an estoppel."

The *Mansell* doctrine has both advantages and disadvantages. The advantages are immediate and substantial. It allows the court that very flexibility which the jurisdictional principle treats as a foregone conclusion. It manifests a willingness to inquire whether the disadvantages to the public interest by allowing estoppel to be pleaded really do outweigh the injustice to the individual. Lord Greene M.R.'s *obiter dictum* has as its hypothesis that the former must necessarily outweigh the latter. The variety of activities brought within the rubric "administrative law" make it doubtful whether so uniform a solution as that proposed in *Minister of Agriculture and Fisheries* v. *Hulkin*[47] can be an accurate evaluation of the conflict between public and individual interests. In many of the areas where the representation relates to a purely financial matter, such as a claim by the government for tax or a citizen seeking social security benefits, the hardship to the individual who has detrimentally relied will outweigh any public disadvantage. There are, of course, many other areas where the balance would be different.[48]

(2) OBJECTIONS TO JUDICIAL BALANCING

The disadvantages of the *Mansell* doctrine are twofold, one practical, the other conceptual. The *practical objection* is uncertainty, particularly in the initial period when the application of the doctrine is being tested in different areas. Any such uncertainty must be weighed against the hardship which the judicial balancing approach alleviates.

The *conceptual objection* is more central. It may be felt that a test akin to that in the *Mansell* case would not fit into the constitutional structure which exists in this country. Our judiciary act against the background of parliamentary sovereignty. If Parliament has laid down certain limits to the powers of a body, or imposed certain duties upon it, are the courts the correct bodies to decide that these limits can be exceeded, or that a statutory duty should not be performed, by determining that the detriment

---

[46] *Ibid.* p. 448. The court did, however, reserve the question of what would happen where the body totally lacked the power to achieve that which estoppel would accomplish against it, p. 450. See also, *Strong* v. *County of Santa Cruz* 543 P.2d 264 (1975); *Longshore* v. *County of Ventura* 151 Cal. Rptr. 708 (1979); *Lentz* v. *McMahon* 231 Cal. Rptr. 622 (1986).

[47] Above n.2.

[48] See, *e.g.* the fact pattern in *Strong* 543 P. 2d 264 (1975).

to the public interest is minimal compared with that of an individual? The theme that statutory duties simply cannot be affected in this way through the operation of estoppel is one which recurs in the case law.[49]

There is obvious force in this objection. The strength of the argument is, however, diminished quite simply because we do allow such balancing to be undertaken in other areas. There are at least three areas in which the jurisdictional principle is compromised and in all of these the balancing is accepted as legitimate or inevitable. The law relating to invalidity, waiver, and delay all exhibit such an approach.

In the law relating to invalidity there are examples of situations in which the courts have not allowed the concept of retrospective nullity to run to its full effect, however logically beautiful that might be, because the effects of doing so upon the administration or upon an individual are regarded as unacceptable.[50] We allow waiver to operate with the effect that there will be no remedy for what was an *ultra vires* decision.[51] Perhaps most notable of all are the provisions regarding remedies and delay. The precise status of the rules on delay is unclear,[52] but under section 31(6) of the Supreme Court Act 1981 the court can refuse a remedy where there has been undue delay in making the application, if it considers that the granting of relief would cause substantial hardship to, or substantially prejudice the rights of, any person or would be detrimental to good administration. Thus, delay by an individual in seeking review can justify the court in balancing the *ultra vires* nature of the impugned act with the detriment to the administration or to another individual, but no such balancing is countenanced where the innocent individual has been misled by a representation made by a public body. A number of objections might be made to the above analysis.

First, it might be argued that such a balancing is justified in the context of delay because the balancing has legislative sanction. This will not withstand examination. The argument misconstrues the position at common law prior to the passage of the Supreme Court Act 1981. If this argument were correct then it would indicate that until such legislative sanction was forthcoming then no such balancing was or could be undertaken by the courts. This would, however, be to ignore the attitude of the courts prior to the passage of that statute.[53] The courts have in fact taken a wide variety of factors into account in determining whether to withhold a remedy or not. Although the courts have not always been uniform in their response, many courts have taken account of considerations of administrative convenience, effectiveness, hardship to third parties, and broad notions of justice.[54] In substance, if not in form, the courts have, in such instances, been balancing the *ultra vires* nature of the conduct against the consequences of granting a remedy. Viewed in this way section 31(6) seems little more than a declaration of the previous common law position.

---

[49] See above n. 2.
[50] Chap. 12.
[51] Chap. 14.
[52] *Ibid.* pp. 585-586.
[53] Moreover, if legislative sanction were held to be required then Order 53, r. 4 would have been *ultra vires* prior to the passage of the Supreme Court Act 1981.
[54] See Chap. 14.

A second objection to the analogies drawn from invalidity, waiver and delay might be cast as follows. In all of the examples given the *ultra vires* nature of the act is not touched. It is simply the remedy which is refused or modified in its operation. This will not do. There may well be a whole variety of reasons why we would wish the courts to exercise their balancing discretion at the remedial level rather than by manipulating *vires* itself.[55] Let us not, however, allow form to blind us to substance: in whichever way the balancing is expressed it is still balancing. The full effects of the *ultra vires* principle are still being compromised. There is in any event no reason to suggest that the balancing which would take place in the context of representations could not be expressed in the same way. If such balancing were allowed we would not have to say, nor would we intend to say, that "you the public body can now lawfully do something which is outside your powers." What we would be saying is that "you the public body have made a representation beyond your powers, but that in this instance because of the detrimental reliance by an individual and the minimal effect on the public interest, compared to the harm suffered by the representee, we are going to hold you to your word."

A third possible objection is contained in the judgment of Megaw L.J. in the *Western Fish*[56] case. Megaw L.J. points out that there may be interests of third parties affected by a decision to permit the estoppel to bind the public body, and those third parties might have had no opportunity to put their views. This is quite correct, but it is not a convincing general objection to balancing. There will of course be cases where third parties might be affected, and this will indeed be one of the factors to be taken into account in the balancing process.[57] Moreover, the problem of third party interests is every bit as real when the balancing takes place in relation to invalidity, waiver or delay, yet in so far as it has received attention in those areas it has not been regarded as a reason for never indulging in balancing at all.

A further objection would be to argue that the balancing within invalidity, waiver and delay is justified because in those areas it is directed towards the factor of administrative convenience. A public body's action might be upheld, or the effects of invalidity would be limited, because of the administrative inconvenience that could thereby be avoided. Balancing of this type is justified because the public body represents a wider public interest. A process of weighing is not, it could be argued, warranted "the other way round", where the only interest affected by the misleading representation is that of the individual. This objection fails to make sense for a number of reasons. Granted that the public body does represent a wider public interest, this does not explain why an *ultra vires* representatfon should never be allowed to bind *if* the detriment to the individual does outweigh the harm to the public interest. Indeed, the balancing approach being advocated will only allow estoppel to be applied when this is the case. In any event the argument is fallacious even in its own terms. When the courts balance within invalidity, waiver, and delay they do not only take

---

[55] See above, Chap. 12.
[56] [1981] 2 All E.R. 204, 221.
[57] *e.g. Raley* v. *California Tahoe Regional Planning Agency* 137 Cal. Rptr. 699 (1977).

account of administrative convenience. They have considered a much broader range of factors, such as effectiveness, third party interests, the detriment to the applicant, and more amorphous considerations of justice.

A fifth, and final, objection might be that to advocate a judicial balancing here is inconsistent with the position taken when discussing negligence.[58] This does not follow. The operation is very different in the two areas. The thesis being advanced in the context of negligence was that there are certain matters which are not justiciable. If a public body has decided to drain areas A and B before C and D, because A and B are more valuable, or if that public body has decided that it can only afford machinery of a certain quality, those decisions should not be reassessed by the courts through the medium of a negligence action, which is what would be happening if the courts were to intervene simply because they believed that other criteria were more reasonable. The balancing within invalidity, waiver and delay, and that being advocated within the context of representations, is wholly different. In each of these areas an *ultra vires* act has occurred. The question which then follows is whether the full effects of retrospective nullity should operate, and whether the logical purity of the jurisdictional principle should be applied with its full force. There is no question here of the courts substituting their view for that of the decision-maker as to how resources ought to be used.

(3) JUDICIAL BALANCING BY UNITED KINGDOM COURTS

There is in fact some positive authority for the balancing approach within our own law. Not surprisingly it comes from Lord Denning M.R. His Lordship stated,[59]

"The underlying principle is that the Crown cannot be estopped from exercising its powers, whether given in a statute or by common law, when it is doing so in the proper exercise of its duty to act for the public good, even though this may work some injustice or unfairness to the private individual...[60] It can, however, be estopped when it is not properly exercising its powers, but is misusing them; and it does misuse them if it exercises them in circumstances which work injustice or unfairness to the individual without any countervailing benefit to the public."[61]

Not only does Lord Denning M.R. provide support for the balancing approach, he conceptualises it in a most interesting manner. When estoppel is allowed to operate it does not do so in derogation from the *ultra vires* principle. The formulation makes the binding nature of the representation flow from fulfilment of that principle: where the public body exercises its

---

[58] See above, pp. 620-623.
[59] *Laker Airways Ltd.* v. *Department of Trade* [1977] Q.B. 643, 707.
[60] Citing *Maritime Electric Co. Ltd.* v. *General Dairies Ltd.* [1937] A.C. 610.
[61] Citing *Robertson* v. *Minister of Pensions* [1949] 1 K.B. 227; *R.* v. *Liverpool Corporation, ex p. Liverpool Taxi Fleet Operators' Association* [1972] 2 Q.B. 299 and *H.T.V. Ltd.* v. *Price Commission* [1976] I.C.R. 170, 185-186.

powers such as to work injustice to the individual without any counter-vailing benefit to the public this is itself a misuse of powers. If the jurisdictional principle is the trump card his Lordship trumps the trump by making this notion of fairness part of the constraints on the use of discretion. The other members of the Court of Appeal were more tradi-tional. Estoppel could not operate so as to ossify governmental policy.[62] While this is indisputable, it does not answer the more general point as to what should happen in cases where there is no such danger. Later authority provides some support for the approach taken by Lord Denning M.R.

In the *Preston*[63] case P made an agreement with the Revenue in 1978 to forgo interest relief which he had claimed and he also paid some capital gains tax; in return, the inspector said that he would not raise any further inquiries on certain tax affairs. In 1982, following the receipt of new information concerning the same transaction, the Revenue decided to apply certain provisions of the tax legislation. P sought judicial review of this decision. Lord Templeman, giving judgment for their Lordships, stated that P would have no remedy for breach of the representation as such, because the Revenue could not bind itself in 1978 not to perform its statutory duty in 1982.[64] Judicial review was, however, available:[65] a court could direct the Revenue to abstain from performing its statutory duties or exercising its powers where the unfairness to the applicant of doing so rendered such insistence an abuse of power.[66] Conduct by the Revenue which was equivalent to a breach of representation could, said Lord Templeman, be one such instance of abuse of power.[67]

How much support the *Preston* case provides remains open to question for a reason mentioned above:[68] the reviewing court may not always make it clear whether it believes that the initial representation was *intra* or *ultra vires*. This is exemplified by the *Preston* case itself in which, although there are statements covering the situation where the representation is *ultra vires* or contrary to a statutory duty, the court does not decide whether the particular representation was in fact of this nature. The assumption in *Preston* itself appears to have been that the representation was *intra vires*.[69] However, if a court believes that no balancing can be undertaken if the representation is *ultra vires*, but it does wish to consider the effects of the representation on the individual affected by it, this may cause the court to categorise the representation as *intra* rather than *ultra vires*, if this is possible on the facts of the case.[70] This is particularly so because, as will be

---

[62] [1977] Q.B. 643, 709, 728.
[63] R. v. *Inland Revenue Commissioners, ex p. Preston* [1985] A.C. 835.
[64] [1985] A.C. 835, 862.
[65] *Ibid.* pp. 862-863.
[66] *Ibid.* p. 864G. And Lord Templeman quotes *H.T.V. v. Price Commission* [1976] I.C.R. 170, 185-186, where Lord Denning M.R. phrased the applicability of estoppel in very similar terms to the quotation given above.
[67] [1985] A.C. 835, 866-867. The applicant failed on the facts, pp. 867-871.
[68] See above, p. 653.
[69] This is the interpretation of the case in R. v. *Inland Revenue Commissioners, ex p. M.F.K. Underwriting Agents Ltd.* [1990] 1 W.L.R. 1545.
[70] See, *e.g.*, the approach in the *M.F.K.* case [1990] 1 W.L.R. 1545.

seen below, if a public authority has made an *intra vires* representation which has created a legitimate expectation, then this may well be enforced to some degree.[71]

Everything said thus far in defence of judicial balancing has drawn only upon overt examples where an *ultra vires* decision is weighed against some other variable. This does not even touch upon the more implicit balancing which goes on within the *ultra vires* principle itself.[72] This can take the form of a value judgment as to whether to categorise an error as one of law, fact, discretion, or no error at all. It can manifest itself in the decision as to whether an error should be characterised as jurisdictional or not. The expansion of the concept of jurisdiction should dispel any illusions that the limits of a public body's jurisdiction are self-defining.

If, despite all of this, it is still felt that the judiciary should not undertake the balancing then this might to some extent be achieved through legislation.

(4) THE RELEVANCE OF LEGITIMATE EXPECTATIONS IN JUDICIAL BALANCING

It is important at this point to clarify the role which the concept of legitimate expectations plays in the type of case under consideration. In short that concept is a necessary, but not sufficient, condition for the application of estoppel. This requires explanation.

Reasonableness of reliance is a *necessary* condition for the existence of a legitimate expectation and for the application of estoppel: only if the representation is made by one on whom it was reasonable to rely, can it be said to give rise to a legitimate expectation that the representation will be followed. The very idea of a legitimate expectation can be said to be inherent in the notion of a binding representation, and this is indeed the normative foundation which justifies the application of estoppel.

The presence of a legitimate expectation is not, however, a *sufficient* condition for the application of estoppel in the type of case which is under consideration for the following reason. Even if the representation does create a legitimate expectation in the above sense, this does not, of itself, remove the difficulty that it may be outside the power of the public body.[73] The articulation of the concept of legitimate expectation is not, therefore, some intellectual panacea which will make the problem of estoppel in public law disappear. To contend otherwise would be to say that any representation which would otherwise raise an estoppel, and in this sense

---

[71] *Att.-Gen. of Hong Kong* v. *Ng Yuen Shiu* [1983] 2 A.C. 629; *R.* v. *Secretary of State for the Home Department, ex p. Khan* [1985] 1 All E.R. 40.
[72] *e.g.* although the *Ng Yuen Shiu* and *Khan* cases both have the qualification that the representation must not be in conflict with a statutory duty of the public body, it seems clear that the courts in these cases would not have readily found this to be so.
[73] It could be argued that a representee could never have a "legitimate" expectation if the representation was *ultra vires*. This, however, merely amounts to a restatement of the rule that *ultra vires* representations cannot generate an estoppel. It adds nothing to that statement. It is also misleading in that it conveys the impression that the individual somehow harboured an illegitimate or unwarranted expectation that the representation would be fulfilled. The reality is rather that the representee is innocent, and has no reason to expect that the representation is outside the complex powers of the public body.

create a legitimate expectation, should do so in public law irrespective of any excess of power by the public body that might thereby be entailed. Thus, in fact situations such as *Lever Finance*,[74] *Robertson*[75] or *Western Fish*[76] it may well be the case that the representation was one on which it was reasonable or legitimate for the representee to rely. *If*, however, that representation was outside the powers of the relevant public body, or its officer, the problem considered above would still be present.

While the existence of a legitimate expectation is not a sufficient condition for the application of estoppel it does serve as a signal that issues of legal certainty are involved in a case, and that these should be weighed or balanced against the fact that the representation was prima facie illegal. The existence of a legitimate expectation should, therefore, operate as a trigger to alert a court that a balance between the principles of legality and legal certainty may be required.

(5) THE LEGISLATURE

Legislative intervention could take one of two forms. A clause dealing with the problem might be inserted in particular statutes.[77] Alternatively, there could be a general statute. This could provide a defence for bona fide reliance upon a rule or opinion, where the rule or opinion was made by the body responsible for administering that law, and the rule was promulgated to guide the class of persons to which the representee belonged. The particular statutes to which this defence would apply could be stipulated and additions could be made.[78]

The deficiency of both of these statutory mechanisms is not in their conception, but in their scope. Both the particular legislative enactments and the general statute provide defences to money claims, or claims for some form of penalty directed against the representee. Although such relief is a valuable first stage in the representee's protection, it will often not be sufficient in itself. The individual may need not just relief from a penalty, but the ability to pursue the course of conduct which he was induced to follow by the representation. The *Mansell* formula would cover this, whereas the statutory examples given above would not.

What is needed is an area by area analysis. The balance between the injustice to the individual and the detrimental effects upon the public interest must be assessed. If it is decided that the former outweighs the latter then a provision should be enacted in the particular statute which not only relieves the representee who had detrimentally relied from a penalty, but actually allows that person to continue with the proposed course of conduct. Where the effects upon the public interest will be in excess of

---

[74] [1971] 1 Q.B. 222.

[75] [1949] 1 K.B. 227.

[76] [1981] 2 All E.R. 204.

[77] *e.g.* in the US see, Portal-to-Portal Act 1947, 29 U.S.C.A. ss. 258, 259; *e.g.* Trust Indenture Act 1939, 15 U.S.C.A. s. 77(c); Public Utility Holding Act 1939, 15 U.S.C.A. s. 79 I(d); Defence Production Act 1950, 50 U.S.C.A. s. 2157.

[78] Newman, "Should Official Advice be Reliable? – Proposals as to Estoppel and Related Doctrines in Administrative Law" 53 Col. L. Rev. 374 (1953).

any harm to the individual then compensation should be given, provided always that the reliance was reasonable in the circumstances. The relationship between compensation and estoppel will now be considered.

4. *The Relationship between Estoppel and Compensation*

An argument that might be made against the suggestions put forward above is that it would be much simpler to give compensation to the aggrieved representee than to allow an *ultra vires* representation to bind. There are two points that should be made in relation to this suggestion.

The first is that in some circumstances it would be tantamount to doing the same thing. Giving compensation in cases like *Robertson* v. *Minister of Pensions*[79] would have the same effect as allowing the representee to plead estoppel.

The second point is far more important. Two examples will serve as illustrations. Let us assume that X has been given an assurance that certain alterations to property do not require further planning permission. X builds the property with the alterations. The assurance given was *ultra vires* the representor. The cost of compensating X will be £20,000.[80] The second example has analogies with the *Skytrain*[81] case. Y has received an assurance that he can operate a new transport service. In reliance thereon he invests £5 million. The assurance turns out to be *ultra vires* the body that made it.

Any system of compensation that is instituted will derive its funds from a certain section of society, directly or indirectly. It may, for example, be through general taxation or from the local rates. It is a trite, though important, proposition that funds for compensation are scarce. The vital question that is not answered by those who advocate compensation, rather than ever allowing an *ultra vires* assurance to bind, is this: if by balancing the public and private interest it can be shown that the detriment to the former by allowing estoppel to bind is outweighed by that of the latter if estoppel were not allowed to operate, why give compensation rather than allow the estoppel to apply? The *ultra vires* principle operates to keep bodies within the ambit of their powers, and does so to protect society or a certain section of it. Yet, if through the balancing process advocated above, it can be shown that society, or a certain section of it, is not going to suffer in comparison with the detriment to the individual, then to insist that X's building should be torn down, or that Y's investment should lay idle, and then to pay X and Y compensation, would be, in a quite literal sense, a waste of these resources. Society is compensating X and Y for the destruction of things the presence of which did not really harm it. It is doubtful if this is the most pressing object on which society can spend its scarce resources devoted to compensation. Compensation for wrongful

---

[79] [1949] 1 K.B. 227.
[80] The example has obvious analogies with *Lever Finance* [1971] 1 Q.B. 222.
[81] *Laker Airways Ltd.* v. *Department of Trade* [1977] Q.B. 643.

administrative action may well be needed.[82] It is not, however, an alternative to allowing estoppel to operate when there has been an *ultra vires* assurance. It can only be a complement.

Section 4. Fettering of Discretion

1. *Changes of Policy and Fettering of Discretion*

Now it might well be thought that whatever difficulties exist in the context of *ultra vires* representations, the situation must be simpler if the representation which has been made and relied upon by the individual is in fact *intra vires*. The matter is, unfortunately, not quite so simple.

It is important to begin by making the factual position clear. A public body has to decide how to disburse certain funds. It might do so either by a series of individual adjudications or by laying down a set of qualifying criteria and then making determinations concerning their applicability. The public body might have made a representation to an individual that the matter would be dealt with in a certain manner; or the individual might have relied upon a public policy statement as to the criteria which would determine the disbursement of the funds. What should happen when the public body makes one determination and then seeks to upset this by making a different decision? The key point here is that both decisions may well be *intra vires*. The reason for the change may be because of a shift in view about policy, or because of an altered perception concerning the factual application of that policy to the individual. Should such a change be allowed and what should be the position of the individual in such a situation?

In *Re 56 Denton Road, Twickenham, Middlesex*[83] the plaintiff's house was damaged during the war and later demolished by the local authority. The preliminary determination by the War Damage Commission was that the property was a total loss. This was later altered, the Commission saying that the loss was non-total. A third turn of the wheel caused them to revert to the categorisation of total loss. Greater compensation would be paid where the loss was non-total. It was held that the second determination was final and that where Parliament had imposed a duty of deciding any question the deciding of which affected the rights of subjects, such a decision, when made and communicated in terms which were not preliminary, was final and conclusive. It could not, in the absence of express statutory power or the consent of the person affected, be withdrawn.[84] The

---

[82] See Chap. 15. There may, *e.g.*, be good reason to compensate Z who has suffered loss of amenity due to the *ultra vires* assurance given to X.

[83] [1953] Ch. 51. See also, *Livingstone* v. *Westminster Corporation* [1904] 2 K.B. 109, 120 where there were special statutory reasons for regarding the decision as final.

[84] *Ibid.* pp. 56-57.

case provides a very neat illustration of our problem. The question here was whether a determination which was *intra vires* would be held to bind the public body. The *Denton Road* case expresses a qualified affirmative answer. The decision was binding as a valid decision, in and of itself.[85]

There is, however, a tension between this principle and the concept that public bodies must not be fettered in the exercise of their discretion. In *Rootkin* v. *Kent County Council*[86] the plaintiff's daughter was given a place at a school which the local authority believed to be over three miles from her home. They thereby came under an obligation to provide transport or to reimburse travelling expenses, and decided upon the latter. They later measured the distance once again and, having decided that the distance was in fact less than three miles, withdrew the funding. The plaintiff relied on the *Denton Road* case and upon estoppel. The former argument was rejected, the court saying that it had no application where the citizen was receiving only a discretionary benefit as opposed to a statutory right. The latter was rejected also because there had been no detrimental reliance and, in any event, estoppel could not fetter the exercise of executive discretion.[87]

2. *Resolution of the Problem*

What should the answer be in circumstances such as those posed above? On principle it should be as follows.

First, when a public body does make what is a lawful final judgment this should be binding upon it even in the absence of detrimental reliance. A citizen should be entitled to assume that such a judgment will not be overturned by a second decision even if the latter is equally lawful. This should be the starting point. The principle of legal certainty has a particularly strong application in these circumstances, and the ideal that there must be an end to litigation seems equally apposite here as elsewhere.

Secondly, it should make no difference whether that initial decision was the determination of a statutory right or the exercise of a discretion. The line between the two may well be hazy.[88] Moreover, once an exercise of discretion is concretised in its application to a particular person the argument that that person should be able to rely upon it is equally strong as in the case of a decision about rights. This is supported by the decision in the *M.F.K.* case.[89] The applicants had approached the Inland Revenue as to whether certain investments would be taxed as capital or income. The initial response from the Revenue convinced the applicants that the investments would be taxed as capital, but the Revenue later resolved to tax

---

[85] *Ibid.* p. 57. No reliance on the original decision will be possible where that decision was based upon facts which have been falsified by the applicant, *R.* v. *Dacorum Borough Council, ex p. Walsh* [1992] C.O.D. 125.

[86] [1981] 1 W.L.R. 1186.

[87] *Ibid.* pp. 1195-1197, 1200.

[88] For example, the distinction drawn between the legislation in the *Denton Road* case and that in *Rootkin* is not as clear on closer examination as it appears at first sight.

[89] [1990] 1 W.L.R. 1545.

the assets as income. Bingham L.J. held that the applicants must fail if the representation was in breach of the Revenue's statutory duty. No such breach was present on the facts of the case, since the Revenue was merely acting in pursuance of its proper *managerial discretion*. In such circumstances the Revenue could not withdraw from its representation *if* this would cause substantial unfairness to the applicant, and *if* the conditions for relying upon any such representation were present. Those conditions were that: the applicant should give full details of the transaction on which the Revenue's ruling was being sought; the applicant should make it apparent that it was seeking a considered ruling which it intended to rely upon; and the ruling itself would have to be clear and unambiguous.[90] On the facts the applicants failed, but the case clearly demonstrates that a representation given by a public body pursuant to the exercise of its statutory discretion can, subject to the above conditions, be relied upon. It will not necessarily be defeated by the argument that to sanction such a result would be a fetter on the general discretion of that body.[91]

Thirdly, where the initial decision is changed because of a mistake or misinterpretation of the facts then if there has been detrimental reliance compensation should be given. Provided that the applicant has not misled the public body then the onus of ensuring that the facts are correctly applied should be on the public body.

Fourthly, the arguments about fettering of discretion must be kept within perspective. Any lawful decision will perforce limit the way in which discretion can be used by ruling out other options. Policies can of course change and in this sense it is true to say that the making of new policy cannot be fettered. But this point must be kept within bounds. Three different situations can be distinguished.

(a) The original decision may only be of limited temporal effectiveness. When that time runs out then it can of course be redetermined differently.

(b) A whole new policy may be introduced shortly after the initial decision. That decision should remain unaffected. If implementation of the new policy necessitates alteration of that decision then, subject to the statutory framework, this must be allowed with compensation for detrimental reliance.[92]

(c) A statute will normally allow a public body to revise its policy. In this situation the decisions in *Ng Yuen Shiu*[93] and *Khan*[94] are to be welcomed. Where a public body has created a legitimate expectation, through an *intra vires* representation based upon an existing policy, that it will apply certain criteria to determine an issue then it should be under a duty to follow such criteria. The public body should only be able to apply new standards to this individual who has relied on the previously published criteria, if the overriding public interest requires it, and then only after a hearing. Legal

---

[90] *Ibid.* pp. 1568-1569.
[91] See also, R. v. *Inland Revenue Commissioners, ex p. Preston* [1985] A.C. 835; *Gillingham Borough Council* v. *Medway (Chatham) Dock Co. Ltd.* [1992] 3 W.L.R. 449.
[92] See the analogous situation in contracts, Chap. 19, pp. 699-707.
[93] [1983] 2 A.C. 629.
[94] [1985] 1 All E.R. 40.

certainty warrants at least this degree of protection for the representee who has reasonably relied on the previous criteria.[95]

When applying this formulation it is important to keep two issues distinct: did the applicant possess any legitimate expectation derived from the representation or policy; and is there an overriding public interest which requires departure from that policy, even in the instant case. The importance of preserving this distinction can be appreciated by contrasting the following two cases.

In the *Ruddock* case[96] the applicant, who had been a prominent member of the Campaign for Nuclear Disarmament, sought judicial review of a decision to intercept her telephone calls on the ground she had a legitimate expectation that the published criteria as to when this would be done would be followed. Taylor J. recognised that in a case such as the present, where *ex hypothesi* there would be no right to be heard before making the interception order, it might be particularly important that the ministerial undertaking should be kept. He accepted that the minister's power could not be fettered, but correctly placed this idea in perspective: the publication of a policy did not preclude any future change; nor did it prevent the non-application of that policy in a particular case for reasons of national security. The minister had not, however, argued that the policy should be dispensed with on these grounds, and therefore the applicant did have a legitimate expectation that the published criteria would be applied.[97]

This reasoning can be compared to that in the *Oral Snuff* case.[98] The applicant manufactured oral snuff and had received a grant from the government for a factory in 1985, even though the government was aware of the health risk from the substance. In 1988 the government, acting on the advice of a committee, stated that it intended to ban such snuff. The court rejected the applicant's arguments based on legitimate expectations, and Taylor L.J. held that the Secretary of State's discretion could not be fettered by a moral obligation to the applicants which was based on the government's earlier favourable treatment of them. The decision may well have been correct on the facts, but the reasoning elides the two issues mentioned above. There may well have been an overriding public interest here which should trump any legitimate expectation which the applicant might have had, but this should not be taken to mean that no such expectation existed.

More recently, Laws J. held in the *Richmond* case that it was not for the court to decide whether the overriding public interest required a change of policy; this was a matter for the public body. However, he also held that this decision to change policy could itself be reviewed on *Wednesbury* grounds.[99]

---

[95] See also, R. v. *Department of Trade and Industry, ex p. Blenheim Queensdale Estates Ltd.* [1992] C.O.D. 453; R. v. *Rochdale Metropolitan Borough Council, ex p. Schemet* [1993] C.O.D. 113, 115; R. v. *Lord Chancellor, ex p. Hibbit and Saunders (a firm)* [1993] C.O.D. 326, 327.

[96] R. v. *Secretary of State for the Home Department, ex p. Ruddock* [1987] 1 W.L.R. 1482.

[97] The applicant failed on the facts because the court held that the minister could have concluded that the criteria were applicable.

[98] R. v. *Secretary of State for Health, ex p. United States Tobacco International Inc.* [1992] Q.B. 353, 369.

[99] R. v. *Secretary of State for Transport, ex p. Richmond upon Thames London B.C.* [1994] All E.R. 577, 596-597.

Section 5. Estoppel by Record

1. *General Principles*

One variety of estoppel which requires special attention, is that of estoppel by record or, as it is often known, estoppel *per rem judicatem*.[100] This type of estoppel is itself of two kinds. One is known as cause of action estoppel. If the same cause of action has been litigated to a final judgment between the same parties, or their privies,[101] litigating in the same capacity, no further litigation is possible, the principle being that there must be an end to litigation. The other form of estoppel by record is issue estoppel. A single cause of action may contain several distinct issues. Where there is a final judgment between the same parties, or their privies, litigating in the same capacity on the same issue, then that issue cannot be reopened in subsequent proceedings. There may be a difference of opinion as to whether an issue is the same as one which has already been litigated.[102]

The application of the *res judicata* doctrine in the public law context was reaffirmed in *Thrasyvoulou* v. *Secretary of State for the Environment*.[103] It was held that in relation to adjudications which were subject to a comprehensive self-contained statutory code the presumption was that where the statute had created a specific jurisdiction for the determination of any issue which established the existence of a legal right, the principle of *res judicata* applied to give finality to that determination, unless an intention to exclude that principle could be inferred as a matter of construction from the statutory provisions.

2. *Application to Administrative Law*

There are two obstacles to the application of *res judicata* in administrative law. These are the necessity to alter policy, which has been considered above, and the *ultra vires* doctrine itself. The present discussion will focus upon the latter issue.

Res judicata expresses the binding nature of a matter litigated to final judgment. In administrative law many matters decided by a tribunal or other public body are not final in this sense. Which matters come within this category? All those which are regarded as jurisdictional. These will be determined by the reviewing court. The limitation on *res judicata* is, therefore, simply the reverse side of the coin called judicial review of jurisdiction. Which issues do and should go to jurisdiction have already been considered.

---

[100] *Cross on Evidence* (7th ed., 1990, by C. Tapper), pp. 74-90.
[101] Privies connotes those claiming through the original party, *Cross*, pp. 76-77.
[102] *Ibid.* pp. 81-84.
[103] [1990] 2 A.C. 273, 289.

In *R. v. Hutchings*[104] a local Board of Health had applied to the justices under the Public Health Act 1875 to recover the expenses of repairing a street from a frontager. The latter contended that it was a public highway repairable by the inhabitants at large. This contention was upheld by the justices. Some years later the Board of Health made an application against the same person, and on this occasion the justices did order payment of expenses. The plea that the matter was *res judicata* because of the earlier decision was rejected. It was held that, on construction, the justices had no power to decide whether the street was or was not a public highway; that was a matter only incidentally cognisable by them. Their only jurisdiction was to determine whether a sum of money should be paid or not.[105]

Even where the subject-matter is clearly within the jurisdiction of the tribunal, there may be a temporal limit to the conclusiveness of that tribunal's findings which limits the application of *res judicata*. This is illustrated by cases concerning rating and taxes.[106]

Provided that the issue is within the subject-matter and temporal jurisdiction of the public body, *res judicata* will prevent the same matter being litigated before the original tribunal over again. Whether the public body is performing administrative rather than judicial tasks is not a relevant criterion for the application of *res judicata*, nor is the existence of a *lis inter partes*.[107]

The label *res judicata* is, however, only required where an applicant does attempt to litigate the matter over again before the original decision-maker. In circumstances where the individual has received one decision from the public body and then attempts to have this reversed on appeal or review the label is not really required. If the original decision is *intra vires* then it is binding simply because it is a lawful decision given by the appropriate body. The term *res judicata* is of use to prevent frequent attempts to determine the same point. Thus, if an applicant attempts to obtain a decision from one tribunal, fails, tries later on the same point, still fails, and then seeks appeal or review, *res judicata* is an appropriate label to apply provided that the original decision was *intra vires*.

---

[104] [1881] 6 Q.B.D. 300, 304-305; *R. v. Secretary of State for the Environment, ex p. Hackney London Borough Council* [1984] 1 W.L.R. 592.
[105] *cf. Wakefield Corporation v. Cooke* [1904] A.C. 31.
[106] *Society of Medical Officers of Health v. Hope* [1960] A.C. 551; *Caffoor v. Commissioner of Income Tax* [1961] A.C. 584.
[107] *Caffoor* [1961] A.C. 584, 597-599.

19. CONTRACT

We have already encountered the use of contract in various contexts, and we have also considered the extent to which contracts can be subject to judicial review.[1] This chapter will focus on certain more general aspects of the contract relationship.[2] We will begin by looking at the making and terms of the contract and ask whether the person who contracts with government merits some procedural protection in relation to the consideration of the bid. This will be followed by an examination of the constraints which are imposed upon public bodies when they undertake public procurement. There will then be a discussion of the way in which government contracting policy operates in reality, and of the use made by government of contract to obtain other regulatory goals. The final sections of the chapter will focus upon the conflict that can occur between a public body fulfilling its contractual obligations and compliance with its statutory mandate. As we shall see, contractual principles may have to be modified in their application to public bodies.

Section 1. Making the Contract: General

1. *Capacity to Contract*

(1) CROWN

Ministers are often granted a power to conclude contracts by a statute, but in addition the Crown possesses a common law power to contract.[3] It is debatable whether this power should be seen as part of the prerogative.[4] Whatever label is attached, the Crown's contracting power is unconstrained by restrictions as to subject-matter or person.[5]

---

[1] See above, Chap. 15.
[2] Street, *Governmental Liability* (1953), Chap. 3; Mitchell, *Contracts of Public Authorities* (1954); Turpin, *Government Procurement and Contracts* (1989); Arrowsmith, *Civil Liability and Public Authorities* (1992).
[3] *Bankers Case* (1700) 90 E.R. 270. Turpin, *Government Procurement*, pp. 83-84; Arrowsmith, *Civil Liability*, pp. 53-54.
[4] Daintith, "Regulation by Contract: The New Prerogative" (1979) C.L.P. 41, 42-43.
[5] *cf. New South Wales* v. *Bardolph* (1934) 52 C.L.R. 455, 496.

(2) MINISTERS OF THE CROWN

The contractual *capacity* of ministers of the Crown, and other Crown agents, requires separate treatment. It is clear that a minister will normally possess the *authority* to make a contract on behalf of the Crown itself. This will be examined below. What is of relevance here is the question of whether a minister possesses *capacity* to make contracts in his or her own name.

It could be argued either that such agents have no independent contractual capacity, in the sense that the Crown is the only entity which is a party to the contract; or that while the primary liability rests with the Crown, the minister may also be a party to the contract; or that ministers do in fact have an independent contractual capacity within their area of responsibility in the same way as any other artificial legal entity and that while they can contract on behalf of the Crown, they can also choose to make a contract to which the Crown is not a party, and for which the Crown bears no liability.[6]

There is some authority that a minister or other Crown agent can choose to contract in his or her own name, even in relation to those functions which are carried out on behalf of the Crown, and that whether this has occurred depends upon the intent of the parties.[7] The principal motivation behind these cases was, however, to allow plaintiffs to sue without the necessity of using the Petition of Right procedure: this procedure was only necessary in actions against the Crown, not when suits were brought against individual ministers.

Other cases have adopted a different approach. In *Town Investments*[8] certain rent legislation only gave protection from rent increases where the tenant and the occupier were the same person. The Department of the Environment (DOE) organised accommodation for other departments and had negotiated a lease, but the building was in fact occupied by a different department. The landlord sought to argue that the tenant and occupier were not one and the same, that the DOE had power to make the lease in its own name and hence that the protective rent legislation did not apply. The House of Lords rejected the argument: acts of government which were done by ministers were acts done by the Crown, and the Crown was to be treated as one entity. Although there are ambiguities in the judgments, the general thrust is that ministers do not possess an independent contractual capacity.

A ministerial office may be created at common law or by statute. If the minister's office is one which exists at common law then the minister will, it seems, possess the contractual capacity of the Crown. Thus, a contract made will be valid even if it is outside the specific terms of a statute unless a court construes the statute as imposing a limit on contractual power in the area covered by the enabling instrument. Where a minister is a purely statutory creation the argument for restricting the contracting power by

---

[6] See Arrowsmith, *Civil Liability*, pp. 56-59.
[7] *Graham* v. *Public Works Commissioners* [1901] 2 K.B. 781; *International Railway Co.* v. *Niagara Parks Commission* [1941] A.C. 328.
[8] *Town Investments* v. *Department of the Environment* [1978] A.C. 359.

the *ultra vires* principle is, in theory, stronger. However, as seen above, the effect of the *Town Investments*[9] case appears to be that the contractual capacity and authority of a specific minister merges with that of the Crown.[10] It is unclear whether this will always be the case, but certain dicta suggest an affirmative answer.[11] On this view any contract made by the minister in a public capacity will bind the Crown, and it would also seem to be the case that the minister has no separate contractual capacity as such, unless this is specifically conferred by statute. Other jurisdictions have, however, not adopted this approach,[12] nor as will be seen below, does it sit easily with the approach of our own courts in other areas. Three comments may be made on the foregoing.

First, it is doubtful whether anything should in fact turn upon whether the minister's office existed at common law or was the creation of a statute. There is no reason in principle why there should be any difference in their respective contractual capacities.

Secondly, the argument for saying that the minister possesses the contractual capacity of the Crown is that the Crown in its governmental capacity operates through individual ministers or other Crown servants. It has to do so. It is, therefore, thought to be unrealistic to speak of the Crown in a governmental sense which is divorced from those servants. Having said this our courts *have* recognised that ministers and departments can be regarded as separate from the Crown. This is commonly acknowledged in judicial review proceedings where the orthodox view is that the prerogative orders will not lie against the Crown itself, but will lie against individual ministers.[13] Thus in the context of such proceedings, it has been recognised that ministers can act in an *official* capacity separate from the Crown itself: the statute will be construed as giving powers to a particular minister to be exercised in his or her own name as *persona designata*, and not as agent for the Crown.[14] The "logic" of merging the capacity of the minister with that of the Crown is not pursued remorselessly in this context.[15] It is clear, therefore, that on some occasions our courts have chosen to regard the Crown and its ministers as one and indivisible, while on others they have accepted that they can be treated as separate entities for many important purposes.

Thirdly, given that this is so, a preference for one of these theories should not be allowed to dictate a conclusion which is unacceptable in substantive terms. For example, even if one does subscribe to the *Town Investments* approach and believes that the contractual capacity of the minister merges with that of the Crown, this should not enable clear delimitations of a minister's contracting power laid down in a statute to be circumvented by

---

[9] [1978] A.C. 359.

[10] *Town Investments Ltd.* v. *Department of the Environment* [1978] A.C. 359.

[11] *Ibid.* pp. 380-382, 400.

[12] *J.E. Verrault & Fils* v. *Quebec* [1971] S.C.R. 41; *Meates* v. *Attorney General* [1979] 1 N.Z.L.R. 415.

[13] Whether this orthodoxy is in fact correct is questionable, see below, pp. 725-726.

[14] *M* v. *Home Office* [1993] 3 All E.R. 537.

[15] Many statutes such as the Ministers of the Crown Act 1975 are premised upon the hypothesis that a minister accepts rights and obligations in his or her own name.

reliance on some more general contractual power of the Crown. Where such a limit is clearly expressed or can be implied then, by analogy with the case law on the royal prerogative, such a limit should be respected and enforced.[16]

(3) STATUTORY BODIES

Authorities which are not Crown agents and which derive their powers from statute are subject to the limitations imposed by the legislation. Thus, a contract which goes beyond the limits imposed by the statute will be *ultra vires*.[17] This is exemplified by the decision in *Hazell* v. *Hammersmith and Fulham London Borough Council*.[18] A local authority was held to have no power to enter into speculative interest rate swap transactions which would result in profits or losses depending upon movements in interest rates.

The scope of such a public body's contractual capacity will, therefore, be dependent upon the construction of the relevant statute. However, many such bodies are granted broad powers to facilitate the carrying out of their tasks: for example section 111 of the Local Government Act 1972 empowers local authorities to do anything which is calculated to facilitate the discharge of any of its functions, or is incidental thereto. Moreover, the courts have held that a power to contract may be implied as an incidence of other powers which the particular body has been given.[19]

(4) THE EFFECT OF AN UNLAWFUL CONTRACT

The precise effects of a contract which is beyond the capacity of the relevant body are unclear. In private law the common law rule was that the unlawful contract was unenforceable against the corporation which made it.[20] The principal rationale behind this rule was to prevent corporate funds from being disbursed on an unauthorised purpose, to the detriment of the share holders and creditors of the company. The common law position has now been amended by statute which, in general, allows such agreements to be enforced against the company.[21]

Whether the old common law rule applies to unlawful contracts entered into by a public body is still not entirely clear. If they are unenforceable then this can cause real hardship to the contractor who may lose any expected profits on the transaction, and may be unable to recover expenses which have been incurred in preparing to perform the contract. As Arrowsmith states,[22]

> "Contracts which are unlawful for a breach of public law should generally be enforceable at least where the contractor is not aware that

---

[16] *Att.-Gen.* v. *De Keyser's Royal Hotel Ltd.* [1920] A.C. 508.

[17] *Att.-Gen.* v. *Manchester Corporation* [1906] 1 Ch. 643; *Att.-Gen.* v. *Fulham Corporation* [1921] 1 Ch. 44.

[18] [1922] 2 A.C. 1.

[19] *Att.-Gen.* v. *Great Eastern Railway* (1880) 5 App. Cas. 473, 478.

[20] *Ashbury Carriage and Iron Co.* v. *Riche* (1875) L.R. 7 H.L. 653.

[21] Companies Act 1985, s.35(1), Companies Act 1989, s.108.

[22] *Civil Liability*, pp. 64–65. For detailed consideration of the problems surrounding recovery in the *Hazell* case [1992] 2 A.C. 1 see, Loughlin, "Innovative Financing in Local Government: The Limits of Legal Instrumentalism – Pt.II" [1991] P.L. 568.

the contract is unlawful: the *prima facie* right of the contractor should prevail over the public interest. This should apply even if, as in *Hazell*, the contract is one which on its face could not have lawfully been made: the onus should be on the authority itself to ensure compliance with its legislative mandate, and not on the contractor. Alternatively, however, the courts might wish to hold that the contract is enforceable only where it is one which might have been lawful if made for a proper purpose, and the other party does not know of the improper purpose."

2. *The Authority of an Agent*

In order to maintain an action not only must the public body have capacity to make the contract, but the agent must have been authorised to do so. Special problems can occur when such an agent purports to act on behalf of a public authority.

(1) THE EXTENT OF THE AGENT'S AUTHORITY: GENERAL

In a contract made between two private parties an agent can bind the principal if the agent has authority, actual or ostensible.[23] There are, however, difficulties in applying these principles to the situation in which a public body makes a contract through an agent. These problems have been considered in the discussion of representations, and reference should be made to that discussion.[24] The principles can be briefly reiterated here.

Actual authority may be given by the terms of a particular statute, and it may equally be precluded where the legislation stipulates that that individual cannot bind the authority in a certain transaction. The fact that the authority has purported to delegate to a particular officer will not legitimate the contract if the statute makes it clear that the function must be performed by a different party. Ostensible authority exists in the situation where a representation is made by the principal that the agent has authority to deal with a certain type of transaction, or perhaps where an agent in that position would normally do so. However, as explained earlier, ostensible authority cannot validate a transaction which is *ultra vires* the public body itself, nor can it validate a delegation of authority to an agent where this is prohibited by the relevant statute. The harsh results which this doctrine can produce have been considered earlier, and the reforms suggested there are equally apposite here.[25]

These principles apply in general to Crown servants and agents. Thus it will normally have to be shown that a minister possesses actual or ostensible authority to enter into a contract of the type in question. These principles have clearly been applied to servants of the Crown who are not ministers.[26] The only difference between such servants and ministers of the

---

[23] See generally, Reynolds, *Bowstead's Law of Agency* (15th ed., 1985).
[24] See above, pp. 653-655.
[25] See above, pp. 661-672.
[26] *Att.-Gen. for Ceylon* v. *A.D. Silva* [1953] A.C. 461. For discussion of this case, see above, pp. 654-655.

Crown is that the latter are likely to have a broader remit of authority than the former.[27]

(2) BREACH OF WARRANTY OF AUTHORITY

In normal circumstances if an agent is duly authorised to make a contract then the principal will be liable but the agent will not; where, however, the agent possesses no authority he or she can be sued for breach of warranty of authority. There is some case law indicating that this action will not lie against a servant who makes a contract on behalf of the Crown. Thus, in *Dunn* v. *MacDonald*[28] the plaintiff was engaged for three years by the defendant on behalf of the Crown. He was dismissed prior to the end of his term and claimed breach of an implied warranty of authority by the defendant. The action failed, but the case is not conclusive authority that such an action could never succeed.

The reasons given for the decision differed. Charles J. believed that such an action would be against public policy,[29] while the Court of Appeal preferred to rest their decision on the fact that there was no breach.[30] The reasoning based upon public policy is unconvincing; it is difficult to see why the agent acting on behalf of the Crown should be in any better position than any other agent.[31]

3. Parliamentary Appropriation

Given the breadth of the Crown's power to contract, the legislature must have power to refuse an appropriation to pay for a contract made by the executive of which it disapproves.[32]

It was at one time thought that unless an express appropriation of money had been made the contract would be invalid and null. This belief was derived originally from the dicta of Shee J. in *Churchward* v. *R.*[33] and statements by Viscount Haldane.[34] However, it is clear from later cases that Viscount Haldane regarded the absence of the requisite appropriation as making the contract unenforceable as there was no *res* against which to enforce it, rather than making the contract null.[35] The view that the absence

---

[27] Unless one were to read the *Town Investments* case to mean that ministers always had the authority of the Crown generally, but this would be an extreme application of the merger theory applied in that case.

[28] [1897] 1 Q.B. 401, 555.

[29] *Ibid.* pp. 404-406.

[30] *Ibid.* pp. 556-558.

[31] Street, *Governmental Liability*, p. 93 makes the further points that the representation may well have been one of law rather than fact and that the plaintiff may not, on the facts, have relied upon it.

[32] Street, *Governmental Liability*, pp. 84-90.

[33] (1865) L.R. 1 Q.B. 173, 209, Cockburn C.J. was clearly of a different opinion, 200-201.

[34] *Commercial Cable Co.* v. *Government of Newfoundland* [1916] 2 A.C. 610, 617.

[35] *Commonwealth of Australia* v. *Kidman* [1926] 32 A.L.R. 1, 2-3; *Att.-Gen.* v. *Great Southern and Western Ry. Co. of Ireland* [1925] A.C. 754.

of appropriation goes to enforceability and not validity is supported by fully reasoned authority in Australia,[36] which also establishes that the appropriation does not have to be specifically directed towards a particular contractual expense.

The meaning of "enforceability" is not entirely clear. If the necessary funds are not appropriated what is the result? In *New South Wales* v. *Bardolph* Evatt J., at first instance, stated that failure to vote the funds would relieve the Crown from performance, the voting being an implied condition of the contract.[37] This comes perilously close to regarding appropriation as a condition of validity by the back door. On appeal, the High Court disagreed with this part of Evatt J.'s judgment, finding that the lack of appropriation did not relieve the Crown from its obligation to perform.[38]

Enforceability could have one of two other meanings. One suggestion is that is should bear the same interpretation as in the Statute of Frauds.[39] There are, however, difficulties in transferring the meaning of unenforceable from a statute concerned with ensuring written evidence for certain transactions, to the different context of the absence of the requisite parliamentary appropriation.[40] Another suggestion is that enforceability is best seen as a condition to the satisfaction of judgment,[41] rather than as to the enforceability of the claim itself. The difficulty with this view is that it amounts to saying no more than that there is no legal right to execute judgment against Crown property which is the general rule for all judgments against the Crown.

Appropriation Acts are, in any event, drawn broadly at present and thus the above problems are unlikely to occur.

4. *Proceedings against the Crown*

In claims brought against public authorities there is, in general, no problem about who to bring an action against or how: public bodies can be sued in their own name. Where the defendant is the Crown the position is different. As seen when considering the liability of the Crown in tort, the petition of right developed as a mechanism whereby actions, including those for breach of contract, could be brought against the Crown.

The Crown Proceedings Act 1947 abolished the petition of right and certain other forms of procedure. Under section 1 any claim against the Crown which could have been enforced, albeit subject to fiat, by petition of right (or under any of the more specialised statutory liabilities prior to the Act) can now be enforced without the fiat, as of right. The defendant is

---

[36] *New South Wales* v. *Bardolph* (1934) 52 C.L.R. 455.
[37] *Ibid.* pp. 483-484.
[38] *Ibid.* pp. 497-498, 508-510.
[39] Street, *Governmental Liability*, pp. 91-92.
[40] *e.g.* would the distinction between law and equity operate here, and would the doctrine of part performance with its specialised meaning be regarded as an exception to the unenforceability?
[41] Hogg, *Liability of the Crown* (1971), Chap. 5.

either the appropriate government department or the Attorney-General. It is clear, therefore, that the substantive areas covered by the old petition of right will still provide the actual scope of actions which can be brought against the Crown. However, apart from actions in tort (and salvage) the coverage of the petition of right appears to be comprehensive. Two qualifications are necessary.

First, the Act is only applicable in relation to the United Kingdom government.[42] A plaintiff seeking redress against the Crown for other areas is dependent upon the petition of right procedure. It has been held that even this pre-1947 procedure is unavailable and that the repeal of the Petitions of Right Act 1860 is total. This conclusion is debatable.[43] Secondly, it is unclear whether the Crown can be sued personally. It was, prior to 1947, possible to bring a petition of right but this, as stated, has been abolished and section 40(1) states that nothing in the 1947 Act shall apply to proceedings by or against the sovereign in his private capacity. It may, however, be that the petition of right survives to the extent of allowing such actions.

Section 2. Making the Contract: Public Procurement and the EC

The principles considered thus far are those to be found in domestic law and govern all contracts which are made by public bodies. There are, in addition, important rules which have emerged from the EC which stipulate how certain types of contract should be advertised and made.[44] The rules which apply in these areas are complex. They are, however, of great practical importance, and also raise interesting conceptual issues. An outline of the main provisions will, therefore, be provided within this section.

1. *The Object of the EC Rules*

One of the main objectives of the EC is to create a single market. Many of the articles of the Treaty are directed towards attainment of this goal, by prohibiting, for example, trade barriers, tariffs, and quantitative restrictions on the free movement of goods within the Community. These provisions by themselves are not, however, sufficient to achieve the desired goal. Member States may inhibit free movement by more subtle means than tariff

---

[42] s.40(2)(b),(c).

[43] *Franklin* v. *Att.-Gen.* [1974] Q.B. 185, 201. The 1947 Act states that nothing in it shall affect proceedings against the Crown relating to non-UK claims. This saving should, in this respect, preserve the 1860 Act.

[44] Turpin, *Government Procurement and Contracts* (1989); Arrowsmith, *Civil Liability and Public Authorities* (1992), Chap. 3 and *Government Procurement and Judicial Review* (1988); Geddes, *Public Procurement* (1993).

barriers. They may, for example, discriminate against companies from other Member States which wish to tender for a contract, favouring instead their own domestic firms. This may be a particular problem during a recession when a country's instinct may be to put its own industry first, and perhaps second and third, at the expense of more Community-minded goals. This is of economic significance because public procurement has been estimated by the Commission to account for 15% of the entire gross domestic product of the EC: if discrimination is not eradicated from this area then the hope of attaining a single market will always remain partially unfulfilled. With this in mind the Community institutions have applied Treaty norms to cases involving public procurement, and they have passed directives which address the issue more specifically. These will be considered in turn.

2. The Application of the Treaty

The articles of the Treaty will be applied to cases involving public procurement where relevant. This can be illustrated through three brief examples.

In *Commission* v. *Ireland*[45] a water company called for tenders for a project, and specified an Irish national standard for pipes which was met by only one firm, which was also Irish. This was held to be prima facie in breach of Article 30 of the Treaty, which prohibits quantitative restrictions on the free movement of goods or measures which have an equivalent effect, since a different specification of pipe might have been just as good for the job at hand and therefore the requirement in the tender document impeded free movement. The ECJ, in the *Du Pont* case[46] similarly invalidated a requirement of national legislation which obliged local authorities to obtain a minimum proportion of their supplies from a particular region or country. Articles 52 and 59 of the Treaty which relate to freedom of establishment and freedom to provide services can also be used in this context. Thus, in *Commission* v. *Italy*[47] it was held that a national rule, whereby only those companies which had a majority of shares owned by the state could tender for certain government contracts, was in breach of these Articles.

3. The Application of the Directives

(1) THE COMMUNITY DIRECTIVES

Notwithstanding the possible application of the Treaty provisions themselves it has long been acknowledged that more detailed regulation of

[45] Case 45/87, [1988] E.C.R. 4929.
[46] Case 21/88, *Du Pont de Nemours Italiana SpA* v. *Unita Sanitaria Locale, No.2 di Carrara* [1990] I E.C.R. 889.
[47] Case 3/88, [1989] E.C.R. 4035.

these areas was needed. To this end the Community enacted the Public Works Directive 71/305 and the Public Supplies Directive 77/62, which have been in force in the UK since 1973 and 1978 respectively. These directives were later strengthened, and they were also supplemented by Directive 89/665 which instituted a more stringent enforcement regime. A separate Directive, 90/531, was made for the utilities sector, covering industries such as water, transport, energy and telecommunications. The rationale for this separate treatment was that these activities are undertaken by a variety of bodies which exist along the public/private spectrum. It would, therefore, have been inappropriate to regulate these areas only when they were undertaken by public bodies *stricto sensu*. The final element of the Community regime is the Public Services Directive 92/50, which applies to the award of public service contracts.

(2) APPLICATION IN THE UK

We have already seen that directives dictate the ends which must be reached while leaving the means to the Member States.[48] The Community directives on public procurement have been given effect in the UK through secondary legislation: the Public Works Contracts Regulations 1991,[49] the Public Supply Contracts Regulations 1991,[50] and the Utilities and Works Contracts Regulations 1992.[51] This legislation will, in line with the *Von Colson*[52] principle, have to be construed so as to effectuate the objects of the directives. Space precludes a detailed examination of the entirety of this legislation. The main provisions of the Public Works regulations will, therefore, be taken by way of example.

The principal objectives of the Community rules in this area are: to ensure that public contracts above a certain value are advertised, thereby enabling all those in the Community who are interested to tender for them; to prohibit the use of technical specifications in the contract documents which could favour domestic firms; to mandate procedures for the award of the contract; and to stipulate the substantive criteria for award of the contract itself.

The Public Works Contracts Regulations apply to *contracting authorities*, which include:[53] ministers of the Crown; government departments; the House of Commons and the House of Lords; local authorities; and fire and police authorities. Regulation 3(1)(r) extends the definition of contracting authorities to include corporations, or groups of individuals, which or who act together for the specific purpose of meeting needs in the public interest, not having an industrial or commercial character, where they are financed wholly or mainly by another contracting authority, or are

---

[48] See above, Chap. 5.
[49] S.I. No. 2680.
[50] S.I. No. 2679.
[51] S.I. No. 3279.
[52] Case 14/83, *Von Colson & Kamaan* v. *Land Nordrhein-Westfalen* [1984] E.C.R. 1891.
[53] S.I. No. 2680 (1991), reg. 3.

subject to management by another contracting authority, or more than half of the members are appointed by another contracting authority.[54]

A *public works contract* is held to be[55] a contract in writing for consideration, for the carrying out of works for a contracting authority or under which the contracting authority engages a person to produce the specified work. The regulation only applies if the contract is worth more than 5 million ECUs, but there are provisions which are designed to prevent the contracting authority from dividing contracts in order to avoid the bite of the regulatory scheme.[56] Subject to this threshold, the regulations pertain whenever a contracting authority offers a public works contract other than one which is expressly excluded from the operation of the regulations, regardless of whether the contract is actually awarded or not.[57]

Regulation 8 then provides a detailed set of rules which relate to the *technical specifications* which are permitted in the tender document, the object being to avoid discrimination against non-domestic companies by the specification of standards which can be more easily met by the domestic operator.

One of the central parts of the regulation concerns *procedures*. There are three such procedures.[58] Under the *open procedure* any interested party can submit a bid; under the *restricted procedure* only those selected by the contracting party can do so; while under the *negotiated procedure* the authority negotiates the terms of the contract with one or more persons who are selected by it. Notice of intent to seek offers in relation to public works must be publicised in the Official Journal.[59] There are further detailed rules which specify when a contractor may be excluded from the tendering process, such as in the event of bankruptcy.[60] The contracting authority is entitled to consider the economic and financial standing of the contractor, but there are limits here too as to the type of information which the contracting authority can have regard to.[61]

The regulation then designates the criteria which must be used when *awarding* the contract. This must be on the basis either of the tender which offers the lowest price, or the offer which is the most economically advantageous, taking account of considerations of price, period for completion, running costs, profitability and technical merit.[62] All the criteria which the contracting authority intends to apply if using the economically advantageous test must be stated in the contract documentation. It may be lawful to specify a policy objective which the contractor should comply with, provided that this is itself compatible with Community law. But

[54] Bodies such as the Health and Safety Executive, the Advisory, Conciliation and Arbitration Service, the National Rivers Authority and the Commission for New Towns have been held to meet these criteria.
[55] Reg. 2(1). Works contracts relating to utilities are dealt with under the separate utilities regulation, and there are exceptions for public works involving state security.
[56] Reg. 7.
[57] Reg. 5.
[58] Regs. 11-13. The negotiated procedure can only be used in limited circumstances.
[59] Reg. 9.
[60] Reg. 14.
[61] Reg. 15.
[62] Reg. 20.

compliance with such an objective is not relevant to the assessment of that contractor's technical capacity to do the work, nor is it part of the actual criteria for deciding upon the award of the contract.[63]

Once the contract has been awarded the regulations then impose a duty to provide *reasons* as to why a particular contractor has been chosen.[64] This duty is owed to any unsuccessful contractor who requests a reasoned explanation. There is, in addition, an obligation to furnish a more general dossier which indicates the procedure which was adopted, the successful applicant, and the reasons for this choice.

We have already seen that one of the defects of the earlier provisions on public procurement concerned enforcement, and the lack of effective *remedies*. This problem was addressed by Directive 89/665, the Compliance Directive, and provisions to effectuate the obligations contained therein have been incorporated in the relevant UK regulations. This is dealt with, in the context of public works, by regulation 31. This provides that the duties under the regulation and under Community law are owed to contractors. A breach of such duties is not a criminal offence, but it does sound as an action for breach of duty, presumably breach of statutory duty, in civil law. The aggrieved contractor must first tell the contracting authority of the apprehended breach of duty and the intention to bring the action.[65] The court has a number of options: it may issue an interim order which, in effect, halts the contract award procedure; it may set aside the decision by the contracting authority and it can award damages to the contractor. However, if a contract has already been entered into pursuant to the contested decision then damages is the only available remedy.[66] The court cannot, therefore, set aside a contract which has been made in breach of the regulations.

The precise *measure of damages* which should be awarded is unclear. The problem for the aggrieved contractor is that it may be uncertain how far a breach of the regulations affected its chances of winning the contract; and it may be equally questionable whether it would have made profits from the contract. One possible solution would be to use doctrines developed within contract law to cope with uncertain losses, and to allow those who would have had a reasonable chance of success to recover a percentage of the likely profit.[67]

Regulation 31 makes it clear that the remedies which are delineated are to be without prejudice to any other powers of the court. This leaves open the possibility of an application for judicial review, and a damages action for breach of the Treaty or norms made thereunder. Both of these issues have been considered above.[68]

---

[63] Case 31/87, *Gebroeders Beentjers BV v. State of the Netherlands* [1988] E.C.R. 4635.
[64] Reg. 22.
[65] The action must be brought within three months from the date when the grounds for bringing it first arose, unless the court believes that there are good reasons for extending the time.
[66] Reg. 31(7).
[67] Arrowsmith, "Enforcing the E.C. Public Procurement Rules: The Remedies System in England and Wales" (1992) 1 P.P.L.R. 92; *Chaplin* v. *Hicks* [1911] 2 K.B. 786; *Hotson* v. *East Berkshire Health Authority* [1987] 1 A.C. 750.
[68] See above, pp. 685-686.

Section 3. Making the Contract: Public Procurement and Domestic Law

In addition to the rules which are derived from Community law there are also domestic norms which govern the making of an important range of contracts by local authorities and some other public bodies.

1. *Competitive Procedures for Contracts*

Local authorities have been under an obligation to employ competitive procedures in the award of their contracts for some considerable time. The Local Government Act 1972, section 135 requires such authorities to promulgate standing orders which make provision for competitive procedures to be used when contracts are awarded. There are, as would be expected, financial thresholds below which this obligation does not bite. The objectives are to ensure value for money and to help to prevent the improper allocation of valuable contracts.

2. *Market Principles and the Prohibition of Non-Commercial Considerations*

We have already seen that one theme of Conservative policy has been to subject public transactions to market principles.[69] It will also be seen below that public bodies, including local authorities, have in the past sought to use their contractual power to attain other socio-political goals. The ability to use contracting power in this manner has now been severely restricted by the Local Government Act 1988.

Section 17 precludes public authorities[70] from taking into account non-commercial matters when exercising their power to make contracts relating to the supply of goods or services, or for the execution of public works. Non-commercial matters are defined in section 17(5). A public authority cannot henceforth take account of any of the following matters: the terms and conditions of employment by contractors of their workers;[71] any involvement of the business activities of contractors with irrelevant fields of government policy;[72] the conduct of contractors or their workers in industrial disputes;[73] the country or territory or origin of supplies to, or

---

[69] See above, Chap. 3.
[70] As defined in Sched. 2, to cover, *inter alia*, local authorities and development corporations. Central government is not included.
[71] s.17(5)(a).
[72] s.17(5)(b), as defined in s.17(8). A contractor could not, *e.g.* be excluded because it had supplied weaponry to the government of a type which the public authority disapproves.
[73] s.17(5)(d).

the location in any country of the business activities of contractors;[74] any political, industrial or sectarian affiliations of contractors or employees;[75] the fact of financial support given to or withheld from an institution to which the public authority gives or withholds support.[76] Special provision is made for matters concerned with race relations.[77]

The obvious question is how does one prove that the public authority has acted on such considerations? The legislation is fierce in this respect. On the one hand, if a public authority asks any question relating to a non-commercial matter, or includes such a matter in a draft contract, it will be deemed to have made its decisions on that forbidden ground.[78] On the other hand, it cannot escape section 17 merely by "keeping quiet" and basing its decision on a non-commercial ground, because the disappointed contractor has a right to a reasoned decision as to why it was not chosen.[79] It may be difficult to formulate such reasons without revealing a "forbidden" consideration.

The aggrieved contractor can seek judicial review of the public authority's decision, and also damages.[80] The damages remedy is limited to reliance type losses: expenditure reasonably incurred for the purpose of submitting the tender.[81]

The legislation is clearly premised upon the idea that contracts made by public authorities should be based solely upon commercial considerations, and is part of the more general Conservative ethos that the "market" should govern allocative decisions wherever possible. Two types of question are thereby raised. The first concerns the difficulties of applying the legislation, given its background aim. The second is whether the general thrust of the legislation is in fact correct.

The principal difficulty with applying the legislation arises from the breadth of the non-commercial considerations. It is easy to envisage situations in which a public authority may wish to ask a question concerning one of the precluded matters precisely because it correctly believes that it will affect the commercial viability of the tender submitted. If, for example, a contractor obtains supplies from, or is located in, a country which is unstable politically this will obviously affect its ability to deliver the goods on schedule. Any such inquiry is, however, precluded by the legislation.[82] The courts would be faced with a difficult choice. Either they apply section 17(5) "formalistically", refusing to listen to any such arguments; but the consequence would be to prevent the authority choosing the bid which really is the best in commercial terms. Or, they are prepared to hear such arguments, the consequence being that the peremptory force of

---

[74] s.17(5)(e). EC law also prohibits discrimination on the grounds of nationality when tendering for public contracts.
[75] s.17(5)(f), defined in s.17(8).
[76] s.17(5)(g).
[77] s.18.
[78] s.19(10).
[79] s.20.
[80] s.19(7).
[81] s.19(8).
[82] s.17(5)(e).

section 17(5) would be weakened, since public authorities would then be able to argue that they were considering section 17(5) matters only in so far as they related to the commercial viability of the tender.[83]

Is then the thrust of the legislation correct? This is a difficult question which is exacerbated by the fact that the answer may differ depending upon the type of non-commercial consideration which is under scrutiny.

The factors in favour of such legislation are as follows. The ability to award contracts gives considerable power to public authorities. This power should, like other exercises of public power, not be used for improper purposes. To place no restrictions upon an authority's contracting power would allow it to pursue a policy which might have no legislative sanction, which might be unrelated to the primary objective for which the contracting power was granted, and which might jeopardise the effective fulfilment of that primary objective. To allow authorities unrestricted freedom could also lead to regional variations in the criteria applied for the award of a contract, and these criteria may not be known to the prospective contractors. Covert blacklists might exist, and the "facts" which justified placing a firm on such a list might not be accurately or fairly determined. Central legislation which establishes contracting criteria serves, moreover, to facilitate the judicial task of deciding whether the conditions employed by a particular authority are valid or not rather than leaving the matter to be dealt with through *ad hoc* applications of tests such as improper purposes or unreasonableness.[84]

A number of arguments can be made against such legislation, or against legislation as broad as section 17(5). Contracts made by public bodies should not be viewed solely as commercial bargains. The very power to grant contracts should be able to be utilised to advance socially desirable objectives, precisely because such authorities cannot be and should not be politically neutral towards such matters. It may not always be possible to pass legislation which enshrines such objectives,[85] and even where this has been attained, the use of contracting power may be an effective method of enforcing such legislative norms.[86] The existence of some regional variations in contracting criteria is on this view not a fact to be deplored, but rather a natural corollary of local autonomy which should be respected. This should be upheld against the centralising tendencies of government legislation which establish the criteria to be applied by all public authorities. This second view does not deny the need for some constraints on contracting power. It would clearly be wrong to blacklist a contractor because he or she held differing political views from that of the authority. Subject to such constraints it should, however, be open to an authority to

---

[83] A further difficulty arises in relation to damages. It seems questionable in principle whether a contractor should be able to recover even reliance losses unless it can prove that but for the non-commercial consideration it would have been given the contract. The solution canvassed above, of assessing the chance of the contractor's success, could, however, be employed here.

[84] *cf. R. v. Lewisham London Borough Council, ex p. Shell UK Ltd.* [1988] 1 All E.R. 938.

[85] Daintith, "The Executive Power Today: Bargaining and Economic Control", *The Changing Constitution* (Jowell and Oliver eds., 1985), Chap. 8.

[86] See *Religious and Political Discrimination and Equality of Opportunity in Northern Ireland, Report on Fair Employment,* Cm. 237 (1987).

decide, for example, to employ a local firm which will give employment to the area even if it does not submit the lowest tender. The line between pursuit of acceptable and unacceptable policies would then have to be determined upon an *ad hoc* basis through techniques such as propriety of purpose or unreasonableness.

3. *Contracting out and Compulsory Competitive Tendering*

The market-oriented strategy of the Conservative government has stretched beyond the commitment to ensuring that procurement is based upon commercial considerations. It has extended to the decision whether a service should be performed "in house", or whether it should be "contracted out" to a private undertaking. The objective, or at least one of the objectives,[87] has been to further market-based practices in order to make sure that the activity is undertaken most efficiently, whether this be in house or through a private firm. Compulsory tendering was made a requirement for local authorities by the Local Government Planning and Land Act 1980, Part III, which applied to construction and maintenance work. The regime was extended by the Local Government Act 1988.

The 1988 Act, section 2, imposes contracting out obligations in relation to matters such as refuse collection, street cleaning, vehicle maintenance and some aspects of catering. This list has been augmented as a result of powers exercised by the Secretary of State, who has added to it the management of sports and leisure facilities.

Where a local authority is contemplating giving work of this kind to its own in house labour organisation it must first publicise the matter and call for bids from interested parties.[88] At least three persons must be allowed to submit bids, and the authority's own labour organisation must do so if it wishes to retain the task. The local authority in reaching any decision must not act so as to restrict, distort or prevent competition.

Section 4. The Reality of Public Contracting:
Government Contracts

The discussion thus far has set out some of the legal principles which apply in the context of contracts which are made by public bodies. These principles are necessary in order to understand the legal structure within which such contracting takes place. They do not, however, convey the full reality of public contracting. The way in which contracting operates will obviously differ depending upon the type of public body in question. Procurement policy which is made and implemented by central government itself will be taken by way of example.

---

[87] See above, pp. 107-113, for the wider context in which such legislation was made.
[88] s.7.

1. The Framing of Government Procurement Policy

Central government spends a very large sum of money on procuring the goods and services which it requires: one estimate for expenditure in 1982 was £15 billion.[89] The principal purchasers of these goods and services have included the Ministry of Defence, the Property Services Agency, HMSO and the Department of Health. Who then determines the principles on which such goods and services are bought?

The *Treasury* will exercise an overall responsibility for public procurement, which is not surprising given that department's role in the management of public expenditure. It is the Treasury which will "distil and promulgate agreed principles",[90] and conduct necessary negotiations with the EC and industry. The principles which emerge from the Treasury will often take the form of guidance issued to departments on matters such as tendering procedures, the conditions to be included in the contract and project management.[91] A link between the Treasury and individual departments has been provided by the *Procurement Policy Committee*, an inter-departmental committee concerned with the maintenance of the principles of government contracting. The application of these principles has been monitored by the *Central Unit on Purchasing* which became part of the Treasury, and which determined, for example, how far the government really is securing value for money in the contracts which it has made. *Individual departments* will each possess a section which is responsible for its own procurement requirements, and there is often a dialogue between the individual department and the Treasury.

The principles which emerge will reflect input by the *Confederation of British Industry*, which is naturally concerned about the terms on which business of the magnitude indicated above is conducted. There is, in addition, the *Review Board for Government Contracts* which was established in 1969. Its members are drawn in part from the CBI and in part from industry, and its original remit was to review the pricing of non-competitive government contracts.

One enduring object of government procurement has been value for money. Another has been a desire to improve the competitiveness of suppliers. Government has also, as will be seen below, sought to use the power which it has through the disbursement of contracts to attain other, less economic goals. How far this is still possible will be considered in due course.

Whenever possible contracts will be put out to competitive tender. It will be important to ensure that there is not a closed list of those who are invited to take part in such a competition, but at the same time there will be advantages to be secured to government by knowing the firms with which it customarily deals. As Turpin notes, the aims of government procurement

---

[89] Turpin, *Government Procurement and Contracts* (1989), p. 1.
[90] *Ibid.* p. 62.
[91] *Ibid.* p. 64.

"require a middle way between a detached, impersonal conduct of business and an almost symbiotic relationship" between the government and the contractor.[92] This preference for competitive tender has been fuelled by other policies of the government, such as the desire to contract out services which had previously been provided in house.[93]

2. *Terms of the Contract*

It is commonplace nowadays to state that the concept of a contract, as a bargain made at arm's length, with the parties negotiating over particular terms, does not reflect actual practice. In many spheres contracts are made upon standard terms to which little if any modification is possible. The degree to which contracts made by public bodies involve standard conditions will obviously differ depending upon the type of public authority involved. It is, however, clear that in one major area the use of such standardised forms predominates. This is in the context of contracts made by the government itself.

Standard forms are used. These do not constitute a blank contract as such, but rather a set of model conditions which can be incorporated into a particular contract. There is a standard form for Works contracts and one for Stores contracts.[94] A sample of these standard clauses will convey a sense of their importance.

Both of the standard forms contain a "break" clause, which allows the government to terminate the contract by written notice to the contractor subject to the payment of compensation.[95] This reflects the need that a government may have to alter policy and to change the direction of public expenditure. There are also provisions relating to equality of information which are designed to ensure that the government has information on the costs of the supplier. Governments have been embarrassed more than once in the past when it has become apparent that a contractor has made excessive profits from a public contract: the provisions on access to information are aimed at making a recurrence of this less likely.[96] Clauses which enable the government to obtain a "post-costing" of completed contracts have a similar objective.[97] Other clauses give the government wide powers to order variations to the original contract specifications, with adjustments being made to the price which was initially agreed.[98]

---

[92] *Ibid.* pp. 70-71.
[93] See above, pp. 107-113.
[94] Turpin, *Government Procurement*, pp. 105-111.
[95] *Ibid.* pp. 243-245.
[96] *Ibid.* pp. 160-161.
[97] *Ibid.* pp. 162-163.
[98] *Ibid.* pp. 186-190.

3. *Conclusions*

The eclectic nature of government contract principles is peculiarly English.
The unwillingness in any sense to codify reflects our dislike of the rigidity
which can be attendant upon such reform. There are clearly advantages
in the flexibility of the present system and it would be wrong to assume
a continuous state of conflict between government and prospective
contractor. Standard terms can save costs, by saving the need for constant
renegotiation of basic contractual terms. They can, moreover, be easily
reviewed and amended to take account of changing circumstances or the
needs of a particular contract.

However, it would be equally incorrect to assume that the system could
not be improved. The very variety of committees which are concerned with
government contracting principles can make it difficult for a contractor, or
a lawyer, to know what the position is.

Street[99] has suggested that certain issues central to the contract such as
agency, building, appropriations, supervision, direction and power to
amend, should be enshrined in a Governments Contracts Act. Other less
immutable terms should be applied to a contract by delegated legislation,
thereby preserving a balance between flexibility, certainty and accessibility.
Turpin, on the other hand, contends that the present system is not any less
satisfactory than those which exist in other countries which do recognise,
in more formal terms, a separate body of government contract law.[100] He
does, however, suggest that the revision of standard forms should only be
undertaken after proper consultation with representative organisations of
contractors, and that more substantial changes in the regime of government
contracting should be open to wider public scrutiny.[101] This reflects the fact
that "contract...is a kind of treaty by which the conditions of a relationship
of interdependence between government and its suppliers are established",
and this is "something of legitimate concern to the public".[102] Thus while
internal management systems are necessary to oversee the operation of
government contracts, these must be supplemented by "arrangements for
external political accountability that are proper to governmental functions
in a parliamentary democracy".[103]

Whichever view is taken on this issue one thing *is* clear: the ordinary
principles of contract play only a limited role in this area. As Turpin
states,[104] "the general law of contract, in short, is only one of the elements,
and not necessarily the most significant, by which the conduct of the parties
to a government contract is regulated." A number of such contracts may be
regarded as a "co-operative programme of work towards a still uncertain
goal rather than as a precise definition of the contractor's obligation", and

---

[99] *Governmental Liability*, pp. 104-105.
[100] *Government Procurement*, p. 114.
[101] *Loc.cit.*
[102] *Ibid.* p. 258.
[103] *Ibid.* p. 260.
[104] *Ibid.* pp. 104-105.

the legal liabilities that may exist under the contract "will not necessarily be decisive of the solution reached".[105]

Section 5. Contract as an Instrument of Policy

The discussion within the previous two sections has touched on the use made by public bodies, whether at the central or local level, of their contracting power in order to achieve certain policy objectives. This issue warrants further examination.

Governments and public bodies disburse extremely large sums through their grant of contracts, and have in the past used such power to attain policy goals other than the provision of goods or services. The power to award contracts has been used to further the Fair Wages Resolution,[106] and policies such as "Buy British". Bargaining has also been a not uncommon feature in the planning context, and the award of contracts has been used as a device to secure compliance with anti-inflation policy.[107]

The legality of such action has always been debatable. Legal control may now be exerted in a variety of ways. Judicial review may be applied in certain circumstances to the exercise of public contractual power. The precise metes and bounds of judicial review in this context have been considered above.[108] Statute now imposes severe constraints upon the range of considerations which public bodies can take into account when awarding contracts, as we have seen in relation to local government. There are, in addition, the controls over public procurement which have emanated from the EC Treaty and the directives made thereunder. The Treaty itself will, as we have seen, impose constraints upon the types of policies which governments can pursue through their contracting power. It is clear, for example, that "Buy British" policies will be illegal under EC law, as an impediment to the free movement of goods.[109] The directives, which apply to a wide range of bodies concerned with the award of contracts for works, supply and services, have, moreover, further restricted the degree to which contracting power can be used to attain other socio-political goals.

Notwithstanding the controls which now exist on the use of contractual power it is important to dwell a little further on the reasons why governments choose to use contract power to achieve these ends. Daintith has

---

[105] *Ibid.* p. 104.
[106] Kahn-Freund, "Legislation through Adjudication, The Legal Aspect of Fair Wages Clauses and Recognised Conditions" (1948) 11 M.L.R. 269, 429.
[107] Jowell, "Bargaining in Development Control" (1977) J.P.L. 414; and "Limits of Law in Urban Planning" (1977) C.L.P. 63; Ferguson and Page, "Pay Restraint; The Legal Constraints" (1978) 128 N.L.J. 515; Daintith, "Regulation by Contract: The New Prerogative" (1979) C.L.P. 41; Daintith, "Legal Analysis of Economic Policy" (1982) 9 Jnl. Law & Soc. 191; Page, "Public Law and Economic Policy: The United Kingdom Experience" (1982) 9 Jnl. Law & Soc. 225.
[108] See above, Chap. 15.
[109] Case 249/81, *Commission* v. *Ireland* [1982] E.C.R. 4005.

produced important work on this issue.[110] He distinguishes two ways in which government can seek to attain its goals. It can do so through what he terms imperium, which is manifested in the ordinary command of law. It can also do so through dominium, which is the use made by government of its power to disburse benefits to those who comply with governmental objectives. There can be both limitations and disadvantages in seeking to pursue objectives through the use of imperium. It may be impracticable to draft the necessary legislation, which may be lengthy, complex and uncertain in its impact. Pursuit of objectives through dominium can, by way of contrast, have positive attractions. Where expenditure does require statutory authorisation the legislation will often leave a broad measure of discretion to the implementing body. Dominium power can also be used in other ways, such as bargaining and informal agreement. This can facilitate short-term experimentation with policy choices and obviate the need for legislative authorisation.

Daintith admits that constitutional problems can occur as a result of the use of dominium power, such as when third parties are affected by agreements of which they had no knowledge, or in areas where an individual had no real choice as to whether to enter such an agreement.[111] He does, however, believe that the development of policy in this manner reflects the fact that government often regards it as the optimum method of attaining its objectives; that those who bargain with them are often under no constraint; and that MPs can call the government to account if they are dissatisfied with this method of policy implementation.[112]

There is, as Daintith himself notes,[113] no ready made solution which will determine the appropriate legal response to the many and varied instances in which dominium power is used as opposed to the more formal exercise of governmental power through imperium. There are a number of options at our disposal. These could include process rights for third parties, and indeed for those more directly involved in the bargaining. There could be an obligation to make the transactions more transparent, open and public to those who are affected by them. There could, as a matter of principle, also be intervention which is designed to safeguard the legislative process itself, by, for example, stipulating that if the executive wishes to achieve certain policy objectives then it must in fact obtain specific legislative authorisation. This is not as strange as it might appear, since much of the history of judicial control over prerogative power has been concerned with just this issue: placing limits upon the policies which the executive can pursue without parliamentary authority. The options at our disposal are, therefore, varied. Their suitability will no doubt depend upon the more particular type of dominium power which is in issue. The importance of the issue should not, however, be doubted.

---

[110] "The Executive Power Today: Bargaining and Economic Control", *The Changing Constitution* (Jowell and Oliver eds., 2nd ed., 1989); "Regulation by Contract: The New Prerogative" (1979) C.L.P. 41; "Legal Analysis of Economic Policy" (1982) 9 J. Law and Soc. 191.

[111] "The Executive Power Today", pp. 208-218.

[112] *Ibid.* pp. 207-208.

[113] *Ibid.* p. 218.

Section 6. Limits on Contractual Effectiveness: General

1. *The Problem*

A public body, whether it be a statutory corporation, governmental department, or local authority, has a variety of statutory powers and duties to perform. The issue that arises here is the effect of a clash between such a power or duty and an existing contractual obligation that the public body has with a private individual. It thus raises problems directly analogous to those dealt with earlier concerning the fettering of discretion, but the solution of the problem where the fetter is a contractual obligation is peculiarly difficult.[114]

In what circumstances will public policy deem that the contractual obligation be declared ineffective as a fetter on the statutory power of duty? If it is declared ineffective should the private individual have any claim to compensation? These are the two questions which will be examined below.[115]

2. *When must the Contract Fall?*

It is clear that a public body cannot escape from a contract merely because it has made a bad bargain.[116]

(1) THE INCOMPATIBILITY TEST

The problem presented above is not a new one; the emergence of the Welfare State and the correlative growth of bodies rendering a public service of some form has merely increased its incidence. The problem was posed clearly in the nineteenth-century case of *R.* v. *Inhabitants of Leake*[117] where the court had to decide whether certain land vested in commissioners responsible for drainage could be deemed to be dedicated to the public as a highway, it having been thus used for 25 years. Parke J. expounded a test based upon compatibility. If the objects prescribed by the statute were incompatible with the land being dedicated as a highway then the commissioners could not in law do such a thing; however, if such use by the public was not incompatible with the statutory purposes then the dedication could take place. On the facts no incompatibility was found to exist.

---

[114] See generally, Street, *Governmental Liability* (1953), Chap. 3; Mitchell, *Contracts of Public Authorities* (1954); Arrowsmith, *Civil Liability and Public Authorities* (1992), pp. 72-79; Rogerson, "On the Fettering of Public Powers" [1971] P.L. 288.

[115] Some of the cases concern, as will be apparent, proprietary rights rather than simple contracts.

[116] *Att.-Gen.* v. *Lindegren* (1819) 6 Price 287; *Municipal Mutual Insurance Co. Ltd.* v. *Pontefract Corporation* (1917) 33 T.L.R. 234; *Commissioners of Crown Lands* v. *Page* [1960] 2 Q.B. 274.

[117] (1833) 5 B. & Ad. 469.

This test clearly has much common sense to recommend it. If the rule were that no contract could stand if it were hypothetically to be a fetter on another of that body's powers then very few contracts could subsist. This would be disadvantageous to the public body as well as the contractor since the former needs to make contracts in many contexts where it may be acting *qua* an ordinary commercial undertaking. A balance is required between the necessity for the public body to make contracts and fairness to the contractor on the one hand, and the need to ensure that contracts thus made do not stifle other statutory powers. The incompatibility test of Parke J. achieves this by allowing the contract to stand unless it is incompatible with another statutory power or duty.

(2) DEVELOPMENT OF THE TEST

Cases after *Leake* may be divided into two groups. The first group concerns decisions which may well have been correct on the facts: the contract may indeed have been incompatible with the statutory power. However, the language in these cases is suggestive of a stricter test, to the effect that whenever a statutory power and a contract touch upon the same subject-matter the latter will inevitably be void. For example, in *Ayr Harbour Trustees* v. *Oswald*[118] trustees were concerned with the management of a harbour and were empowered by statute to take certain lands to carry out specified works. They acquired part of Oswald's land and took a restrictive covenant that they would allow access from his remaining land to the harbour (thereby reducing the amount of compensation that they would have to pay). The House of Lords held that the covenant could not stand. Where the legislature had conferred powers to take land compulsorily (now or in the future) a contract purporting to bind them not to use those powers was void. As stated, on the facts it may well have been that the covenant could be seen as a sterilisation of the "statutory birthright" given to the trustees and hence incompatible with the statute. But the court did not speak in terms of incompatibility; the cases cited used a stricter test[119] and *Oswald* became the cornerstone of any counsel's arguments that a public body should be freed from a private law obligation. Other cases gave the same impression of a test stricter than that in *Leake,* or at least of the application of that test with undue strictness.[120]

The second group of cases represents both a reaffirmation of the incompatibility test and a less strict application of it. The Court of Appeal confirmed that a public body or statutory undertaking could grant an easement,[121] or take a restrictive covenant,[122] provided that these were not incompatible with the statutory powers, emphasising that it could be disadvantageous for a public body not to be able to do so since a potential

---

[118] (1883) 8 App.Cas. 623.

[119] *e.g. Mulliner* v. *Midland Railway* (1879) 11 Ch. D. 611.

[120] *e.g. York Corporation* v. *H. Leetham & Sons Ltd.* [1924] 1 Ch. 557. The decision in the *Amphitrite* [1921] 3 K.B. 500, discussed in the context of Crown liability, could be mentioned here also.

[121] *South Eastern Ry. Co.* v. *Cooper* [1924] 1 Ch. 211.

[122] *Stourcliffe Estates Co. Ltd.* v. *Bournemouth Corporation* [1910] 2 Ch. 12.

vendor would be less likely to agree to a sale. Decisions of the House of Lords were to follow. In *Birkdale District Electricity Supply Co. Ltd* v. *Southport Corporation*[123] Lord Sumner refused to hold *ultra vires* a contract by Birkdale Electricity Supply Co. Ltd that it would not increase the price for electricity higher than that charged by Southport Corporation. His Lordship held that the contract was not incompatible with a statutory power to charge what it wished up to a certain maximum. The *Ayr* case was distinguished as being concerned with proprietary rights and *York Corporation* v. *H. Leetham & Sons Ltd*[124] was disapproved.

This more lenient approach was firmly endorsed in *British Transport Commission* v. *Westmoreland County Council.*[125] The question before their Lordships was whether a footpath across an accommodation bridge could be dedicated to the public. This was opposed by the railway authorities who argued that statutory powers enabled them to discontinue the bridge and therefore the footpath across it could not be dedicated to the public. Viscount Simonds, giving the leading judgment, endorsed the incompatibility test of *Leake*, found that there was no incompatibility on the facts of the *Westmoreland* case, and said of *Ayr Harbour*, which was relied on by the railway authorities,[126]

"It was in fact an example of incompatibility not a decision to the effect that incompatibility does not supply a test."

(3) WHEN WILL INCOMPATIBILITY OCCUR?

The basic test of when incompatibility will be deemed to have occurred was established in the *Westmoreland* case. Compatibility is to be judged by a test of reasonable foresight: is it reasonably foreseeable that a conflict will arise between the contract and the statute? The existence of a mere possibility that this might occur at some future date is insufficient.[127] Clearly, whether incompatibility does exist in a particular case will be a factual question.[128] Two factors which have been held to be of relevance in the determination of incompatibility do, however, require further mention.

(a) Contract and property rights

In the *Birkdale* case[129] Lord Sumner made certain statements which could be interpreted to mean that only where the contract created something akin

---

[123] [1926] A.C. 355.
[124] [1924] 1 Ch. 557.
[125] [1958] A.C. 126.
[126] *Ibid.* p. 143; Lord Radcliffe, pp. 152-153.
[127] *Ibid.* p. 144.
[128] Examples of application of the incompatibility test are *Ransom and Luck Ltd.* v. *Surbiton Borough Council* [1949] Ch. 180; *Marten* v. *Flight Refuelling Ltd.* [1962] Ch. 115; *Triggs* v. *Staines Urban District Council* [1969] 1 Ch. 10. The incompatibility test will also be applied to attempts by the private contractor to imply a term into a contract which is incompatible with a statutory power, *Board of Trade* v. *Temperly Steam Shipping Co. Ltd.* (1927) 27 Ll.L.Rep. 230; *William Cory and Son Ltd.* v. *London Corporation* [1951] 2 K.B. 476; *Commissioners of Crown Lands* v. *Page* [1960] 2 Q.B. 274.
[129] [1926] A.C. 355.

to a property right would it be deemed to be incompatible with the statutory power. When distinguishing the *Ayr* case his Lordship said that in that case the trustees were, by the covenant, forbearing to acquire all that the statute intended them to acquire; they were sterilising part of their birthright. This was distinguished from a mere contract, even if in perpetuity. Thus, Lord Sumner believed that if the trustees had covenanted with Oswald to allow him to moor his barges in perpetuity at any wharf the decision could have been different. It was on this ground also that the *Leetham* case was criticised: there the contract was only concerned with trading profit, not the land itself.[130]

Although one may agree that as a general rule the possibility of incompatibility is increased if the right is proprietary rather than contractual, it is doubtful whether the distinction should be taken any further than that. There may well be cases where even though there is no proprietary right there is a clear incompatibility between the contract and the statutory power.

(b) "Valid exercises of statutory power"

In *Dowty Boulton Paul Ltd* v. *Wolverhampton Corporation*[131] the defendant corporation had in 1936 conveyed to an aircraft company a plot of land for the erection of a factory, together with the right of the company to use the municipal airport for business purposes for 99 years, or so long as the corporation should maintain the airport as a municipal airport, whichever should be the longer. The conveyance also stated that, without prejudice to the Corporation's powers to deal with the airport, it should not, in exercise of its powers, unreasonably affect the plaintiff's rights. The corporation changed its mind in 1970, wishing to use the area for housing, and therefore refused to renew the licence for the airfield. The plaintiff pleaded their lease and the corporation argued that this was *ultra vires* as fettering their statutory powers to provide housing.

Pennycuick V.C. found for the plaintiff, reasoning as follows. The cases on incompatibility were concerned with attempts to fetter in advance the future exercise of statutory powers otherwise than by the valid exercise of a statutory power. They were not concerned with the position where a statutory power has been validly exercised creating a right extending over a term of years. The existence of that right excludes other statutory powers in relation to the same subject-matter, but it could not be held to be a fetter upon the future exercise of powers.[132]

If this means that whenever a contract or lease is created in pursuance of one statutory power it can never be incompatible with a second statutory power, then this must be wrong. A moment's reflection will show that it is quite possible for one statute to give to a public body a general power of leasing land, etc., the lease so granted becoming incompatible with a

---

[130] *Ibid.* p. 371.
[131] [1971] 1 W.L.R. 204.
[132] The case was decided differently, on other grounds, in *Dowty Boulton Paul Ltd.* v. *Wolverhampton Corporation (No. 2)* [1976] Ch. 13.

later statutory power. The point is well illustrated by *Blake* v. *Hendon Corporation*.[133] The corporation had acquired land for a park under a statute of 1875 and claimed that the beneficial ownership was, for rating purposes, in the public. This was contested by the valuation officer who argued that such a dedication would be incompatible with the Local Government Act 1933 which allowed a local authority to grant leases, which of course the corporation could not do *vis-à-vis* the park if the beneficial ownership was in the public. Devlin L.J. (as he then was) rejected the valuation officer's argument, but not in the "blanket" way of Pennycuick V.C. Where two statutory powers might conflict they had, said Devlin L.J. to be construed. Here the power to lease in the 1933 Act was subordinate to that in the 1875 Act. However, Devlin L.J. could envisage a situation in which the plaintiff's argument did work: one in which the 1933 Act would predominate (*e.g.* where the Act contained a specific provision allowing the leasing of parkland), on which hypothesis the beneficial ownership could not be in the public. The approach of Devlin L.J. must be correct. The two statutory powers must be construed, and a decision must be made as to whether the later in time really does render incompatible that which was done under the earlier. It cannot be presumed that the grant of a lease under the first statutory power is immune from the effect of a later statute.

3. *Compensation*

If a contract is found to be incompatible with a statutory power or duty should it merely be declared null, or *ultra vires*? Or should the contractor be entitled to some form of compensation? There are three possible ways in which compensation could be awarded.

(1) DAMAGES FOR BREACH OF CONTRACT

One argument which has been made is that the incompatibility test only tells us that a contract which is incompatible with a statutory power should not be specifically enforced; it does not mean that the contractor should not obtain damages for breach of the contract.[134]

This argument is, however, flawed. A condition precedent to the grant of damages for breach of a contract is that there has been a breach: one party is failing to do something which he or she has expressly or impliedly promised to do. Wherein lies this breach? The loss which is being caused to the private contractor flows from the exercise by the public body of other powers or duties which it possesses. This is simply a manifestation of the dual role which such bodies play, acting both commercially and as a public authority. An allegation of breach would therefore have to be framed in the following terms: "You the public body have promised expressly or

---

[133] [1962] 1 Q.B. 283; *R.* v. *Hammersmith and Fulham London Borough Council, ex p. Beddowes* [1987] Q.B. 1050.
[134] Hogg, *Liability of the Crown* (1971), Chap. 5 argues for this solution.

impliedly that you will do nothing in your public role which is incompatible with our contract." Such a promise is clearly unrealistic and would never be made by a public authority. An express promise would certainly be *ultra vires* and thus *a fortiori* no such promise could be implied.[135]

(2) FRUSTRATION

A second possible way of granting compensation would be to say that the contract had been frustrated. There are, however, a number of difficulties.

First, it is not clear whether on normal principles the contract would be held to be frustrated. For example, in the *Cory* case, although the corporation had conceded frustration the point was not argued, and it is unclear whether the contract would have been frustrated since the essence of the claim was simply that it was now less profitable to do the work.

Secondly, the compensation available under the Law Reform (Frustrated Contracts) Act 1943 might not be adequate or appropriate.

Thirdly, the suggestion that the public body's action in this type of case should be deemed self-induced frustration is misconceived.[136] The premise behind this concept is that a party cannot rely on frustration brought about by his or her own conduct, act or election. The party will still be liable to perform the contract or pay damages for breach because he or she has deliberately, or perhaps negligently, without legal constraint, brought about the event in question. A public body has no freedom in this sense. Either it is exercising a statutory duty with which the contract is incompatible, or it has decided *intra vires* to exercise its statutory powers in a particular way with the same result. The action, unlike that of the private individual, is done under these legal constraints and thus cannot be deemed self-induced frustration.[137]

The fourth difficulty is perhaps the most important. Underlying the frustration solution is the idea that the contract should be at an end, and that neither the public body nor the private party have any interest in its continuity. This was clearly felt to be the case by Lord Sumner in *Birkdale*.[138] With respect, the problem is not so simple or clear-cut.

The *Cory*[139] case provides a good example. The plaintiffs in 1936 made a contract with the defendant corporation to dispose of its refuse. In 1948 the defendant, *qua* Port of London Health Authority, made bylaws which caused refuse disposal to be more expensive. Cory claimed that this was a breach of contract, arguing that the 1936 contract contained an implied term that the defendant would not do anything which made the contract more onerous; this, as seen above, was rejected.

---

[135] *William Cory and Son Ltd.* v. *London Corporation* [1951] 2 K.B. 476; *Commissioners of Crown Lands* v. *Page* [1960] 2 Q.B. 274, 291.

[136] Harlow, "'Public' and 'Private' Law: Definition without Distinction" (1980) 43 M.L.R. 241, 248-249. Harlow implies that self-induced frustration was applied in the *Cory* case. This is not so. The point, conceded without argument by the London Corporation, was commercial frustration of the venture. On frustration generally, see Treitel, *Law of Contract* (7th ed., 1987), Chap. 20.

[137] The argument from self-induced frustration is simply a damages action by the back door.

[138] [1926] A.C. 355, 374-375.

[139] [1951] 2 K.B. 476.

Clearly, what underlies the plaintiff's argument is that it had offered a price presuming that certain costs would be involved and that these costs had risen due to the bylaws. If Cory cannot make any profit at all it will be forced into liquidation. This is of no concern to Lord Sumner since a different company will undertake refuse collection. Yet, presuming that Cory is a reasonably efficient firm, any other firm which tenders for the contract will set its price taking full account of the more expensive nature of the job resulting from the 1948 bylaws. The defendant corporation does, therefore, irrespective of any notions of fairness to the plaintiff, have an interest in the continuity of performance of the task. The simplest solution would be to allow Cory to revise their price upwards to take account of the greater costs incurred. On the actual facts of the *Cory* case it appeared that Cory had made a bad bargain from which it was seeking to escape. The general point being made, that a public body may well have an interest in the continuity of the relationship, is nonetheless still important. If the firm undertaking the refuse collection *had* made a reasonable bargain which was only rendered unreasonable by regulations which applied solely to that firm, then a remedy which would allow revision of the price would be beneficial.

(3) A SPECIALISED REMEDY

The particular problems created by public authority contracts, where the public body may be acting in a "public" and a "private" role, is the key to an understanding of what type of remedy should be given. Just as the problem is one peculiar to public bodies and is not capable of solution by the application of ordinary contractual principles, so the solution must be one tailored to meet those problems. Normal contract principles have as their premise the necessity for one party to show that the other has committed a wrong in order to found a claim for a breach of contract; X has broken his promise so that Y can now claim damages. This does not work here. A public body is not and cannot be promising not to exercise its statutory or common law powers so as not to interfere with a contract which it has. The exercise of such powers is lawful and cannot be hindered by the threat of an action for breach of contract. However, it may be hard upon the private contracting party who may have suffered considerable loss. What is required is a remedy which recognises the legality of the public body's action but which nevertheless accepts that compensation should be payable.

Such remedies exist in France, which country recognises administrative contracts as a separate entity.[140] The central idea is the predominance of the public interest; the realisation that in certain circumstances the public body may in its public role be required to take action which is detrimental to the other contracting party, and can to this end suspend or vary the contract. Three remedies are of a particular interest.

Imprevision is similar to frustration subject to two important differences. It is based upon the continuity of the relationship and not necessarily its

---

[140] Mitchell, *Contracts of Public Authorities*, Chap. 4; Brown and Bell, *French Administrative Law* (4th ed., 1993), pp. 192-201.

termination. It does not require that the contract should have become legally or physically incapable of being performed, and applies when circumstances upset the economic substance of the contract, rendering it more difficult than contemplated, over and beyond the normal risk. When this occurs the contractor may, for example, continue to perform the contract, but at a revised rate.

The second and perhaps most interesting of the three is a remedy called *fait du prince*. An unforeseeable loss may be shared by the two parties and the contractor can obtain an indemnity for increased costs. This applies where the contract is affected by something done by the public body itself in its public role which renders the bargain less profitable. The remedy may constitute an indemnity for the private party or an authorisation to increase the charge. *Fait du prince* will not apply where the loss is caused by legislation affecting all people equally.

A third doctrine, that of *supervision*, allows the administration to modify the contractual terms in the public interest, but it has to pay an indemnity to the other party if, on the facts, that is the fair balance.

The flexibility provided by the French remedies is to be envied. Recognising the specialised nature of the problem, specialised solutions have been found. English law, by way of contrast, is inadequate in this respect. While the rules developed as to when a contract should fall are now satisfactory, the consequences of the demise of the contract are not. Epithets such as *ultra vires*, void or null tend to be attached as if some initial invalidity always existed thereby providing an excuse not to grant compensation. This does not bear examination.[141] Care must be taken to ensure that the person contracting with the public body is not placed in a better position than the party to a purely private contract. However, where action taken by a public authority does not affect people generally then a remedy akin to *fait du prince* would be most welcome.[142]

It is true, as we have seen above, that the standard form contracts made by the government itself go some way to achieving the same result, by allowing the government to vary the contract unilaterally and by recognising that it may have to break the original bargain, subject to adjustments in the recompense paid to the contractor. It would, nonetheless, be of assistance if these principles were recognised in relation to public contracts generally, and enshrined in legal doctrine.

4. A Special Rule for the Crown?

The problems arising when a public body acts in a dual capacity as a contracting party and as the holder of statutory powers and duties is not

---

[141] *e.g.* in *Dowty Boulton Paul* [1971] 1 W.L.R. 204 a decision by a local authority that it now wished to use the land for housing could not be said to render the prior lease of that land for 30 years void *ab initio*.

[142] On the actual facts of *Cory* the plaintiffs should probably not be granted such compensation since it is difficult to see how they were in any worse position than anyone else who would be affected by the new bylaws.

altered by the public body being the Crown. The same principles outlined above should be applied, both as to when any contract should fall, and as to whether compensation should be granted. Rowlatt J.'s decision in the *Amphitrite*[143] does, however, suggest a stricter test.

Neutral shipowners, aware of the danger of their ships being detained in British ports, obtained undertakings from the British government that if the ship carried a particular type of cargo it would not be detained. The ship was nevertheless detained and the shipowners sought damages. Rowlatt J. found against the shipowners. While Rowlatt J. stated that it was competent for the Crown to bind itself by an ordinary commercial contract, the present agreement was not a contract but an arrangement whereby the government purported to say what its future executive action would be. It was in fact an expression of intent and not a contract, the main reason why this was so being that the government could not fetter its future executive action which must be determined by the needs of the community. Reliance was placed upon the cases concerning Crown service.

The case has been criticised in later authorities,[144] and ignored in at least one case to which it might have been applied.[145] On principle the judgment of Rowlatt J. is too extreme. It can be accepted that the Crown, like any other public body, cannot enter into a contract which would be incompatible with its executive powers. However, the judgment implies that any contract which in any way fetters the discharge of any executive power must fall, or be deemed not to be a contract at all. This, like the judgment in the *Ayr Harbour* case, is unnecessarily draconian. The position of the Crown should be brought into line with that of other public bodies and the incompatibility test should be applied.

Section 7. Limits on Contractual Effectiveness: Crown Service[146]

1. *The Existence of a Contract*

The law relating to Crown service has been much criticised, as will be seen in the subsequent discussion. One of the initial questions which must be resolved is whether Crown servants have any actual contract of service at all. This issue has come before the courts on a number of occasions in recent years.

---

[143] [1921] 3 K.B. 500.

[144] *Robertson* v. *Minister of Pensions* [1949] 1 K.B. 227; *Howell* v. *Falmouth Boat Co.* [1951] A.C. 837.

[145] *Steaua Romana* [1944] P.43.

[146] For detailed examination of the various issues which can arise in the area of public sector employment see, Fredman and Morris, *The State as Employer, Labour Law in the Public Services* (1989).

The argument that Crown servants do not have any contract of service as such is based, in part, on the fact that they can be dismissed at will. However, as noted by Lord Atkin in *Reilly* v. *King*,[147] the existence of a power to dismiss such servants at will is not inconsistent with the existence of a contract prior to that dismissal. In the *Bruce* case[148] May L.J. held that there was nothing unconstitutional about civil servants being employed by the Crown pursuant to a contract of service, and that this would be consistent with the modern view of the position of the civil servants *vis-à-vis* the Crown. However, he went on to hold that prior to 1985 the Crown did not intend that civil servants should have such contracts. The point arose once again in *McClaren* v. *Home Office*[149] where a prison officer claimed that the introduction of a new shift system constituted a breach of contract, or of his conditions of service. It was held that it was at least arguable that the relationship between the Home Office and prison officers was a contractual one. The willingness to think of Crown servants as having a contract of service is also apparent in *Nangle*,[150] where the court affirmed the view taken in *Bruce* that the Crown does possess the capacity to make a contract with its staff. It went on to hold that a contract had been created on the facts, and that there was a strong presumption in favour of an intention to create legal relations.

These decisions are to be welcomed. There is no sound reason in the modern day why civil servants should not be employed under a contract of service. It is true that the regime under which such staff have been employed has been based upon the assumption that no such contract existed.[151] It is true also that provision has been made for resolving disputes between the Crown and its staff within this framework, and that statutory protections of varying kinds have been extended to Crown servants.[152] The recognition that Crown servants have a contract of employment would, nonetheless, go some way to demystifying the relationship between the Crown and its employees, and to undermining the idea that such employees should be treated very differently from others. This does not, however, necessarily mean that they should be treated in the identical manner as those in private employment as the following extract from Fredman and Morris demonstrates.[153]

> "We would argue that the major difference is that, while private employers are free to act unless constrained by the law, public employers derive their authority from prerogative or statute. There is a 'public' dimension to the way in which the civil service and the rest of

---

[147] [1934] A.C. 176, 180.

[148] *R.* v. *Civil Service Appeals Board, ex p. Bruce* [1988] I.C.R. 649. The point was not taken before the Court of Appeal, [1989] I.C.R. 171.

[149] [1990] I.C.R. 824.

[150] *R.* v. *Lord Chancellor's Department, ex p. Nangle* [1991] I.R.L.R. 343.

[151] Fredman and Morris, *The State as Employer*, pp. 61-70.

[152] Race Relations Act 1976, ss.75, 76; Sex Discrimination Act 1975, s. 85(2); Equal Pay Act 1970, s.1(8).

[153] *The State as Employer* (1989), p. 66.

the public services are administered, which means that the State owes duties to the general public as well as its workforce. It is necessary to find a balance between these interests. To declare that civil servants have no contract is to give too little emphasis to the rights of the individual employee; but simply to reverse this and declare that they do have contracts is to ignore the public duties of the Crown."

2. *Dismissal of Crown Servants*

One of the main areas in which Crown employees have been in a disadvantageous position concerns dismissal. In *Dunn* v. *Queen*[154] a consular agent was appointed for three years and dismissed before the end of that period. His claim for damages for wrongful dismissal was denied, the court stating that Dunn's office was held at pleasure. This rule was applied by way of analogy with the dismissibility of military servants, the policy behind it being the necessity for the Crown to be able to rid itself of a servant who might otherwise act detrimentally to the interests of the state. There are obvious flaws in this reasoning. While some Crown servants in senior positions might represent a danger of this type, it is difficult to envisage this being so for the majority of such servants. More important is the fact that the above reasoning only goes to preclude specific performance of the contract which would not be given anyway, not to the award of damages.

The rule of dismissibility at pleasure can be excluded by statute.[155] What is less clear is whether it can be excluded by the terms of the contract itself and if so what terms are capable of doing so.[156] In a sequel to the *Dunn* case the Court of Appeal found that a provision for a fixed term would not in itself prevent dismissibility at pleasure,[157] but there are some indications in the case law that appropriate terms in the contract could exclude the general rule,[158] for example, where there is provision for a fixed term and for power to determine for cause.[159] However, a number of authorities support the conclusion that dismissibility at pleasure can only be excluded by statute and that any contractual term purporting to exclude this rule will be disregarded.[160] The reasoning in these latter cases is not convincing,[161] but they have not been overruled.

---

[154] [1896] 1 Q.B. 116.
[155] *Gould* v. *Stuart* [1896] A.C. 575.
[156] Nettheim, "*Dunn* v. *The Queen* Revisited" (1975) 34 C.L.J. 253.
[157] *Dunn* v. *Macdonald* [1897] 1 Q.B. 401, 555.
[158] *Shenton* v. *Smith* [1895] A.C. 229.
[159] *Reilly* v. *King* [1934] A.C. 176; *Robertson* v. *Minister of Pensions* [1949] 1 K.B. 227.
[160] *Rodwell* v. *Thomas* [1944] K.B. 596; *Riordan* v. *War Office* [1959] 1 W.L.R. 1046.
[161] In neither case are the authorities relied on convincing for establishing the propositions laid down. As pointed out above, the provision for a fixed term in the *Dunn* case appears to have been held not to be inconsistent with a power to dismiss at pleasure, rather than a clog upon such power. See also, *Terrell* v. *Secretary of State for the Colonies* [1953] 2 Q.B. 482.

3. *Arrears of Pay*

Until 1943 it was believed that a civil servant would be entitled to salary accrued at the date of dismissal.[162] The point had not, however, been fully argued in any case and in *Lucas* v. *Lucas* Pilcher J.[163] reached the opposite conclusion. The reasoning is, with respect, unconvincing. Starting from the premise that a Crown servant is dismissible at pleasure, Pilcher J. reached the conclusion that therefore arrears of pay were irrecoverable, which is a *non sequitur*. As Lord Atkin stated in *Reilly* v. *King*, a right to terminate the contract at will is not inconsistent with the existence of a contract prior to termination.[164] The decision in *Lucas* has been cogently criticised by the Privy Council[165] which refused to follow it. It is to be hoped that other courts will adopt the same approach.[166]

4. *Statutory Protection*

In the context of Crown service the maxim that the common law will supply the omission of the legislature has been reversed: it is statute which has provided protection. The common law has not been overruled, but rendered less important by the passage of legislation concerning unfair dismissal.[167] The legislation, now contained in the Employment Protection (Consolidation) Act 1978, provides that an employee has the right not to be unfairly dismissed[168] and proceeds to set out what constitutes dismissal.[169] The basic scheme of the legislation is that the employer has to show the reason for the dismissal.[170] In determining whether the dismissal was fair or unfair it is necessary to look to all the circumstances of the case to decide whether the employer acted reasonably or not in treating the reason as sufficient for the dismissal.[171] Specific provisions are made for dismissal for certain causes.[172] Remedies for unfair dismissal are either a monetary award[173] or an order for reinstatement or re-engagement.[174]

---

[162] R. v. *Doutré* (1884) 9 App. Cas. 745; *Sutton* v. *Att.-Gen.* (1923) 39 T.L.R. 294.
[163] [1943] P. 68; *Mulvenna* v. *The Admiralty* 1926 S.C. 842. Logan, "A Civil Servant and his Pay" (1945) 61 L.Q.R. 26.
[164] [1934] A.C. 176. *cf. I.R.C.* v. *Hambrook* [1956] 2 Q.B. 641.
[165] *Kodeeswaran* v. *Att.-Gen. of Ceylon* [1970] A.C. 1111, 1123.
[166] *cf.* Crown Proceedings Act 1947, s.27.
[167] Employment Protection (Consolidation Act) 1978, Pt. V.
[168] s.54.
[169] s.55.
[170] s.57(1).
[171] s.57(3).
[172] *e.g.* s.58, trade union membership (see now Trade Union and Labour Relations (Consolidation) Act 1992, s.152); s.60, pregnancy.
[173] ss.72-76.
[174] ss.69-70. For the limits of enforceability see, s.71. See also, Employment Act 1980, ss.6-13. Certain aspects of unfair dismissal are now covered by the Trade Union and Labour Relations (Consolidation) Act 1992, ss.152, 238.

The general scheme of the legislation relating to unfair dismissal[175] applies to Crown employment,[176] which means employment under or for the purposes of a government department, or any officer or body exercising on behalf of the Crown functions conferred by any enactment. The most important general exception, apart from the military, is where a certificate issued by a minister states that persons of a type specified in the certificate must be excluded from the legislation on grounds of national security.[177] Civil servants also have the benefit of the Equal Pay Act 1970,[178] and the Sex Discrimination Act 1975.[179]

---

[175] On unfair dismissal generally, see Davies and Freedland, *Labour Law* (2nd ed., 1984), pp. 459-521.
[176] s.138. Military servants are excluded, s.138(3) as are the police, s.146(2).
[177] s.138(4).
[178] s.1(8).
[179] s.85.

20. EVIDENCE AND CROWN LIABILITY

The position of the Crown in relation to tortious[1] and contractual[2] liability has already been considered. Three matters will be discussed in this chapter. First, the extent to which evidence may be withheld. As will be seen, evidence may be withheld not only by the Crown, but by certain other public bodies. Secondly, we will examine the law relating to the Crown and statutes. The final topic which will be considered is the position of the Crown in litigation.

Section 1. Public Interest Immunity

1. *"Crown Privilege"*

When an action takes place discovery of documents will often be necessary. One party will ask the other to produce such documents as are in their possession which may be material to any question in issue. Where a party resists disclosure the court will not order the production of the documents unless it believes that the order is necessary either for disposing fairly of the cause or matter, or for saving costs.[3]

Until 1968 the Crown possessed what was known as Crown privilege.[4] It could refuse to reveal certain documents because to do so would be contrary to the public interest. This principle was widely drawn as may be demonstrated by *Duncan* v. *Cammell, Laird & Co. Ltd.*[5] A submarine built by the defendants for the Admiralty sank while on trial. The plaintiff was the widow of one of those drowned who brought an action for negligence. She sought discovery of certain documents including plans of the submarine. The Admiralty withheld them and claimed Crown privilege. The House of Lords found for the Crown and propounded a broad rule allowing the Crown to withhold documents of two types. They could be withheld either if the disclosure of the *contents* of a particular document would injure the public interest, or where the document was one of a *class* of documents which must be withheld in order to ensure the proper functioning of the public service. Moreover, a statement by a minister in the

---

[1] See above, pp. 634–635.
[2] See above, pp. 684–685.
[3] R.S.C., Order 24, r. 13.
[4] Jacob, "From Priviliged Crown to Interested Public" [1993] P.L. 121.
[5] [1942] A.C. 624.

proper form that a document fell into one of these two categories would it seems not be challenged by the courts.

There is little doubt that the *Duncan* case sanctioned the withholding of documents to a greater extent than had been allowed previously.[6] The potential breadth of the "class category" enabled the government to protect documents of a type which may well not have required blanket protection.[7] Dissatisfaction with this state of affairs led the Lord Chancellor in 1956 to announce that the government would henceforth not claim privilege in certain areas. Reports of witnesses of accidents on the road, on government premises, or involving government employees; medical reports concerning civilian employees; medical reports where the Crown was sued for negligence, including reports made by prison doctors; materials required for the defence against a criminal charge and witnesses' statements to the police; certain reports on factual matters relating to liability in contract:[8] in none of these areas would privilege be claimed.

While this self-denying ordinance was to be welcomed, it proved to be a double-edged sword. The areas where privilege would not be claimed had little if any analytic coherence. This prompted reasoning by analogy. Was there such a difference between the matters specified and those still protected to justify the chasm between them? Pressure for judicial reconsideration of the *Duncan* case came from both Scotland[9] and the Court of Appeal.[10] The common link between them was the refusal to accept that the court was bound by every class claim put forward by the government. Despite these promising omens, the Court of Appeal[11] then returned once more to the rigidity of the *Duncan* approach. Happily, the case went on appeal to the House of Lords which took the opportunity for a thorough revision of the law.

2. *From Crown Privilege to Public Interest*

In *Conway* v. *Rimmer*[12] the plaintiff was a former probationary police constable who began an action for malicious prosecution against his former superintendent. The Secretary of State objected to the production of five documents, certifying that they fell within classes of documents disclosure of which would be injurious to the public interest. Four of the reports were made by the defendant about the plaintiff during his probationary period;

---

[6] See, *e.g. Robinson* v. *South Australia (No. 2)* [1931] A.C. 704; *Spiegelman* v. *Hocker* (1933) 50 T.L.R. 87.

[7] See, *e.g. Ellis* v. *Home Office* [1953] 2 Q.B. 135; *Broome* v. *Broome* [1955] P. 190.

[8] H.L. Deb., Vol. 197, col. 741 (June 6, 1956).

[9] *Glasgow Corporation* v. *Central Land Board* 1956 S.C. 1.

[10] *Re Grosvenor Hotel (London) Ltd. (No. 2)* [1965] Ch. 1210; *Merricks* v. *Nott-Bower* [1965] 1 Q.B. 57; *Wednesbury Corporation* v. *Ministry of Housing and Local Government* [1965] 1 W.L.R. 261.

[11] *Conway* v. *Rimmer* [1967] 1 W.L.R. 1031.

[12] [1968] A.C. 910.

the fifth was a report made by him to his chief constable in connection with the prosecution of the plaintiff on a criminal charge on which he was acquitted. It was this criminal charge which was the foundation of the action for malicious prosecution.

The *Duncan* case was overturned.[13] The House of Lords expressly asserted the power of the courts to hold a balance between the public interest as expressed by the minister who wished to withhold certain documents, and the public interest in ensuring the proper administration of justice. While their Lordships were unanimous in this respect, the formulations as to how the balancing was to operate differed somewhat. Two aspects of the balancing operation may be cited by way of example.

First, it is unclear from *Conway* itself whether there are documents of a kind which will always be privileged. Lord Reid thought that Cabinet minutes and high level policy-making should never be disclosed, irrespective of their content.[14] Lord Pearce recognised an exception in similar terms.[15] It is, however, unclear from his judgment whether this meant that the court could in principle inspect the documents, or whether no inspection whatsoever was warranted in these areas. The same is true of Lord Upjohn's judgment.[16] By way of contrast, Lord Morris of Borth-y-Gest[17] began with the principle that the court must always balance the competing interests whatever the type of document, albeit with the recognition that there are certain classes of documents which will by their nature be excluded. As we shall see, this ambiguity has persisted in later cases.

A second aspect of the balancing which is unclear relates to the type of reasons put forward by the minister to justify non-disclosure. Lord Reid stated that if these reasons were such that a court was not competent to weigh them, then the minister's view must prevail.[18] A similar but not identical idea was put forward by Lord Morris of Borth-y-Gest.[19] Lord Pearce agreed[20] with Lord Reid in general terms, but did not allude to this specific point. The issue does not seem to have been specifically addressed by Lord Hodson or Lord Upjohn.

While these ambiguities do permeate the decision in *Conway*, they should not be allowed to cloud the importance of the main principle which was unequivocally asserted: the courts would balance the competing public interests to determine whether disclosure should be ordered. If the court was in doubt as to the outcome of this balancing it could inspect the documents before ordering production. This was in fact done and the court concluded that the documents should be produced.

---

[13] Some of their Lordships preferred to distinguish the case as covering only situations where discovery would involve a real danger to the public interest, *e.g.* Lord Reid, pp. 938-939, Lord Upjohn, pp. 990-991; others, *e.g.* Lord Morris of Borth-y-Gest, preferred a more direct attack, pp. 958-959.

[14] [1968] A.C. 910, 952-953. See also, *Att.-Gen. v Jonathan Cape Ltd.* [1976] Q.B. 752.

[15] [1968] A.C. 910, 986-987. See also, Lord Hodson, p. 973.

[16] *Ibid.* p. 993.

[17] Ibid. p. 971.

[18] *Ibid.* p. 952.

[19] *Ibid.* pp. 971-972.

[20] *Ibid.* p. 980.

Given the nature of the balancing operation which the *Conway* case requires, the name "Crown privilege" is obviously inappropriate. The Crown cannot simply decide whether to withdraw a category of documents from the court. That the title was indeed misleading was recognised in *Rogers* v. *Secretary of State for Home Department*.[21] An application for a gaming certificate had been refused and Rogers wished to know the contents of a letter written by the chief constable to the Gaming Board about him. The Home Secretary sought to prevent discovery of the document and pleaded Crown privilege. While the House of Lords agreed that the letter should not be produced, they disapproved of the term Crown privilege. Lord Reid[22] stated that the term privilege was misleading, and that the real issue was whether the public interest in not disclosing the document outweighed the interest of the litigant in having all the evidence before the court.

3. *Public Interest Immunity: Scope and Nature*

(1) THE TYPE OF BODY WHICH CAN ASSERT PUBLIC INTEREST IMMUNITY

This question arose for consideration in *D.* v. *National Society for the Prevention of Cruelty to Children*.[23] The Court of Appeal had decided that public interest immunity was only available where the public interest related to the effective functioning of departments or other organs of central government. This view was rejected by the House of Lords. The NSPCC was an authorised body for the purpose of bringing care proceedings under the Children and Young Persons Act 1969. Although it was not under a statutory duty to bring such actions, this was not necessary. Ensuring the confidentiality of the information was as important here as it had been in *Rogers*.[24]

How far beyond the organs of central government one may go and still have the defence available is questionable. Their Lordships not only rejected the view that the defence only operated where the effective functioning of departments or other organs of central government was involved; they also rejected the very broad approach posited by the NSPCC that whenever a party to legal proceedings claims that there is a public interest to be served by withholding documents it is the duty of the court to weigh that interest against the countervailing public interest in the administration of justice, and to refuse disclosure if the balance tilts that way. Which bodies are entitled to raise the issue will therefore have to be decided upon a case by case approach.[25]

---

[21] [1973] A.C. 388.
[22] *Ibid.* p. 400. See also, pp. 406, 408, 412.
[23] [1978] A.C. 171.
[24] [1973] A.C. 388.
[25] See, *e.g.* B.L. *Cars Ltd. (Formerly Leyland Cars)* v. *Vyas* [1980] A.C. 1028; *Buckley* v. *Law Society (No. 2)* [1984] 1 W.L.R. 1101; *British Steel Corporation* v. *Granada Television Ltd.* [1981] A.C. 1096.

(2) INFORMATION GIVEN IN CONFIDENCE

A number of cases have concerned the protection of information which has been given in confidence.[26] It is, however, clear that confidentiality is not by itself a separate ground for withholding evidence. This was established by *Alfred Crompton Amusement Machines Ltd* v. *Customs and Excise Commissioners (No. 2)*.[27] The company claimed that the assessment of purchase tax based upon the wholesale value of the machines was too high. As part of their investigation into the matter, the commissioners obtained from Crompton's customers and other sources information concerning the value of the machines. No agreement was reached as to the appropriate tax rate. When the matter went to arbitration the commissioners claimed that the information received from these customers and other sources should be immune from disclosure since it would reveal the commissioners' methods and contained information supplied confidentially. The House of Lords upheld this claim. Disclosure of the information could hinder the commissioners in the discharge of their functions. However, the fact that the information was supplied in confidence was not in itself a reason for non-disclosure; it was not itself a separate head of privilege, but could be a material consideration when privilege was claimed on the ground of public interest.

Confidentiality also played a part in *D.* v. *National Society for the Prevention of Cruelty to Children*.[28] The NSPCC relied heavily upon members of the public coming forward to give information about possible child abuse. In the instant case the society acted upon information which subsequently proved to be untrue. The mother claimed damages against the NSPCC, alleging a failure to take reasonable care before investigating an allegation of maltreatment. She demanded discovery of all the documents which the society had relating to the case. The House of Lords upheld the public interest defence. They reiterated the point that confidentiality is not itself a defence but, reasoning by analogy from the case of police informants, it was decided that the documents did not have to be disclosed. Sources of information would dry up if the names of the informants were to be made public, hampering the society in the discharge of its duties. This was held to outweigh the interest of the individual in knowing the name of the informant.[29]

In deciding whether the public interest demands disclosure or not the court will consider the significance of the documents in relation to their likely effect on the decision in the case and whether their absence will result in a complete or partial denial of justice to one or both of the parties, as well as the importance of the litigation to the parties and the public. This is

---

[26] *Rogers* [1973] A.C. 388. See also, *Lonrho Ltd.* v. *Shell Petroleum Co. Ltd. (No. 2)* [1982] A.C. 173; *Neilson* v. *Laugharne* [1981] Q.B. 736. See Cripps, "Judicial Proceedings and Refusal to Disclose the Identity of Sources of Information" (1984) 43 C.L.J. 266.
[27] [1974] A.C. 405.
[28] [1978] A.C. 171. See also, *Re D. (Infants)* [1970] 1 W.L.R. 599; *Gaskin* v. *Liverpool City Council* [1980] 1 W.L.R. 1549; *Buckley* v. *Law Society (No. 2)* [1984] 1 W.L.R. 1101.
[29] See also, *Norwich Pharmacal Co.* v. *Customs and Excise Commissioners* [1974] A.C. 133.

illustrated by *Campbell* v. *Tameside Metropolitan Borough Council*.[30] The plaintiff, a schoolteacher, was attacked by an 11-year-old pupil. Her injuries forced her to take early retirement. She sought to bring an action against the local authority claiming that they were negligent in allowing a child of such violent disposition to attend an ordinary school. The documents required were psychologists' reports on the child which the local authority refused to disclose because they were highly confidential and those making them would be inhibited if the contents could be used in legal proceedings. The court ordered discovery. The possibility of inhibition by those making such reports was small, whereas the documents could be highly significant for the plaintiff's case.

(3) THE BALANCING PROCESS, EXCLUDED CATEGORIES AND INSPECTION

(a) *The balancing process and excluded categories*

A number of important points concerning the nature of public interest immunity and the balancing process must be distinguished.

First, it has been held in the *Makanjuola* case[31] that public interest immunity cannot be waived. The reasoning behind this is that the litigant who asserts public interest immunity is not claiming a right, but observing a duty. This immunity is an exclusionary rule which is imposed in certain circumstances where this is warranted by the public interest. It is for this reason that the immunity cannot be waived. The court also gave important indications as to when documents should in fact be withheld. The court stated, on the one hand, that documents should not be kept back in every case where they might be prima facie immune if, on any weighting of the public interest for and against disclosure, there would be a clear balance in favour of disclosure. On the other hand, the court also held that where a litigant does possess documents within a class which is or might be prima facie immune from disclosure, then public interest immunity should, save for exceptional cases, be claimed and disclosure should be denied, since the ultimate judge of where the balance of public interest lies is not the litigant but the court itself.

The judgment in the *Makanjuola* case will be of significance for the practical operation of public interest immunity, and may make life more difficult for litigants who seek to sue the government. While it can be accepted that public interest immunity cannot in general be waived, one may expect defendants seeking to deny access to documents to rely on the latter part of the formulation set out above. They will be tempted, in other words, to raise the defence of public interest immunity, decline to disclose the material and then leave the matter to be judged by the court. It may well, in this sense, encourage government departments to withhold documentation and thereby force plaintiffs to overcome the hurdles, considered below, which are a condition precedent to obtaining the documents being

---

[30] [1982] 3 W.L.R. 75. See also, *Peach* v. *Commissioner of Police of the Metropolis* [1986] Q.B. 1064.

[31] *Makanjuola* v. *Commissioner of Police of the Metropolis* [1992] 3 All E.R. 617; *Halford* v. *Sharples* [1992] 1 W.L.R. 736.

sought. Some indications that this is the stance being adopted are to be found in the Matrix Churchill saga, concerning the sale of arms to Iraq, where government ministers were advised by the Attorney-General that they had no discretion and had to sign certificates claiming public interest immunity.[32] Much then depends upon how courts and administrators interpret the two parts of the reasoning in the *Makanjuola* case.[33] It appears however to be the case that the government's approach to claims for public interest immunity is altering in the light of the Scott inquiry into the Matrix Churchill saga: the criticism voiced as to the use of public interest immunity in that case seems to have caused Whitehall to re-think the way in which it operates in this area.

In any event the *Bennett* case[34] makes it clear that there are exceptions to the general rule that immunity cannot be waived. A public body could, in exceptional cases, voluntarily consent to disclosure of documents without first seeking an order of the court, even though the documents would be in a class covered by immunity and even though it would normally be the court's responsibility to decide where the balance of public interest lies. In that case it was held that the Crown Prosecution Service could disclose to the defence documents which would otherwise be covered by public interest immunity. Before doing so the public body should seek the approval of the Treasury Solicitor. The latter would then consult any other government departments which were involved, and the Treasury Solicitor should be satisfied that the balance of interest was in favour of disclosure. In a criminal case the Treasury Solicitor should more readily approve the disclosure of documents which were likely to assist the defence than the prosecution.

Secondly, there is the important issue of whether there are any categories in relation to which balancing does not apply. We have already seen that the members of the House of Lords in *Conway*[35] differed as to whether certain types of documents should automatically be regarded as beyond the reach of the courts and not subject to the balancing approach. The question of whether such a category did exist arose in *Burmah Oil Co. Ltd* v. *Bank of England*.[36] Burmah Oil was in financial difficulty and a rescue package was put together under which Burmah sold its British Petroleum stock to the Bank. The original intent was that, because BP stock was low at the time of the sale, any profit from the resale of the stock would be divided between the Bank and Burmah Oil. The government did not, however, accept this part of the scheme. BP stock did rise in value, and Burmah Oil alleged that the sale of the stock was unconscionable. It sought to discover certain documents including those from meetings at which ministers had been present, and those relating to meetings of government officials. The object of such discovery was to find evidence that the government's rejection of the profit sharing scheme was unfair.

---

[32] Bradley, "Justice, Good Government and Public Interest Immunity" [1992] P.L. 514.
[33] See generally, Tomkins, "Public Interest Immunity after Matrix Churchill" [1993] P.L. 650.
[34] *R.* v. *Horseferry Road Magistrates' Court, ex p. Bennett (No. 2)* [1994] 1 All E.R. 289.
[35] See above, p. 714.
[36] [1980] A.C. 1090.

Their Lordships held that no classes of document were entirely excluded from the balancing process. Even high level governmental policy could be subjected to this process. This emerges most clearly from the judgments of Lord Keith of Kinkel[37] and Lord Scarman;[38] it is accepted, albeit less forcefully, by Lord Wilberforce[39] and is implicit in the judgment of Lord Edmund-Davies.[40] It is, however, clear that the importance of the documents will be a key factor in the balancing process.

Thirdly, the *Burmah Oil* case indicates the way in which the balancing approach is to be conducted.

(i) The person arguing against disclosure raises the public interest in favour of immunity. How strong a case must be made out is not entirely clear.[41] If there is doubt about whether a document should be included within a particular class claim the court may inspect it.[42]

(ii) The person claiming discovery must then show that the documents are necessary for fairly disposing of the cause or matter or for saving costs, within the rules of discovery normally applicable to litigation.[43] It may, however, be unclear whether the documents *are* necessary until they are looked at. The person seeking discovery is in danger of being caught in a "Catch 22" dilemma whereby it can only be shown that they are necessary for disposing of the case by seeing the documents which are the very matter in question. Yet the courts do not wish to sanction fishing expeditions by people who are seeking to establish a cause of action. The way out of this conundrum is for the applicant to prove that the documents may well be of use to the case. The precise standard demanded by their Lordships differed. Lord Wilberforce[44] stated that the court should not inspect the documents unless the party could show a strong positive case that they might be of help to him. Lord Keith of Kinkel[45] used a test of reasonable probability, while Lord Edmund-Davies[46] adopted a test of likelihood. Only if the person seeking access to the documents surmounts this hurdle will the court undertake the balancing operation.

(iii) The ruling in *Makanjuola* exacerbates this problem for the individual who is seeking to sue the government: government departments may now be encouraged to assert the immunity when the document is in a class which would be prima facie immune, and the plaintiff is then faced with the problem of proving that the requisite

---

[37] *Ibid.* pp. 1134-1135.
[38] *Ibid.* pp. 1143-1144.
[39] *Ibid.* p. 1113.
[40] *Ibid.* p. 1129.
[41] *e.g.* Lord Wilberforce speaks of a claim for public interest immunity having been made on a strong and well fortified basis, p. 1112, while Lord Edmund-Davies speaks of the Chief Secretary establishing a good prima facie case for withholding the documents, p. 1125.
[42] *Conway* v. *Rimmer* [1968] A.C. 910, 995; *Burmah Oil* [1980] A.C. 1090.
[43] R.S.C., Order 24, r. 13. See also, *Air Canada* v. *Secretary of State for Trade (No. 2)* [1983] 2 A.C. 394.
[44] [1980] A.C. 1090, 1117.
[45] *Ibid.* pp. 1135-1136.
[46] *Ibid.* p. 1126.

degree of probability exists. It is precisely when the document is one of a class of such documents that it might be most difficult for the individual to meet this standard of proof.

Fourthly, only when it has been found that the materials are necessary for fairly disposing of the case will the court balance the public interest of preventing harm to the state by allowing disclosure with the public interest of preventing the administration of justice from being frustrated.[47] Various types of argument are used to justify non-disclosure, particularly of high policy documents. The two most oft-repeated are the argument that disclosure would place candour within the public service at risk, and that it would fan ill-formed or captious public or political criticism by those without real understanding of how government worked. The candour argument is not now regarded as such an important factor. Judicial opinion does, however, continue to differ as to its relevance. For example, Lord Reid in *Conway*[48] did not believe that the possibility of disclosure would inhibit candour. This sentiment was echoed even more strongly by Lord Keith of Kinkel in *Burmah Oil*[49] who regarded the notion that candour would be diminished by the off-chance of disclosure as grotesque. Similarly dismissive statements are to be found in other cases.[50] To be contrasted with these views are those of Lord Wilberforce in *Burmah Oil*[51] who felt that the candour argument had received an excessive dose of cold water, and Lord Scarman[52] in the same case was of the opinion that both the candour argument and the captious public criticism argument were of importance.[53]

The final point to be made is that it is now clear that a document which is held to be immune from disclosure cannot be used for any purpose in the proceedings to which the immunity applies.[54]

(b) Inspection

We have already touched upon the question of inspection in the context of the preceding discussion. The topic does, however, warrant consideration in its own right. It is important to realise that inspection may be of relevance at four different stages of the proceedings.

First, there may be doubts as to whether a particular document should be included within a class for which immunity has been claimed. Inspection by the judge can resolve this matter. Secondly, it may be necessary to inspect

---

[47] *Evans* v. *Chief Constable of Surrey* [1988] Q.B. 588.
[48] [1968] A.C. 910, 952.
[49] [1980] A.C. 1090, 1133.
[50] *e.g. Science Research Council* v. *Nassé* [1980] A.C. 1028, 1070 (Lord Salmon), 1081 (Lord Fraser); *Campbell* v. *Tameside Metropolitan Borough Council* [1982] 3 W.L.R. 75 where Ackner L.J. regarded the candour doctrine as having been given its quietus; *Williams* v. *Home Office* [1981] 1 All E.R. 1151.
[51] [1980] A.C. 1090, 1112.
[52] *Ibid.* p. 1145. Even where the balance is against disclosure there may be a temporal limit upon the secrecy, *R.* v. *Inland Revenue Commissioners, ex p. Rossminster Ltd.* [1980] A.C. 952.
[53] See also the opinion of Lord Fraser in *Air Canada* [1983] 2 A.C. 394.
[54] *Makanjuola* [1992] 3 All E.R. 617; *Halford* v. *Sharples* [1992] 1 W.L.R. 736.

the documents to determine whether their disclosure is indeed necessary for fairly disposing of the case or for saving costs. This was the question upon which the *Burmah Oil*[55] case ultimately turned. Thirdly, inspection may be required at the balancing stage in order to determine whether the public interest is for or against disclosure. Fourthly, if on balance the court considers that the document should be produced, should it inspect it before ordering production?

Judicial opinion has differed on the desirability of ordering inspection. Comment is rendered more difficult because the judicial statements do not always refer to inspection at the same level, and it is clear that differing policy considerations may apply at the four stages. Some attempt must however be made to disentangle the authorities.

The position with respect to the first level appears both on authority and on principle to be in favour of inspection. If there is doubt as to whether a particular document should or should not be part of a class of documents for which immunity might properly be claimed, not to inspect in order to determine whether the document was properly included would make it possible for the party against disclosure to protect material under the umbrella of a class to which it did not in reality belong. Authority is in favour of inspection in such instances.[56]

Burmah Oil[57] is authority that inspection can be ordered at the second level. On principle this must be correct. Provided that the plaintiff can show that there is a likelihood, or reasonable probability, or strong positive case, to use the different formulations of their Lordships, that there might be documents which are indeed necessary for fairly disposing of the case then, unless inspection is undertaken, the point cannot be answered. There are however two problems in this area.

On the one hand, the degree of likelihood that the plaintiff must show in order for the court to inspect the documents continues to divide the judiciary. Thus in the *Air Canada*[58] case their Lordships refused to inspect on this second level, but their formulations differed. Three of their Lordships held that in order to warrant inspection the plaintiff must show that there was a reasonable probability that the material was necessary for fairly disposing of the case, and that the documents would help his or her case or damage that of the other side.[59] Two of their Lordships held that the plaintiff must show that the documents were likely to be necessary for fairly disposing of the case, and that the court could inspect the documents when it considered that their disclosure might materially assist either of the parties or the court in the determination of the issues.[60] There is a danger

---

[55] [1980] A.C. 1090.
[56] *Conway* v. *Rimmer* [1968] A.C. 910, 995; *Burmah Oil* [1980] A.C. 1090 where it appears to have been accepted that inspection should take place on this first level, see, *e.g.* pp. 1111-1112, 1129.
[57] [1980] A.C. 1090.
[58] [1983] 2 A.C. 394.
[59] The precise degree of probability differed, Lord Fraser, *ibid.* p. 435; Lord Wilberforce, p. 439; Lord Edmund-Davies, pp. 442-443.
[60] Lord Scarman, pp. 445-446; Lord Templeman, pp. 447-449.

in the stricter formulation. If the standard is set too high then we could find ourselves back in a position not very different from that prior to *Conway*. The court will only balance the interest for and against disclosure if the plaintiff surmounts the Order 24, rule 13 hurdle. If the courts refuse to inspect documents in respect of which immunity has been claimed unless, to use one of their Lordships' formulations, the plaintiffs can show that the documents are very likely to contain material which would give substantial support to their contentions, then the plaintiffs are unlikely to reach the balancing stage at all.

On the other hand, some cases object to such inspection at this second level because the court may not be in a good position to assess the relevance of the material for the case.[61] There may indeed be such difficulties, but what is the alternative? Either the court refuses to inspect at all, but then how can the court tell whether the material *is* necessary for fairly disposing of the case? Or having inspected the documents it would then show the material to the plaintiffs to allow them to indicate its importance; but this would automatically answer the case in favour of disclosure, in the sense that the documents would be known.

Disagreement also exists as to whether inspection should take place at the third level. The judgments in *Conway*[62] endorse inspection where necessary in order to decide where the balance lies. In *Burmah Oil*[63] the House of Lords was also willing, if necessary, to inspect the documents to determine whether the balance was in favour of disclosure. Notwithstanding these statements from high authority, other courts have expressed more circumspection about the desirability of such inspection.[64] Varying reasons have been given for this more wary approach. One recurring theme is that to inspect infringes the broad rule of justice that documents should be available to both sides. This point is well answered by Lord Upjohn.[65]

"I do not understand this objection. There is a lis between A and B; the Crown may be A or B...But when the judge demands to see the documents for which privilege is claimed he is not considering that lis but quite a different lis, that is whether the public interest in withholding the document outweighs the public interest that all relevant documents not otherwise privileged should be displayed in litigation. The judge's duty is to decide that lis...."

The House of Lords in *Conway* clearly felt that inspection should take place before ordering production of a document, that is the fourth level indicated above, if the document had not been seen by the court before that stage.

---

[61] *e.g. Gaskin* v. *Liverpool City Council* [1980] 1 W.L.R. 1549, 1555; *Neilson* v. *Laugharne* [1981] Q.B. 736.
[62] [1968] A.C. 910, 953, 972, 980, 989, 995-996.
[63] [1980] A.C. 1090, 1121-1122, 1129, 1134-1135; 1145.
[64] *Gaskin* [1980] 1 W.L.R. 1549; *Neilson* [1981] Q.B. 736.
[65] *Conway* v. *Rimmer* [1968] A.C. 910, 995-996.

Section 2. Statutes and the Crown

1. *Statutes Binding the Crown*

The question of whether the Crown is bound by statutes is one of those areas in which early decisions have been interpreted in a way which they do not warrant and where those subsequent interpretations have become the law. The commonly stated rule is that the Crown is not bound by statute in the absence of express provision or necessary implication. This was not always the case. Street has traced the history of this rule and has demonstrated the subtle change of meaning to which the case law has been subjected.[66] In the sixteenth century the position was that the Crown was bound by a statute which was intended to bind it.[67] Where the statute touched upon the rights of subjects generally then the Crown would normally be bound also. There was, however, a presumption that a general statute would not affect the prerogative rights of the King unless he was named therein. The transition from this position to the commonly stated rule set out above was made, it seems, largely by accident and mis-interpretation.[68] By the twentieth century a rule began to the propounded in texts upon statute law that the Crown, if not named, would be bound by a statute only if that was the necessary implication. Such an implication would only be necessary if to do otherwise would be to render the statute "unmeaning".[69] This test will only be met if it can be affirmed at the time when the statute was passed that it was apparent from its terms that its purpose would be wholly frustrated if the Crown were not to be bound. The House of Lords has recently endorsed this general rule of construction, and has made it clear that it applies irrespective of whether the statute in question has been passed for the public benefit or not.[70]

Who is entitled to take advantage of this immunity? The most appropriate answer is that provided by Hogg.[71] The immunity should be shared by any person who could show that application of the statute to him or her would prejudice the Crown. On this hypothesis being a Crown servant would be neither a sufficient nor necessary condition for immunity. It would not be the former because it would be possible for a person to be a Crown servant, but for the application of the statute not to be prejudicial to the Crown. It would not be the latter because it would be quite possible

---

[66] "The Effect of Statutes upon the Rights and Liabilities of the Crown" 7 U.T.L.J. 357 (1948); *Governmental Liability* (1953), pp. 143-154. I am indebted to Street for the historical material in this section. See also Williams, *Crown Proceedings* (1948), pp. 48-58; Hogg, *Liability of the Crown* (1971), Chap. 7.

[67] *Willion v. Berkley* (1561) 1 Plowden 223.

[68] *Magdalen College Case* (1615) 11 Co. Rep. 66b.

[69] *Province of Bombay v. Municipal Corporation of the City of Bombay* [1947] A.C. 58; *Madras Electric Supply Co. Ltd. v. Boarland* [1955] A.C. 667; *Gorton Local Board v. Prison Commissioners* [1904] 2 K.B. 165; *British Broadcasting Corporation v. Johns* [1965] Ch. 32. cf. *Att.-Gen. v. De Keyser's Royal Hotel Ltd.* [1920] A.C. 508.

[70] *Lord Advocate v. Dumbarton District Council* [1990] 2 A.C. 580.

[71] *Liability of the Crown*, pp. 174-175.

for independent contractors and others to argue that the application of a statute to them would prejudicially affect the Crown.

The present state of the law can hardly be regarded as satisfactory. The shift from a rule sensibly based upon general legislative purpose and intent to the present position has been accomplished partly by accident and partly by misinterpretation of earlier authority. Little thought has been given to the justification, if any, for this position. It might be argued that the present rule gives rise to no great problems because the Crown can easily be expressly included in the statute. This would be oversimplistic. A number of problems do exist.[72]

First, it is unclear when the exception to the present rule will apply. Secondly, the retention of the present presumption creates problems with the application to the Crown of statutes concerning tortious liability. The present presumption was left unaltered by the Crown Proceedings Act 1947, section 40(2)(f), except as otherwise expressly provided. Section 2 of the same legislation imposes liability in tort upon the Crown as if it were a private person. A neat question therefore arises as to whether such statutes passed before and after the 1947 Act are rendered automatically applicable to the Crown through the operation of section 2, or whether express provision in the particular statute is required.[73] Thirdly, and most important, the argument that the present rule produces no problems is premised upon an ideal whereby legislators will carefully weigh the matter to decide whether to extend an Act to the Crown. The legislative process will often not meet these expectations. Whether the Crown should be bound may receive scant attention or simply be forgotten. A reversal of the present presumption would provide a simple solution: the Crown should be bound unless there is a clear indication to the contrary. This would at least force the government to take the initiative in practical terms if it wished to secure immunity, and also place upon it the onus of arguing why immunity was required.

2. *Statutes Benefiting the Crown*

It appears[74] to be the law that the King can take the benefit of statutes even though not named therein. The point has been doubted,[75] but appears to be correct. If on true construction of a statute it seems as if the Crown should receive a benefit, then that benefit should indeed be forthcoming even if the Crown is not named expressly therein. This seems to give the Crown a power to approbate and reprobate, to claim the benefit but not to take the burden. The possibility of this occurring lies not, however, with the fact that the Crown can take a benefit, even though not named, if the statute

---

[72] *Ibid.* pp. 200-202.
[73] For a clear summary of the arguments see Treitel, "Crown Proceedings: Some Recent Developments" [1957] P.L. 321, 322-326.
[74] Street, *Governmental Liability*, pp. 154-156; Hogg, *Liability of the Crown*, pp. 180-183.
[75] *Cayzer, Irvine & Co. Ltd.* v. *Board of Trade* [1927] 1 K.B. 269, 274; *Nisbet Shipping Co. Ltd.* v. *Queen* [1955] 1 W.L.R. 1031, 1035.

was intended to grant the benefit, but with the inflexible rule about the Crown not being bound by statutes unless named therein.

A related but separate question is whether the Crown could take the benefit of certain statutory rights without the restrictions attendant upon them. The answer, on authority, appears to be negative.[76]

The common law position is left unchanged by the Crown Proceedings Act 1947, section 31(1) of which states that the Act shall not prejudice the right of the Crown to take advantage of the provisions of a statute although not named therein and that, in any civil proceedings against the Crown, the Crown, subject to express provision to the contrary, may rely upon the provisions of any Act of Parliament which could, if the proceedings were between subjects, be relied on by the defendant as a defence.

Section 3. Procedure and Remedies

1. General

In general the rules of civil procedure apply to actions by and against the Crown. This general rule is, however, subject to certain modifications.

The Crown is not a party to the proceedings. It is represented whether as plaintiff or defendant by a government department or by the Attorney-General. A list of such departments is provided; where none of these is appropriate, or where there are reasonable doubts as to which is appropriate, the Attorney-General should be made the defendant.[77]

The most notable distinction between ordinary actions and those brought against the Crown is in relation to the remedies available. There are two particular points to note in this context.

The first is that it has been argued by Wade that the prerogative remedies cannot lie against the Crown itself since they emanate from the Crown.[78] This is said, however, to be no impediment to the availability of certiorari or prohibition since these remedies lie to control all inferior jurisdictions and therefore apply to ministers of the Crown on whom powers are conferred by Parliament in their own names. It is said to be a problem in the context of mandamus since the Crown itself has public duties. The consequence, in the context of mandamus, is said to be that where the servant of the Crown is merely an instrument selected by the Crown for the discharge of the Crown's duty, any complaint must lie against the Crown itself. Where, however, Parliament has imposed the duty upon a person acting in a particular capacity mandamus will lie even though such a person is acting upon the Crown's behalf.[79]

---

[76] *Crooke's Case* (1691) 1 Show K.B. 208; *Nisbet* [1955] 1 W.L.R. 1031. Although, as Hogg, p. 182 points out, this would not be logically impossible as Parliament might intend the Crown not to be subject to certain restrictions.

[77] Crown Proceedings Act 1947, s.17.

[78] Wade, *Administrative Law* (6th ed., 1988), p. 662.

[79] *Ibid.* pp. 662-663.

Whether this particular limit upon the availability of mandamus really exists may be doubted. In general terms the prerogative orders will issue to ministers of the Crown, and the previous chapters of this book are replete with examples of this. It is clear also that mandamus can issue to a minister who is acting in an official capacity.[80] The objection to the applicability of the prerogative remedies against the Crown itself is more questionable. The authority cited for this proposition[81] gives two reasons for holding that mandamus cannot apply to the sovereign: that it would be incongruous for the sovereign to command herself, and that disobedience results in a writ of attachment. Both of these arguments would have force if one were thinking in terms of mandamus applying to the sovereign in a personal capacity. They lose much of this force when applied to the sovereign as personified in and through the government of the day. Viewed in this light it does not appear to be so incongruous for the prerogative orders which emanate from the Crown, in the sense that historically the Crown had a judicial capacity, to be applied to the Crown in its governmental capacity. Moreover, as Lord Woolf has noted,[82] when a minister is sued in his or her official capacity then unless the minister is treated as being distinct from the Crown the incongruity of the Crown suing the Crown would still be present.

The second point to note is that much of the machinery for enforcing a judgment is excluded. Thus, no execution or attachment or process can issue for enforcing payment by the Crown,[83] and the Crown is not susceptible to an order for specific performance, or an injunction or for an order compelling the delivery of property. The plaintiff must be content with a declaratory judgment.[84] This will normally create no problem since the Crown will satisfy the judgment. It could, however, give rise to difficulties where the plaintiff is seeking interim relief as will be seen below. Where the redress required is a money payment, the Act states that the appropriate government department shall pay the amount to the person entitled[85] out of moneys provided by Parliament.[86] The normal rules of indemnity and contribution apply.[87]

2. Injunctions and Interim Relief

The root cause of the problem was that injunctions, and therefore interim injunctions, were, until recently, thought not to be available against the Crown or its officers.

---

[80] Padfield [1968] A.C. 997; R. v. Customs and Excise Commissioners, ex p. Cook [1970] 1 W.L.R. 450, 455; M v. Home Office [1993] 3 All E.R. 537, 558-559.
[81] R. v. Powell (1841) 1 Q.B. 352, 361.
[82] M. v. Home Office [1993] 3 All E.R. 537, 559.
[83] Crown Proceedings Act 1947 s.25(4).
[84] s.21. See Williams, Crown Proceedings (1948), Chap. 7, for further matters such as the Crown's privilege in choice of forum.
[85] Crown Proceedings Act 1947, s.25(3).
[86] s.37.
[87] s.4.

(1) EXTENDING THE AVAILABILITY OF INJUNCTIVE RELIEF

The courts have, as will be seen below, adopted differing views as to whether the Crown or its officers are subject to injunctive relief, and hence whether they are also liable for interim injunctive relief. It is necessary to review some of the important case law in this area in order to understand the present position.

(i) Section 21 of the Crown Proceedings Act 1947 allows the court in civil proceedings to award any relief against the Crown as it could in proceedings between subjects, provided that it cannot grant injunctions or specific performance, but can instead make a declaratory order. Section 21(2) further provides that the court should not grant an injunction against an officer of the Crown if the effect of doing so would be to give any relief against the Crown which could not have been obtained in proceedings against the Crown itself. Civil proceedings do not include proceedings for judicial review, but prior to the reform of Order 53 injunctions could not be sought in judicial review actions.[88] The accepted wisdom was, therefore, that injunctive relief could not be sought against the Crown or its officers.

(ii) The reforms in the law of remedies then allowed injunctions to be claimed when applying for judicial review, and this was given statutory force by section 31 of the Supreme Court Act 1981. Certain decisions suggested that the absence of injunctive relief had in fact been cured by these reforms, and that injunctions could be sought against officers of the Crown pursuant to judicial review.[89]

(iii) These decisions were, however, overruled in the first *Factortame* case,[90] where Lord Bridge stated that the reforms in the law of remedies could not be taken to have changed the law in this respect: interim injunctive relief against the Crown or officers of the Crown acting as such was not possible. The reasoning was, in essence, as follows: the Crown Proceedings Act 1947, section 21(1) precluded injunctive relief in civil proceedings against the Crown; this prohibition did not, on its face, extend to proceedings for judicial review,[91] but no such prohibition was, however, necessary because injunctions were, in any event, not available in judicial review proceedings prior to, or even after, 1947; injunctions against officers of the Crown were also prohibited;[92] section 31 of the Supreme Court Act 1981 could not be held to have altered this position, since a more explicit legislative indication of a change was required.

(iv) It was, somewhat paradoxically, the *Factortame* litigation which fuelled the demand for this gap to be filled. The facts of the case have been set out above.[93] In the first *Factortame* case the House of Lords asked the ECJ whether the absence of interim relief against the Crown was *itself* a breach of Community law: the applicants contended that national legal

---

[88] s.38(2).
[89] R. v. *Licensing Authority Established under the Medicines Act, ex p. Smith Kline and French Laboratories Ltd. (No.2)* [1990] 2 Q.B. 574; R. v. *Secretary of State for the Home Department, ex p. Herbage* [1987] Q.B. 872.
[90] R. v. *Secretary of State for Transport, ex p. Factortame Ltd.* [1990] 2 A.C. 85.
[91] Because of the definition of civil proceedings within s.38(2) of the 1947 Act.
[92] By s.21(2) read with s.23(2)(b).
[93] See above, pp. 189-190.

systems must provide protection for Community rights, and that this required the presence of some form of interim protection when those rights were in danger of being irremediably impaired in the period pending the final resolution of the dispute. The ECJ responded by stating that the absence of any such protection was indeed a breach of Community law, and that any national rule which prevented this relief from being claimed must be set aside.[94]

The case then returned to the House of Lords for consideration in the light of the ECJ's opinion. In *Factortame (No.2)*[95] their Lordships accepted the ECJ's ruling and acknowledged that, as a matter of Community law, interim relief had to be applicable against the Crown. The more specific legal manner of reaching this result is not considered in any detail by the court. Lord Goff relied upon the general power to award injunctive relief contained in the Supreme Court Act 1981, and then proceeded to apply the principle to the facts of the case.[96]

In purely formal terms the decision in *Factortame (No.2)* only applies to cases which have a Community law element. Yet it is clear that it created an uneasy dualism: interim injunctive relief would be obtainable in cases which had a Community law element, but not in those which were wholly domestic in character. The very existence of the remedy in the one type of case added weight to the suggestion that it should be equally available in the other. This provides a good example of the indirect influence which Community law can have upon our jurisprudence: it might only apply in certain areas, but this then creates pressure for reform in domestic law.[97]

(v) The matter rested there until the decision of the House of Lords in *M. v. Home Office*.[98] The facts of this case will be set out more fully below. However, the question of injunctive relief came before the court, in essence, because the Home Secretary was being held in contempt of court for action which he had taken in relation to M. who had been refused political asylum. The availability of injunctions against the Crown was of relevance because if the courts had no power to make such coercive orders then the judge who had made the finding of contempt might have done so without jurisdiction.[99] Lord Woolf, giving the judgment of the court, in effect reversed the holding in the first *Factortame* case, and held that injunctions, including interim injunctions, were available against Ministers of the Crown. The reasoning is complex and cannot be fully explored here. The essence of the argument can, however, be conveyed. Lord Woolf's judgment may be conveniently divided into two parts, which deal respectively with the interpretation of the 1947 Act and the 1981 Act.

His Lordship began his interpretation of the 1947 Act by considering the legal position prior to its passage. He held that prior to the 1947 Act a plaintiff could sue the actual wrongdoer, even if this was a minister acting

---

[94] Case 213/89, *R. v. Secretary of State for Transport, ex p. Factortame Ltd.* [1990] 3 C.M.L.R. 867.

[95] *R. v. Secretary of State for Transport, ex p. Factortame Ltd. (No.2)* [1991] 1 A.C. 603.

[96] Craig, "Administrative Law, Remedies and Europe" (1991) 3 E.R.P.L. 521, 527.

[97] See above, pp. 209–210.

[98] [1993] 3 All E.R. 537.

[99] *Ibid.* p. 549.

in his official capacity, and that an injunction could be issued.[100] This was so even after 1947, since section 21(2) of the Act only prevented actions against a minister acting in a representative capacity. If a statute placed a duty on a specific minister, as opposed to the Crown, then an action could be brought and an injunction could be obtained.[101] A minister could, therefore, be personally liable for wrongs done by him or her when acting in an official capacity.[102]

With this reasoning behind him Lord Woolf then turned to the *1981 Act*. The analysis of the 1947 Act was, however, crucial, when interpreting the later legislation because a cornerstone of Lord Bridge's opinion in *Factortame*[103] was that no injunctive relief against ministers had been available under the 1947 regime, and that therefore any change from this position would have been dramatic. Lord Woolf's contrary interpretation of the 1947 legislation blunted the edge of this critique. He further pointed out that prohibition and mandamus were applicable to ministers, so that the only consequence of reading section 31 as enabling injunctions to be granted against ministers would be to provide an alternative to those remedies and to allow interim relief.[104] Lord Woolf's conclusion was that injunctive relief, both final and interim, should be available against officers of the Crown, given the unqualified language of section 31.[105] These remedies could, moreover, be issued even prior to the granting of leave where this was appropriate.[106]

The general jurisdiction to issue injunctions should, however, only be exercised in limited circumstances, and his Lordship left open the possibility of the courts being able to grant interim declarations. It is to this issue that we should now turn.

(2) INTERIM DECLARATIONS

The courts have, in the past, set their face against the grant of interim declarations.[107] In *R. v. Inland Revenue Commissioners, ex p. Rossminster Ltd*[108] their Lordships differed as to whether interim relief should be available against the Crown. Lord Wilberforce, Viscount Dilhorne and Lord Scarman all expressed doubts about the availability of interim relief against the Crown, and about the advisability of providing this remedy.[109] Lord Diplock was of a different view: the absence of such relief was to be regarded as a serious procedural defect.[110] There appear to be three objections to the granting of such relief.

---

[100] *Ibid.* p. 553.
[101] *Ibid.* p. 555-556.
[102] *Ibid.* pp. 557-558, doubting the judgment in *Merricks v. Heathcoat-Amory* [1955] Ch. 567.
[103] [1990] 2 A.C. 85.
[104] [1993] 3 All E.R. 537, 561.
[105] *Ibid.* pp. 563-564.
[106] *Ibid.* p. 564.
[107] *Underhill v. Ministry of Food* [1950] 1 All E.R. 591; *International General Electric Co. of New York Ltd. v. Customs and Excise Commissioners* [1962] Ch. 784.
[108] [1980] A.C. 952.
[109] *Ibid.* pp. 1001, 1007, 1027.
[110] *Ibid.* pp. 1014-1015.

The first is that the very idea of an interim declaration, even between private parties, is simply illogical. A declaration must declare the final rights of the parties and cannot simply preserve the status quo. This reasoning is questionable and is dangerously close to being circular. Thus, it is said that there cannot be an interim declaration because declarations exist to tell people what their rights are and this cannot be achieved until the final judgment.[111] But the whole point is that the plaintiff is not seeking a final determination of his or her rights at this stage. The plaintiff is simply asking the court to preserve the status quo. This objection to the grant of interim declaratory relief has been rejected by some other high authorities which have seen nothing odd or illogical about an interim declaration.[112] Another reason which emerges is that the final declaration when given might be in different terms, or even opposite in effect, from the interim order.[113] Yet it is difficult to see the logic which states that because a final order can differ from the interim relief, therefore the interim relief cannot be given. Final injunctions will often differ from an interim injunction granted to preserve the status quo.

The second argument is that to grant an interim declaration would indirectly infringe against the principle that the decisions of the state are presumptively valid unless and until they are shown to be wrong.[114] This argument is flawed. There is nothing inconsistent in regarding, quite correctly, such decisions as presumptively valid and still leaving open the possibility of granting interim relief. The presumption of validity places the burden of proof upon the party challenging the decision. It does not tell us whether that party should be able to claim interim relief. Provided that the plaintiff is required to show a sufficiently strong prima facie case of invalidity and provided that the balance of convenience is properly assessed, interim relief would not be inconsistent with this principle.[115]

The third of the arguments against the interim declaration is that it would have much the same effect as would the grant of an injunction.[116] This argument is difficult to understand. Section 21 of the Crown Proceedings Act 1947 provides for a declaration to be granted instead of an injunction or specific performance. What does the above objection mean? It might mean that the Crown will feel duty bound to abide by the court's order. This could, however, be said just as much about final declarations. The Crown does comply with them. It might mean a wariness of granting interim relief on incomplete evidence.[117] This is a valid reason for not giving

[111] *International General Electric* [1962] Ch. 784, 789.
[112] *Yotvin v. State of Israel* (1979).
[113] *Underhill* [1950] 1 All E.R. 591, 593; *Rossminster* [1980] A.C. 952, 1027.
[114] See, *e.g. Rossminster* [1980] A.C. 952, 1027, Lord Scarman.
[115] Lord Diplock saw no inconsistency between the presumption of validity and the availability of interim relief, *ibid.* pp. 1013, 1014-1015, and it was Lord Diplock who gave the exposition of that presumption in *Hoffmann-La Roche & Co. A.G. v. Secretary of State for Trade and Industry* [1975] A.C. 295, 366-367.
[116] *Rossminster* [1980] A.C. 952, 1001, 1007.
[117] Lord Wilberforce, *ibid.* p. 1001.

such relief on the facts of a particular case,[118] because the plaintiff cannot meet the required standard of proof. It is difficult to see how it provides an objection in principle to the interim declaration.

(3) GRANTING A STAY

Prior to the decision in M. v. Home Office one way which was suggested of resolving the problem of the inability to obtain interim injunctive relief against the Crown was to grant a stay against the relevant minister. This solution was adopted in R. v. Secretary of State for Education and Science, ex p. Avon County Council[119] where Glidewell L.J. based the court's jurisdiction upon Order 53, rule 3(10)(a) which provides that, once leave has been granted, then if the relief which has been sought is certiorari or prohibition, the grant of leave shall operate as "a stay of the proceedings to which the application relates until the determination of the application or until the court otherwise orders". Glidewell L.J. held that the term "proceedings" was broad enough to cover administrative decisions of ministers, in addition to decisions of tribunals or lower courts.

It is, however, doubtful whether this decision can stand in the light of the dicta of Lord Oliver in Minister of Foreign Affairs, Trade and Industry v. Vehicles and Supplies Ltd[120], where his Lordship indicated that stays were confined to lower courts and tribunals. The decision in the Avon case has, moreover, been subjected to academic criticism.[121]

(4) CONCLUSION

As the Law Commission has stated, the immunity of the Crown from interim relief is not sustainable on grounds of legal principle.[122] The decision in M. v. Home Office is, therefore, to be welcomed, and it is to be hoped that interim declarations will also become available.

3. Contempt

The leading decision upon this point is M. v. Home Office.[123] The applicant, M., arrived from Zaire and sought political asylum in the UK. The claim for asylum was rejected by the Secretary of State and he made a direction for the removal of M. back to Zaire. M. then sought leave to apply for judicial review. The judge thought that there was an arguable

---

[118] As in Rossminster itself where the material necessary to challenge the legality of the seizure was protected by public interest immunity at the time of the action.

[119] [1991] 1 Q.B. 558.

[120] [1991] 1 W.L.R. 550, 556.

[121] Sir John Laws, "Crown Proceedings", Judicial Review (Supperstone Q.C. and Goudie Q.C. eds., 1992), pp. 248-252; Administrative Law, Judicial Review and Statutory Appeals, Law Com. Consultation Paper No. 126, pp. 39-41. There are, however, indications in the M. case that Lord Woolf might have a broader view of the power to award a stay, [1993] 3 All E.R. 537, 561B.

[122] L.C.C.P. No. 126, p. 46.

[123] [1993] 3 All E.R. 537.

point and wished M. to remain in the UK until the following day when the point could be fully argued. Counsel for the Secretary of State then gave what the judge believed to be an undertaking that M. would not be removed from the UK pending the hearing. There followed a series of mistakes and mishaps which culminated in M. being returned to Zaire. The judge then issued a mandatory order to the Home Secretary demanding that M. be returned to the UK. The Home Secretary challenged this order, after taking legal advice, and the judge, at a hearing on the issue, discharged the order on the basis that he, the judge, had no power to make it. An action was then brought on behalf of M. for contempt of court by the Home Secretary on the basis that he had broken the undertaking and the judge's order while it was in force.

The House of Lords held both that coercive orders, such as injunctions, could lie against ministers of the Crown, and also that if a minister did act in disregard of an injunction made against him in his official capacity the court did have jurisdiction to make a finding of contempt against him or his department, albeit not against the Crown itself. The contempt proceedings would, however, differ from normal proceedings of this kind, in that they would not be either personal or punitive: fines and sequestration of assets would not be appropriate in cases involving departments or ministers, although they might be necessary in other instances.[124] There would, said Lord Woolf, still be a point in the finding of contempt since "such a finding would vindicate the requirements of justice",[125] and this could be underlined by awarding costs against the government. It would then be for Parliament to decide upon the consequences of the contempt. Any such finding of contempt would be against the authorised department, the minister or the Attorney-General, rather than the Crown. It would, moreover, be more normal to make the finding of contempt against the department as opposed to the minister personally. The constitutional precept that the Crown itself can do no wrong was preserved, by presuming that the minister had acted without the authority of the Crown in such circumstances.[126]

The decision in the case is undoubtedly of significance in emphasising that the government must obey the law not just as a matter of choice, but ultimately by way of compulsion. Instances of contempt are likely to be rare in practice, but this should not diminish the important point of principle in the House of Lords' ruling. It is fitting to conclude this discussion with the following words of Lord Templeman.[127]

"My Lords, the argument that there is no power to enforce the law by injunction or contempt proceedings against a minister in his official capacity would, if upheld, establish the proposition that the executive obey the law as a matter of grace and favour and not as a matter of necessity, a proposition which would reverse the result of the Civil War."

---

[124] *Ibid.* pp. 566-567.
[125] *Ibid.* p. 566.
[126] *Ibid.* pp. 553, 566.
[127] *Ibid.* p. 541.

APPENDIX
DEREGULATION AND CONTRACTING OUT
BILL 1994[1]

Section 1. Introduction

One piece of legislation which is of great importance both conceptually and pragmatically is the Deregulation and Contracting Out Bill which is currently working its way through Parliament.[2] The Bill emerged too late to be integrated into the main text, but its significance warrants mention here. As is apparent from the title to the Bill it deals with two main issues, Deregulation and Contracting Out, and these issues will be considered in turn.

Section 2. Deregulation

1. *The Deregulatory Provisions*

Part I of the Bill deals with Deregulation. It gives broad powers to a Minister of the Crown to remove certain statutory burdens on business.

Clause 1 provides that if a Minister is of the opinion that the effect of a provision is such as to impose a burden affecting any person in the carrying on of any trade, and that by repealing or amending the enactment concerned it would be possible to remove or reduce the burden without removing any necessary protection then he may amend or repeal the enactment. The Minister may remove the burden entirely or put in its place a less restrictive alternative. Various limits are provided for the situation in which new or modified criminal offences are created.[3]

There is a duty to consult.[4] If the Minister then wishes to proceed he must, according to Clause 3(4), lay a document before Parliament which contains a draft order together with details of the following matters: the burden which is to be reduced; any protections which will thereby be

---

[1] I have benefited greatly from discussions with Mark Freedland on the Bill.
[2] The numbering of the clauses is taken from the version of the Bill as it has been amended in Standing Committee.
[3] Clause 2.
[4] Clause 3(1).

removed, and if this is so how the protection is to be continued in a different form; the cost savings; any other benefits from the removal of the restriction; the consultation exercise which has been undertaken and the extent to which the Minister has modified his original proposals in the light of the representations which he has received.

Deregulation orders are statutory instruments and are subject to the affirmative procedure.[5] There is, in addition, a period of 40 days during which the order has to be laid before Parliament.

The Bill also contains a number of miscellaneous deregulatory provisions.

2. *The Deregulatory Provisions: An Assessment*

The provisions of the Bill on Deregulation continue the Government's philosophy of removing burdens on industry whenever possible.[6] Two features of these provisions are noteworthy.

One is that they have come in for a good deal of criticism from the Opposition which regards the Bill as one big Henry VIII clause, in the sense that it enables a Minister to suspend any Act of Parliament by Order. There is some measure of truth in this proposition in that the Bill does give a Minister very wide powers to modify existing legislation.

The other noteworthy feature of these provisions of the Bill to some extent mitigates the concern expressed in the preceding paragraph. The process which the Minister has to go through, both in terms of consultation *and* in terms of the nature of the Order which he has to lay before the House, are to be welcomed. The latter is deserving of particular attention. The difficulties of ensuring effective scrutiny of delegated legislation have been considered fully above. However, Parliament's role in this respect will be strengthened by the duties imposed on the Minister under Clause 3(4). The obligation to supply not just the bare deregulation order, but the detailed information on costings, the consultation exercise, protections which have been removed etc will enhance the scrutiny process.

Section 3. Contracting Out

While considerable attention in the Parliamentary debates on the Bill has focused on those clauses concerned with deregulation the provisions which are of relevance to contracting out are of equal importance. These are to be found in Part II of the Bill. An outline will be given of these provisions to be followed by a brief commentary on them.

---

[5] Clause 1(4).
[6] *Deregulation: Cutting Red Tape*, Department of Trade and Industry.

1. *The Contracting Out Provisions*

The Bill is designed to facilitate contracting out by central and local government.

Clauses 59(1) and (2) provide that any function of a Minister or office holder which is conferred by or under any enactment, and which by virtue of any enactment or rule of law may be exercised by an officer of his, and which is not excluded by Clause 61, may, by order, be exercised by (or by the employees of) such person, if any, as may be authorised by the Minister or office-holder whose function it is.[7] The relevant Minister must consult the office-holder before making an order under the section.[8] Functions may be contracted out either wholly or to the extent specified in the order; and conditions may be attached.[9] The authorisation has a temporal limit of 10 years, can be revoked at any time, and does not prevent the Minister or office-holder from exercising the function to which the authorisation relates.[10]

Analogous provisions are made with respect to contracting out certain functions of local authorities.[11]

Clause 61 prohibits the contracting out of a function if its exercise, or a failure to exercise it, would necessarily interfere with or otherwise affect the liberty of any individual; or where the function entails a power or right of entry, search or seizure; or where it is a power or duty to make subordinate legislation.[12]

Clause 62 deals with the effect of contracting out. It is crucially ambiguous. Clause 62(2) states that anything done or omitted to be done by the authorised person (or an employee of his) in, or in connection with, the exercise or purported exercise of the function shall be treated for all purposes as done or omitted to be done by the Minister, or office-holder in his capacity as such. The same basic principle applies to a local authority. So far so good: the Minister is still responsible for matters which have been contracted out. The confusion is generated by the exceptions to this basic proposition. Clause 62(3)(a) provides that clause 62(2) shall not apply for the purposes of so much of any contract made between the authorised person and the Minister, office-holder or local authority as relates to the exercise of the function. Precisely what this means and how it fits in with the basic principle in Clause 62(2) is by no means clear. This matter will be considered more fully below. Clause 62(3)(b) states that Clause 62(2) shall also not apply for the purposes of criminal proceedings brought in respect of anything done or omitted to be done as mentioned in 62(2).

Clause 63 deals with the effect of termination of contracting out, providing that the revocation of a subsisting contract is to be treated as a

---

[7] See also Clause 64 which enables certain office holders who do not yet have the power to do so, to authorise one of their officers to undertake certain of their functions.

[8] Clause 59(3).

[9] Clause 59(4).

[10] Clause 59(5).

[11] Clause 60.

[12] Clauses 61(2),(3) contain exceptions to this exclusionary rule.

repudiation of the contract by the Minister, as opposed to frustration of the contract.

If functions are contracted out then there may be consequential problems concerning the disclosure of information which is restricted by statute or by duties of confidentiality. These are dealt with in Clause 65 which renders it an implied term of the contract that the information is not disclosed. However, Clause 65(2) makes it clear that disclosure is not to be penalised between the Minister and party to whom the function is contracted out, or between employees of the authorised party, where the disclosure is necessary or expedient in connection with the exercise of the relevant function, or a related function or the performance of ancillary services.

2. The Contracting Out Provisions: An Assessment

(1) THE CONTRACTING OUT MAP

It is now clear that we are faced with an increasingly complex picture in relation to contracting out as a whole. In general terms the position is as follows.

> (a) There are certain instances in which contracting out may have a foundation within a particular statute, such as in the context of the Criminal Justice Act 1991 for prison services, and the legislation on local government which relates to Compulsory Competitive Tendering;
> (b) There are many other instances where the decision to contract out an activity, whether after competition with an in-house unit or not, has no direct statutory foundation as such. Thus much of the Government's policy on Market Testing is based on organisational choice, derived from the more general themes to be found in the Citizen's Charter.[13] The conceptual foundation for the decision to execute policy in this manner would appear to be the power of the Crown to contract, whether this be viewed as an aspect of prerogative power, or as a separate common law power in addition thereto.
> (c) There are now also the provisions of the Bill considered above.

The interrelationship between these provisions is not wholly self-evident. The following options are possible.

> (i) On one view there are two general tracks which a department can follow if it wishes to contract out. It can either do so as a matter of organisational choice independently of the Bill, or it can do so by promoting an Order under the Bill.
> (ii) The argument to the contrary would be that where Parliament has spoken on an issue which was previously regulated by the common law or by prerogative, then the Crown cannot choose to

---

[13] See The Government's Guide to Market Testing (1993).

rely any longer on the non-statutory powers, but must follow the statutory remit.[14] This would however mean that any contracting out would have to be through the promulgation of an Order under the Bill, and it seems unlikely that the Government intended that this should always be required.

(iii) A third possible argument would be that an Order under the Bill would only be required where the Minister wished to imbue the private contractor with the same species of authority as would be possessed if a civil servant were performing the task in-house; or where there are other statutory obstacles to contracting out which necessitate the use of the procedures in the Bill.[15]

(2) THE CARLTONA PRINCIPLE

The object of the Bill is to facilitate contracting out and to extend the *Carltona* principle. That principle establishes, as we have seen, that civil servants can exercise functions which have been conferred on Ministers. The object is to extend this principle so that private sector contractors can also act on behalf of Ministers, office-holders etc. The very ease with which conventional doctrine is extended in this fashion should not, however, conceal the novelty and importance of the development. The *Carltona* principle is based on the sensible idea that a Minister cannot in reality perform all the functions which are nominally ascribed to him or her; civil servants must perforce undertake them on the Minister's behalf. To extend this proposition to the situation of a private contractor who may have no contact with government other than through this one particular contract represents a major extension of established principle.

(3) THE LIMITS OF CONTRACTING OUT

In the earlier discussion of contracting out one of the questions which was posed concerned the types of functions which could be contracted out. As noted above the Bill deals with this issue in Clause 61. The impact of the limits contained within this Clause remains to be seen. On the one hand, the limits themselves are not extensive, and would allow many of what may be regarded as 'core' functions to be contracted out. On the other hand, the limitation which relates to individual rights may well lead to legal challenges to Orders, particularly where it was not clear when the Order was initially promulgated that it would have an effect on such rights.

(4) LEGAL ACCOUNTABILITY AND LIABILITY

The Explanatory Guide on the Bill states that the accountability and legal liability of the Minister or office holder will not be affected by the legislation. Clause 62(2) affirms this view, as indeed it must do if the Bill is

---

[14] It should be noted that Schedule 13 of the Bill contains consequential amendments which facilitate contracting out by amending other particular statutes, but this does not alter the general nature of the point being made above.

[15] The Explanatory Guide to the Bill contains indications that this is the intent of the legislation.

to be seen as an extension of the *Carltona* principle. However, we have also seen the ambiguity of Clause 62(3)(a). The interpretation of this Clause is unclear. It renders Clause 62(2) inapplicable for the purposes of "so much of any contract" as "relates to the exercise of the function". The word "function" means the function which has been assigned to the authorised person by the Order. Why this Clause does not undermine the principle contained in Clause 62(2) is not clear, nor is it immediately apparent what type of situation the drafters have in mind which is intended to come within Clause 62(3)(a). Moreover, Clause 62(3)(b), which states that Clause 62(2) shall not apply for the purposes of criminal proceedings brought in respect of anything done or omitted to be done as mentioned in Clause 62(2), may also serve to limit the extent to which responsibility may be laid at the door of the Minister. Space precludes a detailed analysis of this issue. A brief example will indicate the difficulties which could arise. A function concerning residential care is contracted out and the authorised person is found to be guilty of a common law or statutory crime. It transpires that the terms on which the function was contracted out did not, objectively viewed, enable the care to be undertaken at the proper level. Will any proceedings against the Minister or office-holder be precluded by Clause 62(3)(b)?

INDEX